1985 Annual Edition
West's Federal Taxation:

Individual Income Taxes

1985 Annual Edition
West's Federal Taxation:
Individual Income Taxes

General Editors

WILLIAM H. HOFFMAN, JR., J.D., Ph.D., C.P.A.
EUGENE WILLIS, Ph.D., C.P.A.

Contributing Authors

D. LARRY CRUMBLEY, Ph.D., C.P.A.
Texas A & M University

STEVEN C. DILLEY, J.D., Ph.D., C.P.A.
Michigan State University

PATRICA C. ELLIOTT, D.B.A., C.P.A.
University of New Mexico

WILLIAM H. HOFFMAN, Jr., J.D., Ph.D., C.P.A.
University of Houston

JEROME S. HORVITZ, J.D., LL.M. in Taxation
University of Houston

MARILYN PHELAN, J.D., D.B.A., C.P.A.
Texas Tech University

WILLIAM A. RAABE, Ph.D., C.P.A.
University of Wisconsin-Milwaukee

BOYD C. RANDALL, J.D., Ph.D.
Brigham Young University

W. EUGENE SEAGO, J.D., Ph.D., C.P.A.
Virginia Polytechnic Institute and State University

JAMES E. SMITH, Ph.D., C.P.A.
College of William and Mary

WILLIS C. STEVENSON, Ph.D., C.P.A.
University of Wisconsin-Madison

EUGENE WILLIS, Ph.D., C.P.A.
University of Illinois at Urbana

WEST PUBLISHING CO.

ST. PAUL • NEW YORK • LOS ANGELES • SAN FRANCISCO

Copy editor and indexer: Deborah Smith
Text composition: York Graphic Services, Inc.

COPYRIGHT © 1978, 1979, 1980, 1981, 1982, 1983, 1984 by WEST PUBLISHING CO.
50 West Kellogg Boulevard
P.O. Box 43526
St. Paul, Minnesota 55164

Library of Congress Cataloging inc Publication Data

Main entry under title:
  West's Federal Taxation.
  includes index.
  1. Income tax—United States—Law
I. Hoffman, William H. III. Willis, Eugene
ISBN 0–314–8031–7   KF6369.W47   343'.73'052   77–20656

ISSN 0272–0329

1985 ANNUAL EDITION

PREFACE

The text is intended as a basis for a first course in Federal taxation for undergraduate or graduate accounting, business, and law students. With certain modifications in the coverage of the materials, the text may be used in a survey course on Federal taxation for undergraduate or graduate students. The materials may also be valuable as a tool for self-study, since they contain numerous clarifying examples adaptable to such an approach.

Tax policy considerations and historical developments are introduced in the text only to the extent that they shed light on the reason for a particular rule. The many simple and straightforward examples further clarify the materials by showing how a particular tax rule applies in an actual situation.

Once knowledge of the tax law has been acquired, it needs to be used. The tax reduction process, however, normally requires careful planning. Because we recognize the importance of planning procedures, most chapters include a separate section (designated TAX PLANNING CONSIDERATIONS) illustrating the applications of such procedures to specific areas.

We believe that any basic course in Federal taxation should offer the reader the opportunity to learn and utilize the methodology of tax research. Chapter 3 and Appendix E are devoted to this methodology. Also, most chapters contain a category of problem materials (designated *Research Problems*) that require the use of research tools. The effectiveness of the text does not, however, depend on the coverage of tax research procedures. Consequently, the treatment of this subject may be omitted without impairing the continuity of the remaining textual materials.

Although it was not our purpose to approach the presentation and discussion of taxation from the standpoint of the preparation of tax returns, some orientation to tax forms is necessary. Wherever appropriate, we have incorporated into the 1985 edition extracts from various key forms. In some cases, the form itself is reproduced and explained. Further tax-form orientation is achieved through *Tax Form Problems, Cumulative Tax Return Problems* (Chapters 6, 11, 13, and 17), and *Comprehensive Tax Return Problems* (Appendix F). The difference between the classes of problem materials rests with what is expected of the student. *Tax Form Problems,* for example, merely require the preparation of a specific form, whereas *Cumulative Tax Return Problems* necessitate the preparation of multiple forms and the use of materials covered in preceding chapters.

Appendix F contains three *Comprehensive Tax Return Problems,* two of which are completely new. Each of these problems lends itself for use as a term project because of the sophistication required for satisfactory completion. The new problems were specifically designed to be solved using the tax preparation software we are making available to our users in the fall. The problems may also be solved manually.

For the reader's convenience, Appendix B contains a full reproduction of most of the tax forms frequently encountered in actual practice. Tax forms for student use are available in the publication, *West's Federal Taxation: 1983 Federal Tax Forms.* These forms have been selected to correspond with the various tax return problems throughout the text.

While the primary emphasis of the text is on the income taxation of individuals, Chapter 20 is an overview of the Federal taxation of other forms of business organization (i. e., corporations and partnerships). This chapter could be of particular significance to students who do not plan to take a second course in federal taxation. For others, Chapter 20 may serve as a lead-in to *West's Federal Taxation: Corporations, Partnerships, Estates, and Trusts.*

The Instructor's Guide that accompanies the text (when adopted for classroom use) contains an instructor's summary of each chapter, test questions and solutions, and ancillary materials for classroom use and discussion. The materials in the Instructor's Guide have been expanded and improved in the 1985 edition.

Since the original edition was issued in 1978, we have followed a policy of annually revising the text material to reflect statutory, judicial, and administrative changes in the Federal tax law and to correct any errors or other shortcomings. Because the 1985 edition has not been affected by any major changes in the tax law, we have directed our efforts toward improving the problem materials. Each chapter contains at least ten new questions or problems.

We are most appreciative of the many suggestions that we have received for revising the text, many of which have been incorporated in past editions and in the 1985 edition. Special thanks go to the following reviewers for their excellent suggestions: Ronald Blasi, SUNY—Buffalo; Phil Harper, Middle Tennessee State University; Michael Holland, Georgia State University; Jerrold Stern, Indiana University; and Dan Wade, Indiana State University. Also, we thank Freda Mulhall of the University of Illinois at Urbana. Finally, this 1985 edition would not have been possible without the technical assistance of and manuscript review by Bonnie Hoffman, CPA.

WILLIAM H. HOFFMAN, Jr.,
EUGENE WILLIS

CONTENTS IN BRIEF

TABLE OF CONTENTS

CHAPTER 1. AN INTRODUCTION TO TAXATION

CHAPTER 2. UNDERSTANDING THE FEDERAL TAX LAW

CHAPTER 3. WORKING WITH THE TAX LAW

CHAPTER 4. TAX DETERMINATION, PERSONAL AND DEPENDENCY EXEMPTIONS, AN OVERVIEW OF PROPERTY TRANSACTIONS

CHAPTER 5. GROSS INCOME:
CONCEPTS AND INCLUSIONS

CHAPTER 7.   DEDUCTIONS AND LOSSES: IN GENERAL

CHAPTER 8.   DEDUCTIONS AND LOSSES: CERTAIN BUSINESS EXPENSES AND LOSSES

CHAPTER 10.   DEDUCTIONS: EMPLOYEE EXPENSES

CHAPTER 11. DEDUCTIONS AND LOSSES:
CERTAIN ITEMIZED DEDUCTIONS

CHAPTER 12. SPECIAL METHODS FOR COMPUTING THE TAX AND PAYMENT PROCEDURES

CHAPTER 13. TAX CREDITS

CHAPTER 14. PROPERTY TRANSACTIONS: DETERMINATION OF GAIN OR LOSS AND BASIS CONSIDERATIONS

CHAPTER 16. PROPERTY TRANSACTIONS: CAPITAL GAINS AND LOSSES

CHAPTER 17. PROPERTY TRANSACTIONS: SECTION 1231 AND RECAPTURE PROVISIONS

CHAPTER 18. ACCOUNTING PERIODS
AND METHODS

CHAPTER 19. DEFERRED COMPENSATION

CHAPTER 20. CORPORATIONS AND PARTNERSHIPS

APPENDIXES

1985 Annual Edition
West's Federal Taxation:

Individual Income Taxes

Chapter 1

An Introduction
to Taxation

Before dealing with specific tax provisions, it is desirable to review
the historical development of the Federal tax law and to understand
the underlying rationale for our tax system. To this end, an initial
review is made of the historical and economic aspects of the tax law.
This chapter also includes a discussion of the major types of taxes and
an introduction to the organizational aspects of administering the
Federal tax law.

HISTORY OF U. S. TAXATION

EARLY PERIODS

The concept of an income tax can hardly be regarded as a newcomer
to the Western Hemisphere. Although an income tax was first enacted
in 1634 by the English colonists in the Massachusetts Bay Colony, it
was not until 1861 that this form of taxation was adopted by
the Federal government. In fact, the income tax was used by both the
Federal Union and the Confederate States of America to provide
funds to finance the Civil War. Although modest in its reach and
characterized by broad exemptions and low rates, the income tax during the Civil War generated $376 million of revenue for the Federal
government.

When the Civil War ended, the need for additional revenue disappeared and the income tax was repealed. As was true before the war, the Federal government was able to finance its operations almost exclusively from customs (i. e., tariff) duties. It is somewhat surprising that no one challenged the constitutionality of the income tax in effect during the Civil War.

One of the reasons the Federal income tax evoked criticism from the outset was the notion that it was an invasion of privacy. In the nineteenth century, financial affairs were regarded as highly personal and concerned only the party involved. Of all things, such matters were none of the business of the U. S. government.

When a new Federal income tax on individuals was enacted in 1894, its opponents were prepared to and did challenge its constitutionality. The U. S. Constitution provided that ". . . No Capitation, or other direct, Tax shall be laid, unless in Proportion to the Census or Enumeration herein before directed to be taken." In *Pollock* v. *Farmers' Loan and Trust Co.*, the U. S. Supreme Court found that the income tax was a direct tax that was unconstitutional, since it was not apportioned among the states in proportion to their populations.[1]

A Federal corporate income tax, enacted by Congress in 1909, fared better in the judicial system. The U. S. Supreme Court found this tax to be constitutional because it was treated as an excise tax.[2] In essence, it was a tax on the right to do business in the corporate form. As such, it was likened to a form of the franchise tax.[3] It should be noted that the corporate form of doing business was developed in the late nineteenth century and was an unfamiliar concept to the framers of the U. S. Constitution. Since a corporation is an entity created under law, jurisdictions possess the right to tax its creation and operation. Using this rationale, many states still impose franchise taxes on corporations.

The ratification of the Sixteenth Amendment to the U. S. Constitution sanctioned both the Federal individual and corporate income taxes and, as a consequence, neutralized the continuing effect of the *Pollock* decision.

REVENUE ACTS

Due to an interpretation of the U. S. Constitution by the Supreme Court, it was necessary to amend the Constitution to permit the enactment of a Federal income tax. Following ratification of the Sixteenth Amendment, Congress enacted the Revenue Act of 1913. Under this Act, a flat one percent tax was levied upon the income of corporations. Individuals paid a normal tax rate of one percent on

---

1. *Pollock v. Farmers' Loan & Trust Co.*, 3 AFTR 2602, 15 S.Ct. 912 (USSC, 1895). See Chapter 3 for an explanation as to how judicial decisions are cited.
2. *Flint v. Stone Tracy Co.*, 3 AFTR 2834, 31 S.Ct. 342 (USSC, 1911).
3. See the discussion of state franchise taxes later in the chapter.

taxable income after deducting a personal exemption of $3,000 for a single individual and $4,000 for a married taxpayer. Surtax rates of one to six percent were applied to high-income taxpayers.

Various revenue acts were passed during the period from 1913 to 1939. In 1939, all of these revenue laws were codified into the Internal Revenue Code of 1939. In 1954, a similar codification of the revenue law took place. The current law consists of the Internal Revenue Code of 1954 as amended by numerous revenue laws passed since 1954.

HISTORICAL TRENDS

The income tax has proved to be a major source of revenue for the Federal government. Figure I contains a breakdown of the major revenue sources. The importance of the income tax is demonstrated by the fact that income tax collections from individuals and corporations amount to approximately 41 percent of the total receipts.

Figure I
FEDERAL BUDGET RECEIPTS—1983[4]

Individual income taxes	36%
Corporation income taxes	5
Social insurance taxes and contributions	26
Excise taxes	4
Borrowing	25
Other	4
	100%

The need for revenues to finance the war effort during WW II converted the income tax into a "mass tax." For example, in 1939, less than six percent of the U. S. population was subject to the Federal income tax. In 1945, over 74 percent of the population was subject to the Federal income tax.[5]

Certain changes in the income tax law are of particular significance in understanding the Federal income tax. In 1943, Congress passed the Current Tax Payment Act, which provided for the first pay-as-you-go tax system. A pay-as-you-go feature of an income tax system compels employers to withhold for taxes a specified portion of an employee's wages. For persons with income from other than wages, periodic (e. g., quarterly) payments must be made to the taxing authority (e. g., the Internal Revenue Service) for estimated taxes due for the year.

---

4. *The United States Budget is Brief,* Office of Management and Budget (Washington, D.C., 1983).
5. Richard Goode, *The Individual Income Tax* (Washington, D.C.: Brookings Institution, 1964), pp. 2–4.

CRITERIA USED IN THE SELECTION OF A TAX BASE

Adam Smith first identified certain "canons of taxation" that are still considered when evaluating a particular tax structure. These canons of taxation follow:[6]

—*Equality*. Each taxpayer enjoys fair or equitable treatment by paying taxes in proportion to his or her income level. Ability to pay a tax is the measure of how equitably a tax is distributed among taxpayers.

—*Convenience*. Administrative simplicity has long been valued in formulating tax policy. If a tax is easily assessed and collected and the costs of administration are low, it should be favored. The withholding (pay-as-you-go) system has been advocated because of its convenience for taxpayers. It should be noted, however, that our Federal income tax laws have become increasingly complex despite outcries from tax specialists, politicians, business executives, et al., regarding the need for administrative simplicity.

—*Certainty*. A "good" tax structure exists if the taxpayer can readily predict when, where, and how a tax will be levied. Individuals and businesses need to know the likely tax consequences of a particular type of transaction.

—*Economy*. A "good" tax system is one which requires only nominal collection costs by the government and involves minimal compliance costs on the part of the taxpayer. Although the government's cost to collect Federal taxes amounts to less than one-half of one percent of the revenue collected, the complexity of our existing tax structure imposes substantial taxpayer compliance costs.

THE TAX STRUCTURE

TAX RATES

Tax rates are applied to the tax base to determine a taxpayer's liability. The tax rates may be proportional or progressive.

A tax is proportional if the rate of tax remains constant for any given income level.

Example 1. T has $10,000 of taxable income and pays a tax of $2,000, or 20%. Y's taxable income is $20,000 and the tax on this amount is $4,000, or 20%. If this constant rate is applied throughout the rate structure, the tax is proportional.

6. *The Wealth of Nations*, Book V, Chapter II, Part II (New York: Dutton, 1910).

The Federal income tax, Federal gift and estate taxes, and most state income tax rate structures are progressive. In the case of the Federal income tax, a higher percentage rate of tax is applied as taxable income increases.

> **Example 2.** If T, a married individual filing jointly, has taxable income of $10,000, the tax is $868 for an effective tax rate of 8.68%. If, however, T's taxable income was $20,000, the tax would be $2,611 for an effective tax rate of 13.055%. The tax is progressive, since higher rates are applied to greater amounts of taxable income.

ADJUSTMENTS TO TAX BASE AND INCIDENCE OF TAXATION

The degree to which the total tax burden is shared by various segments of society is difficult to assess. Assumptions must be made concerning who absorbs the burden for payment of the tax. For example, the corporate tax rate structure is a stair-step progression (e. g., for 1984, 15 percent of the first $25,000 of taxable income, 18 percent of the next $25,000, 30 percent of taxable income in excess of $50,000 up to $75,000, 40 percent in excess of $75,000 up to $100,000, and 46 percent of amounts over $100,000). Since dividend payments to shareholders are not deductible and such amounts are generally taxable income to shareholders, a form of double taxation on the same income is being levied. Concern over double taxation is valid to the extent that corporations are *not* able to shift the corporate tax to the consumer through higher commodity prices. If it can be shifted, the corporate tax becomes merely a consumption tax which is borne by the ultimate purchasers of goods.

The U. S. Federal income tax rate structure for individuals appears to be highly progressive (e. g., rates range from 0 to 50 percent). However, if adjustments to the tax base are taken into account, a different pattern may emerge. Wealthy individuals with high incomes are able to take advantage of certain tax benefits (e. g., tax-sheltered investments, charitable contributions of money and other property, and recognition of long-term capital gains). Studies have indicated that the effective tax rates for Federal and state taxes are generally proportional for almost 90 percent of the population.[7]

MAJOR TYPES OF TAXES

PROPERTY TAXES

Normally referred to as "ad valorem" taxes because they are based on value, property taxes are a tax on wealth, or capital. In this regard,

---

7. Joseph Pechman and Benjamin Okner, *Who Bears the Tax Burden?* (Washington, D.C., The Brookings Institution, 1974).

they have much in common with death taxes and gift taxes discussed later in this chapter. Although property taxes do not tax income, the income actually derived (or the potential for any such income) may be relevant insofar as it affects the value of the property being taxed.

Property taxes fall into two categories: those imposed on realty and those imposed on personalty. Both have added importance, since they usually generate a deduction for Federal income tax purposes (see Chapter 11).

Ad Valorem Taxes on Realty. Property taxes on realty are exclusively within the province of the states and their local political subdivisions (e. g., cities, counties, school districts). They represent a major source of revenue for local governments, but their importance at the state level has waned over the past few years.[8] The trend has been for the states to look to other types of taxes (e. g., sales, income, severance) to meet their fiscal needs. Most of the revenue derived from property taxes on realty are used to provide essential governmental services (e. g., police and fire protection, public education, waste disposal, utility sources).

Particularly in those jurisdictions that do not impose ad valorem taxes on personalty, what is included in the definition of realty could have an important bearing on which assets are or are not subject to tax. Primarily a question of state property law, realty generally includes real estate and any capital improvements thereto that comprise "fixtures." Simply stated, a fixture is something so permanently attached to the real estate that its removal will cause irreparable damage.[9] A built-in bookcase might well be a fixture, whereas a movable bookcase would not. Certainly items like electrical wiring and plumbing when installed in a building have ceased to be personalty and have become realty.

Some of the characteristics of ad valorem taxes on realty are highlighted below:

—Exemption is provided for property owned by the Federal government. Similar immunity usually is extended to property owned by state and local governments and by certain charitable organizations.

—Some states provide for lower valuations on property dedicated to agricultural use or other special uses (e. g., wildlife sanctuaries).

—Some states provide for partial exemption from taxation of the homestead portion of the property. Modern homestead laws

---

8. The furor in California over Proposition 13 (and similar proposals in other states) reflects that the ad valorem tax on realty is not without controversy. It may be that continued taxpayer opposition and resistance will cause such taxes to decline in significance in the years to come.

9. *Black's Law Dictionary,* fifth edition (St. Paul, Minn.: West Publishing Co., 1979), p. 574.

normally operate to protect some or all of a personal residence (including a farm or ranch) from the actions of creditors pursuing claims against the owner.

—Lower taxes may apply as to a residence owned by an elderly taxpayer (e. g., age 65 and older).

—Some jurisdictions extend immunity from tax for a specified period of time (i. e., a "tax holiday") for new or relocated businesses.

—Common in recent years, some states have enacted legislation preventing upward reassessment in value for a specified period of time (unless the property is disposed of during the "freeze" period).

Unlike the ad valorem tax on personalty (see page 8), the tax on realty is difficult to avoid. Since real estate is impossible to hide, a high degree of taxpayer compliance is not surprising. The only avoidance possibility that generally is available lies with the assessed value of the property. For this reason, both the assessed value of the property and, particularly, a reassessed value upward are not without their share of controversy and litigation. For these purposes, at least, everyone is convinced that his or her property is worth less than that belonging to neighbors or near-neighbors.

The four methods currently in use for assessing the value of real estate are summarized below:

1. Actual purchase or construction price.

2. Contemporaneous sales prices or construction costs of comparable properties.

3. Cost of reproducing a building, less allowance for depreciation and obsolescence from the time of actual construction.

4. Capitalization of income from rental property.

Because all of these methods suffer faults and lead to inequities, a combination of one or more is not uncommon. For example, because of rising real estate values and construction costs, the use of actual purchase or construction price (method 1) places the purchaser of a new home at a definite disadvantage with the owner who acquired similar property years before. As another illustration, if the capitalization of income (method 4) deals with property subject to rent controls, then the property may be undervalued.

The history of the ad valorem tax on realty has been marked by inconsistent results in its application due to a lack of competent tax administration and definitive guidelines as to assessment procedures. In recent years, however, significant inroads toward improvement have taken place. Some jurisdictions, for example, have computerized their valuation reassessment procedures so as to have an immediate effect on all property located within any jurisdiction. This has to be a definite move toward equity in tax treatment when one compares the result of the probable previous approach (e. g., because of personnel shortages in tax assessors, one-tenth of the property within the jurisdiction is revalued every ten years).

Ad Valorem Tax on Personalty. Personalty can be defined as all assets that are not realty. At the outset, it may be well to make the distinction between the classification of an asset (i. e., realty or personalty) and the use to which it is placed. Both realty and personalty can be either business use or personal use property. Examples of this distinction include a residence (realty that is personal use), an office building (realty that is business use), surgical instruments (personalty that is business use), and regular wearing apparel (personalty that is personal use).[10]

Personalty can be also classified as tangible property or intangible property. For ad valorem tax purposes, intangible personalty includes stocks, bonds, and various other securities (e. g., bank shares).

Generalizations concerning the ad valorem tax on personalty are listed below:

—Particularly with personalty devoted to personal use (e. g., jewelry, household furnishings) taxpayer compliance ranges from poor to zero. In some jursidictions, enforcement of the tax on these items is not even attempted. In the case of automobiles devoted to personal use, many jurisdictions have converted from value as the tax base to arbitrary license fees based on the weight of the vehicle. Recently, some jurisdictions are taking into consideration the age factor (e. g., automobiles six years or older are not subject to the ad valorem tax as they are presumed to have little, if any, value).

—In the case of personalty devoted to business use (e. g., inventories, trucks, machinery, equipment) taxpayer compliance and enforcement procedures are measurably better.

—Assessed values of personalty may run lower than in the case of realty.

—Which jurisdiction possesses the authority to tax movable personalty (e. g., railroad rolling stock) always has been and continues to be a troublesome issue.

—The ad valorem tax on intangibles, although it still exists in some jurisdictions, largely has fallen into disfavor. Undoubtedly the lack of effective enforcement capability on the part of

10. The distinction, important for ad valorem and for Federal income tax purposes, becomes confused when personalty often is referred to as "personal" property to distinguish it from "real" property. Obviously, such designation does not give a complete picture of what is involved. The description "personal" residence, however, is clearer since one can identify a residence as being realty. What is meant, in this case, is realty that is personal use property.

the taxing authorities has contributed to this decline in use. As in the case of jewelry, ownership of stocks and bonds is information that is difficult to obtain without a substantial investment of time and money. In many cases, this use of time and money is not warranted by the revenue generated from the tax on intangibles.

TRANSACTION TAXES

Characteristically imposed at the manufacturer's, wholesaler's, or retailer's level, transaction taxes cover a wide range of transfers. Like many other types of taxes (e. g., income taxes, death taxes, and gift taxes), transaction taxes usually are not peculiarly within the exclusive province of any level of taxing authority (i. e., Federal, state, local government). As the description implies, these levies place a tax on the transfers of property and normally are determined by a percentage rate multiplied by the value involved.

Federal Excise Taxes. Long one of the mainstays of the Federal tax system, Federal excise taxes had declined in relative importance until recently. It may be that the trend is changing, however, with the enactment of the Crude Oil Windfall Profit Tax Act of 1980. (This legislation imposes a temporary excise tax on the production of domestic crude oil after February 29, 1980.) Furthermore, in late 1982 Congress substantially increased the Federal excise taxes on such items as tobacco products, fuel and gasoline sales, telephone usage, and air travel passenger tickets. Other Federal excise taxes include:[11]

—Manufacturers' excise taxes on trucks, trailers, tires, firearms, sporting equipment, coal, and the gas guzzler tax on automobiles.[12]

—Alcohol taxes.

—Miscellaneous taxes (e.g., the tax on wagering).

The list of transactions covered, although seemingly impressive, has diminished over the years. At one time, for example, there was a Federal excise tax on admission to amusement facilities (e. g., theaters) and on the sale of such "luxury" items as leather goods, furs, jewelry, and cosmetics.

When reviewing the list of both Federal and state excise taxes, one should recognize the possibility that the tax laws may be trying

---

11. Most excise taxes are contained in § § 4041–4998 of the Internal Revenue Code of 1954. Alcohol and tobacco taxes, however, are in § § 5001–5872. The Crude Oil Windfall Profit Tax Act of 1980 was incorporated in new § § 4986–4998. See Chapter 3 for an explanation of how provisions of the Internal Revenue Code of 1954 are cited.
12. The gas guzzler tax is imposed on the manufacturers of automobiles and progresses in amount as the mileage ratings per gallon of gas decrease. See § 4064.

to influence social behavior. Quite obviously, for example, the gas guzzler tax is intended as an incentive for the automobile companies to build cars that are fuel efficient. Since alcohol and tobacco are considered by many to be harmful to a person's health, why not increase their cost with the imposition of excise taxes and thereby discourage their use? Unfortunately, there exists little evidence to support a high level of correlation between the imposition of an excise tax and consumer behavior. This is particularly true where the rate of the excise tax is modest and the demand for the commodity being taxed is relatively inelastic.

State Excise Taxes. Many state and local excise taxes parallel the Federal version. Thus, all states tax the sale of gasoline, liquor, and tobacco products; however, the rates vary significantly. In the case of gasoline products, for example, compare the 18 cents per gallon imposed by the state of Washington with the 5 cents per gallon levied by the state of Texas. For tobacco sales, contrast the two cents per pack of cigarettes in effect in North Carolina with the 26 cents per pack applicable in Massachusetts. In the latter situation, is it surprising that the smuggling of cigarettes from North Carolina for resale elsewhere is so widespread? Here might be a situation where an excise tax probably encourages criminal conduct more than it discourages consumer use.

Other excise taxes found at some state and local levels include those on admission to amusement facilities, hotel occupancy and the rental of various other facilities, the sale of playing cards and oleomargarine products, and the sale of prepared foods. Most states impose a transaction tax on the transfer of property that requires the recording of documents (e. g., real estate sales).[13] Some extend the tax to the transfer of stocks and other securities.

General Sales Taxes. The distinction between an excise tax and a general sales tax is easy to make. One is restricted to a particular transaction (e. g., the 9 cents per gallon Federal excise tax on the sale of gasoline), while the other covers a multitude of transactions (e. g., a 5 percent tax on *all* retail sales). In actual practice, however, the distinction is not always that clear. Some state statutes might exempt certain transactions from the application of the general sales taxes (e. g., sales of food to be consumed off the premises, sales of certain medicines and drugs). Also, it is not uncommon to find that rates vary depending on the commodity involved. In many states, for example, preferential rates are allowed for the sale of agricultural equipment or different rates (either higher or lower than the general rate) apply to the sale of automobiles. With many of these special exceptions and classifications of rates, a general sales tax can take on the appearance

---

13. This type of tax has much in common with the stamp tax levied by Great Britain on the American colonies during the pre-Revolutionary period in U. S. history.

of a collection of individual excise taxes. As noted in Chapter 11, the distinction is very important for Federal income tax purposes. General sales taxes on the purchase of property intended for personal use are normally deductible, while excise taxes usually are not.

State general sales taxes range from a low of 2 percent in Oklahoma to a high of 7.5 percent in Connecticut. Every state that imposes a general sales tax levied on the consumer also has a use tax. The states without either tax are Alaska, Delaware, Montana, New Hampshire, and Oregon.

To prevent the avoidance of a sales tax, a use tax is a necessary complement.

> **Example 3.** T resides in a jurisdiction that imposes a 5% general sales tax but lives near a state that has no tax at all. T purchases for $10,000 an automobile from a dealer located in the neighboring state. Has T saved $500 in sales taxes? The state use tax is designed to pick up the difference between the tax paid in another jurisdiction and what would have been paid in the state where T resides.

The use tax may be difficult to enforce for many purchases and is, therefore, often avoided. In the case of an automobile (see Example 3), however, it probably would be imposed when T registers the car in his or her home state.

Local general sales taxes, over and above those levied by the state, are common. It is not unusual to find taxpayers living in the same state who pay different general sales taxes due to the situs of their residence.

> **Example 4.** R and S, two individuals, both live in a state that has a general sales tax of 3%. S, however, resides in a city that imposes an additional general sales tax of 2%. In spite of the fact that R and S live in the same state, one is subject to a rate of 3% while the other pays a tax of 5%.

The existence of a local (e. g., city, county) sales tax becomes important when working with the Optional State Sales Tax Tables (see Appendix A–3) issued by the IRS. These tables, discussed in Chapter 11, provide a way to determine the sales tax deduction a taxpayer may be entitled to for Federal income tax purposes.

Severance Taxes. An important source of revenue for many states is derived from severance taxes. These transaction taxes are based on the notion that the state has an interest in its natural resources (e. g., oil, gas, iron ore, coal), and therefore, their extraction is an occasion for the imposition of a tax.

DEATH TAXES

A death tax is a tax on the right to transfer property or to receive property upon the death of the owner. Consequently, a death tax falls into the category of an excise tax. If the death tax is imposed on the right to pass property at death, it is classified as an estate tax. If it taxes the right to receive property from a decedent, it is termed an inheritance tax. Typical of other types of excise taxes, the value of the property transferred measures the base for determining the amount of the death tax.

Of the two, inheritance tax and estate tax, the Federal government imposes only an estate tax. State governments, however, levy inheritance taxes, estate taxes, or both.

> **Example 5.** At the time of her death, D lived in a state that imposes an inheritance tax but not an estate tax. S, one of D's heirs, also lives in the same state. D's estate would be subject to the Federal estate tax while S would be subject to the state inheritance tax.

The Federal Estate Tax. The Revenue Act of 1916 incorporated the estate tax into the tax law. Although never designed to generate a large source of revenue, its original purpose was to prevent large concentrations of wealth from being kept within the family for many generations. Whether this objective has been accomplished is debatable. Like the income tax, estate taxes can be reduced significantly through various planning procedures.

The scheme of the Federal estate tax is outlined below:

The gross estate[14]	$ x,xxx,xxx
Less: Deductions[15]	xx,xxx
The taxable estate	$ xxx,xxx
Add: Taxable gifts made after 1976	xx,xxx
The tax base	$ xxx,xxx
Estate tax as derived from the tax rates[16]	$ xx,xxx
Less: Tax credits[17]	x,xxx
Estate tax due	$ x,xxx

The gross estate includes property the decedent owned at the time of death. It also includes life insurance proceeds when paid to

---

14. The relevant portions of the Internal Revenue Code of 1954 dealing with the gross estate are § § 2031–2046.

15. See § § 2051–2056.

16. § 2001(c) contains the tax rates applicable to the estate tax. The rates are progressive and for 1984 range from 18% on a tax base of less than $10,000 to 55%, on a base of over $3,000,000.

17. The credits allowed can be found in § § 2010–2016.

the estate or when paid to a beneficiary other than the estate if the deceased-insured had any ownership rights in the policy. Property owned jointly with others may or may not be included in the gross estate depending on the type of ownership and whether husband and wife are involved.[18] Quite simply, the gross estate represents property interests subject to Federal estate taxation.

All property included in the gross estate is valued as of the date of death or, if the alternate valuation date is elected, six months later.[19]

> **Example 6.** At the time of his death in 1984, D owned the following assets:

	Fair Market Value (on date of death)
Personal and household effects	$ 10,000
Personal residence (original cost of $40,000)	150,000
Stock investments (original cost of $100,000)	80,000
Insurance policy on D's life with S as the designated beneficiary (the policy had a cash surrender value of $20,000 and a maturity value of $100,000)[20]	100,000

In addition, D had made a taxable gift of $20,000 in cash two years prior to death on which no gift tax was due or paid. Presuming the alternate valuation date is not elected, D's gross estate is $340,000 [$10,000 (personal and household effects) + $150,000 (personal residence) + $80,000 (stock investments) + $100,000 (proceeds of life insurance)]. The taxable gift of $20,000 is added to the taxable estate in arriving at the tax base for applying the estate tax rates. Thus, the tax is applied to transfers during the transferor's life plus transfers at death.

Deductions from the gross estate in arriving at the taxable estate include funeral and administration expenses, certain taxes, debts of the decedent, casualty losses[21] incurred during the administration of the estate, transfers to charitable organizations, and in some cases, the marital deduction. The marital deduction is available for amounts actually passing to a surviving spouse (i. e., a widow or widower).

---

18. For further information on these matters see *West's Federal Taxation: Corporations, Partnerships, Estates, and Trusts,* Chapter 10.
19. See the discussion of the alternate valuation date in Chapter 14.
20. The cash surrender value of life insurance is the amount the owner of the policy could obtain upon surrendering it to the insurance company. The maturity value (or face amount) is the amount the insurance company is obligated to pay the beneficiary upon the death of the insured.
21. For a definition of casualty losses, see the Glossary of Tax Terms in Appendix C.

Example 7. At the time of his death, H had a gross estate of $1,000,000. H's will passes $300,000 of this property to W (the surviving spouse). Even though the maximum marital deduction that could have been allowed his estate is $1,000,000, the deduction will be limited to $300,000, since this is all that passes from H to W.

Once the taxable estate has been determined and certain taxable gifts are added thereto, the estate tax can be computed. From the amount derived from the appropriate tax rate schedules, various credits should be subtracted to arrive at what, if any, tax is due.[22] Although many other credits also are available, probably the most significant one is the unified transfer tax credit. The main reason for this credit is to eliminate or reduce the estate tax liability for modest estates. For deaths during 1984, the amount of the credit is $96,300. Based on the estate tax rates, the amount of the credit covers a tax base of $325,000.

Example 8. D has never made any taxable gifts prior to his death in 1984. If D dies with a taxable estate of $325,000 or less, no Federal estate tax will be due because of the application of the unified transfer tax credit.[23]

Another credit that is allowed for Federal estate tax purposes is the credit for state death taxes. As noted in Chapter 2, the reason for the credit is to mitigate the effect of double taxation on the same estate (i. e., the imposition of the Federal estate tax as well as a state death tax). The credit allowed is the lesser of the amount actually paid or the amount derived from a schedule contained in the Internal Revenue Code.[24] It could be, therefore, that the credit proves to be less than the amount paid to the state in the form of a death tax. To avoid the imposition of double taxation, a credit against the estate tax liability is permitted for any transfers previously subject to a gift tax which are included in the tax base (i. e., taxable gifts made after 1976).

Example 9. In 1978 D made a taxable gift of $50,000 upon which she paid a Federal gift tax of $10,000. D dies in 1984 leaving a gross estate of $700,000 and a taxable estate of $600,000. As noted earlier, the $50,000 is added to her taxable estate in arriving at the tax base for Federal estate tax purposes. More-

---

22. For tax purposes it always is crucial to appreciate the difference between a deduction and a credit. A credit is a dollar-for-dollar reduction of tax liability. A deduction, however, only benefits the taxpayer to the extent of his or her tax bracket. An estate in a 50% tax bracket, for example, would need $2 of deductions to prevent $1 of tax liability from developing. In contrast, $1 of credit neutralizes $1 of tax liability.

23. Under § 2001(c), the estate tax on a taxable estate of $325,000 is $70,800 plus 34% of the amount over $250,000. Thus, $70,800 + (34% × $75,000) = $96,300.

24. § 2011(b).

over, D's estate is allowed a $10,000 credit for the Federal gift tax previously paid. This means that whatever tax liability the unified transfer tax rates yields is reduced by $10,000.

State Death Taxes.   As noted earlier, states usually levy an inheritance tax, an estate tax, or both. The difference between the two forms of death taxes depends upon whom the tax is imposed (i. e., the heir or the estate).

Characteristically, an inheritance tax divides the heirs into classes based on their relationship to the decedent. The more closely related the heir, the lower the rates imposed and the greater the exemption allowed.

Example 10.   A particular inheritance tax has the following classes, exemptions, and rates:

	Exemption	Rates
Class A. Surviving spouse, lineal descendants, and lineal ascendants.[25]	$ 25,000	1%–6%
Class B. Brothers, sisters, nephews, and nieces.	10,000	3%–9%
Class C. Uncles, aunts, and cousins.	1,000	4%–15%
Class D. Others (e. g., unrelated)	500	5%–20%

Some inheritance taxes provide for a limited exclusion for life insurance proceeds (usually $40,000) not payable to the estate. Some exempt or provide for partial exclusion of property jointly owned with a surviving spouse. Most state statutes provide for special treatment of gifts made by the decedent within three years of his or her death. Such gifts may or may not be subject to the inheritance tax, depending on the motivation prompting the gift. States with inheritance taxes are about equally divided as to whether an alternate valuation date is permitted in valuing the property subject to tax.

State estate taxes fall into one of two patterns. One form follows much the same approach found in the Federal estate tax. Thus, the gross estate is reduce by such items as the marital deduction, charitable transfers, and other specified deductions. A tax then is imposed on the taxable estate. In most cases, the applicable tax rates are significantly lower than those prescribed for the Federal estate tax.

The more typical type of state estate tax, and the one that seems to be the current trend, often is referred to as a "sponge" tax. Under this version of a death tax, the estate merely remits to the state whatever amount qualifies for the maximum state death tax credit allowed for Federal estate tax purposes.

---

25.   Lineal descendants include sons, daughters, grandchildren, etc. Lineal ascendants include father, mother, grandparents, etc.

Example 11. D's taxable estate is $840,000. If D resided in a state that imposes an estate tax based on the Federal state death tax credit, the state death tax would be $27,600.[26]

States that impose an inheritance tax often have an estate tax to insure that they receive the maximum allowed to the estate as a Federal credit.

Example 12. Assume the same facts as in Example 11 except that D resided in a state that imposes an inheritance tax and an estate tax (i. e., the "sponge" variety). Further assume that the sum of all the inheritance taxes levied on the heirs equals only $25,000. The state estate tax would require that D's estate remit an additional $2,600 to the state, since $27,600 is the amount allowed as the Federal state death tax credit.

GIFT TAXES

Like a death tax, a gift tax is an excise tax levied on the right to transfer property. In this case, however, the tax is directed to transfers made during the owner's life and not at death. Also, a gift tax applies only to transfers that are not supported by full and adequate consideration.

Example 13. D sells to his daughter property worth $20,000 for $1,000. Although property worth $20,000 has been transferred, only $19,000 represents a gift, since this is the portion not supported by full and adequate consideration.

The Federal Gift Tax. First enacted in 1932, the purpose of the Federal gift tax was to complement the estate tax. Without any tax applicable to lifetime transfers by gift, it would be possible, of course, to avoid the estate tax and escape taxation entirely.

Only taxable gifts are subject to the gift tax. For this purpose, a taxable gift is measured by the fair market value of the property on the date of transfer less the annual exclusion of $10,000 per donee and, in some cases, less the marital deduction, which allows tax-free transfers between spouses.[27] Each donor is allowed an annual exclusion of $10,000 for each donee.[28]

Example 14. On December 31, 1984, D (a widow) gives $10,000 to each of her four married children (and their spouses) and her eight grandchildren. On January 3, 1985, she repeats the same

---

26. The $27,600 is the amount allowed by the schedule contained in § 2011(b).

27. The marital deduction is available for gifts between husband and wife.

28. § 2503(b). The purpose of the annual exclusion is to avoid the need of having to report and pay a tax on "modest" gifts. As noted in Chapter 2, the absence of the exclusion could create for the Internal Revenue Service a real problem of taxpayer noncompliance.

procedure. Although D transferred $160,000 [$10,000 × 16 (number of donees)] in 1984 and $160,000 [$10,000 × 16 (number of donees)] in 1985 for a total of $320,000 ($160,000 + $160,000), she has not made a taxable gift.

Once a taxable gift has been made, the cumulative nature of the gift tax requires a special procedure to be followed in determining the current tax. This procedure is as follows:

Taxable gifts in the current year	$ xx,xxx
Add: All taxable gifts in past years	xx,xxx
Total of *all* taxable gifts	$ xxx,xxx
Gift tax on *all* taxable gifts as derived from the tax rates[29]	$ xx,xxx
Less: Gift taxes previously paid[30]	xxx
Gift tax due on current gifts	$ x,xxx

Due to the progressive nature of the tax rates, every subsequent taxable gift places the donor in a higher tax bracket.

Example 15. In 1983, D makes a taxable gift of $250,000 upon which she pays a gift tax of $70,800. In 1984, D makes another taxable gift of $250,000. In determining the gift tax liability for the 1984 transfer, proceed as follows:[31]

Gift tax on $500,000 as derived from the tax rates	$ 155,800
Less: Gift tax paid on the 1983 transfer	70,800
Gift tax due on the 1984 transfer	$ 85,000

Although both gifts were of the same amount (i. e., $250,000), the second gift resulted in a greater gift tax liability by $14,200 ($85,000 − $70,800).

For all taxable gifts made after 1976, the unified transfer tax credit is available. As was true with the Federal estate tax, the

---

29. For taxable gifts made after 1976, the gift tax rate schedule is the same as that applicable to the estate tax. The schedule commonly is referred to as "the unified transfer tax schedule."

30. A special adjustment may be necessary for the gift tax paid on pre-1977 taxable gifts. For further information on this and other matters regarding the Federal gift tax, see *West's Federal Taxation: Corporations, Partnerships, Estates, and Trusts,* Chapter 11.

31. These computations disregard the effect of the unified transfer tax credit.

amount of this credit for 1984 is $96,300.[32] There is, however, only one unified transfer tax credit, and it applies both to taxable gifts and to the Federal estate tax. In a manner of speaking, therefore, once it has been exhausted for Federal gift tax purposes, it is no longer available to insulate a decedent from the Federal estate tax.

A special election applicable to married persons allows one-half of the gift made by the donor-spouse to be treated as being made by the nondonor-spouse.[33] The effect of this election to split the gifts of property made to third persons is to increase the number of annual exclusions available, to allow the use of the nondonor-spouse's unified transfer tax credit, and possibly to lower the tax brackets that will apply.

> **Example 16.** Assume the same facts as in Example 14 except that D is not a widow but is married to H. If H agrees to split any gifts made by D, she could double the amount given each year without making any taxable gifts. Since both D and H would be treated as donors, the annual exclusion per donee becomes $20,000 instead of $10,000.

By now it should be apparent that taxable gifts made after 1976 are subject to the same set of tax rates and the same unified transfer tax credit as applicable to the estate tax.[34] Also, such gifts affect the computation of the estate tax liability, since they have to be added to the tax base.

In the light of these considerations, is there any advantage of making lifetime transfers by gift? The answer has to be *yes* if the following points are kept in mind:

—Only some or none of the gift may be taxable. In making full use of the annual exclusion, consider Examples 14 and 16. How much could be gifted free of any gift tax over a 10-year period?

—Give property that is expected to appreciate in value. A gift of real estate that is worth $50,000 today may be worth $500,000 when the donor dies 10 years later. Compare a gift tax liability on $50,000 with an estate tax liability on $500,000.[35] Besides real estate, other items that can be expected to appreciate in

---

32. The unified transfer tax credit, for both estate and gift taxes, is scheduled to increase to $121,800 in 1985. Other annual increases are prescribed until the credit reaches $192,800 in 1987. The effect of the credit is to exempt transfers from the unified transfer tax. The exemption equivalent of the $192,800 credit is $600,000. As a result, it is expected that fewer taxpayers will be subject to the unified transfer tax when the increase in the credit is fully implemented. §§ 2010 and 2505.
33. § 2513.
34. Before 1977, gifts were subject to a separate set of tax rates which were lower than those applicable to the estate tax. Also, every donor was entitled to a $30,000 specific exemption to cover gifts made in excess of the annual exclusion.
35. One must, however, take into account the time value of any gift tax that has to be paid.

value include antiques, works of art, coin and stamp collections, and life insurance.[36]

—A gift of property normally shifts future income therefrom to the donee. This would be advantageous for income tax purposes if the donee is in a lower tax bracket than the donor.

—All states except Nevada impose some type of state death tax, while only a few impose a state gift tax (see the discussion below). Thus, a gift may escape any state transfer tax.

State Gift Taxes. The states imposing a state gift tax are Delaware, Louisiana, New York, North Carolina, Oregon, Rhode Island, South Carolina, Tennessee, and Wisconsin.

Most of these laws provide for lifetime exemptions and annual exclusions. Like the Federal gift tax, the state taxes are cumulative in effect. But unlike the Federal version, the amount of tax depends on the relationship between the donor and the donee. Like state inheritance taxes, larger exemptions and lower rates apply when the donor and donee are closely related to each other.

INCOME TAXES

Income taxes are levied by the Federal government, most states, and some local governments. Needless to say, the trend in recent years has been to place greater reliance on this method of taxation. The trend is not consistent with what is happening in other countries, and in this sense, our system of taxation is somewhat different.

At least in the Common Market countries of Western Europe, the value-added tax (i. e., VAT) has gained acceptance as a major source of revenue. Although variously classified, VAT seems more like a national sales tax, since it taxes the increment in value as goods move through production and manufacturing stages to the marketplace. VAT has its proponents in the United States as a partial solution to high Federal income tax rates and increases in employment taxes. Its incorporation as part of our tax system in the near future is, however, problematical.

Income taxes generally are imposed on individuals, corporations, and certain fiduciaries (estates and trusts). Most jurisdictions attempt to assure their collection by requiring certain pay-as-you-go procedures (e. g., withholding requirements as to employees and estimated tax prepayments for other taxpayers).

On occasion, Congress has seen fit to impose additional taxes on income. Such impositions were justified either by economic considera-

---

36. The value of a life insurance policy that has not matured usually is its interpolated terminal reserve (i. e., approximately the cash surrender value). This should be compared to its value upon maturity (i. e., at the death of the insured) which normally would be the amount subject to the Federal estate tax.

tions or by special circumstances resulting from wartime conditions.[37] During the period from April 1, 1968, to July 1, 1970, for example, taxpayers were subject to a surcharge of 10 percent of the amount of their regular income tax liability. This led to the strange result that taxpayers had to pay, so to speak, an income tax on their income tax. The justification for the special tax was to place restraints on what was regarded as an overactive economy, to curtail inflation, and to reduce the Federal deficit. In the light of current budget deficits, the surcharge approach has its advocates in Congress and therefore may be of more than historical interest.[38]

Federal Income Taxes. Chapters 4 through 19 deal with the application of the Federal income tax to individuals. The procedure for determining the Federal income tax applicable to individuals is summarized in Figure II.

Figure II

Income (broadly conceived)	$ xx,xxx
Less: Exclusions (income that is not subject to tax)	x,xxx
Gross income (income that is subject to tax)	$ xx,xxx
Less: Business deductions (usually referred to as deductions *for* adjusted gross income)	x,xxx
Adjusted gross income	$ xx,xxx
Less: Certain personal deductions (usually referred to as *itemized deductions* or as deductions *from* adjusted gross income) in excess of the zero bracket amount	x,xxx
Personal and dependency exemptions	x,xxx
Taxable income	$ x,xxx
Tax on taxable income (see tax rate schedules or table in Appendix A)	$ xxx
Less: Tax credits (including Federal income tax withheld and other prepayments of Federal income taxes)	xxx
Tax due (or refund)	$ xx

As explained in Chapter 4, the zero bracket amount represents a deduction allowed to every taxpayer and varies from $3,400 allowed to married persons filing together (i. e., joint return) to $1,700 for married persons filing apart (i. e., separate returns), with $2,300 per-

---

37. During World War II and the Korean conflict, an excess-profits tax was imposed in addition to the regular Federal income tax. The tax was aimed at the profiteering that occurs when the economy is geared to the production of war materials.

38. The advantage of the surcharge approach is that it represents a temporary solution to the problem. Thus, the tax can be imposed on a one-shot basis without compelling Congress to modify the regular income tax rates.

mitted for single (unmarried) taxpayers. (Note: The zero bracket amount has not been separately deducted in Figure II, since the Tax Table and the Tax Rate Schedules are structured such that the respective amounts are taken into account.) The personal exemptions are $1,000 apiece and are allowed for the taxpayer and spouse, for age (65 or over), and for blindness. An exemption of $1,000 is allowed for each dependent of the taxpayer. Both personal and dependency exemptions are explained in Chapter 4.

The rules for the application of the Federal corporate income tax do not require the computation of adjusted gross income and do not provide for the zero bracket amount and personal and dependency exemptions. All allowable deductions of a corporation fall into the business-expense category. In effect, therefore, the taxable income of a corporation is the difference between gross income (net of exclusions) and deductions.

Once the taxable income of a corporation is determined, however, any income tax liability is computed under a set of rates separate from those applicable to individuals. But unlike the tax rates that apply to individuals, the corporate tax rates are progressive only to a mild extent. The rates applicable to 1984 are as follows:[39]

Rate Applicable	Amount of Taxable Income
15%	first $25,000
18	above $25,000 to $50,000
30	above $50,000 to $75,000
40	above $75,000 to $100,000
46	over $100,000

Chapter 20 summarizes the rules relating to corporations. For an in-depth treatment of the Federal income tax as it affects corporations, estates, and trusts, see *West's Federal Taxation: Corporations, Partnerships, Estates, and Trusts,* 1985 Edition, Chapters 2 through 5, 7, and 13.

State Income Taxes. All but the following states impose an income tax on individuals: Alaska, Florida, Nevada, South Dakota, Texas, Washington, and Wyoming. New Hampshire and Tennessee have an income tax, but its application is limited to dividend and interest income.

Some of the characteristics of state income taxes are summarized below:

—With few exceptions, all states require some form of withholding procedures.

—Most states use as the tax base the income determination made for Federal income tax purposes.

---

39. § 11(b).

—A minority of states go even further and impose a flat rate upon adjusted gross income (AGI) as computed for Federal income tax purposes. Several apply a rate to the Federal income tax liability.[40]

—Because of the tie-in to the Federal return, notification to the state of any changes made by the IRS upon audit of a Federal return usually is required.

—Most states allow a deduction for personal and dependency exemptions. Some states substitute a tax credit for a deduction.

—A diminishing minority of states allows a deduction for Federal income taxes.

—Most states allow their residents some form of tax credit for income taxes paid to other states.

—The due date for filing generally is the same as that for the Federal income tax (i. e., the fifteenth day of the fourth month following the close of the tax year).

Nearly all states have an income tax applicable to corporations. It is difficult to determine those that do not, because a state franchise tax sometimes is based in part on the income earned by the corporation.[41]

Corporations that do business or derive income from more than one state could be subject to multiple taxation of the same income or, in some cases, to no taxation at all. To the extent that income and expenses cannot be specifically allocated to sources within any one state, it may be necessary to apportion these items among the states involved. Passive income (e. g., rents, dividends, gains from the sales of investments, interest) that is not considered business income usually is assigned for tax purposes to the state where such income-producing property is located. Business income may be allocated for income taxation among the various states based on a percentage of property owned in the state, on the amount of payroll there, on sales within the state, or on some other reasonable basis.

A related problem arises when a state imposes an income tax on multinational corporations. Known as the unitary tax, the base for the imposition of the tax is founded upon the total income of the corporation from both U. S. and international operations. Again, the major problem arising with this form of taxation rests with how this income is to be allocated to the state imposing the tax.

Local Income Taxes. Cities imposing an income tax include, but are not limited to, Baltimore, Cincinnati, Cleveland, Detroit, Kansas City (Mo.), New York, Philadelphia, and St. Louis.

---

40. This is often referred to as the piggyback approach to state income taxation. Although the term "piggyback" does not lend itself to precise definition, in this sense it means making use, for state income tax purposes, of what was done for Federal income tax purposes.

41. See the discussion of franchise taxes later in the chapter.

EMPLOYMENT TAXES

Classification as an employee usually leads to the imposition of employment taxes and to the requirement that the employer withhold specified amounts for income taxes. The rules governing the withholding for income taxes are discussed in Chapter 12. The material that follows concentrates on the two major employment taxes: FICA (Federal Insurance Contributions Act—commonly referred to as the Social Security tax) and FUTA (Federal Unemployment Tax Act). Both taxes can be justified by social and public welfare considerations: FICA offers some measure of retirement security, while FUTA provides a modest source of income in the event of loss of employment.

Employment taxes come into play only if two conditions are satisfied. First, is the individual involved an "employee" (as opposed to "self-employed")? The difference between an employee and a self-employed person is discussed in Chapter 10.[42] Second, if the individual involved is an employee, is he or she covered under FICA or FUTA? The coverage of both of these taxes is summarized in Figure III in Chapter 12.[43]

FICA Taxes. The tax rates and wage base under FICA are not constant, and as reflected in Figure III below, the increases over the years are quite apparent.[44]

Figure III

FICA RATES AND BASE

Year	Percent	Base Amount	Maximum Tax
1978	6.05%	$ 17,700	$ 1,070.85
1979	6.13%	22,900	1,403.77
1980	6.13%	25,900	1,587.67
1981	6.65%	29,700	1,975.05
1982	6.70%	32,400	2,170.80
1983	6.70%	35,700	2,391.90
1984	6.70%	37,800	2,532.60
1985	7.05%	—*	—**
1986–87	7.15%	—	—
1988–89	7.15%	—	—
1990 on	7.65%	—	—

* Not yet determined by Congress
** Cannot be computed until the wage base is set by Congress

For 1984 only, the rate is 7 percent but the employee is allowed a credit of 0.3 percent, which is to be taken into account in withholding

---

42. See also Circular E, Employer's Tax Guide, issued by the IRS as Publication 15.
43. Chapter 12 deals with the self-employment tax (i. e., the Social Security version of FICA for self-employed persons).
44. The provisions of the Internal Revenue Code dealing with FICA are contained in §§ 3101–3126.

the tax. Thus, the employer's portion is 7 percent, while the employee pays an effective rate of 6.7 percent ($7\% - 0.3\%$).

In at least two situations it is possible for an employee to have paid excess FICA taxes.

> **Example 17.** During 1984, T changed employers in the middle of the year, and from each job he earned $30,000 (all of which was subject to FICA). As a result, each employer withheld $2,010 ($6.7\% \times \$30,000$) for a total of $4,020. Since T has overpaid his share of the FICA taxes by $1,487.40 [$4,020 (amount paid) − $2,532.60 (maximum tax from Figure III)] he should claim this amount as a tax credit when filing an income tax return for 1984.[45]

> **Example 18.** During 1984, E earned $30,000 from her regular job and $10,000 from a part-time job (all of which was subject to FICA). As a result, one employer withheld $2,010 ($6.7\% \times \$30,000$), while the other employer withheld $670 ($6.7\% \times \$10,000$) for a total of $2,680. Since E has overpaid her share of the FICA taxes by $147.40 ($2,680 − $2,532.60), she should claim this amount as a tax credit when filing an income tax return for 1984.

In both Examples 17 and 18 it was not possible for the employee to prevent the overwithholding from taking place. In both cases, however, the employee was able to obtain a credit for the excess withheld. The same result does not materialize as to the portion paid by the employer. Since this amount is not refundable, it leads to a situation where employers pay more FICA taxes than the covered employees.

The mere fact that a husband and wife both are employed does not, by itself, result in overwithholding of FICA taxes.[46]

> **Example 19.** During 1984, H and W (husband and wife) both are employed and each earns wages subject to FICA of $20,000. Accordingly, each has FICA withheld of $1,340 [$6.7\% \times \$20,000$ (wages earned)] for a total of $2,680. Since neither spouse paid FICA in excess of $2,532.60 (see Figure III), there is no overwithholding.

The frequency with which an employer must make payments to the IRS depends on the monthly total of three items: income tax withheld from the employees, FICA taxes withheld from the employees, and the employer's matching share of the FICA taxes. But regardless of whether or not monthly deposits are required, each employer must

---

45. The effect of a tax credit would be to reduce any income tax T might owe or, possibly, to generate a tax refund.

46. However, if a spouse works for his or her spouse, none of the amounts paid are subject to either FICA or FUTA.

file a Form 941, Employer's Quarterly Federal Tax Return, on a quarterly basis.[47] It is important that Form 941 contain the employer's identification number.[48]

The failure to make deposits and to file required employment tax returns on time could result in the imposition by the IRS of various penalties. Additionally, employers are liable for any taxes that should have been, but were not, withheld from their employees.[49]

FUTA Taxes. The purpose of FUTA is to provide funds that the states can use to administer unemployment benefits. This leads to the somewhat unusual situation of one tax being handled by both Federal and state governments. The end product of such joint administration is to compel the employer to observe a double set of rules. Thus, state and Federal returns must be filed and payments made to both governmental units.

FUTA applies at a rate of 3.5 percent on the first $7,000 of covered wages paid during the year to each employee.[50] The Federal government allows a credit for FUTA paid (or allowed under a merit rating system) to the state. The credit cannot exceed 2.7 percent of the covered wages. Thus, the amount required to be paid to the IRS could be as low as 0.8 percent (i. e., 3.5 percent − 2.7 percent).

States follow a policy of reducing the unemployment tax on employers who experience stability in employment. Thus, an employer with little or no turnover among employees might find that the state rate could drop as low as 0.1 percent or, in some states, even to zero. The reason for the merit rating credit is obvious. Steady employment means the state will have lower unemployment benefits to pay.

FUTA is to be distinguished from FICA in the sense that the incidence of taxation falls entirely upon the employer. A few states, however, levy a special tax on employees either to provide disability benefits or supplemental unemployment compensation, or both.

Also distinguishable from FUTA are various union-negotiated plans funded by employers that provide for additional or extended unemployment compensation to workers that have been laid off. Common in certain seasonal industries (e. g., automobile production), these plans are not part of the tax structure but are private sector compensation arrangements.

Every employer subject to FUTA must make an annual accounting to the IRS by filing Form 940, Employer's Annual Federal Unemployment Tax Return, on or before January 31 of the following year.

---

47. For further information on deposit and filing requirements, see Circular E (cited in Footnote 42).
48. An identification number is obtained by filing Form SS–4, Application for Employer Identification Number.
49. § 3403.
50. The provisions of the Internal Revenue Code dealing with FUTA are contained in § § 3301–3311.

The return should be accompanied by the portion of FUTA due and payable to the IRS. State filing and payment requirements also must be satisfied.

OTHER TAXES

In order to complete the overview of the U. S. tax system, some missing links need to be covered which do not fit into the classifications discussed elsewhere in this chapter.

Federal Customs Duties. One tax that has not yet been mentioned is the tariff on certain imported goods.[51] Generally referred to as customs duties or levies, this tax, together with selective excise taxes, provided most of the revenues needed by the Federal government during the nineteenth century and even to the advent of World War I in the early twentieth century. Considering present times, it is remarkable to note that tariffs and excise taxes alone paid off the national debt in 1835 and enabled the U. S. Treasury to pay a surplus of $28 million to the states.

In recent years, tariffs have served the nation more as an instrument for carrying out protectionist policies than as a means of generating revenue. Thus, a particular U. S. industry might be saved, so the argument goes, from economic disaster by placing customs duties on the importation of foreign goods that can be sold at lower prices. The protectionist would contend that the tariff, therefore, neutralizes the competitive edge held by the producer of the foreign goods.[52]

Miscellaneous State and Local Taxes. Most states impose a franchise tax on corporations. Basically, a franchise tax is one levied on the right to do business in the state. The base used for the determination of the tax, of course, varies from state to state. Although corporate income considerations may come into play, this tax most often is based on the capitalization of the corporation (either with or without certain long-term indebtedness).

Closely akin to the franchise tax are occupational taxes applicable to various trades or businesses: a liquor store license, for example, or a taxicab permit or a fee to practice the various professions (e. g., law, medicine, accounting). Most of these are not significant revenue producers and fall more into the category of licenses rather than taxes. The revenue derived is used to defray the cost incurred by the jurisdiction in regulating the business or profession in the interest of the public good.

---

51. Less-developed countries that place principal reliance on one or more major commodities (e. g., oil, coffee) are prone to favor *export* duties as well.

52. Protectionist policies seem more appropriate for less-developed countries whose industrial capacity has not yet matured. In a world where a developed country should have everything to gain from the encouragement of international free trade, such policies may be of dubious value. History proves that tariffs often lead to retaliatory action on the part of the nation(s) affected.

TAX ADMINISTRATION

INTERNAL REVENUE SERVICE

The responsibility for administering the Federal tax laws rests with the Treasury Department. Administratively, the IRS is part of the Department of the Treasury and is responsible for enforcing the tax laws.

The Commissioner of Internal Revenue is appointed by the President. His responsibilities are to establish policy and to supervise the activities of the entire IRS organization. The National Office organization of the IRS includes a Deputy Commissioner and several Assistant Commissioners who have supervisory responsibility over field operations.

The field organization of the IRS consists of the following:

—Service Centers (10) which are primarily responsible for processing tax returns, including the selection of returns for audit.

—District Directors (59) who perform audit work and are responsible for the collection of delinquent taxes.

—Regional Commissioners (7) who are responsible for the settlement of administrative appeals of disputed tax deficiencies.

THE AUDIT PROCESS

Selection of Returns for Audit. The IRS utilizes mathematical formulas and statistical sampling techniques to select tax returns which are most likely to contain errors and to yield substantial amounts of additional tax revenues upon audit.

Though the IRS does not openly disclose all of its audit selection techniques, the following observations may be made relative to the probability of selection for audit:

—Certain groups of taxpayers are subject to audit much more frequently than others. These groups include individuals with gross income in excess of $50,000, self-employed individuals with substantial business income and deductions, taxpayers with prior tax deficiencies, and cash businesses (e. g., cafes and small service businesses) where the potential for avoidance is high.

Example 20. T owns and operates a liquor store on a cash-and-carry basis. As all of T's sales are for cash, T might well be a prime candidate for an audit by the IRS. Obviously, cash transactions are easier to conceal than those made on credit.

—If information returns (e. g., Form 1099, Form W–2) are not in substantial agreement with reported income, an audit can be anticipated.

—If an individual's itemized deductions are in excess of norms established for various income levels, the probability of an audit is increased.

—Filing of a refund claim by the taxpayer may prompt an audit of the return.

—Certain returns are selected on a random sampling basis [known as the Taxpayer Compliance Measurement Program (TCMP)] to develop, update, and improve the mathematical formulas and statistical sampling techniques used by the IRS.

—Information obtained from other sources (e. g., informants, news items).

Example 21. After 15 years of service, F is discharged by her employer, Dr. T. Shortly thereafter, the IRS receives an anonymous letter informing them that Dr. T keeps two separate sets of books, one of which substantially understates his cash receipts.[53]

Example 22. During a divorce proceeding it is revealed that T, a public official, kept large amounts of cash in a shoe box at home. Such information is widely disseminated by the news media and comes to the attention of the IRS. Needless to say, the IRS would be interested in knowing whether such amounts originated from a taxable source and, if so, whether they were reported on T's income tax returns.

Types of Audits. Once a return is selected for audit, the taxpayer is notified accordingly. If the issue involved is minor, it may be that the matter can be resolved simply by correspondence between the IRS and the taxpayer.

Example 23. During 19X0, T received $340 in dividend income from Z Corporation. In early 19X1, Z Corporation reflected the payment on Form 1099DIV (an information return for the reporting of dividend payments), the original being sent to the IRS and a copy to T. When preparing his income tax return for 19X0, T apparently overlooked this particular Form 1099DIV and failed to include the dividend on Schedule B, Interest and Dividend Income, of Form 1040. In 19X2, the IRS sends a notice to T calling his attention to the omission and requesting a remittance of $110 in additional taxes and interest. T promptly mails a check to the IRS for $110 and the matter is closed.

---

53. The tax law permits the IRS to pay rewards to persons who provide information that leads to the detection and punishment of those who violate the tax laws. Such rewards may not exceed 10% of the taxes, fines, and penalties recovered as a result of such information. Code § 7623 and Reg. § 301.7623–1. For an explanation of a Reg. (i. e., U. S. Treasury Department Regulation) see Chapter 3.

Other examinations generally fall into the classification of either office audits or field audits. An office audit usually is restricted in scope and is conducted in the facilities of the IRS. By way of contrast, a field audit involves an examination of numerous items reported on the return and is conducted on the premises of the taxpayer or the taxpayer's representative.

Upon the conclusion of the audit, the examining agent issues a Revenue Agent's Report (i. e., RAR) which summarizes the findings. The RAR will result in a refund (the tax was overpaid), a deficiency (the tax was underpaid), or a "no change" (the tax was correct) finding.

Settlement Procedures. If an audit results in an assessment of additional tax and no settlement is reached with the IRS agent, the taxpayer may attempt to negotiate a settlement with the IRS. If an appeal is desired, an appropriate request must be made to the Appeals Division of the IRS. In some cases, a taxpayer may be able to obtain a percentage settlement or a favorable settlement of one or more disputed issues because the Appeals Division is authorized to settle all disputes based on the hazards of litigation (i. e., the probability of favorable resolution of the disputed issue or issues if litigated).

If a satisfactory settlement is not reached within the administrative appeal process, the taxpayer may wish to litigate the case in the Tax Court, a Federal District Court, or the Claims Court. It should be noted, however, that litigation should be recommended only as a last resort because of the legal costs involved and the uncertainties relative to the final outcome. Tax litigation considerations are discussed more fully in Chapter 3.

STATUTE OF LIMITATIONS

A statute of limitations is a provision in the law which offers a party a defense against a suit brought by another party after the expiration of a specified period of time. Found at the state and Federal levels, such statutes cover a multitude of suits, both civil and criminal.[54] For our purposes, the relevant statutes deal with the Federal income tax. The two categories involved cover both the period of limitations applicable to the assessment of additional tax deficiencies by the IRS and that dealing with claims for refunds by taxpayers.

Assessment by the IRS. Under the general rule, the IRS may assess (i. e., impose) an additional tax liability against a taxpayer within three years of the filing of the income tax return.[55]

---

54. The purpose of a statute of limitations is to preclude parties from prosecuting "stale" claims. The passage of time makes the defense of such claims difficult, since witnesses may no longer be available or evidence may have been lost or destroyed.
55. §§ 6501(a) and (b)(1).

Example 24. T, a calendar year taxpayer, files her income tax return for 19X2 on April 15, 19X3. In completing the return she inadvertently failed to report some interest income from a savings account. Pursuant to the general rule, T may prevent the IRS from assessing a tax on the omitted income any time after April 15, 19X6.

A special six-year period of limitations applies if, on a return, a taxpayer omits an amount of gross income which is in excess of 25 percent of the gross income reported on such return.[56]

Example 25. Assume the same facts as in Example 24 but with the following additional information:

Amount of gross income reported on the 19X2 return	$ 100,000
Amount of interest income inadvertently omitted from the return	26,000

Because T omitted more than 25 percent (i. e., $25,000) from the return, she now becomes subject to the six-year statute of limitations. Thus, she is not "safe" from an assessment of tax on the $26,000 of interest income not reported until after April 15, 19X9.

There is no statute of limitations on assessments of tax if no return is filed or if a fraudulent return is filed.[57]

Example 26. Assume the same facts as in Example 24 except that the omission of the interest income was not inadvertent but deliberate. Since the return was fraudulent, there is no restriction on when the IRS can tax the interest income.

Limitations on Refunds. If a taxpayer believes that an overpayment of Federal income tax was made, a claim for refund should be filed with the IRS. A claim for refund, therefore, is a request to the IRS that it return to the taxpayer the excessive income taxes paid.[58]

A claim for refund generally must be filed within three years from the date the return was filed or within two years from the date the tax was paid, whichever is later.[59] Income tax returns that are filed early are deemed to have been filed on the date the return was due.

Example 27. T, a calendar year taxpayer, files his 19X1 income tax return on March 2, 19X2, although the due date of the return is April 15, 19X2. T later discovers that he failed to include a

---

56. § 6501(e).

57. § 6501(c).

58. The forms to use in filing a claim for refund are discussed in Chapter 4.

59. § 6511(a).

$400 deduction on the return. Under these circumstances, T has through April 15, 19X5, in which to file a claim with the IRS to recover the taxes that would be saved by utilizing the $400 deduction.

INTEREST AND PENALTIES

From July 1, 1983, through June 30, 1984, interest accrues at the rate of 11 percent per year, compounded daily, on both assessments and refunds of income taxes.[60] In the case of assessments of additional taxes, the interest begins running on the unextended due date of the return. With refunds, however, no interest is allowed if the overpayment is refunded to the taxpayer within 45 days of the date the return is filed.[61] For this purpose, returns filed early are deemed to have been filed on the due date.

> **Example 28.** T, a calendar year taxpayer, files her income tax return for 19X0 on March 1, 19X1. T's return reflects that the income taxes withheld from her wages exceeded her tax liability by $450. This amount is refunded to T on May 20, 19X1. No interest is payable on the refund, since the 45-day period did not begin to run until April 15, 19X1 (i. e., the due date of the return).

The tax law provides various penalties for lack of compliance on the part of taxpayers.[62] Some of these penalties are summarized below:

—For a *failure to file* a tax return by the due date (including extension—see Chapter 4) a penalty of 5 percent per month (up to a maximum of 25 percent) is imposed on the amount of tax shown as due on the return.[63] Any fraction of a month counts as a full month.

—A penalty for a *failure to pay* the tax due (as shown on the return) in the amount of 0.5 percent per month (up to a maximum of 25 percent). During any month in which both the failure to file penalty and the failure to pay penalty apply, the failure to file penalty is reduced by the amount of the failure to pay penalty.

> **Example 29.** T files his tax return 18 days after the due date of the return. Along with the return, he remits a check for $1,000

---

60. Since the IRS is required to adjust the interest twice a year (based on an average prime rate formula), the rate applicable after December 31, 1984, cannot yet be ascertained.

61. § 6611(e).

62. As noted in Chapter 12, the big difference between interest paid on an income tax deficiency and a penalty for noncompliance with the tax laws is their treatment for Federal income tax purposes. Interest is deductible, whereas penalties are not.

63. § 6651.

which is the balance of the tax owed by T. Disregarding the interest element, T's total penalties are as follows:

Failure to pay penalty (0.5% × $1,000)		$ 5
Plus:		
Failure to file penalty (5% × $1,000)	$ 50	
Less failure to pay penalty for the same period	5	
Failure to file penalty		45
Total penalties		$ 50

Note that the penalties for one full month are imposed even though T was delinquent by only 18 days. Unlike the method used to compute interest, any part of a month is treated as a whole month.

—A negligence penalty of 5 percent of any underpayment for intentional disregard of rules and regulations without intent to defraud. In addition, new legislation enacted in 1981 imposes a nondeductible addition to tax equal to 50 percent of the interest attributable to that portion of an underpayment caused by the negligence.

Example 30. T underpaid his taxes for 1983 in the amount of $20,000, such underpayment being attributable to negligence. If the interest on the underpayment was $2,000, T's total negligence penalty is determined as follows:

Regular negligence penalty (5% × $20,000)	$ 1,000
Penalty imposed on the interest due as a result of the negligence (50% × $2,000)	1,000
Total negligence penalty	$ 2,000

—Various fraud penalties.[64] Fraud is a deliberate action on the part of the taxpayer evidenced by deceit, misrepresentation, concealment, etc.[65] A taxpayer with limited education and experience may be considered only negligent and not guilty of fraud. On the other hand, a knowledgeable person in the same situation might be subject to fraud penalties. For possible fraud situations, see Examples 21 and 22.

—Various penalties imposed on those who prepare tax returns in a negligent manner or perpetrate other acts related thereto.[66]

---

64. See, for example, § 6653(b) and § § 7201–7207.

65. The burden of proving fraud is on the IRS. This is to be contrasted with the usual deficiency assessment made by the IRS. There, the burden is on the taxpayer to show that he or she does not owe any additional tax.

66. § § 6694 and 6695. For further information on the penalties imposed on the preparers of tax returns see *West's Federal Taxation: Corporations, Partnerships, Estates, and Trusts,* Chapter 14.

PROBLEM MATERIALS

Questions for Class Discussion

1. When and why was the first Federal income tax enacted in the U. S.?

2. Why did the Supreme Court hold that the 1894 income tax was unconstitutional?

3. What is the difference between the Internal Revenue Code of 1939 and the Internal Revenue Code of 1954, as amended?

4. Why are most individuals currently subject to Federal income tax, whereas in 1939 less than 6% of the U. S. population was required to pay Federal income taxes?

5. Do you feel that our Federal government could continue to collect the same amount of tax from its taxpayers if the pay-as-you-go tax system were abolished? Why?

6. Discuss Adam Smith's canons of taxation. Are these criteria for a "good" tax system still appropriate in today's economy?

7. Several proposals have been introduced in Congress that would institute a Federal value added tax (i. e., VAT). Such proposals would impose a tax on the increment in value that is added at each stage of the manufacturing process and would be levied on the party adding such value. Evaluate VAT in terms of Adam Smith's canons of taxation.

8. How would you characterize the Federal income and estate and gift tax rate structure (i. e., progressive or proportional)?

9. T's personal residence is subject to three different and separate ad valorem property taxes. How could this be possible?

10. The use of computers by state and local taxing authorities usually has made the application of the ad valorem tax more equitable. Why is this the case?

11. After T converts her personal residence into a rental house, she finds that the ad valorem taxes on the property increase. Why might this happen?

12. T buys a new home for $150,000, its cost of construction plus the usual profit margin for the builder. The new home is located in a neighborhood largely developed 10 years ago when the homes sold for approximately $50,000 each. Assuming the homes of his neighbors are worth (in current values) in the vicinity of $150,000, could T be at a disadvantage with regard to the ad valorem tax on realty?

13. T, a farmer, lives in a county where a significant amount of property is owned by the Federal government (for use as a military installation) and the state (for use as an experimental agricultural station). If the county assesses and collects an ad valorem tax on realty, what might be T's position?

14. A jurisdiction that is in need of additional (and substantial) revenue is considering imposing an ad valorem tax on personalty devoted to personal use. The tax also would cover intangible property. Any comment on the jurisdiction's realistic expectations on revenue production?

15. T, a resident of Wyoming (which imposes a general sales tax) goes to Montana (which does not impose a general sales tax) to purchase her automobile. Will T successfully avoid the Wyoming sales tax? Explain.

16. T pays $15.90 for a ticket to attend a theatrical production of *Evita*. If $1.90 of the price is for taxes, what are the possibilities in terms of their classification? What type of jurisdiction(s) probably imposed the taxes?

17. Nevada, a state where gambling is legalized and heavily regulated, does not have many of the taxes common to other states. For example, Nevada does not have corporate and individual income taxes, death taxes, and gift taxes. However, it does impose a general sales tax, a gambling tax, and a casino entertainment tax.

    (a) Is there any rationale underlying this scheme of taxation?

    (b) Is the state of Nevada "missing the boat" by not having some type of death tax? Why?

18. Alaska and Texas are leading producers of oil and gas, and neither imposes an individual income tax. Is there any correlation between these two facts? Explain.

19. States that generate a large amount of revenue from severance taxes on oil and gas (e. g., Alaska, Oklahoma, and Texas) are very vulnerable to OPEC pricing and production policies. Explain.

20. The retail purchase price of cigarettes in Kentucky and North Carolina is lower than in other states. Why?

21. Why should some states see fit to impose a tax on oleomargarine products?

22. "There is no national general sales tax." Explain this statement.

23. Why might a person who purchases a product from an establishment located in jurisdiction X desire to take delivery in jurisdiction Y? Would it matter whether or not the person resided in jurisdiction X? Explain.

24. "There is no Federal inheritance tax." Do you agree or disagree with this statement?

25. During his life, T has accumulated considerable wealth as a result of personal service income. T is quite distressed when he learns that upon his death, the wealth will be subject to death taxes. He feels this is unfair, since the wealth accumulated has already been subject to taxation (i. e., the income tax). Please comment.

26. At the time of her death, D owned an insurance policy (maturity value of $200,000) on her own life, with S as the designated beneficiary. Since the policy proceeds will be paid by the insurance company to S and not to D's estate, none of the $200,000 should be subject to the Federal estate tax. Do you agree? Why or why not?

27. Rearrange the following components to show the scheme for arriving at the Federal estate tax due:

    (a) Tax credits

    (b) Gross estate

    (c) Taxable estate

    (d) Deductions

      (e) Tax base

      (f) Post-1976 taxable gifts

      (g) Estate tax as derived from the tax rate schedules

28. A decedent who leaves all of his property to his surviving spouse and to qualified charitable organizations will not be subject to a Federal estate tax. Explain.

29. The estate of Howard Hughes attempted to prove that Mr. Hughes was a resident of Nevada at the time of his death. Why?

30. Under a typical inheritance tax, the decedent's son will not be taxed at the same rate as the decedent's uncle. Why?

31. How much property can D, a widow, give to her three married children (and their spouses) and five grandchildren over a period of 12 years without making a taxable gift?

32. The Federal gift tax is applied on a cumulative basis. Explain.

33. When a donor is married, what is the effect of the election to split gifts?

34. Under present law, what advantages, if any, exist in making lifetime gifts rather than transfers by death?

35. An employee who has more than one job during the year always will have excess FICA withholdings. Do you agree? Why or why not?

36. In connection with FUTA, what purpose is served by a state merit rating system?

37. Compare FICA and FUTA in connection with each of the following:

      (a) Incidence of taxation.

      (b) Justification for taxation.

      (c) Reporting and filing requirements.

      (d) Rates and base involved.

38. T, an individual taxpayer and a resident of Rhode Island, is considering retiring to a warmer climate. At present, T has in mind either Florida or Arizona. What tax factors might affect his decision in making a choice between these two states?

39. What types of taxpayers are most likely to be audited by the IRS? Why does the IRS select returns filed by these taxpayers?

40. T, the owner and operator of a cash-and-carry military surplus retail outlet, has been audited many times by the IRS. When T mentions this fact to his next-door neighbor, an employee with Ford Motor Company, he is somewhat surprised to learn that the neighbor has never been audited by the IRS. Is there any explanation for this apparent disparity in treatment?

41. While Dr. T and his family are out of town on vacation, their home is burglarized. Among the items stolen and reported to the police are $35,000 in cash and gold coins worth $80,000. Shortly after the incident, Dr. T is audited by the IRS. Could there be any causal connection between the burglary and the audit? Explain.

42. What is meant by the phrase "hazards of litigation"? Should the IRS settle or compromise a case based upon the hazards of litigation? Why?

43. In 1980 T, an individual, filed an income tax return for tax year 1979 in which he knowingly overstated certain deductions. Since then, three years have passed and he has heard nothing from the IRS concerning the mis-statement. T concludes that he has successfully beaten the tax system.

    (a) Why does T arrive at this conclusion?

    (b) Is he correct?

44. During 1984, T is employed by X Corporation on a full-time basis with a salary of $50,000. He also has a part-time job with Y Corporation for which he earns $10,000.

    (a) Since T's main salary clearly exceeds the FICA maximum, there is no need for Y Corporation to withhold any amounts for this purpose. Please comment.

    (b) In any event, Y Corporation will be entitled to recover its share of FICA contributions made on behalf of T. Please comment.

45. T overstated his deductions on a prior year's Federal income tax return. Upon audit by the IRS, it is determined that the overstatement was the result of negligence. As a result, T owes additional income taxes of $10,000. The interest attributable to the underpayment amounts to $1,200.

    (a) What is T's negligence penalty?

    (b) Is any such penalty deductible for Federal income tax purposes?

Chapter 2

Understanding the Federal Tax Law

THE WHYS OF THE TAX LAW

The Federal tax law is a mosaic of statutory provisions, administrative pronouncements, and court decisions. Anyone who has attempted to work with this body of knowledge would have to admit to its disturbing complexity. For the person who has to trudge through a myriad of rule upon rule to find the solution to a tax problem, it may be of some consolation to know that the law's complexity can generally be explained. Whether sound or not, there is a reason for the formulation of every rule. Knowing these reasons, therefore, is a considerable step toward understanding the Federal tax law.

At the outset one should stress that the Federal tax law does not have as its sole objective the raising of revenue. Although the fiscal needs of the government are of obvious importance, other considerations do exist which explain certain portions of the law. Economic, social, equity, and political factors also play a significant role. Added to these factors is the marked impact the Internal Revenue Service and the courts have had and will continue to have on the evolution of Federal tax law. These matters are treated in this chapter, and wherever appropriate, the discussion is tied to subjects covered later in the text.

ECONOMIC CONSIDERATIONS

The use of the tax system in an effort to accomplish economic objectives appears to have become increasingly popular in recent years.

Generally, it involves utilization of tax legislation to amend the Internal Revenue Code[1] and looks toward measures designed to help control the economy or to encourage certain activities and businesses.

Control of the Economy. One of the better known provisions of the tax law which purports to aid in controlling the economy is the investment tax credit. By providing a tax credit for investment in qualified property, so the logic goes, businesses will be encouraged to expand.[2] The resulting expansion stimulates the economy and generates additional employment. As a safety valve against over-expansion, the investment credit can be suspended for a period of time or completely terminated.[3]

A further incentive towards capital formation is the degree to which a capital investment can be recovered with a tax benefit. For many years the tax law had recognized this consideration with provisions allowing accelerated methods of depreciation when writing off the cost of most tangible personalty (e. g., machinery, equipment) acquired for use in a trade or business. The Economic Recovery Tax Act of 1981 (ERTA) went much further by generally allowing shorter recovery periods and more generous recovery amounts under a newly established accelerated cost recovery system (ACRS). Additionally, beginning in 1982, taxpayers are allowed to expense certain capital asset acquisitions. In other words, limited amounts (up to $7,500 in 1984) may be deducted in the year the asset is purchased and placed in service. Thus, the taxpayer derives an immediate tax benefit from the property acquisition and does not have to await (under ACRS) recoupment of cost over a prescribed period of time.

> **Example 1.** In 1984, T purchases a machine for $7,500 for use in his trade or business. The machine is classified as five-year property under ACRS. At T's election, he may expense the $7,500 in 1984 rather than capitalize the amount and deduct its cost over a five-year period.

Of more immediate impact on the economy is a change in the tax rate structure. By lowering tax rates, taxpayers are able to retain more spendable funds. An increase in tax rates, moreover, carries the opposite effect. An illustration of this approach was the passage of the Revenue Act of 1978. Among the many changes provided by this legis-

---

1. The Internal Revenue Code is a compilation of Federal tax legislation.
2. Keep in mind that a dollar of tax credit generally means a dollar of income tax savings.
3. Since the investment tax credit first was enacted in 1962, it has been suspended once and repealed once. The credit was reinstated in 1971, and its benefits were expanded under the Tax Reduction Act of 1975 and the Revenue Act of 1978. Some restriction of the credit, however, did occur as the result of the Tax Equity and Fiscal Responsibility Act of 1982 (TEFRA). Except for the TEFRA retrenchment, which was more motivated by budgetary constraints, all of these changes were justified in terms of the effect they would have on the nation's economy.

lation was a decrease (from 48 percent to 46 percent) in the maximum rate of tax applicable to corporations. Also modified was the amount of taxable income (from the excess of $50,000 to the excess of $100,000) to which the maximum rate applies.

The Economic Recovery Tax Act of 1981 indicates that Congress has every intention of pursuing rate reduction as a means of stimulating the economy. The law included a multistage, across-the-board reduction in income tax rates phased in over a period from 1981–1983.

In the same legislation, Congress also recognized the effect that a combination of a progressive income tax system with inflation could have on the purchasing power of taxpayers. What happens, for example, to a taxpayer who receives a pay raise to adjust for the increase in a year when inflation is 10 percent? Although his or her consumption power has not risen, the pay raise will mean additional income taxes. Beginning in 1985, therefore, the tax brackets are to be adjusted upward to compensate for inflation. Also affected are personal and dependency exemptions and the zero bracket amount. The indexation procedure is to be based on the increase in the average consumer price index (CPI) over previous years.

> **Example 2.** For 1985, a 42% rate applies to a joint return where taxable income falls between $60,000 and $85,600. If the CPI adjustment is 10%, the 42% rate now applies to the $66,000–$94,160 bracket. Further, a personal and dependency exemption rises from $1,000 to $1,100 and the zero bracket amount increases from $3,400 to $3,740.

Although indexation has much to commend it, continuing concern over budget deficits may force Congress to change the game plan. Many people thus believe that the proposed change is not likely to take place.

Encouragement of Certain Activities. Without passing judgment on the wisdom of any such choices, it is quite clear that the tax law does encourage certain types of economic activity or segments of the economy. If, for example, one assumes that technological progress is fostered, the favorable treatment allowed research and development expenditures can be explained. Under the tax law such expenditures can be deducted in the year incurred or, as an alternative, capitalized and amortized over a period of 60 months or more. In terms of timing the tax saving, such options usually are preferable to a capitalization of the cost with a write-off over the estimated useful life of the asset created.[4]

The Economic Recovery Tax Act of 1981 further recognized the need to stimulate, through the use of the tax laws, technological prog-

---

4. If the asset developed has an indefinite useful life, no write-off would be available without the two options allowed by the tax law.

ress. In addition to the favorable write-off treatment noted above, certain incremental research and development costs now qualify for a 25 percent tax credit (see Chapter 13).

The encouragement of technological progress can also explain why the tax law places the inventor in an advantageous position. Not only can patents qualify as capital assets, but under certain conditions their disposition automatically carries favorable long-term capital gain treatment.

Is it desirable to encourage the conservation of energy resources? Considering the world energy situation and our own reliance on foreign oil production, the answer to this question has to be obvious. The concern over energy usage was a prime consideration that led to the enactment in 1978 of the Energy Tax Act. The result of this legislation was to make available to taxpayers various tax savings (in the form of tax credits) for energy conservation expenditures made on personal residence and business property.

Are ecological considerations a desirable objective? If they are, this explains why the tax law permits a 60-month amortization period for costs incurred in the installation of pollution-control facilities.

Is it wise to stimulate U. S. exports of goods and services abroad? Considering the pressing and continuing problem of a deficit in the U. S. balance of payments, the answer should be clear. Along this line, Congress has created a unique type of organization designed to encourage domestic exports of goods. Called DISCs (i. e., Domestic International Sales Corporations), such corporations are allowed, under prescribed conditions, to defer for income tax purposes the recognition of a percentage of their income derived from foreign sales. Also in an international setting, Congress has deemed it advisable to establish incentives for those U. S. citizens who accept employment overseas. Under the Economic Recovery Tax Act of 1981, such persons receive generous tax breaks through special treatment of their foreign-source income and certain housing costs.

An item previously mentioned can be connected to the encouragement of U. S. foreign trade. Because one of this country's major exportable products is its technology, can it not be said that the special favoritism accorded to research and development expenditures (see above) also serves to foster international trade?

Encouragement of Certain Industries. No one can question the proposition that a sound agricultural base is necessary for a well-balanced national economy. Undoubtedly this can explain why farmers are accorded special treatment under the Federal tax system. Among these benefits are the following: the election to expense rather than capitalize soil and water conservation expenditures, fertilizers, and land-clearing costs; the possibility of obtaining favorable long-term capital gain treatment on the disposition of livestock held for draft, breeding, or dairy purposes; the availability of the investment tax credit on certain farm structures; and the election to defer the recognition of gain on the receipt of crop-insurance proceeds.

The economic difficulties recently encountered by certain financial institutions (viz., savings and loan associations) can explain, in part, the special tax treatment allowed any All-Savers Certificates purchased through 1982. Under the Economic Recovery Tax Act of 1981, the interest from such certificates (up to $2,000 on a joint return) was not taxed. One should note in passing, moreover, that the "All-Savers" certificates have as a further objective the encouragement of the residential construction industry which, in recent years, has fallen upon hard times. Thus, so the argument goes, more savings lead to additional mortgage funds which, in turn, stimulate home construction.

Concern over capital formation in the public utility sector of the economy led Congress to provide attractive tax advantages for the reinvestment of dividends into the stock of the utility. Normally, if a shareholder in a corporation is given the option of cash or stock, the choice of stock is nevertheless taxable as a dividend. If certain conditions are met, shareholders of public utilities will be exempt from this rule. To the extent stock is chosen, income tax consequences will be deferred until such time as the stock is disposed of in a taxable event.

Encouragement of Small Business. At least in the U. S., a consensus exists that what is good for small business is good for the economy as a whole. Without evaluating its validity, this assumption has led to a definite bias in the tax law favoring small business. How else can one explain why the owner of a family business can elect to write off a capital expenditure for 1984 of up to $7,500 while Exxon is limited to the same amount?

In the corporate tax area, several provisions can be explained by their motivation to benefit small business. One provision permits the shareholders of a small business corporation to make a special election that generally will avoid the imposition of the corporate income tax.[5] Furthermore, such an election enables the corporation to pass through to its shareholders any of its operating losses and investment tax credits.[6]

The tax rates applicable to corporations tend to favor small business insofar as size is relative to the amount of taxable income generated in any one year. Since the full corporate tax rate of 46 percent applies only to taxable income in excess of $100,000, corporations that stay within these limits are subject to lower effective tax rates.

Example 3. For calendar year 1984, X Corporation has taxable income of $100,000 and Y Corporation has taxable income of

---

5. Known as the S election, the subject is discussed in Chapter 20.
6. In general, an operating loss can benefit only the corporation incurring the loss through a carryback or carryforward to profitable years. Consequently, the shareholders of the corporation usually cannot take advantage of any such loss.

$200,000. Based on this information, the corporate income tax is $25,750 for X Corporation and $71,750 for Y Corporation. By comparison, then, X Corporation is subject to an effective tax rate of 25.75% (i. e., $25,750/$100,000) while Y Corporation is subject to a rate of 35.875% (i. e., $71,750/$200,000).

Another provision specifically designed to aid small business is the new LIFO inventory procedure. Enacted in 1981, such procedures are available only to those businesses with average gross receipts of less than two million dollars.[7]

SOCIAL CONSIDERATIONS

Some of the tax laws can be explained by looking to social considerations. This is particularly the case when dealing with the Federal income tax of individuals. Notable examples and the rationale behind each are summarized below:

— The nontaxability of certain benefits provided to employees through accident and health plans financed by employers. It would appear socially desirable to encourage such plans, since they provide medical benefits in the event of an employee's illness or injury.

— The nontaxability to the employee of premiums paid by an employer for group-term insurance covering the life of the employee. These arrangements can be justified on social grounds in that they provide funds for the family unit to help it readjust following the loss of wages caused by the employee's death.

— The tax treatment to the employee of contributions made by an employer to qualified pension or profit sharing plans.[8] The contribution and any income it generates will not be taxed to the employee until the funds are distributed. Private retirement plans should be encouraged, since they supplement the subsistence income level the employee otherwise would have under the Social Security system.[9]

— The deduction allowed for contributions to qualified charitable organizations.[10] The deduction attempts to shift some of the financial and administrative burden of socially desirable programs from the public (the government) to the private (the citizens) sector.

---

7. LIFO inventory and small business accounting are discussed in Chapter 18.
8. These arrangements also benefit the employer by allowing a tax deduction when the contribution is made to the qualified plan. See Chapter 19.
9. The same rationale explains the availability of similar arrangements for self-employed persons (the H.R. 10 or Keogh type of plan).
10. The charitable contribution deduction is discussed in Chapter 11.

—The tax credit allowed for amounts spent to furnish care for certain minor or disabled dependents to enable the taxpayer to seek or maintain gainful employment.[11] Who could deny the social desirability of encouraging taxpayers to provide care for their children while they work?

—The disallowance of a tax deduction for certain expenditures deemed to be contrary to public policy. This disallowance extends to such items as fines, penalties, illegal kickbacks, and bribes to government officials.[12] Social considerations dictate that these activities should not be encouraged by the tax law. Permitting the deduction would supposedly encourage these activities.

—Restrictions on the deductibility of campaign expenditures. Although persons running for public office may offset campaign expenditures against campaign contributions, any excess expenditures cannot be deducted. To allow otherwise, so some believe, would place a tax premium on the use of wealth as a means of winning elections.

Many other examples could be included, but the conclusion would be unchanged: Social considerations do explain a significant part of the Federal tax law.

EQUITY CONSIDERATIONS

The concept of equity is, of course, relative. Reasonable persons can, and often do, disagree about what is fair or unfair. In the tax area, moreover, equity is most often tied to a particular taxpayer's personal situation. To illustrate, it may be difficult for Ms. Jones to understand why none of the rent she pays on her apartment is deductible when her brother, Mr. Jones, is able to deduct a large portion of the monthly payments he makes on his personal residence in the form of interest and taxes.[13]

In the same vein, compare the tax treatment of a corporation with that of a partnership. Although the two businesses may be of equal size, similarly situated, and competitors in production of goods or services, they are not comparably treated under the tax law. The corpo-

---

11. See Chapter 13.
12. Disclosures involving large corporations with international operations have highlighted this policy. It is interesting to note that in the Tax Equity and Fiscal Responsibility Act of 1982, Congress singled out for special treatment those persons who deal in illegal drug operations. Such persons will no longer be able to deduct any related business expenses (except the cost of goods sold) in arriving at taxable income. One must question, however, what deterrent effect (if any) this provision will have on illegal drug trafficking.
13. The encouragement of home ownership can also be justified on both economic and social grounds.

ration is subject to a separate Federal income tax; the partnership is not. Whether the differences in tax treatment logically can be justified in terms of equity is beside the point. The point is that the tax law can and does make a distinction between these business forms.

Equity, then, is not what appears fair or unfair to any one taxpayer or group of taxpayers. It is, instead, what the tax law recognizes. Some recognition of equity does exist, however, and offers an explanation of part of the law. The concept of equity appears in tax provisions that alleviate the effect of multiple taxation, postpone the recognition of gain when the taxpayer lacks the ability or wherewithal to pay the tax, and mitigate the effect of the application of the annual accounting period concept.

Alleviating the Effect of Multiple Taxation. The income earned by a taxpayer may be subject to taxes imposed by different taxing authorities. If, for example, the taxpayer is a resident of New York City, income might generate Federal, state of New York, and city of New York income taxes. To compensate for this apparent inequity, the Federal tax law allows a taxpayer to claim a deduction for state and local income taxes. The deduction, however, does not neutralize the effect of multiple taxation, since the benefit derived depends on the taxpayer's Federal income tax bracket.[14]

Equity considerations can explain the Federal tax treatment of certain income from foreign sources. Since double taxation results when the same income is subject to both foreign and U. S. income taxes, the tax law permits the taxpayer to choose between a credit or a deduction for the foreign taxes paid.

The Wherewithal to Pay Concept. Quite simply, the wherewithal to pay concept recognizes the inequity of taxing a transaction when the taxpayer lacks the means with which to pay the tax. It is particularly suited to situations in which the taxpayer's economic position has not changed significantly as a result of the transaction.

Example 4. T owns unimproved land held as an investment. The land cost T $60,000 and has a fair market value of $100,000. This land is exchanged for a building (worth $100,000) which T will use in his business.[15]

Example 5. T owns a warehouse that she uses in her business. At a time when the warehouse has an adjusted cost of $60,000, it is destroyed by fire. T collects the insurance proceeds of $100,000

---

14. A tax credit, rather than a deduction, would eliminate the effects of multiple taxation on the same income.

15. The nontaxability of like-kind exchanges applies to the exchange of property held for investment or used in a trade or business for property to be similarly held or used. See Chapter 15.

and, within two years of the end of the year in which the fire occurred, uses all of the proceeds to purchase a new warehouse.[16]

In both of the above examples, T had an economic gain of $40,000 [i. e., $100,000 (fair market value of the property received) − $60,000 (cost of the property given up)]. It would seem inequitable to force the taxpayer to recognize any of this gain for two reasons. First, without disposing of the property or interest acquired, the taxpayer would be hard-pressed to pay the tax. Second, the taxpayer's economic situation has not changed significantly.

Mitigating the Effect of the Annual Accounting Period Concept. For purposes of effective administration of the tax law, it is necessary for all taxpayers to report to and settle with the Federal government at periodic intervals. Otherwise taxpayers would remain uncertain as to their tax liabilities, and the government would have difficulty judging revenues and budgeting expenditures. The period selected for final settlement of most tax liabilities, in any event an arbitrary determination, is one year. At the close of each year, therefore, a taxpayer's position becomes complete for that particular year. Referred to as the annual accounting period concept, its effect is to divide, for tax purposes, each taxpayer's life into equal annual intervals.

The finality of the annual accounting period concept could lead to dissimilarity in tax treatment for taxpayers who are, from a long-range standpoint, in the same economic position. Compare, for example, two individual taxpayers, C and D. Over a five-year period, C has annual income of $10,000 for the first four years and $100,000 in the fifth year. During the same period, D has income of $28,000 per year. Which taxpayer is better off? Considering the progressive nature of the Federal income tax, D's overall tax liability will be much less than that incurred by C. Is this a fair result in view of the fact that each taxpayer earned the same total income (i. e., $140,000) over the five-year period? It is easy to see, therefore, why the income averaging provision of the tax law can be explained on the basis of equitable considerations.[17] Keep in mind, however, that the income averaging provision does not violate the annual accounting period concept but merely operates to mitigate its effect. By income averaging, C would compute the tax on the $100,000 received in the fifth year by a special and favorable procedure without disturbing the finality of any of the returns filed or the taxes paid for the preceding four years.

---

16. The nontaxability of gains realized from involuntary conversions applies when the proceeds received by the taxpayer are reinvested within a prescribed period of time in property similar or related in service or use to that converted. Involuntary conversions take place as a result of casualty losses, theft losses, and condemnations by a public authority. See Chapter 15.

17. See Chapter 12.

The same reasoning used to support income averaging can be applied to explain the special treatment accorded by the tax law to net operating losses, excess capital losses, and excess charitable contributions.[18] Carryback and carryover procedures help mitigate the effect of limiting a loss or a deduction to the accounting period in which it was realized. With such procedures, a taxpayer might be able to salvage a loss or a deduction that might otherwise be wasted.

Example 6. R and S are two sole proprietors and have experienced the following results during the past four years:

	Profit (or Loss)	
Year	R	S
1981	$ 50,000	$ 150,000
1982	60,000	60,000
1983	70,000	70,000
1984	50,000	(50,000)

Although R and S have the same profit of $230,000 over the period from 1981–1984, the finality of the annual accounting period concept places S at a definite disadvantage for tax purposes. The net operating loss procedure, therefore, offers S some relief by allowing him to apply some or all of his 1984 loss to the earlier profitable years (in this case 1981). Thus, he would be in a position with a net operating loss carryback to obtain a refund for some of the taxes he paid on the $150,000 profit reported for 1981.

Mitigation of the annual accounting period concept also explains in part the preferential treatment the tax law accords to long-term capital gains. Often the gain from the disposition of an asset is attributable to appreciation that has developed over a long period of time. In view of the impracticality of taxing such appreciation as it occurs, the law looks to the year of realization as the taxable event.[19] Long-term capital gain treatment, therefore, represents a rough means of achieving relief from the bunching effect of forcing a gain to be recognized in the tax year of realization.

Example 7. In 1982, T (a calendar year individual) acquired as an investment shares in X Corporation at a cost of $20,000. The stock had a value of $22,000 as of December 31, 1982, and $25,000 on December 31, 1983. In 1984, T sells the stock for $30,000. Since it is neither practical nor appropriate for the taxpayer to recognize the appreciation as it develops (i. e., $2,000 for

18. The tax treatment of these items is discussed in Chapters 8, 11, and 16.
19. Postponing the recognition of gain until the year it is realized is consistent with the wherewithal to pay concept. It would be difficult, for example, to pay a tax on the appreciation of an asset before its sale or other disposition has provided the necessary funds.

1982, $3,000 for 1983, and $5,000 for 1984), the full $10,000 gain [$30,000 (selling price) − $20,000 (cost)] must be reported for 1984. Consequently, T is provided some measure of relief from this concentration of gain in the year of sale through the availability of the long-term capital gain deduction.[20]

The installment method of recognizing gain on the sale of property allows a taxpayer to spread tax consequences over the payout period.[21] The harsh effect of taxing all the gain in the year of sale is thereby avoided. The installment method can also be explained by the wherewithal to pay concept, since recognition of gain is tied to the collection of the installment notes received from the sale of the property. Tax consequences, then, tend to correspond to the seller's ability to pay the tax.

> **Example 8.** In 1984, T sold real estate (cost of $40,000) for $100,000. Under the terms of the sale, T receives two notes from the purchaser, each for $50,000 (plus interest). One note is payable in 1985 and the other note in 1986. Without the installment method, T would have to recognize and pay a tax on the gain of $60,000 for the year of the sale (i. e., 1984). A rather harsh result, since none of the sale proceeds will be received until 1985 and 1986. With the installment method and presuming the notes are paid when each comes due, T recognizes half of the gain (i. e., $30,000) in 1985 and the remaining half in 1986.

The annual accounting period concept has been modified to apply also to situations in which taxpayers may have difficulty in accurately assessing their tax positions by year-end. In many such cases, the law permits taxpayers to treat transactions taking place in the next year as having occurred in the prior year.

> **Example 9.** T, a calendar year individual taxpayer, is a participant in an H.R. 10 (Keogh) retirement plan. (See Appendix C and Chapter 19 for a definition of a Keogh plan.) Under the plan, T contributes 15% of her net self-employment income, such amount being deductible for Federal income tax purposes. On April 10, 1984, T determines that her net self-employment income for cal-

---

20. As a general rule, only 40% of long-term capital gains are subject to the Federal income tax. Thus, if a taxpayer has a long-term capital gain for the year of $10,000, only $4,000 of this amount is subject to the income tax. See Chapter 16. It has been suggested that a more equitable approach to the problem of bunching of gain in the year of sale would be to vary the amount of the long-term capital gains deduction with the holding period of the property. Undoubtedly, a difference exists between two taxpayers, one who held the property for one year and one day and one who had a ten-year holding period. Yet the tax law allows each the same relief.

21. Under the installment method, each payment received by the seller represents both a return of basis (the nontaxable portion) and profit from the sale (the taxable portion).

endar year 1983 was $40,000, and consequently, she contributes $6,000 (15% × $40,000) to the plan. Even though the $6,000 contribution was made in 1984, the law permits T to claim it as a deduction for tax year 1983. Requiring T to make the contribution by December 31, 1983, in order to obtain the deduction for that year would place the burden on her of arriving at an accurate determination of net self-employment income long before her income tax return needs to be prepared and filed.

POLITICAL CONSIDERATIONS

A large segment of the Federal tax law is made up of statutory provisions. Since these statutes are enacted by Congress, is it any surprise that political considerations do influence tax law? For purposes of discussion, the effect of political considerations on the tax law is divided into the following topics: special interest legislation, political expediency situations, and state and local government influences.

Special Interest Legislation. There is no doubt that certain provisions of the tax law can largely be explained by looking to the political influence some pressure groups have had on Congress. Is there any other realistic reason why, for example, prepaid subscription and dues income are not taxed until earned while prepaid rents are taxed to the landlord in the year received?

One recent example of political pressure as an instrument of tax policy was the fate that befell the withholding procedures on interest and dividends. Enacted as part of the Tax Equity and Fiscal Responsibility Act of 1982, such procedures were to go into effect during 1983. Because of cost considerations and other reasons, financial institutions were strongly opposed to these procedures. It is not surprising, therefore, that Congress had a change of heart, and withholding never came to pass.

The tip-reporting rules enacted in 1982 came about as a compromise between Congress and the restaurant industry. An alternative means of generating additional revenue would have limited the deductibility of business meals by taxpayers. Because the loss of part of the deduction would have reduced business entertainment (with an attendant impairment of food and beverage sales), pursuing the reporting of tip income seemed to Congress to be the less onerous approach.

Along the same line are those tax provisions sponsored by individual members of Congress at the obvious instigation of a particularly influential constituent. In one case, for example, the effective date in proposed legislation that would reinstate the investment tax credit was moved back several months. It was well-known by all that the member of Congress initiating the change had a constituent with substantial capital expenditures that otherwise would not have qualified for the credit.

Special interest legislation is not necessarily to be condemned if it can be justified on economic, social, or some other utilitarian grounds. At any rate, it is an inevitable product of our political system.

Political Expediency Situations. Various tax reform proposals rise and fall in favor depending upon the shifting moods of the American public. That Congress is sensitive to popular feeling is an accepted fact. There are, therefore, certain provisions of the tax law that can be explained on the basis of political expediency existing at the time of enactment.

Measures which deter more affluent taxpayers from obtaining so-called preferential tax treatment have always had popular appeal and, consequently, the support of Congress. Provisions such as the minimum tax, the imputed interest rules, and the limitation on the deductibility of interest on investment indebtedness can be explained on this basis.[22]

Other changes partially founded on the basis of political expediency include the lowering of individual income tax rates, increasing the amount of the dependency exemption, and instituting the earned income credit.

State and Local Influences. Political considerations have played a major role in the nontaxability of interest received on state and local obligations. In view of the furor that has been raised by state and local political figures every time any kind of modification of this tax provision has been proposed, one might well regard it as next to sacred.

Somewhat less apparent has been the influence state law has had in shaping our present Federal tax law. Of prime import in this regard has been the effect of the community property system employed in eight states.[23] At one time the tax position of the residents of these states was so advantageous that many common law states actually adopted community property systems.[24] Needless to say, the political pressure placed on Congress to correct the disparity in tax treatment was considerable. To a large extent this was accomplished in the Revenue Act of 1948 which extended many of the community property tax

---

22. See Chapters 11 and 12.
23. The eight states with community property systems are Louisiana, Texas, New Mexico, Arizona, California, Washington, Idaho, and Nevada. The rest of the states are classified as common law jurisdictions. The difference between common law and community property systems centers around the property rights possessed by married persons. In a common law system, each spouse owns whatever he or she earns. Under a community property system, one-half of the earnings of each spouse is considered owned by the other spouse. Assume, for example, H and W are husband and wife and their only income is the $40,000 annual salary H receives. If they live in New York (a common law state), the $40,000 salary belongs to H. If, however, they live in Texas (a community property state), the $40,000 salary is divided equally, in terms of ownership, between H and W.
24. These states (Michigan, Oklahoma, and Pennsylvania) have since reverted to common law states.

advantages to residents of common law jurisdictions.[25] Thus, common law states avoided the trauma of discarding the time-honored legal system familiar to everyone.

INFLUENCE OF THE INTERNAL REVENUE SERVICE

The influence of the IRS is recognized in many areas beyond its obvious role in the issuance of the administrative pronouncements which make up a considerable portion of our tax law. In its capacity as the protector of the national revenue, the IRS has been instrumental in securing the passage of much legislation designed to curtail the most flagrant tax avoidance practices (to close tax loopholes). In its capacity as the administrator of the tax laws, the IRS has sought and obtained legislation to make its job easier (to attain administrative feasibility).

The IRS as Protector of the Revenue.   Innumerable examples can be given of provisions in the tax law which stemmed from the direct influence of the IRS when it was applied to preclude the use of a loophole as a means of avoiding the tax consequences intended by Congress. Working within the letter of existing law, ingenious taxpayers and their advisers devise techniques which accomplish indirectly what cannot be accomplished directly. As a consequence, legislation is enacted to close the loophole that taxpayers have located and exploited. Some tax law can be explained in this fashion and is discussed in the chapters to follow.

In addition, the IRS has secured from Congress legislation of a more general nature which enables it to make adjustments based on the substance, rather than the formal construction, of what a taxpayer has done. One such provision permits the IRS to make adjustments to a taxpayer's method of accounting when the method used by the taxpayer "does not clearly reflect income."[26]

Administrative Feasibility.   Some of the tax law is justified on the grounds that it simplifies the task of the IRS in collecting the revenue and administering the law. With regard to collecting the revenue, the IRS long ago realized the importance of placing taxpayers on a pay-as-you-go basis. Elaborate withholding procedures apply to wages while the tax on other types of income may be paid at periodic intervals throughout the year. The IRS has been instrumental in convincing the courts that accrual basis taxpayers should pay taxes on prepaid

---

25. The major advantage extended was the provision allowing married taxpayers to file joint returns and compute the tax liability as if the income had been earned one-half by each spouse. This result is automatic in a community property state since half of the income earned by one spouse belongs to the other spouse. The income-splitting benefits of a joint return are incorporated as part of the tax rates applicable to married taxpayers. See Chapter 4.

26. See Chapter 18.

income in the year received and not when earned. The approach may be contrary to generally accepted accounting principles, but it is consistent with the wherewithal to pay concept.

Of considerable aid to the IRS in collecting revenue are the numerous provisions which impose interest and penalties on taxpayers for noncompliance with the tax law. Provisions such as the penalties for failure to pay a tax or to file a return that is due, the negligence penalty for intentional disregard of rules and regulations, and various penalties for civil and criminal fraud serve as deterrents to taxpayer noncompliance.

> **Example 10.** At the instigation of the IRS, Congress in the Economic Recovery Tax Act of 1981 increased the civil penalty for furnishing false withholding information on a Form W–4 from $50 to $500. Apparently, the IRS was concerned that many employees were listing mythical dependents (e. g., 19) so that no income tax would be withheld from their wages. The imposition of the stiffer penalty is an obvious effort to deter noncompliance with the pay-as-you-go withholding procedures.

> **Example 11.** T, a tax protester, files an income tax return but does not reflect any financial information thereon on the grounds that the Federal income tax is unconstitutional. Under a new provision contained in the Tax Equity and Fiscal Responsibility Act of 1982, T's return will be treated as "frivolous," and T will be subject to a penalty of $500 for his actions. This penalty will be imposed in addition to other penalties that normally would result (e. g., failure to pay, negligence—refer to Chapter 1).

One of the keys to an effective administration of our tax system is the audit process conducted by the IRS. To carry out this function, the IRS is aided by provisions which reduce the chance of taxpayer error or manipulation and, therefore, simplify the audit effort that is necessary. An increase in the amount of the zero bracket amount, for example, reduces the number of individual taxpayers who will choose the alternative of itemizing their excess personal deductions.[27] With fewer deductions to check, therefore, the audit function is simplified.[28]

The audit function of the IRS has been simplified by provisions of

---

27. For a discussion of the zero bracket amount, see Chapter 4.

28. The same justification was given by the IRS when it proposed to Congress the $100 limitation on personal casualty and theft losses. Imposition of the limitation eliminated many casualty and theft loss deductions and, as a consequence, saved the IRS considerable audit time. The further curtailment of casualty and theft loss deductions certainly will follow as a result of recent statutory changes. The Tax Equity and Fiscal Responsibility Act of 1982, in addition to retaining the $100 feature, limits deductible losses to those in excess of 10% of a taxpayer's adjusted gross income. See Chapter 8.

the tax law dealing with the burden of proof. Suppose, for example, the IRS audits a taxpayer and questions a particular deduction. Who has the burden of proving the propriety of the deduction? The so-called presumption of correctness that attaches in favor of any deficiency assessed by the IRS can be explained by considering the nature of our tax system. The Federal income tax is a self-assessed tax, which means that each taxpayer is responsible for rendering an accounting to the IRS of all of his or her transactions during the year. A failure to do so means that any doubts will be resolved in favor of the IRS. Only in the case of criminal fraud (which could involve fines and penal sanctions), does the IRS have the burden of proof.

INFLUENCE OF THE COURTS

In addition to interpreting statutory provisions and the administrative pronouncements issued by the IRS, the Federal courts have influenced tax law in two other respects.[29] First, the courts have formulated certain judicial concepts which serve as guides in the application of various tax provisions. Second, certain key decisions have led to changes in the Internal Revenue Code. Understanding this influence helps to explain some of our tax law.

Judicial Concepts Relating to Tax. A leading tax concept developed by the courts deals with the interpretation of statutory tax provisions which operate to benefit taxpayers. The courts have established the rule that these relief provisions are to be narrowly construed against taxpayers if there is any doubt about their application. Suppose, for example, T wants to treat an expenditure as deductible for income tax purposes but has not literally satisfied the statutory requirements covering the deduction. Because income tax deductions are relief provisions favoring taxpayers, chances are the courts will deny T this treatment.

Important in this area is the arm's length concept. Particularly in dealings between related parties, transactions may be tested by looking to whether the taxpayers acted in an "arm's length" manner. The question to be asked is: Would unrelated parties have handled the transaction in the same way?

Example 12. T, the sole shareholder of X Corporation, leases property to it for a yearly rental of $6,000. To test whether the corporation should be allowed a rent deduction for this amount, the IRS and the courts will apply the arm's length concept. Would X Corporation have paid $6,000 a year in rent if the same property had been leased from an unrelated party (rather than from the sole shareholder)? Suppose it is determined that an unrelated

29. A great deal of case law is devoted to ascertaining Congressional intent. The courts, in effect, ask: What did Congress have in mind when it enacted a particular tax provision?

third party would have paid an annual rental for the property of only $5,000. Under these circumstances, X Corporation will be allowed a deduction of only $5,000. The other $1,000 it paid for the use of the property represents a nondeductible dividend. Accordingly, T will be treated as having received rent income of $5,000 and dividend income of $1,000.

Judicial Influence on Statutory Provisions. Some court decisions have been of such consequence that Congress has incorporated them into statutory tax law. One illustration of this influence appears below.

> **Example 13.** In 19X0, T claimed a loss of $100,000 for stock in Z Corporation that had become worthless during the year. Because of the absence of any offsetting gains, the loss deduction produced no income tax savings for T either in 19X0 or in future years. In 19X5, T institutes a lawsuit against the former officers of Z Corporation for their misconduct which resulted in the corporation's failure and, thereby, led to T's $100,000 loss. In settlement of the suit, the officers pay $50,000 to T. The IRS argued that the full $50,000 should be taxed as gain to T. Because the stock in Z Corporation was written off in 19X0 as being worthless, it had a zero value for tax purposes. The $50,000 recovery received by T on the stock was, therefore, all gain. Although the position of the IRS was logical and conformed to the tax statutes as they then existed, it was not equitable. The court stated that T should not be taxed on the recovery of an amount previously deducted unless the deduction produced a tax savings. Since the $100,000 loss deduction in 19X0 produced no tax benefit, none of the $50,000 received in 19X5 results in gain.

The decision reached by the courts in Example 13, known as the tax benefit rule, has since become part of the statutory tax law.[30]

On occasions, however, Congress has reacted in a negative manner with respect to judicial interpretations of the tax law.

> **Example 14.** L leases unimproved real estate to T for 40 years. At a cost of $200,000, T erects a building on the land. The building is worth $100,000 when the lease terminates and L takes possession of the property. Does L have any income either when the improvements are made or when the lease terminates? In a landmark decision, a court held that L must recognize income of $100,000 upon the termination of the lease.

Congress felt that the result reached in Example 14 was inequitable in that it was not consistent with the wherewithal to pay concept. Consequently, the tax law was amended to provide that a landlord

---

30. See Chapter 6.

does not recognize any income either when the improvements are made (unless made in lieu of rent) or when the lease terminates.

SUMMARY

In addition to its obvious revenue raising objective, the Federal tax law has developed in response to several other factors:

—*Economic considerations.* Here, the emphasis is on tax provisions which help regulate the economy and encourage certain activities and types of businesses.

—*Social considerations.* Some tax provisions are designed to encourage (or discourage) certain socially desirable (or undesirable) practices.

—*Equity considerations.* Of principal concern in this area are tax provisions which alleviate the effect of multiple taxation, recognize the wherewithal to pay concept, and mitigate the effect of the annual accounting period concept.

—*Political considerations.* Of significance in this regard are tax provisions which represent special interest legislation, reflect political expediency situations, and exhibit the effect of state law.

—*Influence of the IRS.* Many tax provisions are intended to aid the IRS in the collection of the revenue and in the administration of the tax law.

—*Influence of the Courts.* Court decisions have established a body of judicial concepts relating to tax law and have, on occasion, led Congress to enact statutory provisions to either clarify or negate their effect.

These factors explain various tax provisions and, thereby, help in understanding why the tax law developed to its present state. The next step involves learning to work with the tax law.

PROBLEM MATERIALS

Questions for Class Discussion

1. It has been suggested by some that the current Federal income tax be replaced by a flat rate tax. Under one version of the proposed system, a flat rate would be imposed upon gross income with no deductions (other than business-related) allowed. The income tax rates would be substantially reduced but would remain progressive.

    (a) How would such a system measure up to Adam Smith's canons of taxation (refer to Chapter 1)?

    (b) What would be the major disadvantages to such a system?

2. In connection with a proposed flat rate tax, how would you expect the following parties to react?

   (a) A builder of residential homes.

   (b) A lending institution (e. g., bank, finance company).

   (c) A charitable organization.

   (d) A taxpayer who has large itemized deductions (i. e., *dfrom*) in excess of the zero bracket amount.

3. In what manner does the tax law encourage the international export of U. S. goods and services?

4. Give examples of specific provisions of the tax law which are intended to help control the national economy.

5. In what way does the tax law attempt to encourage technological progress?

6. Suppose Congress decided to use the tax laws to further encourage the installation of pollution-control equipment.

   (a) What type of tax benefit would you suggest?

   (b) What might be more effective, a tax deduction or a tax credit? Explain.

7. In what way does the tax law encourage home ownership?

8. Congress has enacted an income tax credit for the cost of home insulation and certain other energy-saving items. What objective, if any, does such legislation accomplish?

9. Discuss the probable justification for the following provisions of the tax law:

   (a) Multiple tax rates for corporate income tax purposes.

   (b) The election permitted certain corporations to avoid the corporate income tax.

   (c) A provision which allows railroads to amortize the cost of tunnel bores over a period of 50 years.

   (d) A provision which makes nontaxable certain benefits furnished to employees through accident and health plans financed by employers.

   (e) Nontaxable treatment for an employee as to premiums paid by an employer for group-term insurance covering the life of the employee.

   (f) The tax treatment to the employee of contributions made by an employer to qualified pension or profit sharing plans.

   (g) The deduction allowed for contributions to qualified charitable organizations.

10. T owns and operates a trucking firm. During the year his employees incur a substantial number of fines for violating the 55 mile per hour highway speed limitation. T considers these fines as a necessary expense of running the business, as he knows his firm cannot make a profit by observing the posted speed limitation. Are these fines deductible for income tax purposes? Why or why not?

11. Except to the extent that they can offset campaign contributions, the tax law precludes any deduction for expenditures incurred by a candidate running for public office. Can you see any social justification for such a rule? Explain.

12. A provision of the Code allows a taxpayer a deduction for Federal income tax purposes for state and local income taxes paid. Does the provision eliminate the effect of multiple taxation of the same income? Why or why not? In this connection, consider the following:

    (a) Taxpayer, an individual, has itemized deductions less than the zero bracket amount.

    (b) Taxpayer is in the 30% tax bracket for Federal income tax purposes. The 50% tax bracket.

    (c) The state imposing the income tax allows a deduction for Federal income taxes paid.

13. Provide examples of the wherewithal to pay concept operating to insulate a transaction from Federal income tax consequences.

14. Explain the annual accounting period concept. Why is it necessary?

15. During 1984, two different individual taxpayers made the following sales:

Taxpayer	Asset	Cost	Selling Price	Length of Time Asset Was Held
Q	Land held as an investment	$40,000	$100,000	10 years
R	Stock held as an investment	40,000	100,000	13 months

    (a) In what way does the tax law mitigate the effect of the annual accounting period concept?

    (b) Why might such mitigation be described as a "rough means of achieving relief"?

16. T leases a building from L for 20 years. During the term of the lease, T makes significant capital improvements to the property which revert to L on the termination of the lease. Several years after the lease has terminated, L sells the building for a profit, a portion of which is attributable to the value of the improvements made by T.

    (a) Should the improvements made by T be taxed to L?

    (b) If so, when (i. e., at the time when made, on the termination of the lease, on the sale of the property)?

17. State the manner in which the annual accounting period concept is mitigated by the tax provisions relating to:

    (a) Income averaging.

    (b) Net operating loss carrybacks and carryovers.

    (c) Excess charitable contribution carryovers.

    (d) Long-term capital gains.

    (e) Installment sales.

18. H and W are husband and wife and live in Indiana (a common law state). During the year they earn wages as follows: $20,000 for H and $26,000 for W. If H and W file a joint return, their tax will be determined by a schedule based on the tax for $23,000 multiplied by two.

(a) Why is the tax schedule applicable to married taxpayers filing a joint return determined in this manner?

(b) Suppose H and W lived in California (a community property state) and filed separate returns. How would the result compare with that reached under part (a)?

19. T, an individual taxpayer, files a Federal income tax return for the year in which he reports income on a cash basis and expenditures on an accrual basis.

(a) What was T trying to accomplish in reporting as income only the amounts actually received while claiming deductions for amounts due but unpaid?

(b) Does the IRS have any defense against T's approach? Explain.

20. In what way does the wherewithal to pay concept aid the IRS in the collection of tax revenue?

21. T, a calendar year and cash basis taxpayer, operates a sole proprietorship. On December 28, 1984, T signs checks for business bills that are due and payable and instructs her office manager to be sure that the checks are mailed to the payees before year-end. Inadvertently, the office manager disregards T's instructions and does not mail the checks until January 3, 1984. Does T have any hope of deducting the amount of the checks for tax year 1984? Explain why or why not. (Note: A cash basis taxpayer may deduct expenses only in the year in which they are paid.)

22. R, a calendar year taxpayer, purchases § 38 property (i. e., assets for which an investment tax credit is allowed) in September of 1984. The seller assures R that the property can be delivered and placed in service in the business by December 15, 1984. Due to a mix-up in the delivery process on the part of the seller, the property is not received by T and placed in service until January of 1985. Does R have any hope of claiming an investment tax credit for tax year 1984? Explain why or why not. (Note: An investment tax credit is not allowed until the property is placed in service.)

23. On her income tax return for the year, T claims as a deduction certain charitable contributions that she did not make. When you question her about this she responds:

(a) "How is the IRS going to prove that I did not make these contributions?"

(b) "Even if the IRS disallows the deductions, the worst that can happen is that I will owe the same amount of tax I would have paid anyway."

Comment on T's misconceptions about the tax law.

24. Under current tax law, a donor generally can make a gift of $10,000 per year to a donee without having to file a Federal gift tax return and pay a Federal gift tax. How does this provision simplify the administrative responsibility of the IRS for enforcement of the tax laws?

25. "The Federal income tax is more frequently evaded by self-employed taxpayers than by those who are employed."

(a) Do you agree with this statement? Why or why not?

(b) If the statement is true, how might the problem be resolved?

26. T, an employee and a calendar year taxpayer, lives in a state that imposes a state income tax. During 1983 (through the withholding procedure), T pays state income taxes of $1,800. Of this amount, $400 is refunded to T in 1984 by the state as being in excess of the tax that she owed. How should the $400 state income tax refund be handled for Federal income tax purposes? In answering this question evaluate the following alternatives:

    (a) T should limit the deduction for state income taxes on her 1983 Federal income tax return to $1,400.

    (b) T should offset the $400 refund against any state income tax paid in 1984.

    (c) T should disregard the $400 refund.

    (d) Should T include any of the $400 refund in her income for 1984?

27. In the Tax Equity and Fiscal Responsibility Act (TEFRA) of 1982, the tax law was amended to extend income tax withholding procedures to certain interest and dividend payments. In 1983, however, Congress balked at implementing these pay-as-you-go procedures.

    (a) What motivated the original TEFRA legislation?

    (b) Why do you suppose Congress had a change of heart about going through with the new rules?

28. T is the sole shareholder of X Corporation. In connection with the arm's length concept, how could the following transactions be relevant:

    (a) T sells property to X Corporation.

    (b) T buys property from X Corporation.

    (c) T leases property to X Corporation.

    (d) T leases property from X Corporation.

Chapter 3

Working with the Tax Law

TAX SOURCES

Learning to work with the tax law involves the following three basic steps:

—Familiarity with the sources of the law.

—Application of research techniques.

—Effective use of planning procedures.

Statutory, administrative, and judicial sources of the tax law are considered first.

STATUTORY SOURCES OF THE TAX LAW

Origin of the Internal Revenue Code. Prior to 1939, the statutory provisions relating to tax were contained in the individual revenue acts enacted by Congress. Because of the inconvenience and confusion that resulted from dealing with many separate acts, in 1939 Congress codified all of the Federal tax laws. Known as the Internal Revenue Code of 1939, the codification arranged all Federal tax provisions in a logical sequence and placed them in a separate part of the Federal statutes. A further rearrangement took place in 1954 and resulted in the Internal Revenue Code of 1954 which continues in effect to the present day.

The following observations will help clarify the significance of the codification procedure:

—With some exceptions, neither the 1939 nor the 1954 Codes substantially changed the tax law existing on the date of their enactment. Much of the 1939 Code, for example, was incorporated into the 1954 Code; the major change was the reorganization and renumbering of the tax provisions.[1]

—Statutory amendments to the tax law are integrated into the Code. The Tax Equity and Fiscal Responsibility Act of 1982, for example, became part of the Internal Revenue Code of 1954.

The Legislative Process. Federal tax legislation generally originates in the House of Representatives where it is first considered by the House Ways and Means Committee.[2] If acceptable to the Committee, the proposed bill is referred to the whole House of Representatives for approval or disapproval. Approved bills are sent to the Senate where they are referred to the Senate Finance Committee for further consideration.[3] The next step involves referral from the Senate Finance Committee to the whole Senate. Assuming no disagreement between the House and Senate, passage by the Senate means referral to the President for approval or veto. If the bill is approved or if the President's veto is overridden, the bill becomes law and part of the Internal Revenue Code.

When the Senate version of the bill differs from that passed by the House,[4] the Joint Conference Committee, including members of both the House Ways and Means Committee and the Senate Finance Committee, is called upon to resolve these differences. The result, usually a compromise of the two versions, is then voted on by both the House and Senate. Acceptance by both bodies precedes referral to the President for approval or veto.

The typical legislative process dealing with tax bills is summarized as follows:

---

1. This point is important in assessing judicial decisions interpreting provisions of the Internal Revenue Code of 1939. If the same provision was included in the Internal Revenue Code of 1954, the decision has continuing validity.

2. Tax bills do originate in the Senate when they are attached as riders to other legislative proposals.

3. Some tax provisions are commonly referred to by the number of the bill designated in the House when first proposed or by the name of the member of Congress sponsoring the legislation. For example, the Self-Employed Individuals Tax Retirement Act of 1962 is popularly known as H.R. 10 (i. e., House of Representatives Bill No. 10) or as the Keogh Act (i. e., Keogh being one of the members of Congress sponsoring the bill).

4. This is frequently the case with major tax bills. One factor contributing to a different Senate version is the latitude each individual senator has to make amendments to a bill when the Senate as a whole is voting on a bill referred to it by the Senate Finance Committee. Less latitude is allowed in the House of Representatives. Thus, the whole House either accepts or rejects what is proposed by the House Ways and Means Committee, and changes from the floor are not commonplace.

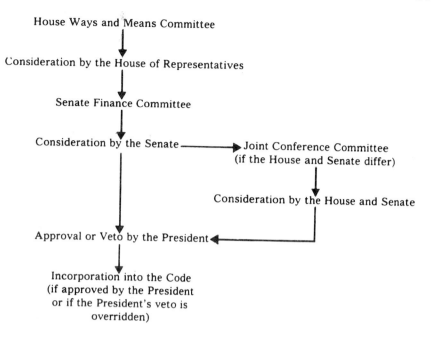

Referrals from the House Ways and Means Committee, the Senate Finance Committee, and the Joint Conference Committee are usually accompanied by committee reports. Because these committee reports often explain the provisions of the proposed legislation, they are a valuable source in ascertaining the intent of Congress. What Congress had in mind when it considers and enacts tax legislation is, of course, the key to interpreting such legislation.

The role of the Joint Conference Committee indicates the importance of compromise to the legislative process. The practical effect of the compromise process is illustrated by reviewing what happened in the Economic Recovery Tax Act of 1981 concerning change in the carryover of unused investment credits.

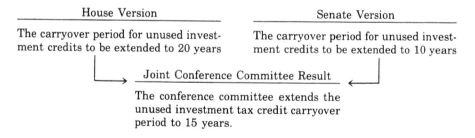

House Version	Senate Version
The carryover period for unused investment credits to be extended to 20 years	The carryover period for unused investment credits to be extended to 10 years

Joint Conference Committee Result

The conference committee extends the unused investment tax credit carryover period to 15 years.

Arrangement of the Code.　In working with the Code it helps to understand the format followed. Note, for example, the following partial table of contents:

Subtitle A. Income Taxes
    Chapter 1. Normal Taxes and Surtaxes
        Subchapter A. Determination of Tax Liability
            Part I. Tax on Individuals
                Sections 1–5
            Part II. Tax on Corporations
                Sections 11–12

*   *   *

In referring to a provision of the Code, the key is usually the section number involved. In designating Section 2(a) (dealing with the status of a surviving spouse), for example, it would be unnecessary to include Subtitle A, Chapter 1, Subchapter A, Part I. Merely mentioning Section 2(a) will suffice, since the section numbers run consecutively and do not begin again with each new Subtitle, Chapter, Subchapter, or Part. However, not all Code section numbers are used. Notice that Part I ends with Section 5 and Part II starts with Section 11 (i. e., at present there are no Sections 6, 7, 8, 9, and 10).[5]

Among tax practitioners, a common way of referring to some specific area of income taxation is by Subchapter designation. More common Subchapter designations include Subchapter C ("Corporate Distributions and Adjustments"), Subchapter K ("Partners and Partnerships"), and Subchapter S ("Election of Certain Small Business Corporations as to Taxable Status"). Particularly in the last situation, it is much more convenient to describe the effect of the applicable Code provisions involved (Sections 1361–1379) as "S corporation status" rather than as the "Election of Certain Small Business Corporations as to Taxable Status."

Citing the Code. Code sections often are broken down into subparts.[6] Section 2(a)(1)(A) serves as an example.

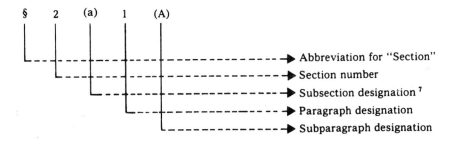

----

5. When the 1954 Code was drafted, the omission of section numbers was intentional. This provided flexibility to incorporate later changes into the Code without disrupting its organization.
6. Some Code Sections do not necessitate subparts. See, for example, § § 211 and 262.
7. Some Code Sections omit the subsection designation and use, instead, the paragraph designation as the first subpart. See, for example, § 212(1) and § 1221(1).

Broken down as to content, § 2(a)(1)(A) becomes:

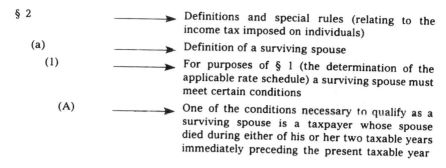

§ 2	Definitions and special rules (relating to the income tax imposed on individuals)
(a)	Definition of a surviving spouse
(1)	For purposes of § 1 (the determination of the applicable rate schedule) a surviving spouse must meet certain conditions
(A)	One of the conditions necessary to qualify as a surviving spouse is a taxpayer whose spouse died during either of his or her two taxable years immediately preceding the present taxable year

Throughout the remainder of the text, references to the Code sections are in the form given above. The symbols "§" and "§ §" are used in place of "Section" and "Sections." Unless otherwise stated, all Code references are to the Internal Revenue Code of 1954. The format followed in the remainder of the text is summarized below.

Complete Reference	Text Reference
Section 2(a)(1)(A) of the Internal Revenue Code of 1954	§ 2(a)(1)(A)
Sections 1 and 2 of the Internal Revenue Code of 1954	§ § 1 and 2
Section 12(d) of the Internal Revenue Code of 1939[8]	§ 12(d) of the Internal Revenue Code of 1939

ADMINISTRATIVE SOURCES OF THE TAX LAW

The administrative sources of the Federal tax law can be grouped as follows: Treasury Department Regulations, Revenue Rulings and Procedures, and other administrative pronouncements (see Figure I on page 64). All are issued either by the U. S. Treasury Department or one of its instrumentalities [e. g., the Internal Revenue Service (IRS), or a District Director].

Treasury Department Regulations. Regulations are issued by the U. S. Treasury Department under authority granted by Congress.[9] Interpretative by nature, they provide taxpayers with considerable guidance on the meaning and application of the Code. Although not issued by Congress, Regulations do carry considerable weight and are an important factor to consider in complying with the tax law.

---

8. § 12(d) of the Internal Revenue Code of 1939 is the predecessor to § 2 of the Internal Revenue Code of 1954. Keep in mind that the 1954 Code has superseded the 1939 Code. The reason that a provision of the 1939 Code may be referred to is set forth in Footnote 1 of this chapter.

9. § 7805.

Figure I

ADMINISTRATIVE SOURCES

Source	Location	Authority
Legislative Regulations	Federal Register*	Higher than most Regulations
Regulations	Federal Register*	Force and effect of law
Proposed Regulations	Federal Register Internal Revenue Bulletin Cumulative Bulletin*	Preview of final Regulations
Revenue Rulings Revenue Procedures	Internal Revenue Bulletin Cumulative Bulletin	Do not have the force and effect of law
Letter Ruling	Prentice-Hall and Commerce Clearing House loose-leaf services	Applicable only to taxpayer addressed

*Finalized and proposed Regulations are published in soft-cover form by several publishers.

Since Regulations interpret the Code, they are arranged in the same sequence. Regulations are, however, prefixed by a number which designates the type of tax or administrative, procedural, or definitional matter to which they relate. For example, the prefix 1 designates the Regulations under the income tax law. Thus, the Regulations under Code § 2 would be cited as Reg. § 1.2 with subparts added for further identification. These subparts often have no correlation in numbering pattern with the Code subsections. The prefix 20 designates estate tax Regulations; 25 covers gift tax Regulations; 31 relates to employment taxes; and 301 refers to procedure and administration. This listing is not all-inclusive.

Sometimes temporary regulations are issued by the Treasury relating to elections and other matters where speed is important. For example, Temp. Reg. § 9.3 provides the requirements for the one percent additional investment credit with respect to an employee stock ownership plan under § 46(a).

New Regulations and changes to existing Regulations are usually issued in proposed form before they are finalized. The time interval between the proposal of a Regulation and its finalization permits taxpayers and other interested parties to comment on the propriety of the proposal. Proposed Regulations under Code § 2, for example, would be cited as Prop.Reg. § 1.2.

Proposed and final Regulations are published in the *Federal Register* and are reproduced in major tax services. Final regulations are issued as Treasury Decisions (T.D.).

Revenue Rulings and Revenue Procedures. Revenue Rulings are official pronouncements of the National Office of the IRS and, like Regulations, are designed to provide interpretation of the tax law. However, they do not carry the same legal force and effect of Regulations and usually deal with more restricted problems. Both Revenue Rulings and Revenue Procedures serve an important function in that they afford guidance to both IRS personnel and taxpayers in handling routine tax matters.

Although letter rulings (as discussed below) are not the same as Revenue Rulings, a Revenue Ruling often results from a specific taxpayer's request for a letter ruling. If the IRS believes that a taxpayer's request for a letter ruling deserves official publication, the specific request will be made anonymously. Names, identifying descriptions, and money amounts are changed to disguise the identity of the requesting taxpayer. The IRS will then issue a written statement for information and guidance of taxpayers, practitioners, and IRS personnel.

Revenue Procedures are issued in the same manner as are Revenue Rulings, but they deal with the internal management practices and procedures of the IRS. Familiarity with these procedures can increase taxpayer compliance and assist the efficient administration of the tax laws by the IRS.

Revenue Rulings and Revenue Procedures are published weekly by the U. S. Government in the *Internal Revenue Bulletin* (I.R.B.). Semiannually, the Bulletins for a six-month period are gathered together, reorganized by Code Section classification, and published in a bound volume designated *Cumulative Bulletin* (C.B.).[10] The proper form for citing Rulings and Procedures depends on whether the item has been published in the *Cumulative Bulletin* or is available in I.R.B. form. Consider, for example, the following transition:

Temporary Citation	Rev.Rul. 83–20, I.R.B. No. 4, 13. *Explanation:* Revenue Ruling Number 20, appearing on page 13 of the 4th weekly issue of the *Internal Revenue Bulletin* for 1983.
Permanent Citation	Rev.Rul. 83–20, 1983–1 C.B. 231. *Explanation:* Revenue Ruling Number 20, appearing on page 231 of Volume 1 of the *Cumulative Bulletin* for 1983.

---

10. Usually only two volumes of the *Cumulative Bulletin* are published each year. However, when major tax legislation has been enacted by Congress, a third volume may be published containing the Congressional Committee Reports supporting the Revenue Act. See, for example, the third volume for 1974 dealing with the Employee Retirement Income Security Act of 1974 (ERISA). The 1974–3 *Cumulative Bulletin* contains the text of the Act itself and two House Reports plus the Conference Committee Report; 1974–3 Supp. contains additional Committee Reports and Congressional Record Excerpts relating to ERISA. This makes a total of four volumes of the *Cumulative Bulletin* for 1974: 1974–1, 1974–2, 1974–3, and 1974–3 Supp.

Since the first volume of the 1983 *Cumulative Bulletin* was not published until the end of 1983, the I.R.B. citation must be used until that time. After the publication of the *Cumulative Bulletin,* the C.B. citation is proper. The basic portion of both citations (i. e., Rev.Rul. 83–20) indicates that this was the 20th Revenue Ruling issued by the IRS during 1983.

Revenue Procedures are cited in the same manner, except that "Rev.Proc." is substituted for "Rev.Rul." Procedures, like Rulings, are published in the *Internal Revenue Bulletin* (the temporary source) and later transferred to the *Cumulative Bulletin* (the permanent source).

Other Administrative Pronouncements. Treasury Decisions (T.D.) are issued by the Treasury Department to promulgate new Regulations, amend or otherwise change existing Regulations, or announce the position of the Government on selected court decisions. Like Revenue Rulings and Revenue Procedures, T.D.s are published in the *Internal Revenue Bulletin* and subsequently transferred to the *Cumulative Bulletin.*

The IRS publishes other administrative communications in the *Internal Revenue Bulletin* such as Announcements, Notices, LRs (proposed regulations), Prohibited Transaction Exemptions, and T.D.s (final regulations).

Individual rulings are issued upon a taxpayer's request and describe how the IRS will treat a proposed transaction for tax purposes. These apply only to the taxpayer who asks for and obtains the ruling.[11] Though this procedure may sound like the only real way to carry out effective tax planning, the IRS limits the issuance of individual rulings to restricted, preannounced areas of taxation. Thus, it is not possible to obtain a ruling on many of the problems that are particularly troublesome for taxpayers.[12]

Individual rulings are not published and at one time were "private" (i. e., the content of the ruling was made available only to the taxpayer requesting the ruling). However, Federal legislation and the courts have forced the IRS to modify its position on the confidentiality of individual rulings.[13] The Tax Reform Act of 1976 now requires the IRS to make individual rulings available for public inspection after identifying details are deleted.[14] Published digests of private letter

---

11. In this regard, individual rulings differ from Revenue Rulings which are applicable to *all* taxpayers. Individual rulings may later lead to the issuance of a Revenue Ruling if the holding involved affects many taxpayers.
12. Rev.Proc. 83–22, 1983-1 C.B. 680 contains a listing of areas in which the IRS will not issue advance rulings. From time to time, subsequent Revenue Procedures are issued that modify or amplify Rev.Proc. 83–22.
13. The Freedom of Information Act as interpreted by *Tax Analysts and Advocates v. U. S.,* 74–2 USTC ¶ 9635, 34 AFTR2d 74–5731, 505 F.2d 350 (CA–DC, 1974) and *Tax Analysts and Advocates v. U. S.,* 75–2 USTC ¶ 9869, 37 AFTR2d 76-352, 405 F.Supp. 1065 (D.Ct.D.C., 1975).
14. § 6110.

rulings may be found in *Private Letter Rulings* (published by Prentice-Hall), BNA *Daily Tax Reports,* and Tax Analysts & Advocates *TAX Notes. IRS Letter Rulings Reports* (published by Commerce Clearing House) contains both digests and full texts of all letter rulings.

The National Office of the IRS releases Technical Advice Memoranda weekly. Although letter rulings are responses to requests by taxpayers, Technical Advice Memoranda are initiated by the IRS during its audit activities. Each memorandum applies only to the taxpayer it addresses, and § 6110(j)(3) indicates that a memorandum may not be used or cited as precedent. Both letter rulings and Technical Advice Memoranda are issued multi-digit file numbers. Consider, for example, the following Technical Advice Memorandum dealing with the completed contract method of accounting: DOC. 8329002. The first two digits refer to the year (83 = 1983), the next two digits indicate the week of issuance (29 = the twenty-ninth week), and the last three digits represent the number of ruling issued during such week (second ruling during the twenty-ninth week).

Like individual rulings, determination letters are issued at the request of taxpayers and provide guidance concerning the application of the tax law. They differ from individual rulings in that the issuing source is the District Director rather than the National Office of the IRS. Also, determination letters usually involve completed (as opposed to proposed) transactions. Determination letters are not published but are made known only to the party making the request.

The distinction between individual rulings and determination letters is illustrated below:

Example 1. The shareholders of X Corporation and Y Corporation want assurance that the consolidation of these corporations into Z Corporation will be a nontaxable reorganization. The proper approach would be to request from the National Office of the IRS an individual ruling concerning the income tax effect of the proposed transaction.

Example 2. T operates a barber shop in which he employs eight barbers. To properly comply with the rules governing income tax and payroll tax withholdings, T wants to know whether the barbers working for him are "employees" or "independent contractors." The proper procedure would be to request from the appropriate District Director a determination letter on the status of such persons.

JUDICIAL SOURCES OF THE TAX LAW

The Judicial Process in General. After a taxpayer has exhausted some or all of the remedies available within the IRS (i. e., no satisfactory settlement has been reached at the agent or at the Appeals Division level), the dispute can be taken to the Federal courts. The dispute

Figure II

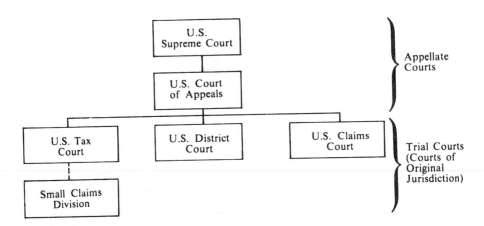

is first considered by a court of original jurisdiction (known as a trial court) with any appeal (either by the taxpayer or the IRS) taken to the appropriate appellate court. In most situations the taxpayer has a choice of any of four trial courts: a Federal District Court, the U. S. Claims Court, the U. S. Tax Court, or the Small Claims Division of the U. S. Tax Court. The trial and appellate court scheme for Federal tax litigation is illustrated in Figure II.

The broken line between the U. S. Tax Court and the Small Claims Division indicates that there is no appeal from the Small Claims Division. The jurisdiction of the Small Claims Division is limited to cases involving amounts of $5,000 or less.

American law, following English law, is frequently "made" by judicial decisions. Under the doctrine of *stare decisis,* each case (except in the Small Claims Division) has precedential value for future cases with the same controlling set of facts. Most Federal and state appellate court decisions and some decisions of trial courts are published. More than 3,000,000 judicial opinions have been published in the United States; over 30,000 cases are published each year.[15] Published court reports are organized by jurisdiction (Federal or state) and level of court (appellate or trial).

Trial Courts. Differences between the various trial courts (courts of original jurisdiction) are summarized below:

      —There is only one U. S. Claims Court and only one Tax Court, but there are many Federal District Courts. The taxpayer does not select the District Court which will hear the dispute but must sue in that one which has jurisdiction.

---

15. E. H. Pollack, *Fundamentals of Legal Research,* 4th Edition (Mineola, N.Y.: The Foundation Press, Inc., 1973).

—Each District Court has only one judge, the Claims Court has 16 judges, and the Tax Court has 19. In the case of the Tax Court, however, the whole court will decide a case (i. e., the court sits *en banc*) only when more important or novel tax issues are involved. Most cases will be heard and decided by one of the 19 judges.

—The Claims Court meets most often in Washington, D. C., while a District Court meets at a prescribed seat for the particular district. Since each state has at least one District Court and many of the more populous states have more, the problem of travel inconvenience and expense for the taxpayer and his or her counsel (present with many suits in the Claims Court) is largely eliminated. Although the Tax Court is officially based in Washington, D.C., the various judges travel to different parts of the country and hear cases at predetermined locations and dates. While this procedure eases the distance problem for the taxpayer, it could mean a delay before the case comes to trial and is decided.

—The U. S. Claims Court has jurisdiction in judgment upon any claim against the United States which is based upon the Constitution, any Act of Congress, or any regulation of an executive department.

—The Tax Court hears only tax cases; the Claims Court and District Courts hear nontax litigation as well. This difference, plus the fact that many Tax Court justices have been appointed from IRS or Treasury Department positions, has led some to conclude that the Tax Court has more expertise in tax matters.

—The only court in which a taxpayer can obtain a jury trial is in a District Court. But since juries can decide only questions of fact and not questions of law, even those taxpayers who choose the District Court route often do not request a jury trial. In such event, the judge will decide all issues. Note that a District Court decision is controlling only in the district in which the court has jurisdiction.

—In order for the Claims Court or a District Court to have jurisdiction, the taxpayer must pay the tax deficiency assessed by the IRS and sue for a refund. If the taxpayer wins (assuming no successful appeal by the Government), the tax paid plus appropriate interest thereon will be recovered. In the case of the Tax Court, however jurisdiction is usually obtained without first paying the assessed tax deficiency. In the event the taxpayer loses in the Tax Court (and no appeal is taken or any such appeal is unsuccessful), the deficiency must be paid with appropriate interest.

—The Claims Court does not have the power to fine or imprison for contempt of its order. Thus, a taxpayer will have to seek enforcement of the Claims Court's orders against nonparties in district courts.

Appellate Courts. Regarding appeals from a trial court, the following listing indicates the Court of Appeals of appropriate jurisdiction:

First	Seventh
Maine	Illinois
Massachusetts	Indiana
New Hampshire	Wisconsin
Rhode Island	
Puerto Rico	Eighth
	Arkansas
Second	Iowa
Connecticut	Minnesota
New York	Missouri
Vermont	Nebraska
	North Dakota
Third	South Dakota
Delaware	
New Jersey	Ninth
Pennsylvania	Alaska
Virgin Islands	Arizona
	California
District of Columbia	Hawaii
Washington, D.C.	Idaho
	Montana
Fourth	Nevada
Maryland	Oregon
North Carolina	Washington
South Carolina	Guam
Virginia	
West Virginia	Tenth
	Colorado
Fifth	Kansas
Canal Zone	New Mexico
Louisiana	Oklahoma
Mississippi	Utah
Texas	Wyoming
Sixth	Eleventh
Kentucky	Alabama
Michigan	Florida
Ohio	Georgia
Tennessee	
	Federal[16]
	U.S. Claims Court

---

16. The Court of Appeals for the Federal Circuit was created, effective October 1, 1982, by P.L. 97–164 (4/2/82) to hear decisions appealed from the U. S. Claims Court.

If the Government loses at the trial court level (i. e., District Court, Tax Court, or Claims Court), it need not (and frequently does not) appeal. The fact that an appeal is not made, however, does not indicate that the IRS agrees with the result and will not litigate similar issues in the future. There could be a number of reasons for the Service's failure to appeal. First, the current litigation load may be heavy, and as a consequence, the IRS may decide that available personnel should be assigned to other, more important, cases. Second, the IRS may determine that this is not a good case to appeal. Such might be true if the taxpayer is in a sympathetic position or the facts are particularly strong in his or her favor. In such event, the IRS may wait to test the legal issues involved with a taxpayer who has a much weaker case. Third, if the appeal is from a District Court or the Tax Court, the Court of Appeals of jurisdiction could have some bearing on whether or not the decision is made to go forward with an appeal. Based on past experience and precedent, the IRS may conclude that the chance for success on a particular issue might be more promising in another Court of Appeals. The IRS will wait for a similar case to arise in a different appellate court.

With the establishment of the new Federal Circuit at the appellate level, a taxpayer has an alternative forum to the court of appeals. Appeals from both the Tax Court and the District court go to a taxpayer's home circuit. Now, where a particular circuit has an adverse decision, the taxpayer may wish to select the Claims Court route, since any appeal will be to the Federal Circuit.

District Courts, the Tax Court, and the Claims Court must abide by the precedents set by the Court of Appeals of jurisdiction. A particular Court of Appeals need not follow the decisions of another Court of Appeals. All courts, however, must follow the decisions of the U. S. Supreme Court.

Because the Tax Court is a national court (i. e., it hears and decides cases from all parts of the country), the observation made in the previous paragraph has caused problems. For many years the Tax Court followed a policy of deciding cases based on what it thought the result should be, even though the appeal of its decision may have been to a Court of Appeals that had previously decided a similar case differently. A few years ago this policy was changed in the *Golsen*[17] decision. Now the Tax Court will still decide a case as it feels the law should be applied *only* if the Court of Appeals of appropriate jurisdiction has not yet passed on the issue or has previously decided a similar case in accord with the Tax Court's decision. If the Court of Appeals of appropriate jurisdiction has previously held otherwise, the Tax Court will conform even though it disagrees with the holding.

Example 3. Taxpayer T lives in Texas and sues in the Tax Court on Issue A. The Fifth Court of Appeals, the appellate court

---

17. *Jack E. Golsen*, 54 T.C. 742 (1970).

of appropriate jurisdiction, has already decided, based on similar facts and involving a different taxpayer, that Issue A should be resolved against the Government. Although the Tax Court feels that the Fifth Court of Appeals is wrong, under its *Golsen* policy it will render judgment for T. Shortly thereafter, Taxpayer U, a resident of New York, in a comparable case, sues in the Tax Court on Issue A. Assume further that the Second Court of Appeals, the appellate court of appropriate jurisidiction, has never expressed itself on Issue A. Presuming the Tax Court has not reconsidered its position on Issue A, it will decide against Taxpayer U. Thus, it is entirely possible for two taxpayers suing in the same court to end up with opposite results merely because they live in different parts of the country.

Appeal to the U. S. Supreme Court is by Writ of Certiorari. If the Court accepts jurisdiction, it will grant the Writ (i. e., *Cert. Granted*). Most often, it will deny jurisdiction (i. e., *Cert. Denied*). For whatever reason or reasons, the Supreme Court rarely hears tax cases. The Court usually grants certiorari to resolve a conflict among the Courts of Appeals (e. g., two or more appellate courts have assumed opposing positions on a particular issue). The granting of a Writ of Certiorari indicates that at least four members of the Supreme Court believe that the issue is of sufficient importance to be heard by the full court.

The role of appellate courts is limited to a review of the record of trial compiled by the trial courts. Thus, the appellate process usually involves a determination of whether or not the trial court applied the proper law in arriving at its decision. Rarely will an appellate court disturb a lower court's fact-finding determination.

Both the Code[18] and the Supreme Court[19] indicate that facts are binding on Federal courts of appeals unless clearly erroneous. This appellate process is illustrated by a recent District of Columbia Circuit decision involving whether a taxpayer was engaged in an activity for profit under § 183.[20] This Circuit Court specifically held that the "Tax Court's findings of facts are binding on Federal courts of appeals unless clearly erroneous."[21] The Circuit Court applauded the Tax Court for the thoroughness of its factual inquiry but could "not place the stamp of approval upon its eventual legal outcome."[22] In reversing and remanding the decision to the Tax Court, the appellate court said that "the language of § 183, its legislative history and the applicable Treasury regulation combine to demonstrate that the court's [Tax

---

18. § § 7482 (a) and (c).
19. *Commissioner v. Duberstein*, 363 U. S. 278, 80 S.Ct. 1190 (1960).
20. *M. C. Dreicer v. Comm.*, 81-2 USTC ¶ 9863, 48 AFTR2d 5884, 665 F.2d 1292 (CA–DC 1981).
21. *Ibid*, p. 1293.
22. *Ibid*, p. 1297.

Court's] standard is erroneous as a matter of law."[23] The appeals court held that this taxpayer's claims of deductibility were to be evaluated by proper legal standards.[24]

The result of an appeal could be any of a number of possibilities. The appellate court could approve (affirm) or disapprove (reverse) the lower court's finding, and it could also send the case back for further consideration (remand). When many issues are involved, it is not unusual to encounter a mixed result. Thus, the lower court could be affirmed (i. e., *aff'd*) on Issue A, reversed (i. e., *rev'd*) on Issue B, and Issue C could be remanded (i. c., *rem'd*) for additional fact finding.

When more than one judge is involved in the decision-making process, it is not uncommon for them to disagree with one another. In addition to the majority view, there could be one or more judges who "concur" (i. e., agree with the result reached but not with some or all of the reasoning) or "dissent" (i. e., disagrcc with the result). In any one case it is, of course, the majority view that controls. But concurring and dissenting views may have influence on other courts or, at some subsequent date when the composition of the court has changed, even on the same court.

Having concluded a brief description of the judicial process, it is appropriate to consider the more practical problem of the relationship of case law to tax research. As previously noted, court decisions are an important source of tax law. The ability to cite a case and to locate it is, therefore, a must in working with the tax law.

Judicial Citations—The U. S. Tax Court. A good starting point is with the U. S. Tax Court (formerly the Board of Tax Appeals). The Court issues two types of decisions: Regular and Memorandum. The distinction between the two involves both substance and form. In terms of substance, Memorandum decisions deal with situations necessitating only the application of already established principles of law; however, Regular decisions involve novel issues not previously resolved by the Court. In actual practice, however, this distinction is not always preserved. Not infrequently, Memorandum decisions will be encountered that appear to warrant Regular status and vice versa. At any rate, do not conclude that Memorandum decisions possess no value as precedents. Both represent the position of the Tax Court and, as such, can be relied upon.

Another important distinction between the Regular and Memorandum decisions issued by the Tax Court arises in connection with form. The Memorandum decisions officially are published in mimeograph form only, but Regular decisions are published by the U. S. Government in a series designated *Tax Court of the United States Reports*. Each volume of these *Reports* covers a six-month period

---

23. *Ibid.*
24. *Ibid*, p. 1300.

(April 1 through September 30 and October 1 through March 31) and is given a succeeding volume number. But, as was true of the *Cumulative Bulletins,* there is usually a time lag between the date a decision is rendered and the date it appears in bound form. A temporary citation may be necessary to aid the researcher in locating a recent Regular decision. Consider, for example, the temporary and permanent citations for *Durbin Paper Stock Co., Inc.,* a decision filed on January 20, 1983:

Temporary Citation
{ *Durbin Paper Stock Co., Inc.,* 80 T.C. ___, No. 5 (1983)
Explanation: Page number left blank because not yet known.

Permanent Citation
{ *Durbin Paper Stock Co., Inc.,* 80 T.C. 252 (1983)
Explanation: Page number now available.

Both citations tell us that the case will ultimately appear in Volume 80 of the *Tax Court of the United States Reports.* But until this volume is bound and made available to the general public, the page number must be left blank. Instead, the temporary citation identifies the case as being the fifth Regular decision issued by the Tax Court since Volume 79 ended. With this information, the decision can be easily located in either of the special Tax Court services published by Commerce Clearing House or Prentice-Hall. Once Volume 80 is released, the permanent citation can be substituted and the number of the case dropped.

Before 1943, the Tax Court was called the Board of Tax Appeals, and its decisions were published as the *United States Board of Tax Appeals Reports* (B.T.A.). These 47 volumes cover the period from 1924 to 1942. For example, the citation *Karl Pauli,* 11 B.T.A. 784 (1928) refers to the eleventh volume of the *Board of Tax Appeals Reports,* page 784, issued in 1928.

One further distinction between Regular and Memorandum decisions of the Tax Court involves the IRS procedure of acquiescence (i. e., "A" or "Acq.") or nonacquiescence (i. e., "NA" or "Nonacq."). If the IRS loses in a Regular decision, it will usually indicate whether it agrees or disagrees with the result reached by the Court. The acquiescence or nonacquiescence will be published in the *Internal Revenue Bulletin* and the *Cumulative Bulletin.* The procedure is not followed for Memorandum decisions or for the decisions of other courts. The IRS can retroactively revoke an acquiescence. The IRS sometimes issues an announcement that it will *or* will not follow a decision of another Federal court on similar facts.

Although Memorandum decisions are not published by the U. S. Government, they are published by Commerce Clearing House (CCH) and Prentice-Hall (P–H). Consider, for example, the three different ways that *Walter H. Johnson* may be cited:

Walter H. Johnson, T.C. Memo. 1975–245

> The 245th Memorandum Decision issued by the Tax Court in 1975.

Walter H. Johnson, 34 TCM 1056

> Page 1056 of Vol. 34 of the *CCH Tax Court Memorandum Decisions.*

Walter H. Johnson, P–H T.C. Mem.Dec. ¶ 75,245

> Paragraph 75,245 of the *P–H T.C. Memorandum Decisions.*

Note that the third citation contains the same information as the first. Thus, ¶ 75,245 indicates the following information about the case: year 1975, 245th T.C.Memo. Decision.[25] Although the Prentice-Hall citation does not indicate specifically a volume number, the paragraph citation does indicate that the decision can be found in the 1975 volume of the P-H Memorandum Decision service.

Judicial Citations—The U. S. District Court, Claims Court, and Court of Appeals. District Court, Claims Court, Court of Appeals, and Supreme Court decisions dealing with Federal tax matters are reported in both the CCH, *U. S. Tax Cases* (USTC), and the P-H, *American Federal Tax Reports* (AFTR) series.

Federal District Court decisions, dealing with *both* tax and non-tax issues, also are published by West Publishing Company in its Federal Supplement Series. Examples of how a District Court case can be cited in three different forms appear below:

Simons-Eastern Co. v. U. S., 73–1 USTC ¶ 9279 (D.Ct.Ga., 1972).

Explanation: Reported in the first volume of the *U. S. Tax Cases* (i. e., USTC) published by Commerce Clearing House for calendar year 1973 (i. e., 73–1) and located at paragraph 9279 (i. e., ¶ 9279).

Simons-Eastern Co. v. U. S., 31 AFTR2d 73–640(D.Ct.Ga., 1972).

Explanation: Reported in the 31st volume of the second series of the *American Federal Tax Reports* (i. e., AFTR2d) published by Prentice-Hall and commencing on page 640. The "73" preceding the page number indicates the year the case was published but is a designation used only in recent decisions.

Simons-Eastern Co. v. U. S., 354 F.Supp. 1003 (D.Ct.Ga., 1972).

Explanation: Reported in the 354th volume of the *Federal Supplement Series* (i. e., F.Supp.) published by West Publishing Company and commencing on page 1003.

In all of the above citations note that the name of the case is the same (Simons-Eastern Co. being the taxpayer) as is the reference to

---

25. In this text, the Prentice-Hall citation for Memorandum decisions of the U. S. Tax Court is omitted. Thus, *Walter H. Johnson* would be cited as: 34 TCM 1056, T.C. Memo. 1975–245.

the Federal District Court of Georgia (i. e., D.Ct.Ga.) and the year the decision was rendered (i. e., 1972).[26]

Decisions of the Claims Court and the Courts of Appeals are published in the USTCs, AFTRs, and a West Publishing Company reporter designated as the Federal Second Series (F.2d). Illustrations of the different forms follow:

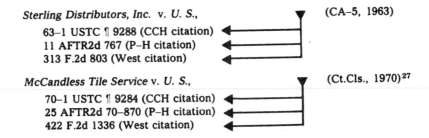

Note that *Sterling Distributors, Inc.* is a decision rendered by the Fifth Court of Appeals in 1963 (i. e., CA–5, 1963), while *McCandless Tile Service* is one rendered by the Court of Claims in 1970 (i. e., Ct.Cls., 1970), the predecessor of the Claims Court.

Judicial Citations—The U. S. Supreme Court. Like all other federal tax cases (except those rendered by the U. S. Tax Court), Supreme Court decisions are published by Commerce Clearing House in the USTCs and by Prentice-Hall in the AFTRs. The U. S. Government Printing Office also publishes these decisions in the *United States Supreme Court Reports* (i. e., U. S.) as does West Publishing Company in its *Supreme Court Reporter* (i. e., S.Ct.) and the Lawyer's Co-Operative Publishing Company in its *United States Reports, Lawyer's Edition* (i. e., L.Ed.). An illustration of the different ways the same case can be cited appears below:

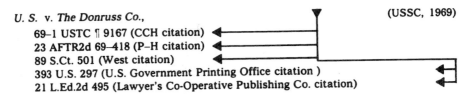

The parenthetical reference (USSC, 1969) identifies the decision as having been rendered by the U. S. Supreme Court in 1969. The citations given in this text for Supreme Court decisions will be limited to the CCH (i. e., USTC), P-H (i. e., AFTR), and the West (i. e., S.Ct.) versions. For a summary, see Figure III.

---

26. In the text the case would be cited in the following form: *Simons-Eastern Co. v. U. S.*, 73–1 USTC ¶ 9279, 31 AFTR2d 73–640, 354 F.Supp. 1003 (D.Ct.Ga., 1972).
27. Before October 1, 1982, the Claims Court was called the Court of Claims.

Figure III

JUDICIAL SOURCES
(DESCENDING ORDER OF AUTHORITY)

Court	Location	Authority
U.S. Supreme Court	S.Ct. Series (West) U.S. Series (U.S. Gov't.) L.Ed. (Lawyer's Co-Op.) AFTR (P–H) USTC (CCH)	Highest authority
U.S. Courts of Appeal	Federal 2nd (West) AFTR (P–H) USTC (CCH)	Next highest appellate court
Tax Court (regular decisions)	U.S. Govt. Printing office PH/CCH separate services	Highest of the trial courts
Tax Court (memorandum decisions)	P–H Memo TC (P–H) TCM (CCH)	Less authority than regular T.C. decision
U.S. Claims Court	Federal 2nd (West) AFTR (P–H) USTC (CCH)	Similar authority as Tax Court
U.S. District Courts	F.Supp. Series (West) AFTR (P–H) USTC (CCH)	Lowest trial court
Small Claims Division of Tax Court	Not published	No precedent value

WORKING WITH THE TAX LAW—TAX RESEARCH

Tax research is the method whereby one determines the best available solution to a situation that possesses tax consequences. In other words, it is the process of finding a competent and professional conclusion to a tax problem. The problem might originate either from completed or proposed transactions. In the case of a completed transaction, the objective of the research would be to determine the tax result of what has already taken place. For example, was the expenditure incurred by the taxpayer deductible or not deductible for tax purposes? When dealing with proposed transactions, however, the tax research process is directed toward the determination of possible tax consequences. To the extent that tax research leads to a choice of

alternatives or otherwise influences the future actions of the taxpayer, it becomes the key to effective tax planning.

Tax research involves the following procedures:

—Identifying and refining the problem.

—Locating the appropriate tax law sources.

—Assessing the validity of the tax law sources.

—Arriving at the solution or at alternative solutions with due
consideration given to nontax factors.

—Effectively communicating the solution to the taxpayer or the
taxpayer's representative.

—Following up on the solution (where appropriate) in the light of
new developments.

These procedures are diagrammed in Figure IV. The broken lines
reflect those steps of particular interest when tax research is directed
towards proposed, rather than completed, transactions.

Figure IV

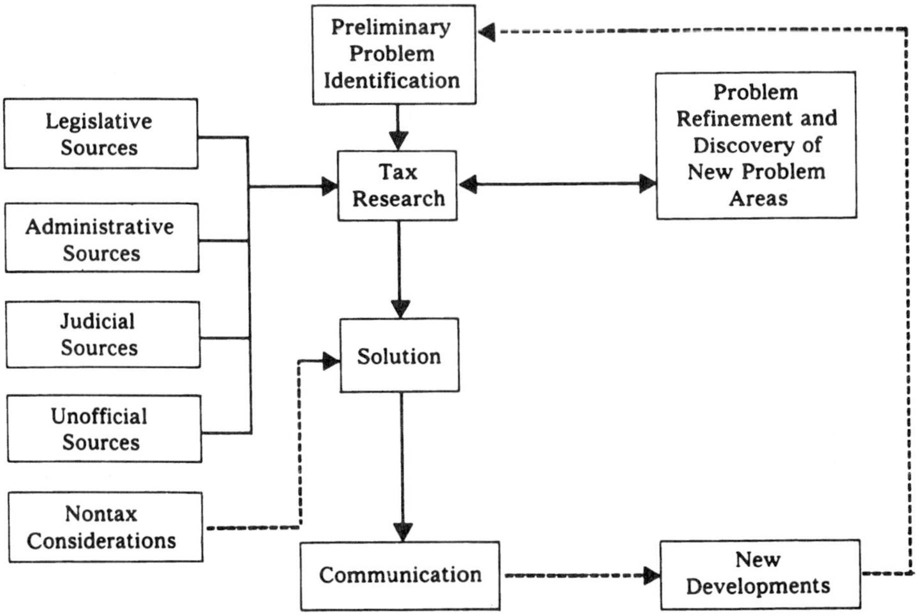

IDENTIFYING THE PROBLEM

Problem identification must start with a compilation of the relevant
facts involved.[28] In this regard, *all* of the facts that may have a bear-

---

28. For an excellent discussion of the critical role of facts in carrying out tax research, see Ray M. Sommerfeld and G. Fred Streuling, *Tax Research Techniques,* Tax
Study No. 5 (New York: The American Institute of Certified Public Accountants,
1981), Chapter 2.

ing on the problem must be gathered because any omission could modify the solution to be reached. To illustrate, consider what appears to be a very simple problem.

> **Example 4.** On December 30, 19X0, X Corporation (a calendar year and accrual basis taxpayer) declares a $20,000 bonus payable to R, one of its employees. The stock of X Corporation is held by R, S, and T, all individuals. The problem: Is the bonus deductible by X Corporation?

Refining the Problem. Initial reaction would be to sanction the deduction in Example 4, since it has long been accepted that salaries or other compensation represent an ordinary and necessary expense in carrying on a trade or business [see § 162(a)]. Further investigation into this area reveals, however, that the accrual of year-end employee bonuses is subject to specific restrictions in § 404. Payments that are not made within a reasonable time period (i. e., by the due date of the tax return including extensions) are deductible only in the year of payment rather than in the year of accrual. Assume, however, further fact gathering reveals the following additional information:

—The bonus was accrued on December 30, 19X0, but not actually paid until July 1, 19X1.

—R uses the cash method of accounting for income tax purposes.

—The stock in X Corporation is owned in equal proportion by R, S, and T (i. e., each owns one-third of the stock).

—R, S, and T are brothers and sisters.

With these new facts, additional research leads to a consideration of § 267(a)(2) which overrides the general rules for deductibility under § 404. Under this Code provision X Corporation would lose the deduction if all of the following three conditions are met:

1. X Corporation uses the accrual method of accounting while R uses the cash method.

2. The bonus is not paid within 2½ months from the end of the tax year in which accrued (in this case no later than March 15, 19X1).

3. R owns, directly or *indirectly,* more than 50 percent in the value of X Corporation's outstanding stock.

Has condition 3 been satisfied, since R owns only 33⅓ percent of the stock in X Corporation? Further research reveals that an individual is deemed, for this purpose at least, to own all of the stock owned by members of his or her family [§ 267(c)(2)]. Because members of the family include brothers and sisters [§ 267(c)(4)], R owns 100 percent of the stock of X Corporation (i. e., 33⅓ percent directly and 66⅔ percent indirectly).[29] All three conditions having been met, it therefore appears that X Corporation will be denied a deduction for the accrued bonus.

Further Refinement of the Problem.   One of the conditions necessary for the disallowance of X Corporation's deduction under § 267 was the failure to pay the bonus to R within 2½ months from the close of the tax year in which it was accrued. Suppose, however, further investigation reveals the following:

—R had the right to receive the bonus once it was authorized (or no later than March 15, 19X1).

—X Corporation had the duty and the financial capacity to pay the bonus when it was authorized.

In the light of this new information, X Corporation's deduction might not be lost. Further research indicates that if R (the payee) is in constructive receipt of the income, X Corporation (the payor) will be considered to have made a constructive payment.[30] Thus, the date of constructive payment, as opposed to the date of actual payment, will control for purposes of applying § 267. If constructive payment occurs no later than March 15, 19X1, the $20,000 bonus will be deductible to X Corporation for tax year 19X0 (the year of the accrual). Additional research would provide judicial authority setting forth guidelines on what does and does not constitute a constructive payment.[31]

Even if the deduction of the bonus is not prevented by § 267, a further refinement of the problem should take into account the possible effect of § 162(a)(1). Under this provision salaries and other compensation can be deducted only if "reasonable" in amount. To properly resolve the question of reasonableness, the researcher would need to gather such facts as the nature and extent of the services performed, the amount of other compensation paid to R in the same year as the bonus, the salaries paid by similar firms for similar services, and the dividend payment record of X Corporation. These facts, when tested by the Regulations under § 162 and court decisions on the subject, would provide the basis for assessing the reasonableness of the bonus and, consequently, its deductibility by X Corporation.

LOCATING THE APPROPRIATE TAX LAW SOURCES

Once the problem is clearly defined, what is the next step? Although this is a matter of individual judgment, most involved tax research

---

29.   By virtue of the family attribution rules of § 267(c)(2), R has constructive ownership of the stock owned by his brother and sister. Thus, "indirect" ownership means "constructive" ownership.

30.   Reg. § 1.267(a)–1(b)(1)(iii). The concept of constructive receipt is explained in Reg. § 1.451–2.

31.   See, for example, *Fetzer Refrigerator Co. v. U. S.,* 71–1 USTC ¶ 9202, 27 AFTR2d 71–613, 437 F.2d 577 (CA–6, 1971); *F. D. Bissett & Son, Inc.,* 56 T.C. 453 (1971); and *Hendershot & Smith, Inc.,* 34 TCM 788, T.C. Memo. 1975–183.

begins with the index volume of the tax service. If the problem is not that complex, the researcher may bypass the tax service and turn directly to the Internal Revenue Code and the Treasury Regulations. For the beginner, this procedure saves time and will solve many of the more basic problems. If the researcher does not have a personal copy of the Code or Regulations, resorting to the appropriate volume(s) of a tax service will be necessary.[32]

The major tax services available are listed below:

Standard Federal Tax Reporter, Commerce Clearing House.

Federal Taxes, Prentice-Hall.

Mertens, *Law of Federal Income Taxation,* Callaghan and Co.

Tax Coordinator, Research Institute of America.

Tax Management Portfolios, Bureau of National Affairs.

Rabkin and Johnson, *Federal Income, Gift and Estate Taxation,* Matthew Bender, Inc.

Working With the Tax Services. In this text it is not feasible to teach the use of any particular tax service—this can be learned only by practice.[33]

There are, however, several important observations about the use of tax services that cannot be overemphasized. First, never forget to check for current developments. The main text of any service is not revised frequently enough to permit reliance on that portion as the *latest* word on any subject. Where such current developments can be found depends, of course, on which service is being used. Both the Commerce Clearing House and Prentice-Hall services contain a special volume devoted to current matters. Second, when dealing with a tax service synopsis of a Treasury Department pronouncement or a judicial decision, remember there is no substitute for the original source.

To illustrate, do not base a conclusion solely on a tax service's commentary on *Simons-Eastern Co. v. U. S.*[34] If the case is vital to the research, look it up! It is possible that the facts of the case are distinguishable from those involved in the problem being researched. This is not to say that the case synopsis contained in the tax service is wrong—it might just be misleading or incomplete.

Tax Periodicals. Additional sources of tax information are the various tax periodicals. The best means of locating a journal article

---

32. Several of the major tax services publish paperback editions of the Code and Treasury Regulations which can be purchased at modest prices. These editions are usually revised twice each year.

33. The representatives of the various tax services are prepared to provide the users of their services with printed booklets or individual instruction, or both, on the utilization of such materials.

34. See Footnote 26.

pertinent to a tax problem is through Commerce Clearing House's *Federal Tax Articles*. This three-volume service includes a subject index, a Code Section number index, and an author's index. Also, the P-H tax service has a topical "Index to Tax Articles" section that is organized using the P-H paragraph index system.

Some of the more useful tax periodicals are listed below:

The Journal of Taxation
Warren, Gorham and Lamont
210 South Street
Boston, MA 02111

Tax Law Review
Warren, Gorham and Lamont
210 South Street
Boston, MA 02111

Taxation for Accountants
Warren, Gorham and Lamont
210 South Street
Boston, MA 02111

TAXES—The Tax Magazine
Commerce Clearing House, Inc.
4025 West Peterson Avenue
Chicago, IL 60646

National Tax Journal
21 East State Street
Columbus, OH 43215

The Tax Adviser
1211 Avenue of the Americas
New York, NY 10036

The Practical Accountant
Institute of Continuing
   Professional Development
964 3rd Avenue
New York, NY 10155

Journal of Corporate Taxation
Warren, Gorham and Lamont
210 South Street
Boston, MA 02111

Trusts and Estates
Communication Channels Inc.
6255 Barfield Road
Atlanta, GA 30328

Estate Planning
Warren, Gorham and Lamont
210 South Street
Boston, MA 02111

Taxation for Lawyers
Warren, Gorham and Lamont
210 South Street
Boston, MA 02111

The Tax Executive
300 N. 17th Street
Arlington, VA 22209

Oil and Gas Tax Quarterly
Matthew Bender & Co.
235 East 45th Street
New York, NY 10017

The International Tax Journal
Panel Publishers
14 Plaza Road
Greenvale, NY 11548

The Tax Lawyer
American Bar Association
1800 M Street, N. W.
Washington, DC 20036

Journal of the American Taxation Association
American Accounting Association
5717 Bessie Drive
Sarasota, FL 33583

ASSESSING THE VALIDITY OF THE TAX LAW SOURCE

Once a source has been located, the next procedure is to assess such source in the light of the problem at hand. Proper assessment involves careful interpretation of the tax law with consideration as to its relevance and validity. In connection with validity, an important step is to check for recent changes in the tax law.

Interpreting the Internal Revenue Code. The language of the Code can be extremely difficult to comprehend fully. For example, a subsection [§ 341(e)] relating to collapsible corporations contains *one* sentence of more than 450 words. Within this same subsection are two other sentences of 300 and 340 words. One author has noted 10 common pitfalls in interpreting the Code:[35]

1. Determine the limitations and exceptions to a provision. Do not permit the language of the Code Section to carry greater or lesser weight than was intended.

2. Just because a Section fails to mention an item does not necessarily mean that the item is excluded.

3. Read definitional clauses carefully.

4. Do not overlook small words such as "and" and "or." There is a world of difference between these two words.

5. Read the Code Section completely; do not jump to conclusions. Return to Example 4 and the bonus X Corporation accrued on behalf of R. If the analysis of § 267 stopped with subsection (b)(1), it would appear that the bonus is deductible, since R owns only one-third of the stock in X Corporation and not "more than 50%." A further reading of § 267, however, reveals that R constructively owns all of the stock of his brother and sister (i. e., S and T). Because R is deemed to own "more than 50%" of X Corporation, the conclusion reached after only a partial examination is invalidated.

6. Watch out for cross-referenced and related provisions, since many Sections of the Code are interrelated.

7. Congress is at times not careful when reconciling new Code provisions with existing Sections. Conflicts among Sections, therefore, do arise.

8. Be alert for hidden definitions; terms in a particular Code Section may be defined in the same Section *or in a separate Section.*

9. Some answers may not be found in the Code; therefore, a researcher may have to consult the Regulations and/or judicial decisions.[36]

10. Take careful note of measuring words such as "less than 50%", "more than 50%", and "at least 80%".

---

35. H. G. Wong, "Ten Common Pitfalls in Reading the Internal Revenue Code," *The Practical Accountant* (July–August, 1972), pp. 30–33.
36. The Code is silent concerning the deductibility of educational expenses. Such deductibility, however, falls under the general provision of § 162(a) (the allowance for "all the ordinary and necessary expenses paid or incurred during the taxable year in carrying on any trade or business . . . "). Guidelines for deductibility of educational expenses can be found in Reg. § 1.162–5. See Chapter 10 for a more complete discussion.

Assessing the Validity of a Treasury Regulation. It is often stated that Treasury Regulations have the force and effect of law. This is certainly true for most Regulations, but there have been judicial decisions which have held a Regulation or a portion thereof invalid, usually on the grounds that the Regulation is contrary to the intent of Congress upon the enactment of a particular Code Section.

Keep in mind the following observations when assessing the validity of a Regulation:

—In a challenge, the burden of proof is on the taxpayer to show that the Regulation is wrong.

—If the taxpayer loses the challenge, the imposition of a penalty under § 6653(a) may result. This provision deals with the "intentional disregard of rules and regulations" on the part of the taxpayer.

—Some Regulations merely reprint or rephrase what Congress has stated in its Committee Reports issued in connection with the enactment of tax legislation. Such Regulations are "hard and solid" and almost impossible to overturn, because they clearly reflect the intent of Congress.

—In some Code Sections, Congress has given to the "Secretary or his delegate" the authority to prescribe Regulations to carry out the details of administration or to otherwise complete the operating rules. Under such circumstances, it could almost be said that Congress is delegating its legislative powers to the Treasury Department. Regulations issued pursuant to this type of authority truly possess the force and effect of law and are often called "legislative regulations."

Assessing the Validity of Other Administrative Sources of the Tax Law. Revenue Rulings issued by the IRS carry less weight than Treasury Department Regulations. Rulings are important, however, in that they reflect the position of the IRS on tax matters. In any dispute with the IRS on the interpretation of tax law, therefore, taxpayers should expect agents to follow the results reached in any applicable Rulings.

Revenue Rulings further tell the taxpayer the IRS's reaction to certain court decisions. Recall that the IRS follows a practice of either acquiescing (i. e., agreeing) or not acquiescing (i. e., not agreeing) with the *Regular* decisions of the U. S. Tax Court. This does not mean that a particular decision of the Tax Court is of no value if, for example, the IRS has nonacquiesced in the result. It does, however, indicate that the IRS will continue to litigate the issue involved.

Assessing the Validity of Judicial Sources of the Tax Law. The judicial process as it relates to the formulation of tax law has already been described. How much reliance can be placed on a particular decision depends upon the following variables:

—The level of the court. A decision rendered by a trial court (e. g., a Federal District Court) carries less weight than one issued by an appellate court (e. g., the Fifth Court of Appeals). Unless Congress changes the Code, decisions by the U. S. Supreme Court represent the last word on any tax issue.

—The legal residence of the taxpayer. If, for example, a taxpayer lives in Texas, a decision of the Fifth Court of Appeals means more than one rendered by the Second Court of Appeals. This is the case, since any appeal from a U. S. District Court or the U. S. Tax Court would be to the Fifth Court of Appeals and not to the Second Court of Appeals.[37]

—Whether the decision represents the weight of authority on the issue. In other words, is it supported by the results reached by other courts?

—The outcome or status of the decision on appeal. For example, was the decision appealed and, if so, with what result?

In connection with the last two variables, the use of a citator is invaluable to tax research.[38] Such use is illustrated in Appendix E.

ARRIVING AT THE SOLUTION OR AT ALTERNATIVE SOLUTIONS

In Example 4 the problem was whether or not X Corporation could deduct a bonus of $20,000, declared on December 30, 19X0, and payable to R, one of its employees. A refinement of the problem added the additional information that the bonus was not paid until July 1, 19X1, and all of the stock of X Corporation was owned by R and his brother and sister. The end result was a disallowance of the deduction unless it could be shown that the bonus was constructively paid to R no later than March 15, 19X1. The solution, therefore, turned on whether the conditions for application of § 267 (i. e., disallowance of expenses involving related parties) were satisfied. But even if § 267 could be avoided, the bonus would have to pass the test of reasonableness set forth in § 162(a)(1). If, when added to the other compensation R received in 19X0 from X Corporation, some or all of the bonus is unreasonable, such amount will be disallowed as a deduction.

In summary, the solution to the problem depends upon the resolution of two questions of fact. First, has a constructive payment occurred? Second, is the compensation R received reasonable in amount? Under such circumstances, a clear-cut answer may not be

---

37. Before October 1, 1982, an appeal from the then named U. S. Court of Claims (i. e., the other trial court) was directly to the U. S. Supreme Court.

38. The major citators are published by Commerce Clearing House, Prentice-Hall, and Shepard's Citations, Inc.

possible. This does not, however, detract from the value of the research. Often, a guarded judgment is the best possible solution that can be given to a tax problem.

COMMUNICATING TAX RESEARCH

Once satisfied that the problem has been researched adequately, the researcher may need to prepare a memo setting forth the result. The form such a memo takes could depend on a number of different considerations. For example, is any particular procedure or format recommended for tax research memos either by an employer or an instructor? Is the memo to be given directly to the client or will it first pass to the researcher's employer? But whatever form it takes, a good research memo should contain the following elements:

— A clear statement of the issue.

— In more complex situations, a short review of the factual pattern which raises the issue.

— A review of the tax law sources (e. g., Code, Regulations, Rulings, judicial authority).

— Any assumptions made in arriving at the solution.

— The solution recommended and the logic or reasoning in its support.

— The references consulted in the research process.

In short, a good tax memo should tell the reader what was researched, the results of that research, and the justification for the recommendation made.[39]

WORKING WITH THE TAX LAW—
TAX PLANNING

Tax research and tax planning are inseparable. The primary purpose of effective tax planning is to reduce the taxpayer's total tax bill. This does not mean that the course of action selected must produce the lowest possible tax under the circumstances; the minimization must be considered in context with the legitimate business goals of the taxpayer.

A secondary objective of effective tax planning works toward a deferment or postponement of the tax. Specifically, this objective aims to accomplish any one or more of the following procedures: eradicating the tax entirely; eliminating the tax in the current year; deferring the receipt of income; converting ordinary income into capital gains; proliferating taxpayers (i. e., forming partnerships and corporations

---

39. See Chapter 6 of the volume referred to in Footnote 28.

or making lifetime gifts to family members); eluding double taxation; avoiding ordinary income; or creating, increasing, or accelerating deductions. However, this second objective should be accepted with considerable reservation. Although the maxim "A bird in the hand is worth two in the bush" has general validity, there are frequent cases in which the rule breaks down. For example, a tax election in one year, although it accomplishes a current reduction in taxes, could saddle future years with a disadvantageous tax position.

NONTAX CONSIDERATIONS

There is an honest danger that tax motivations may take on a significance that is not in conformity with the true values involved. In other words, tax considerations may operate to impair the exercise of sound business judgment by the taxpayer. Thus, the tax planning process may become a medium through which to accomplish ends that are socially and economically objectionable. Ostensibly, there exists a pronounced tendency for planning to go toward the opposing extremes of either not enough or too much emphasis on tax considerations. The happy medium—one that recognizes the significance of taxes, but not beyond the point at which planning serves to detract from the exercise of good business judgment, turns out to be the promised land that is seldom reached.

The remark is often made that a good rule to follow is to refrain from pursuing any course of action which would not be followed were it not for certain tax considerations. This statement is not entirely correct, but it does illustrate the desirability of preventing business logic from being "sacrificed at the altar of tax planning." In this connection, the following comment is significant:

> The lure of a quick tax dollar is often the only justification for a transaction that might have been accomplished with much sounder economic results and equivalent tax savings if more careful and deliberate consideration had been given to the problem. Certainly in this atmosphere of the tax-controlled economy a very heavy obligation is cast upon the tax adviser to give serious consideration as to whether a proposed action achieves a desirable economic result apart from tax savings or whether the immediate tax advantages may be more than offset by later economic or personal disadvantage. We cannot afford to develop successful cures that are killing our patients.[40]

---

40. Norris Darrell, "Some Responsibilities of the Tax Adviser in Regard to Tax Minimization Devices," *Proceedings of the New York University Eighth Annual Institute on Federal Taxation* (Albany, N.Y.: Matthew Bender & Co., 1950), pp. 988–989. For a more detailed discussion of tax planning, see Norwood, Chisholm, Burke, and Vaughn, *Federal Taxation: Research, Planning and Procedure* (Englewood Cliffs, N.J.: Prentice-Hall Inc., 1979), Ch. 6.

TAX EVASION AND TAX AVOIDANCE

There is a fine line between legal tax planning and illegal tax planning—tax avoidance versus tax evasion. Tax avoidance is merely tax minimization through legal techniques. In this sense, tax avoidance becomes the proper objective of all tax planning. Evasion, while also aimed at the elimination or reduction of taxes, connotes the use of subterfuge and fraud as a means to an end. Popular usage—probably because of the common goals that are involved—has linked these two concepts to the extent that any true distinctions have been obliterated in the minds of many. Consequently, the taint created by the association of tax avoidance and tax evasion has deterred some taxpayers from properly taking advantage of the planning possibilities. The now-classic verbiage of Judge Learned Hand in *Commissioner v. Newman* reflects the true values the individual should have. In this opinion Judge Hand declared:

> Over and over again courts have said that there is nothing sinister in so arranging one's affairs as to keep taxes as low as possible. Everybody does so, rich or poor; and all do right, for nobody owes any public duty to pay more than the law demands: taxes are enforced extractions, not voluntary contributions. To demand more in the name of morals is mere cant.[41]

FOLLOW-UP PROCEDURES

Because tax planning usually involves a proposed (as opposed to a completed) transaction, it is predicated upon the continuing validity of the advice based upon the tax research. A change in the tax law (either legislative, administrative, or judicial) could alter the original conclusion. Additional research may be necessary to test the solution in the light of current developments (see one set of broken lines depicted in Figure IV).

TAX PLANNING—A PRACTICAL APPLICATION

Returning to the facts of Example 4, what could have been done to protect X Corporation's deduction for the $20,000 bonus to R had the transaction not been completed? Concerning the § 267 issue (i. e., disallowance of accrued but unpaid expenses among certain related parties), the following steps should be taken:

—Pay the bonus to R by December 31, 19X0.

—If the payment is to be postponed, it should take place no later than March 15, 19X1. In this event, the parties should firmly

---

41. *Comm. v. Newman,* 47–1 USTC ¶ 9175, 35 AFTR 857, 159 F.2d 848 (CA–2, 1947).

establish X Corporation's liability to make the payment before the close of its tax year (i. e., December 31, 19X0).

What about any potential unreasonable compensation issue under § 162(a)(1)? One tax planning aid would be to make the amount of the bonus contingent on a predetermined formula. Bonuses arbitrarily determined at year-end are particularly suspect when paid to an employee-shareholder of a closely-held corporation.[42] Regulation § 1.162–7(b)(2) states in part:

> Generally speaking, if contingent compensation is paid pursuant to a free bargain between the employer and the individual *made before the services are rendered,* not influenced by any consideration on the part of the employer other than that of securing on fair and advantageous terms the services of the individual, it should be allowed as a deduction *even though in the actual working out of the contract it may prove to be greater than the amount which would ordinarily be paid.* [Emphasis added.]

Thus, a contract entered into by R and X Corporation before the services are rendered (in early 19X0) establishing R's bonus as contingent on profits or some other measure of productivity would help justify a larger amount as reasonable than would otherwise be the case.

* * *

Throughout the text, most chapters include observations on TAX PLANNING CONSIDERATIONS. Such observations are not all-inclusive but are intended to illustrate some of the ways in which the material covered can be effectively utilized to minimize taxes.

PROBLEM MATERIALS

Questions for Class Discussion

1. Trace through Congress the path usually followed by a tax bill.
2. What is the final step in the making of a new tax law?
3. Why are committee reports of Congress important as a source of tax law?
4. The Tax Equity and Fiscal Responsibility Act of 1982 (TEFRA) became part of the Internal Revenue Code of 1954. Explain the meaning of this statement.

---

42. The unreasonable compensation issue is essentially a problem restricted to closely-held corporations. A closely-held corporation can be defined as one in which only a few shareholders are in a position to manipulate corporate policy to their own advantage. X Corporation fits this definition, since all of its stock is held by three shareholders (R, S, and T), all of whom are related to one another.

5. Judicial decisions interpreting a provision of the Internal Revenue Code of 1939 are no longer of any value in view of the enactment of the Internal Revenue Code of 1954. Assess the validity of this statement.

6. In tax law, what has the highest tax authority or reliability?

7. What is a Proposed Regulation? How would a Proposed Regulation under § 541 be cited?

8. Distinguish between:

    (a) Treasury Regulations and Revenue Rulings.

    (b) Revenue Rulings and Revenue Procedures.

    (c) Revenue Rulings and individual (i. e., "private") rulings.

    (d) Individual (i. e., "private") rulings and determination letters.

9. Interpret the citation DOC. 8312019.

10. What are the major differences between individual rulings and determination letters?

11. Interpret each of the following citations:

    (a) Rev.Rul. 80–325, 1980–2 C.B. 5.

    (b) Rev.Proc. 80–32, 1980–2 C.B. 767.

12. What are Treasury Decisions (T.D.)?

    (a) What purpose do they serve?

    (b) Where are they published?

13. Summarize the trial and appellate court system for Federal tax litigation.

14. List an advantage and a disadvantage of using the U. S. Tax Court as the trial court for Federal tax litigation.

15. List an advantage and a disadvantage of using a U. S. District Court as the trial court for Federal tax litigation.

16. List an advantage and a disadvantage of using the U. S. Claims Court as the trial court for Federal tax litigation.

17. Taxpayer lives in Michigan. In a controversy with the IRS, taxpayer loses at the trial court level. Describe the appeal procedure under the following different assumptions:

    (a) The trial court was the Small Claims Division of the U. S. Tax Court.

    (b) The trial court was the U. S. Tax Court.

    (c) The trial court was a U. S. District Court.

    (d) The trial court was the U. S. Claims Court.

18. Suppose the U. S. Government loses a tax case in the U. S. District Court of Idaho but does not appeal the result. What does the failure to appeal signify?

19. Because the U. S. Tax Court is a national court, it always decides the same issue in a consistent manner. Assess the validity of this statement.

20. Interpret each of the citations appearing below:

    (a) 54 T.C. 1514 (1970).

    (b) 408 F.2d 117 (CA–2, 1969).

    (c) 69–1 USTC ¶ 9319 (CA–2, 1969).

    (d) 23 AFTR2d 69–1090 (CA–2, 1969).

    (e) 293 F.Supp. 1129 (D.Ct., Miss., 1967).

    (f) 67–1 USTC ¶ 9253 (D.Ct., Miss., 1967).

    (g) 19 AFTR2d 647 (D.Ct., Miss., 1967).

    (h) 56 S.Ct. 289 (USSC, 1935).

    (i) 36–1 USTC ¶ 9020 (USSC, 1935).

    (j) 16 AFTR 1274 (USSC, 1935).

    (k) 422 F.2d 1336 (Ct.Cls., 1970).

21. Explain the following abbreviations:

    (a) CA–2

    (b) Cls.Ct.

    (c) *aff'd*

    (d) *rev'd*

    (e) *rem'd*

    (f) *cert. denied*

    (g) *acq.*

    (h) B.T.A.

    (i) USTC

    (j) AFTR

    (k) F.2d

    (l) F.Supp.

    (m) USSC

    (n) S.Ct.

    (o) D.Ct.

22. What is the difference between a Regular and a Memorandum decision of the U. S. Tax Court?

23. What is a legislative Regulation?

24. In assessing the validity of a prior court decision, discuss the significance of the following on the taxpayer's issue:

    (a) The decision was rendered by the U. S. District Court of Wyoming. Taxpayer lives in Wyoming.

    (b) The decision was rendered by the U. S. Claims Court. Taxpayer lives in Wyoming.

    (c) The decision was rendered by the Second Court of Appeals. Taxpayer lives in California.

    (d) The decision was rendered by the U. S. Supreme Court.

    (e) The decision was rendered by the U. S. Tax Court. The IRS has acquiesced in the result.

    (f) Same as (e) except that the IRS has issued a nonacquiescence as to the result.

25. Where may a researcher locate a 1981 District Court decision?

26. A student/friend majoring in sociology indicates that tax advisers are immoral since they merely help people cheat the government. Defend tax planning by tax advisers.

27. While researching a tax problem, why may the answer not be found in the Internal Revenue Code?

28. When may a researcher have a need to refer to a citator?

29. In the tax research process, what does problem identification involve?

30. Where may you locate a published decision of the Claims Court?

31. What is the purpose of the U. S. Claims Court?

Problems

32. You inherit a problem that was researched four months previously. You believe the answers are correct, but you wish to evaluate the reliability of the authority given in the research report. How do you determine the latest developments with respect to a research problem?

33. T, an individual taxpayer, has just been audited by the IRS and, as a result, has been assessed a substantial deficiency (which has not yet been paid) in additional income taxes. In preparing his defense, T advances the following possibilities:

    (a) Although a resident of Kentucky, T plans to sue in a U. S. District Court in Oregon which appears to be more favorably inclined towards taxpayers.

    (b) If (a) is not possible, T plans to take his case to a Kentucky state court where an uncle is the presiding judge.

    (c) Since T has found a B.T.A. decision that seems to help his case, he plans to rely on it under alternatives (a) or (b).

    (d) If he loses at the trial court level, T plans to appeal either to the U. S. Claims Court or the U. S. Second Court of Appeals. The reason for this choice is the presence of relatives in both Washington, D.C., and Chicago. Staying with these relatives could save T lodging expense while his appeal is being heard by the court selected.

    (e) Whether or not T wins at the trial court or appeals court level, he feels certain of success on an appeal to the U. S. Supreme Court.

    Evaluate T's notions concerning the judicial process as it applies to Federal income tax controversies.

34. Using the legend provided, classify each of the statements appearing below (more than one answer per statement may be appropriate):

Legend

D = Applies to the U. S. District Court
T = Applies to the U. S. Tax Court
C = Applies to the U. S. Claims Court
A = Applies to the U. S. Court of Appeals
U = Applies to the U. S. Supreme Court
N = Applies to none of the above

(a) Decides only Federal tax matters.

(b) Decisions are reported in the F.2d Series.

(c) Decisions are reported in the USTCs.

(d) Decisions are reported in the AFTRs.

(e) Appeal is by Writ of Certiorari.

(f) Court meets most often in Washington, D. C.

(g) A jury trial is available.

(h) Trial courts.

(i) Appellate courts.

(j) Appeal is to the Federal Circuit and bypasses the taxpayer's particular circuit court.

(k) Has a Small Claims Division.

(l) The only trial court where the taxpayer does not have to first pay the tax assessed by the IRS.

Research Problems

35. Locate the following Internal Revenue Code citations and give a brief description of them:

(a) § 43(c)(1)(B).

(b) § 179(b)(2).

(c) § 219(c)(2)(A)(i).

36. Locate the following Regulation citations and give a brief description of them:

(a) Reg. § 1.2–2(a)(i).

(b) Reg. § 1.44–5(c)(1).

(c) Reg. § 1.61–7(b)(1).

37. Determine the acquiescence/nonacquiescence position of the IRS with respect to *Edward A. Moradian,* 53 T.C. 207 (1969).

38. Locate the following tax services in your library and indicate the name of the publisher and whether the service is organized by topic or Code Section.

(a) *Federal Taxes.*

(b) *Standard Federal Tax Reporter.*

(c) *Tax Coordinator 2d.*

(d) *Mertens Law of Federal Income Taxation.*

(e) *Tax Management Portfolios.*

(f) Rabkin & Johnson, *Federal Income, Gift & Estate Taxation.*

39. In the Tax Publications Matrix on page 95, place an X if a court decision can be found in the publication. There may be more than one X along a row for a particular court decision.

40. Complete the citations appearing below to the extent the research materials are available to you:

A. *Midland Ross Corp. v. U. S.*, 73–2 USTC —— (——, 1972).

B. *Midland Ross Corp. v. U. S.*, 32 AFTR2d —— (——, 1972).

C. *Groman v. Comm.*, 86 F.2d ——, (——, 1936).

D. —— v. ——, 49–2 USTC ¶ 9377 (——, ——).

E. —— v. ——, 35 AFTR2d 75–526 (——, ——).

F. *R. J. Nicholl Co.*, 59 T.C. —— (——).

G. *Maresca Trust*, TCM 1983–——.

H. Rev.Proc. 83–71, I.R.B. ——, ——.

I. *Hortense A. Menefee*, —— B.T.A. —— (1941).

J. *Bardahl Manufacturing Co.*, 24 TCM ——.

K. Rev.Proc. 72–51, 1972–—— C.B. ——.

41. By using the research materials available to you, answer the following questions:

    (a) Has Prop. Reg. § 1.482–2 been finalized?

    (b) What happened to *Golconda Mining Corp.*, 58 T.C. 736 (1972) on appeal?

    (c) Does Rev.Rul. 69–185 still represent the position of the IRS on the issue involved?

42. Indicate the disposition of these court decisions by the U. S. Supreme Court:

    A. *Comm. v. Anderson*, 371 F.2d 59 (CA–6, 1966).

    B. *Heard v. Comm.*, 326 F.2d 962 (CA–8, 1964).

    C. *Adolph Coors Co. v. Comm.*, 519 F.2d 1280 (CA–10, 1975).

    D. *Comm. v. Golonsky*, 200 F.2d 72 (CA–3, 1952).

43. Determine the reliability of the following items.

    A. Rev.Rul. 60–97, 1960–1 C.B. 69.

    B. *Berry's Estate v. Comm.*, 372 F.2d 479 (CA–6, 1967).

    C. *Barry D. Pevsner*, ¶ 79,311 P–H Memo TC (1979).

44. During 1984, T lived with and supported a 20-year-old woman who was not his wife. He resides in a state which has a statute that makes it a misdemeanor for a man and woman not married to each other to live together. May T claim his "friend" as a dependent assuming he satisfies the normal tax rules for the deduction? Should T consider moving to another state?

Partial list of research aids:

§ 152(b)(5).

John T. Untermann, 38 T.C. 93 (1962).

S.Rept. 1983, 85th Cong., 2d Sess., reprinted in the 1958 Code Cong. & Adm.News 4791, 4804.

TAX PUBLICATIONS MATRIX

Court	U. S. Govt. Printing Office	West Publishing Company			Prentice-Hall			Commerce Clearing House	
		Federal Supp.	Federal 2d	S.Ct.	BTA Memo	TC Memo	AFTR	TC Memo	USTC
U. S. Supreme Court									
Court of Appeals									
Claims Court									
Distrct Court									
Tax Court (regular decisions)									
Tax Court (memo decisions)									
Board of Tax Appeal									
BTA Memo									

Chapter 4

Tax Determination, Personal and Dependency Exemptions, An Overview of Property Transactions

To understand how the Federal income tax applies to individuals, it is necessary to look into the manner in which the tax is determined. To this end, this chapter will review and develop further some of the components of the tax formula, introduce and explain the concept of the zero bracket amount, and explain the steps involved in the computation of the tax using both the Tax Table and the Tax Rate Schedules.

The role of the deduction for personal and dependency exemptions in the determination of the income tax liability of individuals is covered in this chapter. Justification for these exemptions, as well as the rules governing their application, is included in the discussion.

When property is sold or otherwise disposed of, the result could affect the determination of income tax liability. Although the area of property transactions is covered in detail in Chapters 14–17 of the text, an understanding of certain basic concepts is helpful in working with some of the materials to follow. The concluding portion of this chapter, therefore, furnishes an overview of the area. Here, the distinction is made between realized and recognized gain or loss, the classification of such gain or loss (i. e., ordinary or capital), and its treatment for income tax purposes.

TAX FORMULA

Most individuals will compute taxable income using the tax formula shown in Figure I.[1]

Figure I

TAX FORMULA

Income (broadly conceived)		$ xx,xxx
Less: Exclusions		x,xxx
Gross income		$ xx,xxx
Less: Deductions *for* adjusted gross income		x,xxx
Adjusted gross income		$ xx,xxx
Less: Excess itemized deductions—		
Total itemized deductions	$ x,xxx	
Minus: Zero bracket amount	x,xxx	x,xxx
Personal and dependency exemptions (number of exemptions × $1,000)		x,xxx
Taxable income		$ xx,xxx

Before illustrating the application of the tax formula, a brief introduction to the components of the formula is necessary.

SOME OF THE COMPONENTS

Income (broadly conceived).   This includes all income of the taxpayer, both taxable and nontaxable. It is essentially equivalent to gross receipts, but it does not include a return of capital or receipt of borrowed funds.

Exclusions.   For various reasons[2] Congress has chosen to exclude certain types of income from the income tax base. The principal income exclusions are discussed in Chapter 6. A partial list of these exclusions is shown in Figure II.

---

1.   Certain modifications of the tax formula are sometimes necessary. Some taxpayers are required to compute an unused zero bracket amount in determining taxable income. These taxpayers will use a different tax formula, as shown in Example 5 (to be used by certain dependent children) or Example 7 (to be used by married taxpayers filing separate returns and by all other taxpayers who are required to compute an unused zero bracket amount). Another item that will require a slight modification of the tax formula in certain cases is the direct charitable contribution (discussed in Chapter 11), which is deducted *from* adjusted gross income, but not as an itemized deduction, in computing taxable income.

2.   See Chapter 6 for a discussion of the reasons for some of the principal exclusions from income.

Figure II
PARTIAL LIST OF EXCLUSIONS FROM GROSS INCOME

Accident insurance proceeds
Annuities (to a limited extent)
Bequests
Casualty insurance proceeds
Child support payments
Compensatory damages
Cost-of-living allowance (for military)
Damages for personal injury or sickness
Death benefits (up to $5,000)
Disability benefits
Federal Employee's Compensation Act payments
Fellowship grants (to a limited extent)
Gifts
Group-term life insurance, premium paid by employer (coverage not over $50,000)
Health insurance proceeds not deducted as a medical expense
Inheritances
Life insurance paid on death
Meals and lodging (furnished for employer's convenience)
Military allowances
Minister's dwelling rental value allowance
Railroad retirement benefits (to a limited extent)
Relocation payments
Scholarship grants (to a limited extent)
Social Security benefits (to a limited extent)
Unemployment compensation (to a limited extent)
Veterans' benefits
Welfare payments
Workers' compensation

Gross Income. Gross income is defined broadly in the Code as "all income from whatever source derived."[3] It includes, but is not limited to, the items shown in the partial list in Figure III. It does not include unrealized gains. Gross income is discussed in Chapters 5 and 6.

Figure III
PARTIAL LIST OF GROSS INCOME ITEMS

Alimony
Amounts recovered after being deducted in prior years
Annuities
Awards
Back pay
Bargain purchase from employer
Bonuses
Breach of contract damages
Business income
Clergy fees
Commissions
Compensation for services
Contributions to members of the clergy
Death benefits in excess of $5,000
Debts forgiven
Director's fees
Dividends (subject to a limited exclusion)*
Embezzled funds
Employee awards
Employee bonuses
Employee benefits (except certain fringe benefits)
Estate and trust income

---

3. § 61(a).

Figure III *(continued)*

Farm income	Partnership income
Fees	Pensions
Free tour	Prizes
Gains from illegal activities	Professional fees
Gains from sale of property	Punitive damages
Gambling winnings	Reimbursement for moving
Group-term life insurance,	expenses
premium paid by employer	Rents
(coverage over $50,000)	Retirement pay
Hobby income	Rewards
Incentive awards	Royalties
Interest	Salaries
Jury duty fees	Severance pay
Living quarters, meals (unless	Strike and lockout benefits
furnished for employer's	Supplemental unemployment
convenience)	benefits
Mileage allowance	Tips and gratuities
Military pay (unless combat pay)	Travel allowance
Notary fees	Wages

* For 1984 certain dividends are excluded from gross income of up to $100 ($200 on a joint return).

Deductions for Adjusted Gross Income. There are two categories of deductions for individual taxpayers: (1) deductions *for* adjusted gross income and (2) deductions *from* adjusted gross income. Deductions *for* adjusted gross income include ordinary and necessary expenses incurred in a trade or business, certain employee business expenses, moving expenses, alimony paid, payments to an individual retirement account, forfeited interest penalty for premature withdrawal of time deposits, the capital gain deduction, and others.[4] Deductible employee business expenses include employment-related expenses for travel and transportation. The principal deductions *for* adjusted gross income are discussed in Chapters 7, 8, 9, and 10.

Adjusted Gross Income. This is an important subtotal which serves as the basis for computing percentage limitations on certain itemized deductions, such as medical expenses and charitable contributions. For example, medical expenses are deductible only to the extent they exceed five percent of adjusted gross income.

Itemized Deductions. As a general rule, personal expenditures are disallowed as deductions in arriving at taxable income. However, Congress has chosen to allow certain specified expenses as itemized deductions, even though they are personal in nature. In addition, tax-

---

4.   § 62.

Figure IV

PARTIAL LIST OF ITEMIZED DEDUCTIONS

Medical expenses in excess of 5% of adjusted gross income
State and local income taxes
Real estate taxes
General sales taxes
Personal property taxes
Interest on home mortgage
Interest on credit and charge cards
Interest (in general)
Charitable contributions
Casualty and theft losses
Miscellaneous expenses:
    Union dues
    Professional dues and subscriptions
    Certain educational expenses
    Tax return preparation fee
    Investment counsel fees

payers are allowed to itemize expenses related to (1) the production or collection of income; (2) the management of property held for the production of income; and (3) the determination, collection, or refund of any tax.[5] Itemized deductions (discussed in Chapter 11) include, but are not limited to, the expenses listed in Figure IV.

Zero Bracket Amount. The zero bracket amount is a specified amount set by Congress which is dependent on the filing status of the taxpayer.[6] The effect of the zero bracket amount is to exempt a taxpayer's income, up to the specified amount, from Federal income tax liability.

Filing Status	Zero Bracket Amount[7]
Single	$ 2,300
Married, filing jointly	3,400
Surviving spouse[8]	3,400
Head of household	2,300
Married, filing separately	1,700

Excess Itemized Deductions. Taxpayers are allowed to deduct itemized deductions in excess of the zero bracket amount (see Example 2). Taxpayers whose itemized deductions are less than the zero bracket amount will compute their tax using the zero bracket amount rather than itemizing (see Example 3).

---

5. § 212.
6. Filing status is discussed in a later section of this chapter.
7. § 63(d).
8. This filing status is described on the tax return as "Qualifying widow(er) with dependent child," but is commonly referred to as "surviving spouse" status.

Exemptions. Exemptions of $1,000 each are allowed for the taxpayer, the taxpayer's spouse, and for each dependent of the taxpayer. Additional exemptions are allowed taxpayers and their spouses who are age 65 or older or blind.

APPLICATION OF THE TAX FORMULA

The tax formula shown in Figure I is illustrated in the following example.

> **Example 1.** J, age 25, is single and has no dependents. She is a high school teacher and earned a $16,000 salary in 1984. Her other income consisted of a $1,000 prize won in a sweepstakes contest she had entered and $500 interest on municipal bonds received as a graduation gift in 1981. During 1984 she incurred deductible travel expenses of $100 while attending the annual state teacher's convention. Her itemized deductions, which consisted mostly of interest on the mortgage on her condominium, were $2,750. J's taxable income for 1984 would be computed as follows:

Income (broadly conceived):		
Salary		$ 16,000
Prize		1,000
Interest on municipal bonds		500
		$ 17,500
Less: Exclusion—		
Interest on municipal bonds		500
Gross income		$ 17,000
Less: Deduction *for* adjusted gross income—		
Travel expenses		100
Adjusted gross income		$ 16,900
Less: Excess itemized deductions—		
Total itemized deductions	$ 2,750	
Minus: Zero bracket amount	2,300	450
Personal and dependency exemptions		
(1 × $1,000)		1,000
Taxable income		$ 15,450

The structure of the individual income tax return (Form 1040 or Form 1040A) differs somewhat from the tax formula illustrated above. On the tax return, gross income generally is the starting point in computing taxable income. Exclusions, with few exceptions, are not reported on the tax return at all. Common examples of the few exceptions which are reported on the tax return are the exclusions for dividends and for disability income (see Form 1040 in Appendix B–3).

ZERO BRACKET AMOUNT

General Rule. As a general rule, taxpayers compute their taxable income using the full zero bracket amount. If itemized deductions exceed the zero bracket amount, taxable income is computed as shown in Example 2.

Example 2. H and W are married taxpayers who file a joint return. They have itemized deductions of $5,000 and four personal and dependency exemptions. Assuming they have adjusted gross income of $20,000, their taxable income is computed as follows:

Adjusted gross income[9]		$ 20,000
Less: Excess itemized deductions—		
Total itemized deductions	$ 5,000	
Minus: Zero bracket amount	3,400	1,600
Personal and dependency exemptions		
(4 × $1,000)		4,000
Taxable income		$ 14,400

If itemized deductions are less than the zero bracket amount, the taxpayer will compute taxable income using the zero bracket amount rather than itemizing.

Example 3. Assume the same facts as in the previous example except that H and W have total itemized deductions of only $3,000.

Adjusted gross income		$ 20,000
Less: Excess itemized deductions—		
Total itemized deductions	$ 3,000	
Minus: Zero bracket amount	3,400	–0–[10]
Personal and dependency exemptions		
(4 × $1,000)		4,000
Taxable income		$ 16,000

Structure of the Tax Table and Rate Schedules. To fully understand the role of the zero bracket amount, it is necessary to understand the structure of the Tax Table and Tax Rate Schedules.[11]

---

9. For convenience, adjusted gross income is used as the starting point in this and certain other examples throughout the text. Adjusted gross income is computed as shown in Figure I.

10. Since the taxpayer's total itemized deductions are less than the zero bracket amount, the taxpayer will not itemize. Thus, taxable income equals adjusted gross income minus exemptions.

11. Individuals must compute their tax using either the Tax Table or the Tax Rate Schedules. Procedures for using the Tax Table and Tax Rate Schedules are discussed under TAX DETERMINATION later in this chapter. Some taxpayers are eligible to compute their tax using a special method, income averaging (see Chapter 12).

Careful study of the tax formula shows that the zero bracket amount is not subtracted from adjusted gross income in arriving at taxable income. Instead, the zero bracket amount is subtracted from total itemized deductions in computing excess itemized deductions.

If the zero bracket amount is not subtracted in computing taxable income, how does the taxpayer benefit from the zero bracket amount? The answer is that the zero bracket amount is built into the Tax Table and Tax Rate Schedules, which has the effect of exempting the taxpayer's income, up to the specified zero bracket amount, from Federal income tax liability.

> **Example 4.** R, age 20, is single and has no dependents. In 1983, he earned $3,300. R has no itemized deductions, so his taxable income is $2,300 (i. e., gross income of $3,300 minus R's $1,000 personal exemption). Examination of the Tax Table in Appendix A–2 confirms that R's tax liability is $0.

In the past, Congress has attempted to set the tax-free amount (represented by the zero bracket amount) approximately equal to an estimated poverty level,[12] although it has not always been consistent in doing so.

Through the personal exemption, Congress has exempted an additional $1,000 of income for every taxpayer. The combined effect of the zero bracket amount and the personal exemption is demonstrated in the previous example.

UNUSED ZERO BRACKET AMOUNT

The following taxpayers are ineligible to use the full zero bracket amount and are required to make a special computation which might result in an *unused zero bracket amount:*[13]

—A married individual filing a separate return where either spouse itemizes deductions.

—A nonresident alien.

—A U. S. citizen who is entitled to exemption under § 931 for income from U. S. possessions.

—A dependent child who is either under 19 or a full-time student, who may be claimed as a dependent on his or her parents' return and who has unearned income of $1,000 or more (e. g., dividends or interest).

---

12. S.Rep.No.92–437, 92nd Cong., 1st Sess., 1971, p. 54. Another purpose of the zero bracket amount was discussed in Chapter 2 under the heading of "Administrative Feasibility." The size of the zero bracket amount has a direct bearing on the number of taxpayers who are in a position to itemize excess deductions *from* adjusted gross income. A reduction of the number of such taxpayers, in turn, requires less audit effort on the part of the IRS.

13. § 63(e).

The special computation is required because of the structure of the Tax Table and Tax Rate Schedules. For various reasons, Congress has chosen to limit the zero bracket amount for the taxpayers listed above. Because the Tax Table and Tax Rate Schedules have the full zero bracket amount built in, the portion of the zero bracket amount not allowed must be added to adjusted gross income in arriving at taxable income. The portion of the zero bracket amount which is disallowed is called the unused zero bracket amount. Two situations which require the special computation limiting the zero bracket amount are discussed below and on pages 106 and 107.

Dependent Child. The zero bracket amount is limited for a child who may be claimed as a dependent[14] on his or her parents' tax return and who has <u>unearned</u> income of $1,000 or more.[15] The unused zero bracket amount in this case is equal to the child's zero bracket amount[16] minus the greater of the child's itemized deductions or the child's earned income. Earned income includes salaries, wages, and other forms of compensation. Unearned income includes, but is not limited to, dividends, interest, and distributions from trusts established for the benefit of the child.

Example 5. K is a full-time student who is supported by her parents and is claimed by them as a dependent on their tax return for 1984. K earned $1,800 from a part-time job and has dividend income of $1,200 (after the $100 dividend exclusion). K's itemized deductions amounted to $600. Her taxable income would be computed as follows:

Adjusted gross income ($1,800 + $1,200)		$ 3,000
Plus: Unused zero bracket amount—		
Zero bracket amount	$ 2,300	
Minus: The greater of—		
Itemized deductions ($600) or		
earned income ($1,800)	1,800	500
Total		$ 3,500
Less: Personal and dependency exemptions		
(1 × $1,000)		1,000
Taxable income		$ 2,500

The unused zero bracket amount computation is not required if the dependent child has itemized deductions or earned income in excess of his or her zero bracket amount. In such case the child's taxable income is computed according to the tax formula in Figure I.

---

14. The requirements for claiming a child as a dependent are discussed later in this chapter.

15. § 63(e)(1)(D).

16. A dependent child's zero bracket amount is $2,300 if single or $1,700 if married filing a separate return.

Example 5 shows that the zero bracket amount of a dependent child who does not itemize will be limited to the amount of earned income (or itemized deductions if greater). If it were not for this limitation, up to $3,300 of income could be shifted tax-free from a parent to a child.

Example 6. G is a wealthy taxpayer who is in the 50 percent marginal tax bracket. (The highest rate of tax paid by a taxpayer is referred to as his or her marginal tax rate.) In an attempt to reduce his income tax, G transfers cash to a savings account in the name of S, his son. The bank pays interest of $3,300 to S in 1983. G fully supports S, age 6, and claims S as a dependent on his tax return. Will the $3,300 be tax-free to S? The answer is no, because S must compute an unused zero bracket amount in arriving at taxable income. Assuming S has no itemized deductions and no earned income, taxable income for 1983 is computed as follows:

Adjusted gross income		$ 3,300
Plus: Unused zero bracket amount—		
Zero bracket amount	$ 2,300	
Minus: The greater of—		
Itemized deductions ($0) or		
earned income ($0)	–0–	2,300
Total income		$ 5,600
Less: Personal and dependency exemptions		
(1 × $1,000)		1,000
Taxable income		$ 4,600

The Tax Table in Appendix A–2 shows that the tax on S's income is $285.[17]

Married Taxpayers Filing Separately. The unused zero bracket amount computation also is required of a married taxpayer filing a separate return when either spouse itemizes deductions. The unused zero bracket amount is equal to that portion of the zero bracket amount that exceeds the taxpayer's itemized deductions.[18] This computation differs from the unused zero bracket amount computation of a dependent child in that earned income is of no significance in computing the unused zero bracket amount.

Example 7. H and W are married individuals who file separate returns. H itemizes deductions on his separate return. W's adjusted gross income is $15,000 and she has itemized deductions of $1,400. W's taxable income would be computed as follows:

---

17. A dependent child who is claimed as an exemption on his or her parents' tax return is also allowed to claim an exemption on his or her own return. See discussion later in this chapter.

18. § 63(e).

Adjusted gross income		$ 15,000
Plus: Unused zero bracket amount—		
Zero bracket amount	$ 1,700	
Minus: Itemized deductions	1,400	300
Total		$ 15,300
Less: Personal and dependency exemptions		
(1 × $1,000)		1,000
Taxable income		$ 14,300

The unused zero bracket amount must be added to adjusted gross income, since the zero bracket amount of $1,700 is built into the Tax Table and W is required to itemize her deductions of $1,400 rather than make use of the zero bracket amount. This computation is designed to prevent the double benefit which would result if one spouse were allowed to itemize all deductions of the family while the other spouse used the zero bracket amount.

If the itemized deductions of a married taxpayer filing separately exceed the zero bracket amount, there is no unused zero bracket amount. Instead, taxable income is computed as shown in the tax formula in Figure I.

PERSONAL AND DEPENDENCY EXEMPTIONS

The use of exemptions in the tax system is based in part on the concept that a taxpayer with a small amount of income should be exempt from income taxation. Every individual taxpayer is allowed an exemption which frees $1,000 of income from tax. A broader justification for the use of exemptions is the wherewithal to pay concept. Thus even larger amounts of income are freed from tax by allowing exemptions for dependents of the taxpayer and additional exemptions if the taxpayer or the taxpayer's spouse is age 65 or over, or blind, or both.

PERSONAL EXEMPTIONS

The Code provides a $1,000 personal exemption for the taxpayer and an additional $1,000 exemption for the spouse if a joint return is filed.[19] However, when separate returns are filed, a married taxpayer cannot claim a $1,000 exemption for his or her spouse unless the spouse has no gross income and is not claimed as the dependent of another taxpayer.

The determination of marital status generally is made at the end of the taxable year, except when a spouse dies during the year. If

---

19. § 151(b). For several years prior to 1979 the personal and dependency exemptions were $750.

spouses enter into a legal separation under a decree of divorce or separate maintenance prior to the end of the year, they are considered to be unmarried at the end of the taxable year.

Example 8. The effect of death or divorce upon marital status is illustrated below:

	Marital Status for 19X1
1. W is the widow of H who dies on January 3, 19X1.	They are considered to be married for purposes of filing the 19X1 return.
2. W and H entered into a divorce decree which is effective on December 31, 19X1.	They are considered to be unmarried for purposes of filing the 19X1 return.

In addition to the regular $1,000 exemptions for a taxpayer and his or her spouse, additional exemptions are permitted if either has attained the age of 65 prior to the end of the year and/or if either is blind.[20]

Example 9. The exemptions available to H and W (married and filing a joint return) are illustrated below:

	Regular Exemptions	Additional Exemptions
—H and W are married and file a joint return.	$ 2,000	
—H is 66 years old and W is 62.	$ 2,000	$ 1,000
—H and W file a joint return; W is not totally blind, but she has a doctor's statement that her visual acuity does not exceed 20/200 in her better eye with corrective lenses. She is, however, considered to be blind for purposes of the personal exemptions.[21]	$ 2,000	$ 1,000

Note that personal exemptions for blindness and for age 65 or over are applicable only to the taxpayer and spouse and not to dependents of the taxpayer (e. g., a taxpayer who supports an aged parent cannot claim more than one dependency exemption for the parent).

---

20. §§ 151(c) and (d). For tax purposes, a person becomes 65 on the day before the sixty-fifth birthday. Thus, a taxpayer whose sixty-fifth birthday is January 1, 19X2, is considered to be age 65 for the tax year 19X1.

21. § 151(d)(3).

DEPENDENCY EXEMPTIONS

The Code also allows an individual to claim a dependency exemption of $1,000 for each eligible dependent. To qualify as a dependent, the following five tests must be met:

—Support.

—Relationship or member of the household.

—Gross income.

—Joint return.

—Citizenship or residency.

Support Test. Over one-half of the support of a dependent must be furnished by the taxpayer. Support includes food, shelter, clothing, medical and dental care, education, etc. In testing for the 50 percent requirement, expenditures of nontaxable amounts such as Social Security payments are included.[22] However, a scholarship received by a student is not included for purposes of computing whether the taxpayer furnished more than one-half of the child's support.[23]

Example 10. H contributed $2,500 (consisting of food, clothing, and medical care) toward the support of his son, S, who earned $1,500 from a part-time job and received a $2,000 scholarship to attend a local university. Assuming that the other dependency tests are met, H may claim S as a dependent, since he has contributed more than one-half of S's support. The $2,000 scholarship is not included as support for purposes of this test.

Example 11. S contributed $1,000 to his father's support during 19X3. His father received $800 in Social Security benefits and $300 of dividend income before deducting the $100 dividend exclusion. All of these amounts were used for his support during the year. Since the Social Security payments expended for support are considered in the determination of whether the support test has been met, S cannot claim his father as a dependent because he has not contributed more than one-half of the total support.

If a dependent does not spend funds which have been received from any source, such unexpended amounts are not counted for purposes of the support test (e. g., Social Security benefits received by the dependent are not considered if such amounts are not spent on items considered "support").

Example 12. S contributed $3,000 to her father's support during the year. In addition, her father received $2,400 in Social Secu-

---

22. Reg. § 1.152–1(a)(2). If property or lodging is provided, the amount of support is measured by its fair market value.

23. Reg. § 1.152–1(c).

rity benefits, $200 of interest, and wages of $600. The Social Security benefits, interest, and wages were deposited in the father's savings account and were not used for his support. Thus, the Social Security benefits, interest, and wages are not considered as support provided by her father, and S may claim her father as a dependent if the other tests are met.

Capital expenditures such as furniture, appliances, and automobiles are included in total support if the item does, in fact, constitute support.[24]

> **Example 13.** F purchased a television set costing $150 for his minor daughter. The television set was placed in the child's bedroom and was used exclusively by her. F should include the cost of the television set in determining the support of his daughter.

> **Example 14.** F paid $6,000 for an automobile which was titled and registered in his name. F's minor son is permitted to use the automobile equally with F. Since F did not give the automobile to his son, the $6,000 cost is not includible as a support item. However, the out-of-pocket operating expenses for the benefit of the child are includible as support.[25]

One exception to the support test, which is based on the existence of a multiple support agreement, permits one of a group of taxpayers who furnish more than one-half of the support of a dependent to claim a dependency exemption even when no one person provides more than 50 percent of the support.[26] Any individual who contributed more than 10 percent of the support is entitled to claim the exemption if each person in the group who contributed more than 10 percent files a written consent. This provision frequently enables one of the children of aged dependent parents to claim an exemption when none of the children meets the 50 percent support test. Each person who is a party to the multiple support agreement must meet all other requirements (except the support requirement) for claiming the dependent. A person who does not meet the relationship or member of household requirement, for instance, could not claim the dependency exemption under a multiple support agreement, even though he or she contributed more than 10 percent of the dependent's support.

> **Example 15.** M, who resides with her son, received $2,000 from various sources during 19X2; this constituted her entire support for the year. The support was received from the following:

24. Rev.Rul. 57–344, 1957–2 C.B. 112; Rev.Rul. 58–419, 1958–2 C.B. 57.
25. *Your Federal Income Tax,* IRS Publication 17 (Rev. Oct. 83), p. 21.
26. § 152(c).

	Amount	Percent of Total
A, a son	$ 960	48
B, a son	200	10
C, a daughter	600	30
D, a friend	240	12
	$ 2,000	100

If they file a multiple support agreement, either A or C may claim M as a dependent. B may not claim M as a dependent because he did not contribute more than 10% of her support, nor would B's consent be required in order for A and C to file a multiple support agreement. D does not meet the relationship or member of household test and therefore cannot be a party to the multiple support agreement. The decision as to who claims M will rest with A and C. It is possible for C to claim M as a dependent even though A furnished more of M's support.

A second exception to the 50 percent support requirement can occur in the case of children of divorced or separated parents. Special rules have been established to help resolve disputes and uncertainty relative to the dependency status of these children.[27] Generally, the parent having custody of the child for the greater portion of the year is entitled to the dependency exemption. However, the noncustodial parent may be entitled to the dependency exemption in either of the following situations:

—The noncustodial parent contributed at least $600 support for each child claimed as a dependent, and the divorce or separate maintenance decree or a written agreement between the parents provides that the noncustodial parent is to receive the dependency exemption.

—The noncustodial parent provides $1,200 or more support for each child, and the custodial parent cannot clearly establish that he or she provided more than one-half of the total support.[28] In such cases, each parent is entitled to receive an itemized statement of the expenditures which were made by the other parent.

> **Example 16.** H and W obtain a divorce decree in 19X8. In 19X9 their two children are in the custody of W. H contrib-

---

27. § 152(e); Reg. § 1.152–4. As this book goes to press, a bill is before Congress to simplify the law relating to exemptions for children of divorced parents. See § § 424 and 427 of H.R. 4170, The Tax Reform Act of 1983, contained in H. Rept. 98–432, 98th Cong., 1st Sess., 1983, pp. 213–220 and 224–226.

28. § 152(e)(2)(B)(1). Contrast the result reached in *Lynne T. Robinson,* 37 TCM 140, T.C. Memo. 1978–21 with that in *Nancy Boyd Martin,* 37 TCM 202, T.C. Memo. 1978–37.

uted $700 of child support for each child. Absent any written agreement relative to the dependency exemptions, W should be entitled to the exemptions.

Example 17. Assume the same facts as in Example 16 except that H contributed $3,000 of child support for each child and the divorce decree gives the exemptions to H. H is entitled to the two dependency exemptions, since his contribution was $600 or more for each child.

Relationship or Member of the Household Test. The dependent must be either a relative of the taxpayer or a member of the taxpayer's household. The Code contains a detailed listing of the various blood and marriage relationships which qualify. Note, however, that the relationship test is met if the dependent is a relative of either spouse, and a relationship, once established by marriage, continues regardless of subsequent changes in marital status.

The following individuals may be claimed as dependents of the taxpayer if the other tests for dependency are met.[29]

1. A son or daughter of the taxpayer, or a descendant of either.
2. A stepson or stepdaughter of the taxpayer.
3. A brother, sister, stepbrother, or stepsister of the taxpayer.
4. The father or mother of the taxpayer, or an ancestor of either.
5. A stepfather or stepmother of the taxpayer.
6. A son or daughter of a brother or sister of the taxpayer.
7. A brother or sister of the father or mother of the taxpayer.
8. A son-in-law, daughter-in-law, father-in-law, mother-in-law, brother-in-law, or sister-in-law of the taxpayer.
9. An individual (other than an individual who at any time during the taxable year was the spouse of the taxpayer) who, for the taxable year of the taxpayer, has as his or her principal place of abode the home of the taxpayer and is a member of the taxpayer's household.

The following rules are also prescribed in the Code:[30]

—A legally adopted child is treated as a natural child.

—A foster child qualifies if the child has his or her principal place of abode in the taxpayer's household.

---

29. § 152(a). However, under § 152(b)(5) a taxpayer may not claim someone who is a member of his or her household as a dependent if their relationship is in violation of local law. In a recent case the dependency exemption was denied because the taxpayer's relationship to the person claimed as a dependent constituted "cohabitation," a crime under applicable state law. *Cassius L. Peacock, III,* 37 TCM 177, T.C. Memo. 1978–30.

30. § 152(b)(2).

Gross Income Test. The dependent's gross income must be less than $1,000 unless the dependent is a child of the taxpayer who is under 19 or a full-time student.[31] A parent who provides over one-half of the support of a child who is under 19 at the end of the year or who is a full-time student may claim a $1,000 dependency exemption for such child. In addition, the child is entitled to claim a personal exemption on his or her own income tax return, if one is filed. A child is defined as a son, stepson, daughter, stepdaughter, adopted son or daughter and may include a foster child.[32] In order for the child to qualify as a student for purposes of the dependency exemption, he or she must be a full-time student for at least five months of the year at an educational institution.[33] This exception to the gross income test, for dependent children who are under 19 or full-time students, is intended to permit a child or college student to earn money from part-time or summer jobs without penalizing the parent with the loss of the dependency exemption.

Joint Return Test. If a dependent is married, the supporting taxpayer (e. g., the parent of a married child) is not permitted a dependency exemption if the married individual files a joint return with his or her spouse.[34] An exception to this rule is provided, however, if neither the dependent nor the dependent's spouse is required to file a return but does so solely to claim a refund of tax withheld (i. e., if the dependent and spouse each had gross income of less than $1,000).[35]

Citizenship or Residency Test. A dependent generally must be either a U. S. citizen or a resident of the U. S. or a country which is contiguous to the U. S.[36]

TAX DETERMINATION

Most taxpayers will compute their tax using the Tax Table.[37] Those who are not allowed to use the Tax Table will compute their tax using the Tax Rate Schedules.

TAX TABLE METHOD

Taxpayers who are eligible to use the Tax Table will (1) compute taxable income (as shown in Figure I) and (2) determine their tax by refer-

---

31. § 151(e).
32. Reg. § 1.151–3(a).
33. Reg. § 1.151–3(b) and (c).
34. § 151(e)(2).
35. Rev.Rul. 54–567, 1954–2 C.B. 108; Rev.Rul. 65–34, 1965–1 C.B. 86.
36. § 152(b)(3); *Pir M. Toor,* 36 TCM 1616, T.C. Memo. 1977–399.
37. According to Treasury Department estimates, 96 percent of individual taxpayers would be able to use the Tax Table introduced in the Tax Reduction and Simplification Act of 1977. This percentage should increase as a result of the provisions in the Economic Recovery Tax Act of 1981 which expand the coverage of the tables.

ence to the Tax Table. Since the 1984 Tax Table was not available at the date of publication of this text, the 1983 Tax Table will be used for purposes of illustration in all examples throughout the text in which tax is determined by the Tax Table method. It is expected that the structure of the Tax Table and the method of computing tax will remain in effect in 1984 and future years.

> **Example 18.** J is single and has taxable income of $15,450. She will determine her tax on taxable income of $15,450 using the Tax Table method. J's tax from the 1983 Tax Table (reproduced in Appendix A–2) is $2,211.

TAX RATE SCHEDULE METHOD

Certain taxpayers are not eligible to use the Tax Table for computing their tax.[38]

> —An estate or trust.
>
> —An individual who uses income averaging (discussed in Chapter 12).
>
> —An individual who files a short period return (see Chapter 18).
>
> —Those taxpayers whose taxable income exceeds the maximum amounts in the Tax Table. (In 1983, taxpayers with taxable income of $50,000 or more must use the Tax Rate Schedules rather than the Tax Table.)

The 1984 Tax Rate Schedules (reproduced in Appendix A–1) will be used to illustrate the computation of tax using the Tax Rate Schedule method.

> **Example 19.** Z had taxable income of $65,300 in 1984. Because his taxable income is not less than $50,000, Z is not eligible to use the Tax Table. Therefore, he must compute his tax using the Tax Rate Schedule method. Since Z is single and has no dependents, he will use 1984 Tax Rate Schedule X (see Appendix A–1):

Tax on $55,300	$ 16,115
Plus: Tax at 48%* on $10,000 of taxable income in excess of $55,300	4,800
Total tax	$ 20,915

> * This is the taxpayer's marginal tax rate.

COMPUTATION OF NET TAXES PAYABLE OR REFUND DUE

The pay-as-you-go feature of the Federal income tax system requires payment of all or part of the taxpayer's income tax liability during the year. These payments take the form of Federal income tax withheld

---

38. § 3(b).

by employers or estimated tax paid by the taxpayer or both. These amounts are applied against the tax from the Tax Table or Tax Rate Schedules to determine whether the taxpayer will get a refund or pay additional tax.

Employers are required to withhold income tax on compensation paid to their employees and to pay this tax over to the government. The employer notifies the employee of the amount of income tax withheld on Form W–2, Wage and Tax Statement. The employee should receive this form by January 31 after the year in which the income tax is withheld.

Estimated tax must be paid by taxpayers who receive income that is not subject to withholding or income from which not enough tax is being withheld. These individuals must file Form 1040–ES, Declaration of Estimated Tax for Individuals, and pay in quarterly installments the income tax and self-employment tax estimated to be due (see Chapter 12 for a thorough discussion).

The income tax from the Tax Table or the Tax Rate Schedules is reduced first by the individual's tax credits. There is an important distinction between tax credits and tax deductions. Tax credits reduce the tax liability dollar-for-dollar. Tax deductions reduce taxable income on which the tax liability is based.

> **Example 20.** X is a taxpayer in the 40% marginal tax bracket. As a result of a $100 contribution to the campaign fund of Senator Z, she is entitled to a $50 tax credit for political contributions (see Chapter 13 for details). X also contributed $100 to the American Cancer Society and included this amount in her itemized deductions. The credit for political contributions results in a $50 reduction of X's tax liability for the year. The contribution to the American Cancer Society results in a $40 reduction in X's tax liability ($100 contribution deduction times 40% marginal rate).

Tax credits are discussed in Chapter 13. Some of the more common credits are listed below:

—Credit for contributions to candidates for public office.

—Credit for child and dependent care expenses.

—Credit for the elderly.

—Investment tax credit.

—Foreign tax credit.

—Targeted jobs credit.

—Energy credits for individuals.

Computation of an individual's net tax payable or refund due is illustrated in the following examples.

> **Example 21.** Y, age 30, is a single taxpayer with no dependents. During 1983, Y had the following: taxable income, $22,700;

income tax withheld, $3,000; estimated tax payments, $900; and credit for political contributions, $50. Y's net tax payable is computed as follows:

Income tax (from 1983 Tax Table, Appendix A–2)		$ 4,132
Less: Tax credits and prepayments—		
Credit for political contribution	$ 50	
Income tax withheld	3,000	
Estimated tax payments	900	3,950
Net taxes payable or (refund due)		$ 182

Example 22. Assume the same facts as in Example 21 except that income tax withheld was $3,300. Y's refund due is computed as follows:

Income tax		$ 4,132
Less: Tax credits and prepayments—		
Credit for political contributions	$ 50	
Income tax withheld	3,300	
Estimated tax payments	900	4,250
Net taxes payable or (refund due)		$ (118)

FILING CONSIDERATIONS

Under the category of filing considerations, the following questions need to be resolved:

—Is the taxpayer required to file an income tax return?

—If so, which form should be used?

—When and how should the return be filed?

—In computing the tax liability, which column of the Tax Table or which Tax Rate Schedule should be used?

The first three of these questions are discussed below under the heading of FILING REQUIREMENTS. The last question is treated under the category of FILING STATUS.

FILING REQUIREMENTS

An individual must file a tax return if certain minimum amounts of gross income have been received. A self-employed individual with net earnings from a business or profession of $400 or more must file a tax return regardless of the amount of his or her gross income. Also required to file is an individual who receives any advance earned income credit payments (see Chapter 13) from his or her employer during the year. The other filing requirements for 1984 are as follows:[39]

---

39. § 6012(a).

Single (legally separated, divorced, or married and living apart from spouse) and under 65	$ 3,300
Single (legally separated, divorced, or married and living apart from spouse) and 65 or over	4,300
Single (can be claimed as a dependent on parents' return) with taxable dividends, interest, or other unearned income of $1,000 or more	1,000
Qualified surviving spouse [i. e., widow(er) with dependent child] under 65	4,400
Qualified surviving spouse [i. e., widow(er) with dependent child] 65 or over	5,400
Married couple filing jointly, living together at the end of the year (or at date of death of spouse), and both under 65	5,400
Married couple filing jointly, living together at the end of the year (or at date of death of spouse), and one spouse 65 or over	6,400
Married couple filing jointly, living together at the end of the year (or at date of death of spouse), and both 65 or over	7,400
Married individual filing a separate return	1,000

The filing requirements reflect the zero bracket amount and the allowable personal exemptions (including additional exemptions for taxpayers 65 or older). For example, a single taxpayer under age 65 must file a tax return in 1984 if gross income is $3,300 or greater ($2,300 zero bracket amount plus $1,000 personal exemption).

Even though an individual's gross income is below the required amounts and he or she does not, therefore, owe any tax, it will be necessary to file a return to obtain a tax refund of amounts which have been withheld. A return is also necessary to obtain the benefits of the earned income credit allowed to taxpayers with little or no tax liability. Chapter 13 discusses the earned income credit.

Individual taxpayers file a return on either Form 1040, Form 1040A, or Form 1040EZ. (See Appendixes B–1, B–2, and B–3.) Form 1040A is a short form which is used by many taxpayers who have uncomplicated situations. An individual may be required to use Form 1040 rather than Form 1040A if:[40]

—Taxable income is $50,000 or more.

—The taxpayer has income other than wages, salaries, tips, unemployment compensation, dividends, or interest.

—The taxpayer claims credits other than credits for political conributions, child or dependent care, or the earned income credit.

—The taxpayer is required to use the Tax Rate Schedules.

---

40. *Your Federal Income Tax*, IRS Publication 17 (Rev. Oct. 83), pp. 5–6. *Your Federal Income Tax* lists 22 reasons a taxpayer may not use Form 1040A, including those noted here.

—The taxpayer claims any deductions other than deductions for payments to an IRA, for married couples when both work, or the partial deduction for charitable contributions.

Form 1040EZ, a new form for taxpayers with uncomplicated tax situations, was introduced in 1982. This form, which has only 11 lines, may be used by taxpayers who are single with no dependents and who satisfy all of the following requirements:

—Do not claim exemptions for being 65 or over, or for being blind.

—Have taxable income of less than $50,000.

—Had only wages, salaries, and tips and had interest income of $400 or less.

—Had no dividend income.

—Had no interest from an All-Savers Certificate.

Taxpayers who cannot use Form 1040EZ will use either Form 1040 or Form 1040A.

Tax returns of individuals are due on or before the fifteenth day of the fourth month following the close of the tax year. For the calendar year taxpayer, therefore, the usual filing date is on or before April 15 of the following year.[41] When the due date falls on a Saturday, Sunday, or legal holiday, the last day for filing falls on the next business day. If the return is mailed to the proper address with sufficient postage and is postmarked on or before the due date, it is deemed to be timely filed.

If a taxpayer is unable to file his or her return by the specified due date, a four-month extension of time can be obtained by filing Form 4868, Application for Automatic Extension of Time to File U. S. Individual Income Tax Return.[42] Further extensions of time may be granted by the IRS upon a showing by the taxpayer of good cause. For this purpose, Form 2688, Application for Extension of Time to File U. S. Individual Income Tax Return, should be used. Although obtaining an extension excuses a taxpayer from a penalty for failure to file, it does not insulate against the penalty for failure to pay.[43] If more tax is owed, therefore, the filing of Form 4868 (see above) should be accompanied by an additional remittance to cover the balance due.

The return should be sent or delivered to the Regional Service Center of the IRS for the area where the taxpayer lives.[44]

If it is necessary to file an amended return (e. g., due to a failure to report income or to claim a deduction or tax credit), Form 1040X is filed by individual taxpayers and is generally filed within three years

---

41. § 6072(a).

42. Reg. § 1.6081–4.

43. For an explanation of these penalties, see Chapter 1.

44. The Regional Service Centers and the geographical area each covers can be found on the back cover of *Your Federal Income Tax,* IRS Publication 17 (Rev. Oct. 83).

of the filing date of the original return or within two years from the time the tax was paid, whichever is later.[45]

FILING STATUS

Effective in 1979 the Tax Rate Schedules were widened for all individuals and rate reductions were provided in certain brackets. The Economic Recovery Tax Act of 1981 provided further tax cuts across all brackets, with a reduction of the top rate from 70 percent to 50 percent which took effect in 1982. The Act included a multistage, across-the-board 30 percent reduction in individual income tax rates. These reductions in tax liability were accompanied by a series of withholding adjustments corresponding to the rate changes. The 30 percent tax cut was a key element in the Reagan administration's plan for economic recovery. Much debate has recently taken place concerning the need to raise income taxes to reduce the deficit caused, at least in part, by this 30 percent cut.

The amount of tax will vary considerably depending on which Tax Table or Tax Rate Schedule is used. This is illustrated in the following example.

> **Example 23.** These amounts of tax appear in the 1983 Tax Table for a taxpayer (or taxpayers in the case of a joint return) with $20,000 of taxable income (see Appendix A–2).

Filing Status	Amount of Tax
Single	$ 3,376
Married, filing joint return	$ 2,611
Married, filing separate return	$ 4,161
Head of household	$ 3,128

Rate Schedules and Tax Table for Married Individuals. The joint return [Tax Rate Schedule Y, Code § 1(a)] was originally enacted to establish equity for married taxpayers in common law states because married taxpayers in community property states are able to split their income.

> **Example 24.** A and B are husband and wife. A earns a salary of $40,000. B is not employed. Before enactment of the joint return provisions, their income tax would vary significantly depending on whether they lived in a common law state or a community property state. If they lived in a common law state, A would report $40,000 of income on his tax return. However, if they lived in a community property state, A and B each would report $20,000

---

45. See Rev.Rul. 1981–2 C.B. 243 for the date that the period of limitation for assessment of tax will expire when the date prescribed for filing the original return is a Saturday, Sunday, or legal holiday.

of income. Because the rate structure is progressive (i. e., the higher the income, the higher the tax rate), the tax paid by A and B would be higher in a common law state than in a community property state.

To correct this inequity, in 1948 Congress passed legislation authorizing joint returns. Under the joint return Tax Rate Schedule, the progressive rates are constructed based on the assumption that income is earned equally by the two spouses.

If married individuals elect to file separate returns, both must use a different Tax Rate Schedule [§ 1(d)] which is applied to married taxpayers filing separately. It is generally advantageous for married individuals to file a joint return, since the combined amount of tax is lower. However, special circumstances (e. g., significant medical expenses incurred by one spouse subject to the five percent limitation) may warrant the use of the separate-return election. Note also that the Code places some limitations on deductions, credits, etc., when married individuals file separately.

The joint return rates also apply for two years following the death of one spouse providing the surviving spouse maintains a household for a dependent child.[46] This filing status is commonly referred to as "surviving spouse" status.

> **Example 25.** H dies leaving W with a dependent child. For the year of H's death, W files a joint return with H (presuming the consent of H's executor is obtained). For the next two years, W, as a surviving spouse, may use the joint return rates (i. e., Schedule Y). (Note: In subsequent years, W may use the head-of-household rates if she maintains a household as her home which is the domicile of the child.)

Rate Schedules and Tax Table for Unmarried Individuals. Unmarried individuals who maintain a household for a dependent (or dependents) are entitled to use the head-of-household rates.[47] The head-of-household rates are approximately two-thirds of the way (in terms of progression) between the joint return Tax Rate Schedule and the Tax Rate Schedule for single taxpayers.

As a general rule, to qualify for head-of-household rates, an unmarried taxpayer must maintain a household as his or her home which is the domicile of a relative as defined in § 152(a).[48] Over one-half of the cost of maintaining the household must be furnished by the unmarried taxpayer. One exception to the general rule is that certain unmarried relatives (i. e., a son, stepson, daughter, stepdaughter, or a descendant of a son or daughter) need not qualify as a dependent of the taxpayer.

---

46. § 2(a).
47. § 2(b).
48. § 2(b)(1)(A)(i).

Example 26. M maintains a household in which S, her non-dependent, unmarried son and she reside. Since S is not married, M qualifies for the head-of-household rates. (Note: If S is married, he must qualify as M's dependent in order for M to use the head-of-household rates.)

Another exception to the general rule is that head-of-household status may be claimed if the taxpayer maintains a separate home for his or her parent or parents who also qualify as dependents.[49]

Example 27. S, an unmarried individual, lives in New York City and maintains a household in Detroit for his dependent parents. S may use the favorable head-of-household rates even though his parents do not reside in his New York home.

Mitigation of the Marriage Penalty. Generally, it is advantageous from a tax standpoint to enter into marriage. However, where the former single individuals' incomes are approximately equal, the opposite may be the case. The additional tax which sometimes results from being married and filing jointly, as opposed to being unmarried and filing as two single taxpayers, is commonly referred to as the "marriage penalty."

The roots of this problem can be traced to enactment of the joint return rate schedule (refer to Example 24 and related discussion), followed by a liberalization of the rate schedules for single taxpayers in 1971. This adjustment provided that the tax paid by a single individual would not exceed 120 percent of the comparable rates for married individuals filing jointly. Example 28 illustrates how these and other minor adjustments to the tax structure result in a marriage penalty.

The Economic Recovery Tax Act of 1981 provided some relief from the marriage penalty by providing a deduction for working couples. This deduction, called the two-earner married couples deduction, is equal to 10 percent (5 percent in 1982) of qualified earned income, up to $30,000, of the spouse with the lesser earnings.[50] Generally, qualified earned income is earned income less certain deductions for adjusted gross income, such as employee business expenses and trade or business expenses. The deduction is available both to couples who claim excess itemized deductions and to those who do not (i. e., it is a deduction *for* adjusted gross income). The following two examples illustrate how the tax rate structure results in a marriage penalty and how the two-earner married couples deduction helps to mitigate that penalty. The tax in these examples is computed using the 1984 Tax Rate Schedules (see Appendix A–1).

---

49. § 2(b)(1)(B).
50. § 221. Income items which are not "qualified earnings" are set out in § 221(b)(2)(A).

Example 28. The computation of tax for single and married individuals at the same income level is illustrated below. Assume that in 1984 H and W each have gross income of $25,000 with no itemized deductions or deductions *for* adjusted gross income. Also assume that there is no deduction for two-earner married couples.

		Tax Liability (Using 1984 Tax Rate Schedules)	
		If Unmarried	Married Filing Jointly
H's taxable income	$ 24,000	$ 4,265	
W's taxable income	24,000	4,265	
Total	$ 48,000	$ 8,530	$ 10,608

The marriage penalty without the two-earner married couples deduction is $2,078 (i. e., $10,608 − $8,530).

Example 29. Assuming the same facts as in Example 28, under the ERTA provisions, H and W are entitled to a two-earner married couples deduction of $2,500 (i. e., 10% of $25,000). Thus, their taxable income on a joint return is $45,500 [(i. e., $50,000 − $2,500 (two-earner married couples deduction) − $2,000 (exemptions)] and their tax is $9,673. The marriage penalty under the ERTA provisions will be reduced to $1,143 (i. e., $9,673 − $8,530). Example 28 shows a marriage penalty of $2,078 without the two-earner married couples deduction. The reduction in the marriage penalty is $935 ($2,078–$1,143).

The deduction will benefit married persons who both work and whose combined income is allocated between them more evenly than 80%:20%. Together with the across-the-board tax rate cut, it was expected that the deduction would reduce the marriage penalty by at least 50 percent.

INDEXATION

For tax years beginning after 1984, certain elements in the tax structure are scheduled to be indexed (i. e., adjusted) so that inflation will not result in tax increases. The items to be adjusted are the exemption amount, the zero bracket amount, and the tax rates.[51]

GAINS AND LOSSES FROM PROPERTY TRANSACTIONS—IN GENERAL

Gains and losses from property transactions are discussed in detail in Chapters 14 through 17. Because of their importance in the tax system, however, they will be introduced briefly at this point.

---

51. § § 1(f) and 63(d). Refer to Example 2 in Chapter 2.

On the sale or other disposition of property, gain or loss may result. Such gain or loss has an effect on the income tax position of the party making the sale or other disposition when the *realized* gain or loss is *recognized* for tax purposes. Without realized gain or loss, generally, there can be no recognized gain or loss. The concept of realized gain or loss can be expressed as follows:

Amount realized from the sale − adjusted basis of the property = realized gain (or loss)

The amount realized is the selling price of the property less any costs of disposition (e. g., brokerage commissions) incurred by the seller. Simply stated, adjusted basis of the property is determined as set forth below:

Cost (or other original basis) at date of acquisition[52]

Add: Capital additions

Subtract: Depreciation (if appropriate) and other capital recoveries (see Chapter 9)

Adjusted basis at date of sale or other disposition

All realized gains are recognizable (i. e., taxable) unless some specific provision of the tax law provides otherwise (see Chapter 15 dealing with certain nontaxable exchanges). Realized losses may or may not be recognizable (i. e., deductible) for tax purposes, depending on the circumstances involved. Usually, losses realized from the disposition of personal use property (i. e., property neither held for investment nor used in a trade or business) are not recognizable.

Example 30. During the current year, T (age 50) sells his personal residence (adjusted basis of $40,000) for $100,000. The proceeds from the sale of the residence are not reinvested in a new principal residence, and T moves into a high-rise apartment.[53] T also sells one of his personal automobiles (adjusted basis of $8,000) for $5,000. T's realized gain of $60,000 from the sale of the personal residence is, under these circumstances, recognizable. On the other hand, the $3,000 realized loss on the sale of the automobile is not recognized and will not provide T with any deductible tax benefit.

Once it has been determined that the disposition of property results in a recognizable gain or loss, the next step is to classify such

---

52. Cost usually means purchase price plus expenses incident to the acquisition of the property and incurred by the purchaser (e. g., brokerage commissions). For the basis of property acquired by gift or inheritance and other basis rules, see Chapter 14.
53. If T had reinvested the sale proceeds in a new principal residence, the exchange might have been nontaxable due to the application of § 1034. (See Chapter 15.)

gain or loss as capital or ordinary. Although ordinary gain is fully taxable and ordinary loss is fully deductible, the same may not hold true for capital gains and capital losses.

GAINS AND LOSSES FROM PROPERTY TRANSACTIONS— CAPITAL GAINS AND LOSSES

A sale or exchange of capital assets receives special treatment under the income tax law. Preferential long-term capital gain treatment is accorded to the sale or exchange of capital assets which have been held for more than one year. These favorable long-term capital gain provisions are intended to encourage the formation of private capital investment.

DEFINITION OF A CAPITAL ASSET

Capital assets are defined in the Code as any property held by the taxpayer, other than property listed in § 1221. This list includes inventory, accounts receivable, depreciable property or real estate used in a business, etc. Thus, the sale or exchange of assets in these categories usually results in ordinary income or loss treatment. Note, however that the sale or exchange of § 1231 assets (i. e., assets that are not capital assets, such as machinery, equipment, land, and buildings used in business) may result in favorable long-term capital gain treatment under certain circumstances. (See Chapter 17.)

> **Example 31.** C owns a pizza parlor. During 19X1 C sells two automobiles. The first automobile, used as a pizza delivery car, was sold at a loss of $1,000. Because this automobile is an asset used in his business (i. e., a § 1231 asset), C has an ordinary loss deduction of $1,000, rather than a capital loss deduction. The second automobile, which C had owned for two years, was C's personal car. It was sold for a gain of $800. The personal car is a capital asset. Therefore, C has a capital gain of $800.

The principal capital assets held by an individual taxpayer include assets held for personal (as opposed to business) use, such as a personal residence or an automobile, and assets held for investment purposes (e. g., corporate securities and land).

COMPUTATION OF NET CAPITAL GAINS AND LOSSES

Short-term capital gains and losses (i. e., those on assets held for one year or less) are offset initially, and long-term capital losses are used to offset long-term capital gains. Any net short-term capital losses are used then to offset net long-term capital gains. The same offsetting process is used if a taxpayer has net long-term capital losses and net short-term capital gains.

Example 32. In 19X3, T has the following capital gains and losses: short-term losses of $4,000; short-term gains of $3,000; long-term gains of $6,000; and long-term losses of $2,000. T has net short-term capital losses of $1,000 ($4,000 − $3,000) and net long-term capital gains of $4,000 ($6,000 − $2,000). The $1,000 net short-term capital loss is used to offset the $4,000 net long-term capital gain resulting in an excess of net long-term capital gain over net short-term capital loss of $3,000.

CAPITAL GAIN DEDUCTION AND ALTERNATIVE TAX

Only the amount of net long-term capital gains in excess of net short-term capital losses receives preferential tax treatment. This excess is defined in § 1222 as *net capital gain*. Individuals receive a deduction equal to 60 percent of the net capital gain. Net short-term capital gains are included in gross income in full and do not receive preferential treatment.

Example 33. N has the following capital gains and losses during 19X3: long-term gains of $8,000; long-term losses of $3,000; short-term gains of $2,000; and short-term losses of $6,000. The long-term gains and losses are netted, resulting in net long-term capital gain of $5,000 (i. e., $8,000 − $3,000). The short-term gains and losses are netted, resulting in net short-term capital loss of $4,000. The $1,000 of net long-term capital gain in excess of net short-term capital loss (i. e., $5,000 − $4,000) is the *net capital gain*. N includes the entire $1,000 in gross income and deducts $600 ($1,000 net capital gain times 60% net capital gain deduction) as a deduction for adjusted gross income.

Example 34. During 19X3, F had short-term capital gains of $2,500 and short-term capital losses of $1,000. The short-term gains and losses are netted, resulting in net short-term capital gain of $1,500. Net short-term capital gains do not receive preferential treatment (i. e., there is no net capital gain deduction). The entire $1,500 is included in F's gross income.

Under current law, the maximum *effective* tax rate on net capital gain is 20 percent. This effective tax rate is computed by multiplying the 40 percent of net capital gain included in computing taxable income (i. e., 100 percent minus the 60 percent net capital gain deduction) times the 50 percent maximum marginal tax rate for individuals. For taxpayers who are in a tax bracket below 50 percent, the effective rate on net capital gain can be computed by multiplying their marginal rate by 40 percent. For example, a taxpayer in the 30 percent bracket would pay an effective rate of 12 percent (30 percent times the 40 percent net capital gain remaining after the 60 percent deduction). It is apparent why capital gains are so important in an individual's tax planning.

Corporate taxpayers are not eligible for the long-term capital gain deduction. Net capital gains are included in income in full under the regular tax computation. However, a corporation is entitled to compute its tax under an alternative tax computation which effectively subjects net capital gain to a maximum rate of 28 percent. See Chapter 20 for a discussion of the corporate capital gain tax rules.

TREATMENT OF CAPITAL LOSSES

Capital losses are first offset against capital gains. If an individual taxpayer has net capital losses, such losses are deductible as a deduction *for* adjusted gross income to a maximum of $3,000 per year. Any unused amounts are carried over for an indefinite period. Net short-term capital losses are deductible on a dollar-for-dollar basis. However, $2 of net long-term capital loss must be used to obtain a $1 deduction against ordinary income.

> **Example 35.** In 19X2, T has $1,000 of net long-term capital losses and $2,000 of net short-term capital losses. T's other income is $100,000. T's capital loss deduction for 19X2 is $2,500, which consists of $2,000 short-term capital loss (deductible in full) and $500 long-term capital loss ($\frac{1}{2} \times$ $1,000). T's benefit from the long-term capital loss of $1,000 is only $500. The full $1,000 loss is used up and none is carried forward to 19X3.

When a taxpayer has both short-term and long-term capital losses, the short-term losses must be used first in absorbing the $3,000 limitation.

> **Example 36.** R has short-term capital losses of $2,500 and long-term capital losses of $5,000 in 19X2. R's other income is $50,000. R uses the losses as follows:
>
> | | |
> |---|---:|
> | Short-term loss | $ 2,500 |
> | Long-term loss ($1,000 used because of 2-for-1 reduction) | 500 |
> | Maximum 19X2 capital loss deduction | $ 3,000 |

The remaining long-term capital loss of $4,000 (i. e., $5,000 loss minus $1,000 used in 19X2) may be carried over for an indefinite period. See Chapter 16 for a detailed discussion of capital loss carryovers.

Corporate taxpayers may offset capital losses only against capital gains. Capital losses in excess of capital gains may not be used to reduce ordinary income of a corporation. A corporation's unused capital losses are subject to a carryback and carryover. Capital losses are initially carried back three years and then carried forward five years to offset capital gains that arise in those years. See Chapter 16 for a discussion of capital losses of individual and corporate taxpayers.

SHIFTING INCOME TO LOWER BRACKET FAMILY MEMBERS

The following example illustrates one of the basic principles of income tax planning—shifting of income from high-bracket to low-bracket family members.

> **Example 37.** Referring to Example 6, has G's action resulted in any income tax savings? It has, for two reasons: First, because S is entitled to an exemption on his own tax return, $1,000 of the $3,300 interest income is sheltered from income tax. Second, if G had held the account in his own name, he would have paid income tax of 50% on $3,300. Thus, G's tax on this interest income would have been $1,650 (50% of $3,300) compared to $285 of income tax which will be paid by S.

ALTERNATING BETWEEN ITEMIZED DEDUCTIONS AND THE ZERO BRACKET AMOUNT

When total itemized deductions are approximately equal to the zero bracket amount from year to year, it is possible for cash basis taxpayers, by proper timing of payments, to obtain a deduction for excess itemized deductions in one year and make use of the zero bracket amount in the next year, thereby obtaining a larger benefit over the two-year period than otherwise would be available.

> **Example 38.** T, an unmarried cash-basis and calendar year taxpayer, qualifies as a head of household for income tax purposes. For tax years 19X3 and 19X4, T's itemized deductions are as follows:

	19X3	19X4
Church contribution	$ 1,200	$ 1,200
Other itemized deductions (e. g., interest, taxes)	900	900
Total itemized deductions	$ 2,100	$ 2,100

As presently structured, in neither year will T be able to benefit from these itemized deductions, since they do not exceed the zero bracket amount applicable to a head of household (i. e., $2,300). Thus, T's benefit for both years totals $4,600 (i. e., $2,300 + $2,300), all based on the zero bracket amount.

Example 39. Assume the same facts as in Example 38 except that in late 19X3 T prepays the church contribution for 19X4. With this change, T's position for both years becomes:

	19X3	19X4
Church contribution	$ 2,400	$ –0–
Other itemized deductions	900	900
Total itemized deductions	$ 3,300	$ 900

Under these circumstances, T would claim itemized deductions of $3,300 for 19X3 and make use of the zero bracket amount of $2,300 for 19X4. A comparison of the total benefit of $5,600 (i. e., $3,300 + $2,300) with the result reached in Example 38 of $4,600 (i. e., $2,300 + $2,300) clearly shows the advantage of this type of planning.

DEPENDENCY EXEMPTIONS

The Joint Return Test. In order for a taxpayer to be able to claim a married person as a dependent, such person must not file a joint return with his or her spouse. If a joint return has been filed, however, the damage might be undone if separate returns are substituted on a timely basis (i. e., on or before the due date of the return).

Example 40. While preparing a client's 19X3 income tax return on April 10, 19X4, the tax practitioner discovered that the client's daughter filed a joint return with her husband in late January of 19X4. Presuming the daughter otherwise qualifies as the client's dependent, the exemption will not be lost if she and her husband file separate returns on or before April 15, 19X4.

Keep in mind that the filing of a joint return will not be fatal to the dependency exemption if the parties are filing solely to recover income tax withholdings and neither is required to file a return. In determining whether a return has to be filed, the appropriate test is the one applicable to married persons filing separately (i. e., either spouse has gross income of $1,000 or more). The application of these rules can be interesting when contrasting common law and community property jurisdictions.

Example 41. In 19X3, T furnished 80 percent of the support of his son (S) and daughter-in-law (D). During the year, D earned $1,800 from a part-time job, and as a result, D and S filed a joint return in order to obtain a refund of the income tax withheld. All parties reside in New York (a common law state). Presuming the joint return stands (see Example 40), T cannot claim either S or D as his dependent. Although D and S filed a joint return to recover D's withholdings, D was required to file (i. e., she had gross income of $1,000 or more).

Example 42. Assume the same facts as in Example 41 except that all parties reside in Arizona (a community property state). Under these circumstances T may claim both S and D as dependents. Not only have they filed a joint return to recover D's withholdings, but neither was required to file. Recall that in a community property state (unless otherwise altered by agreement between spouses, if permitted by state law), half of the wages of a spouse are attributable to the other spouse. Thus, S and D each will be treated as having earned $900, or less than the $1,000 gross income filing requirement for married persons filing separate returns.

The Gross Income Test. The exception to the gross income test for a person under the age of 19 or a full-time student applies only to a child of the taxpayer. The term "child" is limited to a son, stepson, daughter, stepdaughter, adopted son, or adopted daughter, and may include a foster child.

Example 43. Assume the same facts as in Example 41 except that S and D (the son and daughter-in-law) do not file a joint return. Further assume that D (the person who had gross income of $1,800) is a full-time student. Even though T may claim S as a dependent, D does not qualify, since she has gross income of $1,000 or more. The student exception to the gross income test does not apply because D is not a "child" of T.

As was true with Example 42, the residence of the parties in a common law or a community property state can produce different results.

Example 44. In 19X3, T furnishes 60% of the support of his son (S) and daughter-in-law (D), both over the age of 19. During the year D earns $3,000 from a part-time job, while S is unemployed and not a full-time student. All parties reside in New Jersey (a common law state). T may claim S as a dependent, but D does not qualify due to the gross income test.

Example 45. Assume the same facts as in Example 44 except that all parties reside in Washington (a community property state). T may not claim either S or D as dependents due to the application of the gross income test. Each spouse is treated as having gross income of $1,500 (i. e., one-half of $3,000) which is not below the $1,000 restriction.

The Support Test. Adequate records of expenditures for support should be maintained in the event a dependency exemption is questioned on audit by the IRS. The maintenance of adequate records is particularly important in situations involving children of divorced or separated parents and for exemptions arising from multiple support agreements.

It may be desirable to provide in a divorce decree or separation agreement that the noncustodial parent is entitled to the dependency exemption if the noncustodial parent is in a higher tax bracket because the relative benefits from the dependency exemptions are, thereby, increased.

Relationship to the Deduction for Medical Expenses. Generally, medical expenses are deductible only if they are paid on behalf of the taxpayer, his or her spouse, and their dependents. Since deductibility may rest on dependency status, planning becomes important in arranging multiple support agreements.

> **Example 46.** During 19X3, M will be supported by her two sons (S_1 and S_2) and her daughter (D), each to furnish approximately one-third of the required support. If the parties decide that the dependency exemption should be claimed by the daughter under a multiple support agreement, any medical expenses incurred by M should be paid by D.

In planning the decision under a multiple support agreement, one should take into account which of the parties is most likely to exceed the five percent limitation (see Chapter 11). In Example 46, for instance, D might be a poor choice if she and her family do not expect to incur many medical and drug expenses of their own.

One exception exists to permit the deduction of medical expenses paid on behalf of someone who is not a spouse or a dependent. If the person could be claimed as a dependent *except* for the gross income or joint return tests, the medical expenses, nevertheless, are deductible.

> **Example 47.** In 19X3, T pays for all of the medical expenses of her uncle (U) and her married son (S). U otherwise qualifies as T's dependent except that he had gross income of $1,200. Also, S otherwise qualifies as a dependent except that he filed a joint return with his wife. Even though T may not claim dependency exemptions for U and S, she can claim the medical and drug expenses she paid on their behalf.

FILING STATUS

When married persons file separate returns, the following unfavorable tax consequences materialize:

—Each spouse is limited to a zero bracket amount of $1,700.

—Both spouses must be consistent in choosing the zero bracket amount or the alternative of itemizing deductions *from* adjusted gross income.

—The highest of all the tax rates relating to individual taxpayers apply.

—The earned income credit and the child care credit (see Chapter 13) are not available.

Section 143(b) mitigates these harsh results by allowing a married taxpayer to be treated as single for income tax purposes if all of the following conditions are satisfied:

(1) A separate return is filed.

(2) The taxpayer furnished more than one-half of the cost of maintaining his or her home during the year.

(3) The other spouse did not live in the home at any time during the year.

(4) The home was, for more than six months of the year, the principal residence of the taxpayer's child or stepchild who qualifies as a dependent.

If the last condition is satisfied for the *entire* year, the taxpayer will qualify as a head of household as well. Otherwise, he or she must use the rates applicable to single persons. This provision is commonly referred to as the abandoned spouse rule.

Example 48. W's husband left W and their three-year-old son in 1982. W had taxable income of $20,000 in 1983. W met requirements (1) through (4) above, and in addition, she maintained a household which was the principal residence of the child for the entire taxable year. Therefore, W was eligible to file as a head of household in 1983. Her tax using the 1983 Tax Table is $3,128. If she had not met the 'abandoned' spouse requirements, she would have been required to file as a married person filing separately and her tax would have been $4,161. Filing as a head of household saved W $1,033 ($4,161 − $3,128).

Example 49. Assume the same facts as in Example 48, except that the child lived with his father for three months during 1983. Since W met the abandoned spouse requirements, she was eligible to file as a single taxpayer rather than as a married taxpayer filing separately. She did not qualify as a head of household, since the child did not live with her for the *entire* year.

PROBLEM MATERIALS

Questions for Class Discussion

1. How is taxable income computed? Describe the components of the tax formula.

2. T, who is unmarried and has no dependents, is doing the preliminary work on his 1984 Federal income tax return in December of 1984. T's total itemized deductions at this time are $2,200. T owes real estate taxes of $600, which may be paid without penalty at any time before January 15, 1985. He also plans to contribute $300 to the American Cancer Society within the next month or two. T's marginal tax rate is 50%. Can you give T any tax planning suggestions? How much income tax would T be able to save for 1984 by following your advice?

3. Why is it necessary for dependent children (who are under 19 or are full-time students) to add back any unused zero bracket amounts to their adjusted gross income in the computation of taxable income?

4. What is the rationale for permitting personal and dependency exemptions?

5. What tests must be met to qualify as a dependent of another person?

6. If an individual who may qualify as a dependent does not spend funds which he or she has received (e. g., wages or Social Security benefits), are such unexpended amounts considered in applying the support test? Are such amounts included in applying the gross income test?

7. F contributed $2,100 toward the support of his son, S, who is 18 years old and a full-time college student. S earned $1,100 interest on a savings account and $900 working at a supermarket during the summer. S used all his earnings for his support. He also received a $1,000 scholarship from the college he attended. Can F claim S as a dependent? Explain.

8. M received $2,200 in Social Security benefits during the year. She spent $1,700 of this amount towards her own support. M lives with her daughter, D, who spent $1,500 towards M's support. Can D claim M as a dependent? Explain.

9. Under what circumstances are capital expenditures, which are incurred for the benefit of a dependent, included in the computation of support?

10. Is a dependent son, a full-time student or under 19 years of age, who earns $1,000 or more permitted a personal exemption for himself even though the supporting parent claims a dependency exemption for him?

11. Assuming the same facts as in question 10, would the supporting parent be able to claim a dependency exemption if the child were 19 years old and not attending school on a full-time basis?

12. What is a multiple support agreement? When is it necessary to file such an agreement with the IRS?

13. Why are special rules relating to dependency exemptions for children of divorced or separated spouses necessary?

14. Under what conditions are individuals ineligible to use the Tax Table?

15. Under certain conditions a married taxpayer is eligible to file as a single taxpayer. What are these conditions?

16. B, who is unmarried, expects to have gross income of $22,000 in 1984. B does not itemize deductions. How much income tax can B save if N, his 10-year-old nephew, moves in with him and qualifies as his dependent in 1984?

17. How was the marriage tax partially rectified by the 1981 changes in the tax law?

18. T and S are engaged to be married. Each has gross income of $20,000 for 1983. Assume that they plan to make use of the zero bracket amount and have no dependency exemptions or tax credits. What is the overall effect on the total Federal income taxes that would be paid if they marry prior to the end of 1983? Use the 1983 Tax Table in your computations.

19. Will married individuals always benefit from using the joint return rate schedules? Why?

20. H, age 67, is married to W, who is age 62. W is blind. H and W file a joint return. How much gross income can they earn before they are required to file an income tax return?

21. When is it desirable to file a tax return even though the filing of such return is not required?

22. Under what circumstances is an individual not eligible to file Form 1040A? Form 1040EZ?

23. If an individual fails to claim a deduction or tax credit on a tax return which has previously been filed with the IRS, what remedy is available?

24. During the current year T has a realized gain of $10,000 and a realized loss of $10,000 from the sale of various properties. Since T figures that losses should offset gains, he plans to report none of these transactions on his Federal income tax return. Do you agree with T's approach? Why or why not?

25. Ten years ago, T purchased a personal residence for $45,000. In the current year, she sells the residence for $150,000. T's friends tell her she has a recognized gain from the sale of $105,000. Do you agree with the friend's comment? Elaborate.

26. Discuss the reasons for according preferential treatment to long-term capital gains.

27. Why is it important to determine whether an asset is an ordinary asset or capital asset?

28. Compare and contrast the treatment of capital gains and capital losses by noncorporate and corporate taxpayers.

29. Discuss the tax treatment of an individual who has both net short-term capital gains and net long-term capital gains.

30. If an individual has net long-term capital losses of $1,500 and net short-term capital losses of $1,500, what amount is deductible? Assume the individual has sufficient amounts of other income.

31. If a corporation has net short-term capital losses of $20,000 and net long-term capital gains of $6,000, what amounts are deductible by the corporation? How are any unused losses treated?

32. T and S, two individual and unrelated taxpayers, have the following gains and losses from the sale of capital assets over a two-year period:

	T	S
For tax year 1983—		
Long-term capital gain	$ 3,000	$ –0–
Short-term capital loss	3,000	3,000
For tax year 1984—		
Long-term capital gain	–0–	3,000

Presuming both taxpayers are in the same tax bracket in both years, does one have a better tax position than the other? Why or why not?

33. In early 1984, T, an individual taxpayer, incurred a long-term capital loss of $6,000. In late 1984, he consults you concerning the advisability of selling some securities for a short-term capital gain of $6,000. Since T has heard that short-term capital gains yield ordinary income and do not qualify for the 60 percent long-term capital gain deduction, he is hesitant about making the sale. What is your advice on this matter?

Problems

Note: Because the 1984 Tax Table was not available at the date of publication of this text, all problems requiring use of the Tax Table are written for 1983. Problems requiring use of the Tax Rate Schedules are written for 1984. The 1984 Tax Rate Schedules and 1983 Tax Table are reproduced in Appendix A–1 and Appendix A–2, respectively.

34. Compute T's taxable income and tax before credits and prepayments for 1983 under the following circumstances (use the 1983 Tax Table):

   (a) T is married and files a joint return with his spouse. They have two dependent children. T and his spouse have adjusted gross income of $15,000 and $3,600 of itemized deductions.

   (b) T is unmarried and has no dependents. He has adjusted gross income of $20,000 and itemized deductions of $2,700.

   (c) T is a full-time college student who is supported by his parents. He earned $2,100 from a part-time job and had interest income of $600. T's itemized deductions amounted to $500.

   (d) T is a full-time college student who is supported by his parents. He earned $1,100 from a part-time job and had interest income of $1,600. T's itemized deductions amounted to $500.

35. Compute T's taxable income and tax before credits and prepayments for 1984 in the following situations (use the 1984 Tax Rate Schedules):

   (a) T is married, files separately, and claims two dependent children. T's adjusted gross income is $60,000, and he claims itemized deductions of $8,700. T's spouse also itemizes her deductions.

   (b) Assume the same facts as (a) except that T's itemized deductions are only $1,500.

36. Which of the following individuals will be required to determine his or her income tax from the Tax Rate Schedules rather than from the Tax Table?

(a) T, single, with no dependents, earned $10,000 and had itemized deductions of $2,400.

(b) H and W are married and file a joint return. They have eight children whom they claim as dependents. His salary was $76,000 and their itemized deductions were $4,500.

(c) B, a bachelor, age 36, earned $57,000. His itemized deductions were $6,400. He had no dependents.

(d) P, single, age 45, earned $58,000 and had itemized deductions of $5,100. She has no dependents. Because of her unusually high earnings, P elects to compute her tax using the income averaging method.

37. Select the appropriate Tax Table or Tax Rate Schedule and compute the tax before prepayments or credits for the taxpayers in parts (a), (b), and (c) of problem 36. If you choose the Tax Table method, use the 1983 Tax Table. If you select the Tax Rate Schedule method, use the 1984 Tax Rate Schedules.

38. X is single, age 30, and has no dependents. In 1983, X earned $20,000, had deductible employee business expenses of $500, and had itemized deductions of $3,800. Compute X's adjusted gross income, taxable income, and tax before prepayments or credits in 1983.

39. T earned $75,000 in 1984. He had deductible employee business expenses of $2,000 and total itemized deductions of $9,200. Compute T's taxable income and tax before prepayments and credits for 1984. Use the 1984 Tax Rate Schedules.

40. R is a wealthy executive who is in the 50 percent marginal tax bracket. He is considering transferring title in a duplex he owns to his son, S, age 6. S has no income and is claimed as a dependent by R. Net rental income from the duplex is $3,000 a year, which S will be encouraged to place in a savings account. How much income tax will the family save in 1983 if R transfers title in the duplex to S? Use the 1983 Tax Table.

41. In each of the following independent cases determine the number of personal and dependency exemptions T may claim. Assume any dependency test not mentioned has been met. Unless otherwise specified, T is not married and is not entitled to a personal exemption for old age or blindness.

Case 1. T provides 80 percent of the support of an uncle who does not live with him. The uncle has gross receipts of $1,100 from rental property. Expenses attributable to this income amounting to $200 are paid by the uncle.

Case 2. T provides 80 percent of the support of his nephew (age 17) who lives with him. During the year the nephew has gross income of $1,000 and is a full-time student.

Case 3. Assume the same facts as in Case 2 except that the $1,000 was paid to the nephew as a scholarship.

Case 4. T provides over 50 percent of the support of his son, S, and his son's wife, D. S is a full-time student at a university. During 19X1, D earned $1,950 on which income taxes were withheld. On January 31, 19X2, D filed a separate return for tax year 19X1. All parties reside in New York.

Case 5. Assume the same facts as in Case 4 except that all parties reside in California.

Case 6. During 19X1, T gave his father, F (age 68), cash of $1,000 and a used automobile (cost of $2,000). F's total expenditures for food, lodging, and clothing for 19X1 amount to $3,000 ($1,000 received from T and $2,000 withdrawn from F's savings account). F meets the test for blindness, although he possesses an unrestricted driver's license. F dies on June 3, 19X1.

Case 7. T and his two brothers each provide 15 percent of the support of their mother. The mother derives the remainder of her support from a Social Security benefit of $1,300.

42. Determine the correct number of personal and dependency exemptions in each of the following situations:

   (a) T, age 66 and disabled, is a widower who maintains a home for his unmarried daughter who is 24 years old. The daughter earned $3,000 and attends college on a part-time basis. T provides more than 50 percent of her support.

   (b) T, a bachelor age 45, provides more than 50 percent of the support of his father, age 70. T's father had gross income of $900 from a part-time job.

   (c) T, age 45, is married and has two dependent foster children who live with him and are totally supported by T. One of the foster children, age 14, had $1,100 of gross income. T and his spouse file a joint return.

   (d) T, age 67, is married and has a married daughter, age 24. T's daughter attended college on a full-time basis and was supported by T. The daughter filed a joint return with her spouse; and T filed a joint return with his spouse, age 62.

43. Compute the number of personal and dependency exemptions in the following independent situations:

   (a) T, a single individual, provides 60 percent of the support of his mother, age 69. She received $800 dividend income and $1,500 in Social Security benefits.

   (b) T, a married individual filing a joint return, provides 100 percent of the support of his son, age 21, who is a part-time student. T's son earned $2,000 during the year from part-time employment.

   (c) T, who is divorced, provides $2,000 child support for his child who is living with her mother. The divorce decree provides that the noncustodial parent is to receive the dependency exemption.

44. Has T provided more than 50 percent support in the following situations?

   (a) T paid $6,000 for an automobile which was titled in his name. His 19-year-old son uses the automobile approximately 50 percent of the time while attending a local college on a full-time basis. The son earned $4,000 from a part-time job which was used to pay his college and living expenses. The value of the son's room and board which was provided by T amounted to $1,200.

   (b) T contributed $4,000 to his mother's support during the year. His mother received $5,000 in Social Security benefits which were placed in her savings account for future use.

(c) Assume the same facts in (b) except that T's mother used the funds for her support during the year.

45.   A, B, and C contribute to the support of their mother, M, age 67. M lives with each of the children for approximately four months during the year. Her total living costs amounted to $6,000 and were paid as follows:

From M's Social Security benefits	$ 1,700
By A	500
By B	1,250
By C	1,250
By T, M's unrelated friend	1,300
	$ 6,000

(a) Which, if any, of these individuals may claim M as a dependent (assume no multiple support agreement is filed)?

(b) If a multiple support agreement is filed, who must be a party to it, and who may claim the exemption for M under the agreement?

46.   Which of the following individuals are required to file a tax return for 1984? Should any of these individuals file a return even if such filing is not required? Why?

(a) T is married and files a joint return with his spouse. Their combined gross income was $6,000.

(b) T is a dependent child under age 19 who received $1,000 in wages from a part-time job and $1,100 of dividend income.

(c) T is single and is 67 years old. His gross income from wages was $4,800.

(d) T is a self-employed single individual with gross income of $12,000 from an unincorporated business. Business expenses amounted to $11,800.

47.   Which of the following individuals may use the short Form 1040A?

(a) T's gross income is solely from wages. His taxable income was $70,000 during the year.

(b) T is a self-employed individual whose income was $30,000 from professional services as an accountant. He also received taxable dividends of $2,000.

(c) T earned wages of $14,000 and received $250 interest from a savings account. T itemizes his deductions during the year.

48.   Which of the following individuals may use Form 1040EZ?

(a) G, who is single, age 67, had taxable income of $42,000. Her gross income included a salary of $48,000 and interest on a savings account of $350.

(b) S, age 32, is divorced. She had taxable income of $26,000. She contributed $1,500 toward the support of B, her son, who lives with F, her former husband. F contributed $1,000 toward B's support. The divorce decree is silent as to which parent may claim the exemption for B. S will claim the exemption if she is allowed to.

(c) M, age 40, is married to W, who left him two years ago and has not returned. W's whereabouts are unknown. M had taxable income of $31,000, which consisted entirely of salary.

(d) K is single, age 29. She had taxable income of $32,500, which included her salary plus interest of $300. She does not claim any dependents.

49. Can T use Tax Rate Schedule Z (head of household) in 19X3?

(a) T's wife died in 19X2. T maintained a household for his two dependent children during 19X3. Over one-half of the cost of the household was provided by T.

(b) T is unmarried and lives in an apartment. He supported his aged parents who live in a separate home. T provides over one-half of the funds used to maintain his parents' home. T also claimed his parents as dependents, since he provided more than one-half of their support during the year.

(c) T is unmarried and maintains a household (over one-half of the cost) for his 18-year-old married daughter and her husband. His daughter filed a joint return with her husband solely for the purpose of obtaining a refund of income taxes that were withheld.

50. Indicate in each of the following situations which of the Tax Rate Schedules that T should use for calendar year 1984. (Assume that T is not eligible to use the Tax Table.)

(a) T, the mother and sole support of her three minor children, was abandoned by her husband in late 1983.

(b) T is a widower whose wife died in 1983. T furnishes all of the support of his household, which includes two dependent children.

(c) T furnishes all of the support of his parents who live in their own home in a different city. T's parents qualify as his dependents. T is not married.

(d) T's household includes an unmarried stepchild, age 18, who has a gross income of $6,000 during the year. T furnishes all of the cost of maintaining the household. T is not married.

51. K, age 39, is single. She maintains a household that is the residence of her two children, B, age 8, and G, age 11. The children are claimed as dependents by their father, who provides $2,000 child support for each of them. During 1984, K earned a salary of $45,000. Other items which affected her taxable income are listed below:

Total itemized deductions	$ 3,800
Employee travel expense (a deduction *for* AGI)	500
Capital gains	
Short-term	900
Long-term	3,500
Capital losses	
Short-term	(300)
Long-term	(700)
Interest income	650

K provides all the support for her mother, M, who lives in a nursing home. M qualifies as K's dependent.

    (a) Compute K's adjusted gross income, taxable income, and income tax before prepayments and credits.

    (b) Assume the same facts as in (a), except K's short-term capital loss was $3,000 and her long-term capital loss was $4,700.

52. H, single with no dependents, had a short-term capital loss of $2,600 in 1983. He earned a salary of $15,000 and had itemized deductions of $2,100.

    (a) Compute H's taxable income for 1983.

    (b) Assume the same facts as in (a) except that H also had a $1,400 long-term capital loss in 1983. Compute H's taxable income and capital loss carryforward to 1984.

53. N, age 67, is married to H, age 65. N and H file a joint return for 1984. During 1984, N's salary was $82,000. He attended a business convention in July, incurring travel expenses of $800, for which he was not reimbursed by his employer. N has an extensive portfolio of stock investments. During 1984, he engaged in several stock transactions, with the following results:

Capital gains	
Short-term	$ 2,500
Long-term	9,000
Capital losses	
Short-term	(3,700)
Long-term	(1,200)

N and H had total itemized deductions of $14,400 during 1984. He received interest of $4,800 on City of Phoenix bonds.

    (a) Compute taxable income for N and H for 1984.

    (b) Assume the same facts as in (a), except that N's long-term capital gain was only $400.

54. T is a cash basis, calendar year taxpayer. For the years 19X1 and 19X2 he expects adjusted gross income of $20,000 and the following itemized deductions:

Church pledge	$ 1,200
Interest on home mortgage	1,500
Other (sales taxes, etc.)	700

Assuming the zero bracket amount for each year is $3,400, discuss the tax consequences of the following alternatives:

    (a) In 19X2, T pays his church pledge for 19X1 and 19X2 ($1,200 for each year).

    (b) T does nothing different (i. e., deductions from adjusted gross income for each year are $3,400).

Cumulative Problems

55. J and K, both age 25, are husband and wife. J is a computer programmer and earned $24,000 during 1983. K is a student at the Ohio State University medical school. They have one child, L, who was born on June 30,

1983. K had taken the summer off from school and returned in the fall. J and K hired a neighbor to care for L during the day from September through December. As a result of the payments made for child care, they are entitled to a tax credit for child and dependent care expenses of $133. J received $10,000 of taxable income from a trust her father had established to pay for her education. In addition, she was awarded a $3,000 scholarship by the medical school in 1983.

In examining their records, you find that J and K are entitled to the following itemized deductions:

Medical expenses (in excess of the percentage limitation)	$ 600
State and local income taxes	550
Real estate taxes on their condominium	1,140
General sales taxes	260
Interest on mortgage on their condominium	3,100
Charitable contributions	400
Tax return preparation fee	100
	$ 6,150

Income tax withheld by J's employer was $2,300. In addition, J and K made estimated tax payments of $2,200 during 1983.

Compute (a) taxable income and (b) net tax payable or refund due for J and K on a joint return. (Use the 1983 Tax Table.)

56. H and W, husband and wife, file a joint return for the tax year 1984. H, who is 66 years old, is a restaurant manager. W, who is 54, is manager of a beauty shop. During 1984, H and W received the following amounts:

H's salary	$ 32,000
W's salary	29,000
Bonus from W's employer	3,000
Net capital gain (excess of net long-term capital gain over net short-term capital loss) on the sale of 50 shares of stock	10,000
Interest on bonds issued by the City of Chicago	700
Life insurance proceeds received on the death of H's mother	50,000
Property inherited from H's mother	80,000

In examining the records of H and W, you find the following items of possible tax consequence (all applicable to 1984):

(a) H attended a convention of restaurant managers in July and incurred $400 travel expenses for which he was not reimbursed by his employer.

(b) H and W subscribe to several professional journals; they paid $140 for these subscriptions.

(c) In April, H and W paid you $100 for preparing their 1983 tax return.

(d) H and W had other itemized deductions, not including any amount mentioned above, of $7,600.

(e) Federal income tax withheld by their employers totaled $10,000; in addition, they made estimated tax payments of $2,000.

(f) H and W are entitled to a political contribution credit of $100 for a contribution they made to the campaign fund of J, a friend of theirs who was elected mayor.

H and W have a son, S, who lived with them during 1984, except for nine months during which he was away at college. S, age 27, is a law student and plans to graduate in 1985. During the summer, S worked and earned $1,100. He used his earnings for school expenses. His parents contributed $2,700 toward his support.

Compute the following amounts for H and W: (a) gross income, (b) adjusted gross income, (c) taxable income, and (d) net tax payable or refund due.

Tax Form Problems

57. Harold Green, age 41, is married to Joan Green, age 38. Harold and Joan have two dependent children, Anthony, age 15, and Lisa, age 13. The Greens live at 121 Barberry Court, Franklin, Anystate, 02816. Harold is a factory worker and earned $14,200 in 1983. Joan worked part-time as a department store clerk and earned $5,200. Their only other income was $500 interest on a joint savings account. Their employers withheld income tax of $2,028 in 1983. They had itemized deductions of $2,800. Harold and Joan file a joint return. Compute their net tax payable or refund due using Form 1040A. On the form, disregard any blanks for which no information is provided.

58. Walter Hankins, age 20, is a full-time student at State University. He is single and is claimed as a dependent by his parents, who provided over half of his support. Walter earned $1,500 working part-time at a department store during 1983. In addition, Walter received $1,200 of taxable income from a trust set up by his grandfather to help pay his college expenses. Walter's itemized deductions for 1983 were $700. His adjusted gross income (from Form 1040, line 32) was $2,700. Walter's Social Security number is 111-01-0001. Compute Walter's tax, before prepayments and credits, for 1983, using lines 33 through 40 of Form 1040.

59. Fred Kennedy, age 40, is married to Irene Kennedy, age 39. They have two dependent children, Deanna, age 14 and Brenda, age 12. During 1983 they had the following items of income:

Fred's salary	$ 14,000
Irene's salary	$ 12,000
Interest on a joint bank account	$ 400

Fred incurred deductible employee business expenses (reported on Form 2106) of $250. They had excess itemized deductions (from Schedule A, line 28) of $2,630. Fred and Irene are entitled to a credit for contributions to a candidate for public office of $100. Their employers withheld Federal income tax of $2,780 in 1983. Compute the Kennedys' net tax payable or refund due on Form 1040. They file a joint return.

Research Problems

60. R was divorced during 19X6. She has custody of two minor children and contributed more than one-half of their support during 19X7. The divorce decree provides that her former husband J is required to pay $400 per month child support and is entitled to the dependency exemptions for income tax purposes. J paid the child support payments for the first six months of 19X7. However, J was unable to make the child support payments during the last six months of 19X7. R has little hope of receiving any future payments or a recovery of the unpaid amounts.

(a) Is R entitled to claim the children as dependents in 19X7?

(b) Is R entitled to claim the children in 19X8 and future years if the divorce decree is not modified and J does not make any child support payments?

Partial list of research aids:

R. A. Gordon, 33 TCM 732, T.C. Memo. 1974–169.

61. W was the owner-operator of several mobile home parks. He employed his three young children to assume certain duties, such as maintenance of the swimming pool, landscaping, office duties and other odd jobs. In 19X1, the youngest child (then age 7) was paid $1,600 and in 19X3 was paid $2,100. The IRS disallowed W a deduction for 90 percent of the wages paid to the youngest child. Would you advise W to contest the ruling? If so, what arguments should W make in support of the deduction?

62. H and W were married in 19X1 and in the next three years had two small children. On January 9, 19X5, H and W entered into a written separation agreement covering child custody and a property settlement. Their agreement established child support payments and provided that H was to be entitled to claim the children as dependents. The agreement stipulated that (1) H was to be allowed the dependency exemptions subject to the regulations of the IRS and (2) the agreement was to be governed by laws of the state of Maryland (of which H and W were residents).

H and W received a final decree of divorce on January 25, 19X6. The divorce decree gave custody of the children to W, awarded child support, and incorporated the provisions of the January 9, 19X5, separation agreement.

H provided over $600 support for each child during 19X8. W claimed the children as dependents on her 19X8 return, and the IRS disallowed the exemptions.

W argued that the agreement was unfair, that it was not incorporated into the divorce decree, that H had failed to comply with some of its provisions, and that she had provided over half of the support of the children. Should W challenge the action of the IRS?

Chapter 5

Gross Income: Concepts and Inclusions

Computation of the income tax liability of an individual or a corporation begins with the determination of "gross income." Section 61 provides an all-inclusive definition of gross income: "gross income means all income from whatever source derived." Section 61 supplements this definition with a list of items (not necessarily all-inclusive) which are includible in gross income (e. g., compensation for services, rents, interest, dividends, alimony). Other Code sections contain specific rules for particular types of income.

Congress has provided that certain items are exempt from taxation. These items include interest on certain governmental obligations (state and municipal bonds). The exemptions appear in § § 101–131 of the Code and are discussed in Chapter 6.

GROSS INCOME—WHAT IS IT?

GENERAL DEFINITION

Section 61(a) of the Internal Revenue Code defines the term "gross income" as follows:

> Except as otherwise provided in this subtitle, gross income means all income from whatever source derived.

Since the sweeping scope of the definition is apparent, the Supreme Court has stated:

The starting point in all cases dealing with the question of the scope of what is included in "gross income" begins with the basic premise that the purpose of Congress was to use the full measure of its taxing power.[1]

The clause, "Except as otherwise provided in this subtitle," refers to sections of the Code in which Congress has exempted certain types of income from the tax base. Such exclusions are discussed in Chapter 6.

ECONOMIC AND ACCOUNTING CONCEPTS

The term "income" is used in the Code but is not separately defined. Thus, early in the history of our tax laws, the courts were required to interpret "the commonly understood meaning of the term which must have been in the minds of the people when they adopted the Sixteenth Amendment to the Constitution."[2] In determining the definition of income, the Supreme Court rejected the economist's concept of income.

For the economist, measuring economic income requires a determination of the fair market value of the taxpayer's net assets at the beginning and end of the year. After this determination is made, economic income is defined as the sum of the taxpayer's change in net worth plus actual consumption of goods and services for the tax period. Economic income also includes imputed values for such items as the rental value of an owner-occupied home and the value of food a taxpayer might grow for personal consumption.[3] The use of these and other market values would present difficult problems in administering the tax laws and would produce endless controversies between the taxpayer and the IRS. Thus, the economist's concept of income has been rejected by the courts simply on the grounds of its impracticality.

In contrast, the accountant's concept of income is founded on the realization principle.[4] According to this principle, income is not recognized until it is realized. Realization entails (1) an exchange of goods and services between the accounting entity and some independent, external group and (2) assets received in the exchange that are capable of being objectively valued. The mere appreciation in the market value of assets prior to a sale or other disposition is not sufficient to warrant income recognition. Also, imputed savings arising from the self-construction of assets to be used in one's own operations is not income because there is no exchange.

1. *James v. U. S.*, 61–1 USTC ¶ 9449, 7 AFTR2d 1361, 81 S.Ct. 1052 (USSC, 1961).
2. *Merchants Loan and Trust Co. v. Smietanka*, 1 USTC ¶ 42, 3 AFTR 3102, 41 S.Ct. 386 (USSC, 1921).
3. See Henry C. Simons, *Personal Income Taxation* (University of Chicago Press, 1933), Ch. 2–3.
4. See the American Accounting Association Committee Report on the "Realization Concept," *The Accounting Review* (April 1965), pp. 312–322.

The Supreme Court in *Eisner v. Macomber*[5] added the realization requirement to a judicial definition of income which had been formulated in early cases:

> Income may be defined as the gain derived from capital, from labor, or from both combined, provided it is understood to include profit gained through a sale or conversion of capital assets. . . . Here we have the essential matter: not a gain accruing to capital; not a *growth* or *increment* of value *in* investment; but a gain, a profit, something of exchangeable value, *proceeding from* the property, *severed from* the capital, however, invested or employed, and *coming in,* being *"derived"*—that is, *received* or *drawn by* the recipient for his separate use, benefit and disposal—*that* is, income derived from the property.

Thus, the early Supreme Court definition of income can simply be restated as the gain realized from capital, from labor, or from a combination of the two.

As a result of cases subsequent to *Eisner v. Macomber,* the "from capital, from labor . . ." phrases can be deleted. For example, in *Glenshaw Glass Co.,*[6] the taxpayer received punitive damages from a supplier who had committed fraud and violated federal antitrust laws. Clearly, the damages were intended to be a punishment and, therefore, were not gain realized from capital, from labor, or from both combined. Nevertheless, the Supreme Court held that the punitive damages received by Glenshaw were income:

> Here we have instances of undeniable accessions to wealth, clearly realized, and over which the taxpayers have complete dominion.

In other cases the Supreme Court reasoned similarly that embezzlement[7] and extortion proceeds[8] were income.

In summary, "income" represents an increase in wealth which is recognized for tax purposes only upon realization.

COMPARISON OF ACCOUNTING AND TAXABLE INCOME

Although income tax rules frequently parallel financial accounting measurement concepts, differences do exist. Of major significance, for example, is the fact that unearned (i. e., prepaid) income received by an accrual basis taxpayer is taxed in the year of receipt. For financial accounting purposes, such prepayments are not treated as income

---

5. 1 USTC ¶ 32, 3 AFTR 3020, 40 S.Ct. 189 (USSC, 1920).
6. 55–1 USTC ¶ 9308, 47 AFTR 162, 75 S.Ct. 473 (USSC, 1955).
7. *Supra,* Footnote 1.
8. *Rutkin v. U. S.,* 52–1 USTC ¶ 9260, 41 AFTR 596, 72 S.Ct. 571 (USSC, 1952).

until earned.[9] Because of this and other differences, many corporations report financial accounting income which is substantially different from the amounts reported for tax purposes. (See Chapter 20, Reconciliation of Taxable Income and Accounting Income.)

The explanation for some of the variations between accounting and taxable income was given in a recent Supreme Court decision involving inventory and bad debt adjustments.[10] The relevant portion of the opinion is reproduced below:

> The primary goal of financial accounting is to provide useful information to management, shareholders, creditors, and others properly interested; the major responsibility of the accountant is to protect these parties from being misled. The primary goal of the income tax system, in contrast, is the equitable collection of revenue. . . . Consistently with its goals and responsibilities, financial accounting has as its foundation the principle of conservatism, with its corollary that 'possible errors in measurement [should] be in the direction of understatement rather than overstatement of net income and net assets.' In view of the Treasury's markedly different goals and responsibilities, understatement of income is not destined to be its guiding light.
>
> . . . Financial accounting, in short, is hospitable to estimates, probabilities, and reasonable certainties; the tax law, with its mandate to preserve the revenue, can give no quarter to uncertainty.

FORM OF RECEIPT

Gross income is not limited to cash received. "It includes income realized in any form, whether in money, property, or services. Income may be realized [and recognized], therefore, in the form of services, meals, accommodations, stock or other property, as well as in cash."[11]

Example 1. If an employer allows an employee to use a company car for his or her vacation, then the employee realizes income. Income realized by the employee is equal to the rental value of a car for the trip.

Example 2. A stockholder realizes income (i. e., a constructive dividend) when a corporation sells him or her property for less

---

9. Similar differences exist in the deduction area. Goodwill, for example, can be amortized for financial accounting purposes but cannot be deducted under the Federal income tax.

10. *Thor Power Tool Co. v. Comm.*, 79–1 USTC ¶ 9139, 43 AFTR2d 79–362, 99 S.Ct. 773 (USSC, 1979).

11. Reg. § 1.61–1(a).

than its market value. The income is the difference between the market value of the property and the price paid by the stockholder.

Example 3. A debtor generally realizes income if debt is discharged for less than the amount due the creditor.[12]

EXCEPTIONS TO THE INCOME REALIZATION DOCTRINE

Indirect Economic Benefits to Employee. Over the years the courts have developed an exception to the rule that any economic gain realized by the taxpayer is recognized as taxable income. Benefits received by the employee when the goods or services were actually provided for the convenience of the employer and when the employee had no control over their receipt are not taxable income. An early case involved meals and lodging for a hotel manager who was required by his employer to live in the hotel and take his meals on the premises. In *Van Rosen,* the Tax Court held that the value of the meals and lodging was not taxable income:

> Though there was an element of gain to the employee, in that he received subsistence and quarters which otherwise he would have had to supply for himself, he had nothing he could take, appropriate, use and expend according to his own dictates, but rather, the ends of the employer's business dominated and controlled, just as in the furnishing of a place to work and in the supplying of the tools and machinery with which to work. The fact that certain personal wants and needs of the employee were satisfied was plainly secondary and incidental to the employment.[13]

In 1954, Congress enacted § 119 (discussed in Chapter 6), which excludes the value of meals and lodging from the employee's income in cases such as *Van Rosen.* However, the Tax Court's reasoning in that case can be applied to indirect economic benefits received by employees in a number of situations not addressed by § 119. For example, the employee has no taxable income from the following:

—An employer requires the employee to attend a convention in Hawaii to perform significant services.

—The employee is required to undergo an annual physical examination, the cost of which is paid by the employer.

—The employer furnishes uniforms that must be worn on the job.

—The employee consumes food and beverages while entertaining a customer, and the expenses are paid by the employer.

---

12. Reg. § 1.61–12. See *U. S. v. Kirby Lumber Co.,* 2 USTC ¶ 814, 10 AFTR 458, 52 S.Ct. 4 (USSC, 1931). Exceptions to this general rule are discussed in Chapter 6.
13. *Gunnar Van Rosen,* 17 T.C. 834 (1951).

—The employer provides the employee with an expensive automobile for visiting customers.

It takes very little imagination to envision various significant nontaxable fringe benefits available to employees. However, the expenditure must serve a business purpose of the employer, other than to compensate the employee, if the benefit is to be considered a tax-free item.[14]

The Recovery of Capital Doctrine. The Constitution grants Congress the power to tax "income" but does not define the term. Because the Constitution does not define income, it would seem that Congress could simply tax gross receipts. And while Congress can allow certain deductions, none are constitutionally required. However, the Supreme Court has held that there can be no income subject to tax until the taxpayer has recovered the capital invested.[15]

> . . . We must withdraw from the gross proceeds an amount sufficient to restore the capital value that existed at the commencement of the period under consideration.

In its simplest application, the recovery of capital doctrine means a seller can reduce the gross receipts (i. e., selling price) by the adjusted basis in the property sold.[16] This net amount, in the language of the Code, is gross income. But the doctrine also has subtle implications.

Example 4. In 19X3 B paid $5,000 additional taxes because his accountant did not maintain proper documentation of expenses. B's loss was only temporary, because he collected the $5,000 from the accountant after threatening a negligence suit. The $5,000 received from the accountant is not income, because it merely replaces the capital taken by the tax collector as a result of the accountant's negligence.[17] B also lost one day's pay, $100, for time spent at the local office of the IRS protesting the additional taxes. The accountant reimbursed B for his loss of wages. The $100 is not a recovery of capital, because no capital was formed until either the income or its substitute (payment from the accountant) was received.

Example 5. Z Corporation recovered $150,000 as damages inflicted by a competitor on the goodwill of the corporation. The goodwill was the product of fast and efficient services to its customers, and no cost of the asset was reflected on the corporation's balance sheet. Because the company has no capital invested in its goodwill, the $150,000 is taxable.[18]

---

14. *Patterson v. Thomas,* 61–1 USTC ¶ 9310, 7 AFTR2d 862, 289 F.2d 108 (CA–2, 1960). See Chapter 19 for a discussion of deferred compensation.
15. *Doyle v. Mitchell Bros. Co.,* 1 USTC ¶ 17, 1 AFTR 235, 38 S.Ct. 467 (USSC, 1916).
16. For a definition of adjusted basis see the Glossary of Tax Terms in Appendix C.
17. *Clark v. Commissioner,* 40 B.T.A. 333 (1939).
18. *Raytheon Production Corp. v. Commissioner,* 44–2 USTC ¶ 9424, 32 AFTR 1155, 144 F.2d 110 (CA–1, 1944).

Example 6. In 19X1 the taxpayer, C, purchased an acre of land for $10,000. In 19X2, A Electric Company paid C $1,000 for a permanent easement to run an underground cable across his property. The easement prevents C from making certain uses of his property (e. g., it affected where a house could be located and where trees could be planted) but C can still make some use of the property. The costs of the interests in the property C gave up for the $1,000 cannot be determined; therefore, C may treat the $1,000 as a recovery of his original cost of the property and reduce his basis to $9,000. If C later sells the property for more than $9,000 he will recognize a gain.

YEAR OF INCLUSION

ANNUAL ACCOUNTING PERIOD

The annual accounting period is a basic component of our tax system.[19] All taxable entities may use a calendar year to report income. Those who keep adequate books and records may use a fiscal year (i. e., a period of 12 months ending on the last day of any month other than December) or a 52-53 week year which ends on the same day of the week nearest the last day of the same month each year.[20] A retailer considering a 52-53 week year might choose a year ending in January so that he or she can properly account for Christmas returns, and on a Saturday so that inventory can be taken on Sunday. Automobile dealers often select a fiscal year ending in September, since the taxable year corresponds with their natural business year (i. e., the change in car models).

Since the lifetime earnings of a taxable entity must be divided into these 12-month intervals and a progressive tax rate schedule must be applied to the taxable income for each interval, it is often of more than just academic interest to determine the period into which a particular item of income is allocated. Determining this period is important because (1) Congress may change the tax rate schedule, (2) the entity's income may rise or fall between years so that placing the income in a particular year may mean that the income is taxed at a different marginal rate, or (3) the entity may undergo a change in its status and a different tax rate schedule may apply (e. g. an individual might marry or a proprietorship may incorporate).

ACCOUNTING METHODS

The year an item of income is subject to tax often depends upon which acceptable accounting method the taxpayer regularly employs.[21] Most

---

19. See "Accounting Periods" in Chapter 18.
20. § § 441(a) and (d).
21. See "Accounting Methods" in Chapter 18.

individuals and many businesses use the cash receipts and disbursements method of accounting, whereas most corporations use the accrual method. Section 1.446 of the Regulations requires the accrual method for determining purchases and sales when a taxpayer maintains inventory.[22] Therefore, some businesses employ a hybrid method which reflects a combination of the cash and accrual methods of accounting.

In addition to these overall accounting methods, a taxpayer may choose to spread the gain from the sale of property over the collection periods by electing the installment method of income recognition;[23] contractors may either spread profits from contracts over the periods in which the work is done (the percentage of completion method) or defer all profit until the year in which the project is completed (the completed contract method).[24]

The Commissioner has the power to prescribe the accounting method to be used by the taxpayer. Section 446(b) grants the Commissioner broad powers to determine if the accounting method used clearly reflects income:

> Exceptions—If no method of accounting has been regularly used by the taxpayer, or *if the method used does not clearly reflect income, the computation of taxable income shall be made under such method as, in the opinion of the Secretary or his delegate, does clearly reflect income.*

Also, a change in the method of accounting requires the consent of the Commissioner.[25]

Cash Receipts Method. Under the cash receipts method, property or services received are included in the taxpayer's gross income in the year of actual or "constructive" receipt by the taxpayer or agent, regardless of whether the income was earned in that year.[26] The receipt of income need not be reduced to cash in the same year; rather, all that is necessary for income recognition is that property or services received have a fair market value—a cash equivalent.[27] Thus, if a cash basis taxpayer receives a note in payment for services, he or she has income in the year of receipt equal to the value of the note. However, a creditor's mere promise to pay (e. g., an account receivable), with no supporting note, is not usually considered to have a fair mar-

---

22. Reg. § 1.446–1(c)(2)(i). See the Glossary of Tax Terms in Appendix C for a discussion of the terms "accrual method," "accounting method," and "accounting period."
23. §§ 453(a) and (b) and § 453A.
24. Reg. § 1.453–3.
25. § 446(e). See Chapter 18.
26. *Julia A. Strauss,* 2 B.T.A. 598 (1925). See the glossary for a discussion of the terms "cash equivalent doctrine" and "constructive receipt."
27. Reg. §§ 1.446–1(a)(3) and (c)(1)(i).

ket value.[28] Thus, the cash basis taxpayer defers income recognition until the account receivable is collected.

> **Example 7.** D, an accountant, reports his income by the cash method. In 19X1 he performed an audit for X and billed the client $5,000 which was collected in 19X2. In 19X1, D also performed an audit for Y, and because of Y's precarious financial position, D required Y to issue an $8,000 secured negotiable note in payment of the fee. The note had a fair market value of $6,000. D collected $8,000 on the note in 19X2. D's gross income for the two years is as follows:

	19X1	19X2
Fair market value of		
note received from Y	$ 6,000	
Cash received:		
From X on account receivable		$ 5,000
From Y on note receivable		8,000
Less: Recovery of capital		(6,000)
Total gross income	$ 6,000	$ 7,000

Accrual Method. Under accrual accounting, an item is generally included in the gross income for the year in which it is earned, regardless of when the income is collected. The income is earned when (1) all the events have occurred which fix the right to receive such income and (2) the amount thereof can be determined with reasonable accuracy.[29]

Generally, the taxpayer's rights to the income accrue when title to property passes to the buyer or the services are performed for the customer or client.[30] If the rights to the income have accrued but are subject to a potential refund claim (e. g., under a product warranty), the income is reported in the year of sale and a deduction is allowed in subsequent years when actual claims accrue.[31]

Where the taxpayer's rights to the income are being contested (e. g., a contractor who fails to meet specifications), the year in which the income is subject to tax depends upon whether payment has been received. If payment has not been received, no income is recognized until the claim has been settled; only then is the right to the income established.[32] However, if the payment is received before the dispute

---

28. *Bedell v. Comm.,* 1 USTC ¶ 359, 7 AFTR 8469, 30 F.2d 622 (CA–2, 1929).
29. Reg. § 1.451–1(a).
30. *Lucas v. North Texas Lumber Co.,* 2 USTC ¶ 484, 8 AFTR 10276, 50 S.Ct. 184 (USSC, 1929).
31. *Brown v. Helvering,* 4 USTC ¶ 1223, 12 AFTR 128, 54 S.Ct. 356 (USSC, 1933).
32. *Burnet v. Sanford and Brooks,* 2 USTC ¶ 636, 9 AFTR 603, 51 S.Ct. 150 (USSC, 1931).

is settled, the court-made claim of right doctrine requires the taxpayer to recognize the income in the year of receipt.[33]

> **Example 8.** A contractor completed a building in 19X1 and presented a bill to the customer. The customer refused to pay the bill and claimed that the contractor had not met specifications. A settlement with the customer was not reached until 19X2. Assuming the customer had a valid claim, no income would accrue to the contractor until 19X2. If the customer paid for the work and then filed suit for damages, the contractor could not defer the income (i. e., the income would be taxable in 19X1).

The measure of accrual basis income is generally the amount the taxpayer has a right to receive. Unlike the cash basis, the fair market value of the customer's obligation is irrelevant in measuring accrual basis income.

> **Example 9.** Assume the same facts as in Example 7, except D is an accrual basis taxpayer. D must recognize $13,000 ($8,000 + $5,000) income in 19X1, when his rights to the income accrued.

EXCEPTIONS APPLICABLE TO CASH BASIS TAXPAYERS

Constructive Receipt. The doctrine of constructive receipt places certain limits upon the ability of cash basis taxpayers to arbitrarily shift income from one year to another in an effort to minimize total taxes. Regulation § 1.451–2(a) provides:

> (a) *General Rule.* Income although not actually reduced to the taxpayer's possession is constructively received by him in the taxable year during which it is credited to his account, set apart for him or otherwise made available so that he could have drawn upon it during the taxable year if notice of intention to withdraw had been given. However, income is not constructively received if the taxpayer's control of its receipt is subject to substantial limitations or restrictions.

A taxpayer who is entitled to receive income made available to him or her cannot "turn his or her back" on it. A taxpayer is not permitted to defer income for December services by refusing to accept payment until January.

Some other examples of the application of the constructive receipt doctrine follow:

---

33. *North American Oil Consolidated Co. v. Burnet,* 3 USTC ¶ 943, 11 AFTR 16, 52 S.Ct. 613 (USSC, 1932); see the glossary for a discussion of the term "claim of right doctrine."

Example 10. A salary check received by T on December 31, 19X8, but after banking hours, was taxable in 19X8. The check was property with a market value.[34]

Example 11. T, the controlling shareholder of a corporation, accrued a bonus to himself on December 31, 19X8, but he waited until the following year to have the check written. Since T could control when the payment was to be made, the bonus was constructively received on December 31, 19X8.[35]

Example 12. T is a member of a barter club. In 19X1 T performed services for other club members and earned 1,000 points. Each point entitles him to $1 in goods and services sold by other members of the club, and the points can be used at any time. In 19X2, T exchanged his points for a new color TV. T must recognize $1,000 income in 19X1 when the 1,000 points were credited to his account.[36]

Example 13. On December 31, 19X8, an employer issued a bonus check to an employee but asked him to hold it for a few days until the company could make deposits to cover the check. The income was not constructively received on December 31, 19X8, since the issuer did not have sufficient funds in its account to pay the debt.[37]

Example 14. Interest coupons which have matured and are payable, but which have not been cashed, are constructively received in the taxable year during which the coupons mature, unless it can be shown that there are no funds available for the payment of the interest.[38]

Example 15. Interest on bank savings accounts and dividends on savings and loan deposits (treated as interest for tax purposes) are income to the depositor for the tax year when credited to his or her account.

Example 16. Dividends on stock are not taxed until the check is received if the corporation, as a regular business policy, mails year-end dividends so that they cannot be received by the shareholder until January.

However, the constructive receipt doctrine does not reach income that the taxpayer is not yet entitled to receive even though he or she could have contracted to receive the income at an earlier date.

---

34. *C. F. Kahler,* 18 T.C. 31 (1952).
35. *W. C. Leonard & Co. v. U. S.,* 71–1 USTC ¶ 9290, 27 AFTR2d 964, 324 F. Supp. 422 (D.Ct.Miss., 1971).
36. Rev.Rul. 80–52, 1980–1 C.B. 100.
37. L. M. Fischer, 14 T.C. 792 (1950).
38. Reg. § 1.451–2(b).

Example 17. X offered to pay Y $100,000 for land in December 19X1. Y refused but offered to sell the land to X on January 1, 19X2, when Y would be in a lower tax bracket. If X accepted Y's offer, gain would be taxed in 19X2 when the sale was completed.[39]

Example 18. T is a professional athlete and reports his income by the cash method. In negotiating a contract, the club owner made two alternative offers to T:

   (1) $1,000,000 cash upon signing in 19X1.

   (2) $100,000 per year plus 10% interest for 10 years.

T accepted the second offer. The income is taxed according to the amount he actually receives (i. e., $100,000 per year plus interest). The $1,000,000 T could have contracted to receive in 19X1 is not constructively received in that year because he accepted the alternative offer.[40]

If the final contract had provided that T could receive either the lump sum or installment payments, the $1,000,000 would have been constructively received in 19X1.

Finally, income set apart or made available is not constructively received if its actual receipt is subject to "substantial restrictions." The life insurance industry has used "substantial restrictions" as a cornerstone for designing life insurance contracts with favorable tax features.

Example 19. R sells ordinary life insurance. The policy provides for current protection (an amount payable in the event of death) and a savings feature (a cash surrender value payable to R if he terminates the policy during his life).

Each year the cash surrender value of the policy increases, much the same as interest would accrue on a savings account. However, the increase in cash surrender value, unlike the interest on the savings account, is not taxable because the policyholder must cancel the policy to actually receive the increase in value.[41] Because the cancellation requirement is a substantial restriction, the policyholder does not constructively receive the annual increase in cash surrender value.

According to R, individuals should purchase a more expensive ordinary life insurance policy instead of purchasing a cheaper term insurance policy (current protection only) and placing the premium savings in a savings account paying taxable

---

39. *Cowden v. Comm.,* 61–1 USTC ¶ 9382, 7 AFTR2d 1160, 289 F.2d 20 (CA–5, 1961).

40. Rev.Rul. 60–31, 1960–1 C.B. 174, further discussed in Chapter 19.

41. *Theodore H. Cohen,* 39 T.C. 1055 (1963).

interest. Wheter R is correct depends upon a number of variables (e. g., the difference in premiums, alternatives available, interest, and the taxpayer's marginal tax rate).

Series E and Series EE Bonds. Certain U. S. Government savings bonds [Series E (before 1980) and Series EE (after 1979)] are issued at a discount and are redeemable for fixed amounts which increase at stated intervals. No interest payments are actually made; rather, the difference between the purchase price and the amount received on redemption is the bondholder's interest income from the investment.

The income from these savings bonds is generally deferred until the bonds are redeemed or mature. There are three maturity dates: the original maturity date (at which time the bond can be redeemed for its face amount), an extended maturity date (at which time the bond can be redeemed for more than its face amount), and a final maturity date (at which time the total interest accumulated must be reported in income unless the bond is exchanged for a new Series HH bond within one year of the final maturity date). No such deferral is available for corporate bonds or savings accounts. The savings bonds may, therefore, be especially attractive to taxpayers who are in high tax brackets but approaching retirement years and expect to be in lower tax brackets. The bonds can be used to shift income to the low bracket years.

The date of *final* maturity will soon come for the earliest issues of Series E bonds (i. e., those issued during the period May 1, 1941, through April 30, 1952). For these bonds, the final maturity date is 40 years after the date of issue. Series E bonds issued after April 30, 1952, and through November 30, 1965, will reach final maturity 30 years after the issue date. Suppose the taxpayer at the time he or she purchased the bonds was overly pessimistic about his or her earnings in the years of final maturity and unaware of the consequences of 30 or 40 years' interest becoming taxable on the date of reckoning (*final* maturity).

> **Example 20.** In May 1944, R purchased Series E bonds with a total face amount of $10,000 at a cost of $7,500. At *final* maturity in 1984 R will receive $32,760 and will have taxable income of $25,260 ($32,760 − $7,500).

Fortunately, the government has provided R a means of further deferring the tax. If these early issue Series E bonds are exchanged *within one year of the final maturity date* for new Series HH bonds, the accumulated interest will be deferred until the Series HH bonds are redeemed, reach final maturity, or otherwise are disposed of.[42] In the meantime, interest is paid at semiannual intervals on the Series HH

---

42. Treas. Dept. Circulars No. 1–80 and No. 2–80, 1980–1, C.B. 714, 715.

bonds and must be included in income as received. One important advantage of the rollover of Series E into Series HH bonds is that it allows the taxpayer to choose the year in which to report his or her income from the Series E bonds.

Of course, the deferral feature of government bonds issued at a discount is not an advantage if the investor has insufficient income to be subject to tax as the income accrues. In fact, the deferral may work to the investor's disadvantage if he or she has other income in the year the bonds mature or the bunching of the bond interest into one tax year creates a tax liability. But the sellers of U. S. Government bonds have a provision for these investors. A cash basis taxpayer can elect to include in gross income the annual increment in redemption value.[43] The election is frequently useful for minors who have less than enough income to offset their personal exemption and receive the bonds as gifts.

When the election is made to report the income from the bonds on an annual basis, it applies to all such obligations the taxpayer owns at the time of the election and all such securities acquired subsequent to the election. A change in the method of reporting the income from the bonds requires permission of the IRS.

Crop Insurance Proceeds.   Another exception to the general rules of cash basis accounting is a provision which allows farmers to defer the recognition of crop insurance proceeds until the tax year following the year in which the crop was destroyed, if the crop would ordinarily have been sold in the following year.[44] This provision protects the farmer from reporting the income from two years in one tax year.

> **Example 21.**   T, a cash basis farmer, completes his harvest in October 19X1 but does not collect the sales proceeds until January 19X2. In March 19X2, T plants a crop which is destroyed in August 19X2. He collects the crop insurance proceeds in September of 19X2. Under the usual applications of accounting, the income from the 19X1 harvest and the 19X2 crop insurance would be reported in 19X2. However, T may elect under § 451(d) to defer the 19X2 income from the insurance until 19X3.

Amounts Received Under an Obligation to Repay.   The receipt of funds with an obligation to make repayment in the future is the essence of borrowing. Because the taxpayer's assets and liabilities increase by the same amount, no income is realized when the borrowed funds are received. Because amounts paid to the taxpayer by mistake and customer deposits are often classified as borrowed funds, receipt of the funds is not a taxable event.

---

43.   § 454(a).
44.   § 451(d).

Example 22. A customer erroneously paid a utility bill twice. The utility company does not recognize income from the second payment because it has a liability to the customer.[45]

Example 23. A lessor received a damage deposit from a tenant. No income would be recognized by the lessor prior to forfeiture of the deposit because the lessor has an obligation to repay the deposit if no damage occurs.[46] However, if the deposit is in fact a prepayment of rent, it is taxed in the year of receipt.

Payment-in-Kind (PIK). The Department of Agriculture has adopted a payment-in-kind (PIK) program under which farmers are paid with commodities for diverting farmland from production. Under the general rules of tax accounting, the farmer would have income when the commodities are received. However, to avoid the hardships associated with paying taxes in respect to the unsold commodities, in 1983 Congress allowed PIK receipts to be deferred from income until the crops are actually sold; thus, the tax was deferred until the farmer had the cash to pay the tax.[47] In 1984, Congress will decide whether the PIK deferral will be extended to 1984 receipts.

EXCEPTIONS APPLICABLE TO ACCRUAL BASIS TAXPAYERS

Prepaid Income. For financial reporting purposes, advance payments received from customers are reflected as prepaid income and as a liability of the seller. However, for tax purposes, the prepaid income often is taxed in the year of receipt. For example, if a tenant pays the January rent in the preceding December, an accrual or cash basis landlord must report the income as earned in December for tax purposes.

Taxpayers have repeatedly argued that deferral of income until it is actually earned properly matches revenues and expenses; moreover, a proper matching of income with the expenses of earning the income is necessary to clearly reflect income, as required by the Code. The Commissioner responds that § 446(b) grants him broad powers to determine whether an accounting method clearly reflects income. He further argues that generally accepted financial accounting principles should not dictate tax accounting for prepaid income because of the practical problems of collecting federal revenues. Collection of the tax is simplest in the year the taxpayer receives the cash from the customer or client.

Over a 40-year period of litigation, the Commissioner had less than complete success in the courts. In cases involving prepaid income

---

45. *Comm. v. Turney,* 36–1 USTC ¶ 9168, 17 AFTR 679, 82 F.2d 661 (CA–5, 1936).
46. *John Mantell,* 17 T.C. 1143 (1952).
47. For a further discussion of the PIK program, see 1983 IRB No. 34, 17.

from services to be performed at the demand of customers (e. g., dance lessons to be taken at any time in a 24-month period), the Commissioner's position has been upheld.[48] In these cases, the taxpayer's argument that deferral of the income was necessary to match the income with expenses was not persuasive, because the taxpayer did not know precisely when each customer would demand services and, thus, when the expenses would be incurred. However, taxpayers have had some success in the courts when the services were performed on a fixed schedule (e. g., a baseball team's season-ticket sales).[49] In some cases involving the sale of goods, taxpayers have successfully argued that the prepayments were mere deposits[50] or in the nature of loans.[51]

In addition, Congress has intervened in the controversy. In 1958 and 1961, § § 455 and 456 were enacted. Section 455 allows the taxpayer to prorate subscription income over the subscription period, and § 456 allows certain membership organizations to prorate dues over the membership period.

Against this background of mixed results in the courts, Congressional intervention, and taxpayers' strong resentment to the IRS's position, in 1971 the IRS modified its prepaid income rules, as explained below.

Deferral of Advance Payments for Goods. Under Reg. § 1.451–5, a taxpayer can elect to defer advance payments for goods under the following conditions:

—The goods are not on hand on the last day of the year.

—The amount collected is less than the seller's cost of the goods.

—The taxpayer's method of accounting for the sale is the same for tax and financial reporting purposes.

The first two conditions would be satisfied in the commonly encountered situation where the buyer makes a partial payment but the seller is out of stock.[52]

---

48. *Automobile Club of Michigan v. U. S.,* 57–1 USTC ¶ 9593, 50 AFTR 1967, 77 S.Ct. 707 (USSC, 1957); *American Automobile Association v. U. S.,* 61–2 USTC ¶ 9517, 7 AFTR2d 1618, 81 S.Ct. 1727 (USSC, 1961); *Schlude v. Comm.,* 63–1 USTC ¶ 9284, 11 AFTR2d 751, 83 S.Ct. 601 (USSC, 1963).

49. *Artnell Company v. Comm.,* 68–2 USTC ¶ 959, 22 AFTR2d 5590, 400 F.2d 981 (CA–7, 1968). See also, *Automated Marketing Systems, Inc. v. Comm.,* 74–2 USTC ¶ 9711, 34 AFTR2d 74–5427 (S.Ct. Ill., 1974); *Boise Cascade Corp. v. U. S.,* 76–1 USTC ¶ 79–195, 1979–1 C.B. 177.

50. *Vernstra & DeHavaan Coal Co.,* 11 T.C. 964 (1948).

51. *Consolidated-Hammer Dry Plate & Film Co. v. Comm.,* 63–1 USTC ¶ 9494.11 AFTR2d 1518, 317 F.2d 829 (CA–7, 1963).

52. See Reg. § 1.451–5(c)(4), for an illustration of additional deferral rules where conditions (1) and (2) are not satisfied. Condition (3) is not applicable to contractors who use the completed contract method. Reg. § 1.451–5(b).

Deferral of Advance Payments for Services. Revenue Procedure 71–21[53] permits an accrual basis taxpayer to defer advance payments for services to be performed by the end of the tax year following the year of receipt. No deferral is allowed if the taxpayer may be required to perform the services, under the agreement, after the tax year following the year of receipt of the advance payment.

> **Example 24.** X Corporation, an accrual basis taxpayer, sells its services under 12-, 18-, and 24-month contracts. The corporation services each customer every month. In April of 19X8, X Corporation sold the following customer contracts:

Length of Contract	Total Proceeds
12 months	$ 6,000
18 months	3,600
24 months	2,400

> Fifteen hundred dollars of the $6,000 may be deferred ($\frac{3}{12} \times$ $6,000) and $1,800 of the $3,600 may be deferred because it will not be earned until 19X9. However, the entire $2,400 received on the 24-month contracts is taxable in the year of receipt, since a part of the income will still be unearned by the end of the tax year following the year of receipt.

Revenue Procedure 71—21 does not apply to prepaid rent, prepaid interest, or amounts received under guarantee or warranty contracts. Thus, the income will still be taxed in the year of receipt if collected before the income is actually earned. However, there is a special condition on the definition of the term "rent":

> "Rent" does not include payments for the use or occupancy of rooms or other space where significant services are also rendered to the occupant . . . .

The effect of the definition is to allow hotels, motels, tourist homes, and convalescent homes to defer the recognition of income under the rules discussed above.

In summary, Revenue Procedure 71–21 will result in conformity of tax and financial accounting in a very limited number of prepaid income cases. It is not apparent why prepaid rents and interest cannot be deferred, why revenues under some service contracts may be spread over two years, and why revenues under longer service contracts must be reported in one year. Revenue Procedure 71–21 will lessen the number of controversies involving prepaid income, but a consistent policy has not yet evolved.

---

53. 1971–2 C.B. 549.

INCOME SOURCES

PERSONAL SERVICES

It is a well-established principle of taxation that the income from personal services must be included in the gross income of the person who performs the services. This principle was first established in a Supreme Court decision, *Lucas v. Earl*.[54] Mr. Earl entered into a binding agreement with his wife whereby she was to receive one-half of his salary. Justice Holmes used the celebrated "fruit and tree" metaphor to explain that the fruit (income) must be attributed to the tree from which it came (Mr. Earl's services). A mere assignment of income does not shift the liability for the tax.

In the case of a child, § 73 specifically provides that amounts earned from his or her personal services must be included in the child's gross income, even though the income is paid to other persons (e. g., the parents).

INCOME FROM PROPERTY

Income from property (e. g., interest, dividends, rent) must be included in the gross income of the owner of the property.[55] If a father clips interest coupons from bonds shortly before the interest payment date and gives the coupons to his son, the interest will still be taxed to the father.[56] Also, a father who assigns rents from rental property to his son will be taxed on the rent, since he retains ownership of the property.[57]

Who is to pay the tax on income accrued at the time of the transfer of income-producing property, and when does the income accrue? The position of the IRS is that in the case of a gift, interest accrues on a daily basis; but the cash basis donor does not recognize the income until it is collected by the donee.[58]

> **Example 25.** F, a cash basis taxpayer, gave S $10,000 face amount bonds with an 8% stated rate of interest. The gift was made on November 30, and the interest is payable each January 1. When S collects the interest in January, F must recognize $732 interest income (8% × $10,000 × 334/365). The son will recognize $68 interest income ($800 − $732).

When there is a sale of property which has accrued interest, a portion of the selling price is treated as interest and is taxed to the seller in the year of sale.

---

54. 2 USTC ¶ 496, 8 AFTR 10287, 50 S.Ct. 241 (USSC, 1930).
55. *Galt v. Comm.,* 54–2 USTC ¶ 9457, 46 AFTR 633, 216 F.2d 41 (CA–7, 1954).
56. *Helvering v. Horst,* 40–2 USTC ¶ 9787, 24 AFTR 1058, 61 S.Ct. 144 (USSC, 1940).
57. *Supra,* Footnote 55.
58. Rev.Rul. 72–312, 1972–1 C.B. 22.

Dividends, unlike interest, do not accrue on a daily basis because the declaration of the dividend is at the discretion of the board of directors of the corporation. Generally, the dividends are taxed to the person who is entitled to receive them, the stockholder of record as of the corporation's record date.[59] However, the Tax Court has held that a donor does not shift the dividend income to the donee if a gift of stock is made after the date of declaration but before the date of record.[60] The "fruit" has sufficiently ripened as of the declaration date to tax the dividend to the donor of the stock.

Example 26. On June 20, 19X1, the board of directors of Z Corporation declares a $10 per share dividend. The dividend is payable on June 30, 19X1, to shareholders of record on June 25, 19X1. As of June 20, 19X1, M owned 200 shares of Z Corporation's stock. On June 21, 19X1, M sold 100 of the shares to N for their fair market value and gave 100 of the shares to S. Assume both N and S are shareholders of record as of June 25, 19X1. N (the purchaser) will be taxed on $1,000, since he is entitled to receive the dividend. However, M (the donor) will be taxed on the $1,000 received by S (the donee), because the gift was made after the declaration date of the dividend.

INCOME FROM PARTNERSHIPS, S CORPORATIONS, TRUSTS, AND ESTATES

Each partner must report his or her distributive share of the partnership's income and deductions for the partnership's tax year ending within or with his or her tax year.[61] The income must be reported by each partner as if earned even if such amounts are not actually distributed.

Example 27. T owned a one-half interest in the capital and profits of T & S Company (a partnership). For tax year 19X1, the partnership earned revenue of $150,000 and had operating expenses of $80,000. During the year, T withdrew from his capital account $2,500 per month (for a total of $30,000). For 19X1, T must report $35,000 as his share of the partnership's profits [½ × ($150,000 − $80,000)] even though he received a distribution of only $30,000.

A small business corporation may elect to be taxed as a partnership, and thus the shareholders pay the tax on the corporation's income.[62] The electing corporation is referred to as an "S corporation."

---

59. Reg. § 1.61–9(c).
60. *M. G. Anton,* 34 T.C. 842 (1960). The record date is the cutoff for determining the shareholders who are entitled to receive the dividend.
61. § 706(a) and Reg. § 1.706–1(a)(1). For a further discussion see Chapter 20.
62. §§ 1361(a) and 1366. For a further discussion see Chapter 20.

Generally, the shareholder reports his or her proportionate share of the corporation's income and deductions for the year, whether or not any distributions are actually made by the corporation.

> **Example 28.** Assume the same facts as in Example 27, except that T & S Company is an S corporation. T's income for the year is his share of the net taxable income earned by the corporation, i. e., $35,000, rather than the amount actually distributed to him.

The beneficiaries of estates and trusts generally are taxed on the income earned by the estates or trusts that is actually distributed or required to be distributed to them.[63] Any of the income not taxed to the beneficiaries is taxable to the estate or trust.

INCOME IN COMMUNITY PROPERTY STATES

State law in Louisiana, Texas, New Mexico, Arizona, California, Washington, Idaho, and Nevada is based upon a community property system. The basic difference between common law and community property systems centers around the property rights possessed by married persons.

Under a community property system, all property is deemed to be either separately owned by the spouse or belonging to the marital community. Property may be held separately by a spouse if it was acquired prior to marriage or received by gift or inheritance following marriage. Otherwise, any property is deemed to be community property. For Federal tax purposes, each spouse is taxable on one-half the income from property belonging to the community.

The laws of Texas, Louisiana, and Idaho distinguish between separate property and the income it produces. In these states, the income from separate property belongs to the community. Accordingly, for Federal income tax purposes, each spouse is taxed on one-half the income. In the remaining community property states, separate property produces separate income that the owner-spouse must report as his or her Federal taxable income.

What appears to be income, however, may really represent a recovery of capital. A return of capital and gain realized on separate property retains its identity as separate property. Items such as nontaxable stock dividends, royalties from mineral interests, and gains and losses from the sale of property take on the same classification as the assets to which they relate.

> **Example 29.** H and W are husband and wife and reside in a community property state. Among other transactions during the year, the following occurred:

---

63. § § 652(a) and 662(a).

—Nontaxable stock dividend received by W on stock that was given to her by her mother after her marriage.

—Gain of $10,000 on the sale of unimproved land purchased by H before his marriage.

—Oil royalties of $15,000 from a lease W acquired after marriage with her separate funds.

Since the stock dividend was distributed on stock held by W as separate property, it also is her separate property. The same result occurs as to the oil royalties W receives. All of the proceeds from the sale of unimproved land (including the gain of $10,000) are H's separate property.

Income from personal services (e. g., salaries, wages, income from a professional partnership) is generally treated as one-half earned by each spouse in all community property states.

Example 30. H and W are married but file separate returns. H received $25,000 salary and $300 taxable interest on a savings account he established in his name. The deposits to the savings account were made from H's salary earned since the marriage. W collected $2,000 taxable dividends on stock she inherited from her father. W's gross income is compared below under three assumptions as to the state of residency of the couple.

	California	Texas	Common Law States
Dividends	$ 2,000	$ 1,000	$ 2,000
Salary	12,500	12,500	–0–
Interest	150	150	–0–
	$ 14,650	$13,650	$ 2,000

ITEMS SPECIFICALLY INCLUDED IN GROSS INCOME

The general principles of gross income determination (discussed above) as applied by the IRS and the courts have on occasion yielded results Congress found unacceptable. Thus, Congress has set forth more specific rules for determining the gross income from certain sources. Some of these special rules are clustered in §§ 66–86 of the Code.

COMMUNITY PROPERTY SPOUSES LIVING APART

The general rules for taxing the income from services performed by residents of community property states can create complications and even inequities for spouses who are living apart.

Example 31. D and C were married but living apart for the first nine months of 19X1 and were divorced as of October 1, 19X1. In December 19X1 C married E, who was married but living apart from F prior to their divorce in June 19X1. C and F had no income from personal services in 19X1.

C brought into the C–E marriage a tax liability on one-half of D's earnings for the first nine months of the year. However, E left with F a tax liability on one-half of E's earnings for the first six months of 19X1.

In circumstances such as depicted in Example 31, the accrued tax liability could be factored into a property division being negotiated at a time when the parties did not need further complications. In other cases, an abandoned spouse could be saddled with a tax on income earned by a spouse whose whereabouts are unknown.

In 1980 Congress developed a simple solution to the many tax problems of community property spouses living apart. In 1981 and thereafter a spouse (or former spouse) will be taxed only on his or her actual earnings from personal services under the following circumstances:[64]

—The individuals live apart for the entire year.

—They do not file a joint return with each other.

—No portion of the earned income is transferred between the individuals.

It should be noted that the exception only applies to income from personal services and thus does not apply to income from property.

Example 32. H and W reside in a community property state and both are gainfully employed. On July 1, 19X1, they separated and on June 30, 19X2, they were divorced. Presuming their only source of income is wages, one-half of such income for each year is earned by June 30, and the spouses did not file a joint return for 19X1, each should report the following gross income:

	H's Separate Return	W's Separate Return
19X1	One-half of H's wages One-half of W's wages for the year	One-half of H's wages One-half of W's wages for the year
19X2	All of H's wages	All of W's wages

The results would be the same if H married another person or W married another person in 19X2, except the newlyweds would probably file a joint return.

---

64. § 66.

ALIMONY AND SEPARATE MAINTENANCE PAYMENTS

Alimony and separate maintenance payments made by one spouse to another result in a shifting of income from the payor to the recipient spouse. Before 1942 the Code contained no special rules for alimony.

> **Example 33.** Before 1942, H and W were divorced. Under the terms of the divorce, H was required to pay $500 per month to W. H's only source of income was a salary of $1,000 per month. Under the general income from services principle, because H earned the $1,000 per month, H was required to pay the tax on the entire amount. Conversely, W had no tax liability from receipt of the $500 per month.[65]

In 1942, the Code was amended to alleviate this inequity by making the alimony taxable to the recipient and deductible by the payor. Alimony received and alimony paid are reported on page 1 of Form 1040.

Under current law, payments to a spouse or partner spouse will be classified as alimony only if all the conditions set forth in § 71 are satisfied:

1. The payments must be made pursuant to either (a) a court order (i. e., a decree of divorce, separate maintenance decree, or decree for support) or (b) a written separation agreement (i. e., an enforceable contract between the spouses or former spouses).

2. The payments must be periodic (see discussion below).

3. The payments must be in "discharge of a legal obligation arising from the marital or family relationship."[66]

Requirements 2 and 3 present the most difficult problems in practice, because the requirements often overlap, as will be seen below.

Periodic Payments. Often a decree or agreement will provide for a payment of a principal amount. Installment payments of the principal amount will satisfy the periodic requirement if (1) the principal sum is paid over a period ending more than 10 years from the date of the agreement or (2) the payments are subject to a contingency such as the death of either spouse, remarriage of the recipient, or change in the economic status of either spouse.[67]

> **Example 34.** The divorce decree provides that H is to pay W a principal sum of $60,000 payable in the amount of $1,000 per month for five years. If W dies before the end of the fifth year, W's

---

65. *Gould v. Gould,* 1 USTC 13, 3 AFTR 1958, 38 S.Ct. 53 (USSC, 1917).

66. § § 71(a) and (b).

67. § 71(c); Reg. § 1.71–1(d)(1)–(3). See Rev. Proc. 82–53, 1982–2 C.B. 842, for further examples.

estate is to receive the balance of the payments. The payments are not periodic and are not income to W or deductible by H, since W's estate will continue to receive the payments.

Example 35. The separation agreement requires H to pay W a principal sum of $108,000 in the amount of $1,000 per month for nine years or until W's remarriage, whichever occurs first. The payments satisfy H's obligation of support. Since the payments are subject to a contingency and in the nature of a support payment, they are periodic.

Example 36. The separation agreement provides that W will receive $1,000 per month for five years in satisfaction of H's obligation of support. The payments are not treated as alimony, since they are neither subject to a contingency nor paid over more than 10 years.

If the installment payments are to extend for more than 10 years, only payment of up to 10 percent of the principal sum can be considered alimony in any one year.[68]

Example 37. The decree of divorce provides that H is to pay W a principal sum in installments of $15,000 per year for five years and $5,000 per year for the next 10 years. The total amount to be received, $125,000, is considered a principal sum. Therefore, in each of the first five years W must include in income $12,500 (10% of $125,000). W must include the entire $5,000 per year in the sixth through the fifteenth year.[69] Comparable treatment is accorded to H.

The apparent reason for the periodic payment requirement is to limit the paying spouse's ability to control his or her taxable income, as determined after deducting alimony paid.

Marital or Family Obligation. Satisfying the periodic payment requirement is a necessary, but not a sufficient, condition for classifying the payment as alimony. The payments must also satisfy a marital or family obligation. Reg. § 1.71–1(b)(4) defines the marital or family obligation as an obligation for support. Since the support obligation must arise under state law (because there is no federal obligation for support), the alimony issue becomes deeply entangled in state laws.

Many states require that a spouse be paid for his or her "fair share" of the property that has been accumulated during the marriage but retained by the other spouse. Additionally, the state may impose a support obligation on the spouse. Thus, a cash payment may be (1) solely for support, (2) solely for property, or (3) in part for sup-

68. § 71(c)(2).
69. Reg. § 1.71–1(d)(5), Ex. (4).

port and in part for property. Moreover, the labels the spouses attach to the payments (e. g., by agreement) do not control the payments' classification. The IRS and the courts consider the following factors in classifying the payments.[70]

—Whether the paying spouse receives other property from the other spouse (i. e., a sale occurred).

—Whether the spouse received temporary alimony during the separation or divorce proceedings and, if so, the amount received.

Example 38. R and S are residents of a community property state that recognizes a spouse's obligation for support. Upon divorce, they divide the community property equally. In addition, R agrees to pay S $500 per month until S's remarriage or the death of either R or S. Because R and S each received his or her share of the marital property, the additional $500 per month would probably be deemed as being for S's support, and because the payments are periodic, they are treated as alimony.

Example 39. T and U are co-owners of a condominium, with a basis of $50,000 and a fair market value of $70,000. No other property is jointly owned by T and U. Under an agreement incorporated in their divorce decree, T will pay U $35,000 plus interest over 121 months and T will become the sole owner of the condominium. No other payments are to be made by T and U. The payments are periodic, but they are for U's interest in property; thus, they cannot be classified as alimony. (U must recognize a gain of $10,000 [½ ($70,000 − $50,000)] from the sale of his interest in the condominium.)

Example 40. V and W live in a noncommunity property state, and none of their property is jointly owned. Upon divorce, the court orders V to pay W $50,000 over 121 months for W's fair share of the property accumulated by V during the marriage. The payments are periodic, but they are for W's equitable share of the property, rather than for support, and thus will not qualify as alimony.

Example 41. X and Y live in a noncommunity property state, and none of their property is jointly owned. Under the relevant state laws, Y is entitled to payments for her fair share of the property accumulated during the marriage. Y is also entitled to support. During a separation period, the court had ordered X to pay Y $300 per month as temporary support. X and Y enter into an agreement incorporated into the divorce decree. The agreement provides that Y is to receive $500 per month for 121 months

---

70. A. C. Warnack, 71 T.C. 541 (1979).

but does not specify how much of that amount is for support. Most likely, $300 per month (an amount equal to the temporary support) would be treated as alimony and $200 per month would be treated as a property settlement.

Child Support. Amounts expended for the support of a dependent child of the taxpayer represent a nondeductible personal expense, regardless of whether the payments are made in the typical family setting or pursuant to a decree of divorce or a separation agreement.[71] Undoubtedly, the need for funds to support a child must enter into the bargaining between a husband and wife contemplating divorce or separation. The Supreme Court has held that unless the decree or agreement specifically provides for child support payments, none of the payments actually made will be regarded as such.[72] Therefore, the agreement should specifically identify the portion of the payment which is for child support.

> **Example 42.** The divorce agreement provides that H is required to make periodic alimony payments of $500 per month. However, when H and W's child reaches age 21, marries, or dies (whichever should occur first), the payments will be reduced to $300 per month. W has custody of the child. Although it is reasonable to infer that $200 ($500 − $300) is for child support, cause no payments are specified as child support, the $500 is alimony.

Other Tax Consequences of Divorce Settlements. A transfer of appreciated property to a former spouse in satisfaction of the transferee's marital rights is generally treated as a taxable exchange.[73]

> **Example 43.** Upon divorce, H transferred stock to W in satisfaction of her marital rights (e. g., rights to support, intestate succession, a fair share at divorce). H's basis in the stock was $75,000, and the value of the stock was $100,000. H realized, and must recognize, a $25,000 gain on the transfer.

INCOME FROM ANNUITIES

The tax accounting problem associated with annuities is one of apportioning the amounts received between recovery of capital and income.

> **Example 44.** In 19X1, T purchased for $15,000 an annuity intended as a source of retirement income. In 19X3, when the cash value of the annuity was $17,000, T collected $1,000 on the contract. Is the $1,000 gross income, or recovery of capital, or a combination of capital and income?

---

71. § 71(b).
72. *Comm. v. Lester,* 61–1 USTC ¶ 9463, 7 AFTR2d 1445, 81 S.Ct. 1343 (USSC,1961).
73. *U. S. v. Davis,* 62–2 USTC ¶ 9509, 9 AFTR2d 1625, 82 S.Ct. 1190 (USSC, 1962). But see *Charles D. Cook,* 80 T.C. 512 (1983).

The statutory solution to this problem depends upon whether the payments began before or after the annuity starting date, and when the policy was acquired.

Collections Before the Annuity Starting Date. Generally an annuity contract specifies a date on which monthly or annual payments will begin—the annuity starting date. Often the contract will also allow the annuitant to collect a limited amount before the starting date.

For contracts issued before August 14, 1982, prestarting date collections are treated first as a recovery of capital. Thus, in Example 44, if the $1,000 was received before the starting date, the $1,000 would be a nontaxable recovery of T's investment. For contracts issued after August 13, 1982, the order of distribution is reversed: prestarting date collections are first considered income to the extent of the increase in the cash value of the contract.[74] Thus, the $1,000 prestarting date collection by T in Example 44 would be income if the policy was purchased after August 13, 1982, because the increase in values ($17,000 − $15,000 = $2,000) exceeded the amount received.

The new rules were enacted in 1982 because Congress perceived abuse of the recovery of capital rule. Formerly, individuals could purchase annuity contracts that guaranteed an annual increase in cash value, withdraw the equivalent of interest on the contract, but recognize no income. This is no longer possible. Moreover, the individual must recognize income from borrowing on the contract (e. g., pledging the contract as security for a loan) as well as from an actual distribution.

Collections On and After the Annuity Starting Date. The annuitant can exclude from income (as a recovery of capital) the proportion of each payment that the investment in the contract bears to the expected return under the contract.

The expected return is the annual amount to be paid to the annuitant multiplied by the number of years the payments will be received. The payment period may be fixed, i. e., a "term certain," or based on the life expectancy of the individual as determined from tables published in the Regulations.[75]

> **Example 45.** The taxpayer purchased an annuity from an insurance company for $60,000. He was to receive $500 per month for life, and his life expectancy was 15 years from the annuity starting date. Thus, his expected return is $500 × 12 × 15 = $90,000.

---

74. Section 72(e). The new rules also apply to contracts purchased before August 14, 1982, if a part of the cost on the contract is paid after the effective date. However, the statute is unclear as to how the new rules will apply in these cases. Regulations will have to address the transitional problems.

75. Section 72(c)(3); Reg. § 1.72–9.

$$\frac{\$60,000}{\$90,000} \times \$6,000 = \$4,000$$

The $4,000 is a nontaxable return of capital, and $2,000 is taxable income.

The exclusion ratio remains the same and continues to be applied to annuity payments even if the annuitant outlives his life expectancy.[76] Thus, if in Example 45, the taxpayer lived 20 years after the payments began, he could still exclude two-thirds of each payment from income even though the entire investment was recovered after 15 years. On the other hand, if he lived less than 15 years, the annuitant would have been taxed on some amounts that were actually a return of capital.

Employee Annuities. An exception is provided in § 72(d) for employee annuities. Under a qualified pension or profit sharing plan, amounts contributed by the employer to a retirement fund may subsequently be used to acquire annuity contracts for retired employees.[77] The employer contributions to the retirement fund are not included in the employee's income and are not, therefore, considered to be part of the employee's investment in the contract.[78] Thus, for noncontributory plans, the entire amount received by the employee from the retirement annuity is taxable income. However, if the plan is contributory (i. e., the employee contributes after-tax dollars to the cost of the annuity), amounts received represent a return of capital and are included in the employee's investment in the contract. When the employee's contributions are insignificant relative to the value of the annuity, Congress has provided a substitute approach to the regular recovery exclusion ratio. If an employee will receive retirement amounts during the first three years that are equal to or exceed his or her investment, such amounts are treated as a tax-free return of capital until the investment is reduced to zero. Subsequent amounts received are fully taxable.[79] Income from pensions and annuities is reported on page 1 of Form 1040.

> **Example 46.** S, an employee of XYZ Company, made contributions of $10,000 to a qualified pension plan. Upon retirement S is to receive annual pension benefits of $5,000. Since the amounts that will be received during the first three years ($15,000) exceed S's contributions to the plan ($10,000), the three-year return of capital special rule applies. Thus, the $10,000 received during the first two years is treated as a tax-free return of capital. All subsequent pension payments are fully taxable to S.

---

76. Reg. § 1.72–4(a)(4).

77. See Chapter 19.

78. See § § 401–404.

79. § 72(d). See Chapter 19 for a discussion of qualified employee annuities including the treatment of lump-sum distributions.

Example 47. Assume the same facts as in Example 46 except that S's total contributions are $30,000. Since the amounts received in the first three years ($15,000) do not equal or exceed the employee contributions ($30,000), the three-year rule does not apply. Instead, the regular annuity rules illustrated in Example 45 must be used.

PRIZES AND AWARDS

Prior to 1954 there was uncertainty relative to the taxability of prizes and awards. Taxpayers often sought to treat prizes and awards as nontaxable gifts. In many situations it was difficult to determine whether the prize or award was in the nature of a gift. In 1954 Congress added § 74 to eliminate this uncertainty.

Under § 74, the fair market value of prizes and awards (other than fellowships and scholarships that are exempted under § 117, to be discussed subsequently) is includible in income. Therefore, TV giveaway prizes, door prizes, and awards from an employer to an employee in recognition of achievement are fully taxable to the recipient.[80]

An exception is provided if the award is received in recognition of religious, charitable, scientific, educational, artistic, literary, or civic achievement. In such cases, the recipient must be selected without any action on his part to enter a contest or proceeding, and the recipient must not be required to render substantial future services as a condition to receiving the prize or award.[81] Awards such as the Nobel and the Pulitzer prizes qualify for the exclusion.[82]

The definition of "artistic" achievement has been narrowly construed by the Courts. Thus, athletes have been unsuccessful in their attempts to exclude from their income outstanding player awards as recognition for artistic achievement.[83]

GROUP-TERM LIFE INSURANCE

Prior to the passage of § 79 in 1964, the premiums paid by employers for group-term life insurance on the life of employees were totally excluded from the employee's income. Some companies took undue advantage of the exclusion by providing large amounts of group-term insurance for executives. Current law, therefore, sanctions an exclusion only for the premiums paid on the first $50,000 of group-term life protection. For each $1,000 of coverage in excess of $50,000, the employee must include the following amounts of premiums paid by the employer in gross income:[84]

---

80. Reg. § 1.74–1(a)(1).
81. § 74(b).
82. Reg. § 1.74–1(b).
83. *P. V. Hornung,* 47 T.C. 428 (1967).
84. Reg. § 1.79–3(d)(2).

Uniform Premiums for $1,000 of Group-Term
Life Insurance Protection

Attained Age Last Day of the Employee's Tax Year	Cost Per $1,000 of Protection for One-Month Period
Under 30	8 cents
30–34	9 cents
35–39	11 cents
40–44	17 cents
45–49	29 cents
50–54	48 cents
55–59	75 cents
60–64	$1.17

Example 48. XYZ Corporation has a group-term life insurance policy with coverage equal to the employee's annual salary. Mr. A, age 52, is president of the corporation and receives an annual salary of $75,000. Mr. A must include $144 in gross income from the insurance protection for the year.

$$\frac{(\$75,000-\$50,000)}{\$1,000} \times (.48) \times (12 \text{ months}) = \$144$$

Generally, the amount that must be included in income, computed from the above table, is much less than the price an individual would pay for the same amount of protection. Thus, even the excess coverage provides some tax-favored income for employees when group-term life coverage in excess of $50,000 is desirable.

The benefits under § 79 are available only to employees. Proprietors and partners are not employees; therefore, the premiums paid on the life of the proprietor or a partner are not deductible. In addition, to prevent a company from providing coverage solely to a select few highly paid officers or shareholders, the Regulations generally require broad scale coverage of employees to satisfy the "group" requirement.[85] For example, shareholder-employees would not constitute a qualified group. If premium coverage were confined solely to this group, the $50,000 exclusion on group-term life insurance coverage for each employee would not apply.

The taxation of group-term life insurance becomes very complicated where a single policy has both permanent and term benefits. Further complications arise when the employee contributes toward the cost of the protection. In these types of situations, therefore, the Regulations under § 79 should be checked carefully.

---

85. Reg. § 1.79–1(b)(1)(iii)(b). § 79(d), effective for tax years beginning after December 31, 1983.

UNEMPLOYMENT COMPENSATION

In a series of rulings over the past 40 years, the IRS has exempted unemployment benefits from tax. These payments are considered social benefit programs for the promotion of the general welfare. As previously discussed, the scope of § 61, gross income, is probably broad enough to include unemployment benefits (since an increase in wealth is realized when the payments are received). Nevertheless, the IRS had chosen to exclude such benefits.[86]

Congress addressed the unemployment compensation issue and enacted § 85.[87] The section provides that unemployment benefits are taxable only if the recipient's adjusted gross income exceeds certain levels. The taxable portion (i. e., excess unemployment compensation) is computed by the following formula for a single individual:

Taxable   Portion = 50% × [(Net   Unemployment   Benefits* + Adjusted Gross Income Without Including Benefits + Disability Income Deducted in Arriving at Adjusted Gross Income) − $12,000]

*Net unemployment benefits are total benefits received less any overpayments of benefits during the tax year that were paid back during the tax year.

In the case of a married individual filing a joint return, $18,000 is substituted for $12,000 in the preceding formula. If the married individual files a separate return, zero is substituted for $12,000.

> **Example 49.** T is a bricklayer. He was unemployed during January and February when a severe cold spell halted construction activities. T received $800 in unemployment benefits, and he and his wife had adjusted gross income of $21,000 before unemployment benefits for the year. They received no disability income. Taxable portion = 50% [($800 + $21,000 − $18,000)] = $1,900. Since the taxable portion is greater than the unemployment benefits ($1,900 > $800), the taxpayer must include $800 in gross income.

SOCIAL SECURITY BENEFITS

Beginning in 1984 as much as one half of Social Security retirement benefits must be included in gross income. Under § 86, the taxable amount of Social Security benefits is the lesser of:

---

86. See pp. 47–49 of H.Rpt. 95–1445, 95th Cong., 2nd Sess. (1978); 1978–3 C.B. (Vol. 1) 221. These benefits refer to unemployment compensation paid under government programs. Supplemental unemployment benefits received from a company-financed supplemental unemployment benefit fund are not considered unemployment compensation but are wages and are fully taxable as such.

87. § 85 was added by the Revenue Act of 1978.

(1)   .50 (Social Security benefits)

(2)   .50 [modified adjusted gross income + .50 (Social Security benefits) − base amount]

"Modified adjusted gross income" is, generally, the taxpayer's adjusted gross income from all sources (other than Social Security), plus the two-earner married couple's deduction and any tax-exempt interest received. The "base amount" is as follows:

—$32,000 for married taxpayers who file a joint return

—$0 for married taxpayers who do not live apart for the entire year but file separate returns

—$25,000 for all other taxpayers

For example, a married couple with adjusted gross income of $40,000, no two-earner deduction, no tax-exempt interest, and $11,000 of Social Security benefits must include one-half of the benefits in gross income. This works out as the lesser of:

(1)   .50 ($11,000) = $5,500

(2)   .50 [($40,000 + .50 ($11,000) − $32,000] = .50 ($13,500) = $6,750

If the couple's adjusted gross income were $15,000 and Social Security benefits totaled $5,000, none of the benefits would be taxable, since .50 [$15,000 + .50 ($5,000) − $32,000] = $0.

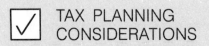

TAX PLANNING CONSIDERATIONS

The materials in this chapter focused on the all-inclusive concept of gross income. With the exception of the discussion of the employee's indirect benefits of the employer's mandates (e. g., "you must go to the trade show in Hawaii at my expense, you must take clients to nice restaurants at my expense, and you must visit customers in the company's Mercedes Benz"), not much was discussed concerning ways to minimize taxable income. However, a few observations can be made regarding timing the recognition of income and shifting income to relatives.

TAX DEFERRAL

Since deferred taxes are tantamount to interest-free loans, the deferral of taxes is a worthy goal of the tax planner. However, the tax planner must also consider the marginal tax rates for the years the income is shifted from and to. For example, a one-year deferral of income from a year in which the taxpayer's marginal rate was 30 percent to a year in which his or her marginal tax rate will be 50 percent would not be advisable if the taxpayer expects to earn less than a 20 percent after-tax return on the deferred tax dollars.

The taxpayer can often defer the recognition of income from appreciated property by postponing the event triggering realization (i. e., the final closing on a sale or exchange of property). If the taxpayer needs cash, obtaining a loan by using the appreciated property as collateral may be the least costly alternative.

Series E and EE bonds may be purchased for long-term deferrals of income. As was discussed in the chapter, Series E bonds can be exchanged for new Series HH bonds to further postpone the tax. In situations where the taxpayer's goal is merely to shift income one year into the future, bank certificates of deposit are useful tools. If the maturity date is one year or less, all interest is reported in the year of maturity. Time certificates are especially useful for a taxpayer who realizes an unusually large gain from the sale of property in one year (and thus is in a high marginal tax bracket) but expects his or her income to be less the following year.

The timing of income from services can often be controlled through the use of the cash method of accounting. Although taxpayers are somewhat constrained by the constructive receipt doctrine ("they cannot turn their backs on income"), seldom will customers and clients offer to pay before they are asked. The usual lag between billings and collections (e. g., December's billings collected in January) will result in a continuous deferring of some income until the last year of operations. A salaried individual approaching retirement may contract with his or her employer before the services are rendered to receive a portion of compensation in the lower tax bracket retirement years.

Moreover, a cash basis taxpayer has some control over the year he or she deducts expenses. At year-end, he or she may pay all outstanding expenses or pay and deduct the expenses in the following year. The choice would be made on the basis of the taxpayer's expected marginal tax brackets in the two years.

In the case of the accrual basis taxpayer who receives advance payments from customers, the transactions should be structured to avoid payment of tax on income prior to the time the income is actually earned. Revenue Procedure 71–21 provides the guidelines for deferring the tax on prepayments for services, and Reg. § 1.451–5 provides the guidelines for deferrals on sales of goods. In addition, with respect to both the cash and accrual basis taxpayer, income can sometimes be deferred by stipulating that the payments are deposits rather than prepaid income. For example, a landlord should require an equivalent damage deposit rather than require prepayment of the last month's rent under the lease.

SHIFTING INCOME TO RELATIVES

The tax liability of a family can be minimized by shifting income from higher- to lower-bracket family members. This can be accomplished through gifts of income-producing property. Furthermore, in many cases, the shifting of income can be accomplished with no negative effect on the family's investment plans.

> **Example 50.** Mr. Brown, who is in the 40 percent marginal tax bracket, is saving for his eight-year-old child's college education. At his current level of income, he can save $100 per month. If he invests the savings at 16% interest, his after-tax yield is only 9.6% ($(1 - .40) \times 16\%$) and he will accumulate $20,000 at the end of 10 years. In contrast, his child can earn up to $1,000 per year with no tax liability; thus, if the savings are given to the child he can earn 16% after-tax return on the first $1,000 interest each year. By this method, the child's savings will total $29,200 at the end of 10 years.

The Uniform Gifts to Minors Act, a model law adopted by all states (but with some variations among the states), facilitates income shifting. Under the Act, a gift of intangibles (e. g., bank accounts, stocks, bonds, life insurance contracts) can be made to a minor but with an adult serving as custodian. Usually, a parent who makes the gift is also named as custodian. The state laws allow the custodian to sell or redeem and reinvest the principal and to accumulate or distribute the income, practically at the custodian's discretion provided there is no commingling of the child's income with the parent's property. Thus, the parent can give appreciated securities to the child, and the donor custodian can then sell the securities and reinvest the proceeds, thereby shifting both the gain and annual income to the child.

U. S. Government bonds (Series E and EE) may be purchased by the parent for his or her children. When this is done, the children should file a return and elect to report the income on the accrual basis.

> **Example 51.** F (father) pays $7,500 for Series E bonds and immediately gives them to S (son), who will enter college the same year the bonds originally mature. The bonds have a maturity value of $10,000. S elects to report the annual increment in redemption value as income for each year the bonds are held. The first year the increase is $250, and S includes that amount in his gross income. If S has no other income, no tax will be due on the $250 bond interest, since such amounts will be more than offset by S's personal exemption. The following year, the increment is $260, and S includes this amount in income. Thus, over the life of the bonds, S will include $2,500 in income ($10,000 − $7,500), none of which will result in a tax liability, assuming S has no other income. However, if the election had not been made, S

would be required to include $2,500 in income on the bonds in the year of original maturity, if redeemed as planned; and this amount of income might result in a tax liability.

ACCOUNTING FOR COMMUNITY PROPERTY

The classification of income as community or separate property becomes important when either of two events occurs:

—Husband and wife, married taxpayers, file separate income tax returns for the year.

—Husband and wife obtain a divorce and, therefore, have to file separate returns for the year (see Chapter 4).

For planning purposes, it behooves married persons to keep track of the source of income (i. e., community or separate). To be in a position to do this effectively when income-producing assets are involved, it may be necessary to distinguish between separate and community property.[88]

EMPLOYEE ANNUITIES

Qualified pension and profit sharing plans often allow employees options for receiving retirement benefits, e. g., payments for life or for a fixed number of years. If the employee has made substantial contributions to the plan, the rule that allows the employee to treat payments as a return of capital should be factored into the decision.

> **Example 52.** T has contributed $15,000 to his employer's qualified plan. At retirement, T has two options for receiving his benefits, and the before-tax present values of the options are the same:
>
> (1) $4,400 per year for 15 years.
> (2) $5,500 per year for 10 years.
>
> The exclusion ratio for alternative (1) is $15,000 divided by ($4,400 × 15 years) = .22727. Thus, the annual exclusion is .22727 × $4,400 = $1,000 (rounded).
>
> Under alternative (2), T will recover his cost in the first three years (3 × $5,500 = $16,500 > $15,000). Therefore, the first $15,000 received will be a nontaxable recovery of capital.
>
> Assuming T does not expect his marginal tax rate to increase, benefit option (2) should be accepted, because the before-tax present values of the alternatives are the same, the recovery of capi-

---

88. Being able to distinguish between separate and community property is crucial to the determination of a property settlement incident to a divorce. It also is vital in the estate tax area (Chapter 1) since the surviving wife's or husband's share of the community property is not included in the gross estate of the deceased spouse.

tal exclusion is used more quickly under (2), and the tax deferral is thus greater.

ALIMONY

The person making the alimony payments favors a divorce settlement which includes provision for deductible alimony payments. On the other hand, the recipient prefers that the payments do not qualify as alimony. If the payor is in a higher tax bracket than the recipient, both parties may benefit after-tax by increasing the payments and constructing them so that they qualify as periodic.

> **Example 53.** H and W are in the process of reaching a divorce agreement. W has asked for $100,000 to be paid in four equal annual installments of $25,000 each. W is in a 30% marginal tax bracket. H, who is in a 50 percent marginal bracket, agrees on the total amount but would like the agreement to stipulate that the payments cease in the event W remarries before the end of the four years (so that the payments will qualify as alimony). W agrees to accept the remarriage contingency provided she receives $40,000 each year for four years. Under the $25,000 per year alternative, W would have $25,000 per year in nontaxable income at an after-tax cost to H of $25,000 per year. Under the $40,000 per year alternative, she would receive $28,000 [(1 − .30) × $40,000] at an after-tax cost to H of $20,000 [(1 − .50) × $40,000].

The parties should be aware of the potential tax consequences of property transfers at divorce. Generally, if property owned by one spouse is transferred to the other spouse, the transferor must recognize a gain (fair market value less basis).

PROBLEM MATERIALS

Questions for Class Discussion

1. Comment on the following formula: Accounting Income ± Adjustments = Taxable Income.

2. What are some of the differences between accounting, tax, and economic concepts of income?

3. Which of the following would be considered "income" for the current year by an economist but would not be gross income for tax purposes? Explain.

   (a) Securities acquired two years ago for $10,000 had a value at the beginning of the current year of $12,000 and a value at the end of the year of $13,000.

   (b) An individual lives in the home he owns.

(c) A corporation obtained a loan from a bank.

(d) A shareholder paid a corporation $3,000 for property valued at $5,000.

(e) An individual owned property which was stolen. The cost of the property three years ago was $2,000 and an insurance company paid the owner $6,000, the value of the property on the date of theft.

(f) At the end of the current year a shareholder sold stock for 200% of all dividends to be paid on the stock from the date of sale until the shareholder's death.

(g) An individual was involved in an automobile accident and lost the use of an arm. The injured party sued and was awarded $25,000 for physical damages. *not income*

(h) An individual found a box of seventeenth century Spanish coins while diving off the Virginia coast.

(i) An individual received a $200 price rebate from the manufacturer upon the purchase of a new car.

4. T is in the 40% marginal tax bracket. He has the following alternative uses of his time: (1) T can work and earn $600 (before tax), or (2) T can stay at home and paint his house. If T selects (1) he must pay $500 to have his house painted. Which alternative would our tax laws encourage T to select?

5. What are some nontaxable fringe benefits an employer can provide employees?

6. Does an attorney realize income upon preparation of a medical doctor's will in exchange for a "free" physical examination? Explain.

7. What are the possible consequences of shifting taxable income from one tax year to the next?

8. Under what conditions must the taxpayer use the accrual method of accounting?

9. A corporation pays all of its monthly salaried employees on the last Friday in each month. What would be the tax consequences to the employees if the date of payment were changed to the first Monday of the following month?

10. What are some possible tax advantages from the use of the cash method of accounting?

11. What is the constructive receipt doctrine?

12. When is income that has been received, but which is being contested, subject to tax if the taxpayer is on the accrual basis?

13. What alternatives are available for reporting interest income from Series E or Series EE U. S. Government bonds?

14. Compare the accounting and tax treatment of income collected by an accrual basis taxpayer prior to the time it is earned.

15. The taxpayer is in the wholesale hardware business. His customers pay for the goods at the time they place the order. Often, the taxpayer is out of stock on particular items and must back order the goods. When this occurs, the taxpayer usually retains the customer's payment, orders the goods from the manufacturer, and ships them to the customer within a

month. At the end of the year there were several unfilled orders. Is it possible to defer the recognition of income from the receipt of advance payments on the unfilled orders?

16. F, a cash basis taxpayer, gave bonds to S in 19X1. At the time of the gift the accrued interest on the bonds was $500 and the interest was payable in 19X2. Does F realize taxable income in 19X1 as a result of the gift?

17. Who pays the tax on dividends when the stock is given away after the date of declaration but before the date of record?

18. Who pays the tax on undistributed income of (a) an S corporation and (b) an estate?

19. H and W were residents of a community property state. In 19X1, H left W for parts unknown. H and W were still married at year-end. How will H's absence complicate W's 19X1 tax return?

20. Critique this comment. "I was a tax practitioner in Texas for 25 years, so I know community property laws."

21. What are the tax advantages of group-term life insurance?

22. What are the possible income tax consequences of a divorce agreement for the husband and wife if they have minor children?

23. What special tax treatment is afforded an individual who collects on an employee annuity?

24. What conditions must be satisfied for a prize to be excluded from income?

25. Why do you suppose that no more than one-half of a recipient's Social Security benefits are taxable?

Problems

26. Does the taxpayer realize gross income from the following events?

    (a) T bought a used piano for $50. When he started repairing the piano he discovered it was stuffed with Confederate notes with a face amount of $10,000. T knows that collectors will pay him $30 for the Confederate notes.

    (b) Same as (a), except the notes have a value of $500.

    (c) T also discovered oil on his property during the year, and the value of the land increased from $10,000 to $5,000,000.

27. Determine the taxpayer's income for tax purposes in each of the following cases:

    (a) In the current year, the RST Corporation purchased $1,000,000 par value of its own bonds and paid the bondholders $980,000 plus accrued interest. The bonds had been issued 10 years ago at par and were to mature 25 years from the date of issue. Does the corporation realize income from the purchase of the bonds?

    (b) A shareholder of a corporation sold property to that corporation for $60,000 (the shareholder's cost). The value of the property on the date of sale was $50,000. Does the taxpayer have any taxable income from the sale?

    (c) T was a football coach at a state university. Because of his disappointing record, he was asked to resign and accept one-half of his pay for the remaining three years of his contract. The coach resigned accepting $75,000.

(d) T, a cash basis taxpayer, transferred some of his farm land (cost of $8,000) to a creditor in satisfaction of a $12,000 debt he owed. The debt represented $11,000 in principal and $1,000 in accrued interest.

28. Determine the taxpayer's income for tax purposes in each of the following cases:

(a) R borrowed $30,000 from the First National Bank. R was required to deliver to the bank stocks with a value of $30,000 and a cost of $10,000. The stocks were to serve as collateral for the loan.

(b) P owned a lot on Sycamore Street which measured 100 feet by 100 feet. His cost of the lot is $10,000. The city condemned a 10 foot strip of the land so that it could widen the street. P received a $2,000 condemnation award.

(c) M owned land zoned for residential use only. The land cost $5,000, and it had a market value of $7,000. M spent $500 and several hundred hours petitioning the county supervisors to change the zoning to A–1 commercial. The value of the property immediately increased to $20,000 when the county approved the zoning change.

29. X, Inc., is a dance studio and sells lessons for cash, on open account, and for notes receivable. During 19X1 the company's cash receipts from customers totaled $150,000:

Cash sales	$ 90,000
Collections on accounts receivable	35,000
Collections on notes receivable	25,000
Total cash receipts	$ 150,000

The balances in accounts and notes receivable at the beginning and end of the year were as follows:

	1-1-X1	12-31-X1
Accounts receivable	$ 15,000	$ 24,000
Notes receivable	20,000	15,000

The fair market value of the notes is equal to 80% of their book value. There were no bad debts for the year, and all notes were for services performed during the year.

Compute the corporation's gross income:

(a) Using the cash basis of accounting.

(b) Using the accrual basis of accounting.

30. When would a cash basis taxpayer recognize income in each of the following independent situations?

(a) The taxpayer's payroll check is mailed from the home office on December 31 and is delivered to her in a local office on January 3 of the following year.

income now   √ set up before earned ?, no security then o.k.

(b) The taxpayer, who was entitled to a $10,000 bonus on December 15 of the current year, asked his employer to place the bonus in an escrow account on his behalf. The taxpayer would be unable to withdraw the bonus until age 65 (in 10 years). If the taxpayer dies before age 65, the $10,000 will be paid to his heirs.

(c) A medical doctor had several Blue Cross claims which, if mailed in by the end of November, would be paid in December. However, he told his office manager not to process the claims until December 1 so payment would not be received until January of the following year.

31. What would be the tax effects to cash basis employees of the following transactions?

(a) The employer's computer made an error and printed T two payroll checks for the week ended December 28, 19X1. The checks were automatically deposited to T's bank account on December 29, 19X1. T discovered the error in January 19X2, informed the employer of the mistake, and paid the company the excess amount received.

(b) On December 31, an employee received a $500 advance for estimated traveling expenses for the following January. The employee actually spent $480 in January and retained the $20 to apply to February expenses.

32. What would be the tax effects of the following transactions on an accrual basis taxpayer?

(a) On December 15, 19X1, B signed a contract to purchase land from T. Payment for the land was to be made on closing, January 15, 19X2. During the interval between the contract and the closing dates, B's attorney was to verify that T had good title to the land. The closing was completed on January 15, 19X2.

(b) M collected $1,500 for services rendered the client in 19X1. Late in 19X1 the client complained that the work was not done in accordance with contract specifications. Also in 19X1 the parties agreed to allow an arbitrator to settle the dispute. In January 19X2 the arbitrator ordered M to refund $500 to the client.

33. The XYZ Apartments, an accrual basis taxpayer, requires each new tenant to make a $200 deposit upon signing a lease. If the tenant breaks the lease, the deposit is forfeited. Also, when a tenant moves (upon expiration of the lease), the apartment is inspected, and any damages are deducted from the deposit. During the current year XYZ collected $15,000 in deposits from new tenants, withheld $9,000 for damages and forfeitures from old tenants, and refunded $5,000. What are the effects of these items on XYZ's taxable income? Assume the same facts except the $15,000 collected was for a payment of the last month's rent under the lease. Would the $15,000 be taxable in the year of receipt?

34. G purchased U. S. Series EE bonds for S, his son, and, A and B, his grandsons. S is in the 30% marginal tax bracket. A is 21 years old and is a senior in college; he has no income for the current year but will become an officer in the family-owned business and will earn $40,000 per year soon after he graduates from college. B is 6 years old and has no other income. Each bond had an original cost of $6,000, and the final maturity

value is $10,000 in 8 years. The donees have never owned any other U. S. bonds. When should the donees report their $4,000 ($10,000 − $6,000) interest income from the bonds?

35. (a) An automobile dealer has several new cars in inventory, but often does not have the right combination of body style, color, and accessories. In some cases the dealer makes an offer to sell a car at a certain price, accepts a deposit, and then orders the car from the manufacturer. When the car is received from the manufacturer, the sale is closed, and the dealer receives the balance of the sales price. At the end of the current year, the dealer has deposits totaling $8,200 for cars that have not been received from the manufacturer. When is the $8,200 subject to tax?

(b) T Corporation, an exterminating company, is a calendar year taxpayer. It contracts to service homeowners once a month under a one- or two-year contract. On April 1 of the current year, the company sold a customer a one-year contract for $60. How much of the $60 is taxable in the current year if the company is an accrual basis taxpayer? If the $60 is payment on a two-year contract, how much is taxed in the year the contract is sold?

(c) X, an accrual basis taxpayer, owns an amusement park whose fiscal year ends September 30. To increase business during the fall and winter months, X sold passes that would allow the holder to ride free during the months of October through March. During the month of September $6,000 was collected from the sale of passes for the upcoming fall and winter. When will the $6,000 be taxable to X?

(d) The taxpayer is in the office equipment rental business and uses the accrual basis of accounting. In December he collected $5,000 in rents for the following January. When is the $5,000 taxable?

36. (a) T is a cash basis taxpayer. On December 1, 19X1, T gave a corporate bond to his son, S. The bond had a face amount of $10,000 and paid $1,200 each January 31. Also on December 1, 19X1, T gave common stocks to his daughter, D. Dividends totaling $720 had been declared on the stocks on November 30, 19X1, and were payable on January 15, 19X2. D became the stockholder of record in time to collect the dividends. What is T's 19X2 gross income from the bond and stocks?

(b) In 19X2, T's mother was unable to pay her bills as they came due. T, his employer, and his mother's creditors entered into an arrangement whereby T's employer would withhold $500 per month from T's salary and the employer would pay the $500 to the creditors. In 19X2, $3,000 was withheld from T's salary and paid to the creditors. Is T required to pay tax on the $3,000?

37. T owns 100% of the stock of T, Inc., an S corporation. For 19X1 the corporation earned $100,000 taxable income but paid only $30,000 dividends to T. T is also a beneficiary of a trust. The trustee can distribute or withhold income "according to the needs of the beneficiary." In 19X1 the trust earned $20,000 but distributed only $5,000 to T because he had adequate income from other sources. What is T's taxable income from the S corporation and trust for 19X1?

38. H and W lived together for part of the year but were divorced on December 31, 19X1. H earned $30,000 salary from his employer during the year; W's salary was $16,000. W also received $8,000 in taxable dividends from stock which is held as separate property.

    (a) If H and W reside in Texas, how much income should be reported by each on their separate tax returns for 19X1?

    (b) If amounts are withheld from their salaries, how are these amounts reported on H and W's separate returns?

    (c) If H and W reside in a common law state, how much income should be reported by each on their separate returns?

39. H and W were married on June 30, 19X2, and resided in Dallas, Texas. In December 19X2 they separated and on March 31, 19X3, they were divorced. On July 1, 19X3, H moved to Grundy, Virginia, and remarried in December 19X3. W did not remarry. H's and W's incomes for the relevant periods were as follows:

Salary	H	W
January 1-June 30, 19X2	$ 23,000	$ 15,000
July 1-December 31, 19X2	24,000	16,000
January 1-March 31, 19X3	25,000	18,000
April 1-December 31, 19X3	40,000	20,000

    In addition to the salaries listed above, on January 31, 19X3, H received $2,400 interest on savings certificates acquired on February 1, 19X2. What is W's gross income for 19X2 and 19X3 as computed on separate returns?

40. H and W were divorced on July 1 of the current year after 10 years of marriage. Their current year's income received before the divorce was as follows:

H's salary	$20,000
W's salary	25,000
Rent on apartments purchased by W 15 years ago	6,000
Dividends on stock H inherited from his mother 4 years ago	1,200
Interest on a savings account in W's name funded with her salary	600

    Allocate the income to H and W assuming they live in:

    (a) California

    (b) Texas

41. Mr. and Mrs. X are in the process of negotiating their divorce agreement. What would be the tax consequences to Mr. X and Mrs. X if the following, considered individually, become part of the agreement:

    (a) Mrs. X is to receive $1,000 per month until she dies or remarries. She also is to receive $500 per month for 12 years for her one-half interest in their personal residence. She paid for her one-half interest out of her earnings.

(b) Mrs. X is to receive a principal sum of $50,000 as part of a property settlement, plus $1,600 per month. The payments will cease if she dies or remarries but will continue for not more than 60 months.

(c) Mrs. X is to receive a principal sum of $100,000. Of this amount $50,000 is to be paid in the year of the divorce and $5,000 per year will be paid to her in each of the following 10 years.

(d) Mrs. X is to receive the family residence (value of $120,000 and basis of $75,000). The home was jointly owned by Mr. and Mrs. X. In exchange for the residence, Mrs. X relinquished all of her rights to property accumulated during the marriage. She also is to receive $1,000 per month until her death or remarriage but for a period of not longer than 10 years.

42. Under the terms of their divorce agreement, H is to transfer common stocks (cost of $25,000, market value of $60,000) to W in satisfaction of her property rights. W is also to receive $15,000 per year until her death or remarriage. W originally asked for $9,000 alimony and $5,000 child support. It was the understanding between H and W that she would use $5,000 of the amount received for the support of the children. How will the terms of the agreement affect H's taxable income?

43. T purchased an annuity from an insurance company for $12,000 on January 1, 19X1. The annuity was to pay him $1,500 per year for life. At the time he purchased the contract, his life expectancy was 10 years.

(a) Determine T's taxable income from the annuity in the first year.

(b) Assume he lives 20 years after purchasing the contract. What would be T's taxable income in the nineteenth year?

(c) Same as (a), except the annuity was received from a qualified pension plan and T had contributed $3,000 toward the cost of the annuity.

44. T purchased an annuity for $50,000. Determine the tax consequences of the following transactions under the assumptions stated:

(a) The contract was purchased in 1981, and monthly payments were to begin in 1985. In 1984, when the cash value of the contract was $55,000, T pledged the annuity as collateral for a $20,000 loan.

(b) Same as (a), except the annuity contract was purchased in 1983.

45. Indicate whether the following items result in taxable income to the recipient. If the item is not taxable, explain why.

(a) S won the Miss Centerville beauty contest and received a $1,000 cash prize.

(b) L won the master's mile run. As the winner, L received a $1,000 cash prize paid by a philanthropist who sponsored the race to encourage running.

(c) C, a part-time student, received a $500 award from his employer for being named to the Dean's list. The employer frequently makes such payments to encourage employees to further their education.

(d) Mr. and Mrs. D are married and file a joint return. In 19X3, they had adjusted gross income of $19,000 before considering unemployment benefits of $1,800.

46. R is unmarried. During 19X1 (after 1983), R received $7,200 in Social Security benefits. R also received taxable interest of $21,400 during the year.

Compute R's adjusted gross income for the year under the following assumptions:

(a) R's only sources of income were the Social Security benefits and interest.

(b) In addition to the Social Security benefits and interest, R earned $1,500 from a part-time job.

(c) In addition to the Social Security benefits and taxable interest, R received $1,500 tax-exempt interest from Montgomery County school bonds.

47. In the following problems, assume the married taxpayer has no tax-exempt interest income and receives $6,000 per year in Social Security benefits:

(a) Compute the maximum adjusted gross income from other sources the taxpayer can receive without including any of the Social Security benefits in adjusted gross income.

(b) How much adjusted gross income from other sources must the taxpayer receive before $3,000 Social Security benefits are included in adjusted gross income?

(c) What complications would be created in calculating the taxpayer's adjusted gross income if he also received $1,000 unemployment compensation?

48. The RST general partnership has a group-term life insurance plan. Each partner has $100,000 protection, and each employee has protection equal to twice his or her annual salary. R is a general partner and is 50 years old. V is a 35-year-old employee whose annual salary is $50,000. The partnership pays an average of $.23 per month per $1,000 of insurance protection for partners and employees.

(a) Compute taxable income for R and V from the group-term life insurance plan.

(b) Would incorporating the business affect R's taxable income from the insurance protection?

Cumulative Problems

49. T is single, age 42, and is employed as a plumber. In 1984, T earned wages of $36,000 and a bonus of $2,000 under his employer's incentive plan. He received the bonus check on December 30, 1984, but did not deposit it in his bank account until January 3, 1985. He held the check until January 3 because he did not want to report it as income in 1984.

T's mother, age 68, lives in a small house he bought for her in Florida. She has no income of her own and is totally dependent on T for her support. To provide his mother with some spending money, T assigned to her the income from some corporate bonds he owns. The interest received by T's mother was $1,050. T retained ownership of the bonds but surrendered all rights to the interest on the bonds.

Over the years, T and his physician, Z, have become good friends. During 1984, T incurred doctor bills of $350. Instead of paying Z in cash, T did the plumbing work for a new bar Z had installed in his basement in September 1984. T and Z agreed that the value of T's services was equal to the $350 in medical bills.

In September 1984, T sold 100 shares of corporate stock for $3,100. He had acquired the stock four years ago for $1,600.

T's itemized deductions for 1984 total $5,800. His employer withheld income tax of $7,400, and T made estimated tax payments of $200.

Compute the following for T:

(a) Adjusted gross income.

(b) Taxable income.

(c) Net tax payable or refund due.

50. D and F, age 48 and 44, respectively, are married and file a joint return. During 1984, they furnished over half of the total support of the following individuals:

(1) G, their daughter, age 22, who was married on December 21, 1984, has no income of her own and for 1984 files a joint return with her husband, who earned $8,000 during 1984.

(2) S, their son, age 17, who had gross income of $2,500. S dropped out of high school in February 1984.

(3) B, F's brother, age 27, who is a full-time college student with gross income of $1,200.

(4) N, their neighbor's son, age 15, who has lived with them since March 1984 (while his parents are in Japan on business) and has no gross income.

D is a radio announcer and earned a salary of $32,000 in 1984. F was employed part-time as a real estate salesperson and was paid commissions of $18,000 in 1984. She incurred automobile expenses of $900 while showing property to her clients. She was not reimbursed by her employer for these expenses. F sold a house on December 30, 1984, and will be paid a commission of $1,500 (not included in the $18,000) on the January 10, 1985, closing date.

D and F own 500 shares of stock in Q Corporation. Q declared a dividend of $2 per share on the stock on December 15, 1984, and mailed dividend checks on December 31. D and F received their dividend check on January 4, 1985. D and F had total itemized deductions of $8,200, not including the following expenditures:

(5) Interest on credit card accounts	$ 450
(6) F's dues in the local realtor's association	$ 40
(7) Charitable contribution to the Boy Scouts	$ 100

Their employers withheld income tax of $7,700, and they paid estimated tax of $800.

Compute the following for the joint return of D and F:

(a) Adjusted gross income.

(b) Taxable income.

(c) Net tax payable or refund due.

Research Problems

51. T is the vice-president of a large publicly held corporation. As an officer, T has participated in the company's bonus plan for several years. In a previ-

ous year, the bonuses given were in the form of annuity contracts purchased from an insurance company. The contracts were nontransferable, and payments did not begin until the employee reached age 65. T's return was examined, and the revenue agent contended that T should include the purchase price of the annuity in income in the year the contract was received. Since the annuity is nontransferable and T does not have the option to receive cash, T does not think income should be recognized until collection on the annuity contract begins. The taxpayer asks your opinion on the matter.

52. R's Casino in Atlantic Beach, New Jersey, reports its income under the accrual method of accounting. At year-end, the casino had $150,000 accounts receivable from customers who, in effect, gambled on credit. Under New Jersey law, the receivables are gambling debts; thus, if the casino attempted to use the courts to collect the debts, the customers could defeat the casino's claim. However, as a practical matter, customers rarely employ the gambling debt defense, and the casino collects over 95% of its receivables.

According to the casino's accountant, the year-end receivables need not be included in income until collected; that is, the gambling debts are not enforceable, and all events have therefore not occurred to fix the casino's right to the income until it is actually collected. The IRS disagrees. Who is right?

53. Mr. A is a commissioned agent for a large insurance company. During the year he purchased a policy on his life and the lives of his children and received a commission. Mr. A treated the commission on these policies as a reduction in cost rather than as income. However, during an audit the revenue agent indicates that Mr. A must include the commission in his gross income. The taxpayer seeks your assistance in resolving the matter with the agent.

Partial list of research aids:

Ostheimer v. U. S., 59–1 USTC ¶ 9300, 3 AFTR2d 886, 264 F.2d 789 (CA–3, 1959).

Rev.Rul. 55–273, 1955–1 C.B. 221.

54. On January 1, 19X2, W filed suit for divorce from H. While awaiting the decree of divorce, H moved into the attic apartment of H and W's home. W continued to occupy the remainder of the house. The attic apartment had a separate entrance, and H and W could remain in the same house without communicating with each other. Along with her petition for support, W requested that H be required to pay utilities on the home as temporary support. The court entered a support decree as W requested. H paid $1,200 for utilities until the final decree for divorce was entered in June 19X1. The court awarded W the home, and H immediately moved out under threat of eviction. W did not report the $1,200 as income on her 19X1 return. According to Reg. Section 1.71–1(b)(3), the temporary support payments are alimony if H and W were living apart. W contends that because she and H occupied the same house they were not living apart. Is W required to include the $1,200 in her 19X1 gross income?

Partial list of research aids

Alexander Washington v. Comm., 77 T.C. 610 (1981) Sydnes v. Comm., 78–2 USTC ¶ 9487, 42 AFTR2d 78–5143, 577 F.2d 60 (CA–8, 1978).

55. B is employed by T Laboratories, a think tank. While employed at the laboratories, B made several scientific breakthroughs and patented several inventions. In recognition of his outstanding contributions to science, T Laboratories made a $5,000 cash award to B. Is the award taxable?

56. H and W were divorced in 19X1. Under a written agreement, W was to pay H $500 per month for his support. The agreement was incorporated into the final divorce decree. H moved to another city, and in December 19X1 he remarried. W was unaware of H's marriage and continued to pay H $500 a month. H's and W's tax returns were examined for 19X2. H did not include the $6,000 (12 × $500) in his gross income. He contended the $6,000 was not alimony, because under state law W was not required to continue paying alimony after H remarried. Is H required to include the $6,000 in his 19X2 gross income?

Chapter 6

Gross Income: Exclusions

ITEMS SPECIFICALLY EXCLUDED FROM GROSS INCOME

Chapter 5 discussed the concepts and judicial doctrines that affect the determination of gross income. As demonstrated, the § 61 definition of gross income is all-inclusive. Chapter 6 focuses on specific items that Congress or, in some cases, the IRS has chosen to exclude from the tax base.

STATUTORY AUTHORITY

Sections 101 through 131 provide the authority for excluding specific items from gross income. In addition, other exclusions are scattered throughout the Code. Each exclusion has its own legislative history and reason for enactment. Certain exclusions are intended as a form of indirect welfare payments. Other exclusions prevent double taxation of income or provide incentives for socially desirable activities (i. e., nontaxable scholarships for educational activities).

In some cases exclusions have been enacted by Congress to rectify the effects of judicially imposed decisions. For example, § 109 was enacted to exclude the value of improvements made by a lessee from the lessor's income upon termination of the lease. Previously, the Supreme Court held that such amounts were taxable income.[1] In this court decision, the lessor was required to include the fair market

---

1. *Helvering v. Bruun,* 40–1 USTC ¶ 9337, 24 AFTR 652, 60 S.Ct. 631 (USSC, 1940).

191

value of the improvements in income upon the termination of the lease despite the fact that there had been no sale or disposition of the property. Congress provided relief in this situation by deferring the value of the improvements until the property was sold, unless the improvements were made by the lessee in lieu of rent.[2]

Section 123 was enacted to counter a District Court's decision in *Arnold v. U. S.*[3] In *Arnold,* the court included in gross income insurance proceeds paid to the taxpayer as reimbursement for temporary housing expenses incurred as a result of a fire in the taxpayer's home. Similar payments made by a government agency to families displaced by urban renewal projects had been held nontaxable in a previous Revenue Ruling.[4] Dissatisfied with the results in *Arnold,* Congress exercised its authority by exempting from tax the insurance proceeds received in circumstances similar to that case. The exclusion is described in § 123.

ADMINISTRATIVE POLICY

Administrative actions of the IRS, expressed through the issuance of interpretive Rulings and Regulations, occasionally have resulted in the exclusion of an item from gross income. For example, the IRS has excluded "supper money" paid to employees who work after regular hours.[5] In addition, the IRS has excluded welfare payments as essentially in the nature of gifts.[6]

SUMMARY OF PRINCIPAL EXCLUSIONS

Figure I is a listing of the principal exclusions from gross income.

Figure I

PRINCIPAL EXCLUSIONS FROM GROSS INCOME

1. Donative Items
   Gifts, bequests, inheritances, and employee death benefits (§ § 102 and 101(b))
   Life insurance proceeds paid by reason of death (§ 101)
   Scholarships and fellowships (§ 117)
   Certain prizes and awards (§ 74(b))
2. Personal and Welfare Items
   Injury or sickness payments (§ 104)
   Public assistance payments (Rev.Rul. 71–425, 1971–2 C.B. 76)
   Amounts received under insurance contracts for certain living expenses (§ 123)
   Reimbursement for the costs of caring for a foster child (§ 131)

---

2. § 109.
3. 68–2 USTC ¶ 9590, 22 AFTR2d 5661, 289 F.Supp. 206 (D.Ct.N.Y.1968).
4. Rev.Rul. 60–279, 1960–2 C.B. 11.
5. O.D. 514, 2 C.B. 90 (1921).
6. Rev.Rul. 71–425, 1971–2 C.B. 76.

3. Wage and Salary Supplements
   (a) Fringe benefits:
      Accident and health benefits (§ § 105 and 106)
      Disability pay (§ 105).
      Lodging and meals furnished for the convenience of the employer (§ 119)
      Rental value of parsonages (§ 107)
      Employer contributions to employee group-term life insurance (§ 79)
      Employee discounts and the use of the employer's facilities and services
      Amounts received under qualified group legal service plans (§ 120)
      Qualified transportation provided by employer (§ 124)
      Cafeteria plans (§ 125)
      Child or dependent care (§ 129)
   (b) Military benefits
      Combat pay (§ 112)
      Mustering-out pay (§ 113)
   (c) Foreign earned income (§ 911)
4. Investor Items
      Net interest exclusion (§ 128, effective in 1985)
      Interest on state and local government obligations (§ 103)
      Dividend exclusion (§ 116)
      Stock dividends from public utilities reinvestment plans (§ 305(e))
5. Benefits for the Elderly
      Social Security benefits (except in the case of certain higher income taxpayers)
      Gain from the sale of personal residence for elderly taxpayers (§ 121)
6. Other
      Recovery of a prior year's deduction which yielded no tax benefits (§ 111)

GIFTS AND INHERITANCES

Beginning with the Income Tax Act of 1913 and continuing to the present, Congress has allowed the recipient of a gift to exclude the value of the property from gross income.[7] The exclusion applies to gifts made during the life of the donor (*inter vivos* gifts) and transfers that take effect upon the death of the donor (bequests and inheritances). However, as discussed in Chapter 5, the recipient of a gift of income-producing property is subject to tax on the income subsequently earned from the property.

In numerous cases, gifts are made in a business setting. For example, a salesman gives a purchasing agent free samples; an employee receives cash from his or her employer on retirement; a corporation makes payments to employees who were victims of a natural disaster; a corporation makes a cash payment to a former employee's widow. In these and similar instances, it is frequently unclear whether a gift was made or the payments represent compensation for past, present, or future services.

The courts have defined a gift as "a voluntary transfer of property by one to another without adequate [valuable] consideration or com-

---

7. § 102(a).

pensation therefrom.[8] If the payment is intended to be for services rendered, it is not a gift, even though the payment is made without legal or moral obligation and the payor receives no economic benefit from the transfer. To qualify as a gift, the payment must be made "out of affection, respect, admiration, charity or like impulses."[9] Thus, the cases on this issue have been decided on the basis of the donor's intent.

In a landmark case, *Comm. v. Duberstein*,[10] the taxpayer (Duberstein) received a Cadillac from a business acquaintance. Duberstein had supplied the businessman with the names of potential customers with no expectation of compensation. The Supreme Court concluded:

> . . . despite the characterization of the transfer of the Cadillac by the parties [as a gift] and the absence of any obligation, even of a moral nature, to make it, it was at the bottom a recompense for Duberstein's past service, or an inducement for him to be of further service in the future.

Therefore, Duberstein was required to include the fair market value of the automobile in gross income.

Similarly, a bequest may be taxable if it represents a disguised form of compensation for services.

> **Example 1.** An attorney entered into an agreement whereby the client would bequeath to the attorney certain securities in consideration for services rendered during the client's life. The value of the securities on the date of the client's death is taxable income to the attorney.[11]

LIFE INSURANCE PROCEEDS

Generally, insurance proceeds paid to the beneficiary on the death of the insured are exempt from income tax.[12] Insurance proceeds are excluded from income because their payment is similar to the receipt of a nontaxable inheritance. In addition, social policy considerations suggest that favorable tax treatment should be granted to the beneficiaries of life insurance following the death of the insured, who is frequently the sole provider for the family. It should be noted, however, that life insurance proceeds are generally subject to the Federal estate tax.

8. *Estate of D. R. Daly*, 3 B.T.A. 1042 (1926).

9. *Robertson v. U. S.*, 52–1 USTC ¶ 9343, 41 AFTR 1053, 72 S.Ct. 994 (USSC, 1952).

10. 60–2 USTC ¶ 9515, 5 AFTR2d 1626, 80 S.Ct. 1190 (USSC, 1960).

11. *Wolder v. Comm.*, 74–1 USTC ¶ 9266, 33 AFTR2d 74–813, 493 F.2d 608 (CA–2, 1974).

12. § 101(a). Certain *flexible premium contracts* issued before 1984 are not eligible for the exclusion. See § 101(f).

Section 101(a)(2) provides an exception to the general rule that life insurance proceeds are excluded from income. This exception is applicable to a life insurance contract that has been transferred for valuable consideration to another individual who assumes ownership rights. The insurance proceeds are income to the assignee to the extent that the proceeds exceed the amount paid for the policy plus any subsequent premiums paid.

Example 2. A pays premiums of $500 for an insurance policy in the face amount of $1,000 upon the life of B and, subsequently, transfers the policy to C for $600. C receives the proceeds of $1,000 on the death of B. The amount which C can exclude from gross income is limited to $600 plus any premiums paid by C subsequent to the transfer.[13]

The Code, however, provides exceptions to the rule illustrated in the preceding example. The four exceptions include transfers to:[14]

—A partner of the insured.

—A partnership in which the insured is a partner.

—A corporation in which the insured is an officer or shareholder.

—A transferee whose basis in the policy is determined by reference to the transferor's basis.

The first three exceptions facilitate the use of insurance contracts to fund buy-sell agreements.

Example 3. R and S are equal partners who have an agreement that allows either partner to purchase the interest of a deceased partner for $50,000. Neither partner has sufficient cash to actually buy the other partner's interest, but each has a life insurance policy on his own life in the amount of $50,000. R and S could exchange their policies (usually at little or no taxable gain) and, upon the death of either partner, the surviving partner could collect tax-free insurance proceeds which could then be used to purchase the decedent's interest in the partnership.

The fourth exception noted above applies to policies that were transferred pursuant to a tax-free exchange (e. g., a transfer of insurance policies to a corporation by its controlling shareholders in exchange for the corporation's stock or securities).[15]

INTEREST ON LIFE INSURANCE PROCEEDS

Investment earnings arising from the reinvestment of life insurance proceeds are generally subject to income tax. However, § 101(d) pro-

---

13. Reg. § 1.101–1(b)(5), Ex. 1.
14. § 101(a)(2)(A) and (B).
15. § 351. See Chapter 20.

vides favorable tax advantages for a surviving spouse who elects to receive the insurance proceeds in installments. The surviving spouse may exclude the first $1,000 of interest income collected on the proceeds each year.

> **Example 4.** Mrs. T was the beneficiary of her husband's $100,000 life insurance policy. She elected to receive the principal in 10 installments of $10,000 each plus interest on the unpaid principal. The first year she received $13,600, which included $3,600 interest. She must recognize interest income of $2,600.

The $1,000 interest exclusion offers a tax advantage if the election is made to receive the proceeds in the form of installment payments; however, it may be possible to earn a greater after-tax return by investing the lump-sum proceeds in other types of investments (e. g., stocks or tax-free municipal bonds).

EMPLOYEE DEATH BENEFITS

Frequently an employer makes payments to a deceased employee's widow, children, or other beneficiaries. If the payments are made out of a legal obligation (e. g., the decedent's accrued salaries), the amounts are generally taxable to the recipient just the same as had the employee lived and collected on the obligation. But where the employer makes voluntary payments, the gift issue arises. Generally, the IRS considers such payments to be compensation for prior services rendered by the deceased employee.[16] However, some courts have held that payments to an employee's widow or other beneficiaries are gifts if:[17]

—The payments were made to the widow and children, rather than to the employee's estate.

—There was no obligation on the employer's part to pay any additional compensation to the deceased.

—The employer derived no benefit from the payment.

—The widow and children performed no services for the employer.

—The decedent had been fully compensated for services rendered.

—Compensation payments were made pursuant to a board of directors' resolution which followed a general company policy of providing such payment for families of deceased employees (but not exclusively for families of shareholder-employees).

---

16. Rev.Rul. 62–102, 1962–2 C.B. 37.
17. *Estate of Sydney J. Carter v. Comm.*, 71–2 USTC ¶ 9129, 29 AFTR2d 332, 453 F.2d 61 (CA–2, 1972) and cases cited therein.

These factors, together, indicate whether the payment was made as an act of "affection or charity." The widow's case for exclusion is greatly strengthened if the payment is made in "light of her financial needs."[18]

Section 101(b) attempts to eliminate or reduce controversy in this area by providing an automatic exclusion of the first $5,000 paid by the employer to the employee's beneficiaries "by reason of the death of the employee." The $5,000 exclusion must be apportioned among the beneficiaries on the basis of each beneficiary's percentage of the total death benefits received.[19] When the employer's payments exceed $5,000, the beneficiaries may still be able to exclude the entire amount received as a gift if they are able to show gratuitous intent on the part of the employer.

Besides avoiding the gift issue in many cases, the employee death benefit exclusion is also intended to allow a substitute for tax-exempt life insurance proceeds.

> **Example 5.** B Company carries a $5,000 life insurance policy on each of its employees. Because the company owns the policy, the employee does not include in his or her gross income the premiums paid by the employer. The employer names the employee's spouse as the beneficiary of the policy. When the employee dies, the spouse collects the tax-exempt life insurance proceeds. In contrast, C Company does not carry life insurance on its employees but pays the surviving spouse $5,000, which is also tax-exempt as an employee death benefit.

PENSION AND PROFIT SHARING BENEFITS

The *substitute for life insurance* rationale is reflected in the taxation of lump-sum (i. e., all benefits in one year) distributions from qualified pension and profit sharing plans. A lump-sum receipt of the benefits is similar to a collection of life insurance proceeds; thus, § 101 allows the $5,000 employee death benefits exclusion for lump-sum pension and profit sharing benefits.[20]

Annuity payments from a qualified plan and all payments from nonqualified plans are subject to the general rule (previously discussed) that amounts *owed* to the employee are not employee death benefits. Thus, the beneficiary can exclude only amounts received in excess of the deceased employee's nonforfeitable interest in the plan.

> **Example 6.** At the time of his death, employee D had nonforfeitable pension benefits with a value of $6,000. His entire bene-

---

18. *Simpson v. U. S.*, 58–2 USTC ¶ 9923, 2 AFTR2d 6036, 261 F.2d 497 (CA–7, 1958), *cert. denied*, 79 S.Ct. 724(USSC, 1958).
19. Reg. § 1.101–2(c)(1).
20. Reg. § 101(b)(1)–(3). See Chapter 19 for further discussion of qualified plans.

fits were financed by employer contributions. The plan also included survivor benefits that allowed D's spouse to collect either a lump sum of $8,000 or an annuity of $1,500 for 12 years. The present value of the annuity was also $8,000.

If the spouse collected the lump sum, her taxable income would be $3,000.

Total amount received	$ 8,000
Less: Employee death benefits	(5,000)
	$ 3,000

Example 7. Assume the same facts as in Example 6, except the surviving spouse selects the annuity option. The death benefit exclusion would bc limited to $2,000 ($8,000 − $6,000 employee's nonforfeitable benefits). Generally, the excluded amount would be treated as the surviving spouse's cost of the annuity and prorated (as discussed in Chapter 5). However, because the surviving spouse will collect more than her cost ($2,000) within three years, she could exclude the first $2,000 received from the qualified plan as a recovery of capital (discussed in Chapter 5).

If payments in excess of $5,000 are treated as compensation and are taxable income of the beneficiaries, such amounts are deductible by the employer as ordinary and necessary business expenses.[21] However, if such excess amounts represent gifts, the employer is entitled to a maximum deduction of only $5,025 ($5,000 as a death benefit plus a $25 ceiling amount for a business gift).[22]

SCHOLARSHIPS AND FELLOWSHIPS

Prior to 1954, there was no specific provision in the Code concerning scholarships and fellowships. Generally, a grant was considered taxable unless the grant's recipient could show that such amounts were nontaxable gifts. The enactment of § 117 was intended to provide some general rules for determining the taxability of scholarships and fellowships. However, the new provision did little more than codify existing case law and treasury decisions and has left many issues unresolved.[23] Thus, each year there are several cases before the courts involving scholarships and fellowships.

The Regulations define a scholarship as "an amount paid or allowed to, or for the benefit of, a student, whether an undergraduate or a graduate, to aid such individual in pursuing his studies." A fellow-

---

21. Reg. § 1.404(a)–(12).
22. § 274(b). See the discussion of business gifts in Chapter 10.
23. See *Elmore L. Reese, Jr.*, 45 T.C. 407 (1966) for a discussion of the history of the scholarship provisions.

ship is "an amount paid or allowed to, or for the benefit of, an individual in the pursuit of study or research."[24] The term "fellowship" includes amounts received to cover the expenses of travel, research, clerical help, and equipment as well as the individual's general living expenses (provided the expenses are related to the individual's studies).[25] However, the payments are compensation and are therefore taxable if they represent payment for past, present, or future services or are primarily for the benefit of the grantor.[26]

Often payments are made for dual motives (i. e., to aid the recipient and to benefit the grantor). The courts have adopted a "purpose of the expenditure" test to decide such cases.

> It is apparent from the above cited regulations and rulings that whether a payment qualifies as a scholarship or fellowship grant excludable from gross income under Section 117 of the 1954 Code depends upon whether the primary purpose of the payment is to further the education and training of the recipient or whether the primary purpose is to serve the interest of the grantor. The problem is usually somewhat difficult of solution because of the fact that in most of the situations there is a dual or mutual benefit involved. The question of necessity must be resolved on a factual basis and depends upon the facts and circumstances in each particular case.[27]

Many graduate students receive payments for teaching or assisting in research. Generally, the payments are compensation for services and, therefore, taxable. However, in some degree programs all students are required to do some teaching or research (e. g., an internship in education or research in the physical sciences). In these cases, the requirements to perform services will not prevent the payment from being excluded as a scholarship;[28] but an institution cannot bring all of its payments to graduate students under the scholarship exclusion by simply making some teaching or research a requirement for a degree. The primary purpose of the payment must be to further the education and training of the recipient rather than "to serve the interest of the grantor." Whether this test is satisfied is "basically a question of fact."[29]

---

24. Reg. § 1.117–3(a).
25. § 117(a)(2).
26. Reg. § 1.117–4(c). Rev.Rul. 68–20, 1968–1 C.B. 55 held that a scholarship awarded to a contestant was compensation for participating in the televised pageant and for performing subsequent services for the sponsor.
27. *C. P. Bhalla,* 35 T.C. 13 (1960).
28. § 117(b)(1).
29. *Bingler v. Johnson,* 69–1 USTC ¶ 9348, 23 AFTR2d 1212, 89 S.Ct. 1439 (USSC, 1969).

A hospital's payments to interns and residents are often the subject of litigation under the fellowship provision. Generally, the payments are considered compensation if the interns' duties are geared to the operational needs of the hospital rather than the interns' research and study needs.[30] However, in some cases the courts have ruled that the payments were primarily to further the educational needs of the student when:[31]

—The principal purpose of the institute was training medical specialists rather than providing patient care.

—The recipient of the funds did not replace personnel who otherwise would have been employed for the care of patients.

A special provision in the Code exists for an individual who receives a fellowship or scholarship when the recipient is *not* a candidate for a degree. The "noncandidate" must meet the same requirements as the degree candidate; the payments cannot be made for services of the recipient nor be primarily for the benefit of the grantor. In addition, the payments must be received from a government or other nonprofit organization. If these requirements are satisfied, the exclusion for the nondegree candidate is limited to $300 times the number of months during which the recipient receives payments in the taxable year (subject to a maximum of 36 total months).[32] Amounts received for expenses incidental to the scholarship do not enter into the calculation of the monthly exclusion.[33]

> **Example 8.** T, calendar year taxpayer, received a post-doctoral fellowship of $4,500 from a qualifying nonprofit organization in March 19X1. The grant commences on September 1, 19X1, and ends on May 31, 19X2 (a period of nine months). T is also to be reimbursed for up to $1,500 in laboratory expenses. If T receives $4,500 on September 1, 19X1, he can exclude $2,700 ($300 × 9) from his 19X1 income, since the amount received is for the full term of the fellowship grant (nine months). The remaining $1,800 must be included in T's gross income for 19X1. The $1,500 reimbursement for laboratory expenses is excludible to the extent that it is offset by T's actual laboratory expenses. Alternatively, if T receives a total of $2,000 ($500 per month for the four-month period from September through December 19X1), he may exclude a maximum of $1,200 ($300 × 4) and must include $800 in his gross income for 19X1.

---

30. *A. J. Prosky,* 51 T.C. 918 (1969).

31. *Wrobleski v. Bingler,* 58–2 USTC ¶ 9556, 1 AFTR2d 1987, 161 F.Supp. 901 (D.Ct.Pa., 1958); to the contrary, Rev.Rul. 57–386, 1957–2 C.B. 105; but under facts similar to the above, payments to student nurses and anesthetists were excludible according to the IRS in Rev.Rul. 58–338, 1958–2 C.B. 54; Rev.Rul. 72–568, 1972–2 C.B. 48.

32. § 117(b)(2)(B).

33. Rev.Rul. 59–81, 1959–1 C.B. 37.

Some employers have made scholarships available solely to the children of key employees. The tax objective of these plans was to provide a nontaxable fringe benefit to the executives by making the payment to the child in the form of an excludible scholarship. However, the IRS has ruled that the payments are generally taxable income to the parent-employee.[34]

COMPENSATION FOR INJURIES AND SICKNESS

DAMAGES

A person who suffers physical or emotional harm caused by another is often entitled to monetary damages. The legal theory of damages is that the amount awarded is intended "to make the plaintiff [the injured party] whole as before the injury."[35] It follows that if the damages received were subject to tax, the after-tax amount received would be less than the actual damages incurred and the injured party would not be "whole as before the injury."

Thus, Congress has specifically excluded from income "the amount of any damages received (whether by suit or agreement) on account of personal injuries or sickness."[36] The courts have applied the exclusion to any personal wrong committed against the taxpayer (e. g., breach of promise to marry, invasion of privacy, libel, slander, battery).

The personal wrong may result in an economic loss as well as a personal loss. An individual hurt in an automobile accident may suffer physical injury, mental anguish, and a reduction in earning power. Generally, damages received as a substitute for a loss of income are taxable (because the income, if it had been earned, would have been taxable). However, the courts have interpreted the personal injury exclusion to be applicable to the economic loss; that is, if the personal injury results in a loss of earnings and the victim receives an amount in respect of the loss of income, the damages are nevertheless nontaxable because they resulted from a personal injury.[37]

As a further complication, in cases involving damages to an individual's reputation, the courts and the IRS have distinguished between damages to a personal reputation and damages to a business reputation. According to the IRS, personal and business reputations

---

34. Rev.Rul. 75–448, 1975–2 C.B. 55. *Richard T. Armantrout,* 67 T.C. 996 (1977).

35. *C. A. Hawkins,* 6 B.T.A. 1023(1928).

36. § 104(a)(2).

37. *Roemer v. Comm.,* 83–2 USTC ¶ 9600, 52 AFTR2d 83–5954 (CA–9, 1983), rev'g 79 T.C. 398 (1982).

can be separated, and damages received in respect to the business reputation are taxable compensation for a loss of income.[38]

> **Example 9.** P, a television news announcer, was dissatisfied with the manner in which R, an attorney, was defending the television station in a libel case. P stated on television that R was "botching the case." R filed a suit against P for damages to R's business reputation. While attempting to negotiate a settlement, R threatened physical harm to P, who became so frightened he developed a speech impediment which forced him to leave his job.
>
> Any damages received by P are nontaxable, because his claim is based on emotional injury (assault) to him. R's damages would be taxable, because they relate to his business reputation— an income-producing asset.

In addition to compensatory damages for the personal harm and loss of income, the plaintiff in some cases may seek punitive damages, an amount awarded to punish the defendant for gross negligence or intentional infliction of harm. Generally, punitive damages are treated the same as the compensating damages. Thus, punitive damages awarded in a claim for personal injury are nontaxable,[39] but punitive damages awarded in a claim for loss of income are taxable.[40]

> **Example 10.** E Company brought suit against F Company for antitrust damages. E Company proved that its income was reduced by $1,000,000 because of F Company's illegal acts. Under federal law, E Company can recover $1,000,000 actual damages plus $2,000,000 punitive damages. The $1,000,000 is taxable, because it replaces income. The $2,000,000 punitive damages are taxable, because they are based on the claim for lost profits.[41]

Amounts received as damages to property generally are treated as a recovery of capital, and any excess amount received is taxable gain.

> **Example 11.** M sued D for placing underground electrical wires on M's side of their adjoining property lines. Amounts received by M will be considered as a recovery of the cost of his land. Amounts received by M in excess of his basis in the land will be taxable gain.

WORKERS' COMPENSATION

State workers' compensation laws require the employer to pay fixed amounts for specific job-related injuries. The state laws were enacted

38. *Wade E. Church,* 80 T.C. 1104 (1983).
39. Rev.Rul. 75–45, 1975–1 C.B. 47.
40. *Glenshaw Glass v. Comm.,* 55–1 USTC ¶ 9308, 47 AFTR 162, 75 S.Ct. 473 (USSC 1955).
41. Id.

so that the employee will not have to go through the ordeal of a law-suit (and possibly not collect damages because of some defense available to the employer) to recover the damages. Although the payments are intended, in part, to compensate for a loss of future income, Congress has, nevertheless, specifically exempted workers' compensation benefits.[42]

ACCIDENT AND HEALTH INSURANCE BENEFITS

Section 104(a)(3) excludes from income benefits collected under an accident and health insurance policy purchased by the taxpayer. Moreover, benefits collected under the taxpayer's insurance policy are exempted even though the payments are a substitute for income.

> **Example 12.**   B purchased a medical and disability insurance policy. The insurance company paid B $200 per week to replace wages he lost while in the hospital. Although the payments serve as a substitute for income, the amounts received are tax-exempt benefits collected under B's insurance policy.

> **Example 13.**   J's injury resulted in a partial paralysis of his left foot. He received $5,000 from his accident insurance company for the injury. The $5,000 accident insurance proceeds are tax-exempt.

A different set of rules applies if the accident and health insurance protection was purchased by the individual's employer, as discussed below.

EMPLOYER-SPONSORED ACCIDENT AND HEALTH PLANS

Congress encourages employers to provide employees and their dependents with accident and health and disability insurance plans. The premiums are deductible by the employer and excluded from the employee's income.[43] Although § 105(a) provides the general rule that the employee has taxable income when he or she collects the insurance benefits, § § 105(b) and (c) provide exceptions:

> § 105(b)   Excludes payments received for medical care of the employee, spouse, and dependents except to the extent such amounts relate to medical expenses which were deducted by the taxpayer in a prior year.

> § 105(c)   Excludes payments for the permanent loss or the loss of the use of a member or function of the body or the permanent disfigurement of the employee, spouse, or a dependent.

---

42. § 104(a)(1).
43. § 106.

Example 14. D incurred $2,000 medical expenses in 19X1. D claimed the medical expenses as an itemized deduction on his 19X1 return. D's adjusted gross income for 19X1 was $30,000, and he had no other medical expenses. Because only medical expenses in excess of 5% of adjusted gross income may be claimed as an itemized deduction on D's 19X1 return, the expense reduced taxable income by only $500 [$2,000 − .05($30,000) = $500]. In 19X2, D received a $2,000 reimbursement from his employer-sponsored health insurance plan. The general rule of Section 105(b) excludes the $2,000 from D's income. However, because D deducted the medical expenses on his return, the exception in § 105(b) applies. D is required to include in 19X2 gross income the $500 deducted on his 19X1 return.

Example 15. E lost an eye in an automobile accident unrelated to his work. As a result of the accident, E incurred $2,000 of medical expenses which he deducted on his return. He collected $10,000 from an accident insurance policy carried by his employer. The benefits were paid according to a schedule of amounts that varied with the part of the body injured (e. g., $10,000 for loss of an eye, $20,000 for loss of a hand).

Because the payment was for loss of a *member or function of the body,* § 105(c) applies and the $10,000 is excluded from income. Moreover, § 105(b) does not apply, because the payment was not specifically for medical care. Thus, the $2,000 deducted is not included in gross income under § 105(b).

MEDICAL REIMBURSEMENT PLANS

In lieu of, and in some cases in addition to, providing the employee with insurance coverage for hospital and medical expenses, the employer may agree to reimburse the employee for these expenses. The amounts received through the insurance coverage (i. e., "insured" plan benefits) are excluded from income under § 105 (as discussed above). Unfortunately in terms of cost considerations, the insurance companies that issue these types of policies usually require a broad coverage of employees. An alternative would be to have a plan that is not funded with insurance (i. e., a "self-insured" arrangement). Here, the employer can single out a group of employees (e. g., management level only) for sole coverage under the plan. Obviously, such plans might prove to be discriminatory in their effect.

Congress addressed this problem with the enactment of § 105(h). This provision requires the employee to include in gross income the medical benefits received from a "self-insured" arrangement if the plan discriminates in favor of "highly compensated individuals."

Example 16. F Corporation carries a Blue Cross medical care policy (i. e., an insured plan) that covers all employees and their dependents. Further, F Corporation has a self-insured arrangement whereby it reimburses its management-level employees for any medical expenses not absorbed by the Blue Cross policy.

T is the president and major shareholder of F Corporation. During the current year, the corporation paid $600 Blue Cross premiums for T and his dependents. T incurred and paid $1,500 medical expenses. He was fully reimbursed for these expenses as follows: $1,200 from Blue Cross and $300 from F Corporation.

The reimbursement from F Corporation is taxable under § 105(h). The Blue Cross premiums are excluded from gross income under § 106, and the Blue Cross reimbursement is excluded under § 105(b).

MEALS AND LODGING FURNISHED FOR THE CONVENIENCE OF THE EMPLOYER

As was discussed in Chapter 5, income can take any form, including meals and lodging. However, § 119 excludes from income the value of meals and lodging, under the following conditions:[44]

—The meals and/or lodging are *furnished* by the employer, on the employer's *business premises,* for the *convenience of the employer.*

—In the case of lodging, the employee is *required* to accept the lodging as a condition of employment.

Each of these requirements has been strictly construed by the courts.

The IRS and some courts have reasoned that a partner is not an employee, and therefore, the exclusion does not apply to the partner. However the Tax Court and the Fifth Circuit Court have ruled in favor of the taxpayer on this issue.[45]

The Supreme Court held a cash meal allowance was ineligible for the exclusion because the employer did not actually furnish the

---

44. § 119(a)(1). The meals and lodging are also excluded from FICA and FUTA tax. *Rowan Companies, Inc. v. U. S.,* 81–1 USTC ¶ 9749, 48 AFTR2d 81–5115, 101 S.Ct. 2288 (USSC. 1981).

45. Rev.Rul. 80, 1953–1 CB 62; *Comm. v. Doak,* 56–2 USTC ¶ 9708, 49 AFTR 1491, 234 F.2d 704 (CA–4, 1956); *Moran v. Comm.,* 56–2 USTC ¶ 9789, 50 AFTR 64, 236 F.2d 53 (CA–8, 1956); *Robinson v. U. S.,* 60–1 USTC ¶ 9152, 273 F.2d 503 (CA–3, 1960). *Briggs v. U. S.,* 56–2 USTC ¶ 10020, 50 AFTR 667, 238 F.2d 53 (CA–10, 1956). But see *G. A. Papineau,* 16 T.C. 130 (1956). *Armstrong v. Phinney,* 68–1 USTC ¶ 9355, 21 AFTR2d 1260, 394 F.2d 661 (CA–5, 1968).

meals.[46] Similarly, one court denied the exclusion where the employer paid for the food and supplied the cooking facilities, but the employee prepared the meal.[47]

The *on the business premises of the employer* requirement, applicable to both meals and lodging, has resulted in much litigation. The Regulations define business premises as simply "the place of employment of the employee."[48] Thus, in *Commissioner v. Anderson*[49] the Sixth Court of Appeals held that a residence, owned by the employer and occupied by Anderson, two blocks from the motel which Anderson managed was not part of the business premises. However, in *J. B. Lindeman*,[50] the Tax Court considered an employer-owned house across the street from the hotel that was managed by the taxpayer to be on the business premises of the employer. Perhaps these two cases can be reconciled by comparing the distance from the lodging facilities to the place where the employer's business was conducted. The closer the lodging to the business operations, the more likely the convenience of the employer is served.

The *convenience of the employer* test is intended to focus the analysis on the employer's motivation for furnishing the meals and lodging, rather than focusing on the benefits received by the employee. If the employer furnishes the meals and lodging primarily to enable the employee to properly perform his or her duties, it does not matter that the employee considers these benefits to be a part of his or her compensation.[51]

The employer *required* test, applicable to lodging but not meals, overlaps with the convenience of the employer test. The employer requires that the employee live on the premises, apparently, so that he or she can properly perform the duties of the job. But making meals available at no charge may induce a sufficient number of employees to remain on the premises to meet the employer's operational needs as illustrated in Reg. § 1.119–1(d):

—A hospital provides a free cafeteria for its staff. The employees are not required to eat on the premises, but the hospital's business purpose in providing the meals is to induce employees to stay on the premises in case an emergency arises. The value of the meals may be excluded from income.

The Regulation gives the following additional examples in which the tests for excluding meals are satisfied:

---

46. *Comm. v. Kowalski,* 77–2 USTC ¶ 9748, 40 AFTR2d 6128, 98 S.Ct. 315 (USSC. 1977).

47. *Tougher v. Comm.,* 71–1 USTC ¶ 9398, 27 AFTR2d 1301, 441 F.2d 1148 (CA–9, 1971).

48. Reg. 1.119–1(c)(1).

49. 67–1 USTC ¶ 9136, 19 AFTR2d 318, 371 F.2d 59 (CA–6, 1966).

50. 60 T.C. 609 (1973).

51. S. Rep. No. 1622, 83d Cong. 2d Sess., 19 (1954).

—A waitress is required to eat her meals on the premises during the busy lunch and breakfast hours.

—A bank furnishes a teller meals on the premises to limit the time the employee is away from his or her booth during the busy hours.

—A worker is employed at a construction site in a remote part of Alaska. The employer must furnish meals and lodging due to the inaccessibility of other facilities.

OTHER EMPLOYEE FRINGE BENEFITS

In 1976 and 1978 Congress enacted various exclusions that have become popular forms of nontaxable fringe benefits. These provisions are summarized below:

—The employee does not have to include in gross income the value of child and dependent care services paid for by the employer and incurred to enable the employee to work. In the case of married couples, the exclusion generally cannot exceed the earned income of either spouse.[52]

—Any benefit received by employees from coverage under qualified group legal service plans provided by the employer is excluded.[53]

Example 17. X Corporation, under its qualified group legal service plan, has established a trust fund to pay for its employees' personal legal expenses. In 19X1, the company contributed $5,000 to the fund. Also in 19X1, employee T incurred $150 in legal fees in connection with updating his will. The trust fund paid T's legal expenses. T is not required to recognize income.

Note that this provision parallels the treatment of medical reimbursement plans pursuant to §§ 105 and 106 (discussed above).

—Qualified transportation provided by employers will be nontaxable to the employees. As mentioned in Chapter 10, commuting expenses (i. e., the cost of going from home to work and back) normally are personal in nature and, therefore, are not deductible. Thus, if these expenses were furnished by the employer, income resulted to the employees. Section 124 now enables employers to furnish commuting-van services for employees without the recognition of income by the employees.

---

52. § 129. The exclusion applies to the same types of expenses which, if they were paid by the employee (and not reimbursed by the employer), would be eligible for the Credit for Child and Dependent Care Expense, discussed in Chapter 13.
53. § 120.

—Until recently, if an employee was granted a choice between cash and a nontaxable fringe benefit, the better view was that the option of cash made the fringe benefit taxable. Section 125 permits this option (called "cafeteria" plans) if certain conditions are met.

Example 18. Y Corporation offers its employees a choice of a cash payment of $1,800 or coverage in its group-term life insurance and medical reimbursement plans. An employee who accepts the cash alternative, of course, will be taxed on the $1,800. By way of contrast, an employee choosing participation in the fringe benefit program will be accorded the typical exclusion from gross income. Cafeteria plans provide tremendous flexibility in tailoring the employee-pay package to fit individual needs. Some employees (usually the younger group) prefer cash, while others (usually the older group) will opt for the fringe benefit programs.

The financing of these fringe benefits will result in a tax deduction to the employer. However, requirements for extensive coverage of employees are imposed in order for the plans to qualify. Therefore, even considering the tax deduction that is generated, cost considerations will play a role regarding which, if any, of these fringe benefits an employer decides to adopt.

Other employee benefits that are not generally includible in gross income are discounts on the employer's merchandise, free parking, payment of the employee's dues in vocational or professional organizations, supper money, and nonbusiness use of the employer's facilities where no additional cost is incurred by the employer.

Example 19. Z Airlines allows its employees to fly on a standby basis on any scheduled flight at no charge. Since the seats the employees occupy would otherwise be empty, the airline incurs no additional cost due to employee use. Consequently, the IRS will not require the employee to include the fair market value of the transportation in his or her gross income.

It should be recalled that in cases such as employee discounts, the value received by the employee probably is within the ambit of § 61 (gross income broadly defined), but the IRS, as a matter of policy, has chosen not to enforce inclusion in gross income where the benefits are made available to all employees.[54]

One fringe benefit that has been subject to repeated attacks by the IRS is loans to employees at less than the market rate of interest

---

54. In the late 1970s, the IRS indicated it intended to issue new regulations which would tax fringe benefits such as illustrated in Example 19. But in 1978 and again in 1981, Congress established a statutory barrier prohibiting any fringe benefit regulations before 1984, when Congress will consider new legislation addressing the fringe benefits issue.

(or at no interest at all). The Tax Court has refused to impose a tax on the difference between the market rate of interest and the rate, if any, actually charged to the employee. However, the Tax Court's rationale for its position is not that the employee did not realize any income but rather that the income realized (actually imputed) is offset by an allowable deduction for interest deemed paid.[55]

> **Example 20.** X Corporation loaned its president $100,000 for one year but did not charge any interest, although the market rate for interest on such loans was 14%. According to the IRS, the president must recognize income of $14,000. The Tax Court holds that if the $14,000 interest is included in income, the president would be entitled to a deduction of $14,000 for the interest deemed paid. Thus, the imputed income and deduction offset each other.

FOREIGN EARNED INCOME

A U. S. citizen is generally subject to U. S. tax on his or her income regardless of its geographic origin. The income may also be subject to tax in the foreign country, and thus the taxpayer must carry a double tax burden. Out of a sense of fairness and to encourage U. S. citizens to work abroad (so that exports might be increased), Congress has provided alternative forms of relief from taxes on foreign earned income. The taxpayer can elect to either (1) include the foreign income in his or her taxable income and then claim a credit for foreign taxes paid or (2) exclude the foreign earnings from his U. S. gross income.[56] The foreign tax credit option is discussed in Chapter 13, but as is apparent from the discussion below, most taxpayers will choose the exclusion.

Foreign earned income consists of the earnings from the individual's personal services rendered in a foreign country (other than as an employee of the U. S. Government).[57] To qualify for the exclusion the taxpayer must be either a bona fide resident of the foreign country or present in the country for 330 days during any 12 consecutive months.[58]

---

55. *J. Simpson Dean,* 35 T.C. 1083 (1961), *nonacq.* 1973–2 C.B. 4. Also see, *Max Zager,* 72 T.C. 1009 (1979) which involved a borrower who was an employee-shareholder. See also *W. L. Hardee v. U. S.,* 83–1 USTC ¶ 9353, 52 AFTR2d 83–5022, 708 F2d 661 (CA–Fed.Cir., 1983).

56. § 911(a). These rules became effective January 1, 1982, and substantially changed the foreign earned income exclusion. Once the election is made to exclude income, it cannot be revoked without the consent of the IRS. See § 911(e).

57. § 911(d)(2).

58. § 911(c). For the definition of resident, see Reg. § 1.871–2(b). Under the regulations a taxpayer is not a resident if he or she is there for a definite period (e. g., until completion of a construction contract).

The exclusion is limited to $85,000 in 1984 and increases by $5,000 per year until 1986, when it reaches $95,000. For married persons, both of whom have foreign earned income, the exclusion is computed separately for each spouse. Also, the community property rules do not apply (i. e., the community property spouse is not deemed to have earned one-half of the other spouse's foreign earned income). A taxpayer who is present in the country for less than the entire year must compute the maximum exclusion on a daily basis (e. g., in 1984, $85,000 divided by the number of workdays present).[59]

In addition to the exclusion for foreign earnings, the reasonable housing costs incurred by the taxpayer and the taxpayer's family in a foreign country in excess of a base amount may also be excluded from gross income. The base amount is 16 percent of the U. S. Government pay scale for a GS–14 (Step 1) employee, which varies from year to year.[60]

As previously mentioned, the taxpayer may elect to include the foreign earned income in federal adjusted gross income and claim a credit (an offset against U. S. tax) for the foreign tax paid. The credit alternative may be advantageous if the individual's foreign earned income far exceeds the excludible amount so that the foreign taxes paid exceed the U. S. tax on the amount excluded. However, once an election is made, it applies to all subsequent years, unless affirmatively revoked. Moreover, the revocation is effective for the year of the change and the four subsequent years.[61]

INTEREST EXCLUSIONS

INTEREST ON CERTAIN STATE AND LOCAL GOVERNMENT OBLIGATIONS

At the time the Sixteenth Amendment was ratified by the states there was some question as to whether the Federal government possessed the constitutional authority to tax interest on state and local government obligations. Taxing the interest on these obligations was thought to violate the doctrine of intergovernmental immunity in that the tax would impair the state and local government's ability to finance its operations.[62] Thus, interest on state and local government obligations was specifically exempted from Federal income taxation. The exemption is still part of our tax laws, but most commentators agree that the exclusion of such interest is based upon political rather than constitutional requirements.

---

59.   § § 911(b)(2)(A), (B) and (C).
60.   § 911(c).
61.   § 911(e).
62.   *Pollock v. Farmer's Loan & Trust Co.,* 3 AFTR 2557, 15 S.Ct. 912 (USSC, 1895).

Obviously, the exclusion of the interest reduces the cost of borrowing for the state and local governments. A taxpayer in the 50 percent marginal tax bracket requires only a four percent yield on a tax-exempt bond to obtain the same after-tax income as a taxable bond paying eight percent interest [$4\% \div (1 - .5) = 8\%$].

However, the lower cost for the state and local government is more than offset by the revenue loss of the Federal government. Also, tax-exempt interest is considered to be a substantial loophole for the very wealthy. For this reason, bills have been proposed to Congress calling for Federal government subsidies to those state and local governments which voluntarily choose to issue taxable bonds. Under these proposals, the tax-exempt status of existing bonds would not be eliminated.

The current exempt status applies solely to the obligations of state and local governments (e. g., interest on bonds and notes). Thus, income received from the accrual of interest on an overpayment of state income tax is fully taxable.[63] Nor does the exemption apply to gains on the sale of tax-exempt securities.

During recent years, state and local governments have developed sophisticated financial schemes to attract new industry. For example, local municipalities have issued bonds to finance the construction of plants to be leased to private enterprise. Because the financing could be arranged with low interest rate municipal obligations, the plant could be leased at a lower cost than the private business could otherwise obtain. State and local governments have also issued tax-exempt bonds and have invested the proceeds in higher-yield Federal and corporate bonds (so-called arbitrage transactions). Sections 103(c) and (d) were enacted in 1969 to place limitations on the use of industrial development and arbitrage bonds by state and local governments.

Under § 103(b), the tax exemption does not apply to interest on bonds whose proceeds will be used directly or indirectly by a business. However, exemptions are provided in the Code for (1) small issues, $1,000,000 or less; (2) obligations whose proceeds are used to finance an industrial park; and (3) obligations whose proceeds are used to finance certain public goods and services such as public transportation, airports, water, sewage, sports facilities, parks, conventions or trade show facilities, and public housing projects.[64]

---

63. *Kieselbach v. Comm.,* 43–1 USTC ¶ 9220, 30 AFTR 370, 63 S.Ct. 303 (USSC, 1943). *U. S. Trust Co. of New York v. Anderson,* 3 USTC ¶ 1125, 12 AFTR 836, 65 F.2d 575 (CA–2, 1933).

64. § 103(b)(4), (5) and (6). In certain instances the limitation on small issues is $5,000,000. The limitation is increased to $10,000,000 for obligations issued after 1978 by the Revenue Act of 1978, amending § 103(b)(6)(D). The Tax Equity and Fiscal Responsibility Act of 1982, § 214(c), placed additional limitations on the industrial development exemption. Moreover, because the exemption is set to expire in 1986, industrial development bonds issued after December 31, 1986, will be taxable.

PARTIAL INTEREST EXCLUSION FOR INDIVIDUALS

In the early 1980s, Congress began to accept the economists' arguments that an increase in savings by individuals would reduce the general rate of inflation and, in particular, reduce interest rates charged borrowers. Lower interests rates were deemed necessary for economic growth. One means of encouraging savings is to increase its after-tax return. Congress did this in 1981–83 by allowing exclusion of the interest on certain savings certificates issued by financial institutions (through the now-expired All-Savers provisions).

Beginning in 1985, a new type of interest exclusion will be available.[65] Individuals (but not corporations) will be allowed to exclude the lesser of (1) 15 percent of interest income reduced by interest expense (other than interest on a home mortgage and interest incurred in a trade or business) or (2) $450 ($900 on a joint return). The law is intended to encourage the flow of savings into the capital markets. Generally, to be eligible for the exclusion, the interest must have been paid by a financial institution (e. g. a bank, insurance company, savings and loan association) or the U. S. government. Corporate bonds and notes may also qualify for the exclusion if they are publicly traded.

As discussed earlier in this chapter, in the case of interest on life insurance proceeds payable in installments, a $1,000 annual interest exclusion is allowed under § 101(d). Apparently, the $1,000 exclusion is first claimed, and the 15 percent limit is applied to the taxable portion of the interest.

DIVIDEND EXCLUSION FOR INDIVIDUALS

Section 116 provides some relief from the double taxation of corporate income (i. e., the income is initially subject to the corporate income tax and the subsequent dividend distributions are taxed to the shareholders). Unmarried individuals and married individuals who file separate returns may exclude the first $100 of dividends received from domestic (U. S.) corporations during the year. On a joint return, a maximum of $200 of dividends may be excluded, regardless of which spouse owns the stock on which the dividends are paid.

> **Example 21.** Mr. and Mrs. A received dividends in the current year as follows:

---

65. § 128.

	Dividends Received on Stock Owned by			
	Mr. A	Mrs. A	Jointly	Total
X Corporation	$ 40	$ 150		$ 190
Y Corporation		90		90
Z Corporation			$ 30	30
	$ 40	$ 240	$ 30	$ 310

On a joint return Mr. and Mrs. A would report $310 minus a $200 exclusion. On a separate return, Mr. A would report $55 [$40 + ½ ($30)] of dividends, but because the total is less than $100, none would be taxable. Mrs. A would report $255 [$240 + ½ ($30)] of dividends and a $100 exclusion on a separate return. Thus, their total taxable income is $155 on separate returns but only $110 on a joint return.

As might have been expected, the community property rules affect the dividend exclusion. Each spouse is taxed on one-half of the dividends on stocks owned by the community, the same as jointly owned stock in a common law state. But the treatment of dividends on separately owned stocks differs among the community property states.

Example 22. The facts are the same as in Example 21, except Mr. and Mrs. A reside in a community property state.

	Separate Property			
	Mr. A	Mrs. A	Community	Total
X Corporation	$ 40	$ 150		$ 190
Y Corporation		90		90
Z Corporation			$ 30	30
	$ 40	$ 240	$ 30	$ 310

In Texas and in other states following the Texas rule,[66] the $280 of dividends from separate property is deemed to be community income. Therefore, Mr. A's income for purposes of the $100 dividend exclusion on a separate return would be ½ ($40 + $240 + $30) = $155. Mrs. A's income would be the same as Mr. A's.

In California and in other states following the California rule,[67] Mr. A's income would be $40 from his separate property plus $15 from his share of the community property income ($40 + $15 = $55), and his dividend exclusion would be limited to

---

66. Louisiana and Idaho.
67. Arizona, Nevada, New Mexico, and Washington follow the California rule.

this amount. Mrs. A's income would be $240 from her separate property plus $15 from the community property. She would be allowed the full $100 exclusion.

NONQUALIFYING DIVIDENDS AND THOSE REQUIRING SPECIAL TREATMENT

A dividend is a payment to a shareholder in respect of his or her stock. The dividend exclusion does not apply to some items which are frequently referred to as dividends.

—Dividends received on deposits with savings and loan associations, credit unions, and banks are actually interest (a contractual rate paid for the use of money).

—Patronage dividends paid by cooperatives (i. e., for farmers) are rebates made to the users and are considered reductions in the cost of items purchased from the association. The rebates are usually made after year-end (after the cooperative has determined whether it has met its expenses) and are apportioned among members on the basis of their purchases.

—Mutual insurance companies pay dividends on unmatured life insurance policies that are considered rebates of premiums.

—Shareholders in mutual investment funds are allowed to report as capital gains their proportionate share of the fund's gains realized and distributed. The capital gain and ordinary income portions are reported on the Form 1099 which the fund supplies its shareholders each year.

Dividends to shareholders are taxable only to the extent the payments are made from either the corporation's current earnings and profits (in many cases the same as before tax net income per books) or its accumulated earnings and profits (in many cases the same as retained earnings per books).[68] Distributions to shareholders that exceed earnings and profits are treated as a nontaxable recovery of capital and reduce the shareholder's basis in the stock. Once the shareholder's basis is reduced to zero, any subsequent distributions in excess of the corporation's earnings and profits are taxed as capital gains.[69]

STOCK DIVIDENDS AND DIVIDEND REINVESTMENT PLANS

When a corporation issues a simple stock dividend (e. g., common stock issued to common stockholders), the shareholder has merely received additional shares to represent the same total investment; thus,

---

68. § 316(a).

69. § 301(c). See Chapter 3, *West's Federal Taxation: Corporations, Partnerships, Estates, and Trusts,* for a detailed discussion of corporate distributions.

the shareholder does not realize income.[70] However, if the share-holder has the option of receiving either cash or stock in the corporation, then the individual realizes taxable income whether he or she receives stock or cash. A taxpayer who elects to receive the stock could be deemed in constructive receipt of the cash he or she rejected.[71] Under § 305(b), the stock dividend is taxable and the amount of income is the value of the stock received, rather than the cash the share-holder rejected.

In recent years many public utilities corporations have adopted dividend policies that allow the shareholder to choose between cash or additional shares of stock. These stocks in lieu of cash schemes are commonly referred to as "dividend reinvestment plans." Dividends from these plans received by individuals are eligible for an exclusion of $750 per year ($1,500 on a joint return).[72] The exclusion is elective (made by indicating on the tax return that the election is being made). If the individual elects to exclude the value of the stock from income, the taxpayer's cost basis in the stock is zero. The proceeds from the sale of the stock are taxed as ordinary income if the sale occurs within one year after receipt of the dividend. A sale more than one year after receipt of the stock will produce a long-term capital gain equal to the proceeds.[73]

> **Example 23.** In 1983, individuals C and D each received shares of stock under a public utility dividend reinvestment plan. C and D each received stock with a value of $200. C elected to exclude his dividends from income, but D included her dividends in gross income for 1983. In 1985, C and D each sold the shares received in 1983 for $300. C's and D's long-term capital gain for 1985 would be computed as follows:

	C	D
Sales price	$ 300	$ 300
Basis	–0–	200
Long-term capital gain	$ 300	$ 100

The exclusion is available from 1982 to 1985. As the short life of the dividend reinvestment plan exclusion indicates, Congress is experimenting. The objective of the exclusion is to assist public utilities in meeting capital needs for the future. The availability of the exclu-

---

70. *Eisner v. Macomber,* 1 USTC ¶ 32, 3 AFTR 3020, 40 S.Ct. 189 (USSC, 1920); § 305(a).
71. See the discussion of constructive receipt in Chapter 5.
72. § 305(e).
73. § 305(e).

sion allows public utilities to remain competitive in the capital markets without having to distribute cash to shareholders and thus permits the industry to expand through internally generated funds.

TAX BENEFIT RULE

Generally, if a taxpayer obtains a deduction for an item in one year and later recovers a portion of the prior deduction, the recovery produces taxable income in the year it is received.[74]

> **Example 24.** A taxpayer who uses the direct charge-off method[75] for bad debts deducted as a loss a $1,000 receivable from a customer when it appeared the amount would never be collected. The following year the customer paid $800 on the receivable. The taxpayer must report as income the $800 in the year it is received.

However, § 111 provides that no income is recognized upon the recovery of a deduction, or the portion of a deduction, that did not yield a tax benefit in the year it was taken. Thus, if the taxpayer in the above example had no tax liability in the year of the deduction (e. g., the excess itemized deductions, the zero bracket amount, and personal exemptions exceeded adjusted gross income), the recovery would be partially or totally excluded from income in the year of the recovery.

> **Example 25.** T has adjusted gross income of $2,500 after deducting a $1,000 uncollectible receivable. T's zero bracket amount and personal exemptions for that year were $3,300. Of the $1,000, $800 would not be taxable income in the year it was collected, since the taxpayer did not receive a tax benefit for this amount in the year of the write-off ($2,500 + $800 − $3,300 = 0). However, if $1,000 were collected on the account, T would have to report $200 income in the year of collection ($2,500 + $1,000 − $3,300 = $200). (This example assumes that the taxpayer received no benefit from the carryback or carryover of the $800 loss under the net operating loss provisions.)[76]

The Code specifically mentions "bad debts, prior taxes and delinquency amounts" as items subject to the tax benefit rule. However, due to a Supreme Court decision,[77] the Regulations have been expanded to make § 111 applicable to recoveries "with respect to all

---

74. § 111(a). See the Glossary of Tax Terms (Appendix C) for a discussion of the term "tax benefit rule" and its application to medical expenses.

75. See Chapter 8 for a discussion of bad debts.

76. See Reg. 1.111–1(b)(3) Example for the computation of tax benefit arising from the utilization of net operating losses. Net operating losses are discussed in Chapter 8.

77. *Dobson v. Comm.*, 44–1 USTC ¶ 9108, 31 AFTR 773, 64 S.Ct. 239 (USSC, 1944).

losses, expenditures, and accruals made the basis of deductions from gross income for prior taxable years."[78]

> **Example 26.** T, a cash basis taxpayer, received a state income tax refund in 19X2 relating to her 19X1 state income taxes. The refunded amount was deductible on T's 19X1 Federal income tax return (assuming T itemized her deductions in 19X1). Thus, the state income tax refund must be included in T's gross income for 19X2. If T used the zero bracket amount in 19X1, the refund is not includible in gross income because she did not receive a tax benefit in 19X1.[79]

> **Example 27.** T, a cash basis taxpayer, is a member of a farmers' cooperative. At the end of the year the cooperative sends a rebate (a patronage dividend) to its members on the basis of each member's purchases during the year. For 19X1, 25% of T's total purchases of $10,000 was for personal (nondeductible) items, and the other 75% represented deductible business expenditures (e. g., seed, feed, and fertilizer). T had taxable income in 19X1 and deducted the business expenses. In 19X2, T received a $500 rebate based on the 19X1 purchases. Of this amount, $375 (75% × $500) must be included in gross income as a recovery of the prior deduction.

INCOME FROM DISCHARGE OF INDEBTEDNESS

A transfer of appreciated property in satisfaction of a debt is an event which triggers the realization of income. The transaction is treated as a sale of the appreciated property followed by a payment of the debt.[80]

Frequently the transfer occurs as a result of foreclosure by the creditor. But in many cases, the creditor will not foreclose and will even forgive a portion of the debt to insure the vitality of the debtor.

> **Example 28.** X Corporation is unable to meet the mortgage payments on its factory building. Both the corporation and the mortgage holder are aware of the depressed market for industrial property in the area. Foreclosure would only result in the creditor's obtaining unsalable property. To improve X Corporation's financial position, and thus improve its chances of obtaining the additional credit from other lenders necessary for survival, the

---

78. Reg. § 1.111–1(a).
79. Itemized deductions are discussed in Chapter 11, and the zero bracket amount was discussed in Chapter 4.
80. *Crane v. Commissioner*, 47–1 USTC ¶ 9217, 35 AFTR 776, 67 S.Ct. 1047 (USSC, 1947).

creditor agrees to forgive all amounts past due and to reduce the principal amount of the mortgage.

Prior case law had held that the reduction in indebtedness was a taxable event.[81] The rationale of these cases was that the debt adjustment was a transaction that increased the taxpayer's net worth. However, the courts also developed numerous exceptions to this general rule.

The Bankruptcy Tax Act of 1980[82] established an almost uniform rule of nonrecognition of income from the discharge of indebtedness.[83] The gain realized but not recognized (the reduction in indebtedness) is applied against the taxpayer's basis (cost less depreciation) in assets.[84] Thus, the gain is merely deferred until the assets are sold (or depreciated).

> **Example 29.** X, Inc., issued bonds for $1,000,000. Two years later the corporation repurchased the bonds on the open market for $900,000. X, Inc., realized a $100,000 gain on the retirement of the debt. The corporation may exclude the gain from income and reduce the bases in assets by $100,000.

The following discharge of indebtedness situations are subject to special treatment:

—Creditor's gifts.[85]

—Shareholder's cancellation of the corporation's indebtedness.[86]

—The discharge of an individual's nonbusiness indebtedness for less than the amount due.

If the creditor reduces the debt as an act of "love, affection or generosity," the debtor has simply received a nontaxable gift. Rarely will a gift be found to have occurred in a business context. A businessperson may settle a debt for less than the amount due, but as a matter of business expediency (e. g., high collection costs or disputes as to contract terms) rather than generosity.[87] If the reduction is not a gift,

---

81. *U. S. v. Kirby Lumber Co.,* 2 USTC ¶ 814, 10 AFTR 458, 52 S.Ct. 4 (USSC, 1931), codified in § 61(a)(12).

82. §§ 108 and 1017.

83. Income must be recognized if the debtor is a solvent (assets exceed liabilities) individual and the indebtedness was not incurred to finance property used in a trade or business. § 108(a). In the case of corporate and individual's business indebtedness, the taxpayer must elect nonrecognition of gain [§ 108(d)(4)(B)]. According to FASB Statement No. 4, the gain must be recognized for financial reporting.

84. § 1017. Forthcoming regulations will explain how the total nonrecognized gain will be allocated among assets. Insolvent and bankrupt taxpayers have additional options for allocating the gain to tax attributes other than bases (e. g., net operating loss carryovers and investment credit). § 108(b).

85. *Helvering v. American Dental Co.,* 43–1 USTC ¶ 9318, 30 AFTR 397, 63 S.Ct. 577 (USSC, 1943).

86. § 108(e)(6).

87. *Comm. v. Jacobson,* 49–1 USTC ¶ 9133, 37 AFTR 516, 69 S.Ct. 358 (USCC, 1949).

generally a debtor can elect to reduce his or her basis in the property unless one of the two other exceptions applies.

A shareholder's cancellation of the corporation's indebtedness to him or her (the second exception) is considered a contribution of capital to the corporation. Thus, the corporation's paid-in capital is increased and its liabilities are decreased by the same amount.

The final exception is very narrow but has frequently encountered applications. If the debt was not incurred in a trade or business (i. e., the debt was incurred for personal or investment purposes) and the debtor is solvent after the indebtedness is reduced, the debtor must recognize income.[88]

> **Example 30.** In 19X1, T borrowed $20,000 from the National Bank to purchase her personal residence. T agreed to make monthly principal and interest payments for 120 months. The interest rate on the note was 8%. In 19X4, when the balance on the note had been reduced through monthly payments to $18,000, the bank agreed to accept $15,000 in full settlement of the note. The bank made the offer because interest rates had increased to 15%. T accepted the bank's offer. As a result, T must recognize $3,000 ($18,000 − $15,000) income.[89]

TAX PLANNING CONSIDERATIONS

The present law excludes certain types of economic gains from taxation. Therefore, tax planning techniques may be useful to assist taxpayers in obtaining the maximum benefits from the exclusion of such gains. Below are some of the tax planning opportunities made available by the exclusions described in the preceding sections of this chapter.

GIFTS AND INHERITANCES

Family tax planning is largely concerned with shifting income-producing property among family members. The gift and inheritance exclusions facilitate these intrafamily transfers.

It should be recognized that the exclusions apply only to the recipient of the gift. The donor generally recognizes no income from the gift, because he or she realizes nothing; however, the donor may be subject to a gift tax on the transfer.[90] In a recent Supreme Court deci-

---

88. §§ 108(a)(1) and 108(d)(4).
89. Rev.Rul. 82–202, 1982–1 C.B. 35.
90. See Chapters 11–13 of *West's Federal Taxation: Corporations Partnerships, Estates, and Trusts* for a detailed discussion of the gift tax.

sion, the gift tax and income tax rules overlapped and the donor was required to recognize income.[91]

> **Example 31.** F gave S stock with a cost to F of $30,000 and a value of $300,000. S accepted the property on the condition that he would pay F's $40,000 gift tax on the transfer. F was required to recognize a $10,000 gain ($40,000 − $30,000) from the transfer of appreciated property in satisfaction of his liability.

Income must also be recognized if the donee assumes a mortgage in excess of the donor's basis in the property.

LIFE INSURANCE

Life insurance offers several favorable tax attributes. As discussed in Chapter 5, the annual increase in the cash surrender value of the policy is not taxable (because no income has been actually or constructively received). By borrowing on its cash surrender value, the owner can actually receive in cash the increase in value of the policy but without recognition of income. Beneficiaries can collect the proceeds of the policy without recognition of gain. And a beneficiary can even receive an additional $1,000 per year of tax-exempt interest income from the insurance company if the life insurance proceeds are collected in installments and the beneficiary is the insured decedent's spouse.

Whether collecting proceeds in installments is preferable depends upon the interest rate paid by the insurance company, alternative rates of return, and the spouse's marginal tax rate.

> **Example 32.** Mrs. T is the beneficiary of her husband's $50,000 life insurance policy. She can elect to receive the face amount of the policy or $7,500 ($2,500 interest) per year for 10 years which will yield 8% before-tax interest. Assume she can invest the $50,000 in savings certificates yielding 12% and is in the 30% marginal tax bracket. Mrs. T's effective tax rate on the installment payments is 18% [[($2,500 − $1,000) ÷ $2,500] × .30 = .18]; thus, her after-tax rate of return is 6.56% [(1 − .18)(.08)]. The after-tax rate of return on the time certificates is 8.4% [(1 − .30)(.12)]. Therefore, the insurance company will have to present some reasons, other than rate of return on investment, to make the installment payments the preferable option.

EMPLOYEE BENEFITS

Generally, employees view accident and health insurance, as well as life insurance, as necessities. Employees can obtain group coverage at

---

91. *Diedrich vs Comm.*, 82–1 USTC ¶ 9419, 50 AFTR2d 82–5053, 102 S.Ct. 2414 (USSC, 1982).

much lower rates than individuals would have to pay for the same protection. Moreover, premiums paid by the employer can be excluded from gross income. Because of the exclusion, employees will have a greater after-tax and after-insurance income if the employer pays a lower salary but also pays the insurance premiums.

Example 33. Individual A receives a salary of $30,000. The company has group insurance benefits, but A was required to pay his own premiums as follows:

Hospitalization and medical insurance	$ 1,400
Term life insurance ($30,000)	200
Disability insurance	400
	$ 2,000

To simplify the analysis, assume A's average and marginal tax rate on income is 25%. After paying taxes of $7,500 (.25 × $30,000) and $2,000 for insurance, A has $20,500 ($30,000 − $7,500 − $2,000) for his other living needs.

If A's employer reduced A's pay by $2,000 (to $28,000) but paid A's insurance premiums, A's tax liability would be only $7,000 ($28,000 × .25). Thus, A would have $21,000 ($28,000 − $7,000) to meet his living needs other than insurance. The change in the compensation plan would save $500 ($21,000 − $20,500).

Similarly, the employer's payment of the employee's child care and group legal services are attractive nontaxable employee fringe benefits.

The meals and lodging exclusion enables the employee to receive from his or her employers what he or she ordinarily must purchase with after-tax dollars. While the requirements that the employee live and take his or her meals on the employer's premises limit the tax planning opportunities, in certain situations, the exclusion is an important factor in the employer's compensation (e. g., hotels, motels, restaurants, farms, and ranches).

It should be recognized that the exclusion of benefits discussed above are generally available only to employees. Proprietors and partners must pay tax on the same benefits their employees receive tax-free. By incorporating and becoming an employee of the corporation, the former proprietor or partner can also receive these tax-exempt benefits. Thus, the availability of employee benefits is a consideration in the decision to incorporate.

Nonstatutory Fringe Benefits. Generally, an employer can provide a variety of incidental benefits which, if made available to all employees, will not be taxable income. Examples of these benefits are company-provided recreational facilities, travel passes for airline employees, and limited personal use of company telephones. However, it should be recognized that the tax treatment of nonstatutory fringe benefits may be changed in the near future, and abuses of the exclusion will not be tolerated by the IRS.

INVESTOR ITEMS

The investor can choose from a variety of tax-favored investments discussed in this chapter. Funds can be invested in stocks paying annual dividends until the $100 ($200 on a joint return) exclusion is reached. Then funds can be invested in public utilities reinvestment plans until $750 ($1,500 on a joint return) in stock dividends have been received. Once these exclusions have been exhausted, tax-exempt state and local bonds can be purchased.

Public utilities reinvestment plans offer both a tax exemption and a tax deferral. The exemption is not the entire amount of dividends. Assuming the shareholder holds the stocks received as a dividend for more than one year, the gain on the sale is a long-term capital gain; thus, 60 percent of the income is excluded. But the shareholder has control over when he or she recognizes the gain. Thus, the investor may defer the income indefinitely or sell the stock and recognize the gain in a year when he or she has capital losses to offset the income. Over a period of years, the investor could accumulate sufficient deferred capital gains from these stocks that capital losses would never exceed the limitation of $3,000 per year.

PROBLEM MATERIALS

Questions for Class Discussion

1. What are the possible tax consequences to an owner of land when a tenant constructs a permanent building on the property?

2. Who pays the tax on a gift of the income from a certain piece of property —the donee or the donor?

3. What is a gift?

4. (a) A served as chairman of the local school board. Upon completion of his term in office, the organization awarded him a silver serving tray in recognition of his outstanding service to the organization. The value of the tray is $200. Is A required to include the value of the tray in his income?

   (b) Assume the employees took up a collection and purchased the tray for A.

5. Under what conditions can payments to the family of a deceased employee be excluded from gross income?

6. What types of payments made by the employer to the family of a deceased employee would not be eligible for the employee death benefit exclusion?

7. Under what conditions are life insurance proceeds subject to taxation?

8. How do the tax laws influence a survivor's choice of a settlement option under a life insurance policy on the life of his or her deceased spouse?

9. In cases involving doctors serving an internship or residency in a hospital, what criteria are used to determine whether the pay received by the doctor is an excludible scholarship or fellowship?

10. X Company has a scholarship program for children of its employees. Employees with more than four years of service can receive up to $1,000 as reimbursement of college tuition paid by the employee. Are the payments excludible as scholarships?

11. If a taxpayer receives damages to compensate for injuries suffered in an automobile accident, the payment is generally excludible from taxable income. Is the tax treatment of payments for personal injury and damages to property consistent?

12. What nontaxable fringe benefits are available to employees that are not available to partners and proprietors?

13. What are the possible tax consequences for a corporation that establishes a medical expense reimbursement plan covering only one employee who also owns all of the corporation's outstanding stock?

14. S earned $400 in the month of June. J received $400 in disability pay. If the tax formula reflects the taxpayer's ability to pay, why should S pay tax when J pays no tax?

15. How does one determine if the meals and lodging supplied by the employer is to serve a valid business purpose? Is the tax treatment of meals and lodging affected if the employer advertises that the meals and lodging provided are one of the employees' fringe benefits?

16. What special tax treatment is available to U. S. citizens who work abroad?

17. What would be the social and economic consequences of eliminating the tax exemption now granted for interest on state and local government bonds?

18. What alternative means could be used to accomplish the purpose of the dividends received exclusion for individuals?

19. What are the tax consequences of recovering an amount deducted on a previous year's tax return?

20. How does the tax treatment of a corporation's income generated by the retirement of bonds for less than book value (issue price plus amortized discount or less amortized premium) differ from the income derived from a shareholder's forgiveness of the corporation's indebtedness?

21. Does the receipt of stock dividends under a public utilities reinvestment plan result in tax-exempt income or merely tax-deferred income?

Problems

22. Determine whether the following may be excluded from gross income as gifts, bequests, scholarships, prizes, or life insurance proceeds.

    (a) Uncle told Nephew, "Come live with me and take care of me in my old age and you can have all my property after my death." Nephew complied with Uncle's request. Uncle's will made Nephew sole beneficiary of the estate.

(b) Uncle told Nephew, "If you study hard and make the Dean's List this year, I will pay your tuition for the following year." Nephew made the Dean's List and Uncle paid the tuition.

(c) Uncle told Nephew, "If you make the Dean's List this year, I will pay you $500." Nephew made the Dean's List and Uncle paid the $500.

(d) D cashed in her life insurance contract and collected $10,000. She had paid premiums totaling $7,000.

23. R Company has a qualified pension plan with survivor's benefits. Mr. K was employed by R company at the time of his death. He had contributed $4,000 to the plan, and his nonforfeitable benefits were valued at $15,000. Mrs. K had the option of receiving $21,000 in a lump sum or an annuity of $2,400 per year for 20 years. The present value of the annuity was also $21,000.

(a) Assuming Mrs. K elected the lump-sum option, compute her taxable income from receipt of the $21,000.

(b) Assuming Mrs. K elected the annuity option, compute her taxable income from collection of the first $2,400.

24. T died during 1984 at age 64. T was hospitalized for the six weeks before his death, and he continued to receive his regular salary of $200 per week. Total salary received during the year until his death was $9,000, with the last paycheck being paid to his spouse. T and his wife had other income of $6,000 for the year, before considering the data below:

(a) At the time of T's death, he had accumulated $20,000 in a qualified employee retirement plan to which he had contributed $5,000. None of T's benefits were forfeitable. T's wife elected to collect the benefits as an annuity of $150 per week and received $1,050 in the year T died.

(b) The employer also paid the wife $2,000 "in appreciation of T's past services to the company."

(c) The wife also was the beneficiary of T's $10,000 life insurance policy and elected to leave the proceeds with the insurance company. She received $155 interest on the proceeds in the calendar year of T's death.

Compute Mr. and Mrs. T's adjusted gross income assuming a joint return is filed in 1984.

25. Determine the taxable life insurance proceeds in the following case.

(a) In 19X1, B purchased a sports franchise and player contracts from S. As part of the transaction, B purchased from S, for $50,000, a life insurance contract on a key player. One month later, the player was killed in an automobile accident and B collected $500,000 on the life insurance contract.

(b) P and R formed a partnership and agreed that upon the death of either partner, the surviving partner would purchase the decedent's partnership interest. P purchased a life insurance policy on R's life and paid $5,000 in premiums. Upon R's death, P collected $100,000 on the life insurance policy and used the proceeds to purchase R's interest in the partnership.

(c) Same as (b), except the partnership was incorporated and P and R owned all the stock. Upon incorporation, P and R transferred their life insurance policies to the corporation in exchange for stock. When R died, the corporation redeemed (purchased) R's stock using the $100,000 life insurance proceeds.

26. The taxpayer was a chemist working for a large corporation when he decided to return to a university to earn a Ph.D. He discussed his plans with his supervisor who encouraged him to pursue his studies but said the company could not pay him or hold his job while he was gone. However, the supervisor said the company was interested in any type of research concerned with controlling air pollutants because of the potential commercial markets, and the company would sponsor his dissertation if it were in the area of pollution. The taxpayer wrote a dissertation proposal, the company reviewed it, and they awarded him a $10,000 scholarship. Under the agreement, the company had no rights to the taxpayer's research effort. Because of the taxpayer's new area of expertise, the employer offered him a new higher paying job when he completed his degree requirement. His first assignment was to develop his dissertation into a new product. Is the $10,000 an excludible fellowship?

27. T served as the manager of an orphanage is 19X8. In this connection he had the following transactions:

    (a) He received no salary from his job but was given room and board (valued at $3,600) on the premises. No other person was employed by the orphanage which is a tax-exempt organization.

    (b) The orphanage paid $300 in tuition for a night course T took at a local university. The course was in the field of philosophy and dealt with the meaning of life. The payment was authorized by the orphanage's trustees in a written resolution.

    (c) The orphanage paid $500 of the premiums on T's life insurance policy and all of his medical expenses of $1,800. Again, the payment was made pursuant to a resolution approved by the trustees.

    (d) T received $1,000 as a cash award in recognition of his services to the orphanage. The award is given each year by a local civic organization to a "great humanitarian."

    Determine the effect of these transactions on T's gross income.

28. A, age 40, is an officer of the XYZ Company which provided the following fringe benefits in 1984:

    (a) Group-term life insurance protection of $80,000.

    (b) Group hospitalization insurance, $1,080.

    (c) Reimbursement of $2,800 from an uninsured medical reimbursement plan maintained exclusively for highly compensated employees.

    (d) Salary continuation payments for $3,000 while A was hospitalized for an illness.

    (e) In addition, $1,800 was collected from a wage continuation policy purchased by A.

    Which items are includible in gross income?

29. Which of the following payments for damages would be taxable?

(a) A corporation received $100,000 from a competitor for infringement of its patent rights.

(b) A woman is paid $60,000 because her personal files were incorporated in a biography without her consent.

(c) A client is paid $12,000 by an investment counselor as reimbursement for a loss resulting from the counselor's poor advice.

30. An overly aggressive bill collector broke K's arm. As a result of the break, K lost 25% of the use of the arm and incurred $3,000 medical expenses.

(a) K filed suit against the collector and received $75,000 for the disability, $3,000 medical expenses, and $15,000 punitive damages (based on the collector's outrageous behavior). The disability damages ($75,000) were based on the estimated decrease in K's future income.

(b) K collected $3,000 on his health insurance policy for the medical expenses.

(c) K's employer also covered K's medical expenses under a group hospitalization insurance policy. K collected $3,000 on the employer's policy.

What is K's gross income from the receipts related to the injury?

31. R was injured in an accident that was not related to his employment. He incurred $10,000 in medical expenses and collected $7,500 on a medical insurance policy he purchased. He also collected $9,500 in medical benefits under his employer's group plan. Originally the doctor diagnosed R's injury as requiring no more than three months of disability. Because of subsequent complications, R was unable to return to work until 14 months after the accident. While away from the job, R collected $200 per week on his employer's wage continuation plan. R also owned an insurance policy which paid him $100 per week while he was disabled. What are the tax consequences of the receipts of the

(a) $17,000 medical benefits?

(b) $300 per week to replace his wages?

32. Does the taxpayer recognize taxable income in the following situations?
(a) A is a registered nurse working in a community hospital. She is not required to take her lunch on the hospital premises, but she can eat in the cafeteria at no charge. The hospital adopted this policy to encourage employees to stay on the premises and be available in case of emergencies. During the year, A ate most of her meals on the premises. The total value of those meals was $750.

(b) J is the manager of a hotel. His employer will allow him either to live in one of the rooms rent free or to receive a $200 per month cash allowance for rent. J elected to live in the hotel.

(c) S is a forest ranger and lives in his employer's cabin in the forest. He is required to live there, and because there are no restaurants nearby, the employer supplies S with groceries that he cooks and eats on the premises.

(d) T is a partner in the ABC Ranch (a partnership). He is the full-time manager of the ranch, and there is a business purpose for his living on the ranch.

33. Analyze the following in terms of the meals and lodging exclusions.

    (a) During the busy season when employees are required to work 10 to 12 hour days, the employees receive $5 per day as supper money. The employees eat in local restaurants.

    (b) The N Corporation maintains a dining room for its executives so that good business use can be made of the lunch hour. However, executives are not required to eat in the company's dining room.

    (c) The S Corporation pays for its executives' business meals at the C City Club. The company also pays for the executives to stay overnight at the club when they work too late to return home at night.

34. Dr. T received a summer research fellowship from her employer, State University. Dr. T received $5,000 on June 1, 19X1, for her living expenses for the period June through August. However, Dr. T spent approximately 20 hours per week from September through December 19X1 completing the project. The fellowship was awarded on the basis of a research proposal submitted by Dr. T. The fellowship program was instituted to stimulate research efforts by new faculty members. What is Dr. T's gross income from the above transactions?

35. R is a U. S. citizen and a production manager for the XYZ Company. On May 1, 1984, he was temporarily assigned to the Monterrey, Mexico, plant. On August 6, 1984, he returned to the United States for medical treatment. On September 1, 1984, he returned to his duties in Monterrey. Except for a two-week period in the United States (December 16–31, 1984), he worked in Monterrey until December 1, 1985, when he was transferred to Boston, Massachusetts. R's salary was $4,000 per month in 1984 and $5,000 per month in 1985. His housing expense did not exceed the base amount. Compute R's foreign earned income exclusion in 1984 and 1985.

36. (a) If state government bonds are yielding 5%, what rate of interest would have to be paid on a taxable bond of comparable risk in order to attract investors who are in the 40% marginal tax bracket?

    (b) J's home was condemned by the state for a highway right-of-way. J contested the valuation placed on his property. It took two years to settle the case. Upon settlement, J received $40,000 for his property and $3,000 interest on the condemnation award. He also collected $4,000 interest on the city's industrial development bonds. The proceeds of the bonds were used to finance construction of a municipal airport. Which, if any, of the above are includible in gross income?

37. Assume Congress is considering eliminating the partial interest exclusion (scheduled to take effect in 1985) and adding an exclusion for the first $100 ($200 on a joint return) of interest income, as is allowed for dividends.

    (a) Which income group (high, low) would benefit from the change?

    (b) Is the rationale for the dividends exclusion also applicable to interest income (and thus supportive of the net interest exclusion)?

38. During 1984 A received $60 in dividends on stock she owned in AT Company. A's spouse also owned shares in the same corporation and received $120 in dividends. They jointly owned stock in another domestic corporation which paid $50 in dividends and stock in a French corporation which paid $40 in dividends. They also have a joint account in a savings and loan

association which paid $80 in dividends, and A collected a $30 dividend on her life insurance policy.

    (a) Calculate the § 116 exclusion for Mr. and Mrs. A on a joint tax return, assuming they reside in a common law state.

    (b) Calculate the § 116 exclusion if Mr. and Mrs. A file separate returns.

39. Determine a cash basis taxpayer's gross income for 19X2 from the following transactions:

    (a) Redemption of Series E U. S. savings bonds for $8,750. The cost of these bonds was $6,250, and no income previously had been recognized on the bonds.

    (b) Sale of state of New York bonds for $10,500 plus $200 in accrued interest. The bonds cost $10,000.

    (c) Receipt of $1,680 from the state of New York which represented a state income tax refund for tax year 19X0 of $1,500 plus $180 in interest. The taxpayer had itemized deductions of $7,000 on the 19X0 Federal income tax return which reported over $60,000 in taxable income.

40. During 1984 H(husband) and W(wife) had dividends and other receipts from investments as follows:

July 2   H received two shares of A Manufacturing Company common stock as a stock dividend. H had the option of receiving $150 cash.

Sept. 30 H received two shares of C Electric Corporation common stock under a dividend reinvestment plan. He had the option of receiving $150 cash, which was the value of the shares received.

Oct. 15 H sold two shares of C Electric stock for $160. The shares were received in December 1983 and treated as dividends received under a public utilities reinvestment plan on his 1983 return.

Dec. 15 They received $70 cash dividends from B Manufacturing Company on stock owned jointly by H and W.

Dec. 31 W collected $120 cash dividends from CD Company, a Canadian corporation.

Dec. 31 W received notice from the bank that $120 had been credited to her savings account. She did not withdraw the interest.

Compute gross income for H and W on a joint return.

41. In a previous year, a cash basis taxpayer took a deduction for an $8,000 commission paid to a broker who supposedly located a customer for the taxpayer's products. Actually, the customer did not have the necessary capital to buy the taxpayer's product, and the broker was aware of this at the time he collected his commission. In the current year, following the threat of a suit, the broker refunded the commission. The taxpayer is in a higher marginal tax bracket in the current year than he was in the year the commission was deducted. Can he obtain any relief under § 111?

42. T, who is in the 40% marginal tax bracket, recently collected $100,000 on a life insurance policy she carried on her father. She presently owes $120,000 on her personal residence and $120,000 on business property. The National Bank holds the mortgage on both pieces of property and has agreed to accept $100,000 in complete satisfaction of either mortgage.

The interest rate on the mortgages is 8%, and both mortgages are payable over 10 years. T can also purchase Montgomery County school bonds yielding 8%. What would be the tax consequences of each of the following alternatives, assuming T presently deducts the mortgage interest on her tax return?

(a) Retire the mortgage on the residence.

(b) Retire the mortgage on the business property.

(c) Purchase tax-exempt bonds but not pay off either mortgage.

Which alternative should T select?

Cumulative Problems

43. H was divorced from F on May 12, 1983. On September 6, 1984, he married W, with whom he files a joint return for 1984.

    H is 49 and is employed as an electrical engineer. His salary for 1984 was $46,200. W is 30 and earned $24,000 as a marriage counselor in 1984.

    The decree of divorce required H to pay F a principal sum of $100,000 in installments of $12,000 a year for the first 5 years and $8,000 a year for the next 5 years and 1 month. He was also required to pay $200 a month in child support for D, their daughter, age 11. F was granted custody of D and can document that she provided $2,000 of support for D.

    H's employer provided him with group-term life insurance coverage in the amount of $90,000 in 1984.

    W's employer provided her with free parking in a parking garage adjacent to their office building. The monthly charge to the general public is $50.

    H received dividends of $40 on stock he owned before marriage, and W received dividends of $50 on her separately owned stock. They received dividends of $100 on jointly owned stock which they had acquired after marriage. H and W live in a common law state.

    Combined itemized deductions for H and W in 1984 were $6,400, not including state income taxes withheld by their employers. H's employer withheld $810 for state income taxes, and W's employer withheld $430. W received a refund of 1983 state income taxes of $250. She had deducted state income taxes withheld as an itemized deduction on her 1983 return.

    Compute income tax, before prepayments or credits, for H and W for 1984.

44. T, who is single, age 44, provided over half the support for the following individuals during 1984.

    (a) M, her widowed mother, age 67, who received $1,000 of dividend income in 1984; M lived in an apartment rented for her by T.

    (b) S, her 19-year-old son, who earned $2,500 during 1984 working part-time as a busboy; S is not a student, lived at home with T, and put all of his earnings into a savings account.

    (c) F, a friend of T who lived in T's home all year, free of charge, while recovering from a serious illness; F had no income.

    (d) U, her unmarried sister, who lives in England; U is a citizen of England, where she has lived all her life.

T is a college professor and earned $29,100 in 1984. She was married to D, who died on September 30, 1984. D was a salesman and earned $22,000 in 1984 before his death. On December 20, 1984, T received a $7,000 death benefit from D's employer as a result of his death.

T was the beneficiary of a $200,000 life insurance policy on D. Instead of taking the entire $200,000 in 1984, T elected to receive the principal in 10 installments of $20,000 each plus interest on the unpaid principal. In 1984, she received $24,000 from the insurance company.

T and D filed their 1983 state income tax return on April 15, 1984. They received a state income tax refund of $800 on May 25, 1984. They did not itemize deductions on their 1983 Federal income tax return.

On February 15, 1984 T and D received 10 shares of stock under a public utility dividend reinvestment plan. You are to handle this in a way which will minimize taxable income for 1984.

Prior to D's death, D and T had received dividends of $100 on jointly owned stock. On D's death, T became sole owner of the stock. On December 15, T received additional dividends of $100.

On May 15, 1984, T and D sold 100 shares of stock for $20 a share. They had acquired the stock on June 1, 1983, for $30 a share.

T and D had itemized deductions of $7,800 before D's death. After D's death, T incurred additional itemized deductions of $1,200.

T has asked you to compute her income tax for 1984. As a competent tax practitioner, you will compute the lowest legal tax liability based on the above information. Use the 1984 Tax Rate Schedule.

Tax Form Problems

45. K retired on June 30, 1980, and started receiving pension payments of $300 a month on July 15, 1980. During 1983, K received $3,600 in pension payments. He had contributed $9,315 to the employer/employee-financed pension fund. Compute his taxable pension for 1983 on lines 16 and/or 17 of Form 1040.

Cumulative Tax Return Problem

46. T, age 45, is married and has two dependent children. In 1983, he had the following transactions:

1.	Salary received from his employer	$ 60,000
2.	Interest received on state of Nebraska General Obligation Bonds	8,000
3.	Group-term life insurance premiums paid by his employer (coverage of $40,000)	80
4.	Annual increment in the redemption value of Series E Government savings bonds (T has not previously included the accrued amounts in gross income)	400

5.	Taxable dividends received from U. S. companies (held jointly). Of the $5,900 in dividends, $1,000 was mailed by a company on December 31, 1983, and received by T on January 2, 1984	5,900
6.	Alimony payments made to T's former wife under a divorce decree	6,000
7.	Itemized deductions	6,800
8.	Federal income tax withheld and quarterly estimated tax payments	14,000

Required:

(a) Determine T's adjusted gross income and taxable income for 1983. Preparation of pages 1 and 2 of Form 1040 and Schedule B is suggested. Assume that T files a joint return with his wife who has no other items of income or deductions.

(b) Determine T's tax liability and net tax payable (or refund due) for 1983.

Research Problems

47. S was asked by the M County School Board to resign her position as superintendent of public schools. She refused and submitted to the board a list of grievances. She also alleged that the board had damaged her professional reputation. S was later fired, but after threatening suit she was paid $20,000 by the board.

    S has supplied a doctor's testimony clearly showing that the dispute with the board caused her to become physically and mentally ill.

    Is the $20,000 taxable?

48. The taxpayer, a resident of Nevada, appeared on a television quiz program and won a new sailboat. The producer of the program had paid $7,500.00 for the boat. However, the taxpayer had no interest in sailing, lived 400 miles from the nearest large body of water, and needed cash. Therefore, the taxpayer visited several boat dealers offering the boat for sale. He eventually sold the boat to a dealer for $5,500.00. The IRS contends the taxpayer's income from the prize is $7,500.00. Is the IRS correct?

49. Mr. B is president of Family Entertainment Centers, Inc. The company owns and franchises combination pizza and video game parlors. The company's major market is families with children under 15. Mr. B frequently makes trips to the centers to discuss business with the operators and to visit with customers to see what they like and dislike about the centers. It is consistent with the company image for Mr. B's wife to accompany him on these trips. Although she is not employed by the company, Mrs. B frequently asks questions during the customer interviews and discusses the results of the interviews with her husband.

    The IRS contends that Mr. B must include in his gross income the trip expenses the company pays for Mrs. B to accompany him. Is there any authoritative support for Mr. B to exclude such amounts from income?

50. In 19X1, C was unemployed and in dire need of money. D offered to pay C $100 if he would sign a statement to the effect that D had loaned C $5,000 and that he would never be able to pay the funds. D deducted the $5,000 as a bad debt on his tax return. C had actually borrowed the $5,000 from D. According to the IRS, C must recognize $5,000 income from discharge of indebtedness as evidenced by the statement he signed for D. Should C challenge the IRS position?

    Research Aid:

    William J. Patterson, 36 TCM 1189, T.C.Memo 1977–300.

Chapter 7

Deductions and Losses: In General

GENERAL TESTS FOR DEDUCTIBILITY

Following the discussion of gross income and inclusions and exclusions from gross income, it is necessary to review deductions and losses. Understanding the manner in which expense items are classified is a necessary prelude to the discussion of specific tax rules. Therefore, this chapter includes the initial discussion of the classification of expenses under the tax law.

As previously discussed, § 61 provides an all-inclusive definition of gross income. Deductions, however, must be specifically provided for in the statute.[1] The courts have established the doctrine that an item is not deductible unless a specific Code section provides for its deduction (i. e., whether and to what extent deductions shall be allowed depends on "legislative grace").[2]

SCHEME OF THE TREATMENT OF DEDUCTIONS AND LOSSES

There are three Code sections dealing with deductions and losses that have widespread applicability and as such, can be compared with Code § 61. These Code sections are § § 162, 165, and 212.

---

1. § 63(b).
2. *New Colonial Ice Co. v. Helvering*, 4 USTC ¶ 1292, 13 AFTR 1180, 54 S.Ct. 788 (USSC, 1934).

233

Section 162 allows a deduction for "all the ordinary and necessary expenses paid or incurred during the taxable year in carrying on any trade or business . . ." Section 165 provides a deduction for losses incurred in a trade or business, losses incurred in any transaction entered into for a profit (even though it is not a trade or business), and casualty losses. Section 212 allows deductions for expenses incurred in the production or collection of income; for expenses incurred in the management, conservation, or maintenance of property held for the production of income; and for expenses in connection with the determination, collection, or refund of any tax.

Section 162 deductions (i. e., trade or business deductions) are deductions *for* adjusted gross income and can be taken whether or not one itemizes. Section 212 deductions, on the other hand, are itemized deductions with the sole exception of expenses incurred in producing rental or royalty income, which are deductions *for* adjusted gross income. Section 165 deductions can be either *for* adjusted gross income or itemized. For example, a business casualty loss is deductible *for* adjusted gross income; a personal casualty loss is an itemized deduction.

The relationship between the three general expense classifications (§ § 162, 165, and 212) and § 62 is crucial in determining where a deduction is taken on the income tax return. Section 62 specifies which deductions are *for* adjusted gross income and includes (in addition to trade or business deductions) certain employee business expenses, the long-term capital gains deduction, rent and royalty expenses, alimony, and certain other expenses. The employee business expenses that are deductible *for* adjusted gross income are travel and transportation expenses (whether or not reimbursed), all expenses of an outside salesperson, and other reimbursed expenses. All other employee business expenses (e. g., unreimbursed dues and subscriptions) are itemized deductions. Contributions to retirement plans (Keogh Plans and Individual Retirement Accounts) are deductions *for* adjusted gross income. Moving expenses incurred in connection with a job in a new location are also deductions *for* adjusted gross income. Employee expenses, which are deductions *for* adjusted gross income, are discussed in detail in Chapter 10.

These three general expense classifications are supplemented by many Code sections dealing with specific expenses such as interest (§ 163), taxes (§ 164), and bad debts (§ 166). Such expenses are discussed later in this chapter and in following chapters.

Trade or Business Expenses. Section 162(a) permits a deduction for all "ordinary and necessary" expenses paid or incurred in carrying on a trade or business. These include reasonable salaries paid for personal services, traveling expenses incurred while away from home overnight in the pursuit of a business, and expenses for the use of business property.

The term "trade or business" is not defined in the Code or Regulations, and the courts have not provided a satisfactory definition. Therefore, it is usually necessary to ask one or more of the following questions to determine whether an item qualifies as a trade or business expense:

—Was the use of the particular item related to a business activity? If funds are borrowed for use in a business, the interest should be deductible as a business expense. However, if the funds were used to acquire passive investments (e. g., stocks and taxable bonds), the interest expense is an itemized deduction.

—Was the expenditure incurred with the intent to realize a profit or to produce income? Expenses in excess of the income from raising horses would not be deductible if the activity were conducted as a personal hobby.

—Were the taxpayer's operation and management activities extensive enough to indicate the carrying on of a trade or business?

Certain employee expenses are treated as § 162 expenses, since employment status is regarded as a trade or business. See Chapter 10 for further discussion.

Section 162 excludes the following items from classification as a trade or business expense:

—Charitable contributions or gifts.

—Illegal bribes and kickbacks and certain treble damage payments.

—Fines and penalties.

The Tax Equity and Fiscal Responsibility Act of 1982 relaxed the rules on so-called grease payments by making such a payment deductible unless it is unlawful under the Foreign Corrupt Practices Act of 1977. Formerly, any bribe was disallowed if it was paid to a foreign official and if it was illegal under the laws of the United States. The former law ignored the fact that bribes are accepted business practice in certain foreign countries and that U. S. businesses had to engage in such practices to do business abroad.

Business and Nonbusiness Losses. Section 165 provides for a deduction for losses sustained which are not compensated for by insurance, to the extent of the adjusted basis of the property involved.

For individual taxpayers, losses which result in a deduction are limited to those incurred in a trade or business or in a transaction entered into for profit. The only personal losses allowed are those that are the result of a casualty. Casualty losses include, but are not limited to, fire, storm, shipwreck, and theft (see Chapter 8 for a further discussion of this area). Deductible personal casualty losses are reduced by $100 per casualty and by 10 percent of adjusted gross income. The excess is an itemized deduction.

Expenses Attributable to the Production or Collection of Income. Section 212 provides for the deductibility of ordinary and necessary expenses which are paid or incurred:

—For the production or collection of income.

—For the management, conservation, or maintenance of property held for the production of income.

—In connection with the determination (including preparation), collection, or refund of any tax.

According to this definition, the following items would not be deductible:

—Expenses related to the management, conservation, or maintenance of a personal residence.[3]

—Expenses related to tax-exempt income.[4]

—Hobby, sport, or recreation expenses.[5]

Investment-related expenses (e. g., safe deposit box rentals) are deductible under § 212[6] as deductions attributable to the production of investment income. Investment-related expenses are deducted *from* adjusted gross income (i. e., itemized deductions) with the exception of rent and royalty expenses, which are deductible *for* adjusted gross income.[7]

To qualify for a deduction under § 212, it is not necessary for the property to be currently producing taxable income.[8] For example, a taxpayer who holds a former residence with the expectation of realizing appreciation in the market value may be entitled to expense deductions such as maintenance and depreciation even though the property is not held for rental purposes.[9]

Example 1. T moves into a new residence. Since real estate values in the area are rising rapidly, T decides to rent the former residence in anticipation of future appreciation. T rents the property on a break-even basis (i. e., the rent is equal to cash outlay). T is entitled to deduct depreciation, maintenance, and other related expenses.

Classification of Deductible Expenses. For individual taxpayers deductions are either (1) *for* adjusted gross income or (2) *from* adjusted

---

3. Reg. § 1.212–1(h).
4. Reg. § 1.212–1(e).
5. Reg. § 1.183–2(a).
6. Reg. § 1.212–1(g).
7. § 62(5).
8. Reg. § 1.212–1(b).
9. See *Frank A. Newcombe*, 54 T.C. 1298 (1970).

gross income (i. e., itemized deductions). Corporations are not subject to this separate classification scheme, since the term "adjusted gross income" does not appear in the corporate tax formula.[10] In the computation of taxable income for corporate taxpayers, items of expense either are deductible or are not deductible (e. g., certain corporate expenses which are unreasonable would not be deductible).

The most frequently encountered deductions *for* adjusted gross income of individual taxpayers include:

—Expenses of a trade, business, or profession (usually reported on Schedule C of Form 1040);

—Rent and royalty expenses. However, expenses attributable to the production or collection of income or to the management, conservation, or maintenance of property held for the production of income other than rent or royalty income are *from* adjusted gross income—i. e., itemized deductions.

—Certain employment-related expenses (e. g., traveling expenses including meals and lodging while away from home, transportation, moving, and employee expenses which are reimbursed by the employer).

—Alimony payments.

Some of the more frequently encountered deductions *from* adjusted gross income (itemized deductions) include the following:

—Contributions to qualified charitable organizations.

—Medical expenses in excess of five percent of adjusted gross income.

—State and local taxes (e. g., sales, real estate, and state and local income taxes).

—Investment-related expenses (e. g., safe deposit box rental and investment counsel or custodian fees).

The distinction between deductions *for* and *from* adjusted gross income is significant, since many tax calculations are based on the amount of adjusted gross income (e. g., medical expenses and contribution deduction limitations). Further, if an item is deductible *from* adjusted gross income as an itemized deduction, a taxpayer would not be able to benefit from such deduction unless the total of such deductions exceeds the zero bracket amount.

Example 2. T is married and files a joint return with his spouse in 19X4. He and his wife have adjusted gross income of $30,000 and have $2,400 of itemized deductions during the year. In December T asks you whether he should pay his real estate taxes of $400 in December or wait until the following January. Since the

---

10. See the discussion of corporate taxation in Chapter 20.

zero bracket amount for 19X4 is $3,400 and the real estate taxes are deductible only as itemized deductions, T would obtain no tax benefit from paying the real estate taxes in December and should, therefore, make the payment in January of the following year. Recall from Chapter 4 the tax planning opportunities in timing these deductions.

ORDINARY AND NECESSARY EXPENSES

The terms "ordinary" and "necessary" are found in both § § 162 and 212. Section 162 governs the deductibility of trade or business expenses. To be deductible under this provision of the Code, any trade or business expense must be "ordinary and necessary." In addition, salaries must be "reasonable" in amount. The Regulations under § 212 require that expenses must bear a reasonable and proximate relationship to the production or collection of income or to the management, conservation, or maintenance of property held for the production of income.[11]

> **Example 3.** W owned a small portfolio of investments left to her by her late husband. Part of this portfolio included 100 shares of T, Inc., common stock. W incurred $350 in travel expenses to attend the annual shareholders' meeting at which she voted her 100 shares against the current management group. Were W's expenses deductible under § 212? No deduction would be permitted, because the expenses must bear a reasonable and proximate relation to the value of the property investment.[12]

The words "ordinary and necessary" are not defined in the Code or Regulations. An expenditure must be both ordinary and necessary, but many expenses which are necessary are *not* ordinary. The courts have held that an expense is necessary if a prudent businessperson would incur the same expense which is expected to be appropriate and helpful in the taxpayer's business.[13]

An expense is ordinary if it is normal, usual, or customary in the type of business conducted by the taxpayer and is not capital in nature.[14] However, the courts have also held that an expense need not be recurring to be deductible as ordinary.[15]

> **Example 4.** T purchased a manufacturing concern which has just been adjudged bankrupt. Because the business has a poor financial rating, T satisfies some of the obligations incurred by its

---

11. Reg. § 1.212–1(d).
12. *J. Raymond Dyer,* 36 T.C. 456 (1961); Reg. § 1.212–1(d).
13. *Welch v. Helvering,* 3 USTC ¶ 1164, 12 AFTR 1456, 54 S.Ct. 8 (USSC, 1933).
14. *Deputy v. DuPont,* 40–1 USTC ¶ 9161, 23 AFTR 808, 60 S.Ct. 363 (USSC, 1940).
15. *Dunn and McCarthy, Inc. v. Comm.,* 43–2 USTC ¶ 9688, 31 AFTR 1043, 139 F.2d 242 (CA–2, 1943).

former owners. Although there existed no legal obligation to pay these debts, T felt this was the only way to reestablish a source of credit for future inventory purchases. The Supreme Court found that such payments were necessary in that they were both appropriate and helpful.[16] The Court held that such payments were *not* ordinary but were in the nature of capital expenditures to build a reputation (i. e., goodwill—see the Glossary of Tax Terms in Appendix C for a definition of this term).

REASONABLENESS REQUIREMENT

The Code refers to reasonableness solely with respect to salaries and other compensation for personal services.[17] The courts, however, have held that for a business expense to be "ordinary and necessary" it must also be "reasonable" in amount.[18]

What constitutes reasonableness is a "question of fact." If an expense is unreasonable, the excess amount is not allowed as a deduction. The question of reasonableness generally arises with respect to closely-held corporations where there is no separation of ownership and management. In such cases, transactions between the shareholders and the company may result in the disallowance of excessive salaries and rent expense to the corporation. However, an unusually large salary will be viewed by the Courts in light of all relevant circumstances, and such a salary may be found reasonable despite its size.[19] If excessive payments for salaries and rents bear a close relationship to the percentage of stock ownership of the recipients, such amounts are treated as dividends to the shareholders and are not deductible by the corporation.[20] However, deductions for reasonable salaries will not be disallowed on the sole ground that the corporation has paid insubstantial portions of its earnings as dividends to its shareholders.[21]

> **Example 5.** XYZ Corporation is closely held in equal ownership interests by X, Y, and Z. The company has been highly profitable for several years and has not paid dividends. X, Y, and Z are key officers of the company, and each receives a salary of $200,000. Salaries for similar positions in comparable companies average only $100,000. Amounts paid to X, Y, and Z in excess of $100,000 may be deemed unreasonable, and a total of $300,000 in

---

16. *Supra*, note 13.

17. § 162(a)(1).

18. *Comm. v. Lincoln Electric Co.*, 49–2 USTC ¶ 9388, 38 AFTR 411, 176 F.2d 815 (CA–6, 1949).

19. *James D. Kennedy, Jr., v. Comm.*, 49 AFTR2d 82–628, 671 F2d 167 (CA–6, 1982), Rev'g 72 T.C. 793 (1979).

20. Reg. § 1.162–8.

21. Rev.Rul. 79–8, 1979–1 C.B. 92.

salary deductions may be disallowed. The excess amounts may be treated as dividends rather than salary income to X, Y, and Z, because such amounts are proportional to stock ownership.

DEDUCTIONS AND LOSSES—TIMING OF EXPENSE RECOGNITION

Importance of Taxpayer's Method of Accounting. A taxpayer's method of accounting is a major factor in the determination of taxable income. The method used determines when an item is includible in income and when an item is deductible on the tax return. Usually the taxpayer's regular method of record keeping is used for income tax purposes.[22] The taxing authorities do not require uniformity among all taxpayers, but they do require that the method used clearly reflects income and that items be handled consistently.[23] The most common methods of accounting are the cash method and the accrual method. In most instances, individuals and professional service organizations use the cash method, while most corporations use the accrual method.

Cash Method Requirements. The expenses of cash basis taxpayers are deductible only when they are actually paid with cash or other property. Promising to pay or issuing a note does not satisfy the "actually paid" requirement.[24] However, the payment can be made with borrowed funds. Thus, at the time taxpayers charge expenses on their bank credit cards, they are allowed to claim the deduction because they are deemed to have simultaneously borrowed money from the credit card issuer and paid the expenses.[25]

Although the cash basis taxpayer must have actually paid the amount, payment does not assure a current deduction. Cash basis taxpayers, as well as accrual basis taxpayers, cannot take a current deduction for capital expenditures, except through amortization or depreciation over the life of the asset. The regulations set forth the general rule that an expenditure that creates an asset having a useful life that extends "substantially beyond" the end of the tax year must be capitalized.[26]

> **Example 6.** T, a cash basis taxpayer, rents property from L. On July 1, 19X4, T paid $2,400 rent for the 24 months ending June 30, 19X6. The prepaid rent extends 18 months—substantially beyond the year of payment. Therefore, T must capitalize the pre-

---

22. § 446(a).

23. § 446(b) and (e); Reg. § 1.446–1(a)(2).

24. *Page v. Rhode Island Trust Co., Exr.,* 37–1 USTC ¶ 9138, 19 AFTR 105, 88 F.2d 192 (CA–1, 1937).

25. Rev.Rul. 78–39, 1978–1 C.B. 73. See also, Rev.Rul. 80–335, 1980–2 C.B. 170, which applies to pay-by-phone arrangements.

26. Reg. § 1.461–1(a).

paid rent and amortize the expense on a monthly basis. His deduction for 19X4 is $600.

The Tax Court and the IRS take the position that an asset that will expire, or will be consumed, by the end of the tax year following the year of payment has a life that extends substantially beyond the year of payment and must be prorated. However, the Ninth Circuit Court has held that the expenditures are currently deductible, and should be treated as shown in the following example.[27]

> **Example 7.** Assume the same facts as in Example 6 except that T was required to pay only 12 months rent in 19X4. T paid $1,200 on July 1, 19X4. The entire $1,200 is deductible in 19X4 according to the minority view of the Ninth Circuit Court.

However, the payment must be required and not a voluntary prepayment to obtain the current deduction under the one-year rule.[28]

Rather than adopting the objective one-year rule, the Tax Court looks to the facts and circumstances of each case.

To obtain a current deduction for an asset, the taxpayer must demonstrate to the Court that an allowance of the current deduction will not result in a material distortion of income. Generally, the deduction will be allowed if the item is recurring (e. g., rent) or was made for a business purpose (rather than to manipulate income).[29] Deduction of prepaid interest is disallowed by § 461(g).

Accrual Method Requirements. The period in which an accrual basis taxpayer can deduct an expense is determined by applying the "all events" test:

> An expense is deductible for the taxable year in which (1) all the events have occurred that determine the fact of the liability and (2) the amount thereof can be determined with reasonable accuracy.[30]

Reserves for estimated expenses that are frequently employed for financial accounting purposes generally are not allowed for tax purposes, because the all events test cannot be satisfied.

> **Example 8.** T Air Line is required by federal law to conduct tests of its engines after 3,000 flying hours. Aircraft cannot return to flight until the tests have been conducted. An unrelated garage does all of the company's tests for $1,500 per engine. For

27. *Martin J. Zaninovich*, 80–1 USTC ¶ 9342, 45 AFTR2d 80–1442, 616 F.2d 429 (CA–9, 1980), reversing 69 T.C. 605 (1978).
28. *Bonaire Development Co. v. Comm.*, 82–2 USTC ¶ 9428 (CA–9), 50 AFTR2d 82–5167 (CA–9, 1982).
29. *Stephen A. Keller v. Comm.*, 79 T.C. No. 2 (1982).
30. Reg. § 1.461–1(a)(2).

financial reporting purposes, the company accrues an expense based upon $.50 per hour of flight and credits an allowance account. The actual amounts paid the garage are offset against the allowance account. However, for tax purposes, the all events test is not satisfied until the company has incurred a liability to the garage (i. c., when the work is done).[31]

Example 9. R Co. is in the business of strip mining for coal. State law requires the company to refill, grade, and re-sort the land within 12 months after the mining operations have been completed. The company is also required to post bond as assurance that the reclamation work will be performed.

During the current year, the company completed mining operations. Engineers have prepared reasonably accurate estimates of the costs of reclaiming the stripped land.

The liability under state law becomes fixed as soon as the land is stripped and the amount of the liability has been determined with reasonable accuracy. Therefore, the estimated expense can be deducted before the reclamation work has actually been performed.[32]

DISALLOWANCE POSSIBILITIES

The tax law provides for the disallowance of certain types of expenses. Without specific restrictions in the tax law, taxpayers might be able to deduct certain items which in reality are personal, nondeductible expenditures. For example, specific tax rules are provided to determine whether an expenditure is for trade or business purposes or whether it is related to a personal hobby and is, therefore, nondeductible.

Certain disallowance provisions represent a codification or extension of prior court decisions (e. g., the courts had denied deductions for payments which were deemed to be in violation of public policy). Thus, the tax law was changed to provide specific authority for the disallowance of such deductions.

The following material includes a detailed discussion of specific disallowance provisions in the tax law.

PUBLIC POLICY LIMITATION

Justification for Denying Deductions.   The courts have developed the principle that a payment which is in violation of public policy is

---

31.   *World Airways, Inc. v. Comm.,* 41 AFTR2d 78–323 (CA–9, 1977), aff'g 62 T.C. 786 (1976).
32.   *Ohio River Collierres Co. v. Comm.,* 77 T.C. 1369 (1981).

not a necessary expense and is, therefore, not deductible.[33] If the law were to permit such deductions, the government would, in effect, be subsidizing a taxpayer's wrongdoing. As a result of these judicial interpretations, § 162 now denies a deduction for bribes and kickbacks (only if the payments violate the U. S. Foreign Corrupt Practices Act of 1977 in the case of foreign bribes and kickbacks), fines and penalties paid to a government for violation of law, and two-thirds of the treble damage payments made to claimants resulting from violation of the antitrust law.[34] Section 162(c) states that no deduction is permitted for a kickback which is illegal under state law (if such state law is generally enforced) and which subjects the payor to a criminal penalty or the loss of license or privilege to engage in a trade or business.

Example 10. During the year T, an insurance salesman, paid $5,000 to U, a real estate broker. The payment represented 20% of the commissions earned by T from policies referred by U. Under state law, the splitting of commissions by an insurance salesperson is an act of misconduct which could warrant a revocation of the salesperson's license. Thus, the payments of $5,000 by T to U are not deductible if the state law is generally enforced.

Example 11. Y Company, a moving company, consistently loads its trucks with weights in excess of the limits allowed by state law because the additional revenue more than offsets the fines levied. Because the fines are in violation of public policy (and, therefore, not a necessary expense), they are not deductible.

Legal Expenses Incurred in Defense of Civil or Criminal Penalties. Generally, legal expenses are deductible (*for* adjusted gross income) as ordinary and necessary business expenses if incurred in connection with a trade or business activity. Legal expenses may also be deductible (*for* adjusted gross income) under § 212 as expenses incurred in conjunction with rental property which is held for the production of income or (*from* adjusted gross income) as fees for tax advice relative to the preparation of the taxpayer's income tax returns. Personal legal expenses are not deductible.

Legal fees pursuant to a criminal defense are deductible if the crime is associated with the taxpayer's trade or business activity.[35] Previously, the position of the IRS was that the legal fees were deductible only if the taxpayer was successful in the criminal suit.

In determining whether legal expenses are deductible, the tax-

---

33. *Tank Truck Rentals, Inc. v. Comm.,* 58–1 USTC ¶ 9366, 1 AFTR2d 1154, 78 S.Ct. 507 (USSC, 1958).
34. § 162(c), (f), and (g).
35. *Comm. v. Tellier,* 66–1 USTC ¶ 9319, 17 AFTR2d 633, 86 S.Ct. 1118 (USSC, 1966).

payer must be able to show that the origin and character of the claim are directly related to a trade or business or an income-producing activity. Otherwise, the legal expenses are personal and nondeductible.

> **Example 12.** T, a financial officer of X Corporation, incurred legal expenses in connection with the defense in a criminal indictment for evasion of X Corporation's income taxes. T may deduct her legal expenses because she is deemed to be in the trade or business of being an executive, and such legal action impairs her ability to conduct this business activity.[36]

Expenses Relating to an Illegal Business. The usual expenses of operating an illegal business (e. g., a numbers racket) are deductible. However, those expenses that are contrary to public policy (e. g., fines, bribes to public officials) are not deductible.[37]

> **Example 13.** S owns and operates an illegal gambling establishment. In connection with this activity, he had the following expenses during the year:

Rent	$ 60,000
Payoffs to the police	40,000
Depreciation on equipment	100,000
Wages	140,000
Interest	30,000
Criminal fines	50,000
Illegal kickbacks	10,000
Total	$ 430,000

All of the usual expenses (i. e., rent, depreciation, wages, and interest) are deductible, while the expenses that are contrary to public policy (i. e., payoffs, fines, and kickbacks) are not deductible. Of the $430,000 spent, therefore, $330,000 is deductible while $100,000 is not.

An exception was made under TEFRA for amounts paid with regard to illegal trafficking in drugs.[38] Drug dealers are no longer allowed a deduction for ordinary and necessary business expenses incurred in such a business. A deduction for cost of goods sold is still allowed, however.

> **Example 14.** If S (in Example 13) were in the business of drug dealing, none of the expenses would be deductible except those that constituted cost of goods sold.

---

36. Rev.Rul. 68–662, 1968–2 C.B. 69.

37. *Supra*, Footnote 35.

38. § 280E.

POLITICAL CONTRIBUTIONS AND LOBBYING ACTIVITIES

Political Contributions. Generally, no business deduction is permitted for direct or indirect payments for political purposes.[39] Historically, the government has been reluctant to grant favorable tax treatment to business expenditures for political purposes because of the possible abuses and the need to prevent undue influence upon the political process. However, since 1979 a tax credit has been allowed for political contributions. Tax credits are discussed in Chapter 13.

Lobbying Expenditures. A deduction for certain expenses incurred in the influence of legislation is allowed provided that the proposed legislation is of direct interest to the taxpayer.[40] A "direct" interest exists if the legislation is of such a nature that it will, or may reasonably be expected to, affect the trade or business of the taxpayer.[41] Any dues and expenses paid to an organization which consists of individuals with a common direct interest in proposed legislation also are deductible.[42] A "common direct" interest exists where an organization consists of persons with the same direct interests in legislation or proposed legislation. However, no deduction is allowed for any expenses incurred to influence the public on legislative matters or for any political campaign.

> **Example 15.** T, a contractor, drove to his state capitol to testify against proposed legislation that would affect building codes. T believes that the proposed legislation is unnecessary and not in the best interest of his company. The expenses are deductible because the legislation is of direct interest to T's company. If T later journeyed to another city to make a speech concerning the legislation at a Lion's Club meeting, the expenditures would not be deductible because the expenses were incurred to influence the public on legislative matters.

INVESTIGATION OF A BUSINESS

Investigation expenses are those expenses paid or incurred to determine the feasibility of entering a new business or expanding an existing business. They include such costs as travel, engineering and architectural surveys, marketing reports, and various legal and accounting services. How such expenses are treated for tax purposes depends on a number of variables, some of which are:

—The current business, if any, of the taxpayer.

—The nature of the business being investigated.

---

39. § 276.
40. § 162(e)(1)(A).
41. Reg. § 1.162–20(c)(2)(ii)(b)(1).
42. § 162(e)(1)(B).

—The extent to which the investigation has proceeded.

—Whether or not the acquisition actually takes place.

If the taxpayer is in a business which is similar to or the same as that being investigated, all expenses in connection therewith are deductible in the year paid or incurred.[43] The tax result would be the same whether the taxpayer did or did not acquire the business being investigated.[44]

> **Example 16.** T, an accrual basis sole proprietor, owns and operates three motels in Georgia. In 19X4, T incurs expenses of $8,500 in investigating the possibility of acquiring several additional motels located in South Carolina. The $8,500 is deductible in 19X4 whether or not T chooses to acquire the motels in South Carolina.

When the taxpayer is not in a business that is the same as or similar to the one being investigated, the tax result usually depends on whether the new business is acquired. If not, all investigation expenses generally become nondeductible.[45] They cannot be deducted under § 162, since the taxpayer is not in a trade or business. Such expenses cannot fall under § 212 (i. e., "for the production or collection of income" or "for the management, conservation, or maintenance of property held for the production of income") because the property never was acquired and no income resulted.

> **Example 17.** R, a retired merchant, incurs expenses in traveling from Rochester, New York, to California in order to investigate the feasibility of acquiring several auto care centers. If no acquisition takes place (i. e., the project is abandoned), none of the expenses are deductible.

When the investigation effort actually leads to the acquisition of a new business, the expenses must be capitalized and, at the election of the taxpayer, amortized over a period of 60 months or more.[46]

HOBBY LOSSES

Rationale for § 183. Deductions under § 162 for business expenses and § 212 for expenses attributable to the production of income are permitted only if the taxpayer can show that the business or in-

---

43. Throughout the portions of the Internal Revenue Code dealing with deductions, the phrase "paid or incurred" is used. "Paid" has reference to the cash basis taxpayer who gets a deduction only in the year of payment. "Incurred" concerns the accrual basis taxpayer who obtains the deduction in the year in which the liability for the expense becomes certain (see Chapter 5).

44. *York v. Comm.,* 58–2 USTC ¶ 9952, 2 AFTR2d 6178, 261 F.2d 421 (CA–4, 1958).

45. Rev.Rul. 57–418, 1957–2 C.B. 143; *Morton Frank,* 20 T.C. 511 (1953); and, *Dwight A. Ward,* 20 T.C. 332 (1953).

46. § 195.

vestment activity was entered into for the purpose of making a profit and not for personal pleasure. Certain activities may have profit-seeking or personal attributes depending upon individual circumstances (e. g., raising horses and operating a farm which is used as a weekend residence). Since personal losses are not deductible, while losses attributable to profit-seeking activities may be deducted and used to offset a taxpayer's other income, it was necessary to develop tax rules to prevent possible tax avoidance.

General Rules. If a taxpayer (an individual or an S corporation) can show that an activity has been conducted with the intent to earn a profit, any losses from the activity are fully deductible and § 183 is not applicable. The hobby loss rules apply only if the activity is not engaged in for profit. Section 183 provides that hobby expenses are deductible only to the extent of hobby income.[47]

The Regulations stipulate the following relevant factors which are to be considered in making the determination of the nature of an activity—profit-seeking or a hobby.[48]

—Whether the activity is conducted in a businesslike manner.

—The expertise of the taxpayers or their advisers.

—The time and effort expended.

—The expectation that the assets of the activity will appreciate in value.

—The previous success of the taxpayer in the conduct of similar activities.

—The history of income or losses from the activity.

—The relationship of profits earned to losses incurred.

—The financial status of the taxpayer (e. g., if the taxpayer does not have substantial amounts of other income, this fact may indicate that the activity is engaged in for profit).

—Elements of personal pleasure or recreation in the activity.

Presumptive Rule of § 183. The Code provides a rebuttable presumption that an activity is profit-seeking if it shows a profit in at least two of any five consecutive years (seven years for activities involving horses) ending with the taxable year in question.[49] For example, if these profitability tests have been met, the activity is presumed to be a trade or business rather than a personal hobby. In effect, the IRS bears the burden of proving that the activity is personal rather than trade or business related.

A taxpayer can elect to postpone this presumption until five or seven years from the time the activity began by filing a statement

---

47. § 183(b).
48. Reg. § 1.183–2(b)(1) through (9).
49. § 183(d).

with the Internal Revenue Service within three years of the commencement of the activity.[50] This election automatically extends the statute of limitations. The extension of the statute of limitations is necessary, because otherwise the normal three-year statute of limitations might run out before the taxpayer has had two gain years to meet the presumption of § 183.

> **Example 18.** T began an activity in 1982 and incurred losses in 1982, 1983, and 1984. If the activity earns profits in 1985 and 1986, T would be presumed to be in a trade or business. However, if T showed losses in 1985 and 1986, the IRS would be barred from collecting deficiencies resulting from losses disallowed in 1982 because the normal statute of limitations is three years. Therefore, the election (which can be in T's favor) extends the statute at least two years to allow the IRS to collect deficiencies if T does not show a profit in two out of five years. This also gives T two more years in which to show a profit and meet the presumption that he is in a trade or business.

> **Example 19.** N is an executive for a large corporation and is paid a salary of $200,000. His wife is a collector of antiques. Several years ago she opened an antique shop in a local shopping center and spends most of her time buying and selling antiques. She occasionally earns a small profit from this activity but more frequently incurs substantial losses. If such losses are business related, they are fully deductible against N's salary income if a joint return is filed.

> —As a tax adviser you should initially determine if the antique "business" has met the two of five years profit test in § 183.

> —If the presumption is not met, the activity may nevertheless qualify as a business if the taxpayer can show that the intent is to engage in a profit-seeking activity. It is not necessary to show actual profits.

> —Attempts should be made to fit the operation within the nine criteria which are prescribed in the Regulations and listed above.

If an activity is deemed to be a hobby, the expenses are deductible only to the extent of the income from the hobby. These expenses must be deducted in the following order: (1) amounts deductible under other sections of the Code without regard to the nature of the activity, such as interest expense; (2) amounts deductible under other sections of the Code had the activity been engaged in for profit, but only if those amounts do not affect adjusted basis (e. g., maintenance); and (3) amounts deductible under other sections of the Code had the activ-

---

50.   § 183(e).

ity been engaged in for profit, which amounts do affect adjusted basis (e. g., depreciation).[51]

> **Example 20.** T, the vice-president of an oil company, decides to pursue painting in his spare time. During the current year, T incurs the following expenses:
>
> | | |
> |---|---:|
> | Correspondence study course | $ 350 |
> | Art supplies | 200 |
> | Cost of converting attic in family residence to a studio | 3,000 |
> | Interest on $3,000 borrowed from a bank—the proceeds were used to convert the attic to a studio | 240 |
> | Fees paid to models | 450 |
>
> During the year T sold three paintings to close friends for $100 each. In the event the activity is deemed a hobby, the $240 of interest expense (which is fully deductible without regard to the nature of the activity) must first be offset against the $300 of income. Thus, only $60 of other hobby expenses are deductible. The net result is that T must include $300 in his gross income and may deduct $240 of interest and $60 of other expenses *from* adjusted gross income. The remaining expenditures are not deductible. All deductible hobby-related expenses are deductions *from* adjusted gross income. Therefore, such expenses are deductible only if the taxpayer itemizes.

Rental of Vacation Homes. Section 280A places restrictions on taxpayers who rent residences (including vacation homes) for part of the tax year. The following rules apply, depending on the extent to which the home is rented during a particular year:

1. If the residence is rented for less than 15 days, all rentals are excluded from gross income and rent expenses are disallowed.[52] However, the taxpayer may still claim deductions for real estate taxes, interest, etc., which would otherwise be deductions *from* adjusted gross income (itemized deductions).

2. If the dwelling is not used more than 14 days for personal use (or more than 10 percent of the total days rented), it is not considered a residence, and the allocations and limitations discussed in item 3 do not apply.[53]

3. If the residence is rented for 15 or more days and is used for personal purposes for the greater of (1) more than 14 days or (2) more than 10 percent of the rental days (the usual case), deductions are applied *for* adjusted gross income and are de-

---

51. § 183(b)(2) and Reg. § 1.183–1(b)(1).

52. § 280A(g).

53. § 280A(d).

ducted in the same order as are hobby loss expenses.

A recent court ruling held that real estate taxes and mortgage interest may be allocated to the rental period using the fraction: $\dfrac{\text{number of rental days}}{\text{number of days in year}}$, rather than the fraction proposed by the IRS: $\dfrac{\text{number of rental days}}{\text{number of days of use}}$.[54] This increases the taxpayer's chances of being able to deduct other expenses, such as maintenance and depreciation.

Example 21. S rents her vacation home for two months and lives in the home for one month (a total of three months—one-third personal and two-thirds rental). Rules outlined in item 3 apply. S's gross rental income is $5,000. For the entire year, the real estate taxes are $2,000; S's mortgage interest expense is $10,000; utilities and maintenance expense equals $2,400; and depreciation is $9,000. These amounts are deductible in this specific order:

Gross Income	$ 5,000
Deduct: Taxes and interest ($2/12 \times$ $12,000)	2,000
Remainder to apply to rental operating expenses and depreciation	$ 3,000
Deduct: Utilities and maintenance ($2/3 \times$ $2,400)	1,600
Balance applicable to depreciation	$ 1,400
Deduct: Depreciation ($2/3 \times$ $9,000 = $6,000 but is limited to above balance)	1,400
Net Income	$ -0-

The nonrental use portion of taxes and interest ($10/12$ in this case) is deductible if the taxpayer elects to itemize (see Chapter 11); the personal use portion of utilities, maintenance, and depreciation is not deductible in any case. Also note that the basis of the property is not reduced by the $4,600 depreciation not allowed ($6,000 − $1,400) because of the above limitation. (See Chapter 14 for discussion of reduction in basis for depreciation allowed or allowable.)

The Revenue Act of 1978 amended § 280A(d) to resolve the problem of whether or not a taxpayer's primary residence was subject to the above rules in the year it was converted to rental property. The deduction for expenses of the property incurred during a qualified rental period is not subject to the personal use test of the vacation home rules. A "qualified rental period" is a consecutive period of 12 or

---

54. *Dorance D. Bolton v. Comm.*, 51AFTR2d 83–305 (CA–9, 1982), disagreeing with proposed Reg. § 1.280A–3(d)(4).

more months and begins or ends in the taxable year in which the *residence* is rented to other than a related party [as defined in § 267(c)(4)] or is held for rental at a fair rental price. If the property is sold before 12 months, the qualified rental period is the actual time rented.

EXPENDITURES INCURRED FOR TAXPAYER'S BENEFIT OR TAXPAYER'S OBLIGATION

Generally, an expense must be incurred for the taxpayer's benefit or arise from the taxpayer's obligation; an individual cannot claim a tax deduction for the payment of the expenses of another individual.

> **Example 22.** During the current year, F pays the interest on his son, T's, home mortgage. Neither F nor T can take a deduction for the interest paid because the obligation is not F's and his son did not pay the interest. The tax result might have been more favorable if F had made a cash gift to T and let him pay the interest. The interest then could have been deducted by the son, and (depending upon other gifts and the amount involved) F may not have been liable for any gift taxes. A deduction would have been created with no cash difference to the family. One exception to this rule is the payment of medical expenses for a dependent. Such expenses are deductible by the payor.[55]

> **Example 23.** T's daughter, D, is a full-time student at a university. During the year she earned $4,000 from a part-time job. D would qualify as T's dependent but for the fact that he contributed only 40% of D's support. Any of D's medical expenses paid by her father would not be deductible by T, since these expenses are neither for his benefit nor his obligation. However, if T contributed more than 50% of D's support to qualify D as his dependent, such expenses would be deductible under the exception noted in Example 22.

DISALLOWANCE OF PERSONAL EXPENDITURES

Section 262 states that "except as otherwise expressly provided in this chapter, no deduction shall be allowed for personal, living, or family expenses." Thus, an individual must be able to identify a particular section of the Code which sanctions the deductibility of an otherwise nondeductible personal expenditure (e. g., charitable contributions, § 170; medical expenses, § 213; moving expenses, § 217). In addition, an individual may deduct ordinary and necessary expenses paid or incurred (1) for the production or collection of income; (2) for the man-

---

55. § 213(a)(1).

agement, conservation, or maintenance of property held for the production of income; or (3) as expenses in connection with the determination, collection, or refund of any tax.[56]

Sometimes the character of a particular expenditure is not easily determined.

> **Example 24.** During the current year, H pays $1,500 in legal fees and court costs to obtain a divorce from his wife, W. Involved in the divorce action is a property settlement which concerns the disposition of income-producing property owned by H. In a similar situation, the Tax Court[57] held that H could not deduct any of the $1,500 costs. "Although fees primarily related to property division concerning his income-producing property, they weren't ordinary and necessary expenses paid for conservation or maintenance of property held for production of income. Legal fees incurred in defending against claims that arise from a taxpayer's marital relationship aren't deductible expenses regardless of possible consequences on taxpayer's income-producing property."

The IRS has clarified the issue of the deduction of legal fees incurred in connection with a divorce.[58] To be deductible, an expense must relate solely to tax advice in a divorce proceeding. For example, legal fees attributable to the determination of dependency exemptions of children, the creation of a trust to make periodic alimony payments, or determination of the tax consequences of a property settlement are deductible if the fees are distinguishable from the general legal fees incurred in obtaining a divorce.

DISALLOWANCE OF DEDUCTIONS FOR UNREALIZED LOSSES

One of the basic concepts in the tax law is that a deduction can be taken only when a loss has actually been realized. For example, a drop in the market price of securities held by the taxpayer does not result in a loss until the securities are actually sold or exchanged at the lower price. Furthermore, any deductible loss is limited to the taxpayer's cost basis in the asset.

> **Example 25.** Early this year T purchased a home in a new residential subdivision for $50,000. Shortly thereafter, heavy spring rains led to severe flooding which indicated that the subdivision's drainage facilities were inadequate. Because the subdivision now has a reputation for poor drainage, T estimates that he could receive only $30,000 on the sale of his home. He has the written appraisal reports of several reputable real estate brokers to sup-

56. § 212.
57. *Harry H. Goldberg,* 29 TCM 74, T.C.Memo., 1970–27.
58. Rev.Rul. 72–545, 1972–2 C.B. 179.

port the $20,000 loss in value. Although § 165 allows a deduction for casualty losses, this loss is based on actual physical loss and not the decline in value that may be a "fluctuation in market value not attributable to any actual physical depreciation."[59]

If T later sells his house for $30,000, he will have a $20,000 nondeductible loss. The loss is not deductible because the house is a personal asset, and the decline in value is not the result of a casualty. Casualty losses are discussed in Chapter 8.

DISALLOWANCE OF DEDUCTIONS FOR CAPITAL EXPENDITURES

The Code specifically disallows a deduction for "any amount paid out for new buildings or for permanent improvements or betterments made to increase the value of any property or estate."[60] The Regulations further define capital expenditures to include those expenditures which add to the value or prolong the life of property or adapt the property to a new or different use.[61] Incidental repairs and maintenance of the property are not capital expenditures and can be deducted as ordinary and necessary business expenses. Repairing a roof is a deductible expense, but replacing a roof is a capital expenditure subject to depreciation deductions over its useful life. The tune-up of a delivery truck is an expense; a complete overhaul is probably a capital expenditure.

Exceptions. There are several exceptions to the general rule regarding capitalization of expenditures. Taxpayers can elect to expense certain mineral developmental costs and intangible drilling costs.[62] Certain farm capital expenditures (such as soil and water conservation, fertilizer, and land clearing costs) and certain research and experimental expenditures may be immediately expensed.[63]

In addition, § 179 now permits an immediate write-off of certain amounts of depreciable property. These provisions are discussed more fully in Chapter 9.

Capitalization Versus Expense. When an expenditure is capitalized rather than expensed, the deduction is at best deferred and at worst lost forever. Although an immediate tax benefit for a large cash expenditure is lost, the cost can be deducted in increments over a longer period of time. If the expenditure is for some improvement that has an ascertainable life, it can be capitalized and depreciated or amortized over that life. Costs that can be amortized include copyrights

59. *Joe B. Thornton,* 47 T.C. 1 (1966).

60. § 263(a).

61. Reg. § 1.263(a)–1(b).

62. § § 263(c) and 616.

63. § § 174, 175, 180 and 182.

and patents. However, there are many other expenditures, such as land and payments made for goodwill, that cannot be amortized or depreciated. Goodwill has an indeterminate life, and land is not a depreciable asset, since its value does not generally decline.

Example 26. T purchased a prime piece of land located in an apartment zoned area. T paid $500,000 for the property which had an old, but usable, apartment building on it. T immediately had the building demolished at a cost of $100,000. The $500,000 purchase price and the $100,000 demolition costs must be capitalized, and the basis of the land is $600,000. Since land is a nondepreciable asset, no deduction is allowed. More favorable tax treatment might result if T rented the apartments in the old building for a period of time to attempt to establish that there was no intent to demolish the building. If T's attempt is successful, it might be possible to allocate a substantial portion of the original purchase price of the property to the building (a depreciable asset). When the building is later demolished, any remaining adjusted cost basis can be taken as an ordinary (§ 1231) loss. See Chapter 17 for a discussion of the treatment of § 1231 assets.

Example 27. During the year T pays $3,000 in legal fees incurred in connection with the defense of a will contest suit. In an action brought by her brothers, T was successful in protecting the inheritance left to her by her mother. T must capitalize the $3,000 of legal fees unless the contested items were income items which must be included in her gross income when received. The capitalized fees are, of course, not deductible by her.[64]

In some cases a taxpayer might prefer to capitalize rather than expense a particular item if the property is depreciable. An immediate deduction may create a net operating loss which (unless utilized) expires in 15 years. No tax benefit (or a smaller tax benefit) would be derived from an immediate deduction. The same expenditure, if capitalized and depreciated over a longer future period, could be offset against taxable income later (or against higher tax bracket income in future years) resulting in a greater tax benefit.

Capitalization Elections. Because of the tax avoidance possibilities inherent in allowing elective "capitalize or expense" decisions, the treatment of most expenditures is, by law, not elective. However, in certain cases it is permissible to elect to capitalize *or* to immediately expense a particular item. For example, § 266 allows taxpayers (but not individuals, S corporations, or personal holding companies) an opportunity to capitalize certain "taxes and carrying charges." This election applies to carrying charges, interest on indebtedness,

64. Reg. § § 1.212–1(k) and 1.263(a)–2(c).

and certain taxes (such as property and employer-paid payroll taxes) paid during the construction period on realty (buildings and land) or personalty (such as machinery and equipment) whether the property is business or nonbusiness in nature.[65] A taxpayer may elect to capitalize some expenditures and not others. For example, one could elect to capitalize property taxes and expense interest on the construction indebtedness. A new election may be made for each project. One could elect to capitalize expenditures on a factory being constructed and expense the same type of items on a constructed machine. On unimproved and unproductive real estate (land held for later sale, for example) a new election must be made for each year.

Section 189 now requires individuals, S corporations, and personal holding companies to capitalize construction period interest and taxes, subject to specific rules for amortizing such amounts (see Chapter 9). This Code section was intended both to match expenses with income in accordance with the traditional accounting principle and to restrict tax shelter opportunities for individuals.

TRANSACTIONS BETWEEN RELATED PARTIES

The Code places restrictions on the recognition of gains and losses between related parties. Because of relationships created by birth, marriage, and business, there would be endless possibilities for engaging in various types of financial transactions which would produce tax savings with no real economic substance or change. For example, a wife could sell property to her husband at a loss and deduct the loss on their joint return, and her husband could hold the asset indefinitely. This illustrates the creation of an artificial loss. Such "sham" transactions have resulted in a complex set of laws designed to eliminate these abuses.

Losses. Section 267 provides for the disallowance of any "losses from sales or exchanges of property . . . directly or indirectly," between related persons.[66] Upon the subsequent sale of such property to a nonrelated party, any gain recognized is reduced by the loss which was previously disallowed.

> **Example 28.** F sells common stock with a basis of $1,000 to his son, T, for $800. T sells the stock several years later for $1,100. F's $200 loss is disallowed upon the sale to T, and only $100 of gain is taxable to T upon the subsequent sale. See Chapter 14 for a further discussion of the treatment of disallowed losses.

> **Example 29.** F sells common stock with a basis of $1,000 to his son, T, for $800. T sells the stock to an unrelated party for $900.

---

65. Reg. § 1.266–1(b).
66. § 267(a)(1).

T's gain of $100 is eliminated due to F's previously disallowed loss of $200. Note that the offset may result in only partial tax benefit upon the subsequent sale. If the property had not been transferred to T, F could have recognized a $100 loss upon the subsequent sale to the unrelated party ($1,000 basis − $900 selling price).

Example 30. F sells common stock with a basis of $1,000 to an unrelated third party for $800. F's son repurchased the same stock in the market on the same day for $800. The $200 loss is not allowed because the transaction is an indirect sale between related parties.[67]

Unpaid Expenses and Interest. Section 267 also operates to prevent related taxpayers from engaging in tax avoidance schemes in which one related taxpayer uses the accrual method of accounting and the other is on the cash basis. For example, an accrual basis closely-held corporation could borrow funds from a cash basis individual shareholder. At the end of the year the corporation would accrue and deduct the interest, but the cash basis lender would not recognize interest income since no interest had been paid. Section 267 specifically disallows a deduction to the accruing taxpayer unless the interest is paid within 2½ months after the end of the borrower's taxable year.[68] This rule applies to interest as well as other expenses, such as salaries and bonuses. Section 267 is particularly burdensome for owner-employees of closely-held corporations, since the accrual basis corporation will never be entitled to the deduction if the payment is not made within the 2½ month period.[69] This stipulation remains in effect even if the payment is made during a subsequent period and the cash basis individual is required to include the payment in income.

Relationships and Constructive Ownership. Section 267 operates to disallow losses and deductions only between related parties. Losses or deductions generated by similar transactions with an unrelated party are allowed. Related parties include the following:[70]

—Siblings and half-siblings, spouses, ancestors (i. e., parents, grandparents) and lineal descendants (i. e., children, grandchildren) of the taxpayer.

—A corporation owned more than 50 percent (directly or indirectly) by the taxpayer.

—Two corporations owned more than 50 percent (directly or indirectly) by the taxpayer if either corporation is a personal holding company or a foreign personal holding company.

---

67. *McWilliams v. Comm.*, 47–1 USTC ¶ 9289, 35 AFTR 1184, 67 S.Ct. 1477 (USSC, 1947).
68. § 267(a)(2).
69. Reg. § 1.267(a)–1(b). See Example 4 in Chapter 3.
70. § 267(b).

—A series of other complex relationships between trusts, corporations, and individual taxpayers.

The law provides that constructive ownership rules are applied to determine whether the taxpayers are "related."[71] Constructive ownership rules state that stock owned by certain relatives or related entities is deemed to be owned by the taxpayer for loss and expense deduction disallowance purposes. For example, a taxpayer is deemed to own not only his or her stock but the stock owned by his or her lineal descendants, ancestors, brothers and sisters or half-brothers or -sisters, and spouse. The taxpayer is also deemed to own his or her proportionate share of stock owned by any partnership, corporation, estate, or trust of which he or she is a member. Additionally, an individual is deemed to own any stock owned, directly or indirectly, by his or her partner. However, constructive ownership by an individual of the partnership's and the other partner's shares does not extend to the individual's spouse or other relatives.

> **Example 31.** The stock of V Corporation is owned 20% by T, 30% by T's father, 30% by T's mother, and 20% by T's sister. On July 1 of the current year, T loaned $10,000 to V Corporation at 7% annual interest, principal and interest payable on demand. V Corporation uses the accrual basis and T uses the cash basis for tax purposes. Both are on a calendar year. Since T is deemed to own the 80% owned by her parents and sister, she constructively owns 100% of V Corporation. If the corporation accrues but does not pay the interest within the taxable year or within 2½ months thereafter (i. e., by March 15 of next year), no deduction is allowed to V. If T were an accrual basis taxpayer or if payment were actually or constructively received by T, the deduction would be allowed.

SUBSTANTIATION REQUIREMENTS

The tax law is built on a voluntary system: Taxpayers file their tax returns, report income and take deductions to which they are entitled, and pay their taxes through the withholding method (on salaries and wages) or by making estimated tax payments throughout the year. Some events throughout the year should be documented as they occur. For example, it is generally advisable to receive a pledge payment statement from one's church, in addition to a cancelled check, for proper documentation of a charitable contribution. Other types of deductible expenditures may require receipts or some other type of support.

Some areas of deductible expenditures such as business entertainment, gifts, and travel have been subject to abuse. Prior to 1962,

---

71. § 267(c).

taxpayers could rely on the so-called Cohan rule, which provided that a taxpayer could deduct travel or entertainment expenses based on an approximation of the actual amounts if the exact amount was not determinable. In *Cohan v. Comm.*, the Court permitted a partial deduction for entertainment expenses of a playwright who kept no records.[72] The law now provides that no deduction will be allowed for any travel, entertainment, or business gift expenditure unless properly substantiated by "sufficient evidence corroborating [the taxpayer's] own statements" of the following information:[73]

—The amount of the expense.

—The time and place of travel or entertainment (or date of gift).

—The business purpose of such expense.

—The business relationship of the taxpayer to the person entertained (or receiving the gift).

"Adequate records" can be a diary, account book, or other expense record, provided the record is made at or near the time of the expenditure. Furthermore, documentary evidence (e. g., receipts, paid bills) is required for lodging and any other expenditure of $25 or more.[74]

> **Example 32.** B had entertainment expenses which were substantiated only by credit card receipts. The receipts established the time, place, and amount of the expenditure. Because neither the business relationship nor the business purpose was established, the deduction may be disallowed.[75]

> **Example 33.** D had entertainment expenses which were substantiated by a diary showing the time, place, amount of the expenditure, business relationship, and business purpose. However, since he had no receipts, any expenditures of $25 or more may be disallowed.[76]

Specific rules for deducting travel and entertainment expenses are discussed in Chapter 10.

EXPENSES AND INTEREST RELATING TO TAX-EXEMPT INCOME

Since certain income, such as interest on municipal bonds, is tax-exempt, and § 212 allows one to deduct expenses incurred for the production of income, it might be possible to make money at the expense of the government by excluding interest income and deducting interest expense.

---

72. *Cohan v. Comm.*, 2 USTC ¶ 489, 8 AFTR 10552, 39 F.2d 540 (CA-2, 1930).
73. § 274(d).
74. Reg. § 1.274–5(c)(2)(iii)(a) and (b).
75. *Frank J. Borsody*, 35 TCM 214, T.C.Memo. 1976–47.
76. *Quen W. Young*, 37 TCM 131, T.C.Memo. 1978–19.

Example 34. P, a taxpayer in the 50% bracket, purchased $100,000 of 9% municipal bonds. At the same time, she used the bonds as collateral on a bank loan of $100,000 at 14% interest. A positive cash flow would result from the tax benefit as follows:

Cash paid out on loan	($ 14,000)
Cash received from bonds	9,000
Tax savings from deducting interest expense (50% of $14,000 interest expense)	7,000
Net positive cash flow	$ 2,000

Specific Disallowance Under the Law. In order to eliminate the possibility outlined above, § 265 specifically disallows as a deduction the expenses of producing tax-exempt income. Interest on any indebtedness incurred or continued to purchase or carry tax-exempt obligations is disallowed under § 265. There is an exception for nonbanking financial institutions.[77]

Judicial Interpretations. It is often difficult to show a direct relationship between borrowings and investment in tax-exempt securities. Suppose, for example, that a taxpayer borrows money, adds it to existing funds, buys inventory and stocks, then later sells the inventory and buys municipal bonds. A series of transactions such as these can completely obscure any relationship between the loan and the tax-exempt investment. One solution would be to disallow any interest on any debt to the extent that any tax-exempt securities were held. This kind of approach would preclude individuals from deducting part of their home mortgage interest if they owned any municipal bonds. Obviously, the law was not intended to go to such extremes. As a result, judicial interpretations have tried to show reasonableness in the disallowance of interest deductions under § 265.

In one case,[78] a company used municipal bonds as collateral on short-term loans to meet seasonal liquidity needs. The Court disallowed the interest deduction on the grounds that the company could predict its seasonal liquidity needs and, therefore, knew it would have to borrow the money to continue to carry the tax-exempt securities. The same company *was* allowed an interest deduction on a building mortgage, even though tax-exempt securities it owned could have been sold to pay off the mortgage. The Court reasoned that short-term liquidity needs would have been impaired if the tax-exempt securities were sold, and bore no relationship to the long-term financing of a construction project.

---

77. § 265(2); Reg. § 1.265–2.
78. *The Wisconsin Cheeseman, Inc. v. U. S.,* 68–1 USTC ¶ 9145, 21 AFTR2d 383, 388 F.2d 420 (CA–7, 1968).

In another case,[79] the Court disallowed an interest deduction to a company that refused to sell tax-exempt securities it had received from the sale of a major asset, which necessitated large borrowings to finance the operation. The Court found that the primary reason that the company would not sell its bonds to reduce its bank debt was the tax savings. Other business reasons existed for holding the municipal bonds, but the dominant reason was for the tax savings. Moreover, there was a direct relationship between the bonds and the debt, because they both arose from the same transaction.

> **Example 35.** In January of the current year, T borrowed $100,000 at 8% interest, which she used to purchase 5,000 shares of stock in P Corporation. In July of the same year she sold the stock for $120,000 and reinvested the proceeds in City of Denver bonds, the income from which is tax-exempt. Assuming the $100,000 loan remained outstanding throughout the entire year, the interest attributable to the period in which the bonds were held cannot be deducted.

TAX PLANNING CONSIDERATIONS

TIME VALUE OF TAX DEDUCTIONS

Cash basis taxpayers often have the ability to make early payments for their expenses at the end of the tax year. This permits such payments to be deducted currently instead of in the following tax year. Because of the time value of money, a tax deduction this year may be worth more than the same deduction next year. Before employing this strategy, the taxpayer must consider next year's expected income and tax rates and whether a cash flow problem may develop from early payments.

The time value of money, as well as tax rate changes, must be taken into consideration when an expense can be paid and deducted in either of two years.

> **Example 36.** T, a cash basis taxpayer, wishes to make a $10,000 charitable contribution in December 1983 or in January 1984. Assuming that T has taxable income of $60,000 before the contribution and is married filing jointly, the net present value of tax savings in making the contribution in 1983 is $607 ($4,000 − $3,393), as follows:

---

79. *Illinois Terminal Railroad Co. v. U. S.*, 67–1 USTC ¶ 9374, 19 AFTR2d 1219, 375 F.2d 1016 (Ct.Cls., 1967).

	1983	1984
Taxable income before contribution	$ 60,000	$ 60,000
Charitable contribution taken	(10,000)	(10,000)
Taxable income after contribution	$ 50,000	$ 50,000
Tax on $60,000	$ 16,014	$ 15,168
Tax on $50,000	12,014	11,368
Tax savings each year	$ 4,000	$ 3,800
Time value factor (@ 12%)	1.0	.893
Net present value of tax savings	$ 4,000	$ 3,393

It should be noted that part of the tax savings results from lower rates in 1984 than in 1983.

> **Example 37.** Assume the same facts as in Example 36, except that the years involved arc 1984 and 1985. The net present value of the tax savings is now only $407, since there is no tax rate change between 1984 and 1985.

	1984	1985
Taxable income before contribution	$ 60,000	$ 60,000
Charitable contribution taken	(10,000)	(10,000)
Taxable income after contribution	$ 50,000	$ 50,000
Tax on $60,000	$ 15,168	$ 15,168
Tax on $50,000	11,368	11,368
Tax savings each year	$ 3,800	$ 3,800
Time value factor (@ 12%)	1.0	.893
Net present value of tax savings	$ 3,800	$ 3,393

If T's income is expected to increase in any of the years, the analysis would change.

The analyses in Examples 36 and 37 ignore the interest factor associated with payment of the charitable contribution in the earlier year. Even if this factor is considered, interest on $10,000 from late December to early January would be so minimal that the outcome would not change. However, this factor should be considered in the analysis of situations involving longer-term prepayments.

UNREASONABLE COMPENSATION

In substantiating the reasonableness of a shareholder-employee's compensation, an internal comparison test is sometimes useful. If it can be shown that employees who are nonshareholders receive the same (or more) compensation as shareholder-employees in comparable positions, it is evident that compensation is not unreasonable.

Another possibility is to demonstrate that the shareholder-employee has been underpaid in prior years. For example the share-holder-employee may have agreed to take a less-than-adequate salary during the unprofitable formative years of the business, provided this "postponed" compensation will be paid in later, more profitable years. This agreement should be documented, if possible, in the corporate minutes.

It is important to keep in mind that in testing for reasonableness, it is the *total* pay package that must be taken into account. One must look at all fringe benefits or perquisites, such as contributions by the corporation to a qualified pension plan (even though those amounts are not immediately available to the covered employee-shareholder).

PERSONAL EXPENDITURES

Section 262 disallows a deduction for legal fees that are personal in nature. Legal fees are deductible under § 212(3), however, to the extent such services represent the rendering of tax advice (e. g., the tax consequences of a property settlement or child support payments). Therefore, it is advisable to request an itemization of attorney's fees to substantiate a partial deduction for the tax-related amounts.

RELATED TAXPAYERS

If an accrual basis corporation accrues salary, bonus, interest, etc. to a related shareholder-employee, the corporation must be careful to pay these amounts within 2½ months of the end of the year. Payments not made within the 2½-month period are not allowed as a deduction in any year, even though the payments are subsequently made. If a company is unable to pay the accrued amounts (or does not do so because of an oversight), it may still be possible to show that the amounts have been constructively received in the year of accrual. In such event, the shareholder-employee should include the accrued amounts in income in the year of accrual, and the corporation should claim a deduction in the same period. A corporation which is temporarily short of funds should consider borrowing money to pay the accrued amounts to insure against loss of the deduction.

Note that an extension of time to file an income tax return does not extend the 2½-month period for payment of accrued items to related shareholder-employees.

> **Example 38.** In February, Y Corporation was granted an extension of time to file its corporate tax return to June 15, 1985, (rather than March 15). An accrued bonus of $20,000 to an employee-shareholder was paid on June 1, 1985. Y Corporation cannot deduct the bonus in its calendar year 1984 return, nor can it deduct the bonus in 1985 when paid, even though the employee-shareholder must report it on his 1985 return.

SHIFTING DEDUCTIONS

Taxpayers should manage their obligations to avoid the loss of a deduction. Deductions can be shifted among family members, depending upon who makes the payment. For example, a father buys a car for his daughter and both sign the note. If either one makes the payment, that person gets the deduction for the interest. If the note is signed by the daughter only and her father makes the payment, neither is entitled to a deduction.

HOBBY LOSSES

To demonstrate that an activity has been entered into for the purpose of making a profit (i. e., not a hobby), a taxpayer should treat the activity as a business. The business should engage in advertising, use business letterhead stationery, and maintain a business phone.

If a taxpayer's activity earns a profit in two out of five consecutive years, the presumption is that the activity is engaged in for profit. It may be possible for a cash basis taxpayer to meet these requirements by timing the payment of expenses or the receipt of revenues. The payment of certain expenses incurred prior to the end of the year may be made in the following year, or the billing of year-end sales may be delayed so that collections are received in the following year.

It should be kept in mind that the two-out-of-five year rule under § 183 is not absolute. All it does is shift the presumption. If a profit is not made in two out of five years, the losses may still be allowed if the taxpayer can show that they are due to the nature of the business. For example, success in artistic or literary endeavors can take a long time. Also, due to the present state of the economy, full-time farmers and ranchers are unable to show a profit; how can one expect a part-time farmer or rancher to do so?

On the other hand, merely satisfying the two-out-of-five year rule does not guarantee that one is automatically "home free" either. If the two years of profits are insignificant relative to the losses of other years, or if the profits are not from the ordinary operation of the business, the Internal Revenue Service can still establish that the taxpayer is not engaged in an activity for profit.[80]

Example 39. A taxpayer had the following gains and losses:

1980	$(50,000)
1981	(35,000)
1982	(60,000)
1983	200
1984	125

---

80. *Hunter Faulconer, Sr.,* 45TCM 1084, T.C.Memo. 1983–165.

Under these circumstances, the IRS should have a relatively easy time proving that the operation is *not* a bona fide business.

PROBLEM MATERIALS

Questions for Class Discussion

1. T and S are unrelated individual single taxpayers, and each has gross income of $20,000 and deductions of $3,000 for the current year. However, T's deductions are *for* adjusted gross income while S's are *from* adjusted gross income. Are these taxpayers in the same position? Why or why not?

2. Are the following items deductible *for* adjusted gross income, deductible *from* adjusted gross income, or nondeductible personal items?

    (a) Unreimbursed travel expenses of an employee.

    (b) Alimony payments.

    (c) Charitable contributions.

    (d) Medical expenses.

    (e) Safe deposit box rentals.

    (f) Repairs made on a personal residence.

    (g) Expenses related to tax-exempt municipal bonds.

3. Explain how an expense may be necessary but not ordinary.

4. Discuss the implications of "reasonable" compensation. Does it make a difference if the corporation is owned by the taxpayer and his or her immediate family? What are the tax consequences to the corporation and shareholder-employee?

5. Is a taxpayer permitted to deduct bribes, kickbacks, or fines and penalties? Why or why not?

6. Are legal expenses deductible if they are incurred to obtain a divorce? Are they deductible if they are incurred in connection with a trade or business? Why is this distinction made?

7. How are expenses (e. g., travel, meals, and lodging) incurred in connection with the investigation of a new business opportunity treated if the new business is acquired? If the new business is *not* acquired?

8. What factors should be considered to determine whether an activity is a legitimate business activity or a hobby?

9. If a taxpayer is unable to meet the requirements of § 183 relative to earning a profit in at least two of five consecutive years, is it possible to qualify the activity as a business? Why or why not?

10. If a taxpayer meets the requirements of § 183 relative to earning a profit in at least two of five consecutive years, is it still possible for the IRS to treat the activity as a hobby of the taxpayer?

11. Why has the Code placed restrictions upon deductions relating to the rental of vacation homes?

12. Can a cash basis taxpayer take a current deduction for the cost of a building used in a business?

13. When can prepaid expenses be deducted by a cash basis taxpayer? Explain.

14. Contrast the accrual method and cash method as they are defined for tax purposes. What are their differences? What are their similarities?

15. Is it ever possible to deduct expenditures incurred for another individual's benefit?

16. List five personal expenses that are allowed as deductions by specific provisions of the Code.

17. Why is a loss limited to a taxpayer's basis (even where the fair market value is much higher) or actual outlay?

18. Distinguish between deductible repairs and capital expenditures. Is the distinction dependent upon the dollar amount involved?

19. Would anyone ever *want* to capitalize (rather than expense) an item? Explain.

20. Discuss the reasons for the disallowance of losses between related parties. Would it make any difference if a parent sold stock to an unrelated third party and the child repurchased the same number of shares of the stock in the market the same day?

21. What is constructive ownership? Discuss.

22. Discuss the substantiation requirements for deductible expenditures, particularly those for travel and entertainment.

23. Would a record of the past year's travel expenses meet the substantiation requirements if the record were compiled at the time the tax return for that year was prepared?

24. Discuss the tracing problems which are encountered in the enforcement of the restrictions of § 265 which disallow a deduction for the expenses of producing tax-exempt income.

Problems

25. T is engaged in an illegal numbers racket. His expenses are as follows:

Cost of goods sold	$ 15,000
Rent and utilities	20,000
Salaries	40,000
Bribes to police	10,000

How much can he deduct on his tax return?

26. If T's business in (25) is a cocaine selling operation, what items could he deduct?

27. T owns .05% of the stock of XYZ Airlines, a widely held corporation. T becomes disgruntled with the existing management of the airlines and attempts to remove the management through proxy. Although she spent a considerable amount of time and money, her endeavor was unsuccessful. Can she deduct the expenditures? Explain. Can she deduct the expenses incurred in traveling to the corporation's annual shareholder's meeting?

28. T, a cash basis taxpayer, rented a building from J on October 1, 1984, paying $12,000 (one full year's rent) in advance and a $10,000 deposit. The lease is for 15 years. T proceeds to add improvements costing $40,000 which have a 20-year life and which will revert to J upon termination of the lease.

    (a) How much rent can T deduct in 1984?

    (b) How much does J include in income if he is an accrual basis taxpayer? A cash basis taxpayer?

    (c) How is the deposit of $10,000 treated to both?

    (d) How are the improvements treated to both?

29. X borrowed $200,000 from a bank in December 1984. She prepaid the interest of $2,000 per month for the period from December 1, 1984, through September 30, 1985. The prepayment of $20,000 was deducted on her 1985 tax return.

    (a) How much of the interest is deductible in 1984?

    (b) How much is deductible in 1985?

    (c) Would your answer be different if the prepayment resulted in a material distortion of income during the two years?

30. T operates a trucking company in Kansas and Nebraska. T's financial records indicate quite clearly that he can stay in business (on a profitable basis) only if his trucks operate at 65 miles per hour during the runs. In the current year T's firm was fined $10,000 by the Kansas and Nebraska authorities for violations of the 55 mile per hour speed limit. Comment on the deductibility of the fines.

31. T owns a restaurant that has a limited liquor license (beer and wine only) under state law. He travels to the capital to testify against a proposed bill that would eliminate such limited licenses. Are his travel expenses deductible?

32. L is a housewife who makes pottery items at home for sale to friends. She had the following income and expenses for the year:

Sales	$ 1,000
Expenses:	
Materials	400
Advertising	250
Travel	350
Classes in ceramics	500
	$ 1,500
Net loss	$ (500)

Comment on whether her activities constitute a "trade or business."

33. T, the owner of a chain of motels in Ohio, travels to Florida to investigate the possible acquisition of a motel chain located in the South. T incurred travel, legal, and financial expenses of $5,000 in the course of the investigation.

    (a) Discuss the tax treatment of T's expenses in the event the investment is made.

(b) In the event the investment is not made.

(c) Assume that T takes another trip during the current year to check on the rental property and spends one half of a day checking the property and 12 days on a vacation. Is any portion of the trip deductible?

34. T owns and operates a dry cleaning business. He pays $500 in legal and accounting fees in the investigation of a possible purchase of the movie theater next door.

(a) Discuss the tax treatment of the $500 if T does not buy the theater.

(b) Discuss the tax treatment of the $500 if T buys and operates the theater.

35. Taxpayer is engaged in horse breeding activities in addition to his regular executive position with a large corporation. He had three years of operations with losses of $120,000, $100,000, and $130,000, respectively. Upon audit by the IRS, he demands a chance at the presumption period of two out of seven years. In the fourth and fifth years, he sustained losses of $90,000 and $126,000. In the sixth and seventh years, he showed net profits of $1,500 and $1,000, respectively.

(a) Is he "safe" under § 183?

(b) Can he claim the statute of limitations bars the loss disallowances for the earlier years?

36. During the current year, P's vacation home was used as follows: one month of occupancy by P, four months of rental to unrelated parties, and seven months of vacancy. Further information concerning the property is summarized below:

Rental income	$ 4,500
Expenses	
Real estate taxes	$ 1,000
Interest on mortgage	2,600
Utilities and maintenance	1,200
Repairs	400
Landscaping	1,700
Depreciation	3,000

Compute P's net rental income or loss and the amount(s) that can be itemized on his income tax return.

37. Indicate whether each expenditure below is deductible by F, who paid the items in question:

(a) Interest on his dependent son's auto loan.

(b) Medical expenses of his mother who furnishes 60% of her own support.

(c) Property taxes on his wife's summer home. They are filing a joint return.

(d) Business lunches for F's clients.

38. H obtained a divorce in 1984 and paid the following fees:

Court costs and legal fees of obtaining divorce	$	200
Rewriting of will		150
Detective fees paid for obtaining evidence of infidelity		500
Legal fees to determine who may claim the children as dependents		500
Legal fees to determine the basis of settlement property		1,500

How much can H deduct on his 1984 return?

39. Discuss the tax treatment of each of the following items paid by T, an individual taxpayer:

    (a) T paid the real estate taxes on her mother's home.

    (b) An analysis of T's stock portfolio revealed a $10,000 decrease in value during the year.

    (c) T paid $3,000 to execute a new will.

40. R bought an old house and turned it into a rental property. Before renting out the house, R incurred the following expenditures. Discuss the tax treatment of each expenditure:

    (a) Replacement of broken fixtures in kitchen.

    (b) Modification of walls and construction of second bathroom so the house could be rented to two separate tenants instead of to one family.

    (c) Addition of a backyard patio.

    (d) Painting of the exterior of the house.

41. J sold stock (basis of $20,000) to her brother, B, for $16,000.

    (a) What are the tax consequences to J?

    (b) What are the tax consequences to B if he later sells the stock for $21,000?

    (c) If B sells it for $14,000?

    (d) If B sells it for $18,000?

42. What is R's constructive ownership of X Corporation, given the following information?

Shares owned by R	450
Shares owned by S, R's uncle	300
Shares owned by T, R's partner	15
Shares owned by U, a partnership owned by R and T equally	150
Shares owned by V, R's granddaughter	285
Shares owned by unrelated parties	300

43. J is the sole owner of X Corporation (an accrual basis taxpayer). X Corporation owes J $125,000 and accrues $10,000 of interest expense on December 31, 1984.

    (a) What are the tax consequences to J and X Corporation if the interest is paid on January 15, 1985?

    (b) On March 20, 1985?

44. D, the dependent daughter of F, bought a new car and obtained a loan on the car. During the current tax year, D made the first six monthly loan

payments and F made the last six. Who can deduct the interest on the payments under the following different assumptions:

(a) D, but not F, signed the loan contract.

(b) F, but not D, signed the loan contract.

(c) Both F and D signed the loan contract.

Cumulative Problems

45. Z, age 36, is married to M. They have no dependents. Z is employed as manager of a large apartment complex. His salary for 1984 was $30,000, and he was provided with an apartment free of rent. The apartment Z and M live in would rent for $400 a month. Z's contract with his employer requires him to live on the premises. M earned $18,000 as an office manager.

In July 1984, M was injured in an automobile accident. In November, she received a settlement for damages of $20,000 from the other driver's insurance company. As a result of her injuries, M incurred medical expenses of $2,500. In September, she received reimbursement of $2,500 from the insurance company under an accident and health policy provided by her employer.

Over the years, Z had developed a close working relationship with B, who owns a moving company. On his recommendation, several tenants hired B to move them. As an expression of his appreciation, on December 24, 1984, B gave Z a stereo system for which he had paid $1,500 on December 23.

Z had the following interest items in 1984:

$200—interest received from United States Series H savings bonds
$100—interest credited to Z's savings account but not withdrawn in 1984
$250—interest received on City of Miami General Obligation Bonds

On April 14, Z sold some stock to pay Federal income tax they owed for 1983. The stock, which they had acquired on January 12, 1984, for $1,000, was sold for $1,500. On November 5, 1984, he sold 50 shares of stock for $43 a share. They had acquired the stock on February 16, 1983, for $27 a share. They received $600 dividends on their stock investments in 1984.

Z made a preliminary computation of their tax liability late in December and realized he needed to take some action to reduce their taxable income. His first move was to sell 100 shares of stock to his father, with the understanding that he would buy the stock back in January, 1985. He sold the stock, which had been acquired on August 23, 1984, at $36 a share, for $2,000. His next action was to delay depositing his December 1984 salary check until January 4, 1985. His net pay for December, after withholding and other deductions, was $1,731.

In examining their receipts, canceled checks, and other documents, you have ascertained that Z and M have various itemized deductions of $4,300, not including any amount described below:

(a) In connection with their stock investments, Z paid an investment counselor $300 in 1984. He also rented a safe deposit box, in which he kept the stocks, for $50.

(b) As part of his year-end tax planning strategy, Z decided to increase their charitable contributions. Because they were short of cash at the end of the year, he charged contributions of $800 on his bank credit card.

(c) Z and three of his friends decided to investigate the possibility of acquiring an apartment complex. The plan was for Z to resign from his present employment and manage the complex. After a thorough investigation, the group decided, based on their CPA's analysis, that the investment would not be profitable. Z's share of the expenses of the investigation was $800.

(d) Z's father was ill for three months in 1984 and was unable to work. To help his father during this time, Z made three of his father's mortgage payments, which included interest of $950.

Z and M file a joint return. You are to compute their taxable income for 1984.

46. X is a bachelor, age 60. He is employed as a vice-president of First National Bank. He provides over half the support for his brother, M, age 74, who resides in a nursing home. M's only source of income is $2,400 of Social Security benefits. X also provides 90% of the support of P, his shell-shocked sergeant from World War II, who has lived with him since his release from a veteran's hospital in 1975. P's only income is a $3,600 pension from the Army. X's salary is $78,500. In addition, he had the following receipts in 1984:

(a) $200 received for jury duty.

(b) $300 state income tax refund. X had total itemized deductions of $4,000 in 1983.

(c) $5,000 death benefit received from his brother B's employer as a result of B's death.

(d) $1,000 gain on sale of State of Virginia bonds he had owned for two years.

(e) $2,000 interest on the bonds in (d) and $2,000 interest on a savings account.

(f) $1,500 kickback he received from a contractor to whom he granted a $50,000 bank loan, even though the contractor was a questionable credit risk.

(g) $25,000 award for defamation of character in a libel suit X brought against a newspaper which had erroneously reported that he had received kickbacks from a construction contractor for a loan he had approved in 1983.

(h) $8,400 rental income from a duplex X owns. Deductible expenses related to the rental property were $6,000.

(i) $11,000 selling price of an antique automobile. X had acquired the auto four years ago for $7,000.

Examination of X's records indicates that he had various itemized deductions of $4,800, not including the following items:

(j) $1,100 travel expenses incurred while attending a banker's convention. Although First National Bank gave him time off to attend the convention, X was not reimbursed for the expenses.

(k) $3,500 legal expenses incurred in connection with the lawsuit described in (g).

(l) $50 safe deposit box rental related to investment activities.

(m) $3,000 interest on funds used to acquire the State of Virginia bonds [see (d) and (e)].

You are to compute X's income tax liability before prepayments or credits.

Research Problems

47. Taxpayer is in the wholesale liquor business in California where a posting of prices is required and no kickbacks or discounts are allowed. The taxpayer devised a system whereby he would issue "credits" to certain customers when they purchased liquor. These credits could be used to buy more liquor (i. e., an additional bottle with each case of liquor purchased). When customers cashed in their credits for additional liquor, the liquor was removed from inventory and became a part of cost of goods sold. Is the taxpayer entitled to the deduction for cost of goods sold?

Partial list of research aids:

§ 162(c)(2).

James Alex, 70 T.C. 322 (1978).

48. Taxpayer, a certified public accountant, gave the wrong advice to a client. As a result, the client incurred an additional $75,000 of costs. The CPA reimbursed the client and, although he had malpractice insurance, failed to file a claim for fear of either having his insurance cancelled or having the premiums drastically increased. Can the taxpayer deduct the $75,000 as a loss incurred in a trade or business under § 165(c) or as an ordinary and necessary business expense under § 162 of the Code?

49. R and S were plumbers working for the same company, and they became close friends. In 19X4, they decided to open their own business, a plumbing store offering parts and advice to "do-it-yourself" homeowners. R and S shared equally in the ownership and management. The store was immediately successful, and R and S shared about $100,000 in profits the first year. During the second year, as the business became more hectic, R realized that S was hurting profits. S was a terrible manager, and his increasingly erratic behavior was driving away customers. R offered to buy S's share of the business to R, but S refused to sell. R then offered to pay S a $20,000 annual salary If S would stay away from the store and leave the management of the store to R. S agreed. Is the $20,000 salary payment deductible?

Partial list of research aids:

Aitkin v. Commissioner, 12 B.T.A. 692 (1928). § 162(a).

50. T and his wife file joint tax returns. Mr. and Mrs. T jointly own a personal residence and an apartment building which are *not* subject to mortgages. During 1984, Mrs. T mortgaged the personal residence and received $100,000. These funds were invested in tax-free municipal bonds earning 7% interest. The mortgage interest on the home is 8%, or $8,000.

The apartment was also mortgaged during the year and the funds ($200,000) were invested in Mr. T's business. The interest on this mortgage was $15,000 in 1984. How much interest, if any, can be deducted in 1984? (Ignore any potential gift tax consequences.)

Partial list of research aids:

§ 163

51. Dr. Johnson regularly purchases his lunch and that of his assistants at the hospital. The cashier is forbidden by hospital rules to issue receipts, but orally substantiated Dr. Johnson's claim that he purchased lunch for himself and his assistants daily. Would the testimony of the taxpayer and that of the cafeteria cashier fulfill the substantiation requirements of § 1.274–5(c)(3)?

Partial list of research aids:

§ 274(d).

La Forge v. Comm., 70–2 USTC ¶ 9694, 26 AFTR2d 70–5768, 434 F.2d 370 (CA–2, 1970).

52. T operates a factory that empties its waste material into a nearby stream. A new state law requires T to add a waste treatment facility to the factory. If T does not comply, the factory must cease operations. The waste treatment facility will not improve, increase, or extend the useful life or productive capacity of the factory. Thus, T wishes to deduct the cost of the waste treatment facility as an expense of the period in which it is built. Will the deduction be allowed?

Partial list of research aids:

Woolrich Woolen Mills v. U. S., 4 AFTR2d 5929, 178 F.Supp. 875 (D.C. Penn., 1959).

53. In 1980, T became interested in raising and showing dogs. After discussing the costs of producing and marketing the dogs with professional dog breeders, T made some calculations and determined that he could make a profit on a dog breeding operation within a few years. T named the operation P Kennels and had stationery, business cards, and pedigree forms made up using that name. T advertised and also hired a professional trainer. T maintained a separate checking account for the kennels. The cancelled checks served as the primary records of the enterprise.

The calculations from 1980 did not materialize. Some of the dogs suffered from unexpected injuries and illnesses. On two occasions, an entire litter of pups died because of the mother's "bad milk." T sold a few dogs without replacing them and retained others that were clearly not championship material. Despite T's degree in animal breeding and the two to three hours per day spent with the dogs, the operation sustained a loss for the next eight years. Gross income over the period totaled $4,000 while deductions claimed amounted to $52,000. Fortunately T had a full-time job in another field during this period and his job earnings increased annually. Can T deduct the losses incurred in the dog breeding operation?

54. Taxpayer was engaged in the business of selling marijuana. He imported his merchandise from both Colombia and Hawaii. His expenses included paying growers and dealers for the merchandise, bribes to various officials and border guards, costs incurred in flying the merchandise into the coun-

try via rented small planes, and other ordinary and necessary expenses (e. g., rent, salaries). What items can he deduct?

55. J owns a farm upon which a mobile home is parked. He rents the mobile home to R (his brother) for a fair rental to have R keep an eye on the other farm property. J stipulates that if R rents it for five years, the mobile home becomes his. Otherwise, it reverts back to J. The trailer is not fully depreciated. How should the payments be treated by J on his return?

Chapter 8

Deductions and Losses: Certain Business Expenses and Losses

Working with the tax formula for individuals requires the proper classification of items which are deductible *for* adjusted gross income and items which are deductions *from* adjusted gross income (itemized deductions). Business expenses and losses, discussed in this chapter, are reductions of gross income to arrive at the taxpayer's adjusted gross income. The one exception, however, might be casualty losses, which could be either deductions *for* adjusted gross income or deductions *from,* depending on the circumstances.

Itemized deductions (in excess of the zero bracket amount) and a taxpayer's personal and dependency exemptions are subtracted *from* adjusted gross income in the determination of taxable income. Itemized deductions are discussed in Chapter 11; the zero bracket amount and the personal and dependency exemptions were discussed in Chapter 4.

BAD DEBTS

If a taxpayer sells goods or provides services on credit and the account receivable subsequently becomes worthless, a bad debt deduction is permitted only if income arising from the creation of the debt (accounts receivable) was previously included in income.[1] No deduction is allowed, for example, for a bad debt arising from the sale of a product or service when the taxpayer is on the cash basis, because no

---

1. Reg. § 1.166–1(e).

income is reported until the cash has been collected. A bad debt deduction for a cash basis taxpayer would amount to a double deduction, because the expenses of the product or service rendered are deducted when payments are made to suppliers and to employees.

> **Example 1.**   T, an individual engaged in the practice of accounting, performed accounting services for X for which he charged $8,000 ($7,700 for services and $300 materials). X never paid the bill, and his whereabouts are unknown.
>
> If T is an accrual basis taxpayer, the $8,000 would be included in income when the services were performed. The $300 would be a business expense when the costs were incurred. When it is determined that X's account will not be collected, the $8,000 will be expensed as a bad debt.
>
> If T is a cash basis taxpayer, the $8,000 would not be included in income until payment is received. However, the $300 would be a business expense at the time the expense was incurred. When it is determined that X's account will not be collected, the $8,000 will not be a bad debt expense, since it was never recognized as income.

A deduction is allowed during the taxable year for any debt that becomes wholly worthless during the year or any business debt that becomes partially worthless during the taxable year.[2] The taxpayer must be able to demonstrate to the satisfaction of the IRS the amount which is worthless and the amount charged off on the taxpayer's books.[3] If the debt previously deducted as partially worthless becomes totally worthless in a future year, only the remainder not previously deducted can be written off.

One of the more difficult tasks is determining if and when a bad debt is, in fact, worthless, since the loss is deductible solely in the year of partial or total worthlessness. Legal proceedings need not be initiated against the debtor when the surrounding facts indicate that such action will not result in collection.[4]

> **Example 2.**   In 19X1, J loaned $1,000 to K, who agreed to repay the loan in two years. In 19X3, K disappeared after the note became delinquent. If a reasonable investigation by J indicates that he cannot find K or a suit against her would not result in collection he can deduct the $1,000 in 19X3.

Bankruptcy is generally an indication of at least partial worthlessness of a debt. Bankruptcy may create worthlessness before the settlement date. If this is the case, the deduction must be taken in the year of worthlessness, not in the later year upon settlement.

---

2.   § 166(a); Reg. § 1.166–3.
3.   Reg. § 1.166–3(a)(2)(iii).
4.   Reg. § 1.166–2(b).

Example 3. In Example 2, assume K filed for personal bankruptcy in 19X2. At that time J learned that unsecured creditors (including J) were expected to receive ultimately 20¢ on the dollar. In 19X3, settlement is made and J receives only $150. He should deduct $800 ($1,000 loan less $200 expected settlement) in 19X2 and $50 in 19X3 ($200 balance less $150 proceeds). J is not permitted to wait until 19X3 to deduct the entire $850.

ALLOWABLE METHODS

A taxpayer may use the reserve for bad debts method or the specific charge-off method in accounting for bad debts. However, a deduction for partial worthlessness of a business bad debt is permitted only if the specific charge-off method is being used.[5] Under the reserve for bad debts method, a deduction is allowed for a reasonable addition to the reserve.[6]

A taxpayer using the specific charge-off method receives a deduction when a specific business debt becomes either partially or wholly worthless or when a specific nonbusiness debt becomes wholly worthless. The taxpayer must satisfy the IRS that a debt is partially worthless and must demonstrate the amount of worthlessness. In the case of total worthlessness, a deduction is allowed for the entire amount in the year the debt becomes worthless. The amount of the deduction depends on the taxpayer's basis in the bad debt. If the debt arose from the sale of services or products and the face amount was previously included in income, this amount is deductible. If the taxpayer purchased the debt, the deduction is equal to the amount the taxpayer paid for the debt instrument.

Under the reserve method of accounting for bad debts, the taxpayer's deduction is based on a "reasonable addition" to the reserve. This may be contrasted with the specific charge-off method. A taxpayer using this method bases the bad debt deduction on the actual write-off of specific accounts. What constitutes a "reasonable addition" to the reserve is largely a matter of judgment and depends on individual facts and circumstances. The Regulations recognize that the reasonableness of an addition to the bad debt reserve is dependent on business prosperity and individual differences among businesses, for example.[7] The determining factors are the total amount of debts outstanding and the balance in the reserve account at the end of the year. If the taxpayer's estimated bad debts are more (or less) than actual losses, the reserve must be adjusted downward (or upward) in the future year.

The specific charge-off method is consistent with the all events

---

5. Reg. § 1.166–3(a).
6. Reg. § 1.166–4(a).
7. Reg. § 1.166–4(b)(1).

test (discussed in Chapter 5) as it is applied to deductions. Congress, in sanctioning the reserve approach, chose to allow a deduction to be anticipated even though all events have not occurred to make the loss a certainty. Thus, the reserve method is a statutory exception to the all events test.

DETERMINING RESERVE ADDITIONS

The courts have generally applied a formula approach for determining a "reasonable addition" to the bad debt reserve. The IRS frequently uses an approach which was derived from the *Black Motor Co.* case.[8] The formula approach is based on a weighted average of the ratio of bad debts to accounts and notes receivable for the current year and preceding five years. This percentage is then applied to the ending balance of accounts and notes receivable to determine the required amount in the reserve at the end of the year. The bad debt deduction represents the amount necessary to bring the reserve up to its required balance at the end of the year.

Example 4. Black Motor Co. formula approach

1. $\dfrac{\text{Bad debts—current year plus five preceding years}}{\text{Total accounts and notes receivable at the end of each of these years}} \quad \dfrac{20{,}000}{500{,}000} = 4\%$

2. 4% × accounts and notes receivable at the end of
   the current year ($80,000) .... $ 3,200*

3. Beginning balance in the reserve for doubtful
   accounts .... $ 3,000
      + Recoveries of previous accounts written off 300
      − Write-off of specific accounts during the year .... (600)
      + Bad debt deduction (addition to reserve) 500
   Ending balance in the reserve .... $ 3,200

*This amount represents the required balance in the reserve at the end of the year.

It should be noted that the formula approach is not mandatory; individual facts and circumstances must be taken into account. In addition, the IRS now agrees that the formula outlined above is not controlling and that the bad debt addition may be more or less depending on the facts and circumstances.[9]

FILING REQUIREMENTS

The taxpayer using the reserve method must attach a statement with the following information to every return:[10]
> —The volume of charge sales during the year and the percentage of the reserve to such amount.

---

8. *Black Motor Co. v. Comm.*, 42–1 USTC ¶ 9265, 28 AFTR 1193, 125 F.2d 977 (CA–6, 1942).
9. Rev.Rul. 76–362, 1976–2 C.B. 45.
10. Reg. § 1.166–4(c).

—The total amount of notes and accounts receivable at the beginning and at the close of the taxable year.

—The amount of debts which have been charged against the reserve.

—The computation of the addition to the reserve for bad debts.

ELECTION OF METHODS

Subject to the approval of the IRS, a taxpayer may elect to use either the reserve or specific charge-off method of accounting. However, the taxpayer can elect the reserve method without the consent of the IRS if the election is made in the first taxable year that a bad debt occurs.[11] The election is subject to the approval of the District Director upon examination of the return. Once an election is made, that method must be followed in all future years unless the taxpayer receives permission to change. A request for a change in method must generally be made within 270 days of the start of the tax year for which the change is sought.[12]

BUSINESS VERSUS NONBUSINESS BAD DEBTS

A nonbusiness bad debt is a debt unrelated to the taxpayer's trade or business either when it was created or when it became worthless. The nature of a debt depends on whether the lender was engaged in the business of lending money or if there is a proximate relationship between the creation of the debt and the lender's trade or business. The use to which the borrowed funds are put by the debtor is of no consequence.[13] Loans to relatives or friends are the most common type of nonbusiness bad debt.

> **Example 5.** J loaned his friend, S, $1,500. S used the money to start a business which subsequently failed. Even though proceeds of the loan were used in a business, the loan is a nonbusiness bad debt because the business was S's, not J's.

> **Example 6.** J loaned another friend, T, $500. T was unable to repay J because of financial difficulties. The loss is attributable to a nonbusiness bad debt.

The distinction between a business bad debt and a nonbusiness bad debt is important: A business bad debt is deductible as an ordinary loss in the year incurred, whereas a nonbusiness bad debt is always treated as a short-term capital loss.[14] Thus, regardless of the age of a nonbusiness bad debt, the deduction is of limited benefit due to the capital loss limitations on deductibility in any one year. The

11. Reg. § 1.166–1(b).
12. § 446(e); Rev.Proc. 82–19.
13. Reg. § 1.166–5(b)(2).
14. § 166(d)(1)(B).

maximum amount of a net short-term capital loss that an individual can deduct against ordinary income in any one year is $3,000. The excess (if any) can be carried over and deducted in future years subject to the same annual limitation. Capital loss rules are more fully discussed in Chapter 16. In addition, no deduction is allowed for the partial worthlessness of a nonbusiness bad debt, and no deduction is permitted if the lender receives a partial recovery of the debt.[15] However, the taxpayer is entitled to deduct the net amount of the loss upon final settlement of the debt.

The following are illustrations of business bad debts adapted from the Regulations.

> **Example 7.**   In 19X1, L sold his business but retained a claim (i. e., note or account receivable) against B. The claim became worthless in 19X2. L's loss is treated as a business bad debt because the debt was created in the conduct of L's former trade or business. Business bad debt treatment is accorded to L despite the fact that he was holding the note as an investor and was no longer in a trade or business when the claim became worthless.[16]

> **Example 8.**   In 19X1, L died and left his business assets to his son, S. One of the business assets inherited by S was a claim against B which became worthless in S's hands in 19X3. S's loss is a business bad debt, since "the loss is sustained as a proximate incident to the conduct of the trade or business in which he is engaged at the time the debt becomes worthless."[17]

The nonbusiness bad debt provisions are not applicable to corporations; it is assumed that any loans made by a corporation are related to its trade or business.

LOANS BETWEEN RELATED PARTIES

Loans between relatives always raise the issue of whether the loan was bona fide or was a gift. The Regulations state that a bona fide debt arises from a debtor-creditor relationship based on a valid and enforceable obligation to pay a fixed or determinable sum of money.[18] Thus, individual circumstances must be examined to determine whether advances between related parties are gifts or loans. Some considerations are these: Was a note properly executed? Is there collateral? What collection efforts were made? What was the intent of the parties?

> **Example 9.**   L loans $2,000 to his widowed mother for an operation. L's mother owns no property and is not employed, and her only income consists of the Social Security benefits. No note is

---

15. Reg. § 1.166–5(a)(2).
16. Reg. § 1.166–5(d), Example 1.
17. Reg. § 1.166–5(d), Example 3.
18. Reg. § 1.166–1(c).

issued for the loan, no provision for interest is made, and no repayment date is mentioned. In the current year, L's mother dies leaving no estate. Assuming the loan is not repaid, L cannot take a deduction for a nonbusiness bad debt, because the facts indicate that no debtor-creditor relationship existed.

SUMMARY OF BAD DEBT PROVISIONS

Figure I
BAD DEBT DEDUCTIONS

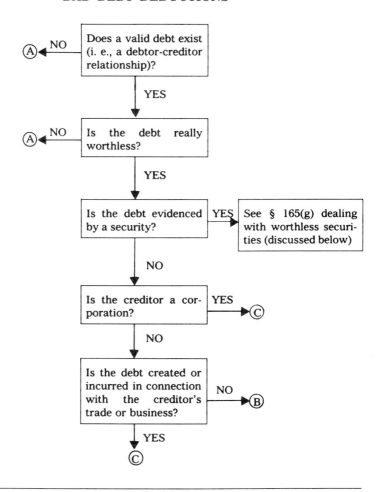

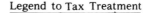

Legend to Tax Treatment

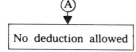

No deduction allowed

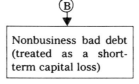

Nonbusiness bad debt (treated as a short-term capital loss)

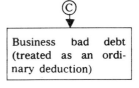

Business bad debt (treated as an ordinary deduction)

WORTHLESS SECURITIES

A loss is allowed under § 165 for a security that becomes worthless during the year.[19] Such securities are usually shares of stock or some form of indebtedness, and the losses generated are usually treated as capital losses which are deemed to have occurred on the last day of the taxable year. Capital losses may be of limited benefit due to the capital loss limitation provisions (discussed in Chapter 16).

> **Example 10.** T, a calendar year taxpayer, owns stock in X Corporation (a publicly held company). The stock was acquired as an investment on November 30 of last year at a cost of $5,000. On July 1 of this year, the stock became worthless. Since the stock is deemed to have become worthless as of December 31 of this year, T has a capital loss from an asset held for 13 months (i. e., a long-term capital loss).

SECURITIES IN AFFILIATED CORPORATIONS

Special treatment is provided for corporations that own securities in affiliated companies.[20] Ordinary loss treatment is granted for such worthless securities if the corporate holder owns 80 percent of the voting power of all classes of stock and at least 80 percent of each class of nonvoting stock of the affiliated company.

SMALL BUSINESS STOCK

The general rule is that shareholders receive capital gain or loss treatment upon the sale or exchange of stock. However, it is possible to receive an ordinary loss deduction if the loss is sustained on small business stock—"§ 1244 stock." Only individuals are eligible to receive the ordinary loss treatment under § 1244, and the loss is limited to $50,000 ($100,000 for married individuals filing jointly) per year. The corporation must meet qualifications (such as capitalization not exceeding $1,000,000) for the worthlessness of § 1244 stock to be treated as an ordinary—rather than a capital—loss.[21]

> **Example 11.** On July 1, 19X1, T, a single individual, purchased 100 shares of X Corporation common stock for $100,000. The X stock qualified as § 1244 stock. On June 20, 19X3, T sold all of the X stock for $20,000. Because the X stock is § 1244 stock, T would have $50,000 of ordinary loss and $30,000 of long-term capital loss.

---

19.   § 165(g).
20.   § 165(g)(3).
21.   "Individuals" include a partnership but not a trust or an estate.

CASUALTY AND THEFT LOSSES

An individual may deduct a loss under § 165(c) in the following circumstances: (1) the loss is incurred in a trade or business; (2) the loss is incurred in a transaction entered into for profit; and (3) the loss is caused by fire, storm, shipwreck, or other casualty or by theft. A taxpayer suffering losses from damage to nonbusiness property can deduct only those losses attributable to fire, storm, shipwreck, or other casualty or theft. While the meaning of the terms "fire, storm, shipwreck, and theft" are relatively free from dispute, the term "other casualty" needs further clarification. The term "other casualty" means casualties analogous to fire, storm, or shipwreck. The term also includes accidental loss of property provided the loss qualifies under the same rules as any other casualty. These rules are that the loss must result from an event that is (1) identifiable; (2) damaging to property; and (3) sudden, unexpected, and unusual in nature. A sudden event is one that is swift and precipitous and not gradual or progressive. An unexpected event is an event that is ordinarily unanticipated and occurs without the intent of the one who suffers the loss. An unusual event is one that is extraordinary and nonrecurring, one that does not commonly occur during the activity in which the taxpayer was engaged when the destruction occurred.[22] Examples include hurricanes, tornadoes, floods, storms, shipwrecks, fires, auto accidents, mine cave-ins, sonic booms, and vandalism. Weather that causes damages (drought, for example) must be unusual and severe for the particular region. Damage must be to the taxpayer's property to qualify as a casualty loss.

The deduction for a casualty loss in the case of an automobile accident can be taken only if the damage was not caused by the taxpayer's willful act or willful negligence.[23]

> **Example 12.** T parks her car on a hill and fails to set the brake properly and to curb the wheels. As a result of T's negligence, the car rolls down the hill, damages U's front porch, injures U who was sitting on the porch, and damages T's car. Due to the accident, T is forced to pay the following amounts:
>
> | | |
> |---|---:|
> | Medical expenses for U's injuries | $ 350 |
> | Repairs to T's car | 400 |
> | Repairs to U's porch | 300 |
> | Fine for moving traffic violation | 30 |
>
> The $400 repairs to T's car should qualify for casualty loss treatment, since T's act of negligence appears to be simple rather than willful. The other expenses are not for damage to T's property and are, therefore, not deductible by T.

---

22. Rev.Rul. 72–592, 1972–2 C.B. 101
23. Reg. § 1.165–7(a)(3)(i).

EVENTS THAT ARE NOT CASUALTIES

Not all "acts of God" are treated as casualty losses for income tax purposes. Because a casualty must be sudden, unexpected, or unusual, progressive deterioration (such as erosion due to wind or rain) is not a casualty, because it does not meet the suddenness test.

Examples of nonsudden events are in the area of disease and insect damages. In the past, some courts have held that termite damage over periods of up to 15 months after infestation constituted a sudden event and was, therefore, deductible as a casualty loss.[24] On the other hand, when the damage was caused by termites over periods of several years, some courts have disallowed a casualty loss deduction.[25] Despite the existence of some judicial support for the deductibility of termite damage as a casualty loss, the current position of the IRS is that termite damage is not deductible.[26]

THEFT LOSSES

Theft includes, but is not necessarily limited to, larceny, embezzlement, and robbery.[27] Theft does not include misplaced items.[28]

Theft losses are computed like other casualty losses (discussed below), but the timing for recognition of the loss differs. A theft loss is taken in the year of discovery, not the year of the theft (unless, of course, the discovery occurs in the same year as the theft). If, in the year of the discovery, a claim exists (e. g., against an insurance company) and there is a reasonable expectation of recovering the fair market value of the asset from the insurance company, no deduction is permitted.[29] If, in the year of settlement, the recovery is less than the asset's fair market value, a partial deduction may be available.

> **Example 13.** J's new sailboat was stolen from the storage marina in December 19X1. He discovered the loss on June 3, 19X2, and filed a claim with his insurance company that was settled on January 30, 19X3. Assuming there is a reasonable expectation of full recovery, no deduction is allowed in 19X2. A partial deduction may be available in 19X3 if the actual insurance proceeds are less than the fair market value of the asset. (Loss measurement rules are discussed in a later section of this chapter.)

---

24. *Rosenberg v. Comm.,* 52–2 USTC ¶ 9377, 42 AFTR 303, 198 F.2d (CA–8, 1952); *Shopmaker v. U. S.,* 54–1 USTC ¶ 9195, 45 AFTR 758, 119 F.Supp. 705 (D.Ct.Mo., 1953).

25. *Fay v. Helvering,* 41–2 USTC ¶ 9494, 27 AFTR 432, 120 F.2d 253 (CA–2, 1941); *U. S. v. Rogers,* 41–1 USTC ¶ 9442, 27 AFTR 423, 120 F.2d 244 (CA–9, 1941).

26. Rev.Rul. 63–232, 1963–2 C.B. 97.

27. Reg. § 1.165–8(d).

28. *Mary Francis Allen,* 16 T.C. 163 (1951).

29. Reg. §§ 1.165–1(d)(2) and 1.165–8(a)(2).

WHEN TO DEDUCT CASUALTY LOSSES

Disaster Area Losses. Generally, a casualty loss is deducted in the year the loss occurs. An exception is allowed for casualties sustained in an area designated as a disaster area by the President of the United States.[30] In those cases, the taxpayer may elect to treat the loss as having occurred in the taxable year immediately preceding the taxable year in which the disaster actually occurred. The rationale for this exception is to provide immediate relief to disaster victims in the form of accelerated tax benefits.

The taxpayer makes this election to claim the disaster area loss on his or her tax return for the prior year (i. e., if the due date, plus extensions, for the prior year's return has not passed). If the disaster occurs after the prior year's return has been filed, it is necessary to file either an amended return or a refund claim. In any case, the taxpayer must show clearly that such an election is being made.[31] The election should show the date(s) of the disaster, the location of the property destroyed, and other pertinent facts. The election must be made by the later of the due date (exclusive of extensions) of the income tax return for the year in which the disaster occurred or the due date (including extensions) of the income tax return for the year immediately preceding the year in which the disaster occurred.

> **Example 14.** During the first week in April 19X2, unusually heavy rainfall caused severe flooding in a large region of southeast Louisiana. Shortly thereafter, the region was designated by the President of the United States as a disaster area and, therefore, eligible for assistance by the Federal government under Chapter 15, Title 42 of the U. S. Code. T, a resident of the affected area, suffered $3,000 in damage to her property due to the flooding. T is a calendar year taxpayer and has already filed her income tax return for the prior year (19X1). T can file either an amended return or refund claim for 19X1, or she can wait until filing the 19X2 return in 19X3 and claim a loss on her 19X2 return.

No casualty loss is permitted if there exists a reimbursement claim with a "reasonable prospect of [full] recovery."[32] If the taxpayer has a partial claim, only part of the loss can be claimed in the year of the casualty, and the remainder is deducted in the year the claim is settled.

> **Example 15.** G's new sailboat was completely destroyed by fire in 19X3. Its cost and fair market value was $10,000. Her only claim against the insurance company was on a $7,000 policy

---

30. § 165(h).
31. Reg. § 1.165–11(e).
32. Reg. § 1.165–1(d)(2)(i).

which was not settled by year-end. The following year, 19X4, G settled with the insurance company for $6,000. G is entitled to a $3,000 deduction in 19X3 and a $1,000 deduction in 19X4. If the sailboat was held for personal use, the $3,000 deduction in 19X3 would be reduced by $100 and then 10% of G's 19X3 adjusted gross income. The $1,000 deduction in 19X4 would be reduced by 10% of G's 19X4 adjusted gross income (see the following discussion).

If a taxpayer receives subsequent reimbursement for a casualty loss previously sustained and deducted, an amended return is not filed. Instead, the taxpayer must include the reimbursement in gross income on the return for the year in which it is received (to the extent that the previous deduction resulted in tax benefit).[33]

MEASURING THE AMOUNT OF LOSS

The amount of the loss for partial losses to business property, property held for the production of income, and personal use property, and for the complete destruction of personal use property is the lower of (1) the adjusted basis of the property or (2) the difference between the fair market value of the property before the event and the fair market value immediately after the event.[34] If business property or property that is held for the production of income (e. g., rental property) is completely destroyed, the measure of the deduction is always the adjusted basis of the property at the time of the destruction.[35] The deduction for the loss of property that is part business and part personal must be computed separately for the business portion and the personal portion.

Any insurance recovery reduces the loss for business, production of income, and personal use losses. In fact, a taxpayer may realize a gain on a casualty if the insurance proceeds exceed the amount of the loss. Chapter 17 discusses the treatment of net casualty gains and losses.

The amount of the loss for personal use property must be further reduced by a $100 per event floor and a 10 percent of adjusted gross income aggregate floor.[36] The $100 floor applies separately to each casualty and applies to the entire loss from each casualty (e. g., if a storm damages both a taxpayer's residence and automobile, only $100 is subtracted from the total amount of the loss).[37] The losses are then added together, and the total is reduced by 10 percent of the taxpay-

---

33.   Reg. § 1.165–1(d)(2)(iii). See also Example 5 in Chapter 2.
34.   Reg. § 1.165–7(b)(1).
35.   Reg. § 1.165–7(b)(1)(ii).
36.   § 165(c)(3).
37.   Reg. § 1.165–7(b)(4)(ii).

er's adjusted gross income.[38] The resulting loss is the taxpayer's itemized deduction for casualty and theft losses.

When a nonbusiness casualty loss is spread between two taxable years because of the "reasonable prospect of recovery" doctrine, the loss in the second year is not reduced by the $100 floor because this floor is imposed per event and has already reduced the amount of the loss in the first year. However, the loss in the second year is still subject to the 10 percent floor based on the taxpayer's second year adjusted gross income. This concept was illustrated in Example 15.

Taxpayers who suffer qualified disaster area losses can still elect to deduct such losses in the year preceding the year of occurrence. The disaster loss will be treated as having occurred in the preceding taxable year, and hence, the 10 percent of adjusted gross income floor will be determined by using the adjusted gross income of the year for which the deduction is claimed.[39]

Example 16. This year T had the following casualty losses:

Asset	Adjusted Basis	Fair Market Value of Asset Before the Casualty	Fair Market Value of Asset After the Casualty	Insurance Recovery
A	$ 900	$ 200	$ –0–	$ 400
B	300	800	250	100

Assets A and B were used in T's business at the time of the casualty.

The following losses are allowed:

Asset A: $500. The complete destruction of a business asset results in a deduction of the adjusted basis of the property (reduced by any insurance recovery) regardless of its fair market value.

Asset B: $200. The partial destruction of a business (or personal) asset results in a deduction equal to the lesser of the adjusted basis ($300) or the loss in value ($550), reduced by any insurance recovery ($100). Both asset A and B losses are deductions for adjusted gross income, and no $100 floor (or 10% floor) applies, because they are business assets.

Example 17. This year T had adjusted gross income of $20,000 and the following casualty losses:

---

38. § 165(h)(1)(B).
39. § 165(i).

		Fair Market Value of Asset		
Asset	Adjusted Basis	Before the Casualty	After the Casualty	Insurance Recovery
A	$ 900	$ 600	$ –0–	$ 200
B	2,500	4,000	1,000	0
C	800	400	100	250

Assets A, B, and C were held for personal use, and the losses to these three assets are from three different casualties.

The computation of the loss created by each asset is as follows:

Asset A: $300. The lesser of the adjusted basis of $900 or the $600 loss in value reduced by the insurance recovery of $200, minus the $100 floor.

Asset B: $2,400. The lesser of the adjusted basis of $2,500 or the $3,000 loss in value, minus the $100 floor.

Asset C: $–0–. The lesser of the adjusted basis of $800 or the $300 loss in value, reduced by the insurance recovery of $250, minus the $100 floor.

T's itemized casualty loss deduction for the year is $700:

Asset A loss	$ 300
Asset B loss	2,400
Asset C loss	–0–
Total loss	$ 2,700
Less: 10% of adjusted gross income (10% × 20,000)	(2,000)
Itemized casualty loss deduction	$ 700

Generally, an appraisal before and after the casualty is needed to measure the amount of the loss. However, the cost of repairs to the damaged property is acceptable as a method of establishing the loss in value provided the following criteria are met:

—The repairs are necessary to restore the property to its condition immediately before the casualty.

—The amount spent for such repairs is not excessive.

—The repairs do not care for more than the damage suffered.

—The value of the property after the repairs does not, as a result of the repairs, exceed the value of the property immediately before the casualty.[40]

---

40.   Reg. § 1.165–7(a)(2)(ii).

RESEARCH AND
EXPERIMENTAL EXPENDITURES

Section 174 sets forth the treatment accorded to "research and experimental expenditures." The Regulations define research and experimental expenditures as:

> All such costs incident to the development of an experimental or pilot model, a plant process, a product, a formula, an invention, or similar property, and the improvement of already existing property of the type mentioned. The term does not include expenditures such as those for the ordinary testing or inspection of materials or products for quality control or those for efficiency surveys, management studies, consumer surveys, advertising, or promotions.[41]

Expenses in connection with the acquisition or improvement of land or depreciable property are not research and experimental expenditures; they increase the basis of the land or depreciable property. However, depreciation on a building used for research may be a research and experimental expenditure.[42]

The law permits three alternatives for the handling of research and experimental expenditures. These expenditures may be expensed in the year paid or incurred or they may be deferred and amortized. If neither of these two methods is elected, the research and experimental costs must be capitalized.[43] If the costs are capitalized, a deduction may not be available until the research project is abandoned or is deemed worthless. Since many products resulting from research projects do not have a definite and limited useful life, a taxpayer should ordinarily elect to write off the expenditures immediately or to defer and amortize them. It is generally preferable to elect an immediate write-off of the research expenditures due to the time value of the tax deduction.

A credit for research and experimentation was introduced in 1981. The credit amounts to 25 percent of certain excess research and experimentation expenditures made after June 30, 1981, and before 1986.[44] The credit is discussed more fully in Chapter 13.

EXPENSE METHOD

A taxpayer can elect to expense all of the research and experimental expenditures incurred in the current year and all subsequent years.[45] The consent of the IRS is not required if the method is adopted for the first taxable year in which such expenditures were paid or incurred.

41. Reg. § 1.174–2(a)(1).
42. Reg. § 1.174–2(b)(1).
43. Reg. § 1.174–1.
44. § 44F
45. § 174(a)(1).

Once such an election is made, the taxpayer must continue to expense all qualifying expenditures unless a request for a change is made to the IRS.[46] In certain instances a taxpayer may incur research and experimental expenditures prior to actually engaging in any trade or business activity. The Supreme Court has applied, in such instances, a liberal standard of deductibility and permitted a deduction in the year of incurrence.[47]

DEFERRAL AND AMORTIZATION METHOD

The deferral and amortization method is allowed for the treatment of research and experimental expenditures, provided the taxpayer makes a binding election[48] (permission to change must be obtained from the IRS) to treat such expenditures as a ratable deduction over a period of not less than 60 months, beginning with the month in which the taxpayer first realizes benefits from such expenditures.[49]

The option to treat research and experimental expenditures as deferred expense is usually employed when a company does not have sufficient income to offset the research and experimental expenses. Rather than create net operating loss carryovers which might not be utilized due to the 15-year limitation on such carryovers, the deferral and amortization method may be used.

> **Example 18.** R Corporation, a manufacturer of plastic products, uses the accrual method and files its return on a calendar year basis. On January 1, 19X1, work is started on a special research project which, if successful, would result in a manufacturing process that would streamline the production of plastic products and effect a considerable cost saving. On this same day, a building is acquired for $60,000; 30% of the building will be used in connection with the research project. Assume the building is to be depreciated under the ACRS optional straight-line method over a 15-year period (see discussion of depreciation methods in Chapter 9). During the year, the following additional expenditures are made in connection with the research project:
>
> | | |
> |---|---:|
> | Salaries | $ 12,000 |
> | Heat, light, and power | 1,000 |
> | Drawings | 2,500 |
> | Models | 7,500 |
> | Lab materials | 9,000 |
>
> The project is concluded successfully on December 30, 19X1, and results in a process which is marketable (but not patentable) and which possesses an indefinite useful life. R Corporation first realizes the benefits from the new process in 19X2.

---

46. § 174(a)(3).
47. *Snow v. Comm.*, 74–1 USTC ¶ 9432, 33 AFTR2d 74–1251, 94 S.Ct. 1876 (USSC, 1974).
48. § 174(b)(2).
49. § 174(b)(1); Reg. § 1.174–4(b)(2).

The R Corporation can (1) capitalize all the expenses and leave them on the balance sheet indefinitely; (2) elect to expense all the expenditures and the depreciation attributable to the project under § 174 in year 19X1; or (3) elect to capitalize all expenditures, including the depreciation under § 174 and amortize it as follows:

Depreciation (30% of one year's depreciation of $4,000)	$ 1,200
Salaries	12,000
Heat, light, and power	1,000
Drawings	2,500
Models	7,500
Lab material	9,000
Total	$ 33,200

Monthly amortization beginning January 1, 19X2:

$$\frac{\$33,200}{60} = \qquad \$ 553.33$$

NET OPERATING LOSSES

The requirement that every taxpayer file an annual income tax return (whether on a calendar year or a fiscal year) may result in certain inequities for taxpayers who experience cyclical patterns of income or expense. Inequities result from the application of a progressive rate structure to amounts of taxable income applied on an annual basis. A net operating loss in a particular tax year would produce no tax benefit if the Code did not include provisions for the carryback and carryforward of such losses to profitable years.

Example 19. J has a business which realizes the following taxable income or loss over a five-year period: 19X1, $50,000; 19X2, ($30,000); 19X3, $100,000; 19X4, ($200,000); and 19X5, $380,000. She is married and files a joint return. P, on the other hand, has a taxable income pattern of $60,000 every year. He, too, is married and files a joint return. A comparison of their five-year tax bills follows:

Year	J's Tax	P's Tax
19X1	$ 11,368	$ 15,168
19X2	–0–	15,168
19X3	32,400	15,168
19X4	–0–	15,168
19X5	171,400	15,168
	$ 215,168	$ 75,840

*The computation of tax is made without regard to any tax credits, income averaging or net operating loss benefits. Rates applicable to 1984 are used to compute the tax.

Even though J and P realized the same total income ($300,000) over the five-year period, J had to pay taxes of $215,168 while P paid taxes of $75,840.

To provide partial relief from this inequitable tax treatment, a deduction is allowed for net operating losses.[50] This provision permits the offset of net operating losses for any one year against taxable income of other years. A net operating loss is intended as a relief provision for business income and losses; therefore, only losses from the operation of a trade or business (or profession), casualty losses, or losses from the confiscation of a business by a foreign government can create a net operating loss. In other words, a salaried individual with itemized deductions and personal exemptions in excess of income is not permitted to deduct such excess amounts as a net operating loss. On the other hand, a personal casualty loss is treated as a business loss and can, therefore, create (or increase) a net operating loss for a salaried individual.[51]

CARRYBACK AND CARRYOVER PERIODS

A net operating loss must be applied initially to the three taxable years preceding the year of the loss.[52] It is carried first to the third prior year, then the second prior year, then the immediately preceding tax year (or until used up). If the loss is not fully used in the carryback period, it must be carried forward to the first year after the loss year, and then forward to the second, third, etc., year after the loss year. For years ending with 1975, the carryover period is 15 years. If a loss is sustained in 1984, it is used in this order: 1981, 1982, 1983, 1985 through 1999.

For taxable years ending after December 31, 1975, a taxpayer can elect not to carry back a net operating loss to any of the three prior years. In such case, the loss is available as a carryforward to the next year. A taxpayer would make the election if it is to his or her tax advantage. For example, a taxpayer might be in a very low marginal tax bracket in the carryback years but expect to be in a high marginal tax bracket in future years. Therefore, it would be to the taxpayer's tax advantage to use the net operating loss to offset income in years when the marginal tax rate is high rather than use it when the marginal tax rate is relatively low. The election might also be advantageous if the taxpayer has taken investment tax credit in the carryback years. If the net operating loss is carried back and the tax liability reduced or eliminated, the benefit of the investment tax credit could be lost because of the expiration of its carryover time limit.

---

50. § 172.
51. § 172(d)(4)(C); Reg. § 1.172–3(a)(3)(iii).
52. § 172(b)(1) and (2).

If the loss is being carried to a preceding year, an amended return is filed on Form 1040X or a quick refund claim is filed on Form 1045. In any case, a refund of taxes previously paid is requested. When the loss is carried forward, the current return shows a net operating loss deduction for the prior year's loss.

Where there are net operating losses in two or more years, the rule is always to use the earliest loss first until it is completely absorbed; then the later loss(es) can be used until they also are absorbed or lost. Thus, one year's return could show net operating loss carryovers from two or more years; each loss is computed and applied separately.

COMPUTATION OF THE NET OPERATING LOSS

Since the net operating loss provisions apply solely to business-related losses, certain adjustments must be made to reflect a taxpayer's "economic" loss. The required adjustments for corporate taxpayers are usually insignificant, because a corporation's taxable loss is generally similar to its economic loss.[53] However, individual taxpayers are allowed deductions for such items as personal and dependency exemptions, itemized deductions, and long-term capital gains which do not reflect actual business-related economic losses.

When computing a net operating loss, the law allows the deduction of total itemized deductions or the zero bracket amount. However, because the zero bracket amount is built into the Tax Table and Rate Schedules, it has not been deducted in computing taxable income. Therefore, the appropriate zero bracket amount must be deducted from taxable income in computing the net operating loss.[54] This resulting amount will be called "modified taxable income."

To arrive at the net operating loss (economic loss) for an individual, modified taxable income must be adjusted by adding back the following items:[55]

—The net operating loss carryover or carryback from another year is not allowed in the computation of taxable income (loss) for the year. The net operating loss for each year must be separate for purposes of the carryback and carryforward provisions discussed above.

—Capital losses may not exceed the amount of capital gains included in income. Since capital losses can be carried forward for individuals, these losses cannot be "mixed" with net operating losses.

—Nonbusiness capital losses may not exceed nonbusiness capital gains. Business capital losses are granted § 1231 treatment

53. Reg. § 1.172–2.
54. § 172(d)(8).
55. § 172(d); Reg. § 1.172–3(a).

(described in Chapter 17) and are fully allowed as deductions, since they reflect the business, or economic, loss. In other words, a nonbusiness capital loss cannot be used to offset a business capital gain.

—No deduction is allowed for 60 percent of the excess of long-term capital gains over short-term capital losses. This 60 percent deduction does not require an outlay of assets, so it does not reflect an economic loss.

—No deduction is allowed for personal and dependency exemptions. These amounts do not reflect economic, or business, outlays.

—Nonbusiness deductions (itemized deductions less personal casualty losses) may not exceed nonbusiness income. Note that a casualty loss, if large enough, can create a net operating loss, since it is not considered a nonbusiness deduction. The theory is that nonbusiness income may be offset by business deductions, but that nonbusiness deductions cannot offset business income. Nonbusiness deductions such as medical expenses and charitable contributions are really items of personal consumption, not business expenses or losses. The deduction for a contribution to a self-employment retirement plan is treated as a nonbusiness deduction.[56] Nonbusiness income includes such passive items as dividends and interest. Business income (or losses) includes salaries, rents, and gains and losses on the sale or exchange of business assets. A taxpayer who does not itemize deductions may use the zero bracket amount to offset nonbusiness income. Therefore, in computing the excess of nonbusiness deductions over nonbusiness income, the taxpayer may use the greater of total itemized deductions or the appropriate zero bracket amount. This concept is illustrated in Examples 20 and 21.

Example 20. If taxpayer and spouse have $2,000 of interest income and no itemized deductions, they must add back $1,400 ($3,400 zero bracket amount less $2,000 interest income) in determining the excess of nonbusiness deductions over nonbusiness income.

Example 21. If taxpayer and spouse have $4,000 of interest income and no itemized deductions, no adjustment is required in computing a net operating loss, because the nonbusiness deductions ($3,400 zero bracket amount) do not exceed the nonbusiness income ($4,000 interest income).

Example 22. T began the operation of a retail store in 1983 and experienced a net operating loss of $185 for that year. T had no taxable income for 1980, 1981, or 1982. T is married, has no de-

---

56. Reg. § 1.172–3(a)(3)(iv).

pendents, and files a joint return. For 1984, T and his wife had the following taxable income:

Gross income from the business	$ 67,000	
Less: Business expenses	71,000	$ (4,000)
Salary from a part-time job		875
Interest on savings account		525
Nonbusiness long-term capital gain	$ 1,000	
Less: Long-term capital gain deduction	600	400
NOL carryover from 1983		(185)
Net loss on rental property		(100)
Adjusted gross income		$ (2,485)
Less: Itemized deductions in excess of zero bracket amount		
Interest expense	$ 3,000	
Taxes	4,300	
Casualty loss	2,000	
Total itemized deductions	$ 9,300	
Zero bracket amount	(3,400)	
Excess itemized deductions		(5,900)
Exemptions (2)		(2,000)
Taxable income		$ (10,385)

T's net operating loss is computed as follows:

Taxable income				$ (10,385)
Less: Zero bracket amount				(3,400)
Modified taxable income				$ (13,785)
Add:				
Net operating loss from 1983		$ 185		
Long-term capital gain deduction		600		
Personal exemptions (2)		2,000		
Excess of nonbusiness deductions over nonbusiness income				
Total itemized deductions		$ 9,300		
Less: Casualty loss		(2,000)		
		$ 7,300		
Less: Interest	$ 525			
Less: Long-term capital gain	1,000	(1,525)	5,775	8,560
Net operating loss				$ (5,225)

Note: The economic loss can be thought of as follows:

Business loss	$ (4,000)
Rental loss	(100)
Casualty loss	(2,000)
Salary income	875
Net economic (operating) loss	$ (5,225)

RECOMPUTATION OF TAX LIABILITY FOR YEAR TO WHICH NET OPERATING LOSS IS CARRIED

When a net operating loss is carried back to a non-loss year, the taxable income and income tax must be recomputed. Several deductions (such as medical expenses) are based on the amount of adjusted gross income. When a net operating loss is carried back, all such deductions except the charitable contribution deduction must be recomputed on the basis of the new adjusted gross income after the net operating loss has been applied.[57] Furthermore, any tax credits limited by or based upon the tax must be recomputed, based on the recomputed tax.

> **Example 23.** J sustained a net operating loss of $11,000 in 1984. Because J had no taxable income in 1981 or 1982, the loss is carried back to 1983. For 1983 his income tax return was as follows:

Salary income			$ 10,000
Dividends (net of exclusion)			2,000
Net long-term capital gain		$ 1,400	
Less: 60% net long-term capital gain deduction		(840)	560
Adjusted gross income			$ 12,560
Excess itemized deductions			
Charitable contributions		$ 1,700	
Medical expenses	$ 1,151		
Less: 5% of adjusted gross income	(628)	523	
Interest		800	
Taxes		420	
Other		100	
		$ 3,543	
Less: Zero bracket amount		(3,400)	(143)
Exemptions (2)			(2,000)
			$ 10,417
Tax (married filing jointly)			$ 928

J's new tax liability for the carryback year is computed as follows:

---

57. Reg. § 1.172–5(a)(3)(ii).

Adjusted gross income			$ 12,560
Less: Net operating loss			11,000
Recomputed adjusted gross income			$ 1,560
Excess itemized deductions			
Charitable contributions		$ 1,700	
Medical expenses	$ 1,151		
Less: 5% of adjusted gross income ($1,560)	(78)	1,073	
Interest		800	
Taxes		420	
Other		100	
		$ 4,093	
Less: Zero bracket amount		(3,400)	(693)
Exemptions (2)			(2,000)
Recomputed taxable income			$ (1,133)
Tax			–0–
Tax originally paid and refund claim			$ 928

In determining the recomputed taxable income, the entire amount of the net operating loss is used, and after computing the amount of refund claim for the initial carryback year, it is then necessary to determine the extent to which any loss remains for carryover to future years. Since only the economic loss may be carried back, the economic (net operating) loss can be used only to offset economic gains. To determine if any net operating loss remains to carry forward, the following adjustments must be made to the recomputed taxable income of the year to which the loss was carried:

—The applicable zero bracket amount must be subtracted.

—Exemptions must be added back.

—The 60 percent net capital gain deduction must be added back.

—An adjustment must be made for any percentage limitations based on the new adjusted gross income. This adjustment is determined by (1) computing a new adjusted gross income plus the capital gain or loss adjustment and any other adjustments to adjusted gross income and (2) computing the new medical (or other) deduction limitation based on the new adjusted gross income. Subtract from the newly computed deduction the amount taken in determining the recomputed taxable income.

Since the figure to which the above adjustments are being added is a negative figure (i. e., there is no net operating loss or net operating loss carryover if there is a positive taxable income), these adjustments serve to reduce the net operating loss available for carryover to the next year.

Example 24. Referring to the facts in Example 23, the adjustments necessary to determine any net operating loss carryover from 1983 available for future years are as follows:

Recomputed taxable income			$ (1,133)
Zero bracket amount			(3,400)
Exemptions (2)		$ 2,000	
Net capital gain deduction		840	
Medical expenses	$ 1,151		
Less: 5% of new AGI			
($12,560 + $840 = $13,400)	670		
	$ 481		
Less: Medical expense taken in determining recomputed taxable income	1,073	592	3,432
Net operating loss to carry forward			$ (1,101)

Since the ending figure is negative, this represents the net operating loss remaining to carry over to 1985 or later years.

The following page shows what the net operating loss carryback would look like on a Form 1045.

Form **1045**
(Rev. December 1983)
Department of the Treasury
Internal Revenue Service

Application for Tentative Refund
(See instruction C for when to file)
Do Not Attach to Your Income Tax Return—File Separately to Expedite Processing
▶ For use by taxpayers other than corporations.

OMB No. 1545-0098

Name J. Taxpayer	Employer identification number
Number and street 100 Main Street	Your social security number 603-24-8163
City or town, State, and ZIP code Anywhere, U.S.A.	Spouse's social security number 603-48-2716

1 This application is filed to carryback: (If no entry in 1(a) skip lines 9 to 15) . . ▶	**(a)** Net operating loss (from page 2, line 10) $ 11,000	**(b)** Unused investment credit $	**(c)** Unused jobs credit $	**(d)** Unused research credit $
2 Return for year of loss, unused credit, or over-payment under section 1341(b)(1) . . . ▶	**(a)** Tax year ended 12/31/84	**(b)** Date filed 3/3/85	**(c)** Service center where filed Ogden, Utah	

3 If this application is for an unused credit created by another carryback, give year of the first carryback ▶

4 (a) Preceding tax year(s) affected by carryback	**(b)** Did spouse file a separate return?	**(c)** Service center where return(s) were filed (City and State)
3rd	☐ Yes ☐ No	
2nd	☐ Yes ☐ No	
1st Dec. 31, 1983	☐ Yes ☒ No	Ogden, Utah

5 If you changed your accounting period, give date permission to change was granted ▶

6 Have you filed a petition in Tax Court for the year or years to which the carryback is to be applied?   ☐ Yes   ☒ No

7 If this carryback is from a loss or investment credit from a Schedule C, state the principal business activity ▶

8 If this carryback is from a loss or investment credit from a Schedule E, state the names and principal business activities of the conduits ▶

Computation of Decrease in Tax	3rd preceding tax year ended		2nd preceding tax year ended ▶		1st preceding tax year ended ▶ 12/31/83	
	(a) Before carryback ▶	**(b)** After carryback	**(c)** Before carryback	**(d)** After carryback	**(e)** Before carryback	**(f)** After carryback
9 Adjusted gross income from tax return . . .					12,560	12,560
10 Net operating loss deduction after carryback (See Instructions—Attach computation)						11,000
11 Subtract line 10 from line 9					12,560	1,560
12 Deductions (see instructions).					143	693
13 Subtract line 12 from line 11					12,417	867
14 Exemptions					2,000	2,000
15 Taxable income (subtract line 14 from line 13) .					10,417	(1,133)
16 Income tax					928	-0-
17 Investment credit						
18 Jobs credit						
19 Research credit						
20 Other credits (identify)						
21 Total credits (add lines 17 through 20)					-0-	-0-
22 Subtract line 21 from line 16					928	-0-
23 Recapture of investment credit						
24 Minimum tax						
25 Alternative minimum tax						
26 Self-employment tax						
27 Other taxes						
28 Total tax liability (add lines 22 through 27) . . .					928	-0-
29 Enter amount from line 28, cols. (b), (d) and (f) . .					-0-	
30 Decrease in tax (subtract line 29 from line 28) . .					928	

31 Overpayment of tax due to a claim of right adjustment under section 1341(b)(1)—attach computation . . . . .

Under penalties of perjury, I declare that I have examined this application (including any accompanying schedules and statements), and to the best of my knowledge and belief, it is true, correct, and complete.

(Your signature and date)   (If application is filed jointly, both you and your spouse must sign)   (Spouse's signature and date)

For Paperwork Reduction Act Notice, see page 3.   Form **1045** (Rev. 12-83)

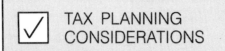

TAX PLANNING CONSIDERATIONS

BAD DEBTS

It is generally preferable to elect the reserve method for bad debts, since the taxpayer is permitted a deduction (in the calculation of the addition to the reserve) for amounts which would not be deductible until subsequent periods if the specific charge-off method were used. In addition, the reserve method may mitigate conflicts with the IRS with respect to the exact year of worthlessness, since under the specific charge-off method, a deduction is available only in such year. The IRS may determine that the loss took place during periods prior to the year in which the deduction was claimed, and a refund adjustment relating to these earlier years may be barred by the statute of limitations.

If the reserve method is employed, the taxpayer should generally use an approach similar to the *Black Motor Company* formula which is based on the history of bad debt losses of the business. If an alternative approach is used, the taxpayer should be prepared to justify this method by providing specific documentation relative to the nature and risks of the business and the character of the receivables.

> **Example 25.** T, an accrual and calendar year taxpayer, employs the reserve method for handling bad debts. Applying the formula set forth in *Black Motor Company* would provide T with an addition to the reserve for bad debts account of $40,000 for 19X1. Instead, T claims $50,000 as a bad debt deduction for 19X1. T should be prepared to justify the additional $10,000 claimed in the event it is questioned by the IRS. A justification, for example, might be T's recent institution of a more liberal credit policy.[58]

If a taxpayer is starting a new business and initial net operating losses are anticipated, the direct charge-off method may be preferable during the initial years. If the reserve method is used, the additional bad debt expense deductions allowed may increase the taxpayer's net operating losses. Because net operating losses may be carried forward for only 15 years, the tax benefits of the bad debt deduction may be lost. The reserve method may be elected after the business has become profitable.

---

58. *Thor Power Tool Co. v. Comm.,* 79–1 USTC ¶ 9139, 43 AFTR2d 79–362, 99 S.Ct. 773 (USSC, 1979) and *Mills & Lupton Supply Co., Inc.,* 36 TCM 1173, T.C.Memo. 1977–294.

DOCUMENTATION OF RELATED-TAXPAYER LOANS, CASUALTY LOSSES, AND THEFT LOSSES

Since non-bona fide loans between related taxpayers may be treated as gifts, adequate documentation is needed to substantiate a bad debt deduction if the loan subsequently becomes worthless. Documentation should include proper execution of the note (legal form) and the establishment of a bona fide purpose for the loan. In addition, it is desirable to stipulate a reasonable rate of interest and a fixed maturity date.

Since a theft loss is not permitted for misplaced items, a loss should be documented by a police report and evidence of the value of the property (e. g., appraisals, pictures of the property, newspaper clippings). Similar documentation of the value of property should be provided to support a casualty loss deduction because the amount of loss is measured by the decline in fair market value of the property.

Casualty loss deductions must be reported on Form 4684 (see Appendix B).

NET OPERATING LOSSES

In certain instances, it may be advisable for a taxpayer to elect not to carry back a net operating loss to a particular year. For an individual, the benefits from the loss carryback may be scaled down or lost due to the economic adjustments which must be made to taxable income for the year to which the loss is carried. The election not to carry back the loss to a particular year may be advantageous in certain circumstances.

> **Example 26.** T sustained a net operating loss of $10,000 in 19X4. His marginal tax bracket in 19X1 was 20%. In 19X5, however, he expects his bracket to be 50% due to a large profit he will make on a business deal. If T carries his loss back, his refund will be $2,000 (i. e., 20% × $10,000). If he elects not to carry it back to 19X1 but chooses, instead, to carry it forward, his savings will be $5,000 (50% × $10,000). Even considering the time value of an immediate tax refund, T appears to be better off by using the carryforward approach.

The 15-year net operating loss carryover provision is effective for losses created in taxable years ending after December 31, 1975. Thus, an NOL sustained in 1976 can be carried forward as far as 1991. In the case of 1976 net operating losses not used up by 1983 (the old expiration date), the carryover period rules allow an additional eight years in which to use up the loss.

In the event a taxpayer incurs a net operating loss which can be carried back to a previous year with a tax benefit, careful consideration should be given to the quick refund procedure of Form 1045

(Form 1139 in the case of a corporate taxpayer). Under this procedure the IRS normally will act on the application for a refund within 90 days from the day it is filed. However, the quick refund procedure is available only if the Form 1045 is filed within 12 months of the year of the loss.

> **Example 27.** T, a calendar year individual, suffers a net operating loss in 1984 which she desires to carry back to 1981. The use of the quick refund procedure would require that T file Form 1045 on or after January 1, 1985 but not later than December 31, 1985.

CASUALTY LOSSES

A special election is available for taxpayers who sustain casualty losses in an area designated by the President as a disaster area. This election affects only the timing, not the calculation, of the deduction. The deduction can be taken in the year prior to the year in which the loss occurred. Thus, an individual can take the deduction on the 1983 return for a loss occurring between January 1 and December 31, 1984. The benefit, of course, is a faster refund (or reduction in tax).

To find out if an event qualifies as a disaster area loss, one can look in any of the major tax services or in the Weekly Compilation of Presidential Documents or the Internal Revenue Bulletin.

PROBLEM MATERIALS

Questions for Class Discussion

1. Dr. T, an individual and cash basis taxpayer engaged in the general practice of dentistry, performed extensive bridge and crown work on Mr. S. for which he charged $3,500 ($2,500 for services and $1,000 for materials and lab work). Since Mr. S never paid the bill and has left for parts unknown, Dr. T feels that he is entitled to a bad debt deduction of $3,500. Comment on Dr. T's tax position on this matter.

2. Under what circumstances may a taxpayer take a deduction for partial worthlessness of a bad debt?

3. Why is it important to determine the exact year of worthlessness for a bad debt?

4. Compare and contrast the reserve and the direct charge-off methods. Which method is generally preferred by most businesses? Why?

5. Is it necessary for the taxpayer to adhere strictly to the *Black Motor Co.* formula approach in computing the addition to the bad debt reserve? Explain.

6. Discuss the difference(s) between business and nonbusiness bad debts? How is the distinction determined? How is each treated on the return?

7. What factors are to be considered in determining if a bad debt arising from a loan between related parties is, in fact, a bad debt?

8. Under what circumstances may a worthless security be treated as a short-term capital loss?

9. Compare the tax treatment of losses on § 1244 stock with the usual treatment of losses on capital stock.

10. What acts of God give rise to a casualty loss? Which ones do not? Discuss.

11. How are thefts treated differently from acts of God for casualty loss purposes?

12. When is a casualty loss deductible? What is the exception and how is it elected? Discuss.

13. How is a personal casualty loss computed? A business casualty loss? What effect do insurance proceeds have on both types of losses?

14. Is it possible to have a casualty gain? How is it taxed?

15. Discuss whether an individual taxpayer may take a deduction for a loss for termite damage to a building used in the taxpayer's business.

16. What is a disaster area loss? Why might a taxpayer benefit from making the disaster area loss election?

17. Why do most taxpayers elect to write off research and experimental expenditures rather than capitalize and amortize such amounts? Are there some situations in which the capitalization approach would be preferable?

18. What is the rationale behind the net operating loss deduction? Who benefits from this provision?

19. Why are such items as nonbusiness deductions and the long-term capital gain deduction not allowed in computing the net operating loss?

20. Discuss the periods to which net operating losses may be carried. Can the taxpayer elect not to carry a net operating loss back to any one year? What possible benefit might result from not carrying a loss back to a particular year?

21. Discuss why the dividend exclusion is not added back in computing an individual's net operating loss.

22. Discuss why deductions *for* adjusted gross income, such as moving expenses and employee business expenses, do not have to be added back in computing an individual's net operating loss.

Problems

23. M loaned T $10,000 on April 1, 19X4. In 19X5 T filed for bankruptcy. At that time it was revealed that T's creditors could expect to receive 60¢ on the dollar. In February 19X6 final settlement was made and M received $3,000. How much loss can M deduct and in which year? How is it treated on M's return?

24. X Company employs the allowance method for its bad debts. At the beginning of the current year, the credit balance in the allowance account was $120,000. Based on an aging of the accounts receivable at the end of the current year, it was determined that a reasonable balance in the allowance account, as of the end of the current year, would be $150,000. During the current year, X wrote off $70,000 against the allowance account and collected $5,000 that had been written off in a previous year. Determine the amount of X's bad debt deduction for the current year.

25. Determine the amount of the addition to the reserve for bad debts of the J Company as of December 31, 19X6, using the *Black Motor Co.* formula and given the following information:

    (a) Net bad debts for the current year and five preceding years is $60,000.

    (b) Total accounts and notes receivable outstanding at the end of the year are as follows:

19X1	$ 167,000
19X2	183,000
19X3	150,000
19X4	133,000
19X5	200,000
19X6	167,000

    (c) Beginning balance in the reserve for bad debts in 19X6 is $20,000.

    (d) In 19X6 recoveries of previous accounts written off equals $3,333.

    (e) Specific write-offs during 19X6 equal $13,328.

26. T, a single taxpayer, bought stocks for $65,000 on June 3, 19X8. On May 15, 19X9, the company went bankrupt and the stock became worthless.

    (a) Does the taxpayer have a deduction?

    (b) When?

    (c) What is the character of the loss?

    (d) If the stock qualified as § 1244 stock, when is the taxpayer allowed the deduction, what is the amount of the loss, and what is the character of the loss?

27. B had the following items for the current year:

    —A nonbusiness bad debt of $2,000.

    —A business bad debt of $5,000.

    —A bond acquired for $1,500 on August 8 of the prior year that became worthless on June 20 of the current year.

    —Salary of $35,000.

    Determine B's adjusted gross income for the current year.

28. When J returned from a vacation in Hawaii on November 8, 19X4, she discovered that a burglar had stolen her silver, stereo, and color television. In the process of removing these items, the burglar damaged some furniture which originally cost $1,400. J's silver cost $3,640 and was valued at $6,500; the stereo system cost $8,400 and was valued at $6,200; the television cost $840 and was worth $560. J filed a claim with her insurance company and was reimbursed in the following amounts on December 20, 19X4:

Silver	$ 2,800
Stereo	5,600
Television	490

    The insurance company disputed the reimbursement claimed by J for the damaged furniture, but she protested and was finally paid $280 on January 30, 19X5. The repairs to the furniture totaled $448. J's adjusted gross income for 19X4 was $12,000, and it was $15,000 for 19X5. How much can J claim as a casualty loss? In which year?

29. K owned an acre of land in Kansas upon which he had his home, two rental houses, an apartment building, and his construction company. A tornado hit the area and destroyed one of the rental houses, damaged the apartment building, and destroyed some of K's construction equipment. The tenant of K's other rental house moved out for fear of another tornado and K lost $450 in rent. The local real estate appraiser told K his personal residence (with an adjusted basis of $52,500) had been worth $75,000 until the disaster and was now worth only $45,000 (although it was undamaged) because it had been established that the house was in a tornado path. Other losses were as follows:

Item	Adjusted Basis	FMV Before	FMV After	Insurance Proceeds
Rental house # 1	$ 34,500	$ 43,500	$ –0–	$ 37,500
Apartment building	100,000	225,000	180,000	31,500
Equipment	90,000	112,500	–0–	75,000

(a) How much is K's casualty loss before applying any limitation?

(b) Assuming the loss occurred on March 3, 19X7, and that the area was designated by the President as a disaster area, what options are open to K with respect to the timing of the loss?

30. On January 7 of the current year, T dropped off to sleep while driving home from a business trip. Luckily, she was only slightly injured in the resulting accident, but her car was completely destroyed.

T had purchased the car new two years ago and had driven it 64,000 miles at the time of the accident. Of these miles, 28,000 were business miles; the remaining miles were personal miles. The car cost $7,200 new. T has taken $1,985 of depreciation for the business use of the car. She carried $1,000 deductible collision insurance on the car. Her insurance company settled her claim by paying her $2,400 for the car (fair market value before the wreck was $3,400).

After T's release from the hospital the day after the accident, she could not find her purse (cost $65, fair replacement value $30) or its contents, which included $350 in cash and $500 in travelers checks. The travelers checks were replaced by the issuing company. She also was unable to locate the stone from her diamond engagement ring. The stone cost her husband $2,500 when purchased nine years ago and was worth $6,400 at the time of the loss.

(a) Determine the amount of T's deductible loss *for* adjusted gross income.

(b) Determine the amount of the loss deductible *from* adjusted gross income, assuming adjusted gross income for the year is $25,000.

31. During the current year, H and W, married with three dependent children, had the following items of income and expense:

Gross receipts from business	$ 85,000
Business expenses	97,000
Last year's net operating loss carried to the current year	4,800
W's salary	13,000
Gain on sale of stock purchased three years ago	2,000
Interest from bank account	1,000
Itemized deductions	3,000

(a) Determine the amount of H and W's current year's taxable net income.

(b) Determine the amount of the current year's net operating loss.

32. G, who is married filing jointly, owns a grocery store. In 19X1, his gross sales were $286,000 and operating expenses were $310,000. Other items on his 19X1 return were as follows:

Nonbusiness capital gains (long-term)	$ 6,000
Nonbusiness capital losses (short-term)	9,000
Itemized deductions	10,000
Ordinary nonbusiness income	4,000
Salary from part-time job	2,000
Personal exemptions	2,000

What is G's 19X1 net operating loss?

33. During 19X3 T, married with one dependent child, had the following items of income, expense, and loss to report:

Gross receipts from business	$ 250,000
Business expenses	274,000
Interest received from State of Utah bonds	8,000
Interest received from bank savings account	2,000
Wife's salary from part-time work	6,000
Long-term capital gain on sale of stock held as an investment	9,000
Short-term capital loss on sale of State of Utah bonds	8,000
Itemized deductions	2,700

(a) Assuming T files a joint return, what is T's taxable income for 19X3?

(b) What is the amount of T's net operating loss for 19X3?

34. H, married and filing jointly, has two dependent children. He had the following income and deductions for 19X4:

Salary	$ 36,000
Gross dividends from domestic corporations	800
Interest received from bank savings account	6,000
19X3 net operating loss carried to 19X4	6,000
Itemized deductions	5,000

In addition to the above information, H's uninsured personal residence was damaged by fire during the year. The home had a value of $240,000 before the fire, but it was worth only $80,000 after the fire. H's basis in the home was $200,000.

(a) What is H's taxable income for 19X4?

(b) What is H's net operating loss for 19X4?

35. T had the following income tax return for 1981:

Salary		$ 15,000	
Interest		1,000	
Long-term capital gain	$ 2,000		
Less 60% net capital gain deduction	1,200	800	
Adjusted gross income			$ 16,800
Itemized deductions:			
Charitable contributions		$ 2,000	
Medical expenses	$ 1,204		
Less: 3% AGI	504	700	
Interest and taxes		3,000	
Other		2,100	
		$ 7,800	
Less: Zero bracket amount		(3,400)	(4,400)
Exemptions (2)			(2,000)
Taxable income			$ 10,400

In 1984, T sustained a net operating loss of $51,000.

(a) What is his recomputed taxable income for 1981?

(b) What is his amount of net operating loss remaining to carry over?

Cumulative Problems

36. Y is single, age 40, and has no dependents. She is employed half-time as a legal secretary. In addition, she owns and operates a typing service located in the campus area of Florida State University. She is a cash basis taxpayer. During 1984, Y had the following receipts:

(a) $10,000 salary as a legal secretary.

(b) $32,000 gross receipts from her typing service business.

(c) $500 cash dividend from Buffalo Mining Company, a Canadian corporation.

(d) $1,000 Christmas bonus from her employer for outstanding work as a legal secretary.

(e) $10,000 life insurance proceeds on the death of her sister.

(f) $5,000 check given by her wealthy aunt.

(g) $100 won in a bingo game.

Y had various business deductions of $18,680, not including any of the items below.

(h) $4,000 net operating loss carryover from 1983; this is the remaining amount of a $10,000 net operating loss, $6,000 of which has been carried back to 1980, 1981, and 1982.

After examining Y's records, you have determined that she has various itemized deductions of $3,100, not including any of the following amounts.

(i) $5,000 fair market value of silverware stolen from her home by a burglar. She had paid $4,000 for the silverware 8 years ago. She was reimbursed $1,500 by her insurance company, having neglected to increase the insurance coverage as the price of silver increased.

(j) She had loaned $2,100 to a friend, K, a year ago. K declared bankruptcy in August 1984 and was unable to repay the loan.

You are to compute Y's taxable income for 1984.

37. (a) On January 27, 1983, S deposited $8,000 in a savings account at the ABC Finance Company. The savings account bore interest at 15% compounded semiannually. S received a $600 interest payment on July 27, 1983, but received no interest payments thereafter. The finance company filed for bankruptcy on January 12, 1984, and was adjudicated bankrupt on April 7, 1984. S received a $710 check in final settlement of his account from the bankruptcy trustee on December 20, 1984.

(b) S purchased 500 shares of XYZ Airlines common stock on March 3, 1984, for $7 a share. The purchase was made from an original stock offer of the airline, which consisted of a single class of 135,000 shares of common stock, all issued at $7 per share. By October 31, 1984, the airline was defunct and the stock was worthless.

(c) A $10,000 face amount, 8½% bond of the PDQ Company which S purchased for $320 on July 20, 1976, was due to be paid on September 30, 1984. On presentation of the bond for payment to the MT Bank, S found that PDQ had folded in 1979 and there had been insufficient company assets at that time to pay even legal and court costs; no company creditor received any payment on corporate debts.

(d) On August 7, 1984, a fire severely damaged a two-story building owned by S, who occupied the second story of the building as a residence and operated a liquor store on the ground level. The following information is available with respect to the incident:

	Adjusted Basis	Fair Market Value Before Fire	Fair Market Value After Fire
Building	$ 64,000	$ 130,000	$ 50,000
Inventory	35,000	55,000	none
Store equipment	3,000	1,800	none
Home furnishings	12,600	6,000	800
Personal auto	8,900	7,800	7,600
Stamp collection	7,700	82,000	none

S's fire insurance policy paid the following:

Building	$50,000 (policy maximum)
Equipment	none
Inventory	$33,000
Home furnishings	$1,000 (policy maximum)
Personal auto	none
Stamp collection	none

Completely destroyed in the fire was a mattress on a spare bed. Unfortunately, S had stashed $150,000 in $100 bills in the mattress. S's insurance company denied any liability for the burned money. S did not believe in banks and handled all his transactions in cash.

(e) In March 1980 S loaned a neighboring businessman $15,000. The debtor died of a heart attack on June 21, 1984. S had no security and was unable to collect anything from the man's estate.

(f) In addition to the events in items (a) through (e), S had taxable income from investments of $72,000 in 1984. He also sold a piece of real estate he had been holding for speculation on which he had a $37,200 long-term capital gain.

Required:

(1) Determine the amount of S's taxable income, assuming he is single, has no dependents, and is age 69.

(2) Determine the amount of S's 1984 net operating loss, if any.

38. T had the following transactions during the current year:

1. Sold X Corporation stock for $6,000. He had purchased the stock two years earlier for $4,000.

2. Sold a computer to his brother for $1,000. He had purchased the computer two years earlier for $4,500. He had used the computer in his business and had taken $1,665 of depreciation.

3. On September 1 of the current year, he found out that A had been sentenced to jail in a foreign country for 20 years. T had loaned A $20,000 on June 1 of last year. The loan was due on June 1 of the current year, and T has not been able to collect.

4. On August 15 of the current year, T's broker informed T that the Y stock that he owned was completely worthless. T had purchased the stock on December 23 of last year for $3,000.

5. On April 15 of the current year, T sold W Corporation stock to an unrelated party for $12,000. T's basis in the stock was $17,000. T had organized W Corporation three years ago, but the business never really got off the ground. The stock was § 1244 stock.

6. Sold D Corporation stock for $11,000. T had purchased the stock six years ago for $3,000.

7. T's salary for the current year was $60,000.

Determine the amount of T's adjusted gross income for the current year.

Research Problems

39. T lives in Florida and recently suffered a loss of pine trees due to a rapid invasion of the southern pine beetle. The pine trees were destroyed within 10 days even though the area was previously not known for such devastating attacks. T also lost some coconut palm trees due to lethal yellowing, a disease which destroyed T's palms some 9 to 10 months after the disease was transmitted to the palms by insects. Can T claim a § 165(c)(3) casualty loss deduction for the value of either the pine trees or the palms?

40. On June 6 of the current year, G was preparing for bed; because of an

injury to her ring finger earlier in the day, she took off her diamond ring and wrapped it in tissues and placed it on the bathroom countertop. The next morning G's husband arose very early, and in the process of preparing himself for the day, he disposed of the tissues, not knowing they contained the ring, by flushing them down the toilet. Later in the day when G discovered what had happened she immediately called a plumber, and the sewer traps were searched. All of the efforts to recover the ring were unavailing. The ring was not insured, and the loss amounted to $5,000. Discuss whether G and her husband can claim a Sec. 165(c)(3) casualty loss for the loss of the ring.

41. T's son, S, entered the U. S. Navy on May 23, 19X1. At the time he was 19 years old. In 19X2, as a result of financial pressures, S was in need of funds. After unsuccessfully attempting to secure a loan from a financial institution, S borrowed $2,000 from T, with the understanding that the loan was to be repaid when S got on his feet. In 19X3, S was incarcerated in a military stockade. During the next five years, S was in and out of prison at various times. In 19X9, S violated restrictions of his prison work-release program and was returned to prison. Discuss whether T is entitled to a nonbusiness bad debt deduction in 19X9.

Chapter 9

Depreciation, Cost Recovery, Amortization, and Depletion

The Internal Revenue Code provides for a deduction for the consumption of the cost of an asset through depreciation, cost recovery, amortization, or depletion. Before discussing each cost consumption method, however, it may be well to review the difference between the classification of an asset (i. e., realty or personalty) and the use to which it is placed (i. e., business or personal). Personalty can be defined as all assets that are not realty.[1] Both realty and personalty can be either business use or personal use property. Examples of this distinction include a residence (realty that is personal use), an office building (realty that is business use), a dump truck (personalty that is business use), and regular wearing apparel (personalty that is personal use).

A further distinction is made between tangible and intangible property. Tangible property is any property with physical substance (e. g., equipment, buildings), while intangible property lacks such substance (e. g., goodwill, patents).

A write-off of the cost (or other adjusted basis) of an asset is known as the process of depreciation, depletion, or amortization. Depreciation relates to tangible property, depletion refers to certain natural resources (e. g., oil, coal, gravel), and amortization concerns intangible property. As is noted later, a write-off for income tax purposes is not allowed when an asset lacks a determinable useful life (e. g., land, goodwill) or when it is not business use property.

---

1. Refer to Chapter 1 for a further discussion.

The depreciation rules were completely overhauled by the Economic Recovery Tax Act of 1981 (ERTA); hence, property acquired after December 31, 1980, is subject to the accelerated cost recovery system (ACRS). However, property acquired before January 1, 1981, is still subject to the pre-ERTA depreciation rules. Therefore, this chapter first discusses the pre-ERTA depreciation rules, including the amortization rules not changed by ERTA, and follows with a discussion of ACRS.

DEPRECIATION AND AMORTIZATION

Section 167 permits a depreciation deduction in the form of a reasonable allowance for the exhaustion, wear and tear, and obsolescence of business property and property which is held for the production of income (e. g., rental property held by an investor).[2] Obsolescence refers to normal technological change due to reasonably foreseeable economic conditions. If rapid or abnormal obsolescence occurs, a taxpayer may change to a shorter estimated useful life if there is a "clear and convincing basis for the redetermination."[3]

The taxpayer must adopt a reasonably consistent plan for depreciating the cost or other basis of assets over the estimated useful life of the property (e. g., the taxpayer cannot arbitrarily defer or accelerate the amount of depreciation from one year to another). In addition, the basis of the depreciable property must be reduced by the depreciation allowed and not less than the allowable amount.[4] For example, if the taxpayer does not claim any depreciation on property during a particular year, the basis of the property is nevertheless reduced by the amount of depreciation which should have been deducted.

> **Example 1.** On January 1, 19X1, T paid $6,000 for a truck to be used in his business. He chose a four-year estimated useful life, no salvage value, and straight-line depreciation. Thus, the allowable depreciation deduction was $1,500 per year. However, depreciation actually taken was as follows:
>
> | | |
> |---|---|
> | 19X1 | $ 1,500 |
> | 19X2 | –0– |
> | 19X3 | –0– |
> | 19X4 | 1,500 |
>
> The adjusted basis of the truck must be reduced by the full amount of allowable depreciation of $6,000 ($1,500 × 4 years) despite the fact that T claimed only $3,000 depreciation during

---

2. § 167(a); Reg. § 1.167(a)–1(a).
3. Reg. § 1.167(a)–1(b).
4. § 1016(a)(2); Reg. § 1.167(a)–10(a).

the four-year period. Therefore, if T sold the truck at the end of 19X4 for $1,000, a $1,000 gain would be recognized, since the adjusted cost basis of the truck is zero.

The depreciation rules have been revised significantly during the past several years to reflect fiscal and social policy objectives of Congress. For example, a rapid recovery of capital is accomplished by allowing accelerated depreciation methods or by permitting taxpayers to use artificially shortened useful life estimates. In certain periods, Congress has deemed it necessary to stimulate private investment in capital assets and therefore has permitted businesses to use methods which assure a rapid recovery of capital. For example, Congress attempted to stimulate increased investment in low-income housing by permitting rapid amortization of certain rehabilitation expenditures.[5] The Economic Recovery Tax Act of 1981 made perhaps the most significant revision ever with respect to the rapid recovery of capital. This accelerated cost recovery system (ACRS) is discussed later in the chapter.

QUALIFYING PROPERTY

As mentioned earlier, the use rather than the character of property determines whether a depreciation deduction is permitted. Property must be used in a trade or business or held for the production of income to qualify as depreciable.

> **Example 2.** T is a self-employed CPA who uses her automobile for both personal and business purposes. A depreciation deduction is permitted only for the property used in business. Assuming the automobile was acquired at a cost of $12,000 and T's mileage during the year was 10,000 miles, of which 3,000 miles were for business, only 30% of the cost, or $3,600, would be subject to depreciation.

The basis for depreciation is generally the adjusted cost basis used to determine gain if the property is sold or disposed of.[6] However, if personal use assets are converted to business or income-producing use, the basis for depreciation is the lower of the adjusted basis or fair market value when the property is converted.[7]

> **Example 3.** T acquires a personal residence in 19X1 for $30,000. In 19X4 he converts the property to rental use when the fair market value is only $25,000. The basis for depreciation is $25,000, since the fair market value is less than the adjusted basis. The $5,000 decline in value is deemed to be personal (since

---

5. § 167(k).

6. § 167(g).

7. Reg. § 1.167(g)–1.

it occurred while the property was held for personal use) and therefore nondeductible.

The Regulations provide that tangible property is depreciable only to the extent that the property is subject to wear and tear, to decay or decline from natural causes, to exhaustion, and to obsolescence.[8] Thus, land and inventory are not depreciable, but land improvements are depreciable (e. g., paved surfaces, fences, landscaping).

Depreciation or amortization of intangible property is not permitted unless the property has a definite and limited useful life.[9] For example, patents and copyrights have a definite and limited legal life and are therefore eligible for amortization. Goodwill is not amortizable, since its life extends for an unlimited period.[10]

Other types of intangible assets which may or may not be subject to amortization include the cost of acquiring customer and subscription lists. The IRS has held that such assets are generally not subject to amortization.[11] However, the courts have permitted a deduction for amortization when the taxpayer has been able to establish an ascertainable life separate and distinct from goodwill and show that the asset had a limited useful life which could be ascertained with reasonable accuracy.[12]

OTHER DEPRECIATION CONSIDERATIONS

Under pre-1981 depreciation rules, taxpayers had to take into account the salvage value (assuming there was a salvage value) of an asset in calculating depreciation. An asset could not be depreciated below its salvage value.[13]

However, the Code permitted a taxpayer to disregard salvage value for amounts up to 10 percent of the basis in the property.[14] This rule applied to tangible personal property (other than livestock) with an estimated useful life of three years or more.

> **Example 4.** The XYZ Company acquired a machine for $10,000 in 1980 with an estimated salvage value of $2,000 after 10 years. The company may disregard salvage value to the extent of $1,000 and compute its depreciation based upon a cost of $10,000 less $1,000 salvage. The adjusted basis may be reduced to $1,000 (depreciation of $9,000 may be taken) despite the fact that the actual salvage value is $2,000. This rule was incorporated into the law

---

8. Reg. § 1.167(a)–2.
9. Reg. § 1.167(a)–3.
10. Ibid.
11. Rev.Rul. 74–456, 1974–2 C.B. 65.
12. *Manhattan Co. of Virginia, Inc.,* 50 T.C. 78 (1968); *Houston Chronicle Publishing Co. v. U. S.,* 73–2 USTC ¶ 9537, 32 AFTR2d 73–5312A, 481 F.2d 1240 (CA–5, 1973).
13. Reg. § 1.167(a)(1)(c).
14. § 167(f).

to reduce the number of IRS and taxpayer disputes relative to the salvage value which should be used.

Another consideration before ERTA was the choice of depreciation methods from among the several allowed. The Code provided for the following alternative depreciation methods for property placed into service before January 1, 1981:[15]

—The straight-line method (cost basis less salvage ÷ estimated useful life).

—The declining-balance method (i. e., DB) using a rate not to exceed twice the straight-line rate. Common methods included 200 percent DB (double-declining balance), 150 percent DB, and 125 percent DB. Salvage value is not taken into account under any of the declining-balance methods. However, no further depreciation can be claimed once net book value (i. e., cost minus depreciation) and salvage value are the same.

—Any other consistent method which did not result in greater total depreciation being claimed during the first two-thirds of the useful life than would have been allowable under the double-declining balance method. Permissible methods included sum-of-the-years' digits (i. e., SYD), machine-hours, and the units-of-production method.

Example 5. T acquired a new automobile on January 1, 1980, to be used in his business. The asset cost $10,000 with an estimated salvage value of $2,000 and a four-year estimated useful life. The following amounts of depreciation could be deducted, depending on the method of depreciation used (note that pre-ERTA rules continue to apply for the entire useful life of assets acquired prior to 1981):

	1980	1981	1982	1983
1. Straight-line: $10,000 cost less ($2,000 salvage reduced by 10% of cost) ÷ 4 years	$ 2,250	$ 2,250	$ 2,250	$ 2,250
2. Double-declining balance:				
a. $10,000 × 50% (twice the straight-line rate)	$ 5,000			
b. ($10,000 − $5,000) × 50%		$ 2,500		
c. ($10,000 − $5,000 − $2,500) × 50%			$ 1,250	
d. ($10,000 − $5,000 − $2,500 − $1,250) × 50%				$ 250[16]

---

15. § 167(b).
16. Total depreciation taken cannot exceed cost minus estimated salvage value (i.e., $1,000 in this example).

	1980	1981	1982	1983
3. Sum-of-the-years' digits:*				
$10,000 cost less ($2,000 salvage reduced by 10% of cost) or $9,000				
a. $9,000 × ⁴⁄₁₀	$ 3,600			
b. $9,000 × ³⁄₁₀		$ 2,700		
c. $9,000 × ²⁄₁₀			$ 1,800	
d. $9,000 × ¹⁄₁₀				$ 900

*The sum-of-the-years' digits (SYD) method formula is

$$\text{Cost minus salvage} \times \frac{\text{remaining life at the beginning of the year}}{\text{sum-of-the-years' digits of the estimated life}}$$

In this example, the denominator for SYD is $1 + 2 + 3 + 4$, or 10. The numerator is 4 for year 1 (i. e., the number of years left at the beginning of year 1), 3 for year 2, etc. The denominator can be calculated by the following formula:

$$S = \frac{Y(Y + 1)}{2} \text{ where } Y = \text{estimated useful life}$$

$$\text{e. g., } S = \frac{4(4 + 1)}{2} = 10$$

Example 6. Using the depreciation calculations in the prior example, the following is a comparison of the depreciation reserve at the end of 1983.

	Cost	− Depreciation	= Book Value of Residual*
Straight-line	$ 10,000	$ 9,000	$ 1,000
Double-declining balance	10,000	9,000	1,000
Sum-of-the-years' digits	10,000	9,000	1,000

*Note that an asset may not be depreciated below its salvage value even when a declining-balance method is used.

The Tax Reform Act of 1969 placed certain restrictions on the use of accelerated methods for new and used realty placed in service prior to January 1, 1981. These restrictions were imposed to reduce the opportunities for using real estate investments as tax shelters; the use of accelerated depreciation frequently resulted in the recognition of ordinary tax losses on economically profitable real estate ventures.[17]

The following methods were permitted for commercial and residential real property acquired prior to ERTA:[18]

---

17. S.Rep. 91–552, 91st Cong., 1st Sess., 1969, p. 212.
18. § 167(j).

	Nonresidential Real Property (commercial and industrial buildings, etc.)	Residential Real Property (two-family houses, etc.)
New property acquired after July 24, 1969, and prior to January 1, 1981	150% DB, SL	200% DB, SYD, 150% DB or SL
Used property acquired after July 24, 1969, and prior to January 1, 1981	SL	125% DB if estimated useful life is 20 years or greater; SL

Restrictions on the use of accelerated methods were not imposed on new tangible personalty (e. g., machinery, equipment, and automobiles). However, 200 percent declining-balance and sum-of-the-years' digits were not permitted for used tangible personal property. The 150 percent declining-balance method was permitted for used tangible personalty which had a useful life of at least three years.[19] Since the acquisition of used property did not result in any net addition to gross private investment in our economy, Congress chose not to provide as rapid accelerated depreciation for used property. It should be noted that accelerated methods (i. e., 200 percent declining-balance and sum-of-the-years' digits) were permitted for new residential rental property. Presumably, the desire to stimulate construction of new housing units justified the need for such accelerated methods.

Another consideration for pre-ERTA property was the additional first-year depreciation allowed. This so-called bonus depreciation was limited to 20 percent of the cost of new or used tangible depreciable personalty, with a ceiling $10,000 of basis ($20,000 if a joint return was filed). Thus, the maximum deduction per year was $2,000 ($4,000 on a joint return). Bonus depreciation was replaced by a direct write-off under ERTA (discussed later in the chapter).

A pre-ERTA consideration which often caused disagreement between taxpayers and the IRS was the determination of a useful life for a depreciable asset. One source of information was the company's previous experience and policy with respect to asset maintenance and utilization. Another source was the guideline lives issued by the IRS.[20] In 1971, the IRS guideline life system was modified and liberalized by the enactment of the Asset Depreciation Range (ADR) system. The ADR rules were extremely complex[21] and have been eliminated by ERTA.

---

19. Rev.Rul. 57–352, 1957–2 C.B. 150.
20. Rev.Proc. 77–10, 1977–1 C.B. 548.
21. Reg. § 1.167(a)(ii).

SPECIAL DEPRECIATION AND AMORTIZATION PROVISION

Rehabilitation Expenditures for Low-income Housing. The Code provides a special five-year amortization election for rehabilitation expenditures on low-income housing.[22] The rehabilitation expenditures must exceed $3,000 per dwelling unit over two consecutive years and in the aggregate may not exceed $20,000 per dwelling unit.[23] Any cost in excess of the $20,000 ceiling is subject to the regular depreciation rules.

> **Example 7.** In the current year, T incurred $30,000 of rehabilitation expenditures to renovate an old home which qualifies as low-income housing. Of this $30,000 investment, $20,000 may be amortized on a straight-line basis over 60 months using the elective provisions of § 167(k); $10,000 must be depreciated under the § 167 regular depreciation rules.

Construction Period Interest and Taxes. Section 189 requires the capitalization of certain construction period interest and taxes. These charges must be capitalized in the year they are paid or accrued for the construction of real property or improvements thereto. Such amounts can be amortized over a period that usually extends for 10 years. However, before the 10-year period amortization rules take full effect, a transition schedule must be followed for nonresidential real property and residential real property.[24] This transition period is completed for nonresidential real property in 1981 and for residential real property in 1983.

S corporations and personal holding companies are required to capitalize construction period interest and taxes with respect to residential real property, and all corporations are required to capitalize interest and taxes paid or incurred in tax years beginning after 1982 for construction of nonresidential real property begun after 1982.

The provision does not apply to low-income housing or to any amount that is capitalized at the election of a taxpayer as a carrying charge under § 266. In addition, it does not apply to interest or taxes paid or incurred with respect to property not held for business or investment purposes (e. g., a taxpayer's personal residence).

In the case of a sale or exchange of property, the unamortized balance of the construction period interest and taxes is to be added to the basis of the property for purposes of determining gain or loss on the sale or exchange. In a case of a nontaxable transfer or exchange

---

22. § 167(k). ERTA amended this section to increase the $20,000 limit to $40,000 if certain conditions are met. The conditions relate to government certification, rights of tenants to acquire the property, etc.

23. § 167(k)(2)(A) and (B).

24. § 189(b).

(e. g., a transfer to a partnership or a controlled corporation, a like-kind exchange, or a gift), the transferor is to continue to deduct the amortization allowed over the period remaining.[25]

ACCELERATED COST RECOVERY SYSTEM (ACRS)

GENERAL CONSIDERATIONS

The depreciation rules prior to ERTA were designed to allocate depreciation deductions over the period the asset is used in business so that the deductions for the cost of an asset are matched with the income produced by the asset (the so-called matching concept).

Often this led to controversies between taxpayers and the IRS concerning the estimated useful life of an asset, and it delayed the tax benefit to be derived from the recoupment of a capital investment in the form of a deduction for depreciation.

One way to resolve the estimated useful life problem was to utilize the Asset Depreciation Range (ADR) system, which specified ranges for particular assets. Taxpayers could select a useful life for an asset within the specified range for that particular asset. However, many assets were not eligible for ADR or taxpayers saw fit not to elect the system. In such cases, useful lives were determined according to the facts and circumstances pertaining to each asset or by agreement between the taxpayer and the IRS.

ERTA replaced the ADR system for property placed in service after December 31, 1980, with the accelerated cost recovery system (ACRS). Under ACRS, the cost of an asset is recovered over a predetermined period generally shorter than the useful life of the asset or the period the asset is used to produce income.[26] The change was designed to encourage investment, improve productivity, and simplify the law and its administration.

Eligible Property Under ACRS. Assets used in a trade or business or for the production of income are depreciable if they are subject to wear and tear, decay, or decline from natural causes or obsolescence. Assets that do not decline in value on a predictable basis or that do not have a determinable useful life (e. g., land, goodwill, stock) are not depreciable.

Under ERTA, most tangible depreciable property (real and personal) is covered by ACRS. However, ACRS does not apply to (1) property not depreciated in terms of years (e. g., units-of-production method) except for certain railroad property or (2) property that is

---

25.   See pp. 25–29 of the Joint Committee Report on P.L. 94–455 as reported in 1976–3 C.B. Vol. 2, 37–41.
26.   § 168(b)(1).

amortized (e. g., leasehold improvements and certain rehabilitation expenditures).[27]

PERSONALTY: RECOVERY PERIODS AND METHODS

ACRS provides that the cost of eligible personalty (and certain realty) is recovered over 3, 5, 10, or 15 years. The classification of property by recovery period is as follows:[28]

3 years . . . . . Autos, light-duty trucks, R & D equipment, race horses over 2 years old and other horses over 12 years old, and personalty with an ADR midpoint life of 4 years or less.

5 years . . . . . Most other equipment except long-lived public utility property. Also includes single-purpose agricultural structures and petroleum storage facilities, which are designated as § 1245 property under the law.

10 years . . . . . Public utility property with an ADR midpoint life greater than 18 but not greater than 25 years, burners and boilers using coal as a primary fuel if used in a public utility power plant and if replacing or converting oil- or gas-fired burners or boilers, railroad tank cars, mobile homes, and realty with an ADR midpoint life of 12.5 years or less (e. g., theme park structures).

15 years . . . . . Public utility property with an ADR midpoint life exceeding 25 years (except certain burners and boilers using coal as a primary fuel).

Under ACRS, taxpayers have the choice of using (1) the straight-line method over the regular or optional (see below) recovery period or (2) a prescribed accelerated method over the regular recovery period.[29] These two methods are both part of the ACRS system enacted in new § 168. However, § 168 does not provide a convenient name for either of the two methods. Hereafter, the straight-line method will be referred to as the optional (or elective) straight-line method. The method using percentages prescribed in the Code will be referred to as the statutory percentage method.

The rates to be used in computing the deduction under the statutory percentage method are prescribed in § 168.[30] These rates are shown in Figure I. The rates are based on the 150 percent declining-balance method, using the half-year convention and an assumption of zero salvage value.

---

27. § 168(e).
28. § 168(c).
29. § 168(b)(3)(A).
30. § 168(b)(1)(A), (B), and (C).

Figure I

ACRS STATUTORY PERCENTAGES
FOR PROPERTY OTHER THAN 15-YEAR REAL PROPERTY

For Property Placed in Service After December 31, 1980

The applicable percentage for the class of property is:

If the recovery year is:	3-year	5-year	10-year	15-year public utility
1	25	15	8	5
2	38	22	14	10
3	37	21	12	9
4		21	10	8
5		21	10	7
6			10	7
7			9	6
8			9	6
9			9	6
10			9	6
11				6
12				6
13				6
14				6
15				6

Example 8. In December 1982, T buys the following business assets: $34,000 of machinery, $6,000 of office furniture, and $16,000 of light-duty trucks. The machinery and office furniture are five-year properties and the trucks are three-year properties. T's depreciation deductions using the statutory percentage method are as follows:

1982

25% of $16,000 (trucks)	$ 4,000
15% of $40,000 (machinery and furniture)	6,000
	$ 10,000

1983

38% of $16,000	$ 6,080
22% of $40,000	8,800
	$ 14,880

1984

37% of $16,000	$ 5,920
21% of $40,000	8,400
	$ 14,320

1985

21% of $40,000 $ 8,400

1986

21% of $40,000 $ 8,400

Note that in 1982, T got a half year's depreciation deduction (since the half-year convention is reflected in the percentages in Figure I) although she held the property only one month.

Reduction of Basis for Investment Tax Credit.   For personalty placed in service after 1982, TEFRA requires that the basis of the property for the ACRS write-off must be reduced by one-half the amount of the investment tax credit taken on the property.[31] Investment credit is not allowed on realty. (See Chapter 13 for details.)

> **Example 9.**   In 1984, T purchases a machine, which is five-year ACRS property, for $10,000. T takes a $1,000 investment credit on the property (10% of $10,000). Under the TEFRA provision, the basis of the property must be reduced by $500 (½ of the $1,000 investment tax credit). Thus, T's cost recovery allowance will be based on $9,500 [$10,000 (cost) − $500 (reduction for investment credit)]. T's cost recovery deduction for 1984 will be $1,425 (15% of $9,500).

The 50 percent basis reduction rule applies to regular investment tax credit property, energy credit property, and certified historic property. However, the basis of properties to which the 15 or 20 percent rehabilitation credit applies (see Chapter 13) is reduced by the full amount of the credit.

As an alternative to reducing the basis of the property, a taxpayer may elect to take a reduced investment credit. Under this election, the investment credit is eight percent (rather than ten percent) for recovery property that is not three-year property and four percent (instead of six percent) for three-year property.[32]

> **Example 10.**   In 1984, T purchases a machine, which is five-year ACRS property, for $10,000. T elects to take an $800 investment credit on the property (8% × $10,000). Under the elective provision, the basis of the property need not be reduced by any of the investment credit taken. Thus, T's cost recovery allowance will be based on $10,000 (cost), and T's cost recovery deduction for 1984 will be $1,500 (15% × $10,000).

Upon the future sale of the asset, the reduction in basis will be treated as depreciation for purposes of applying the depreciation re-

---

31.   § 48(q)(1).
32.   § 48(q)(4).

capture provisions. However, the basis of the property disposed of will be increased by one-half the amount of the investment credit to be recaptured. This increase occurs immediately before the disposition (or other event) that triggers recapture of depreciation. See Chapter 17.

REALTY: RECOVERY PERIODS AND METHODS

Under ACRS, realty is assigned a 15-year recovery period. Component depreciation generally is no longer allowed. Given a new 15-year

Figure II

ACRS STATUTORY PERCENTAGES FOR 15-YEAR-
REAL PROPERTY

15-year Real Property Table (other than low-income housing)

Year	Month Placed in Service											
	1	2	3	4	5	6	7	8	9	10	11	12
1st	12%	11%	10%	9%	8%	7%	6%	5%	4%	3%	2%	1%
2d	10%	10%	11%	11%	11%	11%	11%	11%	11%	11%	11%	12%
3d	9%	9%	9%	9%	10%	10%	10%	10%	10%	10%	10%	10%
4th	8%	8%	8%	8%	8%	8%	9%	9%	9%	9%	9%	9%
5th	7%	7%	7%	7%	7%	7%	8%	8%	8%	8%	8%	8%
6th	6%	6%	6%	6%	7%	7%	7%	7%	7%	7%	7%	7%
7th	6%	6%	6%	6%	6%	6%	6%	6%	6%	6%	6%	6%
8th	6%	6%	6%	6%	6%	6%	6%	6%	6%	6%	6%	6%
9th	6%	6%	6%	6%	6%	6%	5%	5%	5%	6%	6%	6%
10th	5%	6%	5%	6%	5%	5%	5%	5%	5%	5%	6%	5%
11th	5%	5%	5%	5%	5%	5%	5%	5%	5%	5%	5%	5%
12th	5%	5%	5%	5%	5%	5%	5%	5%	5%	5%	5%	5%
13th	5%	5%	5%	5%	5%	5%	5%	5%	5%	5%	5%	5%
14th	5%	5%	5%	5%	5%	5%	5%	5%	5%	5%	5%	5%
15th	5%	5%	5%	5%	5%	5%	5%	5%	5%	5%	5%	5%
16th	—	—	1%	1%	2%	2%	3%	3%	4%	4%	4%	5%

15-year Real Property Low-Income Housing Table

Year	Month Placed in Service											
	1	2	3	4	5	6	7	8	9	10	11	12
1st	13%	12%	11%	10%	9%	8%	7%	6%	4%	3%	2%	1%
2d	12%	12%	12%	12%	12%	12%	12%	13%	13%	13%	13%	13%
3d	10%	10%	10%	10%	11%	11%	11%	11%	11%	11%	11%	11%
4th	9%	9%	9%	9%	9%	9%	9%	9%	10%	10%	10%	10%
5th	8%	8%	8%	8%	8%	8%	8%	8%	8%	8%	8%	9%
6th	7%	7%	7%	7%	7%	7%	7%	7%	7%	7%	7%	7%
7th	6%	6%	6%	6%	6%	6%	6%	6%	6%	6%	6%	6%
8th	5%	5%	5%	5%	5%	5%	5%	5%	5%	5%	6%	6%
9th	5%	5%	5%	5%	5%	5%	5%	5%	5%	5%	5%	5%
10th	5%	5%	5%	5%	5%	5%	5%	5%	5%	5%	5%	5%
11th	4%	5%	5%	5%	5%	5%	5%	5%	5%	5%	5%	5%
12th	4%	4%	4%	5%	4%	5%	5%	5%	5%	5%	5%	5%
13th	4%	4%	4%	4%	4%	4%	5%	4%	5%	5%	5%	5%
14th	4%	4%	4%	4%	4%	4%	4%	4%	4%	5%	4%	4%
15th	4%	4%	4%	4%	4%	4%	4%	4%	4%	4%	4%	4%
16th	—	—	1%	1%	2%	2%	2%	3%	3%	3%	4%	4%

recovery period, real estate (e. g., rental property) is immediately more attractive as an investment than it was under the old law.

Real property other than low-income housing can be depreciated using the 175 percent declining-balance method, changing to the straight-line method to maximize acceleration. Low-income housing is depreciated using the 200 percent declining balance method, changing to straight-line.[33] Statutory percentages for real property are shown in Figure II, which contains rates for low-income housing as well as other 15-year real estate.

Since the half-year convention does not apply to 15-year real property, these tables are structured differently than those in Figure I. The cost recovery deduction for 15-year real property is based on the month the asset is placed in service, rather than on the half-year convention.[34]

> **Example 11.** T purchased a warehouse for $100,000 on January 1, 1984. The first year's cost recovery allowance using the statutory percentage method is $12,000 (12% of $100,000). Cost recovery deductions for 1985, 1986, and 1987 are, respectively, $10,000, $9,000, and $8,000. (See Figure II for percentages.)

> **Example 12.** Assume the same facts as in Example 11, except the property is low-income housing. Cost recovery deductions for 1984 through 1987 are $13,000, $12,000, $10,000 and $9,000.

STRAIGHT-LINE ELECTION UNDER ACRS

Under ACRS, taxpayers may elect to write off an asset using the straight-line method rather than the statutory percentage method. The straight-line recovery period may be equal to the prescribed recovery period under the statutory percentage method, or it may be a longer period. Allowable straight-line recovery periods for each class of property are summarized below:[35]

  3-year property.......... 3, 5, or 12 years
  5-year property.......... 5, 12, or 25 years
  10-year property.......... 10, 25, or 35 years
  15-year property.......... 15, 35, or 45 years

If the straight-line option is elected, the half-year convention is applied in computing the cost recovery deduction in the case of property other than 15-year real property. There is no cost recovery deduction in the year of disposition of property other than 15-year real property. This rule is applicable to both the statutory percentage method and the optional straight-line method.

---

33. § 168(b)(2).
34. § 168(b)(2)(A).
35. § 168(b)(3).

Example 13. J acquired a light-duty truck (three-year property) on March 1, 1984, at a cost of $10,000. J elects to write off the cost of the truck using the optional straight-line method, with a recovery period of five years. Assume J makes the reduced credit election and takes a $400 investment credit ($10,000 × .04). Because the half-year convention applies, J can deduct only $1,000 [($10,000 ÷ 5) × ½] in 1984.

Example 14. Assume the same facts as in Example 13. If J disposes of the truck at any time during 1985, no cost recovery deduction is allowed for 1985, the year of disposition.

The half-year convention does not apply in the case of 15-year real property for which the straight-line option is elected. Nor is the cost recovery deduction disallowed in the year of disposition. The first year's deduction and the deduction for the year of disposition are computed on the basis of the number of months the property was in service during the year.[36]

Example 15. K acquired a store building on October 1, 1984, at a cost of $150,000. K elects the straight-line method using a recovery period of 15 years. K's cost recovery deduction for 1984 is $2,500 (($150,000 ÷ 15) × 3/12).

Example 16. Assume the same facts as in Example 15 and that K disposes of the asset on September 30, 1986. K's cost recovery deduction for 1986 would be $7,500 (($150,000 ÷ 15) × 9/12).

For each class of property other than 15-year real estate, the straight-line election applies to all assets in a particular class that are placed in service during the year for which the election is made, and later to the entire recovery period for those vintage assets.[37] The election may be changed for property of the same class placed in service in other taxable years. By contrast, the straight-line election for 15-year real property may be made on a property by property basis within the same year.[38]

ELECTION TO EXPENSE ASSETS

Prior to ERTA, taxpayers were allowed additional first-year (or "bonus") depreciation of 20 percent of up to $10,000 ($20,000 on a joint return) of qualifying § 179 property (see page 317). ERTA repealed § 179 as then worded and substituted new § 179. Entitled "Election to Expense Certain Depreciable Business Assets," the new

---

36. § 168(b)(2).
37. § 168(b)(3)(B)(i).
38. § 168(b)(3)(B)(ii).

§ 179 permits an immediate write-off based on the following amounts and phase-in periods:[39]

Year	Amount of Write-off
1982 1983	$ 5,000
1984–1985	7,500
1986 and thereafter	10,000

Thus, such amounts may not be capitalized and depreciated. Also, no investment tax credit is allowed for items expensed under new § 179.[40] The election applies to purchased tangible personal property used in a trade or business.

> **Example 17.** T acquires machinery (five-year property) on February 1, 1984, at a cost of $40,000 and elects to expense $7,500 under the § 179 provisions. T takes $3,250 investment credit on the machine [10% of $32,500 ($40,000 cost − $7,500 § 179 expense not eligible for investment credit)]. T's statutory percentage cost recovery deduction for 1984 is $4,631.25 [$32,500 ($40,000 cost − $7,500 expensed) − $1,625 (½ × $3,250 investment credit) × .15]. T's total write-off in 1984 is $12,131.25 ($7,500 expensed + $4,631.25 cost recovery deduction).

OTHER ASPECTS OF ACRS

Because the ACRS deduction may be larger than the depreciation deduction under pre-1981 rules, there was concern that some taxpayers might engage in transactions that did not result in an actual ownership change in an attempt to change pre-1981 property into post-1980 recovery property. To prevent this, ACRS contains "anti-churning" rules that prevent the use of ACRS on personal property acquired after 1980 if the property was owned or used during 1980 by the taxpayer or a related person (i. e., "churned" property).[41] Hence, the taxpayer must use pre-1981 depreciation rules on churned property.

> **Example 18.** T began renting a tractor to use in his farming business in 1979. T used the tractor until 1982, at which time he purchased it. T is not entitled to use ACRS, because he used the tractor in 1980. Instead, he must use the pre-1981 depreciation rules.

In addition, ACRS does not apply to real property if:

---

39.   § 179(b)(1). The amount shown is per taxpayer, per year.
40.   § 179(c)(9).
41.   § 168(e)(4)(A).

—The property was owned by the taxpayer or a related person at any time during 1980.

—The taxpayer leases the property to a person, or a person related to such person, who owned the property at any time during 1980.

—The property is acquired in nonrecognition transactions, such as certain like-kind exchanges or involuntary conversions. However, this applies only to the extent that the basis of the property includes an amount representing the adjusted basis of other property owned by the taxpayer or a related person during 1980.[42]

Example 19. In 1984, J made a nontaxable like-kind exchange (see Chapter 15). He gave an apartment building, held since 1978, with an adjusted basis of $300,000 and a fair market value of $400,000. He also gave $200,000 in cash. In exchange, J received an apartment building worth $600,000. The basis of the new building is $500,000 [$300,000 (basis of old building) + $200,000 (cash paid)], but only $200,000 of the basis is subject to the ACRS rules.

A person is considered related to a previous user or owner if there exists a family or fiduciary relationship or if there exists ownership of 10 percent of a corporation or partnership.

DEPLETION

In developing an oil or gas well, four types of expenditures must be made by the producer. The first type is the payment for the natural resource (the oil under the ground). Because natural resources are physically limited, these costs are recovered through depletion, which is discussed below. The second type occurs when the property is made ready for drilling: the cost of labor in clearing the property, erecting derricks, and drilling the hole. These costs, called intangible drilling and development costs, generally have no salvage value and are a lost cost if the well is dry. The treatment of these costs is discussed below. The third type of cost is for tangible assets such as tools, pipes, and engines. Such costs are capital in nature and must be capitalized and recovered through depreciation. Finally, there are costs that are incurred after the well is producing, including such items as labor, fuel, and supplies. They are clearly operating expenses which are deductible currently when incurred (on the accrual basis) or when paid (on the cash basis).

The expenditures for depreciable assets and operating expenses pose no unusual problems for producers of natural resources. The tax treatment of depletable costs and intangible drilling and development costs is quite a different matter.

---

42. § 168(e)(4)(B) & (C).

INTANGIBLE DRILLING AND DEVELOPMENT COSTS (IDC)

Intangible drilling and development costs can be handled in one of two ways, at the option of the taxpayer. They can be either charged off as an expense in the year in which they are incurred or capitalized and written off through depletion. The election is made in the first year that such expenditures are incurred either by taking a deduction on the return or by adding them to the depletable basis. No formal statement of intent is required, and once made, the election is binding on both the taxpayer and the Commissioner for all such expenditures in the future. If the taxpayer fails to make the election to expense such costs on the original timely filed return the first year such expenditures are incurred, an automatic election to capitalize them has been made and is irrevocable.

As a general rule, it is more advantageous to expense intangible drilling and development costs. The obvious benefit of an immediate write-off (as opposed to a deferred write-off through depletion) is not the only advantage. Since a taxpayer can use percentage depletion which is calculated without reference to basis (see Example 20), the intangible drilling and development costs may be completely lost as a deduction if they are capitalized.

DEPLETION METHODS

Wasting assets (e. g., oil, gas, coal, gravel) are subject to depletion, which simply is a form of depreciation applicable to natural resources. Land generally cannot be depleted.

The owner of an interest in the wasting asset is entitled to deduct depletion. An owner is one who has an "economic interest" in the property.[43] An economic interest requires the acquisition of an interest in the minerals in place and the receipt of income from the extraction or severance of such minerals. Like depreciation, depletion is a deduction *for* adjusted gross income.

There are two methods of calculating depletion: cost and percentage. Cost depletion can be used on any wasting asset (and is the only method allowed for timber). Percentage depletion is subject to a number of limitations, particularly as to oil and gas deposits. Depletion should be calculated both ways, and generally the method that results in the largest deduction is used. The choice between cost and percentage depletion is an annual election.

Cost Depletion   Cost depletion is determined by using the adjusted basis of the asset.[44] Such basis is divided by the estimated recoverable units of the asset (e. g., barrels, tons) to arrive at the depletion per unit. The depletion per unit then is multiplied by the

---

43. Reg. § 1.611–1(b).
44. § 612.

number of units sold (*not* the units produced) during the year to arrive at the cost depletion allowed. Cost depletion, therefore, resembles the units-of-production method of calculating depreciation.

> **Example 20.** On January 1, 19X1, T purchased the rights to a mineral interest for $1,000,000. At that time, the remaining recoverable units in the mineral interest were estimated to be 200,000. Under these circumstances, the depletion per unit becomes $5 [$1,000,000 (adjusted basis) ÷ 200,000 (estimated recoverable units)]. If during the year 60,000 units were mined and 25,000 were sold, the cost depletion would be $125,000 [$5 (depletion per unit) × 25,000 (units sold)].

If later it is discovered that the original estimate was incorrect, the depletion per unit must be redetermined based on the revised estimate.[45]

> **Example 21.** Assume the same facts as in Example 20. In 19X2, T realizes that an incorrect estimate was made. The remaining recoverable units now are determined to be 400,000. Based on this new information, the revised depletion per unit becomes $2.1875 [$875,000 (adjusted basis) ÷ 400,000 (estimated recoverable units)]. Note that the adjusted basis is the original cost ($1,000,000) reduced by the depletion claimed in 19X1 ($125,000). If 30,000 units are sold in 19X2, the depletion for this year would be $65,625 [$2.1875 (depletion per unit) × 30,000 (units sold)].

Percentage Depletion. Percentage depletion (also referred to as statutory depletion) is a specified percentage provided for in the Code. The percentage varies according to the type of mineral interest involved. A sample of these percentages is shown in Figure III. The rate is applied to the gross income from the property, but in no event may percentage depletion exceed 50 percent of the taxable income from the property before the allowance for depletion.

> **Example 22.** Assuming gross income of $100,000, a depletion rate of 22%, and other expenses relating to the property of $60,000, the depletion allowance is determined as follows:

Gross income	$ 100,000
Less: Other expenses	60,000
Taxable income before depletion	$ 40,000
Depletion allowance [the lesser of $22,000	
(22% × $100,000) or $20,000 (50% × $40,000)]	20,000
Taxable income after depletion	$ 20,000

---

45. § 611(a).

Figure III

SAMPLE OF PERCENTAGE DEPLETION RATES

22% Depletion

Antimony	Nickel
Beryllium	Platinum
Cadmium	Sulfur
Cobalt	Tin
Lead	Titanium
Manganese	Tungsten
Mercury	Uranium
Molybdenum	Zinc

15% Depletion

Copper mines	Oil and gas
Gold mines	Oil shale
Iron mines	Silver mines

14% Depletion

Borax	Magnesium carbonates
Calcium carbonates	Marble
Dolomite	Phosphate rock
Feldspar	Potash
Gilsonite	Quartzite
Granite	Slate
Limestone	Soapstone

10% Depletion

Coal	Perlite
Lignite	Sodium chloride

5% Depletion

Gravel	Pumice
Peat	Sand

The adjusted basis of the property would be reduced by $20,000, the depletion allowed. If the other expenses had been only $55,000, the full $22,000 could have been deducted and the adjusted basis would have been reduced by $22,000.

Note that percentage depletion is based on a percentage of the gross income from the property and makes no reference to cost. When percentage depletion is used it is possible, therefore, to deduct more than the original cost of the property. If percentage depletion is used, however, the adjusted basis of the property (for computing cost depletion) must be reduced by the amount of percentage depletion taken until basis reaches zero.

Effect of Intangible Drilling Costs on Depletion. The treatment of intangible drilling and development costs has an effect on the depletion deduction in two ways. If the costs are capitalized, the basis for cost depletion is increased, and as a consequence, the cost depletion is increased. If intangible drilling and development costs are expensed, they reduce the taxable income from the property, which may result in application of the provision which limits depletion to 50 percent of taxable income before deducting depletion.

> **Example 23.** J purchased the rights to an oil interest for $1,000,000. The recoverable barrels were estimated to be 200,000. During the year, 50,000 barrels were sold for $1,500,000. Regular expenses amounted to $800,000, and intangible drilling and development costs were $250,000. If the intangible drilling and development costs are capitalized, the depletion per unit is $6.25 ($1,000,000 plus $250,000 divided by 200,000 barrels), and the following taxable income results:

Gross income	$ 1,500,000
Less: Expenses	800,000
Taxable income before depletion	$ 700,000
Cost depletion ($6.25 × 50,000) = $312,500	
Percentage depletion (15% × $1,500,000) = $225,000	
Greater of cost or percentage depletion	312,500
Taxable income	$ 387,500

If the costs are expensed, the taxable income becomes $200,000, as follows:

Gross income		$ 1,500,000
Less: Expenses, including IDC		1,050,000
Taxable income before depletion		$ 450,000
Cost depletion (($1,000,000 ÷ 200,000 barrels) × 50,000 barrels) =	$ 250,000	
Percentage depletion (15% of $1,500,000, limited to 50% of $450,000 taxable income before depletion) =	225,000	
Greater of cost or percentage depletion		250,000
Taxable income after depletion		$ 200,000

For further restrictions on the use or availability of the percentage depletion method, see § 613.

REPORTING PROCEDURES

Sole proprietors engaged in a business should file a Schedule C, Profit or (Loss) From Business or Profession, to accompany the Form 1040.

The top part of page 1 requests certain key information about the taxpayer (e. g., name, address, Social Security number) and the business methods involved (e. g., accounting method and inventory method used). Part I provides for the reporting of items of income. If the business requires the use of inventories and the computation of cost of goods sold (see Chapter 18 for when this is necessary), Schedule C–1 on page 2 must be completed and the cost of goods sold amount transferred to line 2.

Part II allows for the reporting of deductions. Some of the deductions discussed in Chapters 8 and 9 and their location on the form are bad debts (line 7), depletion (line 11), and depreciation (line 12). Other expenses (line 30) include those items not already covered (see lines 6–29). An example would be research and experimental expenditures.

If depreciation is claimed, it should be supported by completing Form 4562. The amount listed on line 10 of Form 4562 is then transferred to line 12 of page 1 of Schedule C.

> **Example 24.** T was employed as an accountant until July 1982, when he opened his own practice. T keeps his books on the accrual basis and had the following business expenses in 1983:
>
> (a) Revenue from accounting practice, $80,000.
>
> (b) Bad debts, $2,000.
>
> (c) Automobile expenses, $3,000.
>
> (d) Insurance, $800.
>
> (e) Office supplies, $4,000.
>
> (f) Rent, $12,000.
>
> (g) Furniture and fixtures acquired on July 15, 1982, for $8,000. T used the ACRS statutory percentage cost recovery method.
>
> (h) Business automobile acquired on November 20, 1982, for $10,000. T used the ACRS statutory percentage cost recovery method.
>
> (i) Microcomputer acquired on May 7, 1983, for $9,000. T elects § 179 and uses the ACRS statutory percentage cost recovery method. T also takes $400 of investment credit on the computer.
>
> T would report the above information on Schedule C and Form 4562 as follows on pp. 333–335.

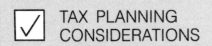

TAX PLANNING
CONSIDERATIONS

DEPRECIATION, ACRS, AND AMORTIZATION

A taxpayer who starts a new business and anticipates initial losses or has a net operating loss that is going to expire in the next few years should consider the use of cost recovery and amortization methods which produce smaller deductions in the early years. The taxpayer might elect under § 174 to capitalize and amortize research and experimental costs over a period of not less than 60 months instead of elect-

SCHEDULE C (Form 1040) Department of the Treasury Internal Revenue Service	**Profit or (Loss) From Business or Profession** (Sole Proprietorship) Partnerships, Joint Ventures, etc., Must File Form 1065. ▶ **Attach to Form 1040 or Form 1041.** ▶ **See Instructions for Schedule C (Form 1040).**	OMB No 1545-0074 19**83** 09

Name of proprietor		Social security number of proprietor 123 45 6789

A   Main business activity (see Instructions) ▶ Accounting Services   ; product ▶

B   Business name and address ▶ T Accounting Services
     297 Mountainview, Ogden, Utah 84201   **C** Employer identification number

D   Method(s) used to value closing inventory:
     (1) ☐ Cost   (2) ☐ Lower of cost or market   (3) ☐ Other (attach explanation)

E   Accounting method: (1) ☐ Cash   (2) ☐ Accrual   (3) ☐ Other (specify) ▶ ....

		Yes	No
F Was there any major change in determining quantities, costs, or valuations between opening and closing inventory?			X
If "Yes," attach explanation.			
G Did you deduct expenses for an office in your home?			X

PART I.—Income

1	a	Gross receipts or sales	**1a**	80,000 00
	b	Less. Returns and allowances	**1b**	
	c	Subtract line 1b from line 1a and enter the balance here	**1c**	80,000 00
2		Cost of goods sold and/or operations (Part III, line 8)	**2**	
3		Subtract line 2 from line 1c and enter the **gross profit** here	**3**	80,000 00
4	a	Windfall Profit Tax Credit or Refund received in 1983 (see Instructions)	**4a**	
	b	Other income	**4b**	
5		Add lines 3, 4a, and 4b. This is the **gross income** ▶	**5**	80,000 00

PART II.—Deductions

6 Advertising		23 Repairs		
7 Bad debts from sales or services (Cash method taxpayers, see Instructions)	2,000 00	24 Supplies (not included in Part III)		
		25 Taxes (Do not include Windfall Profit Tax here. See line 29.)		
8 Bank service charges		26 Travel and entertainment		
9 Car and truck expenses	3,000 00	27 Utilities and telephone		
10 Commissions		28 a Wages		
11 Depletion		b Jobs credit		
12 Depreciation and Section 179 deduction from Form 4562 (not included in Part III)	11,130 00	c Subtract line 28b from 28a		
		29 Windfall Profit Tax withheld in 1983		
13 Dues and publications		30 Other expenses (specify):		
14 Employee benefit programs		a		
15 Freight (not included in Part III)		b		
16 Insurance	800 00	c		
17 Interest on business indebtedness		d		
18 Laundry and cleaning		e		
19 Legal and professional services		f		
20 Office expense	4,000 00	g		
21 Pension and profit-sharing plans		h		
22 Rent on business property	12,000 00	i		

31	Add amounts in columns for lines 6 through 30i. These are the **total deductions** ▶	**31**	32,930 00
32	Net profit or (loss). Subtract line 31 from line 5 and enter the result. If a profit, enter on Form 1040, line 12, and on Schedule SE, Part I, line 2 (or Form 1041, line 6). If a loss, go on to line 33	**32**	47,070 00

33 If you have a loss, you must answer this question: "Do you have amounts for which you are not at risk in this business (see Instructions)?" ☐ Yes ☐ No
If "Yes," you must attach Form 6198. If "No," enter the loss on Form 1040, line 12, and on Schedule SE, Part I, line 2 (or Form 1041, line 6)

PART III.—Cost of Goods Sold and/or Operations (See Schedule C Instructions for Part III)

1 Inventory at beginning of year (if different from last year's closing inventory, attach explanation)	**1**	
2 Purchases less cost of items withdrawn for personal use	**2**	
3 Cost of labor (do not include salary paid to yourself)	**3**	
4 Materials and supplies	**4**	
5 Other costs	**5**	
6 Add lines 1 through 5	**6**	
7 Less Inventory at end of year	**7**	
8 Cost of goods sold and/or operations. Subtract line 7 from line 6. Enter here and in Part I, line 2, above.	**8**	

For Paperwork Reduction Act Notice, see Form 1040 Instructions.   Schedule C (Form 1040) 1983

Form **4562** Department of the Treasury Internal Revenue Service	**Depreciation and Amortization** ▶ See separate instructions. ▶ Attach this form to your return.	OMB No. 1545-0172 19**83** 67

Name(s) as shown on return	Identifying number
T	123-45-6789

Business or activity to which this form relates

Accounting Services

PART I.—Depreciation

Section A.—Election to expense recovery property (Section 179)

A. Class of property	B. Cost	C. Expense deduction
5-Year Class Property-Microcomputer	9,000.00	5,000.00

1 Total (not more than $5,000). Enter here and on page 2, line 8 (Partnerships or S corporations—see the Schedule K and Schedule K-1 Instructions of Form 1065 or 1120S)		5,000.00

Section B —Depreciation of recovery property

A. Class of property	B. Date placed in service	C. Cost or other basis	D. Recovery period	E. Method of figuring depreciation	F. Percentage	G. Deduction for this year
2 Accelerated Cost Recovery System (ACRS) (See instructions):						
	11/20/82	10,000.00	3 YR	PRE	38%	3,800.00
(a) 3-year property						
	7/15/82	8,000.00	5 YR	PRE	22%	1,760.00
	5/7/83	3,800.00	5 YR	PRE	15%	570.00
(b) 5-year property						
(c) 10-year property						
(d) 15-year public utility property						
(e) 15-year real property— low-income housing						
(f) 15-year real property other than low-income housing						
3 Property subject to section 168(e)(2) election (See instructions):						

4 Total column G. Enter here and on page 2, line 9	6,130.00

See Paperwork Reduction Act Notice on page 1 of the separate Instructions.   Form **4562** (1983)

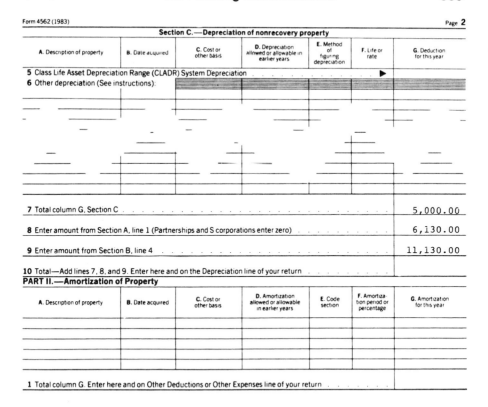

Form 4562 (1983)   Page **2**

Section C.—Depreciation of nonrecovery property

A. Description of property	B. Date acquired	C. Cost or other basis	D. Depreciation allowed or allowable in earlier years	E. Method of figuring depreciation	F. Life or rate	G. Deduction for this year
5 Class Life Asset Depreciation Range (CLADR) System Depreciation					▶	
6 Other depreciation (See instructions):						
7 Total column G, Section C						5,000.00
8 Enter amount from Section A, line 1 (Partnerships and S corporations enter zero)						6,130.00
9 Enter amount from Section B, line 4						11,130.00
10 Total—Add lines 7, 8, and 9. Enter here and on the Depreciation line of your return						

PART II.—Amortization of Property

A. Description of property	B. Date acquired	C. Cost or other basis	D. Amortization allowed or allowable in earlier years	E. Code section	F. Amortization period or percentage	G. Amortization for this year
1 Total column G. Enter here and on Other Deductions or Other Expenses line of your return						

ing the expense method. In addition, it may be preferable to elect straight-line ACRS instead of the statutory percentage ACRS method. The straight-line election of ACRS allows the taxpayer to use a longer life than the prescribed life under ACRS, thereby decreasing the early years' deductions.

Depreciation schedules should be reviewed annually for possible retirements, abandonments, obsolescence, and changes in estimated useful lives.

Example 25. An examination of the depreciation schedule of X Company reveals the following:

—Asset A was abandoned when it was discovered that the cost of repairs would be in excess of the cost of replacement. Asset A had an adjusted basis of $3,000.

—Asset D was being depreciated over a period of 10 years, but a revised estimate showed that its estimated remaining life is only two years. Its original cost was $60,000 and it had been depreciated under the straight-line method for three years. It was a pre-ERTA asset and was not subject to ACRS provisions.

—Asset J had become obsolete this year, at which point, its adjusted basis was $8,000.

The depreciation expense on Asset D should be $21,000 [$60,000 (cost) − $18,000 (accumulated depreciation) = $42,000 ÷ 2 (remaining estimated useful life)]. Assets A and J should be written off for an additional expense of $11,000 ($3,000 + $8,000).

Because of the deductions for depreciation, interest, and ad valorem property taxes, investments in real estate can be highly attractive. In figuring the economics of such investments, one should be sure to take into account any tax savings that result.

Example 26. In early January 1980, T (an individual in the 50% marginal tax bracket) purchased rental property for $125,000 (of which $20,000 was allocated to the land and $105,000 to the building). The building had an estimated useful life of 25 years and no anticipated salvage value. T made a down payment of $25,000 and assumed the seller's mortgage for the balance. Under the mortgage agreement, monthly payments of $1,000 are required and are applied toward interest, taxes, insurance, and principal. As the property was already occupied, T continued to receive from the tenant rent of $1,200 per month.

During the first year of ownership, T's expenses were as follows:

Interest	$ 10,000
Taxes	800
Insurance	1,000
Repairs and maintenance	2,200
Depreciation (under the straight-line method)	4,200
Total	$ 18,200

The deductible loss from the rental property is computed below:

Rental income ($1,200 × 12 months)	$ 14,400
Less expenses (see above)	18,200
Net loss	$ 3,800

But what is T's overall position for the year when the tax benefit of the loss is taken into account? Considering just the cash intake and outlay, this is summarized as follows:

Intake—		
Rental income	$ 14,400	
Tax savings [50% (income tax bracket) × $3,800 (loss from the property)]	1,900	$ 16,300
Outlay—		
Mortgage payments ($1,000 × 12 months)	$ 12,000	
Repairs and maintenance	2,200	14,200
Net cash benefit		$ 2,100

In taking the expensing election under ACRS, timing is of utmost importance. A mere purchase at December 31 is not enough, as the asset has to be placed in service during the year.[46] A similar, and usually more significant, problem arises in terms of the availability of the investment tax credit (see Chapter 13).

The new expensing procedure under § 179 is not available for property acquired from a related party, as defined in § 267. This is to prevent a taxpayer from buying property, expensing the allowable portion of it, then selling it to a relative (spouse, ancestor, or descendant) who makes another expense election for it. Thus, if a father sells his son a machine, the son cannot elect the expensing procedure. Brothers and sisters are not related parties for purposes of § 179.

The taxpayer should also consider the benefits of current expensing under § 179 with the ACRS statutory percentage method. To do this, the taxpayer must consider the tax savings generated by the alternatives. Current expensing may initially seem to be the best. However, no investment credit may be taken on any amount that has been expensed under § 179. In addition, if the investment credit is taken, the basis of the property must be reduced by 50 percent of the investment credit unless the taxpayer elects to reduce the credit by two percent.

The following illustration compares the tax savings generated by the alternatives.

Example 27.　Assume that in 1983 a taxpayer invests $5,000 in personal property. Since the comparison is of cash flow from tax savings over a period of time, the time value of money must be considered. Assume 15% is the appropriate rate. The present values of the tax savings generated if (1) the capital asset is expensed immediately, (2) ACRS and the total investment credit is taken, or (3) ACRS and the reduced investment credit is taken are compared in the following table:

Three-Year Class Property

Marginal Tax Rate	Section 179 Expensing	ACRS AND ITC 6% ITC	4% ITC
20%	$ 870	$ 986	$ 922
30%	1,304	1,349	1,296
40%	1,739	1,712	1,670
50%	2,174	2,075	2,044

---

46. § 179.

Five-Year Class Property

		ACRS AND ITC	
Marginal Tax Rate	Section 179 Expensing	10% ITC	8% ITC
20%	$ 870	$ 1,061	$ 1,007
30%	1,304	1,374	1,337
40%	1,739	1,688	1,667
50%	2,174	2,011	1,996

From the figures, it can be seen that with respect to both three-year and five-year class property, the taxpayer should elect ACRS with the full investment credit if his or her marginal tax rate is 30% or less. However, if the marginal tax rate is 40% or more, the taxpayer is better off to elect to expense the $5,000 under § 179.[47]

DEPLETION

Since the election to use the cost or percentage depletion method is an annual election, a taxpayer can use cost depletion (if higher) until the basis is exhausted, then switch to percentage depletion in the following years.

Example 28. Assume the following facts for T:

Remaining depletable basis	$ 11,000
Gross income (10,000 units)	100,000
Expenses (other than depletion)	30,000
Depletion per unit	4

Since cost depletion is limited to the basis of $11,000 and if the percentage depletion is $22,000, T would choose the latter. His basis is then reduced to zero; in future years, however, he can continue to take percentage depletion, since percentage depletion is taken without reference to the remaining basis.

The election to expense intangible drilling and development costs is a one-time election. Once the election is made to either expense or capitalize the intangible drilling and development costs, it is binding on all future expenditures. The permanent nature of the election makes it extremely important for the taxpayer to determine which treatment will provide the greatest tax advantage. (Refer to Example 23 for an illustration of the effect of using the two different alternatives for a given set of facts.)

---

47. Gardner and Stewart, "Decision to Expense or Capitalize Property Affected by Several Changes Made by TEFRA," *Taxation for Accountants* (December 1982), p. 364.

PROBLEM MATERIALS

Questions for Class Discussion

1. What depreciation methods can be used for the following assets which were acquired after 1969 and before January 1, 1981?

    (a) Used machinery and equipment used in the business.

    (b) New apartment building held for investment.

    (c) Land held for business use.

    (d) Used apartment building held for investment.

    (e) New factory used for business.

    (f) New automobile used in the business.

2. Discuss the § 179 election to expense assets. Should all taxpayers who qualify make the election?

3. If a taxpayer does not claim depreciation in one year, can an excess amount be claimed during a subsequent year? How is the basis for depreciable property affected by the failure to claim depreciation during any one year?

4. What may a taxpayer to do avoid reducing the basis of an asset by 50% of the investment tax credit for purposes of computing the cost recovery allowance?

5. XYZ Corporation acquired the assets of ABC Company for $1,000,000 in cash. The book value of the tangible assets was $400,000; their fair market value was $600,000. XYZ Corporation was willing to pay $400,000 for the ABC Company's goodwill, since the company's operations have been extremely profitable. For accounting purposes, XYZ Corporation will amortize the goodwill over a period of 40 years as prescribed by Accounting Principles Board Opinion No. 17. Is this procedure acceptable for income tax purposes? Explain.

6. If a personal use asset is converted to business use, why is it necessary to compute depreciation on the lower of fair market value or adjusted basis at the date of conversion?

7. Why is a patent subject to amortization while goodwill is not amortizable?

8. What is the difference between the terms "depreciation" and "amortization"?

9. Why is the basis of an asset reduced by the § 179 amount before the amount of the cost recovery allowance is computed?

10. When can a taxpayer disregard salvage value on property acquired prior to 1981?

11. If real property is placed in service in the sixth month of year one and is sold in the third month of year nine, determine and explain the percentage of the basis that can be recovered in the year of the sale.

12. Why would a taxpayer elect the optional straight-line method for an asset acquired after 1980?

13. Briefly discuss the differences between cost depletion and percentage depletion.

Problems

14. On January 1, 1979, X Company acquired an automobile for use in its business for $9,000. No depreciation was taken in 1979 or 1980, since the company had net operating losses and wanted to "save" the deductions for later years. In 1981, the company claimed a three-year life for the auto-mobile (and no salvage value) and deducted $3,000 of depreciation using a straight-line rate. On January 1, 1982, the automobile was sold for $4,500. Calculate the gain or loss on the sale of the automobile in 1982.

15. X acquired a personal residence in 1978 for $60,000. In January 1980, he converted the residence to rental property when the fair market value was $64,000.

    (a) Calculate the amount of depreciation which can be taken in 1980, as-suming that the straight-line rate is used, there is no salvage value, and the residence has a 30-year estimated useful life.

    (b) What would your answer be if the property were worth only $40,000 in 1980?

16. T, who is single, acquired a new machine for $30,000 on January 1, 1979. Assuming bonus depreciation is taken, calculate the total depreciation deduction allowed in the first year if the estimated useful life is 10 years (salvage value of $4,000) under each of the following methods:

    (a) 200 percent declining-balance.

    (b) Sum-of-the-years' digits.

    (c) 150 percent declining-balance.

    (d) Straight-line.

17. Assume the same facts as in Problem 16, except that T acquired the new machine on March 2, 1983, and claimed $2,500 of investment credit on the machine. What is the maximum amount that T can write off in 1983?

18. K acquired a machine on September 5, 1984, for $100,000. The machine has a recovery period of five years. Calculate K's write-off for 1984 assum-ing the following:

    (a) K elects the straight-line method over the longest permissible recovery period and does not elect immediate expensing under § 179. K claims $10,000 of investment tax credit on the machine.

    (b) K elects immediate expensing under § 179 and does not elect the straight-line recovery method. K claims $9,250 of investment tax credit on the machine.

    (c) K does not elect immediate expensing under § 179, nor does he elect the straight-line recovery method. However, K does claim $10,000 of investment tax credit on the machine.

19. C acquired a building on July 1, 1984, at a cost of $200,000.

    (a) Calculate C's cost recovery allowance for 1984, assuming the building is a warehouse and C does not elect the straight-line recovery method.

(b) Calculate C's cost recovery allowance for 1984, assuming the building is low-income housing and C does not elect the straight-line recovery method.

20. X acquired a low-income housing apartment in January 1980 and incurred $25,000 in rehabilitation expenditures for each of the 10 housing units. These expenditures have an estimated useful life of 20 years with no salvage value. Calculate the amount of amortization which may be claimed if the rapid amortization election is made.

21. During 1984, T bought the following business assets:
    Factory machinery (five-year class property), $50,000
    Light-duty trucks (three-year class property), $20,000
    The investment credit on the factory machinery is 10% of the qualifying cost and on the light-duty trucks, 6% of the qualifying cost. Calculate T's cost recovery allowances for 1984.

    (a) Using the statutory percentage method, assuming T does not make the § 179 election.

    (b) Using the statutory percentage method, assuming T does make the § 179 election.

22. Taxpayer acquired a building for $250,000 (exclusive of land) on January 1, 1984. Calculate the depreciation using the statutory percentage method for 1984 and 1985 if:

    (a) The real property is low-income housing.

    (b) The real property is a factory building.

23. U acquires a warehouse on March 1, 1984, at a cost of $2,000,000 and does not elect the straight-line recovery method. On August 30, 1991, U sells the warehouse.

    (a) Calculate U's cost recovery allowance for 1984.

    (b) Calculate U's cost recovery allowance for 1991.

24. Assume the same facts as in problem 23, except U elects to use the straight-line recovery method over 35 years.

    (a) Calculate U's cost recovery allowance for 1984.

    (b) Calculate U's cost recovery allowance for 1991.

25. B acquired a business car on December 1, 1984, at a cost of $15,000. B did not elect § 179 expensing, but she did elect to use the straight-line recovery method over 5 years. B also took $900 of investment tax credit on the car.

    (a) Calculate B's cost recovery allowance for 1984.

    (b) Calculate B's cost recovery allowance for 1989.

    (c) Assuming B sells the car on May 15, 1987, calculate B's cost recovery allowance for 1987.

26. H acquired a small delivery truck on April 4, 1984, at a cost of $20,000. H elected to take an expense deduction under § 179; however, he did not elect to use the straight-line recovery method. H elected to take a 4% investment tax credit of $500 [($20,000 − $7,500) × .04] on the truck. Calculate H's total deduction with respect to the truck for 1984.

27. On September 16, 1984, T purchased and placed into service a new car. The purchase price was $18,000. T drove the car 12,000 miles during the remainder of the year, with 9,000 miles being business miles and 3,000 miles being personal miles. T elected to expense the maximum amount under § 179. He also used the percentage method of cost recovery and took an investment tax credit of $360 on the car. Calculate the total deduction T may take for 1984 with respect to the car.

28. T acquired a mineral interest during the year for $5,000,000. A geological survey estimated that 250,000 tons of the mineral remained in the deposit. During the year, 70,000 tons were mined and 45,000 tons were sold. Calculate the depletion allowance based on the cost method.

29. X had gross income from a gravel pit of $60,000. Assuming the depletion rate allowed by law is 5% and other expenses relating to the property are $40,000, calculate X's depletion allowance under the percentage method.

30. T purchased an oil interest for $2,000,000. Recoverable barrels were estimated to be 500,000. During the year, 120,000 barrels were sold for $3,840,000, regular expenses (including depreciation) were $1,240,000, and IDC were $1,000,000. Calculate the taxable income under the expensing and capitalization methods of handling IDC.

Cumulative Problem

31. B, age 30, is single and has no dependents. He was employed as a barber until October 1984, when he opened his own hair styling salon. B had the following receipts in 1984.

(a) Salary (January 1 to September 30) $ 10,800
(b) Dividend from domestic corporation $ 350
(c) Net long-term gain on the sale of stock $ 3,000
(d) Receipts from hairstyling business $ 2,400

B presents you with the following information for 1984.

(e) Installed a barber chair and other equipment
with a cost recovery period of five years (B has asked
you to maximize his cost recovery allowance
but not to elect immediate expensing; B takes
investment credit of $640 on the chair). $ 6,400
(f) Business expenses (not including depreciation) $ 3,700
(h) Itemized deductions $ 2,100

Compute B's taxable income for 1984.

Research Problems

32. Dr. T, a surgeon, paid a fee of $40,000 to practice in a private hospital. This fee is nonrefundable and nontransferable. It lasts for the lifetime of the physician. Dr. T wants to deduct currently the $40,000. He is 40 years old and plans to retire at age 65.

(a) Can he deduct the fee currently?

(b) Can he amortize the fee over 25 years?

(c) If he became prematurely disabled and unable to practice medicine, what would happen to the unamortized balance of the fee?

33. X acquired an old apartment building and land for $100,000 in 19X1. The land was appraised at $50,000, and the apartment building was worth $50,000. X demolished the apartment building at a cost of $20,000 and constructed a new building for $300,000.

(a) Calculate the cost basis for depreciation of the new apartment building.

(b) Would your answer be different if X had rented the old building for a period of five years prior to its demolition and the construction of the new building?

34. D, a dentist, purchased five paintings for a total of $17,000. D displayed the paintings on her business premises as part of the office decor. Discuss whether D can depreciate the paintings using the accelerated cost recovery system (ACRS) with the paintings being classified as five-year property.

Chapter 10

Deductions:
Employee Expenses

Following the discussion of business expenses and losses in Chapter 8, and various types of cost recovery in Chapter 9, it is now appropriate to discuss employment-related expenses. The Code provides that certain employee expenses are deductible *for* adjusted gross income and treated as expenses incurred in a trade or business. Other types of employee expenses are deductible *from* adjusted gross income (as itemized deductions). Chapter 10 gives consideration to the proper classification of employee expenses before discussing specific items.

CLASSIFICATION OF EMPLOYMENT-RELATED EXPENSES

SELF-EMPLOYED VERSUS EMPLOYEE STATUS

In many instances it is difficult to distinguish between an individual who is self-employed and one who is performing services as an employee. Expenses of self-employed individuals are deductible as trade or business expenses (*for* adjusted gross income). However, if the expenses are incurred as the result of an employment relationship, they are deductible subject to limitations in the Code relative to employee expenses.

Generally, an employer-employee relationship exists when the employer has the right to specify the end result and the ways and

345

means by which the end result is to be attained. Thus, an employee is subject to the will and control of the employer with respect to not only what shall be done but also how it shall be done.[1] If the individual is subject to the direction or control of another only to the extent of the end result (e. g., the preparation of a taxpayer's return by an independent CPA) but not as to the means of accomplishment, an employee relationship does not exist. Other factors may indicate an employer-employee relationship. These factors include the right to discharge without legal liability the person performing the service, the furnishing of tools or a place to work, and payment based on time spent rather than the task performed. However, each case is tested on its own merits, and the right to control the means and methods of accomplishment is the definitive test. Generally, physicians, lawyers, dentists, contractors, subcontractors, et al., who offer services to the public are not classified as employees.[2]

Real estate agents and direct sellers are classified as self-employed persons if two conditions are met: (1) substantially all their income for services must be directly related to sales or other output and (2) their services must be performed under a written contract that specifies that they are not to be treated as employees for tax purposes.[3] The Internal Revenue Service is prohibited from issuing any rulings or regulations dealing with classification as employees or independent contractors until Congress enacts legislation clarifying the employment tax issue.[4]

> **Example 1.** D is a lawyer whose major client accounts for 60% of her billings. She does the routine legal work and income tax returns at their request. She is paid a monthly retainer in addition to amounts charged for extra work. D is a self-employed individual. Even though most of her income is from one client, she still has the right to determine how the end result of her work is attained.

> **Example 2.** E is a lawyer hired by D to assist her in the performance of services for the client mentioned in Example 1. E is under D's supervision; D reviews E's work; D pays E an hourly fee. E is an employee of D.

> **Example 3.** F is a practical nurse who works as a live-in nurse. She is under the supervision of the patient's doctor and is paid by the patient. F is not an employee of either the patient (who pays her) or the doctor (who supervises her), because the ways and means of attaining the end result (care of the patient) are under her control.

---

1. Reg. § 31.3401(c)–(1)(b).
2. Reg. § 31.3401(c)–(1)(c).
3. § 3508(b).
4. § 530 of the Revenue Act of 1978, as modified by P.L. 97–248.

A self-employed individual is required to file Schedule C of Form 1040, and all allowable expenses related to the Schedule C activity are deductions *for* adjusted gross income.[5]

DEDUCTIONS FOR OR FROM AGI

The Code specifies those employee expenses which are deductible *for* adjusted gross income as follows:[6]

—Reimbursed expenses.

—Expenses for travel away from home.

—Transportation expenses.

—Expenses of outside salespersons.

—Moving expenses.

All other employee expenses are deductions *from* adjusted gross income which can be deducted only if the employee-taxpayer itemizes his or her deductions. Certain activities require an apportionment of expenses among these two categories (*for* and *from* AGI).

The distinction between *for* and *from* AGI is important because no benefit is received for an item which is deductible *from* adjusted gross income if a taxpayer's itemized deductions are less than the zero bracket amount. In addition, certain deductions are based on the amount of adjusted gross income (e. g., medical expenses are deductible to the extent they exceed five percent of adjusted gross income).

Besides the employee expenses listed above, the only deductions allowed *for* adjusted gross income are specified in § 62, as follows:

—Trade or business deductions (more fully defined in § 162).

—The long-term capital gains deduction.

—Losses from the sale or exchange of property (no losses are allowed for personal use property).

—Deductions attributable to rents and royalties.

—Certain deductions of life tenants and income beneficiaries of property.

—Certain retirement plan contributions of a self-employed individual (e. g., a Keogh plan).

—Pension plans of electing small business corporations.

—Certain retirement plan contributions of an employee (e. g., an IRA).

—A portion of certain lump-sum distributions from certain pension plans.

---

5. § § 62(1) and 162(a). See Chapter 9 for a partial reproduction and explanation of Schedule C.

6. § 62(2).

—Interest forfeited due to early withdrawal of deposits.

—Alimony paid.

—A deduction for two-earner married couples.

Code § 212 specifies the deductible expenses for the production of income, which are itemized (*from* AGI) deductions, as follows:

—Ordinary and necessary expenses paid or incurred for the production or collection of income (except expenses related to rent and royalty income, which are deductions *for* adjusted gross income[7]).

—Expenses for the management, conservation, or maintenance of property held for the production of income.

—Expenses in connection with the determination, collection, or refund of any tax.

Other itemized deductions (medical expenses, charitable contributions, interest, taxes, etc.) are discussed in Chapter 11.

SPECIAL TREATMENT FOR OUTSIDE SALESPERSONS

If an employee qualifies as an outside salesperson, all employment-related expenses are deductible *for* adjusted gross income and may be claimed even if the taxpayer uses the zero bracket amount.[8]

Congress apparently considers that an outside salesperson's activities resemble those of a self-employed individual more than they resemble those of an employee and, therefore, should receive comparable treatment.

Definition of an Outside Salesperson.   An outside salesperson is one who solicits business away from an employer's place of business on a full-time basis.[9] An employee who performs service or delivery functions from an employer's place of business is not an outside salesperson. However, outside salesperson status is not lost if the employee performs incidental tasks (such as writing up orders, picking up mail or phone messages) at the employer's office.

The question of whether an employee is an outside salesperson has been the subject of extensive litigation. Each case has been decided on its own merits, and quite often, different interpretations have been given to similar fact patterns.

Example 4.   The following are illustrations of employees who qualify as outside salespersons, since the performance of office duties is incidental to their primary outside sales job:

—G is a real estate agent who reports to his office on a daily basis to check new listings, current sales, etc.

---

7. § 62(5).
8. § 62(2)(D).
9. Reg. § 1.62–1(h).

—R is an employee who sells burglar alarm systems to local businesses. She checks into her office periodically to obtain new leads and to write up orders.

The following are illustrations of employees who are not outside salespersons, since the nature of their jobs is primarily service or delivery rather than sales:

—B is a bread deliveryman who makes regular rounds after picking up fresh bread at his employer's bakery. He uses the company office to do his daily accounting and cash checkout.

—Q is a television repairman who is dispatched from his employer's shop to perform service repair calls for customers.

REIMBURSED EXPENSES

It has been stressed in this chapter that certain expenses of an employee are deductions *for* adjusted gross income: travel, transportation, and moving expenses, and the expenses of an outside salesperson. Other expenses of an employee, such as professional dues and subscriptions, entertainment, and uniforms, must be deducted *from* adjusted gross income. If reimbursement is received, however, the expense deduction will be *for* adjusted gross income.

Reimbursements are included in an employee's gross income. Congress apparently felt that because the reimbursements were income, an offsetting deduction should be allowed. Therefore, the law allows an employee to deduct any bona fide employee expense *for* adjusted gross income if that expense is reimbursed by the employer.[10] An employee who receives reimbursement for employee expenses is allowed to offset the expenses incurred against the reimbursement (income) whether or not the election to itemize is made.

When reimbursements are present, there are three distinct possibilities: (1) the expenses and the reimbursement are equal, (2) the reimbursement exceeds the expenses, or (3) the expenses exceed the reimbursement. The treatment of these possibilities depends on whether the employee has made an "adequate accounting" to the employer.

Recordkeeping Requirements. An adequate accounting means that the employee has submitted a record (with receipts and other substantiation) to the employer with the following pertinent facts: amount, place and date of expenditure, and the business purpose and business relationship of the expenditure.[11] The use of a reasonable per diem (currently $44 per day except in an area where the Federal government allows its employees a higher per diem) and mileage allowance (currently 20.5 cents per mile) does constitute an adequate

---

10. § 62(2)(A).
11. Reg. § 1.162–17(b)(4).

accounting, unless the employer and employee are related. Any employee who does not adequately account to his or her employer must submit a detailed statement with his or her return showing expense categories, reimbursements, etc.[12] The following situations may be encountered:

— Expenses and reimbursements are equal. If an adequate accounting has been made, the employee may omit both the reimbursement and the expenses from the tax return.

— Reimbursements exceed expenses. If an adequate accounting has been made, the employee may report the excess as miscellaneous income and ignore expenses and reimbursements up to the amount of the expenses.

— Expenses exceed reimbursements. Regardless of whether an adequate accounting is made to the employer, if the employee deducts the excess expenses, a statement of all expenses (by category) and all reimbursements must be attached to the income tax return.[13]

Example 5. M, an employee of an unrelated corporation, incurred the following expenses which were carefully documented and submitted for complete reimbursement:

Travel:	
Transportation	$ 1,600
Meals and lodging	980
Other:	
Dues and subscriptions	70
Entertainment	350
Total reimbursed	$ 3,000

M can ignore both the reimbursement and the expenditures on her tax return because she made an adequate accounting to her employer.

Example 6. Assume the same facts as in Example 5, except that M did not make an adequate accounting to her employer but instead received an expense account allowance of $5,000. The $5,000 is included in M's gross income and the expenses must be reported on her return.

Allocation Problems. A further problem exists when reimbursements are intended to cover all employee expenses and the total reimbursement is less than the total expense. Travel and transportation are deductible *for* adjusted gross income, whether or not they are reimbursed. Other expenses of an employee (except an outside salesper-

---

12. Reg. § 1.162–17(c) and Rev.Rul. 80–203, 1980–2 C.B. 101.
13. Reg. § 1.162–17(b)(1), (2) and (3).

son) are deductible *for* adjusted gross income only to the extent that they are reimbursed. When all expenses are partially reimbursed, the whole problem is solved by using a simple pro rata procedure. All travel and transportation expenses are deductible *for* adjusted gross income, but only the pro rata share of other expenses that have been reimbursed is deductible *for* adjusted gross income. The remaining expenses (the unreimbursed other expenses) are itemized deductions. The formula for computing the other expenses deductible *for* adjusted gross income is:[14]

$$\frac{\text{Total other expenses}}{\text{Total expenses (including travel + transportation)}} \times \text{Reimbursement}$$

Example 7. Assume an employee incurs a total of $3,750 in business expenses consisting of transportation expenses of $500; meals and lodging away from home of $2,500; and dues, subscriptions, and entertainment expenses amounting to $750. The reimbursement which is intended to cover all of the expenses amounts to $2,500. The deductions *for* and *from* adjusted gross income are computed as follows:

Travel (100%)	$ 2,500
Transportation (100%)	500
Other $\left(\dfrac{\$750}{\$3,750} \times \$2,500\right)$	500 ← reimburse portion
Deductible *for* AGI	$ 3,500
Less: Reimbursements	2,500
Net deductible *for* AGI	$ 1,000 Jlob
Total other	$ 750 → pro tanto
Less: Deducted *for* AGI	500 → already deducted
Deductible *from* AGI	250 Sch. A reimburse
Total deductible	$ 1,250

TRANSPORTATION EXPENSES

QUALIFIED EXPENDITURES

An employee is permitted a deduction *for* adjusted gross income for transportation expenses paid in connection with services performed as an employee.[15] Transportation expense includes only the cost of transporting the employee from one place to another in the course of employment when the employee is not "away from home" in a travel status.[16] Such costs include taxi fares, automobile expenses, tolls, and parking.

---

14. Reg. § 1.62–1(f).
15. § 62(2)(C).
16. Reg. § 1.62–1(g).

Commuting from home to one's place of employment is a personal, nondeductible expense. The fact that one employee drives 30 miles to work and another employee walks 6 blocks is of no significance.[17]

Example 8. G is employed by the X Corporation. He drives 22 miles each way to work. One day G drove to a customer's office from his place of work. It was a 14-mile round trip to the customer's office. G can take a deduction for 14 miles of business transportation. The remaining 44 miles are a nondeductible commuting expense.

There are several exceptions to the general rule which disallows a deduction for commuting expenses. An employee who uses an automobile to transport heavy tools to work, and who otherwise would not drive to work, will be allowed a deduction. However, the deduction is allowed only for the additional costs incurred to transport work implements. Additional costs are those exceeding the cost of commuting by the same mode of transportation without the tools (e. g., the rental of a trailer but *not* the expenses of operating the automobile).[18] The Supreme Court has held that a deduction is permitted only if the taxpayer can show that he or she would not have used the automobile were it not necessary to transport tools or equipment.[19]

Another exception is provided for an employee who has a second job. The expenses of getting from one job to another are deductible. If the employee goes home between jobs, the deduction is limited to the lesser of (1) the cost of the transportation (or mileage) between the two jobs or (2) the actual expenditure.

Example 9. In the current year T holds two jobs, a full-time job with B Corporation and a part-time job with C Corporation. During the 250 days T works (adjusted for weekends, vacation, and holidays), she customarily leaves home at 7:30 a.m. and drives 30 miles to the B Corporation plant where she works until 5:00 p.m. After dinner at a nearby cafe, T drives 20 miles to C Corporation and works from 7:00 to 11:00 p.m. The distance from the second job to T's home is 40 miles. Only 20 miles (the distance between jobs) is allowed as a deduction.

It is sometimes difficult to distinguish between a nondeductible commuting expense and a deductible transportation expense necessary to the taxpayer's business. If the taxpayer is required to incur a transportation expense to travel between work stations, that expense should be deductible, but the commuting costs from home to the first

17. *Tauferner v. U. S.*, 69–1 USTC ¶ 9241, 23 AFTR2d 69–1025, 407 F.2d 243 (CA–10, 1969).
18. Rev.Rul. 75–380, 1975–2 C.B. 59.
19. *Fausner v. Comm.*, 73–2 USTC ¶ 9515, 32 AFTR2d 73–5202, 93 S.Ct. 2820 (USSC, 1973).

work station and from the last work station to home should not be deductible. Also deductible is the reasonable travel cost between the general working area and a temporary work station outside that area. What constitutes the general working area depends on the facts and circumstances of each situation. For example, a bank manager who must spend an occasional day at a remote branch office in the suburbs can deduct transportation expenses (or mileage) as an employee expense. If an employee is permanently reassigned to a new location, however, the assignment is deemed to be for an indefinite period and the expenses are nondeductible commuting expenses. Furthermore, if an employee customarily works on several temporary assignments in a localized area, that localized area becomes the "regular place of employment" and transportation from home to these locations becomes a personal, nondeductible commuting expense.

> **Example 10.** V works for a firm in downtown Denver, and he commutes to work. V occasionally works in a customer's office. On one such occasion, he drove directly to the customer's office (a round-trip distance from his home of 40 miles). He did not go into his office, which is a 52-mile round-trip distance. None of his mileage is deductible.

> **Example 11.** T, a general contractor, drove from his home to his office, then drove to three building sites to perform his required inspections, and finally drove home. The costs of driving to his office and driving home from the last inspection are nondeductible commuting expenses. The other transportation costs are deductible.

COMPUTATION OF AUTOMOBILE EXPENSES

Basically, a taxpayer has two choices in computing automobile expenses. The actual operating cost, which includes depreciation, gas, oil, repairs, licenses, and insurance, may be used. Records should be kept which detail the automobile's personal and business use. Only the percentage (based upon the ratio of business miles to total miles) which is allocable to business transportation and travel is allowed as a deduction.

Use of the automatic mileage method is the second alternative. The deduction is based upon 20.5 cents per mile for the first 15,000 business miles driven. Eleven cents per mile is allowed for any miles in excess of 15,000.[20] Parking fees, tolls, and the investment tax credit are allowed in addition to expenses computed using the automatic mileage method.[21]

Generally, a taxpayer may elect either method for any particular year. However, the following restrictions apply:

---

20. Rev.Proc. 82–61, 1982–2 C.B. 849, as modified by Rev. Proc. 83– 74, 1983 IRB No. 41, 16.
21. Rev.Rul. 73–91, 1973–1 C.B. 71.

—If two or more vehicles are in use (for business purposes) at the *same* time (not alternately), a taxpayer may not use the automatic mileage method.

—If the taxpayer changes from the automatic mileage method to the actual operating cost method, the cost basis of the automobile must be reduced by the amount of straight-line depreciation that would have been allowed had the automatic mileage method not been used. Note that use of the standard mileage rate in the first year the auto is placed in service is considered an election to exclude the auto from the accelerated cost recovery system of depreciation (discussed in Chapter 9).[22]

—A taxpayer cannot switch to the automatic mileage method if the ACRS statutory percentage method has been used or if the taxpayer elected immediate expensing of the automobile under § 179.

—If an automobile has been fully depreciated, the standard mileage rate of 11 cents per mile is used for all miles thereafter.

Example 12. W uses her automobile 60% for business and 40% for pleasure. During 19X5 she drove a total of 40,000 miles. W had purchased the automobile for $8,000 on January 1, 19X2, and has depreciated it on the straight-line method over its three-year useful life. She can use the automatic mileage method, but because the automobile has been fully depreciated, she is limited to 11 cents per mile, or $2,640 (.11 × 40,000 × 60%).

Any reimbursement for auto expenses must be reported on the tax return to reduce the deduction if the automatic mileage method is used. If an employee receives a reimbursement for transportation expenses from his or her employer, it may still be possible to claim a deduction if there is an excess of actual expenses over the reimbursed amounts. Also, if the standard mileage rate (20.5 cents) exceeds the reimbursed rate (e. g., 15 cents), the taxpayer is entitled to a deduction for the difference when the optional method is elected. Frequently, taxpayers discover that actual automobile expenses for depreciation, gas, oil, repairs, etc., exceed the amount of expense calculated under the standard mileage rate prescribed by the IRS.

TRAVEL EXPENSES

DEFINITION OF TRAVEL EXPENSES

A deduction *for* adjusted gross income is allowed for travel expenses related to a trade or business or employment.[23] Travel expenses are

---

22. Rev.Proc. 82–61, 1982–2 C.B. 849.
23. § § 62(2)(B) and 162(a)(2).

more broadly defined in the Code than are transportation expenses. Travel expenses include, in addition to transportation expenses, meals and lodging that are not lavish or extravagant under the circumstances while away from home in the pursuit of a trade or business, including that of being an employee. Transportation expenses are deductible even though the taxpayer is not away from home; a deduction for travel expenses is available only if the taxpayer is away from his or her tax home. Travel expenses also include reasonable laundry and incidental expenses.[24] Entertainment expenses are not a travel expense even if incurred while traveling. They are treated as an "other employee expense" and, unless fully reimbursed, are an itemized deduction.

AWAY-FROM-HOME REQUIREMENT

The crucial test of the deductibility of travel expenses is whether the employee is "away from home overnight." "Overnight" need not be a 24-hour period, nor from dusk to dawn, but it must be a period substantially longer than an ordinary day's work and require rest, sleep, or a relief-from-work period.[25] A one-day or intracity business trip is not travel; therefore, meals and lodging are not deductible.

The employee must be away from home for a temporary period. If the taxpayer-employee is reassigned to a new post for an indefinite period of time, that new post becomes his or her "tax home." Temporary indicates that the assignment's termination is expected within a reasonably short period of time. The position of the IRS is that the "tax home" is the business location, post, or station of the taxpayer. Thus, travel expenses are not deductible if a taxpayer is reassigned for an indefinite period and does not move his or her place of residence to the new location.

Under ordinary circumstances, there is no problem in determining the location of a taxpayer's tax home and whether the taxpayer is on a temporary work assignment away from that tax home. Under other circumstances, however, this is a controversial problem that has found the IRS and various courts in conflict.[26] An example of this problem is the situation in which a construction worker cannot find work in the immediate area and takes work several hundred miles away, with the duration of that work uncertain. The IRS has published criteria for determining whether such a work assignment is temporary, as opposed to permanent or indefinite.[27]

In general, a work assignment of less than a year is regarded as temporary, while a work assignment of more than two years is re-

24. Rev.Rul. 63–145, 1963–2 C.B. 86.
25. *U. S. v. Correll,* 68–1 USTC ¶ 9101, 20 AFTR2d 5845, 88 S.Ct. 445 (USSC, 1967); Rev.Rul. 75–168, 1975–1 C.B. 58.
26. Rev.Rul. 73–529, 1973–2 C.B. 37.
27. Rev.Rul 83–82, 1983 I.R.B. No. 22, 5.

garded as indefinite or permanent, regardless of the facts and circumstances. The nature of a work assignment expected to last between one and two years will be determined on the basis of the facts and circumstances of the specific case.

The following objective factors are to be used in determining whether the abode that the taxpayer claims to be away from is the taxpayer's actual tax home:

—Whether the taxpayer has used the claimed abode for lodging purposes while performing work in the vicinity thereof immediately before the current job and the taxpayer continues to maintain bona fide work contacts (such as job seeking, leave of absence, on-going business) in that area during the alleged temporary employment.

—Whether the taxpayer's living expenses at the claimed abode are duplicated because work requires the taxpayer to be away from the abode.

—Whether the taxpayer has a family member or members (marital or lineal only) currently residing at the claimed abode or continues to currently use the claimed abode frequently for the purposes of his or her own lodging.

To be allowed to deduct travel expenses while away from home on a temporary assignment, a taxpayer must clearly demonstrate the existence of a realistic expectation as to the temporary nature of the job and must satisfy all three of the above requirements. If the taxpayer clearly demonstrates the expectation that the job is of a temporary nature and satisfies two of the above requirements, the deductibility question will be decided on the basis of all the facts and circumstances of the case.

Even if the requisite expectation as to the temporary nature of the job is demonstrated, the IRS will hold that the taxpayer is on indefinite assignment unless the taxpayer can satisfy two of the three requirements. If it is determined that the assignment is indefinite rather than temporary, no deduction will be allowed for the traveling expenses.

An employee whose living expenses are increased due to a work assignment should be able to deduct those duplicated expenses. If there is no duplication of expenses (i. e., an employee establishes a new home as the result of a work assignment), those living expenses are of a personal nature and are, therefore, nondeductible.

> **Example 13.** H is employed as a long-haul truck driver. He stores his clothes, etc., at his parents' home and stops there for periodic visits. The rest of the time, H is on the road, sleeping in his truck and in motels. His meals, lodging, laundry, and inciden-

tal expenses are not deductible because he has no tax home from which he can be absent.[28]

Example 14. T is employed as a short-distance hauler. His wife and children live in Chicago. T makes trips of both long and short duration. These short trips are often one-day trips in the surrounding area. His meals on a one-day trip are not deductible. If he makes a 10-day trip to Florida, he is "away from home" and his meals are deductible.

COMBINED BUSINESS AND PLEASURE TRAVEL

To be deductible, travel expenses need not be incurred in the performance of specific job functions. For example, travel expenses incurred in attending a professional convention are deductible by an employee, if attendance is connected with services as an employee. Thus, an employee of a CPA firm could deduct travel expenses incurred in attending a meeting of the American Institute of Certified Public Accountants. Unfortunately, this deduction has been abused in the past by persons who claimed a tax deduction for what was essentially a personal vacation. As a result, several provisions have been enacted to govern deductions associated with combined business-pleasure trips. If the business-pleasure trip is within the United States (i. e., the trip is from one point in the U. S. to another point in the U. S.), the transportation expenses are deductible only if the trip is primarily business.[29] If the trip is primarily for pleasure, no transportation expenses can be taken as a deduction. Even if the trip is primarily for pleasure (or other personal reasons), any expenses incurred at the destination that are properly allocable to business are deductible.

Example 15. J traveled from Seattle to New York on a combined business-pleasure trip. She spent five days conducting business and three days sightseeing and seeing shows. Her plane and taxi fare amounted to $560. Her meals, lodging, and incidental expenses amounted to $120 per day. Since the trip was primarily business (five days versus three days) the transportation is fully deductible. Only $600 of the other expenses (five days) is deductible.

Example 16. Assume the same facts as in the previous example. How much would be deductible if J conducted business for two days and vacationed the remaining six days? Since the trip is then primarily personal, no transportation expenses are deductible. However, $120 per day for two days can be deducted.

---

28. *Moses Mitnick*, 13 T.C. 1 (1949).
29. Reg. § 1.162–2(b)(1).

If an employee-taxpayer is accompanied by one or more family members, the incremental costs paid for the family's travel cannot be deducted unless the family members' presence has a bona fide business purpose. Incidental services performed by family members do not constitute a bona fide business purpose.[30]

When the trip is outside the United States, special rules apply.[31] If the taxpayer is away from home for seven days or less or if less than 25 percent of the time was for personal purposes, no allocation of transportation expenses need be made. No allocation is required if the taxpayer has no substantial control over arrangements for the trip or the desire for a vacation is not a major factor in taking the trip. If the trip is primarily for pleasure, none of the transportation charges are deductible. In all other cases, all travel expenses must be allocated between business and personal expenses. Days devoted to travel are considered as business days. Weekends, legal holidays, and intervening days are considered business days, provided that both preceding and succeeding days were business days.[32]

> **Example 17.** K took a trip from New York to Japan primarily for business purposes. He was away from home from June 10 through June 19. He spent three days vacationing and seven days conducting business (including two travel days). K's air fare was $2,500 and his meals and lodging amounted to $150 per day. K can deduct only 70% of his transportation expenses and $150 per day for seven days, since he was away from home for more than seven days and more than 25% of his time was devoted to personal purposes.

> **Example 18.** In Example 17, if K had been required to take the trip (i. e., had no substantial control over arrangements for the trip) and had no desire for a vacation, all of his transportation expenses ($2,500) and $150 per day for seven days would be deductible. The burden of proof is on the taxpayer to prove he or she had no control or desire for a vacation.

> **Example 19.** L, a fashion buyer for a large department store, travels to London primarily to view the spring collections. She is gone 10 days (including two days of travel). She spent eight days (including travel time) engaged in business and two days sightseeing. Since less than 25 percent of the total time was spent vacationing, all her transportation expenses and all but two days of meals and lodging are deductible.

> **Example 20.** If L, in Example 19, had spent six days vacationing, two days traveling, and two days conducting business, the

30. Reg. § 1.162–2(c).
31. § 274(c); Reg. § 1.274–4.
32. Reg. § 1.274–4(d)(2)(v).

trip probably would be primarily for pleasure and none of the transportation expenses would be deductible. Two days of meals and lodging expenses would be deductible.

Example 21. M flew to Paris, traveling two days, vacationing two days, and conducting business two days. Since he was gone less than seven days, all transportation expenses and all but two days of meals and lodging expenses would be deductible.

Example 22. N flew to Paris from New York on Tuesday to conduct business every day (except the weekend) through the following Wednesday and flew back to New York on Thursday. All the days, including the weekend, were business days.

Example 23. If N, in Example 22, had flown to Paris on Sunday, conducted business through Friday and had flown home the following Monday, the two weekend days would be personal days.

FOREIGN CONVENTION EXPENSES

Certain restrictions are imposed on the deductibility of expenses paid or incurred to attend conventions located outside the North American area. For this purpose, the North American area includes the United States, its possessions (including the Trust Territory of the Pacific Islands), Canada, and Mexico. The expenses will be disallowed unless the taxpayer establishes that the meeting is directly related to a trade or business or to an activity described in § 212 (i. e., for the production or collection of income or for the management, conservation, or maintenance of property held for the production of income). Disallowance also will occur unless the taxpayer shows that it is as reasonable for the meeting to be held in a foreign location as within the North American area. The deduction for a convention, seminar, or other meeting held on a cruise ship is limited to $2,000 per individual per year, and this deduction is restricted to U. S. cruise ships traveling within the United States.[33]

The foreign convention rules will not operate to bar a deduction to an employer if the expense is compensatory in nature and, as such, is included in the gross income of the employee.[34]

MOVING EXPENSES

GENERAL REQUIREMENTS

Moving expenses are deductible *for* adjusted gross income (see Form 3903) for moves in connection with the commencement of work (either as an employee or as a self-employed individual) at a new principal

---

33. §§ 274(h)(1) and (2). See § 274(h)(3)(B) for the definition of a "cruise ship."
34. § 274(h)(1)(B).

place of work.[35] Reimbursement from employers must be included in gross income under § 82. To be eligible for a moving expense deduction, a taxpayer must meet two basic tests: distance and time.[36]

DISTANCE TEST

The distance test requires that the taxpayer's new job location must be at least 35 miles farther from the taxpayer's old residence than the old residence was from the former place of employment. In this regard, the minimum distance requirement does not apply to the location of the new residence. This eliminates a moving deduction for taxpayers who purchase a new home in the same general area without changing place of employment or accept a new job in the same general area as the old job location. If a new job does not necessitate moving or if the move is for personal reasons (e. g., a better neighborhood), the taxpayer is not permitted a tax deduction.

> **Example 24.** J was permanently transferred to a new job location. J has met the distance requirements for a moving expense deduction. (Refer to the diagram below.) The distance from J's former home to his new job (80 miles) exceeds the distance from his former home to his old job (30 miles) by more than 35 miles. If J was not employed prior to the move, his new job must be at least 35 miles from his former residence. In this instance, the distance requirements also would be met if J had not been previously employed.

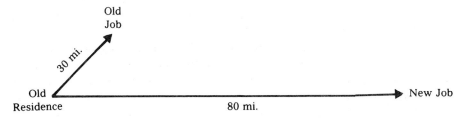

TIME REQUIREMENTS

To be eligible for a moving expense deduction, the employee must be employed on a full-time basis at the new location for 39 weeks in the 12-month period following the move. If the taxpayer is a self-employed individual, he or she must work (either as a self-employed individual or as an employee of another) in the new location for 78 weeks during the next two years. (The first 39 weeks must be in the first 12 months.) The time requirement is suspended if the taxpayer dies, be-

---

35. § § 62(8) and 217(a).
36. § 217(c).

comes disabled, or is discharged or transferred by the new employer through no fault of the employee.[37]

It is obvious that an employee might not be able to meet the 39-week requirement by the end of the tax year. For this reason, there are two alternatives allowed. The taxpayer can take the deduction in the year the expenses were incurred even though the 39-week test has not been met. If the taxpayer later fails to meet the test, the income of the first year that the test cannot be met (i. e., the following year) must be increased by an amount equal to the deduction previously claimed for moving expenses. The second alternative is to wait until the test is met and then file an amended tax return for the prior year.

WHEN DEDUCTIBLE

The general rule is that expenses of a cash basis taxpayer are deductible only in the year of payment. However, if reimbursement is received from the employer, an election may be made to deduct the moving expenses in the year subsequent to the move in the following circumstances.[38]

—The moving expenses are incurred and paid in 1984, and the reimbursement is received in 1985.

—The moving expenses are incurred in 1984 and are paid in 1985 (on or before the due date including extensions for filing the 1984 return) and the reimbursement is received in 1984.

The election to deduct moving expenses in the year the reimbursement is received is made by claiming the deduction on the return, amended return, or claim for refund for the taxable year the reimbursement is received.

The moving expense deduction is allowed regardless of whether the employee is transferred by the existing employer, is employed by a new employer, moves to a new area and obtains employment, or switches from self-employed status to employee status (or vice versa). The moving expense deduction is also allowed if an individual is unemployed prior to obtaining employment in a new area.

Example 25. The following taxpayers moved during the year:

—A is transferred by her employer from Wichita to Santa Barbara.

—B obtains a job with a new employer in Phoenix, terminates his employment in Omaha, and moves to Phoenix.

—C terminates his employment in New York, moves to Miami, and obtains a job in Miami.

---

37.   Reg. § 1.217–2(d)(1).
38.   Reg. § § 1.217–2(a)(2) and 1.217–2(d)(1).

—D resigns her position in Chicago, moves to San Diego, and opens a small business in the area.

—E graduates from college in Boston, obtains a job in Portland, and moves to the new location.

Assuming the distance and time requirements are met, all of the above individuals may deduct moving expenses.

CLASSIFICATION OF MOVING EXPENSES

There are five classes of moving expenses, and different limitations and qualifications apply to each class.[39] Direct moving expenses include:

1. The expense of moving household and personal belongings. This class includes fees paid to a moving company for packing, storing, and moving possessions and the rental of a truck if the taxpayer moves his or her own belongings. Also included is the cost of moving household pets. Reasonableness is the only limit on these direct expenses. Expenses of refitting rugs or draperies, losses on the disposal of club memberships, etc., are not deductible as moving expenses.

2. Travel to the new residence. This includes the cost of transportation, meals, and lodging of the taxpayer and the members of the taxpayer's household en route, but does not include the cost of moving servants or others who are not members of the household. The taxpayer can elect to take actual auto expenses (no depreciation is allowed) or the automatic mileage method. In this case, moving expense mileage is limited to nine cents per mile for each car. These expenses are also limited only by the reasonableness standard. For example, if one moves from Texas to Florida via Maine and takes six weeks to do so, the transportation, meals, and lodging must be allocated between personal and moving expenses.

Indirect moving expenses include the following:

3. House-hunting trips. Expenses of traveling (including meals and lodging) to the new place of employment to look for a home are deductible only if the job has been secured in advance of the house-hunting trip. The dollar limitation is explained below.

4. Temporary living expenses. Meals and lodging expenses incurred while living in temporary quarters in the general area of the new job while waiting to move into a new residence are deductible within certain dollar limits (see below). However,

---

39. § 217(b)(1)(A),(B),(C),(D), and (E).

these living expenses are limited to any consecutive 30-day period commencing after employment is secured.

5. Certain residential buying and selling expenses. Buying and selling expenses include those that would normally be offset against the selling price of a home and those expenses incurred in buying a new home. Examples are commissions, escrow fees, legal expenses, points paid to secure a mortage, transfer taxes, and advertising. Also deductible are costs involved in settling an old lease or acquiring a new lease or both. Fixing up expenses, damage deposits, prepaid rent, and the like are not deductible.

Since buying and selling expenses of any asset normally increase the basis or reduce the selling price of that asset, such expenses on the sale or purchase of a personal residence can be considered in computing basis or selling price or as a moving expense under item 5. Any buying or selling expenses claimed as a moving expense deduction cannot be added to the basis of a new home or subtracted from the amount realized on the sale of an old home. This restriction eliminates any possible double benefit of deducting the costs at both points. Generally, since the taxpayer can defer the gain on the sale of a personal residence, the election to take the maximum amount as a moving expense deduction will be preferable. The dollar limits are discussed below.

Indirect moving expenses are limited to a total of $3,000. Furthermore, house-hunting and temporary living expenses may not exceed $1,500 in the aggregate.[40] Again, direct moving expenses are unlimited.

Items 1[41] + 2   = No limit   ✳
Items 3 + 4   = $1,500 limit
Items 3 + 4 + 5 = $3,000 limit

Generally, the dollar limitations apply equally, regardless of filing status. If both spouses change jobs and file separate returns, the limitations are $1,500 and $750, unless only one spouse makes a job change (the spouse who makes the change gets the full amount) or if both change jobs, do not live together, and work at job sites at least 35 miles apart.[42] In the latter case, whether the married couple files jointly or separately, each spouse gets the $3,000 and the $1,500 limits.

Example 26. T, an employee of X Corporation, is hired by Y Corporation at a substantial increase in salary. T is hired in Feb-

---

40. § 217(b)(3)(A).
41. The numbers refer to the types of moving expenses outlined above.
42. Reg. § 1.217–2(b)(9)(v).

ruary 19X4 and is to report for work in March 19X4. The new job requires a move from Los Angeles to New York City. Pursuant to the move, T incurs the following expenses:

February 19X4 house-hunting trip	$ 600
Temporary living expenses in New York City incurred by T and family from March 10–30, 19X4, while awaiting the renovation of their new apartment	1,000
Penalty for breaking lease on Los Angeles apartment	2,400
Charge for packing and moving household goods	4,200
Travel expense during move (March 5–10)	700

Assuming there is no reimbursement of any of these expenses by T's new employer, she can deduct the following amount:

Moving household goods			$ 4,200
Travel expense			700
House-hunting trip	$ 600		
Temporary living expense	1,000		
	$ 1,600		
Limited to:		$ 1,500	
Lease penalty		2,400	
		$ 3,900	
Limited to:			3,000
Moving expense deduction allowed			$ 7,900

A statement should be attached to the tax return showing the detailed calculations of the ceiling limitations, reimbursements, change in job locations, etc. Form 3903 may be used for this purpose.

EDUCATION EXPENSES

GENERAL REQUIREMENTS

An employee may deduct expenses incurred for education as ordinary and necessary business expenses provided such items were incurred either (1) to maintain or improve existing skills required in the present job or (2) to meet the express requirements of the employer or the requirements imposed by law to retain his or her employment status.

Education expenses are not deductible if the education either (1) is required to meet the minimum educational standards for qualification in the taxpayer's existing job or (2) qualifies the taxpayer for a new trade or business.[43] Thus, fees incurred for professional qualifica-

---

43. Reg. § 1.162–5(b)(2) and (3).

tion exams (the bar exam, for example) and fees for review courses (such as a CPA review course) are not deductible.[44] If the education incidentally results in a promotion or raise, the deduction can still be taken so long as the education maintained and improved existing skills and did not qualify a person for a new trade or business. A change in duties is not always fatal to the deduction if the new duties involve the same general work.[45] For example, the IRS has ruled that a practicing dentist's education expenses incurred to become an orthodontist are deductible.[46]

REQUIREMENTS IMPOSED BY LAW OR BY THE EMPLOYER FOR RETENTION OF EMPLOYMENT

Teachers often qualify under the provision that permits the deduction of the education expenses if they are required by the employer or if the requirements are imposed by law. Many states require a minimum of a bachelor's degree and a specified number of additional courses to retain a teaching job. In addition, some public school systems have imposed a master's degree requirement and have required teachers to make satisfactory progress toward a master's degree in order to keep their position. An instructor with a master's degree who is teaching at a college where the minimum degree for a permanent post is a doctorate is not permitted to deduct the expenses of obtaining a PhD.; the instructor is obtaining the minimum education required for that position.[47]

MAINTAINING OR IMPROVING EXISTING SKILLS

The "maintaining or improving existing skills" requirement in the Code has been difficult for both taxpayers and the courts to interpret. For example, a business executive may be permitted to deduct the costs of obtaining an M.B.A. on the grounds that the advanced management education is undertaken to maintain and improve existing management skills. However, if the business executive incurred the expenses to obtain a law degree, the expenses would not be deductible because they constitute training for a new trade or business. For example, the Regulations deny the deduction by a self-employed accountant of expenses relating to law school.[48] In addition, several courts have disallowed deductions to IRS agents for the cost of obtaining a law degree, since the degree was not required to retain employment; the education qualified the agent for a new profession.[49]

---

44. Reg. § 1.212–1(f); Rev.Rul. 69–292, 1969–1 C.B. 84.
45. Reg. § 1.162–5(b)(3).
46. Rev.Rul. 74–78, 1974–1 C.B. 44.
47. Reg. § 1.162–5(b)(2)(iii) Example (2); *Kenneth C. Davis,* 65 T.C. 1014 (1976).
48. Reg. § 1.162–5(b)(3)(ii) Example (1).
49. *J. L. Weiler,* 54 T.C. 398 (1970).

Clearly, the executive mentioned previously would be eligible to deduct the costs of specialized, nondegree management courses which were taken for continuing education or to maintain or improve existing skills.

CLASSIFICATION OF SPECIFIC ITEMS

Education expenses include books, tuition, typing, and transportation (e. g., from the office to night school) and travel (e. g., meals and lodging while away from home at summer school). Transportation and travel are deductible *for* adjusted gross income (whether or not reimbursed) and all other educational expenses are deductions *from* adjusted gross income (unless such expenses are reimbursed by the employer or incurred by a self-employed individual or an outside salesperson).

> **Example 27.** T holds a bachelor of education degree. T is a teacher of secondary education in the Los Angeles, California, school system. Last year the school board changed its minimum education requirement for new teachers by prescribing five years of college training instead of four. Under a grandfather clause, teachers who have only four years of college (such as T) would continue to qualify if they show satisfactory progress toward a graduate degree. Pursuant to this new requirement, T enrolls at the University of Southern California and takes three graduate courses. T's unreimbursed expenses for this purpose are as follows:

Books and tuition	$ 250
Meals and lodging while in travel status (June–August)	1,150
Laundry while in travel status	220
Transportation	600

> T can claim the meals and lodging, laundry, and transportation as a deduction *for* adjusted gross income (as a travel expense). The books and tuition are deductible *from* adjusted gross income on Schedule A of Form 1040 if T itemizes her deductions.

ENTERTAINMENT EXPENSES

In 1962 Congress enacted § 274 of the Code to place restrictions on the deductibility of entertainment expenses. This provision was in response to the alleged abuses by business executives and other employees of entertainment expense deductions. The law now contains strict recordkeeping requirements and provides restrictive tests for the deduction of certain types of entertainment expenses.

CLASSIFICATION OF EXPENSES

Entertainment expenses may be categorized as follows: those *directly related to* business and those *associated with* business.[50] Directly related expenses are related to an actual business meeting or discussion. These expenses may be contrasted with entertainment expenses that are often incurred to promote goodwill. To obtain a deduction for directly related entertainment, it is not necessary to show that actual benefit resulted from the expenditure as long as there was a "reasonable" expectation of benefit. To qualify as directly related, the expense should be incurred in a clear business setting. If there is little possibility of engaging in the active conduct of a trade or business due to the nature of the social facility, it may be difficult to qualify the expenditure as "directly related to" business.

Expenses associated with, rather than directly related to, business entertainment must serve a specific business purpose, such as obtaining new business or continuing existing business. These expenditures qualify only if the expenses directly precede or follow a bona fide business discussion. Entertainment occurring on the same day as the business discussion meets the test.

RESTRICTIONS UPON DEDUCTIBILITY

Business Meals. Section 274(e) allows the deduction of certain entertainment expenses that would otherwise not be deductible. The cost of meals or beverages served in surroundings which are conducive to a business discussion (the so-called quiet business meal rule) is deductible.[51] There is no requirement that business actually be discussed. The taxpayer need only demonstrate a business relationship for the entertainment and a reasonable expectation of business benefit. This quiet business meal rule also extends to the furnishing of meals or beverages at business programs, conventions, etc. (e. g., a dental equipment supplier may purchase meals or buy drinks for dentists at a convention).

> **Example 28.** T, a sales representative, took a customer to dinner at a local restaurant. After dinner, T took the customer to a nearby nightclub where they had drinks and watched a floor show. The cost of dinner is deductible because it meets the "directly related" test. This is true whether or not business was actually discussed because of the "quiet business meal" rule. The cost of entertainment at the nightclub is also deductible, since it meets the "associated with" test (i. e., the nightclub entertainment directly followed the business dinner, which meets the "directly related" test).

---

50. § 274(a)(1)(A).
51. Reg. § 1.274–2(f)(2)(i).

Example 29. S, a sales representative, took a customer to a nightclub where they had drinks and watched a floor show. Business was not discussed during the evening. The expenses incurred by S are not deductible. The entertainment does not satisfy the "associated with" test, since it did not precede or follow a bona fide business discussion (nor does it meet the "quiet business meal" requirement). Contrast this result with the result in Example 28, where both the "directly related" and "associated with" tests were met.

Entertainment Facilities. If certain conditions were met, prior to 1979 all or part of the cost of maintaining an entertainment facility (e. g., hunting lodge, fishing camp, yacht, country club) could be deducted as a business expense. In this connection, the amount deductible included such items as depreciation, maintenance and repairs, and annual membership dues. Apparently fearful that taxpayer abuse was taking place, Congress narrowed the categories of entertainment facilities that qualify for the deduction. As to amounts paid or incurred after December 31, 1978, only "dues or fees to any social, athletic, or sporting club or organization" can be considered.[52]

To obtain a deduction for the dues paid or incurred to maintain a club membership, a "primary use" test is imposed. Unless it can be shown that over 50 percent of the use of the facility was for business purposes, no deduction is permitted. In meeting the primary use test, the following rules govern:

—Consider only the days the facility is used. Thus, days of nonuse do not enter into the determination.[53]

—A day of both business and personal use counts as a day of business use.

—Business use includes entertainment that is *associated with* and *directly related to.*

But even if the primary use test is satisfied, only the portion of the dues attributable to the *directly related to* entertainment qualify for the deduction. For this purpose, however, quiet business meals are treated as *directly related to* entertainment.[54]

Example 30. T is the sales manager of an insurance agency and as such, is expected to incur entertainment expenditures in connection with the sale of insurance to existing and potential clients. None of these expenses are reimbursed by his employer. During the year, T paid the following amounts to the Leesville Country Club:

---

52. § 274(a)(2)(A) and (C).
53. Reg. § 1.274–2(e)(4)(iii).
54. Rev.Rul. 63–144, 1963–2 C.B. 129.

Membership fee (refundable upon termination of membership)	$ 2,000
Annual dues	1,200 *prorated*
Meals and other charges relating to business use	900
Meals and other charges relating to personal use	400

The club was used 120 days for purposes *directly related to* business and 80 days for personal use. The club was not used at all during the remaining days of the year. Since the facility was used for business more than 50% of the time (i. e., 120 days out of 200 days), the "primary use" test is satisfied. The portion of the annual dues that can be deducted is $720 (120/200 = 60% × $1,200). None of the membership fee is deductible, since it is refundable. In summary, a total deduction of $1,620 [$720 (club dues) + $900 (meals and other charges relating to business use)] is allowed.

Example 31. Assume the same facts as in Example 30 except that the business use was made up as follows: 30 days of *directly related to* entertainment, 70 days of *associated with* entertainment, and 20 days of quiet business meals. The deduction for dues now would be $300 (50/200 = 25% × $1,200). The total deduction, therefore, becomes $1,200 [$300 (club dues) + $900 (meals and other charges relating to business use)].

Recordkeeping Requirements. Prior to 1962, the courts frequently permitted a deduction for entertainment expenses under the Cohan rule. Under this rule, deduction of a portion of the taxpayer's expenses was permitted where the exact amount could not be determined due to incomplete records.[55]

Section 274(d) now provides that no deduction is permitted unless adequate substantiation is maintained including:

—The amount of the expense.

—The time and place of the expense.

—The business purpose.

—The business relationship.

It is not necessary to report the expenses and employer reimbursements on the employee's tax return if the reimbursement is equal to the expenses and if the employee furnishes an adequate accounting to the employer. The employee is only required to state on the return that the reimbursements did not exceed the allowable expenses.[56] In all other cases, it is necessary to submit a statement with

---

55. *Cohan v. Comm.,* 2 USTC ¶ 489, 8 AFTR 10552, 39 F.2d 540 (CA–2, 1930); in Rev.Rul. 75–169, 1975–1 C.B. 59, the IRS held that due to the passage of § 274(d) no deduction will be allowed on the basis of the Cohan rule or unsupported testimony.
56. Reg. § § 1.162–17(b)(1) and 1.274–5(e)(2).

the return (i. e., when the reimbursements exceed the allowable expenses or when the expenses exceed the reimbursement and the taxpayer deducts such excess amounts on the return, the excess must be included in income).[57] In all cases involving a shareholder-employee relationship (i. e., where the employee owns more than 10 percent of the employer corporation's stock), a statement of the employee's expenses must be submitted with the tax return.[58]

Business Gifts. Business gifts are deductible to the extent of $25 per donee per year.[59] An exception is made for gifts costing $4 or less (e. g., pens with the employee's or company's name on them) or promotional materials. Such items are not treated as business gifts (subject to the $25 limitation). In addition, incidental costs such as engraving of jewelry and nominal charges for giftwrapping, mailing, and delivery are not included in the cost of the gift for purposes of applying the $25 per gift limitation.[60] The $25 limitation applies to both direct and indirect gifts. A gift is indirect if it is made to a person's spouse or other family member or to a corporation or partnership on behalf of the individual. All such gifts must be aggregated in applying the $25 limit. Excluded from the $25 limit are gifts or awards to employees for length of service, etc., that are under $400.[61] Prior to August 13, 1981, the limit for awards to employees was $100.[62]

It is necessary to maintain records substantiating the gifts. These substantiation requirements are similar to the rules applying to entertainment expenses discussed above.

If the taxpayer is an outside salesperson or if the expenses are reimbursed by an employer, employee gifts are deductible *for* adjusted gross income; in all other cases, the deduction is *from* adjusted gross income and can be taken only if the employee itemizes deductions.

Example 32. T, an outside salesperson, makes the following gifts, none of which are reimbursed during the year:

P (a client)	$ 20	
Q (a nonclient and the husband of P)	10	
X (a client)	30	
A (T's supervisor)	15	
L (T's secretary)	26	(includes a $1 charge for gift wrapping)

---

57. Reg. § 1.274–5(e)(2)(ii) and (iii); Rev.Rul. 73–191, 1973–1 C.B. 151.
58. Reg. § 1.274–5(e)(5)(ii).
59. § 274(b)(1).
60. Reg. § 1.274–3(c).
61. § 274(b)(1)(C).
62. § 274(b)(3)(C) allows a deduction for gifts to employees of up to $1,600 under a *qualified plan* as long as the average cost of all awards under the qualified plan does not exceed $400. Qualified plans are described in § 274(b)(3).

The gifts to P and Q must be combined and are limited to $25. The gift to X is likewise limited to $25. The $15 to A is not deductible, since a gift by an employee to his supervisor does not qualify as a business gift; such gifts are personal nondeductible expenditures. The $26 to L is not limited to $25 due to the nominal gift-wrapping charge. T must maintain adequate records to substantiate the business relationships and the amounts of the gifts. Since T is an outside salesperson, all these gifts are deductible *for* adjusted gross income.

OTHER EMPLOYEE EXPENSES

OFFICE IN THE HOME

No deduction is permitted for an office in the home unless a portion of the residence is used exclusively on a regular basis (1) as the principal place of business for any trade or business of the taxpayer or (2) as a place of business which is used by patients, clients, or customers. Employees must meet an additional test: the use must be for the convenience of the employer as opposed to being merely "appropriate and helpful." [63]

The exclusive use requirement means that a specific part of the home must be used solely for business purposes. Since the office in the home must be used exclusively for business, a deduction, if permitted, will require an allocation of total expenses of operating the home between business and personal use based on floor space or number of rooms.

Even if the taxpayer meets the above requirements, the allowable business expenses may not exceed the gross income from the business activity reduced by an allocable portion of expense deductions which would otherwise qualify as personal itemized deductions (e. g., mortgage interest and real estate taxes). [64]

Example 33. T is a self-employed CPA who maintains an office in his home which is devoted exclusively to client work. Clients regularly visit this office. The gross income from his practice was $2,000 during 19X4. The portion of mortgage interest and real estate taxes allocated to business use amounted to $1,500; an allocable portion of maintenance expenses, utilities, maid service, and depreciation on the house was $1,000. As shown below, his other business expenses of $1,000 are limited, therefore, to $500, which is the excess of gross income of $2,000 over the allocable portion of expenses otherwise deductible as itemized deductions.

---

63. § 280A(c)(1).
64. § 280A(c)(5).

Gross income from self-employment		$ 2,000
Less:	Allocable portion of itemized deduction items—interest and taxes	1,500
	Balance	$ 500
Less:	Other deductions ($1,000, limited to the balance of $500)	500
	Net income from self-employment	$ –0–

Example 34. T, an accountant for the XYZ Corporation, maintains an office in her home. She uses the office primarily for reading professional journals, and her family uses the office for personal reasons. T occasionally brings work relating to XYZ Corporation home and uses the office at home on weekends and during the evenings. Her outside consulting activities are limited to the preparation of a few tax returns from which she received $1,000 gross income during 19X1. Mortgage interest and real estate taxes allocable to the office amounted to $1,500; and an allocable portion of other household expenses, including utilities, depreciation, etc., was $1,000. The $1,500 mortgage interest and real estate taxes are deductible *from* adjusted gross income as itemized deductions. None of the other expenses are deductible, because the office in T's home is not used exclusively and on a regular basis by T as a place of business. In addition, an employee must show that the office is used for the convenience of the employer. It appears that T's office is merely appropriate and helpful in the performance of her duties as an employee. This situation does not permit a deduction.

MISCELLANEOUS EMPLOYEE EXPENSES

Other employee expenses which are deductible include special clothing and its upkeep;[65] union dues;[66] professional expenses, such as dues and attendance at professional meetings;[67] and employment agency fees for seeking employment in the same trade or business, whether or not a new job is secured.[68] These deductions are *for* adjusted gross income only if the employee is an outside salesperson, if the expenses are travel or transportation, or if they are reimbursed. In all other cases, they are deductions *from* adjusted gross income.

To be deductible, special clothing must be both specifically required as a condition of employment and not generally adaptable to

---

65. Rev.Rul. 70–474, 1970–2 C.B. 34.
66. Rev.Rul. 72–463, 1972–2 C.B. 93.
67. Reg. § 1.162–6.
68. Rev.Rul. 75–120, 1975–1 C.B. 55 as clarified by Rev.Rul. 77–16, 1977–1 C.B. 37. However, such expenses are not deductible, according to the IRS, if an individual is seeking employment in a new trade or business.

regular wear (e. g., a police officer's uniform is not suitable for off-duty activities) or continually used to the extent that the clothing takes the place of regular clothing (e. g., military uniforms).

Regulation § 1.212–1(f) disallows a deduction for job-hunting expenses. The current position of the IRS, however, is that expenses incurred in seeking employment (e. g., travel, employment agency fees) are deductible if the taxpayer is seeking employment in the same trade or business in which he or she is currently employed (or, if unemployed, there has been no substantial lack of continuity since the last job and the search for a new position) even if the attempts to secure the job are unsuccessful. However, no deduction is allowed for persons seeking their first job or seeking employment in a new trade or business (whether or not successful).

Other employee expenses which are not deductible include regular clothes, commuting expenses, and any other expenditures of a personal nature.

EXPENSES OF EMPLOYEES WORKING OUTSIDE THE U. S.

The U. S. income tax applies to the worldwide income of its citizens and residents. Since most other countries also have an income tax, expatriates (Americans working abroad) were at the distinct disadvantage of having to pay two income taxes on foreign earned income. The increased cost of living in some foreign countries plus the scarcity of adequate housing in less-developed countries made working abroad even more disadvantageous to Americans. To induce U. S. citizens and residents to accept employment or relocation overseas, U. S. companies were compelled to offer various cost differentials and tax equalization assurances, which increased their labor costs and placed U. S. concerns at an economic disadvantage with their foreign competitors. To equalize the situation, Congress passed favorable legislation for foreign earned income.

The expatriate has the option of a generous flat-dollar exclusion (discussed in Chapter 6), a considerably simplified excess housing allowance, or both.[69] The new provisions are summarized below:

—To qualify, the taxpayer must satisfy either the bona fide residence test or the physical presence test—330 full days of foreign residency out of 12 consecutive months. An exception to the 330-day rule is provided for expatriates who are forced to leave a country because of civil unrest or similar conditions (e. g., the recent widespread civil disorder in Lebanon).

—In addition to electing the foreign earned income exclusion, an expatriate may elect to exclude an amount determined on the basis of housing costs incurred. For this purpose, the housing

---

69. §§ 119 and 911.

cost amount consists of reasonable housing costs, including rent, insurance, and utilities (but not interest and taxes that are independently deductible). The amount to be excluded is the excess of these costs over 16 percent of the salary of a government employee holding grade GS–14. (At present salary levels, this would cover amounts in excess of approximately $6,000.) For those expatriates who are not reimbursed for housing costs, a special rule would substitute a deduction for the exclusion.

—Deductions or credit for foreign taxes attributable to the excluded income are not allowable. Consequently, the expatriate is placed in a position of having to forego the foreign tax credit of § 901 in order to obtain the § 911 exclusion.

—The exclusions are elective. Taxpayers are able to elect the income and housing-reimbursement exclusions separately, together, or not at all. Once elected, however, the exclusions are binding upon subsequent years unless affirmatively revoked. Revocation places the taxpayer in a five-year holding period during which the exclusions cannot be reelected.

The exclusion rule for expatriates is generally advantageous for those working in countries with little, if any, income taxes. If, on the other hand, the country imposes a high income tax, it may be preferable not to elect the exclusions and use the foreign tax credit route to reduce or eliminate U. S. income taxes.

CONTRIBUTIONS TO INDIVIDUAL RETIREMENT ACCOUNTS

An important and popular deduction *for* adjusted gross income is the amount contributed to an Individual Retirement Account (IRA). This amount may be as great as $2,000 per year for an individual. IRAs are covered in detail in Chapter 19.

REPORTING PROCEDURES

Form 2106 is used for reporting employee business expenses. Keep in mind that no reporting is required where the employee renders an adequate accounting to the employer and is reimbursed fully for all legitimate expenses. Form 2106 also need not be used where the reimbursement is less than the amount spent but the employee chooses to forego the excess deduction.

Page 1 of Form 2106 is reproduced on p. 375. Part I of page 1 covers those expenses that are treated as deductions *for* adjusted gross income. Transportation and travel are reflected on lines 1–3, while all of the employee expenses of an outside salesperson are grouped on line 4. Car expenses are computed in Part II and the total is transferred to line 3 of Part I. In computing car expenses, Part II provides

Form **2106**	**Employee Business Expenses**	OMB No. 1545-0139
Department of the Treasury Internal Revenue Service	(Please use Form 3903 to figure moving expense deduction.) ► **Attach to Form 1040.**	19**83** 54

Your name	Social security number	Occupation in which expenses were incurred
Employer's name	Employer's address	

PART I.—Employee Business Expenses Deductible in Figuring Adjusted Gross Income on Form 1040, Line 32

1 Reimbursed and unreimbursed fares for airplane, boat, bus, taxicab, train, etc..	**1**	
2 Reimbursed and unreimbursed meal, lodging, and other expenses while away from your tax home. . .	**2**	
3 Reimbursed and unreimbursed car expenses from Part II.	**3**	
4 Reimbursed and unreimbursed outside salesperson's expenses other than those shown on lines 1 through 3. **Caution:** *Do not use this line unless you are an outside salesperson (see instructions)*		

---	**4**	
5 Reimbursed expenses other than those shown on lines 1 through 3 (see instructions)	**5**	
6 Add lines 1 through 5	**6**	
7 Employer's payments for these expenses only if not included on Form W-2	**7**	
8 If line 6 is more than line 7, subtract line 7 from line 6. Enter here and on Form 1040, line 24 . . .	**8**	
9 If line 7 is more than line 6, subtract line 6 from line 7. Enter here and on Form 1040, line 7	**9**	

PART II.—Car Expenses (Use either your actual expenses or the mileage rate.)

	Car 1	Car 2	Car 3
A. Number of months you used car for business during 1983 .	_____ months	_____ months	_____ months
B. Total mileage for months on line A	_____ miles	_____ miles	_____ miles
C. Business part of line B mileage	_____ miles	_____ miles	_____ miles

Actual Expenses (Include expenses on lines 1 and 2 only for the months shown on line A, above.)

		Car 1	Car 2	Car 3
1 Gasoline, oil, lubrication, etc.	**1**			
2 Other	**2**			
3 Total (add lines 1 and 2)	**3**			
4 Divide line C by line B, above	**4**	%	%	%
5 Multiply line 3 by line 4	**5**			
6 Depreciation (see instructions)	**6**			
7 Section 179 deduction (see instructions)	**7**			
8 Business parking fees and tolls.	**8**			
9 Total (add lines 5 through 8). Enter here and in Part I, line 3	**9**			

Mileage Rate

10 Enter the smaller of (a) 15,000 miles or (b) the total mileage (Car 1+ Car 2+ Car 3) from line C, above	**10**	miles
11 Multiply line 10 by 20½¢ (11¢ if applicable, see instructions)	**11**	
12 Enter the total mileage, if any (Car 1 + Car 2 + Car 3) from line C that is over 15,000 miles	**12**	miles
13 Multiply line 12 by 11¢ and enter here	**13**	
14 Business part of car interest, parking fees, tolls, and State and local taxes (except gasoline tax) . . .	**14**	
15 Total (add lines 11, 13, and 14). Enter here and in Part I, line 3	**15**	

PART III.—Information About Educational Expenses Shown in Part I or on Schedule A (Form 1040)

1 Did you need this education to meet the basic requirements for your business or profession? . . . . □ Yes □ No
2 Will this study program qualify you for a new business or profession? . . . . □ Yes □ No
Note: *If your answer to question 1 or 2 is "Yes," stop here. You cannot deduct these expenses, even if you do not intend to change your business or profession.*
3 If "No," list the courses you took and their relationship to your business or profession ►-------------------------------
----

For Paperwork Reduction Act Notice, see instructions on back.　　　　　　　　　　　　　　Form **2106** (1983)

for the use of the actual expense method or the automatic mileage rate. Although moving expenses also qualify as deductions *for* adjusted gross income, they are reportable on Form 3903—not on Form 2106. Any reimbursements received from the employer (and not included on the employee's Form W–2) are listed on line 7. Deductions in excess of reimbursements (line 8) or reimbursements in excess of deductions (line 9) are transferred to the employee's Form 1040.

Expenses that are deductions *from* adjusted gross income (e. g., entertainment, business gifts, some education costs) are reported on Schedule A if the employee itemizes.

Part III requests information about any education expenses included in either Part I or Part II.

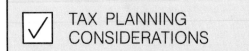

TAX PLANNING CONSIDERATIONS

SELF-EMPLOYED INDIVIDUALS

A taxpayer who has the flexibility to be classified as either an employee or as a self-employed individual (e. g., a real estate agent or a direct seller) should not automatically assume that the latter is better until all factors are considered.

While it is advantageous to deduct one's business expenses *for* adjusted gross income, a self-employed individual may have higher expenses, such as local gross receipts taxes, license fees, franchise fees, personal property taxes, and occupation taxes. One of the most expensive considerations is the Social Security tax versus the self-employment tax. In 1984, for example, the maximum tax on an employee is $2,532.60, while a self-employed individual may be subject to a maximum of $4,271.40.

The recordkeeping and filing requirements for all of these local taxes can be quite burdensome. After analyzing all these factors, a taxpayer may decide that employee status is preferable to self-employed status.

SHIFTING DEDUCTIONS BETWEEN EMPLOYER AND EMPLOYEE

In a closely-held corporation, there is an opportunity for the employee-shareholder to shift deductions from the corporation to the employee if proper advance planning is done. Typically, the shareholder-employee incurs travel and entertainment expenses in the course of employment. The corporation gets the deduction if it reimburses the employee-shareholder. Suppose the employee is in a higher tax bracket than the corporation so that the deduction is more valuable on the employee-shareholder's return. If the employee simply pays the expenses and fails to get reimbursed by the corporation, both the employee and the corporation lose the deduction, since the employee could have been reimbursed by the corporation, and the corporation did not make the payment (see Chapter 7).

However, if there is a resolution by the corporation that employees are expected to absorb such expenses out of their salaries, the employee can take the deduction. Note that such a corporate resolution must be made before such expenses are incurred so that the tax planning (and the corporate resolution establishing this policy) must take place before the beginning of the year.

TRANSPORTATION AND TRAVEL EXPENSES

Adequate detailed records should be kept of all transportation and travel expenses. Since the mileage allowance is 20.5 cents (or 11 cents) per mile, a new expensive automobile which is used primarily for business may generate a higher expense based on actual cost. The election to expense under § 179, ACRS depreciation, insurance, repairs and maintenance, automobile club dues, interest on the auto loan, etc., may result in automobile expenses in excess of the automatic mileage method allowance.

If a taxpayer wishes to sightsee or vacation on a business trip, it would be beneficial to schedule business on both a Friday and a Monday to turn the weekend into business days for allocation purposes. It is especially crucial to schedule appropriate business days when foreign travel is involved.

MOVING EXPENSES

Commissions on the sale of a personal residence may either be treated as indirect moving expenses subject to the overall ceiling limitations or be deducted from the selling price of the residence in arriving at the amount realized. Generally, it is preferable to deduct the commissions as moving expenses, since a deduction from the selling price of the house merely reduces the capital gain on the sale (or increases a nondeductible loss). In addition, such capital gains may be postponed if a new residence is acquired within the prescribed time period and certain other requirements of the Code are met. Postponement of gain rules for the sale of a personal residence are discussed in Chapter 15. Consideration should be given to the fact that sale-related expenses which are not used as moving expenses (due to the ceiling limitations) may be deducted from the selling price of the residence.

Since reimbursements of moving expenses are required to be included in gross income and certain moving expenses may not be deductible due to the ceiling limitations, an employee may be required to pay additional income tax due to the move. Therefore, some employers reimburse their employees for these additional taxes. The additional taxes are estimated and included in the employee's reimbursement.

Persons who retire and move to a new location incur personal nondeductible moving expenses. However, if the retired person accepts a full-time job in the new location prior to moving, the moving expenses become deductible.

> **Example 35.** J retired from the practice of public accounting in New York and moved to Las Cruces, New Mexico, where he became an instructor in accounting at New Mexico State University. If he had acquired the new job prior to the move, his moving expenses would be deductible. Otherwise, they were personal in nature and, therefore, nondeductible.

EDUCATION EXPENSES

Education expenses are treated as nondeductible personal items unless the individual is employed or is engaged in a trade or business. A temporary leave of absence for further education is one way to reasonably assure that the taxpayer is still qualified, even if a full-time student. It has been held that an individual was qualified for the education expense deduction even though he resigned from his job, returned to school full time for two years, and accepted another job in the same field upon graduation. The Court held that the student had merely suspended active participation in his field.[70] In another instance, a nurse had been inactive in her field for 13 years and returned to school to study biology; she was not in a trade or business and the expenses were not deductible.[71] To secure the deduction, an individual should be advised to arrange his or her work situation to preserve employee or business status.

Travel as a form of education is allowed under Reg. § 1.162–5(d) only to "the extent [that] such expenditures are attributable to a period of travel that is directly related to the duties of the individual in his employment. . . ." The travel must directly maintain or improve existing skills, and the major portion of the travel must be primarily for education. General travel that is primarily for pleasure or only indirectly enhances one's existing skills is not deductible.[72] Thus, it is particularly important to document educational travel activities.

70. *Stephen G. Sherman,* 36 TCM 1191, T.CMemo. 1977–301.
71. *Geraldine G. Cannon,* 36 TCM 1130, T.C.Memo. 1977–283; *John M. Cannon,* 40 TCM 541, T.C.Memo. 1980–224, affirmed by court order (CA–7, 1981).
72. *Kenneth W. Allison,* 36 TCM 1114, T.C.Memo. 1977–277, affirmed by court order (CA–9, 1979).

ENTERTAINMENT EXPENSES

Proper documentation of expenditures is essential due to the strict recordkeeping requirements and the restrictive tests which must be met. For example, credit card receipts as the sole source of documentation may be inadequate to substantiate the business purpose and business relationship.[73] Taxpayers should be advised to maintain detailed records of amounts, time, place, business purpose, and business relationships. Since a credit card receipt details the place, date, and amount, a notation made on the receipt at that time of the names of the person(s) attending, the business relationship, and the topic of discussion should constitute proper documentation.

"Associated with" or goodwill entertainment is not deductible unless a business discussion is conducted immediately before or after the entertainment and there is a business purpose for such entertainment. Taxpayers should be advised to arrange for a business discussion before or after such entertainment and to provide documentation of the business purpose (e. g., to obtain new business from a prospective customer).

Since a 50 percent test is imposed for the deductibility of country club dues, it may be necessary to accelerate business use or reduce personal use of a club facility. The 50 percent test is made on a daily use basis; therefore, detailed records should be maintained to substantiate business versus personal use.

> **Example 36.** T confers with his CPA on December 5 and finds that he has used the country club 30 days for business and 33 days for personal use. On the advice of his CPA, T schedules four business lunches between December 5 and December 31 and refrains from using the club for personal purposes until January of the following year. Because of this action, T will meet the 50 percent test and will be permitted a deduction for a portion of the club dues.

PROBLEM MATERIALS

Questions for Class Discussion

1. T owns a barber shop with four chairs, one of which he operates himself. The other three chairs are worked by other persons. What factors should be taken into account in determining whether or not the other barbers are T's employees or independent contractors?

2. What difference does it makes if an individual's expenses are classified as employment related versus expenses from self-employment?

---

73. *George L. Gee,* 36 TCM 327, T.C.Memo. 1977–72.

3. Why did Congress provide special treatment for outside salespersons?

4. Does the outside salesperson classification apply if an employee performs service or delivery functions (e. g., television repair or milk delivery)?

5. Why might it be worthwhile to structure one's employment situation carefully to meet the definition of outside salesperson rather than to be an employee?

6. Why is a taxpayer permitted to take a deduction *for* adjusted gross income for reimbursed expenses that would otherwise be treated as itemized deductions if no reimbursement were received?

7. What tax return reporting procedures must be followed by an employee under the following circumstances?

    (a) Expenses and reimbursements are equal, and an adequate accounting is made to the employer.

    (b) Reimbursements exceed expenses, and an adequate accounting is made to the employer.

    (c) Expenses exceed reimbursements, and no accounting is made to the employer.

8. One employee commutes one block to work; another employee travels 60 miles to his place of employment. Does the distance traveled have any effect upon the deductibility of these transportation expenses?

9. A taxpayer has two jobs. He drives 40 miles to his first job. The distance fom the first job to the second is 32 miles. During the year he worked 200 days at both jobs. On 150 days, he drove from his first job to the second job; on the remaining 50 days, he drove home (40 miles) and then to the second job (42 miles). How much can he deduct?

10. T's job requires her to carry tools and equipment to work every day. If she did not take these tools to work, she would commute by bus at a cost of $1 per day. It costs her $2.50 per day to drive. How much can T deduct?

11. A taxpayer has asked you to determine whether he should use the automatic mileage method or the actual operating cost method to compute his deduction for transportation. He is an outside salesperson and used two cars: one, a Volvo, is used 40% for business and the other, a Lincoln, is used 80% for business. What is your answer and what factors would you consider?

12. If an employee receives a reimbursement of 15 cents per mile for job-related automobile expenses, can he deduct any excess expense amounts on his tax return?

13. If automobile expenses are computed using the automatic mileage method, what expenses are allowed in addition to the mileage allowance?

14. Distinguish between the terms "transportation" expense and "travel" expense.

15. J incurred travel expenses while away from home on company business. These expenses were not reimbursed by his employer. Can J deduct the travel expenses? If so, are they deductions *for* or *from* adjusted gross income (itemized deductions)?

16. If an individual accepts a three-year work assignment in another city, are

the rental payments and meal expenses incurred because of that work assignment deductible as travel expenses?

17. If an employee takes a combined business/pleasure trip, what portion of the expenses is deductible?

18. What restrictions exist on the deductibility of expenses connected with attendance at a convention located in Brazil?

19. Are moving expenses deductible *for* or *from* adjusted gross income?

20. Distinguish between direct moving expenses and indirect moving expenses. Why is it important to classify such items properly?

21. What is the reason for imposing time and distance requirements to determine the deductibility of moving expenses?

22. What difference does it make if a taxpayer is improving existing skills or acquiring new ones for the purpose of the educational deduction? Under what general tax principle does the justification for this rule lie?

23. Discuss whether each of the following employees will be allowed a deduction for education expenses. Why or why not?

    (a) A, a CPA who attended night school in order to take computer courses to improve her auditing skills.

    (b) B, a CPA who is a tax specialist, attended night law school to gain a greater expertise in the tax area.

    (c) C, a computer programmer who attended night school to become a computer analyst for her present employer.

    (d) D, an elementary school teacher who took courses in art appreciation during the summer. D had no art training, and art is taught in his school. It was not a requirement of the employer.

    (e) E, a marketing manager who took a Dale Carnegie course.

    (f) F, a homemaker who took a Dale Carnegie course.

    (g) G, a retired Army officer, who returns to school for business courses to prepare for a civilian job.

    (h) What if G (above) took the courses after he had obtained a civilian business position?

24. Are the following education-related expenses deductible *for* or *from* adjusted gross income?

    (a) taxi fares
    (b) typing fees
    (c) meals while away from home
    (d) books

25. Discuss the difference between "directly related to" and "associated with" entertainment.

26. What is the "quiet business meal" rule?

27. Why is it necessary to maintain detailed records for entertainment expenses?

28. To what extent may a taxpayer make business gifts to a business associate? To an employee? To a superior?

29. What requirements must be met for an employee to deduct expenses for an office in the home?

30. Are the expenses incurred by a college graduate seeking her first full-time job allowed as a deduction?

Problems

31. B incurred the following expenses on a business trip: (It was 100% business and the taxpayer was away from home overnight.)

Air fare	$ 1,082
Taxi	30
Meals	75
Room	105
Entertainment	40
Laundry	25

None of the expenses are reimbursed by B's employer. How much can be deducted, and is the deduction *for* or *from* adjusted gross income if B is not an outside salesperson?

32. In problem 31, assume B took her husband along. His air fare was $541 of the total; they shared the taxi to the hotel (which would have cost $20 for one person); he ate half the meals; and they shared a double room (a single room would have cost $90). All of the laundry and the entertainment expenses were incurred by B, not her husband. What can B deduct on her return, and is the deduction *for* or *from* adjusted gross income?

33. J is a salesman for the XYZ Company. He solicits orders from commercial businesses within the general vicinity of the company office, which is also his tax home. When business is slow, he promotes the company's residential products by making house-to-house calls within the general area. The company provides a desk for J which he occasionally uses to write up an order. On Friday of each week J goes to the company office to pick up his mail. J incurred the following unreimbursed expenses during 1984:

—Automobile (e. g., depreciation, gas, oil)—$5,000.

—Luncheons for clients—$3,000.

J maintains that he "never" eats lunch unless he entertains a client.

(a) Is J classified as an outside salesperson?

(b) Is J entitled to a tax deduction for these expenses? If so, is the deduction *for* adjusted gross income or *from* adjusted gross income?

34. (a) S works for a local government and inspects the electrical wiring in new housing projects. He calls his office each day to receive that day's assignments. On a certain day, he drove his personal car from home to site A (20 miles), from site A to site B (12 miles), and from site B to site C (30 miles), after which he was free to drive home (6 miles). How many, if any, miles driven by S on this day count towards deductible transportation expenses?

(b) Same as (a), except that S drove to site A and then home on day 1, to site B and then home on day 2, and to site C and then home on day 3. The three round trips are 40 miles, 45 miles, and 12 miles. How many, if any, miles driven by S on these days count towards deductible transportation expenses?

35. P is employed by the L Corporation. She drives 12 miles each way to work. After work, she drove by a customer's home to drop off a rush order. The total distance from the office to her home via the customer's home was 20 miles. What, if any, transportation expense can she deduct?

36. T incurred the following employee expenses (he is not an outside salesperson):

Travel while away from home	$ 2,000
Transportation	1,000
Entertainment of customers	900
Professional dues	600
Telephone for business use	500

   T's employer allowed him $4,000 to cover all of these expenses. Calculate T's deduction *for* and *from* adjusted gross income.

37. S received reimbursements of $3,300 after adequately accounting to his employer. His expenses were as follows:

Air fare, taxi, and auto mileage	$ 2,000
Meals and lodging while away from home	2,000
Entertainment while away from home	1,000
Dues, subscriptions, and books	500

   What are S's deductions *for* and *from* adjusted gross income? (Assume S is not an outside salesperson.)

38. P received reimbursements of $6,500 after adequately accounting to her employer. Her expenses were as follows:

Transportation expenses	$ 2,500
Meals and lodging while away from home	1,000
Entertainment	1,500
Other expenses (dues, etc.)	1,000

   How should P treat these expenses on her return, assuming she is not an outside salesperson?

39. T uses his automobile 70% for business and 30% for personal travel. During the year, T traveled a total of 25,000 miles. How much can he deduct using the automatic mileage method?

40. V's records showed that of the 19,000 miles he drove in 1984, 10,000 were business miles. V purchased his auto two years ago for $10,000. It has an estimated useful life of five years and no salvage value. V has used the automatic mileage method in the two prior years. He incurred the following auto expenses this year:

Gas and oil	$ 4,000
Repairs	1,000
License and insurance	400
Business tolls and parking	100

(a) Compute V's deduction under the most favorable method. Assume straight-line depreciation.

(b) Without regard to your answer in (a), compute V's basis in the automobile at the end of year three if he uses the actual cost method. (Assume 19,000 total miles and 10,000 business miles for each of the two prior years.)

41. P took a trip from Los Angeles to Tokyo, primarily on business for the company of which she is president. Eight days were spent on business and two days on sightseeing. P's travel expenses were as follows:

Air fare	$1,200
Meals	750
Lodging	950
Incidental expenses	100

What travel expenses may be deducted by P?

42. J took a trip from Los Angeles to New York. He spent three days conducting business and seven days vacationing and visiting friends. The expenses incurred were as follows:

Air fare	$ 600
Meals and lodging	1,200
Entertainment of clients	400
	$ 2,200

What amounts, if any, can J deduct on his tax return? Is the deduction *for* or *from* AGI?

43. D, a college professor, accepted a position with the GAO in Washington, D.C. The assignment was designated as temporary and was for a 15-month period. The professor left his wife and children in Cleveland and rented an apartment in Washington during the period of employment. He incurred the following expenses, none of which were reimbursed by his employer:

(a) Air fare—weekend trips to and from Washington and Cleveland to visit his family—$7,000.

(b) Rent—Washington apartment—$5,000.

(c) Meals, laundry, etc., in Washington—$4,000.

(d) Entertainment of fellow employees and supervisor in the GAO— $2,000.

Which, if any, of these expenses are deductible by D? Are they deductions *for* adjusted gross income or *from* adjusted gross income?

44. T incurred the following expenses when she was transferred from San Francisco to Dallas:

Loss on the sale of old residence	$ 7,000
Moving company's charges	2,100
House-hunting trip	1,200
Temporary living expenses for 60 days	3,000
Broker's fees on residence sold	5,000
Charges for fitting drapes in new residence	800
Total	$ 19,100

(a) How much can T deduct, assuming no reimbursement?

(b) What would be T's tax consequences if the employer reimburses her for all of the expenses?

45. D graduated from a college in Boston and was hired by a St. Louis CPA firm. She incurred the following moving expenses:

Apartment-hunting trip to St. Louis	$ 1,200
Loss of damage deposit because of ruined carpet in Boston apartment	200
Expense of renting and driving a truck with household goods	2,200
Meals and lodging in St. Louis for one week before apartment was ready	350
Cost of shipping pet cat to St. Louis	150
Payment to real estate firm that located a suitable apartment in St. Louis	75
Cost of refitting drapes for St. Louis apartment	125

What is the most D can deduct?

46. T is a tax specialist for a large CPA firm. During the year, he enrolled in the following course of study to continue his education and incurred the following expenses:

—Business school courses in taxation—enrolled as a nondegree special student—with tuition of $1,500 and transportation expenses of $150.

—Special courses offered by the Kansas Society of CPAs for continuing education. Tuition totaled $1,000 and transportation expenses were $200.

—CPA exam review and CPA license fee. Fees amounted to $800 plus transportation expenses of $100.

(a) Which, if any, of these expenses are deductible by T? *For* adjusted gross income or *from* adjusted gross income?

(b) What would your answer be if T took course work on a PhD. in accounting with the eventual expectation of becoming a college professor?

47. T belongs to a country club which he uses for both business and personal purposes. Assuming none of his expenses are reimbursed, how much can he deduct on his tax return in the two cases outlined below?

Annual dues	$ 5,000
Business meals "directly related to"	400
Business meals "associated with"	300
Business meals "quiet business meals"	350
Personal meals and charges	2,000

Case (a) Days directly related to business	80
Days associated with business	30
Days for quiet business meals	30
Days for personal use	150
Case (b) Days directly related to business	60
Days associated with business	70
Days for quiet business meals	20
Days for personal use	75

48. J is an accountant with the XYZ Company. He is also a self-employed tax consultant with several clients and earns $12,000 per year from his outside consulting. He has an office in his home which is used exclusively for meeting with his consulting clients and for work performed for these clients. Based on square footage, he estimates that total expenses amount to $3,500, including $1,500 of taxes and interest on his home mortgage.

(a) Can J take a deduction for an office in the home? If so, how is it reported and how much can be deducted?

(b) If the office was also used for work he brought home from his regular job, how would your answer to (a) differ? Assume it was used 80% for the consulting business and 20% for his regular job.

Cumulative Problems

49. L, age 23 and single, is an employee of Y Corporation, which specializes in developing and offering adult education courses. Her salary is $21,720, and Y Corporation withheld $4,411 for federal income taxes. L presents the following data to you for 1984:

(1) Expenses of a three-day trip to Washington, D.C. to present a proposal for Federal funds:

Air fare	$ 200
Hotel (2 nights)	118
Meals	65
Taxi fares and tips	14
	$ 397

(2) L accounted to her employer and received the following reimbursements for the Washington trip:

Air fare	$ 200
Per diem—$100/day for three days	300
	$ 500

(3) L made presentations to several local organizations on the adult educational programs offered by Y Corporation. She did not keep records

of out-of-pocket expenses related to transportation but did keep a record indicating she had driven 400 miles on these occasions.

(4) L paid annual dues of $175 to a local members-only nightclub with live entertainment scheduled on weekends. She bought the membership because she knew her boss enjoyed going there occasionally. During the year, she took her boss to the club for dinner three times. The total cost of dinners, for which she paid, was $90.

(5) In connection with her employment, L spent $450 for meals while entertaining customers. L submitted receipts for these meals to Y Corporation, but was reimbursed only $400 because, on several occasions, she had exceeded Y Corporation's limit for reimbursement for meals.

(6) L paid $240 to take an evening course in business administration at the local college. Y Corporation's policy is to reimburse employees 100% for tuition if the employee receives a grade of A, 75% for a grade of B, 50% for a grade of C, and nothing for a grade lower than a C. Unfortunately, L received a grade of C in the course and was reimbursed only $120.

(7) L's deductible medical expenses, interest, taxes, and contributions were $2,770. This $2,770 amount does not include any potential deductions from items (1) through (6).

Compute L's taxable income.

50. H and W. are married. H is an outside salesperson. W is a corporation executive. They have no dependents and are both under 65.

In 1984, H earned $32,000 in commissions and W earned a $62,000 salary, part of which was intended to cover her business expenses. H received no reimbursements for expenses.

H uses his two-year-old car on sales calls and keeps a log of all miles driven. In 1984, he drove 36,000 miles, 25,000 of them for business.

H made several out-of-state sales trips, incurring transportation costs of $1,600 and meals and lodging costs of $750. H also spent $1,400 during the year taking customers to lunch.

W incurred the following expenses related to her work: taxi fares of $125, business lunches of $615, and a yearly commuter train ticket of $800.

During the year, W received $1,200 in interest, $20,000 life insurance proceeds upon the death of her mother, and $500 in dividends from General Motors. She contributed $2,000 to her Individual Retirement Account.

W gave a gift valued at $500 to the president of her firm upon his promotion to that position.

H and W had itemized deductions of $14,250, apart from all items mentioned above.

Compute the adjusted gross income and the taxable income on a joint return for H and W.

Tax Form Problems

51. Steven R. Chandler, Social Security number 215-04-1786, is single. In October 1983, Steve was transferred by his employer from Louisville, Ken-

tucky, to Pittsburgh, Pennsylvania. Steve incurred the following expenses in connection with the move:

Premove house-hunting trip	$ 800
Temporary living expenses in Pittsburgh while waiting for his furniture to arrive (15 days)	900
Travel expenses from old residence to new residence	130
Broker's commission on sale of old residence	1,800
Cost of moving household goods (reimbursed by employer, with reimbursement included on Steve's Form W–2)	1,400
Down payment on new residence	10,000

Steve expects to meet the 39-week, full-time work test. Compute Steve's moving expense deduction using Form 3903.

52. Richard Fuller is a professor of accounting who travels extensively in presenting continuing professional education courses for the university. He is paid by the university. Richard is reimbursed in full for his airplane fares and is reimbursed at the rate of 15¢ a mile for automobile expenses. His reimbursement for meals and lodging is limited to $50 a day. During 1983, Richard incurred the following business-related expenses:

Airplane fares	$ 1,750
Meals and lodging (20 days)	1,360

He drove his automobile 16,000 miles on business but did not keep records of his automobile expenses, except for parking fees and tolls, which totaled $90 in 1983.

In order to keep abreast of recent developments in accounting, Richard attended a three-day workshop sponsored by the American Institute of Certified Public Accountants in June 1983, at his own expense. In connection with this workshop, he incurred the following expenses:

Airplane fare	$ 319
Meals and lodging	186
Enrollment fee	300

Compute Richard's deduction for employee business expenses for 1983, using Form 2106.

Research Problems

53. T was an executive for a savings and loan association. His job entailed obtaining new business and placing new loans. In an attempt to generate new business, T and his wife took vacation trips that were group tours for builders and contractors. Although there were few business meetings, T spent his time during sightseeing trips and entertainment functions becoming acquainted with builders and contractors and renewing old ac-

quaintances. He discussed what services his company had to offer and did, in fact, increase business through these contacts, although no direct relationship could be established. T and his wife did not particularly enjoy these tours but were encouraged to attend by T's employer. In fact, T's employer gave him time off, in addition to his regular vacations, to go on these tours. T incurred the expenses for the actual tours. Because of the increase in business, T received a promotion and increase in salary. Is T allowed a deduction under § § 162 and 274 for these expenditures?

54. (a) M, a self-employed nurse, moved to Phoenix from Baltimore and eventually met the 78-week requirement. She took a deduction for her moving expenses in the year she met the time requirement rather than in the earlier year in which they were incurred. Is this treatment acceptable?

(b) T, a self-employed court reporter, moved from San Francisco to Washington, D.C. After nine months in Washington, she determined that the apartment she had rented was in the path of airplanes landing and taking off from National Airport. The noise so interfered with her work that she moved back to San Francisco without meeting the time requirements. She claimed the airport noise constituted a disability on her part and that her moving expenses should be allowed. Does she get the deduction?

55. T lived in the downtown area of Milwaukee, Wisconsin, and worked in a warehouse five miles from his home. In May, T's employer shifted the location of the entire business to a suburb of Milwaukee and purchased a new warehouse in that suburb. The new warehouse is 30 miles from T's old home, but that 30-mile drive goes through the downtown area and requires 1-1/2 hours in rush hour traffic. T chose a 45-mile route that avoids downtown and requires 45 minutes of driving.

In August, T moved to a new home near the new warehouse. T wishes to deduct the moving expenses, because the reasonable increase in distance from his old home to the new warehouse was 40 miles. Will the deduction be allowed?

Partial list of research aids:
Robert R. Incollingo v. Comm., 45 TCM 350, T.C. Memo. 1982–727.

56. Z, a college professor, accepted a two-year appointment with State University to teach in its overseas program. He would be out of the country for two years. State University has a contract with the U.S. Government to provide college credit courses for service personnel at various U. S. military bases in Europe.

Does Z's income from State University qualify as foreign earned income under § 911? How should he treat his living and traveling expenses while abroad?

57. The Ultra Modern National Bank devoted considerable effort to maintaining the goodwill of the key people (e. g., lawyers, customers, politicians) in the local community. One of its efforts was to invite such individuals to the bank president's home for cocktail parties, dinners, etc. During such occasions, the bank officials were instructed to mingle with the invited guests and to engage in business discussions when warranted by the occasion. The officers maintained detailed records of the business conversations

with the guests, and the bank feels that it is entitled to deduct the full cost of the entertainment expenses as "associated with" entertainment.

Are these expenses deductible under § 274?

Partial list of research aids:

St. Petersburg Bank and Trust Co. v. U. S., 73–2 USTC ¶ 9683, 32 AFTR2d 73–5679, 362 F.Supp. 674 (D.Ct.Fla., 1973).

Chapter 11

Deductions and Losses: Certain Itemized Deductions

GENERAL CLASSIFICATION OF EXPENSES

Personal expenditures are specifically disallowed by § 262 as deductions in arriving at taxable income. Personal expenses may be contrasted with business expenses which are incurred in the production or expectation of profit. Business expenditures are adjustments to gross income in arriving at adjusted gross income and are reported on Schedule C of Form 1040. Certain nonbusiness expenses are also deductible in arriving at adjusted gross income (e. g., expenses attributable to rents and royalties and forfeited interest on a time savings deposit).

This chapter is principally concerned with expenses which are essentially personal in nature but which are deductible due to specific legislative grace (e. g., contributions, medical expenses, and certain state and local taxes). If the Code does not specifically state that a personal type of expense is deductible, no deduction is permitted. Allowable personal expenses are deductible *from* adjusted gross income in arriving at taxable income to the extent that they exceed the zero bracket amount. At this point, it may be helpful to review the computation in the tax formula for individuals which appears in Chapters 1 and 4.

MEDICAL EXPENSES

GENERAL REQUIREMENTS

Medical expenses paid for the care of the taxpayer, spouse, and dependents[1] are allowed under § 213 as an itemized deduction to the extent the expenses are "not compensated for by insurance or otherwise . . ." [i. e., not reimbursed to the taxpayer or paid to anyone else (such as to a doctor or a hospital) by hospital, health, or accident insurance or by an employer]. Further, the medical expense deduction is limited to the amount of such expenses that exceeds five percent (three percent before 1983) of the taxpayer's adjusted gross income. The rationale for allowing a medical deduction solely for amounts in excess of such limits is based on social considerations. Since five percent of adjusted gross income is considered by Congress to be a normal yearly expenditure, only amounts in excess of this percentage are deductible.

The term "medical care" includes expenditures incurred for the "diagnosis, cure, mitigation, treatment, or prevention of disease."[2] The term also includes expenditures incurred for "affecting any structure or function of the body."[3] A taxpayer cannot deduct medical expenses that provide both therapeutic benefits and personal enjoyment unless the expenditure is necessary and is the only method of treating the illness. The IRS has ruled that the cost of a program to stop smoking is not deductible as a medical expense, because the cost is incurred for the purpose of improving the taxpayer's general health and not for the purpose of curing any specific ailment or disease.[4] A similar ruling has been issued denying the cost of a weight reduction program.[5]

The deductibility of nursing home expenses depends on the medical condition of the patient and the nature of the services rendered.[6] If an individual enters a home for the aged for personal or family considerations and not because he or she requires medical or nursing attention, deductions are allowed only for the costs which are attributable to the medical and nursing care (i. e., meals and lodging normally are not considered a cost of medical care).

> **Example 1.** T is totally disabled and has a chronic heart ailment. His children have decided to place T in a nursing home

---

1. To qualify as a taxpayer's dependent for the medical expense deduction, it is not necessary to meet the gross income or joint return test. Reg. § 1.213–(1)(a)(3). Refer to Chapter 4 for a discussion of the dependency tests.
2. Reg. § 1.213–1(e).
3. § 213(e)(1)(A).
4. Rev.Rul. 79–162, 1979–1 C.B. 116.
5. Rev.Rul. 79–151, 1979–1 C.B. 116. However, in IRS Letter Ruling No. 8004111 (October 31, 1979) the taxpayer was allowed a medical deduction for the costs incurred in weight reduction programs for specific diseases (e. g., hypertension, obesity, and hearing problems).
6. Reg. § 1.213–1(e)(1)(v).

which is equipped to provide medical and nursing care facilities. Total nursing home expenses amount to $15,000 per year. Of this amount, $4,500 is directly attributable to medical and nursing care. Since T is in need of significant medical and nursing care and is placed into the facility primarily for this purpose, all $15,000 of the nursing home costs are deductible. Only $4,500 of the expenses would be deductible if T were placed in the home primarily for personal or family considerations.

Tuition expenses of a dependent at a special school may be deductible as a medical expense. The cost of medical care includes the expenses of a special school for a mentally or physically handicapped individual if his condition is such that the resources of the school for alleviating such infirmities are a principal reason for his presence there. If this is the case, the cost of meals and lodging, in addition to the tuition, is a proper medical expense deduction.[7]

> **Example 2.** T's daughter, D, attended public school through the seventh grade. Because D was a poor student, she was tested by a clinical psychologist who diagnosed an organic problem which created a learning disability. D was enrolled in a private school so that she would receive individual attention. Since this school has no special program for students with learning disabilities, nor does it provide special medical treatment, the expenses related to D's attendance are not deductible under § 213(a) as medical expenses.

CAPITAL EXPENDITURES FOR MEDICAL PURPOSES

Normally, capital expenditures for medical purposes are adjustments to basis and are not deductible, because the Code makes no provision for depreciation relative to these capital improvements. However, a capital expenditure for a permanent improvement and expenditures made for its operation or maintenance may both qualify as medical expenses. Some examples of capital expenditures for medical purposes are swimming pools if the taxpayer does not have access to a neighborhood pool, air conditioners if they do not become permanent improvements,[8] dust elimination systems,[9] elevators,[10] and a room built to house an iron lung. These expenditures are medical in nature if they are incurred as a medical necessity upon the advice of a physician, the facility is used primarily by the taxpayer alone, and the expense is reasonable. A capital improvement which otherwise quali-

---

7. *Donald R. Pfeifer,* 37 TCM 817, T.C.Memo. 1978–189. Also see Rev.Rul. 78–340, 1978–2 C.B. 124.
8. Rev.Rul. 55–261, 1955–1 C.B. 307, modified by Rev.Rul. 68–212, 1968–1 C.B. 91.
9. *F. S. Delp,* 30 T.C. 1230 (1958).
10. *Riach v. Frank,* 62–1 USTC ¶ 9419, 9 AFTR2d 1263, 302 F.2d 374.

fies as a medical expenditure is deductible to the extent that the expenditure exceeds the increase in value of the related property.[11] It should be noted that the appraisal costs would also be deductible under § 212(3), since such amounts are expenses incurred in the determination of the taxpayer's tax liability.

> **Example 3.** The taxpayer is advised by his physician to install an elevator in his residence so that the taxpayer's wife, who is afflicted with heart disease, will not be required to climb the stairs. If the cost of installing the elevator is $3,000 and the increase in the value of the residence is determined to be only $1,700, $1,300 is deductible as a medical expense. Additional utility costs to operate the elevator should also be deductible as medical expenses.

TRANSPORTATION AND TRAVEL EXPENSES FOR MEDICAL TREATMENT

Expenditures for a taxi, airplane, train, etc., to and from a point of treatment are deductible as medical expenses. However, the amount allowable as a deduction for "transportation primarily for and essential to medical care" generally does not include meals and lodging while away from home receiving medical treatment.[12]

Food and beverages prescribed for the alleviation or treatment of an illness are deductible if the prescribed food and beverages are not a substitute for food and beverages ordinarily consumed.[13] In the case of lodging, such expenses are generally not deductible under § 213. However, the Regulations under § 213 provide an exception in the case of lodging expenses that result from inpatient hospital care provided in institutions other than hospitals.[14] In some unusual circumstances, lodging expenses are allowed as medical expenses when the taxpayer is not staying overnight at a hospital or other institution that regularly provides medical care. For example, the Seventh Circuit in *Kelly v. Comm.*[15] allowed a deduction for hotel room expenses for a taxpayer who was convalescing in a motel from an appendectomy because he was forced to move out of the hospital due to a shortage of rooms. Consequently, lodging expenses may be deductible if the lodging is a substitute for a hospital room.

---

11. Reg. § 1.213–1(e)(1)(iii).
12. Reg. § 1.213–1(e)(1)(iv); *Comm. v. Bilder,* 62–1 USTC ¶ 9440, 9 AFTR 2d 1355, 82 S.Ct. 881 (USSC, 1962). In this case, a taxpayer who had a history of heart trouble was ordered by his physician to spend the winter months in Florida. The taxpayer was not permitted to deduct rental expenses incurred in Florida as a medical expense.
13. *L.R. Cohn,* 38 T.C. 387(1962).
14. Reg. § 1.213–1(e)(1)(v).
15. 71–1 USTC π 9282, 27 AFTR2d 71–912, 440 F.2d 307; also see *Vowiler v. Comm.* 57 T.C. 367, 371(1971).

The IRS currently allows a deduction of nine cents a mile for the use of an automobile in traveling for medical treatment.[16]

Example 4. T was ordered by his doctor to receive specialized medical care which could only be rendered in a hospital in Boston. T resides in Columbus, Ohio, and incurred transportation costs of $300 to reach the Boston hospital. The transportation costs of $300 are deductible as medical expenses because the expenditure was "primarily for and essential to medical care."

AMOUNTS PAID FOR MEDICAL INSURANCE PREMIUMS

In years before 1983, one-half of the amount paid for medical care insurance for the taxpayer, spouse, or a dependent was not subject to the percentage limitation for total medical expenses. Such amounts were fully deductible up to $150 per year. Premiums paid in excess of $150 (if any) were included with other medical expenses and were subject to the overall percentage limitation rules.

Beginning in 1983, medical insurance premiums are not treated as a separate item. Instead, premiums are included with other medical expenses and subject to the five percent of AGI limit.

If amounts are paid under an insurance contract to cover loss of life, limb, sight, etc., no amount can be deducted unless the coverage for medical care is separately stated in the contract.

EXPENDITURES FOR MEDICINE AND DRUGS

For years before 1984, § 213(b) permitted a deduction for expenses incurred for medicine and drugs to the extent that such amounts were in excess of one percent of adjusted gross income. The one percent floor on medicine and drugs is eliminated after 1983. Through 1983, the term "medicine and drugs" included those drugs that were "legally procured" and were purchased either with or without a prescription. However, expenditures for such items as toothpaste, shaving lotion, face creams, deodorants, and hand lotions were not deductible. Amounts paid for vitamins, iron supplements, and similar items were deductible if recommended by a doctor. Beginning in 1984, the definition of medicine and drugs will be limited to prescription drugs and insulin.

For years before 1984, if the total amount paid for medicine and drugs exceeded one percent of adjusted gross income, the excess was added to other medical expenses for computing the medical expense deduction. Beginning in 1984, the total cost of such items will be added to other medical expenses.

---

16. Rev. Proc. 82-61, I.R.B. No. 46, p. 28.

Example 5. The taxpayer, a single individual with no dependents, had adjusted gross income of $12,000 for the calendar year 1984. During 1984, he paid a doctor $600 for medical services, a hospital $200 for hospital care, and a pharmacy $300 for medicine and drugs. These payments exceeded the amounts compensated by insurance. Health insurance premiums paid during 1984 totaled $700. The deduction allowable under § 213 for the calendar year 1984 is $1,200:

Payments for medical care in 1984	
Doctor	$ 600
Hospital	200
Health insurance premiums	700
Medicine and drugs	300
Total medical expenses	$1,800
Less: Five percent of $12,000 (adjusted gross income)	600
Allowable deduction for 1984	$1,200

To illustrate how the medical expense deduction is reported, these expenses are shown below as they would appear on Schedule A of Form 1040. Since the 1984 Schedule A was not available at the date of publication of this text, the 1983 Schedule A is used. Using the 1983 Schedule A also illustrates the differences between the 1984 law and the 1983 law. Note that in Example 5, which is based on 1984 law, there is no one percent floor on medical expenses. However, as illustrated in this excerpt from the 1983 Schedule A, the one percent floor did apply in 1983. Thus, the taxpayer's medical deduction in 1984 would be $120 more than the 1983 deduction.

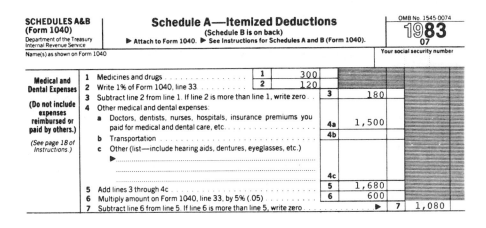

REIMBURSEMENT FOR MEDICAL EXPENSES
PAID IN PRIOR YEARS

When a taxpayer receives an insurance reimbursement for medical expenses deducted in a previous year, the reimbursement must be included in gross income in the year of receipt. Taxpayers are not permitted to include expenses for which reimbursement is anticipated in the computation of the medical expenses for the year such expenses are incurred. Reimbursements in the following year are included in gross income only to the extent that the expenses were deductible in the prior year.[17] If the taxpayer used the zero bracket amount in the year the expenses were incurred rather than itemizing deductions, any reimbursement received in a subsequent year will not be included in gross income. The expenses incurred would not reduce the taxpayer's taxable income for the prior year (i. e., the taxpayer would receive no tax benefit from the deduction).[18]

The following rules apply to reimbursements for medical expenses:[19]

—If the amount of the reimbursement is equal to or less than the amount which was deducted in a prior year, the entire amount is includible in gross income, *or*

—If the amount of the reimbursement is greater than the amount which is deducted, the portion of the reimbursement received which is equal to the deduction taken shall be included in gross income.

Example 6. T has adjusted gross income of $20,000 for 1984. He was injured in a car accident and paid $1,300 for hospitalization expenses and $700 for doctor bills. T also incurred medical expenses of $600 for his child. In 1985, T was reimbursed $600 by his insurance company for his car accident. His deduction for medical expenses in 1984 would be computed as follows:

Hospitalization	$ 1,300
Bills for doctor's services	700
Medical expenses for dependent	600
Total	$ 2,600
Less: Five percent of $20,000	1,000
Medical expense deduction (assuming T itemizes his deductions)	$ 1,600

If medical care reimbursement had occurred in 1984, the medical expense deduction would have been only $1,000 ($1,600 − $600

---

17. Reg. § 1.213–1(g)(1).
18. Reg. § 1.213–1(g)(2). See a discussion of the tax benefit rule in the Glossary of Tax Terms (Appendix C) and in Chapter 6.
19. Reg. § 1.213–1(g)(3).

reimbursement). Since the reimbursement was made in a subsequent year, $600 would be included in gross income for 1985. If T used the zero bracket amount in 1984, the $600 reimbursement would not be included in 1985 gross income, because no tax benefit resulted in 1984.

TAXES

The deduction of state and local taxes paid or accrued by a taxpayer is permitted by § 164. The Committee Reports indicate that the deduction for state and local taxes was created to relieve the burden of multiple taxes upon the same source of revenue.[20] Further, the Committee Reports state that without provision for the deductibility of all non-Federal taxes, state and local governments might be forced to impose additional taxes to generate operating revenues.[21]

DEDUCTIBILITY AS A TAX

One must make a distinction between a "tax" and a "fee," since fees are not deductible unless incurred as an ordinary and necessary business expense under § 162 or as an expense in the production of income under § 212.

The IRS has defined a tax as follows:

> A tax is an enforced contribution exacted pursuant to legislative authority in the exercise of taxing power, and imposed and collected for the purpose of raising revenue to be used for public or governmental purposes, and not as payment for some special privilege granted or service rendered. Taxes are, therefore, distinguished from various other contributions and charges imposed for particular purposes under particular powers or functions of the government. In view of such distinctions, the question whether a particular contribution or charge is to be regarded as a tax depends upon its real nature.[22]

Thus, in accordance with the above definition, fees for dog licenses, automobile inspection, automobile titles and registration, hunting and fishing licenses, bridge and highway tolls, drivers' licenses, parking meter deposits, postage, etc., are not considered to be currently deductible unless incurred as a business expense under § 162 or for the production of income under § 212.

Section 164 lists the following taxes to be deductible whether paid or accrued during the taxable year:

---

20. See Chapter 2 for a discussion of alleviating the effect of multiple taxation.
21. H.R.Rep. No. 749, 88th Cong., 1st Sess., 1964–1 C.B. 171.
22. Rev.Rul. 57–345, 1957–2 C.B. 132 and Rev.Rul. 70–622, 1970–2 C.B. 41.

—State, local, and foreign real property taxes.

—State and local personal property taxes.

—State, local, and foreign income taxes.

—State and local general sales taxes.

—The windfall profit tax.

The following taxes cannot be deducted:[23]

—Federal income taxes, including Social Security and railroad retirement taxes paid by the employee.

—Estate, inheritance, legacy, succession, and gift taxes.

—Foreign income taxes, if the taxpayer claims a foreign tax credit.

—Taxes on real property to the extent that such taxes are to be apportioned and treated as imposed on another taxpayer.

PROPERTY TAXES, ASSESSMENTS, AND APPORTIONMENT OF TAXES

Property Taxes. State, local, and foreign taxes on real and personal property are generally deductible only by the person against whom the tax is imposed. Cash basis taxpayers may deduct these taxes in the year of actual payment, and accrual basis taxpayers may deduct them in the year which fixes the right to deductibility.

Deductible personal property taxes must be ad valorem (i. e., assessed in relation to the value of the property).[24] Therefore, a motor vehicle tax based on weight, model, year, and horsepower is not an ad valorem tax. However, a tax based on value and other criteria may qualify in part.

> **Example 7.** State X imposes a motor vehicle registration tax on 4% of the value of the vehicle plus 40 cents per hundredweight. B, a resident of the state, owns a car having a value of $4,000 and weighing 3,000 pounds. B pays an annual registration fee of $172. Of this amount, $160 (4% of $4,000) would be deductible as a personal property tax. The remaining $12 based on the weight of the car, would not be deductible.

Assessments for Local Benefits. As a general rule, real property taxes do not include taxes assessed for local benefits, since such assessments tend to increase the value of the property (e. g., special assessments for streets, sidewalks, curbing, and other like improvements).[25] A taxpayer cannot deduct the cost of a new sidewalk

---

23. § 164(c)(2) and Reg. § 1.164–2(a) through (e).

24. Reg. § 1.164 3(c). Refer to the discussion of ad valorem taxes on realty and personalty in Chapter 1.

25. Reg. § 1.164–2(g) and 1.164–4(a).

(relative to a personal residence), even though the construction was required by the city and the sidewalk may have provided an incidental benefit to the public welfare.[26] Such assessments are added to the adjusted cost basis of the taxpayer's property.

Assessments for local benefits are deductible as a tax if they are made for maintenance or repair or for meeting interest charges with respect to such benefits. In such cases, the burden is on the taxpayer to show the allocation of the amounts assessed for the different purposes. If the allocation cannot be made, none of the amount paid is deductible.

Apportionment of Taxes on Real Property Between Seller and Purchaser. The real estate taxes for the entire year are apportioned between the buyer and seller on the basis of the number of days the property was held by each in the year of sale.[27] This apportionment is required without regard to whether the tax is paid by the buyer or the seller or is prorated pursuant to the purchase agreement. The rationale for apportioning the taxes between the buyer and seller is based on administrative convenience of the IRS in determining who is entitled to deduct the real estate taxes in the year of sale. In making the apportionment, the assessment date and the lien date are disregarded.

> **Example 8.** The real property tax year in County R is April 1 to March 31. S, the owner on April 1, 19X6, of real property located in County R, sells the real property to B on June 30, 19X6. B owns the real property from June 30, 19X6, through March 31, 19X7. The tax for the real property tax year April 1, 19X6, through March 31, 19X7, is $365. For purposes of § 164(a), $90 (90/365 × $365, April 1 to June 29 of 19X6) of the real property tax is treated as imposed upon S, the seller, and $275 (275/365 × $365, June 30, 19X6, to March 31, 19X7) of such tax is treated as imposed upon B, the purchaser.[28]

If the actual real estate taxes are not prorated between the buyer and seller as part of the purchase agreement, adjustments are required in the determination of the amount realized by the seller and the adjusted cost basis of the property to the buyer.[29] If the buyer pays the entire amount of the tax, he or she has, in effect, paid the seller's portion of the real estate tax and has, therefore, paid more for the property than the actual selling price. Thus, the amount of real estate tax which is apportioned to the seller (for tax purposes) is added to the buyer's adjusted cost basis. The seller must increase the amount realized on the sale by the same amount.

---

26. *Erie H. Rose,* 31 TCM 142, T.C.Memo. 1972–39; Reg. § 1.164–4(a).
27. § 164(d).
28. Reg. § 1.164–6(b)(3) Ex. (1).
29. §§ 1001(b)(2) and 1012; Reg. §§ 1.1001–1(b) and 1.1012–1(b).

Example 9. S sells real estate on June 30, 19X6, for $50,000. The buyer, B, pays the real estate taxes of $1,000 for the calendar year. Of the real estate taxes, $500 is apportioned to and is deductible by the seller, S, and $500 of the taxes is deductible by B. The buyer has, in effect, paid S's real estate taxes of $500 and has therefore paid $50,500 for the property. B's basis is increased to $50,500, and the amount realized by S from the sale is increased to $50,500.

The opposite result occurs if the seller (rather than the buyer) pays the real estate taxes. In this case, the seller reduces the amount realized from the sale by the amount which has been apportioned to the buyer. The buyer is required to reduce his or her adjusted cost basis by a corresponding amount.

Example 10. S sells property for $50,000 on June 30, 19X6. While S held the property, he paid the real estate taxes for the calendar year in the amount of $1,000. Although S paid the entire $1,000 of real estate tax, $500 of that amount is apportioned to B and is therefore deductible by B. The effect is that the buyer, B, has paid only $49,500 for the property. The amount realized by S, the seller, is reduced by $500, and the buyer reduces his cost basis in the property to $49,500.

INCOME TAXES

State, local, or foreign income taxes are not deductible *for* adjusted gross income unless the taxes are incurred in a trade or business or for the production of income. Personal use taxes are deductible only *from* AGI as itemized deductions.[30] It is the position of the IRS that state income taxes imposed upon an individual are deductible only as itemized deductions even if the taxpayer's sole source of income is from business, rents, or royalties.[31]

Cash basis taxpayers are entitled to deduct state income taxes withheld by the employer in the year such amounts are withheld. In addition, estimated state income tax payments are deductible in the year the payment is made by cash basis taxpayers even if the payments relate to a prior or subsequent year.[32] If the taxpayer overpays the state income taxes due to excessive withholdings or estimated tax payments, the refund which is received must be included in gross

30. Rev.Rul. 70–40, 1970–1 C.B. 50; *Tanner v. Comm.,* 66–2 USTC ¶ 9537, 18 AFTR2d 5125, 363 F.2d 36 (CA–4, 1966).
31. *Your Federal Income Tax,* IRS Publication 17 (Rev. Oct. 83), p. 123.
32. *Lillian B. Glassell,* 12 T.C. 232 (1949); *Estate of Aaron Lowenstein, First National Bank of Mobile, Executor,* 12 T.C. 694 (1949); Rev.Rul. 71–190, 1971–1 C.B. 70.

income of the following year to the extent that the deduction provided a tax benefit in the prior year.[33]

> **Example 11.** T is a cash basis taxpayer who had $800 state income tax withheld during 19X7. In addition, she made quarterly estimated payments amounting to $400 in 19X7. These payments and withholdings of $1,200 were deducted on T's 19X7 return which was filed in April 19X8. However, if her actual liability for the 19X7 state income tax was only $1,000, the $200 refund received in 19X8 would be included in gross income on T's Federal income tax return for 19X8.

GENERAL SALES TAXES

State and local sales taxes are deductible by the consumer provided the tax is separately stated and imposed upon the consumer (i. e., the tax is added to the sales price and collected or charged as a separate item).[34] Whether a state or local tax is imposed on the retailer or consumer depends on state and local law. In most instances, state and local sales taxes are deemed to be passed on to the consumer and are therefore deductible.

The tax will be considered separately stated, to meet the requirement noted above, if it clearly appears that at the time of sale to the consumer the tax was added to the sales price and collected or charged as a separate item. It is not necessary that the consumer be furnished with a sales slip, bill, invoice, or other statement on which the tax is separately stated.[35]

To aid the taxpayer, the IRS issues optional state sales tax tables. These tables are reprinted in Appendix A–3. It should be noted that the tables can be used only if deductions are being itemized on Schedule A of Form 1040.

The state sales tax tables are based on the taxpayer's adjusted gross income plus nontaxable items such as tax-exempt interest and Social Security benefits. The table does not include sales taxes on specific purchases such as automobiles, boats, airplanes, and materials for a new home (if the tax is separately stated on the invoice).[36] In addition, the tables generally do not make any provision for county and local sales taxes. Thus, sales tax on specified major purchase items and county and local sales taxes, if not included in the table amount, must be added to the amount which is derived from the sales tax table.

---

33. Rev.Rul. 79–15, 1979–1 C.B. 80 illustrates the application of the zero bracket amount in computing the amount of a state income tax refund that is excludible from gross income under the tax benefit rule.
34. Reg. § 1.164–5.
35. Reg. § 1.164–5.
36. *Your Federal Income Tax,* IRS Publication 17 (Rev. Nov. 83) p. 122.

Example 12. T has a wife and two dependent children and was a resident of Ohio during 1983. His adjusted gross income was $28,000. T received $2,100 of income which was nontaxable during the year (i. e., tax-exempt interest). He had no major purchases during the year. County and local sales taxes are levied at a rate of two percent. T's sales tax deduction using the optional sales tax tables is computed as follows:

Adjusted gross income	$ 28,000	
Add: Nontaxable income	2,100	
Base for sales tax table (total available income)	$ 30,100	
Tax per table		$ 297
Add: County and local sales taxes $\frac{2\%}{4\%}\left(\frac{\text{local and county rate}}{\text{Ohio rate}}\right) \times \$297$		148
Total sales tax deduction		$ 445

If the taxpayer's records indicate that more taxes were paid than the amount shown in the tables, the larger amount may be deducted. However, a taxpayer has the burden of proving that he or she is entitled to the amount claimed as a sales tax deduction. If there is no evidence to indicate that the amount allowed by the IRS is incorrect, the allowance stated in the optional tables will be approved.[37]

FILING REQUIREMENTS

Deductible state and local taxes are reported on Schedule A of Form 1040. For example, if the taxpayer had incurred $1,200 of state and local income taxes, $600 of real estate taxes on his residence, general sales taxes of $420 (as determined by the state sales tax tables), and personal property taxes of $275, these items would appear on Schedule A as noted below.

Taxes				
Taxes	8	State and local income	8	1,200
(See page 19 of Instructions.)	9	Real estate	9	600
	10 a	General sales (see sales tax tables)	10a	420
	b	General sales on motor vehicles	10b	
	11	Other (list—include personal property) ▶	11	275
	12	Add lines 8 through 11. Write your answer here ▶	12	2,495

---

37. *Bradford v. Comm.*, 65–1 USTC ¶ 9401, 15 AFTR2d 1106 (CA–2, 1965) and *Harry A. Koch Co. v. Vinal*, 64–1 USTC ¶ 9401, 13 AFTR2d 1241, 228 F.Supp. 782 (D.Ct.Neb., 1964).

INTEREST

A deduction for interest has been allowed since enactment of the income tax law in 1913. Despite its long history of Congressional acceptance, the interest deduction continues to be one of the most controversial areas in the tax law.

The controversy centers around the propriety of deducting interest charges for the purchase of consumer goods and services and interest on borrowings which are used to acquire investments (i. e., investment interest). Currently, various limitations are imposed on the deductibility of prepaid interest and the deduction of interest on funds which are used to acquire investment property. In addition, no deduction is permitted for interest on debt incurred to purchase or carry tax-exempt securities.

ALLOWED AND DISALLOWED ITEMS

Interest has been defined by the Supreme Court as compensation for the use or forbearance of money.[38] The general rule permits a deduction for all interest paid or accrued within the taxable year on indebtedness.[39] This general rule is modified by other Code provisions which disallow or restrict certain interest deductions.[40] Generally, a deduction is allowed for the following:

—Mortgage interest.

—Loan origination fees (i. e., points paid by the buyer of a principal residence).

—Mortgage prepayment penalty.

—Finance charges separately stated.

—Bank credit card plan interest.

—Note discount interest.

—Penalty for late payment of utility bills.

Generally, a deduction is not allowed for:

—Points if paid by a seller.

—Service charges.

—Credit investigation fees.

—Loan placement fees paid by a seller of property.

—Nonredeemable ground rents.

—Interest relative to tax-exempt income.

---

38. *Old Colony Railroad Co. v. Comm.,* 3 USTC ¶ 880, 10 AFTR 786, 52 S.Ct. 211 (USSC, 1936).
39. § 163(a).
40. § § 163(b) and (d), 264 through 267 and 483.

—Interest paid to carry single premium life insurance.

—Premiums paid on the purchase of a convertible bond arising from the conversion feature.

RESTRICTIONS ON DEDUCTIBILITY AND TIMING CONSIDERATIONS

Taxpayer's Obligation. Interest is deductible if the related debt represents a bona fide obligation for which the taxpayer is liable.[41] Thus, a taxpayer is not allowed a deduction for interest paid on behalf of another individual. To insure the deduction of interest, both debtor and creditor must intend that the loan be repaid. Intent of the parties can be especially crucial between related parties such as a shareholder and a closely-held corporation. A shareholder may not deduct interest paid by the corporation on his or her behalf.[42] Likewise, a husband cannot deduct interest paid on his wife's property if they file separate returns.[43]

Time of Deduction. Generally, interest must be paid to secure a deduction unless the taxpayer uses the accrual method of accounting. Under the accrual method, interest is deductible ratably over the life of the loan.[44]

> **Example 13.** T borrows $1,000 on November 2, 19X6. The loan is payable in 90 days at 6% interest. On February 1, 19X7, T pays the $1,000 note and interest amounting to $15. The accrued portion ($\frac{2}{3} \times \$15 = \$10$) of the interest is deductible by T in 19X6 only if he is an accrual basis taxpayer. Otherwise, the entire amount of interest ($15) is deductible in 19X7.

Prepaid Interest. The Tax Reform Act of 1976 effectively imposes accrual method requirements on cash basis taxpayers relative to interest prepayments which extend beyond the end of the taxable year.[45] Such payments must be capitalized and allocated to the subsequent periods to which the interest payments relate. These restrictions do not apply to points (loan origination fees) paid by the purchaser of a principal residence if charging points is customary and the points do not exceed a normal rate.[46] These changes were intended to prevent cash basis taxpayers from "manufacturing" tax deductions prior to the end of the year by entering into prepayment of interest agreements.

---

41. *Arcade Realty Co.,* 35 T.C. 256 (1960).
42. *Continental Trust Co.,* 7 B.T.A. 539 (1927).
43. *Colston v. Burnet,* 3 USTC ¶ 947, 11 AFTR 606, 59 F.2d 867 (CA–D.C., 1932).
44. Reg. § 1.461–1(a)(2) and *Chas. Schaefer and Son, Inc.,* 20 T.C. 558 (1953).
45. § 461(g).
46. § 461(g)(2).

CLASSIFICATION OF INTEREST EXPENSE

Whether interest is deductible *for* adjusted gross income or as an itemized deduction depends on whether the indebtedness has a business, investment, or personal purpose. If the indebtedness is incurred in relation to a business or for the production of rent or royalty income, the interest is deductible *for* adjusted gross income.[47] However, if the indebtedness is incurred for personal use, the deduction must be reported as an itemized deduction on Schedule A of Form 1040. Schedule A deductions are allowed only if the taxpayer has itemized deductions in excess of the zero bracket amount. See Appendix B–2, Form 1040. Business expenses appear on Schedule C of Form 1040.

The courts have established that the use to which the borrowed funds are put, not the security behind the obligation, governs the nature of the debt (i. e., business or nonbusiness).[48]

> **Example 14.** If T mortgages his home to raise money for his business, the interest is deductible as a business expense. However, if the funds were used to purchase security investments, the interest expense would be deductible only if T elects to itemize his deductions on Schedule A of Form 1040.

The interest expense deduction is reported on Schedule A of Form 1040. Thus, if the taxpayer has interest expense from his home mortgage of $3,500, interest of $110 on credit cards, and $1,150 interest expense from his car loan, these interest charges would appear on Schedule A as shown below.

Interest Expense (See page 20 of Instructions.)	13 a Home mortgage interest paid to financial institutions	13a	3,500	
	b Home mortgage interest paid to individuals (show that person's name and address) ▶	13b		
	14 Credit cards and charge accounts	14	110	
	15 Other (list) ▶	15	1,150	
	16 Add lines 13a through 15. Write your answer here ▶	16	4,760	

DISALLOWANCE POSSIBILITIES

Related Parties. There is nothing to prevent the deduction of interest paid to a related party as long as the payment actually took place and meets the usual requirement for deduction as stated above. Recall from Chapter 7 that there is a special rule for related taxpayers which is applicable when the debtor uses the accrual basis and the related creditor is on the cash basis.[49] If this rule is applicable, interest which has been accrued but not paid at the end of the debtor's tax year must be paid within two and one-half months. Otherwise, no

47. § 62(1) and (5).
48. *Wharton v. U. S.,* 53–2 USTC ¶ 9597, 44 AFTR 512, 207 F.2d 526 (CA–5, 1953).
49. § 267(a)(2).

interest deduction is permitted to the accrual basis debtor even if such amounts are paid following the expiration of the two and one-half month period.

Tax-Exempt Securities. Section 265 provides that no deduction is allowed for interest on debt incurred to purchase or carry tax-exempt securities. A major problem has been for the courts to determine what is meant by the words "to purchase or carry." Refer to Chapter 7 for a detailed discussion of these complex issues.

Interest on Investment Indebtedness. High-income taxpayers frequently borrow funds which are then used to acquire low income-producing assets (e. g., vacant land held for appreciation or low-yield high-growth stocks). The deduction of interest expense coupled with little or no offsetting ordinary income and the eventual sale of the assets at favorable long-term capital gain rates would result in substantial tax benefits. Congress, therefore, has placed limitations on the deductibility of interest when funds are borrowed for the purpose of purchasing or continuing to hold investment property.[50] The limitations do not apply to corporate taxpayers or to interest expense which is incurred for business use. Interest that can be deducted is limited to the following:

—$10,000 plus

—The amount of net investment income (if any).

Amounts which are disallowed may be carried over and treated as investment interest of the succeeding year. Investment income is defined as the gross income from interest, dividends, rents, royalties, net short-term capital gains attributed to the property held for investment, and ordinary income from the recapture of depreciation under § 1245 and § 1250. Investment expenses are deducted from investment income in arriving at net investment income.

> **Example 15.** T had net investment income of $15,000 and paid $60,000 of investment interest. His deduction in the current year is $25,000. This interest deduction is calculated as follows:
>
> | | |
> |---|---:|
> | Floor | $ 10,000 |
> | Net investment income | 15,000 |
> | Current year deduction | $ 25,000 |

[handwritten annotation: so that deduction can't be carried over into other incomes]

T would be allowed a carryover of $35,000.

Form 4952, Investment Interest Expense Deduction, is used to calculate the current deduction and the amount of any carryover. For individuals, if the investment interest expense pertains to rental property, it is reported in Part I of Schedule E, Supplemental Income

---

50. § 163(d).

Schedule; otherwise it is reported in the interest expense section of Schedule A.

Interest Paid for Services. It is common practice in the mortgage loan business to charge a fee for finding, placing, or processing a mortgage loan. Such fees are often called "points" and are expressed as a percentage of the loan amount. In periods of tight money, it may be necessary to pay points to obtain the necessary financing. To qualify as deductible interest, the points must be considered compensation to a lender solely for the use or forbearance of money.[51] The points cannot be a form of service charge or payment for specific services if they are to qualify as deductible interest.[52] Points paid by the seller are not deductible because the debt on which they are paid is not the debt of the seller.[53] Points paid by the seller are treated as a reduction of the selling price of the property. If the points are paid by the buyer and are for the use or forbearance of money, the points are immediately deductible if they are not prepaid interest which must be capitalized and amortized.[54]

The 1968 Federal Truth in Lending Act, which requires disclosure of finance charges as an annual percentage, has simplified the determination of whether a charge is interest or a fee for servicing the account. The IRS has ruled that the following charges are deductible as interest:[55] finance charges on gasoline credit cards, on department store purchases, and on bank credit cards.

INSTALLMENT PURCHASES—INTEREST NOT SEPARATELY STATED

Whenever a taxpayer enters into a contract to purchase personal property (furniture, household appliances, etc.) that requires installment payments and there is a separately stated carrying charge but the interest is not separately stated, interest is imputed (charged) at six percent according to § 163(b). This interest is imputed to the contract regardless of whether payments are made when due or are in default. They are still deductible. The six percent interest charge allowable as an itemized deduction is considerably lower than installment interest presently charged by bank credit cards. Undoubtedly, Congress will update the imputed interest figure to a more realistic amount. This calculation is, however, seldom necessary as a result of the requirement that finance charges be disclosed as an annual percentage (see the preceding discussion of the 1968 Federal Truth in Lending Act).

---

51.   Rev.Rul. 69–188, 1969–1 C.B. 54; amplified by Rev.Rul. 69–582, 1969–2 C.B. 29.
52.   Rev.Rul. 67–297, 1967–2 C.B. 87.
53.   *Robert T. Hunt,* 24 TCM 915, T.C.Memo. 1965–172.
54.   § 461(g)(2).
55.   Rev.Rul. 73–136, 1973–1 C.B. 68; Rev.Rul. 72–315, 1972–1 C.B. 49; and Rev.Rul. 71–98, 1971–1 C.B. 57.

CHARITABLE CONTRIBUTIONS

RATIONALE FOR DEDUCTIBILITY

Section 170 permits the deduction of contributions made to qualified domestic organizations by individuals and corporations. Contributions to qualified charitable organizations serve certain social welfare needs and, therefore, relieve the government of the cost of providing these needed services to the community.[56]

CRITERIA FOR A "GIFT"

Section 170(c) defines "charitable contribution" as a gift made to a qualified organization. The major elements needed to qualify a contribution as a gift are a donative intent, the absence of consideration, and acceptance by the donee. Consequently, the taxpayer has the burden of establishing that the transfer was made from motives of "disinterested generosity" as established by the courts.[57] As one can imagine, this test is quite subjective and has led to problems of interpretation. For example, a taxpayer engaged in a trade or business may attempt to qualify an expenditure as an ordinary and necessary business expense under § 162 rather than as a charitable contribution, since contributions are subject to certain ceiling limitations.

> **Example 16.** X is a travel agent and has for a number of years conducted most of his business with clients who are charitable organizations as described under § 170. At the end of each year, payments were made directly to these organizations, the amount of which depended directly on the volume and profitability of the business relationship. These payments are not charitable contributions but are business expenses under § 162; therefore, the charitable contribution limitations do not apply.[58]

QUALIFIED ORGANIZATIONS

To be deductible, a contribution must be made to one of the following organizations:[59]

—A state or possession of the United States or any subdivisions thereof.

—A corporation, trust, or community chest, fund, or foundation that is situated in the United States and is organized and oper-

---

56. Refer to the discussion of tax policy in Chapter 2.
57. *Comm. v. Duberstein,* 60–2 USTC ¶ 9515, 5 AFTR2d 1626, 80 S.Ct. 1190 (USSC, 1960).
58. *Sarah Marquis,* 49 T.C. 695 (1968).
59. § 170(c).

ated exclusively for religious, charitable, scientific, literary, or educational purpose or for the prevention of cruelty to children or animals.

—A veterans' organization.

—A fraternal organization operating under the lodge system.

—A cemetery company.

The IRS publishes a list of organizations which have applied for and received tax-exempt status under § 501 of the Code.[60] This publication is updated frequently and may be helpful to determine if a gift has been made to a qualifying charitable organization.

Gifts made to needy individuals are generally not deductible; therefore, a deduction will not be permitted if a gift is received by a donee in an individual capacity rather than as a representative of a qualifying organization.

TIME OF PAYMENT

The Code permits a contribution deduction generally in the year the payment is made. This requirement extends to both cash and accrual basis individuals.[61] An accrual basis corporation, however, is permitted a deduction if the contribution is made within two and one-half months of the close of the taxable year and if the board of directors authorizes such payment prior to the end of the taxable year.[62]

A contribution is ordinarily deemed to have been made on the delivery of the property to the donee. For example, if a gift of securities (properly endorsed) is made to a qualified charitable organization, the gift is considered complete on the day of delivery or mailing. However, if the donor delivers the certificate to his bank or broker or to the issuing corporation, the gift is considered complete on the date that the stock is transferred on the books of the corporation.[63]

VALUATION PROBLEMS

Property donated to a charity is generally valued at fair market value at the time the gift is made. The Code and Regulations give very little guidance on the measurement of the fair market value except to say, "The fair market value is the price at which the property would change hands between a willing buyer and a willing seller, neither being under any compulsion to buy or sell and both having reasonable

---

60. Although this *Cumulative List of Organizations* (IRS Publication 78) may be helpful, it is not required that a qualified organization be listed. Not all organizations that qualify are listed in this publication (e. g., American Red Cross, University of Cleveland).

61. § 170(a)(1). Also see *infra,* Footnote 90.

62. § 170(a)(2). See the discussion in Chapter 20.

63. Reg. § 1.170–1(b).

knowledge of relevant facts."[64] The IRS has established guidelines[65] for appraising contributed property, and many established charities offer appraisal services to donors. Contributed property that has a value of $200 or more must be fully described, and a statement of how the property was valued must accompany the taxpayer's return.[66]

LIMITATIONS ON CHARITABLE DEDUCTIONS

In General. Charitable contributions are subject to certain overall ceiling limitations (i. e., contributions for individuals are limited to 50 percent of the taxpayer's adjusted gross income, and in some cases, a 30 percent ceiling limitation is imposed for contributions of capital gain property).[67] Certain contributions of individuals are subject to either a 50 percent or 20 percent limitation for contributions to certain private foundations. The distinction between the ceiling limitations for private foundations is discussed below. Corporations are subject to an overall limitation of 10 percent of taxable income computed without regard to the contributions made and certain other adjustments.[68]

In addition, the contribution of certain types of property (e. g., inventory) may result in a deduction of less than the fair market value of such property.

Ordinary Income Property. Ordinary income property is any property which, if sold, will result in the recognition of ordinary income.[69] The term includes inventory for sale in the taxpayer's trade or business, a work of art created by the donor, a manuscript prepared by the donor, and a capital asset held by the donor for less than the required holding period for long-term capital gain treatment. Also included is property that results in the recognition of ordinary income due to the recapture of depreciation. If ordinary income property is contributed, the deduction is equal to the fair market value of the property less the amount of ordinary income which would have been reported if the property were sold (i. e., in most instances, the deduction is limited to the cost basis of the property to the donor).[70] *basis is deductible*

> **Example 17.** T owned stock in EC Corporation which he donated to a local university on May 1, 19X7. T had purchased the stock for $2,500 on April 3, 19X7, and the stock had a value of

---

64. Reg. § 1.170–1(c)(1).
65. Rev.Proc. 66–49, 1966–2 C.B. 1257.
66. Reg. § 1.170A–1(a)(2)(ii).
67. Under § 170(b) the ceiling limitations apply to the taxpayer's contribution base. Pursuant to § 170(b)(1)(E), the contribution base is defined as adjusted gross income (computed without regard to any net operating loss carryback to the taxable year).
68. § 170(b)(2). See Chapter 20.
69. Reg. § 1.170A–4(b)(1).
70. § 170(e)(1).

$3,600 when he made the donation. Since the property had not been held for a sufficient period to meet the long-term capital gain requirements, a short-term capital gain of $1,100 would have been recognized had the property been sold. Since short-term capital gain property is treated as ordinary income property, T's charitable contribution deduction is limited to the extent of its adjusted basis of $2,500.

A special exception was added by the Tax Reform Act of 1976 which permits a corporation to contribute inventory (ordinary income property) to a public charity or private operating foundation (50 percent charities) and receive a deduction[71] equal to the adjusted basis of the property plus one-half of the difference between the fair market value and the adjusted basis of the property. In no event may the deduction exceed twice the adjusted basis of the property. To qualify for this exception, the inventory must be used by the charity in its exempt purpose for the care of children, the ill, or the needy.

The limitations on ordinary income property were intended to prevent taxpayers from obtaining undue advantage from the contribution of substantially appreciated ordinary income property. For example, a taxpayer (in a 50 percent bracket) who contributed inventory with a fair market value of $100 and an adjusted basis of $40 would receive a tax benefit of $50 (50% × $100) and have a net profit, in effect, of $10 if these limitations did not apply. Application of these rules limits the deduction to $70 [$40 + ½ (100 − 40)] and thus limits the tax benefit to $35 ($70 × 50%).

Capital Gain Property.   Capital gain property is any property that would have resulted in the recognition of long-term capital gain if the property had been sold by the donor.[72] If capital gain property is contributed to a private foundation as defined in § 509(a), the taxpayer must reduce the contribution by 40 percent of the long-term capital gain which would have been recognized if the property had been sold at its fair market value.[73] This reduction was imposed because a taxpayer is not taxed on the appreciated portion of the contributed property at long-term capital gain rates (i. e., 40 percent of the long-term capital gain would have been subject to tax at ordinary rates if the property were sold rather than contributed to the private foundation). It should be noted, however, that contributions of capital gain property to public charities are not generally reduced by 40 percent of the capital gain element.

Example 18.   T purchases stock for $800 on January 1, 1975, and donates it to a private foundation on June 21, 1984, when it

---

71. § 170(e)(3).
72. Reg. § 1.170A–4(b)(2).
73. § 170(e)(1)(B)(ii).

is worth $2,000. T's charitable contribution is $1,520 [$2,000 − (40% × $1,200 appreciation)].

Example 19. Assume the same facts as in the previous example except that T contributed the stock to a public charity (e. g., the YMCA, his church, or a university). T's charitable contribution would be $2,000, since these limitations apply only to private foundations.

Special rules apply to capital gain property which is tangible personalty.[74] If tangible personalty is contributed to a public charity such as a museum, church, or university, the charitable deduction is reduced by 40 percent of the long-term capital gain if the property is put to an <u>unrelated</u> use. A taxpayer in this instance must establish that the property is not in fact being put to an unrelated use by the donee and that at the time of the contribution it was reasonable to anticipate that the property would not be put to an unrelated use. In the case of a contribution of personalty to a museum, if the work of art is the kind of art normally retained by the museum, it will be reasonable for a donor to anticipate that the work of art will not be put to an unrelated use (even if the object is later sold or exchanged).[75]

Example 20. T contributes a Picasso, for which he paid $20,000, to a local museum. It had a value of $30,000 at the time of the donation. The painting was displayed by the museum for a period of two years and subsequently sold for $50,000. The charitable contribution is not reduced by 40 percent of the unrealized appreciation [40% × ($30,000 − $20,000)], since the painting was put to a related use even though it was later sold by the museum.

Contribution of Services. No deduction is allowed under § 170 for a contribution of one's services to a qualified charitable organization. However, unreimbursed expenses related to the services rendered may be deductible. For example, the cost of a uniform (without general utility) which is required to be worn while performing services may be deductible. Deductions are also permitted for transportation and reasonable expenses for meals and lodging while away from home incurred in performance of the donated services.[76]

Example 21. If a delegate representing her church in San Francisco, California, travels to a national meeting in Denver,

---

74. Tangible personalty is all property that is not realty (i. e., land and buildings) and does not include intangible property such as stock or securities.
75. Reg. § 1.170A–4(b)(3)(ii)(b).
76. Reg. § 1.170A–1(g). Under the automatic mileage method, the IRS allows a deduction of nine cents per mile for the use of an automobile in the pursuit of certain charitable activities (e. g., soliciting contributions for a United Fund campaign).

Colorado, the transportation, meals, and lodging would be deductible if the meeting was solely for religious reasons.

Fifty Percent Ceiling Limitation. Contributions made to public charities may not exceed 50 percent of an individual's adjusted gross income for the year.[77] Excess contributions may be carried over to the next five years.[78] The 50 percent ceiling on contributions applies to the following types of public charities:[79]

—A church or a convention or association of churches.

—An educational organization which maintains a regular faculty and curriculum.

—A hospital or medical school.

—An organization supported by the government which holds property or investments for the benefit of a college or university.

—A governmental unit which is Federal, state, or local.

—An organization normally receiving a substantial part of its support from the public or a governmental unit.

—Certain types of private foundations.

Twenty Percent Ceiling. Contributions to most private foundations are limited generally to 20 percent of adjusted gross income. However, a 50 percent limitation generally applies to private foundations that have broad public support.[80] A private foundation is any domestic or foreign organization that is exempt under § 501(c)(3), except an organization that receives more than one-third of its support from the general public, and except churches, schools, hospitals, fund raisers for schools, state and local government units, and publicly supported charities. Contributions to which the 20 percent limitation applies may not be carried forward. Private foundations are described in § 509(a) and are considered public charities or operating foundations for which the 50 percent ceiling applies if they meet the tests of §§ 170(b)(1)(D) and 4942(j)(3). If the tests for an operating foundation are not met, the 20 percent limitation applies.

If substantial contributions are also made to public (50 percent) charities, the limitation to private charities categorized as 20 percent organizations may be less than 20 percent. The deduction for contributions in these cases is the lesser of 20 percent of the taxpayer's contribution base (generally adjusted gross income) or 50 percent × adjusted gross income less the amount of charitable contributions qualifying for the 50 percent deduction ceiling. The excess, if any, cannot be carried over.[81]

---

77. § 170(b).
78. § 170(d)(1).
79. § 170(b)(1)(A).
80. Reg. § 1.509(a)–1.
81. § 170(b)(1)(B).

Example 22. T has adjusted gross income of $15,000. He contributes $5,000 to a local university which is a 50% charity and $4,000 to the XYZ Foundation for the deaf, which is a private foundation. T's contribution deduction is $7,500 (the sum of the $5,000 contribution to the university and $2,500 of the $4,000 contribution to the XYZ Foundation). The lesser of $3,000 (20% × $15,000) or $2,500 [(50% × $15,000) − $5,000] is allowed for the contribution to the XYZ Foundation.

Thirty Percent Ceiling. To prevent possible abuse when a taxpayer contributes appreciated property, specific rules apply to limit the deduction. For example, if capital gain property does not come under the 20 percent limitation for contributions to a private foundation, it is subject to a 30 percent limitation based on the taxpayer's adjusted gross income.[82] Consequently, any capital asset or § 1231 asset that would result in a long-term capital gain if sold is subject to the 30 percent limitation. When applying the limitation rules, contributions to which the 30 percent limit is applicable are the last to be considered.[83]

Example 23. T has adjusted gross income for the taxable year of $20,000. T contributes cash of $6,000 and stock with a cost basis of $3,000 and fair market value of $7,000, which has been held for two years, to a local university. Since the appreciated stock is a capital asset which has been donated to a public charity, it is subject to the 30% limitation of $6,000 (30% of $20,000). Since this contribution plus the cash contribution exceeds 50% of adjusted gross income ($10,000), the actual deduction must be limited to $10,000 or $6,000 cash plus $4,000 in appreciated stock. The $3,000 unused capital gain property contribution can be carried over (subject to the 30% rule) to subsequent years.

According to § 170(e)(1), a taxpayer may elect to reduce the deduction for donated capital gain property by 40 percent of the difference between its fair market value and its adjusted cost basis.[84] In making this election, a taxpayer may receive a larger deduction in the year the contributions are made due to the higher ceiling (i. e., 50 percent in lieu of 30 percent). However, if the property is substantially appreciated, the election will result in a reduction of the contributions which might otherwise be carried forward to subsequent years.

Example 24. In 19X0, T has adjusted gross income of $50,000. During 19X0, T makes charitable contributions to a church of $57,000, consisting of cash of $2,000 and 30% capital gain property with a fair market value of $55,000 and an adjusted basis of $15,000. For 19X0, T elects under § 170(e)(1) to have the 50%

---

82. § 170(b)(1)(D). See the discussion of § 1231 in Chapter 17.
83. § 170(b)(1)(C)(i).
84. § 170(e)(1).

ceiling apply. The appreciation on the 30% property is $40,000 ($55,000 market value − $15,000 basis). The deduction for property that is contributed to the church is reduced by $16,000 ($40,000 appreciation × 40%) and becomes $39,000 ($55,000 − $16,000). Since the 50% ceiling applies to T, T is allowed a $25,000 charitable contribution for 19X0, with a carryover to 19X1 of $16,000 [$41,000 ($2,000 cash + $39,000 property) − $25,000].

Excess Contributions Carryover. Excess contributions to public charities subject to the 50 percent limitation may be carried over for five years.[85] Excess contributions under the 30 percent ceiling are also carried over but are subject to the 30 percent ceiling limitation in the carryover years. In the carryover year, the contributions made during such year are first applied before any carryover amounts are deducted.[86]

> **Example 25.** T, in 19X1, contributes $20,000 cash to a public charity. Her adjusted gross income for 19X1 is $30,000. Since T's contribution ceiling is $15,000 (50% of $30,000), she may carry over $5,000 to 19X2, then, if any remains, to 19X3, etc., through 19X6.

> **Example 26.** Assume the same facts as in the previous example plus for the following information related to 19X2–19X6:

	19X1	19X2	19X3	19X4
Adjusted gross income	$ 30,000	$ 25,000	$ 35,000	$ 40,000
Contributions subject to the 50 percent limitations	20,000	20,000	10,000	10,000
Deductible contributions:				
Current year	15,000	12,500	10,000	10,000
Carryovers from:				
19X1			5,000	
19X2			2,500	5,000
Unused carryovers from:				
19X1	5,000		—	—
19X2		7,500	5,000	—
Total deduction	$ 15,000	$ 12,500	$ 17,500	$ 15,000

Direct Charitable Contributions. Because the zero bracket amount has increased over the past few years, individual taxpayers have found it more difficult to accumulate enough itemized deductions to exceed the zero bracket amount. Consequently, the incentive

---

85. § 170(d)(1).
86. § 170(d)(1)(A).

to make charitable contributions has been reduced. To restore some of this incentive, Congress enacted § 170(i).

According to this provision, a "direct charitable contribution" as defined under § 63(i) will be allowed as a deduction *from* adjusted gross income even by taxpayers who do not itemize. It will be phased in over a five-year period, with a ceiling limitation (i. e., the maximum amount of the contribution that qualifies) for the first three years. The phase-in is scheduled as follows:

Year	Percentage Allowed	Ceiling Limitation
1982	25%	$ 100
1983	25%	$ 100
1984	25%	$ 300
1985	50%	None
1986	100%	None
1987	—Provision Expires—	

Example 27. X and Y are married and file a joint return for 1984. They have $500 in interest expense, $250 in medical expenses after the application of the percentage limitations, and $400 in charitable contributions. Because these expenses do not exceed $3,400 (the zero bracket amount for a joint return), X and Y are not in a position to itemize deductions. However, $75 [$300 ceiling limitation times 25% (percentage allowed)] is permitted as a direct charitable contribution and is deducted *from* adjusted gross income.

The ceiling limitation is not doubled for a married person filing a joint return. Thus, a single taxpayer comes under the same ceiling limitation as a married taxpayer filing a joint return. In the case of a married individual filing a separate return, the ceiling limitation is $50 for tax years beginning in 1982 and 1983 and $150 for tax year 1984. There is no ceiling limitation for tax years beginning in 1985 and 1986. For tax years beginning *after* 1986 the provision for a direct charitable contribution deduction is terminated. Also, there is no carryover provision for excess direct charitable contributions beyond the applicable ceiling limitation.

SUMMARY OF RULES

Figure I reflects a summary of the rules applicable to the contribution of appreciated property by individuals. (Note: the rules for the direct charitable contribution have been omitted.)

SUBSTANTIATION REQUIREMENTS

The IRS has issued Proposed Regulation § 170A–13, which sets out the substantiation requirements for claiming charitable contribu-

Figure I[95]*
DETERMINING THE DEDUCTION FOR CONTRIBUTIONS OF APPRECIATED PROPERTY BY INDIVIDUALS

If the sale of the contributed property by the donor would result in:	and the property is contributed to:	the contribution is measured by:	but the deduction is limited to:	with:
1. Long-term capital gain	a 50 percent organization	fair market value of the property	30 percent of adjusted gross income	a 5-year carryover
2. Ordinary income only	a 50 percent organization	the basis of the property	50 percent of adjusted gross income	a 5-year carryover
3. Long-term capital gain (and the property is tangible personal property put to an unrelated use by the donee)	a 50 percent organization	fair market value minus 40 percent of the appreciation on the property	50 percent of adjusted gross income	a 5-year carryover
4. A portion of ordinary income	a 50 percent organization	fair market value minus ordinary income which would result	50 percent of adjusted gross income	a 5-year carryover
5. Long-term capital gain (and the reduced deduction is elected)	a 50 percent organization	fair market value minus 40 percent of the appreciation on the property	50 percent of adjusted gross income	a 5-year carryover (but no carryover for amount by which deduction is reduced)

6. Long-term capital gain	a 20 percent organization or for the use of a 20 percent or 50 percent organization	fair market value minus 40 percent of the appreciation on the property	the lesser of: 1. 20 percent of adjusted gross income 2. 50 percent of adjusted gross income minus other contributions to 50 percent organizations	no carryover
7. Long-term capital gain (and the property is tangible personal property put to an unrelated use by the donee)	a 20 percent organization or for the use of a 20 percent or 50 percent organization	fair market value minus 40 percent of the appreciation on the property	the lesser of: 1. 20 percent of adjusted gross income 2. 50 percent of adjusted gross income minus other contributions to 50 percent organizations	no carryover
8. Ordinary income only	a 20 percent organization or for the use of a 20 percent or 50 percent organization	the basis of the property	the lesser of: 1. 20 percent of adjusted gross income 2. 50 percent of adjusted gross income minus other contributions to 50 percent organizations	no carryover
9. A portion of ordinary income	a 20 percent organization or for the use of a 20 percent or 50 percent organization	fair market value minus ordinary income which would result from sale of the property	the lesser of: 1. 20 percent of adjusted gross income 2. 50 percent of adjusted gross income minus other contributions to 50 percent organizations	no carryover

95. Adopted with permission of the author and the publisher (*The Accounting Review*) from Eugene Willis, "The Amount of a Charitable Contribution of Property," *The Accounting Review* (April 1977), p. 498.

*Under the Economic Recovery Act of 1981, corporations can make charitable contributions of research property. This provision is omitted from this illustration and is discussed in *West's Federal Taxation: Corporations, Partnerships, Estates, and Trusts.*

tions beginning after 1982. For charitable contributions of money, the taxpayer must maintain one of the following for *each* contribution: (1) a cancelled check; (2) a receipt from the donee showing the date of the contribution, the amount, and the name of the donee; or (3) in the absence of either a cancelled check or a receipt, other reliable written evidence showing the name of the donees and the date and amount of the contribution.

For property other than money, the taxpayer must have a receipt from the donee that contains the name of the donee, the date and the location of the contribution, and a description of the property. If the property contributed results in a contribution in excess of $500, additional records are required regarding the manner of acquisition of the property, and the property's cost or other basis. More stringent requirements must be satisfied for property held for more than a year because of the favorable long-term capital gains rates.

FILING REQUIREMENTS

The deduction for contributions (other than direct charitable contributions) is made as an itemized deduction on Schedule A of Form 1040. Cash contributions which are supported by receipts, cancelled checks, etc., are totaled and listed together on Schedule A. Those cash contributions not supported by cancelled checks or receipts are to be detailed as to payee and amount. Other-than-cash contributions (such as contributions of property or mileage at nine cents per mile incurred in performing charitable work) are reported separately from cash contributions. If the taxpayer makes a gift of property in excess of $200 ($500 under Proposed Regulation § 170A–13), the Regulations require that the taxpayer state the name of each organization to which a contribution was made, the amount of the contribution, and its date. In addition, it is necessary to provide a description of the property, the manner of its acquisition, the fair market value of the property at the time of the gift, the basis of the property, and the terms of any agreement relating to the contribution.[87]

To illustrate the use of Schedule A, assume a taxpayer made the following contributions to qualified charitable organizations during the year:

Payment of a church pledge (cancelled checks retained)	$ 2,800
Donations of cash to door-to-door solicitors—$5 to the March of Dimes, $15 to the Salvation Army Christmas Drive	20

---

87. Reg. § 1.170A–1(a)(2).

Donation of used clothing and certain
household effects (e. g., chairs, table,
baby furniture) to Goodwill Industries.
The property cost $1,200 and had an
estimated fair market value of $300. Re-
ceipts acknowledging the donations
are available.   300

Presuming there is no problem with the percentage limitations, the
completed portion of Schedule A that is relevant is reproduced below.

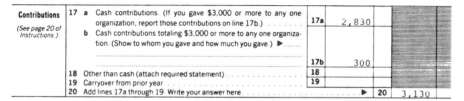

MISCELLANEOUS DEDUCTIONS

According to § 262, no deduction is allowed for personal, living, or
family expenses. However, there are a number of expenditures that
one may incur that are related to employment. If an employee incurs
unreimbursed business expenses other than for travel and transportation, the expenses are deductible as miscellaneous deductions. Beyond
unreimbursed employee expenses, certain other expenses fall into the
category of miscellaneous deductions. In both cases, these expenses
are reported on Schedule A. Deductible miscellaneous expenses include (but are not limited to) the following:[88]

—Professional dues to membership organizations.

—Uniforms or other clothing that cannot be used for normal
wear.

—Fees incurred for the preparation of one's tax return or fees
incurred for tax litigation before the IRS or the courts.

—Subscription costs to professional journals.

—Fee paid for a safe deposit box.

—Section 212 expenses as discussed in Chapter 10.

COMPREHENSIVE EXAMPLE OF SCHEDULE A

T, who is single, had the following transactions for 1983:

—Medicine and drugs	$200
—Other medical expenses	825
—State and local income taxes	1,200
—Real estate taxes	600
—General sales tax (based on T's records)	420
—Personal property taxes	275

88. *Your Federal Income Tax*, IRS Publication 17 (Rev. Oct. 83), p. 136.

—Home mortgage interest	3,500
—Credit cards	110
—Other	1,150
—Cash contributions	2,830
—Contributions other than cash	300
—Union dues	400
—Tax return preparation fee	150

T's adjusted gross income for 1983 is $12,000, and his zero bracket amount is $2,300. The completed Schedule A on the following page shows excess itemized deductions of $8,940.

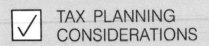

TAX PLANNING CONSIDERATIONS

EFFECTIVE UTILIZATION OF EXCESS ITEMIZED DEDUCTIONS

Since an individual may use the zero bracket amount in one year and itemize his or her deductions in another year, it is frequently possible to obtain maximum benefit by shifting itemized deductions from one year to another. For example, if a taxpayer's itemized deductions and the zero bracket amount are approximately the same for each year of a two-year period, the taxpayer should use the zero bracket amount in one year and shift itemized deductions (to the extent permitted by law) to the other year. The individual could, for example, prepay a church pledge for a particular year or avoid paying end-of-the-year medical expenses to shift the deduction to the following year.

UTILIZATION OF MEDICAL DEDUCTIONS

Because of the percentage limitations on medical and drug expenses, taxpayers may find it worthwhile to delay the processing of year-end medical insurance reimbursement claims.

Example 28. Prior to paying $2,000 for an operation carried out in November of 19X1, T had medical expenses for the year of $800. In late December of 19X1, she files a claim with the insurance company to recover the amount allowed to her under the policy covering her medical care. In January of 19X2, T receives a check from the company in the amount of $2,000. For tax year 19X1, T has adjusted gross income of $30,000 and has itemized deductions in excess of the zero bracket amount. Under these circumstances, T has a medical expense deduction of $1,300 [i. e., ($800 + $2,000) − (5% × $30,000)]. Under the application of the tax benefit rule, she must, however, include in her gross income for 19X2, $1,300 of the $2,000 reimbursement received in January.

SCHEDULES A&B (Form 1040)	Schedule A—Itemized Deductions	OMB No. 1545-0074
Department of the Treasury Internal Revenue Service	(Schedule B is on back) ▶ Attach to Form 1040. ▶ See Instructions for Schedules A and B (Form 1040).	1983 07

Name(s) as shown on Form 1040	Your social security number
John Taxpayer	890 56 3451

Medical and Dental Expenses	1	Medicines and drugs	1	200		
	2	Write 1% of Form 1040, line 33	2	120		
(Do not include expenses reimbursed or paid by others.)	3	Subtract line 2 from line 1. If line 2 is more than line 1, write zero	3	80		
	4	Other medical and dental expenses:				
(See page 18 of Instructions.)	a	Doctors, dentists, nurses, hospitals, insurance premiums you paid for medical and dental care, etc.	4a	825		
	b	Transportation	4b			
	c	Other (list—include hearing aids, dentures, eyeglasses, etc.) ▶				
			4c			
	5	Add lines 3 through 4c	5	905		
	6	Multiply amount on Form 1040, line 33, by 5% (.05)	6	600		
	7	Subtract line 6 from line 5. If line 6 is more than line 5, write zero ▶			7	305
Taxes	8	State and local income	8	1,200		
(See page 19 of Instructions.)	9	Real estate	9	600		
	10 a	General sales (see sales tax tables)	10a	420		
	b	General sales on motor vehicles	10b			
	11	Other (list—include personal property) ▶				
			11	275		
	12	Add lines 8 through 11. Write your answer here ▶			12	2,495
Interest Expense	13 a	Home mortgage interest paid to financial institutions	13a	3,500		
(See page 20 of Instructions.)	b	Home mortgage interest paid to individuals (show that person's name and address) ▶	13b			
	14	Credit cards and charge accounts	14	110		
	15	Other (list) ▶				
			15	1,150		
	16	Add lines 13a through 15. Write your answer here ▶			16	4,760
Contributions	17 a	Cash contributions. (If you gave $3,000 or more to any one organization, report those contributions on line 17b.)	17a	2,830		
(See page 20 of Instructions.)	b	Cash contributions totaling $3,000 or more to any one organization. (Show to whom you gave and how much you gave.) ▶	17b			
	18	Other than cash (attach required statement)	18	300		
	19	Carryover from prior year	19			
	20	Add lines 17a through 19. Write your answer here			20	3,130
Casualty and Theft Losses	21	Total casualty or theft loss(es) (attach Form 4684) (see page 20 of Instructions) ▶			21	–0–
Miscellaneous Deductions	22	Union and professional dues	22	400		
	23	Tax return preparation fee	23	150		
	24	Other (list) ▶				
(See page 21 of Instructions.)			24			
	25	Add lines 22 through 24. Write your answer here ▶			25	550
Summary of Itemized Deductions	26	Add lines 7, 12, 16, 20, 21, and 25			26	11,240
(See page 21 of Instructions.)	27	If you checked Form 1040 { Filing Status box 2 or 5, write $3,400 } { Filing Status box 1 or 4, write $2,300 } { Filing Status box 3, write $1,700 }			27	2,300
	28	Subtract line 27 from line 26. Write your answer here and on Form 1040, line 34a. (If line 27 is more than line 26, see the Instructions for line 28 on page 21.) ▶			28	8,940

For Paperwork Reduction Act Notice, see Form 1040 Instructions.　　　　　　　　Schedule A (Form 1040) 1983

In Example 28, what did the taxpayer accomplish? By delaying the filing of the claim for reimbursement, T obtained the benefit of an additional deduction of $1,300 for 19X1. Although this amount has to be reported as income in 19X2 (to the extent attributable to the deduction taken in 19X1), she obtains the advantage of a tax savings for one year. The advisability of her actions presumes that her income tax bracket in 19X2 will not increase significantly over the 19X1 level.

When a taxpayer anticipates that his or her medical expenses will approximate the percentage limitation, much might be done to generate a deductible excess. Any of the procedures described below can help build a deduction by the end of the year:

—Incur the obligation for or have carried out needed dental work.[89] Orthodontic treatment, for example, may have been recommended for a member of the taxpayer's family.

—Have remedial surgery that may have been postponed from prior years (e. g., tonsillectomies, vasectomies, correction of hernias, hysterectomies).

—Incur the obligation for capital improvements to taxpayer's personal residence recommended by a physician (e. g., an air filtration system to alleviate a respiratory disorder).

As an aid to taxpayers who might experience temporary cash-flow problems at the end of the year, the use of bank credit cards is deemed to be payment for purposes of timing the deductibility of charitable and medical expenses.[90]

Example 29. On December 12, 19X1, T (a calendar year taxpayer) purchases two pairs of prescription contact lenses and one pair of prescribed orthopedic shoes for a total of $305. These purchases are separately charged to T's credit card. On January 6, 19X2, T receives his statement containing these charges and makes payment shortly thereafter. The purchases are deductible as medical expenses in the year charged (i. e., 19X1) and not in the year the account is settled (i. e., 19X2).

Recognizing which expenditures qualify for the medical deduction also may be crucial to exceeding the percentage limitations.

Example 30. T employs E (an unrelated party) to care for her incapacitated and dependent mother. E is not a trained nurse but spends approximately one-half of the time performing nursing duties (e. g., administering injections and providing physical therapy) and the rest of the time doing household chores. An allocable portion of E's wages that T pays (including the employer's portion of FICA taxes) qualifies as a medical expense.[91]

To assure a deduction for the entire cost of a nursing home for an aged dependent, it is helpful if the transfer of the individual to the home is for medical reasons which are recommended by a doctor. In

---

89. Prepayment of medical expenses does not generate a deduction unless the taxpayer is under an obligation to make such payment. *Robert S. Basset,* 26 T.C. 619 (1956).

90. Rev.Rul. 78–38, 1978–1 C.B. 67 and Rev.Rul. 78–39, 1978–1 C.B. 73.

91. These expenditures might qualify for the child and disabled dependent care tax credit discussed in Chapter 13.

addition, the nursing home facilities should be adequate to provide the necessary medical and nursing care. To assure a deduction for all of the nursing care expenses, it is necessary to show that the individual was placed in the home due to required medical care rather than for personal or family considerations.

For tax years beginning after 1982, the separate deductions for one-half (up to $150) of medical insurance expenses is repealed. After 1982 any medical premium expense will be limited by the five percent floor. Since the benefit for deducting medical premiums will be limited, individuals will probably turn more to commercial insurance, since contributions made by employers are excluded from gross income under § 106.

Proper documentation is required to substantiate medical expenses. The taxpayer should keep all receipts for credit card or other charge purchases of medical services and supplies, cash register receipts, etc. In addition medical transportation mileage should be recorded.

PLANNING WITH SALES TAXES

In a year of major purchases such as remodeling or building a new house, individuals should record actual sales tax payments, since such amounts may be in excess of the figure provided by the optional sales tax table issued by the IRS. If a new home or addition is planned, it is possible to receive a sales tax deduction for the building materials if the tax is separately stated and is billed to the taxpayer. If the optional sales tax tables are used, the deduction for building materials should be added to the amount determined by the tables.

PROTECTING THE INTEREST DEDUCTION

Although the deductibility of prepaid interest by a cash basis taxpayer has been severely restricted, a notable exception is contained in § 461(g)(2). Under this provision, points paid to obtain financing for the purchase or improvement of a principal residence may be deductible in the year of payment. However, such points must actually be paid by the taxpayer obtaining the loan and must represent a charge for the use of money. It has been held that points paid from the mortgage proceeds do not satisfy the payment requirement.[92] Also, the portion of the points attributable to service charges does not represent deductible interest.[93] For taxpayers financing home purchases or improvements, planning usually should be directed toward avoiding these two hurdles to immediate deductibility.

---

92. *Alan A. Rubnitz,* 67 T.C. 621 (1977).
93. *Donald L. Wilkerson,* 70 T.C. 240 (1978).

There may be instances when a taxpayer wishes to elect to capitalize points if the points plus other itemized deductions do not exceed the taxpayer's zero bracket amount.

> **Example 31.** X purchases a home on December 15, 19X1, for $95,000 with $30,000 cash and a 30-year mortgage of $65,000 financed by the Greater Metropolis National Bank. X pays two points as a processing fee in addition to interest allocated to the period from December 15 until December 31, 19X1, at an annual rate of 14%. Since X does not have enough itemized deductions to exceed the zero bracket amount for 19X1, this taxpayer should elect to capitalize the interest expense by amortizing the points over 30 years. In this instance, X would deduct $43.33 for 19X1 as an interest expense [$1,300 (two points) divided by 30 years].

Interest is not deductible unless the party making the payment is the party who has the obligation to do so. A proper structuring of the loan agreement may avoid the possible loss of the deduction.

> **Example 32.** As a college graduation present, M makes a down payment on a new automobile for her daughter, D. As there is some doubt as to D's ability to make the earlier monthly payments, M makes herself co-liable on the car loan issued by the finance company. Under these circumstances, M will be entitled to the interest deduction on any car payments she makes. Had the loan listed only D as being liable, the interest portion of any payments made by M would be nondeductible. In that case, the loan is D's, not M's, obligation.

ASSURING THE CHARITABLE CONTRIBUTION DEDUCTION

For a charitable contribution deduction to be available, the recipient must be a qualified charitable organization. Sometimes the mechanics of how the contribution is carried out can determine whether or not a deduction results.

> **Example 33.** T wants to donate $5,000 to her church's mission in Seoul, Korea. In this regard, she considers three alternatives:
> (1) Send the money directly to the mission.
> (2) Give the money to her church with the understanding that it is to be passed on to the mission.
> (3) Give the money directly to the missionary in charge of the mission who is currently in the U. S. on a fund-raising trip.
>
> If T wants to obtain a deduction for the contribution, she would be well advised to choose alternative (2). A direct donation to the mission [alternative (1)] would not be deductible because the mission is a foreign charity. A direct gift to the missionary [alterna-

tive (3)] does not comply, since an individual cannot be a qualified charity for income tax purposes.[94]

When making donations of other than cash, the type of property chosen can have decided implications in measuring the amount, if any, of the deduction.

> **Example 34.** T desires to give $60,000 in value to her church in some form other than cash. In this connection, she considers four alternatives:
>
> (1) Stock held as an investment with a cost basis of $100,000 and a fair market value of $60,000.
>
> (2) Stock held as an investment for more than one year with a cost basis of $10,000 and a fair market value of $60,000.
>
> (3) The rent-free use of a building for a year which normally leases for $5,000 a month.
>
> (4) A valuable stamp collection held as an investment and owned for more than one year with a cost basis of $10,000 and a fair market value of $60,000. The church plans to sell the collection if and when it is donated.

Alternative (1) is ill advised as the subject of the gift. Even though T would obtain a deduction of $60,000, she would forego the potential loss of $40,000 that would be recognized if the property had been sold.[95] Alternative (2) makes good sense, since the deduction still is $60,000 and none of the $50,000 of appreciation that has occurred must be recognized as income. Alternative (3) yields no deduction at all and would not, therefore, appear to be a wise choice.[96] Alternative (4) involves tangible personalty which the recipient does not plan to use. As a result, 40% of the appreciation involved, or $20,000 [40% × ($60,000 − $10,000)], becomes nondeductible. Thus, the amount of the deduction would be limited to $40,000 ($60,000 − $20,000).[97]

In the case of property transfers (particularly real estate) the ceiling limitations on the amount of the deduction allowed in any one year (i. e., 20 percent, 30 percent, or 50 percent of adjusted gross income—as the case may be) could be a factor to take into account. With proper planning, donations can be controlled to stay within the limi-

---

94. *Thomas E. Lesslie,* 36 TCM 495, T.C.Memo. 1977–111.
95. *LaVar M. Withers,* 69 T.C. 900 (1978).
96. Due to abuse on the part of taxpayers, the Tax Reform Act of 1969 eliminated any deduction for allowing a charitable organization free or bargain use of property.
97. The 40% adjustment did not apply to alternative (2), since stock is "intangible" property and not "tangible" personalty.

tations and therefore avoid the need for a carryover of unused charitable contributions.[98]

> **Example 35.** T desires to donate a tract of unimproved land, held as an investment, to the University of Maryland (a qualified charitable organization). The land has been held for more than one year and has a current fair market value of $300,000 and a basis to T of $50,000. T's adjusted gross income for the current year is estimated to be $200,000, and he expects much the same for the next few years. In the current year he deeds (i. e., transfers) an undivided one-fifth interest in the real estate to the University.

What has T accomplished for income tax purposes? In the current year he will be allowed a charitable contribution deduction of $60,000 [i. e., ⅕ (or 20%) × $300,000] which will be within the applicable limitation of adjusted gross income (30% × $200,000). Presuming no other charitable contributions for the year, T has avoided the possibility of a carryover. In future years, T can arrange donations of undivided interests in the real estate to stay within the bounds of the percentage limitations. The only difficulty with this approach is the necessity of having to revalue the real estate each year before the donation, since the amount of the deduction is based on the fair market value of the interest contributed at the time of the contribution.

PROBLEM MATERIALS

Questions for Class Discussion

1. X has a history of heart disease. Upon the advice of his doctor, he installs an elevator in his residence so he does not have to climb stairs. Is this a valid medical expense? If it is, how much of the expense is deductible?

2. T, a self-employed individual taxpayer, prepared his own income tax return for the past year and asked you to check it over for accuracy. A review by you indicates that he failed to claim certain business entertainment expenses.

   (a) Would the correction of this omission affect the amount of medical expenses T can deduct? Explain.

   (b) Would it matter if T were employed rather than self-employed?

---

98. The carryover approach may be dangerous in several respects. First, the carryover period is limited to five years. Depending on the taxpayer's projected adjusted gross income as opposed to actual adjusted gross income, some of the amount carried over may expire without tax benefit after the five-year period has ended. Second, unused charitable contribution carryovers do not survive the death of the party making the donation and, as a consequence, are lost.

3. If a taxpayer incurred medical expenses of $500 and deducted such amounts in 19X1, how would a $300 insurance reimbursement be treated if received in 19X2? Received in 19X1? What if the taxpayer had no excess itemized deductions in 19X1 and received the $300 reimbursement in 19X2?

4. What is an ad valorem tax? Why should a distinction be made between an ad valorem tax (based on value) and a tax based on other factors such as weight, year, model?

5. Why is it necessary to make an apportionment of real estate taxes between the buyer and the seller of a home in the year of sale? What effect does the apportionment have upon the adjusted basis of the property to the buyer if the seller pays the real estate taxes?

6. If a taxpayer overpays his or her state income tax due to excessive with-holdings or estimated tax payments, how is the refund check treated when received in the subsequent year? Are the excess amounts paid deductible in the current year?

7. Are there any restrictions placed on the deductibility of sales taxes incurred during the tax year? If so, what are the restrictions and how can a taxpayer avoid them?

8. If a taxpayer's records indicate that state sales taxes in excess of the amount allowed per the sales tax tables were paid, is such excess amount deductible? Do the IRS sales tax tables include major purchase items such as automobiles and appliances? Is it necessary to make adjustments for local and county sales taxes? Why?

9. Which of the following is generally deductible as interest:

    (a) Bank credit card interest.

    (b) Service charges.

    (c) Points paid by the seller of property.

    (d) Finance charges separately stated.

    (e) Late payment fees on the payment of utility bills.

10. Discuss the special problems that arise with respect to the deductibility of interest on a debt between related parties. How does § 267 of the Code relate to this problem?

11. If a taxpayer pays interest on behalf of another, is the payment deductible under § 163?

12. How and why does the tax treatment of interest expense differ when borrowed funds are used for business versus nonbusiness purposes?

13. Why has Congress imposed limitations on the deductibility of interest when funds are borrowed for the purpose of purchasing or continuing to hold investment property?

14. When an installment contract results from a purchase and the buyer incurs a separate carrying charge but the actual interest cannot be ascertained, how much interest can the buyer deduct under § 163?

15. Why is it necessary for a charitable organization to receive qualified status under § 501 of the Code?

16. What is ordinary income property? If inventory with an adjusted cost basis of $60 and fair market value of $100 is contributed to a public charity, how much is deductible? (Assume that the inventory is not used by the charity for the care of children, the ill, or the needy.)

17. What is capital gain property? What tax treatment is required if capital gain property is contributed to a private foundation? To a public charity? What difference does it make if the contribution is tangible personalty and it is put to a use unrelated to the donee's business?

18. An accountant normally charges $50 an hour when preparing financial tatements for clients. If the accountant performs accounting services for a church without charge, can the value of the donated services be deducted on his or her tax return?

19. Compare the deductibility of contributions made to private foundations with contributions made to public charities (i. e., with respect to percentage limitations and carryover rules).

20. Discuss the filing requirements for contributions of property in excess of $200.

21. Name some of the miscellaneous deductions that are reported on Schedule A. What happens to these deductions if the taxpayer does not itemize?

Problems

22. H and W are married and together have adjusted gross income of $24,000. They have no dependents, and they filed a joint return in 1984. Each pays $450 for hospitalization insurance. During the year, they paid the following amounts for medical care: $1,900 in doctor and dentist bills and hospital expenses and $310 for medicine and drugs. An insurance reimbursement for hospitalization was received in December 1985, for $700. Determine the deduction allowable under § 213 for medical expenses paid in 1984.

23. X lives in Arkansas and discovers that he has a rare disease that can be treated only with surgery by a surgeon in France. X incurs $1,500 in air fare, $200 in meals, and $800 in lodging expenses related to his medical care in France. What amount, if any, of these expenses is deductible under § 213?

24. H and W, who have a dependent child, C, were both under 65 years of age at the close of calendar year 1984 and filed a joint return for that year. During the year 1984, H's mother, M, attained the age of 65 and qualified as a dependent of H. The adjusted gross income in 1984 of H and W was $14,000. During 1984, H and W paid the following amounts for medical care: $700 for doctors and hospital expenses and $145 for medicine and drugs for themselves, $375 for doctors and hospital expenses and $70 for medicine and drugs for C, and $500 for doctors and hospital expenses and $125 for medicine and drugs for M. No insurance reimbursements were received for these expenses. How much is allowed as a deduction for medical expenses for the taxable year 1984?

25. Upon the advice of his physician, T, a heart patient, installs an elevator in his personal residence at a cost of $8,000. The elevator has a cost recovery period of five years. A neighbor who is in the real estate business

charges T $40 for an appraisal which places the value of the residence at $50,000 before the improvement and $55,000 after. The value increases because T lives in a region where many older people retire and, therefore, would find the elevator an attractive feature in a home. As a result of the operation of the elevator, T noticed an increase of $55 in his utility bills for the current year. Disregarding percentage limitations, which of the above expenditures qualify as a medical deduction?

26. The City of Houston adopted a zoning ordinance that requires a minimum number of off-street parking spaces for each building. To finance the parking lots, the city levied an assessment of $1,000 against each commercial property in each district. These funds were used to construct off-street parking for the commercial property. Is the $1,000 assessment deductible?

27. T uses the cash method of accounting and lives in a state that imposes an income tax (including withholding from wages). On April 14, 19X2, he files his state return for 19X1 paying an additional $500 in income taxes. During 19X2, his withholdings for state income tax purposes amount to $2,750. On April 13, 19X3, T files his state return for 19X2 claiming a refund of $125. The refund is received by T on August 3, 19X3.

    (a) If T itemizes his deductions, how much may he claim as a deduction for state income taxes on his Federal return for calendar year 19X2 (filed in April 19X3)?

    (b) How will the refund of $125 received in 19X3 be treated for Federal income tax purposes?

28. In County Z the real property tax year is the calendar year. The real property tax becomes a personal liability of the owner of real property on January 1 in the current real property tax year 19X1. The tax is payable on July 1, 19X1. On May 1, 19X1, A sells his house to B, who uses the cash method of accounting, but B reports his income on the basis of a fiscal year ending July 31. On July 1, 19X1, B pays the entire real estate tax for the year ending December 31, 19X1. How much of the real estate tax for 19X1 is considered to be imposed on B?

29. X is married, has two dependent children, and files a joint return with his wife. During 19X1, their adjusted gross income was $35,000, which included 40% of a $2,000 net capital gain (i. e., $800 was included). He also had $2,000 of tax-exempt interest income. X acquired a new automobile during the year; and he paid $550 of state, county, and local sales tax on the purchase. X is a resident of Texas, which imposes a four percent general state sales tax. County and local sales taxes (not included in the table) amount to a total of two percent of consumer purchases.

    (a) Calculate X's sales tax deductions using the table in Appendix A–3.

    (b) If X's actual payments of sales tax were greater than the amount determined above, which amount should be deducted?

30. On July 1, 19X2, T borrows $15,000 at 10% for one year; interest is discounted in advance. Under the loan agreement, T receives the net proceeds of $13,500 and repays $15,000 on July 1, 19X3. T uses the calendar year for tax purposes.

    (a) Assume T is a cash basis taxpayer. Discuss the tax treatment of the interest deduction.

(b) Discuss the treatment of the interest deduction assuming T is an accrual basis taxpayer.

(c) Assume that T is required to repay the loan in 12 monthly payments of $1,250 starting on August 1, 19X2. Presuming the repayment takes place as scheduled and T uses the cash basis of accounting, what are the allowable interest deductions for 19X2 and 19X3?

31. On January 20, 19X5, C purchases a television set for $400, which includes a carrying charge of $25. C makes a down payment of $50, and the balance is paid in 12 monthly installments beginning in February. What amount of each payment is considered deductible interest?

32. X is married and files a joint tax return for 19X5. X has investment interest expense of $95,000 for a loan made to him in 19X5 to purchase a parcel of unimproved land. His income from investments (dividends, capital gains, and interest) totaled $15,000 and investment expenses amounted to $2,500. Consequently, his net investment income is $12,500 ($15,000 less $2,500). X also has $3,000 as a net long-term capital gain from the sale of another parcel of unimproved land. Calculate X's investment interest deduction for 19X5.

33. A, B, and C are equal owners in the X Corporation. All three shareholders make loans to X Corporation in 19X1 and receive interest-bearing notes. A and B are brothers, and C is their uncle. All three owners are on the cash method of accounting, while X Corporation is on the accrual method. A, B, C, and X Corporation use a calendar year for tax purposes. Can X Corporation deduct the interest payments made to A, B, and C on April 1, 19X2, for 19X1?

34. Dr. X, a famous heart surgeon practicing in Chicago, performs heart surgery in charitable hospitals around the state during one day of each week. He incurs $250 per week in travel and related expenses pursuant to the rendition of these services. He receives no compensation for the services, nor is he reimbursed for the travel expenses. Assume his professional fees average $3,000 per operation and that he normally performs two operations each day. Based on these facts, what is Dr. X's charitable contribution deduction for the year?

35. Determine the amount of the charitable deduction allowed in each of the following situations:

(a) Donation of X Corporation stock (a publicly traded corporation) to taxpayer's church. The stock cost the taxpayer $2,000 four months ago and has a fair market value of $3,000 on the date of the donation.

(b) Donation of a painting to the Salvation Army. The painting cost the taxpayer $2,000 five years ago and has a fair market value of $3,500 on the date of the donation.

(c) The local branch of the American Red Cross uses a building rent-free for half of the current year. The building normally rents for $500 a month.

(d) Donation by a cash basis farmer to a church of a quantity of grain worth $900. The grain was raised by the farmer in the preceding year at a cost of $650, all of which was deducted for income tax purposes.

36. T, an individual with an adjusted gross income of $60,000 in 19X3, contributed 100 shares of IBM stock to a local college. The adjusted basis of the IBM stock was $250 per share, and its fair market value was $400 per share on the date of the gift. The stock was acquired in 19X1 and contributed to the college in 19X3.

    (a) Calculate the amount of the gift which qualifies for the charitable contribution deduction.

    (b) How are excess amounts, if any, treated?

37. An individual taxpayer, M, had adjusted gross income of $30,000. She contributed $12,000 to a public charity and $9,000 to a private foundation in 19X1.

    (a) Calculate the total contribution deduction for 19X1.

    (b) How are any excess amounts treated?

38. On December 30, 19X1, T purchased four tickets to a charity ball sponsored by the City of Mobile and for the benefit of underprivileged children. Each ticket cost $100 and had a fair market value of $25. On the same day as their purchase, T gave the tickets to the minister of her church for the personal use by his family. At the time of the gift of the tickets, T pledged $1,000 to the building fund of her church. The pledge was satisfied by check dated December 31, 19X1, but not mailed until January 3, 19X2.

    (a) Presuming T is a cash basis and calendar year taxpayer, how much can be deducted as a charitable contribution for 19X1?

    (b) Would the amount of the deduction be any different if T is an accrual basis taxpayer? Explain.

39. Classify each of the independent expenditures appearing below as nondeductible (ND) items, business (*dfor*) deductions, or itemized (*dfrom*) deductions. (Note: In many cases it may be necessary to refer to the materials contained in the earlier chapters of the text.)

    (a) Interest on home mortgage accrued by a cash basis taxpayer.

    (b) State income taxes paid by a sole proprietor of a business.

    (c) Subscription to *The Wall Street Journal* paid by a vice-president of a bank and not reimbursed by her employer.

    (d) Automobile mileage for attendance at weekly church services.

    (e) Street paving assessment paid to the county by a homeowner.

    (f) Speeding ticket paid by the owner-operator of a taxicab.

    (g) Interest and taxes paid by the owner of residential rental property.

    (h) Business entertainment expenses (properly substantiated) paid by a self-employed taxpayer.

    (i) State and Federal excise taxes on tobacco paid by a self-employed taxpayer who gave his clients cigars as Christmas presents. The business gifts were properly substantiated and under $25 each.

    (j) State and Federal excise taxes on cigarettes purchased by a heavy smoker for personal consumption.

    (k) Federal excise taxes (i. e., four cents per gallon) on the purchase of gasoline for use in the taxpayer's personal automobile.

(l) Theft loss of personal jewelry worth $300 but which originally cost $75.

(m) Maternity clothing purchased by a taxpayer who is pregnant.

(n) Stretch bandage purchased by a taxpayer with a "trick" knee.

(o) An electric toothbrush purchased by a taxpayer whose dentist recommended its use to alleviate a gum disorder.

(p) Medical expenses paid by an employer on behalf of an employee.

(q) Interest paid by a taxpayer on a loan obtained to build an artist studio in his personal residence. Assume that taxpayer's art activities are classified as a hobby.

(r) Assume the same facts as in (q) except that the art activities are classified as a trade or business.

Cumulative Problems

40. A and N, both 27, are married with one dependent child. They file a joint return. A and N had the following receipts in 1984.

(1) A's salary.	$ 20,000
(2) N's salary.	15,000
(3) Dividends on domestic stock owned by A	200
(4) Reimbursement of 1984 medical bills by insurance company.	1,600
(5) Expense allowance from A's employer to cover business expenses incurred by A.	750
(6) Selling price of a parcel of land they had held for two years as an investment (basis was $5,000).	7,000
(7) Reimbursement by A's employer of A's dues in a professional organization related to A's work.	150
(8) Dividends received on X Corporation stock owned by N before marriage (A and N live in a common law state). X Corporation is a domestic corporation.	200
(9) Dividends on Y Corporation stock (jointly owned). Y Corporation is a domestic corporation.	100
(10) Interest on corporate coupon bonds owned by N's father, who clipped the coupons shortly before the interest payment date and gave them to N. *gift*	500
(11) Payment to A by insurance company of disability benefits under a medical and disability insurance policy; A, who *not income* was injured and unable to work for four weeks, had acquired and paid the premiums on the policy.	800
(12) Refund of Federal income tax withheld in 1983.	400

A and N had receipts and other documentary evidence for the following disbursements made in 1984:

(13) Business expenses incurred by A [see (5) for reimbursement information] included business travel, $600, and business entertainment, $400.	$ 1,000
(14) Contribution to United Way. *charity*	520
(15) Premiums for health insurance coverage.	400
(16) Prescription drugs and medicines.	420
(17) Nonprescription drugs and medicines.	60

(18) Doctor bills.	800
(19) Hospital bills.	2,200
(20) Contact lenses for N.	150
(21) Interest on home mortgage.	3,000
(22) Interest on charge accounts.	120
(23) Real property taxes on their residence.	729
(24) State sales tax on new automobile purchased in December 1984 (A and N live in West Virginia).	325
(25) State income tax paid in April 1984 when they filed their state income tax return for 1983.	70
(26) Fee for preparation of 1983 tax returns.	100
(27) Professional dues and subscriptions for N.	85

A's personal automobile was totaled in November 1984 when it caught fire because of a leak in the fuel line. A had paid $2,200 for the auto two years ago. Its fair market value on the date of the fire was $1,400. A carried only liability insurance on the auto and received no reimbursement from his insurance company. He sold the auto to a salvage company for $500.

Federal income tax withheld by their employers totaled $5,033, and state income tax withheld totaled $700. Estimated federal tax payments were $400. They are entitled to a political contributions credit of $100.

Compute taxable income for 1984 for A and N (Use the 1983 sales tax table for computing the sales tax deduction, since the 1984 sales tax table was not available at the date of publication of this text.) Assume A does not render an adequate accounting to his employer but has the records necessary to substantiate employee expenses.

41. H and W are married taxpayers, age 44 and 42, respectively, who file a joint return. In 1984, H was employed as an assistant manager of a department store at a salary of $26,000. W is a high school teacher and earned $16,000. W has two children, ages 13 and 15, from a previous marriage. The children reside with H and W throughout the school year and reside with F, W's former husband, during the summer. Pursuant to the divorce decree, F pays $100 per month per child for each of the nine months during which W has custody of the children, but the decree is silent as to which parent may claim the exemptions. F claims that he spends $200 a month supporting each child during the three summer months when the children live with him. W can document that she and H provided support of $1,600 for each child in 1984.

In August H and W decided to add a "mother-in-law" suite to their home to provide more comfortable accommodations for M, W's mother who had moved in with them the preceding February after the death of W's father. Not wanting to borrow the money for this addition at the current high interest rates, H and W sold 400 shares of stock for $30 a share and used the $12,000 to cover construction costs. They had purchased the stock four years before for $20 a share. They received dividends of $100 on the jointly owned stock prior to the sale.

W's mother is 66 years old and drew $3,600 in Social Security benefits during the year, of which she gave H and W $1,200 to use toward household expenses and deposited $2,400 in her personal savings account. H and W estimate that they spent a minimum of $1,500 of their own money for food, clothing, medical expenses, and other items for M, not counting the rental value of the portion of the house she occupies.

H and W received $1,600 interest on some municipal bonds they had bought in 1984. H had heard from a friend that municipal bonds were paying good rates and that municipal bond interest was not taxable. To finance the purchase of the bonds, he borrowed $20,000 from the bank at 10% interest, figuring the deduction for interest would save him enough income tax to make the investment worthwhile. He paid the bank $2,000 interest during 1984.

Other interest paid during the year included $3,530 on their home mortgage and $106 on various charge accounts.

W's favorite uncle died in October and willed W 50 shares of stock worth $25 per share. She received a dividend of $2 a share on the stock late in the year.

In December 1984, H was riding a snowmobile he had just acquired for $4,200. In his eagerness to try it out, he neglected two things. First, he had forgotten to insure it. Second, he had not taken time to read the operating instructions. As a result of his lack of familiarity with the snowmobile, he lost control of it as he was headed toward a large, concrete barn. Fortunately, H was able to jump off before the crash and escaped injury. The barn was not damaged. The snowmobile, however, was demolished. H sold it back to the dealer for parts for $200.

W incurred travel expenses of $600 while attending a teacher's convention. On the second day of the convention, she attended a workshop for which she paid an enrollment fee of $50. The school district which employs her does not reimburse her for either travel expenses or educational expenses.

H and W paid doctor and hospital bills of $2,800 and were reimbursed by their insurance company for $1,400. Medicines and drugs cost them $600, and premiums on their health insurance policy were $450. Included in the amounts paid for hospital bills was $800 for W's mother; and of the $600 spent for medicines and drugs, $300 was for W's mother.

Taxes paid during the year included $1,120 property taxes on their home, sales tax of $325 on the purchase of a new automobile, and state income taxes (withheld) of $840. In March 1984, H and W received a refund on their 1983 state income taxes of $140. They reside in Wisconsin. They had itemized deductions on their 1983 return and had received a tax benefit for the full amount of state income taxes reported. (Use the 1983 sales tax table for computing the sales tax deduction, since the 1984 sales tax table was not available at the date of publication of this text.)

H and W contribute $20 a week to their church and have cancelled checks for these contributions totaling $1,040. In addition, H's employer withheld $260 from his check, per his instructions, as a contribution to United Way. H and W also have a receipt from the Salvation Army for some used clothing the family had contributed. H and W estimated the value of the clothes at $200.

H and W had $5,773 of Federal income tax withheld in 1984 and paid estimated Federal income tax of $800.

Compute taxable income for H and W for 1984.

Cumulative Tax Return Problem

42. T, age 45, is married and has two dependent children. In 1983, he incurred the following:

(1) Salary received from his employer	$ 60,000
(2) Cost of art supplies. T took up painting as a hobby and plans to sell the paintings to friends and art galleries but had no willing purchasers during 1983.	1,000
(3) Contribution of 20 shares of X Corporation stock to his church (fair market value of $1,000, cost of $400, and acquired in 1976).	1,000
(4) T's wife had a diamond ring which was stolen in April 1983. A police report was filed but the ring was not recovered. It is not covered by insurance. The ring had been recently appraised at $2,000, which was also its original cost.	2,000
(5) Travel and auto expenses incurred in connection with T's employment (none of which were reimbursed)	2,500

(6) T and his family moved from Nashville to Providence during the year and incurred the following unreimbursed expenses:

Moving van	$ 2,500	
Temporary relocation and house-hunting expenses	1,800	
Selling commissions on the former home	3,500	7,800

(7) T paid and incurred the following personal expenses:

Medical and dental bills for the family	1,500
State and local income taxes	4,500

Required:

Determine T's adjusted gross income and taxable income for 1983, assuming that a joint return is filed and that there are no other items of income or deduction. Preparation of pages 1 and 2 and Schedules A and B of Form 1040 and Forms 3903 and 2106 is suggested.

Research Problems

43. Taxpayers have a daughter who has been diagnosed as having a learning disability and is approximately two years behind in her cognitive skills as compared to other children her age. Taxpayers have decided to send their daughter to a special school to enhance her education. In doing this, taxpayers are willing to pay tuition for their daughter to attend a private school. Can the tuition be deducted as a medical expense under § 213 of the Code?

44. T suffers from a degenerative spinal disorder. Her physician, therefore, recommended the installation of a swimming pool at her residence for her use to prevent the onset of permanent paralysis. T's residence had a market value of approximately $500,000 before the swimming pool was installed. The swimming pool was built, and an appraiser estimated that the value of T's home increased by $98,000 due to the addition.

The pool cost $194,000 and T claimed a medical deduction on her tax return of $172,000. Upon audit of the return, the IRS determined that an adequate pool should have cost $70,000 and would increase the property value by only $31,000. Thus, the IRS claims that T should be entitled to a deduction of only $39,000.

(a) Is there any ceiling limitation on the amount deductible as a medical expense?

(b) Can capital expenses be deducted as medical expenses?

(c) What is the significance of a "minimum adequate facility"? Should aesthetic or architectural qualities be considered in this determination?

Partial list of research aids:

Reg. § 1.213–1(e)(1)(iii).

Ferris v. Comm., 36 TCM 765, T.C.Memo. 1977–186.

45. Taxpayer has one of his children attending a school operated by a society for religious instruction associated with a local church. The society was an exempt organization under § 170(c)(2). Tuition for the school was based on what a parent could afford. The question posed is whether or not the payments made to the society are deductible as a charitable contribution.

46. The taxpayer suffered from a disease known as hypoglycemia, which is a condition caused by abnormally low blood sugar in the body. The taxpayer's doctor prescribed frequent feedings of a high protein diet as the major treatment for the condition.

Taxpayer compared her food bills with those of her friends and estimated that the cost of her food with high protein supplements was much greater than that of ordinary food bought at the grocery store. In 1982, taxpayer paid $3,483 for food and estimated that 30 percent of this sum was attributable to extra protein required to treat her disease. Is this extra sum deductible as a medical expense?

47. Taxpayers, husband and wife, filed joint tax returns for 19X2 and 19X3. On August 15, 19X0, the taxpayers' parents transferred to them $4,000 with the understanding that they would repay $8,000 sometime in the future. No specific interest rate was agreed to, nor was any specific date set for repayment. The taxpayer was an attorney, and he intended to repay his parents from fees that would be earned with funds generated by development of a residential subdivision located in Akron, Ohio. In 19X2 and 19X3, the taxpayers deducted $2,168 for 19X2 and $2,114 for 19X3 as interest incurred on the repayment of the loan to their parents.

Were the deductions taken allowable as interest?

48. A and B are the sole members of a limited partnership. The partnership is formed for the purpose of developing and constructing apartment complexes. In 19X4, the A-B partnership obtains a loan of $3 million from the First Ohio Bank. The loan is nonrecourse, because it is to be secured by the properties that are being financed. According to the loan agreement, the partnership is required to pay a finance charge or fee to the bank of $62,000. The loan agreement provides that the financing fee will be advanced *with* the loan proceeds. The A-B partnership wants to deduct the finance charge in 19X4 under § 163.

(a) Is the finance charge deductible under § 163?

(b) If the finance charge is not deductible, is there any way to cure the problem so that the fee can be an allowable deduction under § 163?

49. T enters into a contract for the construction of a personal residence on land which he had acquired previously. Under the terms of the contract, T agrees to reimburse the contractor for the cost of work plus a contractor's fee of $20,000. The contract specified that the cost of work included any sales, use, or similar taxes imposed by any governmental authority for which the contractor was liable. Under a mortgage financing arrangement between T and a bank, the contractor was paid in full as the work progressed.

Of the amount paid to the contractor, $5,000 was for sales taxes imposed on the purchase of materials, supplies, fixtures, and equipment used in the construction of the residence. On his individual income tax return, T deducted the $5,000 in sales taxes paid by the contractor as an itemized deduction. Upon audit, the IRS disallowed the deduction on the grounds that the contractor, and not T, was the proper party upon which the sales taxes were imposed.

(a) What arguments can T raise to demonstrate that the sales tax was imposed upon him?

(b) What arguments can the IRS use to refute T's position?

Partial list of research aids:

Rogers v. Comm., 60–2 USTC ¶ 9602, 6 AFTR2d 5187, 281 F.2d 233 (CA–4, 1960).

Jerry M. Petty, 77 T.C. 482(1981).

William F. Armentrout, 43 T.C. 16 (1964).

Chapter 12

Special Methods
for Computing the Tax
and Payment Procedures

Once gross income has been determined (refer to Chapters 5 and 6) and various deductions accounted for (refer to Chapters 7–11), the income tax liability can be computed. Generally the computation procedure requires only familiarity with the Tax Table and Tax Rate Schedule methods (discussed in Chapter 4). Some taxpayers, however, may qualify for certain beneficial computation methods (e. g., income averaging) or may be subject to taxes in addition to the regular income tax (e. g., the alternative minimum tax, the self-employment tax). This chapter deals with the special methods available for determining the income tax and the various other taxes imposed.

Also covered in this chapter are the means by which taxes are collected and paid. If an employment arrangement is involved, compliance by employers with specified withholding procedures is necessary. Self-employed taxpayers have their own pay-as-you-go set of rules. Generally, this requires the filing of a declaration of estimated tax (Form 1040-ES) and the making of periodic payments. Such prepayments should take into account the estimated income tax liability for the year and any self-employment tax that will be due.

441

SPECIAL METHODS
FOR COMPUTING THE TAX

INCOME AVERAGING

The finality of the annual accounting period concept, when considered along with the progression of the income tax rates, could cause real hardship in a rags-to-riches type of situation.[1]

> **Example 1.** Over a five-year period, R and T (each is a married individual filing a joint return) have the following income tax results:[2]

	R		T	
Year	Taxable Income	Tax Due	Taxable Income	Tax Due
19X1	$ 14,000	$ 1,510	$ 5,000	$ 179
19X2	14,000	1,510	5,000	179
19X3	14,000	1,510	5,000	179
19X4	14,000	1,510	5,000	179
19X5	14,000	1,510	50,000	12,014
Totals	$ 70,000	$ 7,550	$ 70,000	$ 12,730

> Although both R and T have the same taxable income over a five-year period (i. e., $70,000), T pays additional income taxes of $5,180 ($12,730 − $7,550).[3]

The purpose, then, of the income averaging provisions is to provide relief from the bunching effects of *unusual* amounts of income received in any one year. As noted below, the tax law quantifies what is *unusual* by applying a percentage (i. e., the 120 percent rule) to the average income of the past four years and requiring that the current income exceed this average by a specified amount (i. e., the $3,000 rule).

At the outset, it is important to recognize that the income averaging provisions do not violate the finality of the annual accounting period concept. Thus, income averaging does not call for the filing of amended tax returns for the base period (i. e., the past four years), but merely considers the base period average in arriving at how the income tax for the current year is to be computed. Nor does the income

---

1. The annual accounting period concept requires that each taxpayer's income and expenses be determined at periodic intervals (usually annually). For a further discussion of this concept and the problems it can cause in terms of inequity, refer to Chapter 2 under the heading *Mitigating the Effect of the Annual Accounting Period Concept.*
2. The tax due amounts on taxable income up to $50,000 are based on the 1983 Tax Table. The tax on $50,000 taxable income is based on the 1983 Tax Rate Schedule.
3. The tax savings by R should not be taken in isolation. After all, R has lost the use of the extra tax dollars paid from 19X1–19X4.

averaging procedure call for the use of special tax rates. It merely determines how the tax is to be computed in working with the regular Tax Rate Schedules. It is important to note that the Tax Rate Schedules must be used in computing the tax using the income averaging method. The Tax Table cannot be used if income averaging is elected.

In order to qualify for income averaging, the following two requirements must be met:[4]

—The taxpayer must be an eligible individual.

—Averageable income must be more than $3,000.

Eligible Individual. An eligible individual is one who meets the citizenship or residence test and the support test. The first test requires U. S. citizenship or resident status throughout the computation year (i. e., the year income averaging is elected) and the base period years (i. e., the four preceding years).[5]

Under the support test, the taxpayer must have provided at least 50 percent of his or her own support in each of the base period years.[6] If married in any base period year, both spouses must have provided at least 50 percent of their combined support.

The support test is waived in the following situations:

1.   If the taxpayer is at least 25 years old in the computation year and not a full-time student for any four tax years after reaching age 21.[7]

2.   If more than one-half of taxable income for the computation year is attributable to work done largely during two or more of the taxpayer's base period years.[8]

3.   If a joint return is filed in the computation year and the taxpayer who had been supported by another in any base period year does not provide more than 25 percent of the combined adjusted gross income of both spouses for such computation year.[9]

The support test and some of the exceptions thereto are illustrated below:

Example 2. While attending college on a full-time basis from 19X4–19X7, T (age 25) was supported by her parents. Based on

----

4. § 1301.
5. § § 1303(a) and (b).
6. § 1303(c)(1). Were it not for the support test, many could use income averaging upon completing school and commencing full-time employment.
7. § 1303(c)(2)(A). For a definition of student, see § 1303(d).
8. § 1303(c)(2)(B). One of the reasons for this exception is to recognize the problem often encountered in the creation of artistic and literary works. Here, the period of creativity may span several years during which the taxpayer may not be self-supporting.
9. § 1303(c)(2)(C). For this purpose, community income that results from personal services is treated as the separate income of the spouse who performed the services.

these facts, T does not meet the support test and, therefore, cannot make use of income averaging for 19X8. She does not fit within exception 1 because of the full-time student restriction.

Example 3. In 19X8, P receives 90% of her taxable income from a novel written by her during 19X4–19X7. Even if P were the dependent of another during the base period, the support test is waived through the application of exception 2.

Example 4. H and W were married in 19X8. Although H supported himself during the base period of 19X4–19X7, W was a dependent of her parents. During 19X8, their combined adjusted gross income was earned 80% by H and 20% by W. If H and W file a joint return for 19X8, the support test is waived for W under exception 3.

Averageable Income. Presuming an eligible individual is involved, income averaging is available only if the averageable income exceeds $3,000. Averageable income is defined by the Code as being the taxable income for the computation year less 120% of average base period income.[10] In arriving at average base period income, add the taxable income for each of the prior four years and divide the result by four. Because the determination of taxable income was not necessary for taxpayers using the Tax Table for years 1977 through 1980, a special computation is required by such taxpayers to determine taxable income for those base period years that are applicable.[11] This computation is illustrated in the following example.

Example 5. H and W, who are married and have no dependents, had Tax Table income[12] of $22,000 in 1980. They had taxable income of $22,800 in 1981, $24,000 in 1982, and $26,000 in 1983. Their base period income is computed as shown below.

Year	Tax Table Income	Exemptions	Taxable Income
1980	$ 22,000	$ 2,000	$ 20,000
1981			22,800
1982			24,000
1983			26,000
		Total	$ 92,800

---

10. § 1302(a)(1). By virtue of § 1302(a)(2), certain adjustments to taxable income for the computation year may have to be made. For further information see *Your Federal Income Tax*, IRS Publication 17, (Rev. Oct. 83), p. 141.

11. See Schedule G (reproduced in Appendix B).

12. Tax Table income, which is described on Schedule G as "amount from Form 1040 —line 34" equals taxable income plus the deduction for exemptions, since exemptions were not subtracted in computing Tax Table income. Tax Table income was computed for tax years 1977 through 1980.

Example 6. Assume the same facts as in Example 5 and that H and W had taxable income of $43,200 in 1984. Averageable income is computed as shown below:

Taxable income for the computation year	$ 43,200
Less: Nonaverageable income [$23,200 (average base period income) × 120%]	27,840
Averageable income	$ 15,360

Since averageable income exceeds $3,000, and assuming all other conditions are met, H and W may use income averaging for 1984.

In determining averageable income, Schedule G (Income Averaging) of Form 1040 deviates from the procedure followed above by introducing a shortcut approach.[13] Instead of dividing total base period income by four and multiplying the quotient by 120 percent, total base period income is multiplied by 30 percent.

Computation Procedure. Once the key amounts have been determined (e. g., base period income, taxable income for the computation year, averageable income), income averaging proceeds as follows:[14]

Step 1. Determine the nonaverageable income. Using the Schedule G shortcut approach, this would be 30 percent of total base period income.

Step 2. Add 20 percent of averageable income.

Step 3. Using the appropriate Tax Rate Schedule (i. e., X, Y, or Z in Appendix A–1), compute the tax on the sum reached in Step 2.[15]

Step 4. Compute the tax on the Step 1 amount.

Step 5. Subtract the tax computed in Step 4 from that computed in Step 3 and multiply the difference by four.

Step 6. Add the product determined in Step 5 to the tax determined in Step 3.[16]

Step 6, then, yields the amount of tax due by using the income averaging procedure.

---

13. The procedure used in Example 6, however, follows that specified in the Internal Revenue Code [§ 1302(a)(1)].
14. § 1301.
15. For married taxpayers living in community property states who file separate returns, an adjustment for excess community income may be necessary and should be added to the result reached in Step 2. See § 1304(c)(3) and *Your Federal Income Tax* as cited in Footnote 10.
16. For a limited adjustment, see § 1304(e).

Example 7. Assume the same facts as in Example 5. Determine the income tax liability of H and W both without and with the use of income averaging.

Without income averaging:

> The tax on $43,200 [see 1984 Schedule Y (Appendix A–1)] is $6,274 + $2,800 [33% of $8,000 (taxable income in excess of $35,200)] $ 8,914

With income averaging:

Step 1. $92,800 (base period income) × 30% (Schedule G shortcut approach) = $27,840 (nonaverageable income).

Step 2. $27,840 (nonaverageable income) + $3,072 [20% × $15,360 (averageable income)] = $30,912.

Step 3.   Tax on Step 2 amount of $30,912 [see 1984 Schedule Y, first column (Appendix A–1)] is $4,790 + $283 [28% × $1,012 (the amount computed at Step 2 in excess of $29,900)], or $5,073.

Step 4.   Tax on Step 1 amount of $27,840 [see Schedule Y, first column (Appendix A–1)] is $3,465 + $810 [25% × $3,240 (the amount of nonaverageable income in excess of $24,600)], or $4,275.

Step 5. $5,073 (Step 3) − $4,275 (Step 4) = $798 × 4 = $3,192.

Step 6. $3,192 (Step 5) + $5,073 (Step 3) = income tax liability with income averaging $ 8,265

Thus, Mr. and Mrs. T would save $649 [$8,914 (tax without) − $8,265 (tax with) by using income averaging].

The tax computations in this Example are rounded to the nearest dollar.

Reporting Procedures.   Income averaging is elected by completing Schedule G of Form 1040. Schedule G is reproduced in Appendix B. To illustrate, a completed 1983 Schedule G is shown below. Assume that John and Betty Doe are a married couple, with no dependents, filing a joint return. Their Tax Table income (amount from Form 1040, line 34) was $18,000 in 1979 and $20,000 in 1980. Their taxable income was $20,000 in 1981, $26,000 for 1982, and $50,000 for 1983. Note that the computation procedures are slightly different from those in Example 7, which is based on 1984 as the computation year.

Schedule G
(Form 1040)
Department of the Treasury
Internal Revenue Service

Income Averaging

▶ See instructions on back.   ▶ Attach to Form 1040.

OMB No. 1545-0074

1983

17

Name(s) as shown on Form 1040
    John and Betty Doe

Your social security number
123 45 6789

Step 1   Figure your income for 1979—1982

1979	1	Fill in the amount from your 1979 Form 1040 (line 34) or Form 1040A (line 11)	1	18,000	
	2	Multiply your total exemptions in 1979 by $1,000	2	2,000	
	3	Subtract line 2 from line 1. If less than zero, enter zero	3		16,000
1980	4	Fill in the amount from your 1980 Form 1040 (line 34) or Form 1040A (line 11)	4	20,000	
	5	Multiply your total exemptions in 1980 by $1,000	5	2,000	
	6	Subtract line 5 from line 4. If less than zero, enter zero	6		18,000
1981	7	Fill in the amount from your 1981 Form 1040 (line 34) or Form 1040A (line 12). If less than zero, enter zero	7		20,000
1982	8	Fill in the amount from your 1982 Form 1040 (line 37), Form 1040A (line 16), or Form 1040EZ (line 7). If less than zero, enter zero	8		26,000
Total	9	Fill in all income less deductions earned outside of the U.S. or within U.S. possessions and excluded for 1979 through 1982 (include housing exclusion in 1982)	9		
	10	Add lines 3, 6, 7, 8 and 9	10		80,000

Step 2   Figure your averageable income

	Multiply the amount on line 10 by 30% (.30)		x .30	
11	Write in the answer	11	24,000	
12	Fill in your taxable income for 1983 from Form 1040, line 37	12	50,000	
13	If you received a premature or excessive distribution subject to a penalty under section 72, see instructions	13		
14	Subtract line 13 from line 12	14	50,000	
15	If you live in a community property state and are filing a separate return, see instructions	15		
16	Subtract line 15 from line 14. If less than zero, enter zero	16	50,000	
17	Write in the amount from line 11 above	17	24,000	
18	Subtract line 17 from line 16. This is your averageable income	18	26,000	

~ IRA, Keogh (handwritten annotation)

If line 18 is $3,000 or less, do not complete the rest of this form. You do not qualify for income averaging.

Step 3   Figure your tax

	Multiply the amount on line 18 by 20% (.20)			x .20	
19	Write in the answer	19		5,200	
20	Write in the amount from line 11 above	20		24,000	
21	Add lines 19 and 20	21		29,200	
22	Write in the amount from line 15 above	22			
23	Add lines 21 and 22	23		29,200	
24	Tax on amount on line 23 (from Tax Rate Schedule X, Y, or Z)	24		4,852	
25	Tax on amount on line 21 (from Tax Rate Schedule X, Y, or Z)	25	4,852		
26	Tax on amount on line 20 (from Tax Rate Schedule X, Y, or Z)	26	3,518		
27	Subtract line 26 from line 25	27	1,334		
	Multiply the amount on line 27 by 4		x 4		
28	Write in the answer	28		5,336	
	If you have no entry on line 13, skip lines 29 through 31 and go to line 32.				
29	Tax on amount on line 12 (from Tax Rate Schedule X, Y, or Z)	29			
30	Tax on amount on line 14 (from Tax Rate Schedule X, Y, or Z)	30			
31	Subtract line 30 from line 29	31			
32	Add lines 24, 28, and 31. Write the result here and on Form 1040, line 38. Be sure to check the Schedule G box on that line	32		10,188	

Paperwork Reduction Act Notice, see Form 1040 instructions.   Schedule G (Form 1040) 1983

Other Considerations. Income averaging is an elective provision which generally must be elected by the taxpayer within the period of limitations applicable to claims for refunds.[17]

---

17. § 1304(a). For a special set of circumstances dealing with the statute of limitations restriction, see *Louis R. Hosking,* 62 T.C. 635 (1974).

Example 8. T, a calendar year taxpayer, files his return for 1982 on March 3, 1983. When preparing his return for 1983, T discovers that the use of income averaging would have reduced his income tax liability for 1982 by $920. On April 3, 1984, T files an amended return (Form 1040X) for 1982 electing the income averaging provisions. As T's amended return is timely (i. e., not barred by the statute of limitations), the utilization of income averaging is proper.[18]

Income averaging cannot be elected, however, if the taxpayer claims an exclusion from earned income while employed outside the U. S.[19]

The income averaging provisions can become very complex when the marital status of a taxpayer changes for any of the base period years or the computation year. Special allocation procedures may be necessary, but a discussion of these rules is beyond the scope of this text.[20]

ALTERNATIVE MINIMUM TAX

Historical Development. The tax laws give preferential treatment to certain kinds of income, such as long-term capital gains. Certain deductions, such as accelerated depreciation on real property, also receive favorable treatment. These special benefits are referred to as tax preference items. To insure that taxpayers who benefit from these and other special provisions pay at least a minimum amount of tax, Congress enacted two special taxes. One of these taxes, called the minimum tax, applies only to corporations (see Chapter 20). The other, called the alternative minimum tax, applies to individuals, trusts, and estates. Unlike income averaging, the alternative minimum tax is not beneficial to taxpayers. Instead of saving tax dollars through special computation procedures, it could result in additional tax liability.

In enacting the first minimum tax, Congress was concerned over statistical data compiled by the Department of the Treasury which revealed that some taxpayers with large economic incomes were able to avoid the usual tax associated with such amounts. This reduction in income taxes was being accomplished legally through various in-

---

18. For a brief discussion of the nature and purpose of a statute of limitations, refer to Chapter 1 under TAX ADMINISTRATION.

19. Section 911 allows an exclusion from gross income of up to $80,000 in 1983 (increasing by $5,000 a year until 1986 when it reaches $95,000) for certain U. S. citizens or resident aliens who work in foreign countries. Section 1304(b)(1) provides that taxpayers who claim this exclusion cannot use income averaging.

20. See "Income Averaging," IRS Publication 506 (Rev. Nov. 83), p. 3, which contains a helpful table for use in computing base period income in 20 different marital and filing status situations.

vestments that resulted in preferential treatment for tax purposes (i. e., items of tax preference). That Congress was distressed with the inequity that resulted from such tax avoidance is a point clearly made by the following extract from the Report by the Ways and Means Committee of the House of Representatives on the Tax Reform Act of 1969:

> This is obviously an unfair situation. In view of the tax burden on our citizens, at this time, it is particularly essential that our taxes be distributed in a fair manner. Your committee believes that no one should be permitted to avoid his fair share of the tax burden—to shift his tax load to the backs of other taxpayers.[21]

Thus, the minimum tax on items of tax preference that came about was intended as a means of accomplishing more equitable distribution of the tax burden among taxpayers. Originally, it was a special tax of 10 percent levied against specified items of tax preference in excess of $30,000.[22]

Before 1983, the tax law included two forms of the minimum tax applicable to individuals: the regular minimum tax and the alternative minimum tax. The Tax Equity and Fiscal Responsibility Act of 1982 repealed the regular minimum tax, while retaining and expanding the scope of the alternative minimum tax. The regular minimum tax was often referred to as the add-on minimum tax, since the effect of its application was to "add" the amount of the tax "on" to the income tax as usually determined. By way of contrast, the alternative minimum tax is a substitute for the income tax and must be used when it produces a greater tax liability (see Example 11).

COMPUTATION OF THE ALTERNATIVE MINIMUM TAX

Coping with the new alternative minimum tax for individuals is a difficult task that requires an understanding of the formula for computing the tax (see Figure I).

Also required is an understanding of each component of the formula. The more complex of these components are discussed in detail in the sections that follow.

Alternative Tax Net Operating Loss Deduction. In computing taxable income, taxpayers are allowed to deduct net operating loss (NOL) carryovers and carrybacks (refer to Chapter 8). The income tax

---

21. 1969–3 C.B. 249.
22. Interest income on state and local bonds, probably one of the grandest of all tax-free sources of income, was considered for inclusion in the list of tax preference items. Ultimately, it was omitted, undoubtedly due to the objections by representatives of state and local governments.

Figure I

FORMULA FOR COMPUTING ALTERNATIVE
MINIMUM TAX

Adjusted gross income (computed without regard to any net operating loss)
Minus:
   Alternative tax net operating loss deduction
   Alternative tax itemized deductions
   Amounts included in income under § 667 (i. e., income included due to a distribution
     of accumulated trust income)
Plus:
   Tax preference items (§ 57)
Equals:
   Alternative minimum taxable income (AMTI)
Minus:
   Exemption amount
Equals:
   Alternative minimum tax base
Times:
   Rate (20%)
Equals:
   Total
Minus:
   Regular tax on taxable income
Equals:
   Alternative minimum tax

NOL must be modified, however, in computing alternative minimum taxable income (AMTI).[23] The starting point in computing the alternative tax NOL is the regular NOL computed for income tax purposes. The income tax NOL must be reduced for tax preference items deducted in the NOL year.

> **Example 9.** In 1983, T, who does not itemize, incurred a net operating loss of $10,000. T's deductions in 1983 included tax preference items of $1,800. His alternative tax NOL for 1984 will be $8,200 [$10,000 (NOL for 1983) − $1,800 (tax preferences deducted in computing the 1983 NOL)].

In Example 9, if the adjustment were not made to the income tax NOL, the $1,800 in tax preference items deducted in 1983 would have the effect of reducing AMTI in 1984. This would weaken the entire concept of the alternative minimum tax as a tax on preference items.

An additional limitation on the alternative tax NOL is that it must be computed taking into account only those itemized deductions that are allowed as alternative tax itemized deductions (see the following section) in the NOL year.

If a taxpayer has an alternative tax NOL that is carried back or over to another year, such alternative tax NOL must be used against

---

23. § 55(d).

AMTI in the carryback or carryover year, even if the regular tax, rather than the alternative minimum tax, applies.

> **Example 10.** K's alternative tax NOL for 1984 (carried over from 1983) is $10,000. Her AMTI before considering the alternative tax NOL is $25,000. K's regular income tax exceeds the alternative minimum tax, thus the alternative minimum tax does not apply. Nevertheless, K's alternative tax NOL of $10,000 is "used up" in 1984 and is not available for carryover to a later year.

The above rules apply to post-1982 net operating losses. Special transitional rules apply to pre-1983 net operating losses.

Alternative Tax Itemized Deductions. Some itemized deductions that are allowed in computing taxable income are not allowed in computing AMTI. Allowable alternative tax itemized deductions are limited to casualty losses, gambling losses, charitable contributions, medical expenses in excess of 10 percent of adjusted gross income (although the floor is five percent for income tax purposes), estate tax on income in respect of a decedent, and qualified interest.

The alternative tax itemized deduction for qualified interest includes qualified housing interest plus other interest to the extent of qualified net investment income included in the alternative minimum tax base. The items needed to compute the deduction for qualified interest are defined in Figure II.

Figure II

DEFINITIONS OF TERMS[24]

Qualified housing interest—interest paid or accrued during the taxable year on indebtedness incurred in acquiring, constructing, or substantially rehabilitating any property used (1) as the principal residence of the taxpayer at the time the interest is paid or accrued or (2) as a qualified dwelling of the taxpayer or any member of his or her family [within the meaning of § 267(c)(4)].

Qualified dwelling—any house, apartment, condominium, or mobile home (not used on a transient basis) used by the taxpayer or any member of his or her family [within the meaning of § 267(c)(4)] during the taxable year.

Qualified net investment income—the excess of qualified investment income over qualified investment expenses.

Qualified investment income—includes (1) gross income from interest, dividends, rents, and royalties; (2) amounts recaptured as ordinary income under §§ 1245, 1250, and 1254, but only to the extent such income is not derived from the conduct of a trade or business; (3) any capital gain net income attributable to the disposition of property held for investment; and (4) any dividends excluded under § 116 (i. e., $100 on a single return, $200 on a joint return) or any interest excluded under the All-Savers provisions.

Qualified investment expenses—deductions directly connected with the production of qualified investment income to the extent that (1) such deductions are allowable in computing adjusted gross income and (2) such deductions are not items of tax preference.

---

24. § 55(e).

Tax Preference Items. An important step in computing the alternative minimum tax is to arrive at the sum of the items of tax preference.[25] The most commonly encountered items of tax preference are summarized below.

—The 60 percent capital gain deduction.

—Accelerated depreciation on realty in excess of what would have been allowed under the straight-line method.

—The bargain element in certain stock options in the year the options are exercised.

—The excess of the depletion deduction over the adjusted basis of the property at the end of the year (figured before deducting the depletion for the year).

—Amounts for amortization of certified pollution control facilities and child care facilities in excess of the depreciation normally allowable.

—Depreciation or amortization for leased personalty in excess of the amount that would have been allowed under the straight-line method.

—The excess of intangible drilling and development costs of oil, gas, and geothermal wells deducted during the year minus the sum of (1) the amount allowed if the costs had been capitalized and written off under the straight-line method and (2) the net income for the year from oil, gas, and geothermal properties.

—For cost recovery property (i. e., property placed in service in 1981 and later) subject to a lease, the excess of the cost recovery allowance over the deduction which would have been allowable had the property been depreciated using the straight-line method and the half-year convention for a period of years specified in § 57(a)(12).

—Dividends excluded from gross income under § 116 ($100 on a single return, $200 on a joint return).

—Interest excluded from gross income under § 128 (All-Savers interest).

—Interest excluded from gross income under the 15 percent net interest exclusion rule (which takes effect after 1984).

—Excess deductions for mining exploration and development expenditures (i. e., deductions in excess of ratable amortization over 10 years).

—Bargain element at the date of exercise of incentive stock options (i. e., the excess of the fair market value of the stock over the option price at the date the option is exercised).

---

25. All tax preference items are specified in § 57.

Exemption Amount. The exemption amount is $40,000 for married taxpayers filing joint returns, $30,000 for single taxpayers, and $20,000 for married taxpayers filing separate returns.[26]

Alternative Minimum Tax Rate. The rate for the alternative minimum tax is a flat 20 percent. It replaces the two-tier rate structure (10 percent and 20 percent) under prior law.

Illustration of the Alternative Minimum Tax Computation. The complex provisions for computation of the alternative minimum tax are illustrated in the following example.

Example 11. T, who is single, had taxable income for 1984 as shown below:

Salary		$ 102,000
Interest		8,000
Capital gain ($250,000 net capital gain from sale of stocks—$150,000 capital gain deduction)		100,000
		$ 210,000
Less: Employee business expenses		10,000
Adjusted gross income		$ 200,000
Less: Excess itemized deductions –		
medical expenses ($35,000 – 5% of $200,000 AGI)	$ 25,000*	
Taxes	10,000	
Interest		
Home mortgage	30,000*	
Other	5,300*	
Contributions	7,000*	
Casualty losses	4,000*	
	$ 81,300	
Less: Zero bracket amount	2,300	$ 79,000
		$ 121,000
Less: Exemption		1,000
Taxable income		$ 120,000

Deductions marked by an asterisk are allowed as *alternative tax itemized deductions.* Alternative minimum taxable income is computed as follows:

Adjusted gross income		$200,000
Less: Alternative tax itemized deductions		
Medical expenses	$15,000[a]	
Interest	35,300[b]	
Contributions	7,000	
Casualty losses	4,000	61,300
		$138,700

---

26.   § 55(f).

Plus:	Tax preferences (capital gain deduction)	150,000
	Alternative minimum taxable income	$288,700
Less:	Exemption	30,000
	Minimum tax base	$258,700
	Rate	.20
		$ 51,740
Less:	Regular tax on $120,000 taxable income	47,935
	Alternative minimum tax	$ 3,805

[a]Total medical expenses were $35,000, reduced by 5% of AGI, resulting in an itemized deduction of $25,000. However, for alternative minimum tax purposes, the reduction is 10%, which leaves an alternative minimum tax itemized deduction of $15,000 ($35,000 − 10% of $200,000 AGI).

[b]In this illustration, all interest is deductible in computing alternative minimum taxable income. Home mortgage interest is always deductible. Other interest ($5,300) is deductible to the extent of net investment income included in the minimum tax base. For this purpose, interest income and capital gain net income are treated as net investment income.

Although there are many other detailed rules in the TEFRA provisions, space limitations require that some be omitted in this discussion. However, there are two additional features which require comment.

First, nonrefundable credits other than the foreign tax credit are not allowed as offsets against the alternative minimum tax. The foreign tax credit may be utilized, but it is subject to a limitation based on income from sources outside the United States.[27]

Second, individuals may avoid having a tax preference item on certain *qualified expenditures*. This is accomplished by an election to amortize such expenditures ratably over a 10-year period in lieu of expensing such amounts in the year incurred.[28]

PAYMENT PROCEDURES

The tax law contains elaborate rules which require the prepayment of various Federal taxes. Consistent with the pay-as-you-go approach to the collection of taxes, these rules carry penalties for lack of compliance.[29] Prepayment procedures fall into two major categories: those applicable to employers and those applicable to self-employed persons. In the case of employers, both payroll taxes (i. e., FICA and FUTA) and income taxes may be involved. With self-employed taxpayers, the focus is on the income tax and the self-employment tax.[30]

---

27. § 55(c)(2).

28. See § 58(i) for details.

29. See, for example, § 3403 (employer liable for any taxes withheld and not paid over to the IRS), § 6656 (5% penalty on amounts withheld and not paid over and 25% penalty for overstated deposit claims), and § 6654 (20% charge for failure to pay estimated income taxes).

30. For the distinction between employees and self-employed persons, refer to Examples 1–3 in Chapter 10.

PROCEDURES APPLICABLE TO EMPLOYERS

As noted in Chapter 1, employment taxes include FICA (Federal Insurance Contributions Act) and FUTA (Federal Unemployment Tax Act). The employer usually is responsible for withholding the employee's share of FICA (commonly referred to as Social Security tax) and appropriate amounts for income taxes. In addition, the employer must match the FICA portion withheld and fully absorb the cost of FUTA. The sum of the employment taxes and the income tax withholdings must be paid to the IRS at specified intervals.

The key to employer compliance in this area involves the resolution of the following points:

—Ascertaining which employees and wages are covered by employment taxes and subject to withholding for income taxes.

—Arriving at the amount to be withheld.

—Reporting and paying employment taxes and income taxes withheld to the IRS on a timely basis through the use of proper forms.

Coverage Requirements. Circular E (Employer's Tax Guide), Publication 15, issued by the IRS contains a complete list of which employees and which wages require withholdings for income taxes and employment taxes. Figure III extracts a portion of this list and is reproduced on the following pages.

In working with Figure III, consider the following observations:

—The designation "exempt" in the income tax withholding column does not mean that the amount paid is nontaxable to the employee. It merely relieves the employer from having to withhold.

Example 12. T works for X Corporation and has the type of job where tips are not common but do occur. If the total tips T receives are less than $20 per month, X Corporation need not withhold Federal income taxes on these amounts. Nevertheless, the tips should be included by T in his gross income.

—Notice that in some cases, income tax withholding is not required but is voluntary. This is designated "Exempt (taxable if both employer and employee voluntarily agree)."

Example 13. T is employed as a gardener by a wealthy family. In the past, he has encountered difficulty in managing his finances so as to be in a position to pay the income tax due every April 15. To ease the cash flow problem that develops in April, T requests that the employer withhold income taxes from his wages.

—The FICA column relates to the employer's share. The same holds true with FUTA, since the employee does not contribute to this tax.

Figure III

Special classes of employment and special types of payment	Treatment under different employment taxes		
	Income tax withholding	Social Security	Federal unemployment
Dismissal or severance pay............	Taxable................	Taxable................	Taxable
Educational assistance program payments by employer under § 127.	Exempt..............	Exempt..............	Exempt
Family employees: a. Son or daughter under 21 employed by parent (or by partnership consisting only of parents); wife employed by husband or husband employed by wife.	Taxable............	Exempt.............. {Taxable if in course of the son or daughter's business; exempt if not in the course of the son or daughter's business. For household work in private home of son or daughter, refer to section 13 in Circular E (Rev. October 1981).	Exempt
b. Parent employed by a son or daughter.	Taxable............		Exempt
Household workers (domestic service in private homes).	Exempt (taxable if both employer and employee voluntarily agree).	Taxable if paid $50 or more in cash in quarter.	Taxable if employer paid cash wages of $1,000 or more in any calendar quarter in the current or preceding year.
Interns working in hospitals	Taxable............	Taxable if hospital is subject to Social Security.	Exempt

Meals and lodging including those furnished at a bargain charge to the employee.		(a) Meals—taxable unless furnished for employer's convenience and on the employer's premises. (b) Lodging—taxable unless furnished on employer's premises, for the employer's convenience, and as condition of employment.
Ministers of churches performing duties as such.	Exempt..............	Exempt
Moving expenses: a. Reimbursement for moving expenses you believe are deductible by employee.	Exempt..............	Exempt
b. Reimbursement for moving expenses you believe are not deductible by employee.	Taxable.............	Taxable
Newspaper carrier under age 18 delivering to consumers.	Exempt (taxable if both employer and employee voluntarily agree).	Exempt
Tips, if less than $20 in a month..........	Exempt from withholding. Taxable to employee.	Exempt
Workers' compensation.................	Exempt..............	Exempt

Amount of Withholding. In the case of FICA, withholdings from employees must continue until the base amount is reached (refer to Figure III in Chapter 1). In tax year 1984, for example, withholding would cease once the employee has earned wages subject to FICA in the amount of $37,800.

Arriving at the amount to be withheld for income tax purposes is not so simple. Basically, it involves three steps:[31]

—Have the employee complete Form W–4, Employee's Withholding Allowance Certificate.

—Determine the employee's payroll period.

—Compute the amount to be withheld, usually using either the wage-bracket tables or the percentage method.

Form W–4 reflects the employee's marital status, withholding exemptions, and allowances. Generally, it need not be filed with the IRS and is retained by the employer as part of the payroll records.[32] The employer need not verify the number of exemptions claimed. Any misinformation contained therein will be attributed to the employee. However, if the employer has reason to believe that the employee made a false statement, the IRS District Director should be notified. In the meantime, the Form W–4 should be honored.

Employees are subject to penalties for filing false withholding statements. Because many employees (particularly tax protestors) were claiming excessive withholding allowances, the penalty was increased by the Economic Recovery Tax Act of 1981.[33] The civil penalty for filing false information with respect to wage withholding is now $500.

On Form W–4 an employee may claim withholding allowances for the following: personal and dependency exemptions, the zero bracket amount allowance, and additional allowances (e. g., because of unusually large deductions *from* adjusted gross income, alimony deductions, child and dependent care credit, earned income credit, and credit for the elderly).[34] The zero bracket amount allowance (designated as a "special withholding allowance" on Form W–4) can be claimed only if the employee has one job or, if married, his or her spouse is not employed. Tables for determining the proper number of withholding allowances based on the additional allowances appear on page 2 of Form W–4. If the taxpayer is married and both spouses are employed, the total allowances may be allocated between them as

---

31. The withholding provisions are contained in §§ 3401–3402. These sections will not be referenced specifically in the discussion that follows.

32. Filing a copy of Form W–4 with the IRS may be necessary if the employee claims more than 14 exemptions or, in certain cases, claims exempt status. The IRS is aware that some employees deliberately avoid income tax withholding through the use of either of these procedures.

33. § 6682.

34. Tax credits are discussed in Chapter 13.

they see fit. The same allocation procedure is required if a taxpayer has more than one job. In no event should the same allowance be claimed more than once at the same time.[35]

Example 14. H and W are married and have three dependent children. Both are employed and have no additional allowances. Together they should be entitled to five allowances [2 (for personal exemptions) + 3 (for dependency exemptions)]. The zero bracket amount allowance is not available, since both spouses are employed. If H was the spouse first employed and his Form W–4 reflects five allowances, W's Form W–4 should claim none. They could, however, reallocate their allowances between them as long as the total claimed does not exceed five.

Example 15. Assume the same facts as in Example 14 except that W is not employed. H, however, has a full-time and a part-time job. If H's Form W–4 filed with his full-time employer reflects five allowances, he should be claiming none as to the part-time job. In this case, the zero bracket amount allowance is not available since H has two jobs at the same time.

The period of service for which an employee is paid is known as the payroll period. Daily, weekly, biweekly, semimonthly, and monthly periods are the most common arrangements. If an employee has no regular payroll period, then he or she is considered to be paid on a daily basis.

Once the allowances are known (as reflected on Form W–4) and the payroll period determined, the amount to be withheld for Federal income taxes can be computed. The computation usually is made through the use of the wage-bracket tables or by the percentage method.

Wage-bracket tables are available for daily, weekly, biweekly, semimonthly, and monthly payroll periods as to single (including heads of household), and married taxpayers. An extract of the tables dealing with married persons on a monthly payroll period is reproduced in Figure IV.

The table in Figure IV is for the period from after June 1983 and before January 1985. The use of withholding tables is illustrated in Examples 16 and 17.

Example 16. T is married and has three dependent children and no additional allowances. In his job with X Corporation, T earns $2,770 in May 1984. Presuming T's wife is not employed

---

35. It is permissible, of course, to declare *fewer* allowances than the taxpayer is entitled to in order to increase the amount of withholding. Doing so, however, does not affect the number of exemptions allowable on the employee's income tax return. Also, provision is made to permit an employee to have the employer withhold a certain dollar amount in addition to the required amount.

Figure IV

MARRIED Persons—MONTHLY Payroll Period
(For Wages Paid After June 1983 and Before January 1985)

And the wages are—		And the number of withholding allowances claimed is—										
At least	But less than	0	1	2	3	4	5	6	7	8	9	10
		The amount of income tax to be withheld shall be—										
$1,760	$1,800	$247.70	$229.40	$211.00	$196.10	$181.90	$167.80	$153.60	$139.40	$125.30	$111.10	$96.90
1,800	1,840	256.50	238.20	219.80	202.90	188.70	174.60	160.40	146.20	132.10	117.90	103.70
1,840	1,880	265.30	247.00	228.60	210.30	195.50	181.40	167.20	153.00	138.90	124.70	110.50
1,880	1,920	274.10	255.80	237.40	219.10	202.30	188.20	174.00	159.80	145.70	131.50	117.30
1,920	1,960	282.90	264.60	246.20	227.90	209.60	195.00	180.80	166.60	152.50	138.30	124.10
1,960	2,000	292.10	273.40	255.00	236.70	218.40	201.80	187.60	173.40	159.30	145.10	130.90
2,000	2,040	302.10	282.20	263.80	245.50	227.20	208.80	194.40	180.20	166.10	151.90	137.70
2,040	2,080	312.10	291.30	272.60	254.30	236.00	217.60	201.20	187.00	172.90	158.70	144.50
2,080	2,120	322.10	301.30	281.40	263.10	244.80	226.40	208.10	193.80	179.70	165.50	151.30
2,120	2,160	332.10	311.30	290.40	271.90	253.60	235.20	216.90	200.60	186.50	172.30	158.10
2,160	2,200	342.10	321.30	300.40	280.70	262.40	244.00	225.70	207.40	193.30	179.10	164.90
2,200	2,240	352.10	331.30	310.40	· 289.60	271.20	252.80	234.50	216.20	200.10	185.90	171.70
2,240	2,280	362.10	341.30	320.40	299.60	280.00	261.60	243.30	225.00	206.90	192.70	178.50
2,280	2,320	372.10	351.30	330.40	309.60	288.80	270.40	252.10	233.80	215.40	199.50	185.30
2,320	2,360	382.10	361.30	340.40	319.60	298.80	279.20	260.90	242.60	224.20	206.30	192.10
2,360	2,400	392.10	371.30	350.40	329.60	308.80	288.00	269.70	251.40	233.00	214.70	198.90
2,400	2,440	402.40	381.30	360.40	339.60	318.80	297.90	278.50	260.20	241.80	223.50	205.70
2,440	2,480	413.60	391.30	370.40	349.60	328.80	307.90	287.30	269.00	250.60	232.30	214.00
2,480	2,520	424.80	401.50	380.40	359.60	338.80	317.90	297.10	277.80	259.40	241.10	222.80
2,520	2,560	436.00	412.70	390.40	369.60	348.80	327.90	307.10	286.60	268.20	249.90	231.60
2,560	2,600	447.20	423.90	400.60	379.60	358.80	337.90	317.10	296.30	277.00	258.70	240.40
2,600	2,640	458.40	435.10	411.80	389.60	368.80	347.90	327.10	306.30	285.80	267.50	249.20
2,640	2,680	469.60	446.30	423.00	399.60	378.80	357.90	337.10	316.30	295.40	276.30	258.00
2,680	2,720	480.80	457.50	434.20	410.80	388.80	367.90	347.10	326.30	305.40	285.10	266.80
2,720	2,760	492.00	468.70	445.40	422.00	398.80	377.90	357.10	336.30	315.40	294.60	275.60
2,760	2,800	503.20	479.90	456.60	433.20	409.90	387.90	367.10	346.30	325.40	304.60	284.40
2,800	2,840	514.40	491.10	467.80	444.40	421.10	397.90	377.10	356.30	335.40	314.60	293.80
2,840	2,880	526.10	502.30	479.00	455.60	432.30	409.00	387.10	366.30	345.40	324.60	303.80
2,880	2,920	539.30	513.50	490.20	466.80	443.50	420.20	397.10	376.30	355.40	334.60	313.80
2,920	2,960	552.50	525.00	501.40	478.00	454.70	431.40	408.00	386.30	365.40	344.60	323.80
2,960	3,000	565.70	538.20	512.60	489.20	465.90	442.60	419.20	396.00	375.40	354.60	333.80
3,000	3,040	578.90	551.40	523.90	500.40	477.10	453.80	430.40	407.10	385.40	364.60	343.80
3,040	3,080	592.10	564.60	537.10	511.60	488.30	465.00	441.60	418.30	395.40	374.60	353.80
3,080	3,120	605.30	577.80	550.30	522.80	499.50	476.20	452.80	429.50	406.20	384.60	363.80
3,120	3,160	618.50	591.00	563.50	536.00	510.70	487.40	464.00	440.70	417.40	394.60	373.80
3,160	3,200	631.70	604.20	576.70	549.20	521.90	498.60	475.20	451.90	428.60	405.20	383.80
3,200	3,240	644.90	617.40	589.90	562.40	534.90	509.80	486.40	463.10	439.80	416.40	393.80
3,240	3,280	658.10	630.60	603.10	575.60	548.10	521.00	497.60	474.30	451.00	427.60	404.30
3,280	3,320	671.30	643.80	616.30	588.80	561.30	533.80	508.80	485.50	462.20	438.80	415.50
3,320	3,360	684.50	657.00	629.50	602.00	574.50	547.00	520.00	496.70	473.40	450.00	426.70
3,360	3,400	697.70	670.20	642.70	615.20	587.70	560.20	532.70	507.90	484.60	461.20	437.90
3,400	3,440	710.90	683.40	655.90	628.40	600.90	573.40	545.90	519.10	495.80	472.40	449.10
3,440	3,480	724.10	696.60	669.10	641.60	614.10	586.60	559.10	531.60	507.00	483.60	460.30
3,480	3,520	737.30	709.80	682.30	654.80	627.30	599.80	572.30	544.80	518.20	494.80	471.50
3,520	3,560	750.50	723.00	695.50	668.00	640.50	613.00	585.50	558.00	530.50	506.00	482.70
3,560	3,600	763.70	736.20	708.70	681.20	653.70	626.20	598.70	571.20	543.70	517.20	493.90
3,600	3,640	776.90	749.40	721.90	694.40	666.90	639.40	611.90	584.40	556.90	529.40	505.10
3,640	3,680	790.10	762.60	735.10	707.60	680.10	652.60	625.10	597.60	570.10	542.60	516.30
3,680	3,720	803.30	775.80	748.30	720.80	693.30	665.80	638.30	610.80	583.30	555.80	528.30
3,720	3,760	816.80	789.00	761.50	734.00	706.50	679.00	651.50	624.00	596.50	569.00	541.50
3,760	3,800	831.60	802.20	774.70	747.20	719.70	692.20	664.70	637.20	609.70	582.20	554.70
3,800	3,840	846.40	815.60	787.90	760.40	732.90	705.40	677.90	650.40	622.90	595.40	567.90
3,840	3,880	861.20	830.40	801.10	773.60	746.10	718.60	691.10	663.60	636.10	608.60	581.10
3,880	3,920	876.00	845.20	814.30	786.80	759.30	731.80	704.30	676.80	649.30	621.80	594.30
3,920	3,960	890.80	860.00	829.10	800.00	772.50	745.00	717.50	690.00	662.50	635.00	607.50
3,960	4,000	905.60	874.80	843.90	813.20	785.70	758.20	730.70	703.20	675.70	648.20	620.70
4,000	4,040	920.40	889.60	858.70	827.90	798.90	771.40	743.90	716.40	688.90	661.40	633.90
4,040	4,080	935.20	904.40	873.50	842.70	812.10	784.60	757.10	729.60	702.10	674.60	647.10
4,080	4,120	950.00	919.20	888.30	857.50	826.70	797.80	770.30	742.80	715.30	687.80	660.30
4,120	4,160	964.80	934.00	903.10	872.30	841.50	811.00	783.50	756.00	728.50	701.00	673.50
4,160	4,200	979.60	948.80	917.90	887.10	856.30	825.40	796.70	769.20	741.70	714.20	686.70
4,200	4,240	994.40	963.60	932.70	901.90	871.10	840.20	809.90	782.40	754.90	727.40	699.90
4,240	4,280	1,009.20	978.40	947.50	916.70	885.90	855.00	824.20	795.60	768.10	740.60	713.10
4,280	4,320	1,024.00	993.20	962.30	931.50	900.70	869.80	839.00	808.80	781.30	753.80	726.30
4,320	4,360	1,038.80	1,008.00	977.10	946.30	915.50	884.60	853.80	823.00	794.50	767.00	739.50
4,360	4,400	1,053.60	1,022.80	991.90	961.10	930.30	899.40	868.60	837.80	807.70	780.20	752.70
4,400	4,440	1,068.40	1,037.60	1,006.70	975.90	945.10	914.20	883.40	852.60	821.70	793.40	765.90
4,440	4,480	1,083.20	1,052.40	1,021.50	990.70	959.90	929.00	898.20	867.40	836.50	806.60	779.10
4,480	4,520	1,098.00	1,067.20	1,036.30	1,005.50	974.70	943.80	913.00	882.20	851.30	820.50	792.30
4,520	4,560	1,112.80	1,082.00	1,051.10	1,020.30	989.50	958.60	927.80	897.00	866.10	835.30	805.50
4,560	4,600	1,127.60	1,096.80	1,065.90	1,035.10	1,004.30	973.40	942.60	911.80	880.90	850.10	819.30
		37 percent of the excess over $4,600 plus—										
$4,600 and over		1,135.00	1,104.20	1,073.30	1,042.50	1,011.70	980.80	950.00	919.20	888.30	857.50	826.70

and all available allowances are claimed on Form W–4, X Corporation should withhold $367.10 a month from T's wages. This amount is taken from the six allowances column in the wage bracket of $2,760–$2,800. The six allowances result from personal exemptions (two) plus the special zero bracket amount allowance (one) plus dependency exemptions (three).

Example 17. Assume the same facts as in Example 16 except that T's salary is $5,000 per month. The amount of the monthly income tax withholding becomes $1,098 [$950 + (37% × $400)]. Because T's monthly salary is more than $4,600, the excess is subject to a flat 37%.

Although the wage-bracket table requires little, if any, calculations, the percentage method is equally acceptable and sometimes is used by employers.[36] It is particularly useful when payroll computations are computerized. The use of the percentage method, however, requires use of a conversion chart. The following amounts apply to taxpayers with one withholding allowance.

Payroll Period	Amount of One Allowance
Daily	$ 3.85
Weekly	19.23
Biweekly	38.46
Semimonthly	41.66
Monthly	83.33
Quarterly	250.00
Semiannual	500.00
Annual	1,000.00

Under the percentage method, proceed as follows:

Step 1. Multiply the amount of one allowance (as specified in the conversion chart) by the employee's total allowances (taken from Form W–4).

Step 2. Reduce the employee's wages by the product reached in Step 1. This remainder is called "amount of wages."

Step 3. Using the result derived in Step 2, compute the income tax withholding under the proper percentage-method table.

The table that should be used in applying the percentage method for those with monthly payroll periods is reproduced in Figure V.

An illustration of the percentage method follows:[37]

Example 18. Assume the same facts as in Example 16 except that T's income tax withholding is determined using the percentage method.

---

36. Its use may be necessary for payroll periods where no wage-bracket tables are available (i. e., quarterly, semiannual, and annual payroll periods).

37. Its use may be necessary for payroll periods where no wage-bracket tables are available (i. e., quarterly, semiannual, and annual payroll periods).

Figure V

TABLES FOR PERCENTAGE METHOD OF WITHHOLDING[38]

TABLE 4—If the Payroll Period With Respect to an Employee is Monthly

(a) SINGLE person—including head of household:			(b) MARRIED person—		
If the amount of wages is:	*The amount of income tax to be withheld shall be:*		*If the amount of wages is:*	*The amount of income tax to be withheld shall be:*	
Not over $117 0			Not over $200 0		
Over—	**But not over—**	**of excess over—**	**Over—**	**But not over—**	**of excess over—**
$117	—$342 ....12%	—$117	$200	—$800 ....12%	—$200
$342	—$792 ...$27.00 plus 15%	—$342	$800	—$1,598...$72.00 plus 17%	—$800
$792	—$1,200...$94.50 plus 19%	—$792	$1,598	—$1,967...$207.66 plus 22%	—$1,598
$1,200	—$1,833...$172.02 plus 25%	—$1,200	$1,967	—$2,408...$288.84 plus 25%	—$1,967
$1,833	—$2,317...$330.27 plus 30%	—$1,833	$2,408	—$2,850...$399.09 plus 28%	—$2,408
$2,317	—$2,758...$475.47 plus 34%	—$2,317	$2,850	—$3,733...$522.85 plus 33%	—$2,850
$2,758	.........$625.41 plus 37%	—$2,758	$3,733	...........$814.24 plus 37%	—$3,733

Step 1. $83.33 (amount of one allowance for a monthly payroll period) × 6 (total allowances) = $499.98.

Step 2. $2,770 (monthly salary) − $499.98 (step 1) = $2,270.02 (amount of wages).

Step 3.   Referring to Figure V: $288.84 + (25% × $303.02) = $364.60.

By way of comparison, the wage-bracket tables yielded an amount for income tax withholding of $367.10 (see Example 16) while the percentage method resulted in $364.60 (see Example 18). The difference is explained by the fact that the wage-bracket table amounts are derived by computing the withholding on the median wage within each bracket.[39]

Reporting and Payment Procedures. Proper handling of employment taxes and income tax withholdings requires considerable compliance effort on the part of the employer. Among the Federal forms which will have to be filed are the following:

Form Designation	Title
SS–4	Application for Employer Identification Number
W–2	Wage and Tax Statement
W–3	Transmittal of Income and Tax Statements
940	Employer's Annual Federal Unemployment Tax Return
941	Employer's Quarterly Federal Tax Return

Form SS–4 is the starting point, since it provides the employer with an identification number that must be used on all of the other

---

38.   This table is for wages paid after June 1983 and before January 1985.

39.   The same result can develop when comparing the income tax liability yielded by the Tax Table as opposed to the Tax Rate Schedules.

forms filed with the IRS and the Social Security Administration. The number that will be issued (usually in about 10 days after the filing of form SS–4) will consist of nine digits and is hyphenated between the second and third digits (e. g., 72–1987316).

Form W–2 furnishes essential information to employees concerning wages paid, FICA, and income tax withholdings. The multiple copies of Form W–2 are distributed as follows: Copy A is sent by the employer to the Social Security Administration office which services the area, Copy B goes to the employee and is to be attached to his or her income tax return, Copy C also goes to the employee for retention in personal records, and Copy D is kept by the employer as part of the usual payroll records. Extra copies of Form W–2 may have to be prepared for state and local use.[40] Form W–2 must be furnished to an employee not later than January 31 of the following year. If an employee leaves an employment before the end of the year, the time for delivery is not later than 30 days after the last payment of wages.

Form W–3 should accompany the Copy A of Form W–2 filed by the employer. Its basic purpose is to summarize and reconcile the amounts withheld for FICA and income taxes from *all* employees.

Form 940 constitutes the employer's annual accounting for FUTA purposes. It must be filed on or before January 31 of the following year and must be accompanied by the payment of any undeposited FUTA due the Federal government.[41]

Regardless of whether or not monthly deposits are required (see below) each employer must settle his or her employment taxes every quarter. To do this, Form 941 must be filed on or before the last day of the month following the end of the quarter. Due dates for the filing of Form 941 for each quarter are as follows:

Quarter	End of Quarter	Due Date
January, February, March	March 31	April 30
April, May, June	June 30	July 31
July, August, September	September 30	October 31
October, November, December	December 31	January 31

Form 941 lists the wages subject to FICA, provides for the computation of the tax, and summarizes the income tax withholdings. Any balance due over prior deposits must be remitted with the form.

The frequency with which an employer must make payments to the IRS depends on the monthly total of three items: the income tax withheld from the employees, the FICA taxes withheld from the employees, and the employer's share of FICA. When the cumulative total

---

40. An employee, for example, who lives in New York City, would require additional copies of Form W–2 for state and city income tax purposes.

41. For a discussion of state involvement in FUTA, refer to Chapter 1.

of these three items is $500 or more but less than $3,000 for any month other than March, June, September, or December, the amount must be deposited within 15 days after the close of the month.[42]

Example 19. E, an employer, had total taxes (amounts withheld plus employer's portion of FICA) of $450 on wages paid in October and $550 on wages paid in November. No deposit is required for October, but the total amount of $1,000 ($450 + $550) must be deposited by December 15.

The payment should be sent or taken to any commercial bank qualified as a depository for Federal taxes or to the nearest Federal Reserve bank. The mailing date determines the deposit date. A deposit received by the bank after the due date will be considered timely if it was mailed on or before the second day before the due date. Since proof of mailing should be available, certified or registered mail should be used.

As soon as the cumulative total of FICA and income taxes withheld is $3,000 or more in any eighth-monthly period, the employer must deposit the taxes within three banking days after the close of such period.[43] The monthly or eighth-monthly period deposit, when required, must be accompanied by Form 501 (Federal Tax Deposit). When the employer files Form 941 (see above), he or she will claim the payments as a reduction of tax due.

Example 20. T, an employer, had $3,500 of taxes on wages paid from the first through the third of May. T must deposit these taxes within three banking days after May 3.

For those employers who are not required to make deposits, the payment of payroll taxes and income tax withholdings is postponed to the time of filing Form 941 if the balance due is less than $500. If the balance due is $500 or more, the entire amount must be deposited on or before the fifteenth day of the first month following the close of the quarter.

WITHHOLDING ON PENSIONS

The Tax Equity and Fiscal Responsibility Act of 1982 contained numerous provisions to increase the level of taxpayer compliance. Among the most important of these is the provision requiring withholding at the source on pensions. In the past, no income tax withholding was required for pension payments unless the payee so requested. TEFRA made such withholding mandatory unless the taxpayer affirmatively elects out. Part of the reason for the new law is to

---

42. *Employer's Tax Guide,* IRS Publication 15 (Rev. July 83), p. 7.
43. An eighth-monthly period is the period that ends on the 3rd, 7th, 11th, 15th, 19th, 22nd, 25th, and the last day of each month.

ease the burden on the retiree of filing and paying quarterly estimated tax payments.

The amount of the withholding (presuming the payee has not elected out) depends on whether the payments are periodic (e. g., an annuity) or nonperiodic (e. g., a lump-sum distribution). If periodic, the payments are treated as wages and the regular payroll withholding procedures apply as to the taxable portion. The payee informs the payor concerning his or her marital status and exemptions by filing Form W-4P, Withholding Certificate for Pension or Annuity Payments. When the payee does not furnish any information or furnishes inadequate information concerning his or her tax status, he or she will be treated by the payor as being married with three exemptions. If not periodic, a 10 percent rate of withholding generally applies to pension distributions. Recipients may elect to have no income tax withheld on pension or annuity payments. However, such taxpayers may be required to make estimated tax payments on the amounts received.

PROCEDURES APPLICABLE TO SELF-EMPLOYED PERSONS

Although the discussion to follow largely centers on self-employed taxpayers, some of the procedures may be applicable to employed persons. In many cases, for example, employed persons may be required to file a declaration of estimated tax. Along the same vein, an employee may have a second trade or business which is conducted in a self-employment capacity. Depending upon the circumstances, the second job may require the payment of a self-employment tax.

Declaration of Estimated Tax by Individuals. Any individual who reasonably expects his or her gross income to exceed the following amounts must file a declaration of estimated tax (Form 1040–ES):[44]

—$20,000 for single individuals, heads of households, and surviving spouses.

—$20,000 for married individuals entitled to make joint estimated tax payments, if one spouse has not received wages during the year.

—$10,000 for married individuals entitled to file a joint declaration when both spouses have wages.

—$5,000 for married individuals not entitled to file a joint declaration.

Regardless of the above guidelines, a declaration of estimated tax is required if more than $500 of income is received from sources not subject to withholding (e. g., dividends and interest). The declaration

---

44. § 6015.

is not required, however, if the estimated tax can reasonably be expected to be less than $400 ($500 in 1985 and thereafter).[45] Therefore, it is possible for an employee to avoid these filing requirements by requesting his or her employer to increase the amounts of Federal income tax withheld.

Declarations of estimated tax are due when an individual first meets these filing requirements. Payments may be made in quarterly installments beginning on April 15 for calendar year taxpayers. The installment payments are due on April 15, June 15, September 15, and January 15 of the following year. An amended estimate is required if the taxpayer discovers that the original estimate was inaccurate. The newly determined tax amount (less amounts previously paid) is spread equally over the remaining installments.

Married taxpayers may file a joint declaration of estimated tax even though a joint income tax return is not subsequently filed. In such event, the estimated tax payments may be applied against the separate return liability of the spouses as they see fit.[46] If a husband and wife cannot agree on a division of the estimated tax payments, the Regulations provide that the payments are to be allocated in proportion to the tax paid on the separate returns.[47]

Penalty on Underpayments. A nondeductible penalty is imposed on the amount of underpayment of estimated tax. The rate for this penalty is adjusted semiannually to reflect changes in the average prime rate. From July 1, 1983, to April 15, 1984, the annual rate was 11 percent. The rate after April 15, 1984, had not been set at the date of this writing.

Note that there is no additional penalty for failure to file a declaration of estimated tax; the only penalty which is imposed is the underpayment penalty. An underpayment occurs when any installment (the sum of estimated tax paid and income tax withheld) is less than 80 percent of the total tax shown on the return for the year, divided by the number of installments that should have been made (usually four).[48]

In recognition of the inherent difficulty associated with the estimation of income, the following exceptions are provided which will prevent the imposition of the penalty for underpayment of estimated tax.[49]

1. Installment payments (including amounts withheld) are equal to or exceed the amount of the tax liability on the prior year's return. (The prior year's return must cover a period of 12 months and show a tax liability.)

---

45. § 6654(f).
46. § 6015(b).
47. Reg § 1.6015(b)–1(b).
48. *Your Federal Income Tax,* IRS Publication 17 (Rev. Oct. 83), p. 29.
49. § 6054(d).

2. Installment payments (including amounts withheld) are equal to or exceed the prior year's tax liability using current year's rates and exemptions.

3. Installment payments (including amounts withheld) are equal to or exceed 80 percent of the tax due for the current year based upon the annualization of current year's income.

4. Such payments are equal to or exceed 90 percent of the tax computed by applying current year rates to actual taxable income and self-employment income for the months preceding the month in which the installment is due.

Example 21. During the current year, T made quarterly estimated tax payments of $250 each and $5,000 was withheld from her salary. Since income tax withheld is considered paid equally on each installment date,[50] each quarterly installment was $1,500 [$250 + $1,250 (one-fourth of $5,000)] for a total of $6,000. T's tax liability amounted to $10,000 for the current year and was $5,000 for the prior year. T is subject to the underpayment penalty because she has paid in quarterly less than one-fourth of 80% of the total tax liability shown on her return [¼ of $8,000 (80% × $10,000) = $2,000]. However, she can avoid the penalty by filing Form 2210 and claiming Exception 1 because each installment was equal to or greater than one-fourth of her prior year's tax of $5,000.

To avoid the underpayment penalty, it is advisable to base the estimated payments upon one of the exceptions (e. g., estimated tax payments should be based upon an amount which is equal to the prior year's tax liability). If a possible underpayment of estimated tax is indicated, Form 2210 should be filed to compute the penalty due or to justify qualification under one or more of these exceptions.

Self-Employment Tax. The tax on self-employment income is levied to provide Social Security benefits for self-employed individuals. Individuals with net earnings from self-employment of $400 or more are subject to the self-employment tax.[51] For 1984, the self-employment tax is 14 percent on self-employment income up to $37,800. However, the self-employed taxpayer is allowed a credit of 2.7 percent of self-employment income up to $37,800, resulting in a net rate of 11.3 percent. The rate is scheduled to increase as follows:

1985	14.1%
1986–1987	14.3%
1988–1989	15.02%
1990 and later	15.30%

---

50. § 6654(e)(2). Other dates can be established for payment of income tax withheld.
51. § 6017.

For 1985, the credit will be 2.3 percent, and for 1986 through 1989, it will be 2 percent. Beginning in 1990, there will be no credit, but self-employed taxpayers will be allowed an income tax deduction for one-half the amount of self-employment taxes paid.

If an individual also receives wages subject to FICA tax, the $37,800 cciling amount upon which the self-employment tax is computed is reduced. Thus, no self-employment tax is due if a self-employed individual also receives FICA wages of $37,800.

> **Example 22.** In 1984, T had $24,000 of net earnings from the conduct of a bookkeeping service (trade or business activity). He also received wages as an employee amounting to $15,000 during the year. T's taxable self-employment income for the year is $22,800 [$37,800 (maximum subject to FICA) − $15,000 (wages)].

Net earnings from self-employment include gross income from a trade or business less allowable trade or business deductions, the distributive share of any partnership income or loss derived from a trade or business activity, and net income from the rendering of personal services as an independent contractor. Gain or loss from the disposition of property (including involuntary conversions) is excluded from the computation of self-employment income unless the property involved is inventory.[52]

The IRS has ruled that director's fees, which are paid to a non-employee, are self-employment income, since a director is considered to be engaged in a trade or business activity.[53] An employee who performs services on a part-time basis as an independent contractor or an employee who is engaged in a separate trade or business activity may be subject to the self-employment tax.

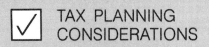

TAX PLANNING CONSIDERATIONS

INCOME AVERAGING

A taxpayer who anticipates that he or she may be able to income average in either the current year or the near future should have available the necessary information regarding the base period years.

> **Example 23.** Because T has received a substantial raise in her job, she believes that she will qualify for income averaging in 19X8. In checking her personal files, however, T is able to locate

---

52. Reg. § 1.1402(a)–6. Involuntary conversions are discussed in Chapter 15. For the present, see the Glossary of Tax Terms in Appendix C.
53. Rev.Rul. 57–246, 1957–1 C.B. 388 and Rev.Rul. 68–595, 1968–2 C.B. 378.

only the copies of the income tax returns for 19X5–19X7. Apparently, the tax return for 19X4 either has been misplaced or destroyed.

What should T do? In no event, should she proceed to income average without accurate information on *all* base period years. Thus, an estimate as to her taxable income for 19X4 would not be proper. It behooves her, therefore, to obtain a copy of her 19X4 return.[54] She can do this by filing Form 4506, Request for Copy of Tax Form, with the IRS.

One should recognize that the income averaging procedure may not be confined to a single year but may benefit the taxpayer in several successive years.

> **Example 24.** Through 19X8, T had yearly taxable income as follows:

Year	Taxable Income
19X3	$ 10,000
19X4	10,000
19X5	10,000
19X6	10,000
19X7	50,000
19X8	50,000

Based on these facts, it is quite clear that T should qualify for income averaging for tax year 19X7.[55] But what about tax year 19X8? Although the tax savings will not be as large, income averaging should be available.[56] The reason the tax savings will not be as large is that 19X3 (taxable income of $10,000) is dropped and 19X7 (taxable income of $50,000) is added as one of the base period years.

ALTERNATIVE MINIMUM TAX

For most taxpayers, the alternative minimum tax probably will not pose any threat for any of several reasons.

—Absent significant amounts of items of tax preference, the alternative minimum tax will not apply. Items of tax preference result from certain investments, and investments require capital. Many taxpayers do not have this kind of capital available.

---

54. If the 19X4 return was prepared by someone else, T might obtain a copy from the preparer. This, of course, assumes that the preparer is still in business, can be located, and has retained a copy in his or her files.

55. Averageable income for 19X7 is $38,000 ($50,000 − $12,000), and this is in excess of $3,000.

56. Averageable income for 19X8 is $26,000 ($50,000 − $24,000) which is greater than $3,000.

—The amount of the exemption allowed often will keep items of tax preference from being subject to the alternative minimum tax. Recall that the exemption is $20,000, $30,000, or $40,000 (depending on filing status). For example, a single taxpayer could absorb up to $30,000 in items of tax preference without having to worry about the alternative minimum tax.

The alternative minimum tax can prove troublesome when taxpayers have large amounts of long-term capital gains in any single year.

Example 25. During 1984, T sells real estate held as an investment (adjusted basis of $40,000) for $200,000 and thereby recognizes a long-term capital gain of $160,000.

Example 26. Assume the same facts as in Example 25 except that the sale is structured as follows: $40,000 down payment with the balance payable in equal annual installments (at 12% interest) over the next four years. As a result of the sale, T recognizes a long-term capital gain of $32,000 in the year of the sale and in each of the next four years.[57]

In order to circumvent or control the alternative minimum tax, the procedure followed in Example 26 usually is to be preferred. Unlike the result that took place in Example 25, the bunching of large amounts of long-term capital gain in a single year can be avoided.

ADJUSTMENT TO INCREASE WITHHOLDING

The penalty for underpayment of estimated tax by individuals is computed for each quarter of the tax year. A taxpayer cannot play "catch-up" and avoid the penalty by making additional estimated payments near the end of the year. Such payments will be applied to the quarter in which they are made and will not reduce the underpayment for prior quarters. However, income tax withheld will be assumed to have been paid evenly throughout the year and will be allocated equally among the four installments in computing any penalty. Therefore, a taxpayer who would otherwise be subject to a penalty for underpayment should increase withholdings late in the year. This can be done by changing the number of exemptions claimed on Form W–4 or by special arrangement with the employer to increase the amount withheld.

ADJUSTMENTS TO AVOID OVERWITHHOLDING

Publication 505, Tax Withholding and Estimated Tax, contains a worksheet that taxpayers may use to take advantage of special provi-

---

57. Under the installment method of reporting gain on the sale of property (see Chapter 18), the recognition of gain is spread over the payment period.

sions for avoiding overwithholding. Extra exemptions for withholding purposes are allowed if the taxpayer has unusually large itemized deductions, deductions for adjusted gross income, or tax credits. Net losses from Schedules C, D, E, and F may be considered in computing the number of extra withholding exemptions. Net operating loss carryovers may also be considered in the computation. Expected tax savings from using the income averaging computation may result in an increase in the number of withholding exemptions the taxpayer may claim. A taxpayer who is entitled to extra withholding exemptions for any of these reasons should file a new Form W-4 (Employee's Withholding Allowance Certificate) with his or her employer.

PROBLEM MATERIALS

Questions for Class Discussion

1. A taxpayer makes the following remark: "Although I was able to use income averaging last year, this year it appears to be out of the question since my income has not increased." Do you agree? Why or why not?

2. Could a taxpayer be eligible for income averaging in a year in which he or she was not gainfully employed? Explain.

3. T, a college friend of yours majoring in engineering, has an excellent job offer after graduation. T has heard that he can save a significant amount of income tax by using the income averaging method in filing his tax return. What information should you give to T?

4. What are the general requirements for using the income averaging method?

5. While being supported by others, during a six-year period T created a musical composition which proved to be a large financial success. Could T qualify for income averaging? What further information, if any, would you want to know before resolving this question?

6. In using the income averaging method, it is necessary to make an adjustment for the taxpayer's exemptions for years 1979 and 1980, but not for years after 1980. Why?

7. H and W are married and file a joint return in 1984. H was self-supporting during the base period years 1980–1983. W was a college student during the entire base period and was claimed as a dependent by her parents. Is there any possibility H and W can use the income averaging method for 1983?

8. List and discuss the items of tax preference subject to the alternative minimum tax.

9. A wealthy acquaintance of yours is concerned about the alternative minimum tax on tax preference items and is thinking about selling all of his municipal bonds to prevent the interest from being subject to the tax. What advice should you give him?

10. If the employer is not required to withhold income taxes on an item of income paid to an employee, does this mean that the item is nontaxable? Explain.

11. Why did Congress enact a tax on tax preference items?

12. Are all itemized deductions that are allowed in computing taxable income also allowed in computing alternative minimum taxable income? Explain any differences.

13. In computing the alternative tax itemized deduction for interest, it is possible that some interest allowed as an itemized deduction for income tax purposes will not be allowed. Explain.

14. The net operating loss for computing taxable income differs from the alternative tax net operating loss. Explain.

15. Under what circumstances will the zero bracket amount allowance be allowed?

16. Although T is entitled to four allowances, just one is claimed on the Form W–4 she completes.

    (a) Why would T claim fewer allowances than she is entitled to?

    (b) Is this procedure permissible?

17. At a social function you overhear one of the guests remark: "If the item of income is subject to the income tax, it will be subject to Social Security taxes." Do you agree or disagree with this statement? Why?

18. At the same social function you hear another guest comment: "I quit paying Social Security taxes in March of this year." Please interpret.

19. If the computation of income tax withholding for employers is to be done manually, the use of the wage-bracket tables is to be preferred over the percentage method. Why?

20. Prior to determining the amount to be withheld for income taxes, why is it essential to determine the payroll period of the employee?

21. When comparing the use of the wage-bracket tables and the percentage method on the same wage, the amount of the income tax to be withheld may not be the same.

    (a) Is there an explanation for this variation in results? Elaborate.

    (b) Make up a hypothetical salary between $2,960 and $3,000 where both approaches will yield the same amount of withholding (refer to Figures IV and V in this chapter).

22. H and W (residents of Louisiana) during 1984 were husband and wife until July 1, when the divorce decree became final and the community was dissolved. Both were employed during the entire year and each received a Form W–2 from the employer. Could there be a problem when H and W file an income tax return for 1984? (Refer to Chapter 5 concerning the community property treatment of wages.)

23. In March of 1984, T, the newly hired payroll officer of Y Corporation carries out the following procedures:

    (a) Gives each employee the Form W–4 that they completed in the past.

    (b) Sends all copies of Form W–2 for 1983 to the local office of the IRS.

(c) Sends Form W–3 and Form 940 for 1983 to the State Collector of Internal Revenue.

(d) Under items (b) and (c), identifies the employer by using the Social Security number of the president of Y Corporation.

What did the payroll officer do wrong?

24. T, a client of yours who is nearing retirement, has come to you for an explanation of the TEFRA provisions relating to withholding on pensions and annuities. Explain the options to T.

25. T, an employee of Z Corporation, has an annual salary of $80,000. Frequently, T turns down offers for outside consulting on the grounds that he does not wish to incur a self-employment tax. Does T's reasoning make sense? Please expand.

26. E, an employee of R Corporation, has an annual salary of $25,000. Until 1984, E's withholdings for income tax purposes always approximated her income tax liability (i. e., either a slight refund resulted or a slight amount of tax was due). In early 1984, however, E inherits $300,000 from an uncle. For tax year 1984, does E have a problem in terms of the declaration of estimated tax by individuals? Why or why not?

27. M is operating on a very tight budget this year. Following a Saturday afternoon of tax planning, she has determined that she will be able to save several hundred dollars of income tax if she uses the income averaging method this year and next year. She has asked you if there is any way she can have her employer decrease the amount withheld from her wages so she can use the money to ease her budget problems, rather than wait until the end of each year for a tax refund. What should you tell her?

Problems

28. In which of the following independent situations are the individuals eligible to use income averaging?

(a) H and W were married during the current year. H provided more than 50% of his own support during the previous four years. W, however, was supported by her parents prior to her marriage. W had adjusted gross income of $20,000 during the current year, and H and W plan to file a joint return. H's adjusted gross income is $40,000.

(b) T, a single individual, is 27 years old. He was supported by his parents during college but has provided all of his own support during the past five years. T attended graduate school on a part-time basis during the past three years to earn an M.B.A.

(c) H and W are 27 years old and were married when they were both 22. During the past four years H has been attending graduate school on a full-time basis to earn a Ph.D. Both H and W were employed on a part-time basis during the base-year period and provided 60% of their own support. During the current year, H received his Ph.D. and was fully employed as a professor. H and W earned $40,000 during the current year and were self-supporting.

29. For calendar year 1984, T has taxable income of $55,000. His taxable income for the four preceding years is as follows:

Year	Taxable Income
1980	$ 14,200
1981	15,000
1982	18,000
1983	22,200

Assume T otherwise meets the requirements for income averaging and is single.

(a) What is T's tax liability for 1984 using income averaging? (Assume he is single during the entire period.)

(b) Without income averaging?

30. T is single and an eligible individual for income averaging. Her only income for the computation and the base period years was from wages. T's taxable income for the past six years is listed below:

Year	Taxable Income
1979	$ 7,200
1980	5,000
1981	11,950
1982	17,000
1983	25,200
1984	37,750

(a) Assume the computation year is 1983. Can T benefit from income averaging?

(b) Assume the computation year is 1984. Can T benefit from income averaging?

31. Mr. and Mrs. V are married, with no dependents, and expect to file a joint return. The relevant information for 1984 is summarized below:

Net income from a consulting practice conducted on a part-time basis	$ 150,000
Interest and dividends (after exclusion)	40,000
Salary from a full-time job	60,000
Items of tax preference which qualify as deductions *for* adjusted gross income	15,000
Unreimbursed employee travel expenses	10,000
Other deductions *for* adjusted gross income	20,000

Taxable income for 1984 proves to be $190,000.

During the period 1980–1983, Mr and Mrs. V had average taxable income of $100,000. Presuming Mr. and Mrs. V are eligible individuals, compute their tax liability under income averaging and under the regular method.

32. T, who is single, has the following items relative to her tax return for 1984:

Bargain element from the exercise of an incentive stock option	$ 50,000
Accelerated depreciation on real estate investments (straight-line depreciation would have yielded $60,000)	80,000
Net capital gain deduction (60% of $150,000)	90,000
Alternative tax itemized deductions	20,000

For 1984, T's adjusted gross income is $150,000 and the Federal income tax liability (as usually determined) is $22,000.

(a) Determine the items of tax preference T has for 1984.

(b) Calculate the alternative minimum tax for 1984.

33. B, who is single, has the following items for 1984:

Income
Salary	$150,000
Interest from bank	5,000
Interest on municipal bonds	10,000
Dividends from domestic corporations	4,100
Short-term capital gain	12,000
Long-term capital gain	200,000

Expenses
Employee business expenses	3,000
Total medical expenses	40,000
State income taxes	8,000
Real property taxes	7,000
Home mortgage interest	5,000

Casualty loss on vacation home
Decline in value	20,000
Adjusted basis	70,000
Insurance proceeds	12,000

Compute B's tax liability for 1984 before credits or prepayments.

34. In each of the independent situations appearing below, determine the maximum withholding allowances permitted T (an employee) on Form W–4:

(a) T is single with no dependents.

(b) T is married to a nonemployed spouse and they have no dependents.

(c) T is married to S, an employed spouse, and they have three dependent children. On the Form W–4 that S filed with the employer she claimed zero allowances.

(d) Assume the same facts as in (c) except that T and S fully support T's mother who lives with them. The mother (age 70 and blind) qualifies as their dependent. (Refer to Chapter 4.)

(e) T is single with no dependents but works for two employers on a full-time and part-time basis. The Form W–4 filed with the first employer (the full-time job) reflects two withholding exemptions.

(f) Assume the same facts as in (e) except that T is married to a non-employed spouse.

35. T is married to a nonemployed spouse and has four dependents. T is employed by Z Corporation and is paid a monthly salary of $3,000 (i. e., $36,000 per year). On these facts, determine the amount to be withheld by Z Corporation for Federal income tax purposes under the:

(a) Wage-bracket tables.

(b) Percentage method.

36. T's calendar year tax liability for 19X1 (as reported on his return filed on April 15, 19X2) was $36,000. T paid $8,000 in estimated tax for 19X1 (four equal installments on the prescribed dates). (Assume 19X2 is not leap year. Use 16% as the penalty rate.)

(a) Compute T's penalty for underpayment of estimated tax (presuming he cannot avoid the penalty through use of one of the four exceptions).

(b) Would any such charge be deductible by T?

37. During 1984, T, the owner of a store, had the following income and expenses:

Gross profit on sales	$ 36,000
Income from part-time job (subject to FICA)	14,000
Business expenses (related to store)	15,000
Fire loss on store building	1,200
Dividend income (unadjusted for any exclusion)	300
Long-term capital gain on the sale of a stock investment	2,000

Compute T's self-employment tax for 1984.

Cumulative Problems

38. X is single, age 46, and has no dependents. In 1984 he earned a salary of $150,000 as vice-president of ABC Manufacturing Corporation. Over the years, he has invested wisely and owns several thousand shares of stock, an apartment complex, and mineral property.

In January 1984, X sold 500 shares of stock for a gain of $50,000. He had owned the stock for 12 years. X received dividends of $15,100 on the stock he retained.

On May 20, 1984, X exercised his rights under ABC's incentive stock option plan. For an option price of $26,000, he acquired stock worth $53,000.

Gross rental income from the apartment complex was $140,000. Deductible expenses for the complex were $105,000, including depreciation of $55,000. If the straight-line method had been used, depreciation would have been $30,000.

X received income of $60,000 from an interest in a mineral property. X's depletion deduction was $40,000 (his basis in the property at the beginning of the year was $24,000).

X received $10,000 interest on corporate bonds in 1984. His itemized deductions were $51,300. X's average base period income for the years 1980, 1981, 1982, and 1983 was $160,000. X's alternative minimum tax itemized deductions were $40,000.

Compute X's lowest legal tax liability, before prepayments or credits, for 1984.

39. R, age 38, is single and has no dependents. He is independently wealthy as a result of having inherited sizable holdings in real estate and corporate stocks and bonds. R is a minister at First Methodist Church, but he accepts no salary from the church. However, he does reside in the church's parsonage free of charge. The rental value of the parsonage is $400 a month. The church also provides R a cash grocery allowance of $50 a week. Examination of R's financial records provides the following information for 1984.

(a) On January 16, 1984, R sold 2,000 shares of stock for a gain of $100,000. The stock was acquired four years ago.

(b) R received gross rental income of $160,000 from an apartment complex he owns.

(c) Expenses related to the apartment complex were $145,000, including declining-balance depreciation of $68,000 (straight-line depreciation would have been $41,000).

(d) R's dividend and interest income was $40,100.

(e) R had the following itemized deductions *from* adjusted gross income:

(1) $7,000 contribution to Methodist church.

(2) $2,000 interest

(3) $8,500 state and local taxes.

(4) $3,000 medical expenses (in excess of 5% of adjusted gross income).

(5) $1,000 casualty loss (in excess of the $100 limitation and the 10% limitation).

Compute R's tax, including minimum tax if applicable, before prepayments or credits for 1984. Use the 1984 Tax Rate Schedule for your computation.

Tax Form Problem

40. James Berry, who is eligible to use income averaging, has never been married. His taxable income in 1983 was $112,000. This was a considerable increase over his income of the four previous years, as shown below:

Year	Taxable Income	Tax Table Income
1982	$ 56,000	
1981	$ 53,000	
1980	$ 49,000	$ 50,000
1979	$ 42,000	$ 43,000

Compute James Berry's income tax, before prepayments or credits, for 1983 using Schedule G of Form 1040.

Research Problems

41. In 19X5, T signed a contract to play professional football with the Cincinnati Bengals. He received a lucrative contract which included a salary in excess of $100,000 a year plus a large bonus for signing. As a result of the significant increase in income over his earnings on summer jobs during his college years (19X1–19X4), T filed his 19X5 tax return using income averaging. IRS declared T ineligible for income averaging, asserting that he had not been self-supporting during the base period years. T argued (1) that an athletic scholarship received during his college years constituted support furnished by him during the base period and (2) that the bonus he received was income attributable to work performed by him in substantial part during the base period years, 19X1–19X4. Will T be allowed to use income averaging in 19X5?

42. H and W realized a large gain on the sale of business machinery and equipment in 19X7. In filing their tax return for 19X7, they did not report the

capital gain deduction related to this gain as a tax preference item. IRS contested this treatment and assessed H and W for minimum tax based on the argument that gain on business assets which is treated as capital gain gives rise to a tax preference item. H and W argued that the gain was § 1231 gain rather than capital gain and that no tax preference existed. Will H and W be successful in contesting the IRS assessment?

43. T is a secretary-stenographer who takes temporary jobs for various law firms and corporations. The duration of her jobs varied during the year. Many jobs were for one day, some were for several days, and some were for a week or longer. Her longest job lasted for five weeks. T did not pay self-employment tax when she filed her tax return for 19X4. IRS assessed a deficiency for self-employment tax for 19X4, claiming that T was a self-employed independent contractor. T claims she is an employee and is not subject to self-employment tax. Should T contest the deficiency assessment?

Chapter 13

Tax Credits

TAX POLICY CONSIDERATIONS

In recent years, Congress has increased its reliance on tax credits as a means of implementing tax policy objectives. This trend is evidenced by numerous provisions in recent tax acts which either modify old credits (such as the investment tax credit, child and dependent care credit, rehabilitation credit, and the targeted jobs credit) or introduce new credits (including the payroll-based ESOP credit and the research and experimentation credit).

A tax credit should not be confused with an income tax deduction. Certain deductions for individuals are permitted as deductions from gross income in arriving at adjusted gross income (e. g., business expenses or certain unreimbursed employee expenses). Additionally, individuals are permitted to deduct nonbusiness personal and investment-related expenses *from* adjusted gross income. A tax credit is worth more to a taxpayer than a deduction, since the credit is directly offset against the tax liability, while a deduction merely reduces taxable income.

> **Example 1.** T has paid a 15 percent Canadian withholding tax in the amount of $3,000 on royalties for books published in that country. This item qualifies as either a business deduction or a tax credit. T's marginal tax rate is 50 percent. Use of the tax as a deduction produces a $1,500 tax reduction ($3,000 × 50%). As a credit, it would provide a $3,000 tax reduction.

Tax credits generally are used by Congress to achieve social or economic objectives or to provide equity for different types of taxpayers. For example, the investment tax credit, introduced by the Kennedy administration in 1962, was expected to encourage growth in the economy, improve the competitive position of American industry at home and abroad, and help alleviate the nation's balance of payments problem.[1]

One reason for the increased popularity of tax credits as a means of implementing tax policy is that tax credits provide benefits on a more equitable basis when compared with tax deductions.

> **Example 2.** Assume Congress wishes to encourage a certain type of expenditure. One way to accomplish this objective would be to allow a tax credit of 25% for such expenditures. Another way to accomplish this objective would be to allow an itemized deduction for the expenditures. Assume taxpayer A's marginal tax rate is 15%, while taxpayer B's marginal rate is 50%. The tax benefits available to each taxpayer, for a $1,000 expenditure, are summarized below.

	Taxpayer A	Taxpayer B
Tax benefit if a 25 percent credit is allowed	$ 250	$ 250
Tax benefit if an itemized deduction is allowed	$ 150	$ 500

These results make it clear that tax credits provide benefits on a more equitable basis than do tax deductions. This is even more apparent considering the fact that the deduction approach would benefit only those taxpayers who itemize deductions, while the credit approach benefits all taxpayers who make the specified expenditure.

SPECIFIC BUSINESS-RELATED TAX CREDIT PROVISIONS

INVESTMENT TAX CREDIT

The investment tax credit was initially enacted in 1962 and has been a significant fiscal policy tool for controlling the economy. The tax credit on the purchase of certain types of business property presumably acts to encourage expansion and investment. The resulting expansion stimulates the economy and generates additional employment. The investment credit has been suspended, reinstated, repealed, and

---

1. Summary of remarks of the Secretary of the Treasury, quoted in S. Rept. 1881, 87th Cong., 2nd Sess., reported in 1962–3 C.B. 707.

reenacted in response to varying economic conditions and political pressures. In addition, many specific operational and definitional rules have been modified.

These changes in the tax law have created a nightmare for tax practitioners. Both suspension and reenactment of the investment credit have necessitated the adoption of special transitional rules relative to qualification and to the carryback and carryover of unused credits. Further complications have been created by modifications of what constitutes qualified investment credit property. As a result of these changes the Code contains numerous provisions relative to specific suspension and reenactment years and other transitional rules.

Amount of the Credit. The Economic Recovery Tax Act of 1981 (ERTA) made several significant changes in the investment tax credit area, some of which were necessary to conform to the new accelerated cost recovery system (ACRS) rules. Under the ACRS provisions, an asset is assigned a recovery period of three, five, ten, or fifteen years, depending on the nature of the asset (see Chapter 9). The normal credit for property placed in service after 1980 is based on the recovery period under ACRS, as shown below.[2] This assumes the reduced credit election (discussed in the next section) is not made by the taxpayer.

ACRS

Recovery Period (in years)	Percentage of Credit
3	6
5, 10, and 15	10

[handwritten: 4% / 8% } election p 322 / no deduction to basis]

The limitation on used property qualifying for the credit is $125,000 for 1981 through 1984 and $150,000 beginning in 1985.[3]

Example 3. In 1984, T acquired and placed in service the following new assets: automobile, $9,000; light-duty truck, $12,000; office furniture, $2,500; and airplane, $120,000. T's tentative investment credit would be computed as follows:

Qualifying Property	Cost	Recovery Period	Percentage of Credit	Investment Tax Credit
Automobile	$ 9,000	3 years	6%	$ 540
Light-duty truck	$ 12,000	3 years	6%	720
Office furniture	$ 2,500	5 years	10%	250
Airplane	$ 120,000	5 years	10%	12,000
Tentative investment credit				$ 13,510

2. § 46(c).
3. § 48(c)(2).

The amount computed above is described as a tentative investment credit because the allowable credit for any year is subject to a ceiling limitation (see Example 6).

Reduced Credit Election. Because Congress felt it had been too generous in the Economic Recovery Tax Act of 1981, the Tax Equity and Fiscal Responsibility Act of 1982 (TEFRA) contained two major provisions to reduce the rate of cost recovery. First, the step-up in rates for computing cost recovery allowances, originally scheduled to be phased in after 1984, was eliminated (refer to Chapter 9). Second, taxpayers are required to reduce the basis for depreciation by 50 percent of the amount of the credit taken, if the full ten percent or six percent credit is taken. This basis reduction requirement applies to property placed in service after 1982.

> **Example 4.** In 1984, T purchases a machine, which is five-year ACRS property, for $10,000. T takes a $1,000 investment credit on the property (10 percent of $10,000). Under the new TEFRA provision, the basis of the property must be reduced by $500 [½ of $1,000 (investment credit)]. Thus, T's cost recovery allowance will be based on $9,500 [$10,000 (cost) − $500 (reduction for investment credit)].

The 50 percent basis reduction rule applies to the following: regular investment credit property, energy credit property, and certified historic property. The basis of properties to which the 15 or 20 percent rehabilitation credit applies is reduced by the full amount of the credit.

As an alternative to reducing the basis of the property, a taxpayer may elect to take a reduced investment credit. Under this election, the investment credit is eight percent (rather than 10 percent) for recovery property that is not three-year property and four percent (instead of six percent) for three-year property.

Upon future sale of the asset, the reduction in basis will be treated as depreciation for purposes of applying the recapture provisions (see Chapter 17, Example 19). However, the basis of the property disposed of will be increased by one-half the amount of the investment credit to be recaptured. This increase occurs immediately before the disposition (or other event) which triggers recapture of depreciation.

Computation of the investment credit under the reduced credit election is illustrated in Example 5.

> **Example 5.** Assume the same facts as in Example 3, except that T elects to take the reduced investment credit to avoid reducing the basis of the properties acquired. T's investment credit decreases from $13,510 (without the election) to $10,640 as shown below:

Qualifying Property	Cost	Recovery Period	Percentage of Credit	Investment Tax Credit
Automobile	$ 9,000	3 years	4%	$ 360
Light-duty truck	$ 12,000	3 years	4%	480
Office furniture	$ 2,500	5 years	8%	200
Airplane	$ 120,000	5 years	8%	9,600
Tentative investment credit				$ 10,640

Ceiling Limitations. The maximum allowable investment credit is 100 percent of the first $25,000 of tax liability plus 85 percent of the tax liability in excess of $25,000.[4] The limitation is imposed on the amount of the tax liability computed in the regular manner without regard to any minimum tax (§ 56) or other special taxes, such as the accumulated earnings tax, which have been imposed. This regular tax liability is reduced by certain tax credits (e. g., the foreign tax credit) to compute the limitation.[5] Controlled corporate groups are required to apportion the basic $25,000 limitation. The basic limitation for married taxpayers filing separately is $12,500 unless one of the spouses is not entitled to the investment credit.

Example 6. T acquired $600,000 of qualified investment credit property (with a five-year recovery period) in 1984. His tax liability, without regard to special taxes, was $50,000. The computation of unused investment credit is illustrated below:

Qualified investment credit ($600,000 × 10 percent)	$ 60,000
Total credit allowed [$25,000 + (85 percent × $25,000)]	46,250
Unused investment credit	$ 13,750

Treatment of Unused Investment Credits. Unused credits are initially carried back three years (to the earliest year in the sequence) and are applied to reduce any amounts in excess of the ceiling during these years. Thus, the taxpayer may receive a refund of tax from the benefits of such carryback. Any remaining unused credits are then carried forward for 15 years.[6] For 1976 and later years, a FIFO method is applied to the carryovers, carrybacks, and utilization of credits earned during a particular year. The oldest credits are used first in determining the amount of investment credit.

The FIFO method minimizes the potential for a loss of investment credit benefit due to the expiration of credit carryovers, since

---

4. § 46(a)(3)(B) as amended by the Tax Equity and Fiscal Responsibility Act of 1982.
5. § 46(a)(4).
6. § 46(b).

the earliest years are used before the current credit for the taxable year.

Example 7. This example illustrates the use of investment credit carryovers:

—Investment credit carryovers		
1981	$ 4,000	
1982	6,000	
1983	2,000	
Total carryovers	$ 12,000	
—1984 investment credit:		
10 percent × $400,000 qualified investment in 5-year property		$ 40,000
—Total credit allowed in 1984 (based on tax liability)	$ 50,000	
Less: Utilization of carryovers		
1981	4,000	
1982	6,000	
1983	2,000	
—Remaining credit allowed	$ 38,000	
Applied against:		
1984 investment credit		(38,000)
1984 unused amount carried forward to 1985		$ 2,000

Recapture of Investment Tax Credit. The amount of the investment tax credit is based on the recovery period of the qualifying property (see Example 3). However, if property is disposed of (or ceases to be qualified investment credit property) prior to the end of the recovery period, the taxpayer must recapture all or a portion of the investment credit originally taken.[7] The amount of investment tax credit which is recaptured in the year of premature disposition (or disqualification as investment credit property) is added to the taxpayer's regular tax liability for that year. Recapture provisions were created to prevent taxpayers from assigning an artificially long useful life to qualified investment credit property in order to maximize the credit.

The portion of the credit recaptured is a specified percentage of the credit which was taken by the taxpayer. This percentage is based on the period the investment credit property was held by the taxpayer, as shown in Figure I on the following page:

Example 8. T acquired an automobile (3-year recovery property) for $10,000 on January 3, 1983, and took an investment tax credit of $600 (6% of $10,000) in that year. T also acquired office furniture (five-year recovery property) on January 3, 1983, at a cost of $5,000. T's investment tax credit on the office furniture

---

7. § 47(a)(5).

Figure I

If the property is held for	The recapture percentage is	
	For 15-year, 10-year, and 5-year property	For 3-year property
Less than 1 year	100	100
One year or more but less than 2 years	80	66
Two years or more but less than 3 years	60	33
Three years or more but less than 4 years	40	0
Four years or more but less than 5 years	20	0
Five years or more	0	0

was $500 (10% of $5,000). T sold both pieces of property in June 1984. Since T held the assets more than one year but less than two, he is required to recapture $396 (66% of $600) of investment tax credit on the automobile and $400 on the office furniture (80% of $500). The effect of the recapture requirement is to increase T's 1984 tax liability by the $796 of investment tax credit recaptured ($396 + $400).

Recapture of investment credit generally is triggered by the following:[8]

—Disposition of property through sale, exchange, or sale-and-leaseback transactions.

—Retirement or abandonment of property or conversion to personal use.

—Gifts of § 38 property.

—Transfers to partnerships and corporations unless certain conditions are met.

—Like-kind exchanges (certain exceptions are provided).

Exceptions are provided for in the Code to prevent inequities. The following transactions illustrate some situations to which the recapture provisions are not applicable:

—A transfer of property to an estate by reason of death.[9]

—A transfer pursuant to certain tax-free reorganizations.[10]

—A liquidation of a subsidiary corporation where the assets are transferred to the parent without receiving a change in basis.[11]

---

8. Reg. § 1.47–2.
9. § 47(b)(1).
10. § 47(b)(2).
11. Ibid. See *West's Federal Taxation: Corporations, Partnerships, Estates, and Trusts.*

Prior to the Economic Recovery Tax Act of 1981, the investment tax credit was computed differently. As a result, the recapture provisions were also different. Even though the 1981 Act changed the investment credit and recapture rules for property placed in service after 1980, the pre-1981 recapture rules continue to apply to premature dispositions of property placed in service before 1981. The pre-1981 rules are covered in a later section of this chapter (see Example 14 and related discussion).

Qualifying Property. Qualifying property (called § 38 property) for 1971 and subsequent years includes the following types of property which is placed in service during the year.[12]

- Tangible personal property (other than an air-conditioning or heating unit) which is depreciable and has a useful life of at least three years.

- Other tangible depreciable property (excluding buildings and their structural components) with a useful life of at least three years if used in manufacturing, production, or extraction, or in furnishing transportation or certain public utility services.[13]

- New elevators and escalators.

- Coin-operated vending and washing machines and dryers.

- Livestock (excluding horses).

The credit is also available for:

- Assets accessory to a business (e. g., grocery store counters, printing presses).

- Assets of a mechanical nature, even though located outside a building (e. g., gasoline pumps).

- Single-purpose livestock and horticulture structures or enclosures.

- Pollution control facilities. Generally, for years after 1978, 100 percent of the credit is available for the portion of the basis of the property that is being rapidly amortized over 60 months.[14] In 1977 and 1978, only 50 percent of such property was eligible for the investment credit; and for years prior to 1977, none of the basis of rapidly amortized pollution control facilities was eligible.

The investment credit is not permitted for the following types of property:

- Intangible property (e. g., patents, copyrights, etc.).

---

12. § 48(a).
13. This category also includes certain research and bulk storage facilities.
14. §§ 169 and 46(c)(5).

—Buildings and their structural components including central air-conditioning, plumbing, and wiring units.

—Property (other than coin-operated vending and washing machines and dryers) used primarily for nontransient lodging (such as the operation of an apartment building).

—Certain property used outside the U. S.

—Foreign-produced property whenever temporary import surcharge is in effect (as determined by the President of the U. S.).

—Property such as rehabilitation expenditures for low-income housing, and certain child care facility expenditures when a special 60-month amortization provision is elected.[15]

—Certain property leased by noncorporate lessors.

—Generally, boilers fueled by oil or gas.

It is sometimes difficult to determine whether an item is tangible personal property, and therefore eligible for the investment credit, or whether such property constitutes a structural component of a building which is not eligible. An item is generally considered to be tangible personal property if it can be removed without causing structural damage to the building. For example, movable partitions are considered tangible personal property if the partitions can be moved without causing injury to the building.[16] Window air-conditioning units no longer are qualified due to specific changes in the Energy Tax Act of 1978 dealing with conservation issues.[17] Also, cinderblock walls, doors, rest rooms, plumbing, office partitions, and electrical wiring do not qualify because they are of a permanent nature.[18]

A functional use test has also been applied to determine whether a special-purpose structure qualifies for the investment credit. For example, the IRS has held that safety equipment units that service an entire building are structural components and, therefore, do not qualify. But comparable equipment which is necessary and used directly in the production process or the operation of a machine will qualify as tangible personal property.[19]

Section 1.48–1 of the Regulations contains detailed rules and examples to assist in determining eligible and excluded property and should be referred to for resolving specific questions.

Computation of Qualified Investment. Qualified investment credit property is the aggregate of new § 38 property which is placed

---

15. § 48(a)(8).
16. Rev.Rul. 75–178, 1975–1 C.B. 9.
17. § 48(a)(1)(A).
18. Rev.Rul. 70–103, 1970–1 C.B. 6.
19. Rev.Rul. 75–78, 1975–1 C.B. 8.

in service during the year.[20] Used § 38 property is included in the above calculation, but the maximum amount of cost is limited to $125,000.[21]

> **Example 9.** In 1984, T acquired used machinery (which was 5-year recovery property) for use in his business. The cost of such property was $200,000. Only $125,000 of the machinery qualifies for the investment credit due to the limitation on used property.

The cost basis of § 38 property is determined under the general rules for determining the basis of property (e. g., basis includes installation and freight costs which are properly included in the depreciable basis of the property). If new § 38 property is acquired in a like-kind exchange, the cost basis of the newly acquired property is equal to the adjusted basis of the property exchanged plus any cash paid.[22]

> **Example 10.** T traded old investment credit property with an adjusted basis of $10,000 plus $15,000 cash for new investment credit property in a like-kind exchange. T's investment credit is based on $25,000 ($10,000 adjusted basis of the old property plus $15,000 cash).

Special rules apply to *used* property acquired in a like-kind exchange. Generally, if old property is traded for used property, only the additional amount spent in the exchange qualifies for the investment credit.[23] The amount qualifying for the investment credit does not include the adjusted basis of the property exchanged.

> **Example 11.** T traded in an automobile used in his business for a used business automobile that had a fair market value of $7,000. T paid the dealer $4,000 cash. The adjusted basis of the automobile exchanged was $1,000. There was no recapture of investment credit, since the automobile had been held for its full cost recovery period. Since the transaction qualifies as a like-kind exchange (see Chapter 14), the basis of the new automobile is equal to the adjusted basis of the old automobile plus cash paid ($1,000 + $4,000). However, the cost for investment credit purposes is only $4,000, the additional amount paid on the exchange.

A different rule applies to used property acquired in a like-kind exchange if disposition of the old property results in recapture of the investment tax credit.[24]

---

20. Reg. § 1.46–3(a)(1).

21. § 48(c)(2). For 1980, the limitation was $100,000. The $125,000 limitation applies to 1981 through 1984. It is scheduled to be increased to $150,000 for years after 1984.

22. Reg. § 1.46–3(c)(1).

23. Reg. § 1.48–3(b)(2).

24. Reg. § 1.48-3(b)(3).

Example 12.   K traded in Machine A, which had an adjusted basis of $20,000, and paid $18,000 cash for Machine B, a used machine. Because Machine A had not been held for its full cost recovery period, K was required to recapture a portion of the investment credit originally taken on Machine A. Since Machine B was acquired in a like-kind exchange, its adjusted basis is $38,000 ($20,000 adjusted basis of Machine A plus $18,000 cash given). K's basis for the investment credit is also $38,000.

Apportionment and limitation rules are provided for married individuals filing separately, controlled corporate groups, and partnerships.

A taxpayer may now elect to claim the investment credit for progress payments for property that is under construction for two or more years if the property will be new § 38 property in the hands of the taxpayer when placed in service.[25] Previously, the credit was not available until the property was placed in service. Special transitional rules are provided if this election is made.[26]

Investment Credit At-Risk Limitation. Before 1981, there was no at-risk limitation on the allowance of investment credits. However, the Economic Recovery Tax Act of 1981 contained an at-risk limitation which applies to business activities, the losses from which are subject to limitation under the at-risk rules of § 465.[27]

Example 13.   T, whose business is subject to the at-risk rules of § 465, bought a machine (five-year recovery property) for $100,000 in 1984. He paid $10,000 cash and negotiated a nonrecourse note of $90,000 for the remainder. Prior to 1981, T's investment tax credit would have been $10,000 (10% of the entire cost of $100,000). However, the at risk provisions will limit T's investment tax credit to $1,000 (10% of the $10,000 T has at risk), since T is not at risk for the nonrecourse debt. (See Appendix C, Glossary of Tax Terms, for definition of nonrecourse debt.)

If the taxpayer's at risk amount increases during the term of the loan, additional investment credit is allowed based on the increase. On the other hand, if the amount at risk decreases, the investment credit recapture provisions will apply to the amount of the decrease.

The at-risk limitations under § 465 are extremely complex and are beyond the scope of this text. Therefore, the preceding discussion of the investment credit at-risk provisions is necessarily brief.

Computation of Investment Credit Under Pre-ERTA Rules. Under pre-ERTA rules (i. e., for years prior to 1981), the full ten percent of the investment credit was allowed (subject to certain limitations) for the acquisition of qualified property with a useful life of

---

25. § 46(d).
26. § 46(d)(7).
27. § 46(c)(8).

seven years or longer. The taxpayer was required to use the same useful life for investment credit purposes which was used for computing depreciation.[28] For property with a useful life of less than seven years, the following percentages were applied to determine the amount of the investment which qualified for the credit (i. e., the "qualified investment"):

—66⅔% for a useful life of five or six years.

—33⅓% for a useful life of three or four years.

Example 14. The computation of the investment credit under pre-ERTA rules is illustrated below:

Qualified Property	Useful Life	Adjusted Cost Basis	Percent	Qualified Investment
Office equipment	7	$ 10,000	100	$ 10,000
Factory machinery	6	$ 30,000	66⅔	20,000
Automobiles	3	$ 18,000	33⅓	6,000
Total qualified investment				$ 36,000
× Investment tax credit rate				10%
= Tentative investment credit				$ 3,600

Recapture of Investment Credit Under Pre-ERTA Rules. Pre-ERTA provisions for recapture of the investment credit were, like the current rules, triggered by premature dispositions (or disqualifying use) of property on which the credit was taken. If investment credit property was prematurely disposed of or ceased to be qualified investment property, investment credit which was previously taken was recaptured in part or in full.[29]

Example 15. The pre-ERTA recapture of investment credit is illustrated below:

Investment credit on machinery—Cost of $10,000, assigned a seven-year estimated useful life in 1978 ($10,000 × 10 percent)	$ 1,000.00
The machinery was sold in 1984 after 6 years. Recomputed credit (66⅔ percent × $10,000 × 10 percent).	(666.67)[30]
Recaptured amount—included in the 1984 tax	$ 333.33

These pre-ERTA recapture provisions still apply to property placed in service prior to 1981. Thus, pre-1981 investment credit prop-

---

28. § 46(c)(2).

29. § 47(a)(1).

30. If the property had been held for 3 or 4 full years, the recomputed credit would be $333.33 (33⅓ percent × $10,000 × 10 percent), and the recaptured amount would be $666.67.

erty which is disposed of prematurely or ceases to be qualifying investment credit property will be subject to recapture as shown in Example 15. Recapture for all investment credit property, whether subject to the old or the new provisions, is reported on Form 4255. A more detailed discussion of the pre-ERTA recapture provisions is contained in the instructions for Form 4255 (see Appendix B).

TARGETED JOBS CREDIT

The targeted jobs credit was enacted to encourage employers to hire individuals from one or more of the following target groups:

—vocational rehabilitation referrals

—economically disadvantaged youths

—economically disadvantaged Vietnam-era veterans

—recipients of certain Social Security supplemental security income benefits

—general assistance recipients

—youths participating in cooperative education programs

—economically disadvantaged ex-convicts

—eligible work incentive employees

—involuntarily terminated CETA employees who began work before January 1, 1983

—qualified summer youth employees

The credit, which was scheduled to expire after December 31, 1981, has been extended through December 31, 1984, by the Tax Equity and Fiscal Responsibility Act of 1982.[31] Computation of the regular targeted jobs credit (see Example 16) differs from the computation of the credit for qualified summer youth employees (see Example 17).

Computation of the Regular Targeted Jobs Credit. The regular targeted jobs credit is equal to 50 percent of the first $6,000 of wages (per eligible employee) for the first year of employment and 25 percent of such wages for the second year.[32] To qualify for the credit, an unemployed individual must be certified by a local jobs service office of a state employment security agency. The former rules which permitted retroactive certification after the employee had been hired have been amended to require certification (or a written request for certification) before the individual begins work.[33] This provision was enacted to insure that employers could claim the credit only for new workers and not for employees who were already on the job before the

---

31.   § 51(c)(3) as amended by the Tax Equity and Fiscal Responsibility Act of 1982.

32.   § 51(a).

33.   § 51(d)(15).

employer learned of the availability of the credit. The intent, obviously, is to allow the credit for new jobs rather than for existing jobs.

There is a ceiling provision which limits the credit to 90 percent of the employer's tax liability (after being reduced by certain specified tax credits).[34] Unused credits may be carried back to the preceding three years and carried forward to the succeeding fifteen years.[35] In addition, the employer's tax deduction for wages is reduced by the amount of the credit.[36]

> **Example 16.** In 1984, T Company hires four handicapped individuals (certified to be eligible employees for the targeted jobs credit). Each of these employees is paid wages of $7,000 during 1984. Assuming the limitation applicable to the jobs credit does not apply (i. e., the 90% limit referred to above), T Company's targeted jobs credit is $12,000 [($6,000 × 50 percent) × 4 employees]. If the tax credit is taken, T Company must reduce its deduction for wages paid by $12,000.

Computation of the Targeted Jobs Credit for Qualified Summer Youth Employees. The credit for qualified summer youth employees is allowed on wages for services during any 90-day period between May 1 and September 15 and applies to certified employees hired on or after May 1, 1983. The maximum wages eligible for the credit are $3,000 per summer employee, and the rate of the credit is 85 percent. Thus, the maximum credit per employee is $2,550 ($3,000 × .85). If the employee continues employment after the 90-day period as a member of another targeted group, the amount of wages subject to the regular targeted jobs credit must be reduced by the wages paid to the employee as a qualified summer employee.

> **Example 17.** X Corporation employs T as a qualified summer youth employee beginning May 1, 1984. After 90 days, T continues his employment as a member of a second targeted group. T was paid $3,000 as a qualified summer employee, for which X Corporation is allowed a $2,550 targeted jobs credit. As a member of the second targeted group, T is paid another $5,000. Of the $8,000 total paid to T, only $6,000 qualifies for the targeted jobs credit. This amount must be reduced by the $3,000 wages paid under the qualified summer employee program. Thus, X Corporation will be allowed an additional credit of $1,500 [($6,000 − $3,000) × .50]. X Corporation's total targeted jobs credit based on wages paid to T in 1984 will be $4,050 ($2,550 + $1,500).

---

34. § 53(a).
35. § 53(b).
36. § 280C.

TAX CREDIT FOR REHABILITATION EXPENDITURES

Taxpayers are allowed a tax credit for expenditures to rehabilitate industrial and commercial buildings and certified historic structures. The operating features of this credit are summarized below:[37]

Rate of the Credit for Rehabilitation Expenses	Nature of the Property
15%	Industrial and commercial buildings at least 30 years of age
20%	Industrial and commercial buildings at least 40 years of age
25%	Residential and nonresidential certified historic structures

A taxpayer is required to depreciate the rehabilitated property over a 15-year period using the straight-line method in order to qualify for the credit.[38] The basis of a rehabilitated building, other than a certified historic structure, must be reduced for the full rehabilitation credit which is taken.[39] In the case of certified historic structures placed in service after 1982, the basis must be reduced by 50 percent of the credit taken. No basis reduction was required for certified historic structures placed in service before 1983.

> **Example 18.** T spent $50,000 to rehabilitate a 40-year-old office building. T is allowed a credit of $10,000 (20% of $50,000) for rehabilitation expenditures. T must reduce the basis of the building by the $10,000 credit and depreciate the building over a 15-year period using the straight-line method.

To qualify for the credit, buildings must be substantially rehabilitated. A building has been substantially rehabilitated if qualified rehabilitation expenditures exceed the greater of (1) the adjusted basis of the property or (2) $5,000.[40]

The rehabilitation credit must be recaptured if the rehabilitated property is disposed of prematurely or if it ceases to be qualifying property. The amount recaptured will be based on a holding period requirement of five years.[41]

The percentage recaptured is based on the period the property was qualified rehabilitation property. These percentages are shown in Figure I (refer to page 485) in the "15-year, 10-year, and 5-year prop-

---

37. § 46(a)(2)(F).
38. § 48(g)(2)(B)(i).
39. § 48(g)(5)(A).
40. § 48(g)(1)(C).
41. § 47(a)(5).

erty" column. In effect, for each year the property is held, the taxpayer earns a credit of 20 percent of the credit originally claimed. Thus, the credit earned each year amounts to 3 percent (15% times 20%), 4 percent (20% times 20%), or 5 percent (25% times 20%) depending on the nature of the property rehabilitated.

RESEARCH AND EXPERIMENTATION CREDIT

To encourage research and experimentation, usually described as research and development (i. e., R&D), § 44F provides a credit of 25 percent for certain qualifying expenditures. The credit, however, applies only to the extent that the current year expenditures exceed the average amount of research expenditures in a base period (usually, the preceding three taxable years). Subject to certain exceptions, this new provision adopts the same definition of research as used for purposes of the special income tax deduction rules under existing § 174.[42]

Research expenditures qualifying for the credit consist of (1) "in-house" expenditures for research wages and supplies, plus certain lease or other charges for research use of computers, laboratory equipment, etc.; (2) 65 percent of amounts paid (e. g., to a research firm or university) for contract research; and (3) 65 percent of corporate grants for basic research to be performed by universities or certain scientific research organizations (or of grants to certain funds organized to make basic research grants to universities). The credit applies to research expenditures made after June 30, 1981, and before 1986.

Qualified research and experimentation expenditures not only are eligible for the 25 percent credit but also can be expensed in the year incurred (or amortized over 60 months if the taxpayer chooses).[43]

> **Example 19.** X Corporation incurred incremental research and experimentation expenditures of $100,000. Assuming X Corporation is in the 46 percent marginal tax bracket and elects to expense the $100,000, the corporation will receive a $71,000 tax benefit for the incremental research and experimentation costs:

Research and experimentation credit ($100,000 × 25%)	$ 25,000
Tax savings from deductions ($100,000 × 46%)	46,000
Total tax benefit	$ 71,000

---

42. § 44F.
43. § 174. Also see discussion of rules for deduction of research and development expenditures in Chapter 8.

Incremental research expenditures are defined as the excess of qualified research expenses for the year over the base period research expenses.[44] Generally the term "base period research expense" means the average of qualified research expenditures for the three years immediately preceding the taxable year for which the computation is being made.[45]

Example 20. Y Corporation incurs qualified research and experimentation expenditures as follows: $70,000 in 1985, $50,000 in 1984, $40,000 in 1983, and $30,000 in 1982. Incremental research expenses for 1985 are computed as shown below:

Expenses in 1985	$ 70,000
Minus: Average base period expenses	
[($50,000 + $40,000 + $30,000) ÷ 3]	40,000
Incremental expenses	$ 30,000

Y Corporation would be entitled to a credit of $7,500 (25% of $30,000) in 1985 (subject to a specified ceiling limitation to be discussed later).

To limit the credit available for taxpayers who have incurred small amounts of research and experimentation costs during the base period, a special rule provides that in no event shall the base period research expenses be less than 50 percent of research expenses in the determination year.[46]

Example 21. Assume the same facts as in Example 20 except that qualified research and experimentation expenses in 1985 were $100,000. Incremental research and experimentation expenditures eligible for the credit are computed as follows:

Expenses in 1985	$ 100,000
Minus: Base period expenses (50% of	
$100,000, since average ex-	
penses for the base period are	
less than 50% of 1985 expenses)	50,000
Incremental expenses	$ 50,000

The research and experimentation credit is nonrefundable, that is, it may not exceed the tax for the year reduced by certain specified

---

44. § 44F(a).
45. § 44F(c).
46. § 44F(c)(3).

credits.[47] Any unused credit is carried back three years and forward fifteen years.[48]

Until the issuance of regulations or other interpretive pronouncements, it is difficult to determine the types of research activities for which Congress intended to allow the credit. According to § 44F(d), the term "qualified research" has the same meaning that the term "research or experimental" has under existing § 174. However, § 174 does not specifically define the term "research or experimental." Responding to this problem, Treasury has issued proposed regulations[49] that define research and experimentation expenditures:

> The term "research or experimental" as used in section 174, means expenditures incurred in connection with the taxpayer's trade or business which represent research and development costs in the experimental or laboratory sense. The term includes generally all such costs incident to the development or improvement of an experimental or pilot model, a plant process, a product, a formula, an invention, or a similar property. It includes research aimed at the discovery of new knowledge and research searching for new applications of either research findings or other knowledge.

The proposed regulations also list numerous types of expenditures that do not qualify as research or experimentation expenditures, including the following:

—Routine or ordinary testing or inspection of materials or products for quality control.

—Routine, periodic, or cosmetic alteration or improvement (such as seasonal design or style changes) of existing products, commercial production lines, or other ongoing operations.

—Routine design of tools, jigs, molds, and dies.

—Construction of copies of prototypes after construction and testing of the original prototype has been completed.

—Costs of acquiring another person's patent, model, or production process.

---

47. § 44F(g)(1). The credits which reduce the tax are those having a lower section number designation than § 44F [except for credits allowable under § 31 (tax withheld on wages), § 39 (certain uses of gasoline, special fuels, and lubricating oil), and § 43 (earned income credit)].

48. § 44F(g)(2).

49. Prop.Reg. § 1.174-2. Another type of cost covered by the proposed regulations is the cost of developing computer software. Generally, such costs are not considered to be research and experimentation expenditures. However, programming costs for the development of "new or significantly improved" computer software are included. See the proposed regulations for examples and additional details.

It should be noted that proposed regulations are not binding regulations until adopted as final regulations and promulgated by Treasury Decisions. However, proposed regulations do reflect Internal Revenue Service thinking on the issues covered.

EMPLOYEE STOCK OWNERSHIP CREDIT

Section 44G provides a payroll-based credit for contributions to employee stock ownership plans (commonly referred to as ESOPs). The investment-based additional tax credit for contributions to ESOPs is repealed after 1982. Beginning in 1983, a tax credit is allowed based on a percentage of the employer's payroll and phased in as follows:[50]

Year	Percentage of Employer's Payroll
1983–1984	0.5%
1985–1987	0.75%
After 1987	None unless extended

The rationale behind these modifications of the ESOP rules is that prior law fell short in spurring ESOP contributions among labor-intensive corporations. Such businesses normally do not make substantial qualified investments in machinery and equipment and, therefore, are not eligible for large investment tax credits.

The amount of the credit is equal to the lesser of (1) the value of employee securities transferred to the tax credit ESOP for the taxable year or (2) the applicable percentage of the amount of compensation paid or accrued to all employees under a tax credit ESOP during the taxable year.[51]

The maximum allowable employee stock ownership credit is 100 percent of the first $25,000 of the employer's tax liability plus 90 percent of the employer's tax liability in excess of $25,000. Tax liability in this regard is defined as the employer's regular tax liability for the year reduced by the total tax credits allowed by Code sections numbered below § 44G (with the exception of those credits provided for by § § 31, 39, and 43).[52]

Excess employee stock ownership credit can be carried back to each of the three preceding taxable years (including taxable years ending before 1983) then carried forward to each of the 15 taxable years following the unused credit year.[53] Any unused credit carryover which would expire at the end of the last taxable year to which it may be carried is allowed as a deduction.[54]

---

50. § 44G(a)(2)(B).
51. § 44G(a)(2).
52. § 44G(b)(1)(A) and (B).
53. § 44G(b)(2).
54. § 404(i).

There are special rules for companies whose rates are regulated (e. g., public utilities) limiting the use of the credit to the degree the credit will influence the rate-setting process.[55]

The employee stock ownership credit is available if the corporation meets certain requirements:

—The corporation's plan must meet the § 409A requirements (qualifications for tax credit employee stock ownership plans).

—No more than one-third of the employer contributions for the taxable year can be allocated to a group of employees consisting of officers, shareholders owning more than 10% of the voting stock or 10% of total value of all stock, and highly compensated individuals as described in § 415(c)(6)(B)(iii) (for 1984, those employees whose annual compensation exceeds $60,000).

—The corporation must make timely transfers of the employer securities (within 30 days after the due date for filing the tax return for the taxable year).[56]

Example 22. In 1984, XYZ Corporation, which files on the calendar year, transfers $4,000 of its corporate stock to its employee stock ownership plan. XYZ Corporation paid gross wages and salaries of $1,200,000, of which $900,000 was paid to employees who qualify under the plan. The credit determined by applying the applicable percentage to qualified compensation is $4,500 (.5% × $900,000). The employee stock ownership credit is limited to the lesser of the value of employer securities transferred to the plan ($4,000) or the amount determined by applying the applicable percentage to qualified compensation ($4,500). Provided that XYZ Corporation has a regular tax liability of at least $4,000 and no other credits to consider, it will be able to currently use the allowable credit of $4,000.

See Chapter 19 for additional discussion of employee stock ownership plans (ESOPs).

OTHER TAX CREDITS

ENERGY TAX CREDITS

Residential. Section 44C provides individual homeowners and renters with two separate tax credits: one for energy conservation expenditures (installation of insulation and other energy-conserving components) and the other for renewable energy source property.[57]

---

55. § 44G(b)(3).
56. § 44G(c).
57. § 44C(a).

All such expenditures must be made for property installed in or on the taxpayer's principal residence. The total credit allowed for the tax year is the sum of the two energy credits.

In addition to the installation of insulation, energy-conserving components include the following:

—Specially designed furnace replacement burners.

—A device for modifying flue openings to increase the efficiency of the heating system.

—Furnace ignition systems which replace a gas pilot light.

—Storm or thermal windows or doors (exterior).

—Energy-saving setback thermostats.

—Caulking or weatherstripping of exterior doors or windows.

—Meters which display the cost of energy usage.

The tax credit for energy conservation expenditures is 15 percent of the first $2,000 of qualifying expenditures, and the maximum credit is $300.

Renewable energy source property expenditures include those for solar, wind, or geothermal energy devices. For years after 1979, the credit is equal to 40 percent of qualifying expenditures up to $10,000, subject to an overall ceiling limitation of $4,000.[58]

To qualify for the credit, expenditures must be incurred on the taxpayer's principal residence and the construction of the residence must have been substantially completed before April 20, 1977. Such expenditures made on or after April 20, 1977, through 1985 will qualify for the credit. No credit is allowed if the credit computed amounts to less than $10. The credits are nonrefundable; but if the total credit exceeds the taxpayer's tax liability, the excess amount is allowed as a credit carryover (but no carryover is allowed to tax years beginning after December 31, 1987).

> **Example 23.** In 1984, T installs the following energy-conserv-ing materials and equipment in his principal residence: insula-tion, $1,200; storm doors, $800; caulking and weatherstripping, $400. (Assume no energy credits were claimed in prior years.) These expenditures qualify for the residential energy credit. However, T's credit is limited to $300 (15% of the first $2,000 of qualifying expenditures). Because the total expenditures amount to $2,400, the $400 excess expenditures are not eligible for the credit. If T's tax liability (before deduction of the credit) was only $200, a tax credit of $200 will be allowed in 1984, and $100 of the credit will be carried over to 1985.

If a taxpayer acquires another principal residence to replace a former residence during the period the credits are in effect, both cred-

---

58. § 44C(b)(2).

its (energy conservation and renewable energy source) start anew.

For purposes of determining the amount of the residential energy tax credit for a tax year, the maximum qualifying expenditures must be reduced by the amount of the expenditures that qualified for the energy tax credit in previous years.

> **Example 24.** In 1982, K has qualified residential renewable energy source expenditures of $6,000. A credit of $2,400 (40% × $6,000) is allowed for that year. In 1984, K incurs additional renewable energy source expenditures of $5,000 on the same residence. The maximum amount of renewable energy source expenditures which qualify in 1984 is $4,000 ($10,000 − $6,000). Thus, of the $5,000 of expenditures in 1984, $4,000 is subject to the 40% credit (for a total residential energy credit in 1984 of $1,600). K receives no energy tax credit for the remaining $1,000 of 1984 expenditures, and no further renewable energy source expenditures by K on the same residence are eligible for the tax credit.

If any of the energy conservation expenditures or the renewable energy source expenditures result in an addition to the basis (see Chapter 14) of the residence, the amount of such addition is reduced by the energy tax credit allowed.[59]

Form 5695, Energy Credits, is used to claim the energy credits (see Appendix B).

Business. Energy tax credits are also extended to businesses to create incentives for conservation and to penalize increased use of oil or gas. The investment credit provisions have been amended to include additional tax credits of 10 to 15 percent for certain energy property.[60] If the property also qualifies as investment credit property, a total credit of 20 to 25 percent is allowed. Qualifying energy property generally must be completed or acquired new after September 30, 1978, and before 1986.

The business energy tax credit applies to the following:[61]

—Solar, wind, or geothermal property 15 percent for periods after 1979 through 1985).

—Ocean thermal property (15 percent for periods after 1979 and through 1985 only).

—Small-scale hydroelectric generating property (11 percent for periods after 1979 and through 1985 only).

—Intercity buses (10 percent for periods after 1979 and through 1985 only).

---

59. § 1016(a)(21).
60. § 46(a).
61. § 46(a)(2)(c).

—Biomass property (e. g., boilers, burners, and related pollution control and fuel-handling equipment) (10 percent for periods from October 1, 1978, through 1985).

—Certain other business energy property not included in the above categories (10 percent for periods from October 1, 1978, through 1985).

The business energy credit is limited to 100 percent of tax liability.[62] It is deducted after the regular investment credit and is subject to the same carryover rules as the regular investment credit.

If property is disposed of prior to the end of its useful life, the credit is recaptured in the same manner as the investment credit. This additional energy credit differs from the regular investment credit, however, in that it is available for qualifying property even though the property is considered a structural component of a building or is otherwise not eligible for the regular investment credit.[63]

EARNED INCOME CREDIT

Taxpayers whose income is below a specified level may be eligible for the earned income credit. The earned income credit is 10 percent of the first $5,000 of earned income.[64] If an individual's adjusted gross income is greater than $6,000, the earned income credit of $500 is reduced by 12.5 percent of the amount of adjusted gross income (or, if greater, earned income) that exceeds $6,000.[65]

> **Example 25.** In 1984, T who otherwise qualifies for the earned income credit, receives wages of $7,200 and has $700 of unreimbursed employee expenses which are deductible in arriving at adjusted gross income. T's earned income credit is $500 (10% × $5,000 earned income) reduced by $150 [12.5% × ($7,200 earned income − $6,000)]. Thus, T's earned income credit is $350 ($500 − $150) for 1984.

It is not necessary to compute the earned income credit. As part of the simplification process, the IRS has issued an Earned Income Credit Table[66] for the determination of the appropriate amount of earned income credit. The table is constructed in income increments of $50 from $0 through $5,000 and from $6,000 through $9,999. This table, along with a worksheet, is included in the instructions to both Form 1040 and Form 1040A and is reproduced in Appendix A.

If adjusted gross income is $6,000 or less, the appropriate earned income credit is found in the table on the same line and to the right of the taxpayer's earned income amount.

---

62. § 46(a)(4).
63. Tax Guide for Small Business, IRS Publication 334 (Rev. Oct. 83), p. 130.
64. § 43(c)(2).
65. § § 43(a) and (b).
66. § 43(f).

If adjusted gross income is greater than $6,000, three steps are required:

1. Determine the earned income credit by locating the appropriate amount of income that represents the taxpayer's earned income.

2. Determine the earned income credit by locating the appropriate amount that represents the taxpayer's adjusted gross income.

3. Claim the allowed earned income credit by taking the smaller of the Step 1 amount or the Step 2 amount.

To be eligible for the credit, the taxpayer must be either (1) married and entitled to a dependency exemption for a child; (2) a surviving spouse; or (3) a head of household with an unmarried (need not be a dependent) child, stepchild, or grandchild or a married (must be a dependent) child, stepchild, or grandchild.[67] Such child, stepchild, or grandchild must reside with the taxpayer in the United States. Married individuals must file a joint return to receive the benefits of the credit.[68]

The earned income credit is a form of negative income tax (i. e., a refundable credit for taxpayers who do not have a tax liability). An eligible individual may elect to receive advance payments of the earned income credit from his or her employer (rather than to receive the credit from the IRS upon filing of the tax return.[69] If this election is made, the taxpayer must file a certificate of eligibility (Form W–5) with his or her employer and *must* file a tax return for the year the income is earned.[70]

TAX CREDIT FOR THE ELDERLY

Retirement income credit provisions were originally enacted in 1954 to provide tax relief for certain elderly taxpayers who were not receiving substantial benefits from tax-free Social Security payments. In 1976, the retirement income credit provisions were substantially modified to include earned income (e. g., salaries and professional fees) as well as retirement income (e. g., dividends and interest). The credit is 15 percent of the taxpayer's income subject to specific ceiling limitations as indicated below.

Many elderly taxpayers receive Social Security benefits in excess of the ceiling limitations and, therefore, are ineligible to receive the credit. The revised eligibility requirements and the tax computation are highly complicated. Therefore, the Code permits an individual to

---

67. § 43(c)(1).
68. § 43(d).
69. § 3507.
70. § 6012(a)(8).

elect to have the IRS compute his or her tax and the amount of the tax credit.[71]

The credit is based on an initial ceiling amount of $2,500 (designated as the § 37 amount) for a single taxpayer. This initial ceiling amount is reduced by (1) Social Security, Railroad Retirement, and certain excluded pension benefits and (2) one-half of the taxpayer's adjusted gross income in excess of $7,500. The remainder is multiplied by 15 percent to compute the credit.

The § 37 amount is also $2,500 for married taxpayers filing a joint return when only one spouse is 65 or older. This increases to $3,750 for married taxpayers filing jointly when both spouses are 65 or older. For married individuals filing separately, the § 37 amount is $1,875.

The adjusted gross income factor of $7,500 for single taxpayers mentioned above is increased to $10,000 for married taxpayers filing jointly. This amount is $5,000 for married taxpayers filing separately.

Beginning in 1984, individuals under age 65 are eligible for this credit only if they retired with a permanent and total disability and have disability income from a public or private employer on account of that disability. For these individuals, the initial §37 amounts are twice the amounts discussed previously (e.g., $7,500 rather than $3,750 on a joint return where both spouses are eligible). This initial amount, however, is limited to disability income. In other respects, the new rules follow the law in effect for 1983. A related provision repeal the disability income exclusion for taxable years beginning after December 31, 1983.

Special Rules. A multitude of special rules is provided by the Code:

—If both spouses are 65 or older and file a joint return, a ceiling amount of $3,750 is permitted for the combined retirement income of both spouses. To qualify for the credit, married taxpayers generally must file a joint return. However, if the married individuals live apart, under certain conditions they may each claim a maximum base for the tax credit of $1,875 on separate returns.

—Special rules for determining the credit are provided for taxpayers who receive pensions from a Federal, state, or local government retirement system.[72]

—The maximum amount of the credit is reduced by FICA and Railroad Retirement benefits received and by pension amounts which are excludible from gross income.

---

71.   § 6014.
72.   § 37(e).

—All types of taxable income qualify for the tax credit (e. g., salaries, wages, and investment income).

Example 26. H and his wife W are both over 65 and received FICA benefits of $2,000 in 1984. On a joint return, H and W reported adjusted gross income of $12,000.

Initial § 37 amount		$ 3,750.00[73]
Less: FICA benefits	$ 2,000	
(One-half of the excess of adjusted gross income of $12,000 over $10,000)	1,000	(3,000.00)
Balance subject to credit		$ 750.00
Tax credit allowed ($750 × 15 percent)		$ 112.50[74]

FOREIGN TAX CREDIT

Both individual taxpayers and corporations may claim a foreign tax credit on income earned and subject to tax in a foreign country or U. S. possession.[75] As an alternative to the credit, a taxpayer may claim a deduction under § 164 of the Code. In most instances the tax credit is advantageous, since it is a direct offset against the tax liability.

The purpose of the foreign tax credit is to eliminate double taxation, since income earned in a foreign country is subject to both U. S. and foreign taxes. However, the operation of the ceiling limitation formula may result in some form of double taxation or taxation at rates in excess of U. S. rates when the foreign tax rate is in excess of U. S. rates. In addition, recent changes in the law now place added restrictions upon the benefits of the credit.

Computation. For years ending after 1975, taxpayers are required to compute the foreign tax credit based upon an "overall" limitation.[76] Formerly, a taxpayer could elect to compute the credit on a per country basis. The "per country" method is still available for taxpayers with income from U. S. possessions.

Example 27. Computation of the foreign tax credit follows: in 1984, T Corporation has $10,000 of income from Country Y, which imposes a 15% tax, and $20,000 from Country Z, which imposes a 50% tax. T Corporation has taxable income of $70,000 from within the U. S. The U. S. tax before the credit is $25,750. Overall limitation:

---

73. § 37(b)(2).
74. § 37(c)(2) limits the tax credit to the amount of the tax liability.
75. § 901(b).
76. § 904.

$$\frac{\text{Foreign income}}{\text{Total U. S. taxable income}} = \frac{\$30,000}{\$100,000} \times \$25,750 = \underline{\underline{\$\ 7,725}}$$

The foreign tax credit, therefore, is the lesser of the foreign taxes imposed ($11,500) or the overall limitation ($7,725). In this case, $7,725 is the amount allowed.

Unused foreign taxes may be carried back two years and then forward five years. Special transitional rules are applied for carry-overs from pre-1976 years for taxpayers who were using the per country limitation method.[77]

Form 1116, Computation of Foreign Tax Credit, is used to compute the limitation on the amount of foreign tax credit.

The foreign earned income exclusion is discussed in Chapter 6, and expenses of employees working outside the United States are discussed in Chapter 10.

CREDIT FOR CHILD AND DEPENDENT CARE EXPENSES

This credit was enacted to benefit taxpayers who incur employment-related expenses for child or dependent care. The credit is a specified percentage of expenses incurred to enable the taxpayer to work or to seek employment. Expenses on which the credit is based are subject to limitations (see Examples 28 and 29).

Eligibility. An individual must maintain a household for:[78]

—a dependent[79] under age 15, *or*

—a dependent or spouse who is physically or mentally incapacitated.

Generally, married taxpayers must file a joint return to obtain the credit.

Eligible Employment-Related Expenses. Eligible expenses include amounts paid for household services and care of a qualifying individual which are incurred to enable the taxpayer to be employed. Child and dependent care expenses include expenses incurred in the home, such as payments for a housekeeper. Out-of-the-home expenses that qualify for the credit include those for the care of a dependent

---

77. § 904(e)(2).

78. § 44A(c).

79. In the case of divorced or legally separated taxpayers, the child [as defined in § 151(e)(3)] need not be the taxpayer's dependent. The child care credit belongs to the parent who has custody of the child for the longer period during the year, provided the child (1) received over one-half of the support from the parents, (2) had been in the custody of one or both parents for more than one-half of the year, and (3) is under 15 or physically or mentally unable to care for himself or herself [§ 44A(a)(f)(5)]. Allocation of expenses is required in case a child turns 15 during the year.

under the age of 15 and those incurred for an older dependent or spouse who is physically or mentally incapacitated as long as he or she regularly spends at least 8 hours each day in the taxpayer's household. This makes the credit available to taxpayers who keep handicapped or older children and elderly relatives in the home instead of institutionalizing them. Out-of-the-home expenses incurred for services provided by a dependent care center will qualify only if the center complies with all applicable laws and regulations of a state or unit of local government.[80]

Child care payments to a relative are eligible for the credit unless the relative is a dependent or is a child (under 19) of the taxpayer.[81]

The total for qualifying employment-related expenses is limited to an individual's earned income. For married taxpayers, this limitation applies to the spouse with the least amount of earned income.

Special rules are provided for taxpayers with nonworking spouses who are disabled or are full-time students.[82] If a nonworking spouse is physically or mentally disabled or is a full-time student, such spouse is deemed to have earned income of $200 per month if there is one qualifying individual in the household (or $400 per month if there are two or more qualifying individuals in the household).

Allowable Amounts.   In general, the credit is equal to 30 percent of employment-related expenses up to $2,400 for one qualifying individual and $4,800 for two or more individuals.[83] The 30 percent rate is reduced one percent for each $2,000 (or fraction thereof) of additional adjusted gross income in excess of $10,000 (but not below 20 percent). The following chart shows the applicable percentage for taxpayers with adjusted gross income greater than $10,000.

Adjusted Gross Income in Excess of	Applicable Credit Percentage
$ 10,000	29%
12,000	28%
14,000	27%
16,000	26%
18,000	25%
20,000	24%
22,000	23%
24,000	22%
26,000	21%
28,000	20%

Example 28.   H and W are married and file a joint return. They have two children under 15 and incurred $6,000 of child care ex-

---

80. § 44A(c)(2).
81. § 44A(f)(6).
82. § 44A(e)(2).
83. § 44A.

penses (for a housekeeper) during the year. H and W were fully employed with H earning $10,000 and W earning $3,000. They have no other income or deductions *for* AGI. The maximum amount of child care expenses for two or more dependents is $4,800, but this amount is further limited by the earned income of W (the spouse with the least amount). In this case, the amount allowed as child care expenses would be $3,000 (earned income of W). H and W have combined AGI of $13,000 which reduces their applicable credit percentage to 28% (see chart above). H and W would be entitled to a tax credit of $840 (28% × $3,000) for the tax year.

Example 29. W has two children under 15 and worked full-time while her spouse, H, was attending college for 10 months during the year. W earned $10,000 and incurred $5,000 of child care expenses. H is deemed to be fully employed and to have earned $400 for each of the 10 months (or a total of $4,000). Since H and W have adjusted gross income of $10,000, they will not have to make an adjustment to the maximum credit rate of 30%. H and W are limited to $4,000 in qualified child care expenses (the lesser of $4,800 or $4,000). They are entitled to a tax credit of $1,200 (30% × $4,000) for the year.

The credit should be claimed by completing and filing Form 2441, Credit for Child and Dependent Care Expenses. A copy of this form appears in Appendix B.

POLITICAL CAMPAIGN CONTRIBUTIONS

Individuals are eligible to receive a tax credit for one-half of qualifying political contributions. This credit is subject to an overall limit of $50 ($100 on a joint return.)[84]

Example 30. T files a joint return for 1984 and makes qualifying political contributions of $400. T's tax credit for 1984 is $100 (one-half of $400, subject to an overall limit of $100 since a joint return is filed). If T had made qualifying political contributions of only $150, the credit allowed would be limited to $75 (one-half of $150). In this latter case, the overall limitation does not apply.

Contributions qualify for the credit if they are made to the following persons or organizations:[85]

—A candidate for nomination to any Federal, state, or local office.

—A political campaign committee sponsoring such individual.

---

84.   § 41(b)(1).
85.   § 41(c).

—A national, state, or local committee of a national political party.

PRIORITY OF CREDITS

Certain credits are refundable while others are nonrefundable. Refundable credits include tax withheld on wages, the credit for non-highway use of certain fuels, and the earned income credit. These credits are refunded to the taxpayer even if the amount of the credit (or credits) exceeds the taxpayer's tax liability.

> **Example 31.** T, who is single, had taxable income of $20,000 in 1983. His income tax from the 1983 Tax Table (see Appendix A) is $3,376. During 1983, T's employer withheld income tax of $3,450. T is entitled to a refund of $74, since the credit for tax withheld on wages is a refundable credit.

Nonrefundable credits are not refunded if they exceed the taxpayer's liability.

> **Example 32.** T is single, age 67, and retired. T's taxable income for 1983 is $2,500, and the tax on this amount is $23. T's tax credit for the elderly is $65. This credit can be used to reduce T's net tax liability to zero, but it will not result in a refund, even though the credit ($65) exceeds the tax liability ($23). This result occurs because the tax credit for the elderly is a nonrefundable credit.

Some nonrefundable credits, such as the investment tax credit, are subject to carryover provisions if they exceed the amount allowable as a credit in a given year. Other nonrefundable credits, such as the tax credit for the elderly (see Example 32), are not subject to carryover provisions and are lost if they exceed the limitations. Because some credits are subject to carryover provisions while others are not, it is important to determine the order in which credits are offset against the tax liability. A specific order of priority is given in various sections of the Code,[86] as shown below:

—Tax credit for the elderly

—Foreign tax credit

—Investment tax credit

—Political contributions credit

—Child and dependent care credit

—Targeted jobs credit

—Residential energy credit

---

86. §§ 904(g), 41(b)(2), 44A(b), 53(a), 44C(b)(5), 44D(b)(5), 44E(e)(1), and 44F(g)(1)(A).

—Alternative fuel source credit

—Alcohol fuels credit

—Research and experimentation credit

—Payroll-based ESOP credit

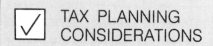

INVESTMENT CREDIT

The optimal utilization of investment credits, including unused carryovers, should be considered by management in the formulation of capital expenditure and project abandonment decisions. Companies which are frequently subject to the ceiling limitations should be particularly aware of the potential for losing part or all of the tax benefits from investment credits due to the expiration of loss carryovers. It should also be noted that if a company incurs net operating losses which are carried back to prior years, the previously allowed investment credits for such prior years may be scaled down or lost.

For capital expenditure planning purposes, it is important to note that certain expenditures within a project may not qualify for the investment credit (e. g., land, buildings, and structural components). It may be possible to design a capital project so that certain components qualify for the credit. For example, movable partitions are considered tangible personal property (and qualifying investment credit property) if the partitions can be removed without causing injury to the building. Also, note that the cost of used property is subject to a limitation of $125,000. Furthermore, the full amount of the investment tax credit is available for pollution control facility costs.

One common misconception taxpayers have about the investment tax credit concerns timing considerations. The mere purchase and transfer of ownership of eligible property will not be sufficient to make the credit available. In some cases, moreover, even the delivery of the property does not qualify the purchaser for the credit. The critical point is when the property is placed in service. According to the IRS, this occurs when "it is placed in a condition or state of readiness and availability for a specifically assigned function."[87]

> **Example 33.** In December of 1983, T (a calendar year taxpayer) purchased six electric typewriters for use in his business. The typewriters were not delivered by the manufacturer until February of 1984. Any investment tax credit that results from this acquisition must be claimed in tax year 1984.

---

87. Reg. § 1.46–3(d)(1)(ii).

Example 34. In July of 1983, R Corporation (a calendar year taxpayer) purchased a lathe for use in its business. Since the lathe required special construction procedures to meet the agreed-upon specifications, it is not delivered to R Corporation until December of 1983. After several test runs were conducted during January and various modifications made, the lathe was operational and available for use in February of 1984. Because the lathe will not be deemed to have been placed in service until 1984, this is the year that R Corporation should claim any investment tax credit.[88]

As previously mentioned, a $125,000 limitation is placed on the amount of used property qualifying for the investment credit. A taxpayer whose investment in used property exceeds the $125,000 limitation may be able to maximize the investment credit by carefully selecting the property on which the credit is taken.

Example 35. In 19X4, T acquired two used assets qualifying for the investment credit. Asset A, which had a cost recovery period of three years, cost $80,000. Asset B, which had a five-year cost recovery period, cost $100,000. Assume T does not make the reduced credit election. A has two alternatives in computing the investment credit.

Alternative 1		
Asset A ($80,000 × .06)	$	4,800
Asset B ($45,000 × .10)		4,500
Total ITC	$	9,300
Alternative 2		
Asset B ($100,000 × .10)	$	10,000
Asset A ($25,000 × .06)		1,500
Total ITC	$	11,500

This illustration makes it clear that the investment credit can be maximized by selecting the asset with the longer recovery period, since the higher rate applies (10% for five-year property versus 6% for three-year property).

REDUCED CREDIT ELECTION

A taxpayer who elects to take a reduced investment credit avoids reducing the basis of the asset by 50 percent of the investment credit. The tradeoff if the election is made is lower investment credit in the year of acquisition in exchange for higher cost recovery allowances over the life of the asset.

Example 36. T Corporation acquires a heavy-duty truck (5-year recovery property) for $20,000 in 1984. If the reduced credit

---

88. Rev.Rul. 79–40, 1979–1 C.B. 13.

election is not made, the credit will be $2,000 (10% of $20,000). The basis of the property will be $19,000. If the reduced credit election is made, T's credit will be $1,600 (8% of $20,000) and the basis of the property will be $20,000.

It is clear that present value analysis should be considered in deciding whether to make the reduced credit election. Factors which must be built into this analysis include (1) T Corporation's marginal tax bracket and (2) the time value of money.

JOBS TAX CREDIT

Employers should evaluate their personnel needs relative to the targeted jobs tax credit. To be eligible for the credit, an expanding work force is required. Also, the decision whether to hire eligible employees should take into account the fact that the benefits of the targeted jobs tax credit are less than the full amount of the credit because the employer's wage deduction is reduced by the amount of the credit.

The new credit for qualified summer youth employees should be utilized when appropriate. The 85 percent rate is higher than the 50 percent rate for the regular targeted jobs credit. Thus, a greater tax credit will result if employees who are members of other targeted groups can be hired initially under the qualified summer youth employee program.

ENERGY TAX CREDITS

Individual homeowners and renters who are faced with rapidly increasing home heating costs should investigate potential cost saving benefits (including tax credits) from energy conservation measures. Although the ceiling limitations (i. e., 15 percent of the first $2,000 of qualifying energy conservation expenditures, subject to a maximum total credit of $300) may restrict the potential tax benefits, many states permit comparable tax credits for state income taxes. In addition, alternative energy sources (e. g., solar heat) should be considered, because this form of credit has been increased to 40 percent of qualifying expenditures up to $10,000 with an overall ceiling limitation of $4,000.

Business capital budgeting decisions should take into account the availability of tax credits for qualifying energy-related expenditures.

FOREIGN TAX CREDITS

Individuals who intend to take a job assignment in a foreign country and companies who have international operations should take into account the related income tax effect. Companies should consider the adoption of an equitable reimbursement policy for employees who are given a foreign assignment. Otherwise, such individuals may be subject, in part, to the effects of double taxation.

An expatriate taxpayer may elect to take either the foreign tax credit or the foreign earned income exclusion. It is obvious that the taxpayer should elect the credit if the rate of tax in the foreign country is higher than the rate of tax in the United States. On the other hand, the exclusion should be elected if the U. S. tax rate is higher than the tax rate in the foreign country. Once the election is made, however, it is binding on future years. Thus, it is necessary that the expatriate taxpayer predict his or her future job track. If the taxpayer is likely to be assigned to a country with a rate higher than the U. S. rate, the credit should be elected. If it is expected that future assignments will be in countries with low tax rates, the exclusion should be elected.

RESEARCH AND EXPERIMENTATION EXPENDITURES

Research and experimentation expenditures are fully deductible if the taxpayer so elects under § 174. Prior to the Economic Recovery Tax Act of 1981 (ERTA), there was no particular motivation to segregate these expenditures from other expenditures. For example, salaries incurred in research and experimentation activities could be left in the salaries account and deducted as salaries expense.

To provide a basis for the new research and experimentation credit added by ERTA, taxpayers should consider establishing a separate account for accumulating research and experimentation expenditures. It is likely that many businesses, particularly small businesses, do not currently have such an account.

Taxpayers should also study the new credit provisions carefully to determine the types of activities for which the credit is allowed. The Congressional committee reports are a good source of information. As an example, the committee reports point out that the credit is allowed for certain research and experimentation expenses incurred to develop computer software. This might be of particular interest, for instance, to accounting firms faced with developing new software to cope with changes in the tax law. The proposed regulations under § 174 provide an additional source of information regarding what constitutes qualifying research and experimentation expenditures.

CREDIT FOR CHILD AND DEPENDENT CARE EXPENSES

Upper-middle and upper income level taxpayers, who were formerly ineligible for a child care deduction due to the ceiling limitations, may now qualify for the tax credit. Thus, if a nonworking spouse is considering full-time employment or if the nonworking spouse is attending college on a full-time basis, the availability of the child care credit should not be overlooked.

If the taxpayer incurs employment-related expenses that also qualify as medical expenses (e. g., a nurse is hired to provide in-the-home care for an ill and incapacitated dependent parent), such expenses may be either deducted as a medical expense (subject to the five percent limitation) or utilized in determining the child and dependent care credit. If the choice is to take the dependent care credit and the employment-related expenses exceed the limitation ($2,400; $4,800; or earned income, as the case may be) the excess may be considered a medical expense. If, however, the choice is made to deduct such qualified employment-related expenses as medical expenses, any portion that is not deductible because of the five percent limitation may not be used in computing the child and dependent care credit.

Example 37. T, a single individual, has the following tax position for tax year 1984:

Gross income from wages		$ 30,000
Deductions *for* adjusted gross income		–0–
Adjusted gross income		30,000
Itemized deductions *from* adjusted gross income—		
Other than medical expenses	$ 2,300	
Medical expenses	6,000	$ 8,300

All of T's medical expenses were incurred to provide nursing care for her disabled father while she was working. The father lives with T and qualifies as her dependent.

What should T do in this situation? One approach would be to use $2,400 of the nursing care expenses to obtain the maximum dependent care credit allowed. Under § 44A, this would be $480 (20% × $2,400). The balance of these expenses should be claimed under § 213. After a reduction of 5% of adjusted gross income, this would produce a medical expense deduction of $2,100 [$3,600 (remaining medical expenses) − (5% × $30,000)].

Another approach would be to claim the full $6,000 as a medical expense and forego the § 44A credit. After the 5% adjustment of $1,500 (5% × $30,000), a deduction of $4,500 remains.

The choice, then, is between a credit of $480 plus a deduction of $2,100 and a credit of $0 plus a deduction of $4,500. Which is better, of course, depends upon the relative tax savings involved.

PROBLEM MATERIALS

Questions for Class Discussion

1. Discuss the underlying rationale of the enactment of the following tax credits:

   (a) Investment credit.

   (b) Foreign tax credit.

   (c) Tax credit for the elderly.

(d) Earned income credit.

(e) Credit for child and dependent care expenses.

(f) Targeted jobs credit.

(g) Energy tax credit.

2. Which of the following is correct?

(a) The investment credit is not available for the purchase of buildings used in a trade or business.

(b) The recovery period for investment credit property must be the same as that used for cost recovery purposes.

(c) Investment credit is allowed for a year in which the corporation incurs a net operating loss.

(d) Unused investment credits are carried back three years and are generally carried forward for fifteen years.

(e) Conversion of qualified investment credit property to personal use may result in recapture of the credit in part or in full.

3. T acquired new investment credit property for $500,000 in 1984. The property has a cost recovery period of five years. T does not make the reduced credit election. T may claim an investment credit of at least $50,000 in 1984. True or false? Explain.

4. Which of the following dispositions of investment credit property will trigger recapture of investment credit?

(a) X Corporation scraps a machine after using it for three years. The machine had a cost recovery period of five years.

(b) T, a self-employed individual, gave a four-year-old truck that he had used in his business to his son, B. The truck had a cost recovery period of three years.

(c) D, a self-employed individual, died. He left to his daughter, G, an automobile that he had used in his business for two years. The automobile had a cost recovery period of three years.

5. In general, what kinds of property qualify for the investment credit? What kinds of property do not qualify?

6. What general limitations are imposed upon the amount of investment credit which may be taken in any one year?

7. The FIFO method is now applied to investment credit carryovers, carrybacks, and the utilization of credits generated during a particular year. What effect does the FIFO method have on the utilization of investment credit carryovers?

8. How will recent changes in the investment credit carryover rules affect the utilization of current and unused investment credits?

9. What limitations have been placed upon used investment credit property? Why did Congress impose such limitations?

10. F, a self-employed individual, acquired a machine for $200,000 in 1984, paying $20,000 cash and signing a nonrecourse note for $180,000. F does not make the reduced credit election. The machine has a cost recovery period of five years. Assuming that this machine is F's only investment in

property qualifying for the investment credit and that the 85% limitation does not apply, what is the maximum investment credit F may take in 1984?

11. How is the investment credit computed if new § 38 property is acquired in a like-kind exchange? If used § 38 property is acquired?

12. If investment credit property is prematurely disposed of or ceases to be qualified property, how is the tax liability affected in the year of the disposition?

13. What factors should a taxpayer consider in deciding whether to make the reduced investment credit election?

14. X acquired a machine for use in her business on December 15, 1984. The machine, which cost $20,000, has a cost recovery period of five years. Installation of the machine was completed on December 30. After an adjustment and break-in period, X began using the machine on January 5, 1985. X does not make the reduced credit election. Assuming no limitations apply, how much investment credit may X claim in 1984?

15. Discuss the general requirements for obtaining the jobs tax credit.

16. What is the purpose of the targeted jobs credit for summer youth employees? Do all youths qualify?

17. May an employer take both the regular targeted jobs credit and the credit for qualified summer youth employees for the same employee? Explain.

18. In 1984, Z Corporation hired C, who is certified as a member of a targeted group for purposes of the targeted jobs credit. C was paid $12,000 during the year. How much is Z Corporation's deduction for wages paid to C during 1984?

19. What provisions in the tax law were enacted to encourage technological development in the United States?

20. Distinguish between the terms "energy conservation expenditures" and "renewable energy source property" for the purpose of computing the amount of residential energy tax credits. Are these two residential energy tax credits computed separately or are they subject to one overall computation and ceiling limitation rule?

21. Y Corporation plans to hire a new employee on May 1, 1984. Two individuals, A and B, have been interviewed. A is an economically disadvantaged ex-convict who is certified as an eligible individual for purposes of the targeted jobs credit. B is certified as an economically disadvantaged youth as well as a qualified summer youth employee. Y Corporation will pay its new employee $1,000 per month, and the job will begin on May 1. Y Corporation is in the 46% marginal tax bracket. Assuming A and B are equally qualified for the job, what tax factors should be considered in the hiring decision? If Y Corporation makes its decision on the basis of tax factors, how much tax will the corporation save?

22. Which of the following taxpayers are eligible for the earned income credit?

(a) H and W are married and have a dependent child. H earned $5,900 and W earned $5,400 during 1984.

(b) A, who is divorced from B, maintains a household for her son, J. J is claimed as a dependent by B, his father, who contributes $2,000 toward his support.

23. Which of the following is correct?

    (a) Individuals who receive substantial Social Security payments are usually not eligible for the tax credit for the elderly, since the FICA payments effectively eliminate the base upon which the credit is computed.

    (b) A taxpayer may claim a foreign tax credit under § 901 or a deduction under § 164.

    (c) Taxpayers are now required to compute the foreign tax credit on a "per country" basis.

24. Discuss the requirements for obtaining a tax credit for child and dependent care expenses.

25. Do child care payments to relatives qualify for the child care credit?

26. What is a refundable credit? Give examples. What is a nonrefundable credit? Give examples.

27. Would a high income level individual generally receive greater benefit from a deduction or a credit?

Problems

28. In 1984, XYZ Corporation made the following purchases:

	Recovery Period	Cost Basis
New factory building	15	$ 600,000
Land for future building site	—	400,000
New auto and trucks used in business	3	100,000
Used equipment	5	150,000
Plant machinery (new)	5	300,000

XYZ Corporation's tax liability (before investment credit) was $50,000 for 1984. Assume XYZ Corporation does not make the reduced credit election.

Compute the following:

(a) Tentative investment credit for 1984.

(b) The credit allowed in 1984.

(c) The 1984 cost recovery allowance for the plant machinery using the statutory percentage method.

29. Assume the same facts as in problem 28 except that XYZ Corporation makes the reduced credit election.

Compute the following:

(a) Tentative investment credit for 1984.

(b) The credit allowed in 1984.

(c) The 1984 cost recovery allowance for the plant machinery using the statutory percentage method.

30. XYZ Corporation acquired the following new properties during 1984:

	Recovery Period	Cost Basis
Office equipment	5 years	$ 140,000
Trucks	3 years	150,000
Factory building	15 years	410,000
		$ 700,000

XYZ's tax liability for 1984 was $35,000 (before investment credit). XYZ has an unused investment credit of $18,000 from 1983 which is carried over to 1984. Assume XYZ Corporation does not make the reduced credit election.

(a) Calculate the amount of tentative investment credit for 1984.

(b) Calculate the amount of investment credit carryover to 1985 and identify the years to which the carryover relates.

31. During 1984, T sells for $10,000 some investment credit property acquired four and one-half years ago at a cost of $15,000. An investment credit of $1,500 was claimed (based on an estimated life of 10 years) in the year the property was acquired. At the time of its disposition, the property has an adjusted basis of $12,000.

(a) How much, if any, of the original credit must be recaptured?

(b) Suppose the property was sold by the executor of T's estate four months after T's death. Would investment credit recapture be required?

32. XYZ Corporation acquired used machinery for use in its business. The machinery cost $200,000, and had a recovery period of five years. XYZ also acquired a new machine by paying the vendor $40,000 and trading in an old machine which had an adjusted cost basis of $20,000. The new machine had a fair market value of $70,000 and a five-year recovery period. XYZ's tax liability in 1984 (before being reduced by the investment credit) was $25,500. Assume the XYZ Corporation does not make the reduced credit election.

(a) Calculate the tentative investment credit for 1984.

(b) Calculate the amount of investment credit allowed during 1984.

(c) How does the tax law treat any unused investment credit amounts during the year?

33. B, a 50% bracket taxpayer, acquired a light-duty truck for use in his business. The truck cost $10,000. B can earn a 16% pre-tax return on any funds he has available to invest. In computing the investment credit on the truck, should B make the reduced credit election? Support your answer with computations.

34. T is a CPA who uses his automobile totally for business purposes. On January 1, 1980, he acquired a new Lincoln for $12,000 and estimated it would have a five-year life. T claimed investment credit on the car on his tax return for 1980. On April 1, 1984, T acquired a new automobile for use in his business and kept the Lincoln for use as a second car for his wife.

(a) Calculate the amount of investment credit recapture, if any, for tax year 1984.

(b) Would your answer be different if T traded in the Lincoln on the new car?

(c) Would your answer be different if T gave the car to his son?

35. B claimed the investment tax credit on the following property acquired in 1982:

Asset	Recovery Period	Cost
Truck	3 years	$ 20,000
Machinery	5 years	$ 80,000

(a) Compute B's tentative investment tax credit for 1982.

(b) Assume B sells both assets in 1984 after holding them for two full years. What is the amount of investment tax credit B must recapture in 1984.

(c) Assume the same facts as in (b) and that B also sells a machine acquired in 1979 after holding it for five full years. In 1979, B had claimed an investment credit based on a useful life of seven years and cost of $30,000. What is the total amount of investment tax credit B must recapture in 1984?

36. X Company hired four handicapped individuals (qualifying X Company for the targeted jobs credit) in 1984. Each of these individuals received wages of $7,000 during 1984. X Company's tax liability for 1984 (after deducting certain tax credits) amounted to $40,000.

(a) Calculate the amount of the jobs tax credit for 1984.

(b) Assume X Company paid total wages of $120,000 to its employees during the year. How much of this amount is deductible in 1984 if the jobs credit is elected?

(c) Calculate the amount of T's jobs credit if the company's tax liability is only $2,000 in 1984.

37. On May 15, 1984, Y Corporation hired four handicapped individuals (A, B, C, and D), all of whom qualified Y Corporation for the targeted jobs credit. A and B also were certified as qualified summer youth employees. D moved out of state in September, quitting his job after earning $4,000 in wages. A, B, and C all continued as employees of Y Corporation. During 1984 each earned $6,500. A and B each earned $3,500 during their first 90 days of employment. Compute Y Corporation's targeted jobs credit, without regard to the ceiling limitation, for 1984. Also compute Y's deduction for wages paid to A, B, C, and D during 1984.

38. Assume the same facts as in Problem 37 and that A, B, and C continue working for Y Corporation in 1985. Each is paid $12,000 wages during the year. What is Y Corporation's targeted jobs credit in 1985 (assuming Congress extends the credit beyond its scheduled expiration date of 1984)?

39. T acquired a 30-year-old office building for $50,000 and spent $60,000 to rehabilitate it. The building was placed in service on January 1, 1984. Compute T's credit for rehabilitation expenditures, basis in the building, and cost recovery allowance for 1984.

40. P incurred research and experimentation expenses as follows:

1984	$ 100,000
1983	$ 80,000
1982	$ 60,000
1981	$ 40,000

(a) Compute P's credit for research and experimentation expenditures in 1984.

(b) Assume the same facts as above except that P incurs $160,000 research and experimentation expenses in 1984. Compute P's research and experimentation credit for 1984.

41. T incurred the following expenditures on his principal residence in 1983 and 1984. He acquired the residence in 1976.

	1983	1984
Caulking and weatherstripping	$ 400	$ 200
Insulation	100	–0–
Storm doors	–0–	300
Solar heating system	6,000	8,000

(a) Calculate the amount of T's allowable residential energy credits for 1983 and 1984 (assuming no energy credits in prior years).

(b) How much unused energy tax credit is available for 1985 and subsequent years?

42. T incurred the following expenditures with respect to her principal residence in 1984. She acquired the residence in 1976.

Insulation materials to reduce heating bills, $2,000.

Storm windows and doors, $1,200.

New roof, $3,000.

(a) Which of the above expenditures qualify for the residential energy credit?

(b) Calculate the amount of T's allowable residential energy credit for 1984 (assuming no energy credits in prior years).

(c) If T's energy credit exceeds the amount of the tax liability, is a carryover of any unused amounts allowed? Explain.

43. Which of the following individuals qualify for the earned income credit for 1984?

(a) T is single and has no dependents. His income consisted of $6,000 wages and taxable interest of $1,000. T's adjusted gross income is $7,000.

(b) T maintains a household for a dependent unmarried child and is eligible for head-of-household rates. Her income consisted of $6,000 salary and $500 taxable interest. T incurred $400 unreimbursed employment-related expenses and her adjusted gross income is $6,100.

(c) T is married and files a joint return with his wife. They have no dependents. Their combined income consisted of $6,000 salary and $600 taxable interest. Adjusted gross income is $6,600.

44. T, a widower, lives in an apartment with his three minor children whom he supports. T earned $7,600 during 1984. He incurred $1,000 of unreimbursed employee business expenses and uses the zero bracket amount. Calculate the amount, if any, of T's earned income credit.

45. H, age 67, and W, age 66, are married retirees who received the following income and retirement benefits during 19X1:

Fully taxable pension income from H's former employer	$ 9,000
Dividends and interest (after exclusion)	2,000
FICA payments	4,000
	$ 15,000

Assume H and W file a joint return and have no deductions *for* adjusted gross income and do not itemize. Are they eligible for the tax credit for the elderly? If so, calculate the amount of the credit.

46. H, age 67, and W, age 66, are married retirees who received the following income and retirement benefits during 19X1:

Fully taxable pension from H's former employer	$ 3,000
Dividends and interest (after exclusion)	8,000
FICA payments	1,750
	$ 12,750

Assume H and W file a joint return and have no deductions *for* adjusted gross income. Are they eligible for the tax credit for the elderly? If so, calculate the amount of the credit assuming their actual tax liability (before credits) is $400.

47. X, a U. S. citizen, had taxable income of $50,000 from sources within the U. S. and $10,000 foreign income from investments in France. X paid a tax of $1,200 to the French government. X files a joint return with his wife, and X and his wife have two minor children. X and his spouse use the zero bracket amount and have no other items of income or deductions. Compute the net tax payable if X elects to take the foreign tax credit in 1984.

48. XYZ Corporation is a U. S. corporation which has foreign operations (a division) in England. XYZ had U. S. taxable income of $200,000, which included $100,000 from the foreign division. XYZ paid foreign taxes of $60,000. XYZ's U. S. tax liability was $71,750 before deducting any foreign tax credit. Compute the amount of XYZ Corporation's foreign tax credit for 1984.

49. H and W are married and have two dependent children under age 15. W works full time and earned $27,000 during 1984 (and had no deductions *for* AGI) while her husband attended college on a full-time basis for the entire year. H and W incurred child care expenses of $4,000 during the year, filed a joint return, and used the zero bracket amount. Calculate the amount, if any, of their child care credit for 1984.

50. In 1984, W hired a domestic worker to enable her to be employed on a full-time basis. W made salary payments of $7,000 to the housekeeper during the year and earned $6,000 from her employer. W's husband

earned $58,000 from his employer. W and her husband have two dependent children under 15, elected the zero bracket amount, and filed a joint return. Compute the amount of child and dependent care credit, if any, for the current year.

51. H and W maintain a household for two minor children under age 15. H is employed on a full-time basis; W held a part-time job during the entire year. H's gross earned income was $30,000, and W earned $3,500. H incurred $2,000 unreimbursed employee expenses (automobile travel while attending job-related meetings). H and W incurred $7,000 of child care expenses. H and W file a joint return for 1984 and have itemized deductions of $6,000.

    (a) Calculate the amount, if any, of the credit for child care expenses.

    (b) Calculate the amount, if any, of the credit if H and W have only one child.

52. During 1984, X made a political campaign contribution of $600 to her next-door neighbor who was running for a local political office in the community. X had adjusted gross income of $110,000, itemized deductions of $12,000, and personal and dependency exemptions of $3,000. X files a joint return with her spouse.

    (a) Compute the amount of the tax credit without regard to any ceiling limitations.

    (b) Compute the amount of the tax credit allowed in 1984.

Cumulative Problems

53. H and W are married, ages 38 and 36, and file a joint return. Their household includes S, their 10-year-old son, and F, who is H's 76-year-old father. F is very ill and has been confined to bed for most of the year. He has no income of his own and is fully supported by H and W. H and W had the following amounts of income during 1984:

(a) H's wages	$ 9,800
(b) W's salary	17,200
(c) Interest from First National Bank	250
(d) Unemployment compensation received by H, who was laid off for 5 months during 1984	4,000
(e) Dividends received on January 3, 1985; the corporation mailed the check on December 31, 1984	250

The following expenses were incurred by H and W during 1984.

(f) Amounts paid to N, H's niece, for household help and caring for S and F while H and W were working	$ 3,000
(g) Contribution to Senator X's campaign for re-election	200
(h) Unreimbursed travel expenses incurred by W in connection with her job	450
(i) Itemized deductions	4,600
(j) Insulation added to their home to reduce heating costs	1,200
(k) Federal income taxes withheld by their employers	2,900

Compute net tax payable (or refund due) for H and W for 1984. (Use the 1984 Tax Rate Schedules. The 1984 Tax Table was not available at the date of publication of this text.)

54. H and W are married and file a joint return. They have two dependent children, S and D, ages 14 and 16, respectively. H is a self-employed businessman (sole proprietor of an unincorporated business), and W is a corporate executive.

    H has the following results from his business activities:

(a) Gross income	$ 280,000
(b) Business expenses (including additional depreciation on real property of $26,000)	166,000

    Additional information pertaining to H's business:

(c) Cost of new machine placed in service during 1984 (recovery period of five years). [The appropriate cost recovery allowance on this machine is included in (b).] H does not make the reduced credit election.	$ 15,000
(d) Proceeds from sale of business automobile on January 3, 1984 (original cost of $10,000, accumulated depreciation of $6,300). The automobile was acquired on January 10, 1981 and an investment credit of $600 was taken in that year.	3,000
(e) Wages of $8,000 each for two new employees hired in 1984 (certified to be eligible employees for the targeted jobs tax credit). Total wages for all employees are included in (b).	16,000

    Records related to W's employment provide the following information.

(f) Salary	$ 130,000
(g) Unreimbursed travel expenses	1,000
(h) Unreimbursed entertainment expenses	600

    Other pertinent information relating to 1984 is given below.

(i) Proceeds from sale of stock acquired on March 15, 1984 (cost of $10,000)	$ 8,000
(j) Proceeds from sale of stock acquired in 1976 (cost of $6,000)	4,800
(k) Wages paid to full-time domestic worker for housekeeping and child supervision	10,000
(l) Cost of insulation installed in personal residence	2,500
(m) Dividends ($6,000) and interest ($2,000) received	8,000
(n) Itemized deductions (including any potential deductions above)	26,900
(o) Federal income tax withheld	27,000
(p) Estimated payments on Federal income tax	60,000

    Compute the lowest net tax payable (or highest refund due) for H and W for 1984.

Tax Form Problem

55. Jim Green is 67 years of age and files a joint return with his wife, Helen, age 65. Their adjusted gross income for 1983 was $11,100, and they received $3,000 in FICA (Social Security) benefits. The amount of their tax from Form 1040 is $410. Compute their credit for the elderly on Schedule R of Form 1040.

Cumulative Tax Return Problem

56. Mr. T acquired a new automobile used solely in his business on January 1, 1983, for $6,000. The recovery period is three years. T and his spouse maintained a household for two dependent children (Julia, age 14, and Laura, age 17) and incurred eligible child care expenses of $6,000 during the year. T had earned income of $40,000 from his business, and Mrs. T had earned income of only $5,000. During the year, Mr. T made a political campaign contribution of $500 to the State Committee of the Democratic Party. Mr. and Mrs. T filed a joint return for 1983.

    Compute the total amount of tax credit allowed for 1983. Assume that none of the credit is limited by the amount of their tax liability. Preparation of page 2 (Tax Credits section) of Form 1040 and Forms 2441, Credit for Child and Dependent Care Expenses, and 3468, Computation of Investment Credit, is suggested. Mr. T does not elect to take the reduced investment credit.

57. James R. Jordan lives at 2322 Branch Road, Mesa, AZ 85202. He is a tax accountant with Mesa Widget Manufacturing Company. He also writes computer software programs for tax practitioners and has a part-time tax practice. James is single, age 35, and has no dependents. His Social Security number is 111-35-2222. He wants to have one dollar directed to the Presidential Election Campaign Fund.

    During 1983, James earned a salary of $45,680 from his employer. He received interest of $890 from Home Federal Savings and Loan and $435 from Home State Bank. He received dividends of $620 from Acme Corporation, $470 from Jason Corporation, and $360 from General Corporation.

    James received a $1,600 income tax refund from the state of Arizona on May 12, 1983. On his 1982 Federal income tax return, he reported total itemized deductions of $3,700, which included $2,000 of state income tax withheld by his employer.

    Fees earned from his part-time tax practice in 1983 totaled $4,200. He paid $500 to have the tax returns processed by a computerized tax return service.

    On February 1, 1983, James bought 500 shares of Acme Corporation common stock for $17.60 a share. Acme suffered serious financial setbacks, and on July 16, James sold the stock for $15 a share.

    James bought a used pickup truck for $3,000 on March 5, 1983. He purchased the truck from his brother-in-law, who was unemployed and was in need of cash. On November 2, 1983, he sold the truck to a friend for $3,400.

    On January 2, 1976, James acquired 100 shares of Jason Corporation common stock for $30 a share. He sold the stock on December 19, 1983, for $75 a share.

    During 1983, James received royalties of $15,000 on a software program he had written. (In preparing James's return, keep in mind that royalties are not subject to self-employment tax.) James incurred the following expenditures in connection with his software writing activities:

Cost of microcomputer	$ 8,000
Cost of printer	2,000
Supplies	650
Fee paid to computer consultant	3,500

James elected to expense $5,000 of the cost of the microcomputer under the provisions of § 179. He also elected to take the reduced rate in computing the amount of the investment credit on the microcomputer and the printer, both of which were placed in service on January 10, 1983.

Although his employer suggested that James attend a convention on current developments in corporate taxation, James was not reimbursed for the travel expenses of $1,360 he incurred in attending the convention.

On December 15, 1983, James opened an Individual Retirement Account, in which he deposited $2,000.

Since his income has increased rather sharply this year, James believes his tax will be lower if he elects to compute the tax using the income averaging method. His tax returns for the past four years show the amounts (from line 34) of $22,000 in 1979, $32,000 in 1980, and $33,000 in 1981, and the amount (from line 37) of $36,000 in 1982. These figures will be needed in the income averaging computation.

James contributed $100 to the campaign fund of a friend who ran for the state senate. He made the contribution on March 4, 1983.

During 1983, James paid $300 for prescription medicines and $2,875 in doctor bills, hospital bills, and medical insurance premiums. His employer withheld state income tax of $1,954. James paid real property taxes of $1,766 on his home and $600 sales tax on a new automobile he purchased in 1983. Interest on his home mortgage was $3,845, and interest to credit card companies was $320. James contributed $20 each week to his church and $10 each week to the United Way. Professional dues and subscriptions totaled $350.

James's employer withheld $11,180 during 1983. James paid estimated taxes of $1,600. What is the amount of James Jordan's net tax payable or refund due for 1983? If James has a tax refund due, he wants to have it credited toward his 1984 income tax. You will need the following forms and schedules: Forms 1040, 2106, 3468, and 4562, and Schedules A, B, C, D, E, G, and SE.

Research Problems

58. T acquired an automobile for $10,000 on January 1, 1979. During 1979, she used the automobile 50 percent for business and claimed investment credit of $167 ($5,000 × ⅓ × 10%) based on a three-year life. In 1980 and 1981, T used the automobile only 20 percent for business.

    (a) Is any amount of the original investment credit recaptured? If so, in what year?

    (b) Would your answer be different if T continued to use the automobile for business purposes and increased its business use to 60 percent during 1982?

Partial list of research aids:

Reg. § 1.47–2(e).

J. Wade Harris, 34 TCM 1192, T.C.Memo. 1975–276.

59. XYZ Company, a retailer, is planning to acquire a department store from its current owners for $1,200,000. The purchase price is allocated to the following items:

Land	$ 200,000
Building	400,000
Components	
Central air conditioning	100,000
Wiring	60,000
Elevators	120,000
Fixtures, lighting, etc.	80,000
Movable partitions	40,000
Carpeting	40,000
Office furniture	60,000
Storage sheds for inventory	100,000
	$ 1,200,000

What items, if any, will qualify for the investment credit?

Partial list of research aids:

Minot Federal Savings and Loan v. U. S., 71–1 USTC ¶ 9131, 27 AFTR2d 71–335, 435 F.2d 1368 (CA–8, 1971).

Rev.Rul. 75–178, 1975–1 C.B. 9.

60. T is a CPA employed by an international accounting firm. In 19X1, the accounting firm asked T to transfer to its Paris office. As part of the inducement to get T to accept the transfer, the accounting firm agreed to reimburse him for all expenses incurred in the move. The firm also agreed to pay all of T's moving expenses on his eventual return to the United States. Reimbursement of moving expenses for the return move was not contingent on T's continued employment by the firm. In 19X5, T returned to the United States and was assigned to the firm's New York office. T properly included the reimbursement in gross income in 19X5. In computing his foreign tax credit, T treated the reimbursement as income earned from personal services performed outside the United States. IRS treated the income as earned from services performed within the United States and reduced T's foreign tax credit. Should T contest the IRS treatment of the moving expense reimbursement?

61. In 1983 T, who is single, paid $1,500 in child care expenses for the care of her son, age 10. T lives in a state that reimburses eligible parents for child care expenses. T was reimbursed by the state agency for $1,200 of the child care expenses incurred in 1983. T properly excluded this reimbursement from gross income on her 1983 tax return, on which she claimed a credit for child care expenses based on the $1,500 expenditure. The Internal Revenue Service disallowed the child care credit for $1,200 of the expenses, allowing a credit only for the $300 not reimbursed by the state agency. T has asked your advice as to whether she should challenge this action by the Internal Revenue Service. What advice will you give her?

Chapter 14

Property Transactions: Determination of Gain or Loss and Basis Considerations

This chapter and the following three chapters are concerned with the income tax consequences of property transactions. This term includes the sale or other disposition of property. The questions to be considered with respect to the sale or other disposition of property are:

—Is there a realized gain or loss?

—If so, is the gain or loss recognized?

—If the gain or loss is recognized, is it ordinary or capital?

Chapters 14 and 15 are concerned with the determination of realized and recognized gain or loss, whereas Chapters 16 and 17 are concerned with the classification of the recognized gain or loss as ordinary or capital.

DETERMINATION OF GAIN OR LOSS

REALIZED GAIN OR LOSS

Realized gain or loss is measured by the difference between the amount realized from the sale or other disposition of property and its adjusted basis on the date of disposition. If the amount realized exceeds the property's adjusted basis, the result is a realized gain. Conversely, if the property's adjusted basis exceeds the amount realized, the result is a realized loss.[1]

---

1. § 1001(a) and Reg. § 1.1001-1(a).

Example 1. T sells X Corporation stock with an adjusted basis of $3,000 for $5,000. T's realized gain is $2,000. If T had sold the stock for $2,000 he would have had a $1,000 realized loss.

Sale or Other Disposition. The term "sale or other disposition" is defined broadly in the tax law and includes virtually any disposition of property. Thus, transactions such as trade-ins, casualties, condemnations, thefts, and bond retirements are treated as dispositions of property. The most common disposition of property arises from a sale or exchange.[2] The key factor in determining whether a disposition has taken place usually is whether an identifiable event has occurred[3] as opposed to a mere fluctuation in the value of the property.[4]

Example 2. T sells X Corporation stock, which cost $3,000, for $5,000 on December 1, 19X2. This is a disposition, and T realizes a $2,000 gain in 19X2.

Example 3. T exchanges X Corporation stock, which cost $3,000, for another taxpayer's S Corporation stock worth $5,000 on December 1, 19X2. This is a disposition, and T realizes a $2,000 gain in 19X2.

Example 4. T does not dispose of the X Corporation stock, and it has appreciated in value by $2,000 during 19X2. T has no realized gain, since mere fluctuation in value is not a disposition or identifiable event for tax purposes.

Example 5. T does not dispose of the X Corporation stock, and it has declined in value by $2,000 during 19X2. T has no realized loss, since mere fluctuation in value is not a disposition or identifiable event for tax purposes.

Amount Realized. The amount realized from a sale or other disposition of property is the sum of any money received plus the fair market value of other property received. The amount realized also includes amounts representing real property taxes treated under § 164(d) as imposed on the taxpayer (i.e., the seller) if they are to be paid by the buyer.[5] The reason for including these taxes in the

---

2. Certain transactions are treated as deemed sales or exchanges. For example, a taxpayer who makes a charitable contribution of property for which the associated mortgage exceeds the property's adjusted basis is deemed to have a sale or exchange to the extent of the excess. (*Leo G. Ebben,* T.C.Memo 1983–200.) Likewise, if a donor makes a gift of property with the condition that the donee pay the gift tax, the donor has realized gain to the extent the gift tax paid exceeds the donor's adjusted basis for the property. [*Diedrich v. Comm.,* 82–1 USTC ¶ 9419, 50 AFTR2d 82–5054, 102 S.Ct. 2414 (USSC, 1982)].

3. Reg. § 1.1001–1(c)(1).

4. *Lynch v. Turrish,* 1 USTC ¶ 18, 3 AFTR 2986, 38 S.Ct. 537 (USSC, 1918).

5. § 1001(b) and Reg. § 1.1001–1(b). Refer to Chapter 11 for a discussion of this subject.

amount realized is that their payment by the purchaser is, in effect, an additional amount paid to the seller of the property. The seller is relieved of paying the taxes, in addition to receiving money or other property.

The amount realized also includes any liability on the property disposed of, such as a mortgage debt, if the buyer assumes the mortgage or the property is sold subject to the mortgage.[6] The amount of such liability is included in the amount realized even if the debt is nonrecourse and the amount of the debt is greater than the fair market value of the mortgaged property.[7]

> **Example 6.** T sells property on which there is a mortgage of $20,000 to U for $50,000 cash. T's amount realized from the sale is $70,000 if the mortgage is assumed by U or if U takes the property subject to the mortgage.

The fair market value of property received in a sale or other disposition has been defined by the courts as the price at which property will change hands between a willing seller and a willing buyer when neither is compelled to sell or buy.[8] Fair market value is determined by considering the relevant factors in each case.[9] An expert appraiser is often required to evaluate these factors in arriving at fair market value. When the fair market value of the property received cannot be determined, the value of the property surrendered may be used.[10]

Finally, the amount realized is reduced by selling expenses such as advertising, commissions, and legal fees relating to the disposition.[11] The amount realized is the net amount received directly or indirectly by the taxpayer from the disposition of property regardless of whether it is in the form of cash.

Adjusted Basis. The adjusted basis of the property disposed of is its original basis adjusted to the date of disposition.[12] Original basis is the cost or other basis of the property on the date it is acquired by the

---

6. *Crane v. Comm.,* 47–1 USTC ¶ 9217, 35 AFTR 776, 67 S.Ct. 1047 (USSC, 1947). A legal distinction exists between the direct assumption of a mortgage and taking property subject to a mortgage. The original mortgagee is no longer secondarily liable if the mortgage is assumed. However, if property is taken subject to the mortgage, the original party holding the mortgage may be liable if, upon default, the proceeds from the sale of the property are insufficient to satisfy the mortgage debt in full.

7. *Tufts v. Comm.,* 83–1 USTC ¶ 9328, 51 AFTR2d 83–1132, 103 S.Ct. 1826 (USSC, 1983).

8. *Comm. v. Marshman,* 60–2 USTC ¶ 9484, 5 AFTR2d 1528, 279 F.2d 27 (CA–6, 1960).

9. *O'Malley v. Ames,* 52–1 USTC ¶ 9361, 42 AFTR 19, 197 F.2d 256 (CA–8, 1952).

10. *U. S. v. Davis,* 62–2 USTC ¶ 9509, 9 AFTR2d 1625, 82 S.Ct. 1190 (USSC, 1962).

11. For certain installment sales, selling expenses are required to be added to the adjusted basis rather than reducing the amount realized. For other installment sales, the selling expenses are deducted as a period expense rather than reducing the amount realized. See Chapter 18 for a discussion of installment sales.

12. § 1011(a) and Reg. § 1.1011–1.

taxpayer. Capital additions increase and recoveries of capital decrease the original basis so that on the date of disposition the adjusted basis reflects the unrecovered cost or other basis of the property.[13] Adjusted basis is determined as follows:

Cost (or other adjusted basis) on date of acquisition
+ Capital additions
− Capital recoveries
= Adjusted basis on date of disposition

Capital Additions. Capital additions include the cost of capital improvements and betterments made to the property by the taxpayer. These expenditures are distinguishable from expenditures for the ordinary repair and maintenance of the property which are neither capitalized nor added to the original basis (refer to Chapter 7). The latter expenditures are deductible in the current taxable year if they are related to business or income-producing property.[14] Amounts representing real property taxes treated under § 164(d) as imposed on the seller, but paid or assumed by the buyer, are part of the cost of the property.[15] Any liability on property transferred to the taxpayer upon purchase is also included in the original basis of the property to the buyer. Amortization of the discount on bonds increases the adjusted basis of the bonds.[16]

Capital Recoveries. Examples of capital recoveries are:

(1) *Depreciation.* The original basis of depreciable property is reduced by the annual depreciation charges while the property is held by the taxpayer. The amount of depreciation which is subtracted from the original basis is the greater of the allowed or allowable depreciation on an annual basis.[17] In most circumstances, the allowed and allowable depreciation amounts are the same.

Allowed depreciation is the amount actually deducted on the taxpayer's return.[18] Allowable depreciation is the amount the taxpayer should have deducted given the useful life and salvage value of the property and the method of depreciation

---

13. § 1016(a) and Reg. § 1.1016–1.
14. Refer to the discussion of capital expenditures versus repairs in Chapter 7.
15. Reg. § § 1.1001–1(b)(2) and 1.1012–1(b). Refer to Chapter 11 for a discussion of this subject.
16. § § 1232(a)(2)(A) and 1232A(a) and (c)(5). See Chapter 16 for a discussion of bond discount and the related amortization.
17. § 1016(a)(2) and Reg. § 1.1016–3(a)(1)(i). Basis is reduced for allowable depreciation only to the extent of any tax benefit which would result.
18. But only to the extent resulting in a reduction of the taxpayer's income taxes. § 1016(a)(2)(B) and Reg. § 1.1016–3(a)(1)(i).

used.[19] The application of the greater of allowed or allowable rule is illustrated as follows:

Example 7. T purchased depreciable property (which was not ACRS recovery property) on January 2, 19X2, at a cost of $100,000. The property had a 10-year useful life and no salvage value. T used the straight-line method of depreciation and deducted the following amounts of depreciation for taxable years 19X2 through 19X4:

19X2	$ 10,000
19X3	10,000
19X4	None

T sold the property on January 2, 19X5, for $90,000. T reported a gain of $10,000 on the 19X5 tax return (amount realized of $90,000 less adjusted basis of $80,000). The proper gain is $20,000. The reason is that the adjustment for depreciation is $30,000, the greater of allowed or allowable depreciation on an annual basis. Thus, the adjusted basis is $70,000 [$100,000 (cost) − $30,000 (allowable depreciation)] when the property is sold, and the gain is $20,000 ($90,000 − $70,000).[20]

(2) *Cost Recovery Allowances.* For property placed in service after December 31, 1980, the Economic Recovery Tax Act of 1981 has replaced the concept of depreciation with the concept of cost recovery. The cost or other adjusted basis of the property is deducted over the statutory recovery period or the optional recovery periods.[21] The previously used depreciation system will continue to apply to property placed in service prior to January 1, 1981, and to property for which the depreciation calculation is not based on the number of years (e. g., unit-of-production method).[22]

---

19. Reg. § 1.1016–3(a)(1)(ii). If no depreciation deductions have been taken by the taxpayer, the amount allowable is determined by using the straight-line method of depreciation. Reg. § 1.1016–3(a)(2)(i). Note, that for purposes of computing the amount subject to depreciation recapture under § 1245 (see Chapter 17), Reg. § 1.1245–2(a)(3) states that the amount taken into account shall be the amount allowed if the taxpayer can establish by adequate records or other sufficient evidence that the amount allowed was less than the amount allowable.

20. The taxpayer could file an amended return and claim depreciation not taken for any taxable years within the statute of limitations, which is generally three years from the date the original return was filed. § 6511(a) and Reg. § 301.6511(a)–1. Among the potential reasons for the taxpayer's foregoing the depreciation deduction in 19X4 are oversight, low effective tax rates for 19X4 versus expected higher tax rates in future years, and the taxpayer's not needing additional deductions in 19X4 (e. g., NOL for 19X4).

21. § 168. Refer to the discussion of the accelerated cost recovery system (ACRS) in Chapter 9.

22. § 168(e).

(3) *Investment Tax Credit.* For property placed in service after 1982, the taxpayer may be required to reduce the adjusted basis of the property by 50 percent of the available investment tax credit. Such reduction in the adjusted basis of the property is required unless the taxpayer elects to take a reduced investment tax credit (refer to Chapter 13).[23]

(4) *Casualties and Thefts.* A casualty or theft may result in the reduction of the adjusted basis of property.[24] The adjusted basis is reduced by the amount of the deductible loss. In addition, the adjusted basis is reduced by the amount of insurance proceeds received. However, the receipt of insurance proceeds may result in a recognized gain rather than in a deductible loss. Such gain increases the adjusted basis of the property.[25]

Example 8. An uninsured truck used in a trade or business is destroyed in an accident. The adjusted basis is $8,000, and the fair market value is $6,500. The amount of the casualty loss is $8,000, and the adjusted basis is reduced by $8,000 to $0.

Example 9. Assume the same facts as in Example 8, except that the truck is insured. The amount of the casualty loss is $1,500 ($6,500 insurance proceeds − $8,000 adjusted basis). The adjusted basis is reduced by the $1,500 casualty loss and the $6,500 of insurance proceeds received.

Example 10. Assume the same facts as in Example 8, except that the truck is damaged rather than destroyed. The fair market value after the accident is $4,200. The amount of the casualty loss is $2,300 (i. e., lesser of decline in value of $2,300 or adjusted basis of $8,000), and the adjusted basis is reduced by $2,300.

Example 11. An insured truck used in a trade or business is damaged in an accident. The adjusted basis is $8,000, and the fair market value is $14,000. The fair market value after the accident is $4,200. The amount of the casualty gain is $1,800 ($9,800 insurance proceeds − $8,000 adjusted basis). The adjusted basis is increased by the $1,800 casualty gain and is decreased by the $9,800 of insurance proceeds.

(5) *Certain Corporate Distributions.* A corporate distribution to a shareholder which is not taxable is treated as a return of capital, and it reduces the basis of the shareholder's stock in the corporation.[26] For example, if a corporation distributes

---

23. §§ 48(q)(1) and (4) and 1016(a)(24).
24. Refer to Chapter 8 for the discussion of casualties and thefts.
25. Reg. § 1.1016–6(a).
26. § 1016(a)(4) and Reg. § 1.1016–5(a).

cash dividends to its shareholders and has no earnings and profits, such distributions are treated as a return of capital. If the corporation does have earnings and profits, but makes a distribution in excess of such earnings and profits, the excess distribution is treated as a return of capital. Once the basis of the stock is reduced to zero, the amount of any subsequent distributions usually is a capital gain.

(6) *Amortizable Bond Premium.*   The basis in a bond which is purchased at a premium is reduced by the amortizable portion of the bond premium.[27] Investors in taxable bonds may elect to amortize the bond premium, but the premium on tax-exempt bonds must be amortized.[28] The amount of the amortized premium on taxable bonds is permitted as an interest deduction. Therefore, the election produces the opportunity for an annual interest deduction to offset ordinary income in exchange for a larger capital gain or smaller capital loss on the disposition of the bond. No such interest deduction is permitted for tax-exempt bonds. The amortization deduction is allowed for taxable bonds because the premium is viewed as a cost of earning the taxable interest from the bonds. The reason the basis of taxable bonds is reduced is that the amortization deduction is a recovery of the cost or basis of the bonds. The basis of tax-exempt bonds is reduced even though the amortization is not allowed. No amortization deduction is permitted on tax-exempt bonds, since the interest income is exempt from tax and the amortization of bond premium merely represents an adjustment of the effective amount of such income. The tax treatment is illustrated in the following example:

Example 12.   T purchases S Corporation taxable bonds with a face value of $100,000 for $110,000, thus paying a premium of $10,000. The annual interest rate is 7%, and the bonds mature 10 years from the date of purchase. If T elects to amortize the bond premium, the annual interest income is $7,000 (7% × $100,000) and the annual amortization deduction is $1,000. Each year the basis of the bonds will be reduced by the $1,000 premium amortization. After T holds the bonds for one year, their basis will be $109,000 (original basis of $110,000 less $1,000 first-year premium amortization). Note

27.   § 1016(a)(5) and Reg. § 1.1016–5(b). The accounting treatment of bond premium amortization is the same as for tax purposes. The amortization results in a decrease in the bond investment account. See Chapter 16 for a discussion of bond discount and the related amortization.
28.   § 171(c).

that if the bonds were tax-exempt, amortization of bond premium and the basis adjustment would be mandatory. However, no deduction would be allowed for the amortization.

RECOGNIZED GAIN OR LOSS

Recognized gain is the amount of the realized gain that is included in the taxpayer's gross income.[29] A recognized loss, on the other hand, is the amount of a realized loss that is deductible for tax purposes.[30] As a general rule, the entire amount of a realized gain or loss is recognized.[31]

Figure I summarizes the realized gain or loss and recognized gain or loss concepts.

Figure I

RECOGNIZED GAIN OR LOSS

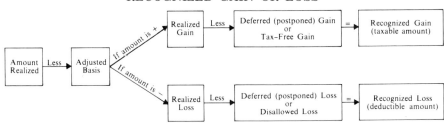

NONRECOGNITION OF GAIN OR LOSS

In certain cases, a realized gain or loss is not recognized upon the sale or other disposition of property.[32] One of the exceptions to the recognition of gain or loss involves nontaxable exchanges, which are covered in Chapter 15. Additional exceptions include losses realized upon the sale, exchange, or condemnation of personal use assets (as opposed to business or income-producing property) and gains realized upon the sale of a residence by taxpayers 55 years of age or older.[33] In addition, realized losses from the sale or exchange of business or income-producing property (as opposed to personal use assets) between certain related parties are not recognized.[34]

The sale of a residence by taxpayers 55 years of age and older is covered in Chapter 15, and the nonrecognition of realized losses from sales or exchanges between related parties is discussed subsequently in this chapter.

---

29. § 61(a)(3) and Reg. § 1.61–6(a).
30. § 165(a) and Reg. § 1.165–1(a).
31. § 1001(c) and Reg. § 1.1002–1(a).
32. Reg. § 1.1002–1(b) and (c).
33. § 121(a), Reg. § § 1.165–1(e) and 1.262–1(b)(4).
34. § 267(a)(1).

Sale, Exchange, and Condemnation of Personal Use Assets. A realized loss from the sale, exchange, or condemnation of personal use assets (e. g., a personal residence or an automobile which is not used at all for business or income-producing purposes) is not recognized for tax purposes. An exception is provided to this rule for casualty or theft losses from personal use assets. In contrast, any gain realized from the sale or other disposition of personal use assets is, generally, fully taxable. The following examples illustrate the tax consequences of the sale of personal use assets.

Example 13. T sells an automobile, which is held exclusively for personal use, for $6,000. The adjusted basis of the automobile is $5,000. T has a realized and recognized gain of $1,000.

Example 14. T sells the automobile in Example 13 for $4,000. T has a realized loss of $1,000, but the loss is not recognized.

Example 15. T sells an automobile which is held exclusively for personal use for $6,000. The adjusted basis is $5,000. In addition, T sells a personal use boat for $2,500. The adjusted basis is $4,000. T has a realized and recognized gain on the sale of the automobile of $1,000 ($6,000 − $5,000). The realized loss on the boat is $1,500 ($2,500 − $4,000), but it is not recognized. T is not permitted to offset the realized loss against the realized gain.

Example 16. T sells an automobile for $4,000. It was used 60% for personal use and 40% for business use. The adjusted basis for the personal use part is $6,000, and the adjusted basis for the business use part is $2,500. The sale is treated as the disposition of two assets. The sales price is allocated between the two assets based on the usage percentage (i. e., $2,400 to the personal use portion and $1,600 to the business use portion). The realized loss of $3,600 ($2,400 − $6,000) on the personal use portion is not recognized, whereas the realized loss of $900 ($1,600 − $2,500) on the business use portion is deductible.

RECOVERY OF CAPITAL DOCTRINE

Doctrine Defined. The recovery of capital doctrine pervades all the tax rules relating to property transactions and is very significant with respect to these transactions. The doctrine derives its roots from the very essence of the income tax law—a tax on income. Therefore, as a general rule, a taxpayer is entitled to recover the cost or other original basis of property acquired and is not taxed on that amount.

The cost or other original basis of depreciable property is recovered through annual depreciation deductions. The basis is reduced as the cost is recovered over the period the property is held. Therefore, when property is sold or otherwise disposed of, it is the adjusted basis (unrecovered cost or other basis) which is compared to the amount realized from the disposition to determine realized gain or loss.

Relationship of the Recovery of Capital Doctrine to the Concepts of Realization and Recognition. It follows by definition that if a sale or other disposition results in a realized gain, the taxpayer has recovered more than the adjusted basis (unrecovered cost or other basis) of the property. Conversely, if a sale or other disposition results in a realized loss, the taxpayer has recovered less than the adjusted basis (unrecovered cost or other basis).

The general rules for the relationship between the recovery of capital doctrine and the realized and recognized gain and loss concepts can be summarized as follows:

Rule 1. A realized gain that is never recognized (e. g., all or a portion of the realized gain on the sale of a personal residence by taxpayers 55 years of age and older is excluded from tax) results in the permanent recovery of more than the taxpayer's cost or other basis for tax purposes.

Rule 2. A realized gain on which recognition is postponed (e. g., an exchange of like-kind property under § 1031, an involuntary conversion under § 1033, or a replacement of a personal residence under § 1034) results in the temporary recovery of more than the taxpayer's cost or other basis for tax purposes.

Rule 3. A realized loss that is never recognized (e. g., a nondeductible loss from the sale of an automobile held for personal use) results in the permanent recovery of less than the taxpayer's cost or other basis for tax purposes.

Rule 4. A realized loss on which recognition is postponed (e. g., an exchange of like-kind property under § 1031) results in the temporary recovery of less than the taxpayer's cost or other basis for tax purposes.

These rules are illustrated in discussions to follow in this and the next chapter.

BASIS CONSIDERATIONS

DETERMINATION OF COST BASIS

The basis of property is generally its cost. Cost is the amount paid for the property in cash or other property.[35] This general rule follows logically from the recovery of capital doctrine. That is, the cost or other basis of property is to be recovered tax-free by the taxpayer.

A bargain purchase of property is an exception to the general rule for determining basis. A bargain purchase may result when an em-

---

35. § 1012 and Reg. § 1.1012–1(a).

ployer transfers property to an employee as compensation for services at less than its fair market value or when a corporation transfers property to a shareholder as a dividend at less than its fair market value. The basis of property acquired in a bargain purchase is its fair market value.[36]

> **Example 17.** T buys a machine from her employer for $10,000 on December 30, 19X2. The fair market value of the machine is $15,000. T must include the $5,000 difference between cost and the fair market value of the machine in gross income for the taxable year 19X2. The bargain element represents additional compensation to T. T's basis for the machine is $15,000, the machine's fair market value.

Identification Problems. Cost identification problems are frequently encountered in securities transactions. For example, the Regulations require that the taxpayer must adequately identify the particular stock which has been sold.[37] A problem arises when the taxpayer has purchased separate lots of stock on different dates or at different prices and cannot adequately identify the lot from which a particular sale takes place. In this case, the stock is presumed to come from the first lot or lots purchased (i. e., a FIFO presumption).[38] When securities are left in the custody of a broker, it may be necessary to provide specific instructions and receive written confirmation as to which securities are being sold.

> **Example 18.** T purchases 100 shares of S Corporation stock on July 1, 19X2, for $5,000 ($50 a share), and another 100 shares of the same stock on July 1, 19X3, for $6,000 ($60 a share). She sells 50 shares of the stock on January 2, 19X4. The cost of the stock sold, assuming T cannot adequately identify the shares, is $50 a share or $2,500. This is the cost she will compare to the amount realized in determining the gain or loss from the sale.

Allocation Problems. When a taxpayer acquires multiple assets in a lump-sum purchase, it is necessary to allocate the total cost among the individual assets.[39] Allocation is necessary because some of the assets acquired may be depreciable (e. g., buildings) and others not (e. g., land), a portion of the assets acquired may be sold, or some of the assets may be capital or § 1231 assets which receive special tax treatment upon subsequent sale or other disposition. A lump-sum cost is allocated on the basis of the fair market values of the individual assets acquired.

36. Reg. §§ 1.61–2(d)(2)(i) and 1.301–1(j).
37. Reg. § 1.1012–1(c)(1).
38. *Kluger Associates, Inc.,* 69 T.C. 925 (1978).
39. Reg. § 1.61–6(a) and Reg. § 1.61–6(a), Example (2).

Example 19. T purchases a building and land for $800,000. Because of the depressed nature of the industry of the seller, T was able to negotiate a very favorable purchase price. Appraisals of the individual assets indicate that the fair market value of the building is $600,000 and that of the land is $400,000. T's basis for the building is $480,000 ($600,000/$1,000,000 × $800,000), and the basis for the land is $320,000 ($400,000/$1,000,000 × $800,000).

Allocation is also necessary in certain nonpurchase situations such as the receipt of nontaxable stock dividends and rights under § 305(a). Sections 307(a) and (b), respectively, stipulate the rules for allocation in these cases.

In the case of nontaxable stock dividends, the allocation depends upon whether the dividend is a common stock dividend on common stock or a preferred stock dividend on common stock. If the dividend is common on common, the cost of the original common shares is allocated to the total shares owned after the dividend.[40]

Example 20. T owns 100 shares of S Corporation common stock for which he paid $1,100. He receives a 10% common stock dividend giving him a new total of 110 shares. Before the stock dividend, T's basis was $11 per share ($1,100 divided by 100 shares). The basis of each share after the stock dividend is $10 ($1,100 divided by 110 shares).

If the dividend is preferred stock on common, the cost of the original common shares is allocated between the common and preferred shares on the basis of their relative fair market values on the date of distribution.[41]

Example 21. S owns 100 shares of X Corporation common stock for which she paid $1,000. She receives a stock dividend of 50 shares of preferred stock on her common stock. The fair market values on the date of distribution of the preferred stock dividend are $30 a share for common and $40 a share for preferred. Thus, the total fair market value is $3,000 ($30 × 100) for common and $2,000 ($40 × 50) for preferred. The basis of S's common after the dividend is $600, or $6 a share ($3,000/$5,000 × $1,000), and the basis of the preferred is $400, or $8 a share ($2,000/$5,000 × $1,000).

In the case of nontaxable stock rights, the cost basis of the rights is zero unless the taxpayer elects or is required to allocate a portion of the cost of the stock to the rights. If the fair market value of the rights

---

40. The holding period of the new shares includes the holding period of the old shares. § 1223(5) and Reg. § 1.1223–1(e).
41. Reg. § 1.307–1(a).

is 15 percent or more of the fair market value of the stock, the taxpayer is required to allocate. If the value of the rights is less than 15 percent of the value of the stock, the taxpayer may elect to allocate.[42] The result is that the rights will either have no basis or the cost of the stock on which the rights are received will be allocated between the stock and rights on the basis of their relative fair market values.

> **Example 22.** T receives nontaxable stock rights with a fair market value of $1,000. The fair market value of the stock on which the rights were received is $8,000 (cost $10,000). T does not elect to allocate. The basis of the rights is zero. If the rights are exercised, the basis of the new stock would be the exercise (subscription) price.

> **Example 23.** Assume the same facts as in Example 22, except the fair market value of the rights is $3,000. T must allocate because the value of the rights is more than 15% of the value of the stock ($3,000/$8,000 = 37.5%). The basis of the rights is $2,727 ($3,000/$11,000 × $10,000); the basis of the stock is $7,273 ($8,000/$11,000 × $10,000). If the rights are exercised, the basis of the new stock would be the exercise (subscription) price plus the basis of the rights. If the rights are sold, gain or loss is recognized. This allocation rule applies only when the rights are exercised or sold. Therefore, if the rights are allowed to lapse (i. e., expire), the rights have no basis, and the basis of the original stock is its cost, $10,000.

The holding period of nontaxable stock rights includes the holding period of the stock on which the rights were distributed.[43] If the rights are exercised, the holding period of the newly acquired stock begins with the date the rights are exercised.[44] The significance of the holding period for capital assets is discussed in Chapter 16.

In the case of stock received as a qualified reinvestment dividend from a qualified public utility, the cost basis is zero and the holding period begins with the date of receipt.[45]

GIFT BASIS

When a taxpayer receives property as a gift, there is, of course, no cost to the recipient. Thus, under the cost basis provision, the donee's basis would be zero. However, this would violate the statutory intent that gifts are not subject to the income tax. With a zero basis, a sale by the donee would result in all of the amount realized being treated as realized gain. Therefore, a basis is assigned to the property received de-

---

42. § 307(b).
43. § 1223(5) and Reg. § 1.1223–1(e).
44. Reg. § 1.1223–1(f).
45. § 305(e). Refer to the discussion of qualified reinvestment dividends in Chapter 6.

pending on the date of the gift, the basis of the property to the donor, and the fair market value of the property.[46]

Gifts Prior to 1921. If the gift property was acquired prior to 1921, its basis for income tax purposes is its fair market value on the date of the gift.[47]

Present Gift Basis Rules If No Gift Tax Is Paid. The present basis rules for gifts of property may be described as follows:

—If the donee subsequently disposes of gift property in a transaction which results in a gain, the basis to the donee is the same as the donor's adjusted basis (i. e., gain basis).[48] Therefore, *a gain results* if the amount realized from the disposition exceeds the donor's adjusted basis.

Example 24. T purchased stock in 19X2 for $10,000. He gave the stock to his son, S, in 19X3, when its fair market value was $15,000. Assuming no gift tax was paid on the transfer and the property is subsequently sold by S for $15,000, S's basis would be $10,000 and S would have a realized gain of $5,000.

—If the donee subsequently disposes of gift property in a transaction which results in a loss, the basis to the donee is the lower of the donor's adjusted basis or fair market value on the date of the gift (i. e., loss basis). Therefore, *a loss results* if the amount realized from the disposition is less than the lower of the donor's adjusted basis or fair market value at the date of the gift.

Example 25. T purchases stock in 19X2 for $10,000. T gives the stock to his son, S, in 19X3 when its fair market value is $7,000. S later sells the stock for $6,000. S's basis is $7,000 (fair market value is less than donor's adjusted basis of $10,000), and the loss from the sale is $1,000 ($7,000 basis less the $6,000 amount realized).

Note that the loss rule prevents the donee from receiving a tax benefit from the decline in value while the donor held the property. Therefore, in the previous example, S has a loss of $1,000 and not $4,000. The $3,000 difference represents the decline in value while T held the property. It is perhaps ironic, however, that the basis for gain rule may eventually result in the donee's being subject to income tax on the appreciation which occurs while the donor held the property.

If the amount realized from sale or other disposition is between the basis for loss and the basis for gain, no gain or loss is realized. See Example 28.

---

46. § 102(a). See the Glossary of Tax Terms (Appendix C) for a definition of the term "gift."

47. § 1015(c) and Reg. § 1.1015–3(a).

48. § 1015(a) and Reg. § 1.1015–1(a)(1). See Reg. § 1.1015–1(a)(3) for cases in which the facts necessary to determine the donor's adjusted basis are unknown.

Adjustment for Gift Tax. If gift taxes are paid by the donor, the donee's gain basis may exceed the adjusted basis of the property to the donor. This will occur only if the fair market value of the property at the date of the gift is greater than the donor's adjusted basis (i. e., the property has appreciated in value.) The portion of the gift tax paid that is associated with the appreciation is added to the donor's basis in calculating the donee's gain basis for the property. The formula, in this circumstance, for calculating the donee's gain basis is as follows:[49]

$$\text{Donee's gain basis} = \text{Donor's adjusted basis} + \frac{\text{Unrealized appreciation}}{\text{Fair market value}} \times \text{Gift tax paid}$$

Example 26. F made a gift of stock to S in 1984 when the fair market value of the stock was $40,000. F had purchased the stock in 1978 for $10,000. Since the unrealized appreciation is $30,000 ($40,000 fair market value less $10,000 adjusted basis) and the fair market value is $40,000, three-fourths ($30,000/$40,000) of the gift tax paid is added to the basis of the property. If the gift tax is $4,000, S's basis in the property is $13,000 [$10,000 + $3,000 (¾ of the $4,000 gift tax)].

Example 27. F made a gift of stock to S in 1984 when the fair market value of the stock was $40,000. F had purchased the stock in 1978 for $45,000. Since there is no unrealized appreciation at the date of the gift, none of the gift tax paid of $4,000 is added to the donor's basis in calculating the donee's gain basis. Therefore, the donee's gain basis is $45,000.

For gifts made prior to 1977, the full amount of the gift tax paid is added to the donor's basis. However, the ceiling on this total is the fair market value of the property at the date of the gift. Thus, in Example 26, if the gift was made prior to 1977, the basis of the property would be $14,000 ($10,000 + $4,000). In Example 27, the basis would still be $45,000 ($45,000 + 0).

Holding Period. The holding period of property acquired by gift begins on the date the property was acquired by the donor if the donor's adjusted basis is the basis to the donee (i. e., gain basis rule).[50] The holding period starts on the date of the gift if fair market value is the basis to the donee (i. e., loss basis rule).[51] The significance of the holding period for capital assets is discussed in Chapter 16.

The following example summarizes the basis and holding period rules for gift property:

---

49. § 1015(d)(6).
50. § 1223(2) and Reg. § 1.1223–1(b).
51. Rev.Rul. 59–86, 1959–1 C.B. 209.

Example 28. T acquires 100 shares of X Corporation stock on December 30, 1978, for $40,000. On January 3, 1984, when the stock has a fair market value of $38,000, T gives it to S. Gift tax of $4,000 is paid by the donor. There is no increase in basis for a portion of the gift tax paid, since the property has not appreciated in value at the time of the gift. S's basis for determining loss is $38,000 (fair market value), since the fair market value on the date of the gift is less than the donor's adjusted basis.

—If S sells the stock for $45,000, he has a recognized gain of $5,000. The holding period for determining whether the capital gain is short-term or long-term begins on December 30, 1978, the date the property was acquired by the donor.

—If S sells the stock for $36,000, he has a recognized loss of $2,000. The holding period for determining whether the capital loss is short-term or long-term begins on January 3, 1984, the date of the gift.

—If S sells the property for $39,000, there is no gain or loss, since the amount realized is less than the gain basis of $40,000 and more than the loss basis of $38,000.

PROPERTY ACQUIRED FROM A DECEDENT

General Rule. The basis of property acquired from a decedent is generally its fair market value at the date of death (referred to as the primary valuation amount).[52] The property's basis is its fair market value six months after the date of death if the executor or administrator of the estate elects the alternate valuation date for estate tax purposes (referred to as the alternate valuation amount). The alternate valuation date and amount determine the beneficiary's basis only if the executor or administrator of the estate elects the alternate valuation date for estate tax purposes. Thus, if an estate tax return does not have to be filed because the estate is below the threshhold amount for taxability, the alternate valuation date and amount are not available. The limitation is intended to prevent small estates from further increasing the income tax basis of the property. Even if an estate tax return is filed and the executor elects the alternate valuation date, the six months after death date is available only for property which the executor has not distributed before this date. Any property distributed or otherwise disposed of during this six-month period will have an adjusted basis equal to the fair market value on the date of distribution or other disposition.[53]

While the primary fiduciary responsibility of the executor is conservation of the assets of the estate, there is no necessary conflict between this responsibility and the minimization of the beneficiary's

---

52. § 1014(a).
53. § 2032(a)(1) and Rev.Rul. 56–60, 1956–1 C.B. 443.

eventual income tax liability. For example, if the property increases in value during the six-month period following the decedent's death, the election of the alternate valuation date will result in a higher basis for the property to the beneficiary with no additional tax cost to the estate if the estate can offset the increased estate tax value with available estate tax deductions or credits. Likewise, if the property declines in value during the six-month period, the executor can minimize the estate tax liability by electing the alternate valuation date. This can be particularly fruitful when the estate's marginal tax rate is greater than that of the beneficiary.

Thus, for inherited property, both unrealized appreciation and decline in value are taken into consideration in determining the basis of the property for income tax purposes.

Example 29. D inherited property from her father, who died in 19X3. Her father's adjusted basis for the property at date of death was $35,000. The property's fair market value at date of death was $50,000. The alternate valuation date was not elected. D's basis for income tax purposes is $50,000. This is commonly referred to as the stepped-up basis rule.

Example 30. Assume the same facts as in Example 29, except the property's fair market value at date of death was $20,000. D's basis for income tax purposes is $20,000.

Example 31. Assume the same facts as in Example 29, except that the alternate valuation date is elected and the fair market value six months after death is $55,000. D's basis for income tax purposes is $55,000.

Example 32. Assume the same facts as in Example 29, except that the alternate valuation date is elected and the property is distributed four months after the date of decedent's death. At the distribution date, the property's fair market value is $51,000. D's basis for income tax purposes is $51,000.

The Economic Recovery Tax Act of 1981 contained a provision designed to eliminate a tax avoidance technique referred to as deathbed gifts. Under this provision, if the time period between the date of the gift of appreciated property and the date of the donee's death is not greater than one year, the adjusted basis of such property inherited by the donor or his or her spouse from the donee shall be the same as the decedent's adjusted basis for the property rather than the fair market value at the date of death or the alternate valuation date. The provision is applicable in the case of decedents dying after December 31, 1981.[54]

---

54. § 1014(e).

Example 33. N gives stock to his uncle, U, in 1984. N's basis for the stock is $1,000, and the fair market value is $9,000. No gift tax is paid. Eight months later, N inherits the stock from U. At the date of U's death, the fair market value of the stock is $12,000. N's adjusted basis for the stock is $1,000.

Survivor's Share of Property. Both the decedent's share and the survivor's share of community property have a basis equal to fair market value on the date of the decedent's death.[55] This result is produced for the decedent's share of the community property in that it flows to the surviving spouse from the estate (i. e., fair market value basis for inherited property). Likewise, the surviving spouse's share of the community property is deemed to be acquired by bequest, devise, or inheritance from the decedent. Therefore, it will also have a basis equal to fair market value.

Example 34. H and W reside in a community property state. H and W own community property (200 shares of XYZ stock) which was acquired in 1973 for $100,000. Assume that H dies in 1984 when the securities are valued at $300,000. One-half of the XYZ stock is included in H's estate. If W inherits H's share of the community property, the basis for determining gain or loss is:

—$300,000 [$150,000 (W's share of one-half of the community property) plus $150,000 (one-half × $300,000, the value of XYZ stock at date of death)] for the 200 shares of XYZ stock.

In a common law state, only one-half of jointly held property of spouses (tenants by the entirety or joint tenants with rights of survivorship) is includible in the estate.[56] In such a case, no adjustment of the cost basis is permitted for the excluded property interest.

Example 35. Assume the same facts as in the prior example except that the property is jointly held by H and W who reside in a common law state. Also assume that H purchased the property and made a gift of one-half of the property when the stock was acquired with no gift tax being paid. Only one-half of the XYZ stock is included in H's estate, and W's basis (for determining gain) in the excluded half is not adjusted upward for the increase in value to date of death.Therefore, W's basis would be $200,000 ($50,000 + $150,000).

Holding Period of Property Acquired from a Decedent. Under § 1223 the holding period of property acquired from a decedent is deemed to be long-term (i. e., held for more than one year). This provision is applicable regardless of whether the property is disposed of at a gain or a loss.[57]

---

55. § 1014(b)(6).

56. § 2040(a).

57. § 1223(11).

Example 36. D purchases property on December 6, 19X2, and dies on January 10, 19X3. The executor of D's estate sells the property on October 20, 19X3, to pay expenses of the estate. For purposes of determining whether any gain or loss recognized on the sale by the estate is long-term or short-term (see Chapter 16), the law treats the property as having been held by the estate for more than one year. Thus, any such gain or loss would be long-term gain or loss.

Example 37. Assume the same facts as in Example 36 except that the executor distributes the property on October 20, 19X3, to a beneficiary. The beneficiary sells the property on December 1, 19X3. The holding period results are the same as those in the previous example (i. e., long-term holding period).

DISALLOWED LOSSES

Related Taxpayers. Section 267 provides that realized losses from sales or exchanges of property, directly or indirectly, between certain related parties are not recognized. Section 267 applies to several types of related-party transactions, but the most common involve (1) members of a family and (2) those between an individual and a corporation in which the individual owns, directly or indirectly, more than 50 percent in value of the corporation's outstanding stock. Section 707 provides a similar loss disallowance provision if the related parties are a partner and a partnership in which the partner owns, directly or indirectly, more than 50 percent of the capital interests or profits interests in the partnership. The rules governing the relationships covered by § 267 have been discussed previously in Chapter 7.

If income-producing or business property is transferred to a related taxpayer and a loss is disallowed, the basis of such property to the recipient is its cost to the transferee. However, if a subsequent sale or other disposition of the property results in a realized gain, the amount of gain is reduced by the loss which was previously disallowed.[58] This right of offset is not applicable if the original sale involved the sale of a personal use asset (e. g., the sale of a personal residence between related taxpayers). Likewise, this right of offset is available only to the original transferee (i. e., the related-party buyer).[59]

Example 38. F sells business property (adjusted basis of $50,000) to his daughter, D, for its fair market value of $40,000.

—F's realized loss of $10,000 is not recognized.

---

58.   § 267(d) and Reg. § 1.267(d)–1(a).
59.   Reg. § 1.267(d)–1(a)(3).

—How much gain will D recognize if she sells the property for $52,000? D recognizes a $2,000 gain. Her realized gain is $12,000 ($52,000 less her basis of $40,000), but she can offset F's $10,000 loss against the gain.

—How much gain will D recognize if she sells the property for $48,000? D recognizes no gain or loss. Her realized gain is $8,000 ($48,000 less her basis of $40,000), but she can offset $8,000 of F's $10,000 loss against the gain. Note that F's loss can only offset D's gain; it cannot create a loss for D.

—How much loss will D recognize if she sells the property for $38,000? D recognizes a $2,000 loss, the same as her realized loss ($38,000 less $40,000). F's loss does not increase D's loss. F's loss can be offset only against a gain. Since D had no gain, F's loss cannot be used and is never recognized. Of course, it is assumed in this example that the property is business or income-producing to D. If not, D's $2,000 loss would be personal and would not be recognized.

The loss disallowance rules are designed to achieve two objectives. First, the rules prevent a taxpayer from directly transferring an unrealized loss to a related taxpayer (in a higher tax bracket) who could receive a greater tax benefit from the recognition of the loss. This result is accomplished by providing that the purchaser's basis is his cost. Any indirect tax benefit that the purchaser receives by being able to offset the seller's disallowed loss against his or her realized gain is dependent on the property's appreciating in value in the hands of the purchaser. Second, the rules eliminate a substantial administrative burden on the Internal Revenue Service in terms of the appropriateness of the selling price (i. e., fair market value or not). It should be noted that application of the loss disallowance rules is comprehensive. That is, the rules are applicable even in those cases where the selling price is equal to fair market value and can be validated (e. g., listed stocks).

The holding period of the buyer for the property is not affected by the holding period of the seller. That is, the buyer's holding period includes only the period of time he or she has held the property.[60]

Wash Sales. Section 1091 stipulates that in certain cases, a realized loss on the sale or exchange of stock or securities is not recognized. Specifically, if a taxpayer sells or exchanges stock or securities and within 30 days before or after the date of such sale or exchange acquires substantially identical stock or securities, any loss realized from the sale or exchange is not recognized.[61] The term "acquire" means acquire by purchase or in a taxable exchange and includes an

---

60. § 267(d), § 1223(2), and Reg. § 1.267(d)–1(c)(3).
61. § 1091(a) and Reg. § 1.1091–1(a).

option to purchase substantially identical securities.[62] "Substantially identical" means the same in all important particulars. Corporate bonds and preferred stock are normally not considered substantially identical to the corporation's common stock; however, if the bonds and preferred stock are convertible into common stock, they may be considered substantially identical under certain circumstances.[63] Attempts to avoid the application of § 1091 by having a related taxpayer repurchase the securities have been unsuccessful.[64] These wash sale provisions do not apply to gains.

Recognition of the loss is disallowed because the taxpayer is considered to be in substantially the same economic position after the sale and repurchase as before the sale and repurchase. However, this rule does not apply to taxpayers engaged in the business of buying and selling securities.[65] The average investor, however, is not allowed to create losses through wash sales to offset income for tax purposes.

Realized loss that is not recognized is added to the basis of the substantially identical stock or securities whose acquisition resulted in the nonrecognition of loss.[66] In other words, the basis of the replacement stock or securities is increased by the amount of the unrecognized loss.[67] If the loss were not added to the basis of the newly acquired stock or securities, the taxpayer would never recover the entire basis of the old stock or securities. By adding the unrecognized loss to the basis of the newly acquired stock or securities, the taxpayer is able to recover the cost of the new stock or securities plus the unrecovered cost or other basis of the old stock or securities. That is, the taxpayer will have a greater loss or lesser gain from the subsequent disposition of the new stock or securities to the extent of the unrecognized loss from the wash sale.

Since the basis of the new stock or securities includes the unrecovered portion of the basis of the formerly held stock or securities, the holding period of the new stock or securities begins on the date the old stock or securities were acquired.[68] The following examples illustrate the application of the wash sale rules:

Example 39. T owns 100 shares of A Corporation stock (adjusted basis of $20,000), 50 shares of which she sells for $8,000. Ten days later, T purchases 50 shares of the same stock for $7,000. T's realized loss of $2,000 ($8,000 less $10,000 adjusted basis of 50 shares) is not recognized because it resulted from a

---

62. Reg. § 1.1091–1(f).

63. Rev.Rul. 56–406, 1956–2 C.B. 523.

64. *McWilliams v. Comm.*, 47–1 USTC ¶ 9289, 35 AFTR 1184, 67 S.Ct. 1477 (USSC, 1947).

65. Reg. § 1.1091–1(a).

66. § 1091(d).

67. Reg. § 1.1091–2(a).

68. § 1223(4) and Reg. § 1.1223–1(d).

wash sale. Her basis in the newly acquired stock is $9,000 ($7,000 purchase price plus $2,000 unrecognized loss from the wash sale).

When the taxpayer acquires less than the number of shares sold in a wash sale, the loss from the sale is prorated between recognized and unrecognized loss on the basis of the ratio of the number of shares acquired to the number of shares sold.[69]

> **Example 40.** In the previous example, if T had purchased 25 new shares for $3,500, only $1,000 of the loss ($25/50 \times $2,000 loss) would be disallowed, and the basis of the new shares would be $4,500 ($3,500 purchase price plus $1,000 unrecognized loss from the wash sale).

Tax Straddles. Before the Economic Recovery Tax Act of 1981, it was possible to use commodity tax straddles to shelter income through the recognition of losses and the deferral of unrealized gains. With only a six-month holding period requirement, it was likely that the unrealized gain, when eventually realized, would be taxed as favorable long-term capital gain.[70]

A straddle is defined as offsetting positions with respect to personal property (e. g., buy and sell orders in the same commodity or a sell order with physical possession of the commodity).[71] While a fluctuation in the market price may leave the taxpayer's economic position unchanged, an unrealized loss occurs on one position and an unrealized gain on the other. The liquidation of the loss position by the taxpayer would produce realized loss (probably a short-term capital loss), whereas the unrealized gain would not be realized until a subsequent taxable year when the taxpayer closed that position (probably resulting in long-term capital gain).

As a general rule, the recognition of any loss with respect to one or more positions established after June 23, 1981, in taxable years ending after such date is limited in any taxable year to an amount equal to the excess of such loss over any unrealized gain with respect to one or more positions which were acquired before the disposition which resulted in such loss and were offsetting positions to the loss position. Nonrecognized losses under this provision are treated as having occurred in the following taxable year and are subject to the deferral rule for that taxable year.[72]

> **Example 41.** T purchases two gold futures contracts, one to buy and the other to sell, for $10,000 each in November 1984. T's position is a straddle, because he has offsetting positions. When

---

69. § 1091(b) and Reg. § 1.1091–1(c).
70. It should be noted that this was the position of the taxpayer and not necessarily that of the Internal Revenue Service. For example, see the position to the contrary taken in Rev.Rul. 77–185, 1977–1 C.B. 48.
71. § 1092(c).
72. § 1092(a)(1)(A) and (B).

the market fluctuates, one position shows a gain and the other a loss. Before the end of 1984, T liquidates one position and realizes a $1,000 loss. At the same time, he has an unrealized gain of $1,000 on the offsetting position which he does not liquidate. T's recognized loss is limited to the excess of the realized loss over the unrealized gain with respect to the offsetting position. In this example, T has no recognized loss (realized loss of $1,000 less unrealized gain of $1,000).

CONVERSION OF PROPERTY FROM PERSONAL USE TO BUSINESS OR INCOME-PRODUCING USE

As discussed previously, losses from the sale of personal use assets are not recognized for tax purposes, but losses from the sale of business and income-producing assets are deductible. Can a taxpayer convert a personal use asset which has declined in value to business use and then sell the asset to recognize a business loss? The law prevents this by requiring that the original basis for loss on personal use assets converted to business or income-producing use is the lower of the property's adjusted basis or fair market value on the date of conversion.[73] Thus, if a taxpayer whose personal residence had an adjusted basis of $100,000 converted it to rental use when it was worth $60,000, it would have a basis of $60,000 for purposes of determining the loss upon its subsequent sale. The $40,000 decline in value is a personal loss and can never be recognized for tax purposes. The gain basis for converted property is its adjusted basis on the date of conversion. The law is not concerned with gains on converted property, because gains are recognized regardless of whether property is business, income-producing, or personal use.

The basis for loss is also the basis for depreciating the converted property.[74] This is an exception to the general rule which provides that the basis for depreciation is the gain basis (e. g., property received by gift). This exception prevents the taxpayer from recovering a personal loss indirectly through depreciation of the higher original basis. Finally, after the property is converted, both its basis for loss and its basis for gain are adjusted for depreciation deductions from the date of conversion to the date of disposition to determine realized gain or loss. These rules apply only if a conversion from personal to business or income-producing use has actually occurred.

The following two examples illustrate the application of these rules:

> **Example 42.** At a time when her personal residence (adjusted basis of $40,000) is worth $50,000, T converts one-half of it to rental use. (Assume the property is not ACRS recovery property.)

---

73. Reg. § 1.165–9(b)(2).
74. Reg. § 1.167(g)–1.

At this point, the estimated useful life of the residence is 20 years and there is no estimated salvage value. After renting the converted portion for five years, T sells the property for $44,000. Assume all amounts relate only to the building; the land has been accounted for separately. T has a $2,000 realized gain from the sale of the personal use portion of the residence and a $7,000 realized gain from the sale of the rental portion. These gains are computed as follows:

	Personal Use	Rental
Original basis for gain and loss— adjusted basis on date of conversion (Fair market value is greater than the adjusted basis)	$ 20,000	$ 20,000
Depreciation—five years	None	5,000
Adjusted basis—date of sale	$ 20,000	$ 15,000
Amount realized	22,000	22,000
Realized gain	$ 2,000	$ 7,000

As discussed in Chapter 15, T may be able to defer recognition of part or all of the $2,000 gain from the sale of the personal use portion of the residence under § 1034. The $7,000 gain from the business portion is recognized.

Example 43. Assume the same facts as in the previous example except that the fair market value on the date of conversion is $30,000 and the sales proceeds are $16,000. T has a $12,000 realized loss from the sale of the personal use portion of the residence and a $3,250 realized loss from the sale of the rental portion. These losses are computed as follows:

	Personal Use	Rental
Original basis for loss—fair market value on date of conversion (Fair market value is less than the adjusted basis)		$ 15,000
Depreciation—five years	None	3,750
Adjusted basis—date of sale	$ 20,000	$ 11,250
Amount realized	8,000	8,000
Realized loss	$ 12,000	$ 3,250

The $12,000 loss from the sale of the personal use portion of the residence is not recognized. The $3,250 loss from the business portion is recognized.

Example 44. Assume the same facts as in Example 43 except that the sales proceeds are $38,000.

	Personal Use	Rental
Original basis for loss—fair market value on date of conversion (Fair market value is less than the adjusted basis)		$ 15,000
Gain basis—adjusted basis on date of conversion	$ 20,000	$ 20,000
Depreciation—five years	None	3,750
Adjusted basis—date of sale	$ 20,000	$ 16,250
Amount realized	19,000	19,000
Realized loss	$ 1,000	
Realized gain		$ 2,750

The loss of $1,000 from the sale of the personal use portion is not recognized. The gain of $2,750 associated with the business portion is recognized. Note that in calculating the depreciation deductions associated with the rental property, the loss basis of $15,000 is used rather than the gain basis of $20,000.

ADDITIONAL COMPLEXITIES IN DETERMINING REALIZED GAIN OR LOSS

Amount Realized. The calculation of the amount realized may appear to be one of the least complex areas associated with property transactions. However, because of the numerous positive and negative adjustments that may be required in calculating this amount, the calculation can be complex and confusing. In addition, the determination of the fair market value of the items received by the taxpayer can be a difficult task. The following example provides insight into various items that can have an impact on the amount realized.

Example 45. T sells an office building and the associated land on October 1, 19X3. Under the terms of the sales contract, T is to receive $600,000 in cash. The purchaser is to assume T's mortage of $300,000 on the property. To enable the purchaser to obtain adequate financing to pay the $600,000, T is to pay the points charged by the lender of $15,000. The broker's commission on the sale is $45,000. The purchaser agrees to pay the property taxes for the entire year (i. e., $12,000). The amount realized by T is calculated as follows:

Selling price:		
Cash	$ 600,000	
Mortgage assumed by purchaser	300,000	
Seller's property taxes paid by		
purchaser ($12,000 × 9/12)	9,000	$ 909,000
Less:		
Broker's commission	$ 45,000	
Points paid by seller	15,000	60,000
Amount realized		$ 849,000

Adjusted Basis. Three types of items tend to complicate the determination of adjusted basis. First, the applicable tax provisions for calculating the adjusted basis are dependent on how the property was acquired (e. g., purchase, taxable exchange, nontaxable exchange, gift, inheritance). Second, if the asset is subject to depreciation, cost recovery, or amortization, adjustments must be made to the basis during the time period the asset is held by the taxpayer. Upon disposition of the asset, the taxpayer's records associated with both of these items may be deficient (e. g., donee does not know the amount of the donor's basis or the amount of gift tax paid by the donor, or taxpayer does not know how much depreciation he or she has deducted). Third, the same type of problem encountered in calculating the amount realized associated with various positive and negative adjustments is also encountered in calculating the adjusted basis.

Example 46. P purchased a personal residence in 19X1. The purchase price and the related closing costs were as follows:

Purchase price	$ 125,000
Recording costs	140
Title fees and title insurance	815
Survey costs	115
Attorney's fees	750
Appraisal fee	60

Other relevant tax information associated with the house during the time it was owned by P is as follows:

—Constructed a swimming pool for medical reasons. The cost was $10,000, of which $3,000 was deducted as a medical expense.

—Added a solar heating system. The cost was $15,000, of which $4,000 was deducted as a residential energy credit (i. e., a renewable energy source expenditure).

—Deducted home office expenses of $18,000. Of this amount, $8,000 was for depreciation.

—None of the closing costs were deducted as moving expenses.

The adjusted basis for the house is calculated as follows:

Purchase price	$ 125,000
Recording costs	140
Title fees and title insurance	815
Survey costs	115
Attorney's fees	750
Appraisal fee	60
Swimming pool ($10,000 − $3,000)	7,000
Solar heating system ($15,000 − $4,000)	11,000
	$ 144,880
Less: Depreciation deducted on home office	8,000
Adjusted basis	$ 136,880

SUMMARY OF BASIS ADJUSTMENTS

Some of the more common items that either increase or decrease the basis of an asset appear in Figure II.

Figure II

ADJUSTMENTS TO BASIS

Item	Effect	Refer to Chapter	Explanation
Amortization of bond discount	Increase	16	Amortization is mandatory for certain taxable bonds and elective for tax-exempt bonds.
Amortization of bond premium	Decrease	14	Amortization is mandatory for tax-exempt bonds and elective for taxable bonds.
Amortization of covenant not to compete	Decrease		Covenant must be for a definite and limited time period.
Amortization of intangibles	Decrease	9	Not all intangibles can be amortized (e. g., goodwill).
Assessment for local benefits	Increase	11	To the extent not deductible as taxes (e. g., assessment for streets and sidewalks that increase the value of the property versus one for maintenance or repair or for meeting interest charges).
Bad debts	Decrease	8	Timing of the deduction is dependent on whether the taxpayer uses the specific charge-off or the reserve method.
Capital additions	Increase	14	Certain items, at the taxpayer's election, can be capitalized or deducted (e. g., selected indirect moving expenses and medical expenses).

Figure II *(continued)*

Casualty	Decrease	8	For a casualty loss, the amount of the adjustment is the summation of the deductible loss and the insurance proceeds received. For a casualty gain, the amount of the adjustment is the insurance proceeds received reduced by the recognized gain.
Cost recovery	Decrease	9	§ 168 is applicable to tangible assets placed in service after 1980 whose useful life is expressed in terms of years.
Condemnation	Decrease	15	See casualty explanation.
Depletion	Decrease	9	Use the greater of cost or percentage depletion. Percentage depletion can still be deducted when the basis is zero.
Depreciation	Decrease	9	§ 167 is applicable to tangible assets placed in service before 1981 and to tangible assets not depreciated in terms of years.
Easement	Decrease		If no use of the land is retained by the taxpayer, all of the basis is allocable to the easement transaction. However, if only part of the land is affected by the easement, only part of the basis is allocable to the easement transaction.
Improvements by lessee to lessor's property	Increase	6	Adjustment occurs only if the lessor is required to include the fair market value of the improvements in gross income under § 109.
Imputed interest	Decrease	18	Amount deducted is not part of the cost of the asset.
Inventory: lower of cost or market	Decrease	18	Not available if the LIFO method is used.
Investment tax credit	Decrease	13	Amount is 50% of the investment tax credit. If the election to reduce the investment tax credit is made, no adjustment is required.
Investment tax credit recapture	Increase	13	Amount is 50% of the investment tax credit recaptured. If the election to reduce the investment tax credit was made, no adjustment is required.
Limited expensing under § 179	Decrease	9	Occurs only if the taxpayer elects § 179 treatment.

Medical: capital expenditure permitted as a medical expense	Decrease	11	Adjustment is the amount of the deduction (i. e., the effect on basis is to increase it by the amount of the capital expenditure net of the deduction).
Moving: capital expenditure permitted as a moving expense	Decrease	10	Adjustment is for the amount the taxpayer elects to deduct as an indirect moving expense (i. e., the effect on basis is to increase it by the amount of the capital expenditure net of the deduction).
Real estate taxes: apportionment between the buyer and seller	Increase or Decrease	11	To the extent the buyer pays the seller's pro rata share, the buyer's basis is increased. To the extent the seller pays the buyer's pro rata share, the buyer's basis is decreased.
Rebate from manufacturer	Decrease		Since the rebate is treated as an adjustment to the purchase price, it is not included in the buyer's gross income.
Residential energy credits	Decrease	13	While the credits are available for both an owner's residence and a lessee's residence, the basis adjustment is applicable only for an owner.
Stock dividend	Decrease	6	Adjustment occurs only if the stock dividend is nontaxable.
Stock rights	Decrease	14	Adjustment occurs only for non-taxable stock rights and only if either the fair market value of the rights is at least 15% of the fair market value of the stock or (if less than 15%) the taxpayer elects to allocate the basis between the stock and the rights.
Theft	Decrease	8	See casualty explanation.

In discussing the topic of basis, a number of specific techniques for determining basis have been presented. While the various techniques are responsive to and mandated by transactions occurring in the marketplace, they do possess enough common characteristics to be categorized as follows:

—The basis of the asset may be determined by reference to its cost.

—The basis of the asset may be determined by reference to the basis of another asset.

—The basis of the asset may be determined by reference to its fair market value.

—The basis of the asset may be determined by reference to the basis of the asset to another taxpayer.

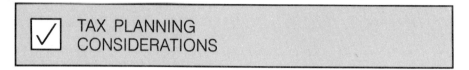

☑ TAX PLANNING
CONSIDERATIONS

COST IDENTIFICATION AND DOCUMENTATION CONSIDERATIONS

It is important for taxpayers to identify the cost of properties and securities for future documentation of a sale or other disposition. If multiple assets are acquired in a single transaction, the purchase agreement should specify the separate values of individual assets. If separate values are not provided in the purchase agreement, the taxpayer should obtain appraisals of the properties to establish their value.

The allocation of the contract price for multiple assets acquired in a single transaction is needed for several reasons. First, some of the assets may be depreciable while others are not. From the different viewpoints of the buyer and the seller, this may produce a tax conflict that will need to be resolved; that is, the seller will prefer a high allocation for nondepreciable assets, whereas the purchaser will prefer a high allocation for depreciable assets (see Chapters 16 and 17). Second, the seller will need to know the amount realized on the sale of the capital assets and the ordinary income assets to classify the recognized gains and losses as capital or ordinary, for example, the sale of goodwill versus a covenant not to compete (see Chapters 16 and 17). Third, the buyer will need the adjusted basis of each asset to calculate the realized gain or loss on the sale or other disposition of a specific asset.

SELECTION OF PROPERTY FOR MAKING GIFTS

A donor can achieve several tax advantages by making gifts of appreciated property. Income tax on the unrealized gain which would have occurred had the donor sold the property is avoided by the donor. A portion of this amount may be permanently avoided as the result of the donee's adjusted basis being increased by a part of the gift tax paid by the donor. Even absent this increase in basis, the income tax liability on the sale of the property by the donee can be less than the income tax liability that would have resulted from the donor's sale of the property. Such reduced income tax liability will occur if the donee is in a lower tax bracket than that of the donor. In addition, any subsequent appreciation during the time it is held by the lower tax bracket donee will result in a tax savings on the sale or other disposition of the property. Such gifts of appreciated property can be an effective tool in family tax planning.

Taxpayers should generally not make gifts of depreciated property (i. e., property that would be sold at a loss), because the donor does not receive an income tax deduction for the unrealized loss element. In addition, the donee will not receive benefit from this unrealized loss upon the subsequent sale of the property because of the loss basis rule (i. e., the donee's basis is the lower of donor's basis or fair market value at the date of the gift). If the donor anticipates that the donee will sell the property upon receiving it, the donor should sell the property and take the loss deduction, assuming the loss is deductible. The donor can then give the proceeds from the sale to the donee.

Two exceptions to the planning rule that the donor should not make gifts of depreciated property deserve mentioning. The first exception occurs when the property is an asset that the donee is not expected to sell (e. g., family farm, family corporation stock). The second exception applies when there is an expectation that the property will appreciate during the time it is held by the donee so that the donee will sell the property at a realized gain (i. e., the selling price will be greater than the donor's adjusted basis).

SELECTION OF PROPERTY FOR MAKING BEQUESTS

A decedent's will should generally make bequests of appreciated property, because income tax is avoided by the decedent and the inheritor of the property on the unrealized gain (since the recipient takes fair market value as his or her basis).

In a community property state, both the decedent's and the survivor's basis in community property is fair market value on the date of the decedent's death. Therefore, income tax is avoided on the unrealized gain attributable to both the decedent's and survivor's share of the community property.

> **Example 47.** H and W reside in a community property state. On the date of H's death, H and W own land held for investment purposes as community property. The land has an adjusted basis of $100,000 and a fair market value of $600,000. If they had sold the property prior to H's death, the recognized gain would have been $500,000. If W inherits H's share of the property and sells the property for $700,000, the recognized gain will be $100,000, only the appreciation since H's death.

Taxpayers generally should not make bequests of depreciated property (i. e., property which could be sold at a loss), because the decedent does not receive an income tax deduction for the unrealized loss element. In addition, the inheritor will not receive benefit from this unrealized loss upon the subsequent sale of the property.

Example 48. On the date of her death, W owned land held for investment purposes with an adjusted basis of $600,000 and a fair market value of $100,000. If W had sold the property prior to her death, the recognized loss would have been $500,000. If H inherits the property and sells it for $50,000, the recognized loss will be $50,000, only the decline in value since W's death. In addition, regardless of the period of time the property is held by H, the holding period is long-term.

From an income tax perspective, it is preferable to transfer appreciated property as a bequest rather than as a gift.[75] This results from the step-up in basis for inherited property, whereas for property received by gift, the donee has a carryover basis.

Example 49. W owns property with an adjusted basis of $40,000 and a fair market value of $100,000. If W sells the property, W will have a recognized gain of $60,000. If W makes a gift of the property to C and C sells the property for $100,000, C will have a recognized gain of $60,000 (because C has a carryover basis of $40,000). Thus, in deciding whether W should sell the property and make a gift of the net proceeds (i. e., reduced by the income tax on the sale) to C or whether W should make a gift of the property to C followed by C's sale of the property, the critical factor is the effective income tax rate of W versus that of C. If W makes a bequest of the property to C, neither W nor C will pay any income tax on the $60,000 of unrealized gain, since the transfer is not a taxable event to either W or C for income tax purposes, and C's basis will be $100,000.

DISALLOWED LOSSES

Section 267 Disallowed Losses. Taxpayers should be aware of the desirability of avoiding transactions that activate the loss disallowance provisions for related parties. This is so, even in light of the provision that permits the related-party buyer to offset his or her realized gain by the related-party seller's disallowed loss. Even with this offset, several inequities exist. First, the tax benefit associated with the disallowed loss ultimately is realized by the wrong party (i. e., the related-party buyer rather than the related-party seller). Second, the tax benefit to the related-party buyer associated with the offset does not occur until he or she disposes of the property. Therefore, the longer the time period between the purchase and disposition of the property by the related-party buyer, the less will be the economic benefit. Third, if during the time period the related-party buyer holds the property it does not appreciate to at least the adjusted basis of the

---

75. Consideration must also be given to the estate tax consequences of the bequest versus the gift tax consequences of the gift.

property to the related-party seller, part of all of the disallowed loss will be permanently lost. Fourth, since the right of offset is available only to the original transferee (i. e., the related-party buyer), all of the disallowed loss will be permanently lost if the original transferee subsequently transfers the property by gift or bequest.

Example 50. T sells property with an adjusted basis of $35,000 to B, his brother, for $25,000, the fair market value of the property. The $10,000 realized loss to T is disallowed by § 267. If B subsequently sells the property to an unrelated party for $37,000, B will have a recognized gain of $2,000 (i. e., realized gain of $12,000 reduced by disallowed loss of $10,000). Therefore, from the perspective of the family unit, the original $10,000 realized loss ultimately is recognized. However, if B sells the property instead for $29,000, he will have a recognized gain of $0 (i. e., realized gain of $4,000 reduced by disallowed loss of $4,000 necessary to offset the realized gain). From the perspective of the family unit, $6,000 of the realized loss of $10,000 is permanently wasted (i. e., $10,000 realized loss minus $4,000 offset permitted).

Example 51. T sells property with an adjusted basis of $35,000 to B, his brother, for $25,000, the fair market value of the property. The $10,000 realized loss to T is disallowed by § 267. During the time that B holds the property, the fair market value increases to $35,000. B is going to make a gift of $35,000 to S, his son. Assume no gift tax will be paid on the gift. If B makes a gift of the property to S, the disallowed loss offset is lost. If S then sells the property for $35,000, his recognized gain will be $10,000 (i. e., $35,000 − $25,000 adjusted basis). If B instead sells the property in the marketplace for $35,000, his recognized gain will be $0 ($35,000 − $25,000 adjusted basis − $10,000 disallowed loss). Therefore, the second option produces superior income tax consequences for the related parties when compared with the first option. Thus, the availability of the disallowed loss offset is a relevant factor in selecting the method of disposition if the property in the hands of the related-party buyer (i. e., B) has appreciated above his adjusted basis (i. e., cost).

Example 52. Assume the same facts as in Example 51 except that during the time that B holds the property, the fair market value declines to $23,000 and the amount of the gift B is going to make to S is $23,000. If B makes a gift of the property to S, the disallowed loss offset is lost. If S then sells the property for an amount greater than $25,000, he will have a recognized gain. Conversely, if S sells the property for an amount less than $23,000, he will have a recognized loss. If B instead sells the property in the marketplace for $23,000, his recognized loss is $2,000 (i. e., $23,000 − $25,000 adjusted basis) and the disallowed loss offset is lost. Therefore, while the second option does produce a potential income tax benefit to the related parties when compared with the first option (i. e., B's basis for loss is $25,000 whereas S's basis for loss is $23,000), the disallowed loss offset is forfeited under both options. Thus, the availability of the disallowed loss offset is not a relevant factor in selecting the method of disposition if the property in the hands of the related-party buyer (i. e., B) has not appreciated above his adjusted basis (i. e., cost).

Example 53. T sells property with an adjusted basis of $35,000 to B, his brother, for $25,000, the fair market value of the property. The $10,000 realized loss to T is disallowed by § 267. S, who is B's son, receives the property by bequest. The bequest results in the disallowed loss offset's being lost (i. e., the right of offset does not pass from B to S). Whether this is of any significance depends on the fair market value of the property for estate tax purposes (i. e., primary valuation amount or alternate valuation amount). If such amount is at least $35,000, the loss of the offset will not produce adverse income tax consequences to the family unit. If such amount is greater than $25,000 but less than $35,000, part of the offset effectively is wasted. If such amount is $25,000 or less, all of the offset effectively is wasted.

All of the disallowed loss will be permanently lost if adequate communication does not occur between the related parties. Only the related-party seller is aware of his adjusted basis for the property and the related amount of his disallowed loss. Therefore, he needs to inform the related-party buyer of the amount of the disallowed loss offset available to the buyer.

Wash Sales. If the wash sale loss disallowance provisions are applicable, the taxpayer must be careful to make the proper positive basis adjustment to the substantially identical property. Otherwise, the effect of the loss disallowance will be permanent rather than temporary.

Example 54. L sells 50 shares of stock at a realized loss of $12,000. The realized loss is disallowed because L purchases substantially identical property within 30 days. The cost of the replacement stock is $50,000. The adjusted basis of the stock is $62,000 ($50,000 + $12,000 disallowed loss).

The wash sale provisions can be avoided even if the security is replaced within the statutory time period with a similar rather than a substantially identical security (e. g., a sale of Bethlehem Steel common stock and a purchase of U.S. Steel common stock would not be treated as a wash sale). Such a procedure can enable the taxpayer to use an unrealized capital loss to offset a recognized short-term capital gain. The taxpayer can sell the security before the end of the taxable year, offset the recognized capital loss against the short-term capital gain, and invest the sales proceeds in a similar security.

Because the wash sale provisions do not apply to gains, it may be desirable to engage in a wash sale before the end of the taxable year. This recognized capital gain may be used to offset capital losses or capital loss carryovers from prior years.

PROBLEM MATERIALS

Questions for Class Discussion

1. Upon the sale or other disposition of property, what three questions should be considered for income tax purposes?

2. When will a property transaction result in a realized gain? A realized loss?

3. What is included in the amount realized from a sale or other disposition of property?

4. What is the definition of fair market value?

5. If the buyer of property assumes the seller's mortgage, why is the amount of the mortgage included in the amount realized by the seller? What effect does the mortgage assumption have on the seller's (a) adjusted basis for the mortgaged property and (b) realized gain or loss?

6. Explain the relationship between the recovery of capital doctrine and (a) realized gain or loss and (b) recognized gain or loss.

7. Explain the relationship of depreciation (or the cost recovery allowance under ERTA) to adjusted basis and implementation of the recovery of capital doctrine.

8. B owns a machine that he uses in his trade or business. He sells the machine on the last day of his taxable year. If the machine was placed in service before 1981 (i. e., subject to § 167 depreciation), what effect does the depreciation in the year of sale have on the adjusted basis of the machine? If the machine was placed in service after 1980 (i. e., subject to § 168 ACRS), what effect does cost recovery in the year of sale have on the adjusted basis of the machine? What would the results be if the asset were a building rather than a machine?

9. A taxpayer who acquires a taxable bond at a discount is required to amortize the discount, whereas a taxpayer who acquires a tax-exempt bond at a discount may elect to amortize the discount. What effect does the amortization have on the adjusted basis for the bonds? Why is the amortization for the taxable bond mandatory whereas that for the tax-exempt bond is elective?

10. Why is the amortization of bond premiums considered a capital recovery?

11. Define recognized gain and recognized loss.

12. Why is it necessary to calculate both the amount of the realized gain or loss and the recognized gain or loss?

13. Why are gains from the sale or exchange of personal use assets recognized when such losses are never recognized?

14. Why is the recovery of capital doctrine generally not applicable for personal use property? Under what circumstances is it applicable to personal use property?

15. When, as a general rule, does a taxpayer recover more than cost? Less than cost? Give some examples.

16. How is the basis of the property determined in a bargain purchase, and why is this method used?

17. Outline the general rules for determining the adjusted basis of stock which is sold if the owner holds more than one lot of the stock.

18. How is cost allocated for lump-sum purchases?

19. Discuss the differences in tax treatment when stock rights are allocated a cost basis and when stock rights have no cost basis. When does each of the above situations occur?

20. Why must gifts of property be given a basis to the donee?

21. What is the basis for gifts prior to 1921?

22. Under what circumstances is it possible to recognize no gain or loss on the sale of an asset which was previously received as a gift?

23. How do gift taxes paid by the donor affect the income tax rules for gift property?

24. The gain basis for gift property is a carryover basis (i. e., determined by the donor's basis). If the donee pays the gift tax, what effect does this have on his or her basis for the property?

25. Outline the rules concerning depreciation (or cost recovery allowance) and holding period for gift property. Why are these rules important?

26. Discuss the differences in tax treatment between property sold prior to death and property which is inherited. Why is this important?

27. R makes a gift of an appreciated building to E. E dies three months later, and R inherits the building from E. During the period that E held the building, he deducted depreciation and made a capital expenditure. What effect might these items have on R's basis for the inherited building?

28. Immediately prior to his death in 1984, H sells securities (adjusted basis of $100,000) for their fair market value of $20,000. The sale was not to a related party. The securities were community property, and H is survived by his wife, W.

   (a) Did H act wisely? Why or why not?

   (b) Suppose the figures are reversed (i. e., sale for $100,000 of property with an adjusted basis of $20,000). Would the sale be wise? Why or why not?

29. At the time of T's death, the value of his gross estate, much of which is comprised of marketable securities, was $700,000. Six months later, the fair market value had increased to $740,000.

   (a) Why might the executor of T's estate elect to use the alternate valuation date for estate tax purposes?

   (b) Suppose part of T's gross estate includes his share of community property. What effect, if any, would the election of the alternate valuation date have on his surviving spouse's share of the community property?

30. What are related-party transactions and why are they important?

31. When is it possible to offset an unrecognized loss against a realized gain? Are there any exceptions? Explain.

32. What is a wash sale? Why isn't a realized loss recognized on a wash sale? How is the recovery of capital doctrine maintained?

33. What is the basis for property which is converted from personal use to business or income-producing use when there is a loss? When there is a gain? Why is there a difference? How does conversion affect depreciation and why?

34. For both property received by gift and property converted from personal use to business or income-producing use, it may be necessary to calculate the basis under two different formulas. Discuss the similarities and differences as they relate to the basis for gain, loss, and depreciation.

Problems

35. A sold her home for $350,000 in 19X3. She had purchased it in 19X0 for $90,000. During the period of ownership, A had:

    —Deducted $57,500 office-in-home expenses ($17,500 depreciation). Refer to Chapter 10.

    —Deducted a casualty loss to residential trees due to a hurricane. The total loss was $12,000 (after the $100 floor and the 10% of adjusted gross income floor) and A's insurance company reimbursed her for $7,500. Refer to Chapter 8.

    —Claimed maximum allowable credit for energy conservation capital expenditures totaling $2,500. Refer to Chapter 13.

    —Paid street paving assessment of $5,000 and added sidewalks for $7,000.

    —Installed an elevator for medical reasons. The total cost was $20,000, and she deducted $6,500 as medical expense. Refer to Chapter 11.

    —Paid legal expenses in connection with the move to the home in 19X0 of $3,000. A deducted these expenses as moving expenses. Refer to Chapter 10.

    —Received $2,500 from a utility company for an easement to install underground utility lines across the property.

    How much is the realized gain?

36. T owns a personal use automobile that has an adjusted basis of $8,000. The fair market value of the automobile is $4,500.

    (a) Calculate the realized and recognized loss if T sells the automobile for $4,500.

    (b) Calculate the realized and recognized loss if T exchanges the automobile for another automobile worth $4,500.

    (c) Calculate the realized and recognized loss if the automobile is stolen and T receives insurance proceeds of $4,500.

37. R bought a rental house at the beginning of 19X2 for $80,000, of which $10,000 is allocated to the land and $70,000 to the building. Early in 19X4, he had a tennis court built in the backyard at a cost of $5,000. Depreciation

is $2,000 a year on the house and $200 a year on the court. At the beginning of 19X7, R sells the house and tennis court for $125,000 cash.

(a) What is his realized gain (loss)?

(b) If an original mortgage of $20,000 is still outstanding and the buyer assumes the mortgage in addition to the cash payment, what is the realized gain (loss)?

(c) If the buyer takes the property subject to the mortgage, what is R's realized gain (loss)?

38. D's residence, with a basis of $80,000 and a fair market value of $100,000, is damaged by fire. After the fire, the fair market value is $45,000. D receives insurance proceeds of $55,000. His adjusted gross income is $40,000.

(a) What effect does the casualty have on the adjusted basis?

(b) What effect does the casualty have on the adjusted basis if the residence is uninsured?

39. C owns all the stock of a corporation. The earnings and profits of the corporation are $25,000. C's adjusted basis for his stock is $40,000. He receives a cash distribution of $50,000 from the corporation.

(a) What effect does the distribution have on the adjusted basis of C's stock?

(b) What effect would the distribution have on the adjusted basis of C's stock if the earnings and profits of the corporation were $80,000?

40. B paid $270,000 for bonds with a face value of $250,000 at the beginning of 19X2. The bonds mature in 10 years and pay 9% interest per year.

(a) If B sells the bonds for $255,000 at the beginning of 19X6, does she have a realized gain (loss)? How much?

(b) If she trades them at the beginning of 19X8 for stock worth $262,500, does she have a realized gain (loss)? If so, how much?

41. Which of the following would definitely result in a recognized gain (loss)?

(a) K sells his lakeside cabin, which has an adjusted basis of $10,000, for $15,000.

(b) A sells his personal residence, which has an adjusted basis of $15,000, for $10,000.

(c) C's personal residence is on the site of a proposed airport and is condemned by the city. He receives $55,000 for the house, which has an adjusted basis of $65,000.

(d) B sells his personal residence, which has an adjusted basis of $80,000, for $90,000.

42. A machine was purchased January 1, 19X2, at a cost of $50,000. The useful life of the asset is five years with no salvage value. Depreciation was deducted and allowed for 19X2 through 19X6 as follows:

19X2	$ 10,000
19X3	–0–
19X4	10,000
19X5	–0–
19X6	10,000

What is the adjusted basis of the asset as of December 31, 19X6?

43. T buys a watch from his employer for $2,500. The fair market value of the watch is $6,000. Assuming that the excess amount of $3,500 represents compensation for services rendered:

   (a) What is T's basis in the watch?

   (b) Why?

44. R makes the following purchases and sales of stock:

Transaction	Date	No. of Shares	Company	Price per Share
Purchase	1-1-X3	300	MDG	$ 75
Purchase	6-1-X3	150	RU	300
Purchase	11-1-X3	60	MDG	60
Sale	12-3-X3	180	MDG	60
Purchase	3-1-X4	120	RU	375
Sale	8-1-X4	90	RU	330
Sale	1-1-X5	150	MDG	90
Sale	2-1-X5	75	RU	420

   Assuming that R is unable to identify the particular lots which are sold with the original purchase, what is the realized gain (loss) on each type of stock as of:

   (a) 7-1-X3

   (b) 12-31-X3

   (c) 12-31-X4

   (d) 7-1-X5

45. During the year F received the following dividends on her stock portfolio:

   (a) Five shares of common stock in U Company on 10 shares of common stock she already owns. F paid $30 a share for the original 10 shares.

   (b) Twenty shares of preferred stock in X Company on 200 shares of common stock for which F paid $10,000. The fair market value of the preferred stock on the date of distribution was $40, and the fair market value of the common stock was $60.

   What is the basis per share for each of the common shares and the preferred shares?

46. K receives nontaxable stock rights with a fair market value of $1,800. The fair market value of the stock on which the rights were received is $12,000. The cost of the stock was $11,000. What is the basis of the rights for purposes of exercise or sale?

47. T received various gifts over the years. He has decided to dispose of the following assets that he received as gifts:

   (a) In 1923, he received land worth $20,000. The donor's adjusted basis was $24,000. He sells the land for $15,000 in 1984.

   (b) In 1935, he received stock in G Company. The donor's adjusted basis was $1,000. The fair market value on the date of the gift was $2,000. T sells the stock for $2,500 in 1984.

(c) In 1920, he received a Rolls Royce worth $22,000. The donor's adjusted basis for the auto was $16,000. He sells the auto for $35,000 in 1984.

(d) In 1951, he received land worth $12,000. The donor's adjusted basis was $9,000. He sells the land for $4,000 in 1984.

What is the realized gain (loss) from each of the above transactions? Assume in each of the gift transactions that no gift tax was paid.

48. A received a car from Z as a gift in 19X0. Z paid $7,000 for the car. She had used it for business purposes and had deducted $2,000 for depreciation up to the time she gave the car to A. The fair market value of the car is $3,500.

(a) Assuming A uses the car for business purposes, what is his basis for depreciation?

(b) If the estimated useful life is two years (from the date of the gift), what is his depreciation deduction for each year? Use the straight-line method.

(c) If he sells the car for $800 one year after receiving it, what is his gain (loss)?

(d) If he sells the car for $4,000 one year after receiving it, what is his gain (loss)?

49. L receives a gift of income-producing property which has an adjusted basis of $20,000 on the date of the gift. The fair market value of the property on the date of the gift is $18,000. Gift tax amounting to $400 was paid by the donor. L later sells the property for $19,000. Determine L's recognized gain or loss.

50. R receives a gift of property (after 1976) which has a fair market value of $100,000 on the date of gift. The donor's adjusted basis for the property was $40,000. Assume the donor paid gift tax of $16,000 on the gift. What is R's basis for gain or loss and for depreciation?

51. U is going to make a gift to N, his daughter. U is undecided as to whether he should give N $10,000 in cash or give her stock worth $10,000. The adjusted basis of the stock is $13,000. U anticipates that N will sell the stock.

(a) Should U make a gift of the stock or should he sell the stock and give the cash proceeds to N?

(b) If the fair market value of the stock is $15,000, what factors are relevant to U's decision as to whether he should make a gift of the stock or sell the stock and give the cash proceeds to N?

(c) Assume the stock is family corporation stock and that N is not expected to sell it. The fair market value is $10,000. What are the tax consequences to U if he gives N $10,000 in cash and then sells the stock to N for $10,000.

52. D bought a hotel for $720,000 on January 1, 19X0. In January 19X2, she died and left the hotel to E. D had deducted $42,000 depreciation on the hotel prior to her death. The fair market value in January 19X2 was $780,000.

(a) What is the basis of the property to E?

(b) If the land is worth $240,000, what is E's basis for depreciation?

53. R owns three pieces of land in west Texas. Parcel A has an adjusted basis of $75,000; Parcel B, $125,000; Parcel C, $175,000. R sells Parcel A to his father-in-law for $50,000. He sells Parcel B to his partner for $120,000, and Parcel C is sold to his mother for $150,000.

    (a) What is the recognized gain (loss) from the sale of each of the parcels of land?

    (b) If R's father-in-law sells his land for $90,000, what is his recognized gain (loss)?

    (c) If R's partner sells his land for $130,000, what is his recognized gain (loss)?

    (d) If R's mother sells her land for $165,000, what is her recognized gain (loss)?

54. H sells to his wife, W, two city lots for $35,000 with an adjusted basis for determining loss to him of $42,000.

    (a) Is the loss allowable as a deduction to H?

    (b) If W sells the city lots for $39,000, what is her realized gain or loss? Her recognized gain or loss?

55. M owns land with an adjusted basis of $30,000. M sells the land to her sister Q for its fair market value of $26,000. Q makes a gift of the land to her nephew N. Q pays gift tax of $1,000. At the date of the gift, the fair market value of the land is $29,000.

    (a) What is the realized and recognized gain or loss to N if he sells the land for $36,000?

    (b) What is the realized and recognized gain or loss to N if he sells the land for $23,000?

    (c) How would the results in (a) and (b) differ if N had inherited the property from Q?

56. On September 15, 19X3, S decides to revise his stock holdings.

Date	Company	No. of Shares	Transaction	Price	Cost
9-10-X3	PAN AM	100	Buy	$25/Share	
9-15-X3	KODAK	120	Sell	20/Share	$25/Share
9-15-X3	FORD	70	Sell	25/Share	20/Share
9-15-X3	IBM	95	Sell	5/Share	10/Share
9-15-X3	XEROX	220	Sell	8/Share	5/Share
9-15-X3	PAN AM	100	Sell	20/Share	30/Share
10- 4-X3	FORD	100	Buy	20/Share	
10- 8-X3	ABC	120	Buy	7/Share	
10-25-X3	KODAK	95	Buy	30/Share	
10-14-X3	AMERICAN	50	Buy	4/Share	

    (a) What is the recognized gain (loss) for each of the stocks sold on September 15?

    (b) Explain why the gain (loss) is or is not recognized on each sale.

57. W purchased 50 shares of A Corporation common stock for $2,500 on May 12, 19X4. On August 12, 19X4, W purchased 25 additional shares for

$1,375; on August 27, 19X4, W purchased 10 additional shares for $500. On September 3, 19X4, he sold the 50 shares purchased on May 12, 19X4, for $2,000.

(a) What is W's realized gain or loss on September 3, 19X4?

(b) What is his recognized gain or loss?

(c) What is the basis of W's remaining shares after the sale on September 3?

58. J purchases two wheat futures contracts, one to buy and one to sell, for $5,000 each in August of 1984. In November 1984, J liquidates the position, showing a loss of $1,000. At the same time, the offsetting position is showing a gain of $950.

(a) What is J's recognized loss?

(b) Would liquidating the offsetting position in November 1984 affect the recognized loss?

59. A retires from a public accounting firm to enter private practice. He bought a home five years earlier for $40,000 and, upon beginning his business, converts one-fourth of his home into an office. The fair market value of the home on the date of conversion (January 1, 19X8, which was prior to 1981) was $75,000; the adjusted basis was $56,000 (ignore land). A lives and works in the home for five years (after converting it to business use) and sells it at the end of the fifth year. The home had an estimated useful life of 20 years (from the date of conversion) with no salvage value anticipated. A used straight-line depreciation.

(a) How much gain (loss) is recognized if A sells the property for $44,000?

(b) If he sells the property for $70,000?

60. Residential property is purchased by D in 19X0 as a personal residence. The residential property was acquired at a cost of $75,000, of which $45,000 is allocable to the building. D uses the property as his personal residence until January 1, 19X6 (which was prior to 1981), at which time its fair market value is $66,000, of which $36,000 is allocable to the building. D rents the property from January 1, 19X6, until January 1, 19X9, at which time it is sold for $48,000. On January 1, 19X6, the building has an estimated useful life of 20 years. Depreciation is computed on the straight-line method. Disregard salvage value.

(a) What is D's realized gain or loss from the sale?

(b) What is D's recognized gain or loss?

Cumulative Problems

61. G, age 28, is single and has no dependents. Her salary in 1984 was $25,000. She incurred unreimbursed expenses of $800 for travel and $500 for entertainment in connection with her job as an assistant personnel director. In addition, she had the following items of possible tax consequence in 1984.

(a) Itemized deductions (not including any potential deductions mentioned previously) $ 4,800

(b) Proceeds from the sale of land inherited from her father on June 15, 1984 (fair market value on June 15 was $35,000, while the father's adjusted basis was $15,000) 38,000

(c) Proceeds from the sale of 50 shares of X Corporation stock received as a gift from her father in 1976 when their fair market value was $6,000 (the father's adjusted basis in the stock was $5,500, and he paid gift tax of $800 on the transfer) 7,500

(d) Proceeds from the sale of her personal automobile, for which she had paid $4,500 in 1982 3,100

(e) Proceeds from sale of 10 shares of Y Corporation stock to her brother (she had paid $85 per share for the stocks in February 1984) 600

(f) Cost of exterior storm door for her house 65

(g) Dividends received from a domestic corporation 120

G's employer withheld Federal income tax of $4,580. Compute her net tax payable (or refund due) for 1984. (Use the 1983 Tax Table. The 1984 Tax Table was not available at the date of publication of this text.)

62. R, age 67, is married and files a joint return with his wife, W, age 65. R and W are both retired. In 1984, they received Social Security benefits of $2,400.

R, who retired on January 1, 1982, receives benefits from a qualified pension plan of $600 a month for life. His total contributions to the plan were $18,000. He treated all retirement benefits received in 1982 and 1983 as a tax-free return of his investment.

W, who retired on December 31, 1983, received benefits of $800 a month beginning on January 1, 1984. Her life expectancy was 18 years from the annuity starting date, and her investment in the qualified pension plan was $57,600.

On September 27, 1983, R and W received a 10% stock dividend on 50 shares of stock they owned. They had paid $11 a share for the stock in 1976. On December 15, 1984, they sold the five shares received as a stock dividend for $30 a share.

Shortly after her retirement, W sold the car she had used in commuting to and from work. She paid $5,000 for the car in 1981 and sold it for $2,000. R and W received a gift of 100 shares of stock from their son X, in 1976. X's basis in the stock was $30 a share, and its fair market value at the date of gift was $25 a share. No gift tax was paid. R and W sold the stock in October 1984 for $15 a share.

R and W paid estimated Federal income tax of $200 and had itemized deductions of $3,800.

Compute their net tax payable (or refund due) for 1984. (Use the 1983 Tax Table for this computation. The 1984 Tax Table was not available at the date of publication of this text.)

Research Problems

63. On January 1, 19X5, X, a major shareholder in H Corporation, purchased land from the company for $300,000. The fair market value of the land is

$1,200,000, and its adjusted basis in the hands of the corporation is $400,000.

(a) What are the possible tax consequences to X?

(b) What is the basis of the land to X?

(c) What is the tax consequence to H Corporation?

64. W is advised by his broker to sell some of his investments at a loss prior to year-end to offset $20,000 of short-term capital gain which was recognized earlier in the year. W has unrealized losses from the following securities:

—a municipal bond investment fund, seventeenth monthly series ($8,000)

—U. S. Steel common stock ($9,500)

Since W feels that both investments are desirable and wants to maintain an equivalent position in each, the following alternatives have been suggested:

(a) Sell the municipal bond fund investment and immediately acquire an equivalent amount of the eighteenth monthly series of a similar bond fund.

(b) Sell U. S. Steel and immediately acquire a call option to buy an equivalent number of shares.

Will either of these two proposals result in a wash sale under § 1091?

Partial list of research aids:

Rev.Rul. 58–210, 1958–1 C.B. 523.

Frank Stein, 36 TCM 992, T.C.Memo. 1977–241.

65. T owns real estate with an adjusted basis of $600,000 and a fair market value of $1,100,000. The amount of the nonrecourse mortgage on the property is $2,500,000. Because of substantial past and projected future losses associated with the real estate development (i. e., occupancy rate of only 37% after three years), T deeds the property to the creditor.

(a) What are the tax consequences to T?

(b) Assume the data are the same, except the fair market value of the property is $2,525,000. Therefore, T also receives $25,000 from the creditor when he deeds the property to the creditor. What are the tax consequences to T?

Partial list of research aids:

Rev.Rul. 76–111, 1976–1 C.B. 214.

Crane v. Comm., 47 USTC ¶ 9217, 35 AFTR 776, 67 S.Ct. 1047 (USSC, 1947).

Chapter 15

Property Transactions: Nontaxable Exchanges

In a nontaxable exchange, realized gains or losses are not recognized.[1] However, the nonrecognition is usually temporary; the recognition of gain or loss is merely postponed (i.e., deferred) until the property received in the nontaxable exchange is subsequently disposed of in a taxable transaction. This is accomplished by assigning a carryover basis to the replacement property.

> **Example 1.** T exchanges property with an adjusted basis of $10,000 and a fair market value of $12,000 for property with a fair market value of $12,000. The transaction qualifies for nontaxable exchange treatment. T has a realized gain of $2,000 ($12,000 − $10,000). His recognized gain is $0. His basis for the replacement property is a carryover basis of $10,000. Therefore, assuming the replacement property is nondepreciable, if T subsequently sells the replacement property for $12,000, his realized and recognized gain will be the $2,000 gain that was postponed (i. e., deferred) in the nontaxable transaction. If the replacement property is depreciable, the carryover basis of $10,000 is used in calculating depreciation.

The tax law recognizes that nontaxable exchanges result in a change in the form but not in the substance of the taxpayer's relative

---

1. Reg. § 1.61–6(b).

economic position. The replacement property received in the exchange is viewed as substantially a continuation of the old investment.[2] In other words, the taxpayer has merely replaced existing property with other property and is in substantially the same relative economic position after the transaction as before the transaction. Additional justification for nontaxable exchange treatment is that this type of transaction does not provide the taxpayer with the wherewithal to pay the tax on any realized gain.[3] It should be noted that the nonrecognition provisions do not apply to realized losses from the sale or exchange of personal use assets. Such losses are not recognized because they are personal in nature, not because of any nonrecognition provision.

In some nontaxable exchanges, only part of the property involved in the transaction will qualify for nonrecognition treatment. If the taxpayer receives cash or other nonqualifying property, part or all of the realized gain from the exchange is recognized. In these instances, gain is recognized because the taxpayer has changed or improved his or her relative economic position and has the wherewithal to pay income tax to the extent of cash or other property received.

The major types of transactions that receive nontaxable exchange treatment are as follows:

—Like-kind exchanges.

—Involuntary conversions.

—Sale of a residence.

—Exchange of stock for property by a corporation.

—Exchange of stock for stock of the same corporation by a shareholder.

—Certain reacquisitions of real property.

—Contribution of property by a partner to a partnership in exchange for a partnership interest.

—Contribution of property by a shareholder to a controlled corporation in exchange for stock.

With the exception of the last two types, which are covered in Chapter 20, each of these types of nontaxable exchanges is covered in this chapter.

It is important to distinguish between a nontaxable disposition, as the term is used in the statute, and a tax-free transaction. First, a direct exchange is not required in all circumstances (e. g., an involuntary conversion or a sale of a residence). Second, as previously mentioned, the term "nontaxable" refers to postponement of recognition via a carryover basis. In a tax-free transaction, the nonrecognition is

---

2. Reg. § 1.1002–1(c).
3. Refer to the discussion of the wherewithal to pay concept in Chapter 2.

permanent and the basis of any property acquired is not dependent on that of the property disposed of by the taxpayer (e. g., § 121 election by a taxpayer age 55 or over to exclude gain on sale of residence).

LIKE-KIND EXCHANGES

Section 1031 provides that "no gain or loss shall be recognized if property held for productive use in trade or business or for investment . . . is exchanged solely for property of a like-kind to be held either for productive use in trade or business or for investment."[4]

Like-kind exchanges include business for business, business for investment, investment for business, or investment for investment property. Property held for personal use, inventory, and securities do not qualify under the like-kind exchange provisions.

The nonrecognition provision for like-kind exchanges is mandatory rather than elective. That is, if the taxpayer wants to recognize a realized gain or loss, it is necessary for him or her to structure the transaction in a form so it does not satisfy the statutory requirements for a like-kind exchange.

LIKE-KIND PROPERTY

"The words 'like-kind' have reference to the nature or character of the property and not to its grade or quality. One kind or class of property may not . . . be exchanged for property of a different kind or class."[5]

While it is intended that the term "like-kind" be interpreted very broadly, there are two categories of exchanges that are not included in this broad definition. First, real estate can be exchanged only for other real estate and personalty can be exchanged only for other personalty. For example, the exchange of a machine (i. e., personalty) for an office building (i. e., realty) is not a like-kind exchange. Real estate includes principally rental buildings, office and store buildings, manufacturing plants, warehouses, and land. It is immaterial whether real estate is improved or unimproved. Thus, unimproved land can be exchanged for an apartment house. Personalty includes principally machines, equipment, trucks, automobiles, furniture, and fixtures. Second, livestock of different sexes does not qualify as like-kind property.[6]

Example 2. T made the following exchanges during the taxable year:

(a) Inventory for a machine used in business.

(b) Land held for investment for a building used in business.

---

4. § 1031(a) and Reg. § 1.1031(a) 1(a).
5. Reg. § 1.1031(a)–1(b).
6. § 1031(e).

(c) Stock held for investment for equipment used in business.

(d) A business truck for a business machine.

(e) An automobile used for personal transportation for a machine used in business.

(f) Livestock for livestock of a different sex.

Exchanges (b), investment real property for business real property, and (d), business personalty for business personalty, qualify under § 1031(a). Exchanges (a), inventory; (c), stock; (e), personal use automobile (which is not held for business or investment purposes); and (f), livestock of different sexes, do not qualify.

MUST BE AN EXCHANGE

The transaction must actually involve a direct exchange of property to qualify as a like-kind exchange. Thus, the sale of old property and the purchase of new property, even though like-kind, is generally not an exchange. However, if the two transactions are mutually dependent, the IRS may treat the two interdependent transactions as a like-kind exchange. For example, if the taxpayer sells an old business machine to a dealer and purchases a new one from the same dealer, a like-kind exchange could result.[7]

The taxpayer might want to avoid nontaxable exchange treatment. Recognition of gain gives the taxpayer a higher basis for depreciation (see Example 39). To the extent that such gains would, if recognized, receive favorable capital gain treatment, it may be preferable to avoid the nonrecognition provisions through an indirect exchange transaction (i. e., by the sale of property to one individual followed by a purchase of similar property from another individual). However, in many instances, it is not possible to recognize capital gain on the sale of depreciable property, since part or all of the gain is recaptured as ordinary income. If gain recognition is postponed, the recapture potential carries over to the new property received in the like-kind exchange.[8] The taxpayer also may want to avoid nontaxable exchange treatment so that a realized loss can be recognized.

BOOT

If the taxpayer in a like-kind exchange gives or receives some property that is not like-kind property, recognition may occur.[9] Property that is not like-kind property, including cash, is labeled boot.

The receipt of boot will trigger recognition of gain if there is realized gain. The amount of the recognized gain is the lesser of the boot

---

7.   Rev.Rul. 61–119, 1961–1 C.B. 395.

8.   §§ 1245, 1250, 1245(a)(2), and 1250(b)(3) and Reg. §§ 1.1245–2(a)(4) and 1.1250–2(d)(1). See Chapter 17 for an explanation of these Code provisions.

9.   § 1031(c) and Reg. § 1.1031(c)–1.

received or the realized gain (i. e., realized gain serves as the ceiling on recognition).

> **Example 3.** T and S exchange machinery, and the exchange qualifies as like-kind under § 1031. Since T's machinery (adjusted basis of $20,000) is worth $24,000, while S's machine has a value of $19,000, S also gives T cash of $5,000. T's recognized gain is $4,000, the lesser of the realized gain ($24,000 − $20,000 = $4,000) or the value of the boot received ($5,000).

> **Example 4.** Assume the same facts as in the previous example except that S's machine is worth $21,000 (not $19,000). Under these circumstances, S gives T cash of $3,000 to make up the difference. T's recognized gain is $3,000, the lesser of the realized gain ($4,000) or the value of the boot received ($3,000).

The receipt of boot does not result in recognition if there is realized loss.[10]

> **Example 5.** Assume the same facts as in Example 3 except the adjusted basis of T's machine is $30,000. T's realized loss is $6,000 ($24,000 − $30,000 = $6,000). The receipt of the boot of $5,000 does not trigger recognition. Therefore, the recognized loss is $0.

The giving of boot usually does not trigger recognition. If the boot given is cash, any realized gain or loss will not be recognized.

> **Example 6.** T and S exchange equipment, and such exchange qualifies as like-kind under § 1031. T receives equipment with a fair market value of $25,000. T transfers equipment worth $21,000 (adjusted basis of $15,000) and cash of $4,000. T's realized gain is $6,000 ($25,000 − $19,000). However, none of the gain is recognized.

However, if the boot given is appreciated or depreciated property (i. e., adjusted basis is not equal to fair market value), gain or loss is recognized to the extent of the differential between the adjusted basis and the fair market value of the boot.[11]

> **Example 7.** Assume the facts are the same as in the previous example except that T transfers equipment worth $10,000 (adjusted basis of $12,000) and boot worth $15,000 (adjusted basis of $9,000). T's realized gain appears to be $4,000 ($25,000 − $21,000). Since realization previously has served as a ceiling on recognition, it appears that the recognized gain is $4,000 (i. e., lower of $4,000 or amount of appreciation on boot of $6,000). However, the recognized gain is $6,000 (i. e., full amount of the

---

10. § 1031(b) and Reg. § 1.1031(b)–1(a).
11. Reg. § 1.1031(d)–1(e).

appreciation on the boot). In effect, T is calculating the like-kind and boot parts of the transaction separately. That is, the realized loss of $2,000 on the like-kind property is not recognized ($10,000 − $12,000), and the $6,000 realized gain on the boot is recognized ($15,000 − $9,000).

One other similar circumstance exists in which realization does not serve as a ceiling on recognition. This is illustrated in the following example.[12]

> **Example 8.** T and S exchange equipment, and the exchange qualifies as like-kind under § 1031. T receives from S like-kind equipment with a fair market value of $25,000 and boot with a fair market value of $6,000. T gives up like-kind equipment with an adjusted basis of $12,000 and boot with an adjusted basis of $8,000. Although T's realized gain appears to be $11,000 ($25,000 + $6,000 − $12,000 − $8,000), he must report the like-kind and boot elements separately. It is therefore necessary to know the fair market value of the like-kind property and the boot transferred by T. Assume the fair market value of the like-kind equipment given up by T is $9,000 and that of the boot is $22,000. The realized loss of $3,000 on the like-kind property is not recognized ($9,000 − $12,000), and the $14,000 realized gain on the boot is recognized ($22,000 − $8,000).

If the transferee either assumes a liability or takes property subject to a liability, the amount of the liability is treated as boot received by the transferor (i.e., increases the amount realized). This concept is illustrated later in this chapter in Example 12.

BASIS OF PROPERTY RECEIVED

If an exchange does not qualify as nontaxable under § 1031, gain or loss is recognized and the basis of property received in the exchange is its fair market value.[13] If the exchange qualifies for nonrecognition, the basis of property received must be adjusted to reflect any postponed (i. e., deferred) gain or loss. The basis of like-kind property received in the exchange is its fair market value less postponed gain or plus postponed loss. If the exchange partially qualifies for nonrecognition (i. e., if there is recognition associated with boot), the basis of like-kind property received in the exchange is its fair market value less postponed gain or plus postponed loss. The basis of any boot received is its fair market value.

If there is a postponed loss, nonrecognition creates a situation in which the taxpayer has recovered less than the cost or other basis of the property exchanged in an amount equal to the unrecognized loss.

---

12. Reg. § § 1.1031(a)–1(a) and 1.1031(d)–1(e).
13. § 1031(d) and Reg. § 1.1031(d)–1(a), (b), and (c).

If there is a postponed gain, the taxpayer has recovered more than the cost or other basis of the old property exchanged in an amount equal to the unrecognized gain.

> **Example 9.** T exchanges a building (used in his business) with an adjusted basis of $30,000 and fair market value of $38,000 for land with a fair market value of $38,000 which will be held as an investment. The exchange qualifies as like-kind (i. e., an exchange of business real property for investment real property). Thus, the basis of the land is its fair market value of $38,000 less the $8,000 postponed gain on the building. If the land is later sold for its fair market value of $38,000, the $8,000 postponed gain will be recognized.

> **Example 10.** Assume the same facts as in the previous example except that the building has an adjusted basis of $48,000 and fair market value of only $38,000. The basis in the newly acquired land is $48,000 (its fair market value of $38,000 plus the $10,000 unrecognized loss on the building). If the land is later sold for its fair market value of $38,000, the $10,000 postponed loss will be recognized.

The Code provides an alternative approach for determining the basis of like-kind property received:

> Adjusted basis of property surrendered
> + Adjusted basis of boot given
> + Gain recognized
> − Fair market value of boot received
> − Loss recognized
> = Basis of like-kind property received

This approach is logical in terms of the recovery of capital doctrine. That is, the unrecovered cost or other basis is increased by additional cost (boot given) or decreased by cost recovered (boot received). Any gain recognized is included in the basis of the new property, because the taxpayer has been taxed on that amount and is now entitled to recover it tax-free. Any loss recognized is deducted from the basis of the new property, because the taxpayer has received tax benefit on that amount.

The holding period of the property surrendered in the exchange carries over and "tacks on" to the holding period of the like-kind property received.[14] The logic of this rule is derived from the basic concept

---

14.   § 1223(1) and Reg. § 1.1223–1(a). For this carryover holding period rule to apply in the case of like kind exchanges after March 1, 1954, the like-kind property surrendered must have been either a capital asset or § 1231 property. See Chapters 16 and 17 for the discussion of capital assets and § 1231 property.

of the new property as a continuation of the old investment. For the boot received, there will be a new holding period (i. e., from the date of exchange) rather than a carryover holding period.[15]

The following comprehensive example illustrates the like-kind exchange rules:

Example 11. T exchanged the following old machines for new machines in five independent like-kind exchanges:

Exchange	Adjusted Basis of Old Machine	Fair Market Value of New Machine	Boot Given	Boot Received
1	$ 4,000	$ 9,000	$ –0–	$ –0–
2	4,000	9,000	3,000	–0–
3	4,000	9,000	6,000	–0–
4	4,000	9,000	–0–	3,000
5	4,000	3,500	–0–	300

T's realized and recognized gains and losses and the basis of each of the like-kind properties received are:

Exchange	Realized Gain (Loss)	Recognized Gain (Loss)	New Basis Calculation				
			Old Adj. Basis +	Boot Given +	Gain Recognized –	Boot Received =	New Basis
1	$ 5,000	$ –0–	$ 4,000 +	$ –0– +	$ –0– –	$ –0– =	$ 4,000*
2	2,000	–0–	4,000 +	3,000 +	–0– –	–0– =	7,000
3	(1,000)	–(0)–	4,000 +	6,000 +	–0– –	–0– =	10,000**
4	8,000	3,000	4,000 +	–0– +	3,000 –	3,000 =	4,000
5	(200)	–(0)–	4,000 +	–0– +	–0– –	300 =	3,700

*Basis may be determined in gain situations under the alternative method by subtracting the gain not recognized from the fair market value o the new property, i. e.,
$9,000 – $5,000 = $4,000 for Exchange 1.
$9,000 – $2,000 = $7,000 for Exchange 2.
$9,000 – $5,000 = $4,000 for Exchange 4.
**In loss situations, basis may be determined by adding the loss not recognized to the fair market value of the new property, i. e.,
$9,000 + $1,000 = $10,000 for Exchange 3.
$3,500 + $200 = $3,700 for Exchange 5.
The basis of the boot received is its fair market value.

Example 12 illustrates the like-kind exchange rules for both parties involved in the transaction and illustrates the effect of a liability associated with the like-kind property.

Example 12. X and Y exchange real estate investments. X gives up property with an adjusted basis of $250,000 (fair market value $400,000) which is subject to a mortgage of $75,000 (assumed by Y). In return for this property, X receives property with a fair market value of $300,000 (adjusted basis $200,000) and cash of $25,000.

---

15. § 1223 and Reg. § 1.1223–1(a).

(a) X's realized gain is $150,000. X gave up property with an adjusted basis of $250,000 and received $400,000 from the exchange [$300,000 fair market value of like-kind property plus $100,000 boot received (in addition to the cash received from Y, the mortgage assumed by Y is also treated as boot received by X)].

(b) X's recognized gain is $100,000. The realized gain of $150,000 is recognized to the extent of boot received.

(c) X's basis in the real estate received from Y is $250,000. This basis can be computed either by subtracting the postponed gain ($50,000) from the fair market value of the real estate received ($300,000) or by adding the recognized gain ($100,000) to the adjusted basis of the real estate given up ($250,000) and subtracting the boot received ($100,000).

(d) Y's realized gain is $100,000. Y gave up property with an adjusted basis of $200,000 plus boot of $100,000 ($75,000 mortgage assumed plus $25,000 cash) or a total of $300,000, and received $400,000 from the exchange (fair market value of like-kind property received).

(e) Y has no recognized gain because he did not receive any boot. The entire gain of $100,000 is postponed.

(f) Y's basis in the real estate received from X is $300,000. This basis can be computed either by subtracting the postponed gain ($100,000) from the fair market value of the real estate received ($400,000) or by adding the boot given ($75,000 mortgage assumed by Y plus $25,000 cash) to the adjusted basis of the real estate given up ($200,000).[16]

INVOLUNTARY CONVERSIONS

GENERAL SCHEME

Section 1033(a) provides that a taxpayer who suffers an involuntary conversion of property may postpone recognition of gain realized from the conversion. The objective of this provision is to provide relief to the taxpayer who has suffered hardship and who does not have the wherewithal to pay the tax on any gain realized from the conversion to the extent he or she reinvests the amount realized from the conversion in replacement property. The rules for nonrecognition of gain are as follows:

---

16. Example (2) of Reg. § 1.1031(d)–2 illustrates a special situation where both the buyer and seller transfer liabilities which are assumed or property is acquired subject to a liability by the other party.

—If the amount reinvested in replacement property equals or exceeds the amount realized, realized gain is not recognized.

—If the amount realized exceeds the amount reinvested in replacement property, realized gain is recognized to the extent of the excess.[17]

The following three examples illustrate the application of these rules:

> **Example 13.** T's property, which has an adjusted basis of $20,000 is condemned by the state. T is awarded $50,000 as compensation for the involuntarily converted property. T elects to postpone gain under § 1033. T's realized gain is $30,000 ($50,000 amount realized less $20,000 adjusted basis). T reinvests $40,000 in replacement property. The recognized gain under § 1033 is $10,000 (excess of $50,000 amount realized over $40,000 reinvested). The remaining $20,000 of realized gain is postponed.

> **Example 14.** Assume the same facts as in the previous example except that T reinvests $60,000 in replacement property. Since T reinvested an amount at least equal to the condemnation award, T's entire realized gain of $30,000 is not recognized and is postponed.

> **Example 15.** Assume the same facts as in Example 13 except that T reinvests $18,000 in replacement property. The deficiency in the required reinvestment (i. e., excess of amount realized of $50,000 over the reinvestment of $18,000) is $32,000. However, the realized gain of $30,000 serves as a ceiling on recognition. Therefore, the recognized gain is $30,000.

If a loss occurs on an involuntary conversion, § 1033 does not modify the normal rules for loss recognition. That is, if realized loss otherwise would be recognized, § 1033 does not change the result.

INVOLUNTARY CONVERSION DEFINED

An involuntary conversion is the result of the destruction (complete or partial), theft, seizure, requisition or condemnation, or the sale or exchange under threat or imminence of requisition or condemnation of the taxpayer's property.[18] To prove the existence of a threat or imminence of condemnation, the taxpayer must obtain confirmation that there has been a decision to acquire the property for public use and that the taxpayer has reasonable grounds to believe the property will be taken.[19] The sale of property to a party other than the author-

---

17. § 1033(a)(2)(A) and Reg. § 1.1033(a)–2(c)(1). This excess of the amount realized over the amount reinvested is analogous to boot under § 1031.

18. § 1033(a) and Reg. § § 1.1033(a)–1(a) and –2(a).

19. Rev.Rul. 63–221, 1963–2 C.B. 332 and *Joseph P. Balistrieri*, 38 TCM 526, T.C.Memo. 1979–115.

ity threatening to condemn it, by a taxpayer with reasonable grounds to believe that the necessary steps to condemn the property eventually will be instituted, qualifies as an involuntary conversion under § 1033.[20] The sale of property to a condemning authority by a taxpayer who acquired the property from its former owner with the knowledge that the property was under threat of condemnation also qualifies as an involuntary conversion under § 1033.[21] A voluntary act, such as an act of arson by a taxpayer to his or her own property, is not an involuntary conversion.[22]

Although most involuntary conversions are casualties or condemnations, there are some special situations included within the definition. Involuntary conversions, for example, include livestock destroyed by or on account of disease or exchanged or sold because of disease or solely on account of drought.[23]

COMPUTING THE AMOUNT REALIZED

The amount realized from the condemnation of property usually includes only the amount received as compensation for the property.[24] Any amount received which is designated as severance damages by both the government and the taxpayer is not included in the amount realized.[25] Severance awards usually occur when only a portion of the entire property is condemned (e. g., a strip of land is taken to build a highway). Severance damages are awarded because the value of the taxpayer's remaining property has declined as a result of the condemnation. Such damages reduce the basis of the property. However, (1) if severance damages are used to restore the usability of the remaining property[26] or (2) if the usefulness of the remaining property is destroyed by the condemnation and it is sold and replaced at a cost equal to or exceeding the sum of the condemnation award, severance damages, and sales proceeds,[27] the nonrecognition provision of § 1033 applies to the severance damages.

> **Example 16.** A portion of T's farmland is condemned by the government to build part of an interstate highway. Because the highway denies T's cattle access to a pond and some grazing land, T receives severance damages in addition to the condemnation proceeds for the land taken. T must reduce the basis of the prop-

20.   Rev.Rul. 81–180, 1981–2 C.B. 161.
21.   Rev.Rul. 81–181, 1981–2 C.B. 162.
22.   Rev.Rul. 82–74, 1982–1 C.B. 110.
23.   § 1033(d) and (e). See the Glossary of Tax Terms (Appendix C) for the definition of the term "condemnation." See also Reg. § § 1.1033(d)–1 and 1.1033(e)–1.
24.   *Pioneer Real Estate Co.,* 47 B.T.A. 886 (1942), *acq.* 1943 C.B. 18.
25.   Rev.Rul. 59–173, 1959–1 C.B. 201.
26.   Rev.Rul. 53 271, 1953–2 C.B. 36 and Rev.Rul. 83–49, I.R.B. No. 12, 8.
27.   Rev.Rul. 73–35, 1973–1 C.B. 367.

erty by the amount of the severance damages. If the amount of the severance damages received exceeds the adjusted basis, gain is recognized.

Example 17. Assume the same facts as in the previous example except that T used the proceeds from the condemnation and the severance damages to build another pond and to clear woodland for grazing. Therefore, all the proceeds are eligible for § 1033 treatment. Thus, there is no possibility of gain recognition as the result of the amount of the severance damages received exceeding the adjusted basis.

REPLACEMENT PROPERTY

The requirements for replacement property under § 1033 are generally more restrictive than those for like-kind property under § 1031. The basic requirement is that the replacement property be "similar or related in service or use" to the involuntarily converted property.[28]

Until 1964, the IRS held the position that "similar or related in service or use" meant that replacement property must be functionally the same as the involuntarily converted property (the functional use test). In 1964, however, the IRS changed its position with respect to owner-investors (such as lessors) as opposed to owner-users to conform with several appellate court decisions.[29] The test for owner-investors is referred to as the taxpayer use test.[30]

Taxpayer Use Test. This test would be met if an investor replaced a manufacturing plant with a wholesale grocery warehouse if both properties were held for the production of rental income.[31] A rental residence replaced by a personal residence does not meet this test.[32] Essentially, the properties must be used by the taxpayer in similar endeavors.

Functional Use Test. This test requires that the taxpayer's use of the replacement property and the involuntarily converted property must be the same. A rental residence replaced by a personal residence does not meet this test either. The manufacturing plant replaced by a wholesale grocery warehouse, whether rented or not, does not meet this test; but as indicated above, the IRS applies the taxpayer use test to owner-investors. However, the functional use test still applies to owner-users (i. e., a manufacturer whose manufacturing plant is destroyed by fire is required to replace the plant with another facility of similar functional use).

---

28. § 1033(a) and Reg. § 1.1033(a)–1.
29. *Liant Record, Inc. v. Comm.,* 62–1 USTC ¶ 9494, 9 AFTR2d 1557, 303 F. 2d 326 (CA–2, 1962); *Loco Realty Co. v. Comm.,* 62–2 USTC ¶ 9657, 10 AFTR2d 5359, 306 F.2d 207 (CA–8, 1962).
30. Rev.Rul. 64–237, 1964–2 C.B. 319.
31. *Loco Realty Co. v. Comm.,* cited in Footnote 29.
32. Rev.Rul. 70–466, 1970–2 C.B. 165.

Special Rules. Under one set of circumstances, the broader replacement rules for like-kind exchanges are substituted for the narrow replacement rules normally used for involuntary conversion. This beneficial provision applies if business real property or investment real property is condemned.[33] Therefore, the taxpayer has substantially more flexibility in terms of his or her selection of replacement property. For example, improved real property can be replaced with unimproved real property. Another special rule provides that proceeds from the involuntary conversion of livestock due to soil or other environmental contamination need only be expended for any property to be used for farming, including real property.[34] Finally, another special rule permits an indirect replacement approach under which the taxpayer acquires controlling interest (i. e., 80 percent) in a corporation that owns property that qualifies as replacement property in lieu of purchasing the replacement property directly. However, the aforementioned special rule that substitutes the broader replacement rules for like-kind exchanges cannot be used in conjunction with this indirect replacement approach.[35]

The rules concerning the nature of replacement property are illustrated in Example 18.

Example 18.

Type of Property and User	Like-kind Test	Taxpayer Use Test	Functional Use Test
—Land used by a manufacturing company is condemned by a local government authority	x		
—Apartment and land held by an investor is sold due to the threat or imminence of condemnation	x		
—An investor's rented wholesale grocery warehouse is destroyed by fire; therefore, the warehouse may be replaced by other rental properties (e. g., an apartment)		x	
—A manufacturing plant was destroyed by fire; therefore, replacement property must consist of another manufacturing plant which is functionally the same as the property converted			x

TIME LIMITATION ON REPLACEMENT

The taxpayer has a two-year period (three years for condemnations of real property used in a trade or business or held for investment) after

---

33. § 1033(g).
34. § 1033(f).
35. § 1033(a)(2) and (g)(2).

the close of the taxable year in which any gain is realized from the involuntary conversion to replace the property.[36] This rule affords as much as three years from the date of realization of gain (or possibly as much as four years in the case of condemnation of business or investment real property) to replace the property if the realization of gain took place on the first day of the taxable year.[37] The rule was changed from one year to two years, and the replacement period was extended to three years for real property condemnations to permit adequate time to acquire replacement property.[38]

> **Example 19.** T's warehouse is destroyed by fire on December 16, 19X2. The adjusted basis is $325,000. Proceeds of $400,000 are received from the insurance company on January 10, 19X3. T is a calendar year taxpayer. The latest date for replacement is December 31, 19X5 (i. e., end of the taxable year in which realized gain occurred plus two years). The critical date is not the date the involuntary conversion occurred, but rather the date of gain realization.

> **Example 20.** Assume the same facts as in the previous example except T's warehouse is condemned. The latest date for replacement is December 31, 19X6 (i. e., end of taxable year in which realized gain occurred plus three years).

The earliest date for replacement typically is the date the involuntary conversion occurs. However, if the property is condemned, it is possible to replace the condemned property before this date. In this case, the earliest date is the date of the threat or imminence of requisition or condemnation of the property.[39] The purpose of this provision is to enable the taxpayer to make an orderly replacement of the condemned property.

NONRECOGNITION OF GAIN

Nonrecognition of gain can be either mandatory or elective depending upon whether the conversion is direct (into replacement property) or into money.

Direct Conversion. If the conversion is directly into replacement property rather than into money, nonrecognition of realized gain is mandatory and the basis of the replacement property is the same as the adjusted basis of the converted property.[40] Direct conversion is

---

36. § 1033(a)(2)(B) and § 1033(g)(4) and Reg. § § 1.1033(a)–2(c)(3) and 1.1033(f)–1(b).

37. The taxpayer can apply for an extension of this time period anytime prior to its expiration. Reg. § 1.1033(a)–2(c)(3). Also, the period for filing the application for extension can be extended if the taxpayer shows reasonable cause.

38. Reg. § 1.1033(a)–2(c)(3).

39. § 1033(a)(2)(B).

40. § 1033(a)(1) and (b) and Reg. § 1.1033(a)–2(b).

rare in practice and usually involves condemnation. The following example illustrates the application of the rules for direct conversions.

Example 21. T's property with an adjusted basis of $20,000 is condemned by the state. T receives property with a fair market value of $50,000 as compensation for the property taken. Since the nonrecognition of realized gain is mandatory for direct conversions, T's realized gain of $30,000 is not recognized and the basis of the replacement property is $20,000 (adjusted basis of the condemned property).

Conversion into Money. If the conversion is into money, "at the election of the taxpayer the gain shall be recognized only to the extent that the amount realized upon such conversion . . . exceeds the cost of such other property or such stock."[41] This is the usual case, and nonrecognition (postponement) is elective.

The basis of the replacement property is its cost less postponed (i. e., deferred) gain.[42] The holding period of the replacement property, if the election to postpone gain is made, includes the holding period of the converted property.[43]

Section 1033 applies only to gains and not to losses. Losses from involuntary conversions are recognized if the property is held for business or income-producing purposes. Personal casualty losses are recognized, but condemnation losses related to personal use assets (e. g., a personal residence) are neither recognized nor postponed.

Example 22. T's residence, which has an adjusted basis of $50,000, is condemned by the state. T receives $20,000 from the state. T's realized loss of $30,000 is neither recognized nor postponed regardless of how much T reinvests in replacement property, because losses from the condemnation of personal use property are never recognized. If the property were business or income-producing, the loss would be recognized. If the personal loss were a casualty loss (e. g., a loss from fire, storm, or theft), it would be recognized subject to the limitations of § 165(c)(3) and Reg. § 1.165–7. See Chapter 8 for a detailed discussion of the casualty loss provisions.

Examples 23 and 24 illustrate the application of the involuntary conversion rules:

Example 23. T's building (used in his trade or business activity), with an adjusted basis of $50,000, is destroyed by fire in

---

41. § 1033(a)(2)(A) and Reg. § 1.1033(a)–2(c)(1).

42. § 1033(b).

43. § 1223(1)(A) and Reg. § 1.1223–1(a). For this carryover holding period rule to apply in the case of involuntary conversions after March 1, 1954, the involuntarily converted property must have been either a capital asset or § 1231 property. See Chapters 16 and 17 for the discussion of capital assets and § 1231 property.

19X2. In 19X2, T receives an insurance reimbursement for the loss in the amount of $100,000. T invests $75,000 in a new building.

(a) T has until December 31, 19X4, to make the new investment and qualify for the nonrecognition election under § 1033(a)(2)(A).

(b) T's realized gain is $50,000 ($100,000 insurance proceeds less $50,000 adjusted basis of old building).

(c) Assuming the replacement property qualifies under § 1033(a)(2), T's recognized gain is $25,000. He reinvested $25,000 less than the insurance proceeds ($100,000 proceeds minus $75,000 reinvested); therefore, his realized gain is recognized to that extent.

(d) T's basis in the new building is $50,000. This is its cost of $75,000 less the postponed gain of $25,000 (realized gain of $50,000 less recognized gain of $25,000).

(e) The computation of realization, recognition, and basis would apply even if T were a real estate dealer and the building destroyed by fire were part of his inventory. Section 1033 does not generally exclude inventory, as does § 1031.[44]

Example 24. Assume the same facts as in the previous example except that T receives only $45,000 (instead of $100,000) of insurance proceeds. T would have a realized and recognized loss of $5,000, and the basis of the new building would be its cost of $75,000. Of course, if the building destroyed was held for personal use, the recognized loss would be subject to the limitations of § 165(c)(3) and Reg. § 1.165–7. That is, the loss would be limited to the decline in fair market value of the property and the amount of the loss would be reduced by $100. The Tax Equity and Fiscal Responsibility Act of 1982 modifies this result effective for taxable years beginning after 1982 for personal use property. Under the act provision, after the loss is reduced by the $100 amount, it is then reduced by 10 percent of adjusted gross income (see Chapter 8).[45]

While the previous discussion describes an indirect conversion as a conversion into money, § 1033 refers to indirect conversions as conversions "into money or other property not similar or related in service or use to the converted property . . . ."[46] An indirect conversion

---

44. The exception is that the real property in § 1033(g) cannot be inventory. § 1033(g)(1) and Reg. § 1.1033(g)–1(a).

45. § 165(h) after amendment by the Tax Equity and Fiscal Responsibility Act of 1982. The 10% floor is applied to total casualties and thefts for the taxable year rather than to each casualty and theft.

46. § 1033(a)(2).

into other than money would be rare, but it could occur and is treated the same as a conversion into money.

INVOLUNTARY CONVERSION OF A PERSONAL RESIDENCE

The tax consequences of the involuntary conversion of a personal residence depend upon whether the conversion is a casualty or condemnation and whether a realized loss or gain results.

Loss Situations. If the conversion is a condemnation, the realized loss is not recognized. Loss from the condemnation of a personal use asset is never recognized. If the conversion is a casualty (i. e., a loss from fire, storm), the loss is recognized subject to the personal casualty loss limitations.

Gain Situations. If the conversion is a condemnation, the gain may be postponed under either § 1033 or § 1034. That is, the taxpayer may elect to treat the condemnation as a sale under the deferral of gain rules relating to the sale of a personal residence under § 1034 which are presented subsequently.[47] If the conversion is a casualty, the gain can be postponed only under the involuntary conversion provisions of § 1033.

REPORTING CONSIDERATIONS

If the taxpayer elects to postpone gain because he or she either has replaced or intends to replace the converted property within the prescribed time period, supporting details should be included in a statement attached to the return for the taxable year in which gain is realized. If the property has not been replaced before filing the return for the taxable year in which gain is realized, the taxpayer should attach a supporting statement to the return for the taxable year in which the property is replaced.

If the property either is not replaced within the prescribed period or is replaced at a cost less than anticipated, an amended return must be filed for the taxable year in which the election was made. A taxpayer who has elected § 1033 postponement and makes an appropriate replacement may not later revoke the election.[48] In addition, once the taxpayer has designated qualifying property as replacement property, he or she cannot later change the designation.[49] If no election is made in the return for the taxable year in which gain is realized, an election may still be made within the prescribed time period by filing a claim for credit or refund.[50]

---

47. § 1034(i)(2) and Reg. §§ 1.1033(b)–1 and 1.1034–1(h)(2)(i).
48. Reg. § 1.1033(a)–2(c)(2) and *John McShain,* 65 T.C. 686(1976).
49. Rev.Rul. 83–39, I.R.B. No. 10, 14.
50. Reg. § 1.1033(a)–2(c)(2).

Involuntary conversions from casualty and theft are reported first on Form 4684, Casualties and Thefts. Casualty and theft losses on personal use property for the individual taxpayer are carried from Form 4684 to Schedule A of Form 1040. For other casualty and theft items, the Form 4684 amounts are reported generally on Form 4797, Supplemental Schedule of Gains and Losses, unless Form 4797 is not required. In the latter case, the amounts are reported directly on the tax return involved.

Except for personal use property, recognized gains and losses from involuntary conversions other than by casualty and theft are reported on Form 4797. As stated previously, if the property involved in the involuntary conversion (other than by casualty and theft) is personal use property, any loss is not recognized; any gain is treated as a voluntary sale.

SALE OF A RESIDENCE—SECTION 1034

A realized loss from the sale of a personal residence is not recognized because the residence is personal use property.[51] A realized gain is, however, subject to taxation.[52] There are two provisions in the tax law whereby all or part of the realized gain is either postponed or excluded from taxation. The first of these, § 1034, is discussed below. The second, § 121, is discussed later in this chapter.

Section 1034 provides for the mandatory nonrecognition of gain from the sale or exchange of a personal residence. Both the old and new residences must qualify as the taxpayer's principal residence.[53] A houseboat or house trailer qualifies if used by the taxpayer as his or her principal residence.[54]

The reason for not recognizing gain from the sale or exchange of a residence which is replaced by a new residence within the prescribed time period (discussed below) is that the new residence is viewed as a continuation of the investment. Also, if the proceeds from the sale are reinvested, the taxpayer does not have the wherewithal to pay tax on the gain. Beyond these fundamental concepts, Congress, in enacting § 1034, was concerned with the hardship of involuntary moves and the socially desirable objective of encouraging the mobility of labor.

REPLACEMENT PERIOD

For the nonrecognition treatment to apply, the old residence must be replaced with a new residence during a period beginning two years

---

51. Reg. § § 1.165–9(a) and 1.262–1(b)(4).

52. § 1001(c). Gain from the sale of a principal residence is not a tax preference item for purposes of computing the alternative minimum tax. Refer to Chapter 12.

53. § 1034(a) and Reg. § 1.1034–1(a) and (b)(1) and (2).

54. Reg. § 1.1034–1(c)(3)(i).

before the sale of the old residence and ending two years after such sale.[55] This four-year period applies regardless of whether the new residence is purchased or constructed. In addition to acquiring the residence during this period, the taxpayer must occupy and use the new residence as the principal residence during this same time period.[56] The occupancy requirement has been strictly construed by both the IRS and the courts, and even circumstances beyond a taxpayer's control do not excuse noncompliance.[57]

> **Example 25.** T sells her personal residence from which she realizes a gain of $50,000. Although the construction of a new residence begins immediately after the sale, unstable soil conditions and a trade union strike cause unforeseen delays in construction. The new residence ultimately is completed and occupied by T 25 months after the sale of the old residence. Since the occupancy requirement has not been satisfied, § 1034 is inapplicable and T must recognize a gain of $50,000 on the sale of the old residence.

Taxpayers might be inclined to make liberal use of § 1034 as a means of speculating when the price of residential housing is rising. Without any time restriction on its use, § 1034 would permit deferral of gain on multiple sales of principal residences, each one of which would result in an economic profit. The Code curbs this approach by precluding the application of § 1034 to any sales occurring within two years of its last use.[58]

> **Example 26.** After T sells his principal residence (hereinafter designated as the first residence) in March of 19X2 for $150,000 (realized gain of $60,000), he buys and sells the following (all of which qualify as principal residences):
>
> | | Date of Purchase | Date of Sale | Amount Involved |
> |---|---|---|---|
> | Second residence | April of 19X2 | | $ 160,000 |
> | Second residence | | May of 19X3 | 180,000 |
> | Third residence | June of 19X3 | | 200,000 |

Because multiple sales have occurred within a period of two years, § 1034 does not apply to the sale of the second residence. Thus, the realized gain of $20,000 [$180,000 (selling price) − $160,000 (purchase price)] must be recognized.

---

55. § 1034(a).
56. Rev.Rul. 69–434, 1969–2 C.B. 163 and § 1034(a).
57. *Joseph T. Galinas,* 35 TCM 448, T.C.Memo. 1976–103, *Helen M. Welch,* 38 TCM 26, T.C.Memo. 1979–9, *James A. Henry,* 44 TCM 844, T.C.Memo. 1982 469, and *William F. Peck,* 44 TCM 1030, T.C.Memo. 1982–506.
58. § 1034(d)(1) and (2).

The two-year rule precluding multiple use of § 1034 could work a hardship where a taxpayer has been transferred by his or her employer and therefore has little choice in the matter. For this reason, § 1034 was amended to provide an exception to the two-year rule when the sale results from a change in the location of employment. To qualify for the exception, a taxpayer must meet the distance and length-of-employment requirements specified for the deduction of moving expenses under § 217.[59]

> **Example 27.** Assume the same facts as in the previous example except that in February of 19X3, T's employer transfers him to a job in another state. Consequently, the sale of the second residence and the purchase of the third residence were due to the relocation of employment. If T satisfies the conditions of § 217, no gain will be recognized on the sale of the first and second residences.

> **Example 28.** Assume the same facts as in Example 26 except that in March of 19X2, T's employer transfers him to a job in another state. Consequently, the sale of the first residence and the purchase of the second residence were due to the relocation of employment. However, the sale of the second residence in May of 19X3 and the purchase of the third residence in June of 19X3 were not job related. Therefore, the exception provision does not apply, and the results are the same as in Example 26.

The running of the time periods specified above is suspended during any time the taxpayer or spouse is on extended active duty (over 90 days or for an indefinite period) with the Armed Forces of the United States after the date the old residence is sold.[60] This suspension is limited to four years after the date the old residence is sold. A similar suspension is available to U. S. citizens who are employed outside the U. S. by nongovernmental employers (i. e., expatriates). In no event, however, may § 1034 apply unless the replacement occurs within four years of the date when the principal residence was sold.[61]

> **Example 29.** T, an employee of F corporation, sold his principal residence in Baltimore on July 5, 19X2, because he had been transferred to the Berlin office on a one-year assignment. T returns to the United States after completion of the assignment on July 1, 19X3. The latest date for a qualifying replacement is July 1, 19X5 (i. e., two years after the end of the suspension period).

> **Example 30.** Assume the same facts as in the previous example except that the assignment is for a three-year period. Therefore,

---

59. Refer to Chapter 10 for the discussion of the rules governing the deduction for moving expenses.
60. § 1034(h) and Reg. § 1.1034–1(g)(1).
61. § 1034(k).

T returns to the United States after completion of the assignment on July 1, 19X5. Two years after the end of the suspension period is July 1, 19X7. However, since the suspension period exception cannot result in extending the replacement time period beyond four years after the date the principal residence was sold, the latest date for a qualifying replacement is July 5, 19X6.

PRINCIPAL RESIDENCE

As indicated above, both the old and new residences must be the taxpayer's principal residence. Whether property is the taxpayer's principal residence is dependent ". . . upon all the facts and circumstances in each case."[62]

> **Example 31.** T sells his principal residence and moves to Norfolk, Virginia, where he is employed. He decides to rent an apartment in Norfolk because of its proximity to his place of employment. He purchases a beach house at Virginia Beach which he occupies most weekends. T does not intend to live in the beach house other than on weekends. The apartment in Norfolk is his principal place of residence. Therefore, the purchase of the beach house does not qualify as an appropriate replacement.

If the old residence ceases to be the taxpayer's principal residence prior to its sale or the new residence ceases to be the principal residence before the taxpayer occupies it, the nonrecognition provision does not apply. For example, if the taxpayer abandons the old residence prior to its sale, it no longer qualifies as a principal residence.[63] If the old residence is converted to other than personal use (e. g., rental) prior to its sale, the nonrecognition provision, of course, does not apply. If only partially converted to business use, gain from the sale of the personal use portion still qualifies for nonrecognition.[64] It is possible to convert part of a principal residence to business use and later to convert that part back to being part of the principal residence (e. g., a home office).[65]

Temporarily renting out the old residence prior to sale does not necessarily terminate its status as the taxpayer's principal residence,[66] nor does temporarily renting out the new residence before it is occupied by the taxpayer.[67]

---

62. Reg. § 1.1034–1(c)(3).
63. *Richard T. Houlette*, 48 T.C. 350 (1967) and *Stolk v. Comm.*, 64–1 USTC ¶ 9228, 13 AFTR2d 535, 326 F.2d 760 (CA–2, 1964).
64. Reg. § 1.1034–1(c)(3)(ii).
65. Rev.Rul. 82–26, 1982–1 C.B. 114.
66. *Robert W. Aagaard*, 56 T.C. 191 (1971), *acq.* 1971–2 C.B. 1; *Robert G. Clapham*, 63 T.C. 505 (1975); Rev.Rul. 59–72, 1959–1 C.B. 203; and Rev.Rul. 78 146, 1978–1 C.B. 260.
67. Reg. § 1.1034–1(c)(3)(i).

NONRECOGNITION OF GAIN REQUIREMENTS

Under § 1034(a) realized gain from the sale of the old residence is not recognized if the taxpayer reinvests an amount at least equal to the adjusted sales price of the old residence. Realized gain is recognized to the extent the taxpayer does not reinvest the adjusted sales price in a new residence. Therefore, the amount not reinvested is treated similarly to boot received in a like-kind exchange. Adjusted sales price is the amount realized from the sale of the old residence less fixing-up expenses.[68]

The amount realized is calculated by reducing the selling price by the selling expenses.[69] Selling expenses include items such as advertising the property for sale, real estate broker commissions, legal fees in connection with the sale, and loan placement fees paid by the taxpayer as a condition of the arrangement of financing for the buyer.[70] To the extent that the selling expenses are deducted as moving expenses, they are not allowed as deductions in the computation of the amount realized.[71]

While selling expenses are deductible in calculating the amount realized, fixing-up expenses are not. Therefore, fixing-up expenses do not have an impact on the calculation of realized gain or loss. However, since fixing-up expenses are deductible in calculating the adjusted sales price, they do have the potential for producing tax benefit in that they reduce the amount of the required reinvestment to qualify for nonrecognition treatment. Conversely, if a replacement residence is not acquired, the fixing-up expenses produce no tax benefit.

Fixing-up expenses are personal in nature and are incurred by the taxpayer to assist in the sale of the old residence.[72] Fixing-up expenses include such items as ordinary repairs, painting, and wallpapering. To qualify as a fixing-up expense, the expense must (1) be incurred for work performed during the 90-day period ending on the date of the contract of sale, (2) be paid within 30 days after the date of the sale, and (3) not be a capital expenditure.[73]

The treatment of fixing-up expenses (i. e., reducing the amount of the required reinvestment) is another illustration of the wherewithal to pay concept. To the extent that the taxpayer has expended part of the funds received on the sale of the old residence in preparing the old residence for sale, he or she does not have the funds available to reinvest in the new residence.

As previously mentioned, fixing-up expenses are not considered in determining realized gain. They are considered only in determining how much realized gain is to be postponed. In addition, fixing-up

---

68. § 1034(b)(1) and Reg. § 1.1034–1(b)(3).

69. Reg. § 1.1034–1(b)(4)(i) and Rev.Rul. 54–380, 1954–2 C.B. 155.

70. Reg. § 1.1034–1(b)(4)(i) and Rev.Rul. 68–650, 1968–2 C.B. 78.

71. § 217(b)(2). Refer to the discussion of moving expenses in Chapter 10.

72. § 1034(b)(2) and Reg. § 1.1034–1(b)(6).

73. § 1034(b)(2) and Reg. § 1.1034–1(b)(6).

expenses have no direct effect on the basis of the new residence. Indirectly, through their effect on postponed gain, they can bring about a lesser basis of the new residence. The effects of fixing-up expenses on the computation of gain realized and recognized and on the basis of the new residence are illustrated in Figure I and in Example 33.

CAPITAL IMPROVEMENTS

Capital improvements are added to the cost basis of a personal residence for the purpose of computing gain or loss on a subsequent sale or other disposition of the property.[74] However, the cost of a replacement residence (for determining the nonrecognition of gain under § 1034) includes only capital improvements incurred during the period beginning two years before the date of sale of the old residence and ending two years after such date (i. e., the time period during which the old residence can be replaced).[75]

> **Example 32.** T purchases a replacement residence on January 2, 19X2, and sells her former residence on January 16, 19X2. T makes capital improvements to the replacement residence over a three-year period beginning on January 4, 19X2. The improvements made prior to the date of sale (from January 4, 19X2, to January 16, 19X2) are added to the cost basis of the replacement residence for computing the nonrecognized gain on the sale of the former residence, because these costs were incurred during the two-year period prior to January 16, 19X2. The improvements incurred within two years following the date of the sale (January 16, 19X2) are also capitalized in determining the cost of the replacement residence under § 1034. Capital improvements made after the two-year period are added to the cost basis solely for determining gain or loss upon a subsequent sale of the replacement residence.

If the taxpayer receives a residence by gift or inheritance, such residence will not qualify as a replacement residence. However, if the taxpayer makes substantial capital expenditures (i. e., reconstruction) to such property within the replacement time period, these expenditures do qualify.[76]

BASIS OF THE NEW RESIDENCE

The basis of the new residence is its cost less the realized gain not recognized (postponed gain).[77] If there is any postponed gain, the hold-

---

74. § 1034(c)(2).

75. *Charles M. Shaw*, 69 T.C. 1034 (1978); Reg. § 1.1034–1(c)(4)(ii); and, Rev.Rul. 78–147, 1978–1 C.B. 261.

76. Reg. §§ 1.1034–1(b)(7) and (9) and 1.1034–1(c)(4)(i).

77. § 1034(e) and Reg. §§ 1.1034–1(e) and 1.1016–5(d).

ing period of the new residence includes the holding period of the old residence.[78]

Figure I summarizes the sale-of-residence concepts. Example 33 illustrates these concepts and the application of the nonrecognition provision.

Example 33. T sells her personal residence (adjusted basis of $36,000) for $44,000. She receives only $41,400 after payment of a brokerage fee of $2,600. Ten days before the sale, T incurred and paid for qualified fixing-up expenses of $1,400. Two months later T acquires a new residence. Determine the gain, if any, T must recognize and the basis of the new residence under each of the following circumstances:

—The residence acquired two months after the sale of the old residence cost $60,000. The cost of the new residence has no effect on determining the realized gain from the sale of the old residence. The realized gain is $5,400 ($41,400 amount realized less $36,000 adjusted basis of old residence). None of the gain is recognized, because T reinvested at least $40,000 (the adjusted sales price of $41,400 − $1,400 fixing-up ex-

Figure I

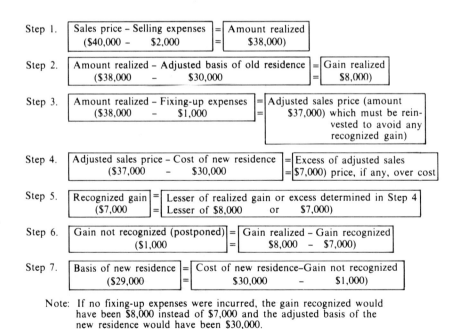

Note: If no fixing-up expenses were incurred, the gain recognized would have been $8,000 instead of $7,000 and the adjusted basis of the new residence would have been $30,000.

---

78. § 1223(7) and Reg. § 1.1223–1(g).

penses) in the new residence. The $5,400 gain is postponed and the basis of the new residence is $54,600 ($60,000 cost less $5,400 postponed gain).

—The new residence cost $38,000. Of the realized gain of $5,400, $2,000 is recognized because T reinvested $2,000 less than the adjusted sales price of $40,000. The remaining gain of $3,400 is not recognized and is postponed. The basis of the new residence is $34,600 ($38,000 cost less $3,400 postponed gain).

—The new residence cost $32,000. All of the realized gain of $5,400 is recognized because T reinvested $8,000 less than the adjusted sales price of $40,000. Since the amount not reinvested exceeds the realized gain, the entire gain is recognized and § 1034 does not apply. The basis of the new residence is simply its cost of $32,000 because there is no postponed gain.

REPORTING PROCEDURES

The taxpayer is required to report the details of the sale of the residence in the tax return for the taxable year in which gain is realized even if all of the gain is postponed. If a new residence is acquired and occupied before filing, a statement should be attached to the return showing the purchase date, its cost, and date of occupancy. Form 2119, Sale or Exchange of Principal Residence, may be used to show the details of the sale and replacement, and a copy should be retained by the taxpayer as support for the basis of the new residence. If a replacement residence has not been purchased when the return is filed, the taxpayer should submit the details of the purchase in the return of the taxable year during which it occurs. If the old residence is not replaced within the prescribed time period, or if some recognized gain results, the taxpayer must file an amended return for the year in which the sale took place.

In any case, it is necessary to report the sale for the statute of limitations to begin running. If the taxpayer has an unreported recognized gain (either because a new residence was not purchased or because the taxpayer is otherwise not entitled to postpone the gain), the statute of limitations does not expire until three years after the date the taxpayer notifies the IRS in writing of (1) the cost of the new residence which results in nonrecognition of gain, (2) the intention not to purchase a new residence, or (3) failure to purchase a new residence within the prescribed period.[79]

79.　§ 1034(j) and Reg. § 1.1034–1(i)(1).

SALE OF A RESIDENCE—SECTION 121

Taxpayers age 55 or older who sell or exchange their principal residence may elect to exclude up to $125,000 ($62,500 for married individuals filing separate returns) of realized gain from the sale or exchange.[80] The election can be made only once.[81] This provision is contrasted with § 1034 where nonrecognition is mandatory and may occur many times during a taxpayer's lifetime. Section 121 also differs from § 1034 in that it does not require the taxpayer to purchase a new residence. The excluded gain is never recognized, whereas the realized gain not recognized under § 1034 is postponed by subtracting it from the cost of the new residence in calculating the adjusted basis.

This provision is the only case in the tax law where a realized gain from the disposition of property that is not recognized is excluded rather than merely postponed. In other words, the provision allows the taxpayer a permanent recovery of more than the cost or other basis of the residence tax-free.

The reason for § 121 is simply the desire of Congress to relieve older citizens of the large capital gains tax they might incur from the sale of a personal residence. The dollar and age limitations restrict the benefit of § 121 to taxpayers who presumably have a greater need for increased tax-free dollars.

REQUIREMENTS

The taxpayer must be at least 55 before the date of the sale and have owned and used the residence as a principal residence for at least three years during the five-year period ending on the date of sale.[82] The ownership and use periods do not have to be the same period of time. Short temporary absences (e. g., vacations) count as periods of use. If the residence is owned jointly by husband and wife, only one of the spouses is required to meet these requirements if a joint return is filed for the taxable year in which the sale took place. Taxpayers age 65 or older who sold or exchanged their principal residence prior to July 26, 1981, may elect to substitute "five years during the eight-year period" for the "three years during the five-year period" test.

If a former residence is involuntarily converted and any gain is postponed under § 1033, the holding period of the former residence is added to the holding period of the replacement residence in determining whether the ownership and use period requirements are satisfied. However, if the realized gain is postponed under § 1034 (i. e., sale of residence provision) rather than postponed under § 1033 (i. e., involuntary conversion provision), the holding period of the replacement

---

80. § 121(a), (b), and (c). For married taxpayers, each spouse must consent.
81. § 121(b)(2) and Reg. § 1.121–2(b). Only one election may be made by married individuals.
82. § 121(a)(2) and (d), Reg. § 1.121–1(b), and Rev.Rul. 80–172, 1980–2 C.B. 56.

residence, in determining whether the ownership and use period requirements are satisfied, begins with the acquisition date of the replacement residence.

> **Example 34.** T has lived in his residence since 19X0. His residence is involuntarily converted in July 19X6. T purchases a replacement residence in August 19X6. In determining whether T can satisfy the ownership and use requirements at the time of the subsequent sale of the residence purchased in 19X6, he includes the holding period of the involuntarily converted residence.

> **Example 35.** Assume the facts are the same as in the previous example except that T's residence was not involuntarily converted. Instead, he sold it so that he could move into a larger house. In determining whether T can satisfy the ownership and use requirements at the time of the subsequent sale of the residence purchased in 19X6, he is not permitted to include the holding period of the old residence.

RELATIONSHIP TO OTHER PROVISIONS

The taxpayer can treat an involuntary conversion of a principal residence as a sale for purposes of § 121(a). Any gain not excluded under § 121 is then subject to postponement under § 1033 or 1034 (condemnation only) assuming the requirements of those provisions are met.[83]

Any gain not excluded under § 121 from the sale of a residence is subject to postponement under § 1034, assuming the requirements of that provision are met. This relationship is illustrated in Examples 37 and 38.

MAKING AND REVOKING THE ELECTION

The election not to recognize gain under § 121 may be made or revoked at any time before the statute of limitations expires.[84] Therefore, the taxpayer generally has until the later of (1) three years from the due date of the return for the year the gain is realized or (2) two years from the date the tax is paid to make or revoke the election. Making the election is accomplished by attaching a signed statement (showing all the details of the sale) to the return for the taxable year in which the sale took place. Form 2119 may be used for this purpose. Revocation is accomplished by filing a signed statement (showing the taxpayer's name, Social Security number, and taxable year for which the election was made) indicating such revocation.[85]

---

83. §§ 121(d)(4) and (7) and 1034(i).
84. § 121(c) and Reg. § 1.121–4(a).
85. Reg. § 1.121–4(b) and (c).

COMPUTATION PROCEDURE

The following example illustrates the application of § 121.

> **Example 36.** Assume the same facts as in Example 33 except T does not acquire a new residence and meets the requirements of § 121. T may elect not to recognize any of the $5,400 realized gain, since the realized gain is not in excess of $125,000.

The following examples illustrate the application of both the § 121 and § 1034 provisions:

> **Example 37.** T sells his personal residence (adjusted basis of $32,000) for $205,000, of which he receives only $195,400 after the payment of selling expenses. Ten days before the sale, T incurred and paid for qualified fixing-up expenses of $6,400. T is age 55 and elects the exclusion of gain under § 121. He does not acquire a replacement residence.

> **Example 38.** Assume the same facts as in the previous example except that T acquires a new residence for $40,000 within the prescribed time period.

The solutions to Examples 37 and 38 are as follows:

	Example 37	Example 38
Amount realized ($205,000 − $9,600)	$ 195,400	$ 195,400
Adjusted basis	32,000	32,000
Realized gain	$ 163,400	$ 163,400
§ 121 exclusion	125,000	125,000
Realized gain after exclusion	$ 38,400	$ 38,400
Amount realized	$ 195,400	$ 195,400
Fixing-up expenses	6,400	6,400
Adjusted sales price	$ 189,000	$ 189,000
§ 121 exclusion	125,000	125,000
Adjusted sales price after exclusion	$ 64,000	$ 64,000
Cost of new residence	0	40,000
Excess of adjusted sales price after the exclusion over reinvestment	$ 64,000	$ 24,000
Recognized gain (lower of realized gain after exclusion or above excess)	$ 38,400	$ 24,000
Realized gain after exclusion	$ 38,400	$ 38,400
Recognized gain	38,400	24,000
Postponed gain	$ 0	$ 14,400
Cost of new residence	$ 0	$ 40,000
Postponed gain	0	14,400
Basis of new residence	$ 0	$ 25,600

Comparing the results of Examples 37 and 38 provides insight into the relationship between § 1034 and § 121. If T had not made the election to postpone gain under § 121 in Example 37, his recognized gain would have been $163,400 (i. e., the realized gain). Thus, the election resulted in the permanent exclusion of the $125,000 of realized gain by reducing the recognized gain to $38,400. Further documentation of the permanent nature of the § 121 exclusion is provided in the calculation of the basis of the new residence in Example 38. The $40,000 cost of the residence is reduced only by the postponed gain of $14,400. That is, it is not reduced by the amount of the § 121 exclusion. To postpone all of the $38,400 realized gain after the exclusion, T would have needed to reinvest $64,000 (i. e., the adjusted sales price after the exclusion). Also, note that the Example 37 results demonstrate that the realized gain after the exclusion is the ceiling on recognition.

OTHER NONRECOGNITION PROVISIONS

Several additional nonrecognition provisions, which are not as common as those already discussed, are treated briefly in the remainder of this chapter.

EXCHANGE OF STOCK FOR PROPERTY—SECTION 1032

Under this section, no gain or loss is recognized to a corporation on the receipt of money or other property in exchange for its stock (including treasury stock).[86] In other words, no gain or loss is recognized by a corporation when it deals in its own stock. This provision is consistent with the accounting treatment of such transactions.

CERTAIN EXCHANGES OF INSURANCE POLICIES— SECTION 1035

Under this provision, no gain or loss is recognized from the exchange of certain insurance contracts or policies.[87] The rules relating to exchanges not solely in kind and the basis of the property acquired are the same as under § 1031. Exchanges qualifying for nonrecognition include (1) the exchange of life insurance contracts, (2) the exchange of a life insurance contract for an endowment or annuity contract, (3) the exchange of an endowment contract for another endowment contract which provides for regular payments beginning at a date not later than the date payments would have begun under the contract exchanged, (4) the exchange of an endowment contract for an annuity contract, or (5) the exchange of annuity contracts.

---

86. § 1032(a) and Reg. § 1.1032–1(a).
87. § 1035(a) and (c) and Reg. § 1.1035–1.

EXCHANGE OF STOCK FOR STOCK OF THE SAME CORPORATION—SECTION 1036

No gain or loss is recognized from the exchange of common stock solely for common stock in the same corporation or from the exchange of preferred stock for preferred stock in the same corporation.[88] Exchanges between individual shareholders as well as between a shareholder and the corporation are included. The rules relating to exchanges not solely in kind and the basis of the property acquired are the same as under § 1031. For example, a nonrecognition exchange occurs when common stock with different rights, such as voting for nonvoting, is exchanged. Gain or loss from the exchange of common for preferred or preferred for common usually is recognized even though the stock exchanged is in the same corporation.

CERTAIN REACQUISITIONS OF REAL PROPERTY— SECTION 1038

Under this provision, no loss is recognized from the repossession of real property which is sold on an installment basis.[89] Gain is recognized to a limited extent.

Chapter 15 has covered certain situations in which realized gains or losses are not recognized (i. e., nontaxable exchanges). Chapters 16 and 17 are concerned with the classification of recognized gains and losses. That is, if a gain or loss is recognized, is it an ordinary or capital gain or loss? Chapter 16 discusses the tax consequences of capital gains and losses.

☑ TAX PLANNING CONSIDERATIONS

LIKE-KIND EXCHANGES

Since application of the like-kind provisions is mandatory rather than elective, in certain instances it may be preferable to avoid qualifying for § 1031 nonrecognition. If the like-kind provisions do not apply, the end result may be the recognition of long-term capital gain in exchange for a higher basis for the newly acquired asset. Also, the immediate recognition of gain may be preferable in certain situations (e. g., if the taxpayer has unused net operating loss carryovers or investment tax credit carryovers or if the taxpayer's effective tax rate is expected to increase in the future).

---

88. § 1036(a) and (b) and Reg. § 1.1036–1(a) and (b).
89. § 1038(a) and (b) and Reg. § 1.1038–1(a) and (b).

Example 39. T disposes of a machine (used in his business) with an adjusted basis of $3,000 for $4,000. T also acquires a new business machine for $9,000. If § 1031 applies, the $1,000 realized gain is not recognized and the basis of the new machine is reduced by $1,000. If § 1031 does not apply, a $1,000 gain is recognized and may receive favorable long-term capital gain treatment to the extent that the gain is not recognized as ordinary income due to the depreciation recapture provisions (see Chapter 17). In addition, the basis for depreciation on the new machine is $9,000 rather than $8,000, since there is no unrecognized gain.

Another time for avoiding the application of § 1031 nonrecognition treatment is when the adjusted basis of the property being disposed of exceeds the fair market value.

Example 40. Assume the facts are the same as in the previous example except the fair market value of the machine is $2,500. If § 1031 applies, the $500 realized loss is not recognized. Therefore, to recognize the loss, T should sell the old machine and purchase the new one. The purchase and sale transactions should be with different taxpayers.

On the other hand, the like-kind exchange procedure can be utilized to control the amount of recognized gain.

Example 41. S has property with an adjusted basis of $40,000 and a fair market value of $100,000. P wants to buy S's property, but S wants to limit the amount of recognized gain on the proposed transaction. P acquires other like-kind property (from an outside party) for $80,000. P then exchanges this property and $20,000 cash for S's property. The results are a $20,000 recognized gain for S and a basis for the like-kind property of $40,000 ($40,000 adjusted basis + $20,000 gain recognized – $20,000 boot received). If S had sold the property to P for its fair market value of $100,000, the result would have been a $60,000 recognized gain to S. It is permissible for S to identify the like-kind property which he wants P to purchase.[90]

INVOLUNTARY CONVERSIONS

In certain cases a taxpayer may prefer to recognize gain from an involuntary conversion. Keep in mind that § 1033, unlike § 1031 (dealing with like-kind exchanges), is an elective provision.

---

90. *Franklin B. Biggs*, 69 T.C. 905 (1978), Rev.Rul. 57–244, 1957–1 C.B. 247, Rev.Rul. 73–476, 1973–2 C.B. 300, *Starker vs. U. S.*, 602 F.2d 1341 (CA–9, 1979), and *Baird Publishing Co.*, 39 T.C. 608 (1962).

Example 42. T has a $40,000 realized gain from the involuntary conversion of an office building. The entire proceeds of $450,000 are reinvested in a new office building. T, however, does not elect to postpone gain under § 1033 because of an expiring net operating loss carryover which is offset against the gain. Therefore, none of the realized gain of $40,000 is postponed. Furthermore, by not electing § 1033, T's basis in the replacement property will be its cost of $450,000 rather than the $450,000 reduced by the postponed gain.

SALE OF A PERSONAL RESIDENCE

Replacement Period Requirements. Several problems arise in avoiding the recognition of gain on the sale of a principal residence. Most of these problems can be resolved favorably through appropriate planning procedures, while a few represent situations where the taxpayer has to accept the adverse tax consequences and possesses little, if any, planning flexibility. One pitfall concerns the failure to reinvest *all* of the proceeds from the sale of the residence into a new principal residence.

Example 43. R sells her principal residence in January 19X2 for $150,000 (adjusted basis of $40,000). Shortly thereafter, R purchases a 50-year-old house in a historical part of the community for $100,000 which she uses as her principal residence. It was R's intention to significantly renovate the property over a period of time and thereby make it more suitable to her living needs. In December 19X4, R enters into a contract with a home improvement company to carry out the renovation at a cost of $60,000.

Example 44. Assume the same facts as in the previous example except that the contract is entered into in June 19X2 (rather than December 19X4). To finance the renovation, at the same time R obtains a mortgage on the property from a local savings and loan association.

The difference between the results reached in Examples 43 and 44 turns on the full or partial application of § 1034. In Example 43, it is clear that only $100,000 of the proceeds from the sale of the old residence has been reinvested in a new principal residence on a *timely* basis. Of the realized gain of $110,000, therefore, $50,000 ($150,000 adjusted sales price − $100,000 reinvested) must be recognized.[91] In Example 44, however, all of the proceeds should be treated as having been reinvested within the prescribed period of time. Consequently, none of the realized gain will be recognized.

---

91. It has been assumed that § 121 did not apply.

One problem that a taxpayer may not be in a position to do anything about concerns the acquisition of property *prior* to the beginning of the replacement period. In this regard, recall that the replacement period begins two years prior to the sale and ends two years after such sale.[92]

> **Example 45.** Three years before S sells her principal residence, she purchased a tract of undeveloped land for $80,000. It was S's intention to use some or all of this land as the site for her new home, when and if she decided to sell her old home and move. Upon the sale of the principal residence, a new residence is constructed on the land (now worth $150,000). None of the cost of the land can be counted towards the replacement amount, since it did not satisfy the two-year rule.[93]

> **Example 46.** T's employer transfers him to a different city in July 19X2. T lists his house for sale with a realtor in July 19X2. T purchases a principal residence in the city to which he is transferred in September 19X2. Because of market conditions, T is unable to sell his original residence until December 19X5. Since this is not within the two-year time of the purchase period, the purchase of the residence in September 19X2 will not be a qualifying replacement residence.

Although the result reached in Example 45 could have been avoided through the proper timing of the purchase of the land, nontax considerations probably will dictate how the transaction is handled. One would not expect S to postpone the making of an attractive investment in land that she wants merely because its cost *might* not qualify in the application of § 1034. The results produced in Example 46 were caused by market conditions. T needed a place to live in the new city, and he did not anticipate that he would encounter such difficulty in selling his old residence.

Principal Residence Requirement. Section 1034 will not apply unless the property involved is the taxpayer's principal residence. In this connection, one potential hurdle can arise in cases where the residence has been rented and has not been occupied by the taxpayer for an extended period of time. Depending on the circumstances, the IRS might contend that the property has been abandoned by the taxpayer as his or her principal residence. The key to the abandonment issue is whether or not the taxpayer intended to reoccupy the property and use it as a principal residence upon his or her return to the locale. If the residence, in fact, is not reoccupied, the taxpayer should have a good reason to explain why this did not take place.

---

92. § 1034(a).
93. Rev.Rul. 78–147, 1978–1 C.B. 261.

Example 47. T is transferred by her employer to another office out of the state on a three-year assignment. It is the understanding of the parties that the assignment is temporary, and upon its completion, T will return to the original job site. During her absence, T rents her principal residence and lives in an apartment at the new location. Although T had every intention of reoccupying her residence, when she returns from the temporary assignment she finds that it is no longer suited to her needs. Specifically, the public school located nearby where she planned to send her children has been closed. As a consequence, T sells the residence and replaces it with one more conveniently located to a public school. Under these circumstances, it would appear that T is in an excellent position to show that the property never was abandoned as her principal residence. The reason it was not reoccupied prior to sale can be explained satisfactorily.[94]

The principal residence requirement could cause difficulty where a taxpayer works in two places and maintains multiple households. In such cases, the principal residence will be the location where the taxpayer lives most of the time.[95]

Example 48. E is a vice-president of Z Corporation and in this capacity spends about an equal amount of time in the company's New York City and Miami offices. E owns a house in each location and expects to retire in about five years. At that point, he plans to sell his New York home and use some of the proceeds to make improvements on the Miami property. Both homes have appreciated in value since their acquisition, and such appreciation can be expected to continue.

From a tax planning standpoint, E should be looking toward the use of § § 121 and 1034 to shelter some or all of the gain he will realize on the future sale of the New York City home.[96] To do this, he should arrange his affairs so as to spend more than six months each year at that location. Upon its sale, therefore, the New York home will be his principal residence.

Section 121 Considerations. Older individuals who may be contemplating a move from their home to an apartment should consider the following possibilities for minimizing or deferring taxes:

—Wait until age 55 to sell the residence and elect under § 121 to exclude up to $125,000 of the realized gain.

---

94. Rev.Rul. 78–146, 1978–1 C.B. 260. Compare *Rudolph M. Stucchi,* 35 TCM 1052, T.C.Memo. 1976–242.

95. Rev.Rul. 77–298, 1977–2 C.B. 308.

96. If E qualifies, § 121 would allow the first $125,000 of gain to be nontaxable. Further gain might be avoided under § 1034 to the extent the sale proceeds are applied toward improvements on the Miami home.

—Sell the personal residence under an installment contract to spread the gain over several years.[97]

—Sell the personal residence and purchase a condominium instead of renting an apartment, thereby permitting further deferral of the cumulative unrecognized gain.

The use of § 121 should be carefully considered. Although such use avoids the immediate recognition of gain, the election expends the full $125,000 allowed.

Example 49. In 19X2 T, age 55, sells his personal residence for an amount that yields a realized gain of $5,000. Presuming T does not plan to reinvest the sale proceeds in a new principal residence (i. e., take advantage of the deferral possibility of § 1034), should he avoid the recognition of this gain by utilizing § 121? Electing § 121 would mean that T would waste $120,000 of his lifetime exclusion.

In this connection, the use of § 121 by one spouse precludes the other spouse from later taking advantage of the exclusion.

Example 50. Assume the same facts as in the previous example except that T was married to W at the time of the sale. Later, T and W are divorced and W marries R. If T used the § 121 exclusion (i. e., for T to make the election for the 19X2 sale, it was necessary for W to join with him in making the election even if the residence was owned separately by T), it is unavailable to W and R even though either one of them may otherwise qualify.[98] For W and R to be able to make the § 121 election, it would be necessary for W and T to revoke their prior election. Another planning approach would be for R to sell his residence prior to the marriage to W and to elect the exclusion on that sale.

If a taxpayer who could elect § 121 exclusion treatment chooses not to do so to remain eligible to elect it in the future, consideration must be given to the probability that the taxpayer will satisfy the three out of five-year ownership and use period requirements associated with a residence sale in the future. As previously mentioned, the holding period for the occupancy and use requirements does carry over for a § 1033 involuntary conversion but does not carry over for a § 1034 sale.

Taxpayers should maintain records of both the purchase and sale of personal residences, since the sale of one residence results in an adjustment of the basis of the new residence if the deferral provisions of § 1034 apply. Form 2119 should be filed with the tax return and a copy retained as support for the basis of the new residence. Detailed cost records should be retained for an indefinite period.

---

97. § 453(a). See the discussion of the installment method in Chapter 18.

98. § 121(c) and Reg. § 1.121–2(b).

PROBLEM MATERIALS

Questions for Class Discussion

1. In general, what is a nontaxable exchange? Are nontaxable exchanges ever taxed? If so, how?

2. Distinguish between

   (a) a nontaxable exchange and a tax-free transaction.

   (b) a nontaxable exchange and a taxable transaction.

3. Why would a taxpayer want to avoid like-kind exchange treatment?

4. What is boot and how does it affect the recognition of gain or loss on a like-kind exchange when received by the taxpayer? When boot is given?

5. In a like-kind exchange, the basis of the property received is the same as the adjusted basis of the property transferred. If boot is received, what effect does the boot have on the basis of the like-kind property received? If boot is given, what effect does the boot have on the basis of the like-kind property received?

6. Discuss the relationship between the recovery of capital doctrine and the rules for the basis of property received and the recognition of gain (loss) in like-kind exchanges.

7. Can inventory ever qualify for like-kind exchange treatment? Why? For § 1033 involuntary conversion treatment?

8. Can the exchange of property held for productive use in a trade or business for investment property qualify for like-kind exchange treatment?

9. What is the holding period of like-kind property received in a like-kind exchange? For boot received? Why?

10. In connection with like-kind exchanges discuss each of the following:

    (a) Realized gain.

    (b) Realized loss.

    (c) Recognized gain.

    (d) Recognized loss.

    (e) Postponed gain.

    (f) Postponed loss.

    (g) Basis of like-kind property received.

    (h) Basis of boot received.

11. What are the rules for determining nonrecognition of gain from an involuntary conversion under § 1033? Is it elective?

12. What constitutes an involuntary conversion?

13. What are severance damages and when are they included in determining nonrecognition of gain from an involuntary conversion?

14. Explain the differences between the two tests that are usually applicable for replacement property in involuntary conversions. Under what circumstance is a third test applicable rather than either of these two?

15. How long does a taxpayer have to replace involuntarily converted property and still qualify for nonrecognition of gain under § 1033?

16. When does the holding period begin in an involuntary conversion for which the similar property rule is applicable? The like-kind property rule?

17. Taxpayer's warehouse is destroyed by fire. Discuss the different tax options available to the taxpayer if he has a realized gain. If he has a realized loss.

18. When a residence is involuntarily converted and a gain results, under what conditions can either § 1033 or § 1034 be applied to postpone recognition of the gain? How is § 1034 applied? Is there any significant difference between applying § 1033 and applying § 1034?

19. How are corrections made when a taxpayer elects to postpone gain and then does not reinvest within the time limits or does not reinvest a sufficient amount? How is postponement accomplished if reinvestment is made but postponement was not elected in the return for the taxable year in which gain was realized?

20. Discuss the justification for nonrecognition of gain on the sale or exchange of a principal residence. Disallowance of loss.

21. Discuss all of the requirements for the replacement period of both purchased and constructed residences. Are there any exceptions?

22. Extensions beyond the two-year replacement period are not granted by the IRS for principal residences. Yet extensions are granted by the IRS in connection with § 1033 involuntary conversions. What is the justification for this difference in tax treatment?

23. What is meant by principal residence in the sale or exchange of a residence?

24. What is adjusted sales price? What are fixing-up expenses? Selling expenses?

25. If the taxpayer elects to deduct selling expenses on the sale of his or her principal residence as indirect moving expenses, what effect does this election have on the realized and recognized gain or loss on the sale of the residence?

26. Discuss fixing-up expenses in relation to:

    (a) Postponed gain.

    (b) Realized gain.

    (c) Basis of new residence.

    (d) Date of contract to sell.

    (e) Date of sale.

27. Explain how the following are determined on the sale or exchange of a residence:

    (a) Realized gain.

    (b) Recognized gain.

    (c) Postponed gain.

    (d) Basis of new residence.

28. Discuss the basis calculation formula as it applies to a new residence if

(a) Realized gain is postponed.

(b) Realized loss is disallowed.

(c) Realized gain is recognized because the new residence is not acquired within the two-year time period from the sale of the old residence.

29. What are the requirements for the statute of limitations to begin running on the sale or exchange of a residence?

30. What does the § 121 exclusion cover? Is it elective? Does the old residence have to be replaced?

31. Why was § 121 enacted?

32. How many times can § 121 exclusion treatment be elected by a taxpayer? If the taxpayer is filing a joint return with his or her spouse, do both taxpayers have to meet the age requirement?

33. Taxpayer converts her principal residence to rental property at the beginning of 19X3 and sells the property on the last day of 19X4. Under what circumstances can the taxpayer qualify for the § 121 exclusion?

34. How does the statute of limitations apply to the § 121 exclusion?

35. Can any other provision or provisions be applied to any remaining gain which is not excluded under § 121?

36. How do fixing-up expenses affect the application of the § 121 exclusion?

37. Distinguish between the effect of the § 121 exclusion and the § 1034 postponement on the basis of a replacement residence.

Problems

38. Which of the following qualify as like-kind exchanges under § 1031?

    (a) Improved for unimproved real estate.

    (b) Crane (used in business) for inventory.

    (c) Rental house for truck (used in business).

    (d) Business equipment for securities.

    (e) Delicatessen for bakery (both used for business).

    (f) Personal residence for apartment building (held for investment).

    (g) Rental house for land (both held for investment).

39. What is the basis of the new property in each of the following exchanges?

    (a) Apartment building held for investment (adjusted basis $160,000) for lake-front property held for investment (fair market value $160,000).

    (b) Barber shop (adjusted basis $30,000) for grocery store (fair market value $24,000), both held for business use.

    (c) Drug store (adjusted basis $30,000) for bulldozer (fair market value $20,000), both held for business use.

    (d) IBM common stock (adjusted basis $2,500) for shoe shine stand used in business (fair market value $5,000).

    (e) Rental house (adjusted basis $20,000) for land held for investment (fair market value $22,500).

40. F buys a warehouse with a 30-year life for $90,000 (ignore land) in January 19X2. The warehouse is not ACRS recovery property. Its estimated salvage value is zero, and F uses the straight line method of depreciation. She exchanges the warehouse at the beginning of 19X6 for an office building, to be used in a business, which has a fair market value of $84,000. The newly acquired office building is depreciated at the rate of $3,000 a year. At the beginning of 19X8, F sells the office building for $75,000. What is the realized, recognized, and postponed gain (loss) and the new basis for each of these transactions?

41. Determine the realized, recognized, and postponed gain (or loss) and the new basis for each of the following like-kind exchanges:

	Adjusted Basis of Old Asset	Boot Given	Fair Market Value of New Asset	Boot Received
(a)	$ 7,000	–0–	$ 4,000	$ 4,000
(b)	4,000	2,000	5,000	–0–
(c)	3,000	7,000	8,000	500
(d)	8,000	–0–	10,000	–0–
(e)	10,000	–0–	11,000	1,000
(f)	10,000	–0–	9,000	–0–

42. B received a truck (used in business) with a six-year useful life and a fair market value of $12,000 in a like-kind exchange in January 19X1. He has a postponed loss of $3,000. At the beginning of 19X4, he exchanges it for another truck to be used in his business with a three-year useful life and a fair market value of $6,000. After two years, he sells the second truck for $2,000. What is the realized, recognized, and postponed gain (loss) and the new basis for each transaction? Assume straight-line depreciation and no salvage value for both trucks.

43. K owns an apartment house which has an adjusted basis of $700,000 but which is subject to a mortgage of $210,000. On September 1, 19X4, she transfers the apartment house to D. K receives from D $70,000 in cash and an office building with a fair market value at the time of the exchange of $840,000. D assumes the $210,000 mortgage on the apartment house.

    (a) What is K's realized gain or loss?

    (b) Her recognized gain or loss?

    (c) The basis of the newly acquired office building?

44. G exchanges real estate held for investment plus stock for real estate to be held for investment. The stock transferred has an adjusted basis of $5,000 and a fair market value of $2,500. The real estate transferred has an adjusted basis of $12,500 and a fair market value of $13,750. The real estate acquired has a fair market value of $16,250.

    (a) What is G's realized gain or loss?

    (b) His recognized gain or loss?

    (c) The basis of the newly acquired real estate?

45. H exchanges a machine (adjusted basis of $32,000 and fair market value of $40,000) and undeveloped land held for investment (adjusted basis of $50,000 and fair market value of $200,000) for land worth $180,000 to be

used in her business. The undeveloped land has a mortgage of $60,000 on it that the other party to the exchange assumes.

(a) What is H's realized gain or loss?

(b) Her recognized gain or loss?

(c) The basis of the newly acquired real estate?

46. Do the following qualify for involuntary conversion treatment?

(a) Purchase of a sporting goods store as a replacement for a bookstore (used in business) which was destroyed by fire.

(b) Sale of a home because a neighbor converted his residence into a nightclub.

(c) Purchase of an airplane to replace a shrimp boat (used in business) which was wrecked by a hurricane.

(d) Taxpayer's residence destroyed by a tornado.

(e) Purchase of an apartment building to replace a rental house by an investor. The rental house was destroyed by flood.

47. What is the *maximum* postponed gain (loss) and the basis for the replacement property for the following involuntary conversions:

Property	Type of Conversion	Amount Realized	Adjusted Basis	Amount Reinvested
(a) Drugstore (business)	condemned	$ 160,000	$ 120,000	$ 100,000
(b) Apartments (investment)	casualty	100,000	120,000	200,000
(c) Grocery store (business)	casualty	400,000	300,000	350,000
(d) Residence (personal)	casualty	16,000	18,000	17,000
(e) Vacant lot (investment)	condemned	240,000	160,000	240,000
(f) Residence (personal)	casualty	20,000	18,000	19,000
(g) Residence (personal)	condemned	18,000	20,000	26,000
(h) Apartments (investment)	condemned	150,000	100,000	200,000

48. A taxpayer realizes $50,000 from the involuntary conversion of a factory. The adjusted basis of the factory was $25,000, and in the same year he spends $40,000 for a new factory.

(a) What is the realized gain or loss?

(b) What is the recognized gain or loss?

(c) What is the basis of the new factory?

(d) If taxpayer does not elect nonrecognition, what is the recognized gain and the basis of the new factory?

49. For each of the following, indicate the earliest and latest dates that qualifying replacement property can be acquired under § 1033.

(a) Business property that is stolen or destroyed.

(b) Personal use property that is stolen or destroyed.

(c) Business property that is condemned.

(d) Personal use property that is condemned.

50. Which of the following are selling expenses, fixing-up expenses, or neither?

(a) New swimming pool.

(b) Legal fees to clear title to residence.

(c) Painting outside of residence.

(d) Repair of leaky plumbing.

(e) New roof.

(f) Advertising the residence for sale.

(g) Painting living and dining rooms.

(h) Broker commissions.

51. On January 1, 19X4, the taxpayer, a 48-year-old widow, buys a new residence for $148,000. On March 1, 19X4, she sells for an adjusted sales price of $150,000 her old residence, which has an adjusted basis to her of $50,000 (no fixing-up expenses are involved, so that $150,000 is the amount realized as well as the adjusted sales price). Between April 1 and April 15 an addition to the new house is constructed at a cost of $5,000. Between May 1 and May 15 a garage is added at a cost of $2,000.

(a) What is taxpayer's realized gain or loss?

(b) The recognized gain or loss?

(c) The basis of the residence?

52. What are the realized, recognized, and postponed gain (loss), the new basis, and the adjusted sales price for each of the following? Assume that none of the taxpayers are 55 years of age or older.

(a) R sells her residence for $90,000. The adjusted basis was $55,000. The selling expenses were $5,000. The fixing-up expenses were $3,000. She did not reinvest in a new residence.

(b) D sells his residence for $170,000. The adjusted basis was $120,000. The selling expenses were $4,000. The fixing-up expenses were $6,000. D reinvested $160,000 in a new personal residence.

(c) M sells her residence for $65,000. It had an adjusted basis of $35,000. The selling expenses were $1,000. The fixing-up expenses were $2,000. She reinvested $40,000.

(d) B sells his residence for $70,000. It has an adjusted basis of $65,000. The selling expenses were $6,000. He reinvested $80,000.

(e) C sells his residence for $100,000 and his mortgage was assumed by the buyer. The adjusted basis was $80,000; the mortgage, $50,000. The selling expenses were $4,000. The fixing-up expenses were $2,000. He reinvested $120,000.

53. J, age 40, sold his residence that he had owned and occupied for 12 years. His original cost was $200,000. Ten percent of the house has been used during the past four years as a qualifying home office under § 280A. J deducted $4,000 of depreciation associated with the portion of the house used as a home office. The selling price was $300,000, and the selling expenses were $18,000. J purchases a new residence costing $325,000 during the statutory two-year period.

(a) What is J's realized gain or loss?

(b) His recognized gain or loss?

(c) The basis of the new residence?

54. L sold his residence which he had owned and occupied for 20 years. The adjusted basis is $36,000, and the selling price was $250,000. The selling expenses were $4,000, and the fixing-up expenses were $8,000. He reinvested $60,000 in a new residence. L is 57 years old. What are the realized, recognized, and postponed gain (loss), the new basis, and the adjusted sales price if his objective is to minimize the recognized gain?

55. Mr. T, age 57, is the sole owner of his principal residence. He has owned and occupied it for 10 years. Mrs. T, his spouse, refuses to join with him in making the § 121 election.

   (a) Can Mr. T elect the § 121 exclusion if he and Mrs. T file a joint return? If so, what is the available amount of the exclusion?

   (b) Can Mr. T elect the § 121 exclusion if he files a separate return? If so, what is the available amount of the exclusion?

   (c) If Mrs. T joins with Mr. T in making the election, what is the available amount of the exclusion on a joint return? On a separate return?

Cumulative Problems

56. G, age 41, is single and has no dependents. She is a self-employed operator of a sole proprietorship. During 1984, gross income from her business was $120,000 and business expenses were $65,000. In addition, she had several property transactions related to her business. These transactions are not reflected in the above income and expense figures.

   (a) Cash received on trade of a parcel of land on the outskirts of town (held for two years as a site for a new warehouse) for a lot near G's store. G intends to build a new warehouse on the lot. The old parcel has a fair market value of $28,000 and adjusted basis of $25,000. The fair market value of the new lot was $24,000. $ 4,000

   (b) Condemnation award from state for an acre of unimproved land (used for parking delivery vans) adjacent to the store (adjusted basis of the land was $12,000).   30,000

   (c) Cost of an acre of unimproved land across the street from the store (the land is to be used for parking delivery vans). G's personal transactions for 1984 are these: 25,000

   (d) Cash received on exchange of 50 shares of X Corporation stock (adjusted basis of $20 a share, fair market value of $50 a share) for 50 shares of Y Corporation stock (fair market value of $40 a share). X Corporation and Y Corporation are not related, and G had held the X Corporation stock for two years.   500

   (e) Amount realized on the sale of a condominium G used as her personal residence. The condominium, which was built in 1975, was acquired in 1980 as a replacement for the house in which she formerly resided. She paid $60,000 for the condominium, and the amount realized for the house she sold was $80,000 (no fixing-up expenses and adjusted basis was $50,000). G is moving into an apartment and does not intend to replace the condominium.   65,000

   (f) Cost of insulation installed in the condominium six months before it was sold. In 1979, G spent $1,300 to insulate the house she had owned prior to acquiring the condominium.   1,600

(g) Loss of amount G loaned to a friend in 1980 (the friend declared bankruptcy in 1984).   3,000
(h) G's interest income on personal savings accounts.   500
(i) Itemized deductions in 1984.   3,900
(j) Estimated Federal income tax payments.   19,000

Compute G's lowest net tax payable (or refund due) for 1984, assuming G makes any available election(s) which will reduce the tax. [Any gain recognized from items (a), (b), or (c) is § 1231 gain, which is discussed in Chapter 17, and this gain is to be treated as long-term capital gain.]

57. T is single, age 65, and has no dependents. He retired on June 30, 1984 (his 65th birthday). He had earned $115,000 in 1984 prior to retirement. In July he began receiving a retirement annuity of $18,000 per month. His life expectancy was 15 years from the annuity starting date, and his investment in the contract was $600,000. T is a 10-percent shareholder in an S corporation. The corporation, which is a calendar year taxpayer, made no distributions during 1984, although it had taxable income of $100,000.

Before retirement T incurred the following expenses in connection with his job: transportation, $2,500; meals and lodging while away from home overnight, $2,000; and entertainment, $1,500. T received an expense allowance, for which he accounted to his employer, of $5,000.

In November, T sold his home in Minnesota and moved to Florida where he bought a new home. The amount realized (and adjusted sales price) for the old home was $205,000. T had acquired the home 20 years earlier for $45,000 and added an extra room at a cost of $5,000 10 years earlier. He paid $60,000 for a small condominium in Florida. He asks you to report the transaction using any provisions which will minimize his tax.

On May 15, T exercised an incentive stock option at a cost of $45,000. The fair market value of the stock at the date of exercise was $65,000.

T incurred the following expenses on his move from Minnesota to Florida: transportation in moving household goods and personal effects, $9,500; travel, meals, and lodging expenses in moving from former to new residence, $1,100; temporary living expenses for 20 days while waiting for furniture to arrive, $2,000; and expenses incurred in selling his old residence, $2,800.

Itemized deductions, not counting any potential deductions above, were $15,600.

Compute T's lowest legal tax liability, before prepayments or credits, for 1984.

Tax Form Problem

58. Ted Black, age 64, sold his personal residence on October 16, 1983, for $180,000. To make the house more attractive to buyers, he incurred fixing-up expenses of $1,000 on September 12, 1983. He paid a real estate broker's commission of $9,000 on the sale. Ted had paid $60,000 for his home and had lived in it for the past eight years. In December, he bought a much smaller home for $55,000. Ted elects to exclude gain under § 121. Compute the gain recognized (if any) on the sale of Ted's old residence and determine the basis of his new residence. Use Form 2119 for your computations.

Research Problems

59. Ms. G had owned and used her house as her principal residence since 1946. However, 20% of the house had been used for business purposes as an office. On January 1, 1984, when Ms. G was over 55, she retired and moved to North Carolina. Ms. G rented her former residence for six months before its sale, since no qualified buyer could be found. She purchased a new residence in North Carolina at a price which exceeded the adjusted sales price of the former residence.

    (a) What treatment should be given to the portion of the former residence used for business? Rental property?

    (b) May Ms. G make an election under § 121(a)?

    (c) Are the nonrecognition of gain provisions of § 1034 available to Ms. G?

    Partial list of research aids:

    Robert G. Clapham, 63 T.C. 505 (1975).

60. F sold his personal residence in Oregon for $70,000 on December 31, 19X3. The following additional data are available:

Selling expenses	$ 10,000
Moving expenses (part of $10,000 selling expenses)	4,000
Cost basis	40,000
Depreciation from 10% business use	3,000

    The reason F sold his home in Oregon was to enable him and his wife to acquire a new residence in Alaska, which they did on April 1, 19X3. The home was badly in need of repair. F's wife planned to redecorate the house, and F therefore purchased a home for $40,000 which F's wife could remodel. Comparable houses in the neighborhood not in need of repair were selling for $70,000. During the rest of 19X3, Mr. and Mrs. F spent the following amounts on remodeling and redecorating:

Carpeting	$ 4,000
Addition to family room	3,000
Remodel kitchen and bathrooms	3,000
Custom drapes	2,000
New fence	2,000
New roof	4,000
Wallpaper, paint, and repairs	5,000
Total expenditures	$ 23,000

    In filing his tax return, F claims that the new residence cost $40,000 plus $23,000 of expenditures which should be capitalized, or $63,000. Therefore, F deferred the entire amount of gain realized on the Oregon home.

    The realized and recognized gain was calculated by F as follows:

Selling price	$ 70,000
Less: Selling expenses	(10,000)
Adjusted sales price	60,000
Less: Adjusted basis	(37,000)
	$ 23,000
Cost of new residence (appraised value)	63,000
Adjusted sales price	60,000
Gain recognized	$ –0–

An IRS agent now contends that the business portion of the former residence does not qualify for nonrecognition under § 1034. Further, he contends that the $23,000 of expenditures should not be capitalized. Thus, the full amount of the realized gain should have been recognized in 19X3.

(a) Was F entitled to capitalize the $23,000 of expenditures on the new residence?

(b) Are the selling expenses deductible in arriving at the adjusted sales price?

(c) Is § 1034 nonrecognition of gain applicable to the business portion of the former residence?

61. T exchanged a partnership interest in an unencumbered building for a partnership interest in unimproved land which was subject to a 99-year lease.

(a) Does the exchange qualify as a like-kind exchange under § 1031(a)?

(b) Would the answer be any different if the building were held primarily for resale? If so, how?

Partial list of research aids:

Carl E. Koch, 71 T.C. 54 (1978).

Gulfstream Land and Development Corporation, 71 T.C. 587 (1979).

62. T owned property which had an adjusted basis of $125,000 of which $100,000 was allocated to the land and $25,000 to the building. The property was condemned by the state, and T received a $275,000 condemnation award. T spent $400,000 for new property, of which $100,000 was allocable to the land and $300,000 to the building. What is the basis of the replacement property, and how is it allocated to the land and the building?

Partial list of research aids:

Reg. § 1.1033(c)–1(a)

Rev.Rul. 73–18, 1973–1 C.B. 368.

63. D held a building which she transferred to a revocable trust. Prior to her death, the building was condemned by a public authority. Using the proceeds of the condemnation award and after D's death, the trustee of the trust replaced the property.

(a) Can the replacement by the trustee qualify the condemnation for nonrecognition of gain treatment under § 1033(a)?

    (b) Would the replacement qualify under § 1033(a) if the trustee replaced the building by acquiring control of a newly formed corporation that subsequently purchased the replacement property?

Partial list of research aids:

Estate of Harry A. Gregg, 69 T.C. 468 (1977).

Rev.Rul. 77–422, 1977–2 C.B. 307.

64.   N exchanged currency (Swiss francs) having a dollar value of $25,000 for numismatic coins (United States Double Eagle gold coins) having a face value of $5,000 and a fair market value of $25,000.

    (a) Are the gold coins considered "money" or "property" under § 1001(b), and why does the distinction make any difference?

    (b) If the gold coins are "property," does the exchange of currency for numismatic coins constitute a nontaxable like-kind exchange?

Partial list of research aids:

§ 1031(a)

California Federal Life Insurance Co., 76 T.C. 107 (1981).

Chapter 16

Property Transactions: Capital Gains and Losses

GENERAL CONSIDERATIONS

RATIONALE FOR FAVORABLE CAPITAL GAIN TREATMENT

Given that a gain or loss is recognized, is it capital or ordinary? The capital gain provisions are intended to encourage the formation of private capital investment and to encourage risk taking by investors. In addition, preferential capital gain treatment is, in part, a recognition that appreciation in value over a long period should not be taxed in full in the year of realization. Favorable capital gain rates, in effect, offset the adverse "bunching effect" caused by recognition of all the gain in one year.[1]

GENERAL SCHEME OF TAXATION

Recognized gains and losses must be properly classified. Proper classification depends upon the tax status of the property, the manner of the property's disposition, and the holding period of the property. The asset may have capital asset, § 1231 asset, or ordinary asset status. The manner of property disposition may be by sale, exchange, casualty, theft, or condemnation. The two important holding periods are one year or less (short-term) and more than one year (long-term).

   The major focus of this chapter is capital gains and losses. Such

---

1. Refer to the discussion under "Mitigating the Effect of the Annual Accounting Period Concept" in Chapter 2.

gains and losses usually result from the sale, exchange, or condemnation of a capital asset. Capital gains and losses may also result (in certain circumstances) from the sale, exchange, or condemnation of § 1231 assets or from casualty (or theft) dispositions of capital assets or § 1231 assets. Except in very limited circumstances, capital gains and losses cannot result from the disposition of ordinary assets.

All taxpayers net their capital gains and losses. Short-term gains and losses (if any) are netted against one another, and long-term gains and losses (if any) are netted against one another. The results will be net short-term gain or loss and net long-term gain or loss. If these two net positions are of opposite sign (one is a gain and one is a loss), they may be netted against one another. Six possibilities exist for the result after all possible netting has been completed. Three of these final results are gains, and three are losses. One possible result is a long-term capital gain (LTCG). This is defined as the "net capital gain."[2] Net capital gains of noncorporate taxpayers are subject to a 60 percent capital gain deduction for gains recognized. A second possibility is a net short-term capital gain (STCG), which is an ordinary gain and is taxable in full and subject to the taxpayer's regular tax rates. Third, the netting may result in both LTCG and STCG. Each part of this result is treated separately; i. e., the LTCG is eligible for the 60 percent capital gain deduction and the STCG is taxed as ordinary income. The preferential treatment given LTCGs is discussed in more detail later in this chapter.

The last three results of the capital gain and loss netting process are losses. Thus, a fourth possibility is a net long-term capital loss (LTCL). A fifth result is a net short-term capital loss (STCL). Finally, a sixth possibility includes both a net LTCL and a net STCL. Neither LTCLs nor STCLs are treated as ordinary losses. Treatment as an ordinary loss generally is preferable to capital loss treatment, since ordinary losses are deductible in full while the deductibility of capital losses is subject to certain limitations. An individual taxpayer may deduct a maximum of $3,000 of capital losses for a taxable year.[3] Net STCLs are preferable to net LTCLs, because the latter are deductible to the extent of only fifty cents on the dollar (e. g., a $1,000 LTCL would result in a $500 deduction). The capital loss rules are discussed in more detail later in this chapter.

Before all the netting of capital gains and losses just discussed can occur, the amount of the capital gains and losses must be determined. Chapter 15 discussed how to compute these amounts. It is now necessary to determine what capital assets are.

---

2. § 1222(11).
3. § 1211(b).

WHAT IS A CAPITAL ASSET?

DEFINITION OF A CAPITAL ASSET

Capital assets are not directly defined in the Code. Rather, § 1221 defines a capital asset as property held by the taxpayer (whether or not connected with his or her trade or business), but *not* including:

—Stock in trade, inventory, or property held primarily for sale to customers in the ordinary course of a trade or business. The Supreme Court, in *Malat v. Riddell,* defined primarily as meaning "of first importance" or "principally."[4]

—Accounts or notes receivable acquired in the ordinary course of a trade or business for services rendered or from the sale of inventory.

—Depreciable property or real estate used in a trade or business.

—Certain copyrights, literary, musical, or artistic compositions, letters or memorandums, or similar property, with the following exceptions. (a) These assets are not capital assets if they are held by a taxpayer whose efforts created the property. (b) A letter, memorandum, or similar property is not a capital asset if it is held by a taxpayer for whom it was produced. (c) In addition, the asset is not a capital asset when the basis of such property is determined, for purposes of determining gain from a sale or exchange, in whole or part by reference to the basis of such property in the hands of a taxpayer described in (a) or (b).

—Certain U. S. government publications. U. S. publications that are not capital assets are those (a) received by a taxpayer from the U. S. government other than by purchase at the price at which they are offered for sale to the public or (b) held by a taxpayer whose basis is determined by reference to a taxpayer described in (a).

The Code defines what is not a capital asset. From the preceding list, it is apparent that inventory, accounts and notes receivable, and most fixed assets of a business are not capital assets. A brief discussion follows to provide further detail on each part of the capital asset definition.

Inventory. What constitutes inventory is determined by the taxpayer's business.

Example 1. T Company buys and sells used cars. T's cars would be inventory. T's gains from sale of the cars would be ordinary income.

---

4.   66–1 USTC ¶ 9317, 17 AFTR2d 604, 86 S.Ct. 1030 (USSC, 1966).

Accounts and Notes Receivable. Usually no gain or loss results from the collection of a business receivable of an accrual taxpayer, because the basis is equal to the amount collected. However, if such a taxpayer sells his or her receivables, an ordinary gain or loss may result. A cash basis taxpayer usually does not have a basis for his or her receivables. Thus, a gain will result from the sale of the receivables.

> **Example 2.** T Company has accounts receivable of $100,000. Because it needs working capital, the receivables are sold for $83,000 to a financial institution. T Company would have a $17,000 ordinary loss if it was an accrual basis taxpayer (it would have earlier recorded $100,000 of revenue when the receivable was established). T Company would have $83,000 of ordinary income if it was a cash basis taxpayer, because it would not have recorded any revenue earlier and because the receivable has no tax basis.

Business Fixed Assets. Depreciable property and real estate used by a business are not capital assets. The Code has a very complex set of rules pertaining to such property. The discussion of real property subdivided for sale later in this chapter and most of Chapter 17 discuss those rules.

Copyrights and Creative Works. Generally, the person whose efforts led to the copyright or creative work has an ordinary asset, not a capital asset. Also, the person for whom such works were created or who received such works from the creator by gift has an ordinary asset.

> **Example 3.** T is a part-time music composer. One of her songs was purchased by a music publisher for $5,000. T would have a $5,000 ordinary gain from the sale of an ordinary asset.

> **Example 4.** T gives a song she composed to her son. The son sells the song to a music publisher for $5,000. The son has $5,000 ordinary gain from the sale of an ordinary asset.

> **Example 5.** T received a letter from the President of the United States in 1944. In the current year, T sells the letter to a collector for $300. T has a $300 ordinary gain from the sale of an ordinary asset (because the letter was created for T).

(Patents are subject to special statutory rules discussed later in the chapter.)

Certain U.S. Government Publications. U.S. government publications received from the U.S. government (or its agencies) for a reduced price are not capital assets. The reason for this is to prevent such assets from later being donated to charity and resulting in a charitable contribution equal to the full fair market value of the publications. (For a fuller explanation of charitable contributions of property, refer to Chapter 11.)

As a result of the above discussion, it should be apparent that the principal capital assets held by an individual taxpayer include personal use (as opposed to business) assets, such as a personal residence or an automobile, and assets held for investment purposes (e. g., land and corporate stock). Of course, losses from the sale or exchange of a taxpayer's personal use assets (as opposed to business or investment assets) are not recognized; therefore, their classification as capital assets is irrelevant for capital loss purposes.

EFFECT OF JUDICIAL ACTION

Court decisions are especially important in the capital gain and loss area because the Code's definition of a capital asset is very broad and it does not specifically define what constitutes a sale or exchange.

> **Example 6.** T Corporation, a large manufacturer of products made from corn, engaged in futures operations (i. e., contracts calling for delivery in the future) in corn in order to protect itself from a price rise and a short supply (its storage facilities were adequate for its production requirements for only a short period). As it turned out, some of the futures were not needed and were sold at a gain.

This example is based on a landmark Supreme Court case, *Corn Products Refining Co.*[5] The question was whether the corn futures were inventory or investment property. Section 1221(1) indicates that inventory is not a capital asset. If the corn futures were considered inventory, the gain from their sale would be ordinary gain rather than capital gain. The Court held that the sales were an integral part of the company's business and the futures were not held for investment; therefore, the gain was an ordinary gain.

The above case points out the need to look beyond the broad definition of a capital asset in the Code. The crux of the problem of determining whether an asset is capital or not usually is whether it is held for investment purposes or for business purposes.[6] Congress did not intend to exempt profits from the ordinary operations of a business from ordinary income treatment.

---

5.   55–2 USTC ¶ 9746, 47 AFTR 1789, 76 S.Ct. 20 (USSC, 1955).
6.   If stock is purchased with a "substantial" investment purpose, however, it will be considered to be a capital asset even though the business motive also was "substantial" and "predominated." *W. W. Windle Co.*, 65 T.C. 694 (1976) and Rev.Rul. 78–94, 1978–1 C.B. 58.

STATUTORY EXPANSIONS

In many cases Congress has felt it necessary to expand the general definition of a capital asset as contained in § 1221.

Dealers in Securities. As a general rule, securities held by a dealer are considered to be inventory and are not, therefore, subject to capital gain or loss treatment. A dealer in securities is a merchant (e. g., a brokerage firm) that regularly engages in the purchase and resale of securities to customers. The dealer must identify any securities being held for investment. Prior to August 13, 1981, if a dealer clearly identified certain securities as held for investment purposes within 30 days after their acquisition, and they were not held at any time after such identification primarily for sale to customers in the ordinary course of business, gain from their sale was capital gain.[7] Generally, since August 13, 1981, for tax years ending after August 12, 1981, if a dealer clearly identifies certain securities as held for investment purposes by the close of business on the date of their acquisition, gain from their sale will be capital gain. Losses are capital losses if at any time the securities have been clearly identified by the dealer as held for investment.

Real Property Subdivided for Sale. Substantial development activities relative to real property may result in the owner's being considered a dealer for tax purposes. Thus, income from the sale of real estate property lots is treated as the sale of inventory (ordinary income) if the owner is considered to be a dealer. Section 1237 provides relief for investors in real estate who engage in limited development activities by allowing capital gain treatment if the following requirements are met:

—The taxpayer cannot be a corporation.

—The taxpayer cannot be a real estate dealer.

—No substantial improvements can be made to the lots sold. Substantial generally means more than a 10 percent increase in the value of a lot. Shopping centers and other commercial or residential buildings are considered substantial, while filling, draining, leveling, and clearing operations are not.[8]

—The taxpayer must hold the lots sold for at least five years, except for inherited property. The substantial improvements test is less stringent if the property is held at least 10 years.

If the above requirements are met, all gain is capital gain until the tax year in which the taxpayer sells the sixth lot. Starting in the tax year that the sixth lot is sold, the taxpayer's gains will be ordinary income to the extent of five percent of the selling price, but all selling

---

7.   § 1236(a) and Reg. § 1.1236–1(a).
8.   Reg. § 1.1237–1(c)(4).

expenses offset the five percent of selling price ordinary income portion of the gain. Since many real estate commissions are at least five percent of selling price, the result often is that none of the gain is ordinary income. Also, in counting the number of lots sold, sales of contiguous lots to a single buyer in a single sale count as the sale of one lot.

A loss from the sale of subdivided real property is an ordinary loss unless the property qualifies as a capital asset under § 1221.[9] A gain which does not qualify under § 1237 may qualify as a capital gain under § 1221 or § 1231 if the requirements of those sections are satisfied. The following example illustrates the application of § 1237.

> **Example 7.** T owns a large tract of land and subdivides it for sale. Assume T meets all the requirements of § 1237 and sells the first 10 lots to 10 different buyers in 19X4 for $10,000 each. T's basis of each lot sold is $3,000 and he incurs total selling expenses of $4,000 on the sales. T's gain is computed as follows:

Selling price (10 × $10,000)		$ 100,000	
Basis (10 × $3,000)		30,000	
Excess over basis		$ 70,000	
Five percent of selling price	$ 5,000		
Selling expenses	(4,000)		
Amount of ordinary income			$ 1,000
Five percent of selling price	$ 5,000		
Excess of expenses over five percent of selling price	–0–	(5,000)	
Capital gain			65,000
Total gain ($70,000 – $4,000 selling expenses)			$ 66,000

Lump-sum Distributions. Section 402(a)(2) provides that lump-sum distributions from qualified pension and profit sharing plans are treated as long-term capital gain to the extent that the distribution exceeds the taxpayer's contributions to the plan.[10] However, the amount treated as capital gain is limited to the portion of the excess which is attributable to participation in the plan prior to January 1, 1974. The amount attributable to participation after December 31, 1973, is ordinary income. A lump-sum distribution is defined generally as a distribution of the employee's entire balance within one taxable year following any of the following: death or disability of the employee, age 59½, or separation from service with the employer. The amount treated as ordinary income is subject to a special elective 10-year forward averaging procedure which can somewhat lighten the burden of this ordinary income treatment. See Chapter 19 for a further discussion of lump-sum distributions.

---

9. Reg. § 1.1237–1(a)(4)(i).
10. § 402(a)(2) and (e)(4)(D).

Nonbusiness Bad Debts. As discussed in Chapter 8, nonbusiness bad debts are treated as short-term capital losses in the taxable year in which they become completely worthless, regardless of how long the debt has been outstanding.[11] This is an excellent example of statutory expansion in the capital gain and loss area. Determining whether the property involved is a capital asset or not, whether a sale or exchange has taken place, and the holding period involved is not a problem, because the Code automatically provides that nonbusiness bad debts are, in all cases, short-term capital losses.

SALE OR EXCHANGE

Recognition of capital gain or loss requires a sale or exchange of a capital asset. Section 1222 uses the term "sale or exchange" but does not define it. Generally, a sale involves the receipt of money or the assumption of liabilities for property, and an exchange involves the transfer of property for other property. Thus, an involuntary conversion (casualty, theft, or condemnation) is not a sale or exchange. In several situations, the determination of whether a sale or exchange has taken place has been clarified by the enactment of Code sections which specifically provide for sale or exchange treatment.

Recognized gains or losses from the cancellation, lapse, expiration, or any other termination of a right or obligation with respect to personal property (other than stock) which is or would be a capital asset in the hands of the taxpayer are capital gains or losses. This provision applies to property acquired and positions established after June 23, 1981, and taxable years ending after June 23, 1981.[12] See the discussion under Options later in this chapter for more details.

WORTHLESS SECURITIES

Section 165(g)(1) provides that "if any security which is a capital asset becomes worthless during the taxable year, the loss resulting therefrom shall . . . be treated as a loss from the sale or exchange, on the last day of the taxable year, of a capital asset." For a more detailed discussion of worthless securities, refer to Chapter 8.

SPECIAL RULE—RETIREMENT OF CORPORATE OBLIGATIONS

When a debt obligation has a tax basis that is more or less than its redemption value, a gain or loss may result from the collection of the redemption value. Under the general rule, the collection of a debt obligation does not constitute a sale or exchange. Therefore, any gain or loss on the collection of a note or other obligation cannot be capital

---

11. § 166(d)(1)(B) and Reg. § 1.166–5(a)(2).
12. § 1234A.

gain or loss, since no sale or exchange has taken place. Section 1232 provides an exception for corporate and certain government obligations, the collection of which is considered to be an exchange and is therefore usually subject to capital gain or loss treatment.[13]

Example 8. T acquires XYZ Corporation bonds at $980 in the open market. If the bonds are held to maturity, the $20 difference between T's collection of the $1,000 maturity value and T's cost of $980 is treated as capital gain because of § 1232. If the obligation were owed to T by an individual instead of by a corporation, T's $20 gain would be ordinary, since there is no sale or exchange of the debt by T.

Original Issue Discount. Most new bond issues do not carry original issue discount, since the stated interest rate is set to make the market price on issue the same as the bond's face amount. In addition, even if the issue price is less than the face amount, the difference is not considered to be original issue discount (OID) if the difference is less than one-fourth of one percent of the redemption price at maturity multiplied by the number of years to maturity.

Example 9. X corporation issues 20-year bonds at 96% of the maturity price (face amount). There is no original issue discount, since the issue price (96%) is in excess of 95% of the maturity price [100% − (1/4% × 20 years = 95%). Therefore, an investor in X's bonds would not be required to amortize the 4% discount over the bond's life. If the bonds are held to maturity, the difference between the maturity price and the taxpayer's basis (cost) is granted capital gain treatment by § 1232.

In the case where OID does exist, it may or may not have to be amortized, depending upon the date the bond was issued. When the OID is amortized, the gain from sale or exchange of the bond is sometimes ordinary income to the extent of the remaining OID or the gain, whichever is smaller. Thus, if at the time of original issue there was an intention to call the obligations before maturity, the gain will be ordinary income to the extent of original issue discount not already included in the gross income of any holder.[14]

The law prior to TEFRA which still applies generally to corporate obligations issued after May 27, 1969, and before July 2, 1982, provided that the issuer of an OID bond must amortize the OID ratably over the life of the bond. Likewise, the holder of the bond spreads the OID ratably over the life of the bond, with corresponding adjustment to the basis of the bond.

For obligations issued after July 1, 1982, a new method of discount amortization applies. The discount amortization each period

---

13. § 1232(a)(1).
14. § 1232(a)(2)(A) and Reg. § 1.1232–3(a)(1)(i).

will be the increase in the value of the instrument. The new rules are in § 1232A and extend the OID requirements to noncorporate obligations such as U.S. government bonds. However, short-term government obligations, tax-exempt state or local government bonds, bonds issued by individuals, most insurance company bonds, and U.S. savings bonds are not subject to the OID rules.

The new OID amortization method reduces the income of the holder and the deduction of the issuer in the early life of the bond but increases both of them in the later years. Example 10 illustrates the ratable method of amortizing OID. Example 11 illustrates the value increase method of amortizing OID.

> **Example 10.** T acquires a $5,000, 6% corporate bond at issue on December 31, 1981, for $2,316. The bond issuer makes annual payments of interest, and the bond matures in five years. The OID is $2,684 ($5,000 − $2,316). Since the bond was issued before July 2, 1982, the old OID rules apply and the monthly amortization would be $44.73 ($2,684 ÷ 60 months) or $537 per year (rounded). The effects of the amortization on the issuer, holder, and tax basis of the bond are summarized below:

	Issuer			Holder			Holder's Tax Basis
Day	Interest Paid* +	OID Amort. =	Total Ded.	Interest Rec'd* +	OID Amort. =	Interest Income	$2,316
12/31/82	$ 300	$ 537	$ 837	$ 300	$ 537	$ 837	+ 537
12/31/83	300	537	837	300	537	837	+ 537
12/31/84	300	537	837	300	537	837	+ 537
12/31/85	300	537	837	300	537	837	+ 537
12/31/86	300	536	836	300	536	836	+ 536
Totals	$1,500	$2,684	$4,184	$1,500	$2,684	$4,184	$5,000

*$5,000 × 6%.

If T holds the bond to maturity, he will realize no gain or loss from redemption of the bond, because his basis for the bond equals the maturity price of $5,000.

> **Example 11.** The facts are the same as in Example 10, except that the bond is issued on December 31, 1982. The bond's yield to maturity would be 26.63%. (The bond is selling at a steep discount because of its high-risk and below-market interest rate.) Since the bond was issued after July 1, 1982, the yield to maturity rate (26.63%) is used to amortize the discount. That rate times the bond's tax basis yields the total interest. The total interest less the stated interest equals the OID amortization. The effects of the amortization on the issuer, holder, and tax basis of the bond are summarized below:

	Issuer			Holder			Holder's Tax Basis
Day	Interest Paid* +	OID Amort.**	Total Ded. −	Interest Rec'd* +	OID Amort.** =	Interest Income	$2,316
12/31/83	$ 300	$ 317	$ 617	$ 300	$ 317	$ 617	+ 317
12/31/84	300	401	701	300	401	701	+ 401
12/31/85	300	508	808	300	508	808	+ 508
12/31/86	300	643	943	300	643	943	+ 643
12/31/87	300	815	1,115	300	815	1,115	+ 815
Totals	$1,500	$2,684	$4,184	$1,500	$2,684	$4,184	$5,000

* $5,000 × 6%.

**(Tax basis of bond × yield to maturity) − stated interest amount = OID amortization. 1983: ($2,316 × 26.63%) − $300 = $317. 1984: [($2,316 + $317) × 26.63%] − $300 = $401. 1985: [($2,316 + $317 + $401) × 26.63%] − $300 = $508. 1986: [($2,316 + $317 + $401 + $508) × 26.63%] − $300 = $643. 1987: [($2,316 + $317 + $401 + $508 + $643) × 26.63%] − $300 = $815.

Once again, T realizes no gain upon redemption, since his tax basis equals the redemption price. The old and new OID rules yield the same total amount of interest income, but the allocation of that income between periods is substantially different.

Special rules apply to original issue discount corporate and government obligations issued before May 28, 1969. Since the holders of such securities are not required to include the amortized discount in income, the sale or exchange of such securities generally results in capital gain treatment. However, all or a portion of the OID may be treated as ordinary income, if (as noted previously) the bonds were issued with an intention to call them before maturity. If there were no such intention, there would be ordinary income from any remaining unamortized OID after imputing OID amortization using the ratable amortization approach.

Short-term Government Bonds. Before July 23, 1981, short-term taxable government bonds issued at a discount were not considered capital assets. The Economic Recovery Tax Act of 1981 provided changes with respect to these bonds:

—If the bonds are issued at a discount and are payable without interest in less than one year, they are capital assets.

—Any gain from the sale or exchange of these obligations is ordinary to the extent of the ratable share of the acquisition discount.

Any remaining gain is short-term capital gain.[15] Recognized losses from the sale or exchange of these obligations are short-term capital losses.

---

15. § 1232(a)(4).

OPTIONS

As a general rule, § 1234 provides that the sale or exchange of an option to buy or sell property results in capital gain or loss if the subject property is (or would be) a capital asset to the option holder.[16]

Failure to Exercise Options. If an option holder (grantee) fails to exercise the option, the lapse of the option is considered a sale or exchange on the option expiration date.[17] Thus, the loss is a capital loss if the property subject to the option is (or would be) a capital asset in the hands of the grantee.

The grantor of an option on stocks, securities, commodities, or commodity futures receives short-term capital gain treatment upon the expiration of the option. Options on property other than stocks, securities, commodities, or commodity futures result in ordinary income to the grantor when the option expires.[18] For example, an individual investor who owns certain stock (a capital asset) may sell a call option which entitles the buyer of the option to acquire the stock at a specified price that is higher than the value at the date the option is granted. The writer of the call receives a premium (e. g., 10 percent) for writing the option. If the price of the stock does not increase during the option period, the option will expire unexercised. Upon the expiration of the option, the grantor must recognize short-term capital gain. The provisions of § 1234 do not apply to options held for sale to customers (i. e., the inventory of a securities dealer).

Exercise of Options by Grantee. If the option is exercised, the amount paid for the option is added to the selling price of the property subject to the option. This increases the gain to the grantor upon the sale of the property. The gain is capital or ordinary depending on the nature of the property sold. The grantee, of course, adds the cost of the option to the basis of the property.

> **Example 12.** On September 1, 1976, X purchases 100 shares of Y Company stock for $5,000. On January 1, 1984, he writes a call option on the stock which gives the option holder the right to buy the stock for $6,000 during the following six-month period. X receives a call premium of $500 for writing the call.
>
> —If the call is exercised by the option holder on August 1, 1984, X has $1,500 ($6,000 + $500 − $5,000) of long-term capital gain from the sale of the stock.

---

16. § 1234(a) and Reg. § 1.1234–1(a)(1). See the Glossary of Tax Terms (Appendix C) for a definition of "stock options". Stock options are discussed in Chapter 19.
17. § 1234(b) and Reg. § 1.1234–1(b).
18. Options granted before September 2, 1976, required the grantor (seller) of the option to recognize ordinary income. Reg. § 1.1234–1(b) and Rev. Rul. 57–40, 1957–1 C.B. 266.

—Assume that X decides to sell his stock prior to exercise for $6,000 and enters into a closing transaction by purchasing a call on 100 shares of Y Company stock for $5,000. Since the Y stock is selling for $6,000, X must pay a call premium of $1,000. He recognizes a $500 short-term capital loss [$1,000 (call premium paid) − $500 (call premium received)] on the closing transaction. On the actual sale of the Y Company stock, X has a long-term capital gain of $1,000 [$6,000 (selling price) − $5,000 (cost)].

—Assume that the original option expired unexercised. X has a $500 short-term capital gain equal to the call premium received for writing the option. This gain is not recognized until the option expires.

Figure I summarizes the option rules.

FIGURE I
OPTIONS SUMMARY

| Event | Effect on | |
	Grantor	Grantee
Option is granted	Receives value and has a contract obligation (a liability)	Pays value and has a contract right (an asset).
Option expires	Has a short-term capital gain if the option property is stocks, securities, commodities, or commodity futures. Otherwise, gain is ordinary income.	Has a loss (capital loss if option property had been a capital asset for the grantee).
Option is exercised	Amount received for option increases proceeds from sale of the option property.	Amount paid for option becomes part of basis of the option property purchased.
Option is sold or exchanged	Result depends upon whether option later expires or is exercised (see above).	Could have gain or loss (capital gain or loss if option property would have been a capital asset for the grantee).

PATENTS

Rationale for Capital Gain Treatment. In certain circumstances, § 1235 may result in long-term capital gain treatment upon the sale of a patent. The justification for § 1235 is primarily to encourage technological progress. This is perhaps ironic if the provision is contrasted with the treatment of authors, composers, and artists. The latter do not qualify for capital gain treatment in any case, because the results of their efforts are not capital assets and do not qualify under § 1231. Presumably, Congress did not choose to use the tax law to encourage cultural endeavors.[19] The following example illustrates the application of § 1235:

> **Example 13.** T, a druggist, invents a pill-counting machine which he patents. In consideration of a lump-sum payment of $200,000 plus $10 per machine sold, T assigns the patent to Drug Products, Inc. Assuming T has transferred all substantial rights, the question of whether the transfer is a sale or exchange of a capital asset is not relevant. T automatically has a long-term capital gain from both the lump-sum payment and the $10 per machine royalty to the extent these proceeds exceed his basis for the patent.

Statutory Requirements. The key issues relating to the transfer of patent rights are (1) whether the patent is a capital asset, (2) whether the transfer is a sale or exchange, and (3) whether all substantial rights to the patent (or an undivided interest therein) are transferred. Section 1235 was enacted primarily to resolve the issue of whether the transfer is a sale or exchange of a capital asset. This Section provides that:

> a transfer . . . of property consisting of all substantial rights to a patent, or an undivided interest therein which includes a part of all such rights, by any holder shall be considered the sale or exchange of a capital asset held for more than one year, regardless of whether or not payments in consideration of such transfer are (1) payable periodically over a period generally coterminous with the transferee's use of the patent, or (2) contingent on the productivity, use, or disposition of the property transferred.[20]

If the transfer meets the requirements of § 1235, any gain or loss is automatically a long-term capital gain or loss regardless of whether the patent is a capital asset, whether the transfer is a sale or exchange, and how long the patent was held by the transferor.

Substantial Rights. To receive favorable capital gain treatment under § 1235, "all substantial rights" to the patent must be transferred. The transfer of patent rights which are limited geographically within the country of issuance or of rights which are limited in duration to a period less than the remaining life of the patent does not constitute the transfer of all substantial rights.[21]

---

19. Refer to Chapter 2 for a discussion of how the tax law encourages certain economic activities.

20. § 1235(a) and Reg. § 1.1235–1(a).

21. Reg. § 1.1235–2(b)(1).

Example 14. T sells certain patent rights to a manufacturing process to S. The rights conveyed to S, however, limit the use of the process to the northeastern section of the United States. T's sale of the patent rights does not qualify for capital gain treatment under § 1235 because the rights are limited geographically within the United States. Since § 1235 does not apply, T's gain is ordinary.

Holder Defined. Section 1235 applies to the creator or inventor and to anyone who purchases the patent rights from the creator, except for the creator's employer and certain related parties. Thus, in the common situation where an employer has the rights to all inventions of its employees, the employer's patents would not be eligible for § 1235 treatment. Also, a transfer by a holder to a related party does not qualify.[22]

Example 15. T sells patent rights to his mother. The transfer does not qualify under § 1235 because the rights are transferred to a related party.

If the transfer does not qualify under § 1235, the taxpayer must look elsewhere for long-term capital gain treatment. That is, the transfer would have to be the sale or exchange of a capital asset or § 1231 asset held for the required long-term holding period.

FRANCHISES

Prior to the enactment of § 1253 in 1969, there was a great deal of controversy in the courts with respect to the proper tax treatment relative to transfers of franchises. The key issue was whether the transfer was a sale or exchange as opposed to a license. Section 1253(a) generally solves this problem by providing that "a transfer of a franchise, trademark, or trade name shall not be treated as a sale or exchange of a capital asset if the transferor retains any significant power, right, or continuing interest with respect to the subject matter of the franchise, trademark, or trade name." Payments contingent on productivity, use, or disposition of the franchise, trademark, or trade name also are not treated as a sale or exchange of a capital asset.

A franchise is defined as an agreement which gives the transferee the right to distribute, sell, or provide goods, services, or facilities within a specified area.[23] A transfer includes the granting of a franchise, the transfer of a franchise by a grantee to a third party, or the renewal of a franchise.

Significant Power, Right, or Continuing Interest. Significant powers, rights, or continuing interests include control over assign-

---

22. Reg. § 1.1235 1(a).
23. § 1253(b)(1). See the Glossary of Tax Terms (Appendix C) for a definition of the term "franchise".

ment, quality of products and services, sale or advertising of other products or services, and the right to require that substantially all supplies and equipment be purchased from the transferor. Also included are the right to terminate the franchise at will and the right to substantial contingent payments. It is apparent that most modern franchising operations involve some or all of these powers, rights, or continuing interests.

Transferee Deduction.   Section 1253 is unique in that it covers the tax consequences to both the transferor and the transferee. Section 1253(d) indicates the tax treatment of amounts paid by the transferee. Contingent payments are deductible as business expenses. Other payments are deductible either currently or over a longer period of time depending on the nature of the payment and the tax treatment afforded the transferor on the payments. The transferee's tax treatment is consistent with the transferor's (e. g., if the payment is ordinary income to the transferor of the franchise, it is an ordinary deduction to the transferee).

> **Example 16.**   T grants a franchise to U to sell fast foods. Payments to T are contingent on the profitability of the franchise outlet. The payments are ordinary income to T and deductible as a business expense by U.

> **Example 17.**   T, a grantee of a franchise, sells the franchise to a third party. Payments to T are not contingent, and all significant powers, rights, and continuing interests are transferred. The payments are capital gain to T if the franchise is a capital asset.

Sports Franchises.   Section 1253 does not apply to professional sports franchises.[24] However, the Tax Reform Act of 1976 imposed certain restrictions upon the allocation of the costs of acquiring a sports franchise to the cost basis of player contracts.[25] In addition, if a sports franchise is sold, gain from the sale of the player contracts is now subject to depreciation recapture as ordinary income under § 1245.[26]

LEASE CANCELLATION PAYMENTS

The tax treatment of payments received in consideration of a lease cancellation depends on whether the recipient is the lessor or the lessee and whether the lease is a capital asset or not.[27]

---

24.   § 1253(e).
25.   § 1056.
26.   § 1245(a)(4). Refer to Chapter 17 for a discussion of the recapture provisions.
27.   See the Glossary of Tax Terms (Appendix C) for definitions of the terms "lessor" and "lessee".

Lessee Treatment. Payments received by a lessee in consideration of a lease cancellation are capital gains if the lease is a capital asset or § 1231 asset.[28] Generally, a lessee's lease would be a capital asset if the property was used for the lessee's personal use (e. g., his or her residence). A lessee's lease would be an ordinary asset if the property was used in the lessee's trade or business.[29]

Lessor Treatment. Payments received by a lessor in consideration of a lease cancellation are always ordinary income because they are considered to be in lieu of rental payments.[30]

> **Example 18.** T owns an apartment building which he is going to convert into an office building. S is one of the apartment tenants and receives $1,000 from T in cancellation of S's lease. S would have a capital gain of $1,000 (which would be long- or short-term depending upon how long S had held the lease). T would have an ordinary deduction of $1,000.

> **Example 19.** M owns an apartment building near a university campus. P is one of the tenants. P is graduating early and offers M $800 to cancel P's lease. M accepts the offer. M has ordinary income of $800. P has a nondeductible payment, since the apartment was personal use property.

HOLDING PERIOD

The required holding period for long-term capital gain or loss treatment is "more than one year" for 1978 and subsequent years. (The holding period was "more than nine months" for 1977, and "more than six months" for prior years.[31]) Conversely, gains or losses from the sale or exchange of capital assets not held for more than one year are short-term capital gains or losses.[32] In computing the holding period, start counting on the day after the property was acquired. In subsequent months, this same day is the start of a new month.[33] The following example illustrates the computation of the holding period:

> **Example 20.** T purchases a capital asset on March 15, 19X3, and sells it on March 16, 19X4. T's holding period is more than one year. If T had sold the asset on March 15, 19X4, the holding period would have been one year and the gain or loss would have been short-term.

---

28. § 1241 and Reg. § 1.1241–1(a).

29. Reg. § 1.1221–1(a).

30. *Hort v. Comm.,* 41–1 USTC ¶ 9354, 25 AFTR 1207, 61 S.Ct. 757 (USSC, 1941).

31. § 1223(3) and (4).

32. § 1222(1) and (2).

33. *Your Federal Income Tax,* IRS Publication 17 (Rev. Oct. 83), p. 77.

A capital asset acquired on the last day of any month must not be disposed of until on or after the first day of the thirteenth succeeding month to be held for more than one year.[34]

Example 21. T purchases a capital asset on January 31, 19X3, and sells it on February 1, 19X4. T's holding period is more than one year, and any gain or loss on the sale is long-term.

REVIEW OF VARIOUS HOLDING PERIOD RULES

Section 1223 provides detailed rules for determining holding period. The application of these rules depends on the type of asset and how it was acquired.

Tax-free Exchanges. The holding period of property received in a nontaxable exchange includes the holding period of the former asset if the property which has been exchanged is a capital asset or § 1231 asset.[35] In certain nontaxable transactions involving a substituted basis, the holding period of the former property is "tacked on" to the holding period of the newly acquired property.

Example 22. X exchanges a business truck for another truck in a like-kind exchange under § 1031. The holding period of the truck exchanged tacks on to the holding period of the new truck.

Example 23. T sells his former personal residence and acquires a new residence. If the transaction qualifies under § 1034 for non-recognition of gain on the sale of a residence, the holding period of the new residence includes the holding period of the former residence.[36]

Certain Nontaxable Transactions Involving a Carryover of Basis. The holding period of a former owner of property is tacked on to the present owner's holding period if the transaction is nontaxable and the basis of the property to the former owner carries over to the new owner.

Example 24. T transfers land to a controlled corporation in exchange for its common stock. If the transaction is nontaxable under § 351 (discussed more fully in Chapter 20), the corporation's holding period for the land includes the period the land was held by T.

Example 25. T acquires 100 shares of A Corporation stock for $1,000 on December 31, 19X2. The shares are transferred by gift to S on December 31, 19X3, when the stock is worth $2,000. S's holding period begins with the date the stock was acquired by T,

34. Rev.Rul. 66–7, 1966–1 C.B. 188.
35. § 1223(1).
36. § 1223(7).

since the donor's basis of $1,000 becomes the basis for determining gain or loss on a subsequent sale by S.

Example 26. Assume the same facts as in Example 25 except that the fair market value of the shares is only $800 on the date of the gift. The holding period begins on the date of the gift if S sells the stock for a loss, since the value of the shares at the date of the gift is used in the determination of basis.[37] If the shares are sold for $500 on April 1, 19X4, S has a $300 recognized capital loss and the holding period is from December 31, 19X3, to April 1, 19X4 (thus, the loss is short-term).

SPECIAL RULES FOR SHORT SALES

The holding period of property sold short is determined under special rules provided in § 1233. A short sale occurs when a taxpayer sells borrowed property and repays the lender with substantially identical property either held on the date of the sale or purchased after the sale. Short sales usually involve corporate stock. The seller's objective is to make a profit in anticipation of a decline in the price of the stock. If the price declines, the seller in a short sale recognizes a profit equal to the difference between the sales price of the borrowed stock and the price paid for the replacement stock.

Section 1233(a) provides that "gain or loss from the short sale of property shall be considered as gain or loss from the sale or exchange of a capital asset to the extent that the property . . . used to close the short sale constitutes a capital asset in the hands of the taxpayer." No gain or loss is recognized until the short sale is closed.[38]

The general rule is that the holding period of the property sold short is determined by the length of time the seller held the property used to repay the lender when closing the short sale.

If substantially identical property has been held for less than the required long-term holding period (i. e., one year or less) on the date of the short sale, the gain or loss is short-term. If substantially identical property is acquired after the date of the short sale and on or before the closing date, the gain or loss is also short-term. If, however, substantially identical property has been held for the required long-term holding period on the date of the short sale, a gain on closing is long-term if the substantially identical property is used to close the sale, but a loss on closing is long-term regardless of whether the substantially identical property is used to close the sale. Figure II summarizes the short sale rules.

The purpose of these special rules is to prevent the taxpayer from engaging in short sales in order to convert short-term capital gains to long-term capital gains or convert long-term capital losses to short-

---

37. § 1223(2) and Reg. § 1.1223–1(b).
38. Reg. § 1.1233–1(a)(1).

FIGURE II

SHORT SALES OF SECURITIES

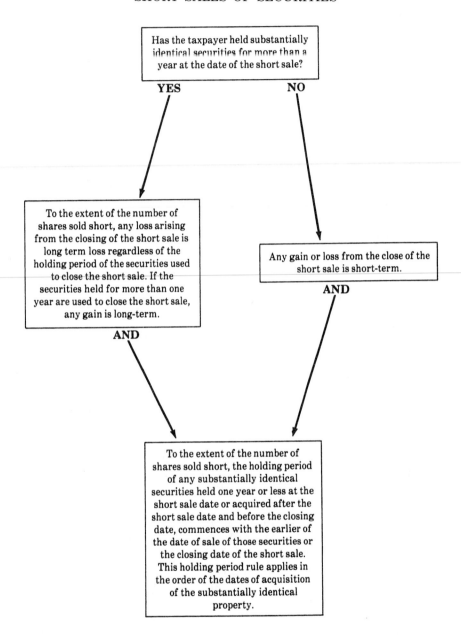

term capital losses. The discussion of capital gains and losses later in this chapter points out the advantage of long-term capital gains and short-term capital losses over short-term capital gains and long-term capital losses. The following examples illustrate the application of the special rules for short sales:

Example 27. On January 2, 19X4, T purchases five shares of XYZ Corporation common stock for $100. On April 14, 19X4, she engages in a short sale of five shares of the same stock for $150. On August 15, T closes the short sale by repaying the borrowed stock with the five shares purchased on January 2. T has a $50 short-term capital gain from the short sale because she held substantially identical shares for less than the required long-term holding period on the date of the short sale.

Example 28. Assume the same facts as in the previous example, except that T closes the short sale on August 30 by repaying the borrowed stock with five shares purchased on August 29 for $200. The stock used to close the short sale was not the property purchased on January 2, but since T held short-term property at the April 14 short sale date, the gain or loss from closing the short sale is short-term. T has a $50 short-term loss ($200 cost of stock purchased August 29 and a short sale selling price of $150).

Example 29. Assume the same facts as in Example 28. On August 31, T sells for $200 the stock purchased January 2. T's holding period for the stock begins August 30, because the holding-period portion of the short sale rules applies to the substantially identical property in order of acquisition. T has a short-term gain of $100 ($100 cost of stock purchased January 2 and a selling price of $200).

Example 30. On January 2, 19X2, T purchases five shares of X Corporation common stock for $100. She purchases five more shares of the same stock on April 14, 19X4, for $200. On August 15, 19X4, she sells short five shares of the same stock for $150. On September 30, she repays the borrowed stock with the five shares purchased on April 14 and sells the five shares purchased on January 2, 19X2, for $200. T has a $50 long-term capital loss from the short sale because she held substantially identical shares for more than one year on the date of the short sale. T has a $100 long-term capital gain from the sale of the shares purchased on January 2, 19X2.

TAX TREATMENT OF CAPITAL GAINS AND LOSSES OF NONCORPORATE TAXPAYERS

TREATMENT OF CAPITAL GAINS

Computation of Net Capital Gain. As discussed earlier in this chapter, the first step in the computation is to net all long-term capital gains (LTCG) and losses (LTCL) and all short-term capital gains

(STCG) and losses (STCL). The result is the taxpayer's net long-term capital gain (NLTCG) or loss (NLTCL) and net short-term capital gain (NSTCG) or loss (NSTCL).[39]

Example 31. Some possible results of the first step in netting capital gains and losses are shown below. Assume that each case is independent (i. e., assume the taxpayer's only capital gains and losses are those shown in the given case).

Case	STCG	STCL	LTCG	LTCL	Result of Netting	Description of Result
A	$ 8,000	($ 5,000)			$ 3,000	NSTCG
B	$ 2,000	($ 7,000)			($ 5,000)	NSTCL
C			$ 9,000	($ 1,000)	$ 8,000	NLTCG
D			$ 8,800	($ 9,800)	($ 1,000)	NLTCL

The second step in netting capital gains and losses requires offsetting any positive and negative amounts which remain after the first netting step. This procedure is illustrated in the following examples.

Example 32. Assume that T had all the capital gains and losses specified in Cases B and C in Example 31:

Case C ($9,000 LTCG − $1,000 LTCL)	$ 8,000	NLTCG
Case B ($2,000 STCG − $7,000 STCL)	($ 5,000)	NSTCL
Excess of NLTCG over NSTCL	$ 3,000	

The $3,000 excess of NLTCG over NSTCL in Example 32 is defined as *net capital gain* (NCG).[40] Section 1202(a) provides favorable tax treatment for net capital gain. Noncorporate taxpayers are allowed to deduct 60 percent of net capital gain as a deduction *for* adjusted gross income. Thus, T may deduct $1,800 (60 percent of $3,000 NCG) in arriving at adjusted gross income, which means that only 40 percent of net capital gain is taxable.

Example 33. Assume that U had all the capital gains and losses specified in Cases A and D in Example 31:

Case A ($8,000 STCG − $5,000 STCL)	$ 3,000	NSTCG
Case D ($8,800 LTCG − $9,800 LTCL)	($ 1,000)	NLTCL
Excess of NSTCG over NLTCL	$ 2,000	

There is no special name for the excess of NSTCG over NLTCL, nor is there any special tax treatment. The nature of the gain is short-term, and the gain is treated as ordinary gain and is included in U's

---

39. § 1222(5), (6), (7) and (8).
40. § 1222(11).

gross income. The 60 percent capital gain deduction applies only to net capital gain (NCG). A review of Example 32 indicates that the nature of NCG is long-term while the nature of the gain in Example 33 is short-term.

Capital gain planning is an important element in the development of an overall tax plan. Because of the 60 percent capital gain deduction, only 40 percent of net capital gain is taxable. This lowers the effective tax rate on net capital gain. To illustrate, assume a noncorporate taxpayer in the 50 percent bracket has $10,000 of ordinary income (e. g., interest). The effective rate on this ordinary income is 50 percent. On the other hand, assume the $10,000 is net capital gain. Only $4,000 of the net capital gain is taxable ($10,000 NCG − $6,000 capital gain deduction). The tax on net capital gain is only $2,000 ($4,000 × 50%), which results in an effective tax rate of 20 percent ($2,000 tax ÷ $10,000 NCG).

The effective rate on net capital gain for individuals can be computed by multiplying the individual's marginal tax rate by 40 percent (since only 40 percent of NCG is taxable). Thus, in the previous illustration, the taxpayer's effective rate on net capital gain of 20 percent could have been computed by multiplying the marginal rate of 50 percent by 40 percent. A taxpayer in the 30 percent bracket, for example, would pay an effective rate on net capital gain of 12 percent (30% × 40%).

Items of Tax Preference.   The 60 percent capital gain portion of the net capital gain is a tax preference item under the alternative minimum tax calculation. Refer to the discussion of the alternative minimum tax in Chapter 12.

TREATMENT OF CAPITAL LOSSES

Computation of Net Capital Loss.   The computation of a taxpayer's *net capital loss* involves the same netting process used for computing capital gain net income. A net capital loss results if the taxpayer's capital losses exceed the capital gains for the taxable year.[41] Again, it is necessary to differentiate between long-term and short-term capital losses. Both long-term and short-term capital losses offset either long-term or short-term capital gains. Losses remaining after such offset are treated differently depending on whether they are long-term or short-term.[42]

---

41.   § 1222(10) defines a net capital loss as the net loss after the deduction from ordinary taxable income (discussed later in this chapter). But this definition confuses the discussion of the treatment of capital losses, and therefore, capital loss is defined for practical purposes as the net loss before the deduction from ordinary taxable income.

42.   § 1211(b)(1) and Reg. § 1.1211–1(b)(1).

Example 34. Three different individual taxpayers have the following capital gains and losses during the year:

Taxpayer	LTCG	LTCL	STCG	STCL	Result of Netting	Description of Result
R	$ 1,000	($ 2,800)	$ 1,000	($ 500)	($ 1,300)	NLTCL
S	1,000	(500)	1,000	(2,800)	(1,300)	NSTCL
T	400	(1,200)	500	(1,200)	(1,500)	NLTCL ($800) NSTCL ($700)

R's net capital loss of $1,300 is all long-term. S's net capital loss is all short-term. T's net capital loss is $1,500, $800 of which is long-term and $700 of which is short-term.

Treatment of Net Capital Loss. The general rule is that a net capital loss is deductible from gross income up to an amount equal to the lower of (1) the taxpayer's "taxable income, as adjusted" [taxable income figured without regard to gains or losses from sales or exchanges of capital assets and reduced (but not below zero) by the appropriate zero bracket amount] or (2) $3,000.[43] As a practical matter, the taxpayer's "taxable income, as adjusted" usually will exceed these dollar limitations and subsequent discussion assumes that it does. Married persons filing separate returns are each limited to one-half of the allowable amounts.

Special Limitation for Long-term Capital Loss After 1969. Prior to 1970, both long-term and short-term capital losses offset ordinary taxable income dollar for dollar up to $1,000. Since net capital gains were previously subject to a 50 percent capital gain deduction, Congress changed the law effective January 1, 1970, to give a similar effect to long-term net capital losses. The change causes taxpayers to permanently lose a dollar of long-term net capital loss for every dollar of such loss deducted from ordinary taxable income.

Example 35. T has a net capital loss of $5,000 in 1983 of which $3,000 is long-term and $2,000 is short-term. Since short-term capital losses are always deducted first[44] and the total amount which is deductible is limited to $3,000, T deducts the $2,000 of net short-term loss and $1,000 of net long-term loss. The $1,000 deduction effectively uses up $2,000 of the net long-term loss. Therefore, only $1,000 of long-term net capital loss is carried over to 1984 as a long-term capital loss.

Carryovers. Taxpayers are allowed to carry over indefinitely unused capital losses, short-term or long-term (except for amounts of long-term capital loss permanently lost as a result of the 50% reduc-

---

43. § 1211(b) and Reg. § 1.1211–1(b)(2) and (6).
44. Reg. § 1.1211–1(b)(4)(i).

tion).[45] Unused capital losses are carried over according to their original nature. That is, if a short-term capital loss is carried over to the following year it is treated the same as a short-term capital loss occurring in that year. Accordingly, such a loss first would be used to offset short-term capital gains occurring in the following year.

> **Example 36.** In 1983, T incurred a LTCL of $11,000 and a STCL of $1,000. In 1984, T has no capital gains or losses.
>
> —T's capital loss for taxable year 1983 is $12,000. T deducts $3,000 [$1,000 (short-term) and $2,000 (long-term) in 1983]. The long-term portion ($2,000) of the loss deducted uses up $4,000 of the total long-term capital loss; thus, T has $7,000 (long-term) to carry over to 1984.
>
> —T deducts $3,000 (long-term) in 1984, using up $6,000 of the $7,000 long-term loss carried over from 1983, and carries over $1,000 (long-term) to 1985.

REPORTING PROCEDURES

Capital gains and losses are reported on Schedule D of Form 1040. Part I of Schedule D provides for the reporting of short-term capital gains and losses while Part II deals with long-term transactions (see below). On page 2 of Schedule D, Part III summarizes the results of Parts I and II and, as appropriate, allows for the 60 percent long-term capital gain deduction or applies the limitations on the deduction for capital losses. Part V (not reproduced) concerns post-1969 capital loss carryovers, both short- and long-term.

> **Example 37.** During 1983, Erlyne Smith (Social Security number, 466-36-4596) had the following sales of capital assets (a 1983 example has been used, since a 1984 form was unavailable):

Description	Date Acquired	Date Sold	Selling Price	Cost Basis*
100 shares of W Corp. common stock	10/21/83	12/3/83	$ 11,000	$ 10,000
300 shares of X Corp. preferred stock	7/29/83	11/25/83	5,000	5,500
2,000 shares of Y Corp. common stock	1/31/81	2/12/83	8,000	7,000
40 shares of Z Corp. common stock	6/11/81	9/5/83	16,000	18,800

*Includes selling expenses (e. g., brokerage commissions).

> Please note that Erlyne's tax position is the same as that of R in Example 34 (page 640). Thus, she has a net LTCL of $1,800

---

45. § 1212(b) and Reg. § 1.1212–1(b).

(Part II of Schedule D) and a net STCG of $500 (Part I of Schedule D). These amounts are combined (see Part III on page 2 of Schedule D) for a net long-term capital loss of $1,300 of which, after proper adjustment for the 50 percent rule, $650 is deductible. In completing a Schedule D for Erlyne Smith it was assumed that she had no capital loss carryovers from prior years and that her taxable income (as adjusted) was at least $650.

SCHEDULE D (FORM 1040)
Department of the Treasury
Internal Revenue Service

Capital Gains and Losses   (Examples of property to be reported on this Schedule are gains and losses on stocks, bonds, and similar investments, and gains (but not losses) on personal assets such as a home or jewelry.)
▶ Attach to Form 1040. ▶ See Instructions for Schedule D (Form 1040).

OMB No. 1545-0074

19 83
11

Name(s) as shown on Form 1040: Erlyne Smith

Your social security number: 466 36 4596

PART I.—Short-term Capital Gains and Losses—Assets Held One Year or Less

a. Description of property (Example, 100 shares 7% preferred of 'Z' Co.)	b. Date acquired (Mo., day, yr.)	c. Date sold (Mo., day, yr.)	d. Gross sales price	e. Cost or other basis, plus expense of sale	f. LOSS If column (e) is more than (d) subtract (d) from (e)	g. GAIN If column (d) is more than (e) subtract (e) from (d)
1 100 shares of W corp. common stock	10/21/83	12/31/83	11,000	10,000		1,000
300 shares of X corp.	7/29/83	11/25/83	5,000	5,500	500	

2 Short-term gain from sale or exchange of a principal residence from Form 2119, lines 7 or 11	**2**			
3 Short-term capital gain from installment sales from Form 6252, line 21 or 29	**3**			
4 Net short-term gain or (loss) from partnerships, S corporations, and fiduciaries	**4**			
5 Add lines 1 through 4 in column f and column g	**5** (	500	)	1,000
6 Combine columns f and g of line 5 and enter the net gain or (loss)	**6**			500
7 Short-term capital loss carryover from years beginning after 1969	**7** (			)
8 Net short-term gain or (loss), combine lines 6 and 7 —————	**8**			500

PART II.— Long-term Capital Gains and Losses—Assets Held More Than One Year

a. Description of property	b. Date acquired	c. Date sold	d. Gross sales price	e. Cost or other basis	f. LOSS	g. GAIN
9 2,000 shares of Y corp. common stock	1/31/81	2/12/83	8,000	7,000		1,000
40 shares of Z corp. common stock	6/11/81	9/15/83	16,000	18,800	2,800	

10 Long-term gain from sale or exchange of a principal residence from Form 2119, lines 7, 11, 16 or 18	**10**			
11 Long-term capital gain from installment sales from Form 6252, line 21 or 29	**11**			
12 Net long-term gain or (loss) from partnerships, S corporations, and fiduciaries	**12**			
13 Add lines 9 through 12 in column f and column g	**13** (	2,800	)	1,000
14 Combine columns f and g of line 13 and enter the net gain or (loss)	**14**			(1,800)
15 Capital gain distributions	**15**			
16 Enter gain from Form 4797, line 6(a)(1)	**16**			
17 Combine lines 14 through 16	**17**			(1,800)
18 Long-term capital loss carryover from years beginning after 1969	**18** (			)
19 Net long-term gain or (loss), combine lines 17 and 18	**19**			(1,800)

Note: Complete the back of this form. However, if you have capital loss carryovers from years beginning before 1970, do not complete Parts III or V. See Form 4798 instead.

For Paperwork Reduction Act Notice, see Form 1040 instructions.   Schedule D (Form 1040) 1983

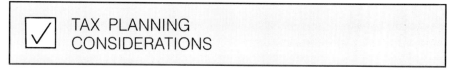

Schedule D (Form 1040) 1983   Page **2**

PART III.—Summary of Parts I and II

20 Combine lines 8 and 19, and enter the net gain or (loss) here	**20** (1,300)
Note: *If line 20 is a loss, skip lines 21 through 23 and complete lines 24 and 25. If line 20 is a gain complete lines 21 through 23 and skip lines 24 and 25.*	
21 If line 20 shows a gain, enter the smaller of line 19 or line 20. Enter zero if there is a loss or no entry on line 19 . . . . **21**	
22 Enter 60% of line 21	**22**
If line 22 is more than zero, you may be liable for the alternative minimum tax. See Form 6251.	
23 Subtract line 22 from line 20. Enter here and on Form 1040, line 13	**23**
24 If line 20 shows a loss, enter one of the following amounts:	
a If line 8 is zero or a net gain, enter 50% of line 20;	
b If line 19 is zero or a net gain, enter line 20; or	
c If line 8 and line 19 are net losses, enter amount on line 8 added to 50% of the amount on line 19	**24** (650)
25 Enter here and as a loss on Form 1040, line 13, the smallest of:	
a The amount on line 24;	
b $3,000 ($1,500 if married and filing a separate return); or	
c Taxable income, as adjusted	**25** (650)

TAX TREATMENT OF CAPITAL GAINS AND LOSSES OF CORPORATE TAXPAYERS

The treatment of a corporation's net capital gain or loss differs from the rules for individuals. Briefly, the differences are:

—There is no 60 percent capital gain deduction.[46]

—An alternative tax rate of 28 percent is allowed in computing the tax on net capital gain.[47]

—Capital losses offset only capital gains; no deduction is permitted against ordinary taxable income (whereas a $3,000 deduction is allowed to individuals).[48]

—There is a five-year carryover and a three-year carryback period for net capital losses.[49] Corporate carryovers and carrybacks are always treated as short-term, regardless of their original nature.

The rules applicable to corporations are discussed in greater detail in Chapter 20.

☑ TAX PLANNING
CONSIDERATIONS

PLANNING FOR CAPITAL ASSET STATUS

It is important to keep in mind that capital asset status often is a question of intent. Thus, property that is not a capital asset to one party may qualify as a capital asset to another party.

---

46. § 1202.
47. § 1201(a)(2).
48. § 1211(a).
49. § 1212(a)(1).

Example 38. T, a real estate dealer, transfers by gift a tract of land to S, her son. The land was part of T's inventory (i. e., it was held for resale) and was therefore not a capital asset to her. S, however, keeps the land as an investment. The land is a capital asset in S's hands, and any later taxable disposition of the property by him will yield a capital gain or loss.

If proper planning is carried out, even a dealer may obtain favorable long-term capital gain treatment on the sale of the type of property normally held for resale.

Example 39. T, a real estate dealer, segregates tract 'A' from the real estate he regularly holds for resale and designates such property as being held for investment purposes. The property is not advertised for sale and is eventually disposed of several years later. The negotiations for the subsequent sale were initiated by the purchaser and not by T. Under these circumstances it would appear that any gain or loss from the sale of tract 'A' should be a capital gain or loss.[50]

EFFECT OF CAPITAL ASSET STATUS IN OTHER THAN SALE TRANSACTIONS

The nature of an asset (i. e., capital or ordinary) is important in determining the tax consequences that result when a sale or exchange occurs. It may, however, be just as significant absent a taxable sale or exchange. When a capital asset is disposed of, the result is not always a capital gain or loss. Rather, in general, the disposition must be a sale or exchange. Collection of a debt instrument having a basis less than its face value would result in an ordinary gain rather than a capital gain even though the debt instrument is a capital asset. The collection is not a sale or exchange. Sale of the debt shortly before the due date for collection will not produce a capital gain.[51] If selling the debt in such circumstances could produce a capital gain but collecting could not, the narrow interpretation of what constitutes a capital gain or loss would be frustrated. Another illustration of the sale or exchange principle could involve a donation of appreciated property to a qualified charity. Recall that the measure of the charitable contribution is fair market value when the property, if sold, would have yielded a long-term capital gain [refer to Chapter 11 and the discussion of § 170(e)].

Example 40. In 1984, T wants to donate a tract of unimproved land (basis of $40,000 and fair market value of $200,000) and

---

50. *Toledo, Peoria & Western Railroad Co.,* 35 TCM 1663, T.C.Memo. 1976–366.
51. *Commissioner v. Percy W. Phillips,* 60–1 USTC ¶ 9294, 5 AFTR2d 855 275 F.2d 33 (CA–4, 1960).

held for more than one year to State University (a qualified charitable organization). However, T currently is under audit by the IRS for capital gains she reported on certain real estate transactions during 1981–1983. Although T is not a licensed real estate broker, the IRS agent conducting the audit is contending that she has achieved dealer status by virtue of the number and frequency of the real estate transactions she has conducted. Under these circumstances, T would be well-advised to postpone the donation to State University until such time as her status is clarified. If she has achieved dealer status, the unimproved land may be inventory (refer to Example 39 for another possible result) and T's charitable contribution deduction would be limited to $40,000. If not, and if the land is held as an investment, T's deduction becomes $200,000 (i. e., the fair market value of the property).

STOCK SALES

The following rules apply in determining the date of a stock sale:

—If the taxpayer is on the accrual basis, the date the sale is executed is the date of the sale. The execution date is the date the broker completes the transaction on the stock exchange.

—If the taxpayer is on the cash basis and the sale results in a gain, the date the sale is settled is the date of the sale.[52] The settlement date is the date the cash or other property is paid for the stock.

—If the taxpayer is on the cash basis and the sale results in a loss, the date the sale is executed is the date of the sale.[53]

Thus, year-end sales at a gain by a cash basis taxpayer will not be recognized in the current year if the settlement date for the sale falls in the following year.

> **Example 41.** T, a cash basis taxpayer, sells stock which results in a gain. The sale was executed on December 29, 19X3, and the settlement date is January 5, 19X4. The date of sale is January 5, 19X4 (the settlement date), because the sale resulted in a gain. If the sale resulted in a loss, the date of sale would be December 29, 19X3. For purposes of determining the holding period, however, the date of sale is December 29, 19X3 (the trade date).[54]

Under the installment sale provisions, recognition of the gain in Example 41 could be shifted to 19X3 by electing not to use the installment method when the taxable year 19X3 income tax return is filed.

---

52. Rev.Rul. 72–381, 1972–2 C.B. 233.
53. Rev.Rul. 70–344, 1970–2 C.B. 50.
54. Rev.Rul. 70–598, 1970–2 C.B. 168.

Installment treatment is automatic unless the taxpayer elects not to have installment treatment apply.[55] See Chapter 18.

MAXIMIZING BENEFITS

Because of favorable tax rates applicable to long-term capital gains, consideration always should be given to the relative tax benefits which accrue from holding a capital asset for the required long-term holding period. Since net short-term capital gains are includible in income in full, consideration should be given before the end of the year to the sale of capital assets at a loss. This approach would help to offset any short-term gains which have been recognized during the year.

Similarly, long-term capital gains are preferable to ordinary income. The new rules on original issue discount (OID) amortization yield a lower amount of interest income in the early years of holding an OID bond than do the old rules. (Review Examples 10 and 11.) If the bond price rises because of a change in market interest rates, the bondholder may realize more long-term capital gain under the new rules than under the old rules. Thus, the purchase of deep discount bonds in anticipation of a favorable swing in interest rates may be a worthwhile strategy. The taxpayer should be careful, however, to purchase bonds that were not issued with an intention to call them before maturity and bonds whose market price will reflect favorable swings in market interest rates.

Ordinary losses generally are preferable to capital losses because of the limitations imposed on the deductibility of net capital losses and the requirement that capital losses be used to offset capital gains. The taxpayer may be able to convert what would otherwise have been capital loss to ordinary loss. For example, business (but not nonbusiness) bad debts, losses from the sale or exchange of small business investment company stock, and losses from the sale or exchange of small business company stock all result in ordinary losses.[56] Also, it should be noted that the acquisition of the stock of a supplier, to assure a source of supply (with no substantial investment motive), should result in ordinary loss treatment if the stock is sold at a loss. Finally, if the taxpayer must generate a capital loss, it is preferable that it be a short-term capital loss.

Although capital losses can be carried over indefinitely, "indefinite" becomes definite when a taxpayer dies. Any loss carryovers not used by such taxpayer are permanently lost; that is, no tax benefit can be derived from the carryovers subsequent to death.[57] Therefore, the potential benefit of carrying over capital losses diminishes when dealing with older taxpayers.

---

55. § 453(d)(1). See the discussion in Chapter 18.

56. §§ 166(d), 1242, and 1244. Refer to the discussion in Chapter 8.

57. Rev.Rul. 74–175, 1974–1 C.B. 52.

SPREADING GAINS

It is usually beneficial to spread gains over more than one taxable year. In some cases, this can be accomplished through the installment sales method of accounting. The bunching of long-term capital gains in one taxable year can be detrimental if the alternative minimum tax applies. Since the alternative minimum tax is applicable only when it exceeds the regular Federal income tax liability, it is possible to spread the long-term capital gains over several years and therefore avoid payment of any alternative minimum tax.

YEAR-END PLANNING

The following general rules can be applied for timing the recognition of capital gains and losses near the end of a taxable year:

—If the taxpayer already has LTCL, recognize STCG.

Example 42. T has already incurred an LTCL of $6,000 for the taxable year. Every dollar of STCG that T recognizes before the end of the year will result in offsetting income (i. e., STCG) which would be fully taxable against loss (i. e., LTCL) which would be deductible at only 50 cents on the dollar. If T's only capital loss is the $6,000 capital loss, only $3,000 would be deductible in the taxable year. On the other hand, if T also recognized an STCG of $6,000, the entire LTCL would be offset against the STCG.

—If the taxpayer already has STCG, recognize LTCL.

—If the taxpayer already has STCL, recognize STCG. Do not recognize LTCG, because the 60 percent capital gains deduction (for the noncorporate taxpayer) or alternative tax benefits (for corporate taxpayers) are then eliminated on the gain which is offset against the STCL.

Example 43. T, who is a 50% bracket taxpayer, has already incurred STCL of $6,000. If T recognizes a $6,000 STCG before the end of the year, he will have used the STCL to offset $6,000 of income which would have been subject to a maximum tax rate of 50%. If T recognizes an LTCG, he will have used the STCL to offset $6,000 of income that would have been subject to a maximum tax rate of 20% (40% of the LTCG times the maximum tax rate of 50%). If T does not recognize any gain, he will be allowed to deduct $3,000 of the STCL this year and carry the remaining $3,000 over to next year.

PROBLEM MATERIALS

Questions for Discussion

1. What type of preferential treatment is afforded long-term capital gains? What is the justification for this treatment?

2. Is there any reason a taxpayer would prefer to recognize a loss as a capital loss rather than as an ordinary loss?

3. Define a short-term capital gain.

4. Under what circumstances are copyrights capital assets?

5. What broad class of assets is excluded from the capital asset category?

6. Compare what would be a "capital asset" for tax purposes with the assets that would be the subject of a "capital asset budgeting" decision in a managerial accounting class. Does capital asset mean the same thing in both contexts?

7. Can the sale of personal use assets result in capital losses?

8. What does "statutory expansion" mean with regard to § 1221?

9. Can a dealer in securities have investments (as opposed to inventory) in securities? Explain.

10. Goods held primarily for sale are not capital assets. There is one exception to this rule.

    (a) What is the exception?

    (b) Why do you think it was enacted?

    (c) To whom is it available?

11. Under what circumstances does § 1237 apply?

12. What are the two requirements for the recognition of a capital gain or loss?

13. Differentiate between the treatment of corporate obligations issued at a discount before July 2, 1982, and those issued after July 1, 1982.

14. Options are capital assets.

    (a) Is this statement true or false?

    (b) Why or why not?

15. If a nonbusiness debt is collected when due, does the taxpayer have gross income? If the debt is not collected when due, what type of loss results when the debt becomes worthless?

16. If an individual pays a $100 premium to acquire an option to buy stock, how does the call premium affect the basis of the stock if the option is exercised?

17. If a grantee of an option exercises the option, do the grantor's proceeds from the sale of the option property increase? Why?

18. When does the transfer of a patent result in long-term capital gain? Short-term capital gain? Ordinary income?

19. What three elements generally are required for capital gain (loss) treatment on a patent? (Do not consider any statutory expansions.)

20. If an inventor's employer automatically has sole patent rights to the inventor's inventions, is the employer a holder of the patent?

21. What is a franchise? In practice, does the transfer of a franchise usually result in capital gain (loss) treatment? Why or why not?

22. Why do you think the Tax Reform Act of 1976 limited the amount of the cost of a sports franchise which could be allocated to player contracts? (*Hint:* Where would the player contracts appear on the books of the owner of the franchise?)

23. When are lease cancellation payments received by a lessee capital in nature?

24. How does one determine if a capital asset has been held for more than one year and is therefore eligible for long-term capital gain (or loss) treatment?

25. Define a short sale. Why does a seller enter into a short sale?

26. What is the general rule used to determine the holding period of property sold short? What is an exception to this rule and why was it enacted?

27. During the Congressional deliberation dealing with the Economic Recovery Tax Act (ERTA) T, an individual taxpayer, became aware of a proposal to change the long-term holding period from "more than one year" to "more than six months." When T learned that this change was not made, he was relieved. Why?

28. Differentiate between the capital loss carryover rules for unused capital losses of individuals and corporations.

29. Do the unused capital losses of individuals retain their same character upon the carryover to succeeding years? Explain.

30. What planning procedures are available to maximize the benefits of a long-term capital loss? Of a short-term capital loss? Why?

Problems

31. T owns the following assets. Which of them are capital assets?

    (a) Ten shares of Standard Motors common stock.

    (b) A copyright on a song T wrote.

    (c) A U. S. savings bond.

    (d) A note T received when he loaned $100 to a friend.

    (e) A very rare copy of "Your Federal Income Tax" (a U. S. government publication that T purchased many years ago from the U. S. Government Printing Office).

    (f) T's personal use automobile.

    (g) A duplex apartment building that T has owned for two years and that he rents to others.

    (h) A letter T received from a former U. S. President. T received the letter because he had complained to the President about the President's foreign policy.

32. G makes a gift to B of the copyright on G's song, "I Love Roses," which has a basis of $20,000 to G. G had owned the copyright for two years. The copyright had a fair market value of $25,000 at the date of the gift. B sells this copyright after one year to C for $30,000.

    (a) What is the recognized gain to B upon the sale?

    (b) What is the nature of B's gain?

    (c) Would your answers to (a) and (b) change if instead B inherited the copyright from G (fair market value at date of death is $25,000)? If so, how?

33. A meets all the conditions of § 1237. In 19X6, she sells four lots to B, C, D, and E and two adjacent lots to F. The sales price of each lot is $20,000, while A's basis is $15,000 for each lot. Sales expenses are $500 per lot.

(a) What is the realized and recognized gain?

(b) Explain its nature (i. e., ordinary income or capital gain).

(c) Would your answers change if, instead, the two lots sold to F were not adjacent? If so, how?

34. R, a calendar-year taxpayer, on January 1, 19X1 (after July 1, 1982) buys a Z Corporation original issue 10-year, 8% bond for $10,000. The bond had a maturity price of $15,000. After holding the bond for several years, R sells the bond to S for $12,000. R had properly amortized $1,000 of the original issue discount.

(a) During the time that R held the bond, how would the amortization of $1,000 of original issue discount affect his gross income?

(b) What is the amount and nature of R's gain or loss when he sells the bond?

35. U purchased a $20,000 face value, five-year, 8% bond on January 1, 19X3. The bond was purchased for $12,418. The yield to maturity is 21%.

(a) For 19X3, what is the amount of U's total interest income if the bond was issued before July 2, 1982? His basis for the bond on January 1, 19X4?

(b) For 19X3, what is the amount of U's total interest income if the bond was issued after July 1, 1982? His basis for the bond on January 1, 19X4?

36. T is looking for vacant land to buy. She would hold the land as an investment. For $1,000, she is granted an eleven-month option to buy 10 acres of vacant land for $25,000. The owner (who is holding the land for investment) paid $10,000 for the land several years ago.

(a) Does the land owner have gross income when $1,000 is received for granting the option?

(b) Does T have an asset when the option is granted?

(c) If the option lapses, does the land owner have a recognized gain? If so, what type of gain? Does T have a recognized loss? If so, what type of loss?

(d) If the option is exercised and an additional $25,000 is paid for the land, how much recognized gain does the seller have? What type of gain? What is T's tax basis for the property?

37. F, an individual, owns a patent on a product that S Corporation wishes to use as a component in another product it manufactures. F had purchased the patent for use in his business from an unrelated inventor. F agrees to let S Corporation use this patent for seven months at $500 a month, with S Corporation's obtaining the right to produce, use, and sell the product within the Los Angeles area. Because many others are designing similar products, the life of the patent is uncertain. Its basis to F is $1,500.

(a) Has a sale or exchange occurred? Explain.

(b) How much income and what kind will F recognize? When will it be recognized?

(c) Suppose F were in the business of buying and selling patents. How do the answers to parts (a) and (b) change?

38. L, Inc., a national franchiser of fried potatoes, transfers to S the right to establish L restaurants in State Q, including the right to franchise others to establish these restaurants in the same state. S uses his right to establish five L restaurants in State Q and franchises two others to do likewise. Neither L nor S retained substantial rights when the transfers were made. Which of S's transfers qualify for purposes of § 1253?

39. T is the owner of numerous office buildings. A major tenant of one of the buildings wishes to cancel its lease because it is moving to another city. After lengthy negotiations, the tenant pays T $50,000, and its obligations under the lease are cancelled. If the tenant had fulfilled the lease terms, T would have received rent of $80,000. How much income does T have, and what is the character of that income?

40. F exchanges a business copying machine for another copier in a § 1031 like-kind exchange. F acquired the machine on March 12, 19X0, and the exchange occurred on July 3, 19X4.

     (a) When does the holding period of the new machine begin?

     (b) How would the answer to (a) change if the transaction were the replacement of a personal residence and the taxpayer qualified under § 1034?

41. K bought 100 shares of X Corporation stock at $10 per share on February 1, 19X1, and sold short 100 shares of X Corporation stock at $15 per share on July 1, 19X4. K closed the short sale on August 1, 19X4, by delivering 100 shares of X Corporation stock bought on that date at $16 per share. On August 2, 19X4, K sells the stock purchased on February 1, 19X1, for $17 per share.

     (a) What is the amount of K's gain or loss upon closing the short sale?

     (b) What is its nature?

     (c) What is the amount and nature of K's gain or loss upon the sale of the stock on August 2, 19X4?

42. T sells short 50 shares of ABC stock at $20 per share on January 1, 19X7. He buys 200 shares of ABC stock on April 1, 19X7, at $15 per share and holds the latter until May 2, 19X8, at which time, 50 shares of the 200-share block are delivered to close the short sale made on January 1, 19X7.

     (a) What is the amount and nature of T's gain or loss upon closing the short sale?

     (b) When does the holding period for the remaining 150 shares begin?

43. U, an unmarried individual with no dependents, has the following transactions in 19X4:

Taxable income (exclusive of capital gains and losses)	$ 15,000
Long-term capital gain	4,000
Long-term capital loss	(900)
Short-term capital gain	1,000
Short-term capital loss	(1,600)

     What is U's net capital gain or loss? What is U's adjusted gross income?

44. R owns an antique shop. She buys property from estates, often at much less than the retail value of the property. Recently, she sold an antique

desk for $4,000 for which she had paid $125. R had held the desk in her shop for 15 months before selling it. How much and what type of gain will be included in her 19X4 tax computation?

45.   X, an unmarried individual with no dependents, has the following 19X4 transactions:

Taxable income (exclusive of capital gains and losses)	$ 15,000
Long-term capital loss	(5,000)
Long-term capital gain	2,000
Short-term capital loss (carried to 19X4 from 19X3)	(2,000)

What is X's net capital gain or loss? What is X's adjusted gross income?

46.   B, an unmarried individual with no dependents, has the following transactions in 19X4:

Taxable income (exclusive of capital gain and losses)	$ 15,000
Long-term capital loss	(3,000)
Long-term capital loss (carried to 19X4 from 19X3)	(1,000)
Short-term capital gain	11,000
Short-term capital loss (carried to 19X4 from 19X3)	(6,000)

What is B's net capital gain or loss? What is B's adjusted gross income?

47.   For 19X4, T, an unmarried individual with adjusted gross income (exclusive of capital gains and losses) of $18,000, has a long-term capital loss of $2,000 and no other capital gains or losses. What is T's net capital loss and adjusted gross income?

48.   S, a married individual filing a separate return, has the following capital gains and losses in 19X4:

Long-term capital loss	$ (3,000)
Short-term capital gain	2,000
Short-term capital loss (carryover from 19X3)	(3,000)

What is S's net capital gain or loss? What is S's adjusted gross income (assume S has no other income)?

49.   In 19X4, W had $10,000 of adjusted gross income (exclusive of capital gains and losses), $500 short-term capital gains, $900 short-term capital losses, $700 long-term capital gains, and $3,500 long-term capital losses. What is W's net capital gain or loss? What is W's adjusted gross income?

50.   In 19X4, K realized a long-term capital gain of $2,000, a short-term capital gain of $12,000, and a long-term capital loss of $1,200. What is K's net capital gain or loss? What is K's adjusted gross income?

Cumulative Problems

51.   T is an automobile mechanic. He is single, age 28, and has no dependents. In April 1984, while tinkering with his automobile, T devised a carburetor modification kit which increases gas mileage by 20%. He patented the invention and in June 1984, sold it to X Corporation for a lump-sum

payment of $250,000 plus $5 per kit sold. Other information of potential tax consequence is given below.

(a) Cash received from X Corporation, which sold 20,000 kits in 1984.	$ 100,000
(b) Wages earned as a mechanic from January 1 through June 17.	4,300
(c) Points paid on a $200,000 mortgage T incurred to buy a luxurious new home (he had previously lived in an apartment).	6,000
(d) State sales taxes paid on four new automobiles T acquired in 1984.	2,200
(e) T has continued his experimental activities and is now working on several potentially patentable automotive devices (costs incurred include rent paid for a garage, materials, supplies, etc.).	14,000
(f) Various itemized deductions (not including any potential deductions above).	9,400
(g) T's total base period taxable income for the four most recent tax years.	32,000
(h) Interest on savings account.	6,200

Compute T's lowest legal tax liability, before prepayments or credits, for 1984.

52. B is single, age 30, and has no dependents. B's salary for 19X4 was $24,000. B inherited a parcel of land from his mother in 19X1, when its fair market value was $50,000 (the mother's basis in the land was $35,000). In 19X3, he subdivided the property into 10 lots, four of which were sold in that year for $10,000 each. B made no improvements on the property. He sold three lots in 19X4 at a price of $12,000 per lot and paid a $1,000 commission to a real estate broker on the sale. In April 19X4, B sold a letter at auction for $8,000. The letter was a handwritten reply from Ronald Reagan to a letter B had written complimenting Mr. Reagan on a campaign speech. B received the letter on March 15, 19X3. On May 14, 19X4, B sold 100 shares of stock he had received from an uncle, U, on May 15, 19X3. He received $5,000 for the stock. U's basis in the stock which he had owned for two years, was $6,000, and its fair market value at the date of gift was $5,500. No gift tax was paid on the transfer. B's itemized deductions for 19X4 were $6,600. Compute his taxable income.

Research Problems

53. P has orally agreed to buy a business conducted by S (as a sole proprietorship) for $500,000. In completing the purchase agreement, S wants $50,000 of the $500,000 allocated to the goodwill of the business. P disagrees and maintains, instead, that the $50,000 should be allocated to S's promise not to compete with P in the same community for a specified period of time.

    (a) Why would P not want the $50,000 allocated to the goodwill of the business?

    (b) Why would S not want the $50,000 allocated to a covenant not to compete?

Partial list of research aids:

Reg. § 1.167(a)–(3).

Gary C. Halbert, 37 TCM 408, T.C.Memo. 1978–88.

General Television, Inc. v. U. S., 79–2 USTC ¶ 9411, 44 AFTR2d 79–5115, 598 F.2d 1148 (CA–8, 1979).

54. In 1978, D (a real estate dealer) acquired a tract of unimproved land in the normal course of his business. Until June of 1979, D attempted to resell the property but without success. Prospective purchasers who D contacted generally were not interested at all because of the remote location of the property. From June of 1979 on, D ceased to advertise the real estate for resale, nor was the property listed with any other broker or dealer. Being busy with other business ventures, D literally forgot about the property. In 1981, and after the county had announced that it would build an access road to the area where the property was located, P contacted D concerning the availability of the real estate. After brief negotiations, the property was sold to P at a price that yielded a considerable gain to D. How might this gain be classified to D?

55. M inherited 600 shares of IBM stock during 1979 with a cost basis of $400 per share. M's broker advises M to write call options on the IBM stock. M can write a six-month option which entitles the holder to acquire the stock at $420. M receives a call premium of $12,000 ($20 × 600 shares) in 1979.

    (a) What are the tax consequences to M upon receipt of the $12,000 call premium in 1979?

    (b) How does this change if the option is exercised in 1981?

    (c) If the option is not exercised, what are M's tax consequences?

    Partial list of research aids:

    § 1001(a).

    Rev.Rul. 58–234, 1958–1 C.B. 279.

56. X Corporation has plants in a number of U. S. cities. It frequently transfers executives between those cities. If the executive cannot sell his or her home, the realty division of X Corporation will buy the home at its appraised value after 90 days. The realty division will then immediately attempt to resell the home. What is the nature of the gains and losses the realty division incurs when it sells the homes?

    Partial list of research aids:

    § 1221

    Rev.Rul. 82–204, 1982–2 C.B. 192.

57. T is a real estate dealer who owns a tract of land that has been subdivided for resale. Before the land was offered for sale as individual lots, the state government condemned the property. Upon being notified of the condemnation, T removed the land from her inventory accounts and listed it with her investment properties. The state purchased the land as park land. Six months later, T reinvested the proceeds in land to be held for investment. What is the nature of T's gain from the sale of the subdivided property?

May T postpone recognition of the gain due to her reinvestment of the proceeds in investment property?

Partial list of research aids:

§§ 1221, 1033

William B. Daugherty 78 TC 623 (1982).

Chapter 17

Property Transactions: Section 1231 and Recapture Provisions

A long-term capital gain was defined in Chapter 16 as the recognized gain from the sale or exchange of a capital asset held for more than one year. This chapter is concerned with § 1231, which applies to the sale or exchange of business properties and to certain involuntary conversions. This chapter is also concerned with recapture provisions that tax as ordinary income certain gains that might otherwise qualify for long-term capital gain treatment.

SECTION 1231 ASSETS

RELATIONSHIP TO SECTION 1221

Section 1221(2) provides that depreciable or real property used in a trade or business is not a capital asset.[1] Thus, recognized gains from the disposition of such types of property (principally machinery and equipment, buildings, and land) would be ordinary income as opposed to capital gain. Section 1231, however, provides that in certain cases (i. e., when a holding period requirement is satisfied and various recapture provisions have been satisfied) long-term capital gain treatment may apply to sales, exchanges, and involuntary conversions of these business assets. Section 1231 also applies in certain cases to

---

1. § 1221(2) and Reg. § 1.1221–1(b).

involuntary conversions of capital assets. The latter would not otherwise qualify for long-term capital gain treatment under § 1222, because an involuntary conversion is not a sale or exchange.

 On the loss side, however, § 1231 may allow for ordinary (as opposed to capital) loss treatment. It seems, therefore, that § 1231 provides for the best of all possible worlds: capital gain treatment for gains and ordinary loss treatment for losses.

JUSTIFICATION FOR FAVORABLE TAX TREATMENT

The highly favorable capital gain/ordinary loss treatment sanctioned by § 1231 can be explained by examining several historical developments. Prior to 1938, business property had been included in the definition of capital assets. Thus, if such property was sold for a loss (not an unlikely possibility during the years of the depression), a capital loss resulted. If, however, such property were depreciable and could be retained for its estimated useful life, much (if not all) of its cost could be recovered in the form of depreciation. Because the allowance for depreciation was fully deductible whereas capital losses were not, the tax law favored those who did not dispose of an asset. Congress recognized this inequity when it removed business property from the capital asset classification. During the period 1938–1942, therefore, all such gains and losses were ordinary gains and losses.

With the advent of World War II, however, several conditions forced Congress to reexamine the situation regarding business assets. First, the tax law did not encourage the sale of such assets if, as was usually the case, the result would be a large gain taxed as ordinary income. This was not a desirable result, since the premium should be on shifting business assets to those who could utilize them more effectively in the war production effort. Second, the government or its instrumentalities were acquiring, through the condemnation process, considerable business property for use by vital industries. Often the condemnation awards resulted in large gains to those taxpayers who were forced to part with their property and deprived them of the benefits of future depreciation deductions. Of course, the condemnations constituted involuntary conversions, the gain from which could be deferred through timely reinvestment in property that was "similar or related in service or use." But where was such property to be found in view of wartime restrictions and other governmental condemnations? The end product did not seem equitable: a large ordinary gain due to government action and no deferral possibility due to government restrictions.

In recognition of these two conditions, in 1942 Congress eased the tax bite on the disposition of some business property by allowing preferential capital gain treatment. Thus, the present scheme of § 1231 and the dichotomy of capital gain/ordinary loss treatment evolved due to a combination of economic considerations existing in 1938 and in 1942.

It is good to keep in mind that the rules regarding § 1231 treatment do not apply to *all* business property. Important in this regard are the holding period requirements (usually more than one year) and the fact that the property must be either depreciable property or real estate used in a trade or business. Nor is § 1231 necessarily limited to business property. Transactions involving certain capital assets may fall into the § 1231 category. Thus, § 1231 singles out only some types of business property and could include personal use property. Although these aspects of § 1231 will be brought out in the discussion that follows, initial mention aids in coping with the nature of the problem.

PROPERTY INCLUDED

Section 1231 property includes:

—Depreciable or real property used in a trade or business (principally, machinery and equipment, buildings, and land).

—Timber, coal, or domestic iron ore to which § 631 applies.

—Livestock (regardless of age) held for draft, breeding, dairy, or sporting purposes. Poultry is not included.

—Unharvested crop on land used in a trade or business.

—Certain capital assets.

PROPERTY EXCLUDED

Section 1231 property does not include:

—Property not held for more than one year. Since the benefit of § 1231 is long-term capital gain treatment, the holding period must correspond to the same holding period that applies to capital assets. Livestock must be held at least 12 months (24 months, in some cases). Unharvested crops do not have to be held for the required long-term holding period, but the land must be held for more than one year.

—Property where casualty losses exceed casualty gains for the taxable year. If a taxpayer has a net casualty loss, the individual casualty gains and losses are treated as ordinary gains and losses.

—Inventory and property held primarily for sale to customers.

—Section 1221(3) property (e. g., copyrights, literary compositions) and § 1221(6) property (i. e., certain U. S. government publications).

SPECIAL RULES FOR CERTAIN SECTION 1231 ASSETS

A rather diverse group of assets is included under § 1231. The following discussion summarizes the special rules for some of those assets.

Timber. A taxpayer can elect to treat the cutting of timber held for sale or for use in a trade or business as a sale or exchange.[2] If the taxpayer makes this election, the transaction qualifies under § 1231. The taxpayer must have owned the timber or a contract to cut it for more than one year prior to the date the cutting takes place. The recognized § 1231 gain or loss is determined at the time the timber is cut and is equal to the difference between the timber's fair market value as of the first day of the taxable year and its adjusted basis for depletion. If a taxpayer sells the timber for more or less than its fair market value as of the first day of the taxable year in which it is cut, the difference is ordinary income or loss.

This provision was enacted to provide preferential treatment relative to the natural growth value of timber, whose maturation is a relatively long-term process. Congress also believed this favorable treatment would encourage reforestation of timber lands. Section 631 also provides that if a taxpayer disposes of timber, held for more than one year, under a royalty contract (where the taxpayer retains an economic interest in the property), the disposal is treated as a sale of the timber. Therefore, any gain or loss qualifies under § 1231.

> **Example 1.** Several years ago, T purchased a tract of land with a substantial stand of trees on it. The land cost $40,000, and the timber cost $100,000. On the first day of 19X4, the timber was appraised at $250,000. In August 19X4, T cut the timber and sold it for $265,000. T elects to treat the cutting as a sale or exchange under § 1231. T has a $150,000 § 1231 gain ($250,000 − $100,000) and a $15,000 ordinary gain ($265,000 − $250,000).

Coal or Domestic Iron Ore. If a taxpayer disposes of coal or domestic iron ore, held for more than one year, under a royalty contract (where the taxpayer retains an economic interest in the property), the disposal is treated as a sale of the coal or domestic iron ore.[3] Therefore, any gain or loss qualifies under § 1231.

The provisions including timber, coal, and domestic iron ore royalties under § 1231 were enacted primarily to encourage the development and preservation of natural resources in the United States and to enable domestic producers to compete more favorably with foreign producers.

Livestock. Cattle and horses must be held 24 months or more and other livestock must be held 12 months or more to qualify under § 1231.[4] The primary reason for enacting this provision was the considerable amount of litigation over the character of livestock [i. e., whether livestock was held primarily for sale to customers (ordinary income) or for use in a trade or business (§ 1231 property)].

---

2. § 631(a) and Reg. § 1.631–1.
3. § 631(c) and Reg. § 1.631–3.
4. § 1231(b)(3) and Reg. § 1.1231–2(a)(1).

Unharvested Crops. An unharvested crop on land used in a trade or business and held for the required long-term capital gain holding period qualifies under § 1231 if the crop and land are disposed of at the same time to the same person.[5] The cost of producing the crop must be capitalized (not expensed) or § 1231 does not apply.[6] This provision was enacted because taxpayers previously were able to recover the costs of producing crops through current deductions and were usually allowed long-term capital gain treatment on the disposition of the crop.

Certain Capital Assets. The peculiar role that personal use capital assets can play in a § 1231 determination probably is the most confusing part of this whole area. Recall that involuntary conversions deal with two major categories: casualties and condemnations. (Throughout this chapter, the term "casualty" means casualty *or* theft.) The casualty gains and losses on involuntary conversions of assets (both business and personal) held for more than one year are combined (see Figure I). If the result is a gain, all of the casualty gains and losses are § 1231 transactions. If the result is a loss, § 1231 classification does not take place. Thus, a personal use capital asset that is subject to a casualty (e. g., a personal residence that is damaged by fire or a personal automobile that is stolen) may or may not be a § 1231 asset, depending on how the netting process works out.

Involuntary conversions due to condemnation are handled differently. If they involve *recognized* gains or losses of assets (both business and personal) held for more than one year, they are considered to be § 1231 assets. But since a loss from the condemnation of a personal use capital asset is not recognized, it cannot be classified as a § 1231 transaction. Consequently, only gains from the condemnation of personal use assets can be covered under § 1231.

When personal use assets are involved, why is it that a casualty loss *might* receive § 1231 treatment whereas a condemnation loss cannot? The answer is quite simple. Section 165(c)(3) allows a deduction for personal casualty losses (refer to Chapter 8) while no provision in the Code accords similar treatment for condemnation losses. Recall that § 1033 (refer to Chapter 15) allows deferral of gains on involuntary conversions (including those resulting from condemnations) but does not apply to losses. This variation in treatment between casualty and condemnation losses sheds considerable light on what § 1231 is all about. Section 1231 has no effect on whether or not realized gain or loss is recognized. Instead, it merely dictates how such gain or loss might be classified (i. e., ordinary or capital) under certain conditions.

---

5. § 1231(b)(4) and Reg. § 1.1231–1(c)(5).
6. § 268 and Reg. § 1.268–1.

GENERAL PROCEDURE FOR SECTION 1231 COMPUTATION

The tax treatment of § 1231 gains or losses depends on the results of a rather complex netting procedure. The steps in this netting procedure are described below.

Step 1. Net all gains and losses from casualties of property held for more than one year. The losses from personal casualties are determined after reduction by the $100 floor. Casualty gains result when insurance proceeds exceed the adjusted basis of the property.

Figure I

SECTION 1231 NETTING PROCEDURE

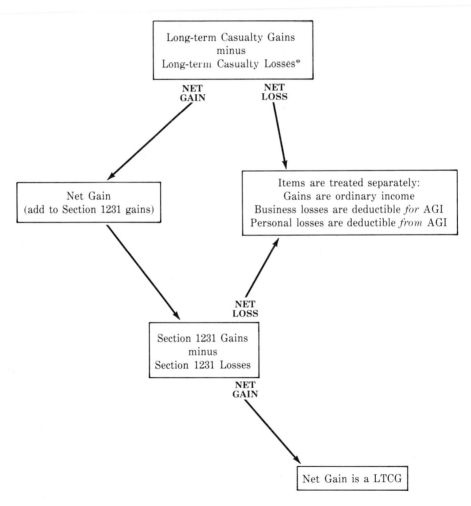

* For personal use property losses: Net of the $100 floor and 10% of AGI reductions.

(a) If the casualty gains exceed the casualty losses, add the excess to the other § 1231 gains for the taxable year.

(b) If the casualty losses exceed the casualty gains, exclude all losses and gains from further § 1231 computation. If this is the case, all casualty gains are ordinary income. Business casualty losses are deductible *for* adjusted gross income. Personal casualty losses in excess of $100 per casualty are deductible *from* adjusted gross income (to the extent they exceed 10 percent of adjusted gross income).

Step 2. After adding any net casualty gain from Step 1(a) to the other § 1231 gains (including recognized gains and losses from condemnations), net all § 1231 gains and losses.

(a) If the gains exceed losses, the excess is a long-term capital gain.[7]

(b) If the losses exceed gains, all gains are ordinary income; business losses are deductible *for* adjusted gross income; and personal casualty losses in excess of $100 per casualty are deductible *from* adjusted gross income (to the extent they exceed 10 percent of adjusted gross income).[8]

If the taxpayer is in a position to recognize § 1231 gains in one year and § 1231 losses in another year, the losses will not have to be offset against the gains. The result is that all the gains in one year are long-term capital gains and all the losses in the other year are ordinary losses deductible against ordinary income. Figure I (see page 662) summarizes the § 1231 computational procedure.

The following examples illustrate the application of the § 1231 computation procedure.

Example 2. During the current year, T had $25,000 of AGI before considering the following recognized gains and losses:

Capital gains and losses	
Long-term capital gain	$ 3,000
Long-term capital loss	(400)
Short-term capital gain	1,000
Short-term capital loss	(200)

Casualties	
Theft of diamond ring (owned four months)	$ (800)*
Fire damage to personal residence (owned 10 years)	(400)*
Gain from insurance recovery on accidental destruction of business truck (owned two years)	200

7. § 1231(a). The gains and losses are reported individually on the tax return.
8. Ibid.

§ 1231 gains and losses from depreciable
business assets held over one year

Asset A	$ 300
Asset B	1,100
Asset C	(500)

Gains and losses from sale of depreciable
business assets held one year or less

Asset D	$ 200
Asset E	(300)

(*As adjusted for the $100 floor on personal casualty losses.)

Disregarding the recapture of depreciation possibility (discussed later in this chapter), the tax treatment of the above gains and losses is as follows:

—The theft of the diamond ring is not a § 1231 transaction, because it was not held for more than one year. The $800 is potentially deductible *from* adjusted gross income.

—The $400 personal casualty loss does not exceed 10% of AGI. (AGI for this purpose is computed by not including any personal casualty gains or losses.) Thus, only the business casualty gain remains. The $200 gain is added to the § 1231 gains.

—The gains from § 1231 transactions (Assets A, B, and C and the business casualty gain) exceed the losses by $1,100 ($1,600 less $500). This excess is a long-term capital gain and is added to T's other long-term capital gains.

—T's net long-term capital gain is $3,700 ($3,000 plus $1,100 from § 1231 transactions less the long-term capital loss of $400). T's net short-term capital gain is $800 ($1,000 less $200). The result is capital gain net income of $4,500. The long-term portion ($3,700) is subject to the 60% capital gains deduction. The $800 short-term portion is ordinary income and subject to T's regular tax rates.

—The gain and loss from Assets D and E (depreciable business assets held for less than the required holding period) are treated as ordinary gain and loss by T.

Results of the gains and losses on
T's tax computation

Included portion of NLTCG [$3,700 − ($3,700 × 60%)]	$ 1,480
STCG	800
Ordinary gain from sale of Asset D	200
Ordinary loss from sale of Asset E	(300)
AGI from other sources	25,000
AGI	$ 27,180

T would have casualty losses of $800 (diamond ring) + $400 (personal residence). A casualty loss is deductible only to the extent it exceeds 10% of AGI. Thus, none of the $1,200 is deductible ($27,180 × 10% = $2,718).

Example 3. Assume the same facts as in the previous example, except the loss from Asset C was $1,700 instead of $500.

—The treatment of the casualty losses is the same as in Example 2.

—The losses from § 1231 transactions now exceed the gains by $100 ($1,700 less $1,600). The result is that the gains from Assets A and B and the business casualty gain are ordinary income and the loss from Asset C is a deduction *for* adjusted gross income (i. e., a business loss). The same result can be achieved by simply treating the $100 net loss as a deduction *for* AGI.

—Capital gain net income is $3,400 ($2,600 long-term plus $800 short-term). The $2,600 long-term portion is subject to the 60% capital gain deduction. The $800 short-term portion is ordinary income.

Results of the gains and
losses on T's tax computation

Included portion of NLTCG [$2,600 − ($2,600 × 60%)]	$ 1,040
STCG	800
Net ordinary loss on Assets A, B, and C and business casualty gain	(100)
Ordinary gain from sale of Asset D	200
Ordinary loss from sale of Asset E	(300)
AGI from other sources	25,000
AGI	$ 26,640

None of the personal casualty loss would be deductible, since $1,200 does not exceed 10% of $26,640.

SECTION 1245 RECAPTURE

Section 1245 was enacted to prevent taxpayers from receiving the dual benefits of depreciation deductions which offset ordinary income plus long-term capital gain treatment under § 1231 on the disposition of the depreciated property.

Example 4. T purchased a business machine for $100,000 and deducted $60,000 of depreciation on the machine before selling it for $80,000. If it were not for § 1245, only 40% of the $40,000 § 1231 gain ($80,000 less $40,000 of adjusted basis) would be subject to tax. Because this § 1231 gain would be treated as a long-term capital gain, the 60% capital gain deduction would result in only $16,000 of gain being taxed. If the depreciation recapture rules were not applicable, T would receive a net tax benefit [($60,000 of depreciation × T's ordinary tax rate) − ($40,000 × T's capital gain tax rate)] by deducting depreciation as an ordinary deduction in the years prior to the sale. Section 1245 prevents this otherwise favorable result by recapturing as ordinary income (not § 1231 gain) any gain to the extent of depreciation taken since 1962. In this example, the entire $40,000 gain would be taxed as ordinary income, assuming the machine was acquired after 1961 or that depreciation taken since 1962 is at least $40,000.

Section 1245 provides, in general, that the portion of recognized gain from the sale or other disposition of § 1245 property which represents depreciation taken since January 1, 1962 (including additional first-year depreciation or immediate expensing under § 179), is recaptured as ordinary income. Any remaining gain after subtracting the amount recaptured as ordinary income will usually be § 1231 gain. The remaining gain would be casualty gain if it was disposed of in a casualty event. Section 1245 provisions also apply to 15-year nonresidential real property if the property's cost is recovered under the statutory percentage method of the accelerated cost recovery system.

The application of § 1245 recapture rules does not mean the depreciation deductions are lost. It means only that to the extent of depreciation taken, the gain does not qualify for potential long-term capital gain treatment under § 1231.

If § 1245 property is disposed of in a transaction other than a sale, exchange, or involuntary conversion, the maximum amount recaptured is the excess of the property's fair market value over its adjusted basis.

SECTION 1245 PROPERTY

Generally, § 1245 property includes all depreciable personalty (e. g., machinery and equipment), including livestock. Buildings and their structural components are not § 1245 property. The following property is also subject to § 1245 treatment:

—Amortizable personalty such as patents, copyrights, and leaseholds of § 1245 property. Professional baseball and football player contracts are § 1245 property.

—Elevators and escalators. However, only depreciation taken after June 30, 1963, is recaptured.

—Certain depreciable tangible real property (other than buildings and their structural components) employed as an integral part of certain activities such as manufacturing and production.

—Pollution control facilities, railroad grading and tunnel bores, on-the-job training, and child care facilities on which amortization is taken are § 1245 property.

—Single-purpose agricultural and horticultural structures and petroleum storage facilities.

—As noted above, 15-year nonresidential real estate for which accelerated cost recovery is used is subject to the § 1245 recapture rules, although it is technically not § 1245 property.

SECTION 1245 POTENTIAL

The following examples express the general application of § 1245.

Example 5. T owns § 1245 property with an estimated useful life of 12 years, acquisition cost on January 1, 1974, of $12,000, and no salvage value. The asset is sold on January 1, 1984, for $13,000. Depreciation amounting to $10,000 has been deducted under the straight-line method.

—The recognized gain from the sale is $11,000. This is the amount realized of $13,000 less the adjusted basis of $2,000 ($12,000 cost less $10,000 depreciation taken).

—Depreciation taken since January 1, 1962, is $10,000. Therefore, $10,000 of the $11,000 recognized gain is ordinary income and the remaining $1,000 gain is § 1231 gain.

Example 6. Assume the same facts as in the previous example except the asset is sold for $9,000 instead of $13,000.

—The recognized gain from the sale is $7,000. This is the amount realized of $9,000 less adjusted basis of $2,000.

—Depreciation taken since January 1, 1962, is $10,000. Therefore, since the $10,000 depreciation taken since January 1, 1962, exceeds the recognized gain of $7,000, the entire $7,000 recognized gain is ordinary income.

Example 7. Assume the same facts as in Example 5 except the asset is sold for $1,500 instead of $13,000.

—The recognized loss from the sale is $500. This is the amount realized of $1,500 less adjusted basis of $2,000.

—§ 1245 does not apply because the recapture rules do not apply to losses. The entire $500 recognized loss is § 1231 loss.

OBSERVATIONS ON SECTION 1245

—In most instances the total depreciation taken since January 1, 1962, will exceed the recognized gain. Therefore, the disposition of § 1245 property usually results in ordinary income rather than gain under § 1231. Thus, generally, there will be no § 1231 gain unless the § 1245 property is disposed of for more than its original cost. Refer to Example 5.

—Recapture applies to the total amount of depreciation allowed or allowable regardless of the depreciation method used.

—Recapture applies regardless of the holding period of the property. Of course, the entire recognized gain would be ordinary income if the property were held for one year or less, because § 1231 would not apply.

—Section 1245 does not apply to losses. Losses receive § 1231 treatment.

SECTION 1250 RECAPTURE PRIOR TO ERTA OF 1981

Section 1250 was enacted in 1964 for depreciable real property. This provision prevents taxpayers from receiving both the benefits of accelerated depreciation deductions and subsequent long-term capital gain treatment upon the sale of real property. As was true in the case of § 1245, § 1250 does not apply to losses.[9]

Section 1250 as originally enacted required recapture of a percentage of the *additional depreciation* deducted by the taxpayer. Additional depreciation is the excess of accelerated depreciation actually deducted over depreciation which would have been deductible if the straight-line method had been used. The percentage of additional depreciation subject to recapture was dependent on the period of time the property was held. Under the original § 1250 provisions, the recapture percentage was 100 percent for assets held for 20 months or less, and zero percent for assets held for 10 years or more. Since the total holding period was used in this computation and these provisions apply to depreciation taken in tax years after 1963 but before 1970, the additional depreciation recapture percentage for this period will always now be zero percent. Thus, practically, there is no longer any § 1250 recapture of pre-1970 additional depreciation.

Numerous changes have been made since the original § 1250 provisions were enacted. Post-1969 additional depreciation on nonresidential real property is now subject to 100 percent recapture (see Example 8). The following discussion describes the computational steps prescribed in § 1250 and reflected on Form 4797 (Supplemental Schedule of Gains and Losses).

If § 1250 property is disposed of in a transaction other than a sale, exchange, or involuntary conversion, the maximum amount recaptured is the excess of the property's fair market value over its adjusted

---

9. Reg. § 1.1250–1(a)(5).

basis.[10] For example, if a corporation distributed property to its shareholders as a dividend, the property would be disposed of by the corporation at a gain if the fair market value is greater than the adjusted basis. The maximum amount of § 1250 recapture would be the gain.

Generally, § 1250 property is depreciable real property (principally, buildings and their structural components) that is not subject to § 1245. Intangible real property such as leaseholds of § 1250 property is also included.[11]

SECTION 1250 POTENTIAL

For § 1250 property other than residential rental property, the potential recapture is equal to the amount of additional depreciation taken since December 31, 1969. (The rules for residential rental housing are discussed later in the chapter.) The lower of the potential § 1250 recapture amount or the gain is multiplied by a percentage to determine the amount of gain recaptured as ordinary income. The following general rules apply:

—Post-1969 additional depreciation is depreciation taken in excess of straight-line after December 31, 1969.

—The post-1969 percentage is 100 percent.

—If the property is held for one year or less (usually not the case), all depreciation taken, even under the straight-line method, is additional depreciation.

—Special rules apply to dispositions of substantially improved § 1250 property. These rules are rather technical, and the reader should consult the examples in the Regulations for illustrations of their application.[12]

It should be observed that the recapture rules under § 1250 are substantially less punitive than the § 1245 recapture rules, since only the amount of additional depreciation is subject to recapture. Straight-line depreciation (except for property held one year or less) is not recaptured.

COMPUTING RECAPTURE ON NONRESIDENTIAL PROPERTY

The following procedure is used to compute recapture on nonresidential real property under § 1250:

—Determine the gain from the sale or other disposition of the property.

—Determine post-1969 additional depreciation.

---

10.   §§ 1250(a)(1) and (2). Reg. §§ 1.1250–1(a)(1) and (4) and –1(b)(1) and (4).
11.   Reg. § 1.1250–1(e)(3).
12.   § 1250(f) and Reg. § 1.1250–5.

—The lower of the gain or the post-1969 additional depreciation is ordinary income.

—If any gain remains (total gain less recapture), it is § 1231 gain. However, it would be casualty gain if the disposition was by casualty, and theft gain if the disposition was by theft.

The following example shows the application of the § 1250 computational procedure:

Example 8. On January 3, 1972, T, an individual, acquired a new building at a cost of $200,000 for use in his business. The building had an estimated useful life of 50 years and no estimated salvage value. Depreciation has been taken under the double-declining balance method through December 31, 1983. Pertinent information with respect to depreciation taken follows:

Year	Undepreciated Balance (Beginning of the Year)	Current Depreciation Provision	Straight-line Depreciation	Additional Depreciation
1972	$ 200,000	$ 8,000	$ 4,000	$ 4,000
1973	192,000	7,680	4,000	3,680
1974	184,320	7,373	4,000	3,373
1975	176,947	7,079	4,000	3,079
1976	169,868	6,795	4,000	2,795
1977	163,073	6,523	4,000	2,523
1978	156,550	6,262	4,000	2,262
1979	150,288	6,012	4,000	2,012
1980	144,276	5,771	4,000	1,771
1981	138,505	5,540	4,000	1,540
1982	132,965	5,319	4,000	1,319
1983	127,646	5,106	4,000	1,106
1984	122,540			
Total 1972–1983		$ 77,460	$ 48,000	$ 29,460

On January 2, 1984, the building was sold for $147,638. Compute the amount of § 1250 ordinary income and § 1231 gain.

—The recognized gain from the sale is $25,098. This is the difference between the $147,638 realized and the $122,540 adjusted basis ($200,000 cost less $77,460 depreciation taken).

—Post-1969 additional depreciation is $29,460.

—The amount of post-1969 ordinary income is $25,098; the post-1969 additional depreciation of $29,460 is more than the recognized gain of $25,098, so the entire gain is recaptured.

—Since all of the $25,098 gain is recaptured as ordinary income under § 1250, there is no § 1231 gain to receive favorable long-term capital gain treatment.

COMPUTING RECAPTURE ON RESIDENTIAL RENTAL HOUSING

Section 1250 recapture applies to the sale or other disposition of residential rental housing. The rules are the same as for other § 1250 property, except that only the post-1975 excess depreciation is recaptured in full.[13] The post-1969 through 1975 recapture percentage is 100 percent less one percentage point for each full month the property is held over 100 months.[14] Therefore, the excess depreciation for periods after 1975 is initially applied against the recognized gain, and such amounts are recaptured in full as ordinary income. Any remaining gain is then tested under the percentage rules applicable to the post-1969 through 1975 period. If any of the recognized gain is not absorbed by the recapture rules pertaining to the post-1969 period, the remaining gain is § 1231 gain. Property qualifies as residential rental housing only if at least 80 percent of gross rental income is rental income from dwelling units.[15]

> **Example 9.** Assume the same facts as in the previous example, except the building is residential rental housing.
>
> —Post-1975 ordinary income is $15,328 (post-1975 additional depreciation of $15,328 is less than the recognized gain of $25,098).
>
> —Post-1969 through 1975 ordinary income is $4,299. The post-1969 through 1975 additional depreciation of $14,132 is more than the remaining gain of $9,770 ($25,098 less $15,328). The post-1969 through 1975 percentage is 44% [100% less (156% less 100%)]. The building was held for 156 months, or 56 months over 100 months. Thus, 44% of $9,770 is $4,299.
>
> —Since only $19,627 ($15,328 plus $4,299) is recaptured as ordinary income under § 1250, the remaining $5,471 ($25,098 − $19,627) of the $25,098 gain is § 1231 gain and may receive favorable long-term capital gain treatment.

ACRS RULES FOR RECAPTURE

The rules for recapture of real estate cost recovery allowances are related to those just discussed for pre-ERTA depreciation recapture. However, there are some important differences for nonresidential real property.

---

13.   § 1250(a)(1)(B)(v).
14.   § 1250(a)(1)(B)(iii) and Reg. § 1.1250–1(d)(1)(i)(c).
15.   § 167(j)(2)(B) and Reg. § 1.167(j)–3(b)(1)(i).

COMPUTING RECAPTURE ON NONRESIDENTIAL REAL PROPERTY

Section 1245 (rather than § 1250) recapture provisions apply to non-residential real property located in the United States for which the ACRS statutory percentage method is used to compute the cost recovery allowance. Nonresidential real property includes buildings such as offices, warehouses, factories, and stores. [Thus, the less severe § 1250 recapture provisions apply to ACRS real property that is (1) residential real property, (2) real property used predominantly outside the United States, (3) real property for which the optional straight-line election is made, and (4) certain government-financed or low income housing (as described in § 1250(a)(1)(B).[16]]

> **Example 10.** T acquired nonresidential real property on January 1, 1981, at a cost of $100,000. She uses the statutory percentage method for computing the cost recovery allowance under ACRS. She sells the asset on January 1, 1984, for $120,000. The amount and nature of T's gain will be computed as follows:

Amount realized			$ 120,000
Adjusted basis			
Cost		$ 100,000	
Minus cost recovery allowances			
1981	$ 12,000		
1982	10,000		
1983	9,000	31,000	69,000
Gain realized			$ 51,000

> The gain of $51,000 will be treated as ordinary income to the extent of all cost recovery allowances previously taken. Thus, T will report ordinary income of $31,000 (total cost recovery allowances) and § 1231 gain of $20,000 ($51,000 gain − $31,000 recaptured as ordinary income).

> **Example 11.** Assume the same facts as in the previous example, except that T elected the optional straight-line method over 15 years. T's total cost recovery would be $20,000 [($100,000/15) × 3 years]. T's entire gain of $40,000 [$120,000 amount realized − ($100,000 cost − $20,000 recovery allowance using straight-line method)] will be § 1231 gain. T will not be required to recognize any ordinary income on this transaction.

COMPUTING RECAPTURE ON RESIDENTIAL REAL PROPERTY

Under ACRS, the treatment of residential real property (e. g., apartment buildings) is unchanged from the post 1975 pre-ERTA rules discussed earlier. Gain is recaptured as ordinary income only to the

---

16. *Riach v. Frank,* 62–1 USTC ¶ 9419, 9 AFTR2d 1263, 302 F.2d 374.

extent of additional depreciation. In this case, additional depreciation is defined as the excess of the ACRS deduction using the statutory percentage method over the deduction that would be allowed using the straight-line method over 15 years.

> **Example 12.** Assume the same facts as in Example 10, except that the property is residential real property. If T had used the straight-line method, total cost recovery allowances would have been $20,000 ($100,000/5) × 3 years). Therefore, T must recapture the excess ACRS deduction of $11,000 ($31,000 − $20,000) as ordinary income. The remaining gain of $40,000 ($51,000 − $11,000) will be § 1231 gain.

CONSIDERATIONS COMMON TO SECTIONS 1245 AND 1250

EXCEPTIONS

Recapture under § § 1245 and 1250 does not apply to the following transactions:

> *Gifts.*[17] However, the recapture potential carries over to the donee.[18]

> **Example 13.** T gives his daughter, D, § 1245 property with an adjusted basis of $1,000. The amount of recapture potential (i. e., depreciation taken since January 1, 1962) is $700. D uses the property in her business and claims further depreciation of $100 before selling it for $1,900. D's recognized gain is $1,000 (amount realized of $1,900 less $900 adjusted basis) of which $800 is recaptured as ordinary income ($100 depreciation taken by D plus $700 recapture potential carried over from T). The remaining gain of $200 is § 1231 gain. Even if D used the property for personal purposes, the $700 recapture potential would still be carried over.[19]

> *Death.* Although not a very attractive tax planning approach, death eliminates all recapture potential.[20] In other words, any recapture potential does not carry over from a decedent to an estate or heir.

> **Example 14.** Assume the same facts as in the previous example, except T's daughter receives the property as a result of T's death. The $700 recapture potential from T is extinguished. D would have a basis for the property equal to the property's fair

---

17. § § 1245(b)(1) and 1250(d)(1) and Reg. § § 1.1245–4(a)(1) and 1.1250–3(a)(1).
18. Reg. § § 1.1245–2(a)(4), 1.1250–2(d)(3) and 1.1250–3(a)(3).
19. Reg. § § 1.1245–3(a)(3) and 1.1250–1(e)(2).
20. § § 1245(b)(2) and 1250(d)(2).

market value ($1,800) at T's death. D would have a $200 gain when the property is sold, because the selling price ($1,900) exceeds the property's adjusted basis ($1,800 original basis to D less $100 depreciation) by $200. Because of § 1245, $100 would be ordinary income.

Charitable Transfers. The recapture potential reduces the amount of the charitable contribution deduction under § 170.[21]

Example 15. T donates to his church § 1245 property with a fair market value of $10,000 and an adjusted basis of $7,000. Assume that the amount of recapture potential is $2,000 (i. e., the amount of recapture that would occur if the property were sold). T's charitable contribution deduction (subject to the limitations discussed in Chapter 11) is $8,000 ($10,000 fair market value less $2,000 recapture potential).

Certain Tax-free Transactions. These are transactions in which the transferor's adjusted basis of property carries over to the transferee.[22] The recapture potential, however, also carries over to the transferee.[23] Included in this category are transfers of property pursuant to (1) tax-free incorporations under § 351, (2) certain liquidations of subsidiary companies under § 338, and (3) tax-free reorganizations. Gain may be recognized in these transactions if boot is received. If gain is recognized, it is treated as ordinary income to the extent of the recapture potential or recognized gain, whichever is lower.[24]

Example 16. T transfers § 1245 property with a fair market value of $12,000 and an adjusted basis of $8,000 to a controlled corporation under § 351. The amount of recapture potential is $3,000. T receives stock of the corporation with a fair market value of $11,000 and cash of $1,000. T's realized gain is $4,000 ($12,000 less $8,000). Gain of $1,000 is recognized because T received boot of $1,000. Since the amount of recapture potential ($3,000) exceeds the recognized gain ($1,000), the entire $1,000 recognized gain is ordinary income. The remaining recapture potential of $2,000 carries over to the corporation.

Like-kind Exchanges (§ 1031) and Involuntary Conversions (§ 1033). Gain may be recognized to the extent of boot received under § 1031, and gain also may be recognized to the extent the proceeds from an involuntary conversion are not reinvested in similar property under § 1033. Such recognized gain is subject to recapture as ordinary income under §§ 1245 and 1250. In

---

21. § 170(e)(1)(A) and Reg. § 1.170–1(c)(3).

22. §§ 1245(b)(3) and 1250(d)(3) and Reg. §§ 1.1245–4(c) and 1.1250–3(c).

23. Reg. §§ 1.1245–2(a)(4) and –2(c)(2), 1.1250–2(d)(1) and (3) and –3(c)(3).

24. §§ 1245(b)(3) and 1250(d)(3); Reg. §§ 1.1245–4(c) and 1.1250–3(c). Some of these special corporate problems are discussed in Chapter 20.

addition, gain may be recaptured to the extent of any non-Section 1245 like-kind property which is received in the exchange.[25]

Example 17. T exchanges § 1245 property with an adjusted basis of $300 for § 1245 property with a fair market value of $6,000. The exchange qualifies as a like-kind exchange under § 1031(a). T also gives $5,000 cash (boot). T's realized gain is $700 [amount realized of $6,000 less $5,300 (adjusted basis of property plus boot given)]. Assuming the recapture potential is $4,500, gain is not recognized because no boot or non-Section 1245 like-kind property is received. The entire recapture potential of $4,500 carries over to the like-kind property received.

OTHER APPLICATIONS

Sections 1245 and 1250 apply notwithstanding any other provisions in the Code.[26] That is, the recapture rules under these sections override all other sections. Special applications include:

> *Installment Sales.* Recapture takes place as cash is received and gain is recognized. Recapture applies first; all gain is ordinary income until the recapture potential is fully absorbed.[27]

Example 18. T sells § 1245 property for $20,000, to be paid in 10 annual installments of $2,000 each plus interest at 10%. T realizes a $6,000 gain from the sale, of which $4,000 is attributable to depreciation taken since January 1, 1962. If T elects the installment method, the entire $600 gain in each of the payments for the first six years plus $400 of the gain in the seventh year is recaptured as ordinary income. The remaining $200 of gain in the seventh year and the entire $600 gain in each of the last three years are § 1231 gain.

Gain is recognized on installment sales in the year of sale (regardless of whether an equal amount of cash is received) in an amount equal to the § 179 (immediate expensing) deductions taken with respect to the property sold.[28]

> *Property Dividends.* Even though gain is otherwise not recognized by a corporation if it distributes property as a dividend, recapture under § § 1245 and 1250 applies to the extent of the lower of the recapture potential or the excess of the property's fair market value over its adjusted basis.[29]

---

25. § 1245(b)(4) and Reg. § 1.1245–4(d). Also, see § 1250(d)(4) and Reg. § 1.1250–3(d)(1) for recapture rules applicable to real property.
26. § § 1245(d) and 1250(i).
27. Reg. § § 1.1245–6(d) and 1.1250–1(c)(6). The installment method of reporting gains on the sale of property is discussed in Chapter 18.
28. § 453(i).
29. Reg. § § 1.1245–1(c) and –6(b), 1.1250–1(a)(4) and –1(b)(4) and –1(c)(2).

Example 19. X Corporation distributes § 1245 property as a dividend to its shareholders. The amount of recapture potential is $300 and the excess of the property's fair market value over its adjusted basis is $800. X Corporation recognizes $300 of ordinary income.

SPECIAL RECAPTURE PROVISIONS

SPECIAL RECAPTURE FOR CORPORATIONS

Under § 291(a)(1), corporations (other than S corporations) selling depreciable real estate may have ordinary income in addition to that required by § 1250. The provisions apply to dispositions of depreciable real estate occurring after December 31, 1982. The "ordinary gain adjustment" is 15 percent of the excess of the § 1245 potential recapture over the § 1250 recapture. The result is that the § 1231 gain is correspondingly decreased by this increase in ordinary income.

Example 20. A corporation purchased a building in 1977 for $200,000. Accelerated depreciation of $110,000 was taken before the building was sold on January 1, 1984. The straight-line depreciation which could have been taken was $80,000. The selling price was $225,000. Section 1250 would recapture $30,000 ($110,000 − $80,000) of the $135,000 gain [$225,000 − ($200,000 − $110,000)] as ordinary income. The § 291 ordinary gain adjustment would be computed as follows:

Section 1245 recapture (lower of depreciation taken or total gain)	$110,000
Less: Gain recaptured by § 1250	(30,000)
Excess of § 1245 gain over § 1250 gain	$ 80,000
Percentage which is ordinary gain	15%
Ordinary gain due to § 291	$ 12,000
Section 1231 gain ($135,000 − $30,000 − $12,000)	$ 93,000

RECAPTURE OF INVESTMENT CREDIT BASIS REDUCTION

The basis reduction under § 48(q) for investment tax credit was discussed in Chapter 13. This basis reduction amount is subject to § 1245 recapture. However, if there is an investment credit recapture upon disposition of the property, one-half of the investment credit recapture is added back to the property's basis before computing gain or loss.

Example 21. B purchased business machinery in January 1983 for $100,000. B took $10,000 of investment credit ($100,000 ×

10%) and $14,250 of cost recovery [$100,000 − ($10,000 × 1/2) = $95,000; $95,000 × 15% = $14,250)] in 1983. In February 1984, B found that the machine was ineffective and sold it for $105,000. B's gain would be $20,250. B would have an investment credit recapture of $8,000. B's recomputed credit is $2,000 (2% × $100,000). The balance of the credit is recaptured. One-half of the $8,000 recaptured would be added back to the machine's basis. Thus, the basis at sale would be $84,750 ($100,000 − $5,000 − $14,250 + $4,000). Gain recaptured by § 1245 would be $15,250 [$14,250 of cost recovery + $1,000 of investment credit basis reduction (the portion of the $5,000 basis reduction that was not added back to basis)]. The remaining $5,000 would be § 1231 gain.

Example 22. Assume the same facts as in the previous example except that B held the machine for six years and then sold it for $96,000. B would have no investment credit recapture, because he held the machine for the ACRS recovery period of at least five full years. His basis at sale would be zero. He would have taken $95,000 of cost recovery and $5,000 of basis reduction because of the investment credit. His gain is $96,000 ($96,000 sale price − zero basis), and it is all recaptured under § 1245 as ordinary income.

GAIN FROM SALE OF DEPRECIABLE PROPERTY BETWEEN CERTAIN RELATED PARTIES

In general, § 1239 provides that in the case of a sale or exchange, directly or indirectly, of depreciable property (principally, machinery, equipment, and buildings, but not land) between spouses or between an individual and his or her controlled corporation, any gain recognized is ordinary income.[30] Depreciable means subject to depreciation in the hands of the transferee.

Example 23. T sells a personal automobile (therefore, it was nondepreciable) to her controlled corporation. The automobile originally cost $5,000 and is sold for $7,000. The automobile is to be used in the corporation's business. If § 1239 did not exist, T would realize a long-term capital gain (assuming the asset is held more than one year) of $2,000. The income tax consequences would be favorable because T's controlled corporation is entitled to depreciate the automobile (assuming business use) based upon the purchase price of $7,000. Under § 1239, the $2,000 gain is ordinary income.

Section 1239 was enacted to prevent certain related parties from enjoying the dual benefits of long-term capital gain treatment (trans-

---

30. § 1239(a) and Reg. § 1.1239–1.

feror) and a step-up in basis for depreciation (transferee). Recapture under § § 1245 and 1250 applies first before recapture under § 1239.[31]

Control for purposes of § 1239 means ownership of 80 percent in value of the corporation's outstanding stock. In determining the percentage of stock owned, the taxpayer must include that owned by related taxpayers as determined under the constructive ownership rules of § 318.

It should be noted that § 267(a)(1) disallows a loss on the sale of property between related taxpayers. Therefore, a sale of property between related parties may result in ordinary income (if the property is depreciable) or a nondeductible loss.

Section 1239 applies regardless of whether the transfer is from a shareholder to the corporation or from the corporation to a shareholder.[32] Ordinary income treatment also applies to transfers (after October 4, 1976) between two corporations controlled by the same shareholder.[33] Prior to the change in the law, the courts held that § 1239 ordinary income treatment was not applicable to transfers between two controlled corporations.

> **Example 24.** T, the sole shareholder of X Corporation, sells a building (adjusted basis of $40,000) to the corporation for $100,000. Since the building was depreciated by T using the straight-line method, none of the depreciation will be recaptured under § 1250. Nevertheless, § 1239 applies to convert T's § 1231 gain of $60,000 to ordinary income. The basis of the building to X Corporation becomes $100,000 (its cost).

REHABILITATION EXPENDITURES FOR LOW-INCOME RENTAL HOUSING

Section 1250 recapture applies to the sale or other disposition of federally assisted housing projects and low-income housing with respect to which rapid amortization of rehabilitation expenditures under § 167(k) has been taken. The rules are generally the same as for residential rental housing except that post-1975 excess depreciation is not recaptured in full (i. e., the post-1969 percentage rules continue to apply.)[34]

This preferential treatment afforded low-income rental housing is the result of Congressional desire to stimulate the construction and reconstruction of such residential rental property. The special rules for depreciating or amortizing these properties are discussed in Chapter 9.

---

31. Reg. § § 1.1245–6(f) and 1.1250–1(c)(4).
32. Reg. § 1.1239–1.
33. § 1239(b)(3) and Rev.Rul. 79–157, 1979–1 C.B. 281.
34. § 1250(a)(1)(B)(iii). See the Glossary of Tax Terms (Appendix C) for a discussion of rehabilitation expenditures.

FARM RECAPTURE PROVISIONS

The cash method of accounting can be and usually is used for farming operations. It should be noted, however, that certain large corporations and partnerships that are engaged in farming are required to use the accrual method of accounting and to capitalize preproductive period expenses.[35] Under the cash method, the taxpayer is allowed the dual benefits of current deductions for the costs of raising livestock and producing crops and long-term capital gain treatment under § 1231 on the sale or other disposition of farm property. Many higher income nonfarmer taxpayers have engaged in farming activities as a hobby. Such activities are particularly attractive if a nonfarmer is permitted a deduction for farm losses as an offset against income from nonfarming sources (e. g., salaries or professional fees). Therefore, Congress enacted two farm recapture provisions in 1969 with an eye toward minimizing the use of farming investments by higher income taxpayers as shelters for their income from other sources. The objective of these provisions was to limit long-term capital gain treatment for such taxpayers on the disposition of certain farm property.

Section 1251. This provision required a cash basis taxpayer to establish an Excess Deductions Account (EDA) to the extent that the taxpayer incurred a net farm loss over $25,000 and his or her nonfarm adjusted gross income exceeded $50,000.[36] In that year and all subsequent years in which the taxpayer's net farm loss exceeded $25,000 and the nonfarm adjusted gross income exceeded $50,000, the taxpayer was required to add the net farm loss over $25,000 to the EDA. Upon the sale or other disposition of certain farm recapture property (e. g., farm machinery and equipment; livestock held for draft, breeding, or sporting purposes; and certain unharvested crops), any gain is recaptured as ordinary income to the extent of the balance in the EDA at the end of the year in which the sale or other disposition took place.[37] The balance of the gain, if any, qualifies under § 1231.[38] The Tax Reform Act of 1976 provides that no additions are made to the Excess Deductions Account for 1976 and subsequent years. The recapture rules continue to apply, however, to amounts in the EDA account.

Recapture under § 1245 takes precedence over recapture under § 1251. Amounts recaptured under § 1245 are reflected as increases in net farm income or decreases in net farm losses.[39]

---

35. §§ 447 and 464.

36. §§ 1251(b)(1) and (2)(A) and (B) and Reg. §§ 1.1251–1(a) and –2(a) and (b)(1) and (2). The amounts for married persons filing separately are $12,500 instead of $25,000 and $25,000 instead of $50,000. These amounts apply only if the taxpayer's spouse has some nonfarm adjusted gross income for the taxable year. § 1251(b)(2)(C) and Reg. § 1.1251–2(b)(4).

37. §§ 1251(c) and (e)(1); Reg. §§ 1.1251 1(b) and –3(a).

38. Reg. § 1.1251–1(e).

39. Reg. §§ 1.1251–1(b)(5) and –3(b)(2).

Example 25. T has an EDA balance of $10,000 on December 31, 1975. T recognized a $5,000 gain from the sale of farm machinery in 1984. Depreciation taken on the machinery since January 1, 1962, is $4,000.

—$4,000 is recaptured as ordinary income under § 1245. The EDA is reduced from $10,000 to $6,000.

—$1,000 is recaptured as ordinary income under § 1251. The EDA is reduced from $6,000 to $5,000.

Section 1252. This section provides for the recapture of a percentage of the total deductions taken for post-1969 soil and water conservation expenditures (§ 175) and land clearing expenditures (§ 182) as ordinary income if farm land held for nine years or less is disposed of in 1970 or later years at a gain.[40] If the land is held five years or less, the applicable percentage is 100 percent. The percentage declines by 20 percent for each year the land is held over five years (e. g., 60 percent for seven years or less and 20 percent for nine years or less). There is no recapture if the land is held more than nine years. Section 1252 applies notwithstanding any other provisions in the Code. The exceptions and limitations under § 1252 are similar to those under § 1245.

Example 26. T purchased farm land in 19X2 for $50,000. T sells the land six years later for $80,000. During the period T held the land, he took $10,000 of deductions under § § 175 and 182.

—T's realized and recognized gain is $30,000 (the $80,000 realized less $50,000 adjusted basis).

—T held the land six years. The applicable percentage is 80%. Therefore, 80% of $10,000, or $8,000, is T's recapture potential under § 1252.

—Since T's gain of $30,000 exceeds the recapture potential of $8,000, $8,000 is recaptured as ordinary income.

INTANGIBLE DRILLING COSTS

Section 263(c) provides that taxpayers may elect to expense or capitalize intangible drilling and development costs. Intangible drilling and development costs (IDC) include all expenditures made by an operator (one who holds a working or operating interest in any tract or parcel of land) for wages, fuel, repairs, hauling, supplies, etc., incident to and necessary for the drilling of wells and preparation of wells for the production of oil or gas.[41] In most instances, taxpayers have elected to expense IDC due to the opportunities for accelerating tax deductions.

Intangible drilling and development costs that are paid or incurred after December 31, 1975, are recaptured if such costs were ex-

---

40. § 1252(a)(1) and Reg. § 1.1252–1(a)(1).
41. Reg. § 1.612–4(a).

pensed rather than capitalized. On the sale or other disposition of such oil or gas properties, the gain is treated as ordinary income to the extent of the lesser of the following.[42]

—IDC expensed after 1975 less amounts which would have been deductible as cost depletion if the IDC had been capitalized.

—The amount realized from the sale, exchange, or involuntary conversion of the property (or fair market value if the property is otherwise disposed of) in excess of the adjusted basis of the property.

Special rules are provided for determining recapture upon the sale or other disposition of a portion or an undivided interest in oil and gas property.

> **Example 27.** X acquired a working interest in certain oil and gas properties for $50,000 during 1983. He incurred $10,000 of intangible development and drilling costs. X elected to expense these costs in 1983. In January 1984, the properties were sold for $60,000. Disregard any depreciation on tangible depreciable properties and assume that cost depletion would have amounted to $2,000. The gain realized and recognized is $10,000 ($60,000 − $50,000). The gain is recaptured as ordinary income to the extent of IDC less the amount which would have been deducted as cost depletion (e. g., $10,000 − $2,000) or $8,000, which is less the amount realized ($10,000). Therefore, $8,000 is recaptured.

REPORTING PROCEDURES

Noncapital gains and losses are reported on Form 4797, Supplemental Schedule of Gains and Losses. Before resorting to Form 4797, however, Form 4684, Casualties and Thefts, must be completed to determine whether or not such transactions will enter into the § 1231 computation procedure. Recall that this will occur only if a net gain results from casualties and thefts of property held for more than one year.

Form 4797 is divided into four parts, summarized as follows:

Part	Function
I	To report regular § 1231 gains and losses [including recognized gains and losses from certain involuntary conversions (i. e., condemnations)].
II	To report ordinary gains and losses.
III	To determine which portion of the gain is subject to recapture (e. g., § § 1245 and 1250 gain).
IV	To elect out of the installment method when reporting a note or other installment obligation at less than full face value.

---

42. § 1254(a)(1).

Generally, the best approach to completing Form 4797 is to start with Part III. Once the recapture amount has been determined, it is transferred to Part II. The balance of any gain remaining after the recapture has been accounted for is transferred from Part III to Part I. Also transferred to Part I is any net gain from certain casualties and thefts as reported on Form 4684 (see above). If the netting process in Part I proves to be a gain, such gain is shifted to Schedule D, Capital Gains and Losses, of Form 1040. If a loss results, it goes to Part II to be treated as an ordinary loss.

Example 28. For 1983, Troy Williams (Social Security number 467-85-3036) had the following recognized gains and losses (a 1983 example has been used, since 1984 forms were unavailable):

Sale of depreciable business assets
held more than one year

Asset A (Note 1)	$ 15,500
Asset B (Note 2)	12,598
Asset C (Note 3)	(1,600)

Sale of depreciable business assets
held one year or less

Asset D (Note 4)	(600)

Capital assets

Long-term gain (Note 5)	$ 3,000
Short-term loss (Note 6)	(200)

Note 1. Asset A was acquired on June 23, 1981, for $50,000. It was 5-year ACRS property, and two years' cost recovery totaled $18,500. The property was sold for $47,000 on August 31, 1983.

Note 2. Asset B was purchased on July 10, 1981, for $37,000. It was 15-year ACRS property. Using the statutory percentage, cost recovery totaled $6,598. The property was sold for $43,000 on January 10, 1983. The building was residential rental property, and straight-line cost recovery for the period of ownership would have totaled $3,906.

Note 3. Asset C was purchased on December 9, 1981, for $16,000. It was 5-year ACRS property, and two years' cost recovery totaled $5,920. The property was sold for $8,480 on December 30, 1983.

Note 4. Asset D was purchased for $7,000 on February 27, 1983. It was 5-year ACRS property but proved unsuitable to T's business. T sold it for $6,400 on November 3, 1983.

Note 5. The LTCG resulted from the sale of 100 X shares purchased for $10,000 on April 5, 1976. The shares were sold on October 21, 1983, for $13,223. Expenses of sale were $223.

Note 6. The STCL resulted from the sale of 50 Y shares purchased for $350 on March 14, 1983. The shares were sold for $170 on August 20, 1983. Expenses of sale were $20.

The sale of Assets A and B at a gain results in the recapture of cost recovery deductions. That recapture is shown in Part III of Form 4797. Some of the gain from the sale of Asset B exceeds the recapture amount and is carried from line 29 to Part I, line 4, of Form 4797. On line 1, the loss on Asset C appears. Part I is where the § 1231 netting process takes place. The net gain on line 6 is transferred to Schedule D, line 16. In Part II of Form 4797, the ordinary gains are accumulated. On line 8, the recapture from line 28 is shown. On line 12, the loss from Asset D is shown. The net gain on line 14 is ordinary income and is transferred to Form 1040, line 15.

Schedule D, Part I, line 1, reports the short-term capital loss from the Y stock. Part II has the net § 1231 gain transferred from the 4797 on line 16 and the X gain on line 9. The net capital gain is determined on line 20, Part III. The capital gain deduction is subtracted from the net capital gain, and the result on Line 23 is then carried to line 13 of Form 1040.

Form **4797**	**Supplemental Schedule of Gains and Losses**	OMB No. 1545-0184
Department of the Treasury Internal Revenue Service	(Includes Gains and Losses From Sales or Exchanges of Assets Used in a Trade or Business and Involuntary Conversions) ▶ To be filed with Form 1040, 1041, 1065, 1120, etc.—See Separate Instructions	19**83** 28

Name(s) as shown on return	Identifying number
Troy Williams	467-85-3036

PART I.—Sales or Exchanges of Property Used in a Trade or Business, and Involuntary Conversions From Other Than Casualty and Theft — Property Held More Than 1 Year (Except for Certain Livestock)

Note: Use Form 4684 to report involuntary conversions from casualty and theft.

Caution: If you sold property on which you claimed the investment credit, you may be liable for recapture of that credit. See Form 4255 for additional information.

a. Description of property	b. Date acquired (mo., day, yr.)	c. Date sold (mo., day, yr.)	d. Gross sales price	e. Depreciation allowed (or allowable) since acquisition	f. Cost or other basis, plus improvements and expense of sale	g. LOSS (f minus the sum of d and e)	h. GAIN (d plus e minus f)
1							
Asset C	12/9/81	12/30/83	8,480	5,920	16,000	(16,000)	

2 Gain, if any, from Form 4684, line 27		
3 Section 1231 gain from installment sales from Form 6252, line 21 or 29		
4 Gain, if any, from line 29, Part III, on back of this form from other than casualty and theft.		9,906
5 Add lines 1 through 4 in column g and column h	(16,000)	9,906
6 Combine columns g and h of line 5. Enter gain or (loss) here, and on the appropriate line as follows: (a) For all except partnership returns:		8,306

(1) If line 6 is a gain, enter the gain as a long-term capital gain on Schedule D. See instruction E.

(2) If line 6 is zero or a loss, enter that amount on line 7. (S corporations, enter on Schedule K (Form 1120S), line 7.)

(b) For partnership returns: Enter each partner's share of line 6 above, on Schedule K-1 (Form 1065), line 8.

PART II.—Ordinary Gains and Losses

a. Description of property	b. Date acquired (mo., day, yr.)	c. Date sold (mo., day, yr.)	d. Gross sales price	e. Depreciation allowed (or allowable) since acquisition	f. Cost or other basis, plus improvements and expense of sale	g. LOSS (f minus the sum of d and e)	h. GAIN (d plus e minus f)
7 Loss, if any, from line 6(a)(2)							
8 Gain, if any, from line 28, Part III on back of this form							18,192
9 Net gain or (loss) from Form 4684, lines 19 and 26a							
10 Ordinary gain from installment sales from Form 6252, line 20 or 28							
11 Recapture of section 179 deduction (see instructions)							
12 Other ordinary gains and losses (include property held 1 year or less):							
Asset D	2/27/83	11/3/83	6,400		7,000	(600)	

13 Add lines 7 through 12 in column g and column h	(600)	18,192
14 Combine columns g and h of line 13. Enter gain or (loss) here, and on the appropriate line as follows:		17,592

(a) For all except individual returns: Enter the gain or (loss) from line 14, on the return being filed. See instruction F for specific line reference.

(b) For individual returns:

(1) If the loss on line 7 includes a loss from Form 4684, Part II, column B(ii), enter that part of the loss here and on line 21 of Schedule A (Form 1040). Identify as from "Form 4797, line 14(b)(1)". . . . . ——

(2) Redetermine the gain or (loss) on line 14, excluding the loss (if any) on line 14(b)(1). Enter here and on Form 1040, line 15 17,592

For Paperwork Reduction Act Notice, see page 1 of separate instructions.	Form **4797** (1983)

Form 4797 (1983)   Page **2**

PART III.—Gain From Disposition of Property Under Sections 1245, 1250, 1251, 1252, 1254, 1255
Skip lines 23 and 24 if you did not dispose of farm property or farmland, or if a partnership files this form.

15	Description of sections 1245, 1250, 1251, 1252, 1254, and 1255 property:	Date acquired (mo., day, yr.)	Date sold (mo., day, yr.)
(A)	Asset A	6/23/81	8/31/83
(B)	Asset B	7/10/81	1/10/83
(C)			
(D)			

	Relate lines 15(A) through 15(D) to these columns ► ► ► ►	Property (A)	Property (B)	Property (C)	Property (D)
16	Gross sales price	47,000	43,000		
17	Cost or other basis plus expense of sale	50,000	37,000		
18	Depreciation (or depletion) allowed (or allowable)	18,500	6,598		
19	Adjusted basis, subtract line 18 from line 17	31,500	30,402		
20	Total gain, subtract line 19 from line 16	15,500	12,598		
21	**If section 1245 property:** (a) Depreciation allowed (or allowable) after applicable date (see instructions)	18,500			
	(b) Enter smaller of line 20 or 21(a)	15,500			
22	**If section 1250 property:** (If straight line depreciation used, enter zero on line 22(f).) (a) Additional depreciation after 12/31/75		2,692		
	(b) Applicable percentage times the smaller of line 20 or line 22(a) (see instruction G.4)		2,692		
	(c) Subtract line 22(a) from line 20. If line 20 is not more than line 22(a), skip lines 22(d) and 22(e)		9,906		
	(d) Additional depreciation after 12/31/69 and before 1/1/76		–0–		
	(e) Applicable percentage times the smaller of line 22(c) or 22(d) (see instruction G.4)				
	(f) Add lines 22(b), and 22(e)		2,692		
23	**If section 1251 property:** (a) If farmland, enter soil, water, and land clearing expenses for current year and the four preceding years				
	(b) If farm property other than land, subtract line 21(b) from line 20; if farmland, enter smaller of line 20 or 23(a)				
	(c) Excess deductions account (see instruction G.5)				
	(d) Enter smaller of line 23(b) or 23(c)				
24	**If section 1252 property:** (a) Soil, water, and land clearing expenses				
	(b) Amount from line 23(d), if none enter zero				
	(c) Subtract line 24(b) from line 24(a). If line 24(b) is more than line 24(a), enter zero				
	(d) Line 24(c) times applicable percentage (see instruction G.5)				
	(e) Subtract line 24(b) from line 20				
	(f) Enter smaller of line 24(d) or 24(e)				
25	**If section 1254 property:** (a) Intangible drilling and development costs deducted after 12/31/75 (see instruction G.6)				
	(b) Enter smaller of line 20 or 25(a)				
26	**If section 1255 property:** (a) Applicable percentage of payments excluded from income under section 126 (see instruction G.7)				
	(b) Enter the smaller of line 20 or 26(a)				

Summary of Part III Gains (Complete Property columns (A) through (D) through line 26(b) before going to line 27)

27	Total gains for all properties (add columns (A) through (D), line 20)	28,098
28	Add columns (A) through (D), lines 21(b), 22(f), 23(d), 24(f), 25(b) and 26(b). Enter here and on Part II, line 8	18,192
29	Subtract line 28 from line 27. Enter the portion from casualty and theft on Form 4684, line 21; enter the portion from other than casualty and theft on Form 4797, Part I, line 4	9,906

PART IV.—Complete this Part Only If You Elect Out of the Installment Method And Report a Note or Other Obligation at Less Than Full Face Value

☐ Check here if you elect out of the installment method.

Enter the face amount of the note or other obligation ► --

Enter the percentage of valuation of the note or other obligation ►

**SCHEDULE D
(FORM 1040)**

Department of the Treasury
Internal Revenue Service

Capital Gains and Losses   (Examples of property to be reported on this Schedule are gains and losses on stocks, bonds, and similar investments, and gains (but not losses) on personal assets such as a home or jewelry.)
▶ Attach to Form 1040. ▶ See Instructions for Schedule D (Form 1040).

OMB No. 1545-0074

1983

11

Name(s) as shown on Form 1040 — Troy Williams

Your social security number — 467 : 85 : 3036

PART I.—Short-term Capital Gains and Losses—Assets Held One Year or Less

a. Description of property (Example, 100 shares 7% preferred of 'Z' Co.)	b. Date acquired (Mo., day, yr.)	c. Date sold (Mo., day, yr.)	d. Gross sales price	e. Cost or other basis, plus expense of sale	f. LOSS If column (e) is more than (d) subtract (d) from (e)	g. GAIN If column (d) is more than (e) subtract (e) from (d)
1 Y Corp. 50 shares	3/14/83	8/20/83	170	370	(200)	

2 Short-term gain from sale or exchange of a principal residence from Form 2119, lines 7 or 11	**2**		
3 Short-term capital gain from installment sales from Form 6252, line 21 or 29	**3**		
4 Net short-term gain or (loss) from partnerships, S corporations, and fiduciaries	**4**		
5 Add lines 1 through 4 in column f and column g	**5** (200	)	
6 Combine columns f and g of line 5 and enter the net gain or (loss)		**6**	(200)
7 Short-term capital loss carryover from years beginning after 1969		**7** (	)
8 Net short-term gain or (loss), combine lines 6 and 7		**8**	(200)

PART II.— Long-term Capital Gains and Losses—Assets Held More Than One Year

a. Description of property	b. Date acquired	c. Date sold	d. Gross sales price	e. Cost or other basis	f. LOSS	g. GAIN
9 X Corp. 100 shares	4/5/76	10/21/83	13,223	10,223		3,000

10 Long-term gain from sale or exchange of a principal residence from Form 2119, lines 7, 11, 16 or 18	**10**		
11 Long-term capital gain from installment sales from Form 6252, line 21 or 29	**11**		
12 Net long-term gain or (loss) from partnerships, S corporations, and fiduciaries	**12**		
13 Add lines 9 through 12 in column f and column g	**13** (	)	3,000
14 Combine columns f and g of line 13 and enter the net gain or (loss)		**14**	3,000
15 Capital gain distributions		**15**	
16 Enter gain from Form 4797, line 6(a)(1)		**16**	8,306
17 Combine lines 14 through 16		**17**	11,306
18 Long-term capital loss carryover from years beginning after 1969		**18** (	)
19 Net long-term gain or (loss), combine lines 17 and 18		**19**	11,306

Note: *Complete the back of this form. However, if you have capital loss carryovers from years beginning before 1970, do not complete Parts III or V. See Form 4798 instead.*

For Paperwork Reduction Act Notice, see Form 1040 instructions.   Schedule D (Form 1040) 1983

Schedule D (Form 1040) 1983   Page **2**

PART III.—Summary of Parts I and II

20 Combine lines 8 and 19, and enter the net gain or (loss) here	**20**	11,106

Note: *If line 20 is a loss, skip lines 21 through 23 and complete lines 24 and 25. If line 20 is a gain complete lines 21 through 23 and skip lines 24 and 25.*

21 If line 20 shows a gain, enter the smaller of line 19 or line 20. Enter zero if there is a loss or no entry on line 19   **21** | 11,106

22 Enter 60% of line 21	**22**	6,664

If line 22 is more than zero, you may be liable for the alternative minimum tax. See Form 6251.

23 Subtract line 22 from line 20. Enter here and on Form 1040, line 13	**23**	4,442

24 If line 20 shows a loss, enter one of the following amounts:
   a   If line 8 is zero or a net gain, enter 50% of line 20;
   b   If line 19 is zero or a net gain, enter line 20; or
   c   If line 8 and line 19 are net losses, enter amount on line 8 added to 50% of the amount on line 19   **24**

25 Enter here and as a loss on Form 1040, line 13, the smallest of:
   a   The amount on line 24;
   b $3,000 ($1,500 if married and filing a separate return); or
   c   Taxable income, as adjusted   **25**

PART IV.—Complete this Part Only If You Elect Out of the Installment Method And Report a Note or Other Obligation at Less Than Full Face Value

☐ Check here if you elect out of the installment method.
Enter the face amount of the note or other obligation ▶ ....
Enter the percentage of valuation of the note or other obligation ▶

PART V.—Computation of Post-1969 Capital Loss Carryovers from 1983 to 1984
(Complete this part if the loss on line 24 is more than the loss on line 25)
Note: *You do not have to complete Part V on the copy you file with IRS.*

Section A.—Short-term Capital Loss Carryover

26 Enter loss shown on line 8; if none, enter zero and skip lines 27 through 30 then go to line 31	**26**	
27 Enter gain shown on line 19. If that line is blank or shows a loss, enter zero	**27**	
28 Reduce any loss on line 26 to the extent of any gain on line 27	**28**	
29 Enter smaller of line 25 or line 28	**29**	
30 Subtract line 29 from line 28. This is your short-term capital loss carryover from 1983 to 1984	**30**	

Section B.—Long-term Capital Loss Carryover

31 Subtract line 29 from line 25 (**Note:** *If you skipped lines 27 through 30, enter amount from line 25*)	**31**	
32 Enter loss from line 19; if none, enter zero and skip lines 33 through 36	**32**	
33 Enter gain shown on line 8. If that line is blank or shows a loss, enter zero	**33**	
34 Reduce any loss on line 32 to the extent of any gain on line 33	**34**	
35 Multiply amount on line 31 by 2	**35**	
36 Subtract line 35 from line 34. This is your long-term capital loss carryover from 1983 to 1984	**36**	

Form **1040**   Department of the Treasury—Internal Revenue Service
U.S. Individual Income Tax Return   **1983**

For the year January 1-December 31, 1983, or other tax year beginning	, 1983, ending	, 19	OMB No. 1545-0074

Use IRS label. Other-wise, please print or type.	Your first name and initial (if joint return, also give spouse's name and initial)	Last name	Your social security number
	Troy	Williams	467 85 3036
	Present home address (Number and street, including apartment number, or rural route)		Spouse's social security number
	City, town or post office, State, and ZIP code	Your occupation	
		Spouse's occupation	

Presidential Election Campaign

Do you want $1 to go to this fund? .... Yes ▦ No ▦
If joint return, does your spouse want $1 to go to this fund? Yes ▦ No ▦

Note: Checking "Yes" will not increase your tax or reduce your refund.

Filing Status

Check only one box.

1 ▢ Single
2 ▢ Married filing joint return (even if only one had income)
3 ▢ Married filing separate return. Enter spouse's social security no. above and full name here. _____
4 ▢ Head of household (with qualifying person). (See page 6 of Instructions.) If the qualifying person is your unmarried child but not your dependent, write child's name here. _____
5 ▢ Qualifying widow(er) with dependent child (Year spouse died ▶ 19___). (See page 6 of Instructions.)

For Privacy Act and Paperwork Reduction Act Notice, see Instructions.

Exemptions

Always check the box labeled Yourself. Check other boxes if they apply.

6a ▢ Yourself   ▢ 65 or over   ▢ Blind
b ▢ Spouse   ▢ 65 or over   ▢ Blind

Enter number of boxes checked on 6a and b ▶ ▢

c First names of your dependent children who lived with you _____

Enter number of children listed on 6c ▶ ▢

d Other dependents		(3) Number of months lived in your home	(4) Did dependent have income of $1,000 or more?	(5) Did you provide more than one-half of dependent's support?
(1) Name	(2) Relationship			

Enter number of other dependents ▶ ▢

Add numbers entered in boxes above ▶ ▢

e Total number of exemptions claimed ....

Income

Please attach Copy B of your Forms W-2, W-2G, and W-2P here.

If you do not have a W-2, see page 5 of Instructions.

Please attach check or money order here.

7	Wages, salaries, tips, etc.	7	
8	Interest income (also attach Schedule B if over $400 or you have any All-Savers interest) ...	8	
9a	Dividends (also attach Schedule B if over $400) _____ , 9b Exclusion _____		
c	Subtract line 9b from line 9a and enter the result	9c	
10	Refunds of State and local income taxes, from worksheet on page 10 of Instructions (do not enter an amount unless you deducted those taxes in an earlier year—see page 10 of Instructions)	10	
11	Alimony received	11	
12	Business income or (loss) (attach Schedule C) .... ▶	12	
13	Capital gain or (loss) (attach Schedule D) .... ▶	13	4,442
14	40% capital gain distributions not reported on line 13 (See page 10 of Instructions)	14	
15	Supplemental gains or (losses) (attach Form 4797)	15	17,592
16	Fully taxable pensions, IRA distributions, and annuities not reported on line 17	16	
17a	Other pensions and annuities, including rollovers. Total received 17a _____		
b	Taxable amount, if any, from worksheet on page 10 of Instructions	17b	
18	Rents, royalties, partnerships, estates, trusts, etc. (attach Schedule E)	18	
19	Farm income or (loss) (attach Schedule F) .... ▶	19	
20a	Unemployment compensation (insurance). Total received ... 20a _____		
b	Taxable amount, if any, from worksheet on page 11 of Instructions	20b	
21	Other income (state nature and source—see page 11 of Instructions) _____	21	
22	**Total income.** Add amounts in column for lines 7 through 21 .... ▶	22	

Adjustments to Income

(See Instructions on page 11)

23	Moving expense (attach Form 3903 or 3903F) 23		
24	Employee business expenses (attach Form 2106) 24		
25a	IRA deduction, from the worksheet on page 12 .... 25a		
b	Enter here IRA payments you made in 1984 that are included in line 25a above ▶ _____		
26	Payments to a Keogh (H.R. 10) retirement plan 26		
27	Penalty on early withdrawal of savings 27		
28	Alimony paid 28		
29	Deduction for a married couple when both work (attach Schedule W) 29		
30	Disability income exclusion (attach Form 2440) 30		
31	**Total adjustments.** Add lines 23 through 30 .... ▶	31	

Adjusted Gross Income

32 Adjusted gross income. Subtract line 31 from line 22. If this line is less than $10,000, see "Earned Income Credit" (line 59) on page 16 of Instructions. If you want IRS to figure your tax, see page 3 of Instructions .... ▶ | 32 |

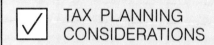

TAX PLANNING CONSIDERATIONS

TIMING OF SECTION 1231 GAIN

Although §§ 1245 and 1250 recapture much of the gain from the disposition of business property, situations exist whereby § 1231 gain will be substantial. For instance, land held as a trade or business asset will generate either § 1231 gain or § 1231 loss. If the taxpayer already has a capital loss for the year, the sale of land at a gain should be postponed so that the net § 1231 gain is not netted against the capital loss. The capital loss deduction will, therefore, be maximized. If the taxpayer already has a § 1231 gain, § 1231 losses should be postponed to maximize the ordinary loss deduction. If the taxpayer already has a § 1231 loss, § 1231 gains should be postponed to maximize the ordinary loss deduction this year and the LTCG deduction next year.

Example 29. T has a net short-term capital loss this year of $2,000. He could sell business land for a § 1231 gain of $3,000. He will have no other capital gains and losses or § 1231 gains and losses this year or next year. T is in the 30% tax bracket. He will have a $1,000 LTCG ($3,000 § 1231 gain − $2,000 STCL) for this year if he sells the land. He will pay a tax of 30% on $400 [$1,000 − ($1,000 × 60% LTCG deduction)], or $120. If T sells the land next year, he will have tax savings of $600 ($2,000 STCL × 30%) this year and pay a tax of 30% on $1,200 [$3,000 LTCG − ($3,000 × 60% LTCG deduction)], or $360, next year. The net tax savings from selling the land next year would be $240 ($600 tax savings this year − $360 tax payments next year). The difference between the two alternatives (sell land this year or sell land next year) is $360 ($120 tax payments from the first alternative plus $240 tax savings from the second alternative).

Example 30. S has a § 1231 loss this year of $15,000. He could sell business equipment for a § 1231 gain of $20,000 and a § 1245 gain of $12,000. S's tax bracket is 50%. If he sells the equipment this year, he will pay a tax of $7,000. He would have a net LTCG of $5,000 ($20,000 § 1231 gain − $15,000 § 1231 loss). The tax on the taxable portion of the LTCG is $1,000 [$5,000 − ($5,000 × 60%) = $2,000; $2,000 × 50% = $1,000]. The tax on the § 1245 gain would be $6,000 ($12,000 × 50%). If S sold the equipment next year, the tax savings this year would be $7,500 ($15,000 × 50%). Next year, the tax would be $10,000 [$20,000 LTCG − ($20,000 × 60%) = $8,000; $8,000 × 50% = $4,000; $12,000 § 1245 gain × 50% = $6,000; $4,000 + $6,000 = $10,000]. For the two years the combined tax would be $2,500. Under the first alternative (sell the equipment this year), the tax was $7,000. Postponing the equipment sale saves $4,500 in tax.

TIMING OF RECAPTURE

Since recapture is usually not triggered until the property is sold or disposed of, it may be possible to plan for recapture in low bracket or in loss years. If a taxpayer has net operating loss carryovers which are about to expire, the recognition of ordinary income from recapture may be advisable to absorb the loss carryovers.

> **Example 31.** T has a $15,000 net operating loss carryover that will expire this year. He owns a machine which he plans to sell in the early part of next year. The expected gain of $17,000 from the sale of the machine will be recaptured as ordinary income under § 1245. T sells the machine prior to the end of this year and offsets $15,000 of the ordinary income against the net operating loss carryover.

It may also be desirable to spread the recaptured income amounts over a number of years. The spreading of such amounts may be accomplished through the use of an installment sale under § 453 (refer to Example 18).

POSTPONING AND SHIFTING RECAPTURE

It is also possible to postpone recapture or to shift the burden of recapture to others. For example, recapture is avoided upon the disposition of a § 1231 asset if the taxpayer replaces the property by entering into a like-kind exchange. In this instance, recapture potential is merely carried over to the newly acquired property (refer to Example 17).

Recapture can be shifted to others through the gratuitous transfer of § 1245 or § 1250 property to family members. A subsequent sale of such property by the donee will trigger recapture to the donee rather than the donor (refer to Example 13). Such procedure would be advisable only if the donee is in a lower income tax bracket than the donor.

AVOIDING RECAPTURE

Since all accelerated ACRS cost recovery allowances using the statutory percentage method must be recaptured on nonresidential real property (refer to Example 10), taxpayers should consider electing the optional straight-line method. If the optional straight-line method is elected, there is no § 1245 or § 1250 recapture on the disposition of the property (refer to Example 11). The immediate expense election (§ 179) is also subject to § 1245 recapture. If the election is not made, the § 1245 recapture potential will accumulate more slowly (refer to

Chapter 11). If the full investment tax credit is taken on other than 30-year or 40-year rehabilitation property, one-half of the credit reduces the basis of the property. The reduction is subject to depreciation recapture upon disposition of the property (refer to Example 21). Not taking the full credit will avoid the recapture, since there will have been no basis reduction for investment tax credit.

Example 32. D bought a nonresidential building in January 1983 for use in his business. He intends to keep the building about three full years and then sell it. The building cost $60,000. Three years' cost recovery would be $18,600 if D used the statutory percentage (accelerated) cost recovery approach. Three years' cost recovery would be $12,000 if D used the straight-line approach. D expects to sell the building for $60,000 and expects to be in the 50% tax bracket through the entire holding period. D would be trading $6,600 ($18,600 − $12,000) additional cost recovery for $18,600 of 1245 gain. The accelerated cost recovery would save $9,300 ($18,600 × 50%), but the § 1245 gain (which equals cost recovery taken) would cost $9,300 ($18,600 × 50%). The net tax cost would be zero. If the straight-line election is used, D would save $6,000 of tax ($12,000 × 50%) because of cost recovery but would pay only $2,400 [$12,000 − ($12,000 × 60%) = $4,800; $4,800 × 50% = $2,400] in tax upon sale. The gain on sale would be $12,000 (which equals depreciation taken), and it would all be § 1231 gain. Thus, D would have a net tax savings of $3,600. If time value of money considerations were injected into this example, the difference between the two alternatives would be less, but it would still be beneficial to elect the straight-line method.

PROBLEM MATERIALS

Questions for Class Discussion

1. What type of transactions involving capital assets are included under § 1231? Why wouldn't they qualify for long-term capital gain treatment without § 1231?

2. Why was § 1231 originally enacted? Why is it still in the law today?

3. If inventory is sold at a loss, what is the nature of the loss?

4. Is it possible to recognize both a gain and a loss on the sale of timber in one taxable year? How? What are the planning implications?

5. How long must a farmer keep a pig before it becomes a § 1231 asset?

6. What circumstances must be met for an unharvested crop to receive preferential treatment under § 1231?

7. What is the effect of an asset's holding period on its ability to qualify for special treatment under § 1231? Why?

8. Under what circumstances is a casualty gain not afforded long-term capital gain treatment? Why?

9. Describe the treatment that results if a taxpayer has net § 1231 losses.

10. What property is excluded from § 1231?

11. Why was § 1245 enacted? How does it achieve this objective?

12. Differentiate between the types of property covered by § § 1245 and 1250.

13. If a farmer buys a pig and uses ACRS, are the cost recovery deductions subject to § 1245 recapture if the pig is sold at a gain?

14. What is recapture potential under § 1245? What factors limit it?

15. What is "additional depreciation"? Why is such a concept necessary?

16. What is recapture potential under § 1250? What factors limit it?

17. What are the two major differences in the computation of depreciation recapture under § § 1245 and 1250? Why do these differences exist?

18. What happens to recapture potential when a gift is involved? What effect does the donee's use have on the recapture potential?

19. Does recapture apply when § 1245 property is donated to charity? Why?

20. List the tax-free transactions which do not cause recapture to be recognized immediately but require it to be carried over to the transferee.

21. What provisions do the recapture rules override?

22. What special recapture provision applies only to regular corporations?

23. Why was § 1239 enacted? How does it accomplish its goals?

24. If the basis of ACRS property was reduced by one-half of the investment tax credit in the year the property was acquired, what impact does this reduction have when the property is later sold?

25. In general, how does § 1239 differ from § § 1245 and 1250?

26. How has residential real estate been granted special treatment under § 1250? What changes were made in 1981, and how will the changes affect subsequent depreciation of residential property?

27. Why are rehabilitation expenditures afforded preferential treatment under § 1250? What is this treatment?

28. What are the dual benefits available to cash method farmers? How have these benefits been restricted by recent changes in the tax law?

29. How does § 1251 attempt to minimize the use of farming investments as tax shelters?

30. If a taxpayer has expensed intangible drilling and development costs, what are the possible future ramifications?

31. What is the purpose of Part I of Form 4797?

32. Would recapture provisions ever affect a decision to maximize depreciation deductions? Why or why not? (Consider tax planning aspects.)

Problems

33. Ms. S purchased a contract to cut timber on a hundred acre tract of land in South Dakota in March of 19X1 for $20,000. On January 1, 19X2, the timber had a fair market value of $50,000. Because of careless cutting in Novem-

ber when the fair market value is $55,000, the wood is sold on January 30, 19X3, for $49,000.

(a) What gain (loss) is realized in 19X1, 19X2, and 19X3? What gain (loss) is recognized in 19X1, 19X2, and 19X3?

(b) What is the nature of the gains (losses) in (a)? What assumption must be made?

(c) Does the answer change if the timber is sold in December of 19X2? Why?

(d) If on January 1, 19X2, the timber was worth only $18,000, was cut in November when worth $21,000, and was sold in December for $19,000, how would the answers to parts (a) and (b) change?

34. T owns an airplane that she uses entirely for pleasure. T's insurance company did not cover $6,000 of damage to T's plane resulting from a tornado. T had paid $350,000 for the plane. T had no other casualty gains and losses for the year and had adjusted gross income of $125,000 (not including any adjustment for the casualty loss). What is T's deduction for the storm damage?

35. D is the sole proprietor of a trampoline shop. During 19X4, the following transactions occurred:

—Unimproved land, adjacent to the store was condemned by the city on February 1. The condemnation proceeds were $25,000. The land, acquired in 19X0, had an allocable basis of $15,000. D has additional parking across the street and plans to use the condemnation proceeds to build his inventory.

—A truck used to deliver trampolines was sold on January 2 for $3,500. The truck was purchased on January 2, 19X1, for $6,000. On the date of sale, the adjusted basis was $2,667.

—D sold an antique rowing machine at an auction. Net proceeds were $3,900. The rowing machine was purchased as used equipment 27 years ago for $5,200 and had been depreciated over a 20-year life using the straight-line method. Depreciation taken after December 31, 1961, was $2,700. The adjusted basis of the machine was $500 (salvage value) on the date of sale.

—D sold an apartment building for $200,000 on September 1. The rental property was purchased on September 1, three years ago, for $150,000 and was being depreciated over a 35-year life using the straight-line method. At the date of sale, the adjusted basis was $135,000.

—D's personal yacht was stolen September 5. It had been purchased in August 19X4 at a cost of $25,000. The fair market value immediately preceding the theft was $20,000. D was insured for 50% of the original cost, and he received $12,500 on December 1, 19X4.

—A Buick was sold by D on May 1 for $9,600. The vehicle was used exclusively for personal purposes. It had been purchased on September 1, 19X1, for $10,800.

—An adding machine used by D's bookkeeper was sold on June 1. Net proceeds of the sale were $135. The machine was purchased on June 2, four years ago, for $350. It was being depreciated over a five-year life employing the straight-line method. The adjusted basis on the date of sale was $70.

—D's trampoline stretching machine (owned two years) was stolen on May 5, but the business's insurance company will not pay any of the machine's value because D failed to pay the insurance premium. The machine had an FMV of $8,000 and an adjusted basis of $6,000 at the time of theft.

—D had 19X4 AGI of $4,000 from sources other than those described above.

(a) For each transaction, what is the amount of recognized gain or loss and what is its nature?

(b) What is D's 19X4 adjusted gross income?

36. V, an individual taxpayer, files her income tax return on the calendar year basis. Her recognized gains and losses for 19X4 are as follows:

(a) $3,000 gain reported in 19X4 (under § 453) on installment sale in 19X2 of warehouse used in business (including land and building held for six years).

(b) $2,000 gain on sale of moving vehicles used in warehouse business and subject to depreciation allowance, held for three years.

(c) $8,000 loss from theft of unregistered bearer bonds, held 18 months.

(d) $2,000 loss in storm of pleasure yacht, purchased in 19X1 for $2,900 and having a fair market value at the time of the storm of $2,000.

What are the tax consequences to V for each of these items?

37. The following transactions were encountered by T during 19X4:

—Damage from wreck of a sailboat held over one year due to hurricane ($5,000 loss).

—Sale of mechanical rake bought on February 1 and sold on September 1 ($600 gain). Disregard recapture.

—Sale of farm land with unharvested crops, held four years ($10,000 gain).

—Recovery on theft of family broach owned for 10 years ($10,000 gain).

—Fire in silo on December 6, purchased May 8 ($1,000 loss).

—Sale of grist mill owned 11 years ($30 loss).

—Sale of 15 shares of Q Corporation stock held three years ($1,500 gain).

(a) How is each transaction treated?

(b) What is T's 19X4 AGI?

38. S Corporation sold machines A and B during the current year. The machines had been purchased for $180,000 and $240,000, respectively. The machines were purchased eight years ago and were depreciated to zero. Machine A was sold for $40,000 and machine B for $260,000. What amount of gain is recognized by S, and what is the nature of the gain?

39. B owns the patent to a rug-cleaning device used by his sole proprietorship to provide services for his customers. This patent was purchased on January 1, 19X1, for $8,000 and is being amortized over 80 months. The cleaning device was built on June 1, 19X1, at a cost of $14,000. It has an

estimated life of seven years and no salvage value. On June 1, 19X5, B sells the patent and the cleaning device for $2,900 and $7,200, respectively. The machine was built before 1981, and straight-line depreciation was used.

(a) What is the amount of the gain or loss which is recognized on the sale?

(b) How is it treated?

(c) Does the answer change if the patent is sold for $100?

40. On March 1, 19X1, N buys and places in service a new machine for $25,000. On April 1, 19X4, N sells the machine for $15,000. Cost recovery deductions to date have been $14,500. The basis of the machine was not reduced because investment tax credit was taken at the reduced rate.

(a) What is N's realized and recognized gain?

(b) What is the nature of the gain?

41. On January 1, 19X1, T acquired a building (not ACRS recovery property) used in his business for $600,000. Later depreciation expense was $150,000. On January 1, 19X9, the building was sold for $800,000. At the time of the sale, additional depreciation taken attributable to periods after December 31, 1969, amounted to $35,000.

(a) What amount is § 1250 ordinary income?

(b) How would the answer change if rehabilitation expenditures were involved?

42. Residential real property (not ACRS recovery property) purchased in 19X0 with an adjusted basis of $60,000 is sold in 19X3 for $78,000. Depreciation attributable to the property for tax years 19X0 through 19X3 is $20,000, of which $4,000 is additional depreciation.

(a) Identify the amount and nature of the gain.

(b) Would the answer change if the property were nonresidential real property?

43. T purchased nonresidential real estate (ACRS recovery property) two years ago for $130,000. T used the statutory percentage ACRS cost recovery method and sold the property for $115,000 after accumulating cost recovery of $28,600.

(a) Identify the amount and nature of the gain or loss.

(b) Assume T used straight-line cost recovery and accumulated $17,333 of cost recovery. Identify the amount and nature of the gain or loss.

(c) Recompute (a) and (b) assuming the sale price was $78,000.

44. Refer to the facts of Problem 43. Rework the problem assuming T was a corporation. The sale date was after 1982.

45. P donated equipment to a qualified charitable organization on January 3, 19X6. P purchased the equipment new on January 1, 19X3, for $100,000 and was taking depreciation under the accelerated cost recovery system (statutory percentage method) for five-year property. At the time of the gift, the property had a fair market value of $130,000. What are the tax consequences to P in the year of the gift?

46. T transferred forklifts used in his factory, with recapture potential of $6,500, to a dealer in exchange for new forklifts worth $8,000 and $1,500 of mar-

ketable securities. The transaction qualified as a § 1031 like-kind exchange. T had an adjusted basis in the equipment of $6,000.

(a) What is T's realized and recognized gain or loss?

(b) What is the nature of the gain or loss?

(c) How would the answer to (a) or (b) change if no marketable securities are involved?

47. In 19X3, C purchased new business equipment for $5,000. On his 19X3 return, C claimed depreciation of $750 using the accelerated cost recovery system (statutory percentage method). On January 1, 19X4, a tornado destroyed the equipment and C received $4,500 from his insurance company. The equipment was replaced for $3,800. What is C's recognized gain or loss and what is the nature of the gain or loss?

48. T sells a business machine on the installment basis. He will recognize $3,000 of gain in each of the next five years. Cost recovery deductions of $12,000 had been taken on the machine. What is the nature of the gain recognized in each of the five years?

49. J acquired a working interest in certain oil and gas properties during 1983 for $125,000. In the same year, she also incurred intangible drilling costs of $60,000 which she elected to expense on her 1983 tax return. If the IDC had been capitalized, cost depletion of $6,000 would have been allowed. In January 1984, J sells her interest in the oil and gas properties for $140,000.

(a) Calculate the amount of gain or loss realized and recognized in 1984. (Ignore any depreciation on tangible depreciable property.)

(b) What amount, if any, is ordinary income?

50. T purchased business machinery on January 1, 19X3, costing $80,000. A full 10% investment tax credit and a $5,000 immediate expense deduction were taken. The property was purchased after December 31, 1982. T used the ACRS statutory percentage method. On January 2, 19X7, T sold the machinery for $38,000.

(a) What are the amounts of investment tax credit, cost recovery, and end-of-year adjusted basis in the year the property is purchased?

(b) What are the amounts of investment tax credit recapture, § 1245 gain, and § 1231 gain in the year of sale?

Cumulative Problems

51. J is a self-employed contractor (single, no dependents) who operates the X Company, a sole proprietorship. During 19X4, X Company had gross sales of $635,000 and business expenses of $550,000, including the cost recovery allowance on the assets bought, sold, or exchanged during 19X4. However, the above income and expense figures do not reflect gains or losses on the following property transactions:

(a) X Company purchased a Model 1200 tractor in 19X2 for $21,000. On July 1, when the adjusted basis of the Model 1200 was $14,000 ($21,000 cost − $7,000 accumulated depreciation), it was traded for a Model 800. The fair market value of the Model 800 tractor was $12,000. X Company received $6,000 cash boot from the dealer.

(b) X Company had a ditch-digging machine which was completely destroyed by fire in October. The machine, which X Company had owned for two years, had an adjusted basis of $6,400 but X Company received only $3,000 from the insurance company. The machine was replaced at a cost of $8,000.

(c) In 19X2, J converted his personal automobile to business use. J had paid $5,400 for the auto, which had a fair market value of $3,800 at the date of conversion. In 19X4, X Company sold the automobile, on which depreciation of $2,200 had been taken, for $1,000.

(d) X Company sold a vacant lot it had been holding for a new store location. Because of a change in plans, the property no longer was needed. The lot, which had an adjusted basis of $15,000, was sold for $17,000. X Company had owned the lot for 14 months.

J had the following transaction involving a personal asset not related to his business:

(e) In December, J sold stock which he had purchased from his brother in October 19X2. His brother's basis for the stock was $3,500. J, who had paid $2,500 for the stock, received $4,000 upon its sale.

J's records reveal the following additional information:

(f) Dividends received on stock in a domestic corporation amounted to $400, and itemized deductions were $6,900.

Compute J's taxable income for 19X4.

52. X is a CPA who owns and operates his own business as a sole practitioner. He is single, age 31, and has no dependents. During 19X4 (a post-1982 year), he had the following items of possible tax consequence:

(a) X's business net earnings were $38,000, not considering the items below.

(b) Property sales:

	Date Acquired	Date Sold	Sales Price	Cost
X Corporation stock	8/6/19X2	9/8/19X4	$ 3,500	$ 1,200
Y Corporation stock	7/4/19X4	10/1/19X4	3,000	5,500

(c) A two-year-old delivery car (adjusted basis of $3,000 and fair market value of $2,600) was stolen. There was no insurance, and the property was not recovered. The delivery car had been used in X's business since the day he purchased it.

(d) A parking lot used in the business was sold on 7/8/19X4 for $36,000. The land was purchased on 1/3/19X0 for $10,000.

(e) A minicomputer was purchased on 10/1/19X3 for $12,000. It was sold for $8,000 on 1/5/19X4 (adjusted basis of $10,800) and was not replaced.

(f) A photocopying machine used in X's business was sold for $6,000. He had purchased it in 19X1 for $12,000. Depreciation allowed since the date of acquisition was $3,000.

(g) An offset printing machine used in his business was sold for $20,000. X had purchased it in 19X2 for $19,000. Depreciation allowed since the date of acquisition was $2,000.

(h) Fire totally destroyed X's pleasure boat, which he purchased in 19X0 and had a basis to him of $10,000. Insurance proceeds were $13,500.

(i) A television set, which cost $600, was stolen from X's home the same day he purchased it.

X had various itemized deductions of $7,400, not including any possible deductions in items (a) through (i). Compute his taxable income for 19X4.

Tax Form Problem

53. Linda Franklin is an attorney. She receives a salary of $45,000. During 1983, she had the following property transactions:

(a) Sales of stock held for investment:

Stock	Selling Price	Basis	Date Sold	Date Acquired
Acme Corporation	$ 2,000	$ 1,400	6/30/1983	8/4/1982
Bareham Corporation	8,000	10,500	12/31/1983	7/15/1983
Cronin, Inc.	9,400	5,400	7/26/1983	5/2/1980
Davis Corporation	1,800	2,900	10/18/1983	10/17/1982

(b) Complete destruction of travel trailer in a wreck on August 1 (basis, $6,500; market value, $5,000; reimbursement for loss by insurance company, $3,000). Linda had bought the trailer on June 12, 1980.

(c) Sale of photocopying machine used in business for $2,800 on November 6. She had acquired the machine on April 29, 1980, for $4,000 and had taken $1,800 depreciation on it.

(d) Sale of typewriter, used in business, on January 15 for $500. The typewriter was acquired on May 8, 1980, at a cost of $1,000; depreciation (including additional first year depreciation) of $440 had been deducted.

Compute Linda Franklin's gains and losses from these transactions using a 1983 Schedule D, Form 4684, Form 4797, and Form 1040.

Cumulative Tax Return Problem

54. T, age 40, operates a retail business as a sole proprietorship. He had the following transactions during the year (1983) regarding his business and personal activities:

(a) A delivery truck was sold for $4,000 on January 1. The truck was acquired on January 1, 1980, at a total cost of $6,000. The truck was depreciated over a three-year life using straight-line depreciation. The adjusted basis on the date of sale was $1,000.

(b) T traded an old office machine used in his business for a new one on December 1. The new machine cost $3,800. T was allowed $1,000 for the old machine which had an adjusted basis of $1,500 and paid $2,800 in cash. The old machine was acquired on December 1, 1979, and straight-line depreciation was taken.

(c) In December, T sold 100 shares of XYZ stock for $3,500 which had been purchased in August of the same year for $3,000.

(d) T sold his personal residence for $60,000 in December which had been acquired in 1979. Selling expenses amounted to $4,000, and the adjusted basis of the house was $46,000. T moved into a rental apartment and does not plan to reinvest the proceeds in a new residence.

Compute T's net gain or loss from the above transactions and describe the nature of the gain or loss. Preparation of Schedule D of Form 1040, Form 2119 (Sale or Exchange of Personal Residence), and Form 4797 (Supplemental Schedule of Gains and Losses) is necessary.

Research Problems

55. T Corporation owns an item of equipment that it uses in its business and that is § 1245 property. The equipment is encumbered by a liability that allows prepayment only if the property is sold. T contributes $100,000 cash to a local charity. The charity immediately purchases the equipment for $100,000 (its fair market value). T has paid $120,000 for the equipment, whose adjusted basis is $75,000. What are the tax consequences to T of these transactions?

    Partial list of research aids:

    Sections 1245(b)(1), 170(c), and 170(e).

    Rev.Rul. 76–151, 1976–1 C. B. 59.

56. Dr. D purchased a personal residence for $150,000 on January 1, 19X1. Ten percent of the residence was converted to a business office, and Dr. D claimed $2,500 total depreciation on the business portion for 19X1 and 19X2. (Straight-line depreciation would have been $2,000 for the two-year period.) On January 1, 19X3, Dr. D sold the home for $180,000 and acquired another personal residence for $140,000.

    (a) Compute realized and recognized gain on the former residence and state the nature of the gain.

    (b) If the requirements for nonrecognition of gain on the sale of a personal residence are met (§ 1034), is it possible to defer the entire amount of the gain? Why or why not?

57. J has purchased a business that erects, maintains, and rents to others outdoor advertising signs. The business owns two types of signs. One type of sign is about 10 feet tall with a display area bolted to a post, which in turn is bolted to a concrete base. The other type is constructed of wood, is very large, and is all one structure. J has determined the cost of each sign purchased and is wondering whether the signs are § 1245 property and therefore eligible for the investment tax credit.

    Partial list of research aids:

    Rev.Rul. 80–151, 1980–1 C. B. 7.

    Whiteco Industries, Inc., 65 T.C. 664 (1975), *acq.*

Chapter 18

Accounting Periods and Methods

An entire subchapter of the Code, Subchapter E, is devoted to accounting periods and accounting methods. Over the long run, the accounting period used by a taxpayer will not affect the aggregate amount of reported taxable income. However, taxable income for any particular year may vary significantly due to the use of a particular reporting period. In addition, because of the progressive nature of tax rates, advantages can be obtained from the use of a particular method of accounting. Through the choice of accounting methods or periods, it is possible to postpone the recognition of taxable income and to enjoy the benefits from such deferral of the related tax.

ACCOUNTING PERIODS

IN GENERAL

Our tax determination and collection system is founded on the concept of an annual reporting by the taxable entity of its income, deductions, and credits. Most individual taxpayers use a calendar year, since the Code and Regulations place restrictions upon the use of a fiscal year for taxpayers who do not keep books.[1] However, both corporate and noncorporate taxpayers may elect to use a fiscal year ending

---

1. § 441(c) and Reg. § 1.441–1(b)(1)(ii).

on the last day of any month (other than December), provided the books of the taxpayer are maintained on the basis of the same fiscal year.[2] Generally, a taxable year may not exceed 12 calendar months. However, if certain requirements are met, a taxpayer may elect to use an annual period which varies from 52 to 53 weeks.[3] In such case, the year-end must be on the same day of the week (e. g., the Tuesday falling closest to October 31 or the last Tuesday in October). The day of the week selected for ending the year would depend upon business considerations. For example, a retail business that is not open on Sundays may end its year on a Sunday so that an inventory can be taken without interrupting business operations.

> **Example 1.** T is in the business of selling farm supplies. His natural business year terminates at the end of October with the completion of harvesting. At the end of the fiscal year it is necessary to take an inventory, and it is most easily accomplished on a Tuesday. Therefore, T could adopt a 52–53 week year ending on the Tuesday nearest October 31. If this method is selected, the year-end date may fall in the following month if closer to October 31. The year ending in 1984 will contain 52 weeks beginning on Wednesday, November 2, 1983, and ending on Tuesday, October 30, 1984. The year ending in 1985 will have also 52 weeks beginning on Wednesday, October 31, 1984, and ending on Tuesday, October 29, 1985.

Partnerships are subject to additional restrictions to prevent partners from deferring partnership income by selecting a different year-end for the partnership (e. g., if the year for the partnership ended on January 31 and the partners used a calendar year, partnership profits for the first 11 months would not be reported by the partners until the following year). In brief, the law provides that the partnership tax year must generally be the same as the year used by its principal partners.[4] Similarly, S corporation shareholders are prevented from deferring from tax their share of the corporation's income. The S corporation must adopt a calendar year unless it has a business purpose for electing a fiscal year.[5]

---

2. Reg. § 1.441–1(e)(2).

3. § 441(f).

4. § 706(b)(2). However, the IRS is authorized to allow the partner's and partnership's tax year to differ if there is a good business purpose for the different years. See Rev.Proc. 72–51, 1972–2 C.B. 832 for the procedure for a change in the partnership year. For a discussion of the S corporation taxable year, see Chapter 7 of *West's Federal Taxation: Corporations, Partnerships, Estates, and Trusts.*

5. Temp.Reg. § 18.1378–(a) applies to post-October 19, 1982, S corporation elections.

MAKING THE ELECTION

A taxpayer elects to use a calendar or fiscal year by the timely filing of his or her initial tax return.[6] For all subsequent years, this same period must be used unless prior approval for change is obtained from the IRS.[7]

Newly formed corporations often fail to make a valid election to use a fiscal year because the company has erroneously concluded that the due date of the election is based on the date the corporation began business rather than the date the corporation comes into existence. Under Reg. § 1.6012–2(a), the election must be keyed to the date the corporation comes into existence, which is usually the date it receives its charter from the state. Failure to make a valid election to use a fiscal year automatically places the corporation on the calendar year.[8]

> **Example 2.** Y Corporation received its charter on June 15, 19X1, but did not begin business until October 2, 19X1. The corporation would like to be on a fiscal year ending September 30. Thus, a short period return should be filed by December 15, 19X1, for the period June 15, 19X1, through September 30, 19X1, even though no business activity was conducted during that time. If Y Corporation's initial return was filed erroneously (e. g., the return included only the period from October 2, 19X1, through September 30, 19X2), the election to use a fiscal year is not valid and the corporation must use a calendar year.

CHANGES IN THE ACCOUNTING PERIOD

A taxpayer must obtain consent from the IRS before changing the tax year.[9] This power to approve or not to approve a change is significant in that it permits the IRS to issue authoritative administrative guidelines which must be met by taxpayers who wish to change their accounting period. An application for permission to change tax years must be made on Form 1128, Application for Change in Accounting Period, and must be filed on or before the fifteenth day of the second calendar month following the close of the short period.[10]

> **Example 3.** Beginning in 19X2, T Corporation, a calendar year taxpayer, would like to switch to a fiscal year ending March 31. The corporation must file Form 1128 by May 15, 19X2.

---

6. Reg. § 1.441–1(b)(3).

7. Reg. § 1.441–(b)(4).

8. See *Calhoun v. U. S.*, 74–1 USTC ¶ 9104, 33 AFTR2d 305, 370 F.Supp. 434 (D.Ct.Va.1973).

9. § 442.

10. Reg. § 1.442–1(b)(1).

IRS Requirements.   The IRS will not grant permission for the change unless the taxpayer can establish a "substantial business purpose" for the change. One "substantial business purpose" is a request to change to a tax year that coincides with the natural business year."[11] Generally, the natural business year will end at or soon after the peak period of business. Thus, a ski lodge may end its year on March 31, a Miami Beach hotel on May 31, a department store on January 31, a soft drink bottler on September 30, and a college textbook publisher on June 30. If a business does not have a peak income period, it may not be able to establish a "natural business year" and may therefore be prevented from changing its tax year.

The IRS usually will establish certain conditions which the taxpayer must accept if the approval for change is to be granted. In particular, if there is a substantial reduction in taxable income in the year of change, the IRS generally will require the spreading of such benefits over a 10-year period beginning in the year following the change.

TAXABLE PERIODS OF LESS THAN ONE YEAR

A short year is a period of less than 12 calendar months. A taxpayer may have a short year for (1) the first tax reporting period, (2) the final income tax return, or (3) a change in the tax year.[12] A taxpayer is not required to annualize the taxable income for the short period for computing the tax liability if the short period constitutes the first or final period (i. e., the computations are the same as for a return filed for a 12-month period).[13]

REQUIREMENT TO ANNUALIZE TAXABLE INCOME

If the short period results from a change in the taxpayer's annual accounting period, the taxable income for such period must be annualized. Due to the progressive tax rate structure, taxpayers could reap substantial tax benefits during the short period if such annualization of income were not required. Once the taxable income is annualized, the tax must first be computed on the amount of annualized income. The annualized tax is then converted to a short period tax. The latter conversion is accomplished as follows:

$$\text{Tax on annualized income} \times \frac{\text{Number of months in the short period}}{12}$$

11.   Rev.Proc. 74–33, 1974–2 C.B. 489.
12.   Reg. § 1.443–1(a).
13.   Reg. § 1.443–1(a)(2).

For individuals, annualizing requires some special adjustments:[14]

—Deductions must be itemized for the short period (the zero bracket amount is not allowed), but itemized deductions are not reduced by the zero bracket amount.

—Personal and dependency exemptions must be prorated.

Example 4. Mr. and Mrs. B obtained permission to change from a calendar year to a fiscal year ending September 30. For the short period, January 1 through September 30, 1984, they had income and deductions as follows:

Gross income (all earned by Mr. B)		$ 28,800
Less: Deductions *for* adjusted gross income		3,000
Adjusted gross income		$ 25,800
Minus:		
Deductions *from* adjusted gross income (itemized deductions)	$ 5,000	
Personal exemptions $\left[3 \times \$1,000 \times \frac{9}{12}\right]$	2,250	7,250
Modified taxable income[(a)]		$ 18,550
Annualized income—		
$\left(\$18,550 \times \frac{12}{9}\right)$	$ 24,733	
Add zero bracket amount	3,400	
	$ 28,133	
Tax on annualized income	$ 4,348[(b)]	
Short period tax $\left(\$4,348 \times \frac{9}{12}\right)$	$ 3,261	

[(a)]Modified taxable income is defined at § 443(b)(3).
[(b)]The tax rate schedules (not the tax tables) must be used. See § 3(b)(2). Tax on $28,133 was computed using the 1984 rate schedule for married taxpayers filing jointly.

MITIGATION OF THE ANNUAL ACCOUNTING PERIOD CONCEPT

There are several provisions in the Code designed to give the taxpayer relief from the seemingly harsh results that may be produced by the combined effects of an arbitrary accounting period and a progressive rate structure.[15] For example, favorable capital gain treatment has been provided, in part, to offset the undesirable effects which may result from the "bunching" of income in one accounting period (i. e., the period in which the capital gains are realized). In addition, income averaging provisions are available for mitigating the adverse effects

---

14. § 443(b)(1).
15. Refer to Chapter 2 for further discussion of mitigating the annual accounting period concept.

which result from other types of income being "bunched up" in any one period.[16] Therefore, an individual receiving substantial amounts of taxable income in one year may be able to obtain the benefits from, in effect, spreading the income over the prior four years and the current year.

The net operating loss carryback and carryover rules also mitigate the effects of a tax based upon one year's income. Under these provisions, a loss in one year can be carried back and offset against taxable income for the preceding three years. Unused net operating losses are then carried over for 15 years.[17] In addition, the Code provides special relief provisions for casualty losses pursuant to a disaster and for the reporting of insurance proceeds from destruction of crops.[18]

Restoration of Amounts Received Under a Claim of Right. The court-made claim of right doctrine applies when the taxpayer has received as income property which he or she treats as his or her own but the taxpayer's rights to the income are disputed.[19] According to the doctrine, the taxpayer must include the amount as income in the year of receipt. The rationale for the doctrine is that the Federal government cannot await the resolution of all disputes before exacting a tax. As a corollary to the doctrine, if the taxpayer is later required to repay the funds, generally, a deduction is allowed in the year of repayment.[20]

> **Example 5.** In 19X1, T received a $5,000 bonus computed as a percentage of profits. In 19X2, it was determined that the 19X1 profits were incorrectly computed, and T had to refund the $5,000 to his employer in 19X2. T was required to include the $5,000 in his 19X1 income, but he can claim a $5,000 deduction in 19X2.

In Example 5 the transactions were a wash, that is, the income and deduction were the same ($5,000). However, suppose T was in the 50 percent marginal tax bracket in 19X1 but in the 30 percent bracket in 19X2. Without some relief provision, the mistake would be costly to T. He paid $2,500 tax in 19X1 (.50 × $5,000), but the deduction reduced his tax liability in 19X2 by only $1,500 (.30 × $5,000). However, the Code does provide the needed relief in this case.

Under § 1341, when income has been taxed under the claim of right doctrine but must later be repaid, in effect, the taxpayer gets the deduction in the year he or she can receive the greater tax benefit.

---

16. §§ 1301–1305. Refer to Chapter 12.

17. § 172. Refer to Chapter 8.

18. §§ 165(h) and 451(d). Refer to Chapter 8.

19. *North American Consolidated Oil Co. v. Burnet,* 49 USTC ¶ 943, 11 AFTR 16, 52 S.Ct. 613 (USSC, 1932). See the glossary for a discussion of the term "claim of right doctrine."

20. *U.S. v. Lewis,* 51–1 USTC ¶ 9211, 40 AFTR 258, 71 S.Ct. 522 (USSC, 1951).

Thus, in Example 5, the repayment in 19X2 would reduce T's 19X2 tax liability by the greater 19X1 rate (.50) applied to the $5,000. However, § 1341 is intended as relief only for cases in which there is a significant difference in the tax; thus, § 1341 applies only to cases in which the deduction for the amount previously included in income exceeds $3,000.

ACCOUNTING METHODS

PERMISSIBLE METHODS

Section 446 requires that taxable income be computed under the method of accounting regularly employed by the taxpayer in keeping his or her books, provided the method "clearly reflects" income. The Code recognizes as generally permissible methods:

—The cash receipts and disbursements method.

—The accrual method.

—A hybrid method (a combination of cash and accrual).

The Regulations refer to the above alternatives as "overall methods" and add that the term "method of accounting" includes not only the overall "method of accounting" of the taxpayer but also the accounting treatment of any item.[21]

Any of the three methods of accounting may be used if the method is consistently employed and clearly reflects income. However, the taxpayer is required to use the accrual method for sales and costs of goods sold if inventories are an income-producing factor to the business.[22] Special methods are also permitted for installment sales, for long-term construction contracts, and for farmers.

A taxpayer who has more than one trade or business may use a different method of accounting for each trade or business activity.[23] Furthermore, a different method of accounting may be used to determine income from a trade or business than is used to compute non-business items of income and deductions.[24] For example, an individual's income from an unincorporated business could be determined under the accrual method, whereas the cash method could be used for all other types of income (e. g., interest and dividends) and deductions (e. g., itemized deductions).

The Code grants the IRS broad powers to determine whether the taxpayer's accounting method clearly reflects income. Thus, if the method employed does not clearly reflect income, the IRS has the power to prescribe the method to be used by the taxpayer. This authority falls under § 446(b) which states:

---

21. Reg. § 1.446–1(a)(1).

22. Reg. § 1.446–1(a)(4)(i).

23. § 446(d).

24. Reg. § 1.446–1(c)(1)(iv)(b).

If no method of accounting has been regularly used by the taxpayer, or if the method used does not clearly reflect income, the computation of taxable income shall be made under such method as, in the opinion of the Secretary or his delegate, does clearly reflect income.

Under these broad powers, the IRS may require that a taxpayer involuntarily change to another method of accounting. For example, the Regulations now require taxpayers to adopt the full absorption inventory costing method if they are not presently using this method.[25]

CASH RECEIPTS AND DISBURSEMENTS METHOD— CASH BASIS

Most individuals and many businesses use the cash basis to report income and deductions. The popularity of this method can largely be attributed to its simplicity and flexibility.

Under the cash method, income is not recognized until the taxpayer receives (actually or constructively) cash or its equivalent.[26] Deductions are generally permitted in the year of payment.[27] Thus, year-end accounts receivable, accounts payable, and accrued income and deductions are not included in the determination of taxable income.

The cash method permits a taxpayer in many cases to choose the year in which he claims the deduction by simply postponing or accelerating the payment of expenses. However, for fixed assets, the cash basis taxpayer claims deductions through depreciation or amortization, the same as is done by an accrual basis taxpayer. Prepaid expenses must be capitalized and amortized if the life of the asset extends "substantially beyond" the end of the tax year.[28] Most courts have applied the one-year rule to determine whether capitalization and amortization are required. According to this rule, capitalization is required only if the asset has a life that extends beyond the tax year following the year of payment.[29]

Restrictions on Use of the Cash Method. The use of the cash method to measure income from a merchandising or manufacturing operation would often yield a distorted picture of the results of operations. Income for the period would largely be a function of when payments were made for goods or materials. Thus, the regulations prohibit the use of the cash method (and require the accrual method)

---

25. Reg. § 1.471–11.
26. Reg. § 1.451–1(a). Refer to Chapter 5 for a discussion of constructive receipt.
27. Reg. § 1.461–1(a)(1).
28. Reg. Section 1.461–1(a)(1).
29. *Martin J. Zaninovich*, 80–1 USTC ¶ 9342, 45 AFTR2d 80–1442, 616 F.2d 429 (CA–9 1980), reversing 60 T.C. 605 (1978). Refer to Chapter 7 for further discussion of the one-year rule.

to measure sales and cost of goods sold if inventories are material to the business.[30]

Although inventories are material to farming operations, the IRS long ago created an exception to its general rule and has allowed farmers to use the cash method of accounting.[31] The purpose of the exception is to relieve the small farmer from the bookkeeping burden of accrual accounting. However, tax shelter promoters recognized, for example, that by deducting the costs of a crop in one tax year and harvesting the crop in a later year, income could be deferred from tax. Thus, § § 447 and 464 were enacted to prevent the use of the cash method by certain farming corporations and limited partnerships (i. e., "farming syndicates").[32]

ACCRUAL METHOD

The Regulations provide that "under the accrual method of accounting, income is includible in gross income when (1) all the events have occurred which fix the right to receive such income and (2) the amount thereof can be determined with reasonable accuracy."[33]

> **Example 6.** A, a calendar year taxpayer who uses the accrual basis of accounting, was to receive a bonus equal to 6% of B Corporation's net income for its fiscal year ending each June 30. For the fiscal year ending June 30, 19X1, B Corporation had net income of $240,000, and for the six months ending December 31, 19X1, the corporation's net income was $150,000. A will report $14,400 (.06 × $240,000) for 19X1, because her rights to the amount became fixed when B Corporation's year closed. However, A would not accrue income based on the corporation's profits for the last six months of 19X1, since her right to the income does not accrue until the close of the corporation's tax year.

In a situation where the accrual basis taxpayer's right to income is being contested and the income has not yet been collected, generally no income is recognized until the dispute has been settled.[34] Prior to the settlement, "all of the events have not occurred which fix the right to receive the income."

As in the case of revenues, Regulation § 1.461–1(a) provides an all events test to determine the year in which a deduction is to be allowed:

---

30. Reg. § 1.446–1(a)(4)(i).
31. Reg. § 1.471–6(a).
32. § 447(c) contains counter-exceptions that allow certain closely-held corporations to use the cash method. See also § 464(c).
33. Reg. § 1.451–1(a). Refer to Chapter 5 for further discussion of the accrual basis.
34. *Burnet v. Sanford & Brooks Co.,* 2 USTC ¶ 636, 9 AFTR 603, 51 S.Ct. 150 (USSC, 1931).

. . . an expense is deductible for the year in which all the events have occurred which determine the fact of the liability and the amount thereof can be determined with reasonable accuracy.

The all events test prevents the use of reserves frequently employed in financial accounting. For example, the deduction for an addition to a reserve for estimated warranty expense may be deemed necessary to properly match income and expenses as computed for financial accounting purposes; however, no tax deduction is allowed until the customer's claims become actual. The filing of the claim is generally the event that triggers the recognition of an expense. The exception to the prohibition of reserves occurs in the case of bad debts. Section 166 authorizes a deduction for a reasonable addition to the bad debt reserve, as discussed in Chapter 8.

HYBRID METHOD

A hybrid method of accounting involves the use of more than one method. For example, a taxpayer who uses the accrual basis to report sales and cost of goods sold but uses the cash basis to report other items of income and expense is employing a hybrid method. The Code permits the use of a hybrid method provided the taxpayer's income is "clearly reflected."[35] A taxpayer who uses the accrual method for business expenses must also use the accrual method for business income (i. e., a cash method for income items may not be used if the taxpayer's expenses are accounted for under the accrual basis.)[36]

It may be preferable for a business which is required to report sales and cost of sales on the accrual method to report other items of income and expense under the cash method. The cash method permits greater flexibility in the timing of income and expense recognition.

CHANGE OF METHOD

The taxpayer, in effect, makes an election to use a particular accounting method when an initial tax return is filed using a particular method.[37] If a subsequent change in method is desired, the taxpayer must obtain the permission of the IRS.[38]

As previously mentioned, the term "accounting method" encompasses not only the overall accounting method used by the taxpayer (i. e., the cash or accrual method), but also the treatment of any mate-

---

35. § 446(c).
36. Reg. § 1.446–1(c)(1)(iv)(a).
37. Reg. § 1.446–1(e)(1).
38. § 446(e).

rial item of income or deduction.[39] Thus, a change in the method of deducting property taxes from a cash basis to an accrual basis which results in a deduction for taxes in a different year would constitute a change in an accounting method. Other examples of accounting method changes include changes involving the method or basis used in the valuation of inventories and a change from the direct charge-off method to the allowance method for deducting bad debts.

Correction of an Error. A change in accounting method should be distinguished from the correction of an error. An error can be corrected (by filing amended returns) by the taxpayer without special permission, and the IRS can simply adjust the taxpayer's liability if an error is discovered on audit of the return. Some examples of errors are incorrect postings; errors in the calculation of the tax liability, tax credits, etc.; deductions of business expense items that are actually personal; and omissions of income and deductions.[40] Furthermore, the Regulations provide that a change in treatment resulting from a change in underlying facts does not constitute a change in the taxpayer's method of accounting. For example, a change in employment contracts so that an employee accrues one day of vacation pay for each month of service, rather than 12 days of vacation pay for a full year of service, is a change in the underlying facts and is not, therefore, an accounting method change.

Change from an Erroneous Method. If a taxpayer is employing an "erroneous method" of accounting, permission must be obtained from the IRS to change to a correct method. An erroneous method is not treated as a mechanical error which can be corrected by merely filing an amended tax return. For example, according to the IRS, the failure to include manufacturing overhead in the computation of inventory is an erroneous method of accounting which can be changed only upon obtaining the consent of the IRS.[41]

Net Adjustments Due to Change in Accounting Method. In the year of change of an accounting method, certain adjustments may be required to items of income and expense to prevent a distortion of taxable income resulting from the change.

> **Example 7.** In 19X3, Z Corporation, with consent from the IRS, switched from the cash to the accrual basis for reporting sales and costs of goods sold.
>
> The corporation's accrual basis gross profit for the year was computed as follows:

---

39. Reg. § 1.446–1(a)(1). See the Glossary of Tax Terms (Appendix C) for a discussion of the term "accounting method."

40. Reg. § 1.446–1(e)(2)(ii)(b).

41. But see *Korn Industries v. U. S.*, 76–1 USTC ¶ 9354, 37 AFTR2d 76–1228, 532 F.2d 1352 (Ct.Cls., 1976).

Sales		$ 100,000
Beginning inventory	$ 15,000	
Purchases	60,000	
Less ending inventory	(10,000)	
Cost of goods sold		(65,000)
Gross profit		$ 35,000

At the end of the previous year, Z Corporation had accounts receivable of $25,000 and accounts payable for merchandise of $34,000. The accounts receivable from the previous year in the amount of $25,000 were never included in gross income, since the taxpayer was on the cash basis and did not recognize the uncollected receivables. In the current year the $25,000 was not included in the accrual basis sales, since the sales were made in a prior year. Therefore, a $25,000 adjustment to income would be required to prevent the omission of the receivables from income. The corollary of failure to recognize a prior year's receivables is the failure to recognize a prior year's accounts payable. The beginning of the year's accounts payable were not included in current or prior year's purchases. Thus, a deduction for the $34,000 was not taken in either year and is therefore included as an adjustment to income for the period of change. An adjustment is also required to reflect the $15,000 beginning inventory which was deducted (due to the use of a cash method of accounting) by the taxpayer in the previous year. In this instance the cost of goods sold during the year of change was increased by the beginning inventory and resulted in a double deduction.

The net adjustment due to the change in accounting method would be computed as follows:

Beginning inventory (deducted in prior and current year)	$ 15,000
Beginning accounts receivable (omitted from income)	25,000
Beginning accounts payable (omitted from deductions)	(34,000)
Net increase in taxable income	$ 6,000

Involuntary Changes—Disposition of Positive Net Adjustment of More Than $3,000. As previously discussed, the IRS has the authority to make a taxpayer change his or her method of accounting if in the Commissioner's opinion the taxpayer's method does not clearly reflect income. Moreover, the general rule of § 481(a) gives the IRS broad discretion for determining how an adjustment due to the change will be "taken into account." Thus, in the absence of some statutory restraints, a taxpayer could be forced to make a change in methods and the IRS could require the taxpayer to increase income for the year of the change by the entire amount of the adjustment. The result could be a bunching of income with adverse tax implications due to the application of progressive tax rates. To prevent this possible hardship, § 481(a) provides for averaging techniques that are available to taxpayers if all the following conditions are met:

— The taxpayer is required by the IRS to change his or her accounting method.

— The adjustment is positive (i. e., an increase in income).

— The amount of the adjustment exceeds $3,000.

The alternatives for making this adjustment include the following:

1. If the taxpayer used the former method of accounting in the two preceding years, the tax is computed by adding one-third of the adjustment to the taxable income for the year of the change and one-third to each of the two preceding years' income. The resulting additional tax for the two preceding years is then added to the current year's tax liability.

2. If the taxpayer can compute taxable income for one or more taxable years consecutively preceding the taxable year of the change, the adjustment may be made to those prior years and the current year.

However, the final tax liability cannot be greater than the tax computed by including the entire adjustment in the taxable income for the year of change.

> **Example 8.** X Corporation has expensed factory overhead each of the four years it has been in existence. Its ending inventory was computed by the FIFO method.

	(a) Amounts Expensed That Should Have Been in Year-end Inventory	(b) Effect on Cost of Goods Sold	(c) Effect on Taxable Income (Understatement)	(d) Marginal Tax Rate
19X1	$ 10,000	$ 10,000	$ (10,000)	.48
19X2	12,000	10,000–12,000	(2,000)	.22
19X3	15,000	12,000–15,000	(3,000)	.46
19X4	16,000	15,000–16,000	(1,000)	.17
19X5			$ (16,000)	.30

> If X Corporation is required to change to full-absorption accounting as of January 1, 19X5, the adjustment due to the change in accounting method will be $16,000. The amount of the beginning inventory for 19X5 is understated. Thus, the amount of prior years' income was (in total) understated. Under method 1, the corporation would (a) add $5,333 ($16,000 × ⅓) to its taxable income as originally reported for years 19X3, 19X4, and 19X5; (b) compute the tax on the increased income for each of the three

years; and (c) pay the excess of the tax computed in step (b) over the amount previously paid. Given the marginal rates above, the corporation would owe an additional $4,960 [(.30 × $5,333) + (.17 × $5,333) + (.46 × $5,333) = $4,960]. However, the tax resulting from including the entire adjustment in income for 19X5 would be $4,800 (.30 × $16,000), which is less than that computed under the first method. Under method 2, the corporation could compute its income for 19X4, which would increase that year's income by $1,000 [see column (c)]. The remaining $15,000 would be included in 19X5 income, and the additional tax would be $4,670 [i. e., (.17 × $1,000) + (.30 × $15,000) = $4,670]. Under method 2, the corporation actually has further flexibility in that it can choose any number of prior years over which to spread the adjustment. Thus, income could be recomputed for years 19X3 and 19X4 and the balance of the adjustment allocated to 19X5, or 19X2 through 19X4 and the balance of the adjustment would be taken in 19X5. Moreover, the corporation could recompute its income for all prior years, in which case there would be no adjustment to 19X5.

Correcting Error vs. Change in Method. As mentioned in the above example, X Corporation could choose, as an alternative for disposing of the adjustment, to recompute its income for all prior years by the new method of accounting. Column (c) in Example 8 shows the amount that would have to be added to each year's income.

Assume that 19X1 was closed by the statute of limitations.[42] If instead of a change in method, the inventory adjustments were deemed to be the correction of an error, the corporation would correct its income for 19X2 through 19X4, but not for 19X1. Thus $10,000 (the amount by which income in 19X1 was understated) would not have to be reported. In many cases, therefore, it is important to know whether the adjustments are to correct errors or are adjustments resulting from change in accounting methods.[43]

Other Involuntary Changes. Where the IRS requires a taxpayer to change his or her method of accounting in order to "clearly reflect" income, any positive adjustment that is attributable to years prior to 1954 is permanently excluded from income.[44] This rule was enacted to facilitate the transition from the 1939 Code to the 1954 Code and applies solely to involuntary changes initiated by the IRS.

Voluntary Changes—Procedure and Disposition of Adjustments. Generally, a taxpayer must file a request to change his or her accounting method (on Form 3115) within the first 180 days after the

---

42. § 6501.
43. *Schuster's Express, Inc.,* 68 T.C. 588 (1976).
44. § 481(a)(2).

beginning of the taxable year of the desired change.[45] However, the IRS has virtually total discretion to accept or reject the proposed change and will not grant permission unless the taxpayer agrees to certain terms or adjustments.[46]

Generally, a taxpayer who makes a timely application for a change in accounting method is allowed to spread the adjustment over ten years, one-tenth allocated to the year of the change and to each of the nine subsequent years. However, under Rev.Proc. 80–51,[47] the prospective period for spreading the adjustment cannot exceed the number of periods over which the adjustment accumulated. Thus, in Example 8, the $16,000 adjustment would be spread over not more than four years (19X5–19X8), since the company used the former method of accounting for only four years.

SPECIAL ACCOUNTING METHODS

Generally, accrual basis taxpayers recognize income when goods are sold and shipped to the customer. Cash basis taxpayers generally recognize income from a sale on the collection of cash from the customer. The tax law provides special accounting methods, however, for unusual situations (e. g., long-term contracts when the contract requires more than 12 months to complete). In addition, the installment method (which is a variation of the cash method) is available to taxpayers if certain conditions are met. These special methods were enacted, in part, to provide equity based on the wherewithal to pay concept (i. e., the taxpayer does not have the cash to pay the tax at the time of sale).

LONG-TERM CONTRACTS

Regulation § 1.451–3(b) defines a "long-term contract" as follows: a building, installation, construction, or manufacturing contract which is not entered into and completed within the same tax year. Furthermore, a manufacturing contract is long-term only if the contract is to manufacture (1) a unique item not normally carried in finished goods inventory or (2) items that normally require more than 12 calendar months to complete.

Example 9. T, a calendar year taxpayer, entered into two contracts during the year. One contract was to construct a building

---

45. Reg. § 1.446–1(e)(3). The deadline may be extended to within the first nine months of the year of the change, if the taxpayer can show good cause for the delay in filing the request.
46. Rev.Proc. 72–52, 1972–2 C.B. 833.
47. Rev.Proc. 80–51, 1980–2 C.B. 818, superseding. Rev.Proc. 70–27, 1970–2 C.B. 509, as clarified in Rev.Proc. 75–18, 1975–1 C.B. 687.

foundation. Work was to begin in October 19X1 and was to be completed by June 19X2. The contract is long-term, because it will not be entered into and completed in the same tax year. The fact that the contract requires less than 12 calendar months to complete is not relevant, because the contract is not for manufacturing. The second contract was for architectural services to be performed over two years. These services will not qualify for long-term contract treatment, because the taxpayer will not build, install, construct, or manufacture a product.

In the year the costs are incurred for such long-term contracts, the taxpayer may elect to use either (1) the completed contract, (2) percentage of completion, (3) cash, (4) accrual, or (5) a hybrid method. Once the election is made, the taxpayer must apply the same method to all subsequent long-term contracts unless permission is obtained for a change in accounting method.[48]

Completed Contract Method. Under the completed contract method, no revenue from the contract is recognized until the contract is completed and accepted. However, a taxpayer may not delay completion of a contract for the principal purpose of deferring tax.[49] Nevertheless, it may be possible for a taxpayer to select the year in which income is recognized by either accelerating or decelerating nearly completed projects prior to the end of the tax year. Some courts have, in effect, applied a *de minimus* rule holding that a contract is complete upon its substantial completion (i. e., minor amounts of work to be completed or defects to be corrected do not postpone the recognition of income if the contract has been accepted).[50] Other courts have applied a literal interpretation to the Regulations and have required total completion and acceptance of the contract.[51] In 1982, Congress directed the IRS to issue new regulations clarifying when a contract is completed.

All costs allocable to the contract are accumulated in a contract-in-progress account (an inventory account) until the revenue is recognized, at which time the costs are offset against the income from the contract. Construction costs such as direct labor and materials must be allocated to individual contracts. In addition, certain indirect costs must be allocated to the extent that they are incident to and necessary for the performance of the long-term contract.[52] Such costs include repairs, maintenance, utilities, rent, and depreciation. Certain of the

48. Reg. § 1.451–3(a).
49. Reg. § 1.451–3(b)(2).
50. *Ehret-Day Co.,* 2 T.C. 25 (1943) *acq.,* 1943 C.B. 7; *Nathan Wohlfeld,* 17 TCM 677, T.C.Memo. 1958–128; *Charles G. Smith,* 66 T.C. 213 (1976).
51. *Thompson-King-Tate v. U. S.,* 62–1 USTC ¶ 9116, 8 AFTR2d 5920, 296 F.2d 290 (CA–6, 1961); *E. E. Black Limited v. Alsup,* 54–1 USTC ¶ 9340, 45 AFTR 1345, 211 F.2d 879 (CA–9, 1954).
52. Reg. § 1.451–3(d)(5)(i) and (ii).

following costs are not required to be allocated to the long-term contracts and may be deducted currently: selling, advertising, distribution, interest, general and administrative, research, depreciation on idle equipment, and pension costs. Complex cost allocation rules apply to contracts that require more than two years to complete. Small contractors (annual gross receipts of less than $25 million) are exempt from the complex cost allocations.[53]

In some instances the original contract price may be disputed or the buyer may desire additional work to be done on a long-term contract. If the disputed amount is substantial (i. e., it is not possible to determine whether a profit or loss will ultimately be realized on the contract), the Regulations provide that no amount of income or loss is recognized until the dispute is resolved. In all other cases, the profit or loss (reduced by the amount in dispute) is recognized in the current period on completion of the contract. However, if additional work is to be performed with respect to the disputed contract, the difference between the amount in dispute and the actual cost of the additional work will be recognized in the year such work is completed rather than in the year in which the dispute is resolved.[54]

> **Example 10.** B, a calendar year taxpayer utilizing the completed contract method of accounting, constructed a building for C pursuant to a long-term contract. The gross contract price was $500,000. B finished construction in 19X2 at a cost of $475,000. When C examined the building, he insisted that the building be repainted or the contract price be reduced. The estimated cost of repainting is $10,000. Since under the terms of the contract, B would be assured of a profit of at least $15,000 ($500,000 − $475,000 − $10,000) even if the dispute was ultimately resolved in favor of C, B must include $490,000 ($500,000 − $10,000) in gross income and is allowed deductions of $475,000 for 19X2.
>
> In 19X3, B and C resolved the dispute, and B repainted certain portions of the building at a cost of $6,000. B must include $10,000 in 19X3 gross income and may deduct the $6,000 expense in that year.
>
> **Example 11.** Assume the same as in the previous example except the estimated cost of repainting the building is $50,000. Since the resolution of the dispute completely in C's favor would mean that there would be a net loss on the contract ($500,000 − $475,000 − $50,000 = − $25,000), no income or loss would be recognized until the year in which the dispute is resolved.

Frequently the contractor will receive payment at various stages of completion. For example, when the contract is 50 percent complete,

---

53. Reg. § 1.451–(b)(3).
54. Reg. § 1.451–3(d)(2)(ii)–(vii), Example(2).

the contractor may receive 50 percent of the contract price less a re-tainage. The taxation of these payments is generally governed by Regulation § 1.451–5 "advanced payments for goods and long-term contracts" (discussed in Chapter 5). Generally, contractors are permitted to defer the advance payments until such payments are recognized as income under the taxpayer's method of accounting.

Percentage of Completion Method. Under the percentage of completion method, a portion of the gross contract price is included in income during each period. The accrued amount represents the percentage of the contract which is completed during the year multiplied by the gross contract price. All of the expenditures made on the contract during the year (after adjustment for variations between the beginning and ending inventories of materials and supplies) are deductible as an offset against the accrued revenue.[55]

The Regulations provide that an estimate of the percentage of completion may be determined by either of the following methods:

—By comparing the costs incurred with the estimated total costs.

—By comparing the work performed with the estimated total work to be performed.

If the estimate is based upon a comparison of work performed, certificates of architects or engineers or other appropriate documentation must be available for inspection on audit by the IRS.[56]

Comparison of the Completed Contract and Percentage of Completion Methods. To illustrate the two methods, assume a contractor agrees to construct a building for $125,000. In the initial year of construction, costs of $80,000 are incurred and the architect estimates the job is 80 percent complete. In the second year the contract is completed at an additional cost of $25,000.

PERCENTAGE OF COMPLETION METHOD

	Year 1	Year 2
Revenue (80% × $125,000 in Year 1)	$ 100,000	$ 25,000
Costs incurred on the contract	(80,000)	(25,000)
Gross profit	$ 20,000	$ –0–

COMPLETED CONTRACT METHOD

	Year 1	Year 2
Revenue	–0–	$ 125,000
Costs incurred on the contract	—	(105,000)
Gross profit	–0–	$ 20,000

---

55. Reg. § 1.451–3(c)(3).
56. Reg. § 1.451–3(c)(2)(i) and (ii).

As illustrated above, an advantage of the completed contract method is the deferral of income. This means that the contractor has the use of funds which would otherwise be paid to the government as income taxes during periods prior to completion. Of course, the completed contract method can result in a bunching of income in one year. However, if the contractor is incorporated and regularly reports taxable income of more than $100,000, the 46 percent rate always will apply. Therefore, the deferral can be accomplished with no increase in total tax. If the taxpayer is an individual, income averaging may afford some relief from the bunched income problem. In addition, the completed contract method may minimize disputes with the IRS since there is no need to make yearly estimates of the percentage of completion.

The taxpayer must also consider the timing of cash receipts from the contract and cash payments for taxes. Under the percentage of completion method, cash may not be available when the tax is due. Such might be the case if advance payments are not received prior to the completion of the contract.

INSTALLMENT METHOD

Under the general rule for computing the gain or loss from the sale of property, the entire amount of gain or loss is recognized upon the sale or other disposition of the property.

> **Example 12.** A sold property to B for $20,000 cash plus B's note (fair market value and face amount of $80,000). A's basis in the property was $40,000. Gain or loss computed under the cash or accrual basis would be as follows:

Amount realized:	
Cash down payment	$ 20,000
Notes receivable	80,000
	$ 100,000
Basis in the property	(40,000)
Realized gain	$ 60,000

In the previous example, the general rule for recognizing gain or loss requires A to pay a substantial amount of tax on the gain in the year of sale even though only $20,000 cash was received. Congress enacted the installment sale provisions to prevent this sort of hardship by allowing the taxpayer to spread the gain from installment sales over the collection period.

The installment sales method is a very important tax planning tool. In addition to its obvious tax deferral possibilities, the installment method can be used to avoid a bunching of income; and in the case of the sale of a capital asset, the installment method may sufficiently spread the capital gain to avoid or reduce any alternative minimum tax (refer to Chapter 12).

Overview of the Installment Sales Provisions. The relevant Code provisions are summarized below:

Section	Subject
453	General rules governing the installment method (e. g., when applicable), related-party transfers, and special situations (e. g., certain corporate liquidations).
453A	Use of the installment method by dealers in personal property (i. e., personalty).
453B	Gain or loss recognition upon the disposition of installment obligations.
1038	Rules governing the repossession of real estate sold under the installment method.

Since the rules governing dealers in personal property (i. e., § 453A) are unique, they are considered first.

INSTALLMENT METHOD—DEALERS IN PERSONAL PROPERTY

To qualify as a dealer in personal property, the taxpayer must regularly sell personal property on the installment plan.[57] "Regularly" would seem to imply a high ratio of installment sales to total sales. However, the Tax Court has interpreted the "regularly sells" requirement to mean that the taxpayer holds him or herself out to the public as selling on the installment plan.[58]

The election may be used to report income both from revolving charge accounts (i. e., consumer charge accounts with extended payment privileges) and traditional installment contracts. At this point, it is not clear whether or not single payment accounts will qualify.[59] Under prior law, more than one payment was necessary before the installment method could be used.[60]

Making the Election. In the case of a new business, the election is made by reporting the income under the installment method. A statement should be attached to the return indicating that the election is being made.[61] If a dealer in personal property has been using the

---

57. § 453A(a)(1).
58. *Davenport Machine & Foundry Co.,* 18 T.C. 38 (1952).
59. Although § 453A is silent on this point, the Senate Finance Committee Report on H.R. 6883 (reported with amendments on September 26, 1980) anticipates that the Regulations issued by the Treasury Department will permit just one payment to qualify.
60. Reg. § 1.453–2(b)(1).
61. Reg. § 1.453–8(a).

accrual method in reporting gains, conversion to the installment method represents a change in an accounting method and requires the consent of the IRS.[62] Under prior law, special adjustments for prior sales were required by the change, which led to a degree of double taxation. Commencing in 1981, no such adjustments are necessary.

> **Example 13.** In 19X1, Z Corporation (a calendar year taxpayer) began its retail operations. In reporting gain on installment sales during 19X1 and 19X2, the accrual method was used. In March of 19X3, Z Corporation decides to adopt the installment method. Pursuant to this decision, a Form 3115 is filed and approval of the change is obtained from the IRS. Z Corporation now will account for the 19X3 sales using the installment method. Any further collections on its 19X1 and 19X2 sales will not result in income, since the gain element already has been recognized.

> **Example 14.** Assume the same facts as in the previous example except that Z Corporation chose to use the installment method when it filed its first income tax return (i. e., for tax year 19X1). Because no change in accounting method is involved, the use of the installment method is automatic and the consent of the IRS is not necessary.

Computing the Realized Gross Profit. The gross profit percentages may be computed for each sale and the percentage can then be applied to each collection. In most instances, however, all of the installment sales for a particular year are grouped and one gross profit percentage for the year is computed.[63]

> **Example 15.** X Company is a new business that sells wood stoves. X Company sells three models on the installment plan. Total sales and cost of goods sold for each model are presented below.

Model	Sales	Cost of Goods Sold	Gross Profit	Gross Profit %	Collections
1	$ 60,000	$ 24,000	$ 36,000	60%	$ 20,000
2	90,000	45,000	45,000	50%	60,000
3	50,000	40,000	10,000	20%	20,000
	$ 200,000	$ 109,000	$ 91,000	45.5%	$ 100,000

> X Company can elect to report its recognized gross profit for the year by relating collections to the particular model using the first method; gross profit is computed to be $46,000 [$20,000 × 60%)

---

62. § 446(e).
63. Reg. § 1.453–2(c).

+ ($60,000 × 50%) + ($20,000 × 20%)]. The gross profit using the average method is $45,500 ($100,000 × 45.5%), computed by applying an average gross profit percentage to total collections.

The dealer may add carrying charges or interest (as determined at the time of the sale) to the cash selling price of the property.[64] Alternatively, the carrying charges may be reported separately (e. g., as interest income) in which case payments received first are applied to the carrying charges (accrued interest).[65]

Example 16. T, a home appliance dealer, had installment sales, cost of goods sold, and gross profit computed under the accrual method as follows:

	Installment Sales (Including Carrying Charges and Interest)	Cost of Goods Sold	Gross Profit	Gross Profit %
19X1	$ 100,000	$ 60,000	$ 40,000	40%
19X2	120,000	90,000	30,000	25%
19X3	150,000	105,000	45,000	30%

In computing the gross profit under the installment method on the 19X3 return, the dealer must take into account collections on current and previous years' installment sales as follows:

Year of Sale	19X3 Collections		Gross Profit %	Gross Profit on Collections
19X1	$ 20,000	×	40%	$ 8,000
19X2	50,000	×	25%	12,500
19X3	60,000	×	30%	18,000
Total 19X3 realized gross profit				$ 38,500

Bad Debts and Repossessions. When the installment method is used by a dealer in personal property and accounts become uncollectible, the vendor receives a bad debt deduction for the unrecovered cost of the merchandise.[66] The deferred gross profit which is included in the receivable cannot be deducted, since it has never been included in gross income.

Example 17. During the current year, T (in Example 16) wrote off, as uncollectible, $10,000 of installment receivables from sales made in 19X2, when the gross profit rate was 25%. The bad debt deduction is $7,500, the balance of the account less the profit included in the receivable [$10,000 − ($10,000 × 25%)].

---

64.   § 453A(a)(2).
65.   § 453A(b).
66.   Reg. § 1.453–1(d).

If the dealer repossesses the merchandise, the value of the merchandise at the time of repossession must be used to reduce the loss (and expenses of repossession which are added to the loss).

> **Example 18.** Assume the property repossessed by T in the previous example had a value of $1,500 at the time it was repossessed. T incurred expenses of $100 in the repossession and later resold the merchandise for $2,000. A loss on repossession of $6,100 would result ($7,500 + $100 − $1,500). T would report a gain of $500 on the subsequent sale of the property ($2,000 − $1,500) since the repossessed goods are included in inventory at their fair market value at the time of repossession.

Repossession of real property is discussed in a subsequent section of this chapter.

Installment Sales—Property Other Than Inventory. As discussed above, the Code contains special rules for installment reporting by dealers in personal property. Other taxpayers who wish to use the installment method must meet the requirements set forth in § 453.

— There must be a sale of property (as contrasted to services).

— The property must not be of a kind which "is required to be included in the inventory of the taxpayer if on hand at the close of the taxable year."[67]

Thus, an engineering firm's income from consulting services and a manufacturer's sale of its products could not be reported by the installment method. However, the wording of the statute regarding inventories apparently means that cash basis farmers are eligible for the installment method. This appears to be true because the statute does not require the cash basis farmer to inventory his or her crops and livestock on hand at year-end.

If the property sold is of the right kind, the next issue is whether there was an installment sale. All that is required to meet the latter requirement is that at least one payment will be received in a tax year other than the year of sale.[68]

> **Example 19.** Z sold land on December 31, 19X1, and received the seller's note receivable. The note was paid in 19X2. Under the installment method, Z would report her entire gain in 19X2 rather than 19X1 (the years she would have reported the gain by the cash or accrual method).

The Nonelective Aspect. Regardless of the taxpayer's method of accounting, as a general rule installment sales must be reported by

---

67. § 453(b)(1)(B).

68. § § 453(b)(1), applicable to sales after October 19, 1980. Under pre-1980 law the IRS took the position that the installment method could not be used if the entire selling price was received in one year.

the installment method.[69] A special election is required to report the gain by any other method of accounting (see further discussion in a subsequent section of this chapter).

> **Example 20.** In December 19X1, S sold land to B. S is an accrual basis taxpayer, but he did not report the sale on his 19X1 return because he was mistaken as to when the sales transaction was completed. B paid some of S's expenses of the sale in 19X1, and these payments were considered collections by S for installment method purposes.
>
> In the process of completing S's 19X2 return, the accountant discovered the installment sale should have been reported on the 19X1 return. Because the installment method is not elective, S must amend his 19X1 return and report the gain attributable to the payments in 19X1. S will not be required to report the entire gain in 19X1 even though it would have been taxable in that year under his overall method of accounting. (Under prior law, S would not have been allowed to use the installment method because he did not make the election on his original 19X1 return.)

Computing the Gain for the Period. The gain reported on each sale is computed by the following formula:

$$\frac{\text{Total gain}}{\text{Contract price}} \times \text{Payments received} = \text{Recognized gain}$$

The computation of the total gain for a taxpayer who is not a dealer in real property is the selling price reduced by selling expenses and the adjusted basis of the property. For a dealer in real property, selling expenses are treated as a business expense and, therefore, are deducted in full in the year of the sale, rather than used to offset the selling price.

The contract price, generally, is the amount (excluding interest) the seller will ultimately collect from the purchaser. Therefore, the contract price is the selling price less the seller's mortgage or notes which are assumed by the buyer. Payments received are the collections on the contract price received in the tax year and thus are generally the cash received (excluding interest income). If the buyer pays any of the seller's expenses, the amount paid is considered constructively received by the seller. Additional items that are considered payments are discussed after the basic calculations have been illustrated.

> **Example 21.** The seller is not a dealer and the facts are as follows:

---

69. § 453(a). Under pre-1980 law the installment method had to be elected.

Sales price:		
Cash down payment	$ 1,000	
Seller's mortgage assumed	3,000	
Notes payable to the seller	13,000	$ 17,000
Selling expenses		(500)
Seller's basis		(10,000)
Total gain		$ 6,500

The contract price is $14,000 ($17,000 − $3,000). Assuming the $1,000 is the only payment in the year of sale, the gain in that year is computed as follows:

$$\frac{\$6,500 \ (\text{total gain})}{\$14,000 \ (\text{contract price})} \times \$1,000 = \underline{\$464} \ \begin{array}{l}(\text{gain recognized} \\ \text{in year of sale})\end{array}$$

If the sum of the nondealer's basis and selling expenses is less than the liabilities assumed by the buyer, the difference must be added to the contract price and to the payments received in the year of sale.[70] This adjustment to the contract price is required so that the ratio of total gain divided by contract price will not be greater than one.

Example 22. Assume the same facts as in the previous example except that the seller's basis in the property is only $2,000. The total gain, therefore, is $14,500. Payments in the year of sale are $1,500.

Down payment	$ 1,000
Excess of mortgage assumed over seller's basis	
and expenses ($3,000 − $2,000 − $500)	500
	$ 1,500

The contract price is $14,500 [$17,000 (selling price) − $3,000 (seller's mortgage assumed) + $500 (excess of seller's expenses and mortgage assumed over seller's basis)], and the gain in the year of sale is computed as follows:

$$\frac{\$14,500 \ (\text{total gain})}{\$14,500 \ (\text{contract price})} \times \$1,500 = \$1,500$$

In subsequent years, all amounts the seller collects on note principal ($13,000) will be recognized gain.

---

70. Reg. § 1.453–1(b)(2)(iii). The dealer adjusts only for the excess of liabilities assumed over his or her basis.

The character of the gain depends on the type of asset sold. When the gain includes some ordinary income under § § 1245 and 1250, as well as § 1231 gain, the Regulations require that all ordinary income be recognized before the § 1231 gain is reported.[71]

Other Amounts Considered Payments Received. Congress and the IRS have added the following items to be considered as payments received in the year of sale:

—Purchaser's evidence of indebtedness payable on demand and certain other readily tradable obligations (e. g., bonds traded on a stock exchange).[72]

—Purchaser's evidence of indebtedness secured by cash or its equivalent.[73]

In the absence of the first adjustments, the seller would have almost complete control over the year he or she reported the gain—whenever he or she demands payment or sells the tradable obligations. Also, the seller receiving the obligations secured by cash can often post them as collateral for a loan and have the cash from the sale; thus, there would be no justification for deferring the tax.

Imputed Interest. Section 483 provides that if a deferred payment contract for the sale of property with a selling price of at least $3,000 does not contain a reasonable interest rate, a reasonable rate is imputed. The imputing of interest effectively restates the selling price of the property to equal the sum of the payments in the year of sale and the discounted present value of the future payments. The difference between the present value of a future payment and its face amount is taxed as interest income when collections are received. Thus, § 483 prevents sellers of capital assets from increasing the selling price to reflect the equivalent of unstated interest on deferred payments and thereby converting ordinary (interest) income into long-term capital gains.

Currently under the Regulations, if a contract entered into on or after July 1, 1981[74], does not provide a simple interest rate of at least nine percent, a rate of 10 percent (compounded semiannually) is imputed. However, the maximum imputed interest rate is only seven percent in the case of sales of land to a family member (the seller's brothers, sisters, spouse, ancestors, or lineal descendants) after June 30, 1981.[75] It seems Congress decided family members should be allowed some of a "good thing"—the ability to convert some interest income into capital gain.

---

71. Reg. § § 1.1245–6(d) and 1.1250–1(b)(6).
72. § 453(2).
73. Reg. § 1.453–1(b)(3).
74. Reg. § 1.483–1(g)(2), Table VII.
75. § 483(g).

Example 23. S sold land to P for $15,000 cash and an installment note with $15,000 due each year for the following nine years. No interest is stated in the agreement, and S's basis in the land is $30,000. In the absence of the imputed interest rules, S's total capital gain would be $120,000 ($150,000 − $30,000).

In the following schedule, the selling price, contract price, and capital gain are calculated with interest imputed at 10% (assuming P is not a family member) and at 7% (assuming P is a family member).

	10%	7%
Present value of $15,000/year for 9 years	$ 86,385	$ 98,923
Down payment	15,000	15,000
Selling price (also contract price)	$ 101,385	$ 113,923
Minus basis	30,000	30,000
Total capital gain	$ 71,385	$ 83,923
Total interest ($120,000 less capital gain)	$ 48,615	$ 36,077

This example demonstrates that the family member has $12,538 more capital gain and $12,538 less interest income than the non-family member under these conditions.

Contingent Payments and Price. Frequently the contract price for the sale of a business or other property will have a contingent element. The total price may be fixed, but the rate at which it is to be paid is unknown.

Example 24. Mr. Z sold his controlling interest in Z Corporation for $150,000. He was to receive $50,000 at the time of the sale plus 30% of annual profit until the total price is collected.

The contingency presents no problem if the contract calls for at least nine percent interest. However, if interest has to be imputed, the seller is faced with a seemingly impossible task. In the year of sale he cannot compute the present value of the selling price because he does not know how much will be collected each year in the future. As a result, he cannot compute the gain and contract price. The Regulations solve the problem by assuming that the price will be paid as soon as possible under the contract.[76] Thus, in the above example, the initial calculation of imputed interest and gains is made on the assumption that 30 percent of the first year's profits will equal $100,000. Interest would then be imputed from the date of sale until the date the first payment is due. Thus, the selling price and contract price are $140,900 ($50,000 plus the present value of $100,000 to be received in one year ($90,900)). The Regulations also illustrate the subsequent

---

76. Reg. § 1.453–1(c)(2).

adjustments that will be necessary if the initial assumption (that 30 percent of the first year's profits is $100,000) proves to be incorrect.

The terms of sale may be fixed in terms of when the payments are due but contingent as to the total selling price.

> **Example 25.** X sold his controlling interest in X Corporation for $50,000 plus 30% of annual profits for the following two years. His basis in the stock was $60,000.

As X collects on the contract, two things must be done to calculate his income: (1) the amount collected must be separated into principal and interest, and (2) a portion of his basis in the property must be allocated. The imputed interest rules are used to separate the interest. Under the installment sales regulations, an equal amount of basis is allocated to each tax year payments are to be received. However, the basis allocated to a particular year cannot exceed the principal collected during the year.[77]

> **Example 26.** X in the previous example collected $20,000 for his share of year 1 profits and $40,000 out of year 2 profits.

Year	Amount Received	Imputed Interest	Recovery of Capital	Capital Gain
1	$ 50,000	$ –0–	$ 20,000*	$ 30,000
2	20,000	1,800	18,200**	–0–
3	40,000	6,400	21,800	11,800
	$ 110,000	$ 8,200	$ 60,000	$ 41,800

*$60,000 (basis) ÷ 3 (years in which payments are to be received).
**Present value (at the date of sale) of $20,000 to be received in one year.

An equal allocation of basis to each of the payment periods can be justified only as simple to apply and as a means for the IRS to prevent taxpayers from applying the open transaction doctrine (under which no gain would be reported until the taxpayer has collected more than his or her total basis in the property, which is year 2.)[78]

Related-Party Sales of Nondepreciable Property. Due to favorable judicial authority, it was possible (with proper planning) to use the installment sales approach in sales between related parties.

> **Example 27.** H and W (husband and wife) each own substantial investment properties. H would like to sell a capital asset that has a basis of $20,000 and a value of $100,000. He could easily sell the property for cash, but that would result in $32,000 taxable gain [.40 (100,000 − 20,000) = $32,000] for the year. To defer

---

77. Reg. § 1.453–1(c)(3).
78. Refer to Chapter 5, Recovery of Capital Doctrine, and the glossary (Appendix C).

the tax while enjoying the proceeds of the sale, H & W could structure transactions as follows:

First Disposition. H sells the assets to W for $100,000 and receives $10,000 cash and a $90,000 interest-bearing long-term note. In the year of the sale he reports a gain of $8,000 (see computation below) of which $3,200 (40%) is taxable.

$$(\frac{\$100,000 - \$20,000}{\$100,000} \times \$10,000 = \$8,000)$$

H has a $72,000 deferred gain.

Second Disposition. W has a basis in the asset of $100,000 (cost). Soon after purchasing the asset from H, W sells it on the open market for $100,000. The net result of the two transactions is that the family unit (H and W) has $100,000 cash and a deferred tax liability that will not come due until the distant future, when W pays H the principal on the notes. The interest payments will be a wash on a joint return—H's income will be offset by W's deduction.

Although transactions as depicted in the previous example had to be carefully planned, before 1980 they could succeed.[79] Obviously, this scheme was too good to be true; thus, in 1980 Congress added § 453(e). The basic approach of the new related-party installment sales rules is to assume that the proceeds of the second sale were used to pay the note owed to the first seller. Thus, the deferred gain from the first disposition is accelerated to the date of the second disposition.

Example 28. Assume the same facts as in the previous example except W sold the asset for $110,000. W realized and must recognize a $10,000 gain, and H must recognize his previously deferred $72,000 gain, even though W did not retire the note payable to H.

A realized loss from the second sale complicates the analysis. The first seller is deemed to have received in the year of the second sale the lesser of the following:[80]

1. The total amount realized from the second disposition.

2. The total contract price reduced by the total amount already received.

Example 29. Assume W, in the previous example, realized only $80,000 from the second disposition when the balance on the contract price was $90,000 ($100,000 selling price − $10,000 down payment). W recognizes a $20,000 loss, and H must recognize a $64,000 gain as computed below:

---

79. For a taxpayer success in this area, see *Rushing v. Comm.*, 1971–1 USTC ¶ 9339, 27 AFTR2d 71–1139, 441 F.2d 593 (CA–5, 1971), *aff'g* 52 T.C. 888 (1969). For examples of where the plan was unsuccessful, see *Paul G. Lustgarten*, 71 T.C. 303 (1978) and *Phillip W. Wrenn*, 67 T.C. 576 (1976).
80. § 453(e)(3).

$$\frac{\$80,000}{\$100,000} \times \$80,000 = \$64,000$$

The \$8,000 balance of H's gain (\$80,000 − \$8,000 − \$64,000 = \$8,000) will be reported as he collects from W on the installment contract.

However, even with this modification of the rules, Congress did not eliminate the benefits of all related-party installment sales:

—Related parties include the first seller's spouse, children, grandchildren, parents, controlled corporations and partnerships, trusts, and estates in which the seller has an interest.[81] But a sale to a grandparent, brother, sister, uncle, aunt, niece, nephew, or cousin is not subject to the rules.

—Except in the case of the sale of marketable securities (securities frequently bought and sold in the open market), there is no acceleration if the second disposition occurs more than two years after the first sale.[82]

Thus, if the taxpayer can sell the property to an unrelated (as defined above) or patient family member, the intrafamily installment sale is still a powerful tax planning tool.

There are other exceptions that can be applied in some circumstances. Gain is not accelerated if the second disposition is an involuntary conversion or a stock redemption or occurs after the death of either of the related parties, or where tax avoidance was not a principal purpose of either the first or second disposition.[83] Obviously, the availability of these exceptions invites the structuring of transactions to come within the exceptions.

Related-Party Sales of Depreciable Property. On the sale of depreciable property, the recapture rules of § § 1245 and 1250 could operate to convert some or all of the § 1231 gain (normally treated as long-term capital gain) into ordinary income. But even absent any § § 1245 or 1250 recapture potential, or if some § 1231 gain remains, when the parties involved in the sale (i. e., the seller and purchaser) are related to each other, they could run afoul of § 1239. Quite simply, § 1239 operates to convert § 1231 gain to ordinary income on the sale of depreciable property between related parties. In spite of these provisions, such sales could be advantageous for tax purposes if they were structured to make use of the installment method of reporting gain.

---

81. § 453(f)(1), cross-referencing § 318(a).
82. § 453(e)(2). But see § 453(e)(2)(B) for extensions of the two-year period and § 453(f)(2) for the definition of "marketable security."
83. § 453(e)(6) and (7).

Example 30. S Corporation sells an apartment building (adjusted basis of $200,000) to P, its sole shareholder, for its fair market value of $500,000. Under the terms of the sale, P makes no down payment but issues notes (face amount of $50,000 each) payable annually (with 12% interest) over a period of 10 years. Even though S Corporation is forced to recognize the $300,000 gain as ordinary income (see § 1239), an election under § 453 would spread the income over the 10-year payout period. Not a bad price to pay when one considers that the transfer results in P's obtaining a building with a step-up in basis to $500,000 for depreciation purposes.

Because Congress felt the deferral of income made possible in situations such as Example 30 constituted a form of unwarranted tax avoidance, it enacted new § 453(g) as part of the Installment Sales Revision Act of 1980. Simply stated, this provision places the related seller of depreciable property on the accrual method of accounting for purposes of timing the recognition of gain. Returning to Example 30, § 453(g) would force S Corporation to recognize the full gain of $300,000 in the year of sale. As noted previously, § 1239 operates to make this gain ordinary income.

For purposes of new § 453(g), related parties include:

—A taxpayer and his or her spouse.

—A taxpayer and a corporation or a partnership in which the taxpayer and/or spouse holds an 80 percent interest.

—A corporation and a partnership in which the taxpayer and/or spouse holds an 80 percent interest.[84]

Disposition of Installment Obligations. Section 453B prevents taxpayers from avoiding the recognition of deferred gross profit on installment obligations through various means (e. g., the sale of installment notes or the distribution of such notes to shareholders). This provision of the Code requires the taxpayer to, in effect, pay the tax on the portion of gross profits which was previously deferred. Section 453B(a) provides as follows:

If an installment obligation is satisfied at other than its face value or distributed, transmitted, sold, or otherwise disposed of, gain or loss shall result to the extent of the difference between the basis of the obligation and either of the following:

1. The amount realized, in the case of satisfaction at other than face value or a sale or exchange.

2. The fair market value of the obligation at the time of distribution, transmission, or disposition, in the case of the distri-

---

84. See § 1239(b) as amended by the Installment Sales Revision Act of 1980.

bution, transmission, or disposition other than by sale or exchange.

The gift of an installment note will be treated as a taxable disposition by the donor. One court, however, has held that no gain will be recognized when the donee also is the obligor.[85] Now § 453B(f)(1) clarifies this matter by making the cancellation a taxable disposition. Furthermore, § 453B(f)(2) holds that the amount realized from the cancellation will be the face amount of the note if the parties (i. e., obligor and obligee) are related to each other.

> **Example 31.** F cancels a note issued by D (F's daughter) that arose in connection with the sale of property. At the time of the cancellation, the note had a basis to F of $10,000, a face amount of $25,000, and a fair market value of $20,000. Presuming the sale fell under § 453, the cancellation now results in gain of $15,000 to F.

Certain exceptions to the recognition of gain provisions are provided for transfers of installment obligations pursuant to tax-free incorporations under § 351, contributions of capital to a partnership, certain corporate liquidations, and transfers due to the taxpayer's death.[86] In such instances, the deferred profit is merely shifted to the transferee who is responsible for the payment of tax on the subsequent collections of the installment obligations.

Repossession of Real Property. Section 1038 limits the gain recognized from the repossession of real property. Generally, this provision prevents the seller from recognizing gain on the appreciation in the value of the property from the date of the sale to the date of repossession and allows the seller to offset any expenses of repossession against the remaining gain recognized.

> **Example 32.** S sold land (basis of $60,000) to P for $100,000, receiving a down payment of $25,000 and three notes of $25,000 per year for three years, plus 10% interest. After paying one note and when the balance due is $50,000, P defaults. At the time of repossession by S, the property is worth $120,000. S's expenses of repossession amounted to $5,000. S's recognized gain on the repossession is $15,000, determined as follows:

Total gain on the installment sale ($100,000 − $60,000)	$ 40,000
Less: Gain previously recognized (40% × $50,000)	(20,000)
Less: Expenses of repossession	(5,000)
Gain on repossession	$ 15,000

---

85. *Miller v. Usry,* 58–1 USTC ¶ 9393, 1 AFTR2d 1295, 160 F.Supp. 368 (D.Ct.L., 1958).

86. § § 453B(c) and (d). See Chapter 20 for a discussion of some of these subjects.

ELECTING OUT OF THE INSTALLMENT METHOD

A taxpayer can elect to not use the installment method. The election is made by reporting on a timely filed return the gain computed by the taxpayer's usual method of accounting (cash or accrual).[87] However, the Regulations provide that the amount realized by a cash basis taxpayer cannot be less than the value of the property sold reduced by the cash down payment.[88] This rule differs from the usual cash basis accounting rules (discussed earlier),[89] which measure the amount realized in terms of the fair market value of the property received. The net effect of the Regulation is to allow the cash basis taxpayer to report his or her gain as an accrual basis taxpayer. The election has frequent application to year-end sales by taxpayers who expect to be in a greater marginal tax bracket in the following year.

> **Example 33.** On December 31, 19X1, T sold to B stock for $20,000 (fair market value). The stock and cash were to be delivered to the buyer and seller on January 4, 19X2 (the settlement date). T is a cash basis taxpayer, and his basis in the stock is $8,000. He expects to have substantially greater taxable income in 19X2 than he did in 19X1.
>
> The transactions constitute an installment sale, because a payment will be received in a tax year after the tax year of disposition. B's promise to pay T is an installment obligation, and under the Regulations, the value of the installment obligation is equal to the value of the property sold ($20,000). If T were to elect out of the installment method, he would report a $12,000 gain ($20,000 − $8,000) in 19X1.

Contingent Payments. Under the Regulations the lower limit on the valuation of rights to contingent payments is the fair market value of the property sold less the sum of the cash and the value of fixed obligations received.[90] As a result, whether the sales price is contingent or fixed, generally the cash basis taxpayer who does not use the installment method must recognize the same amount of gain in the year of sale—the excess of the value of the property sold over the seller's basis.

In the rare situation where the seller receives a contingent obligation and the property sold does not have a fair market value, the taxpayer may treat the transaction as *open* and thus report no income until the basis has been recovered.

> **Example 34.** T sold a mineral interest in land to X Oil Company for 30% of the gross income from the property for the first

---

87. Reg. § 1.453 1(d).

88. Reg. § 1.453–1(d)(2)(ii). See also, Rev.Rul. 82–227, 1982–2, C.B. 89.

89. Refer to Chapter 5, Example 7.

90. Reg. § 1.453–1(d)(3)(iii).

three years of production. She paid $10,000 for the interest 20 years ago. All mineral interests in the area are sold on similar contingent terms; thus, a cash price cannot be determined. Because the venture was so speculative, the contingent payment obligation did not have a fair market value. Over the years T received $35,000 ($5,000, $20,000, and $10,000). T must report gain as follows:

Year	Amount Received	Imputed Interest	Recovery of Capital	Gain
1	$ 5,000	$ 450	$ 4,550	$ –0–
2	20,000	3,200	5,450	11,350
3	10,000	2,400	–0–	7,600
	$ 35,000	$ 6,050	$ 10,000	$ 18,950

[Note: Under the installment method, T would have allocated one-third of her basis to each payment (refer to Example 26)].

Revocation of the Election. Permission of the IRS is required to revoke an election not to use the installment method.[91] The stickiness of the election is an added peril.

Example 35. The taxpayer in the previous example elected to report the transaction as open in the year of sale. Subsequently the IRS brought forth unimpeachable evidence that the mineral interest had a fair market value of $30,000 at the time of the sale. The taxpayer would be required to report a $20,000 gain in the year of sale ($30,000 − $10,000 basis). Moreover, the $5,000 gain from collections ($35,000 − $30,000) would be ordinary income (because collection of a receivable is not a sale or exchange of a capital asset).

Under the installment method, no gain would have been recognized until the first collection was received, at which time $3,333 would be recognized:

$$\frac{\$20,000}{\$30,000} \times \$5,000 = \$3,333$$

Also, except for imputed interest, the entire gain would be capital gain.

In conclusion, before a taxpayer elects out of the installment method, he or she should be confident that his or her valuations will withstand close scrutiny. Also, the taxpayer must consider the effects of converting the capital gain from an installment sale into ordinary income under the alternative methods.

---

91. Reg. § 1.453–1(d)(4).

INVENTORIES

Generally, tax accounting and financial accounting for inventories are much the same:

—The use of inventories is necessary to "clearly reflect" the income of any business engaged in the production and sale or purchase and sale of goods.[92]

—The inventories should include all finished goods, goods in process, and raw materials and supplies which will become part of the product (including containers).

—Inventory rules must give effect to the "best" accounting practice of a particular trade or business, and the taxpayer's method should be consistently followed from year to year.[93]

—All items included in inventory should be valued at either (a) cost or (b) the lower of cost or market value.[94]

The following are not acceptable methods or practices in valuing inventories:[95]

—A deduction for a reserve for anticipated price changes.

—The use of a constant price or nominal value for a so-called normal quantity of materials or goods in stock (e. g., the base stock method).

—The inclusion of stock in transit in inventory to which title is not vested in the taxpayer.

—The direct costing approach (i. e., excluding fixed indirect production costs from inventory).

—The prime costing approach (i. e., excluding all indirect production costs from inventory).

The reason for the similarities between tax and financial accounting for inventories is that § 471 sets forth what appears to be a two-prong test. Under this provision "inventories shall be taken . . . on such basis . . . as conforming as nearly as may be to the *best accounting practice* in the trade or business and as most *clearly reflecting the income*." The best accounting practice is synonymous with generally accepted accounting principles (hereafter referred to as GAAP). However, the IRS determines whether an inventory method clearly reflects income.

In *Thor Power Tool Co. v. Comm.*, there was a conflict between the two tests.[96] The taxpayer's method of valuing obsolete parts was

---

92. Reg. § 1.471–1.
93. Reg. § 1.471–2(b).
94. Reg. § 1.471–2(c).
95. Reg. § 1.471–2(f).
96. 79–1 USTC ¶ 9139, 43 AFTR2d 79–362, 99 S.Ct. 773 (USSC, 1979).

in conformity with GAAP. The IRS, however, successfully argued that the clear reflection of income test was not satisfied because the taxpayer's procedures for valuing its inventories were contrary to the Regulations. Under the taxpayer's method, inventories for parts in excess of estimated future sales were written off (i. e., expensed), although the parts were kept on hand and their asking prices were not reduced. Under Reg. § 1.471–4(b) inventories cannot be written down unless the selling prices also are reduced.

The taxpayer contended that conformity to GAAP creates a presumption that the method clearly reflects income. The Supreme Court disagreed, concluding that the clear reflection of income test was "paramount." Moreover, it is the opinion of the IRS which controls in determining whether the method of inventory clearly reflects income. Thus, the best accounting practice test was rendered practically meaningless. It follows that the taxpayer's method of inventory must strictly conform to the Regulations, regardless of what GAAP might require.

DETERMINING INVENTORY COST

For merchandise purchased, cost is the invoice price less trade discounts, plus freight and other handling charges.[97] Cash discounts approximating a fair interest rate can be deducted or capitalized at the taxpayer's option providing the method used is consistently applied.

The cost of goods produced or manufactured by the taxpayer must be determined by using the full absorption method of inventory costing.[98] Under this method, production costs (e. g., direct materials and labor) must be included in computing the cost of the inventory. In addition, all indirect production costs must be included in inventory except the following:[99]

(1) So-called Category 2 costs need not be included in inventory (e. g., advertising, selling, administrative, distribution, interest).

(2) So-called Category 3 costs may be either included or excluded depending on the taxpayer's treatment of such costs for financial reporting purposes (i. e., property and payroll taxes, depreciation, certain employee benefits).

Category 3 costs may be excluded from inventory only if the treatment of a particular item is consistent with generally accepted accounting principles. Furthermore, the IRS has ruled that the determination of whether the treatment of the item is consistent with gen-

---

97. Reg. § 1.471–3(b).
98. Reg. § 1.471–11(a).
99. Reg. § 1.471–11(c)(2).

erally accepted accounting principles should be decided without regard to the materiality of the item or the consistency of its treatment.[100]

> **Example 36.** The taxpayer is in a manufacturing business and has consistently expensed in the year of accrual the real property tax on the factory. The company accountant recognizes that the property tax should be included in manufacturing overhead (thus, included in the cost of the inventory). However, the item is not material, so the accountant does not require that the financial statements be adjusted. In order to comply with the Regulations, the property tax must be added to the cost of goods sold and ending inventory, rather than deducted currently.

A taxpayer may use the standard cost method to value inventory. However, if indirect production cost variances are significant, a pro rata portion of the variance must be reallocated to the ending inventories.[101]

Lower of Cost or Market. Except for those taxpayers who use the LIFO method, inventories may be valued at the lower of cost or replacement cost (i. e., "market").[102] Those taxpayers using LIFO must value inventory at cost. However, the write-down of damaged or shopworn merchandise and goods which are otherwise unsalable at normal prices is not considered to be an application of the lower of cost or market method. Such items should be valued at bona fide selling price less direct cost of disposal.[103]

In the case of excess inventories (as in *Thor Power Tool Co.,* discussed above), the goods can be written down only to the taxpayer's offering price. If the offering price on the goods is not reduced, the goods must be valued at cost.

> **Example 37.** The Z Publishing Company invested $50,000 in printing 10,000 copies of a book. Although only 7,000 copies were sold in the first three years and none in the next five years, management is convinced that the book will become a classic in 20 years. Z Company leaves the price the same as it was when first distributed (i. e., $15 per copy). The remaining 3,000 books must be valued at cost (i. e., $15,000). It should be noted that the tax law provides an incentive for the taxpayer to destroy or abandon its excess inventory and obtain an immediate deduction rather than wait for the event of future sales.

---

100. TIR 1365, April 17, 1975; modified by Rev.Proc. 75–40, 1975–2 C.B. 571.
101. Reg. § 1.471–11(d)(3).
102. Reg. § 1.472–4.
103. Reg. § 1.471–2(c).

In applying this method, each item included in the inventory must be valued at the lower of its cost or market value.[104]

Example 38. The taxpayer's ending inventory is valued below:

Item	Cost	Market	Lower of Cost or Market
A	$ 5,000	$ 4,000	$ 4,000
B	3,000	2,000	2,000
C	1,500	6,000	1,500
	$ 9,500	$ 12,000	$ 7,500

Under the lower of cost or market method, the taxpayer's inventory would be valued at $7,500 rather than $9,500.

Determining Cost—Specific Identification, FIFO, and LIFO. In some cases it is feasible to determine the cost of the particular item sold. For example, an automobile dealer can easily determine the specific cost of each automobile which has been sold. However, in most businesses it is necessary to resort to a flow of goods assumption such as "first in, first out" (FIFO), "last in, first out" (LIFO), or an average cost method. A taxpayer may use any of these methods provided the method selected is consistently applied from year to year.

During a period of rising prices, LIFO will generally produce a lower ending inventory valuation and will result in a greater cost of goods sold than would be obtained under the FIFO method. The effects on computing costs of goods sold using LIFO and FIFO are illustrated in the following example:

Example 39. On January 1, 19X1, the taxpayer opened a retail store to sell refrigerators. At least 10 refrigerators must be carried in inventory to satisfy customer demands. The initial investment in the 10 refrigerators is $5,000. During the year, 10 refrigerators were sold at $750 each and were replaced at a cost of $6,000 ($600 each). Gross profit under the LIFO and FIFO methods is computed below:

		FIFO			LIFO
Sales (10 × $750)		$ 7,500			$ 7,500
Beginning inventory	$ 5,000		$ 5,000		
Purchases	6,000		6,000		
	11,000		11,000		
Ending inventory:					
10 × $600	(6,000)				
10 × $500			(5,000)		
Cost of goods sold		(5,000)			(6,000)
Gross profit		$ 2,500			$ 1,500

---

104. Reg. § 1.471–4(c).

THE LIFO ELECTION

A taxpayer may adopt LIFO by merely using the method in the tax return for the year of the change and by attaching Form 970 to the tax return.[105] Thus, a taxpayer does not have to request approval for changes within the first 180 days of the tax year. Once the election is made, it cannot be revoked. However, a prospective change from LIFO to any other inventory method can be made if the consent of the IRS is obtained.[106] Currently, the IRS will grant automatic approval if the request is timely filed and the taxpayer agrees to a 10-year spread of any positive adjustment.[107]

The beginning inventory valuation for the first year LIFO is used is computed by the costing method employed in the preceding year. Thus, the beginning LIFO inventory is generally the same as the closing inventory for the preceding year. However, since lower of cost or market cannot be used in conjunction with LIFO, previous write-downs to market for items included in the beginning inventory must be restored to income. The amount the inventories are written up is an adjustment due to a change in accounting method.[108] However, the usual rules for disposition of the adjustments under Rev.Proc. 80–51 are not applicable.[109] Section 472(d), effective for tax years beginning 1982 and thereafter, allows the taxpayer to spread the adjustment ratably over the year of the change and the two succeeding years.

> **Example 40.** In 1982, T used the lower of cost or market FIFO inventory method. The FIFO cost of its ending inventory was $30,000, and the market value of the inventory was $24,000. Therefore, the ending inventory for 1982 was $24,000. T switched to LIFO in 1983 and was required to write up the beginning inventory to $30,000. T must add $2,000 ($6,000 ÷ 3) to his income for each of the years 1983, 1984, and 1985.

Congress added § 472(d) to the Code to overrule the previous IRS policy of requiring that the entire adjustment be included in income for the year preceding the change to LIFO.[110]

Once the LIFO election is made for tax purposes, the taxpayer's financial reports to owners and creditors must also be prepared on the basis of LIFO.[111] The conformity of financial reports to tax reporting is specifically required by the Code and is strictly enforced by the IRS.

---

105. Reg. § 1.472–3(a).
106. Reg. § 1.472–6.
107. Rev.Proc. 72–74, 1972–1 C.B. 749.
108. Reg. § 1.472–2(c). In Rev.Rul. 76–282, 1976–2, C.B. 137, the IRS required the restoration of write-downs for damaged and shopworn goods when the taxpayer switched to LIFO.
109. 1980–1 C.B. 582.
110. See Footnote 109.
111. § 472(c).

However, under Regulations proposed in 1979, the taxpayer is allowed to make a footnote disclosure of the net income computed by another method of inventory valuation (e. g., FIFO).[112]

Simplified LIFO. Although tax practitioners have long been aware of the tax deferrals available under LIFO, prior to 1982 very few companies used LIFO.[113] In the eyes of Congress, LIFO was conspicuous by its absence from the returns of small businesses. For many taxpayers, a series of hurdles in the LIFO Regulations made the cost of compliance outweigh the benefits of LIFO.

As part of the Economic Recovery Tax Act of 1981, Congress ordered the IRS to lower the bars to the LIFO election. The IRS was directed to write regulations which would allow the taxpayer an election to calculate inventory at year-end prices (FIFO) and then convert this value to base-year prices through the use of a government published index.[114] The advantage to using an index is that the taxpayer does not have to determine the actual base period cost of each item in its ending inventory, one of the high compliance costs of the formerly used LIFO valuation methods.

> **Example 41.** In 1984, the L Lawnmower Shop, Inc., adopted the LIFO inventory method. Its equipment inventories at year-end prices (FIFO) were as follows:
>
> | | |
> |---|---|
> | 1983 | $ 30,000 |
> | 1984 | 36,000 |
> | 1985 | 45,000 |
>
> The Producer Price Index values for the classification "lawn equipment, power tools, and other hardware" for all relevant years were 1983: 120.2%; 1984: 129.2%; 1985; 132.7%.
>
> The Company would first convert its ending inventories to LIFO base period prices as follows:
>
> $$1984 \quad \frac{120.2}{129.2} \times \$36,000 = \underline{\underline{\$33,492}}$$
>
> $$1985 \quad \frac{120.2}{132.7} \times \$45,000 = \underline{\underline{\$40,761}}$$

Its ending inventory for 1983 is composed of three layers:

---

112. Reg. § 1.472–2(e).
113. See U. S. Congress, House Committee on Small Business, *Inventory Accounting as a Burden on the Capital Formation Process,* H.Rept. 96–1448, 96th Cong., 2nd sess., 1980.
114. § 472(f).

Base period	$ 30,000

1984 additions at base period prices
    ($33,492 − $30,000 = $3,492)
    converted to 1984 year-end	

prices $= \dfrac{129.2 \ (1982)}{120.2 \ (1983)} \times \$3,492$	3,753

1985 additions at base period prices
    ($40,761 − $33,492 = $7,269)
    converted to 1985 year-end prices	

$\dfrac{132.7 \ (1985)}{120.2 \ (1983)} \times \$7,269 =$	8,025
1985 LIFO Inventory	$ 41,778

The Regulations[115] provide detailed rules for selecting appropriate indexes.

Single Pool LIFO. Taxpayers who elect to use LIFO must divide their inventories into pools. For example, an appliance store may have separate inventory classifications (or pools) for televisions, refrigerators and freezers, laundry equipment, and other appliances. Thus, if at the end of a particular year the television inventory is depleted, the taxpayer must recapture the taxes deferred from that inventory pool.

> **Example 42.** At the beginning of 19X8 the taxpayer had an inventory of televisions with a LIFO cost of $50,000. The FIFO value of the goods would have been $90,000. The difference between the FIFO and LIFO values is income deferred from tax due to the use of LIFO ($90,000 − $50,000 = $40,000). If the company had been out of stock at year-end and purchases were $300,000, its cost of goods sold would have been $300,000 + $90,000 = $390,000 under FIFO but is only $350,000 under LIFO; thus, the deferred taxes on $40,000 ($390,000 − $350,000 = $40,000) would be recaptured.

In the previous example, if the company had only one inventory pool—appliances—there would be less risk of depleting its base stock (e. g., a decrease in televisions could be countered by an increase in refrigerators on hand). It should be apparent that the taxpayer prefers his or her LIFO pools to be as broad as possible. On the other hand, the IRS favors narrow pools.

What constitutes a pool has long been a source of controversy between the IRS and taxpayers.[116] Undoubtedly the potential entanglement with the IRS over the composition of pools has discouraged

---

115.   Reg. § 1.472–8(e)(3)(iii).
116.   See *Kelin Chocolate Co. v. Comm.*, 32 TC 437 (1959).

some taxpayers from using LIFO. In 1981 Congress legislated away these problems for some small businesses by directing the Commissioner to draft regulations which would allow these taxpayers to use a one-pool LIFO inventory method.[117]

ACCOUNTING PERIODS

Practically all individuals adopt calendar year reporting with the filing of their initial returns. And there is no reason to change the year. However, there are often good business and tax reasons to place a corporation on a fiscal year. If a newly formed corporation is profitable in its first year of operation, by closing the tax year before the end of 12 months, the corporation can keep its income in the lower tax brackets.

CHANGES IN ACCOUNTING METHODS

When a taxpayer elects a method of accounting for a particular item of income or deduction, he or she has not made a life-long commitment. Changes are easily made by filing an application with the IRS during the first 180 days of the tax year of the change. In the case of a change to LIFO, advance approval by the IRS is not required.

In the case of a new corporation experiencing losses or earning very little income, tax deferrals may not be in order. However, once the corporation's income begins moving up the rate schedule, accounting methods that defer income or accelerate deductions should be utilized (e. g., installment method, reserve method for bad debts, and LIFO).

Under Rev.Proc. 80–51, the newly profitable business will be allowed to spread its negative adjustments over no more years than the former method was used. Thus, if a business had little or no profits in the first five years but expects profits in the sixth and subsequent years, it could change, for example, to the reserve for bad debts method and spread the adjustment into five profitable years.

INSTALLMENT METHOD

Dealers in personal property can enjoy deferrals of taxes that do not have to be paid until the final year of operations. At the end of each

---

117. § 474. Generally, a small business is a taxpayer with average gross receipts of $2,000,000 per year for the current and two preceding years.

year, some income is always deferred (as compared to the income that would have been paid under the accrual method).

Sale of noninventory property on the installment method allows the taxpayer to accomplish the following goals: (1) defer taxes, (2) avoid bunching of income and resulting application of high progressive rates, and (3) avoid the alternative minimum tax on capital gains. However, in some rare cases, the present value of the tax liability can be reduced by electing to not use the installment method. Electing out of the installment method may be advisable if the taxpayer expects his or her marginal tax bracket to be greater in the years the deferred payments will be collected than his or her marginal tax bracket would be in the year of the sale.

Related Parties. Intrafamily installment sales can still be a useful family tax planning tool in spite of the 1980 changes in the law. Except in the case of marketable securities, if the related party holds the property more than two years, a subsequent sale will not accelerate the gain from the first disposition. Patience and forethought are rewarded. Also, not all relatives are "relatives" for tax purposes.

The seven percent limitation on imputed interest on sales of land between family members enables the seller to convert ordinary income into capital gain, or make what is, in effect, a nontaxable gift. If the selling price is raised to adjust for the low interest rate charges on an installment sale, the seller has more capital gain but less ordinary income than would be realized from a sale to an unrelated party. If the selling price is not raised and the specified interest of seven percent is charged, the seller enables the relative to have the use of the property but without having to pay for its full market value. Moreover, this bargain sale is not a taxable gift.

Disposition of Installment Obligations. A disposition of an installment obligation is also a serious matter. Gifts of the obligations will accelerate income to the seller. The list of taxable and nontaxable dispositions of installment obligations should not be trusted to memory. In each instance where transfers of installment obligations are contemplated, the practitioner should conduct research to be sure he or she knows the consequences.

LIFO

Because inflation is expected for the foreseeable future, and as a result of the new simplified procedures, the use of LIFO will probably become more common. The record-keeping requirements under the simplified procedures are minimal, and the tax savings are obvious. The only major disadvantage to LIFO is the financial-tax conformity requirement. However, this disadvantage can be overcome through footnote disclosure of earnings as computed under FIFO.

PROBLEM MATERIALS

Questions for Class Discussion

1. What taxpayers are eligible to use a fiscal year?

2. When should a business be on a 52–53 week basis?

3. When would a fiscal year be preferable to a calendar year? How is a fiscal year elected?

4. In which of the following situations must a taxpayer annualize income?

   (a) The first tax year.

   (b) The year an individual marries.

   (c) The final return.

   (d) A year of a change in the tax year.

5. What is the procedure for changing a tax year?

6. Is the taxpayer required to use the same method of accounting for all items of income and deductions?

7. Compare the cash basis and accrual basis of accounting as applied to:

   (a) Fixed assets.

   (b) Prepaid rental income.

   (c) Prepaid interest expense.

   (d) A note received for services performed if the market value and face amount of the note differ.

   (e) The deduction for a contested item.

8. What is the general rule as to when income is recognized under the accrual basis of accounting?

9. What is the general rule as to when a deduction will be recognized under the accrual basis of accounting?

10. When are reserves for estimated expenses allowed for tax purposes? What is the role of the matching concept in tax accounting?

11. For several years a taxpayer has consistently used the accrual basis to report income and deductions. During the year she bought some rental property and would like to report the income from the property on the cash method. Would the use of the cash basis to report the rental income constitute a change in accounting method?

12. What is the procedure for obtaining consent to change a method of accounting?

13. Which of the following require the permission of the IRS?

   (a) A change from the cash to the accrual basis for deducting property tax expenses.

   (b) The correction of a prior year's return when the double-declining balance method was incorrectly used to compute the amortization of a patent.

   (c) A change from direct costing to the full absorption method of valuing inventories.

(d) A change from the FIFO to the LIFO inventory method.

(e) A change from cost to the lower of cost or market method of valuing inventories.

(f) A write-down of damaged merchandise to net realizable value when the taxpayer has consistently used cost to value the inventories.

(g) The use of lower of cost or market in conjunction with the LIFO inventory method.

(h) A change from the LIFO to the FIFO inventory method.

14. Why does the Code provide that a greater than $3,000 positive adjustment due to an involuntary change in accounting method can be used to adjust a prior year's income?

15. What difference does it make whether the taxpayer or the IRS initiates the change in accounting method?

16. The taxpayer began work on a contract in June 19X1 and completed the contract in April 19X2.

(a) Can the percentage of completion method be used to report the income from the contract?

(b) If the taxpayer in (a) uses the accrual basis to report income, assuming no advance payments are received, when will the income be recognized?

17. What are the tax advantages of using the completed contract method?

18. T, a cash basis taxpayer, sold land in December 19X1. At the time of the sale, T received $10,000 cash and a note for $90,000 due in 90 days. T expects to be in a much higher tax bracket in 19X2. Can T report the entire gain in 19X1?

19. In 19X1, the taxpayer sold some real estate and received an installment note. The sale met all of the requirements for using the installment method, but the taxpayer did not know that the installment method could be used. Thus, the entire gain was reported in the year of sale. In 19X2, it is discovered that the taxpayer could have used the installment method. Is there anything that can be done? Explain.

20. How does the buyer's assumption of the seller's liabilities in an installment sale affect the:

(a) Selling price.

(b) Contract price.

(c) Buyer's payments in the year of sale.

21. On June 1, 19X1, Father sold land to Son for $100,000. Father reported the gain by the installment method, with the gain to be spread over five years. In May 19X3, Son received an offer of $150,000 for the land, to be paid over three years. What would be the tax consequences of Son's sale?

22. S advertises a tract of land (held as an investment) for sale at a cash price of $100,000. P wishes to purchase the property but requires three years in order to obtain all of the funds. As a compromise, S accepts the three-year arrangement but only if the selling price is raised from $100,000 to $120,000. What is S trying to accomplish for tax purposes?

23. What is the tax effect of a gift of an installment obligation? Suppose the donee is also the obligor?

24. In 19X1, T sold a building to his 100% controlled corporation. The entire purchase price is to be paid in 19X2. When should T report the gain on the sale of the building?

25. For financial reporting purposes, the taxpayer has consistently expensed all payroll taxes on manufacturing salaries and wages rather than including them in inventories and cost of goods sold. Although the accountant recognized the treatment of the taxes was not theoretically correct, he continued to use the incorrect method because its effect on income was not material. Can the IRS require the taxpayer to change the method of accounting for the payroll taxes?

26. What is "cost"? How is "lower of cost or market" computed for purposes of valuing inventories?

27. Explain how inventory regulations provide an incentive for a corporation to dispose of its obsolete excess inventories.

28. Discuss the problems that could result from footnote disclosures of net income computed by the FIFO method when the taxpayer uses the LIFO method to report its taxable income.

29. Contrast the procedures for changing to the LIFO inventory method with the general requirements for making a change in an accounting method.

Problems

30. P Corporation is in the business of sales and home deliveries of fuel oil and currently uses a calendar year for reporting its taxable income. However, P's natural business year ends April 30. For the short period, January 1, 1984, through April 30, 1984, the corporation earned $16,000.

    (a) What must P Corporation do to change its taxable year?

    (b) Compute P Corporation's tax for the short period.

31. X Electric Company is an accrual basis regulated public utility and is allowed to adjust its rates charged to customers in accordance with a fuel adjustment clause. In 19X2, it was determined that the company had incorrectly computed its 19X1 rates and customers were entitled to refunds totaling $25,000. In 19X2, the company refunded the overcharges to customers. Assume the company's tax rates were 46% in 19X1 and 40% in 19X2. In 19X2, the company had $100,000 taxable income before the $25,000 deduction. What is the effect of the refunds on the company's 19X2 tax liability?

32. T receives appliances from the manufacturer on consignment and collects a 5% commission on any sales made during the year. T is an accrual basis taxpayer and made total sales during the year of $750,000. However, the manufacturer is usually a few weeks behind in recording T's sales and at the end of the year recorded only $600,000 in sales.

    T argues that he should report income for the year of only $30,000 (5% × $600,000), since that was all he had a right to receive for the year. T had no right to the commissions on the other $150,000 sales until the manufacturer reported them in the following year. What is T's correct taxable income for the year? Explain.

33. A is an accrual basis taxpayer. Gross income for the year was $85,000, which included $5,000 for services provided a customer. The customer paid with a note. The market value of the note was only $4,000 due to the poor financial condition of the customer. A's accounts receivable of $40,000 include approximately $800 in discounts that will be given for early payments. A's total expenses per books were $50,000. This includes $3,500 of office supplies purchased from a supplier; they have not been paid for as of year-end. A discovered that the supplier had billed him twice for the same $500 order, but the supplier contends that A ordered, and received, two identical shipments. Also included in total expenses per books was $6,000 in addition to the reserve for service under product warranties. An analysis of that account is presented below:

Reserves	
Cost incurred $6,000	$ 15,000 beginning balance
	$ 5,000 additions
	$ 14,000 balance

Compute A's correct taxable income under the accrual basis.

34. T, a cash basis taxpayer, has substantial income from trust funds established for him. He has recently purchased some unincorporated businesses. For each of the businesses described below, explain which accounting method should be used and why that method should be used.

(a) *Cattle raising.* In October, T will purchase cattle that will be shipped to a feed lot operated by an independent party. The feed lot charges will be paid in December, and the cattle will be sold in January. A bank loan (with recourse) will finance the feed lot charges. The loan will be retired out of the proceeds from the sale of the cattle.

(b) *Vegetable growing.* Vegetables will be raised under a contract with a large canner. At the time of delivery, the canner will issue a note to T. The note is due in the year following the year of delivery and has a market value equal to its face amount.

(c) *Land development.* Lots are sold for cash and are fully developed, except for sewerage. For each lot sold, T must pay the City of X $800 for sewerage lines. However, the payment is deferred until the year after the lot is sold.

35. Z Corporation has incorrectly used a reserve for liability under warranties for the three preceding years. The relevant tax rates were 17% on the first $25,000 and 20% on income from $25,000 to $50,000.

	(1) Taxable Income Before Warranty	(2) Net Addition to Reserve	(3) Cost of Warranty Services Rendered	(1)–(2) Taxable Income Reported	(1)–(3) Correct Taxable Income
19X1	$ 20,000	$ 5,000	$ 1,000	$ 15,000	$ 19,000
19X2	30,000	3,000	5,000	27,000	25,000
19X3	40,000	4,000	2,000	36,000	38,000
	$ 90,000	$ 12,000	$ 8,000	$ 78,000	$ 82,000

(a) Compute the adjustment due to change in accounting method as of January 1, 19X4.

(b) Assume the IRS requires Z Corporation to change its method of accounting. What would you recommend with respect to the disposition of the adjustment?

36. In 19X2, the taxpayer was required to switch from the cash to the accrual basis of accounting for sales and cost of goods sold. Taxable income for 19X2 computed under the cash basis was $62,000. There were no pre-1954 adjustments.

	Beginning of the Year	End of the Year
Accounts receivable	$ 5,000	$ 7,000
Accounts payable	15,000	12,000
Inventory	6,200	5,500

Compute the following:

(a) The adjustment due to the change in accounting method.

(b) The accrual basis taxable income for 19X2 (assume the taxpayer agreed to spread the adjustment due to the change over 10 years).

37. C, a cash basis taxpayer, has adjusted gross income of $40,000 before considering the effect of the following payments made on December 31, 19X1 (in connection with business activities):

(a) January 19X2 rent—$1,000.

(b) January 19X2 through June 19X3 property insurance—$2,700.

(c) A refundable deposit for telephone extensions—$300.

(d) 19X2 professional dues and subscriptions—$480.

(e) January through June 19X2 interest on a real estate mortgage—$3,200.

(f) Payment on a lawyer's bill for services rendered in 19X0, net of a $500 refundable deposit made in 19X0—$1,500.

Compute C's adjusted gross income.

38. The R Construction Company reports its income by the completed contract method. At the end of 19X1, the company completed a contract to construct a building at a total cost of $980,000. The contract price was $1,200,000. However, the customer refused to accept the work and would not pay anything on the contract because he claimed the roof did not meet specifications. R's engineers estimated it would cost $140,000 to bring the roof up to the customer's standards. In 19X2, the dispute was settled in the customer's favor; the roof was improved at a cost of $170,000, and the customer accepted the building and paid the $1,200,000.

(a) What would be the effects of the above on R's taxable income for 19X1 and 19X2?

(b) Same as above except R had $1,100,000 accumulated cost under the contract at the end of 19X1?

39. T Corporation is an appliance dealer and reports its sales on the installment method. T groups its sales by years for purposes of computing its realized gross profit for each year. Its collections in the year 19X4 and other relevant information are presented below:

Year of Sale	Current Year Collections	Gross Profit %	Receivables 12-31-X4	Accounts Written off	Value of Repossessions
19X1	$ 10,000	45	$ 5,000	$ 3,000	$ 600
19X2	25,000	40	8,000	4,000	2,000
19X3	70,000	35	40,000	5,000	4,000
19X4	120,000	38	150,000	500	450
	$ 225,000		$ 203,000	$ 12,500	$ 7,050

(a) Compute the realized gross profit for the year.

(b) Compute the loss from repossessions.

(c) In 19X4, T Corporation pledged $100,000 of its 19X4 installment obligations to the bank for $80,000. The bank was to apply collections on the receivables against the loan, but the bank had no recourse against T Corporation if the total collections did not equal $80,000. What are the possible tax consequences of pledging the receivables?

40. S, who is not a dealer, sold an apartment house to P during the current year (19X2). The closing statement for the sale is presented below:

Total selling price		$ 200,000
Add: P's share of taxes (6 months) paid by S		5,000
Less: S's mortgage assumed by P	$ 110,000	
P's refundable binder ("earnest money") paid in 19X1	2,000	
P's 9% installment note given to S	60,000	
S's real estate commissions and attorney's fees	15,000	(187,000)
Cash paid to S at closing		$ 18,000
Cash due from P = $18,000 + $15,000 expenses		$ 33,000

During 19X2 S collected $8,000 in principal on the installment note and $4,000 interest. S's basis in the property was $140,000 [$170,000 − $30,000 (depreciation)], and there was $6,000 in potential depreciation recapture under § 1250.

(a) Compute the following:

    (1) Total gain.

    (2) Contract price.

    (3) Payments received in the year of sale.

    (4) Recognized gain in the year of sale and the character of such gain.

(*Hint*: Think carefully about the manner in which the property taxes are handled before you begin your computations.)

(b) Same as (a)(2) and (3) except S's basis in the property was $90,000.

(c) Assume that S was considering selling the apartment house but there was no mortgage on the property. Would there be any tax benefits if S borrowed on the property prior to the sale?

41. On December 30, 19X1, Father sold land to Son for $10,000 cash and 7% installment notes with a face amount of $190,000. In 19X2, after paying $30,000 on the principal of the note, Son sold the land. In 19X3, Son paid Father $25,000 on the note principal. Father's basis in the land was $50,000.

(a) Assuming Son sold the land for $250,000, compute Father's taxable gain in 19X2.

(b) Assuming Son sold the land for $150,000, compute Father's taxable gain in 19X2.

42. Determine T's gain for 19X4 in each of the following cases, assuming T is a cash basis taxpayer.

(a) On June 1, 19X1, T sold AT&T common stock to his son. T's basis in the stock was $50,000, and T was to receive $70,000 in 19X5 and $80,000 in 19X6, plus 8% interest. In 19X4, T's son sold the stock on the New York Stock Exchange for $125,000.

(b) Same as (a), except the property sold was land rather than stock, and the son resold the land on July 1, 19X4, for $125,000.

(c) On June 1, 19X1, T sold a building to his 100% controlled corporation for $150,000 (plus interest) due in 19X4. T's basis in the building was $50,000. In 19X3, the corporation sold the building to an unrelated third party for $175,000. T collected $150,000 principal and $31,500 interest from the corporation in 19X4.

43. R, a cash basis taxpayer, sold his business for $50,000 plus 50% of the annual profits for the following two years. The total value of the business is $175,000, and R's basis is $90,000. The installment obligation had no market value.

(a) Compute R's gain in the year of the sale by the installment method.

(b) Compute R's gain in the year of sale assuming he elects out of the installment method.

(c) Same as above except the payments in the year of sale were $120,000.

(1) Compute installment gain in the year of sale.

(2) Compute gain in the year of sale if the taxpayer elects out.

(3) Should the taxpayer elect out?

44. X sold land to an unrelated party in 19X1. X's basis in the land was $40,000, and the selling price was $100,000—$25,000 payable at closing and $25,000 (plus 10% interest) due January 1, 19X2, 19X3, and 19X4. What would be the tax consequences of the following? (Treat each part independently and assume (1) X did not elect out of the installment method and (2) the installment obligations have values equal to their face amounts.)

(a) In 19X2, X gave to his daughter the right to collect all future payments on the installment obligations.

(b) In 19X2, after collecting the payment due on January 1, X transferred the installment obligation to his 100% controlled corporation in exchange for additional shares of stock.

(c) X received on December 31, 19X2, the payment due on January 1, 19X3. On December 15, 19X3, X died, and the remaining installment obligation was transferred to X's estate. The estate collected the amount due on January 1, 19X4.

45. T, a cash basis taxpayer, sold stock in 19X1 for $40,000 plus 9% notes with a face amount of $60,000 and a market value of only $40,000. T's basis in the stock was $25,000, and its fair market value was $85,000. In 19X2, she collected the face amounts of the notes. What is T's income in 19X1 and 19X2 from the sale and collections presuming she elects out of the installment method?

46. V, who is not a dealer in real estate, sold land with a basis of $40,000 for a $25,000 down payment and $75,000 due in one year. No interest was specified in the contract, but the market rate of interest on similar contracts was 14%. V's original asking price was $92,000 cash. V reported the gain by the installment method. Compute V's income and indicate its character using the installment method for both the year of sale and the year the note was collected.

47. In 19X2, T changed from the use of the lower of cost or market FIFO method to the LIFO method. The ending inventory for 19X1 was computed as follows:

Item	FIFO Cost	Replacement Cost	Lower of Cost or Market
A	$ 10,000	$ 18,000	$ 10,000
B	25,000	20,000	20,000
			$ 30,000

(a) What is the correct beginning inventory in 19X2 under the LIFO method?

(b) What immediate tax consequences (if any) would result from the switch to LIFO?

Tax Form Problem

48. The Cory Contractors Company has used the percentage of completion method to report its income from long-term contracts for the past 15 years. The company's taxable income (loss) for each of the past five years and gross income reported for contracts in progress at year-end were as follows:

1982	$ 90,000	$ 40,000
1981	50,000	20,000
1980	(20,000)	–0–
1979	30,000	15,000
1978	(10,000)	–0–

John Cory is the sole shareholder of the company and he does not own a controlling interest in any other company. The company is neither a parent nor a subsidiary. Mr. Cory would like to have the company change to the completed contract method. The company will continue to use the percentage of completion method for financial reporting purposes (a condition of a loan agreement with the bank), and it has never before requested a change in accounting method. Complete a Form 3115, Application for Change in Accounting Method.

Research Problems

49. In 19X1, T was granted permission to change from the cash to the accrual basis for reporting the income from his proprietorship. There was a $50,000 positive adjustment due to the change in accounting method, and this adjustment was to be spread over 10 years at $5,000 per year. In 19X4, the taxpayer transferred the assets of the business to a partnership. The transfer was nontaxable. An IRS agent has examined T's tax return and contends that T must report the balance of the adjustment (i. e., $35,000) in 19X4.

    Can you find any authority for the taxpayer's position that the adjustment should be spread over the balance of the original 10-year period?

50. Your client is a dealer in fuel oil. Recently you have been discussing with him a change to the LIFO inventory method. He mentions the likelihood of an oil embargo and the possibility that as a result, he will deplete his base stock. As a result, he may have to recognize the deferred inventory profits and thus have to pay high taxes in a year when he has very little cash coming into the business.

    Is there any tax relief from the involuntary inventory liquidations that might occur to your client?

51. In November 19X1, A agreed to purchase stock from B for $1,000,000. The transaction was to be closed on December 28, 19X1. In early December 19X1, B became concerned about the taxes due on the sale in 19X1. B suggested that the transaction be deferred until January 19X2, but A insisted that the stock should be transferred on December 28, 19X1. A and B agreed that the cash paid by A on December 28, 19X1 would be held by the First Bank as A's escrow agent, and the funds would be dispersed to B on January 4, 19X2. The IRS agent insists that the escrowed amount was constructively received by B in 19X1 and, therefore, B cannot defer his gain until 19X2 under the installment sales rules.

    Is the agent correct?

    Partial list of research aids:

    Reed v. Comm., 83–2 USTC ¶ 9728, 53 AFTR2d 84–335 (CA–1, 1983).

52. In November 19X1, M Corporation's accountant discovered that one of the company's warehouses was empty. The perpetual inventory records indicated $200,000 of merchandise should have been in the warehouse.

    For 19X1 the missing inventory was not included in the company's ending inventory, and thus, the stolen merchandise became a part of cost of goods sold for the year. The IRS claims the missing merchandise should have been deducted as a theft loss and under Reg. § § 1.165–1(d)(2)(i) and 1.165–8(a)(2) is not deductible if there is a reasonable prospect for recovery. Moreover, the company had good prospects of recovery of the loss from the employees, insurance company, or auditors.

Assuming the IRS is correct—that there is a "reasonable prospect for recovery" as of the end of the year—is the taxpayer foreclosed from deducting the $200,000 in 19X1?

Partial list of research aids:

National Home Products, Inc., 71 T.C. 501 (1979).

Chapter 19

Deferred Compensation

This chapter discusses various types of deferred compensation arrangements which are available to employees and self-employed individuals. The tax law encourages employers to offer deferred compensation plans for their employees as a supplement to the Federal Social Security retirement system. For example, contributions to a qualified pension, profit sharing, or stock bonus plan are immediately deductible by the employer. Employees are generally not taxed until the pension funds are made available to them. In addition, the income which is earned on the contributions to the plan is not subject to tax until such amounts are made available to the employees.

The following is a sample of various deferred compensation arrangements which are being offered to employees:

—Qualified profit sharing plans.

—Qualified pension plans.

—Employee stock ownership plans.

—Cash or deferred arrangement plans.

—Tax-deferred annuities.

—Incentive stock option plans.

—Nonqualified deferred compensation plans.

—Restricted property plans.

—Cafeteria benefit plans.

In addition to receiving the various types of deferred compensation, employees may receive other valuable fringe benefits such as group-term life insurance, medical reimbursement plans, company-paid automobiles, and interest-free loans.

The Tax Equity and Fiscal Responsibility Act of 1982 (TEFRA) minimized the differences between corporate pension plans and the HR-10 (Keogh) plans of sole proprietorships, partnerships, and S corporations. The purpose of most of the changes was to bring parity between corporate and noncorporate retirement plans.

QUALIFIED PENSION, PROFIT SHARING, AND STOCK BONUS PLANS

The Federal government has encouraged private pension and profit sharing plans to keep older people from becoming wards of the state. Therefore, the Federal tax law provides substantial tax benefits for plans that meet certain requirements. The major requirement of qualification is that a plan may not discriminate in favor of officers, shareholders, or highly compensated employees.

TYPES OF PLANS

There are three types of qualified plans: pension, profit sharing, and stock bonus plans.

Pension Plans. A pension plan is a deferred compensation arrangement which provides for systematic payments of definitely determinable retirement benefits to employees who meet the requirements set forth in the plan. Benefits are generally measured by, and based on, such factors as years of service and employee compensation. A pension plan may provide for disability payments and incidental death benefit payments through insurance (but not layoff benefits or benefits for sickness, accident, hospitalization, or medical expenses).[1] Employer contributions under a qualified pension plan must *not* depend on profits, but must be sufficient to provide definitely determinable benefits on some actuarial basis.

A pension plan must expressly provide that forfeitures be used to reduce the employer's contributions under the plan.[2] This requirement may be contrasted with the treatment of forfeitures pursuant to a profit sharing or stock bonus plan; these plans may provide that forfeitures are reallocated to increase benefits for the remaining participants.

There are basically two types of qualified pension plans—a defined contribution plan and a defined benefit plan.

---

1. Reg. § 1.401–1(b)(1)(i).
2. Reg. § 1.401–7(a).

A *defined contribution pension plan* (or money purchase plan) requires a separate account for each participant for which benefits are based solely on (1) the amount contributed and (2) income from the fund which accrues to the participant's account.[3] In essence, the plan defines the amount the employer is required to contribute (e. g., a flat dollar amount, an amount based on a special formula, or an amount equal to a certain percentage of compensation). Thus, actuarial calculations are not required to determine the employer's annual contribution. Upon retirement, the employee's pension depends on the value of his or her account. It is possible, although not required, for a plan to require, or permit, employee contributions to the pension fund.

A *defined benefit plan* includes a formula which defines the benefits employees are to receive.[4] Under such a plan an employer must make annual contributions based upon actuarial computations which will be sufficient to pay the vested retirement benefits. Separate accounts are not maintained for each participant. A defined benefit plan provides some sense of security for employees, since the benefits may be expressed in fixed dollar amounts.

> **Example 1.** The qualified pension plan of the X Company calls for both the employer and employee to contribute annually 5% of the employee's compensation to the pension trust. Since the rate of contribution of the employer is fixed, this pension plan is a defined contribution plan. If the plan called for contributions sufficient to provide retirement benefits equal to 30% of the employee's last five years' salary, it would be a defined benefit plan.

Profit Sharing Plans. A profit sharing plan is a deferred compensation arrangement established and maintained by an employer to provide for employee participation in the company's profits. Contributions are paid from the profits of the employer to a trustee and are commingled in a single trust fund. In a profit sharing plan, separate accounts are maintained for each participant. The plan must provide a definite, predetermined formula for allocating the contributions (made to the trustee) among the participants and for distributing the accumulated funds after a fixed number of years or the attainment of a stated age or on the prior occurrence of certain events such as illness, layoff, or retirement. Any amounts allocated to the account of a participant may be used to provide incidental life, accident, or health insurance. A company is not required to contribute a definite, predetermined amount to the plan; but substantial and recurring contributions must be made in order to meet the permanency requirement.[5] Forfeitures arising under this plan do not have to be used to reduce the employer's contribution and may be used to increase the individ-

---

3. § 414(i).
4. § 414(j).
5. Reg. § 1.401–1(b).

ual accounts of the remaining participants as long as such increases do not result in prohibited discrimination.[6] Since the primary emphasis of a profit sharing plan is not necessarily on retirement income, lump-sum payouts may be the normal method of distributing benefits to employees.

An employer may allow an employee to choose between receiving a specified amount of cash as current compensation or having this amount contributed to a qualified profit sharing plan. Such a cash or deferred profit sharing plan must satisfy the pension plan qualification rules and must prohibit the distribution of amounts attributable to employer contributions merely because of the completion of a stated period of plan participation or the passage of a fixed period of time. Also, some nondiscrimination rules require a minimum number of lower-paid individuals to elect deferral.[7]

Stock Bonus Plans. A stock bonus plan is a form of deferred compensation, established and maintained by an employer to provide contributions of the employer's stock to the plan. However, there is no requirement that such contributions be dependent on profits. This plan is subject to the same requirements as a profit sharing plan for purposes of allocating and distributing the stock among the employees.[8] Any benefits of the plan are distributable in the form of stock of the employer company, except that distributable fractional shares may be paid in cash.[9]

Employee Stock Ownership Plan. An employee stock ownership plan (ESOP) is a stock bonus trust that qualifies as a tax-exempt employee trust under § 401(a). Technically, an ESOP is a defined contribution plan which is either a qualified stock bonus plan or a stock bonus and a money purchase plan, both of which are qualified under § 401(a). An ESOP must be designed to invest primarily in qualifying employer securities.[10] Since the corporation can contribute stock rather than cash, there is no cash flow drain. In addition, the tax savings accruing under the plan may have a favorable impact on working capital for the company. This plan provides flexibility, since contributions may vary from year to year and, in fact, may be omitted in any one year.[11]

A corporation can elect a payroll-based tax credit after 1982 if it establishes an ESOP for employees.[12] A company can fund the ESOP by acquiring outstanding shares of stock from its shareholders, who receive favorable capital gain treatment upon the sale of their stock.

---

6. Reg. § 1.401–4(a)(1)(iii).
7. § § 401(k) and 402(a)(8).
8. Reg. § 1.401–1(b)(1)(iii).
9. Rev.Rul. 71–256, 1971–1 C.B. 118; Rev.Rul. 62–195, 1962–2 C.B. 125.
10. § 4975(e)(7).
11. Reg. § 1.401–1(b)(2).
12. § 44G. Refer to the discussion in Chapter 13.

Employees are not subject to tax until they receive a distribution of the stock from the trust. In addition, any distribution of employer securities that is treated as a lump-sum distribution may postpone recognition of the net unrealized appreciation in such securities in the year of distribution. Such net unrealized appreciation is not included in the basis of the securities, and the appreciation is recognized in a subsequent taxable transaction.[13] After December 31, 1978, distributions to employees may be made entirely in cash or partly in cash and partly in employer securities. A participant must have the right to demand the entire distribution in the form of employer securities.[14] Before 1979, only employer securities could be distributed.

> **Example 2.** The ESOP of T Company borrows $100,000 from City Bank & Trust. The loan is secured by the stock interest and is guaranteed by the company. The ESOP buys stock for the trust from a shareholder of T Company for $100,000; the shares are then allocated among the employees' retirement accounts. The shareholder obtains capital gain treatment on the sale. T Company makes deductible contributions to the ESOP, which, in turn, pays off the loan.

The payroll-based tax credit is equal to a percentage of the employer's payroll, to be phased in as follows:[15]

Year	Percentage of Employer's Payroll
1983–1984	0.5%
1985–1987	0.75%
After 1987	None unless extended

The rationale behind this payroll-based tax credit is that the prior investment-based tax credit (in effect before 1983) fell short in spurring contributions among labor-intensive corporations. Keep in mind that such businesses usually do not make substantial qualified investments in machinery and equipment and therefore are not eligible for large investment tax credits.

This additional compensation-based credit is limited to the first $25,000 of tax liability, plus 90 percent of the tax liability over $25,000. The tax liability amount is determined after the investment tax credit, foreign tax credit, and certain other tax credits. Any unused credits may be carried back for three years and carried forward for 15 years. At the expiration of the carryover period, any unused credit may be deducted in full.[16] No additional credit is available if

---

13.   § § 402(e)(4)(D)(ii) and (J).
14.   § 409A(h).
15.   § 44 G(a)(2)(B).
16.   § 44 G(b).

more than one-third of the employer's contributions for the tax year are allocated to officers, highly compensated employees, or shareholders owning more than 10 percent of the employer's stock.[17]

Example 3. S Company has an established ESOP in 1984. During 1984, the company's payroll is $1,300,000, and its tax liability before credits is $252,000. If S contributes employer securities to the ESOP, S is allowed a $6,500 credit (.005 × $1,300,000).

QUALIFICATION REQUIREMENTS

Exclusive Benefit Requirement. Under § 401(a) a pension, profit sharing, or stock bonus trust must be created by an employer for the exclusive benefit of employees or their beneficiaries.

Example 4. The pension trust agreement of P Company provides the trust with complete power to invest funds without regard to whether investments may be new, speculative, hazardous, adventurous, or productive of income. Such a plan is not designed for the exclusive benefit of the employees and would not qualify under § 401(a).[18]

Under a "prudent man" concept, the IRS specifies four investment requirements for meeting this exclusive benefit requirement:[19]

—The cost of the investment must not exceed its fair market value at the time of purchase.

—A fair return commensurate with prevailing rates must be provided.

—Sufficient liquidity must be maintained to permit distributions in accordance with the terms of the qualified plan.

—The safeguards and diversity that a prudent investor would adhere to must be present.

Nondiscrimination Rules. In order to qualify, the contributions or benefits under a plan must not discriminate in favor of employees who are officers, shareholders, or highly compensated individuals.[20] A plan is not deemed to possess this forbidden discrimination "merely because the contributions or benefits of or on behalf of the employees under the plan bear a uniform relationship to the total compensation, or the basic or regular rate of compensation of such employees."[21] Thus, a pension plan which provides for the allocation of the employer contributions based upon a flat three percent of each employee's compensation would not be discriminatory despite the fact that highly

17. § 44 G(c)(1).
18. Rev.Rul. 73–532, 1973–2 C.B. 128.
19. Rev.Rul. 65–178, 1965–2 C.B. 94 and Rev.Rul. 73–380, 1973–2 C.B. 124.
20. § 401(a)(4).
21. § 401(a)(5).

paid employees receive proportionately greater benefits. Furthermore, in determining whether the plan is nondiscriminatory, employer FICA contributions for covered employees may be taken into account.[22] Employees whose total compensation is equal to or less than the Social Security wage base may be excluded from the plan. This exclusion will not label the plan as discriminatory.

> **Example 5.** X Corporation has a retirement plan covering its employees. An employee's retirement income is derived from both Social Security benefits *and* benefits from the retirement plan. Since X bears part of the cost of Social Security benefits, the employer recognizes these benefits in the benefit formula of the plan. The purpose of this integration is to avoid giving lower-level employees proportionately greater benefits or contributions. X is allowed to reduce the contributions or benefits to employees to the extent that they are covered by Social Security.
>
> Rather than exclude employees whose earnings are less than the Social Security taxable wage base, X Corporation provides a level of benefits for compensation above the taxable wage base higher than that provided for compensation below this amount. Although the benefit formula under X's plan favors the higher paid employees, the combined retirement benefits and Social Security benefits produce a total retirement income that is a relatively equal percentage of compensation for all employees. X's plan is nondiscriminatory.

Coverage Requirements. Since a qualified plan must be primarily for the benefit of employees and must be nondiscriminatory, the plan has to cover a reasonable percentage of the company employees. Section 410 provides mathematical tests which may be met in order to satisfy the coverage requirements (i. e., 70 percent and 80 percent tests). To meet these tests, a plan must cover at least (1) 70 percent of all employees or (2) 80 percent of all eligible employees as long as at least 70 percent of the employees are eligible for participation. In determining "all employees," part-time employees and those who have not satisfied the minimum participation requirements as to age and years of service are not counted. Where these tests are not met, a plan can still qualify if the plan does not discriminate in favor of officers, shareholders, or highly compensated employees. It is possible to qualify a plan which covers salaried-only employees if it can be shown that the plan covers a varied cross section of employees.[23]

The 70/80 percent test is not a 56 percent test, because 56 percent is necessary but not a sufficient test. That is, it is possible to meet the 56 percent test but miss either the 70 percent or 80 percent test (e. g., 90 percent are eligible to participate, but only 70 percent participate).

---

22. § 401(a)(5) and Rev.Rul. 81–202, 1981–C.B. 93.

23. Rev.Rul. 66–12, 1966–1 C.B. 72, clarified by Rev.Rul. 68–244, 1968–1 C.B. 158.

Example 6. P Corporation establishes a defined benefit plan with a 25-year minimum age requirement and a one-year service requirement. Of the 1000 employees, 100 are excluded because of the age requirement and 200 are excluded because of the service requirement. Since 700 employees are considered, this plan would meet the 70% test if at least 490 employees participate (700 × .70).

Example 7. T corporation establishes a defined benefit plan. Of the total 1500 employees, 500 do not meet the age or service requirements. The 70/80% test would be met if at least 700 of the employees are eligible to participate and at least 560 actually participate (80% of 700 employees).

Vesting Requirements. An employee's right to accrued benefits derived from his or her own contributions must be nonforfeitable from the date of contribution. The accrued benefits derived from employer contributions must be nonforfeitable in accordance with one of three alternative minimum vesting schedules: 10-year rule, 5-to-15 year rule, or the Rule of 45.[24] The purpose of the vesting requirements is to protect an employee who has worked a reasonable period of time for an employer from losing employer contributions because of being fired or changing jobs.

Under the 10-year rule, an employee with at least 10 years of service must have a nonforfeitable right to 100 percent of accrued benefits derived from employer contributions.[25] Generally, a year of service means a 12-month period during which a participant has completed at least 1,000 hours of service.[26]

The 5-to-15 year vesting rule requires an employee who has at least five years of service to have a nonforfeitable right at least equal to a percentage of the accrued benefits derived from employer contributions determined as follows:[27]

Figure I

Years of Service	Nonforfeitable Percentage
5	25%
6	30%
7	35%
8	40%
9	45%
10	50%
11	60%
12	70%
13	80%
14	90%
15 or more	100%

---

24. § 411(a).
25. § 411(a)(2)(A).
26. § 411(a)(5)(A).
27. § 411(a)(2)(B).

Under the Rule of 45, an employee who has at least five years of service and whose age and service together equal 45 must have at least a nonforfeitable interest in the accrued benefits derived from employer contributions to the extent of the amount determined as follows:[28]

Figure II

If Years of Service Equal or Exceed	And Sum of Age and Service Equals or Exceeds	Then the Minimum Nonforfeitable Percentage Must Be
5	45	50%
6	47	60%
7	49	70%
8	51	80%
9	53	90%
10	55	100%

Notwithstanding the general rule, no plan shall be treated as satisfying the Rule of 45 vesting requirements unless any participant who has completed 10 years of service has a nonforfeitable right to at least 50 percent of accrued benefits derived from employer contributions and to not less than an additional 10 percent for each additional year of service.[29] The Rule of 45 is generally more favorable to older employees.

A major exception permits service prior to age 22 to be disregarded when using the 10-year rule and the 5-to-15 year rule. This exception does not apply when a plan is following the Rule of 45.[30] For example, under the Rule of 45 an employee hired at age 18 would have to be 50 percent vested at the age of 28.

Example 8. R was discharged at age 33 after 10 years of service because of a downturn in the economy. His employer's pension plan provides for vesting under the Rule of 45. Although under the Rule of 45, R has zero vesting, a person with 10 years of service must be 50 percent vested.

Example 9. C resigns at age 30 after 10 years of service with his employer. Under the 10-year rule, C has only eight years of service, since the time before age 22 can be disregarded. Therefore, none of C's interest under the qualified plan is vested under the 10-year rule. Under the 5-to-15 year rule, 40% is vested, since the years before age 22 may be disregarded. Therefore, if the company plan is qualified under the 5-to-15 year rule, C must be entitled to retirement benefits under the plan. Under the Rule of 45, the two years of service prior to age 22 cannot be disregarded and the employee would be 50% vested.

---

28. § 411(a)(2)(C)(i).
29. § 411(a)(2)(C)(ii).
30. § 411(a)(4)(A).

Distribution Requirement. The entire interest of an employee must be distributed no later than (1) the tax year in which the participant attains age 70½ or (2) if later, the year in which the person retires. As an alternative, distributions must begin no later than such tax year and must be made, pursuant to Regulations, over the life of the participant (or lives of the participant and the participant's spouse) or over a period not exceeding the life expectancy of the person (or the life expectancies of the participant and the participant's spouse). Further, under § 401(a)(9)(A), a top-heavy plan must provide that distributions to an individual who is a key employee must begin no later than the tax year in which the key employee attains age 70½, whether or not the key employee separates from service or applies for benefit payments in such year.

TAX CONSEQUENCES TO THE EMPLOYEE AND EMPLOYER

In General. Employer contributions to qualified plans are not subject to taxation until such amounts are distributed to employees.[31] If benefits are paid with respect to an employee, to a creditor of the employee, a child of the employee, etc., the benefits paid would be treated as if paid to the employee. This tax benefit to the employee amounts to a substantial tax deferral and may be viewed as an interest-free loan from the government to the trust fund. Another advantage of a qualified plan is the fact that any income earned by the trust is not taxable to the trust. Employees, in effect, are taxed on such earnings when they receive the retirement benefits.[32]

The taxation of amounts received by employees is generally subject to the annuity rules in § 72 (refer to Chapter 6). Employee contributions have previously been subject to tax and are therefore included in the employee's "investment in contract."

A special three-year rule applies in situations where the employee contributions are nominal relative to the total value of the pension benefits. Under this special rule, if the former employee's pension amounts received during the first three years exceed the total employee contributions to the plan, all such distributions are excludible from income until the basis is recovered.[33] Thereafter, all distributions are fully taxable to the employee. In deciding whether the three-year rule is applicable, no reduction is made for the value of any refund feature.

Example 10. E had contributed $9,000 to a qualified plan when she retired at age 65. E is to receive $300 per month for the re-

---

31. § 402(a)(1). Before 1982, an amount was taxable when "made available" to an employee.

32. § 501(a).

33. § 72(d)(1).

mainder of her life. Since the payments to be received by E during the first three years ($10,800) exceed her total investment ($9,000), the first 30 payments are tax-free ($9,000 ÷ $300), and all subsequent payments are taxable. None of the payments are taxable until the $9,000 investment is recovered.

If the employee does not recover his or her own contributions within three years, the amount excludible is calculated by using the annuity formula under § 72(b):

$$\frac{\text{Investment in contract}}{\text{Annual return} \times \text{Multiple}^{34}} \times \text{Yearly return} = \text{Excluded amount}$$

Any difference between the "annual return" and the "excluded amount" is taxable.[35] A taxpayer does not have a choice as to which of the methods applies.

Example 11. T is to receive $300 per month from his employer's qualified pension plan, beginning at retirement at age 65, for the rest of his life. T contributed $12,000 to the plan. He retires on January 1, and the expected return multiple in Table 1 of Reg. § 1.72–9 for a 65-year-old male is 15.0. Since T will not recover his investment within a three-year period, the exclusion ratio rules apply:

$$\frac{\$12,000}{\$3,600 \times 15.0} \times \$3,600 = \$800.00 \text{ per year or } \$66.67 \text{ per month}$$

Thus, $66.67 of each $300 distribution is excluded from income; $233.33 is taxable as ordinary income.[36]

Lump-sum Distributions from Qualified Plans. Prior to 1969, employees received favorable long-term capital gain treatment for lump-sum distributions from qualified plans. This favorable capital gain treatment has been restricted by legislation which was enacted in 1969 and 1974. Under the current rules, the taxable amount is allocated between a capital gain portion and an ordinary income portion (which may be subject to a special 10-year averaging treatment).[37] That portion attributable to the employee's service after 1973 is included as ordinary income when received and may be taxed under the 10-year averaging provision. An employee must be a plan participant for at least five years to take advantage of the 10-year averaging option. Under current law, it is possible to defer tax on

---

34. The multiple is the life expectancy of the employee determined by using the actuarial tables in Reg. § 1.72–9.
35. § 72(b).
36. § § 72(a) and 402(a)(1).
37. § 402(e)(1)(C).

some or all of the distribution under § 402(a)(5) providing that the employee elects to roll over the distribution by transferring the proceeds to an individual retirement account (IRA).

An employee may elect to treat all of the distribution as ordinary income subject to the 10-year averaging provision.[38] In some instances ordinary income treatment is preferable to long-term capital gains due to the favorable averaging treatment. In general, the 10-year averaging treatment is more attractive as the amount of the ordinary income portion of the distribution increases. Also, it should be kept in mind that long-term capital gains are a tax preference item under the alternative minimum tax provisions.

To determine the tax on a lump-sum distribution, it is necessary to compute the taxable portion of the distribution by subtracting employee contributions and the net unrealized appreciation in the value of any distributed securities of the employer corporation. The taxable amount is then reduced by a "minimum distribution allowance" to arrive at the amount which is eligible for the 10-year income averaging provisions.[39] The portion of the lump-sum distribution which is treated as a long-term capital gain is equal to the following:

$$\text{Taxable amount} \times \frac{\text{Years of service prior to 1974}}{\text{Total years of service}}$$

(computed without being reduced by the minimum distribution allowance)

Example 12. T, age 65 and married, retires at the end of 1985 and receives a lump-sum distribution of $100,000 from his company's profit sharing plan. This plan includes $5,000 of his own contributions and $10,000 of unrealized appreciation on his employer's common stock. The distributee has been a participant in the plan for 20 years.

Taxable portion of the lump-sum distribution [$100,000 − $5,000 (employee contribution) − $10,000 (unrealized appreciation of employer securities)]		$ 85,000
Less: Minimum distribution allowance:		
½ of the taxable amount up to $20,000	$ 10,000	
Less: 20% of the taxable amount in excess of $20,000:		
20% × ($85,000 − $20,000)	(13,000)	
Minimum distribution allowance		−0−
Taxable amount subject to averaging		$ 85,000

---

38. § 402(e)(4)(L).

39. § 402(e)(1)(D).

Computation of tax under 10-year averaging:
    10 times the tax on $10,800
    [(1/10 of $85,000) + $2,300][40] $ 12,030

$12,030 $\times \dfrac{12 \text{ (service after 1973)}}{20 \text{ (total service years)}}$ = $7,218

(ordinary income tax due on ordinary income
    portion)
Long-term capital gain portion

$85,000 $\times \dfrac{8 \text{ (service before 1974)}}{20 \text{ (total service years)}}$ = $34,000

Thus, T's capital gain on the distribution is $34,000. Furthermore, the capital gain on the unrealized appreciation in the employer's common stock is not taxable *until T sells* the stock. In essence, the cost basis of the securities to the trust becomes the tax basis to the employee.[41] If T keeps the securities until he dies, there may be some income tax savings on this gain to the extent the estate or the heirs obtain a step-up in basis. This example illustrates a major advantage of an ESOP.

LIMITATIONS ON CONTRIBUTIONS TO AND BENEFITS FROM QUALIFIED PLANS

Defined Contribution Plans. Under a defined contribution plan (i. e., money purchase pension, profit sharing, or stock bonus plans), the amount of the annual addition to an employee's account cannot exceed the smaller of $30,000 or 25 percent of the employee's compensation. Before 1983, § 415(d) provided that the dollar limitations were to be increased through cost-of-living adjustments. These cost-of-living adjustments have been suspended for 1983 through 1985. They will be resumed in 1986 but will be limited to post-1984 cost-of-living increases. The adjustments will be based on the cost-of-living formula then in effect for Social Security benefits.

> **Example 13.** An employee's compensation was $110,000 during the 1984 plan year of a money purchase pension plan. The maximum annual addition to the participant's account is limited to $27,500 (.25 × $110,000).

Defined Benefit Plans. Under a defined benefit plan, the benefit payable to an employee is limited to the smaller of $90,000 or 100 percent of the employee's average compensation for the highest three

---

40. In making this tax computation, it is necessary to use the Tax Rate Schedule for single taxpayers and to add $2,300 (the zero bracket amount) to the taxable income. The Tax Rate Schedules for taxable years after 1983 were used to compute the tax liability. Thus, tax was computed on $10,800, which is $8,500 (one-tenth of $85,000) plus $2,300.

41. § 402(e)(4)(J).

years of employment.[42] The $90,000 limitation is reduced actuarially where retirement benefits commence before age 62. However, the actuarial reduction cannot reduce the limitation below $75,000 if the benefits commence at or after age 55. The monetary limitation was adjusted for cost of living before 1983. These cost-of-living adjustments, which have been suspended for 1983 through 1985, will again apply in 1986.

Example 14. Employee A's average compensation for the highest three years of employment is $87,000. The § 415(b)(1) limitation does not limit the deductions, but the defined benefit plan would not qualify if the plan provides for benefits in excess of the smaller of (a) $87,000 or (b) $90,000 for Employee A in 1984 (assuming retirement age of 65).

For collectively bargained plans with at least 100 participants, the dollar limitation is the greater of $68,212 or one-half of the $90,000 monetary limit (to be adjusted for cost-of-living increases beginning in 1986).[43]

There are two methods for determining the maximum deduction by a corporation for contributions to pension plans. First, an aggregate cost method allows an actuarially determined deduction based on a level amount, or a level percentage, of compensation over the remaining future service of covered participants. Second, the employer is permitted to deduct the so-called normal cost plus no more than 10 percent of the past service costs.

Example 15. During 19X6, Y Corporation contributes $17,500 to its qualified pension plan. Normal cost for this year is $7,200, and the amount necessary to pay retirement benefits on behalf of employee services before 19X6 is $82,000 (past service costs). The corporation's maximum deduction would be $15,400. This amount consists of the $7,200 normal cost plus 10% ($8,200) of the past service costs. The corporation would have a $2,100 [$17,500(contribution) − $15,400(deduction)] contribution carryover.

Example 16. Assume in the previous example that Y Corporation has normal cost in 19X7 of $7,200 and contributes $10,000 to the pension trust. $12,100 can be deducted which is composed of this year's contribution ($10,000) plus the $2,100 contribution carryover.

The employer's contribution is deductible in the tax year such amounts are paid to the pension trust. However, both cash basis and accrual basis employers may defer the payment of contributions with respect to any fiscal year until the date fixed for filing the taxpayer's

---

42. § 415(b)(1).
43. § 415(b)(7).

Federal income tax return for such year (including extensions thereof).[44] In effect, the corporation is allowed a deduction to the extent it is compelled to make such contributions to satisfy the funding requirement. If an amount is contributed in any tax year which is in excess of the allowable amount, the excess may be carried forward and deducted in succeeding tax years (to the extent such carryover plus that year's contribution does not exceed the deductible limitation for such succeeding year).[45]

Profit Sharing and Stock Bonus Plan Limitations. The maximum deduction permitted each year with respect to contributions to profit sharing and stock bonus plans is 15 percent of the compensation paid or accrued with respect to plan participants.[46] Any nondeductible excess, a so-called contribution carryover, may be carried forward indefinitely and deducted in subsequent years. The maximum deduction in any succeeding year is 15 percent of all compensation paid or accrued during such taxable year. An employer can circumvent the 15 percent limitation by establishing a money purchase pension plan as a supplement to the profit sharing or stock bonus plan. When there are two or more plans, a maximum deduction of 25 percent of the compensation paid is allowable.[47]

Credit Carryovers. Under the 15 percent limitation rule for profit sharing or stock bonus plans, if contributions are less than the allowable amount (15 percent) the difference is defined as a "credit carryover." During subsequent years the employer may contribute amounts in excess of the 15 percent limitation to the extent of any credit carryovers. However, the credit carryover to any one year cannot exceed 10 percent of the compensation paid (i. e., 15 percent is allowed for the current contribution plus 10 percent for the credit carryover contribution). In essence, the maximum deduction is the smaller of (a) 15 percent of compensation and unused credit carryover or (b) 25 percent of compensation.

> **Example 17.** In 19X6 E Corporation had a payroll of $200,000 and made a $24,000 contribution to a qualified profit sharing plan. Since the corporation could have contributed $30,000 (15% × $200,000), it has a $6,000 ($30,000 − $24,000) credit carryover. During 19X7 the payroll was $240,000 and the plan contribution was $52,000. The corporation could deduct a total of $42,000, which is composed of this year's deductible amount of $36,000 ($240,000 × .15) plus the $6,000 credit carryover from 19X6. Furthermore, in 19X7 the corporation has a $10,000 contribution carryover ($52,000 − $42,000). During 19X8 the pay-

---

44. §§ 404(a)(1) and (6).
45. § 404(a)(1)(D).
46. § 404(a)(3)(A).
47. § 404(a)(7).

roll was $300,000 and the plan contribution was $30,000. Thus, for 19X8 the corporation could deduct $40,000, which is composed of this year's contribution of $30,000 plus last year's $10,000 contribution carryover. (The $40,000 amount does not exceed 15% of $300,000.) Note the difference between a "credit carryover" and a "contribution carryover."

TOP-HEAVY PLANS

A new set of rules affecting regular corporations, S corporations, partnerships, and individuals is imposed upon so-called top-heavy plans. Such plans primarily benefit an employer's key employees. Top-heaviness is determined on an annual basis.

Beginning in 1984, top-heavy plans have these additional requirements:

—Only the first $200,000 of an employee's compensation may be taken into account in determining contributions or benefits under the plan.[48] In 1986, this $200,000 limit will be adjusted under the same rules used to adjust the overall limits on contributions and benefits.

—There shall be greater portability for plan participants who are non-key employees. An employee's right to the accrued benefits derived from employer contributions must become nonforfeitable under either of two vesting schedules. Under the first schedule, an employee who has at three years of service with the employer must have a nonforfeitable right to 100 percent of his or her accrued benefits derived from employer contributions. Or under the second schedule, a six-year graded vesting schedule must be met:[49]

Years of Service	Vested Percentage
2	20
3	40
4	60
5	80
6 or more	100

—There must be minimum nonintegrated contributions or benefits for plan participants who are non-key employees. These employees in a defined *benefit* plan must be provided with a minimum nonintegrated normal retirement benefit at two percent of their average monthly compensation (for their high five years of compensation) per year of service. However, this mini-

---

48. § 416(d).
49. § 416(b).

mum benefit does not have to provide more than 20 percent of their high five-year average compensation.[50] In a defined *contribution* plan, non-key employees must receive a minimum nonintegrated contribution of three percent of pay per year.[51]

—There is a reduction in the aggregate limit on contributions and benefits for certain key employees. The aggregate limit for a key employee is the smaller of 1.0 (with respect to the dollar limit) or 1.4 (as applied to the percentage limitation). However, the aggregate limit may be increased to the smaller of 1.25 or 1.4, respectively, if certain conditions are met.[52]

—Additional restrictions are placed upon distributions to key employees. Where a distribution is made to a key employee before he or she attains age 59½, an additional 10 percent penalty tax is imposed upon the premature distribution (except in the case of death or disability). Further, distributions to a key employee must begin no later than the taxable year in which the key employee reaches age 70½.[53] Such required distribution must be made in such a manner that more than 50 percent of the total benefits for the employee are payable to the employee over the employee's life expectancy (or a joint life expectancy). For a plan that is not top-heavy, distributions must begin by the later of age 70½ or separation from employment.[54]

A defined benefit plan is top-heavy if, as of the determination date (1) the present value of the accumulated accrued benefits for participants who are key employees for the plan year exceeds 60 percent of the present value of the accumulated accrued benefits for all employees under the plan or (2) the plan is part of a top-heavy plan.[55] Two or more plans of a single employer may be aggregated to determine whether the plans, as a group, are top-heavy.[56]

A defined contribution plan is top-heavy for a plan year if (1) the sum of the account balances of participants who are key employees for the plan year exceeds 60 percent of the sum of the account balances of all employees under the plan or (2) the plan is part of a top-heavy plan.[57] A simplified employee pension (SEP) is considered a defined contribution plan, and at the election of the employer, the account balance of any employee covered by an SEP is deemed to be the sum of the employer contributions made on the employee's behalf.[58]

---

50. § 416(c)(1).
51. § 416(c)(2).
52. § 415(e).
53. § 401(a)(9)(A).
54. § 401(a)(9).
55. § 416(g)(A)(1)(i).
56. § 416(f).
57. § 416(g)(A)(1)(ii).
58. § 416(i)(6).

Key employees are defined as follows:

—Officers. However, for purposes of this definition, only the smaller of (a) 50 officers or (b) three employees or 10 percent of all employees (whichever is greater) may be considered officers.

—The 10 employees owning the largest interest in the employer.

—A five percent owner of the employer.

—Greater than one percent owner of the employer with annual compensation in excess of $150,000.[59]

An employee need fall within only one of these categories to be classified as a key employee.

To stop an employer from avoiding the top-heavy rules by establishing a one-person corporate shell, new § 269A allows the IRS to allocate any income or deductions between the personal service corporation and its employee-owner. An employee-owner is any employee who owns more than 10 percent of the outstanding stock of the personal service corporation on any day during the tax year.

CASH OR DEFERRED ARRANGEMENT PLANS

A cash or deferred arrangement plan, hereafter referred to as a § 401(k) plan, allows participants to elect to either receive cash or have a contribution made on their behalf to a profit sharing or stock bonus plan.[60] The plan may also be in the form of a salary reduction agreement between an eligible participant and an employer under which a contribution will be made only if the participant elects to reduce his or her compensation or to forego an increase in compensation.[61]

Any pretax amount elected by the employee as a plan contribution is not includible in gross income and is 100 percent vested.[62] Any employer contributions are tax deferred, as are earnings on contributions in the plan.

A § 401(k) plan must meet the general coverage requirements of § 401(b)(1). Further, the plan must be nondiscriminatory under either § 401(k) or § 410(a)(4). There are, however, two safe harbor provisions in § 401(k)(3)(A). First, the actual deferral percentage of the highest paid one-third of the employees must not exceed the actual deferral percentage of the lowest paid two-thirds of the employees by more than one and one-half times. Second, the actual deferral percentage of the highest paid one-third of the employees must (1) not exceed the actual deferral percentage of the lowest paid two-thirds of the employ-

---

59.   § 416(i).

60.   § 401(k)(2).

61.   Prop.Reg. § 1.401(k)–1(a).

62.   § 401(k)(2)(c).

ees by more than three percentage points and (2) not be more than two and one-half times the actual deferral percentage of the lowest paid two-thirds of the employees.[63]

Where a § 401(k) plan is used as a supplement to a defined benefit plan, a contribution to a § 401(k) plan does not cause a decline in the employee's retirement benefits under the defined benefit plan. An employer may determine the benefits from a defined benefit pension plan based upon compensation that includes elective § 401(k) salary reduction contributions.[64]

TAX-DEFERRED ANNUITIES

Since 1958, tax-deferred annuities have been available for employees of public educational organizations and certain other tax-exempt entities. Generally, a tax-deferred annuity (TDA) is an investment vehicle used as a means to achieve tax-sheltered savings for retirement. Only certain individuals are eligible for tax-deferred treatment under § 403(b), and the income to which the deferral will apply is subject to certain limitations.

Basically, contributions to a TDA made by an employer for the benefit of an employee are not included in the employee's gross income. The same treatment is allowed contributions made by the employer using funds provided by a salary reduction agreed to by the employee. The income so invested is not taxable to the employee until later years when the individual receives the money. This deferral provides tax savings because pre-tax dollars are invested, which provides increased funds upon which to earn a return. The tax on the income is paid later, which provides a time value of money advantage. Further, the annuitant's applicable tax rates are likely to be lower in retirement years as opposed to those applicable in peak income years.

Qualified Employers. There are basically two types of organizations whose contributions will qualify for tax deferral under the § 403(b) TDA rules. The first type is the § 501(c)(3) organization exempt from tax under § 501(a).[65] These are organizations operated exclusively for religious, charitable, scientific, testing for public safety, literary, or educational purposes, or to foster national or international amateur sports competition, or for the prevention of cruelty to children and animals.[66]

A second qualifying employer is a state, political subdivision of a state, or an agency or instrumentality of either of the foregoing, whose contributions are for an employee who performs services for an educational institution.[67] An educational institution is an organiza-

---

63. § 401(k)(3).
64. Rev.Rul. 83–89, 1983–1 C.B. 88.
65. § 403(b)(1)(A)(i).
66. § 501(c)(3).
67. § 403(b)(1)(A)(ii).

tion which normally maintains a regular faculty and curriculum and normally has a regularly enrolled body of pupils or students in attendance at the place where its educational activities are regularly carried on.[68] Thus, the second group of employers consists mainly of public schools, state colleges, and universities.

Qualified Employees. Contributions are excludible from gross income only if made on behalf of a present, former, or retired employee.[69] Whether or not this employee-employer relationship exists for federal tax purposes is often not entirely clear. If the individual cannot qualify as an employee, § 403(b) does not apply. An independent contractor does not qualify.

As for employees performing services, either directly or indirectly, for educational institutions, nonacademic staff such as clerical and custodial employees as well as faculty are eligible. However, a person in an elective or appointive public office is not considered an employee performing services for an educational institution unless the individual must have received training or experience in the field of education to be eligible for such election or appointment.[70]

Investment Vehicles. Whatever the form of the tax-deferred annuity, it must be nontransferable[71] and nonforfeitable except for failure to pay future premiums.[72] However, if an individual has a forfeitable annuity which later becomes nonforfeitable, the amount normally includible in the individual's gross income is considered contributed by an employer as of the time the employee's rights under the contract become nonforfeitable.[73] This provision would defer taxation of contributions that were not taxable when made under § 83 because they were not "substantially vested" but would be taxable at a later date when the employee's rights became "substantially vested" or nonforfeitable.[74]

There is no requirement that the purchase of an annuity contract be merely a "supplement to past or current income" for post-1957 rules as there was for pre-1958 rules. Also, contributions to a TDA must be made by the employer if they are to qualify for tax deferral. Therefore, a popular method of funding a TDA is through salary reductions or by foregoing salary increases. The salary reduction or the foregoing of salary increases must be the result of a binding agreement and irrevocable with respect to amounts earned while the agreement is in effect. This provision applies only to amounts contributed after the agreement becomes effective. The employee must not be per-

---

68. § 170(b)(1)(A)(ii).

69. Reg. § 1.403(b)–1(b)(1).

70. Reg. § 1.403(b)–1(b)(5).

71. § 401(g).

72. § 403(b)(1)(c).

73. § 403(b)(6) and Reg. § 1.403(b)–1(b)(2).

74. § 403(c).

mitted to make more than one agreement per taxable year. If an employee has two or more annuity contracts to which the TDA rules would apply, they are treated as a single contract for purposes of the § 403(b) TDA rules.[75]

The investment vehicle may take the form of an individual annuity contract owned by the employee; a group annuity contract with an insurer, providing for a separate account for each participating employee;[76] or an interest in a public retirement system such as a state teachers' retirement system.[77] Contributions to a custodial account, the amounts so contributed to be invested in a regulated investment company stock, the stock to be held in that custodial account, also may qualify if no such amounts may be paid or made available to the distributee before the employee dies, attains age 59½, separates from service, becomes disabled, or encounters financial hardship.[78]

Amounts Excludible from Gross Income. Contributions to a TDA by a qualified employer are excludible from the employee's current gross income up to but not exceeding the "exclusion allowance."[79] The exclusion allowance is 20 percent of the employee's includible compensation (reduced salary), multiplied by the number of years of service with the employer at taxable year-end, less the total amount contributed by the employer to annuity contracts and excludible from gross income in prior years.[80] Includible compensation is generally compensation from an eligible employer includible in the employee's gross income, from the employee's most recent year of service.[81] Employer contributions to qualified plans for the employee are not includible in compensation.[82] If the includible compensation remained constant over the years, so would the excludible amount. For instance, if an employee's includible compensation was $20,000 for years one through three and in each year the employer contributed $4,000 to the employee's TDA, the exclusion allowance would be $4,000. If the contributions in prior years were less than 20 percent of includible compensation in subsequent years or if includible compensation increased in the year under consideration, the exclusion allowance would also be increased due to the cumulative nature of the TDA rules.

This overall exclusion can be calculated from the following formula:

75. Reg. § 1.403(b)–1(b)(3) and (4).
76. Reg. § 1.403(b)–1(c)(3).
77. Rev.Rul. 67–387, 1967–2 C.B. 153.
78. § 403(b)(7)(A).
79. § 403(b)(1).
80. § 403(b)(2).
81. § 403(b)(3).
82. Reg. § 1.403(b)–1(e)(2); Rev.Rul. 79–221, 1979–2 C.B. 188.

$$C = .20(S - C)Y - P$$

where C = allowable exclusion amount
  S = total salary
  Y = years of service at end of year
  P = employer and employee contributions to TDA in prior years

Example 18. Professor O's employer contributes $4,000 to a TDA during the first academic year. If his includible salary is $20,000, the excludible amount is $4,000, calculated from the following formula: C = .20(24,000 − C) 1 − 0. During the second year his total salary is $28,000 and his employer contributes $4,000. His exclusion allowance for the second year is $5,142.86, calculated from the following formula: C = .20 (28,000 − C) 2 − $4,000.

Even though an employer does not contribute to a TDA, an employee may still benefit from a salary reduction TDA. An eligible employee may instruct his or her employer to place part of the compensation into a TDA. An employee is allowed to defer up to one-sixth of the unreduced taxable compensation earned during the tax year.[83] The employee must enter into a legally binding and irrevocable agreement with the employer to take a reduction in salary or to forego an increase in salary before the salary is earned.[84]

Example 19. A teacher began teaching on January 1, 19X0, at a salary of $22,000 per year. The exclusion allowance is $3,667 [C = .20 ($22,000 − C) 1 − 0]. The teacher may enter into a salary reduction agreement whereby her salary may be reduced to $18,333 ($5/6 \times $22,000) and the difference of $3,667 contributed to a TDA. This $3,667 contribution (.20 $\times$ $18,333) is excludible from her gross income.

An annual limitation upon the above exclusion allowance is found in § 415. Under § 415, the maximum employer contribution to a TDA is the lesser of 25 percent of the employee's includible compensation from the employer or $30,000 (to be adjusted by the IRS for increases in the cost of living after 1985).[85] Contributions in excess of the § 415 limitation are included in gross income and also reduce the § 403(b) exclusion allowance dollar for dollar.[86] The 25 percent limit can be calculated from either C = .25 (S − C) or .20 times the total salary.

83. One-sixth of a person's unreduced salary is the same as one-fifth of the employee's salary reduced by the contribution.
84. Reg. § 1.403(b)–1(b)(3).
85. § 415(a)(2)(B).
86. § 415(c)(1).

Example 20. Using the same facts as in Example 18, Professor O's annual limit in the first year is $4,800 ($24,000 × .20). His limit in the second year is $5,600 ($28,000 × .20).

Several other alternatives are available to contributions to a TDA:

—Forget about the overall exclusion allowance and be limited by the smaller of 25 percent of reduced salary or $30,000.

—Raise the exclusion allowance by $4,000, but subject to a $15,000 limit and the exclusion allowance without regard to the § 415 limitation. Use either C = .25 (S − C) + $4,000 or C = .20S + $3200.

—During the final year of employment, disregard the 25 percent annual limitation and be subject only to the exclusion allowance. The contribution cannot exceed $30,000.[87]

RETIREMENT PLANS FOR SELF-EMPLOYED INDIVIDUALS

Since 1962, self-employed individuals and their employees have been eligible to receive qualified retirement benefits under what is known as H.R. 10 (Keogh) plans. Due to contribution limitations and other restrictions, self-employed plans previously were less attractive when compared to corporate plans. But for years beginning after 1983, contributions and benefits of a self-employed person are subject to the general corporate provisions. Basically, self-employed persons are now on the parity with corporate employees. H.R. 10 plans can now provide a self-employed person with an adequate retirement base. In Figure III, it is assumed that the annual contribution at the end of the year is $7,500 or $15,000 with the fund earning 10 or 15 percent, compounded annually. For example, with an annual contribution of $7,500 for 30 years, a total of $1,233,705 would accumulate using a 10 percent rate.

COVERAGE REQUIREMENTS

Before 1984, when an owner-employee[88] participated in an H.R. 10 plan, the plan had to cover all employees with at least three years of service.[89] In addition, before 1984, an employee's rights to contribu-

---

87.   § § 415(c)(4)(A), (B), and (C).
88.   An owner-employee is a self-employed individual who is the sole owner of a proprietorship or, in the case of a partner, owns more than 10% of the profit or capital interest of the partnership. Not all self-employed individuals are owner-employees. The distinction may be significant, since greater restrictions are placed on owner-employees.
89.   § 401(d)(3)(A).

Figure III
H.R. 10 PLAN ACCUMULATIONS

	10% Rate		15% Rate	
Years	$7,500 Annual Contribution	$15,000 Annual Contribution	$7,500 Annual Contribution	$15,000 Annual Contribution
10	$ 119,527	$ 239,055	$ 152,277	$ 304,545
20	429,562	859,125	768,327	1,536,654
30	1,233,705	2,467,410	3,260,587	6,521,175

tions had to be 100 percent vested when the contributions were made.[90] The term "employee" did not include part time employees.[91]

Generally, after 1983, the corporate coverage rules apply to H.R. 10 plans. Thus, the 70 percent and 80 percent tests discussed previously apply also to self-employed plans. However, the more restrictive top-heavy plan rules apply also to H.R. 10 plans.

CONTRIBUTION LIMITATIONS

Through 1983, contributions made on behalf of owner-employees are limited to the lesser of $15,000 or 15 percent of earned income.[92] For tax years beginning after 1983, a self-employed individual may contribute the smaller of $30,000 or 25 percent of earned income to a defined contribution Keogh plan.[93] If the defined contribution plan is a profit sharing plan, the 15 percent deduction limit applies. Under a defined benefit Keogh plan, the benefit payable to an employee is limited to the smaller of $90,000 or 100 percent of the employee's average compensation for the highest three years of employment.[94] More restrictive rules apply to a top-heavy plan.

> **Example 21.** T, an owner-employee, has earned income in 1984 of $40,000 (after Keogh contribution). The maximum contribution to a defined contribution Keogh plan which is deductible for adjusted gross income is $10,000 (25% × $40,000).

Earned income refers to net earnings from self-employment as defined in § 1402(a).[95] "Net earnings from self-employment" means the gross income derived by an individual from any trade or business carried on by such individual, less appropriate deductions, plus the distributive share of income or loss from a partnership.[96] As provided

---

90. § 401(d)(2)(A).
91. § 401(d)(3).
92. § 404(e). For years before 1974, the limitation was the smaller of $2,500 or 10% of earned income, and before 1982, the limitation was $7,500 or 15% of earned income.
93. § 415(c)(1).
94. § 415(b)(1).
95. § 401(c)(2).
96. § 1502(a).

in the Tax Equity and Fiscal Responsibility Act, earned income is reduced by contributions to qualified plans on that individual's behalf.[97]

> **Example 22.** P, a partner, has earned income in 1984 (before any Keogh contribution) of $130,000. The maximum contribution to a defined contribution plan is $26,000, calculated from the following formula: $\$130,000 - .25X = X$, where X is earned income. Solving this equation, $X = \$104,000$; thus, the contribution limit is $.25 \times \$104,000 = \$26,000$. To achieve the maximum contribution of $30,000, P would have to earn at least $150,000.

Many Keogh plans will be top-heavy plans (see previous discussion). For nondiscrimination purposes, the 25 percent limitation on the key employee contribution is computed on the first $200,000 of earned income. In 1986, this $200,000 limit will be adjusted under the same cost-of-living adjustment rules applicable to the overall limits on contributions and benefits.

> **Example 23.** T, a self-employed accountant, has a money purchase plan with a contribution rate of 5% of compensation. T's earned income before the retirement contribution is $220,000. T's contribution would be limited to $9,523.81 ($\$200,000 - .05X = X$), since $X = \$190,476.20$, and $.05 \times \$190,476.20 = \$9,523.81$.

Although an H.R. 10 plan must be established prior to the end of the year in question, contributions may be made up to the normal filing date (plus extensions) for such year. Also, an employee who is covered under a qualified corporate retirement plan, may set up an H.R. 10 plan for earned income from self-employment sources (as well as an IRA).

H.R. 10 PLAN VERSUS CORPORATE PENSION PLAN

Effective for tax years after 1983, the Tax Equity and Fiscal Responsibility Act puts self-employed individuals on an equal basis with individuals covered by corporate plans. Under these new rules, an individual need not incorporate to obtain favorable employee benefit plans. However, a number of minor fringe benefits are available to a corporate employee that are not available to a noncorporate employee (e.g., medical reimbursement plan). Further, some tax deferral can be attained by incorporating and electing a fiscal year.

Before the Tax Equity and Fiscal Responsibility Act, loans to a self-employed individual from a Keogh plan were specifically prohibited. However, effective August 13, 1982, self-employed individuals may borrow from a Keogh plan on the same basis as owner-employees

---

97. § 401(c)(2)(A)(v).

in corporate retirement plans. Now all loans from retirement plans are limited to the greater of (1) $10,000 or (2) the smaller of $50,000 or one-half of vested benefits. Thus, if a Keogh plan provides that all employees are immediately vested, each participant can borrow up to $50,000 so long as such amount does not exceed one-half of their vested benefits.[98]

> **Example 24.** T, in 1984, has vested benefits in his retirement plan of $62,000. He borrows $31,000 from his retirement plan, with the loan being secured and having a reasonable interest rate and a predetermined repayment schedule. He has borrowed from himself and pays tax-deductible interest to himself, and the interest income accumulates free from current taxes in the retirement plan.

INDIVIDUAL RETIREMENT ACCOUNTS (IRA)

GENERAL RULES

Before 1982, persons participating in regular qualified pension or profit sharing plans were precluded from participating in IRAs. Not so after 1981.[99] Employees covered by a qualified plan now may establish their own tax-deductible IRA subject to the smaller of $2,000 (or $2,250 limit for spousal IRAs) or 100% of compensation.[100] Or if an employer retirement plan allows voluntary contributions, an employee may make deductible contributions to the employer plan, subject to the $2,000 or 100% of compensation limits. These IRA contributions are in addition to any nondeductible employee contributions. The deductible contributions may be split between an IRA or an employer plan.

Self-employed persons such as partners and sole proprietors may make additional deductible contributions to an IRA or Keogh plan. Thus, a self-employed person with earned income of $100,000 can contribute a total of $17,000 to a Keogh plan ($15,000 + $2,000). Or the self-employed individual may contribute $15,000 to the Keogh plan and $2,000 to an IRA ($2,250 for spousal IRAs).

After December 31, 1981, any amounts invested in collectibles under a self-directed account in a qualified plan or IRA are treated as distributions for income tax purposes. The term "collectible" refers to rugs, antiques, stamps, coins, guns, works of art, metals, alcoholic beverages, or any other tangible property specified by the IRS.[101]

---

98. § 72(p)(2).
99. § 219(a).
100. § 219(b).
101. § 408(n).

Figure IV indicates the amounts that can be accumulated in two IRAs by a working couple. These figures assume $4,000 is deposited at the end of each year with annual compounding rates of 10, 12, and 15 percent. For example, over a period of 30 years, a total of $657,976 can be accumulated in a couple's IRAs at an annual compounding rate of 10 percent.

Figure IV
IRA ACCUMULATIONS

Years Contributed	10%	12%	15%
10	$ 63,748	$ 70,195	$ 81,212
20	229,100	288,208	409,774
30	657,976	965,328	1,738,980
40	1,770,372	3,068,364	7,116,360

Example 25. K Company contributes $800 to an IRA in 1984 on behalf of F, one of its employees whose earned taxable income is $12,000. K Company may deduct the $800 contribution on its tax return under § 162. F would show $800 of compensation but would be allowed a deduction of $800 *for* adjusted gross income.

Example 26. Assume the same facts as in the previous example except that F also contributes $1,200 to the same IRA (or another IRA). Since F is allowed to deduct the smaller of $2,000 or 100% of compensation ($12,000), F would be allowed to contribute $1,200 to the IRA and deduct a total of $2,000.

Simplified Pension Plans. Beginning in 1984, § 408(j) permits an employer to contribute to an IRA covering an employee an amount equal to the lesser of $30,000 ($15,000 in 1982–83) or 25 percent of the employee's earned income. Under § 408(k)(2) the corporation must make contributions for *each* employee who has reached age 25 and has performed service for the employer during the calendar year and at least three of the five preceding calendar years. Regrettably, the IRA limitation does not increase from $2,000 to $30,000 if less than 100 percent of all eligible employees set up an IRA and receive an allocation of the employer contributions. An employee also can contribute up to $2,000 to an employer's IRA and take an IRA contribution deduction for such amount.

Example 27. During 1984, T was employed by X Corporation at a salary of $30,000. Since X Corporation does not have a regular qualified pension plan, it contributes $4,500 (i. e., 15% of $30,000) to an IRA on behalf of T. An additional contribution of $2,000 can be made by T to the SEP (smaller of $2,000 or 100% of $30,000).

These changes are intended to offer employers an alternative to regular qualified plans. Known as "simplified pension plans," they are subject to many of the same restrictions applicable to qualified plans (e. g., age and period of service requirements and nondiscrimination limitations).

Spousal IRA. If both spouses work, each may establish individually an IRA. However, when only one spouse is employed, an IRA can be established for the nonemployed spouse if the employed spouse is eligible to establish an IRA. Under § 220(b) the maximum deduction for the individual and spouse is the lesser of 100 percent of the compensation income of the working spouse or $2,250. No more than $2,000 can be allocated to the working spouse, and a joint return must be filed.

A divorced or separated spouse may continue to make deductible contributions to such a spousal plan up to the smaller of $1,125 or the sum of the divorced spouse's compensation and taxable alimony. The spousal IRA must have been established at least five years prior to the year of divorce, and the ex-spouse (i. e., the employed spouse) must have contributed to it for at least three of those five years.[102]

> **Example 28.** X, who is married, is eligible to establish an IRA. He received $30,000 in compensation in 1984. He may contribute a total of $2,250 to a spousal IRA, to be divided in any manner between the two spouses. However, no more than $2,000 can be allocated to either working spouse.

For years after 1977, a deductible contribution can be made to an IRA any time prior to the due date of the individual's tax return (including extensions).[103] For example, an individual may contribute to an IRA through April 15, 1984, and deduct this amount on his or her tax return for 1983. An employer may make contributions within three and one-half months after the close of the calendar year and treat such amounts as a deduction for the prior year.[104] As noted earlier, a similar rule applies to H.R. 10 plans. However, the H.R. 10 plan must be established before the end of the tax year. Contributions to the H.R. 10 plan may then be made any time before the due date of the individual's tax return (including extensions).

PENALTY TAXES FOR EXCESS CONTRIBUTIONS

A cumulative, nondeductible six percent excise penalty tax is imposed on the smaller of (1) any excess contributions or (2) the market value

---

102.   § 219(b)(4).
103.   § § 219(c)(3) and (4).
104.   § 404(h)(1)(B).

of the plan assets determined at the end of the due date (including extensions) of the individual's tax return.[105] Excess contributions are any contributions which exceed the maximum limitation and contributions made during or after the tax year in which the individual reaches age 70½.[106] A taxpayer is, of course, not allowed a deduction for excess contributions unless the excess is corrected by contributing less than the deductible amount for a later year. The deduction then is allowable in the later year as a "make-up" deduction.

An excess contribution is taxable annually until returned to the taxpayer or reduced by the underutilization of the maximum contribution limitation in a subsequent year. For taxable years beginning after 1975, the six percent penalty tax can be avoided if the excess amounts are returned.[107]

> **Example 29.** T, age 55, creates an individual retirement plan in 19X1 and contributes $2,300 of cash to the plan. T has earned income of $22,000. T is allowed a $2,000 deduction *for* adjusted gross income for 19X1. Assuming the market value of the plan assets is at least $300, there is a nondeductible 6% excise penalty tax of $18.00 ($300 × 6%). The $300 may be subject to an additional penalty tax in future years if either not returned to T or reduced by underutilization of the $2,000 maximum contribution limitation.

TAXATION OF BENEFITS

A participant has a zero basis in his contributions to an IRA, since they are not taxed currently.[108] Once retirement payments are received, such payments are ordinary income and are not subject to the 10-year averaging allowed for lump-sum distributions. However, a taxpayer can use regular income averaging under § 1301. The value of undistributed proceeds (up to $100,000) of an IRA account is excluded from the gross estate of the participant if the proceeds are payable as an annuity to a beneficiary (other than the estate).[109] Payments made to a participant before he reaches the age 59½ are subject to a nondeductible 10 percent penalty tax on such actual, or constructive, payments.[110]

---

105.   § 4973(a)(1).
106.   § 4973(b).
107.   § § 408(d)(4) and 4973(b)(2).
108.   § 408(d)(1).
109.   § 2039(e).
110.   § 408(f).

NONQUALIFIED
DEFERRED COMPENSATION PLANS

UNDERLYING RATIONALE FOR TAX TREATMENT

Nonqualified deferred compensation (NQDC) plans may be appropriate in certain situations as a compensation tool. Nonqualified plans are frequently used to provide incentives or supplemental retirement benefits for key executives.

The doctrine of constructive receipt is an important concept relating to the taxability of nonqualified deferred compensation.[111] In essence, if a taxpayer irrevocably earns income but may elect to receive it now or at a later date, the income is constructively received and the income is immediately taxed. Income is not constructively received, however, if the taxpayer's control over the amounts earned is subject to substantial limitations or restrictions.

Still another concept is the economic benefit theory. Although a taxpayer does not have a present right to income, the income will be taxable if there exists a right in the form of a negotiable promissory note. Notes and other evidences of indebtedness received in payment for services constitute income to the extent of their fair market value at the time of the transfer.[112]

In Revenue Ruling 60–31,[113] the IRS provided that the constructive receipt doctrine would not cause taxation to employees participating in nonqualified deferred compensation plans as long as certain guidelines were satisfied. On February 3, 1978, the IRS issued Proposed Reg. § 1.61–16. This Regulation states that any compensation deferred at the election of an employee to a tax year later than the year in which it could have been received is taxable in the earlier year. These new Regulations represented a substantial reversal of a long-standing position as outlined in Revenue Ruling 60–31. In the Revenue Act of 1978, Congress indicated that the taxation of any deferred compensation arrangements is to be determined in accordance with Treasury pronouncements made prior to the February 1978 proposed regulations. In essence, the February 3, 1978, Regulations are to be ignored, and Revenue Ruling 60–31 remains the official position of the IRS.

> **Example 30.** R Corporation and B, a cash basis employee, enter into an employment agreement which provides an annual salary of $120,000 to B. Of this amount, $100,000 is to be paid in current monthly installments and $20,000 is to be paid in 10 annual installments beginning at B's retirement or death. A separate account for B is maintained by the corporation. Under § 451(a) and

---

111.   Reg. § 1.451–2.
112.   Reg. § 1.61–2(d)(4).
113.   1960–1 C.B. 174.

Reg. § 1.451–2(a) the $20,000 would not be considered constructively received and would be deferred. Compensation of $100,000 would be currently taxable to B and deductible to R Corporation. The other $20,000 would be taxable and deductible when paid in future years.

TAX TREATMENT TO THE EMPLOYER AND EMPLOYEE

The tax treatment of an NQDC plan depends on whether it is funded or nonfunded and whether it is forfeitable or nonforfeitable. In an unfunded NQDC plan, the employee relies upon the company's mere promise to make the compensation payment in the future. An unfunded, unsecured promise to pay, not represented by a negotiable note, is effective to defer the recognition of income.[114] Thus, the employee is taxed later when the compensation is actually paid or made available.[115] Similarly, the employer is allowed a deduction when the employee recognizes income.

An escrow account can be set up by the employer to accumulate deferred payments on behalf of the employee. These funds may be invested by the escrow agent for the benefit of the employee.[116] By avoiding income recognition until the employee receives the benefits from the escrow custodial account, there is a postponement of tax to the employee. It is usually desirable not to transfer securities to the escrow agent, because the IRS might attempt to treat such transfers as property transferred in connection with the performance of services under § 83. Such a treatment would force the transaction to have a substantial risk of forfeiture and nontransferability (or else the compensation income would be taxable immediately).[117] An escrow arrangement can be well suited for a professional athlete or entertainer whose income is earned in a few peak years.

> **Example 31.** H, a professional athlete, receives a bonus for signing an employment contract. An NQDC plan is established to defer the income beyond his peak income years. The bonus is transferred to an escrow agent who invests the funds in securities, etc., which may act as a hedge against inflation. The bonus is deferred for 10 years and becomes payable gradually from years 11 through 15. The bonus is taxable when H begins to receive the payments.

It is also possible to provide for NQDC through an internally funded revocable trust or through an externally funded nonexempt

---

114. Rev.Rul. 60–31, 1960–1 C.B. 174.

115. Reg. § 1.451–2(a); *U. S. v. Basye,* 73–1 USTC ¶ 9250, 31 AFTR2d 73–802, 93 S.Ct. 1080 (USSC, 1973).

116. Rev.Rul. 55–525, 1955–2 C.B. 543.

117. Reg. § 1.83–1(a).

trust.[118] The detailed requirements relative to such arrangements are beyond the scope of this book. Generally, however, funded nonqualified deferred compensation plans must be forfeitable in order to keep the compensation payments from being taxable immediately. In most instances, employees prefer to have some assurance that they will ultimately receive benefits from the nonqualified deferred compensation (i. e., that the plan provides for nonforfeitable benefits). In such instances, the plan will have to be unfunded to prevent immediate taxation to the employee. Notice that most funded NQDC plans are subject to many of the provisions which apply to qualified plans.

When to Use an NQDC Arrangement. As a general rule, nonqualified deferred compensation (NQDC) plans are more appropriate for executives in a financially secure company. Due to the need for currently disposable income, such plans are usually not appropriate for young employees.

An NQDC plan can reduce an employee's overall tax payments by deferring the taxation of income to later years (possibly when the employee is in a lower tax bracket). In effect, these plans may produce a form of income averaging. Further, NQDC plans may discriminate in favor of shareholders, officers, specific highly compensated key employees, or a single individual.

Certain disadvantages should be noted. Nonqualified plans are usually required to be unfunded, which means that an employee is not assured that funds ultimately will be available to pay the benefits. Also, the employer's tax deduction is postponed until the employee is taxed on such amounts.

RESTRICTED PROPERTY PLANS

GENERAL PROVISIONS

A restricted property plan is an arrangement whereby an employer transfers property (i. e., stock of the employer corporation) to a provider of services at no cost or at a bargain price. Section 83 was enacted in 1969 to provide rules for the taxation of such arrangements which previously were governed by judicial and administrative interpretations. Although the following discussion refers to an employee as the provider of the services, there is no requirement that the services be performed by an employee (i. e., § 83 also is applicable to independent contractors).

As a general rule, if an employee performs services and receives property (e. g., stock), the fair market value of such stock in excess of any amount paid by the employee is includible in gross income of the employee at the earlier of (1) the time the stock is no longer subject to

---

118. See Rev.Rul. 67–289, 1967–2 C.B. 163; Reg. § 1.83–1(a).

a substantial risk of forfeiture or (2) the moment the employee has the right to transfer the property free of the substantial risk of forfeiture. The fair market value of the stock is determined without regard to any restriction, except a restriction which by its terms will never lapse.[119] Since the amount of the compensation is determined at the date that the restrictions lapse or when the property is transferable, the opportunity to generate capital gains on the stock is denied during a period when the ordinary income element is being deferred.

> **Example 32.** On October 1, 19X5, W Corporation sells to J, an employee, 100 shares of W Corporation stock for $10 per share. At the time of the sale, the fair market value of the stock was $100 per share. Under the terms of the sale, each share of stock is nontransferable and subject to a substantial risk of forfeiture (which will not lapse until October 1, 19X9). Evidence of these restrictions is stamped on the face of the stock certificates. On October 1, 19X9, the fair market value of the stock is $250 per share. Since the stock is nontransferable and is subject to a substantial risk of forfeiture, J does not include any compensation in gross income during 19X5 (assuming no special election is made). Instead, during 19X9 J must include $24,000 of compensation in gross income [100 shares × ($250 less $10 per share)]. If for some reason the substantial risk of forfeiture occurs (e. g., the plan requires J to surrender the stock to the corporation if he voluntarily terminates his employment with the company prior to 19X9) and J never gets the stock certificates, he would be allowed a capital loss of $1,000 (the extent of his investment).

SUBSTANTIAL RISK OF FORFEITURE

Under § 83(c) a substantial risk of forfeiture exists if a "person's rights to full enjoyment of such property are conditioned upon the future performance, or the refraining from the performance, of substantial services by an individual." Regulation § 1.83–3(c)(2) includes several examples of restricted property arrangements. For example, if an employee must return the stock (receiving only his original cost, if any) should there be a failure to complete a substantial period of service (for any reason), the property is subject to a substantial risk of forfeiture. Another situation exists in which an employer can compel an employee to return the stock due to a breach of a substantial covenant not to compete. Any substantial risk of forfeiture should be stated on the face of the stock certificates. Assuming that there does not exist a substantial risk of forfeiture, the stock received is valued at its fair market value, ignoring any restrictions, except for one instance dealing with closely held stock.

---

119.   § 83(a)(1); *Miriam Sakol,* 67 T.C. 986 (1977); *T. M. Horwith,* 71 T.C. 932 (1979).

Example 33. On September 1, 19X1, the K Corporation transfers to H 1,000 shares of K Corporation stock at $9.00 per share. Under the terms of the transfer, H is subject to a binding commitment to resell the stock to K Corporation at $9.00 per share if she leaves the employment of K Corporation for any reason prior to the expiration of a 10-year period from the date of such transfer. Since the employee must perform substantial services to K Corporation, H's rights in the stock are subject to a substantial risk of forfeiture.[120]

Special Election Available. An employee may elect within 30 days after the receipt of restricted property to recognize immediately as ordinary income the fair market value in excess of the amount paid for the property. Thus, any appreciation in the value of the property after receipt is taxed as capital gain instead of ordinary income. But no deduction is allowed to the employee for taxes paid on the original amount included in income if the property is subsequently forfeited.[121] Furthermore, the employer must repay taxes saved by any compensation deduction taken in the earlier year.[122] The employee may take a capital loss for any amounts which were actually paid for the stock.[123]

Any increase in value between the time the property is received and the time it becomes either nonforfeitable or transferable is taxed as ordinary income (if no special election is made by the executive). However, if the executive elects to be taxed immediately on the difference between the cost and fair market value on the date of issue, any future appreciation is treated as capital gain. In determining whether the gain is long-term or short-term, § 83(b)(1)(B) indicates that § 83(a) does *not* apply. Thus the holding period for determining whether a gain is long- or short-term starts when the employee is taxed on the ordinary income.[124]

Example 34. On July 1, 1972, F Company sold 100 shares of its preferred stock, worth $15 per share, to D (an employee) for $5 per share. The sale is subject to D's agreement to resell the preferred shares to the company for $5 per share if he terminates employment in the following 10 years. Assume that the stock has a value of $25 per share on July 1, 1984, and D sells the stock for $30 per share on October 10, 1984. D makes the special election to include the original spread, between the value in 1972 of $15 and the amount paid of $5, in income for 1972. D must recognize $1,000 of compensation income in 1972 ($15.00 − $5.00 = $10

---

120.   Reg. § 1.83–3(c)(3), Ex. 3.
121.   § 83(b)(1)(B).
122.   Reg. § 1.83–6(c).
123.   Reg. § 1.83–2(a).
124.   § 1223(6).

× 100 shares), at which time his holding period in his stock begins. D's tax basis in the stock is $1,500 ($1,000 + $500). When the preferred stock is sold in 1984, D will recognize a $1,500 long-term capital gain ($30 × 100 shares − $1,500).

This special provision is usually not elected, since it results in an immediate recognition of income and adverse tax consequences result from a subsequent forfeiture. However, the special election may be attractive in the following situations:

—The bargain element is relatively small.

—Substantial appreciation is expected in the future.

—There is a high probability that the restrictions will be met.

EMPLOYER DEDUCTIONS

The employer is allowed a tax deduction for the same amount, and at the same time, the employee is required to include the compensation in income. The employer must withhold on this amount in accordance with § 3402. In the no-election situation, this deduction is limited to the fair market value of the restricted property (without regard to the restrictions) at the time the restrictions lapse, reduced by the amount originally paid for the stock by the employee.[125] When the employee elects to be taxed immediately, the corporate deduction also is accelerated and deductible in like amount. In those cases of deferred income recognition, employers can receive a very sizable deduction if the property has appreciated.

> **Example 35.** On March 14, 19X1, F Corporation sells to G, an employee, 10 shares of F common stock for $100 per share. The employer corporation and the employee are calendar year taxpayers. The common stock is subject to a substantial risk of forfeiture and is nontransferable; both conditions lapse on March 14, 19X3. At the time of the sale, the fair market value of the common stock (without considering the restrictions) is $1,000 per share. On March 14, 19X3, the restrictions lapse when the fair market value of the stock is $2,000 per share. No special election is made by the employee. In 19X3 G realizes ordinary income of $19,000 (10 shares at $2,000 per share less the $100 per share paid by G). Likewise, F Corporation is allowed a $19,000 compensation deduction in 19X3.

> **Example 36.** In the previous example, assume that the employee makes the election under § 83(b). Since the employee is taxed on $9,000 in 19X1, the corporation is allowed to deduct a like amount in 19X1. No deduction is available in 19X3.

---

125. Reg. § 1.83–6(a).

STOCK OPTIONS

IN GENERAL

There are various equity types of stock option programs available for an employer's compensation package. Some authorities believe that there is a need for some form of "equity kicker" in order to attract new management, to convert key officers into "partners" by giving them a share of the business, and to retain services of executives who might otherwise leave.[126] An "option" gives an individual the right to purchase a stated number of shares of stock from a corporation at a certain price within a specified period of time. The optionee must be under no obligation to purchase the stock, and the option may be revocable by the corporation. The option must be in writing, and its terms must be clearly expressed.[127]

INCENTIVE STOCK OPTIONS

A new equity type of stock option called "incentive stock options" is available for options granted after 1975 and exercised after 1980. Created by the Economic Recovery Tax Act of 1981, these options are designed to replace and improve upon the restricted and qualified stock option provisions[128] that previously existed. The Congressional motivation underlying the reinstitution of a stock option program is to furnish an important incentive device for corporations to attract new management and to retain the services of those already employed. Encouraging the management of a business to have a proprietary interest in its successful operation should provide a key motive to expand and improve the profit position of the companies involved.

An incentive stock option arrangement follows much the same tax treatment previously accorded to restricted and qualified stock option plans. There are no tax consequences when the option is granted, but the "spread" is a tax preference item for purposes of the alternative minimum tax. The spread is the excess of fair market value of the share at the date of exercise over the option price.[129] After the option is exercised and when the stock is sold, any gain therefrom is taxed at long-term capital gain rates if certain holding period requirements are met. To qualify for long-term capital gain treatment, the employee must not dispose of the stock within two years after the option is granted or within one year after acquiring the stock.[130] If the

126. See S.Rep.No.2375, 81st Congress, 2nd Sess., p. 59 (1950).
127. Reg. §§ 1.421–1(a)(1) and –7(a)(1).
128. Qualified stock options were available under § 422 for certain qualified options granted before May 21, 1976. These qualified stock options had many of the statutory requirements of ISOs, but ISOs have a more favorable tax treatment.
129. §§ 422A(a), 421(a)(1) and 57(a)(10).
130. § 422A(a)(1).

employee meets the holding period requirements, none of these transactions generate any business deduction for the employer.[131]

> **Example 37.** E Corporation granted an incentive stock option for 100 shares of its stock to R, an employee, on March 18, 1982. The option price was $100 and the fair market value was $100 on the date of grant. R exercised the option on April 1, 1983, when the market value of the stock was $200 per share. He sold the stock on April 6, 1984, for $300 per share. No ordinary income is recognized by R on the date of the grant or the exercise date, since the option is qualified under § 422A. E corporation received no compensation deduction. R has a $1,000 tax preference item on the exercise date. R has a long-term capital gain upon the sale of the stock in 1984 of $20,000 [($300 − $100) × 100], since the one-year and two-year holding periods and other requirements have been met.

As a further requirement for incentive stock option treatment, the option holder must be an employee of the issuing corporation from the date the option is granted until three months (12 months if disabled) before the date of exercise. Exceptions are made for parent and subsidiary situations, corporate reorganization, and liquidations. The holding period and the employee-status rules described above (i. e., the one-year, two-year, and three-month requirements) are waived in the case of the death of an employee.[132] Also, in certain situations involving an insolvent employee, the holding period rules are modified.[133]

> **Example 38.** Assume the same facts as in the previous example except that R is not employed by E Corporation for six months before the date he exercises the options. R must recognize ordinary income to the extent of the spread, assuming there is no substantial risk of forfeiture. Thus, R would recognize $10,000 [($200 − $100) × 100] of ordinary income on the exercise date, since R was not an employee of E Corporation on the exercise date.

If the holding period requirements are not satisfied but all other conditions are met, the tax is still deferred to the point of the sale. However, the difference between the option price and the value of the stock at the date the option was exercised will be treated as ordinary income. The difference between the amount realized for the stock and the value of the stock at the date of exercise will be short-term or long-term capital gain, depending on the holding period of the stock itself. The employer will be allowed a deduction equal to the amount recognized by the employee as ordinary income.

---

131. § 421(a)(2).
132. § § 422A(a)(2) and 422A(c)(9).
133. § 422A(c)(3).

Example 39. Assume the same facts as in Example 37 except that R sold the stock on March 22, 1984, for $290 per share. Since R did not hold the stock itself for at least one year, $10,000 of the gain is treated as ordinary income in 1984 and E Corporation is allowed a $10,000 compensation deduction in 1984. The remaining $9,000 is a short-term capital gain ($29,000 − $20,000).

Qualification Requirements for Incentive Stock Option Plans. Under § 422A(b), the term "incentive stock option" means an option granted to an individual, for any reason connected with his or her employment, by the employer corporation or by a parent or subsidiary corporation of the employer corporation, to purchase stock of any such corporations. An employee can use company stock to pay for the stock when exercising an option without disqualifying the incentive stock option plan.

For an option to qualify as an incentive stock option, the terms of the option itself must meet the following conditions:[134]

—The option must be granted under a plan specifying the number of shares of stock to be issued and the employees or class of employees eligible to receive the options. The plan must be approved by the shareholders of the corporation within 12 months before or after the plan is adopted.

—The option must be granted within 10 years of the date the plan is adopted or of the date the plan is approved by the shareholders, whichever date is earlier.

—The option must by its terms be exercisable only within 10 years of the date it is granted.

—The option price must equal or exceed the fair market value of the stock at the time the option is granted. This requirement is deemed satisfied if there has been a good faith attempt to value the stock accurately, even if the option price is less than the stock value.

—The option by its terms must be nontransferable other than at death and must be exercisable during the employee's lifetime only by the employee.

—The employee must not, immediately before the option is granted, own stock representing more than 10 percent of the voting power or value of all classes of stock in the employer corporation or its parent or subsidiary. (Here, the attribution rules of § 267 are applied in modified form.) However, the stock ownership limitation will be waived if the option price is at least 110 percent of the fair market value (at the time the option is granted) of the stock subject to the option and the option

---

134. § 422A(b).

by its terms is not exercisable more than five years from the date it is granted.[135]

—The option by its terms is not to be exercisable while there is outstanding any incentive stock option which was granted to the employee at an earlier time. Thus, the periods during which an option may be exercised should be kept reasonably short. If the stock declines in value, a second option at a lower price may be issued and the employee will not have to wait so long to exercise the second option.

An overall limitation is imposed on the amount of incentive stock options (ISOs) which can be issued. This limit is set at $100,000 per year (based on the value of the stock) per employee. Employees, however, can carry forward one-half of the unused value for as long as three years.[136] Further, a company can issue the maximum incentive stock options for an executive and provide the same executive with a nonqualified stock option plan.

> **Example 40.** T is granted ISOs of $40,000 in 1982 and $50,000 in 1983 by X, Inc. During 1984 T can be optioned $100,000 of ISOs plus one-half the amount by which $100,000 exceeds the aggregate value of the stock shares made available in prior years. Thus, in 1984, X, Inc., can option to T $155,000 of ISOs. This amount is composed of $100,000 for 1984 plus unused carryovers of $30,000 from 1982 [½($100,000 − $40,000)] and $25,000 from 1983 [½($100,000 − $50,000)].

NONQUALIFIED STOCK OPTIONS

The IRS has prescribed rules for the treatment of nonqualified stock options.[137] If the nonqualified stock option has a readily ascertainable fair market value (e. g., the option is traded on an established exchange) the value of the option must be included in the employee's income at the date of grant.[138] Thereafter, capital gain or loss is recognized only upon the disposal of the optioned stock.

> **Example 41.** On February 1, 19X1, J is granted a nonqualified stock option to purchase 100 shares of stock from the employer at $10 per share. On this date the option is selling for $2 on an established exchange. J exercised the option on March 30, 19X2, when the stock was worth $20 per share. On June 5, 19X2, J sold the optioned stock for $22 per share.

---

135. § 422A(c)(8).
136. § 422A(c)(4).
137. Reg. § § 1.421–6(c), (d) and (e); Reg. § 1.83–7.
138. Reg. § 1.421–6(c)(1); Reg. § 1.83–7(a).

—J must report ordinary income of $200 ($2 × 100 shares) on the date of grant (February 1, 19X1), since the option has a readily ascertainable market value.

—Upon the sale of the stock, J reports a long-term capital gain of $1,000 [($22 − $12) × 100 shares].

—The employer receives a tax deduction at the date of grant (February 1, 19X1) equal to $200, which is the amount of income reported by J.

If a nonqualified stock option does not have a readily ascertainable fair market value, an employee does not recognize taxable income at the grant date. However, as a general rule, ordinary income must be reported in the year of exercise (i. e., the difference between the fair market value of the stock at the exercise date and option price).[139] The amount paid by the executive for the stock plus the amount reported as ordinary income becomes the basis. Any appreciation above such basis is taxed as a long-term capital gain upon disposition (assuming the stock is held more than the required long-term holding period after exercise).

The corporation receives a corresponding tax deduction at the same time and to the extent that income is recognized by the employee.[140]

Example 42. On February 3, 19X1, S is granted a nonqualified stock option for 100 shares of common stock at $10 per share. On the date of the grant there was no readily ascertainable fair market value for the option. S exercises the options on January 3, 19X2, when the stock was selling for $15 per share. S sells one-half of the shares on April 15, 19X2, and the other half on September 17, 19X3. The sale price on both dates was $21 per share. S would recognize no income on the grant date (February 3, 19X1) but would recognize $500 (i. e., $1,500 − $1,000) of ordinary income on the exercise date (January 3, 19X2). S would recognize a short-term capital gain of $300 on the sale of the first half and a $300 long-term capital gain on the sale of the second batch of stock (½ × $2,100 − $1,500).

The major advantages of nonqualified stock options are summarized below:

—A tax deduction is available to the corporation, without a cash outlay.

—The executive receives capital gain treatment on any appreciation in the stock starting either at the exercise date or at the date of grant if the option has a readily ascertainable fair market value.

---

139. Reg. § 1.83–7(a); Reg. § 1.421–6(d).
140. Reg. § 1.421–6(f).

—Options can be issued at more flexible terms than under incentive stock option plans (e. g., longer exercise period and discount on exercise price).

A major disadvantage is that the executive must recognize ordinary taxable income on exercise of the option or at the date of grant if the option has a readily ascertainable market value, without receiving cash to pay the tax.

QUALIFIED PLANS

Qualified plans provide maximum tax benefits for employers, since the company receives an immediate tax deduction for contributions to such plans and the income which is earned on the contributions is not taxable to the employer. The employer contributions and the trust earnings are not taxed to the employees until such amounts are made available to them.

Qualified plans are most appropriate where it is desirable to provide benefits for a cross section of employees. In some closely-held corporations, the primary objective is to provide benefits for the officer-shareholder group and other highly paid personnel. The nondiscrimination requirements which must be met in a qualified plan may prevent such companies from attaining these objectives. Thus, a non-qualified arrangement may be needed as a supplement to, or used in lieu of, the qualified plan.

Many personal service businesses were incorporated in the past to take advantage of the larger retirement plan deductions. With the reduction in corporate pension plan benefits and the equalization of self-employed plans with corporate plans, many personal service corporations may wish to liquidate. In fact, the Tax Equity and Fiscal Responsibility Act provides a transitional rule for 1983 and 1984 which allows a personal service corporation to liquidate under § 333 (one-month liquidation) without incurring a tax on its unrealized receivables.[141]

TAX-DEFERRED ANNUITIES

Tax-exempt and public educational employers may purchase annuity contracts for their employees without current income tax treatment to the employees. Only employees and not independent contractors are eligible for this tax shelter. See the discussion under "Qualified Em-

---

141. Non-Code provision, Act Section 247.

ployees." However, a tax-deferred annuity (TDA) plan may discriminate in favor of one or more employees. Unlike qualified pension and profit sharing plans, TDA plans may be limited to certain key personnel.

> **Example 13.** A local hospital has two radiologists whom it desperately wants to keep. The hospital cannot afford a tax-deferred annuity for all employees. A TDA plan is established on a purely contributory basis with only the two radiologists as participants. As long as the two doctors are employees (and not independent contractors), the hospital is able to keep the two key employees happy.

Eventual distributions from a TDA are taxed under the annuity rule in § 72. Partial capital gain treatment under a lump-sum distribution and the 10-year averaging method do not apply to TDAs. However, there is no penalty for premature withdrawals from TDAs such as is the case for certain top-heavy pension plans, Keogh plans, or IRAs. Distributions before retirement are merely taxed as ordinary income,[142] and there is no penalty or disqualification from further participation.

Unlike an H.R. 10 or IRA plan, the doctrine of constructive receipt stops a year-end adoption of a TDA and funding with amounts already earned. However, the cumulative nature of the exclusion allowance formula may produce a large exclusion amount for an employee with past services or a large pay raise.

SELF-EMPLOYED RETIREMENT PLANS

If a self-employed individual is considering the incorporation of a business or professional practice, self-employed retirement plans should be reexamined in the light of the changes in the Tax Equity and Fiscal Responsibility Act. The new law has eliminated the large corporate retirement plan deductions and placed H.R. 10 plans on equal footing. In fact, any personal corporation that was formed primarily for tax reasons may wish to liquidate.

A few minor fringe benefits are available to a corporate employee that are not available to a noncorporate employee, such as a medical reimbursement plan. Also, some tax deferral can be attained by incorporating and electing a fiscal year. Further, a loan from an H.R. 10 plan to an owner-employee may be a prohibited transaction.

Certain top-heavy corporate and H.R. 10 plans (and IRAs) provide significant penalties for making excess contributions. Also, the contributions to a top-heavy corporate plan or an H.R. 10 (or IRA) plan are effectively locked in, since the tax law imposes a 10 percent nondeductible penalty on funds that are withdrawn prior to reaching age 59½.

---

142. § 72(e)(1); Reg. § 1.72–11(d).

A Keogh or IRA participant may make a deductible contribution for a tax year up to the time prescribed for filing the individual's tax return, including any extensions of time. However, a Keogh plan must have been established by December 31 in order to obtain a deductible contribution in the subsequent year. An individual can establish an IRA after the end of the tax year and still receive a deductible contribution.

INDIVIDUAL RETIREMENT ACCOUNTS

Even an employee who is an active participant in an employer-sponsored qualified plan or government plan may contribute to an IRA after 1981. Further, Keogh and IRA plans are no longer mutually exclusive.

> **Example 44.** In 1984, B earns a total of $13,000 from director's fees. B may contribute $3,250 to a Keogh plan and $2,000 to an IRA (or $2,250 to a spousal plan). This result is true even if B is an active participant in a corporate retirement plan.

A married person can put $4,000 into an IRA when one spouse works for the other spouse. This requires paying the "employee" spouse $2,000 in salary and have him or her make an independent contribution to an IRA. This extra $2,000 is not subject to FICA or FUTA and does not qualify for Schedule W (i. e., two-earner married couples deduction) purposes. Congress may change the $2,000 IRA limit to $4,000 in 1984.

Distributions from a simplified employee pension (SEP) plan and IRA qualify for exclusion from the estate and gift tax up to an aggregate limit of $100,000 (after 1982). However, SEP and IRA distributions are not eligible for capital gain treatment or the 10-year forward averaging rule available for lump-sum distributions. The regular five-year income averaging rules are available for distributions. Further, under an IRA, distributions must begin by the year in which the participant reaches age 70½ or a 50 percent penalty is applicable. However, deductible SEP contributions are exempt from this rule.

A tax-free rollover for distributions from qualified plans (as well as from another IRA) is an alternative to taxation of a lump-sum distribution or termination distribution.[143] A partial rollover from an IRA after 1982 is also subject to tax-free treatment. A distribution is not included in gross income if transferred within 60 days of distribution to an IRA or another qualified plan. Further, any rollover amount in an IRA can later be rolled over into another qualified plan if the IRA consists of only the amounts from the original qualified plan.[144] Remember that distributions from an IRA are not eligible for lump-sum distribution treatment.

---

143.   § § 402(a)(5) and 408(d)(3).
144.   § 408(d)(3)(ii).

Example 45. Teacher P is a participant in a tax-deferred annuity (TDA), but he quits his job. In order to avoid taxation of the distribution while he is looking for a new job, he rolls over the distribution into an IRA. He makes no other contributions to the IRA. After P finds another teaching position, the assets in the IRA may be rolled over to another TDA.

IRA and Keogh participants may self-direct their investments into a wide variety of assets. The participant self-directs the investments into various assets even though the assets are under the control of a trustee or custodian. For tax years after 1981, the acquisition by an IRA or self-directed Keogh or corporate plan of collectibles (e. g., art, gems, metals) is treated as a distribution (i. e., taxed). For an IRA or Keogh participant under age 59½, there would also be a 10 percent premature distribution penalty.

If an employee makes a voluntary contribution to an employer retirement plan, the employee must notify the employer in writing that the employee does not wish the voluntary contribution to be deductible. Otherwise, the law automatically assumes that the contribution is deductible and the employee will not be able to contribute to an IRA.

NONQUALIFIED DEFERRED COMPENSATION (NQDC) PLANS

Nonqualified deferred compensation arrangements such as restricted property plans may be useful to attract executive talent or to provide substantial retirement benefits for executives. A restricted property plan may be used to retain a key employee of a closely-held company when management continuity problems are anticipated. Such plans may discriminate in favor of officers and other highly paid employees. The employer, however, does not receive a tax deduction until the employee is required to include the deferred compensation in income (upon the lapse of the restrictions).

In the case of a closely-held corporation, NQDC plans could be useful to retain the services of key employees. Without such employees, the untimely death or disability of one of the owners might cause a disruption of the business with an attendant loss in value for his or her heirs.

Example 46. D is the sole shareholder of X Corporation, a profitable company. The success of X Corporation is attributable largely to the efforts of D and, lately, E (a key employee). S, D's son, participates in the business, but due to a lack of experience, D feels that it will be several years before S can assume a major role in the management of X Corporation. To protect against the consequences of D's premature death or disability and to retain the services of E, X Corporation issues restricted stock to E. Under the terms of the restriction, E will forfeit the stock if he terminates employment (except by death or disability) within the next five years. Because the restriction represents a substantial risk of forfeiture, E has no income tax consequences from the transaction until the five-year period has run and the conditions imposed have been satisfied. In the meantime, E will be hesitant about terminating his employment with X Corporation.

The principal advantage of a nonqualified deferred compensation plan is that the employee may defer the recognition of taxable income to future periods when his or her income tax bracket may be lower (e. g., during retirement years). The time value benefits from the deferral of income should also be considered.

The principal disadvantage of NQDC plans could be the bunching effect that takes place on the expiration of the period of deferral. In some cases, planning can alleviate this result.

Example 47. Assume the same facts as in the previous example but with the following modification: the restrictions on the stock issued to E lapse over a period of three years. Thus, one-third of the stock in X Corporation becomes unrestricted after the fifth year, one-third after the sixth year, and one-third after the seventh year. Presuming E did not make the § 83(b) election (i. e., to recognize income when the stock was issued), this modification spreads E's recognition of income over three tax years and avoids the bunching effect of having all of the stock become unrestricted in one year.

STOCK OPTIONS

Nonqualified stock option plans have assumed increasing importance due to tax changes in 1976 which eliminated the qualified stock option. Stock option plans are used more frequently by publicly traded companies than by closely-held private companies. This difference is due to the problems of determining the stock value of a company which is not publicly held.

In a publicly traded company (where the warrant has a readily ascertainable fair market value), the value of the warrant is included in the employee's income at the date of grant. If the stock increases in value, the employee receives favorable capital gain treatment if the stock is later disposed of (subsequent to exercise). This treatment may be contrasted with the situation where the option does not have a readily ascertainable fair market value. In such case, the employee is taxed at ordinary income rates upon the value of the option at the exercise date rather than at the date of grant.

Nonqualified stock options are more flexible and less restrictive than incentive stock options. For example, the holding period for a nonqualified stock option is not as long as an incentive stock option. Further, the option price of a nonqualified stock option may be less than the fair market value of the stock at the time the option is granted. Where a company has issued the maximum incentive stock options for an employee, the company can provide the same employee with nonqualified stock options.

FLEXIBLE BENEFIT PLANS

Employees may be permitted to choose from a package of employer-provided fringe benefits.[145] In these so-called cafeteria benefit plans, some of the benefits chosen by an employee may be taxable and some may be nontaxable (e. g., health and accident insurance, disability benefits, and group-term life insurance). Before 1979, the tax treatment of these cafeteria plans was uncertain.

After 1978, employer contributions made to a flexible plan are included in an employee's gross income only to the extent that the employee actually elects the taxable benefits. Certain nondiscrimination standards with respect to coverage, eligibility for participation, contributions, and benefits must be met. Thus, such a plan must cover a fair cross section of employees. Also, a flexible plan cannot include an election to defer compensation.

VOLUNTARY EMPLOYEE BENEFIT ASSOCIATION TRUST (VEBA)

A company can make currently deductible cash contributions to cover future liabilities by establishing a separate benefit trust called a VEBA.[146] A VEBA is a tax-exempt employee benefit trust formed to provide life and accident benefits to its members and their families. However, VEBAs cannot be used for any type of deferred compensation plan (e. g., pension plan).

The major advantages of a VEBA are as follows:

—The employer is allowed a current deduction.

—The investment income inside the trust is tax-exempt.

—Benefits are not taxable to the employees until paid to them.

—Some benefits may be tax-exempt under other provisions when paid to the employees.

—Benefits may be paid to an employee's dependent.

—A specified group of employees may be covered by the trust.

—Once the VEBA is dissolved, the assets can be used by the members.

Benefits of a VEBA may include the following:

—Death benefits.

---

145. § 125 added by § 134 of the Revenue Act of 1978.
146. § 501(c)(9).

—Temporary or long-term disability benefits.

—Hospital, medical, dental, and surgical benefits.

—Vacation benefits.

—Recreational and vacation facilities.

—Child-care facilities.

—Personal legal services.

—Training or educational courses.

The following benefits are not allowable:

—Loans to members.

—Pension or profit sharing benefits.

—Malpractice insurance.

—Commuting expenses.

—Statutory workers' compensation benefits.

—Employee savings plan.

—Homeowner's insurance.

PROBLEM MATERIALS

Questions for Class Discussion

1. Compare and contrast defined contribution and defined benefit pension plans.

2. Compare and contrast qualified pension and profit sharing plans.

3. List the additional qualification requirements for top-heavy retirement plans.

4. Define "key employee" for purposes of a top-heavy plan.

5. What are the tax and financial advantages accruing to a company which adopts an Employee Stock Ownership Plan (ESOP) for employees?

6. When must distributions start for a key employee of a top-heavy retirement plan?

7. Is it possible to provide greater vested benefits for highly paid employees and still meet the nondiscrimination requirements under a qualified pension plan? Explain.

8. If a plan does not meet the mathematical 70 percent and 80 percent coverage tests, is the plan automatically unable to qualify under the law?

9. What is vesting and how will these requirements help employees who do not remain with one employer during their working years?

10. What is the three-year rule and how does this provision affect the taxation of pension payments to employees? Would this rule apply to noncontributory pension or profit sharing plans?

11. How are lump-sum distributions from qualified plans taxed to the recipients (i. e., capital gain versus ordinary income)? Is income averaging available to an employee who receives a lump-sum distribution?

12. What ceiling limitations have been placed on employer contributions (relative to individual employees) to defined contribution and defined benefit plans?

13. Explain the advantages of a tax-deferred annuity under § 403(b).

14. Discuss the difference between a "credit carryover" and a "contribution carryover" with respect to a profit sharing plan. Can both of these occur in one year?

15. T Corporation is planning to establish a profit sharing plan that will cover all 90 employees. Under the plan, the interest of the participants will vest at the rate of 5% per year. Would the IRS approve this plan? Discuss.

16. Discuss the differences between a Keogh plan and an Individual Retirement Account (IRA).

17. What is meant by a salary reduction TDA?

18. Compare the tax advantages which are available to corporate employees covered under a qualified plan with self-employed retirement plan benefits.

19. Discuss the dilemma of an employee with respect to a nonqualified deferred compensation (NQDC) plan and the following items: funded and nonfunded, forfeitable and nonforfeitable.

20. Explain the differences in tax treatment of an employer and employee (or other provider of services) with respect to the general rule (i. e., no election) and the special election under § 83(b) when dealing with a restricted property plan. Explain the risk aspect of this tax provision.

21. What is a "substantial risk of forfeiture"? Why is it necessary to impose this restriction on the transfer of restricted property?

22. Explain what is meant by a "cafeteria benefit plan."

23. Discuss the advantages of a nonqualified stock option plan versus an incentive stock option plan.

24. Would a 30-year-old executive of T Corporation earning $100,000 prefer an extra $20,000 bonus *or* the option to purchase $20,000 worth of securities for $5,000 from the employer under a nonqualified stock option plan?

25. What factors should the employer and employee consider in determining whether the employee should receive capital gain compensation or ordinary income compensation? Be sure to relate to the timing of income.

26. A calendar year employee realizes compensation income under § 83(a) on January 4, 19X1. His employer is on a fiscal year ending September 30. When does the employee recognize the income, and when does the employer take the related deduction?

27. Compare and contrast an IRA and a § 401(k) plan.

Problems

28. L Company's pension plan provides that any full-time employee is eligible to participate if he or she has at least one year's service and is at least 25

years of age. R, the personnel director, provides you with the following information:

Eligible employees	1350
Ineligible employees because of age	300
Ineligible employees because of length of service	175
Employees with less than 1000 hours	175
Ineligible employees because of salary level	200

(a) Calculate the minimum coverage test for this corporation. § 410(b)(1).

(b) Is there any hope for this company if the minimum coverage test is failed?

29. R is discharged when he is 42 years old and has nine years of service. Determine R's vested portion of his interest in a qualified pension plan under these three alternatives: (a) 10-year rule, (b) 5-to-15 year rule, and (c) Rule of 45. Assume the employer established the rules so as to pay as little as possible.

30. Assume the same facts as in 29 except that R is 32 years old and has 10 years of service with his employer.

31. M is to receive $300 per month from the employer's qualified pension plan for the remainder of her life on retirement. M contributed $10,000 to the plan. When M retires on January 1, her expected return multiple is 17.0. Compute the amount of income taxable to M for each of the first three years and thereafter.

32. In Problem 31, assume the pension trust will pay her only $80 per month. What amount, if any, is taxable each year to M?

33. Q Company's pension plan provides that each employee's rights to his or her employer-derived accrued benefit are nonforfeitable in accordance with the following schedule:

Completed Years of Service	Nonforfeitable Percentage
0–9	0
10	50
11	60
12	70
13	80
14	90
15	100

Does this plan meet the vesting requirements in § 411(a)?

34. When K retires in 1984, he receives a lump-sum distribution of $50,000 from a noncontributory qualified pension plan. His active period of participation was from January 1, 1971, through December 31, 1978. If K files a joint return in 1984 with his wife and elects to use the 10-year averaging provision, calculate (a) his separate tax on this distribution and (b) the capital gain portion.

35. E receives a $150,000 lump-sum distribution in 1984 from a contributory pension plan, which includes employer common stock with net unrealized

appreciation of $20,000. E contributed $20,000 to the qualified plan while he was an active participant from February 10, 1973, to February 10, 1978.

(a) Calculate the total taxable amount.

(b) Calculate the separate tax assuming E elects to use the 10-year averaging provision.

(c) Calculate the capital gain portion. (Treat part of a calendar month as one month.)

36. R has been an active participant in a defined benefit plan for 17 years. During her last five years of employment, R earned $20,000, $30,000, $45,000, $50,000, and $60,000, respectively (representing R's highest income years).

(a) Calculate R's maximum allowable benefits from this qualified plan (assume there are fewer than 100 participants).

(b) Assume that her average compensation for her high three years is $80,000. Calculate R's maximum allowable benefits.

37. During 19X3, PQR Corporation has a total payroll of $2,200,000. The corporation contributes $9,000 of employer securities to an employee stock ownership trust. The company has a tax liability after all tax credits (except this credit) of $17,000. Calculate the company's payroll-based tax credit, if any, for 19X3.

38. A university has contributed $48,000 over 19 years to a professor's tax-deferred annuity (TDA) before 19X2. The university contributes $2,000 during 19X2 to the TDA. The professor would like to calculate the maximum salary reduction contribution that may be excluded from income for 19X2. The professor's includible salary for 19X2 is $26,000.

39. You are provided the following facts concerning a professor at a northeastern university. Determine

(a) The § 403(b) exclusion allowance.

(b) The § 415 limitation.

(c) Amount includible in gross income.

Year	1	2	3	4
Compensation (reduced)	$20,000	$35,000	$55,000	$70,000
Employer contribution	4,000	8,000	15,000	30,000

40. F earns $220,000 of self-employment net income in 1984 in a sole proprietorship.

A. Calculate the maximum amount that F can deduct for contributions to a Keogh plan.

B. Can F safely take a loan from the Keogh plan at an arm's length interest rate?

C. Suppose F contributes more than the allowable amount to the Keogh plan?

D. Can F retire and begin receiving Keogh payments at age 55?

41. Answer the following independent statements with respect to IRA contributions.

(a) During 1984, A earns a salary of $22,000 and his wife has no earned income. What is the maximum total deductible contribution to their IRAs? A wishes to contribute as much as possible to his own IRA.

(b) B has earned income during 1984 of $21,000 and her husband has earned income of $1,700. What is the maximum contribution to their IRAs?

(c) X's employer makes a contribution of $3,500 to X's simplified employee pension (SEP) plan. If X's earned income is $27,000 during 1984, what amount, if any, may X also contribute to an IRA?

42. During 1984, P is a key employee of a top-heavy pension plan. His salary is $240,000. Calculate P's maximum contribution to such a defined benefit plan.

43. In 1984, P earned compensation of $62,000. What is the individual retirement arrangement deduction from gross income on P's income tax return if his employer contributed the maximum amount allowable to a simplified employee pension plan?

44. B, a married individual, decides in 1984 to start an individual retirement account (IRA), even though he is a member of a corporate pension plan. B's total income for 1984 is as follows:

Salary	$ 9,000
Dividends	1,500
Interest	700
Veteran's educational benefits	2,200

If B contributes $1,600 to his IRA on December 20, 1984, what is his allowable IRA deduction for 1984, if any.

45. On September 1, 19X1, D (an author) and V (a publisher) executed an agreement under which the author granted to the publisher the exclusive right to print, publish, and sell a book. The agreement provides that the publisher will (a) pay the author specified royalties based upon the actual cash received from the sale of the published work, (b) render semiannual statements of the sales, and (c) at the time of rendering each statement make settlement for the amount due. On the same day, another agreement was signed by the same parties in which they agreed that in consideration of and notwithstanding any contrary provisions contained in the first contract, the publisher would not pay the author more than $100,000 in any one calendar year. Under the second contract, amounts in excess of $100,000 accruing in any one calendar year are to be carried over by the publisher into succeeding accounting periods. The publisher is not required either to pay interest to the taxpayer on any such excess sums or to segregate any such sums in any manner. Is the second agreement an effective deferral? Why? When would the publisher obtain a deduction?

46. G Company pays bonuses each year to its key executives. The specific employees to receive bonuses and the amount of bonus for each recipient is determined on December 1 of each year. Each employee eligible for a bonus may decide on or before November 15 of each year to postpone the receipt of the bonus until retirement or death. An employee electing to postpone receipt of a bonus is allowed to designate, at any time before

retirement, the time and manner of the post-retirement payments and to designate the persons to receive any amount payable after death. Since most employees elect to defer their bonuses, separate accounts are not maintained for each employee. When would these bonuses be taxed to the executive and be deductible by G Company?

47. On February 20, 19X1, G (an executive of R Corporation) purchased 100 shares of R stock (selling at $20 a share) for $10. A condition of the transaction was that G must resell the stock to R at cost if he leaves his employer voluntarily within five years of receiving the stock (assume this represents a substantial risk of forfeiture).

    (a) Assuming that no election is made under § 83(b), what amount, if any, is taxable to G in 19X1?

    (b) Five years later when the stock is selling for $40 a share, G still is employed by the same firm. What amount of ordinary income, if any, is taxable to G?

    (c) What amount, if any, is deductible by R as compensation expense five years later?

    (d) Assuming G made the § 83(b) special election in 19X1, what amount would be taxable in 19X1?

    (e) In (d), what amount would be deductible by R Corporation five years later?

    (f) Under (d), assume G sold all the stock six years later for $65 per share. How much capital gain is included in G's gross income?

    (g) In (d), what loss is available to G if he voluntarily resigns before the five-year period and does not sell the stock back to the corporation?

    (h) In the year G resigns, what amount, if any, would be taxable to R Corporation?

48. On July 2, 19X2, P Corporation sold 1,000 of its common shares (worth $14 per share) to its employee C for $5 per share. The sale was subject to C's agreement to resell the shares to the corporation for $5 per share if his employment is terminated within the following four years. The shares had a value of $24 per share on July 2, 19X6. C sold the shares for $31 per share on September 16, 19X6. No special election under § 83(b) is made.

    (a) What amount, if any, will be taxed to C on July 2, 19X2?

    (b) On July 2, 19X6?

    (c) On September 16, 19X6?

    (d) What deduction, if any, will P Corporation obtain?

    (e) Assume the same facts but that C makes the election under § 83(b). What amount, if any, will be taxed to C on July 2, 19X2?

    (f) Will the assumption made in (e) have any effect on any deduction P Corporation will receive? Explain.

49. R exercises 100 incentive stock options of X Corporation on May 21, 1984, at the option price of $100 per share when the fair market value is $120 per share. He sells the 100 shares of common stock three and one-half years later for $140.

    (a) Calculate the total long-term capital gain on this sale.

(b) Assume R holds the stock seven months and sells the shares for $140 per share. Calculate any ordinary income on the sale.

(c) In (b), what amount can X Corporation deduct?

(d) Suppose R holds the stock for two years and sells the shares for $115 per share. Calculate any capital gain on this transaction.

(e) In (a), assume the options are nonqualified options with a nonascertainable fair market value on the date of the grant. Calculate total long-term capital gain, if any, in the year of sale.

(f) In (e), assume that each option has an ascertainable fair market value of $10 on the date of the grant and no substantial risk of forfeiture exists. Calculate total long-term capital gain, if any, on the date of the sale.

50. On November 19, 1982, J is granted incentive stock options to purchase 100 shares of S Company (on such date the stock is selling for $8 per share and the option price is $9 per share). J exercises the option on November 21, 1983, when the stock is selling for $10 per share. Four months later, J sells the shares for $9.50 per share.

(a) What amount is taxable to J in 1982?

(b) What amount is taxable to J in 1983?

(c) What amount of ordinary income, if any, is taxable to J in 1984?

(d) What amount of capital gain is taxable to J in 1984?

(e) What amount, if any, is deductible by S Company in 1984?

51. In 1984, T has a yearly salary of $45,000 when he established an individual retirement account (IRA).

(a) What is the maximum amount the employer may contribute to T's IRA?

(b) Suppose T's employer contributes $1,300 to the IRA. What amount, if any, may T contribute?

(c) In (b), assume that the employer contributes $2,100 to the plan in 1984. What amount may T contribute?

(d) Suppose T has a nonemployed spouse and he contributes $770 for his spouse. What total amount can he contribute to the joint IRA?

(e) In (d), assume that T contributes a total of $2,210 to his account in the joint IRA plan. Any problems?

Research Problems

52. S worked for an employer for 17 years until his retirement from full-time employment in 1985. He continued to be a part-time adviser for the company and agreed not to compete with the company. Under the terms of the qualified pension plan, he had two options: (1) withdraw his entire amount as of this date or (2) leave such amount in the trust, with interest, for a period of four years. He chose the latter alternative. S received a series of distributions from the trust constituting his entire balance. He received these distributions within a single year. Do these payments qualify as a lump-sum distribution?

53. An employee of a professional corporation approaches you with a research problem. He needs to know the definition of a key employee for purposes of a top-heavy retirement plan. How will you respond?

54. A potential client walks into your office in March 1985. He is a self-employed individual who is the sole employee of a calendar year small business. He missed the December 31, 1984, deadline for establishing a Keogh plan, yet he wishes to reduce his 1984 taxes by making a contribution to a simplified employee pension (SEP) plan. Can he?

55. Suppose the holding period of an incentive stock option is not met. When and how is the ISO taxed because of the disqualifying disposition?

56. Employee T, age 65, receives a distribution from his employer's noncontributory qualified pension plan. The entire amount was paid to him in 1984. Should he roll this amount over to an IRA? A Keogh plan? Or should he pay a tax on it?

Chapter 20

Corporations
and Partnerships

The purpose of this chapter is to present a general introduction to the Federal income tax provisions which are applicable to corporations and partnerships. Corporate and partnership tax provisions are extremely complex. *West's Federal Taxation: Corporations, Partnerships, Estates, and Trusts* includes detailed coverage of these subject areas.

WHAT IS A CORPORATION?

Initially, a company must comply with the specific requirements for corporate status under state law (e. g., it is necessary to draft and file articles of incorporation with the state regulatory agency, be granted a charter, and issue stock to shareholders).

COMPLIANCE WITH STATE LAW

Compliance with state law, although important, is not the only requirement which must be met to qualify for corporate tax status. For example, a corporation qualifying under state law may be disregarded as a taxable entity if it is a mere "sham" lacking in economic substance. The key consideration is the degree of business activity conducted at the corporate level.

Example 1. C and D are joint owners of a tract of unimproved real estate that they wish to protect from future creditors. Consequently, C and D form R Corporation to which they transfer the land in return for all of the latter's stock. The corporation merely holds title to the land and conducts no other activities. In all respects, R Corporation meets the legal requirements of a corporation under applicable state law. R Corporation probably would not be recognized as a separate entity under the facts set forth in this example.[1]

Example 2. Assume the same facts as in Example 1. In addition to holding title to the land, R Corporation leases the property, collects rents, and pays the property taxes thereon. R Corporation probably would be treated as a corporation for Federal income tax purposes due to the scope of its activities.

In some instances, the IRS has attempted to disregard (or "collapse") a corporation in order to make its income taxable directly to the shareholders.[2] In other cases, the IRS has asserted that the corporation is a separate taxable entity so as to assess tax at the corporate level and to tax corporate shareholder distributions as dividend income.[3]

THE ASSOCIATION APPROACH

An organization not qualifying as a regular corporation under state law may, nevertheless, be taxed as a corporation under the association approach. The designation given to an entity under the state law is not controlling. For example, a partnership of physicians has been treated as an association (therefore taxed under the corporate rules) even though state law prohibited the practice of medicine in the corporate form.[4]

Whether or not an entity will be considered an association for Federal income tax purposes depends upon the number of corporate characteristics it possesses. According to court decisions and the Regulations, corporate characteristics include:[5]

1. Associates.

2. An objective to carry on a business and divide the gains therefrom.

---

1. *See Paymer v. Comm.,* 45–2 USTC ¶ 9353, 33 AFTR 1536, 150 F.2d 334 (CA–2, 1945).
2. *Patterson v. Comm.,* 25 TCM 1230, T.C.Memo. 1966–239, *aff'd.* in 68–2 USTC ¶ 9471, 22 AFTR2d 5810 (CA–2, 1968).
3. *Rafferty Farms Inc. v. U. S.,* 75–1 USTC ¶ 9271, 35 AFTR2d 75–811, 511 F.2d 1234 (CA–8, 1975); *Collins v. U. S.,* 75–2 USTC ¶ 9553, 36 AFTR2d 75–5175, 514 F.2d 1282 (CA–5, 1975).
4. *U. S. v. Kintner,* 54–2 USTC ¶ 9626, 47 AFTR 995, 216 F.2d 418 (CA–5, 1975).
5. Reg. § 301.7701–2(a).

3. Continuity of life.

4. Centralized management.

5. Limited liability.

6. Free transferability of interests.

The Regulations state that an unincorporated organization shall not be classified as an association unless it possesses more corporate than noncorporate characteristics. In making this determination, the characteristics common to both corporate and noncorporate business organizations shall be disregarded.[6] Both corporations and partnerships generally have associates (i. e., shareholders and partners) and an objective to carry on a business and divide the gains. Therefore, if a partnership has three of the last four of the above attributes, it will be treated as an association (taxable as a corporation).

> **Example 3.** The XYZ Partnership agreement provides for the following: the partnership terminates with the withdrawal of a partner; all of the partners have authority to participate in the management of the partnership; all of the partners are individually liable for the debts of the partnership; and a partner may not freely transfer his or her interest in the partnership to another. Since none of the corporate attributes 3 through 6 are present, XYZ is not taxable as an association.

INCOME TAX CONSIDERATIONS

INDIVIDUALS AND CORPORATIONS COMPARED— AN OVERVIEW

Business operations may be conducted as a sole proprietorship, as a partnership, or in corporate form.

—Sole proprietorships are not separate taxable entities. The owner of the business will, therefore, report all business transactions on his or her individual income tax return.

—Partnerships are not subject to the income tax. Under the conduit concept, the various tax attributes of the partnership's operations flow through to the individual partners to be reported on their personal income tax returns.

—The regular corporate form of doing business carries with it the imposition of the corporate income tax. The corporation is recognized as a separate taxpaying entity. Thus, income is taxed to the corporation as earned and taxed again to the shareholders as dividends when distributed.

---

6. Reg. § 301.7701–2(a)(3).

—A regular corporation may elect to be taxed as an S corporation. Such special treatment is similar (although not identical) to the partnership rules. Income tax is generally avoided at the corporate level, and shareholders are taxed currently on the taxable income of the S corporation.

Similarities Between Corporate and Individual Tax Rules. The gross income of a corporation is determined in much the same manner as it is determined for individuals. Both individuals and corporations are entitled to exclusions from gross income, such as interest on municipal bonds. The tax rules for gains and losses from property transactions are also treated similarly. For example, whether a gain or loss is capital or ordinary depends on the nature and use of the asset rather than the type of taxpayer. Upon the sale or other taxable disposition of depreciable personalty, the recapture rules of § 1245 make no distinction between corporate and noncorporate taxpayers. In the case of the recapture of depreciation on real estate (i. e., § 1250), however, corporate taxpayers are treated more severely in terms of tax consequences. Under § 291, corporations must recognize as additional ordinary income 15 percent of what otherwise would qualify as § 1231 gain (refer to Example 20, Chapter 17).

The business deductions of corporations also parallel those available to individuals. Therefore, corporate deductions are allowed for all ordinary and necessary expenses paid or incurred in carrying on a trade or business under the general rule of § 162(a). Corporations may also deduct interest (§ 163), certain taxes (§ 164), losses (§ 165), bad debts (§ 166), depreciation (§ 167), cost recovery (§ 168), charitable contributions subject to corporate limitation rules (§ 170), net operating losses (§ 172), research and experimental expenditures (§ 174), and other less common deductions.

Many of the tax credits available to individuals can be claimed by corporations. The most important of these credits include the investment tax credit (§ 38) and the foreign tax credit (§ 33).

Corporations generally have the same choices of accounting periods and methods as do individuals. Like an individual, a corporation may choose a calendar year or a fiscal year for reporting purposes. Corporations that maintain inventory for sale to customers are required to use the accrual method of accounting for determining sales and cost of goods sold.

Dissimilarities. Corporations and individuals are subject to different tax rate structures. The corporate tax rates reflect a stair-step pattern of progression, whereas individual rates reflect a continual pattern of progression. Corporate tax rates are discussed in a later section of this chapter.

All allowable corporate deductions are treated as business deductions. Thus, the determination of adjusted gross income, so essential in the case of individuals, has no relevance to corporations. As such, corporations need not be concerned with itemized deductions. The zero bracket amount and personal and dependency exemptions are not available to corporations.

SPECIFIC PROVISIONS COMPARED

Corporate and individual tax rules differ in the following areas:

—Capital gains and losses; carryback and carryover provisions.

—Charitable contribution ceiling limitations.

—Net operating loss adjustments.

—Special deductions for corporations (e. g., the 85 percent or 100 percent dividends received deduction).

Capital Gains. Individuals include net long-term capital gains in gross income with an offsetting 60 percent long-term capital gain deduction. Corporations can treat long-term capital gains in either of two ways:

—Include none of the gain in gross income and add to the regular tax liability an alternative tax of 28 percent.[7]

—Include the full gain in gross income and forego the alternative tax computation.

In the latter case, therefore, the long-term capital gain will be subject to the regular income tax rates applicable to corporations. Thus, the choice will depend upon the effective income tax bracket of the corporation.

> **Example 4.** During 19X4, T Corporation has taxable income of $100,000 without the inclusion of a long-term capital gain of $1,000. Since T Corporation has reached the 46% income tax bracket (see the discussion later in this chapter on the corporate income tax rates), it should use the alternative tax. Consequently, $280 (28% of $1,000) should be added to T Corporation's regular income tax liability on $100,000.

> **Example 5.** Assume the same facts as in the previous example except that T Corporation has taxable income of only $24,000. Because it is only at the 15% tax bracket level, the $1,000 long-term capital gain should be included in T Corporation's gross income and the alternative tax method not used.

As was true with individual taxpayers, short-term capital gains are fully included in the gross income of a corporation. The alternative tax method is not applicable to corporate short-term capital gains.

Capital Losses. As discussed in Chapter 16, noncorporate taxpayers can deduct up to $3,000 of net capital losses against ordinary

---

7. § 1201(a).

income. However, if the net capital loss is long-term, it requires $2 of loss to generate $1 of deduction. Noncorporate taxpayers are permitted to carry any remaining capital losses forward to future years until absorbed by capital gains or by the $3,000 deduction.

Unlike individuals, corporate taxpayers are not permitted to claim any net capital losses as a deduction against ordinary income.[8] Capital losses may be used only as an offset against capital gains. Corporations may, however, carry back net capital losses to the three preceding years, applying them initially to the earliest year. Carryovers are allowed for a period of five years from the year of the loss.[9] When carried back or over, a long-term capital loss is treated as a short-term capital loss.

> **Example 6.** T Corporation, a calendar year taxpayer, incurs a long-term net capital loss of $5,000 for 19X4. None of the capital loss may be deducted in 19X4. T Corporation may, however, carry the loss back to years 19X1, 19X2, and 19X3 (in this order) and offset any net capital gains recognized in these years. If the carryback does not exhaust the loss, it may be carried over to 19X5, 19X6, 19X7, 19X8, and 19X9 (in this order). Such capital loss carrybacks or carryovers are treated as short-term capital losses.

Charitable Contributions. Generally, a charitable contribution deduction will be allowed only for the year in which the payment is made. However, an important exception is made in the case of accrual basis corporations. The deduction may be claimed in the year preceding payment if the contribution has been authorized by the board of directors by the end of that year and is, in fact, paid on or before the fifteenth day of the third month of the next year.[10]

> **Example 7.** On December 28, 19X5, the board of directors of the XYZ Company, a calendar year, accrual basis taxpayer, authorizes a $5,000 donation to a qualified charity. The donation is paid on March 14, 19X6. XYZ Corporation may claim the $5,000 donation as a deduction for 19X5. As an alternative, XYZ Corporation may claim the deduction in 19X6 (i. e., the year of payment).

Like individuals, corporations are not permitted an unlimited charitable contribution deduction. For any one year, a corporate taxpayer is limited to 10 percent of taxable income computed without regard to the charitable contribution deduction, any net operating loss carryback or capital loss carryback, and the dividends received deduction.[11] Any contributions in excess of the 10 percent limitation

---

8. § 1211(a).
9. § 1212(a).
10. § 170(a)(2).
11. § 170(b)(2).

may be carried over to the five succeeding tax years. Any carryover must be added to subsequent contributions and will be subject to the 10 percent limitation. In applying this limitation, however, the most recent contributions must be deducted first.[12]

Example 8. During 19X4, T Corporation (a calendar year taxpayer) had the following income and expenses:

Income from operations	$ 140,000
Expenses from operations	110,000
Dividends received	10,000
Charitable contributions made in 19X4	5,000

For the purposes of the 10% limitation only, T Corporation's taxable income is $40,000 ($140,000 − $110,000 + $10,000). Consequently, the allowable charitable deduction for 19X4 is $4,000 (10% × $40,000). The $1,000 unused portion of the contribution may be carried over to 19X5, 19X6, 19X7, 19X8, and 19X9 (in that order) until exhausted.

Example 9. Assume the same facts as in the previous example. In 19X5, T Corporation has taxable income (after adjustments) of $50,000 and makes a charitable contribution of $4,800. The maximum deduction allowed for 19X5 would be $5,000 (10% × $50,000). The first $4,800 of the allowed deduction must be allocated to the 19X5 contributions, and the $200 excess is carried over from 19X4. The remaining $800 of the 19X4 contribution may be carried over to 19X6, etc.

Special rules for property contributions, ordinary income property, long-term capital gain property, etc. apply to both corporate and noncorporate taxpayers. These special rules were discussed in Chapter 11.

Net Operating Losses. The computation of a net operating loss for individuals was discussed in Chapter 8. Corporations are not subject to the complex adjustments required for individuals (e. g., a corporation has no adjustments for nonbusiness deductions or capital gains and losses).

For corporations, the net operating loss is computed by including the dividends received deduction (discussed below) in the amount of the loss.[13] Corporate net operating losses may be carried back three years and over 15 years (or taxpayers may elect to forego the carryback period) to offset taxable income for those years.

Example 10. In 19X5, XYZ Corporation has gross income of $200,000 and deductions of $300,000, excluding the dividends

---

12. § 170(d)(2).
13. § 172(d)(6).

received deduction. XYZ Corporation received taxable dividends of $100,000 from A Corporation, a domestic corporation which is not a member of a controlled group of corporations with XYZ. XYZ Corporation has a net operating loss of $185,000, computed as follows:

Gross income (including dividends)		$ 200,000
Less: Business deductions	$ 300,000	
Dividends received deduction		
(85% × $100,000)	85,000	385,000
Taxable income (loss)		($ 185,000)

Example 11. Assume the same facts as in the previous example and that XYZ Corporation had taxable income of $40,000 in 19X2. The net operating loss of $185,000 is carried back to 19X2 (unless XYZ elects not to carry back the loss to such year). The carryover to 19X3 is $145,000, computed as follows:

Taxable income for 19X2	$ 40,000
Less: Net operating loss carryback from 19X5	185,000
Carryover of unabsorbed 19X5 loss	($ 145,000)

DEDUCTIONS AVAILABLE ONLY TO CORPORATIONS

Dividends Received Deduction. A corporation is allowed a deduction equal to (a) 85 percent of the amount of dividends received from a domestic corporation or (b) 100 percent of the amount of dividends received from a corporation which is a member of a controlled group with the recipient corporation.[14]

The purpose of the 85 percent dividends received deduction is to prevent triple taxation. Absent the deduction, income paid to a corporation in the form of a dividend would be subject to taxation for a second time (once to the distributing corporation) with no corresponding deduction to the distributing corporation. A third level of tax would be assessed when the recipient corporation paid the income to its shareholders. Since the dividends received deduction is usually only 85 percent, only partial relief is provided under the law.

In unusual situations the dividends received deduction may be limited to 85 percent of the taxable income of a corporation computed without regard to the net operating loss deduction, the dividends received deduction, and any capital loss carryback to the current tax year. However, this limitation does not apply if the corporation has a net operating loss for the current taxable year.[15]

---

14. § 243(a).
15. § 246(b)(1) and (2).

Example 12. In the current year, T Corporation has the following income and expenses:

Gross income from operations	$ 400,000
Expenses from operations	340,000
Dividends received from domestic corporations	200,000

The dividends received deduction is $170,000 (85% × $200,000) unless 85% of taxable income is less. Because taxable income (for this purpose) is $260,000 ($400,000 − $340,000 + $200,000) and 85% of $260,000 is $221,000, the full $170,000 will be allowed.

Example 13. Assume the same facts as in the previous example except that T Corporation's gross income from operations is $320,000 (instead of $400,000). The usual dividends received deduction of $170,000 (85% × $200,000) is now limited to 85% of the taxable income. Since 85% of $180,000 ($320,000 − $340,000 + $200,000) is $153,000, this amount is the dividends received deduction (i. e., $153,000 is less than $170,000). The full $170,000 cannot be claimed, because it does not generate or add to a net operating loss. (Taxable income of $180,000 less $170,000 does not result in a net operating loss).

Example 14. Assume the same facts as in Example 12 except that T Corporation's gross income from operations is $300,000 (instead of $400,000). The usual dividends received deduction of $170,000 now can be claimed under the net operating loss exception. Taxable income of $160,000 ($300,000 − $340,000 + $200,000) less $170,000 generates a net operating loss of $10,000.

In summary, Example 12 reflects the general rule that the dividends received deduction is 85 percent of the qualifying dividends. Example 13 presents the exception whereby the deduction may be limited to 85 percent of taxable income. Example 14 indicates the situation in which the taxable income exception will not apply because allowance of the full deduction generates or adds to a net operating loss.

Deduction of Organizational Expenditures. Under § 248, a corporation may elect to amortize organizational expenses over a period of 60 months or more. If the election is not made on a timely basis, such expenditures cannot be deducted until the corporation ceases to conduct business and liquidates. The election is made in a statement attached to the corporation's return for its first taxable year.

Organizational expenditures include:

—Legal services incident to organization (e. g., drafting the corporate charter, bylaws, minutes of organizational meetings, terms of original stock certificates).

—Necessary accounting services.

—Expenses of temporary directors and of organizational meetings of directors and stockholders.

—Fees paid to the state of incorporation.

Expenditures that do not qualify include those connected with issuing or selling shares of stock or other securities (e. g., commissions, professional fees, and printing costs) or with the transfer of assets to a corporation. Such expenditures are generally added to the capital account and are not subject to amortization.

Example 15. T Corporation, an accrual basis taxpayer, was formed and began operations on May 1, 19X5. The following expenses were incurred during its first year of operations (May 1–December 31, 19X5):

Expenses of temporary directors and of organizational meetings	$ 500
Fee paid to the state of incorporation	100
Accounting services incident to organization	200
Legal services for drafting the corporate charter and bylaws	400
Expenses incident to the printing and sale of stock certificates	300

Assume T Corporation makes a timely election under § 248 to amortize qualifying organizational expenses over a period of 60 months. The monthly amortization would be $20 [($500 + $100 + $200 + $400) ÷ 60 months], and $160 ($20 × 8 months) would be deductible for tax year 19X5. Note that the $300 of expenses incident to the printing and sale of stock certificates do not qualify for the election.

DETERMINATION OF TAX LIABILITY

Corporate Income Tax Rates. Unlike the income tax rates applicable to noncorporate taxpayers, the corporate rates are only mildly progressive. The rates applicate to 1984 are as follows:[16]

Rate Applicable	Amount of Taxable Income
15%	first $25,000
18	above $25,000 to $50,000
30	above $50,000 to $75,000
40	above $75,000 to $100,000
46	over $100,000

Example 16. T Corporation, a calendar year taxpayer, had taxable income of $150,000 in 1984. Its income tax liability (disregarding credits) for the year is $48,750, determined as follows:

16. § 11(b).

15% of $25,000	$ 3,750
18% of $25,000	4,500
30% of $25,000	7,500
40% of $25,000	10,000
46% of $50,000	23,000
Total tax	$ 48,750

Minimum Tax. A corporation is subject to the minimum tax on certain tax preferences as are individuals (refer to Chapter 12). However, the tax is computed differently for corporations and is added to a corporation's regular tax liability rather than being an alternative tax as in the case of individuals.

A corporation is liable for a 15 percent minimum tax on tax preferences in excess of the greater of $10,000 or its regular tax liability. The following are included as items of tax preference:

—Accelerated depreciation on real property in excess of the amount that would have been allowed under the straight-line method.

—Deductions for certified pollution control facilities in excess of normal depreciation.

—The excess of the deduction allowed financial institutions for a reasonable addition to a bad debt reserve over the deduction based on actual experience.

—The excess of depletion allowable over the adjusted basis of the property at year-end (figured before deducting depletion for the year).

—Excess of net long-term capital gain over short-term capital loss multiplied by a fraction, the numerator of which is the highest tax rate of the corporation for the taxable year minus the alternative tax of 28 percent and the denominator of which is 46 percent.[17]

For tax years beginning after 1983, only 71.6 percent of the following tax preferences are included in the minimum tax base:

—Accelerated depreciation on real property where there has been a 15 percent increase in depreciation recapture on dispositions after 1982.

—Rapid amortization of certified pollution control facilities placed in service after 1982 where there has been a 15 percent reduction in the rapid amortization.

—A financial institution's excess bad debt deduction where it has been reduced 15 percent after 1982.

—Percentage depletion deduction for coal and iron ore where the depletion deduction has been reduced 15 percent after 1982.

---

17. § 57(a)(9)(B).

Certain modifications in determining the base for the application of the tax are necessary to preclude a double impact. For example, if a tax preference item has been reduced by the 15 percent adjustment previously noted, such adjustment should be taken into account. This can be accomplished by multiplying the tax preference item by 71.6 percent.

A corporation must file Form 4626 if it has tax preferences in excess of $10,000.

Filing Requirements. The corporate income tax return is filed on Form 1120 (see Appendix B–4). Corporations electing under Subchapter S file Form 1120S (see Appendix B–5). The return must be filed on or before the fifteenth day of the third month following the close of the corporation's tax year. A corporation must pay the tax upon filing. Corporations can receive an automatic extension for filing the corporate return by filing form 7004 (Application for Automatic Extension of Time to File Corporation Income Tax Return) by the due date of the return.[18]

A corporation must make payments of estimated tax if its tax liability can reasonably be expected to exceed $40. These payments are made in four installments due on or before the fifteenth day of the fourth month, the sixth month, the ninth month, and the twelfth month of the taxable year.[19]

RECONCILIATION OF TAXABLE INCOME AND ACCOUNTING INCOME

Taxable income and financial net income are seldom the same amount. For example, a difference may arise if the corporation uses accelerated depreciation for tax purposes and straight-line depreciation for financial purposes.

Many items of income for accounting purposes, such as proceeds from a life insurance policy on the death of a corporate officer and interest on municipal bonds, may not be taxable income. Some expense items for financial accounting purposes, such as expenses to produce tax-exempt income, estimated warranty reserves, a net capital loss, and Federal income taxes, may not be deductible for tax purposes.

Schedule M–1 on the last page of Form 1120 is used to reconcile financial net income (net income after Federal income taxes) with taxable income (as computed on the corporate tax return before the deduction for a net operating loss and for the dividends received deduction). In the left-hand column of Schedule M–1, net income per books is added to the Federal income tax liability for the year, the

---

18. § 6081.
19. Reg. § 1.6154.

excess of capital losses over capital gains (which cannot be deducted in the current year), taxable income which is not income in the current year for financial purposes, and expenses recorded on the books which are not deductible on the tax return. In the right-hand column, income recorded on the books which is not currently taxable or is tax-exempt and deductions for tax purposes which are not expenses for financial purposes are totaled and subtracted from the left-hand column total to arrive at taxable income (before the net operating loss or dividends received deductions).

Example 17.

Schedule M–1

Net Income per Books		$ 93,450	Interest on Municipal		
Federal Income Tax		6,450	Bonds	$ 5,000	
Net Capital Loss		2,000	Life Insurance		
Expenses Not Deducted on Return			Proceeds on Death of President	50,000	$ 55,000
Interest Expense to Purchase Tax-exempt Securities	$ 500		Excess of Depreciation Deducted on Return Over Book Depreciation		10,000
Insurance Premiums on Life Insurance Policy on Life of President, Proceeds Payable to Corporation	2,600	3,100	Total		$ 65,000
			Taxable Income [before net operating loss deduction and dividends received deduction		
		$ 105,000	($105,000 − $65,000)]		$ 40,000

FORMING THE CORPORATION

CAPITAL CONTRIBUTIONS

The receipt of money or property in exchange for capital stock produces neither gain nor loss to the recipient corporation.[20] Gross income of a corporation also does not include shareholders' contributions of money or property to the capital of the corporation.[21]

Contributions by nonshareholders, such as land contributed to a corporation by a civic group or a contribution by a municipality to induce the corporation to locate in a particular community, are also excluded from the gross income of a corporation.[22] The basis of such property (capital transfers by nonshareholders) to the corporation is zero.

---

20. § 1032.
21. § 118.
22. *Edwards v. Cuba Railroad Co.,* 1 USTC ¶ 139, 5 AFTR 5398, 45 S.Ct. 614 (USSC, 1925).

Example 18. A city donates land worth $200,000 to X Corporation as an inducement for X to locate in the city. The receipt of the land does not represent taxable income. However, its basis to the corporation is zero.

Thin Capitalization Problem. The advantages of capitalizing a corporation with debt may be substantial. Interest on debt is deductible by the corporation, whereas dividend payments are not. Further, the shareholders are not taxed on loan repayments unless they exceed basis. If a company is capitalized solely with common stock, subsequent repayments of such capital contributions are likely to be treated as dividends to the shareholders.

In certain instances, the IRS will contend that debt is really an equity interest and will deny the shareholders the tax advantages of debt financing. If the debt instrument has too many features of stock, it may be treated as a form of stock, and principal and interest payments will be considered dividends.[23]

Though the form of the instrument will not assure debt treatment, the failure to observe certain formalities in the creation of the debt may lead to an assumption that the purported debt is, in fact, a form of stock. The debt should be in proper legal form, should bear a legitimate rate of interest, should have a definite maturity date, and should be repaid on a timely basis. Payments should not be contingent upon earnings. Further, the debt should not be subordinated to other liabilities, and proportionate holdings of stock and debt should be avoided.

TRANSFERS TO CONTROLLED CORPORATIONS

Absent special provisions in the Code, a transfer of property to a corporation in exchange for its stock would be a sale or exchange of property and would constitute a taxable transaction. Section 351 provides for the nonrecognition of gain or loss upon such transfers of property if the transferors are in control of the corporation immediately after the transfer. Gain or loss is merely postponed in a manner similar to a like-kind exchange.[24] The following requirements must be met to qualify under § 351:

—The transferors must be in control of the corporation immediately after the exchange. Control is defined as ownership of at

---

23. § 385 was added to the Internal Revenue Code in 1969. This provision lists several factors which might be used to determine whether a debtor-creditor relationship or a shareholder-corporation relationship exists. Section 385 also authorizes the IRS to issue Regulations providing guidance to taxpayers as to when debt will be reclassified as equity. After several unsuccessful efforts to issue and complete such Regulations, the IRS gave up in its attempt to provide a workable and equitable solution to the problem. Thus, the standards set forth by case law remain predominant in this area.
24. Refer to the discussion in Chapter 15.

least 80 percent of the total combined voting power of all classes of stock entitled to vote and at least 80 percent of the total number of shares of all other classes of stock.[25]

—Gain (but not loss) is recognized to the extent that the transferors receive property other than stock and securities (e. g., cash or short-term notes).[26] Such nonqualifying property is known as "boot" under the tax law.

Basis Considerations and Computation of Gain. The nonrecognition of gain or loss is accompanied by a carryover of basis. Section 358(a) provides that the basis of stock or securities received in a § 351 transfer is the same as the basis the shareholder had in the property transferred, increased by any gain recognized by the shareholder on the exchange and decreased by boot received. Section 362(a) provides that the basis of properties received by the corporation is the basis in the hands of the transferor increased by the amount of any gain recognized to the transferor shareholder.

> **Example 19.** A and B, individuals, form X Corporation. A transfers property with an adjusted basis of $30,000, fair market value of $60,000, for 50% of the stock. B transfers property with an adjusted basis of $40,000, fair market value of $60,000, for the remaining 50% of the stock. Gain is not recognized on the transfer because the transfer qualifies under § 351. The basis of the stock to A is $30,000, while the basis of the stock to B is $40,000. X Corporation has a basis of $30,000 in the property transferred by A and a basis of $40,000 in the property transferred by B.

> **Example 20.** C and D form Y Corporation with the following investment: C transfers property (basis of $30,000 and fair market value of $70,000) while D transfers cash of $60,000. Each receives 50 shares of the Y Corporation stock, but C also receives $10,000 in cash. Assume each share of the Y Corporation stock is worth $1,200. Although C's realized gain is $40,000 [i. e., $60,000 (the value of 50 shares of Y Corporation stock) + $10,000 (cash received) − $30,000 (basis of the property transferred)], only $10,000 (the amount of the boot) is recognized. C's basis in the Y Corporation stock becomes $30,000 [i. e., $30,000 (basis of the property transferred) + $10,000 (gain recognized by C) − $10,000 (cash received)]. Y Corporation's basis in the property transferred by C is $40,000 [$30,000 (basis of the property to C)

---

25. § 368(c).

26. The courts have required that the definition of a "security" be limited to long-term obligations and exclude short-term notes. See *Turner v. Comm.*, 62–1 USTC ¶ 9488, 9 AFTR2d 1528, 303 F.2d 94 (CA–4, 1962). The required length of maturity to qualify as a security is questionable. Some cases draw the line at five years; others at 10 years. See *Camp Wolters Enterprises, Inc. v. Comm.*, 22 T.C. 737 (1955), *aff'd.* in 56–1 USTC ¶ 9314, 49 AFTR 283, 230 F.2d 555 (CA–5, 1956).

+ $10,000 (gain recognized to C)]. D neither realizes nor recognizes gain or loss and will have a basis in the Y Corporation stock of $60,000.

Example 21. Assume the same facts as in the previous example except that C's basis in the property transferred is $68,000 (instead of $30,000). Because recognized gain cannot exceed realized gain, the transfer generates only $2,000 of gain to C. The basis of the Y Corporation stock to C becomes $60,000 [i. e., $68,000 (basis of property transferred) + $2,000 (gain recognized) − $10,000 (cash received)]. Y Corporation's basis in the property received from C is $70,000 [i. e., $68,000 (basis of the property to C) + $2,000 (gain recognized by C)].

OPERATING THE CORPORATION

DIVIDEND DISTRIBUTIONS

Corporate distributions of cash or property to shareholders are treated as ordinary dividend income to the extent the corporation has accumulated or current earnings and profits (E & P).[27] In determining the source of the distribution, a dividend is deemed to have been made initially from current E & P.

Example 22. As of January 1, 19X1, Y Corporation has a deficit in accumulated E & P of $30,000. For tax year 19X1 it has current E & P of $10,000. In 19X1, the corporation distributed $5,000 to its shareholders. The $5,000 distribution will be treated as a taxable dividend, since it is deemed to have been made from current E & P. This will be the case even though Y Corporation will still have a deficit in its accumulated E & P at the end of 19X1.

Concept of Earnings and Profits. The term "earnings and profits" is not defined in the Code, although § 312 does include certain transactions that affect E & P. While E & P possesses certain similarities to the financial accounting concept of retained earnings, numerous differences may arise. For example, a nontaxable stock dividend is treated for financial accounting purposes as a capitalization of retained earnings, but it does not decrease E & P for tax purposes. Generally, current E & P for a taxable year is taxable income plus or minus certain adjustments (e. g., additions are made for tax-exempt income). Federal income taxes are subtracted from taxable income in arriving at the current E & P. A detailed discussion of the concept of E & P is beyond the scope of this chapter.

---

27. § 316.

Property Dividends. A distribution of property to a noncorporate shareholder is measured by the fair market value of the property on the date of distribution.[28] The noncorporate shareholder's basis in the property received is also its fair market value.[29]

> **Example 23.** P Corporation has E & P of $60,000. It distributes land with a fair market value of $50,000 (adjusted basis of $30,000) to its sole shareholder, T (an individual). T has a taxable dividend of $50,000 and a basis in the land of $50,000.

Special rules apply to property distributions received by corporate shareholders. The amount distributed is the lesser of (a) the fair market value of the property or (b) the adjusted basis of the property in the hands of the distributing corporation increased by the amount of gain recognized (if any) to the distributing corporation. The basis of the property received by the corporate shareholder is also computed under these special rules.

> **Example 24.** All of X Corporation is owned by Y Corporation. X Corporation has ample E & P to cover any distributions made during the year. X Corporation distributed land with an adjusted basis of $5,000 and a fair market value of $3,000 to Y Corporation. Y Corporation has a taxable dividend of $3,000, and its basis in the land becomes $3,000.

> **Example 25.** Assume the same facts as in Example 24 except that the land has an adjusted basis of $3,000 and a fair market value of $5,000. Presuming no gain is recognized by X Corporation as a result of the distribution, Y Corporation has dividend income of $3,000 and its basis in the land becomes $3,000.

The special rules for property distributions to corporate shareholders are due to the 85 percent dividends received deduction which is available to corporate shareholders. The rule prevents a corporate shareholder from obtaining a step-up in basis in appreciated property at a cost of only a 15 percent inclusion in income.

STOCK REDEMPTIONS

If a shareholder's stock is redeemed by the corporation, one of two possible outcomes will occur:

> —The redemption may qualify as a sale or exchange under § 302. In such case, capital gain or loss treatment usually applies to the qualifying shareholders.

> —The redemption will be treated as a dividend under § 301 providing the distributing corporation has earnings and profits.

---

28. § 301(b)(1)(A).
29. § 301(d)(1).

Certain redemptions of corporate stock represent a bona fide contraction of a shareholder's interest in the company and should, therefore, be treated as a sale or exchange of the shareholder's stock. However, absent specific rules in this area, it would be possible to structure a redemption of stock as a dividend in disguise.

Example 26. X and Y each own 100 shares of the voting stock of XY Corporation, which represents 100% of the voting stock. Instead of paying a cash dividend, XY Corporation redeems 10 shares of X's stock and 10 shares of Y's stock for a total of $20,000. Since X and Y each continue to own 50% of the corporation after the distribution, the redemption would be treated as a dividend under § 301 rather than as a sale or exchange of the stock under § 302 if XY Corporation has current and accumulated earnings and profits of at least $20,000.

Requirements for Sale or Exchange Treatment. A redemption of stock qualifies as a § 302 redemption if *any* of the following requirements are met:

—The redemption is not essentially equivalent to a dividend.[30]

—The distribution is substantially disproportionate (i. e., the redeeming shareholder now owns less than 80 percent of his or her total former interest in the corporation and the shareholder owns less than 50 percent of the voting stock of the corporation).[31]

—There is a complete termination of a shareholder's interest.[32]

In most instances, taxpayers should not place significant emphasis upon the first type of redemption, since the Supreme Court has ruled that the existence of a business purpose and the absence of a tax avoidance scheme are insufficient to cause the redemption to be treated as a sale or exchange. There must be a ". . . meaningful reduction of the shareholder's proportionate interest in the corporation."[33] What this means is not entirely clear.

The substantially disproportionate type of redemption is extremely useful, since it provides quantitative safe harbor tests.

Example 27. A, B, and C, unrelated individuals, own 30 shares, 30 shares, and 40 shares, respectively, in X Corporation. X Corporation has E & P of $200,000. The corporation redeems 20 shares of C's stock for $30,000. C paid $200 a share for the stock two years ago. After the redemption, C has a 25% interest in the corporation [20 shares out of a total of 80 shares (100 − 20)]. This

30. § 302(b)(1).
31. § 302(b)(2).
32. § 302(b)(3).
33. *U. S. v. Davis,* 70–1 USTC ¶ 9289, 25 AFTR2d 70–827, 90. S.Ct. 1041 (USSC, 1970).

represents less than 80% of his original ownership (40% $\times$ 80% = 32%) and less than 50% of the total voting power; consequently, the distribution qualifies as a stock redemption. C has a long-term capital gain of $26,000 [$30,000 − $4,000 (20 shares $\times$ $200)].

LIQUIDATING THE CORPORATION

GENERAL RULE OF SECTION 331

Under the general rule, gain or loss is recognized to the shareholders in a corporate liquidation. The amount of recognized gain or loss is measured by the difference between the fair market value of the assets received from the corporation and the adjusted basis of the stock surrendered. Capital gain or loss is recognized by the shareholders if their stock is a capital asset.[34]

> **Example 28.** X Corporation has as its only asset unimproved land (adjusted basis of $100,000 and fair market value of $150,000). T, an individual, owns all of the outstanding stock in X Corporation, such stock having an adjusted basis of $80,000. X Corporation distributes the land to T in complete cancellation of its outstanding stock. Pursuant to the general rule of § 331, T must recognize capital gain of $70,000 [$150,000 (fair market value of the land) minus $80,000 (adjusted basis of the stock)].

EXCEPTIONS TO THE GENERAL RULE

Liquidation of a Subsidiary. Section 332 is an exception to the general rule that the shareholder recognizes gain or loss on a corporate liquidation. If a parent corporation liquidates a subsidiary corporation in which it owns at least 80 percent of the voting stock, no gain or loss is recognized to the parent company. The subsidiary must distribute all of its property in complete liquidation of all of its stock within the taxable year or within three years from the close of the tax year in which the first distribution occurred.

One-Month Liquidation. Section 333 is another exception to the general rule that a shareholder recognizes gain or loss on a corporate liquidation. If shareholders elect and the liquidation is completed within one calendar month, § 333 postpones the recognition of gain on assets which have appreciated in the hands of the liquidating corporation. However, a shareholder does have recognized gain (to the extent

---

34. Stock owned by a broker probably would be inventory and would therefore not constitute a capital asset. Thus, the gain or loss on this type of stock would be ordinary and not capital.

of realized gain) in an amount equal to the greater of (a) the share-holder's portion of earnings and profits accumulated after February 28, 1913, or (b) amounts received by the shareholder consisting of money and stock or securities acquired by the corporation after 1953.[35]

For noncorporate shareholders, recognized gain is treated as dividend income to the extent of the shareholder's pro rata share of the corporate earnings and profits. Any excess amount of recognized gain is treated as capital gain.

For corporate shareholders, gain (to the extent recognized) is all treated as capital gain.[36]

> **Example 29.** The independent cases appearing below illustrate the possible tax consequences to a shareholder under a § 333 liquidation:

Case	Type of Shareholder	E & P	Cash plus Post-1953 Securities	Shareholder's Realized Gain	Shareholder's Recognized Gain	
					Capital	Dividend
A	Corporation	$ 10,000	$ 10,000	$ 5,000	$ 5,000	$ –0–
B	Corporation	10,000	20,000	40,000	20,000	–0–
C	Corporation	20,000	10,000	30,000	20,000	–0–
D	Individual	10,000	10,000	5,000	–0–	5,000
E	Individual	10,000	20,000	40,000	10,000	10,000
F	Individual	20,000	10,000	30,000	–0–	20,000

In Example 29, note that gain recognized for both corporate and noncorporate shareholders can never exceed realized gain (Cases A and D). Also, all recognized gain by a corporate shareholder must be capital gain (Cases A, B, and C). An individual has a capital gain only if the share of the cash plus post-1953 securities exceeds his or her share of the corporation's E & P (contrast Cases E and F).

A corporate shareholder owning 50 percent or more of the stock of a liquidating corporation cannot qualify under § 333. The remaining shareholders are divided into two groups: (a) noncorporate shareholders and (b) those corporate shareholders owning less than 50 percent of the stock in the liquidating corporation. Owners of stock possessing at least 80 percent of the total combined voting power of all classes of stock owned by shareholders in one of the above-mentioned groups must elect the provisions of § 333. If the 80 percent requirement is not met, the one-month liquidation treatment is not available to any member of that group.

---

35. § 333(e).

36. § 333(f) and Reg. § 1.333–4(b). The reason corporate shareholders are forced into capital gain treatment is the 85% dividends received deduction which would otherwise be available if dividend treatment were prescribed. Capital gain treatment, therefore, leads to a harsher tax effect on a corporate shareholder.

BASIS DETERMINATION—SECTION 334

General Rule. Where gain or loss is recognized upon the complete liquidation of a corporation, the basis of the property received by the shareholders is its fair market value.[37] Referring to Example 28, the basis of the land to shareholder T is $150,000 (fair market value) because gain was recognized.

One-Month Liquidation Basis Rules. Since gain is recognized only to a limited extent under § 333, the basis of the property received by the shareholders is the same as the basis of the shares redeemed, decreased by the amount of any money received and increased by gain recognized and liabilities assumed by the shareholders.[38] This amount is allocated to the various assets received on the basis of the relative fair market values of the properties.

Subsidiary Liquidation Basis Rules. The general rule is that the property received by the parent corporation in a complete liquidation of its subsidiary under § 332 has the same basis it had in the hands of the subsidiary.[39] The parent's basis in stock of the liquidated subsidiary disappears.

> **Example 30.** P, the parent corporation, has a basis of $20,000 in stock in S Corporation, a subsidiary in which it owns 85% of all classes of stock. P Corporation purchased the stock of S Corporation 10 years ago. In the current year, P Corporation liquidates S Corporation and acquires assets worth $50,000 with a tax basis to S Corporation of $40,000. P Corporation would have a basis of $40,000 in the assets, with a potential gain upon sale of $10,000. P Corporation's original $20,000 basis in the S Corporation stock disappears.

An exception to the carryover of basis rules is provided in § 338. Under this exception, the parent company may elect to receive a change in basis for the assets equal to the adjusted basis of the stock of the subsidiary. In effect, the initial acquisition of the subsidiary is treated as if the parent company had acquired the assets (rather than the stock) of the subsidiary.

The following requirements must be met:

—The parent must "purchase" at least 80 percent of the total combined voting power of all classes of stock and at least 80 percent of all other classes of stock (except nonvoting preferred) within a 12-month period.

—Within 75 days of meeting the 80 percent control requirement noted above, the parent corporation elects to have § 338 apply.

---

37. § 334(a).
38. § 334(c).
39. § 334(b)(1) and Reg. § 1.334–1(b).

Example 31. P Corporation acquired 100% of the stock of S Corporation for $1,000,000 cash in a taxable purchase transaction on January 1, 19X1. On February 1, 19X1, S Corporation was liquidated into P under § 338. The adjusted basis of S Corporation's net assets is $800,000. Since P acquired at least 80% of the stock in a taxable purchase transaction and made the election under § 338 within 75 days, P Corporation's basis in the net assets of S is $1,000,000 (the amount paid for the S stock). The transaction is treated as if P acquired the S Corporation's assets for $1,000,000 instead of acquiring S's stock for $1,000,000.

THE S ELECTION

JUSTIFICATION FOR THE ELECTION

Since there may be numerous nontax reasons for operating a business in corporate form, the existence of income tax disadvantages (e. g., double taxation of corporate income and shareholder dividends) should not deter business people from using the corporate form. In the interest of preventing tax considerations from interfering with the exercise of sound business judgment, Congress enacted Subchapter S of the Code.

To qualify for S corporation status, the corporation must be a small business corporation.[40] This includes any corporation which:

—Is a domestic corporation.

—Is not a member of an affiliated group.

—Has no more than 35 shareholders.

—Has as its shareholders only individuals, estates, and certain trusts.

—Does not have a nonresident alien as a shareholder.

—Issues only one class of stock.

Making the Election. The election is made by filing Form 2553, and all shareholders must consent. Special rules apply to husbands and wives where stock is jointly held and to minors.

The election must be filed anytime during the preceding taxable year or on or before the fifteenth day of the third month of the current year.[41]

Example 32. T, a calendar year taxpayer, is a regular corporation that desires to elect S status for 19X3. If the election is filed anytime from January 1, 19X3, through March 15, 19X3, it will be effective for 19X3.

---

40. § 1361(b).
41. § 1362(b).

Loss of the Election. Revocation of the S election may occur voluntarily (i. e., a majority of the shareholders file to revoke the election) or involuntarily, in any of the following ways:[42]

—The corporation ceases to qualify as a small business corporation (e. g., the number of shareholders exceeds 35, a partnership becomes a shareholder).

—In certain cases, when the corporation has passive investment income (e. g., interest, dividends) in excess of 25 percent of gross receipts for a period of three consecutive years.

If a majority of the shareholders consent to a voluntary revocation of S status, the election must be made on or before the fifteenth day of the third month of the tax year to be effective for that year.

Example 33. The shareholders of T Corporation, a calendar year S corporation, elect to revoke the election on January 5, 19X3. Assuming the election is duly executed and timely filed, T Corporation will become a regular corporation for calendar year 19X3. If, on the other hand, the election is not made until June 19X3, T Corporation will not become a regular corporation until calendar year 19X4.

In the case where S status is lost because of a disqualifying act, the loss of the election takes effect as of the date on which the event occurs.

Example 34. T Corporation has been a calendar year S corporation for several years. On August 13, 19X3, one of its shareholders sells her stock to Y Corporation. Since T Corporation no longer satisfies the definition of a small business corporation (i. e., it has another corporation as a shareholder), the election has been involuntarily terminated. For calendar year 19X3, therefore, T Corporation will be an S corporation through August 12 and a regular corporation from August 13 through December 31, 19X3.

OPERATIONAL RULES

The S corporation is primarily a tax-reporting rather than a tax-paying entity. In this respect, the entity is taxed much like a partnership. Under the conduit concept, the taxable income and losses of an S corporation flow through to its shareholders and are reported by them on their personal income tax returns.

To ascertain the annual tax consequences to each shareholder, it is necessary to carry out two steps at the S corporation level. First, set aside all corporate transactions that, under the conduit approach, will

---

42. § 1362(d).

flow through to the shareholders on an "as is" basis. Second, what remains is aggregated as the taxable income of the S corporation and is allocated to each shareholder on a per-share and per-day of stock ownership basis.[43]

Separately Stated Items. Summarized below are some of the items that do not lose their identity as they pass through the S corporation and are therefore picked up by each shareholder on an "as is" basis:

—Tax-exempt income.

—Long-term and short-term capital gains and losses.

—Section 1231 gains and losses.

—Charitable contributions.

—Foreign tax credits.

—Basis of § 38 new and used property (for purposes of calculating the investment tax credit or immediate expensing under § 179).

—Dividends.

—Depletion.

—Nonbusiness income or loss under § 212.

—Intangible drilling costs.

The reason that these items are separately stated is that each may lead to a different tax result when combined with a particular shareholder's other transactions.

> **Example 35.** X and Y are equal shareholders in P Corporation (an S corporation). For calendar year 19X3, each must account for one-half of a corporate short-term capital gain of $6,000. X has no other capital asset transactions, while Y has a short-term capital loss of $3,000 from the sale of stock in ABC Corporation. In terms of overall effect, the difference between the two taxpayers should be clear. Although both must report the short-term capital gain pass-through, Y will neutralize its inclusion in gross income through an offset with the $3,000 short-term capital loss from the sale of the stock in ABC Corporation. To X, the short-term capital gain pass-through results in additional ordinary income of $3,000.

Taxable Income. After the separately stated items have been removed, the balance represents the taxable income of the S corporation.[44] In arriving at taxable income, however, the dividends received deduction (§ 243) and the net operating loss deduction (§ 172) are not allowed. Although an S corporation comes under the regular

---

43. § 1366.

44. § 1363.

corporate rules for purposes of amortization of organizational expenditures (§ 248), it is not subject to the special rules regarding corporate tax preferences (§ 291).

Once taxable income has been determined, it passes through to each shareholder as of the last day of the S corporation's tax year.

Example 36. X Corporation, a calendar year S corporation, had the following transactions during 19X3:

Sales		$ 40,000
Cost of goods sold		(23,000)
Other income:		
*Tax-exempt interest	$ 300	
*Dividend income	200	
*Long-term capital gain	500	1,000
Other expenses:		
*Charitable contributions	$ 400	
Advertising expense	1,500	
Other operating expenses	2,000	
*Short-term capital loss	150	(4,050)
Net income per books		$ 13,950

When the items that are to be separately stated [those preceded by an asterisk (*)] and shown "as is" by each shareholder are withdrawn, the taxable income of X Corporation becomes:

Sales		$ 40,000
Cost of goods sold		(23,000)
Other expenses:		
Advertising expense	$ 1,500	
Other operating expenses	2,000	(3,500)
Taxable income		$ 13,500

Example 37. If T owned 10% of the stock in X Corporation (see Example 36) during all of 19X3, he must account for the following:

Separately stated items:	
Tax-exempt interest	$ 30
Dividend income	20
Long-term capital gain	50
Charitable contributions	40
Short-term capital loss	15
Taxable income (10% of $13,500)	1,350

Some of the separately stated items need not be reported on T's individual income tax return (e. g., the tax-exempt interest), while others must be reported but may not lead to tax consequences (e. g., the application of the § 116 dividend exclusion may neutralize the $20 of dividend income). As to T's share of X Corporation's taxable income (i. e., $1,350), this must be picked up by him as ordinary income.

Treatment of Losses. Separately stated loss items (e. g., capital losses, § 1231 losses) will, as noted above, flow through to the shareholders on an "as is" basis. Thus, their treatment to a shareholder will depend on the shareholder's individual income tax position. If, moreover, the S corporation's taxable income determination results in an operating loss, this also will pass through to the shareholders. As is the case with separately stated items, the amount of the loss each shareholder receives depends on the stock ownership during the year.

> **Example 38.** In 19X3, Y Corporation (a calendar year S corporation) incurred an operating loss of $36,500. During 19X3, T's ownership in Y Corporation was as follows: 20% for 200 days and 30% for 165 days. T's share of the loss is $8,950, determined as follows:

$$
\begin{array}{ll}
(\$36{,}500 \times 200/365) \times 20\% = & \$\ 4{,}000 \\
(\$36{,}500 \times 165/365) \times 30\% = & \underline{4{,}950} \\
\text{Total loss} & \underline{\underline{\$\ 8{,}950}}
\end{array}
$$

Presuming the basis limitation does not come into play (see the discussion below), T may deduct $8,950 in arriving at adjusted gross income.

Basis Determination. Like regular corporations, a shareholder's basis in the stock of an S corporation will be the original investment plus additional capital contributions less return of capital distributions. At this point, however, the symmetry disappears. Generally, basis will be increased by the pass-through of income items (including those separately stated) and decreased by the loss items (including those separately stated).[45]

> **Example 39.** In 19X3, M Corporation is formed with an investment of $100,000 of which T contributed $20,000 for a 20% stock interest. A timely S election is made and for 19X3, M Corporation earns taxable income of $15,000. T's basis in her stock investment now becomes $23,000 [$20,000 (original capital contribution) + $3,000 (the 20% share of the corporation's taxable income assigned to T)].

Distributions by an S corporation reduce the basis of a shareholder's stock investment. However, if the amount of the distribution exceeds basis, such excess normally will be accorded capital gain treatment.

---

45. § 1367.

As previously noted, operating losses of an S corporation pass through to the shareholders and reduce the basis in their stock investment. Because the basis of the stock cannot fall below zero, an excess loss is then applied against the basis of any loans the shareholder may have made to the corporation.

Example 40. Z Corporation, a calendar year S corporation, has an operating loss of $60,000 for 19X3. T, a 50% shareholder, has an adjusted basis in his stock investment of $25,000 and has made loans to the corporation of $5,000. Based on these facts, T may take full advantage of the $30,000 loss (i. e., 50% of $60,000) on his 19X3 individual income tax return. T's basis in the stock and the loans must be reduced accordingly, and both will be zero after the pass-through.

In the event the basis limitation precludes an operating loss from being absorbed, the loss can be carried forward and deducted when and if it is covered by basis.

Example 41. Assume the same facts as in the previous example except that T had not made any loans to Z Corporation. Further assume that Z Corporation has taxable income of $15,000 in the following year (i. e., 19X4). T's tax situation for 19X3 and 19X4 is summarized below:

Ordinary loss for 19X3	$ 25,000
Restoration of stock basis in 19X4	
(50% of $15,000)	7,500
Income to be reported in 19X4	7,500
Loss allowed for 19X4 ($30,000 − $25,000)	5,000
Basis in stock account after 19X4	
($7,500 − $5,000)	2,500

Thus, T's unabsorbed loss of $5,000 from 19X3 carries over to 19X4 and is applied against the $7,500 of ordinary income for that year.

PARTNERSHIPS

NATURE OF PARTNERSHIP TAXATION

Unlike corporations, partnerships are not considered separate taxable entities. Instead, each member of a partnership is subject to income tax on his or her distributive share of the partnership's income, even if an actual distribution is not made. Thus, the tax return (Form 1065—see Appendix B–6) required of a partnership serves only to provide information necessary in determining the character and amount of each partner's distributive share of the partnership's income and expense.

Although a partnership is not considered a separate taxable entity for purposes of determining and paying Federal income taxes, it is treated as such for purposes of making various elections and selecting its taxable year, method of depreciation, and accounting methods. Also, a partnership is treated as a separate legal entity under civil law with the right to own property in its own name and to transact business free from the personal debts of its partners.

PARTNERSHIP FORMATION

Recognition of Gain or Loss. Section 721 contains the general rule that no gain or loss is recognized to a partnership or any of its partners on the contribution of property in exchange for a capital interest in the partnership. This general rule also applies to all subsequent contributions of property.

Certain exceptions to the nonrecognition of gain or loss rule include the following:

—If the transfer of property by a partner to the partnership results in the receipt of money or other consideration by the partner, the transaction will be treated as a sale or exchange rather than as a contribution of capital under § 721.

—If a partnership interest is received in exchange for services rendered or to be rendered by the partner to the partnership, the fair market value of the transferred capital interest is considered as compensation for services rendered. In such cases, the recipient of the capital interest must recognize the amount as ordinary income in the year actually or constructively received.

—If property that is subject to a liability in excess of its basis is contributed to a partnership, gain may be recognized to the contributing partner in the amount of such excess.

Basis of a Partnership Interest. The contributing partner's basis in the partnership interest received is the sum of money contributed plus the adjusted basis of any other property transferred to the partnership. However, if gain or loss is recognized on the transfer or if ordinary income results, the basis must be adjusted accordingly.

Example 42. In return for services rendered and the contribution of property (with a basis of $50,000, fair market value of $80,000) to the KLM Partnership, A receives a 25% capital interest valued at $100,000. The contribution of property is nontaxable under § 721. However, the receipt of a partnership interest for services rendered results in compensation to A of $20,000 (value of partnership interest of $100,000 less value of property contributed of $80,000). A's basis in the KLM Partnership interest is $70,000 (basis of property contributed of $50,000 plus ordinary income recognized of $20,000).

A partner's basis in the partnership interest is determined without regard to any amount reflected on the partnership's books as capital, equity, or a similar account.

Example 43. U and V form an equal partnership with a cash contribution of $30,000 from U and a property contribution (adjusted basis of $18,000 and fair market value of $30,000) from V. Although the books of the UV Partnership may reflect a credit of $30,000 to each partner's capital account, only U will have a tax basis of $30,000 in his partnership interest. V's tax basis in his partnership interest will be $18,000, the amount of his tax basis in the property contributed to the partnership.

After its initial determination, the basis of a partnership interest is subject to continuous fluctuations. A partner's basis will be increased by additional contributions and the sum of his or her current and prior years' distributive share of:

—Taxable income of the partnership, including capital gains.

—Tax-exempt income of the partnership.

—The excess of the deductions for depletion over the basis of the partnership's property subject to depletion.[46]

Similarly, the basis of a partner's interest will be decreased, but not below zero, by distributions of partnership property and by the sum of the current and prior years' distributive share of:

—Partnership losses, including capital losses.

—Partnership expenditures which are not deductible in computing taxable income or loss and which are not capital expenditures.

Changes in the liabilities (including trade accounts payable, bank loans, etc.) of a partnership will also affect the basis of a partnership interest. For instance, a partner's basis is increased by his assumption of partnership liabilities and by his or her pro rata share of liabilities incurred by the partnership. Likewise, the partner's basis is decreased by the amount of any of the personal liabilities assumed by the partnership and by the pro rata share of any decreases in the liability of the partnership.

Example 44. X, Y, and Z form the XYZ Partnership with the following contributions: cash of $50,000 from X for a 50% interest in capital and profits, cash of $25,000 from Y for a 25% interest, and property valued at $33,000 from Z for a 25% interest. The property contributed by Z has an adjusted basis of $15,000 and is subject to a mortgage of $8,000 which is assumed by the partnership. Z's basis in his interest in the XYZ Partnership is $9,000, determined as follows:

---

46. § 705(a).

Adjusted basis of Z's contributed property	$ 15,000
Less portion of mortgage assumed by X and Y and treated as a distribution of money to Z (75% of $8,000)	6,000
Basis of Z's interest in XYZ Partnership	$ 9,000

Example 45. Assuming the same facts as in the previous example, X and Y will have a basis in their partnership interest of $54,000 and $27,000, respectively.

	X	Y
Cash contribution	$ 50,000	$ 25,000
Plus portion of mortgage assumed and treated as an additional cash contribution:		
(50% of $8,000)	4,000	
(25% of $8,000)		2,000
Basis of interest in XYZ Partnership	$ 54,000	$ 27,000

Partnership's Basis in Contributed Property. Section 723 states that the basis of property contributed to a partnership by a partner shall be the adjusted basis of such property to the contributing partner at the time of the contribution. Additionally, the holding period of such property for the partnership includes the period during which it was held by the contributing partner. This is true, since the partnership's basis in the property is the same basis the property had in the hands of the partner.[47]

Example 46. In 19X5, R contributed equipment with an adjusted basis of $10,000 and fair market value of $30,000 to the RST Partnership in exchange for a one-third interest in the partnership. If no gain or loss is recognized by R, the basis in the equipment is $10,000 to the RST Partnership. If R had acquired the equipment in 19X1, the holding period for the RST Partnership includes the period from 19X1 through 19X5.

PARTNERSHIP OPERATION

Measuring and Reporting Partnership Income. Although a partnership is not subject to Federal income taxation, it is required to determine its taxable income and file an income tax return for information purposes.[48] The tax return, Form 1065, is due on the fifteenth

---

47. Reg. § 1.723–1 and § 1223(2).
48. § 6031.

day of the fourth month following the close of the taxable year of the partnership.

The measurement and reporting of partnership income requires that certain transactions be segregated and reported separately on the partnership return. Items such as charitable contributions, capital gains and losses, dividends qualifying for the $100 exclusion, and foreign taxes are excluded from partnership taxable income and are allocated separately to the partners.[49] See Appendix B for a sample Form 1065 (the partnership return) and Schedule K–1 (which details each partner's share of income, credits, deductions, etc.). The required segregation and direct allocation of the above items are necessary because they affect the computation of various exclusions, deductions, and credits at the individual partner level. For example, one of the partners may have made personal charitable contributions in excess of the ceiling limitations on his or her individual tax return. Therefore, partnership contributions are excluded from partnership income and are reported separately on the partnership return.

A second step in the measurement and reporting process is the computation of the partnership's ordinary income or loss. In this process, the taxable income of a partnership is computed in the same manner as is the taxable income of an individual taxpayer, except that a partnership is not allowed the following deductions:[50]

—The zero bracket amount.

—The deduction for personal exemptions.

—The deduction for taxes paid to foreign countries or possessions of the United States.

—The deduction for charitable contributions.

—The deduction for net operating losses.

—The personal itemized deductions allowed individuals in § § 211 through 222.

The partnership's ordinary income or loss and each of the items requiring separate treatment are reported in the partnership's information return and allocated to the partners in accordance with the distributive share of each.

Limitation on Partner's Share of Losses. A partner's deduction of the distributive share of partnership losses (including capital losses) is limited to the adjusted basis of the partnership interest at the end of the partnership year in which the losses were incurred.

The limitation for partnership loss deductions is similar to the limitation on losses in the case of S corporations. Like S corporation losses, partnership losses may be carried forward by the partner and utilized against future increases in the basis of the partnership inter-

---

49. § 702(a).
50. § 703(a).

est. Such increases might result from additional capital contributions to the partnership, from additional partnership liabilities, or from future partnership income.

Example 47. C and D do business as the CD Partnership, sharing profits and losses equally. All parties use the calendar year for tax purposes. As of January 1, 19X6, C's basis in his partnership interest is $25,000. The partnership sustained an operating loss of $80,000 in 19X6 and earned a profit of $70,000 in 19X7. For the calendar year 19X6, C may claim only $25,000 of his $40,000 distributive share of the partnership loss (one-half of the $80,000 loss). As a result, the basis in his partnership interest will be reduced to zero as of January 1, 19X7, and he must carry forward the remaining $15,000 of partnership losses.

Example 48. Assuming the same facts as in the previous example, what will be the income tax consequences for C in 19X7? Since the partnership earned a profit of $70,000 for the calendar year 19X7, C will report income from the partnership of $20,000 ($35,000 distributive share of income for 19X7 less the $15,000 loss not allowed for 19X6). The adjusted basis of his partnership interest now becomes $20,000.

Transactions Between Partner and Partnership. A partner engaging in a transaction with the partnership is generally regarded as a nonpartner or outsider. However, certain exceptions have been provided to prevent tax avoidance. For instance, under § 707(b)(1), losses from the sale or exchange of property will be disallowed if they arise in either of the following cases:

—Between a partnership and a partner whose direct or indirect interest in the capital or profits of the partnership is more than 50 percent.[51]

—Between two partnerships in which the same persons own more than 50 percent interest in the capital or profits.

If one of the purchasers later sells the property, any gain realized will be recognized only to the extent that it exceeds the loss previously disallowed.

Example 49. R owns a 60% interest in the capital and profits of the RST Partnership. On September 1, 19X8, R sells property with an adjusted basis of $50,000 to the partnership for its fair market value of $35,000. The $15,000 loss is not deductible, since R's ownership interest is more than 50%. If the RST Partnership later sells the property for $40,000, none of the $5,000 (sale price of $40,000 less adjusted basis to partnership of $35,000) gain will

---

51. Indirect ownership includes constructive ownership by related·partners such as brothers and sisters. § 707(b)(3) and § 267(c)(4).

be recognized. The unused loss of $10,000, however, is of no tax benefit either to the partnership or to R.

Payments made by a partnership to one of its partners for services rendered or for the use of capital, to the extent they are determined without regard to the income of the partnership, are treated by the partnership in the same manner as payments made to a person who is not a partner. Referred to as guaranteed payments under § 707(c), such payments are generally deductible by the partnership as a business expense and must be reported as ordinary income by the receiving partner. Their deductibility distinguishes guaranteed payments from a partner's distributive share of income which is not deductible by the partnership.

Example 50. Under the terms of the LMN Partnership agreement, N is entitled to a fixed annual salary of $18,000, without regard to the income of the partnership. He is also to share in the profits and losses of the partnership as an equal partner. After deducting the guaranteed payment, the partnership has $36,000 of ordinary income. N must include $30,000 as ordinary income in his income tax return for his tax year with or within which the partnership tax year ends ($18,000 guaranteed payment plus his one-third distributive share of partnership income of $12,000).

Taxable Years of Partner and Partnership. In computing a partner's taxable income for a specific year, § 706(a) requires that each partner include in income his or her distributive share of partnership income and any guaranteed payments from a partnership whose tax year ends with or within the partner's taxable year. Thus, a partner reports the share of the income (including guaranteed payments) from the partnership for the year ending on January 31, 19X8, on his or her 19X9 income tax return. Under this provision, there can be an effective deferral of a partner's share of partnership income of up to 11 months. Because of this deferral possibility, a partnership is required to use the same taxable year as that of all its principal partners unless the partnership was formed prior to 1954 or unless the partnership obtains the permission of the IRS to adopt or change its taxable year.[52] When consent is required, it will be conditional on a finding of a business purpose for the adoption or change.

Other Partnership Considerations. Complex tax provisions involving liquidating and nonliquidating distributions and the sale of a partnership interest are beyond the scope of this text and are discussed in depth in *West's Federal Taxation: Corporations, Partnerships, Estates, and Trusts.*

---

52. Reg. § 1.706–1(b).

✓ TAX PLANNING
CONSIDERATIONS

CORPORATE VERSUS NONCORPORATE FORMS OF BUSINESS ORGANIZATION

The decision to use the corporate form in conducting a trade or business must be weighed carefully. Besides the nontax considerations attendant to the corporate form (i. e., limited liability, continuity of life, free transferability of interest, centralized management), tax ramifications will play an important role in any such decision. Close attention should be paid to the following:

—The corporate form means the imposition of the corporate income tax. Corporate-source income will be taxed twice—once as earned by the corporation and again when distributed to the shareholders. Since dividends are not deductible, a strong incentive exists in a closely-held corporation to structure corporate distributions in a deductible form. Thus, profits may be bailed out by the shareholders in the form of salaries, interest, or rents. Such procedures lead to a multitude of problems, one of which, the reclassification of debt as equity, has been discussed. The problems of unreasonable salaries and rents were discussed in Chapter 7.

—Corporate-source income loses its identity as it passes through the corporation to the shareholders. Thus, items possessing preferential tax treatment (e. g., interest on municipal bonds, long-term capital gains) are not taxed as such to the shareholders.

—As noted earlier, it may be difficult for shareholders to recover some or all of their investment in the corporation without an ordinary income result, since most corporate distributions are treated as dividends to the extent of the corporation's earnings and profits. Structuring the capital of the corporation to include debt is a partial solution to this problem. Thus, the shareholder-creditor could recoup part of his or her investment through the tax-free payment of principal. Too much debt, however, may lead to such debt being reclassified as equity.

—Corporate losses cannot be passed through to the shareholders.

—Long-term capital gains and losses generally receive more favorable tax treatment in the hands of noncorporate taxpayers.

—The liquidation of a corporation may generate tax consequences to both the corporation and its shareholders.

—On the positive side, the corporate form may be advantageous for shareholders in high individual tax brackets. With a maximum corporate income tax rate of 46 percent, such shareholders would be motivated to avoid dividend distributions and retain profits within the corporation. If the earnings are reinvested primarily in operating assets, the corporation may safely retain such earnings without being subject to penalty taxes.

—The corporate form does provide the shareholders with the opportunity to be treated as "employees" for tax purposes if they, in fact, render services to the corporation. Such status makes a number of attractive tax-sheltered fringe benefits available (e. g., group-term life insurance, accident and health plans). These benefits are not available to partners and sole proprietors.

REGULAR CORPORATION VERSUS S CORPORATION STATUS

Effective tax planning with S corporations begins with determining whether the election is appropriate. In this context, one should consider the following factors:

—Are losses from the business anticipated? If so, the election may be highly attractive because these losses pass through to the shareholders.

—What are the tax brackets of the shareholders? If the shareholders are in the high individual income tax brackets, it may be desirable to avoid S status and have profits taxed to the corporation at a maximum rate of 46 percent. When the immediate pass-through of taxable income is avoided, profits of the corporation may later be bailed out by the shareholders at capital gain rates through stock redemptions, liquidating distributions, or sales of stock to others; received as dividend distributions, in low tax bracket years; or negated by a step-up in basis at the death of the shareholder. On the other hand, if the shareholders are in low individual income tax brackets, the pass-through of corporate profits does not impact so forcefully and avoidance of the corporate income tax becomes the paramount consideration. Under these circumstances, the S election could be highly attractive. Bear in mind, however, that S corporations escape the Federal corporate income tax but may not be immune from any state and local taxes imposed on corporations.

PROBLEM MATERIALS

Questions for Class Discussion

1. Will a business be treated as a corporation for Federal income tax purposes if the state legal requirements for a corporation are met, even if the business does not possess corporate characteristics?

2. Why would the IRS in some instances assert that an entity is taxable as a corporation rather than being taxed as a noncorporate entity?

3. Section 1250 may compel the recapture of depreciation as ordinary income upon the sale or other taxable disposition of depreciable real estate. In the application of § 1250, are corporate and noncorporate taxpayers treated the same way? Explain.

4. What is the effective corporate tax rate on net long-term capital gains? Are corporations allowed a 60% long-term capital gain deduction?

5. Contrast the corporate tax rules for deducting net capital losses with the rules for individuals. Are the corporate capital loss rules *more* or *less* favorable than the capital loss provisions for individuals? Why?

6. What requirements must be met to properly accrue a charitable contribution, the payment of which is made in the year following the year of the deduction?

7. How are corporate charitable contributions treated if such amounts are in excess of the maximum limitations?

8. Why are the corporate net operating loss adjustments substantially different from the NOL adjustments for individual taxpayers?

9. Why is the 85% dividends received deduction added back to increase an NOL for a corporation?

10. Why would a corporation elect not to carry back an NOL to a particular year?

11. What is the rationale for the dividends received deduction for corporate shareholders?

12. X Corporation makes a timely election to amortize its organizational expenditures over a period of 100 months.

    (a) Is this an allowable procedure?

    (b) Can you think of any reason why this period was selected?

13. Distinguish between expenditures which qualify as organizational expenditures and those which do not qualify.

14. It has been suggested that a shortcut for computing the corporate income tax would be the following formula: $25,750 + (46% of taxable income in excess of $100,000).

    (a) Do you agree? Explain.

    (b) When might the formula not work?

15. Discuss the minimum tax provisions applicable to corporate taxpayers.

16. For many corporations why might taxable income be different from financial accounting income?

17. What purpose does the Schedule M-1 reconciliation of Form 1120 serve (a) for the taxpayer, (b) for the IRS?

18. Why is it usually advantageous to capitalize a corporation by using debt? Is it possible that the debt will be reclassified as equity? Why?

19. What is the rationale for § 351? What is "boot"? Why is gain recognized to the extent of boot received?

20. If appreciated property is transferred to a corporation in a nontaxable exchange under § 351, is gain recognized to the corporation if the property is immediately sold by the corporation at its fair market value? Why?

21. Basis of stock received = basis of property given up − boot received + gain recognized on the transfer. Please comment.

22. It has been said that relying on § 302(b)(1) (a stock redemption that is not essentially equivalent to a dividend) is a "dangerous way to travel." Explain.

23. How do the following transactions affect the earnings and profits of a corporation?

     (a) A nontaxable stock dividend issued to the shareholders.

     (b) Receipt of interest on municipal bonds.

     (c) Federal corporate income tax liability.

24. How is the basis of the assets of a subsidiary determined on the transfer of such assets to the parent in a § 332 liquidation? How is it possible for the parent company to receive a step-up in basis for the subsidiary assets if certain requirements are met?

25. Discuss the requirements of a one-month liquidation. When would the one-month liquidation be preferable to a liquidation under the general rules of § 331?

26. How is the basis determined for assets received by shareholders in a one-month liquidation?

27. What are the requirements to be a small business corporation under Subchapter S?

28. On March 16, 1984, eighty percent of the shareholders of X Corporation, a calendar year taxpayer, elect to terminate S status. For what year will X Corporation first become a regular corporation?

29. What are some examples of separately stated items that pass through "as is" to an S corporation's shareholders? Why is this procedure required?

30. If an S corporation incurs an operating loss, how is such a loss apportioned to the shareholders?

31. Are net operating losses of an S corporation deductible by the shareholders without limit? Why?

32. How are charitable contributions made by an S corporation treated?

33. Compare the nonrecognition of gain or loss on contributions to a partnership with the similar provision found in corporate formation (§ 351). What is (are) the major difference(s)? Similarities?

34. Under what circumstances does the receipt of a partnership interest result in the recognition of ordinary income? What is the effect of this on the partnership and the other partners?

35. How is a contributing partner's basis in a partnership interest determined?

36. What transactions or events will cause a partner's basis in his or her partnership interest to fluctuate continuously?

37. Why is a partnership required to file an information return (Form 1065)?

38. Describe the two-step approach used in determining partnership income. Why is the computation necessary?

39. To what extent can a partner deduct his or her distributive share of partnership losses? What happens to any unused losses?

40. What are guaranteed payments? When might such payments be used?

Problems

41. The XYZ Partnership is engaged in commercial real estate management and investment activities. The partners decided to form the XYZ Corporation, since interest rates were increasing and under state law a corporation lender was exempt from the state usury laws. It was intended that the corporation would be used solely to hold title to the real estate properties and would engage in no other activities. The corporation would act as a nominee or agent for the partners in obtaining adequate financing from banks and other lending institutions.

    It is anticipated that the real estate business will incur losses of $100,000 each year for the next five years. The tax basis in the XYZ Corporation stock for X, Y, and Z would be nominal, since most of the capital would be obtained or contributed by the partnership from outside debt financing.

    (a) What are the possible risks resulting from the creation of a "dummy" corporation?

    (b) If profits were generated after five years and the corporation made distributions to shareholders, how might these distributions be treated?

    (c) Should X, Y, and Z consider the corporate form of organization with an S election?

42. XYZ Corporation, a calendar year taxpayer, was formed in January 19X3. For tax year 19X3 it had taxable income of $25,000, while for tax year 19X4 a net operating loss of $25,000 resulted. It anticipates taxable income of $100,000 for the next tax year (i. e., 19X5). Discuss the disposition of the 19X4 net operating loss under each of the following assumptions:

    (a) XYZ Corporation is an S corporation.

    (b) XYZ Corporation is not an S corporation.

43. XYZ Corporation had taxable income of $80,000 in 19X3, consisting of $40,000 ordinary taxable income and $40,000 long-term net capital gains.

    (a) Compute XYZ's tax under the regular tax computation.

    (b) Compute XYZ's tax by using the alternative tax computation.

    (c) Which method should be used?

44. XYZ Corporation incurred short-term net capital gains of $30,000 and long-term net capital losses of $80,000 during 19X6. Taxable income from other sources was $400,000. Prior years' transactions included the following:

19X2	Long-term net capital gains	$ 80,000
19X3	Short-term net capital gains	20,000
19X4	Long-term net capital gains	10,000
19X5	Long-term net capital gains	10,000

(a) How are the capital gains and losses treated on the 19X6 tax return?

(b) Compute the capital loss carryback to the carryback years.

(c) Compute the amount of capital loss carryover, if any, and designate the years to which the loss may be carried.

45. During the current year, T Corporation has the following transactions:

Gross income	$ 500,000
Allowable business expenses	600,000
Cash dividend received from X Corporation (a domestic corporation not a member of a controlled group)	10,000
Property dividend received from Y Corporation (a domestic corporation not a member of a controlled group)*	15,000
Property dividend received from Z Corporation (a domestic corporation not a member of a controlled group)**	20,000

*The property had a basis to Y Corporation of $10,000 and a fair market value of $15,000. No gain was recognized by Y Corporation as a result of the distribution.
**The property had a basis to Z Corporation of $25,000 and a fair market value of $20,000.

(a) Determine T Corporation's net operating loss.

(b) Determine T Corporation's dividends received deduction.

(c) What basis will T Corporation have in the property it received from Y Corporation?

(d) What basis will T Corporation have in the property it received from Z Corporation?

46. During 19X2, T Corporation, a calendar year taxpayer, had the following income and expenses:

Income from operations	$ 150,000
Expenses from operations	110,000
Dividends from domestic corporations	10,000
NOL carryover from 19X1	3,000

On May 1, 19X2, T Corporation made a contribution to a qualified charitable organization of $7,000 in cash (not included in any of the items listed above).

(a) Determine T Corporation's deduction for charitable contributions for 19X2.

(b) What happens to any portion of the contribution not deductible in 19X2?

47. T Corporation had the following income and expenses for 19X2:

Gross income from operations	$ 300,000
Expenses from operations	350,000
Qualified cash dividends from stock	200,000

(a) Determine T Corporation's dividends received deduction for 19X2.

(b) Suppose the expenses from operations amounted to only $320,000 (instead of $350,000). Determine T Corporation's dividends received deduction for 19X2.

48. T Corporation, an accrual basis taxpayer, was formed and began operations on May 1, 19X2. The following expenses were incurred during its first year of operations (May 1 to December 31, 19X2):

Expenses of temporary directors and of organizational meetings	$ 1,100
Fee paid to the state for incorporation	100
Accounting services incident to organization	200
Legal services for drafting the corporate charter and bylaws	400
Expenses incident to the printing and sale of stock certificates	300
	$ 2,100

Assume T Corporation makes an appropriate and timely election under § 248(c) and the Regulations.

(a) What is the maximum organizational expense T may write off for the calendar year 19X2?

(b) What would be the result if a proper election had not been made?

49. For 19X1, T Corporation, an accrual basis, calendar year taxpayer, had net income per books of $75,050 and the following special transactions:

Prepaid rent received in 19X1 ($10,000 related to 19X2)	$ 15,000
Capital loss in excess of capital gains (no carry-back to prior years)	4,000
Interest on loan to carry tax-exempt bonds	3,500
Interest income on tax-exempt bonds	3,000
Accelerated depreciation in excess of straight-line	5,500
Federal income tax liability for 19X1	35,950

Using schedule M–1 of Form 1120 in Appendix B, compute T Corporation's taxable income for 19X1.

50. X and Y formed XY Corporation with the following investment: X transferred property with a fair market value of $50,000 and basis of $20,000, while Y transferred property with a fair market value of $50,000 and adjusted basis of $70,000. X received $50,000 of XY voting stock and Y received $40,000 of XY voting stock and a demand note for $10,000.

(a) Do the transfers qualify under § 351?

(b) How much gain or loss is recognized by X? By Y?

(c) If Y received $10,000 cash instead of the note, would your answer be different?

(d) Would either X or Y prefer that the transaction be completely taxable? Why?

51. T owns 90 shares of the stock of X Corporation. Unrelated parties own the remaining 10 shares. Since T needs cash for personal reasons, 30 of T's shares were redeemed by the corporation during the year for $50,000. X Corporation has earnings and profits of $150,000.

(a) Is the redemption treated as a sale or exchange of T's stock? If not, what tax treatment is applicable?

(b) Would your answer be different if X Corporation had no earnings and profits?

(c) Would your answer be different if all of T's shares were redeemed?

52. X Corporation was liquidated under the general rules of § 331. The company distributed its only asset (land with a fair market value of $100,000 and adjusted cost basis of $20,000) to T, an individual who held all of the X Corporation stock as an investment. T's basis in the stock of X Corporation was $60,000. X Corporation had earnings and profits of $10,000 which were accumulated since February 28, 1913.

(a) What is the amount and character of gain or loss recognized by T upon the receipt of the land in exchange for his stock?

(b) What is T's basis in the land?

(c) Assume that a one-month plan of liquidation was elected; calculate the amount and character of T's gain or loss and T's basis in the land.

(d) If T were a corporate shareholder and X Corporation was liquidated into T, what liquidation section would apply? How much gain or loss would be recognized by T, and what would be T's basis in the land?

53. T Corporation enters into a plan of complete liquidation under § 333— one-month liquidation rules. T Corporation is owned in equal shares by A, B, and C (who is a corporate shareholder). T Corporation has earnings and profits of $60,000 and distributes two assets, land with a fair market value of $90,000 (adjusted basis of $40,000) and cash of $39,000. T Corporation distributes the land and cash equally to A, B, and C Corporation. A's basis in the T stock is $10,000, B's basis is $30,000, and C Corporation's basis is $20,000.

(a) Are A, B, and C Corporation qualified electing shareholders?

(b) Calculate the amount and character of gain recognized, if any, to A, B, and C Corporation.

(c) Calculate the basis of the land received by A, B, and C Corporation.

54. During 19X4, X Corporation (a calendar year and accrual basis S corporation) had the following transactions:

Sales	$ 300,000
Cost of goods sold	200,000
Interest on municipal bonds	1,000
Long-term capital gain	2,000
Short-term capital loss	3,000
Advertising expense	4,000
Cash dividends on Exxon stock	1,500
Charitable contributions	500
Salaries and wages	40,000
Amortization of organizational expenditures	400

(a) Determine X Corporation's separately stated items for 19X4.

(b) Determine X Corporation's taxable income for 19X4.

55. In 19X5 (a non-leap year), Y Corporation (a calendar year S corporation) had a net operating loss of $109,500. T, a calendar year individual, held stock in Y Corporation as follows: 40% for 300 days and 60% for 65 days. Based on these facts, what is T's loss pass-through for 19X5?

56. B owns 50% of the stock in an S corporation. This corporation sustains a $24,000 operating loss during 19X4. B's adjusted basis in the stock is $2,000, but she has a loan outstanding to the corporation in the amount of $2,000. What amount, if any, is she entitled to deduct with respect to these losses on her Form 1040 in 19X4?

57. A, B, and C form the ABC Partnership on January 1, 19X8. In return for a 30% capital interest, A transfers property (basis of $14,000, fair market value of $25,000) subject to a liability of $10,000. The liability is assumed by the partnership. B transfers property (basis of $24,000, fair market value of $15,000) for a 30% capital interest, and C transfers cash of $20,000 for the remaining 40% interest.

(a) How much gain must A recognize on the transfer?

(b) What is A's basis in his partnership interest?

(c) How much loss may B recognize on the transfer?

(d) What is B's basis in his partnership interest?

(e) What is C's basis in his partnership interest?

(f) What basis will the ABC Partnership have in the property, other than the cash, transferred by A? The property transferred by B?

(g) What would be the tax consequences to A if the basis of the property he contributed is only $9,000.

58. As of January 1, 19X7, D had a basis of $24,000 in his 25% capital interest in the DEF Partnership. He and the partnership use the calendar year for tax purposes. The partnership incurred an operating loss of $120,000 for 19X7 and a profit of $80,000 for 19X8.

(a) How much, if any, loss may D recognize for 19X7?

(b) How much income must D recognize for 19X8?

(c) What basis will D have in his partnership interest as of January 1, 19X8?

(d) What basis will D have in his partnership interest as of January 1, 19X9?

(e) What year-end tax planning would you suggest to ensure that a partner could deduct all of his or her share of any partnership losses?

Research Problems

59. Five years ago, T started a new venture by forming T Corporation with a capital investment of $100,000. The venture did poorly and as a result required additional funds. These were provided by T in the form of direct loans in the amount of $300,000 and were made about equally spaced over the life of the business. In the current year, T Corporation is adjudged bankrupt and T loses all of his $100,000 stock investment and recovers none of the $300,000 debt owed to him. During T Corporation's existence, T was its only shareholder and its principal employee. What is the nature of T's loss?

     Partial list of research aids:

     Code §§ 165(g)(1), 166, and 1244.

     John P. Hollingsworth, 71 T.C. 580 (1979).

     Edward R. Hodgson, 38 TCM 21, T.C.Memo. 1979–8.

60. A cash basis partnership is incorporated. The newly formed corporation elects the cash method of accounting. The partnership transfers $30,000 of accounts receivable along with equipment, land, and cash. The corporation also agrees to pay accounts payable of the partnership in the amount of $40,000. The corporation files its return for its first year of operation and does not report the $30,000 received on accounts receivable of the partnership as income. It does deduct the $40,000 it paid on the partnership's accounts payable. The IRS disallows the deductions totaling $40,000 and increases the corporation's taxable income by $30,000 which represents the collection of partnership accounts receivable. What is the result?

     Partial list of research aids:

     Hempt Bros., Inc. v. U. S., 74–1 USTC ¶ 9188, 33 AFTR2d 74–570, 490 F.2d 1172 (CA–3, 1974).

     Holdcroft Transportation Co. v. Comm., 46–1 USTC ¶ 9193, 34 AFTR 860, 153 F.2d 323 (CA–8, 1946).

61. T is the sole shareholder of B Corporation and of C Corporation. During the current year, she transfers one-half of her stock in B Corporation (basis of $50,000 and fair market value of $200,000) to C Corporation. In return, T receives additional stock in C Corporation (worth $40,000) and cash of $160,000. At the time of the exchange, each corporation had earnings and profits as follows: $400,000 for B Corporation and $300,000 for C Corporation.

     (a) What was T trying to accomplish?

     (b) Will it work?

     Partial list of research aids:

     Code §§ 351 and 304.

     Comm. v. Stickney, 68–2 USTC ¶ 9551, 22 AFTR2d 5502, 399 F.2d 828 (CA–6, 1968).

     Coates Trust v. Comm., 73–2 USTC ¶ 9492, 32 AFTR2d 73–5251, 480 F.2d 468 (CA–9, 1973).

APPENDIX A
TAX RATE SCHEDULES AND TABLES

1983 Tax Rate Schedules   Your zero bracket amount has been built into these Tax Rate Schedules.

Caution: You must use the Tax Table instead of these Tax Rate Schedules if your taxable income is less than $50,000 unless you use **Schedule G** (income averaging), to figure your tax. In that case, even if your taxable income is less than $50,000, use the rate schedules on this page to figure your tax.

Schedule X
Single Taxpayers

Use this Schedule if you checked **Filing Status Box 1** on Form 1040—

If the amount on Form 1040, line 37 is: Over—	But not over—	Enter on Form 1040, line 38	of the amount over—
$0	$2,300	—0—	
2,300	3,400	.......11%	$2,300
3,400	4,400	$121 + 13%	3,400
4,400	8,500	251 + 15%	4,400
8,500	10,800	866 + 17%	8,500
10,800	12,900	1,257 + 19%	10,800
12,900	15,000	1,656 + 21%	12,900
15,000	18,200	2,097 + 24%	15,000
18,200	23,500	2,865 + 28%	18,200
23,500	28,800	4,349 + 32%	23,500
28,800	34,100	6,045 + 36%	28,800
34,100	41,500	7,953 + 40%	34,100
41,500	55,300	10,913 + 45%	41,500
55,300	....	17,123 + 50%	55,300

Schedule Z
Unmarried Heads of Household
(including certain married persons who live apart—see page 6 of the instructions)

Use this schedule if you checked **Filing Status Box 4** on Form 1040—

If the amount on Form 1040, line 37 is: Over—	But not over—	Enter on Form 1040, line 38	of the amount over—
$0	$2,300	—0—	
2,300	4,400	.......11%	$2,300
4,400	6,500	$231 + 13%	4,400
6,500	8,700	504 + 15%	6,500
8,700	11,800	834 + 18%	8,700
11,800	15,000	1,392 + 19%	11,800
15,000	18,200	2,000 + 21%	15,000
18,200	23,500	2,672 + 25%	18,200
23,500	28,800	3,997 + 29%	23,500
28,800	34,100	5,534 + 34%	28,800
34,100	44,700	7,336 + 37%	34,100
44,700	60,600	11,258 + 44%	44,700
60,600	81,800	18,254 + 48%	60,600
81,800	....	28,430 + 50%	81,800

Schedule Y
Married Taxpayers and Qualifying Widows and Widowers

Married Filing Joint Returns and Qualifying Widows and Widowers

Use this schedule if you checked **Filing Status Box 2 or 5** on Form 1040—

If the amount on Form 1040, line 37 is: Over—	But not over—	Enter on Form 1040, line 38	of the amount over—
$0	$3,400	—0—	
3,400	5,500	.......11%	$3,400
5,500	7,600	$231 + 13%	5,500
7,600	11,900	504 + 15%	7,600
11,900	16,000	1,149 + 17%	11,900
16,000	20,200	1,846 + 19%	16,000
20,200	24,600	2,644 + 23%	20,200
24,600	29,900	3,656 + 26%	24,600
29,900	35,200	5,034 + 30%	29,900
35,200	45,800	6,624 + 35%	35,200
45,800	60,000	10,334 + 40%	45,800
60,000	85,600	16,014 + 44%	60,000
85,600	109,400	27,278 + 48%	85,600
109,400	....	38,702 + 50%	109,400

Married Filing Separate Returns

Use this schedule if you checked **Filing Status Box 3** on Form 1040—

If the amount on Form 1040, line 37 is: Over—	But not over—	Enter on Form 1040, line 38	of the amount over—
$0	$1,700	—0—	
1,700	2,750	.......11%	$1,700
2,750	3,800	$115.50 + 13%	2,750
3,800	5,950	252.00 + 15%	3,800
5,950	8,000	574.50 + 17%	5,950
8,000	10,100	923.00 + 19%	8,000
10,100	12,300	1,322.00 + 23%	10,100
12,300	14,950	1,828.00 + 26%	12,300
14,950	17,600	2,517.00 + 30%	14,950
17,600	22,900	3,312.00 + 35%	17,600
22,900	30,000	5,167.00 + 40%	22,900
30,000	42,800	8,007.00 + 44%	30,000
42,800	54,700	13,639.00 + 48%	42,800
54,700	....	19,351.00 + 50%	54,700

Not married but have dependents

1984 Tax Rate Schedules

SCHEDULE X—Single Taxpayers

If taxable income is:		The tax is:	
Over—	but not over—		of the amount over—
$0	$2,300	—0—	
2,300	3,400	------- 11%	$2,300
3,400	4,400	$121 + 12%	3,400
4,400	6,500	241 + 14%	4,400
6,500	8,500	535 + 15%	6,500
8,500	10,800	835 + 16%	8,500
10,800	12,900	1,203 + 18%	10,800
12,900	15,000	1,581 + 20%	12,900
15,000	18,200	2,001 + 23%	15,000
18,200	23,500	2,737 + 26%	18,200
23,500	28,800	4,115 + 30%	23,500
28,800	34,100	5,705 + 34%	28,800
34,100	41,500	7,507 + 38%	34,100
41,500	55,300	10,319 + 42%	41,500
55,300	81,800	16,115 + 48%	55,300
81,800	------	28,835 + 50%	81,800

SCHEDULE Z—Heads of Household

If taxable income is:		The tax is:	
Over—	but not over—		of the amount over—
$0	$2,300	—0—	
2,300	4,400	------- 11%	$2,300
4,400	6,500	$231 + 12%	4,400
6,500	8,700	483 + 14%	6,500
8,700	11,800	791 + 17%	8,700
11,800	15,000	1,318 + 18%	11,800
15,000	18,200	1,894 + 20%	15,000
18,200	23,500	2,534 + 24%	18,200
23,500	28,800	3,806 + 28%	23,500
28,800	34,100	5,290 + 32%	28,800
34,100	44,700	6,986 + 35%	34,100
44,700	60,600	10,696 + 42%	44,700
60,600	81,800	17,374 + 45%	60,600
81,800	108,300	26,914 + 48%	81,800
108,300	------	39,634 + 50%	108,300

SCHEDULE Y—Married Taxpayers and Qualifying Widows and Widowers

Married Filing Joint Returns and Qualifying Widows and Widowers

If taxable income is:		The tax is:	
Over—	but not over—		of the amount over—
$0	$3,400	—0—	
3,400	5,500	------ 11%	$3,400
5,500	7,600	$231 + 12%	5,500
7,600	11,900	483 + 14%	7,600
11,900	16,000	1,085 + 16%	11,900
16,000	20,200	1,741 + 18%	16,000
20,200	24,600	2,497 + 22%	20,200
24,600	29,900	3,465 + 25%	24,600
29,900	35,200	4,790 + 28%	29,900
35,200	45,800	6,274 + 33%	35,200
45,800	60,000	9,772 + 38%	45,800
60,000	85,600	15,168 + 42%	60,000
85,600	109,400	25,920 + 45%	85,600
109,400	162,400	36,630 + 49%	109,400
162,400	--------	62,600 + 50%	162,400

Married Filing Separate Returns

If taxable income is:		The tax is:	
Over—	but not over—		of the amount over—
$0	$1,700	—0—	
1,700	2,750	---------- 11%	$1,700
2,750	3,800	$115.50 + 12%	2,750
3,800	5,950	241.50 + 14%	3,800
5,950	8,000	542.50 + 16%	5,950
8,000	10,100	870.50 + 18%	8,000
10,100	12,300	1,248.50 + 22%	10,100
12,300	14,950	1,732.50 + 25%	12,300
14,950	17,600	2,395.00 + 28%	14,950
17,600	22,900	3,137.00 + 33%	17,600
22,900	30,000	4,886.00 + 38%	22,900
30,000	42,800	7,584.00 + 42%	30,000
42,800	54,700	12,960.00 + 45%	42,800
54,700	81,200	18,315.00 + 49%	54,700
81,200	------	31,300.00 + 50%	81,200

Single Taxpayers [Unmarried Individuals (Other Than Surviving Spouses and Heads of Households)].

If taxable income is:	The tax is:
Not over $2,300	No tax.
Over $2,300 but not over $3,400	11% of the excess over $2,300.
Over $3,400 but not over $4,400	$121, plus 12% of the excess over $3,400.
Over $4,400 but not over $6,500	$241, plus 14% of the excess over $4,400.
Over $6,500 but not over $8,500	$535, plus 15% of the excess over $6,500.
Over $8,500 but not over $10,800	$835, plus 16% of the excess over $8,500.
Over $10,800 but not over $12,900	$1,203, plus 18% of the excess over $10,800.
Over $12,900 but not over $15,000	$1,581, plus 20% of the excess over $12,900.
Over $15,000 but not over $18,200	$2,001, plus 23% of the excess over $15,000.
Over $18,200 but not over $23,500	$2,737, plus 26% of the excess over $18,200.
Over $23,500 but not over $28,800	$4,115, plus 30% of the excess over $23,500.
Over $28,800 but not over $34,100	$5,705, plus 34% of the excess over $28,800.
Over $34,100 but not over $41,500	$7,507, plus 38% of the excess over $34,100.
Over $41,500 but not over $55,300	$10,319, plus 42% of the excess over $41,500.
Over $55,300 but not over $81,800	$16,115, plus 48% of the excess over $55,300.
Over $81,800	$28,835, plus 50% of the excess over $81,800.

Unmarried Heads of Household

If taxable income is:	The tax is:
Not over $2,300	No tax.
Over $2,300 but not over $4,400	11% of the excess over $2,300.
Over $4,400 but not over $6,500	$231, plus 12% of the excess over $4,400.
Over $6,500 but not over $8,700	$483, plus 14% of the excess over $6,500.
Over $8,700 but not over $11,800	$791, plus 17% of the excess over $8,700.
Over $11,800 but not over $15,000	$1,318, plus 18% of the excess over $11,800.
Over $15,000 but not over $18,200	$1,894, plus 20% of the excess over $15,000.
Over $18,200 but not over $23,500	$2,534, plus 24% of the excess over $18,200.
Over $23,500 but not over $28,800	$3,806, plus 28% of the excess over $23,500.
Over $28,800 but not over $34,100	$5,290, plus 32% of the excess over $28,800.
Over $34,100 but not over $44,700	$6,986, plus 35% of the excess over $34,100.
Over $44,700 but not over $60,600	$10,696, plus 42% of the excess over $44,700.
Over $60,600 but not over $81,800	$17,374, plus 45% of the excess over $60,600.
Over $81,800 but not over $108,300	$26,914, plus 48% of the excess over $81,800.
Over $108,300	$39,634, plus 50% of the excess over $108,300.

FOR TAXABLE YEARS BEGINNING AFTER 1983.—

Married Individuals Filing Joint Returns and Surviving Spouses

If taxable income is:	The tax is:
Not over $3,400	No tax.
Over $3,400 but not over $5,500	11% of the excess over $3,400.
Over $5,500 but not over $7,600	$231, plus 12% of the excess over $5,500.
Over $7,600 but not over $11,900	$483, plus 14% of the excess over $7,600.
Over $11,900 but not over $16,000	$1,085, plus 16% of the excess over $11,900.
Over $16,000 but not over $20,200	$1,741, plus 18% of the excess over $16,000.
Over $20,200 but not over $24,600	$2,497, plus 22% of the excess over $20,200.
Over $24,600 but not over $29,900	$3,465, plus 25% of the excess over $24,600.
Over $29,900 but not over $35,200	$4,790, plus 28% of the excess over $29,900.
Over $35,200 but not over $45,800	$6,274, plus 33% of the excess over $35,200.
Over $45,800 but not over $60,000	$9,772, plus 38% of the excess over $45,800.
Over $60,000 but not over $85,600	$15,168, plus 42% of the excess over $60,000.
Over $85,600 but not over $109,400	$25,920, plus 45% of the excess over $85,600.
Over $109,400 but not over $162,400	$36,630, plus 49% of the excess over $109,400.
Over $162,400	$62,600, plus 50% of the excess over $162,400.

. . . .

Married Individuals Filing Separate Returns

If taxable income is:	The tax is:
Not over $1,700	No tax.
Over $1,700 but not over $2,750	11% of the excess over $1,700.
Over $2,750 but not over $3,800	$115.50, plus 12% of the excess over $2,750.
Over $3,800 but not over $5,950	$241.50, plus 14% of the excess over $3,800.
Over $5,950 but not over $8,000	$542.50, plus 16% of the excess over $5,950.
Over $8,000 but not over $10,100	$870.50, plus 18% of the excess over $8,000.
Over $10,100 but not over $12,300	$1,248.50, plus 22% of the excess over $10,100.
Over $12,300 but not over $14,950	$1,732.50, plus 25% of the excess over $12,300.
Over $14,950 but not over $17,600	$2,395, plus 28% of the excess over $14,950.
Over $17,600 but not over $22,900	$3,137, plus 33% of the excess over $17,600.
Over $22,900 but not over $30,000	$4,886, plus 38% of the excess over $22,900.
Over $30,000 but not over $42,800	$7,584, plus 42% of the excess over $30,000.
Over $42,800 but not over $54,700	$12,960, plus 45% of the excess over $42,800.
Over $54,700 but not over $81,200	$18,315, plus 49% of the excess over $54,700.
Over $81,200	$31,300, plus 50% of the excess over $81,200.

1983 Tax Table

Based on Taxable Income
For persons with taxable incomes of less than $50,000.

Example: Mr. and Mrs. Brown are filing a joint return. Their taxable income on line 37 of Form 1040 is $25,325. First, they find the $25,300–25,350 income line. Next, they find the column for married filing jointly and read down the column. The amount shown where the income line and filing status column meet is $3,845. This is the tax amount they must write on line 38 of their return.

At least	But less than	Single	Married filing jointly *	Married filling sepa-rately	Head of a house-hold
			Your tax is—		
25,250	25,300	4,917	3,832	6,117	4,512
25,300	25,350	4,933	3,845	6,137	4,526
25,350	25,400	4,949	3,858	6,157	4,541

If line 37 (taxable income) is— At least	But less than	And you are— Single	Married filing jointly *	Married filing sepa-rately	Head of a house-hold
			Your tax is—		
0	1,700	0	0	0	0
1,700	1,725	0	0	a1	0
1,725	1,750	0	0	4	0
1,750	1,775	0	0	7	0
1,775	1,800	0	0	10	0
1,800	1,825	0	0	12	0
1,825	1,850	0	0	15	0
1,850	1,875	0	0	18	0
1,875	1,900	0	0	21	0
1,900	1,925	0	0	23	0
1,925	1,950	0	0	26	0
1,950	1,975	0	0	29	0
1,975	2,000	0	0	32	0

2,000

At least	But less than	Single	Married filing jointly	Married filing sepa-rately	Head of a house-hold
2,000	2,025	0	0	34	0
2,025	2,050	0	0	37	0
2,050	2,075	0	0	40	0
2,075	2,100	0	0	43	0
2,100	2,125	0	0	45	0
2,125	2,150	0	0	48	0
2,150	2,175	0	0	51	0
2,175	2,200	0	0	54	0
2,200	2,225	0	0	56	0
2,225	2,250	0	0	59	0
2,250	2,275	0	0	62	0
2,275	2,300	0	0	65	0
2,300	2,325	b1	0	67	b1
2,325	2,350	4	0	70	4
2,350	2,375	7	0	73	7
2,375	2,400	10	0	76	10
2,400	2,425	12	0	78	12
2,425	2,450	15	0	81	15
2,450	2,475	18	0	84	18
2,475	2,500	21	0	87	21
2,500	2,525	23	0	89	23
2,525	2,550	26	0	92	26
2,550	2,575	29	0	95	29
2,575	2,600	32	0	98	32
2,600	2,625	34	0	100	34
2,625	2,650	37	0	103	37
2,650	2,675	40	0	106	40
2,675	2,700	43	0	109	43
2,700	2,725	45	0	111	45
2,725	2,750	48	0	114	48
2,750	2,775	51	0	117	51
2,775	2,800	54	0	120	54
2,800	2,825	56	0	124	56
2,825	2,850	59	0	127	59
2,850	2,875	62	0	130	62
2,875	2,900	65	0	133	65
2,900	2,925	67	0	137	67
2,925	2,950	70	0	140	70
2,950	2,975	73	0	143	73
2,975	3,000	76	0	146	76

3,000

At least	But less than	Single	Married filing jointly	Married filing sepa-rately	Head of a house-hold
3,000	3,050	80	0	151	80
3,050	3,100	85	0	158	85
3,100	3,150	91	0	164	91
3,150	3,200	96	0	171	96
3,200	3,250	102	0	177	102
3,250	3,300	107	0	184	107
3,300	3,350	113	0	190	113
3,350	3,400	118	0	197	118
3,400	3,450	124	c3	203	124
3,450	3,500	131	8	210	129
3,500	3,550	137	14	216	135
3,550	3,600	144	19	223	140
3,600	3,650	150	25	229	146
3,650	3,700	157	30	236	151
3,700	3,750	163	36	242	157
3,750	3,800	170	41	249	162
3,800	3,850	176	47	256	168
3,850	3,900	183	52	263	173
3,900	3,950	189	58	271	179
3,950	4,000	196	63	278	184

4,000

At least	But less than	Single	Married filing jointly	Married filing sepa-rately	Head of a house-hold
4,000	4,050	202	69	286	190
4,050	4,100	209	74	293	195
4,100	4,150	215	80	301	201
4,150	4,200	222	85	308	206
4,200	4,250	228	91	316	212
4,250	4,300	235	96	323	217
4,300	4,350	241	102	331	223
4,350	4,400	248	107	338	228
4,400	4,450	255	113	346	234
4,450	4,500	262	118	353	241
4,500	4,550	270	124	361	247
4,550	4,600	277	129	368	254
4,600	4,650	285	135	376	260
4,650	4,700	292	140	383	267
4,700	4,750	300	146	391	273
4,750	4,800	307	151	398	280
4,800	4,850	315	157	406	286
4,850	4,900	322	162	413	293
4,900	4,950	330	168	421	299
4,950	5,000	337	173	428	306

5,000

At least	But less than	Single	Married filing jointly	Married filing sepa-rately	Head of a house-hold
5,000	5,050	345	179	436	312
5,050	5,100	352	184	443	319
5,100	5,150	360	190	451	325
5,150	5,200	367	195	458	332
5,200	5,250	375	201	466	338
5,250	5,300	382	206	473	345
5,300	5,350	390	212	481	351
5,350	5,400	397	217	488	358
5,400	5,450	405	223	496	364
5,450	5,500	412	228	503	371

If line 37 (taxable income) is— At least	But less than	And you are— Single	Married filing jointly *	Married filing sepa-rately	Head of a house-hold
			Your tax is—		
5,500	5,550	420	234	511	377
5,550	5,600	427	241	518	384
5,600	5,660	435	247	526	390
5,650	5,700	442	254	533	397
5,700	5,750	450	260	541	403
5,750	5,800	457	267	548	410
5,800	5,850	465	273	556	416
5,850	5,900	472	280	563	423
5,900	5,950	480	286	571	429
5,950	6,000	487	293	579	436

6,000

At least	But less than	Single	Married filing jointly	Married filing sepa-rately	Head of a house-hold
6,000	6,050	495	299	587	442
6,050	6,100	502	306	596	449
6,100	6,150	510	312	604	455
6,150	6,200	517	319	613	462
6,200	6,250	525	325	621	468
6,250	6,300	532	332	630	475
6,300	6,350	540	338	638	481
6,350	6,400	547	345	647	488
6,400	6,450	555	351	655	494
6,450	6,500	562	358	664	501
6,500	6,550	570	364	672	508
6,550	6,600	577	371	681	515
6,600	6,650	585	377	689	523
6,650	6,700	592	384	698	530
6,700	6,750	600	390	706	538
6,750	6,800	607	397	715	545
6,800	6,850	615	403	723	553
6,850	6,900	622	410	732	560
6,900	6,950	630	416	740	568
6,950	7,000	637	423	749	575

7,000

At least	But less than	Single	Married filing jointly	Married filing sepa-rately	Head of a house-hold
7,000	7,050	645	429	757	583
7,050	7,100	652	436	766	590
7,100	7,150	660	442	774	598
7,150	7,200	667	449	783	605
7,200	7,250	675	455	791	613
7,250	7,300	682	462	800	620
7,300	7,350	690	468	808	628
7,350	7,400	697	475	817	635
7,400	7,450	705	481	825	643
7,450	7,500	712	488	834	650
7,500	7,550	720	494	842	658
7,550	7,600	727	501	851	665
7,600	7,650	735	508	859	673
7,650	7,700	742	515	868	680
7,700	7,750	750	523	876	688
7,750	7,800	757	530	885	695
7,800	7,850	765	538	893	703
7,850	7,900	772	545	902	710
7,900	7,950	780	553	910	718
7,950	8,000	787	560	919	725

*This column must also be used by a qualifying widow(er).

Continued on next page

a If your taxable income is exactly $1,700, your tax is zero.   **c** If your taxable income is exactly $3,400, your tax is zero.
b If your taxable income is exactly $2,300, your tax is zero.

1983 Tax Table (Continued)

If line 37 (taxable income) is—		And you are—			
At least	But less than	Single	Married filing jointly *	Married filing separately	Head of a household
		Your tax is—			
8,000					
8,000	8,050	795	568	928	733
8,050	8,100	802	575	937	740
8,100	8,150	810	583	947	748
8,150	8,200	817	590	956	755
8,200	8,250	825	598	966	763
8,250	8,300	832	605	975	770
8,300	8,350	840	613	985	778
8,350	8,400	847	620	994	785
8,400	8,450	855	628	1,004	793
8,450	8,500	862	635	1,013	800
8,500	8,550	870	643	1,023	808
8,550	8,600	879	650	1,032	815
8,600	8,650	887	658	1,042	823
8,650	8,700	896	665	1,051	830
8,700	8,750	904	673	1,061	839
8,750	8,800	913	680	1,070	848
8,800	8,850	921	688	1,080	857
8,850	8,900	930	695	1,089	866
8,900	8,950	938	703	1,099	875
8,950	9,000	947	710	1,108	884
9,000					
9,000	9,050	955	718	1,118	893
9,050	9,100	964	725	1,127	902
9,100	9,150	972	733	1,137	911
9,150	9,200	981	740	1,146	920
9,200	9,250	989	748	1,156	929
9,250	9,300	998	755	1,165	938
9,300	9,350	1,006	763	1,175	947
9,350	9,400	1,015	770	1,184	956
9,400	9,450	1,023	778	1,194	965
9,450	9,500	1,032	785	1,203	974
9,500	9,550	1,040	793	1,213	983
9,550	9,600	1,049	800	1,222	992
9,600	9,650	1,057	808	1,232	1,001
9,650	9,700	1,066	815	1,241	1,010
9,700	9,750	1,074	823	1,251	1,019
9,750	9,800	1,083	830	1,260	1,028
9,800	9,850	1,091	838	1,270	1,037
9,850	9,900	1,100	845	1,279	1,046
9,900	9,950	1,108	853	1,289	1,055
9,950	10,000	1,117	860	1,298	1,064
10,000					
10,000	10,050	1,125	868	1,308	1,073
10,050	10,100	1,134	875	1,317	1,082
10,100	10,150	1,142	883	1,328	1,091
10,150	10,200	1,151	890	1,339	1,100
10,200	10,250	1,159	898	1,351	1,109
10,250	10,300	1,168	905	1,362	1,118
10,300	10,350	1,176	913	1,374	1,127
10,350	10,400	1,185	920	1,385	1,136
10,400	10,450	1,193	928	1,397	1,145
10,450	10,500	1,202	935	1,408	1,154
10,500	10,550	1,210	943	1,420	1,163
10,550	10,600	1,219	950	1,431	1,172
10,600	10,650	1,227	958	1,443	1,181
10,650	10,700	1,236	965	1,454	1,190
10,700	10,750	1,244	973	1,466	1,199

If line 37 (taxable income) is—		And you are—			
At least	But less than	Single	Married filing jointly *	Married filing separately	Head of a household
		Your tax is—			
10,750	10,800	1,253	980	1,477	1,208
10,800	10,850	1,262	988	1,489	1,217
10,850	10,900	1,271	995	1,500	1,226
10,900	10,950	1,281	1,003	1,512	1,235
10,950	11,000	1,290	1,010	1,523	1,244
11,000					
11,000	11,050	1,300	1,018	1,535	1,253
11,050	11,100	1,309	1,025	1,546	1,262
11,100	11,150	1,319	1,033	1,558	1,271
11,150	11,200	1,328	1,040	1,569	1,280
11,200	11,250	1,338	1,048	1,581	1,289
11,250	11,300	1,347	1,055	1,592	1,298
11,300	11,350	1,357	1,063	1,604	1,307
11,350	11,400	1,366	1,070	1,615	1,316
11,400	11,450	1,376	1,078	1,627	1,325
11,450	11,500	1,385	1,085	1,638	1,334
11,500	11,550	1,395	1,093	1,650	1,343
11,550	11,600	1,404	1,100	1,661	1,352
11,600	11,650	1,414	1,108	1,673	1,361
11,650	11,700	1,423	1,115	1,684	1,370
11,700	11,750	1,433	1,123	1,696	1,379
11,750	11,800	1,442	1,130	1,707	1,388
11,800	11,850	1,452	1,138	1,719	1,397
11,850	11,900	1,461	1,145	1,730	1,406
11,900	11,950	1,471	1,153	1,742	1,416
11,950	12,000	1,480	1,162	1,753	1,425
12,000					
12,000	12,050	1,490	1,170	1,765	1,435
12,050	12,100	1,499	1,179	1,776	1,444
12,100	12,150	1,509	1,187	1,788	1,454
12,150	12,200	1,518	1,196	1,799	1,463
12,200	12,250	1,528	1,204	1,811	1,473
12,250	12,300	1,537	1,213	1,822	1,482
12,300	12,350	1,547	1,221	1,835	1,492
12,350	12,400	1,556	1,230	1,848	1,501
12,400	12,450	1,566	1,238	1,861	1,511
12,450	12,500	1,575	1,247	1,874	1,520
12,500	12,550	1,585	1,255	1,887	1,530
12,550	12,600	1,594	1,264	1,900	1,539
12,600	12,650	1,604	1,272	1,913	1,549
12,650	12,700	1,613	1,281	1,926	1,558
12,700	12,750	1,623	1,289	1,939	1,568
12,750	12,800	1,632	1,298	1,952	1,577
12,800	12,850	1,642	1,306	1,965	1,587
12,850	12,900	1,651	1,315	1,978	1,596
12,900	12,950	1,661	1,323	1,991	1,606
12,950	13,000	1,672	1,332	2,004	1,615
13,000					
13,000	13,050	1,682	1,340	2,017	1,625
13,050	13,100	1,693	1,349	2,030	1,634
13,100	13,150	1,703	1,357	2,043	1,644
13,150	13,200	1,714	1,366	2,056	1,653
13,200	13,250	1,724	1,374	2,069	1,663
13,250	13,300	1,735	1,383	2,082	1,672
13,300	13,350	1,745	1,391	2,095	1,682
13,350	13,400	1,756	1,400	2,108	1,691
13,400	13,450	1,766	1,408	2,121	1,701
13,450	13,500	1,777	1,417	2,134	1,710

If line 37 (taxable income) is—		And you are—			
At least	But less than	Single	Married filing jointly *	Married filing separately	Head of a household
		Your tax is—			
13,500	13,550	1,787	1,425	2,147	1,720
13,550	13,600	1,798	1,434	2,160	1,729
13,600	13,650	1,808	1,442	2,173	1,739
13,650	13,700	1,819	1,451	2,186	1,748
13,700	13,750	1,829	1,459	2,199	1,758
13,750	13,800	1,840	1,468	2,212	1,767
13,800	13,850	1,850	1,476	2,225	1,777
13,850	13,900	1,861	1,485	2,238	1,786
13,900	13,950	1,871	1,493	2,251	1,796
13,950	14,000	1,882	1,502	2,264	1,805
14,000					
14,000	14,050	1,892	1,510	2,277	1,815
14,050	14,100	1,903	1,519	2,290	1,824
14,100	14,150	1,913	1,527	2,303	1,834
14,150	14,200	1,924	1,536	2,316	1,843
14,200	14,250	1,934	1,544	2,329	1,853
14,250	14,300	1,945	1,553	2,342	1,862
14,300	14,350	1,955	1,561	2,355	1,872
14,350	14,400	1,966	1,570	2,368	1,881
14,400	14,450	1,976	1,578	2,381	1,891
14,450	14,500	1,987	1,587	2,394	1,900
14,500	14,550	1,997	1,595	2,407	1,910
14,550	14,600	2,008	1,604	2,420	1,919
14,600	14,650	2,018	1,612	2,433	1,929
14,650	14,700	2,029	1,621	2,446	1,938
14,700	14,750	2,039	1,629	2,459	1,948
14,750	14,800	2,050	1,638	2,472	1,957
14,800	14,850	2,060	1,646	2,485	1,967
14,850	14,900	2,071	1,655	2,498	1,976
14,900	14,950	2,081	1,663	2,511	1,986
14,950	15,000	2,092	1,672	2,525	1,995
15,000					
15,000	15,050	2,103	1,680	2,540	2,005
15,050	15,100	2,115	1,689	2,555	2,016
15,100	15,150	2,127	1,697	2,570	2,026
15,150	15,200	2,139	1,706	2,585	2,037
15,200	15,250	2,151	1,714	2,600	2,047
15,250	15,300	2,163	1,723	2,615	2,058
15,300	15,350	2,175	1,731	2,630	2,068
15,350	15,400	2,187	1,740	2,645	2,079
15,400	15,450	2,199	1,748	2,660	2,089
15,450	15,500	2,211	1,757	2,675	2,100
15,500	15,550	2,223	1,765	2,690	2,110
15,550	15,600	2,235	1,774	2,705	2,121
15,600	15,650	2,247	1,782	2,720	2,131
15,650	15,700	2,259	1,791	2,735	2,142
15,700	15,750	2,271	1,799	2,750	2,152
15,750	15,800	2,283	1,808	2,765	2,163
15,800	15,850	2,295	1,816	2,780	2,173
15,850	15,900	2,307	1,825	2,795	2,184
15,900	15,950	2,319	1,833	2,810	2,194
15,950	16,000	2,331	1,842	2,825	2,205
16,000					
16,000	16,050	2,343	1,851	2,840	2,215
16,050	16,100	2,355	1,860	2,855	2,226
16,100	16,150	2,367	1,870	2,870	2,236
16,150	16,200	2,379	1,879	2,885	2,247
16,200	16,250	2,391	1,889	2,900	2,257

*This column must also be used by a qualifying widow(er).

Continued on next page

1983 Tax Table (Continued)

If line 37 (taxable income) is— At least	But less than	Single	Married filing jointly *	Married filing separately	Head of a household
			Your tax is—		
16,250	16,300	2,403	1,898	2,915	2,268
16,300	16,350	2,415	1,908	2,930	2,278
16,350	16,400	2,427	1,917	2,945	2,289
16,400	16,450	2,439	1,927	2,960	2,299
16,450	16,500	2,451	1,936	2,975	2,310
16,500	16,550	2,463	1,946	2,990	2,320
16,550	16,600	2,475	1,955	3,005	2,331
16,600	16,650	2,487	1,965	3,020	2,341
16,660	16,700	2,499	1,974	3,035	2,352
16,700	16,750	2,511	1,984	3,050	2,362
16,750	16,800	2,523	1,993	3,065	2,373
16,800	16,850	2,535	2,003	3,080	2,383
16,850	16,900	2,547	2,012	3,095	2,394
16,900	16,950	2,559	2,022	3,110	2,404
16,950	17,000	2,571	2,031	3,125	2,415
17,000					
17,000	17,050	2,583	2,041	3,140	2,425
17,050	17,100	2,595	2,050	3,155	2,436
17,100	17,150	2,607	2,060	3,170	2,446
17,150	17,200	2,619	2,069	3,185	2,457
17,200	17,250	2,631	2,079	3,200	2,467
17,250	17,300	2,643	2,088	3,215	2,478
17,300	17,350	2,655	2,098	3,230	2,488
17,350	17,400	2,667	2,107	3,245	2,499
17,400	17,450	2,679	2,117	3,260	2,509
17,450	17,500	2,691	2,126	3,275	2,520
17,500	17,550	2,703	2,136	3,290	2,530
17,550	17,600	2,715	2,145	3,305	2,541
17,600	17,650	2,727	2,155	3,321	2,551
17,650	17,700	2,739	2,164	3,338	2,562
17,700	17,750	2,751	2,174	3,356	2,572
17,750	17,800	2,763	2,183	3,373	2,583
17,800	17,850	2,775	2,193	3,391	2,593
17,850	17,900	2,787	2,202	3,408	2,604
17,900	17,950	2,799	2,212	3,426	2,614
17,950	18,000	2,811	2,221	3,443	2,625
18,000					
18,000	18,050	2,823	2,231	3,461	2,635
18,050	18,100	2,835	2,240	3,478	2,646
18,100	18,150	2,847	2,250	3,496	2,656
18,150	18,200	2,859	2,259	3,513	2,667
18,200	18,250	2,872	2,269	3,531	2,678
18,250	18,300	2,886	2,278	3,548	2,691
18,300	18,350	2,900	2,288	3,566	2,703
18,350	18,400	2,914	2,297	3,583	2,716
18,400	18,450	2,928	2,307	3,601	2,728
18,450	18,500	2,942	2,316	3,618	2,741
18,500	18,550	2,956	2,326	3,636	2,753
18,550	18,600	2,970	2,335	3,653	2,766
18,600	18,650	2,984	2,345	3,671	2,778
18,650	18,700	2,998	2,354	3,688	2,791
18,700	18,750	3,012	2,364	3,706	2,803
18,750	18,800	3,026	2,373	3,723	2,816
18,800	18,850	3,040	2,383	3,741	2,828
18,850	18,900	3,054	2,392	3,758	2,841
18,900	18,950	3,068	2,402	3,776	2,853
18,950	19,000	3,082	2,411	3,793	2,866

If line 37 (taxable income) is— At least	But less than	Single	Married filing jointly *	Married filing separately	Head of a household
			Your tax is—		
19,000					
19,000	19,050	3,096	2,421	3,811	2,878
19,050	19,100	3,110	2,430	3,828	2,891
19,100	19,150	3,124	2,440	3,846	2,903
19,150	19,200	3,138	2,449	3,863	2,916
19,200	19,250	3,152	2,459	3,881	2,928
19,250	19,300	3,166	2,468	3,898	2,941
19,300	19,350	3,180	2,478	3,916	2,953
19,350	19,400	3,194	2,487	3,933	2,966
19,400	19,450	3,208	2,497	3,951	2,978
19,450	19,500	3,222	2,506	3,968	2,991
19,500	19,550	3,236	2,516	3,986	3,003
19,550	19,600	3,250	2,525	4,003	3,016
19,600	19,650	3,264	2,535	4,021	3,028
19,650	19,700	3,278	2,544	4,038	3,041
19,700	19,750	3,292	2,554	4,056	3,053
19,750	19,800	3,306	2,563	4,073	3,066
19,800	19,850	3,320	2,573	4,091	3,078
19,850	19,900	3,334	2,582	4,108	3,091
19,900	19,950	3,348	2,592	4,126	3,103
19,950	20,000	3,362	2,601	4,143	3,116
20,000					
20,000	20,050	3,376	2,611	4,161	3,128
20,050	20,100	3,390	2,620	4,178	3,141
20,100	20,150	3,404	2,630	4,196	3,153
20,150	20,200	3,418	2,639	4,213	3,166
20,200	20,250	3,432	2,650	4,231	3,178
20,250	20,300	3,446	2,661	4,248	3,191
20,300	20,350	3,460	2,673	4,266	3,203
20,350	20,400	3,474	2,684	4,283	3,216
20,400	20,450	3,488	2,696	4,301	3,228
20,450	20,500	3,502	2,707	4,318	3,241
20,500	20,550	3,516	2,719	4,336	3,253
20,550	20,600	3,530	2,730	4,353	3,266
20,600	20,650	3,544	2,742	4,371	3,278
20,650	20,700	3,558	2,753	4,388	3,291
20,700	20,750	3,572	2,765	4,406	3,303
20,750	20,800	3,586	2,776	4,423	3,316
20,800	20,850	3,600	2,788	4,441	3,328
20,850	20,900	3,614	2,799	4,458	3,341
20,900	20,950	3,628	2,811	4,476	3,353
20,950	21,000	3,642	2,822	4,493	3,366
21,000					
21,000	21,050	3,656	2,834	4,511	3,378
21,050	21,100	3,670	2,845	4,528	3,391
21,100	21,150	3,684	2,857	4,546	3,403
21,150	21,200	3,698	2,868	4,563	3,416
21,200	21,250	3,712	2,880	4,581	3,428
21,250	21,300	3,726	2,891	4,598	3,441
21,300	21,350	3,740	2,903	4,616	3,453
21,350	21,400	3,754	2,914	4,633	3,466
21,400	21,450	3,768	2,926	4,651	3,478
21,450	21,500	3,782	2,937	4,668	3,491
21,500	21,550	3,796	2,949	4,686	3,503
21,550	21,600	3,810	2,960	4,703	3,516
21,600	21,650	3,824	2,972	4,721	3,528
21,650	21,700	3,838	2,983	4,738	3,541
21,700	21,750	3,852	2,995	4,756	3,553

If line 37 (taxable income) is— At least	But less than	Single	Married filing jointly *	Married filing separately	Head of a household
			Your tax is—		
21,750	21,800	3,866	3,006	4,773	3,566
21,800	21,850	3,880	3,018	4,791	3,578
21,850	21,900	3,894	3,029	4,808	3,591
21,900	21,950	3,908	3,041	4,826	3,603
21,950	22,000	3,922	3,052	4,843	3,616
22,000					
22,000	22,050	3,936	3,064	4,861	3,628
22,050	22,100	3,950	3,075	4,878	3,641
22,100	22,150	3,964	3,087	4,896	3,653
22,150	22,200	3,978	3,098	4,913	3,666
22,200	22,250	3,992	3,110	4,931	3,678
22,250	22,300	4,006	3,121	4,948	3,691
22,300	22,350	4,020	3,133	4,966	3,703
22,350	22,400	4,034	3,144	4,983	3,716
22,400	22,450	4,048	3,156	5,001	3,728
22,450	22,500	4,062	3,167	5,018	3,741
22,500	22,550	4,076	3,179	5,036	3,753
22,550	22,600	4,090	3,190	5,053	3,766
22,600	22,650	4,104	3,202	5,071	3,778
22,650	22,700	4,118	3,213	5,088	3,791
22,700	22,750	4,132	3,225	5,106	3,803
22,750	22,800	4,146	3,236	5,123	3,816
22,800	22,850	4,160	3,248	5,141	3,828
22,850	22,900	4,174	3,259	5,158	3,841
22,900	22,950	4,188	3,271	5,177	3,853
22,950	23,000	4,202	3,282	5,197	3,866
23,000					
23,000	23,050	4,216	3,294	5,217	3,878
23,050	23,100	4,230	3,305	5,237	3,891
23,100	23,150	4,244	3,317	5,257	3,903
23,150	23,200	4,258	3,328	5,277	3,916
23,200	23,250	4,272	3,340	5,297	3,928
23,250	23,300	4,286	3,351	5,317	3,941
23,300	23,350	4,300	3,363	5,337	3,953
23,350	23,400	4,314	3,374	5,357	3,966
23,400	23,450	4,328	3,386	5,377	3,978
23,450	23,500	4,342	3,397	5,397	3,991
23,500	23,550	4,357	3,409	5,417	4,004
23,550	23,600	4,373	3,420	5,437	4,019
23,600	23,650	4,389	3,432	5,457	4,033
23,650	23,700	4,405	3,443	5,477	4,048
23,700	23,750	4,421	3,455	5,497	4,062
23,750	23,800	4,437	3,466	5,517	4,077
23,800	23,850	4,453	3,478	5,537	4,091
23,850	23,900	4,469	3,489	5,557	4,106
23,900	23,950	4,485	3,501	5,577	4,120
23,950	24,000	4,501	3,512	5,597	4,135
24,000					
24,000	24,050	4,517	3,524	5,617	4,149
24,050	24,100	4,533	3,535	5,637	4,164
24,100	24,150	4,549	3,547	5,657	4,178
24,150	24,200	4,565	3,558	5,677	4,193
24,200	24,250	4,581	3,570	5,697	4,207
24,250	24,300	4,597	3,581	5,717	4,222
24,300	24,350	4,613	3,593	5,737	4,236
24,350	24,400	4,629	3,604	5,757	4,251
24,400	24,450	4,645	3,616	5,777	4,265
24,450	24,500	4,661	3,627	5,797	4,280

*This column must also be used by a qualifying widow(er).

Continued on next page

1983 Tax Table (*Continued*)

If line 37 (taxable income) is—		And you are—			
At least	But less than	Single	Married filing jointly *	Married filing separately	Head of a household
		Your tax is—			
24,500	24,550	4,677	3,639	5,817	4,294
24,550	24,600	4,693	3,650	5,837	4,309
24,600	24,650	4,709	3,663	5,857	4,323
24,650	24,700	4,725	3,676	5,877	4,338
24,700	24,750	4,741	3,689	5,897	4,352
24,750	24,800	4,757	3,702	5,917	4,367
24,800	24,850	4,773	3,715	5,937	4,381
24,850	24,900	4,789	3,728	5,957	4,396
24,900	24,950	4,805	3,741	5,977	4,410
24,950	25,000	4,821	3,754	5,997	4,425
25,000					
25,000	25,050	4,837	3,767	6,017	4,439
25,050	25,100	4,853	3,780	6,037	4,454
25,100	25,150	4,869	3,793	6,057	4,468
25,150	25,200	4,885	3,806	6,077	4,483
25,200	25,250	4,901	3,819	6,097	4,497
25,250	25,300	4,917	3,832	6,117	4,512
25,300	25,350	4,933	3,845	6,137	4,526
25,350	25,400	4,949	3,858	6,157	4,541
25,400	25,450	4,965	3,871	6,177	4,555
25,450	25,500	4,981	3,884	6,197	4,570
25,500	25,550	4,997	3,897	6,217	4,584
25,550	25,600	5,013	3,910	6,237	4,599
25,600	25,650	5,029	3,923	6,257	4,613
25,650	25,700	5,045	3,936	6,277	4,628
25,700	25,750	5,061	3,949	6,297	4,642
25,750	25,800	5,077	3,962	6,317	4,657
25,800	25,850	5,093	3,975	6,337	4,671
25,850	25,900	5,109	3,988	6,357	4,686
25,900	25,950	5,125	4,001	6,377	4,700
25,950	26,000	5,141	4,014	6,397	4,715
26,000					
26,000	26,050	5,157	4,027	6,417	4,729
26,050	26,100	5,173	4,040	6,437	4,744
26,100	26,150	5,189	4,053	6,457	4,758
26,150	26,200	5,205	4,066	6,477	4,773
26,200	26,250	5,221	4,079	6,497	4,787
26,250	26,300	5,237	4,092	6,517	4,802
26,300	26,350	5,253	4,105	6,537	4,816
26,350	26,400	5,269	4,118	6,557	4,831
26,400	26,450	5,285	4,131	6,577	4,845
26,450	26,500	5,301	4,144	6,597	4,860
26,500	26,550	5,317	4,157	6,617	4,874
26,550	26,600	5,333	4,170	6,637	4,889
26,600	26,650	5,349	4,183	6,657	4,903
26,650	26,700	5,365	4,196	6,677	4,918
26,700	26,750	5,381	4,209	6,697	4,932
26,750	26,000	5,397	4,222	6,717	4,947
26,800	26,850	5,413	4,235	6,737	4,961
26,850	26,900	5,429	4,248	6,757	4,976
26,900	26,950	5,445	4,261	6,777	4,990
26,950	27,000	5,461	4,274	6,797	5,005
27,000					
27,000	27,050	5,477	4,287	6,817	5,019
27,050	27,100	5,493	4,300	6,837	5,034
27,100	27,150	5,509	4,313	6,857	5,048
27,150	27,200	5,525	4,326	6,877	5,063
27,200	27,250	5,541	4,339	6,897	5,077

If line 37 (taxable income) is—		And you are—			
At least	But less than	Single	Married filing jointly *	Married filing separately	Head of a household
		Your tax is—			
27,250	27,300	5,557	4,352	6,917	5,092
27,300	27,350	5,573	4,365	6,937	5,106
27,350	27,400	5,589	4,378	6,957	5,121
27,400	27,450	5,605	4,391	6,977	5,135
27,450	27,500	5,621	4,404	6,997	5,150
27,500	27,550	5,637	4,417	7,017	5,164
27,550	27,600	5,653	4,430	7,037	5,179
27,600	27,650	5,669	4,443	7,057	5,193
27,650	27,700	5,685	4,456	7,077	5,208
27,700	27,750	5,701	4,469	7,097	5,222
27,750	27,800	5,717	4,482	7,117	5,237
27,800	27,850	5,733	4,495	7,137	5,251
27,850	27,900	5,749	4,508	7,157	5,266
27,900	27,950	5,765	4,521	7,177	5,280
27,950	28,000	5,781	4,534	7,197	5,295
28,000					
28,000	28,050	5,797	4,547	7,217	5,309
28,050	28,100	5,813	4,560	7,237	5,324
28,100	28,150	5,829	4,573	7,257	5,338
28,150	28,200	5,845	4,586	7,277	5,353
28,200	28,250	5,861	4,599	7,297	5,367
28,250	28,300	5,877	4,612	7,317	5,382
28,300	28,350	5,893	4,625	7,337	5,396
28,350	28,400	5,909	4,638	7,357	5,411
28,400	28,450	5,925	4,651	7,377	5,425
28,450	28,500	5,941	4,664	7,397	5,440
28,500	28,550	5,957	4,677	7,417	5,454
28,550	28,600	5,973	4,690	7,437	5,469
28,600	28,650	5,989	4,703	7,457	5,483
28,650	28,700	6,005	4,716	7,477	5,498
28,700	28,750	6,021	4,729	7,497	5,512
28,750	28,800	6,037	4,742	7,517	5,527
28,800	28,850	6,054	4,755	7,537	5,543
28,850	28,900	6,072	4,768	7,557	5,560
28,900	28,950	6,090	4,781	7,577	5,577
28,950	29,000	6,108	4,794	7,597	5,594
29,000					
29,000	29,050	6,126	4,807	7,617	5,611
29,050	29,100	6,144	4,820	7,637	5,628
29,100	29,150	6,162	4,833	7,657	5,645
29,150	29,200	6,180	4,846	7,677	5,662
29,200	29,250	6,198	4,859	7,697	5,679
29,250	29,300	6,216	4,872	7,717	5,696
29,300	29,350	6,234	4,885	7,737	5,713
29,350	29,400	6,252	4,898	7,757	5,730
29,400	29,450	6,270	4,911	7,777	5,747
29,450	29,500	6,288	4,924	7,797	5,764
29,500	29,550	6,306	4,937	7,817	5,781
29,550	29,600	6,324	4,950	7,837	5,798
29,600	29,650	6,342	4,963	7,857	5,815
29,650	29,700	6,360	4,976	7,877	5,832
29,700	29,750	6,378	4,989	7,897	5,849
29,750	29,800	6,396	5,002	7,917	5,866
29,800	29,850	6,414	5,015	7,937	5,883
29,850	29,900	6,432	5,028	7,957	5,900
29,900	29,950	6,450	5,042	7,977	5,917
29,950	30,000	6,468	5,057	7,997	5,934

If line 37 (taxable income) is—		And you are—			
At least	But less than	Single	Married filing jointly *	Married filing separately	Head of a household
		Your tax is—			
30,000					
30,000	30,050	6,486	5,072	8,018	5,951
30,050	30,100	6,504	5,087	8,040	5,968
30,100	30,150	6,522	5,102	8,062	5,985
30,150	30,200	6,540	5,117	8,084	6,002
30,200	30,250	6,558	5,132	8,106	6,019
30,250	30,300	6,576	5,147	8,128	6,036
30,300	30,350	6,594	5,162	8,150	6,053
30,350	30,400	6,612	5,177	8,172	6,070
30,400	30,450	6,630	5,192	8,194	6,087
30,450	30,500	6,648	5,207	8,216	6,104
30,500	30,550	6,666	5,222	8,238	6,121
30,550	30,600	6,684	5,237	8,260	6,138
30,600	30,650	6,702	5,252	8,282	6,155
30,650	30,700	6,720	5,267	8,304	6,172
30,700	30,750	6,738	5,282	8,326	6,189
30,750	30,800	6,756	5,297	8,348	6,206
30,800	30,850	6,774	5,312	8,370	6,223
30,850	30,900	6,792	5,327	8,392	6,240
30,900	30,950	6,810	5,342	8,414	6,257
30,950	31,000	6,828	5,357	8,436	6,274
31,000					
31,000	31,050	6,846	5,372	8,458	6,291
31,050	31,100	6,864	5,387	8,480	6,308
31,100	31,150	6,882	5,402	8,502	6,325
31,150	31,200	6,900	5,417	8,524	6,342
31,200	31,250	6,918	5,432	8,546	6,359
31,250	31,300	6,936	5,447	8,568	6,376
31,300	31,350	6,954	5,462	8,590	6,393
31,350	31,400	6,972	5,477	8,612	6,410
31,400	31,450	6,990	5,492	8,634	6,427
31,450	31,500	7,008	5,507	8,656	6,444
31,500	31,550	7,026	5,522	8,678	6,461
31,550	31,600	7,044	5,537	8,700	6,478
31,600	31,650	7,062	5,552	8,722	6,495
31,650	31,700	7,080	5,567	8,744	6,512
31,700	31,750	7,098	5,582	8,766	6,529
31,750	31,800	7,116	5,597	8,788	6,546
31,800	31,850	7,134	5,612	8,810	6,563
31,850	31,900	7,152	5,627	8,832	6,580
31,900	31,950	7,170	5,642	8,854	6,597
31,950	32,000	7,188	5,657	8,876	6,614
32,000					
32,000	32,050	7,206	5,672	8,898	6,631
32,050	32,100	7,224	5,687	8,920	6,648
32,100	32,150	7,242	5,702	8,942	6,665
32,150	32,200	7,260	5,717	8,964	6,682
32,200	32,250	7,278	5,732	8,986	6,699
32,250	32,300	7,296	5,747	9,008	6,716
32,300	32,350	7,314	5,762	9,030	6,733
32,350	32,400	7,332	5,777	9,052	6,750
32,400	32,450	7,350	5,792	9,074	6,767
32,450	32,500	7,368	5,807	9,096	6,784
32,500	32,550	7,386	5,822	9,118	6,801
32,550	32,600	7,404	5,837	9,140	6,818
32,600	32,650	7,422	5,852	9,162	6,835
32,650	32,700	7,440	5,867	9,184	6,852
32,700	32,750	7,458	5,882	9,206	6,869

*This column must also be used by a qualifying widow(er).

Continued on next page

1983 Tax Table (Continued)

If line 37 (taxable income) is—		And you are—			
At least	But less than	Single	Married filing jointly *	Married filing separately	Head of a household
		Your tax is—			
32,750	32,800	7,476	5,897	9,228	6,886
32,800	32,850	7,494	5,912	9,250	6,903
32,850	32,900	7,512	5,927	9,272	6,920
32,900	32,950	7,530	5,942	9,294	6,937
32,950	33,000	7,548	5,957	9,316	6,954
33,000					
33,000	33,050	7,566	5,972	9,338	6,971
33,050	33,100	7,584	5,987	9,360	6,988
33,100	33,150	7,602	6,002	9,382	7,005
33,150	33,200	7,620	6,017	9,404	7,022
33,200	33,250	7,638	6,032	9,426	7,039
33,250	33,300	7,656	6,047	9,448	7,056
33,300	33,350	7,674	6,062	9,470	7,073
33,350	33,400	7,692	6,077	9,492	7,090
33,400	33,450	7,710	6,092	9,514	7,107
33,450	33,500	7,728	6,107	9,536	7,124
33,500	33,550	7,746	6,122	9,558	7,141
33,550	33,600	7,764	6,137	9,580	7,158
33,600	33,650	7,782	6,152	9,602	7,175
33,650	33,700	7,800	6,167	9,624	7,192
33,700	33,750	7,818	6,182	9,646	7,209
33,750	33,800	7,836	6,197	9,668	7,226
33,800	33,850	7,854	6,212	9,690	7,243
33,850	33,900	7,872	6,227	9,712	7,260
33,900	33,950	7,890	6,242	9,734	7,277
33,950	34,000	7,908	6,257	9,756	7,294
34,000					
34,000	34,050	7,926	6,272	9,778	7,311
34,050	34,100	7,944	6,287	9,800	7,328
34,100	34,150	7,963	6,302	9,822	7,345
34,150	34,200	7,983	6,317	9,844	7,364
34,200	34,250	8,003	6,332	9,866	7,382
34,250	34,300	8,023	6,347	9,888	7,401
34,300	34,350	8,043	6,362	9,910	7,419
34,350	34,400	8,063	6,377	9,932	7,438
34,400	34,450	8,083	6,392	9,954	7,456
34,450	34,500	8,103	6,407	9,976	7,475
34,500	34,550	8,123	6,422	9,998	7,493
34,550	34,600	8,143	6,437	10,020	7,512
34,600	34,650	8,163	6,452	10,042	7,530
34,650	34,700	8,183	6,467	10,064	7,549
34,700	34,750	8,203	6,482	10,086	7,567
34,750	34,800	8,223	6,497	10,108	7,586
34,800	34,850	8,243	6,512	10,130	7,604
34,850	34,900	8,263	6,527	10,152	7,623
34,900	34,950	8,283	6,542	10,174	7,641
34,950	35,000	8,303	6,557	10,196	7,660
35,000					
35,000	35,050	8,323	6,572	10,218	7,678
35,050	35,100	8,343	6,587	10,240	7,697
35,100	35,150	8,363	6,602	10,262	7,715
35,150	35,200	8,383	6,617	10,284	7,734
35,200	35,250	8,403	6,633	10,306	7,752
35,250	35,300	8,423	6,650	10,328	7,771
35,300	35,350	8,443	6,668	10,350	7,789
35,350	35,400	8,463	6,685	10,372	7,808
35,400	35,450	8,483	6,703	10,394	7,826
35,450	35,500	8,503	6,720	10,416	7,845

If line 37 (taxable income) is—		And you are—			
At least	But less than	Single	Married filing jointly *	Married filing separately	Head of a household
		Your tax is—			
35,500	35,550	8,523	6,738	10,438	7,863
35,550	35,600	8,543	6,755	10,460	7,882
35,600	35,650	8,563	6,773	10,482	7,900
35,650	35,700	8,583	6,790	10,504	7,919
35,700	35,750	8,603	6,808	10,526	7,937
35,750	35,800	8,623	6,825	10,548	7,956
35,800	35,850	8,643	6,843	10,570	7,974
35,850	35,900	8,663	6,860	10,592	7,993
35,900	35,950	8,683	6,878	10,614	8,011
35,950	36,000	8,703	6,895	10,636	8,030
36,000					
36,000	36,050	8,723	6,913	10,658	8,048
36,050	36,100	8,743	6,930	10,680	8,067
36,100	36,150	8,763	6,948	10,702	8,085
36,150	36,200	8,783	6,965	10,724	8,104
36,200	36,250	8,803	6,983	10,746	8,122
36,250	36,300	8,823	7,000	10,768	8,141
36,300	36,350	8,843	7,018	10,790	8,159
36,350	36,400	8,863	7,035	10,812	8,178
36,400	36,450	8,883	7,053	10,834	8,196
36,450	36,500	8,903	7,070	10,856	8,215
36,500	36,550	8,923	7,088	10,878	8,233
36,550	36,600	8,943	7,105	10,900	8,252
36,600	36,650	8,963	7,123	10,922	8,270
36,650	36,700	8,983	7,140	10,944	8,289
36,700	36,750	9,003	7,158	10,966	8,307
36,750	36,800	9,023	7,175	10,988	8,326
36,800	36,850	9,043	7,193	11,010	8,344
36,850	36,900	9,063	7,210	11,032	8,363
36,900	36,950	9,083	7,228	11,054	8,381
36,950	37,000	9,103	7,245	11,076	8,400
37,000					
37,000	37,050	9,123	7,263	11,098	8,418
37,050	37,100	9,143	7,280	11,120	8,437
37,100	37,150	9,163	7,298	11,142	8,455
37,150	37,200	9,183	7,315	11,164	8,474
37,200	37,250	9,203	7,333	11,186	8,492
37,250	37,300	9,223	7,350	11,208	8,511
37,300	37,350	9,243	7,368	11,230	8,529
37,350	37,400	9,263	7,385	11,252	8,548
37,400	37,450	9,283	7,403	11,274	8,566
37,450	37,500	9,303	7,420	11,296	8,585
37,500	37,550	9,323	7,438	11,318	8,603
37,550	37,600	9,343	7,455	11,340	8,622
37,600	37,650	9,363	7,473	11,362	8,640
37,650	37,700	9,383	7,490	11,384	8,659
37,700	37,750	9,403	7,508	11,406	8,677
37,750	37,800	9,423	7,525	11,428	8,696
37,800	37,850	9,443	7,543	11,450	8,714
37,850	37,900	9,463	7,560	11,472	8,733
37,900	37,950	9,483	7,578	11,494	8,751
37,950	38,000	9,503	7,595	11,516	8,770
38,000					
38,000	38,050	9,523	7,613	11,538	8,788
38,050	38,100	9,543	7,630	11,560	8,807
38,100	38,150	9,563	7,648	11,582	8,825
38,150	38,200	9,583	7,665	11,604	8,844
38,200	38,250	9,603	7,683	11,626	8,862

If line 37 (taxable income) is—		And you are—			
At least	But less than	Single	Married filing jointly *	Married filing separately	Head of a household
		Your tax is—			
38,250	38,300	9,623	7,700	11,648	8,881
38,300	38,350	9,643	7,718	11,670	8,899
38,350	38,400	9,663	7,735	11,692	8,918
38,400	38,450	9,683	7,753	11,714	8,936
38,450	38,500	9,703	7,770	11,736	8,955
38,500	38,550	9,723	7,788	11,758	8,973
38,550	38,600	9,743	7,805	11,780	8,992
38,600	38,650	9,763	7,823	11,802	9,010
38,650	38,700	9,783	7,840	11,824	9,029
38,700	38,750	9,803	7,858	11,846	9,047
38,750	38,800	9,823	7,875	11,868	9,066
38,800	38,850	9,843	7,893	11,890	9,084
38,850	38,900	9,863	7,910	11,912	9,103
38,900	38,950	9,883	7,928	11,934	9,121
38,950	39,000	9,903	7,945	11,956	9,140
39,000					
39,000	39,050	9,923	7,963	11,978	9,158
39,050	39,100	9,943	7,980	12,000	9,177
39,100	39,150	9,963	7,998	12,022	9,195
39,150	39,200	9,983	8,015	12,044	9,214
39,200	39,250	10,003	8,033	12,066	9,232
39,250	39,300	10,023	8,050	12,088	9,251
39,300	39,350	10,043	8,068	12,110	9,269
39,350	39,400	10,063	8,085	12,132	9,288
39,400	39,450	10,083	8,103	12,154	9,306
39,450	39,500	10,103	8,120	12,176	9,325
39,500	39,550	10,123	8,138	12,198	9,343
39,550	39,600	10,143	8,155	12,220	9,362
39,600	39,650	10,163	8,173	12,242	9,380
39,650	39,700	10,183	8,190	12,264	9,399
39,700	39,750	10,203	8,208	12,286	9,417
39,750	39,800	10,223	8,225	12,308	9,436
39,800	39,850	10,243	8,243	12,330	9,454
39,850	39,900	10,263	8,260	12,352	9,473
39,900	39,950	10,283	8,278	12,374	9,491
39,950	40,000	10,303	8,295	12,396	9,510
40,000					
40,000	40,050	10,323	8,313	12,418	9,528
40,050	40,100	10,343	8,330	12,440	9,547
40,100	40,150	10,363	8,348	12,462	9,565
40,150	40,200	10,383	8,365	12,484	9,584
40,200	40,250	10,403	8,383	12,506	9,602
40,250	40,300	10,423	8,400	12,528	9,621
40,300	40,350	10,443	8,418	12,550	9,639
40,350	40,400	10,463	8,435	12,572	9,658
40,400	40,450	10,483	8,453	12,594	9,676
40,450	40,500	10,503	8,470	12,616	9,695
40,500	40,550	10,523	8,488	12,638	9,713
40,550	40,600	10,543	8,505	12,660	9,732
40,600	40,650	10,563	8,523	12,682	9,750
40,650	40,700	10,583	8,540	12,704	9,769
40,700	40,750	10,603	8,558	12,726	9,787
40,750	40,800	10,623	8,575	12,748	9,806
40,800	40,850	10,643	8,593	12,770	9,824
40,850	40,900	10,663	8,610	12,792	9,843
40,900	40,950	10,683	8,628	12,814	9,861
40,950	41,000	10,703	8,645	12,836	9,880

*This column must also be used by a qualifying widow(er).

Continued on next page

1983 Tax Table (*Continued*)

If line 37 (taxable income) is— At least	But less than	Single	Married filing jointly *	Married filing separately	Head of a household
41,000					
41,000	41,050	10,723	8,663	12,858	9,898
41,050	41,100	10,743	8,680	12,880	9,917
41,100	41,150	10,763	8,698	12,902	9,935
41,150	41,200	10,783	8,715	12,924	9,954
41,200	41,250	10,803	8,733	12,946	9,972
41,250	41,300	10,823	8,750	12,968	9,991
41,300	41,350	10,843	8,768	12,990	10,009
41,350	41,400	10,863	8,785	13,012	10,028
41,400	41,450	10,883	8,803	13,034	10,046
41,450	41,500	10,903	8,820	13,056	10,065
41,500	41,550	10,924	8,838	13,078	10,083
41,550	41,600	10,947	8,855	13,100	10,102
41,600	41,650	10,969	8,873	13,122	10,120
41,650	41,700	10,992	8,890	13,144	10,139
41,700	41,750	11,014	8,908	13,166	10,157
41,750	41,800	11,037	8,925	13,188	10,176
41,800	41,850	11,059	8,943	13,210	10,194
41,850	41,900	11,082	8,960	13,232	10,213
41,900	41,950	11,104	8,978	13,254	10,231
41,950	42,000	11,127	8,995	13,276	10,250
42,000					
42,000	42,050	11,149	9,013	13,298	10,268
42,050	42,100	11,172	9,030	13,320	10,287
42,100	42,150	11,194	9,048	13,342	10,305
42,150	42,200	11,217	9,065	13,364	10,324
42,200	42,250	11,239	9,083	13,386	10,342
42,250	42,300	11,262	9,100	13,408	10,361
42,300	42,350	11,284	9,118	13,430	10,379
42,350	42,400	11,307	9,135	13,452	10,398
42,400	42,450	11,329	9,153	13,474	10,416
42,450	42,500	11,352	9,170	13,496	10,435
42,500	42,550	11,374	9,188	13,518	10,453
42,550	42,600	11,397	9,205	13,540	10,472
42,600	42,650	11,419	9,223	13,562	10,490
42,650	42,700	11,442	9,240	13,584	10,509
42,700	42,750	11,464	9,258	13,606	10,527
42,750	42,800	11,487	9,275	13,628	10,546
42,800	42,850	11,509	9,293	13,651	10,564
42,850	42,900	11,532	9,310	13,675	10,583
42,900	42,950	11,554	9,328	13,699	10,601
42,950	43,000	11,577	9,345	13,723	10,620
43,000					
43,000	43,050	11,599	9,363	13,747	10,638
43,050	43,100	11,622	9,380	13,771	10,657
43,100	43,150	11,644	9,398	13,795	10,675
43,150	43,200	11,667	9,415	13,819	10,694
43,200	43,250	11,689	9,433	13,843	10,712
43,250	43,300	11,712	9,450	13,867	10,731
43,300	43,350	11,734	9,468	13,891	10,749
43,350	43,400	11,757	9,485	13,915	10,768
43,400	43,450	11,779	9,503	13,939	10,786
43,450	43,500	11,802	9,520	13,963	10,805
43,500	43,550	11,824	9,538	13,987	10,823
43,550	43,600	11,847	9,555	14,011	10,842
43,600	43,650	11,869	9,573	14,035	10,860
43,650	43,700	11,892	9,590	14,059	10,879
43,700	43,750	11,914	9,608	14,083	10,897
43,750	43,800	11,937	9,625	14,107	10,916
43,800	43,850	11,959	9,643	14,131	10,934
43,850	43,900	11,982	9,660	14,155	10,953
43,900	43,950	12,004	9,678	14,179	10,971
43,950	44,000	12,027	9,695	14,203	10,990

If line 37 (taxable income) is— At least	But less than	Single	Married filing jointly *	Married filing separately	Head of a household
44,000					
44,000	44,050	12,049	9,713	14,227	11,008
44,050	44,100	12,072	9,730	14,251	11,027
44,100	44,150	12,094	9,748	14,275	11,045
44,150	44,200	12,117	9,765	14,299	11,064
44,200	44,250	12,139	9,783	14,323	11,082
44,250	44,300	12,162	9,800	14,347	11,101
44,300	44,350	12,184	9,818	14,371	11,119
44,350	44,400	12,207	9,835	14,395	11,138
44,400	44,450	12,229	9,853	14,419	11,156
44,450	44,500	12,252	9,870	14,443	11,175
44,500	44,550	12,274	9,888	14,467	11,193
44,550	44,600	12,297	9,905	14,491	11,212
44,600	44,650	12,319	9,923	14,515	11,230
44,650	44,700	12,342	9,940	14,539	11,249
44,700	44,750	12,364	9,958	14,563	11,269
44,750	44,800	12,387	9,975	14,587	11,291
44,800	44,850	12,409	9,993	14,611	11,313
44,850	44,900	12,432	10,010	14,635	11,335
44,900	44,950	12,454	10,028	14,659	11,357
44,950	45,000	12,477	10,045	14,683	11,379
45,000					
45,000	45,050	12,499	10,063	14,707	11,401
45,050	45,100	12,522	10,080	14,731	11,423
45,100	45,150	12,544	10,098	14,755	11,445
45,150	45,200	12,567	10,115	14,779	11,467
45,200	45,250	12,589	10,133	14,803	11,489
45,250	45,300	12,612	10,150	14,827	11,511
45,300	45,350	12,634	10,168	14,851	11,533
45,350	45,400	12,657	10,185	14,875	11,555
45,400	45,450	12,679	10,203	14,899	11,577
45,450	45,500	12,702	10,220	14,923	11,599
45,500	45,550	12,724	10,238	14,947	11,621
45,550	45,600	12,747	10,255	14,971	11,643
45,600	45,650	12,769	10,273	14,995	11,665
45,650	45,700	12,792	10,290	15,019	11,687
45,700	45,750	12,814	10,308	15,043	11,709
45,750	45,800	12,837	10,325	15,067	11,731
45,800	45,850	12,859	10,344	15,091	11,753
45,850	45,900	12,882	10,364	15,115	11,775
45,900	45,950	12,904	10,384	15,139	11,797
45,950	46,000	12,927	10,404	15,163	11,819
46,000					
46,000	46,050	12,949	10,424	15,187	11,841
46,050	46,100	12,972	10,444	15,211	11,863
46,100	46,150	12,994	10,464	15,235	11,885
46,150	46,200	13,017	10,484	15,259	11,907
46,200	46,250	13,039	10,504	15,283	11,929
46,250	46,300	13,062	10,524	15,307	11,951
46,300	46,350	13,084	10,544	15,331	11,973
46,350	46,400	13,107	10,564	15,355	11,995
46,400	46,450	13,129	10,584	15,379	12,017
46,450	46,500	13,152	10,604	15,403	12,039
46,500	46,550	13,174	10,624	15,427	12,061
46,550	46,600	13,197	10,644	15,451	12,083
46,600	46,650	13,219	10,664	15,475	12,105
46,650	46,700	13,242	10,684	15,499	12,127
46,700	46,750	13,264	10,704	15,523	12,149
46,750	46,800	13,287	10,724	15,547	12,171
46,800	46,850	13,309	10,744	15,571	12,193
46,850	46,900	13,332	10,764	15,595	12,215
46,900	46,950	13,354	10,784	15,619	12,237
46,950	47,000	13,377	10,804	15,643	12,259

If line 37 (taxable income) is— At least	But less than	Single	Married filing jointly *	Married filing separately	Head of a household
47,000					
47,000	47,050	13,399	10,824	15,667	12,281
47,050	47,100	13,422	10,844	15,691	12,303
47,100	47,150	13,444	10,864	15,715	12,325
47,150	47,200	13,467	10,884	15,739	12,347
47,200	47,250	13,489	10,904	15,763	12,369
47,250	47,300	13,512	10,924	15,787	12,391
47,300	47,350	13,534	10,944	15,811	12,413
47,350	47,400	13,557	10,964	15,835	12,435
47,400	47,450	13,579	10,984	15,859	12,457
47,450	47,500	13,602	11,004	15,883	12,479
47,500	47,550	13,624	11,024	15,907	12,501
47,550	47,600	13,647	11,044	15,931	12,523
47,600	47,650	13,669	11,064	15,955	12,545
47,650	47,700	13,692	11,084	15,979	12,567
47,700	47,750	13,714	11,104	16,003	12,589
47,750	47,800	13,737	11,124	16,027	12,611
47,800	47,850	13,759	11,144	16,051	12,633
47,850	47,900	13,782	11,164	16,075	12,655
47,900	47,950	13,804	11,184	16,099	12,677
47,950	48,000	13,827	11,204	16,123	12,699
48,000					
48,000	48,050	13,849	11,224	16,147	12,721
48,050	48,100	13,872	11,244	16,171	12,743
48,100	48,150	13,894	11,264	16,195	12,765
48,150	48,200	13,917	11,284	16,219	12,787
48,200	48,250	13,939	11,304	16,243	12,809
48,250	48,300	13,962	11,324	16,267	12,831
48,300	48,350	13,984	11,344	16,291	12,853
48,350	48,400	14,007	11,364	16,315	12,875
48,400	48,450	14,029	11,384	16,339	12,897
48,450	48,500	14,052	11,404	16,363	12,919
48,500	48,550	14,074	11,424	16,387	12,941
48,550	48,600	14,097	11,444	16,411	12,963
48,600	48,650	14,119	11,464	16,435	12,985
48,650	48,700	14,142	11,484	16,459	13,007
48,700	48,750	14,164	11,504	16,483	13,029
48,750	48,800	14,187	11,524	16,507	13,051
48,800	48,850	14,209	11,544	16,531	13,073
48,850	48,900	14,232	11,564	16,555	13,095
48,900	48,950	14,254	11,584	16,579	13,117
48,950	49,000	14,277	11,604	16,603	13,139
49,000					
49,000	49,050	14,299	11,624	16,627	13,161
49,050	49,100	14,322	11,644	16,651	13,183
49,100	49,150	14,344	11,664	16,675	13,205
49,150	49,200	14,367	11,684	16,699	13,227
49,200	49,250	14,389	11,704	16,723	13,249
49,250	49,300	14,412	11,724	16,747	13,271
49,300	49,350	14,434	11,744	16,771	13,293
49,350	49,400	14,457	11,764	16,795	13,315
49,400	49,450	14,479	11,784	16,819	13,337
49,450	49,500	14,502	11,804	16,843	13,359
49,500	49,550	14,524	11,824	16,867	13,381
49,550	49,600	14,547	11,844	16,891	13,403
49,600	49,650	14,569	11,864	16,915	13,425
49,650	49,700	14,592	11,884	16,939	13,447
49,700	49,750	14,614	11,904	16,963	13,469
49,750	49,800	14,637	11,924	16,987	13,491
49,800	49,850	14,659	11,944	17,011	13,513
49,850	49,900	14,682	11,964	17,035	13,535
49,900	49,950	14,704	11,984	17,059	13,557
49,950	50,000	14,727	12,004	17,083	13,579

*This column must also be used by a qualifying widow(er).

50,000 or over—use tax rate schedules

1983 Optional State Sales Tax Tables

(If you kept records that show you paid more sales tax than the table for your State indicates, you may claim the higher amount on Schedule A, line 10a.)

Your itemized deduction for general sales tax paid can be estimated from these tables plus any qualifying sales taxes paid on the items listed on page 19. To use the tables:

Step 1—Figure your total available income. (See note to the right).

Step 2—Count the number of exemptions for you and your family. Do not count exemptions claimed for being 65 or over or blind as part of your family size.

Step 3 A—If your total available income is not over $40,000, find the income line for your State on the tables and read across to find the amount of sales tax for your family size.

Step 3 B—If your income is over $40,000 but not over $100,000, find the deduction listed on the income line "$38,000-$40,000" for your family size and State. For each $5,000 (or part of $5,000) of income over $40,000, increase the deduction by the amount listed for the line "$40,001-$100,000."

Step 3 C—If your income is over $100,000, your sales tax deduction is limited to the deduction for income of $100,000. To figure your sales tax deduction, use Step 3 B but don't go over $100,000.

Note: Use the total of the amount on Form 1040, line 33, and nontaxable receipts such as social security, veterans', and railroad retirement benefits, workmen's compensation, untaxed portion of long-term capital gains or unemployment compensation, All-Savers interest exclusion, dividends exclusion, disability income exclusion, deduction for a married couple when both work, and public assistance payments.

Income	Alabama [1] 1	2	3	4	5	Over 5	Arizona [2] 1&2	3	4	5	Over 5	Arkansas [1] 1	2	3	4	5	Over 5	California [3] 1&2	3&4	5	Over 5	Colorado [2] 1&2	3&4	5	Over 5	Connecticut 1&2	3,4&5	Over 5	Dist. of Columbia 1	2	3	4	5	Over 5
$1-$8,000	91	113	120	130	141	160	98	113	113	120	126	78	97	102	109	116	132	125	147	155	164	50	59	62	65	126	139	146	94	112	125	125	132	140
$8,001-$10,000	107	129	140	151	164	185	115	133	133	142	148	91	111	118	127	135	152	147	173	183	193	60	70	74	77	150	167	175	110	129	145	146	155	164
$10,001-$12,000	121	144	159	171	185	207	131	152	154	162	169	103	123	134	143	153	170	167	198	208	219	68	81	85	88	172	194	203	125	145	164	166	177	186
$12,001-$14,000	135	158	176	190	204	227	146	170	173	181	188	115	134	148	158	169	187	186	220	232	243	76	91	95	99	194	220	229	139	159	182	186	197	206
$14,001-$16,000	148	170	192	207	223	246	160	186	191	199	207	125	145	161	173	184	202	204	242	255	266	84	101	105	110	214	244	254	152	173	198	205	216	225
$16,001-$18,000	160	182	208	224	240	265	173	202	209	216	224	135	154	174	186	198	217	222	263	276	288	92	110	115	120	234	268	279	165	186	213	223	234	244
$18,001-$20,000	172	193	222	240	257	282	186	218	226	233	241	145	163	186	199	212	231	238	282	297	309	99	119	125	129	253	291	302	177	198	228	240	252	261
$20,001-$22,000	183	204	236	255	273	298	198	233	242	249	257	154	172	198	212	225	245	254	301	317	330	106	128	134	138	271	313	325	189	210	242	256	268	278
$22,001-$24,000	194	214	250	269	288	314	210	247	258	264	273	163	181	209	224	238	258	270	320	336	349	113	136	143	147	289	335	347	200	221	256	272	284	294
$24,001-$26,000	204	224	263	283	303	329	222	261	274	279	288	172	189	220	235	250	270	285	338	355	368	119	144	152	156	306	357	369	211	232	269	287	300	310
$26,001-$28,000	214	234	276	297	317	344	233	274	289	294	303	180	197	230	246	262	282	299	355	373	386	125	152	160	165	323	378	390	222	242	282	302	315	325
$28,001-$30,000	224	243	289	310	331	358	244	287	304	308	317	188	204	240	257	273	294	313	372	391	404	131	160	168	173	340	398	411	232	252	295	317	330	340
$30,001-$32,000	234	252	301	323	344	372	255	300	319	322	331	196	211	250	268	284	305	327	389	408	422	137	168	176	181	356	418	432	242	262	307	332	345	354
$32,001-$34,000	244	261	313	336	357	385	266	313	333	335	345	204	218	260	278	295	316	341	405	425	439	143	176	184	189	372	438	452	252	272	319	346	359	368
$34,001-$36,000	253	269	324	348	370	398	276	325	347	348	359	211	225	270	288	306	326	354	421	441	455	149	183	192	197	388	458	472	262	281	330	360	373	382
$36,001-$38,000	262	277	335	360	383	411	286	337	361	361	372	218	232	279	298	316	336	367	436	457	471	155	190	200	205	403	477	491	271	290	341	373	387	396
$38,001-$40,000	271	285	346	372	395	423	296	349	374	374	385	225	239	288	308	328	346	380	451	473	487	160	197	207	213	418	496	510	280	299	352	386	400	409
$40,001-$100,000 (See Step 3B)	14	14	17	19	20	21	15	17	19	20	21	11	12	14	15	16	17	19	23	24	24	8	10	10	11	21	25	26	14	15	18	19	20	20

Income	Florida Family size 1&2	3	4	5	Over 5	Georgia[1] Family size 1	2	3	4	5	Over 5	Hawaii Family size 1&2	3	4	5	Over 5
$1-$8,000	101	119	120	126	134	82	103	110	116	125	141	158	180	183	190	204
$8,001-$10,000	120	140	141	150	158	95	117	127	135	145	161	181	206	209	219	235
$10,001-$12,000	138	161	163	172	181	107	130	143	152	163	180	201	228	234	245	263
$12,001-$14,000	155	180	183	194	203	118	141	157	167	179	198	220	249	256	269	288
$14,001-$16,000	172	198	203	214	223	129	152	171	182	195	214	238	268	277	292	312
$16,001-$18,000	187	216	223	234	243	139	162	184	196	210	229	254	286	297	313	335
$18,001-$20,000	202	233	242	253	262	149	171	196	209	224	244	270	303	315	333	356
$20,001-$22,000	217	249	260	271	280	158	180	208	222	237	258	285	319	333	352	377
$22,001-$24,000	231	265	278	289	298	167	189	219	234	250	271	299	335	350	371	397
$24,001-$26,000	245	280	295	306	315	176	198	230	246	262	283	313	350	366	389	416
$26,001-$28,000	258	295	312	323	332	184	206	240	258	274	295	326	364	382	406	434
$28,001-$30,000	271	310	328	339	348	192	213	250	269	286	307	339	378	397	423	451
$30,001-$32,000	284	324	344	355	364	200	220	260	280	297	319	351	391	412	439	468
$32,001-$34,000	297	338	360	371	380	208	227	270	290	308	330	363	404	426	454	485
$34,001-$36,000	309	352	376	387	395	215	234	279	300	319	341	375	416	440	469	501
$36,001-$38,000	321	365	392	402	410	222	241	288	310	330	352	386	428	454	484	517
$38,001-$40,000	333	378	407	417	425	229	247	297	320	340	362	397	440	467	499	533
$40,001-$100,000 (See Step 3B)	17	19	20	21	21	11	12	15	16	17	18	20	22	23	25	27

Income	Idaho Family size 1	2	3	4	5	Over 5	Illinois[4] Family size 1	2	3	4	5	Over 5	Indiana Family size 1&2	3&4	5	Over 5
$1-$8,000	94	114	123	133	145	164	109	132	142	148	160	176	117	139	148	157
$8,001-$10,000	110	131	143	155	169	189	128	151	166	173	186	204	137	163	173	183
$10,001-$12,000	125	146	162	175	190	212	145	168	188	196	210	229	156	186	197	207
$12,001-$14,000	139	159	179	194	210	233	162	184	208	218	232	253	173	207	219	230
$14,001-$16,000	152	172	196	212	228	253	177	199	227	238	253	274	189	227	240	252
$16,001-$18,000	165	184	211	229	246	271	192	213	245	258	273	295	205	246	260	272
$18,001-$20,000	177	195	226	245	263	289	206	226	262	276	293	315	220	264	279	291
$20,001-$22,000	188	206	240	260	279	306	220	239	278	294	311	334	234	282	298	310
$22,001-$24,000	199	216	254	275	294	322	233	251	294	312	329	352	248	299	316	328
$24,001-$26,000	210	226	267	290	309	337	246	263	310	328	346	369	261	316	333	346
$26,001-$28,000	221	236	280	304	324	352	258	274	325	344	362	386	274	332	350	363
$28,001-$30,000	231	245	293	317	338	367	270	285	339	360	378	403	287	347	366	379
$30,001-$32,000	241	254	305	330	351	381	282	295	353	376	394	419	299	362	382	395
$32,001-$34,000	251	263	317	343	364	395	293	305	367	391	409	434	311	377	397	411
$34,001-$36,000	260	271	329	356	377	408	304	315	380	406	424	449	323	392	412	426
$36,001-$38,000	269	279	340	368	390	421	315	325	393	420	439	464	334	406	427	441
$38,001-$40,000	278	287	351	380	402	433	326	334	406	434	453	478	345	420	442	456
$40,001-$100,000 (See Step 3B)	14	14	18	19	21	22	16	17	20	22	23	24	17	21	22	23

Income	Iowa Family size 1&2	3,4&5	Over 5	Kansas[1] Family size 1	2	3	4	5	Over 5	Kentucky Family size 1&2	3&4	5	Over 5
$1-$8,000	92	103	110	72	90	95	102	108	122	91	104	109	117
$8,001-$10,000	109	122	130	85	104	112	120	127	142	108	124	130	138
$10,001-$12,000	124	140	149	96	116	127	136	144	160	124	143	150	157
$12,001-$14,000	139	157	167	107	128	141	151	160	177	138	161	168	176
$14,001-$16,000	153	174	183	117	138	155	165	176	193	152	178	186	193
$16,001-$18,000	166	189	199	126	148	168	179	191	208	165	195	203	210
$18,001-$20,000	179	204	215	135	158	180	192	205	222	178	211	219	226
$20,001-$22,000	191	219	230	144	167	192	205	219	236	190	226	235	241
$22,001-$24,000	203	233	244	153	176	203	217	232	249	202	241	250	256
$24,001-$26,000	215	247	258	161	184	214	229	245	262	214	256	265	271
$26,001-$28,000	226	261	272	169	192	225	240	257	274	225	270	280	285
$28,001-$30,000	237	274	285	177	200	235	251	269	286	236	284	294	299
$30,001-$32,000	248	287	298	185	208	245	262	281	298	247	298	308	312
$32,001-$34,000	259	300	311	192	215	255	273	293	309	258	312	322	325
$34,001-$36,000	269	312	324	199	222	265	284	304	320	268	325	336	338
$36,001-$38,000	279	324	336	206	229	275	294	315	330	278	338	349	351
$38,001-$40,000	289	336	348	212	236	284	304	325	340	288	351	362	363
$40,001-$100,000 (See Step 3B)	14	17	17	11	12	14	15	16	17	14	18	18	18

Income	Louisiana[5] Family size 1&2	3&4	5	Over 5	Maine[6] Family size 1&2	3&4	5	Over 5	Maryland Family size 1&2	3	4	5	Over 5	Massachusetts[7] Family size 1&2	Over 2
$1-$8,000	60	67	70	73	89	100	103	109	80	90	90	94	98	58	63
$8,001-$10,000	71	80	84	88	106	120	124	130	95	108	108	113	118	69	76
$10,001-$12,000	82	92	97	101	121	139	144	150	110	125	125	131	136	79	89
$12,001-$14,000	92	104	109	113	135	157	163	169	124	141	143	149	154	89	101
$14,001-$16,000	101	115	121	125	149	175	181	188	137	157	160	166	171	98	113
$16,001-$18,000	110	126	132	137	162	192	198	205	150	172	177	182	188	107	124
$18,001-$20,000	119	136	143	148	175	208	215	222	163	186	193	198	203	116	135
$20,001-$22,000	128	146	153	159	187	224	231	239	175	200	209	213	219	124	146
$22,001-$24,000	136	156	163	169	199	239	247	255	187	214	225	228	234	132	157
$24,001-$26,000	144	166	173	179	211	254	263	271	198	227	240	243	249	140	168
$26,001-$28,000	152	175	183	189	222	269	278	286	209	240	255	257	263	148	178
$28,001-$30,000	160	184	193	199	233	283	293	301	220	253	270	271	278	155	188
$30,001-$32,000	168	193	202	209	244	297	308	316	231	265	285	285	292	162	198
$32,001-$34,000	175	202	211	218	255	311	322	330	242	277	299	299	305	169	208
$34,001-$36,000	182	211	220	227	265	325	336	344	253	289	313	313	319	176	217
$36,001-$38,000	189	219	229	236	275	338	350	358	263	301	327	327	332	183	227
$38,001-$40,000	196	227	238	245	285	351	364	371	273	313	341	341	345	190	236
$40,001-$100,000 (See Step 3B)	10	11	12	12	14	18	18	19	14	16	17	17	17	10	12

[1] Local sales taxes are not included. Add an amount based on the ratio between the local and State sales tax rates considering the number of months the taxes have been in effect.

[2] Local sales taxes are not included. Add the amount paid.

[3] If the State sales tax rate becomes 5¾ percent, November 1, 1983, taxpayers can add three percent to the table amounts. The 1¼ percent local sales tax is included. If a ½ of 1 percent local sales tax for transportation is paid all year (Alameda, Contra Costa, Los Angeles, San Francisco, San Mateo, Santa Clara and Santa Cruz counties) taxpayers can add 8 percent to the table amount.

[4] Local 1 percent sales taxes are included. If public transportation sales taxes are paid, compute the allowable deduction by the method in footnote 1.

[5] If your local sales tax applies to food for home consumption check your local newspaper during mid-January for the correct deduction. Otherwise see footnote 1.

[6] Sales tax paid on purchase of electricity of 750 KWH or more per month, can be added to the table amounts.

[7] Sales tax paid on the purchase of any single item of clothing for $175 or more can be added to the table amounts.

[8] Sales tax paid on purchases of natural gas or electricity can be added to the table amounts. For local sales tax see footnote 1.

[9] Local sales taxes are not included. If paid all year add 26 percent of the table amount for each 1 percent of local sales tax rate. Otherwise use a proportionate amount. For N.Y. City add 107 percent of the table amount.

(Footnotes continued on next page)

1983 Optional State Sales Tax Tables—Continued

Income	Michigan: Family size 1&2	3&4	5	Over 5
$1-$8,000	88	102	108	113
$8,001-$10,000	103	121	127	133
$10,001-$12,000	118	138	145	151
$12,001-$14,000	131	154	161	168
$14,001-$16,000	144	169	177	184
$16,001-$18,000	156	184	192	199
$18,001-$20,000	168	198	207	214
$20,001-$22,000	180	211	221	228
$22,001-$24,000	191	224	234	241
$24,001-$26,000	202	237	247	254
$26,001-$28,000	212	249	260	267
$28,001-$30,000	222	261	272	280
$30,001-$32,000	232	273	284	292
$32,001-$34,000	242	284	296	304
$34,001-$36,000	252	295	308	316
$36,001-$38,000	261	306	319	327
$38,001-$40,000	270	317	330	338
$40,001-$100,000 (See Step 3B)	14	16	17	17

Income	Minnesota[8]: Family size 1&2	Over 2
$1-$8,000	88	101
$8,001-$10,000	104	120
$10,001-$12,000	119	138
$12,001-$14,000	133	155
$14,001-$16,000	146	171
$16,001-$18,000	159	187
$18,001-$20,000	171	202
$20,001-$22,000	183	217
$22,001-$24,000	194	231
$24,001-$26,000	205	245
$26,001-$28,000	216	258
$28,001-$30,000	226	271
$30,001-$32,000	236	284
$32,001-$34,000	246	297
$34,001-$36,000	256	309
$36,001-$38,000	265	321
$38,001-$40,000	274	333
$40,001-$100,000 (See Step 3B)	14	17

Income	Mississippi: Family size 1	2	3	4	5	Over 5
$1-$8,000	137	168	179	189	203	226
$8,001-$10,000	160	193	209	221	236	261
$10,001-$12,000	180	215	236	250	267	293
$12,001-$14,000	200	235	261	276	295	323
$14,001-$16,000	218	254	285	301	322	350
$16,001-$18,000	236	272	307	325	348	377
$18,001-$20,000	252	289	329	348	372	402
$20,001-$22,000	268	305	349	370	395	426
$22,001-$24,000	283	320	369	391	418	449
$24,001-$26,000	298	335	389	411	440	471
$26,001-$28,000	313	349	407	431	461	492
$28,001-$30,000	327	363	425	450	481	513
$30,001-$32,000	341	376	443	469	501	533
$32,001-$34,000	354	389	460	487	521	553
$34,001-$36,000	367	402	477	505	540	572
$36,001-$38,000	380	414	493	522	558	591
$38,001-$40,000	392	426	509	539	576	609
$40,001-$100,000 (See Step 3B)	20	21	25	27	29	30

Income	Missouri[1]: Family size 1	2	3	4	5	Over 5
$1-$8,000	99	119	126	135	145	163
$8,001-$10,000	116	137	147	158	169	188
$10,001-$12,000	132	153	167	178	191	211
$12,001-$14,000	147	168	185	198	211	233
$14,001-$16,000	162	181	202	216	230	253
$16,001-$18,000	175	194	219	234	248	271
$18,001-$20,000	188	207	234	250	266	289
$20,001-$22,000	200	219	249	266	282	306
$22,001-$24,000	212	230	264	282	298	323
$24,001-$26,000	224	241	278	297	314	339
$26,001-$28,000	235	251	291	311	329	354
$28,001-$30,000	246	261	304	325	343	369
$30,001-$32,000	257	271	317	339	357	383
$32,001-$34,000	268	281	330	352	371	397
$34,001-$36,000	278	291	342	365	384	411
$36,001-$38,000	288	299	354	378	397	424
$38,001-$40,000	298	307	366	391	410	437
$40,001-$100,000 (See Step 3B)	15	15	18	20	21	22

Income	Nebraska[1]: Family size 1	2	3	4	5	Over 5
$1-$8,000	91	110	118	124	133	148
$8,001-$10,000	106	126	137	144	154	171
$10,001-$12,000	120	140	154	163	174	191
$12,001-$14,000	133	152	171	181	192	210
$14,001-$16,000	145	164	186	197	209	228
$16,001-$18,000	157	176	200	213	225	245
$18,001-$20,000	168	186	214	228	241	261
$20,001-$22,000	179	196	227	242	256	276
$22,001-$24,000	189	206	240	256	270	290
$24,001-$26,000	199	215	252	269	284	304
$26,001-$28,000	209	224	264	282	297	318
$28,001-$30,000	218	233	276	294	310	331
$30,001-$32,000	227	241	287	306	322	344
$32,001-$34,000	236	249	298	318	334	356
$34,001-$36,000	245	257	309	330	346	368
$36,001-$38,000	253	264	319	341	358	380
$38,001-$40,000	261	271	329	352	369	391
$40,001-$100,000 (See Step 3B)	13	14	16	18	18	20

Income	Nevada[1]: Family size 1&2	3&4	5	Over 5
$1-$8,000	94	106	111	115
$8,001-$10,000	112	128	134	138
$10,001-$12,000	129	148	154	159
$12,001-$14,000	145	167	174	179
$14,001-$16,000	160	186	193	199
$16,001-$18,000	174	204	211	217
$18,001-$20,000	188	221	229	235
$20,001-$22,000	202	238	246	253
$22,001-$24,000	215	254	263	270
$24,001-$26,000	228	270	279	287
$26,001-$28,000	241	286	295	303
$28,001-$30,000	253	301	311	319
$30,001-$32,000	265	316	326	335
$32,001-$34,000	277	331	341	350
$34,001-$36,000	288	346	356	365
$36,001-$38,000	299	360	371	380
$38,001-$40,000	310	374	385	394
$40,001-$100,000 (See Step 3B)	16	19	19	20

Income	New Jersey: Family size 1&2	Over 2
$1-$8,000	79	87
$8,001-$10,000	95	106
$10,001-$12,000	109	123
$12,001-$14,000	122	140
$14,001-$16,000	135	156
$16,001-$18,000	148	172
$18,001-$20,000	160	187
$20,001-$22,000	172	202
$22,001-$24,000	183	217
$24,001-$26,000	194	231
$26,001-$28,000	205	245
$28,001-$30,000	215	259
$30,001-$32,000	225	272
$32,001-$34,000	235	285
$34,001-$36,000	245	298
$36,001-$38,000	255	311
$38,001-$40,000	265	324
$40,001-$100,000 (See Step 3B)	13	16

Income	New Mexico[1]: Family size 1	2	3	4	5	Over 5
$1-$8,000	113	139	145	150	160	173
$8,001-$10,000	131	159	169	176	187	206
$10,001-$12,000	148	177	190	199	212	232
$12,001-$14,000	163	194	210	221	235	256
$14,001-$16,000	178	209	229	241	256	279
$16,001-$18,000	191	224	247	261	277	300
$18,001-$20,000	204	237	264	279	296	321
$20,001-$22,000	217	250	280	297	315	340
$22,001-$24,000	229	263	296	315	333	359
$24,001-$26,000	241	275	311	331	351	377
$26,001-$28,000	252	287	326	347	368	394
$28,001-$30,000	263	298	340	363	385	411
$30,001-$32,000	274	309	354	379	401	428
$32,001-$34,000	284	319	367	394	417	444
$34,001-$36,000	294	329	380	409	432	460
$36,001-$38,000	304	339	393	423	447	475
$38,001-$40,000	313	349	406	437	462	490
$40,001-$100,000 (See Step 3B)	16	17	20	22	23	25

Income	New York[9]: Family size 1&2	3&4	5	Over 5
$1-$8,000	86	99	103	108
$8,001-$10,000	103	118	123	128
$10,001-$12,000	118	136	141	147
$12,001-$14,000	132	152	159	165
$14,001-$16,000	146	168	176	182
$16,001-$18,000	159	183	192	198
$18,001-$20,000	172	198	208	214
$20,001-$22,000	184	212	223	229
$22,001-$24,000	196	226	238	244
$24,001-$26,000	208	240	252	258
$26,001-$28,000	219	253	266	272
$28,001-$30,000	230	266	280	286
$30,001-$32,000	241	278	293	299
$32,001-$34,000	252	290	306	312
$34,001-$36,000	262	302	319	325
$36,001-$38,000	272	314	332	337
$38,001-$40,000	282	326	345	349
$40,001-$100,000 (See Step 3B)	14	16	17	17

Income	North Carolina[10]: Family size 1	2	3	4	5	Over 5
$1-$8,000	92	114	121	130	139	159
$8,001-$10,000	108	131	141	151	162	183
$10,001-$12,000	123	146	159	171	182	204
$12,001-$14,000	137	159	176	189	202	224
$14,001-$16,000	150	172	192	206	220	243
$16,001-$18,000	162	184	207	222	237	261
$18,001-$20,000	174	195	222	237	253	277
$20,001-$22,000	185	206	236	252	268	293
$22,001-$24,000	196	216	249	266	283	308
$24,001-$26,000	207	226	262	280	298	323
$26,001-$28,000	217	236	275	293	312	337
$28,001-$30,000	227	245	287	306	325	351
$30,001-$32,000	237	254	299	319	338	364
$32,001-$34,000	247	263	310	331	351	377
$34,001-$36,000	257	271	321	343	364	390
$36,001-$38,000	266	279	332	355	376	402
$38,001-$40,000	275	287	343	366	388	414
$40,001-$100,000 (See Step 3B)	14	14	17	18	19	21

Income	North Dakota: Family size 1&2	3,4&5	Over 5
$1-$8,000	67	78	84
$8,001-$10,000	80	93	99
$10,001-$12,000	91	107	114
$12,001-$14,000	102	120	127
$14,001-$16,000	113	133	140
$16,001-$18,000	123	146	153
$18,001-$20,000	132	158	165
$20,001-$22,000	141	169	176
$22,001-$24,000	150	180	187
$24,001-$26,000	159	191	198
$26,001-$28,000	168	202	209
$28,001-$30,000	176	213	219
$30,001-$32,000	184	223	229
$32,001-$34,000	192	233	239
$34,001-$36,000	200	243	249
$36,001-$38,000	208	253	258
$38,001-$40,000	215	262	267
$40,001-$100,000 (See Step 3B)	11	13	13

Income	Ohio[1]: Family size 1&2	3&4	5	Over 5
$1-$8,000	90	102	107	112
$8,001-$10,000	107	122	128	134
$10,001-$12,000	123	141	147	154
$12,001-$14,000	138	159	166	172
$14,001-$16,000	153	176	184	191
$16,001-$18,000	167	193	201	208
$18,001-$20,000	180	209	217	225
$20,001-$22,000	193	225	233	241
$22,001-$24,000	206	240	248	257
$24,001-$26,000	218	255	263	272
$26,001-$28,000	230	269	278	287
$28,001-$30,000	242	283	293	302
$30,001-$32,000	253	297	307	316
$32,001-$34,000	264	311	321	330
$34,001-$36,000	275	324	334	344
$36,001-$38,000	286	337	347	357
$38,001-$40,000	297	350	360	370
$40,001-$100,000 (See Step 3B)	15	18	18	19

Income	Oklahoma[1]: Family size 1	2	3	4	5	Over 5
$1-$8,000	49	58	62	65	70	79
$8,001-$10,000	58	67	73	77	82	91
$10,001-$12,000	66	75	82	87	93	103
$12,001-$14,000	73	82	91	97	103	114
$14,001-$16,000	80	89	100	106	113	124
$16,001-$18,000	87	96	108	115	122	133
$18,001-$20,000	93	102	116	123	131	142
$20,001-$22,000	99	108	123	131	139	151
$22,001-$24,000	105	114	130	139	147	159
$24,001-$26,000	111	119	137	147	155	167
$26,001-$28,000	116	124	144	155	163	175
$28,001-$30,000	121	129	151	162	170	183
$30,001-$32,000	126	134	157	169	177	191
$32,001-$34,000	131	139	163	176	184	198
$34,001-$36,000	136	144	169	183	191	205
$36,001-$38,000	141	148	175	189	198	212
$38,001-$40,000	146	152	181	195	205	218
$40,001-$100,000 (See Step 3B)	7	8	9	10	10	11

Income	Pennsylvania: Family size 1&2	Over 2
$1-$8,000	74	81
$8,001-$10,000	89	98
$10,001-$12,000	103	115
$12,001-$14,000	116	130
$14,001-$16,000	129	145
$16,001-$18,000	142	160
$18,001-$20,000	154	174
$20,001-$22,000	165	188
$22,001-$24,000	176	202
$24,001-$26,000	187	215
$26,001-$28,000	198	228
$28,001-$30,000	209	241
$30,001-$32,000	220	253
$32,001-$34,000	230	265
$34,001-$36,000	240	277
$36,001-$38,000	250	289
$38,001-$40,000	260	301
$40,001-$100,000 (See Step 3B)	13	15

Income	Rhode Island		South Carolina						South Dakota[2]						Tennessee[1]						Texas[1]				Utah[11]					
	Family size	Over	Family size					Over	Family size					Over	Family size					Over	Family size			Over	Family size					Over
	1&2	2	1	2	3	4	5	5	1	2	3	4	5	5	1	2	3	4	5	5	1&2	3&4	5	5	1	2	3	4	5	5
$1-$8,000	88	94	101	120	127	135	146	164	109	133	139	148	161	181	114	137	146	155	167	192	67	77	82	87	125	150	158	168	180	203
$8,001-$10,000	104	113	118	138	148	158	169	189	128	152	163	173	187	209	133	157	170	181	194	220	79	92	98	104	146	172	185	197	210	235
$10,001-$12,000	120	131	134	154	168	178	191	211	145	170	184	197	212	234	151	175	191	204	219	245	91	106	113	119	166	192	209	223	237	264
$12,001-$14,000	134	148	149	169	186	198	211	232	161	187	204	218	234	258	167	191	212	225	241	269	102	120	127	134	184	210	232	248	263	290
$14,001-$16,000	148	164	163	182	203	216	230	252	176	202	223	238	256	280	183	207	231	246	263	291	113	133	141	148	202	228	253	271	287	315
$16,001-$18,000	161	180	176	195	219	233	248	271	190	216	241	258	276	301	198	221	249	265	283	311	123	146	154	162	218	244	274	293	310	339
$18,001-$20,000	174	196	189	208	235	250	265	288	204	230	258	276	295	321	212	235	266	283	302	331	133	158	167	175	234	259	293	314	332	361
$20,001-$22,000	187	211	201	219	250	266	281	305	217	243	275	294	314	340	226	248	283	301	321	349	142	170	179	188	250	274	312	334	353	382
$22,001-$24,000	199	225	213	230	264	281	297	321	230	255	291	311	332	359	239	260	299	318	339	367	151	181	191	200	265	288	330	353	374	403
$24,001-$26,000	210	239	224	241	278	296	312	337	242	267	306	328	349	376	252	272	314	334	356	384	160	192	203	212	279	301	348	372	393	422
$26,001-$28,000	221	253	235	251	291	310	327	352	254	279	321	344	366	393	264	284	329	350	372	401	169	203	214	224	293	314	365	390	412	441
$28,001-$30,000	232	267	246	261	304	324	341	367	266	290	336	360	382	410	276	296	344	365	388	417	177	214	225	235	306	327	381	408	431	460
$30,001-$32,000	243	281	256	271	317	337	355	381	277	301	350	375	398	426	288	307	358	380	404	432	185	225	236	246	319	339	397	426	449	478
$32,001-$34,000	254	294	266	280	329	350	369	395	288	311	364	390	414	442	300	317	372	395	419	447	193	235	247	257	332	351	413	443	467	495
$34,001-$36,000	265	307	276	289	341	363	382	408	299	321	377	404	429	457	311	327	385	409	434	462	201	245	257	268	345	363	428	459	484	512
$36,001-$38,000	276	320	286	298	353	376	395	421	310	331	390	418	444	472	322	337	398	423	449	476	209	255	267	279	357	374	443	475	501	529
$38,001-$40,000	286	333	296	307	365	388	407	434	320	341	403	432	458	486	333	347	411	436	463	490	217	265	277	289	369	385	458	491	517	545
$40,001-$100,000 (See Step 3B)	14	17	15	15	18	19	20	22	16	17	20	22	23	24	17	17	21	22	23	25	11	13	14	14	18	19	23	25	26	27

Income	Vermont						Virginia[12]						Washington[13]						West Virginia				Wisconsin[14]				Wyoming[1]					
	Family size					Over	Family size					Over	Family size					Over	Family size			Over	Family size			Over	Family size					Over
	1	2	3	4	5	5	1	2	3	4	5	5	1	2	3	4	5	5	1&2	3&4	5	5	1&2	3&4	5	5	1	2	3	4	5	5
$1-$8,000	44	50	53	58	60	65	88	111	117	127	137	156	143	170	180	184	194	215	102	115	119	124	103	115	119	125	81	98	104	109	117	132
$8,001-$10,000	53	60	63	69	73	77	104	127	137	148	159	179	169	198	213	219	231	252	122	138	142	149	123	137	142	149	95	112	121	127	136	152
$10,001-$12,000	61	68	79	80	84	89	118	141	155	166	179	200	194	223	243	251	264	287	140	159	165	171	141	158	164	171	107	125	136	144	153	170
$12,001-$14,000	68	76	89	91	95	100	131	154	171	184	197	220	217	247	272	281	296	320	157	180	186	193	158	178	185	192	119	136	151	159	169	187
$14,001-$16,000	75	84	98	102	106	110	143	167	187	201	215	238	239	269	299	310	326	351	174	199	206	213	175	197	205	212	130	147	164	173	184	202
$16,001-$18,000	82	92	107	112	116	120	155	178	202	216	231	255	260	290	325	337	355	380	190	217	226	233	191	216	224	231	140	157	176	187	198	217
$18,001-$20,000	89	99	115	122	126	130	166	189	216	231	247	271	280	310	350	364	383	409	205	235	245	252	206	233	242	250	150	167	188	200	212	231
$20,001-$22,000	96	106	123	132	136	139	177	199	230	245	262	286	299	330	374	390	410	436	220	253	263	270	220	251	260	268	159	176	200	213	225	244
$22,001-$24,000	102	113	131	142	145	148	188	209	243	259	276	301	318	348	398	415	436	462	234	270	281	288	234	268	278	285	168	185	211	225	237	257
$24,001-$26,000	108	120	139	151	154	157	198	219	256	273	290	315	336	366	421	439	462	488	248	287	299	306	248	284	295	302	177	193	222	236	249	269
$26,001-$28,000	114	126	147	160	163	166	208	228	268	286	304	329	354	383	443	463	487	513	262	303	316	323	262	300	312	318	186	201	232	247	261	281
$28,001-$30,000	120	132	154	169	172	174	218	237	280	298	317	342	372	400	464	486	511	537	275	319	333	340	275	316	328	334	194	209	242	258	273	293
$30,001-$32,000	126	138	161	178	181	182	227	246	292	310	330	355	389	417	485	508	535	561	288	334	350	356	288	331	344	350	202	216	252	269	284	304
$32,001-$34,000	132	144	168	187	190	190	236	254	303	322	342	368	406	433	506	530	558	584	301	349	366	372	301	346	360	366	210	223	261	280	294	315
$34,001-$36,000	138	150	175	196	198	198	245	262	314	334	354	380	422	448	526	552	581	606	314	364	382	388	313	361	375	381	218	230	270	290	304	326
$36,001-$38,000	143	156	182	204	206	206	254	270	325	345	366	391	438	463	546	573	603	628	326	379	398	404	325	376	390	396	226	237	279	300	314	336
$38,001-$40,000	148	162	188	212	214	214	263	277	336	356	378	402	453	478	566	594	625	650	338	394	413	419	337	390	405	410	233	244	288	310	324	346
$40,001-$100,000 (See Step 3B)	7	8	9	11	11	11	13	14	17	18	19	20	23	24	28	30	31	33	17	20	21	21	17	20	20	21	12	12	14	16	16	17

[10] Local sales taxes are included. Taxpayers not paying local sales taxes (Burke County) should use 75 percent of the table amount allowed.

[11] Local ¾ (⅞ after June 30, 1983) percent taxes are included. Add 5 percent of table amount if the ¼ percent county sales tax for transportation is paid all year. Otherwise add a proportionate amount (see footnote 1).

[12] Local sales taxes are included.

[13] Includes the increase in the State rate to 6.5 percent (3-1-83), plus the local ½ percent sales tax. Border county taxpayers, where the State sales tax rate remained at 5.4 percent, should use 87 percent of the table amount allowed. For each 2/10's of 1 percent of local transit sales tax paid all year you can add 3 percent to the table amount.

[14] Sales tax paid on purchases of natural gas or electricity (May through October) can be added to the table amounts.

APPENDIX B
TAX FORMS

B–1   FORM 1040EZ INCOME TAX RETURN FOR SINGLE FILERS WITH NO DEPENDENTS

Department of the Treasury - Internal Revenue Service

Form 1040EZ Income Tax Return for Single filers with no dependents

1983

OMB No 1545-0675

Name & address	If you don't have a label, please print:

▶

Write your name above (first, initial, last)

Present home address (number and street)

City, town, or post office, state, and ZIP code

Please write your numbers like this.

1 2 3 4 5 6 7 8 9 0

Social security number

Presidential Election Campaign Fund
Check box if you want $1 of your tax to go to this fund. ▶

☐   **Dollars**   **Cents**

Figure your tax

1   Wages, salaries, and tips. Attach your W-2 form(s).   **1**

2   Interest income of $400 or less. If more than $400, you cannot use Form 1040EZ.   **2**

Attach Copy B of Form(s) W-2 here

3   Add line 1 and line 2. This is your **adjusted gross income.**   **3**

4   Allowable part of your charitable contributions. Complete the worksheet on page 19. Do not write more than $25.   **4**

5   Subtract line 4 from line 3.   **5**

6   Amount of your personal exemption.   **6**   1,000.00

7   Subtract line 6 from line 5. This is your **taxable income.**   **7**

8   Enter your Federal income tax withheld. This should be shown in Box 9 of your W-2 form(s).   **8**

9   Use the tax table on pages 29-34 to find the **tax** on your taxable income on line 7. Write the amount of tax.   **9**

Refund or amount you owe

Attach tax payment here

10   If line 8 is larger than line 9, subtract line 9 from line 8. Enter the **amount of your refund.**   **10**

11   If line 9 is larger than line 8, subtract line 8 from line 9. Enter the **amount you owe.** Attach check or money order for the full amount, payable to "Internal Revenue Service."   **11**

Sign your return

I have read this return. Under penalties of perjury, I declare that to the best of my knowledge and belief, the return is true, correct, and complete.

Your signature   Date

X

For IRS Use Only—Please do not write in boxes below.

For Privacy Act and Paperwork Reduction Act Notice, see page 38.

1983   Instructions for Form 1040EZ

You can use this form if:

- Your filing status is single.
- You do not claim exemptions for being 65 or over, OR for being blind.
- You do not claim any dependents.
- Your taxable income is less than $50,000.
- You had **only** wages, salaries, and tips, and you had interest income (other than All-Savers interest) of $400 or less.

  If you can't use this form, you must use Form 1040A or 1040 instead. See pages 4 through 6. If you are uncertain about your filing status, dependents, or exemptions, read the step-by-step instructions for Form 1040A that begin on page 6.

Completing your return

It will make it easier for us to process your return if you do the following:

1. Keep your numbers inside the boxes.

2. Try to make your numbers look like these

3. Do not use dollar signs.

Name and address

Use the mailing label we sent you. After you complete your return, carefully place the label in the name and address area. Correct any errors right on the label. If you don't have a label, print the information on the name and address lines.

Presidential election campaign fund

Congress set up this fund to help pay for Presidential election campaigns. You may have one of your tax dollars go to this fund by checking the box.

Figure your tax

Line 1. Write on line 1 the total amount you received in wages, salaries, and tips. This should be shown on your 1983 wage statement, **Form W-2,** (Box 10). If you don't receive your W-2 form by February 15, contact your local IRS office. Attach the first copy or Copy B of your W-2 form(s) to your return.

Line 2. Write on line 2 the total interest income you received from all sources, such as banks, savings and loans, and credit unions. You should receive an interest statement (usually **Form 1099-INT**) from each institution that paid you interest.

You cannot use Form 1040EZ if your total interest income is over $400, or you received interest income from an All-Savers Certificate.

Line 4. You can deduct 25% of what you gave to qualified charitable organizations in 1983. But if you gave $100 or more, you can't deduct more than $25. Complete the worksheet on page 19 to figure your deduction, and write the amount on line 4.

Line 6. Every taxpayer is entitled to one $1,000 personal exemption. If you are also entitled to additional exemptions for being 65 or over, for blindness, for your spouse, or for your dependent children or other dependents, you cannot use this form.

Line 8. Write the amount of Federal income tax withheld. This should be shown on your 1983 W-2 form(s) (Box 9). If you had two or more employers and had total wages of over $35,700, see page 23. If you want IRS to figure your tax for you, complete lines 1 through 8, sign, and date your return. If you want to figure your own tax, continue with these instructions.

Line 9. Use the amount on line 7 to find your tax in the tax table on pages 29-34. Be sure to use the column in the tax table for **single** taxpayers. Write the amount of tax on line 9. If your tax from the tax table is zero, write 0.

Refund or amount you owe—Compare line 8 with line 9.

Line 10. If line 8 is larger than line 9, you are entitled to a refund. Subtract line 9 from line 8, and write the result on line 10.

Line 11. If line 9 is larger than line 8, you owe more tax. Subtract line 8 from line 9, and write the result on line 11. Attach your check or money order for the full amount. Write your social security number and "1983 Form 1040EZ" on your payment.

Sign your return

You must sign and date your return. If you pay someone to prepare your return, that person must also sign it below the space for your signature and supply the other information required by IRS. See page 25.

Mailing your return

File your return by **April 16, 1984**. Mail it to us in the addressed envelope that came with the instruction booklet. If you don't have an addressed envelope, see page 28 for the address.

B–2 SHORT FORM 1040A U. S. INDIVIDUAL INCOME TAX RETURN

Department of the Treasury—Internal Revenue Service

1983 **Form 1040A US Individual Income Tax Return** OMB No. 1545-0085

Step 1
Name and address

Use the IRS mailing label. If you don't have a label, print or type:

Your first name and initial (if joint return, also give spouse's name and initial)	Last name	Your social security no.

Present home address (number and street)	Spouse's social security no.

City, town or post office. State, and ZIP code

Presidential Election Campaign Fund

Do you want $1 to go to this fund? .... ☐ Yes ☐ No
If joint return, does your spouse want $1 to go to this fund? ☐ Yes ☐ No

Step 2
Filing status
(Check only one)

1 ☐ Single (See if you can use Form 1040EZ.)
2 ☐ Married filing joint return (even if only one had income)
3 ☐ Married filing separate return. Enter spouse's social security number above and spouse's full name here. _____
4 ☐ Head of household (with qualifying person). If the qualifying person is your unmarried child but not your dependent, write this child's name here. _____

Exemptions

Always check the exemption box labeled Yourself. Check other boxes if they apply.

5a ☐ Yourself ☐ 65 or over ☐ Blind
 b ☐ Spouse ☐ 65 or over ☐ Blind
 c First names of your dependent children who lived with you _____

Write number of boxes checked on 5a and b _____

Attach Copy B of Form(s) W-2 here

Write number of children listed on 5c + _____

d Other dependents: 1. Name	2. Relationship	3. Number of months lived in your home.	4. Did dependent have income of $1.000 or more?	5. Did you provide more than one-half of dependent's support?

Write number of other dependents listed on 5d + _____

e Total number of exemptions claimed.

Add numbers entered on lines above = _____

Step 3
Total income

Attach check or money order here

6 Wages, salaries, tips, etc. (Attach Form(s) W-2.) 6 .

7 Interest income. (If line 7 is over $400, also complete Schedule 1, Part I.) 7 .

8a Dividends. (If line 8a is over $400, also complete Schedule 1, Part II.) 8a .

 b Exclusion. See the instructions on page 14. 8b .
 c Subtract line 8b from line 8a. Write the result. 8c .

9a Unemployment compensation (insurance), from Form(s) 1099-G. 9a .
 b Taxable amount, if any, from the worksheet on page 15 of the instructions. 9b .

10 Add lines 6, 7, 8c, and 9b. Write the total. This is your total income. 10 .

Step 4
Adjusted gross income

11a IRA deduction, from the worksheet on page 17. 11a .
 b Write IRA payments made in 1984 that you included on line 11a: ($.)

12 Deduction for a married couple when both work. Complete Schedule 1, Part III. 12 .

13 Add lines 11a and 12. Write the total. These are your total adjustments. 13 .

14 Subtract line 13 from line 10. Write the result. This is your adjusted gross income. 14 .

1983   Form 1040A   Page 2

Step 5 **Taxable income**	**15** Write the amount from line 14.	15	.
	16 Allowable part of your charitable contributions, from the worksheet on page 19 of the instructions.	16	.
	17 Subtract line 16 from line 15. Write the result.	17	.
	18 Multiply $1,000 by the total number of exemptions claimed on line 5e.	18	.
	19 Subtract line 18 from line 17. Write the result. This is your taxable income.	19	.

Step 6
Tax, credits, and payments

If You Want IRS to Figure Your Tax, See Page 19 of the Instructions.

20 Find the tax on the amount on line 19. Use the tax table, pages 29–34. · 20 ·

21a Partial credit for political contributions. See page 20 of the instructions. · 21a ·

b Credit for child and dependent care expenses. Complete Schedule 1, Part IV. · 21b ·

22 Add lines 21a and 21b. Write the total. These are your total credits. · 22 ·

23 Subtract line 22 from line 20. Write the result. This is your total tax. · 23 ·

24a Total Federal income tax withheld. This should be shown in Box 9 of your W-2 form(s). (If line 6 is more than $35,700, see page 23 of the instructions.) · 24a ·

b Earned income credit, from the worksheet on page 24 of the instructions. See page 23 of the instructions. · 24b ·

25 Add lines 24a and 24b. Write the total. These are your total payments. · 25 ·

Step 7
Refund or amount you owe

26 If line 25 is larger than line 23, subtract line 23 from line 25. Write the result. This is the **amount of your refund.** · 26 ·

27 If line 23 is larger than line 25, subtract line 25 from line 23. Write the result. This is the **amount you owe.** Attach check or money order for full amount payable to "Internal Revenue Service." Write your social security number and "1983 Form 1040A" on it. · 27 ·

Step 8
Sign your return

Under penalties of perjury, I declare that I have examined this return and accompanying schedules and statements, and to the best of my knowledge and belief, they are true, correct, and complete. Declaration of preparer (other than the taxpayer) is based on all information of which the preparer has any knowledge.

Your signature	Date	Your occupation
X		

Spouse's signature (if joint return both must sign)	Date	Spouse's occupation
X		

Paid preparer's signature	Date	Preparer's social security no.
X		

Firm's name (or yours, if self-employed)		Employer identification no.
Address and Zip code		Check if self-employed ☐

For **Privacy Act and Paperwork Reduction Act Notice,** see page 38.

Schedule 1
1983 **(Form 1040A)**

Part I—Interest Income
Part II—Dividend Income
Part III—Deduction for a Married Couple When Both Work

OMB No. 1545-0085

Name(s) as shown on Form 1040A.

Your social security number

Test to see when you MUST complete and attach Schedule 1 to Form 1040A

If you—
- Have over $400 of interest income
- Have over $400 of dividend income
- Claim the deduction for a working married couple
- Claim the credit for child and dependent care expenses

Complete the following part of Schedule 1—
- Part I, Interest income
- Part II, Dividend income
- Part III, Deduction for a married couple when both work
- Part IV, Credit for child and dependent care expenses

Part I   **Interest income** (See page 13)

Complete this part and attach Schedule 1 to Form 1040A if you received over $400 in interest income. If you received any interest from an All-Savers Certificate (ASC), use Form 1040 instead of Form 1040A.

1 List names of payers   Amount

	Amount
	$.
	$.
	$.
	$.
	$.
	$.
	$.
	$.

2 Add amounts on line 1. Write the total here and on line 7 of Form 1040A.   2   .

Part II   **Dividend income** (See page 14)

Complete this part and attach Schedule 1 to Form 1040A if you received over $400 in dividends.

1 List names of payers   Amount

	Amount
	$.
	$.
	$.
	$.
	$.
	$.
	$.
	$.

2 Add amounts on line 1. Write the total here and on line 8a of Form 1040A.   2   .

Part III   **Deduction for a married couple when both work** (See page 18)   21

Complete this part to figure the amount you can deduct on line 12 of Form 1040A. Attach Schedule 1 to Form 1040A.

			(a) You	(b) Your spouse
1	Wages, salaries, tips, etc., from line 6 of Form 1040A.	1	.	.
2	IRA deduction, from line 11a of Form 1040A.	2 −	.	− .
3	Subtract line 2 from line 1. Write the result.	3 =	.	= .
4	Write the amount from line 3, column (a) or (b) above, whichever is smaller.		4	.
5	Multiply the amount on line 4 above by 10% (.10).		5	× .10
6	Write your answer here and on line 12 of Form 1040A.		6 =	.

Schedule 1
(Form 1040A)

1983

OMB No. 1545-0085

Part IV—Credit for Child and Dependent Care Expenses

Name(s) as shown on Form 1040A. (Do not complete if name and SSN are shown on other side)   Your social security number

Part IV

Credit for child and dependent care expenses (See pages 20–22)   **24**

Complete this part to figure the amount of credit you can take on line 21b of Form 1040A. Attach Schedule 1 to Form 1040A.

1 Write the number of qualifying persons who were cared for in 1983. (See the instructions for the definition of a qualifying person.)   **1**

2 Write the amount of expenses you incurred and actually paid in 1983, but DO NOT write more than $2,400 ($4,800 if you paid for the care of two or more qualifying persons).   **2** .

3 • If **unmarried** at the end of 1983, write your earned income on line 3, OR
 • If **married,** filing a joint return for 1983,
  a. Write your earned income $ _____ . ____, and
  b. Write your spouse's earned income $ _____ . ____, and
  c. Compare amounts on lines 3a and 3b, and write the **smaller** of the two amounts on line 3.   **3** .

4 Compare amounts on lines 2 and 3. Write the **smaller** of the two amounts here.   **4** .

5 Write the percentage from the table below that applies to the amount on Form 1040A, line 15.

If line 15 is:		Percentage is:	If line 15 is:		Percentage is:
Over—	But not over—		Over—	But not over—	
0—$10,000		30% (.30)	$20,000—22,000		24% (.24)
$10,000—12,000		29% (.29)	22,000—24,000		23% (.23)
12,000—14,000		28% (.28)	24,000—26,000		22% (.22)
14,000—16,000		27% (.27)	26,000—28,000		21% (.21)
16,000—18,000		26% (.26)	28,000		20% (.20)
18,000—20,000		25% (.25)			

     5 × .

6 Multiply the amount on line 4 by the percentage on line 5. Write the result.   **6** = .

7 Write the tax shown on Form 1040A, line 20, minus the amount of any partial credit for political contributions shown on line 21a. (If the result is zero or less, write zero.)   **7** .

8 Compare amounts on lines 6 and 7. Write the **smaller** of the two amounts here. Also write this amount on Form 1040A, line 21b.   **8** .

B–3 FORM 1040 U. S. INDIVIDUAL INCOME TAX RETURN

Form **1040** Department of the Treasury—Internal Revenue Service **U.S. Individual Income Tax Return** **1983**

For the year January 1-December 31, 1983, or other tax year beginning _____ , 1983, ending _____ 19 ___ | OMB No. 1545-0074

Use IRS label. Otherwise, please print or type.	Your first name and initial (if joint return, also give spouse's name and initial) Last name **Your social security number**
	Present home address (Number and street, including apartment number, or rural route) **Spouse's social security number**
	City, town or post office, State, and ZIP code Your occupation Spouse's occupation

Presidential Election Campaign
Do you want $1 to go to this fund? . . . . Yes ☐ No ☐ **Note:** Checking "Yes" will not increase your tax or reduce your refund.
If joint return, does your spouse want $1 to go to this fund? Yes ☐ No ☐

For Privacy Act and Paperwork Reduction Act Notice, see Instructions.

Filing Status

Check only one box.

1 ☐ Single
2 ☐ Married filing joint return (even if only one had income)
3 ☐ Married filing separate return. Enter spouse's social security no. above and full name here. _____
4 ☐ Head of household (with qualifying person). (See page 6 of Instructions.) If the qualifying person is your unmarried child but not your dependent, write child's name here. _____
5 ☐ Qualifying widow(er) with dependent child (Year spouse died ▶ 19 ___). (See page 6 of Instructions.)

Exemptions

Always check the box labeled Yourself. Check other boxes if they apply.

6a ☐ Yourself ☐ 65 or over ☐ Blind
b ☐ Spouse ☐ 65 or over ☐ Blind

Enter number of boxes checked on 6a and b ▶ ☐

c First names of your dependent children who lived with you _____

Enter number of children listed on 6c ▶ ☐

d Other dependents: (1) Name	(2) Relationship	(3) Number of months lived in your home	(4) Did dependent have income of $1,000 or more?	(5) Did you provide more than one-half of dependent's support?

Enter number of other dependents ▶ ☐

e Total number of exemptions claimed . . . .

Add numbers entered in boxes above ▶ ☐

Income

Please attach Copy B of your Forms W-2, W-2G, and W-2P here.

If you do not have a W-2, see page 5 of Instructions.

Please attach check or money order here.

7 Wages, salaries, tips, etc. . . . . | 7 |
8 Interest income (also attach Schedule B if over $400 or you have any All-Savers interest) . . . | 8 |
9a Dividends (also attach Schedule B if over $400) _____ , 9b Exclusion _____
c Subtract line 9b from line 9a and enter the result . . . . | 9c |
10 Refunds of State and local income taxes, from worksheet on page 10 of Instructions (do not enter an amount unless you deducted those taxes in an earlier year—see page 10 of Instructions) . . . . | 10 |
11 Alimony received . . . . | 11 |
12 Business income or (loss) (attach Schedule C) . . . . ▶ | 12 |
13 Capital gain or (loss) (attach Schedule D) . . . . | 13 |
→14 40% capital gain distributions not reported on line 13 (See page 10 of Instructions) . . . . | 14 |
15 Supplemental gains or (losses) (attach Form 4797) . . . . | 15 |
16 Fully taxable pensions, IRA distributions, and annuities not reported on line 17 . . . . | 16 |
17a Other pensions and annuities, including rollovers. Total received | 17a |
b Taxable amount, if any, from worksheet on page 10 of Instructions . . . . | 17b |
18 Rents, royalties, partnerships, estates, trusts, etc. (attach Schedule E) . . . . | 18 |
19 Farm income or (loss) (attach Schedule F) . . . . ▶ | 19 |
20a Unemployment compensation (insurance). Total received . . . | 20a |
b Taxable amount, if any, from worksheet on page 11 of Instructions . . . . | 20b |
21 Other income (state nature and source—see page 11 of Instructions) _____ | 21 |
22 **Total income.** Add amounts in column for lines 7 through 21 . . . . ▶ | 22 |

Adjustments to Income

(See Instructions on page 11)

23 Moving expense (attach Form 3903 or 3903F) . . . . | 23 |
24 Employee business expenses (attach Form 2106) . . . . | 24 |
25a IRA deduction, from the worksheet on page 12 . . . . | 25a |
b Enter here IRA payments you made in 1984 that are included in line 25a above ▶ ☐
26 Payments to a Keogh (H.R. 10) retirement plan . . . . | 26 |
27 Penalty on early withdrawal of savings . . . . | 27 |
28 Alimony paid . . . . | 28 |
29 Deduction for a married couple when both work (attach Schedule W) | 29 |
30 Disability income exclusion (attach Form 2440) . . . . | 30 |
31 **Total adjustments.** Add lines 23 through 30 . . . . ▶ | 31 |

Adjusted Gross Income

32 **Adjusted gross income.** Subtract line 31 from line 22. If this line is less than $10,000, see "Earned Income Credit" (line 59) on page 16 of Instructions. If you want IRS to figure your tax, see page 3 of Instructions . . . . ▶ | 32 |

Form 1040 (1983)

Tax Compu-tation	33	Amount from line 32 (adjusted gross income)	33	
	34a	If you itemize, complete Schedule A (Form 1040) and enter the amount from Schedule A, line 28	34a	
(See Instruc tions on page 13)		**Caution:** If you have unearned income and can be claimed as a dependent on your parent's return, check here ▶ ☐ and see page 13 of the Instructions. Also see page 13 of the Instructions if:		
		• You are married filing a separate return and your spouse itemizes deductions, OR		
		• You file Form 4563, OR		
		• You are a dual-status alien.		
	34b	If you do not itemize deductions on Schedule A (Form 1040), complete the worksheet on page 14. Then enter the allowable part of your charitable contributions here	34b	
	35	Subtract line 34a or 34b, whichever applies, from line 33	35	
	36	Multiply $1,000 by the total number of exemptions claimed on Form 1040, line 6e	36	
	37	Taxable Income. Subtract line 36 from line 35	37	
	38	Tax. Enter tax here and check if from ☐ Tax Table, ☐ Tax Rate Schedule X, Y, or Z, or ☐ Schedule G	38	
	39	Additional Taxes. (See page 14 of Instructions.) Enter here and check if from ☐ Form 4970, ☐ Form 4972, ☐ Form 5544, or ☐ section 72 penalty taxes	39	
	40	**Total.** Add lines 38 and 39. ▶	40	
Credits (See Instruc tions on page 14)	41	Credit for the elderly (attach Schedules R&RP)	41	
	42	Foreign tax credit (attach Form 1116)	42	
	43	Investment credit (attach Form 3468)	43	
	44	Partial credit for political contributions	44	
	45	Credit for child and dependent care expenses (attach Form 2441)	45	
	46	Jobs credit (attach Form 5884)	46	
	47	Residential energy credit (attach Form 5695)	47	
	48	**Total credits.** Add lines 41 through 47	48	
	49	**Balance.** Subtract line 48 from line 40 and enter difference (but not less than zero) . . . . . . ▶	49	
Other Taxes (Including Advance EIC Payments)	50	Self-employment tax (attach Schedule SE)	50	
	51	Alternative minimum tax (attach Form 6251)	51	
	52	Tax from recapture of investment credit (attach Form 4255)	52	
	53	Social security tax on tip income not reported to employer (attach Form 4137)	53	
	54	Uncollected employee social security tax and RRTA tax on tips (from Form W-2)	54	
	55	Tax on an IRA (attach Form 5329)	55	
06	56	**Total tax.** Add lines 49 through 55 . . . . ▶	56	
Payments Attach Forms W-2, W-2G, and W-2P to front.	57	Federal income tax withheld.	57	
	58	1983 estimated tax payments and amount applied from 1982 return	58	
	59	Earned income credit. If line 33 is under $10,000, see page 16 . .	59	
	60	Amount paid with Form 4868	60	
	61	Excess social security tax and RRTA tax withheld (two or more employers)	61	
	62	Credit for Federal tax on special fuels and oils (attach Form 4136)	62	
	63	Regulated Investment Company credit (attach Form 2439)	63	
	64	**Total payments.** Add lines 57 through 63 . . . . ▶	64	
Refund or Amount You Owe	65	If line 64 is larger than line 56, enter amount **OVERPAID** . . . . ▶	65	
	66	Amount of line 65 to be **REFUNDED TO YOU** . . . . ▶	66	
	67	Amount of line 65 to be applied to your 1984 estimated tax . . . . . ▶	67	
	68	If line 56 is larger than line 64, enter **AMOUNT YOU OWE.** Attach check or money order for full amount payable to "Internal Revenue Service." Write your social security number and "1983 Form 1040" on it . . . ▶	68	
		(Check ▶ ☐ if Form 2210 (2210F) is attached. See page 17 of Instructions.) $		

Please Sign Here

Under penalties of perjury, I declare that I have examined this return and accompanying schedules and statements, and to the best of my knowledge and belief, they are true, correct, and complete. Declaration of preparer (other than taxpayer) is based on all information of which preparer has any knowledge.

▶ _____ Your signature | Date | ▶ _____ Spouse's signature (if filing jointly, BOTH must sign)

Paid Preparer's Use Only	Preparer's signature ▶	Date	Check if self-employed ☐	Preparer's social security no.
	Firm's name (or yours, if self-employed) and address ▶		E.I. No.	
			ZIP code	

SCHEDULES A&B (Form 1040)
Department of the Treasury
Internal Revenue Service

Schedule A—Itemized Deductions
(Schedule B is on back)
▶ Attach to Form 1040. ▶ See Instructions for Schedules A and B (Form 1040).

OMB No 1545-0074
1983
07

Name(s) as shown on Form 1040

Your social security number

Medical and Dental Expenses (Do not include expenses reimbursed or paid by others.) (See page 18 of Instructions.)	1	Medicines and drugs	1		
	2	Write 1% of Form 1040, line 33	2		
	3	Subtract line 2 from line 1. If line 2 is more than line 1, write zero . .	3		
	4	Other medical and dental expenses:			
		a Doctors, dentists, nurses, hospitals, insurance premiums you paid for medical and dental care, etc.	4a		
		b Transportation	4b		
		c Other (list—include hearing aids, dentures, eyeglasses, etc.) ▶.................	4c		
	5	Add lines 3 through 4c	5		
	6	Multiply amount on Form 1040, line 33, by 5% (.05)	6		
	7	Subtract line 6 from line 5. If line 6 is more than line 5, write zero . . ▶	7		
Taxes (See page 19 of Instructions.)	8	State and local income	8		
	9	Real estate	9		
	10	a General sales (see sales tax tables)	10a		
		b General sales on motor vehicles	10b		
	11	Other (list—include personal property) ▶................	11		
	12	Add lines 8 through 11. Write your answer here . . . . . . ▶	12		
Interest Expense (See page 20 of Instructions.)	13	a Home mortgage interest paid to financial institutions	13a		
		b Home mortgage interest paid to individuals (show that person's name and address) ▶................	13b		
	14	Credit cards and charge accounts	14		
	15	Other (list) ▶................	15		
	16	Add lines 13a through 15. Write your answer here . . . . . . ▶	16		
Contributions (See page 20 of Instructions.)	17	a Cash contributions. (If you gave $3,000 or more to any one organization, report those contributions on line 17b.)	17a		
		b Cash contributions totaling $3,000 or more to any one organization. (Show to whom you gave and how much you gave.) ▶.........	17b		
	18	Other than cash (attach required statement)	18		
	19	Carryover from prior year	19		
	20	Add lines 17a through 19. Write your answer here . . . . . . ▶	20		
Casualty and Theft Losses	21	Total casualty or theft loss(es) (attach Form 4684) (see page 20 of Instructions) . . . ▶	21		
Miscellaneous Deductions (See page 21 of Instructions.)	22	Union and professional dues	22		
	23	Tax return preparation fee	23		
	24	Other (list) ▶........ *non motion business*	24		
	25	Add lines 22 through 24. Write your answer here . . . . . . ▶	25		
Summary of Itemized Deductions (See page 21 of Instructions.)	26	Add lines 7, 12, 16, 20, 21, and 25	26		
	27	If you checked Form 1040 { Filing Status box 2 or 5, write $3,400 Filing Status box 1 or 4, write $2,300 Filing Status box 3, write $1,700 }	27		
	28	Subtract line 27 from line 26. Write your answer here and on Form 1040, line 34a. (If line 27 is more than line 26, see the Instructions for line 28 on page 21.) . . . . . . ▶	28		

For Paperwork Reduction Act Notice, see Form 1040 Instructions.

Schedule A (Form 1040) 1983

Schedules A&B (Form 1040) 1983   **Schedule B—Interest and Dividend Income**   08   OMB No. 1545-0074   Page 2

Name(s) as shown on Form 1040 (Do not enter name and social security number if shown on other side)	Your social security number

Part I **Interest Income** *(See pages 9 and 21 of Instructions.)* Also complete Part III.	If you received more than $400 in interest or you received any interest from an All-Savers Certificate, you must complete Part I and list ALL interest received. If you received interest as a nominee for another, or you received or paid accrued interest on securities transferred between interest payment dates, see page 22.		

Interest income other than interest from All-Savers Certificates		Amount	
1 Interest income from seller-financed mortgages. (See Instructions and show name of payer.) ▶	1		
2 Other interest income (list name of payer) ▶			
....			
....			
....			
....			
....	2		
....			
....			
....			
....			
3 Add lines 1 and 2	3		

Interest from All-Savers Certificates (ASCs). (See page 22.)		Amount	
4			
....	4		
....			
5 Add amounts on line 4	5		
6 Write the amount of your ASC exclusion from the worksheet on page 22 of Instructions .	6		
7 Subtract line 6 from line 5	7		
8 Add lines 3 and 7. Write your answer here and on Form 1040, line 8 . . . . . . ▶	8		

Part II **Dividend** **Income** *(See pages 9 and 22 of Instructions.)* Also complete Part III.	If you received more than $400 in gross dividends (including capital gain distributions) and other distributions on stock, or you are electing to exclude qualified reinvested dividends from a public utility, complete Part II. If you received dividends as a nominee for another, see page 22.		

Name of payer		Amount	
9			
....			
....			
....			
....	9		
....			
....			
....			
10 Add amounts on line 9	10		
11 Capital gain distributions. Enter here and on line 15, Schedule D.*	11		
12 Nontaxable distributions. (See Instructions for adjustment to basis.)	12		
13 Exclusion of qualified reinvested dividends from a public utility. (See page 22 of Instructions.)	13		
14 Add lines 11, 12, and 13	14		
15 Subtract line 14 from line 10. Write your answer here and on Form 1040, line 9a . . ▶	15		

If you received capital gain distributions for the year and you do not need Schedule D to report any other gains or losses, do not file that schedule. Instead, enter 40% of your capital gain distributions on Form 1040, line 14.

Part III **Foreign** **Accounts** **and** **Foreign** **Trusts** *(See page 22 of Instructions.)*	If you received more than $400 of interest or dividends, OR if you had a foreign account or were a grantor of, or a transferor to, a foreign trust, you must answer both questions in Part III.	Yes	No
	16 At any time during the tax year, did you have an interest in or a signature or other authority over a bank account, securities account, or other financial account in a foreign country? (See page 23 of the instructions for exceptions and filing requirements for Form 90-22.1.)		
	If "Yes," write the name of the foreign country ▶		
	17 Were you the grantor of, or transferor to, a foreign trust which existed during the current tax year, whether or not you have any beneficial interest in it? If "Yes," you may have to file Forms 3520, 3520-A, or 926		

For Paperwork Reduction Act Notice, see Form 1040 Instructions.   Schedule B (Form 1040) 1983

SCHEDULE C (Form 1040)	**Profit or (Loss) From Business or Profession** (Sole Proprietorship)	OMB No. 1545-0074
Department of the Treasury Internal Revenue Service	Partnerships, Joint Ventures, etc., Must File Form 1065. ▶ Attach to Form 1040 or Form 1041. ▶ See Instructions for Schedule C (Form 1040).	1983 09

Name of proprietor	Social security number of proprietor

A Main business activity (see Instructions) ▶ _____ ; product ▶ _____

B Business name and address ▶ ....

C Employer identification number

D Method(s) used to value closing inventory:
   (1) ☐ Cost   **(2)** ☐ Lower of cost or market   **(3)** ☐ Other (attach explanation)

E Accounting method: **(1)** ☐ Cash   **(2)** ☐ Accrual   **(3)** ☐ Other (specify) ▶ ....

F Was there any major change in determining quantities, costs, or valuations between opening and closing inventory? . . . .
   If "Yes," attach explanation.

G Did you deduct expenses for an office in your home? . . . .

		Yes	No

PART I.—Income

1 a	Gross receipts or sales	**1a**	
b	Less: Returns and allowances	**1b**	
c	Subtract line 1b from line 1a and enter the balance here	**1c**	
2	Cost of goods sold and/or operations (Part III, line 8)	**2**	
3	Subtract line 2 from line 1c and enter the **gross profit** here	**3**	
4 a	Windfall Profit Tax Credit or Refund received in 1983 (see Instructions)	**4a**	
b	Other income	**4b**	
5	Add lines 3, 4a, and 4b. This is the **gross income** . . . . ▶	**5**	

PART II.—Deductions

6	Advertising		**23**	Repairs	
7	Bad debts from sales or services (Cash method taxpayers, see Instructions) .		**24**	Supplies (not included in Part III) . .	
8	Bank service charges.		**25**	Taxes (Do not include Windfall Profit Tax here. See line 29.)	
9	Car and truck expenses		**26**	Travel and entertainment . . .	
10	Commissions		**27**	Utilities and telephone . . .	
11	Depletion		**28 a**	Wages	
12	Depreciation and Section 179 deduction from Form 4562 (not included in Part III)		**b**	Jobs credit	
			c	Subtract line 28b from 28a . .	
13	Dues and publications		**29**	Windfall Profit Tax withheld in 1983	
14	Employee benefit programs		**30**	Other expenses (specify):	
15	Freight (not included in Part III) . . .		**a**	....	
16	Insurance		**b**	....	
17	Interest on business indebtedness . .		**c**	....	
18	Laundry and cleaning		**d**	....	
19	Legal and professional services . . .		**e**	....	
20	Office expense		**f**	....	
21	Pension and profit-sharing plans . . .		**g**	....	
22	Rent on business property		**h**	....	
			i		

31	Add amounts in columns for lines 6 through 30i. These are the **total deductions** . . . . ▶	**31**	

32 Net profit or (loss). Subtract line 31 from line 5 and enter the result. If a profit, enter on Form 1040, line 12, and on Schedule SE, Part I, line 2 (or Form 1041, line 6). If a loss, go on to line 33 . . . . | **32** |

33 If you have a loss, you must answer this question: "Do you have amounts for which you are not at risk in this business (see Instructions)?" ☐ Yes ☐ No
If "Yes," you must attach Form 6198. If "No," enter the loss on Form 1040, line 12, and on Schedule SE, Part I, line 2 (or Form 1041, line 6).

PART III.—Cost of Goods Sold and/or Operations (See Schedule C Instructions for Part III)

1	Inventory at beginning of year (if different from last year's closing inventory, attach explanation)	**1**	
2	Purchases less cost of items withdrawn for personal use	**2**	
3	Cost of labor (do not include salary paid to yourself)	**3**	
4	Materials and supplies	**4**	
5	Other costs	**5**	
6	Add lines 1 through 5.	**6**	
7	Less: Inventory at end of year	**7**	
8	Cost of goods sold and/or operations. Subtract line 7 from line 6. Enter here and in Part I, line 2, above. . .	**8**	

For Paperwork Reduction Act Notice, see Form 1040 Instructions.   Schedule C (Form 1040) 1983

**SCHEDULE D
(FORM 1040)**

Department of the Treasury
Internal Revenue Service

Capital Gains and Losses (Examples of property to be reported on this Schedule are gains and losses on stocks, bonds, and similar investments, and gains (but not losses) on personal assets such as a home or jewelry.)
▶ **Attach to Form 1040.** ▶ **See Instructions for Schedule D (Form 1040).**

OMB No. 1545-0074

1983

11

Name(s) as shown on Form 1040   Your social security number

PART I.—Short-term Capital Gains and Losses—Assets Held One Year or Less

a. Description of property (Example, 100 shares 7% preferred of "Z" Co.)	b. Date acquired (Mo., day, yr.)	c. Date sold (Mo., day, yr.)	d. Gross sales price	e. Cost or other basis, plus expense of sale	f. LOSS If column (e) is more than (d) subtract (d) from (e)	g. GAIN If column (d) is more than (e) subtract (e) from (d)
1						

2	Short-term gain from sale or exchange of a principal residence from Form 2119, lines 7 or 11	**2**	
3	Short-term capital gain from installment sales from Form 6252, line 21 or 29	**3**	
4	Net short-term gain or (loss) from partnerships, S corporations, and fiduciaries	**4**	
5	Add lines 1 through 4 in column f and column g	**5** ( )	
6	Combine columns f and g of line 5 and enter the net gain or (loss)	**6**	
7	Short-term capital loss carryover from years beginning after 1969	**7** ( )	
8	Net short-term gain or (loss), combine lines 6 and 7 . . . . . . NSG	**8**	

PART II.— Long-term Capital Gains and Losses—Assets Held More Than One Year

9						

10	Long-term gain from sale or exchange of a principal residence from Form 2119, lines 7, 11, 16 or 18	**10**	
11	Long-term capital gain from installment sales from Form 6252, line 21 or 29	**11**	
12	Net long-term gain or (loss) from partnerships, S corporations, and fiduciaries	**12**	
13	Add lines 9 through 12 in column f and column g	**13** ( )	
14	Combine columns f and g of line 13 and enter the net gain or (loss)	**14**	
15	Capital gain distributions	**15**	
16	Enter gain from Form 4797, line 6(a)(1)	**16**	
17	Combine lines 14 through 16	**17**	
18	Long-term capital loss carryover from years beginning after 1969	**18** ( )	
19	Net long-term gain or (loss), combine lines 17 and 18 . . . . . . NLG	**19**	

Note: *Complete the back of this form. However, if you have capital loss carryovers from years beginning before 1970, do not complete Parts III or V. See Form 4798 instead.*

For Paperwork Reduction Act Notice, see Form 1040 instructions.   Schedule D (Form 1040) 1983

Schedule D (Form 1040) 1983   Page **2**

PART III.—Summary of Parts I and II

20 Combine lines 8 and 19, and enter the net gain or (loss) here . . . . | **20** |

Note: *If line 20 is a loss, skip lines 21 through 23 and complete lines 24 and 25. If line 20 is a gain complete lines 21 through 23 and skip lines 24 and 25.*

21 If line 20 shows a gain, enter the smaller of line 19 or line 20. Enter zero if there is a loss or no entry on line 19 . . . . | **21** |

22 Enter 60% of line 21 . . . . | **22** |

If line 22 is more than zero, you may be liable for the alternative minimum tax. See Form 6251.   *LCG*

23 Subtract line 22 from line 20. Enter here and on Form 1040, line 13 . . . . | **23** |

24 If line 20 shows a loss, enter one of the following amounts:
   a   If line 8 is zero or a net gain, enter 50% of line 20;
   b   If line 19 is zero or a net gain, enter line 20; or
   c   If line 8 and line 19 are net losses, enter amount on line 8 added to 50% of the amount on line 19 . . . | **24** |

25 Enter here and as a loss on Form 1040, line 13, the smallest of:
   a   The amount on line 24;
   b $3,000 ($1,500 if married and filing a separate return); or
   c   Taxable income, as adjusted . . . . | **25** |

PART IV.—Complete this Part Only If You Elect Out of the Installment Method And Report a Note or Other Obligation at Less Than Full Face Value

☐ Check here if you elect out of the installment method.
Enter the face amount of the note or other obligation ▶ . . . .
Enter the percentage of valuation of the note or other obligation ▶

PART V.—Computation of Post-1969 Capital Loss Carryovers from 1983 to 1984
(Complete this part if the loss on line 24 is more than the loss on line 25)
Note: *You do not have to complete Part V on the copy you file with IRS.*

Section A.—Short-term Capital Loss Carryover

26 Enter loss shown on line 8; if none, enter zero and skip lines 27 through 30 then go to line 31. . . . . . | **26** |

27 Enter gain shown on line 19. If that line is blank or shows a loss, enter zero . . . . | **27** |

28 Reduce any loss on line 26 to the extent of any gain on line 27 . . . . | **28** |

29 Enter smaller of line 25 or line 28 . . . . | **29** |

30 Subtract line 29 from line 28. This is your short-term capital loss carryover from 1983 to 1984 . . . . | **30** |

Section B.—Long-term Capital Loss Carryover

31 Subtract line 29 from line 25 (**Note:** *If you skipped lines 27 through 30, enter amount from line 25*) . . . . . . | **31** |

32 Enter loss from line 19; if none, enter zero and skip lines 33 through 36 . . . . | **32** |

33 Enter gain shown on line 8. If that line is blank or shows a loss, enter zero . . . . | **33** |

34 Reduce any loss on line 32 to the extent of any gain on line 33 . . . . | **34** |

35 Multiply amount on line 31 by 2 . . . . | **35** |

36 Subtract line 35 from line 34. This is your long-term capital loss carryover from 1983 to 1984 . . . . | **36** |

| SCHEDULE E
(Form 1040)
Department of the Treasury
Internal Revenue Service | **Supplemental Income Schedule**
(From rents and royalties, partnerships, estates, and trusts, etc.)
▶ Attach to Form 1040.   ▶ See Instructions for Schedule E (Form 1040). | OMB No. 1545-0074
1983
12 |

Name(s) as shown on Form 1040   Your social security number

PART I.—Rent and Royalty Income or Loss

1 Are any of the expenses listed below for a vacation home or other recreational unit (see Instructions)? . . . . . . ☐ Yes ☐ No
2 If you checked "Yes" to question 1, did you or a member of your family occupy the vacation home or other recreational
   unit for more than the greater of 14 days or 10% of the total days rented at fair rental value during the tax year? . . . ☐ Yes ☐ No

Description of Properties (Show kind and location for each)
Property A . . . .
Property B . . . .
Property C

Rental and Royalty Income		Properties			Totals (Add columns A, B, and C)	
		A	B	C		
3 a Rents received . . . . b Royalties received					} 3	
Rental and Royalty Expenses						
4 Advertising	4					
5 Auto and travel	5					
6 Cleaning and maintenance	6					
7 Commissions.	7					
8 Insurance	8					
9 Interest	9					
10 Legal and other professional fees . . .	10					
11 Repairs	11					
12 Supplies	12					
13 Taxes (Do **not** include Windfall Profit Tax here. See Part III, line 37.)	13					
14 Utilities	14					
15 Wages and salaries	15					
16 Other (list) ▶						
. . . .						
. . . .						
. . . .						
. . . .						
. . . .						
. . . .						
. . . .						
. . . .						
17 Total expenses other than depreciation and depletion. Add lines 4 through 16 . . .	17				17	
18 Depreciation expense (see Instructions), or depletion	18				18	
19 Total. Add lines 17 and 18	19					
20 Income or (loss) from rental or royalty properties. Subtract line 19 from line 3a (rents) or 3b (royalties)	20					

21 Add properties with profits on line 20, and write the total profits here . . . . | 21 |
22 Add properties with losses on line 20, and write the total (losses) here . . . . | 22 (   )
23 Combine amounts on lines 21 and 22, and write the net profit or (loss) here . . . . | 23 |
24 Net farm rental profit or (loss) from Form 4835, line 49 . . . . | 24 |
25 Total rental or royalty income or (loss). Combine amounts on lines 23 and 24, and write the total here. If Parts II, III, and IV on page 2 do not apply to you, write the amount from line 25 on Form 1040, line 18. Otherwise, include the amount in line 39 on page 2 of Schedule E . . . . | 25 |

For Paperwork Reduction Act Notice, see Form 1040 Instructions.   Schedule E (Form 1040) 1983

Schedule E (Form 1040) 1983   **12**   Page **2**

Name(s) as shown on Form 1040 (Do not enter name and social security number if shown on other side) | Your social security number

PART II.—Income or Losses from Partnerships, Estates or Trusts, or S Corporations

If you report a loss below, and have amounts invested in that activity for which you are not at risk, you may have to file Form 6198. See instructions.

	(a) Name	(b) Check if foreign partnership	(c) Employer identification number	(d) Net loss (see instructions for at-risk limitations)	(e) Net income
Partnerships					
	26 Add amounts in columns (d) and (e) and write the total(s) here			26 ( )	
	27 Combine amounts in columns (d) and (e), line 26, and write the net income or (loss)			27	
	28 Deduction for section 179 property (from Form 1065, Schedule K-1). (See Instructions for limitations.)			28 (	)
	29 Total partnership income or (loss). Combine amounts on lines 27 and 28. Write the total here and include in line 39 below			29	
Estates or Trusts					
	30 Add amounts in columns (d) and (e) and write the total(s) here			30 ( )	
	31 Total estate or trust income or (loss). Combine amounts in columns (d) and (e), line 30. Write the total here and include in line 39 below			31	
S Corporations					
	32 Add amounts in columns (d) and (e) and write the total(s) here			32 ( )	
	33 Combine amounts in columns (d) and (e), line 32, and write the net income or (loss) here . . .			33	
	34 Deduction for section 179 property (from Form 1120S, Schedule K-1). (See Instructions for limitations.)			34 (	)
	35 Total S corporation income or (loss). Combine amounts on lines 33 and 34. Write the total here and include in line 39 below			35	

PART III.—Windfall Profit Tax Summary

36 Windfall profit tax credit or refund received in 1983 (see Instructions)	36	
37 Windfall profit tax withheld in 1983 (see Instructions)	37 (	)
38 Combine amounts on lines 36 and 37. Write the total here and include in line 39 below	38	

PART IV.—Summary

39 TOTAL income or (loss). Combine lines 25, 29, 31, 35, and 38. Write total here and on Form 1040, line 18 ▶	39	
40 Farmers and fishermen: Write your share of GROSS FARMING AND FISHING INCOME applicable to Parts I and II	40	

PART V.—Depreciation Claimed in Part I.—Complete only if property was placed in service before January 1, 1981. For more space, use Form 4562. If you placed any property in service after December 31, 1980, use Form 4562 for all property; do NOT complete Part V.

	(a) Description of property	(b) Date acquired	(c) Cost or other basis	(d) Depreciation allowed or allowable in prior years	(e) Depreciation method	(f) Life or rate	(g) Depreciation for this year
Property A							
	Totals (Property A)						
Property B							
	Totals (Property B)						
Property C							
	Totals (Property C)						

SCHEDULE F
(Form 1040)

Department of the Treasury
Internal Revenue Service

Farm Income and Expenses

▶ Attach to Form 1040, Form 1041, or Form 1065.
▶ See Instructions for Schedule F (Form 1040).

OMB No. 1545-0074

1983

13

Name of proprietor(s)

Social security number

If you disposed of commodities received under the payments-in-kind (PIK) program, check the box(es) that apply:

☐ Feed for livestock,   ☐ Sold and reported in income.

Employer identification number

PART I.—Farm Income—Cash Method

Do not include sales of livestock held for draft, breeding, sport, or dairy purposes; report these sales on Form 4797.

Sales of Livestock and Other Items You Bought for Resale

a. Description	b. Amount	c. Cost or other basis
1 Livestock ▶ ----------		

-------------------------		
2 Other items ▶ ---------		

-------------------------		
3 Totals		
4 Profit or (loss), subtract line 3, column c, from line 3, column b . . . . ▶		

Sales of Livestock and Produce You Raised and Other Farm Income

Kind	Amount
5 Cattle and calves	
6 Sheep	
7 Swine	
8 Poultry	
9 Dairy products	
10 Eggs	
11 Wool	
12 Cotton	
13 Tobacco	
14 Vegetables	
15 Soybeans	
16 Corn	
17 Other grains	
18 Hay and straw	
19 Fruits and nuts	
20 Machine work	
21 a Patronage dividends . .	
b Less: Nonincome items .	
c Net patronage dividends	
22 Per-unit retains	
23 Nonpatronage distributions from exempt cooperatives . . .	
24 Agricultural program payments: a Cash	
b Materials and services	
25 Commodity credit loans under election (or forfeited) . .	
26 Federal gasoline tax credit	
27 State gasoline tax refund	
28 Crop insurance proceeds	
29 Other (specify) ▶ ---------------------------	
30 Add amounts in column for lines 5 through 29	
31 Gross profits (add lines 4 and 30) . . . . ▶	

PART II.—Farm Deductions—Cash or Accrual Method

Do not include personal or living expenses (such as taxes, insurance, repairs, etc., on your home), which do not produce farm income. Reduce the amount of your farm deductions by any reimbursement before entering the deduction below.

Items	Amount
32 a Labor hired	
b Jobs credit	( )
c Balance (subtract line 32b from line 32a)	
33 Repairs, maintenance	
34 Interest	
35 Rent of farm, pasture	
36 Feed purchased	
37 Seeds, plants purchased	
38 Fertilizers, lime, chemicals . . .	
39 Machine hire	
40 Supplies purchased	
41 Breeding fees	
42 Veterinary fees, medicine	
43 Gasoline, fuel, oil	
44 Storage, warehousing	
45 Taxes	
46 Insurance	
47 Utilities	
48 Freight, trucking	
49 Conservation expenses	
50 Land clearing expenses (see instructions for limitations)	
51 Pension and profit-sharing plans	
52 Employee benefit programs other than line 51	
53 Depreciation and Section 179 deduction (from Form 4562) . .	
54 Other (specify) ▶ ----------	

-------------------------------	
55 Total deductions (add lines 32c through 54) . . . . . . ▶	

---

56 Net farm profit or (loss) (subtract line 55 from line 31). If a profit, enter on Form 1040, line 19, and on Schedule SE, Part I, line 1. If a loss, go on to line 57. (Fiduciaries and partnerships, see the Instructions.) **56**

57 If you have a loss, you must answer this question: "Do you have amounts for which you are not at risk in this farm (see Instructions)?". . ☐ Yes ☐ No
If "Yes," you must attach Form 6198. If "No," enter the loss on Form 1040, line 19, and on Schedule SE, Part I, line 1.

For Paperwork Reduction Act Notice, see Form 1040 Instructions.   Schedule F (Form 1040) 1983

PART III.—Farm Income—Accrual Method (Do not include sales of livestock held for draft, breeding, sport, or dairy purposes; report these sales on Form 4797 and omit them from "Inventory at beginning of year" column.)

a. Kind	b. Inventory at beginning of year	c. Cost of items purchased during year	d. Sales during year	e. Inventory at end of year
58 Cattle and calves				
59 Sheep				
60 Swine				
61 Poultry				
62 Dairy products				
63 Eggs				
64 Wool				
65 Cotton				
66 Tobacco				
67 Vegetables				
68 Soybeans				
69 Corn				
70 Other grains				
71 Hay and straw				
72 Fruits and nuts				
73 Machine work				
74 Other (specify) ▶				
75 Totals (enter here and in Part IV below)	(Enter on line 84)	(Enter on line 85)	(Enter on line 77)	(Enter on line 76)

PART IV.—Summary of Income and Deductions—Accrual Method

76 Inventory of livestock, crops, and products at end of year (line 75, column e)
77 Sales of livestock, crops, and products during year (line 75, column d)
78 Agricultural program payments: a Cash
  b Materials and services
79 Commodity credit loans under election (or forfeited)
80 Federal gasoline tax credit
81 State gasoline tax refund
82 Other farm income (specify) ▶

83 Add lines 76 through 82
84 Inventory of livestock, crops, and products at beginning of year (line 75, column b)
85 Cost of livestock and products purchased during year (line 75, column c)
86 Total (add lines 84 and 85)
87 Gross profits (subtract line 86 from line 83)
88 Total deductions from Part II, line 55 ▶
89 Net farm profit or (loss) (subtract line 88 from line 87). If a profit, enter on Form 1040, line 19, and on Schedule SE, Part I, line 1. If a loss, go on to line 90. (Fiduciaries and partnerships, see the Instructions.) — 89
90 If you have a loss, you must answer this question: "Do you have amounts for which you are not at risk in this farm (see Instructions)?" ☐ Yes ☐ No
If "Yes," you must attach Form 6198. If "No," enter the loss on Form 1040, line 19, and on Schedule SE, Part I, line 1.

Schedule G
(Form 1040)
Department of the Treasury
Internal Revenue Service

Income Averaging

▶ See instructions on back.   ▶ Attach to Form 1040.

OMB No. 1545-0074

1983

17

Name(s) as shown on Form 1040	Your social security number

Step 1   Figure your income for 1979—1982

1979	1	Fill in the amount from your 1979 Form 1040 (line 34) or Form 1040A (line 11)	1	
	2	Multiply your total exemptions in 1979 by $1,000	2	
	3	Subtract line 2 from line 1. If less than zero, enter zero	3	
1980	4	Fill in the amount from your 1980 Form 1040 (line 34) or Form 1040A (line 11)	4	
	5	Multiply your total exemptions in 1980 by $1,000	5	
	6	Subtract line 5 from line 4. If less than zero, enter zero	6	
1981	7	Fill in the amount from your 1981 Form 1040 (line 34) or Form 1040A (line 12). If less than zero, enter zero	7	
1982	8	Fill in the amount from your 1982 Form 1040 (line 37), Form 1040A (line 16), or Form 1040EZ (line 7). If less than zero, enter zero	8	
Total	9	Fill in all income less deductions earned outside of the U.S. or within U.S. possessions and excluded for 1979 through 1982 (include housing exclusion in 1982)	9	
	10	Add lines 3, 6, 7, 8 and 9	10	

Step 2   Figure your averageable income

	Multiply the amount on line 10 by 30% (.30)		x .30
11	Write in the answer	11	
12	Fill in your taxable income for 1983 from Form 1040, line 37	12	
13	If you received a premature or excessive distribution subject to a penalty under section 72, see instructions	13	
14	Subtract line 13 from line 12	14	
15	If you live in a community property state and are filing a separate return, see instructions . .	15	
16	Subtract line 15 from line 14. If less than zero, enter zero	16	
17	Write in the amount from line 11 above	17	
18	Subtract line 17 from line 16. This is your averageable income	18	

If line 18 is $3,000 or less, do not complete the rest of this form. You do not qualify for income averaging.

Step 3   Figure your tax

	Multiply the amount on line 18 by 20% (.20)		x .20
19	Write in the answer	19	
20	Write in the amount from line 11 above	20	
21	Add lines 19 and 20	21	
22	Write in the amount from line 15 above	22	
23	Add lines 21 and 22	23	
24	Tax on amount on line 23 (from Tax Rate Schedule X, Y, or Z)	24	
25	Tax on amount on line 21 (from Tax Rate Schedule X, Y, or Z) .	25	
26	Tax on amount on line 20 (from Tax Rate Schedule X, Y, or Z) .	26	
27	Subtract line 26 from line 25	27	
	Multiply the amount on line 27 by 4		x 4
28	Write in the answer	28	
	If you have no entry on line 13, skip lines 29 through 31 and go to line 32.		
29	Tax on amount on line 12 (from Tax Rate Schedule X, Y, or Z) .	29	
30	Tax on amount on line 14 (from Tax Rate Schedule X, Y, or Z) .	30	
31	Subtract line 30 from line 29	31	
32	Add lines 24, 28, and 31. Write the result here and on Form 1040, line 38. Be sure to check the Schedule G box on that line	32	

For Paperwork Reduction Act Notice, see Form 1040 instructions.   Schedule G (Form 1040) 1983

Instructions

If your income this year is much greater than the average of your income for the past 4 base period years (1979–1982), you may be able to pay less tax by income averaging. To see if you qualify, complete lines 1–18 of this schedule. If line 18 is more than $3,000, fill in the rest of this schedule to see if you will save by income averaging.

If you are eligible, and line 32 of this schedule is less than your tax using other methods, you may choose the income averaging method. You must attach this schedule to your Form 1040 to choose the benefits of income averaging. Generally, you may make or change this choice anytime within 3 years from the date you filed your return.

For more information and a filled-in sample Schedule G, please get **Publication 506,** Income Averaging.

Who Can Income Average?

To be eligible to file Schedule G with Form 1040, you (and your spouse, if you are filing a joint return) must meet the following requirements:

(1) Citizenship or residence.—You must have been a U.S. citizen or resident for all of 1983. You are not eligible if you were a nonresident alien at any time during the 5 tax years ending with 1983.

(2) Support.—You must have furnished at least 50% of your own support for each of the years 1979 through 1982. In a year in which you were married, you and your spouse must have provided at least 50% of the support of both of you. For the definition of support, see Form 1040 Instructions, page 7.

Exceptions: Disregard the support requirement if any one of the three following situations applies to you:

(1) You were 25 or older before the end of 1983 and were not a full-time student during 4 or more of your tax years which began after you reached 21; or

(2) More than 50% of your 1983 taxable income (line 12) is from work you performed in substantial part during 2 or more of the 4 tax years before 1983; or

(3) You file a joint return for 1983 and your income for 1983 is not more than 25% of the total combined adjusted gross income (line 33, Form 1040).

For the definition of full-time student, see Form 1040 Instructions, page 7.

Caution: In the same year you file Schedule G you may not claim the benefits of sections 911 or 931 through 934 (I.R. Code).

Figure Your Income for 1979–1982.

(1) Use your separate income and deductions for all years if you were unmarried in 1979 through 1983.

(2) Use the combined income and deductions of you and your spouse for a base period year:

● if in 1983 you are married and file a joint return, or are a qualifying widow(er), and

● you were not married to any other spouse in that base period year.

(3) If (1) and (2) do not apply, your separate base period income is the largest of the following amounts:

(a) Your separate income and deductions for the base period year;

(b) Half of the base period income from adding your separate income and deductions to the separate income and deductions of your spouse for that base period year; or

(c) Half of the base period income from adding your separate income and deductions to your 1983 spouse's separate income and deductions for that base period year.

Note: *If you were married to one spouse in a base period year and are married and file a joint return with a different spouse in 1983, your separate base period income is the larger of (3)(a) or (b) above. Combine that amount with your 1983 spouse's separate base period income for that base period year.*

Figuring Your Separate Income and Deductions.

The amount of your separate income and deductions for a base period year is your gross income for that year minus your allowable deductions.

If you filed a joint return for a base period year, your separate deductions are:

(1) For deductions allowable in figuring your adjusted gross income, the sum of those deductions attributable to your gross income; and

(2) For deductions allowable in figuring taxable income (exemptions and itemized deductions), the amount from multiplying the deductions allowable on the joint return by a fraction whose numerator is your adjusted gross income and whose denominator is the combined adjusted gross income on the joint return. However, if 85% or more of the combined adjusted gross income of you and your spouse is attributable to one spouse, all deductions allowable in figuring taxable income are allowable to that spouse.

Community property laws.—In figuring your separate taxable income when community property laws apply, you must take into account:

● all of your earned income without regard to the community property laws, or

● your share of the community earned income under community property laws, whichever is more.

If you must figure your separate taxable income for any of the base period years, attach a statement showing the computation and the names under which the returns were filed.

Line-by-Line Instructions

Lines 1–8.—If you did not file a return for any year from 1979 through 1982, enter the amounts that would otherwise be reportable on the appropriate lines. If the amount reported on your return for any of the years was changed by an amended return or by the Internal Revenue Service, enter the corrected amount.

Line 9.—If you excluded any income in any year from 1979 through 1982 because the income was earned from sources outside the United States or within U.S. possessions, fill in the total amount of income (less deductions) that you excluded during that period. Otherwise, leave line 9 blank.

Line 13.—If you are or were an owner-employee, and you received income in 1983 from a premature or excessive distribution from a Keogh (H.R. 10) plan or trust that was subject to a penalty under section 72(m)(5), fill in the amount of that income on this line. Or, if you were an employee in a qualified plan and made deductible voluntary contributions, and received a premature distribution of those contributions subject to a penalty under section 72(o), include that amount on line 13. If you received a premature distribution under an annuity contract subject to a penalty under section 72(q), that amount must also be included on line 13. Otherwise, leave line 13 blank.

Line 15.—You must make this adjustment if you are married, a resident of a community property State, and file a separate return for 1983. Enter the community earned income you reported minus that part of the income which is attributable to your services. Skip this line if the earned income attributable to your services is more than 50% of your combined community earned income.

Example:

Community Earned Income	Attributable to Service of		
	John	Carol	Both
	$40,000	$20,000	$60,000

● **John,** filing a separate return, has no adjustment since the amount of earned income attributable to the services of John ($40,000) is more than 50% of the combined community earned income ($30,000).

Carol, filing a separate return, must include $10,000 in the total for line 15. This is the excess of the 50% of the community earned income reportable by Carol ($30,000) over the amount of community earned income attributable to Carol's services ($20,000).

Line 32.—If the tax on this line is less than the tax figured in any other way, enter the amount from this line on Form 1040, line 38, and check the Schedule G box on that line.

SCHEDULES R&RP	Credit for the Elderly	OMB No. 1545-0074

SCHEDULES R&RP
(Form 1040)
Department of the Treasury
Internal Revenue Service

Credit for the Elderly
▶ See Instructions for Schedules R and RP.
▶ Attach to Form 1040.   ▶ Schedule RP is on back.

OMB No. 1545-0074
1983
18

Name(s) as shown on Form 1040

Your social security number

Please Note: *IRS will figure your Credit for the Elderly and compute your tax. Please see "IRS Will Figure Your Tax and Some of Your Credits" on page 3 of the Form 1040 instructions and complete the applicable lines on Form 1040 and Schedule R or RP.*

Should You Use Schedule R or RP?

If you are:	And were:	Use Schedule:
Single	▶ 65 or over	R
	▶ under 65 and had income from a public retirement system	RP
Married, filing separate return[1]	▶ 65 or over (unless joining in the election to use Schedule RP with your spouse who is under 65 and had income from a public retirement system)	R
	▶ under 65 and had income from a public retirement system (unless your spouse is 65 or over and does not join in the election to use Schedule RP)	RP
Married, filing joint return	▶ both 65 or over	R
	▶ one 65 or over, and one under 65 with no income or income other than from a public retirement system	R
	▶ both under 65 and one or both had income from a public retirement system	RP
	▶ one 65 or over, and one under 65 with income from a public retirement system	R or RP[2]

[1] You can take the credit on a separate return ONLY if you and your spouse lived apart for the whole year. See "Purpose of Schedules" in Schedules R&RP instructions for limitation.
[2] Figure your credit on both schedules to see which gives you more credit.

SCHEDULE R.—Credit for the Elderly—For People 65 or Over

If you received nontaxable pensions (social security, etc.) of $3,750 or more, or your adjusted gross income (Form 1040, line 33) was $17,500 or more, or your tax (Form 1040, line 40) is zero, you cannot take the Credit for the Elderly. Do not file this schedule.

Filing Status and Age
(check only one box)

A ☐ Single, 65 or over
B ☐ Married filing joint return, only one spouse 65 or over
C ☐ Married filing joint return, both 65 or over
D ☐ Married filing separate return, 65 or over, and did not live with spouse at any time in 1983

1 Enter: { $2,500 if you checked box A or B . . . . }
           { $3,750 if you checked box C . . . . } **1**
           { $1,875 if you checked box D . . . . }

2 a Enter amounts you received as pensions or annuities under the Social Security Act, the Railroad Retirement Act (but not supplemental annuities), veterans' pensions (but not military disability pensions), and certain other exclusions from gross income (see instructions).
   Note: *Even though these items of income are not subject to income tax, they **must** be included on line 2a to figure your credit for the elderly.* **If none, you must enter zero** **2a**

   b Enter amount from Form 1040, line 33 . . **2b**

   c Enter: { $7,500 if you checked box A }
            { $10,000 if you checked box B or C } . **2c**
            { $5,000 if you checked box D }

   d Subtract line 2c from 2b. If line 2c is more than line 2b, enter zero **2d**

   e Enter one-half (½) of line 2d **2e**

3 Add lines 2a and 2e. (If line 3 is the same or more than line 1, you cannot take the credit; do not file this schedule. If line 3 is less than line 1, go on to line 4.) **3**
4 Subtract line 3 from line 1 . . . . **4**
5 Multiply line 4 by 15% (.15) **5**
6 Enter amount of tax from Form 1040, line 40 . . . . **6**
7 Enter the amount from line 5 or line 6, above, whichever is less. This is your **Credit for the Elderly.** Enter the same amount on Form 1040, line 41. . . . . ▶ **7**

For Paperwork Reduction Act Notice, see page 1 of separate instructions.   Schedule R (Form 1040) 1983

Schedules R&RP (Form 1040) 1983   OMB No. 1545-0074   Page **2**

Name(s) as shown on Form 1040	Your social security number
	: :

SCHEDULE RP.—Credit for the Elderly—For People Under 65 Who Had Pension or Annuity Income from a Public Retirement System   18

If you are under 72 and received nontaxable pensions (social security, etc.) of $2,500 or more, or your earned income (salaries, wages, etc.) was $3,950 or more, or your tax (Form 1040, line 40) is zero, you cannot take the Credit for the Elderly. Do not file this schedule.

Name(s) of public retirement system(s)

Filing Status and Age (check only one box)

A ☐ Single, under 65

B ☐ Married filing joint return, one spouse is under 65, and that person had income from a public retirement system. (If you checked this box and had community property income, see Community Property Income in the instructions.)

C ☐ Married filing joint return, both under 65. (If you checked this box and had community property income, see Community Property Income in the instructions.)

D ☐ Married filing separate return, under 65, and did not live with your spouse at any time in 1983.

E ☐ Married filing separate return, 65 or over, did not live with your spouse at any time in 1983, and you are joining with your spouse in electing to use Schedule RP.

Column (b)—Fill out column (b) whether you file a separate or joint return.
Column (a)—Fill out column (a) only if you file a joint return and your spouse has retirement income as set forth in line 5. Use it to show amounts for:
- The wife, if both of you were under 65, or
- The spouse who was 65 or over.

	(a)	(b)
1 Enter: a $2,500 if box A; b $2,500 if box B or C (column b, allocate $3,750); c $1,875 if box D or E	1	
2a Amounts received as pensions/annuities under Social Security Act, Railroad Retirement Act, veterans' pensions, etc. If none, enter zero.	2a	
2b(i) If under 62, enter earned income over $900	2b(i)	
2b(ii) If 62 or over but under 72, figure as instructed	2b(ii)	
3 Add lines 2a and 2b	3	
4 Subtract line 3 from line 1	4	
5a If under 65—public retirement income	5a	
5b If 65 or over—total pensions, annuities, etc.	5b	
6 Enter amount from line 4 or line 5, whichever is less	6	
7 Add amounts in columns (a) and (b) of line 6 ▶	7	
8 Multiply line 7 by 15% (.15)	8	
9 Enter amount of tax from Form 1040, line 40	9	
10 Enter amount from line 8 or line 9, whichever is less. Credit for the Elderly. Enter same amount on Form 1040, line 41 ▶	10	

For Paperwork Reduction Act Notice, see page 1 of separate instructions.   Schedule RP (Form 1040) 1983

SCHEDULE SE	**Computation of Social Security Self-Employment Tax**	OMB No. 1545-0074
(Form 1040)	▶ See Instructions for Schedule SE (Form 1040).	19**83**
Department of the Treasury Internal Revenue Service	▶ Attach to Form 1040.	19

Name of self-employed person (as shown on social security card)	Social security number of self-employed person ▶

PART I.—Regular Computation of Net Earnings from Self-Employment

1 Net profit or (loss) from Schedule F (Form 1040), line 56 or line 89, and farm partnerships, Schedule K-1 (Form 1065), line 18b	**1**	
2 Net profit or (loss) from Schedule C (Form 1040), line 32, and Schedule K-1 (Form 1065), line 18b (other than farming). See instructions for kinds of income to report. **Note:** If you are exempt from self-employment tax on your earnings as a minister, member of a religious order, or Christian Science practitioner because you filed Form 4361, check here ▶ ☐ . If you have other earnings of $400 or more that are subject to self-employment tax, include those earnings on this line	**2**	

PART II.—Optional Computation of Net Earnings from Self-Employment

Generally, this part may be used **only** if you meet any of the following tests:

    A Your gross farm profits (Schedule F (Form 1040), line 31 or line 87) were not more than $2,400, or

    B Your gross farm profits (Schedule F (Form 1040), line 31 or line 87) were more than $2,400 and your net farm profits (Schedule F (Form 1040), line 56 or line 89) were less than $1,600, or

    C Your net nonfarm profits (Schedule C (Form 1040), line 32) were less than $1,600 and also less than two-thirds (⅔) of your gross nonfarm income (Schedule C (Form 1040), line 5).

  See instructions for other limitations.

3 Maximum income for optional methods	**3**	$1,600	00
4 Farm Optional Method—If you meet test A or B above, enter: two-thirds (⅔) of gross profits from Schedule F (Form 1040), line 31 or line 87, and farm partnerships, Schedule K-1 (Form 1065), line 18a, or $1,600, whichever is smaller	**4**		
5 Subtract line 4 from line 3	**5**		
6 Nonfarm Optional Method—If you meet test C, enter: the smaller of two-thirds (⅔) of gross nonfarm income from Schedule C (Form 1040), line 5, and Schedule K-1 (Form 1065), line 18c (other than farming), or $1,600, or, if you elected the farm optional method, the amount on line 5	**6**		

PART III.—Computation of Social Security Self-Employment Tax

7 Enter the amount from Part I, line 1, or, if you elected the farm optional method, Part II, line 4	**7**		
8 Enter the amount from Part I, line 2, or, if you elected the nonfarm optional method, Part II, line 6	**8**		
9 Add lines 7 and 8. If less than $400, you are not subject to self-employment tax. Do not fill in the rest of the schedule	**9**		
10 The largest amount of combined wages and self-employment earnings subject to social security or railroad retirement tax (Tier I) for 1983 is	**10**	$35,700	00
11 a Total social security wages from Forms W-2 and railroad retirement compensation (Tier I). **Note:** U.S. Government employees whose wages are only subject to the 1.3% hospital benefits tax (Medicare) should not include those wages on this line (see instructions)	**11a**		
b Unreported tips subject to social security tax from Form 4137, line 9, or to railroad retirement tax (Tier I)	**11b**		
c Add lines 11a and 11b	**11c**		
12 Subtract line 11c from line 10	**12**		
13 Enter the smaller of line 9 or line 12	**13**		
If line 13 is $35,700 or more, fill in $3,337.95 on line 14. Otherwise, multiply line 13 by .0935 and enter the result on line 14		.0935	
14 Self-employment tax. Enter this amount on Form 1040, line 50	**14**		

For Paperwork Reduction Act Notice, see Form 1040 Instructions.   Schedule SE (Form 1040) 1983

Schedule W
(Form 1040)
Department of the Treasury
Internal Revenue Service

Deduction for a Married Couple
When Both Work
▶ For Paperwork Reduction Act Notice, see Form 1040 Instructions.
▶ Attach to Form 1040.

OMB No. 1545-0074

1983
21

Names as shown on Form 1040

Your social security number

Step 1   Figure your earned income

		(a) You		(b) Your spouse	
1	Wages, salaries, tips, etc., from Form 1040, line 7. (Do not include any amount your spouse paid you.) **1**				
2	Net profit or (loss) from self-employment (from Schedules C and F (Form 1040), Schedule K-1 (Form 1065), and any other taxable self-employment or earned income) **2**				
3	Add lines 1 and 2. This is your total earned income **3**				

Step 2   Figure your qualified earned income

		(a) You		(b) Your spouse	
4	Adjustments from Form 1040, lines 24, 25a, 26, 30, and any repayment of sub-pay included on line 31. (See instructions below.) **4**				
5	Subtract line 4 from line 3. This is your qualified earned income. (If the amount in column (a) or (b) is zero (-0-) or less, stop here. You may not claim this deduction.) **5**				

Step 3   Figure your deduction

6	Compare the amounts on line 5(a) and line 5(b) and write the smaller amount here. (Write either amount if 5(a) and 5(b) are exactly the same.) ***Do not write more than $30,000*** .	**6**	
7	Percentage used to figure the deduction (10%)	**7**	x .10
8	Multiply the amount on line 6 by the percentage on line 7. This is the amount of your deduction. Write the answer here and on Form 1040, line 29 . . . . ▶	**8**	

Instructions

Complete this schedule and attach it to your Form 1040 if you take the deduction for a married couple when both work. You may take the deduction if both you and your spouse:

- work and have qualified earned income, and

- file a joint return, and

- do not file **Form 2555** to exclude income or to exclude or deduct certain housing costs, and

- do not file **Form 4563** to exclude income.

There are three steps to follow in figuring the deduction on Schedule W.

Step 1 (lines 1, 2, and 3).—Figure earned income separately for yourself and your spouse.

Step 2 (lines 4 and 5).—Figure qualified earned income separately for yourself and your spouse by subtracting certain adjustments from earned income.

Step 3 (lines 6, 7, and 8).—Figure the deduction based on the **smaller** of:

- the qualified earned income entered on line 5(a) or 5(b) of Schedule W, whichever is less, **OR**

- $30,000.

Earned income.—This is generally income you receive for services you provide. It includes wages, salaries, tips, commissions, disability income, sub-pay, etc. (from Form 1040, line 7). It also includes income earned from self-employment (from Schedules C and F of Form 1040 and Schedule K-1 of Form 1065), and net earnings and gains (other than capital gains) from the disposition, transfer, or licensing of property that you created. Earned income does not include interest, dividends, pensions, annuities, IRA distributions, unemployment compensation, deferred compensation, or nontaxable income.

Caution: *Do not consider community property laws in figuring your earned income.*

Qualified earned income.—This is the amount on which the deduction is based. Figure it by subtracting certain adjustments from earned income. These adjustments (and the related lines on Form 1040) are:

- Employee business expenses (from line 24).

- Payments to an IRA (from line 25a).

- Payments to a Keogh plan (from line 26).

- Disability income exclusion (from line 30).

- Repayment of supplemental unemployment benefits (sub-pay) included in the total on line 31. See the instructions on repayment of sub-pay on page 13 of the Form 1040 Instructions.

Enter the total of any adjustments that apply to your earned income in the appropriate column on line 4.

Example.—You earned a salary of $20,000 and had $6,000 of employee business expenses (line 24 of Form 1040). Your spouse earned $17,000 and put $2,000 into an IRA (line 25a of Form 1040). Your qualified earned income is $14,000 ($20,000 minus $6,000) and your spouse's is $15,000 ($17,000 minus $2,000). Because your qualified earned income is less than your spouse's, the deduction is figured on your income. Therefore, the deduction is $1,400 ($14,000 x .10).

Schedule W (Form 1040) 1983

B–4 FORM 1040–ES DECLARATION OF ESTIMATED TAX AND DECLARATION-VOUCHER FOR INDIVIDUALS

Form **1040-ES**

Department of the Treasury
Internal Revenue Service

Estimated Tax for Individuals

▶ This form is primarily for first-time filers of estimated tax.

OMB No 1545-0087

1984

Instructions

Paperwork Reduction Act Notice.— We ask for this information to carry out the Internal Revenue laws of the United States. We need it to ensure that taxpayers are complying with these laws and to allow us to figure and collect the right amount of tax. You are required to give us this information.

This form is primarily for first-time filers. After your first payment-voucher is received in the Internal Revenue Service Center, IRS will mail you a 1040-ES package. Your name, address, and social security number will be preprinted on the vouchers. You should use these vouchers in making the remaining payments of estimated tax for the year. Using the preprinted vouchers will speed processing, reduce the chance of error, and help save your government processing costs.

This form can also be used if you did not receive a 1040-ES package, or if you lost it. Complete the appropriate payment-voucher and mail it with your payment to your Internal Revenue Service Center (see page 2 for address).

Estimated tax is the amount of tax you expect to owe for the year after subtracting the amount of tax you expect to have withheld and the amount of any credits you plan to take.

You do not have to pay estimated tax if your 1984 income tax return will show (1) a tax refund or (2) a tax balance due of less than $400.

A. Who Must Make Estimated Tax Payments.— The rules below are for U.S. citizens or residents and for residents of Puerto Rico, Virgin Islands, Guam, or American Samoa. (If you are a nonresident alien, use **Form 1040-ES (NR).**) You must make estimated tax payments if your estimated tax balance due is $400 or more **AND** if either item (1) or (2) below applies to you.

You expect your 1984 gross income:

(1) To include more than $500 from sources other than wages subject to withholding; **OR**

(2) To be more than:

- $20,000 if you are single, a head of household, or a qualifying widow or widower;
- $20,000 if you are married, can make joint estimated tax payments, and your spouse has not received wages for 1984;
- $10,000 if you are married, can make joint estimated tax payments, and both of you have received wages for 1984;
- $5,000 if you are married and cannot make joint estimated tax payments. (No joint estimated tax payments may be made if: (1) either you or your spouse is a nonresident alien, (2) you are separated under a decree of divorce or separate maintenance, or (3) you have different years.)

Note: *If you must make estimated tax payments and receive salaries and wages, you may not be having enough tax withheld*

during the year. To avoid making estimated tax payments, consider asking your employer to take more tax out of your earnings. To do this, file a new **Form W-4,** *Employee's Withholding Allowance Certificate,* with your employer and make sure you will not owe $400 or more in tax.

B. How to Figure Your Estimated Tax.— Use the Estimated Tax Worksheet on page 3, the 1984 Tax Rate Schedules on page 4, and your 1983 tax return as a guide for figuring your estimated tax.

Most of the items on the worksheet are self-explanatory. However, the instructions below provide additional information for filling out certain lines.

Caution: Generally, you are required to itemize your deductions if:

- you have unearned income of $1,000 or more and can be claimed as a dependent on your parent's return;
- you are married filing a separate return and your spouse itemizes deductions;
- you file **Form 4563,** Exclusion of Income From Sources in United States Possessions; **OR**
- you are a dual-status alien.

For more information, see the 1983 Instructions for **Form 1040.** If you **MUST** itemize and line 2b of the Estimated Tax Worksheet is more than line 2a, subtract 2a from 2b. Add this amount to line 1 of the worksheet and enter the total on line 3. Disregard the instructions for lines 2c, 2d, and 3 on the worksheet.

The following tax law changes for 1984 may affect your 1984 estimated tax.

1. Medical expense.— The 1% of adjusted gross income (AGI) limitation on medicine and drugs expenses has been eliminated. Only prescription drugs and insulin expenses are deductible and these amounts will now be subject to the overall 5% limitation.

2. Social security and railroad retirement benefits.— These benefits may be includible in your income if your AGI (as adjusted) plus one-half of your benefits exceeds:

(a) $32,000 if you file a joint return;

(b) Zero if you are married, file a separate return, and lived with your spouse at some time during the tax year; or

(c) $25,000 if you have any other filing status.

Tax-exempt interest is includible in AGI for these purposes.

3. Credit for the elderly and the permanently and totally disabled.— The disability income exclusion has been repealed for years beginning after 1983. Beginning with 1984, the credit for the elderly has been expanded to include the permanently and totally disabled. Individuals 65 or older will continue to be able to take the credit. In addition, individuals under 65 who have retired with a permanent and total disability and receive income from a public or private employer because of that disability will be eligible for the credit.

If you are under 65 and receive a taxable pension from a public retirement system, you will no longer be able to take this credit unless you meet the permanent and total disability requirements.

4. Partial deduction for charitable contributions. The amount you can deduct as a charitable contribution if you do not itemize deductions has been increased. You can deduct 25% of the first $300 (the first $150 if married filing separately) of contributions to qualified organizations.

For more details, see **Publication 505,** Tax Withholding and Estimated Tax.

Line 7—Additional taxes.— Enter on line 7 any additional taxes from:

- **Form 4970,** Tax on Accumulation Distribution of Trusts;
- **Form 4972,** Special 10-Year Averaging Method;
- **Form 5544,** Multiple Recipient Special 10-Year Averaging Method; **OR**
- Section 72 penalty taxes.

Line 12—Self-employment tax.— If you and your spouse make joint estimated tax payments and both have self-employment income, figure the estimated self-employment tax separately. Enter the total amount on line 12.

C. How to Use the Payment-Voucher.— Each payment-voucher has the date when the voucher is due for calendar year taxpayers. Please use the correct voucher.

(1) Enter your name, address, and social security number in the space provided on the payment-voucher. If you are filing a joint payment-voucher, your spouse's name and social security number should be included on the voucher. If you file a joint payment-voucher and have different last names, please separate them with an "and." For example, "John Brown and Mary Smith."

(2) Enter the net amount of your payment on line 1 of the payment-voucher. If you paid too much tax on your 1983 Form 1040, you may have chosen to apply the overpayment to your estimated tax for 1984. If so, you may apply all or part of the overpayment to any voucher. Send the payment-voucher to IRS **ONLY** when you are making a payment.

(3) Tear off the voucher at the perforation.

(4) Attach, but do not staple, your check or money order to the payment-voucher. Make check or money order payable to Internal Revenue Service. Please write your social security number and "1984 Form 1040-ES" on your check or money order. Please fill in the Record of Estimated Tax Payments on page 2 so you will have a record of your payments.

(5) Mail your payment-voucher to the Internal Revenue Service Center for the place where you live. Use the address for your State shown on page 2.

D. When to Pay Your Estimated Tax.— The general rule is that you must make your first estimated tax payment by April 16, 1984. You may either pay all of your estimated tax at that time or pay in four equal amounts that are due by April 16, 1984; June 15, 1984; September 17, 1984; and January 16, 1985. Exceptions to the general rule are listed below.

(Continued on page 2)

(1) Other payment dates.—In some cases, such as a change in income, you may have to make your first estimated tax payment after April 16, 1984. The payment dates are as follows:

If the requirement is met after:	Payment date is:
● April 1 and before June 2	June 15, 1984
● June 1 and before Sept. 2	Sept. 17, 1984
● Sept. 1	Jan. 16, 1985

Note: *You may use the "Amended Estimated Tax Schedule" below to figure your amended estimated tax.*

You may pay your estimated tax in equal amounts. If the first payment you are required to make is due:

● June 15, 1984, enter ⅓;

● September 17, 1984, enter ½;

● January 16, 1985, enter all;

of line 17 (less any 1983 overpayment applied to 1984 estimated tax) on line 18 of the worksheet and on line 1 of the payment-voucher.

If you file your 1984 Form 1040 by January 31, 1985, and pay the entire balance due, then you do not have to make the payment which would otherwise be due January 16, 1985.

(2) Farmers and fishermen.—If at least two-thirds of your gross income for 1983 or 1984 is from farming or fishing, you may do one of the following:

● Pay all of your estimated tax by January 16, 1985; **OR**

● File Form 1040 for 1984 by March 1, 1985, and pay the total tax due. In this case, you do not need to make estimated tax payments for 1984.

(3) Fiscal year.—If your return is on a fiscal year basis, your due dates are the 15th day of the 4th, 6th, and 9th months of your fiscal year and the 1st month of the following fiscal year. If any date falls on a Saturday, Sunday, or legal holiday, use the next regular workday.

E. Penalty for Not Paying Enough Estimated Tax.—You may be charged a penalty for not paying enough estimated tax, or for not making the payments on time. The penalty does not apply if each payment is timely and the total tax paid:

● is at least 80% (66 ⅔% for farmers and fishermen) of the amount of income and self-employment taxes due (figured using the taxes and credits specified in **Publication 505**) as shown on your return for 1984; **OR**

● is based on one of the exceptions shown on **Form 2210,** Underpayment of Estimated Tax by Individuals (**Form 2210F,** Underpayment of Estimated Tax by Farmers and Fishermen).

Also the penalty does not apply if you are a U.S. citizen or resident and you had no tax liability for the full 12-month preceding tax year.

Note: *You may be required to make payments of past due amounts to avoid further penalty. You may have to make these payments if you do not make your estimated tax payments on time, or if you did not pay the correct amount for a previous payment date.*

Example: On June 1, 1984, you find out that you should have made an estimated tax payment for April 16. You should immediately fill out the payment-voucher due April 16, 1984, and send in the required amount (¼ × 1984 estimated tax).

If you changed your name because of marriage, divorce, etc., and you made estimated tax payments using your old name, you should attach a brief statement to the front of your 1984 Form 1040. In it explain all the estimated tax payments you and your spouse made during 1984, the name of the Service Center where you made the payments, and the name(s) and social security number(s) under which you made payments.

F. Where to File Your Payment-Voucher.—Mail your payment-voucher to the Internal Revenue Service Center for the place where you live.

If you are located in:	Use this address:
New Jersey, New York City, and counties of Nassau, Rockland, Suffolk, and Westchester	Holtsville, NY 00501
New York (all other counties), Connecticut, Maine, Massachusetts, New Hampshire, Rhode Island, Vermont	Andover, MA 05501
District of Columbia, Delaware, Maryland, Pennsylvania	Philadelphia, PA 19255
Alabama, Florida, Georgia, Mississippi, South Carolina	Atlanta, GA 31101
Michigan, Ohio	Cincinnati, OH 45999
Arkansas, Kansas, Louisiana, New Mexico, Oklahoma, Texas	Austin, TX 73301
Alaska, Arizona, Colorado, Idaho, Minnesota, Montana, Nebraska, Nevada, North Dakota, Oregon, South Dakota, Utah, Washington, Wyoming	Ogden, UT 84201
Illinois, Iowa, Missouri, Wisconsin	Kansas City, MO 64999
California, Hawaii	Fresno, CA 93888
Indiana, Kentucky, North Carolina, Tennessee, Virginia, West Virginia	Memphis, TN 37501
American Samoa	Philadelphia, PA 19255
Guam	Commissioner of Revenue and Taxation Agana, GU 96910
Puerto Rico (or if excluding income under section 933) Virgin Islands: Non-permanent residents	Philadelphia, PA 19255
Virgin Islands: Permanent residents	Bureau of Internal Revenue Charlotte Amalie St. Thomas, VI 00801
A.P.O. or F.P.O. address of:	Miami—Atlanta, GA 31101 New York—Holtsville, NY 00501 San Francisco—Fresno, CA 93888 Seattle—Ogden, UT 84201
Foreign country: U.S. citizens and those excluding income under section 911 or 931, or claiming the housing deduction under section 911	Philadelphia, PA 19255

Note: If you are not required to make the estimated tax payment due April 16, 1984, at this time, you may have to make a payment by a later date. See Instruction D(1).

Record of Estimated Tax Payments

Payment number	(a) Date	(b) Amount	(c)1983 overpayment credit applied	(d) Total amount paid and credited (add (b) and (c))
1				
2				
3				
4				
Total ▶				

Amended Estimated Tax Schedule (Use if your estimated tax changes during the year)

1 Amended estimated tax	**1**	
2 Less: a Amount of 1983 overpayment chosen for credit to 1984 estimated tax and applied to date **2a**		
b Estimated tax payments to date **2b**		
c Total of lines 2a and b	**2c**	
3 Unpaid balance (subtract line 2c from line 1)	**3**	
4 Amount to be paid (line 3 divided by number of remaining payment dates)	**4**	

1984 Estimated Tax Worksheet (Keep for your records—Do Not Send to Internal Revenue Service)

1 Enter amount of Adjusted Gross Income you expect in 1984	**1**	
2 a If you plan to itemize deductions, enter the estimated total of your deductions. (If you do not plan to itemize deductions, skip to line 2c and enter zero) .	**2a**	
b Enter { $3,400 if married filing a joint return (or qualifying widow(er)) $2,300 if single (or head of household) . . . . . . $1,700 if married filing a separate return }	**2b**	
c Subtract line 2b from line 2a (if zero or less, enter zero)	**2c**	
d If you do not itemize deductions, enter your allowable deduction, if any, for charitable contributions (see Instruction B.4 on page 1)	**2d**	
3 Subtract line 2c or 2d, whichever applies, from line 1	**3**	
4 Exemptions (multiply $1,000 times number of personal exemptions)	**4**	
5 Subtract line 4 from line 3	**5**	
6 Tax. (Figure your tax on line 5 by using Tax Rate Schedule X, Y, or Z in these instructions. DO NOT use the Tax Table or Tax Rate Schedule X, Y, or Z in the 1983 Form 1040 Instructions.)	**6**	
7 Enter any additional taxes (see line 7 Instruction)	**7**	
8 Add lines 6 and 7	**8**	
9 Credits (credit for the elderly, credit for the permanently and totally disabled, credit for child and dependent care expenses, investment credit, residential energy credit, etc.)	**9**	
10 Subtract line 9 from line 8	**10**	
11 Tax from recapture of investment credit	**11**	
12 Estimate of 1984 self-employment income $_____ ; if $37,800 or more, enter $4,271.40; if less, multiply the amount by .113 (see line 12 instruction for additional information)	**12**	
13 Tax on premature distributions from an IRA	**13**	
14 Add lines 10 through 13	**14**	
15 a Earned income credit **15a**		
b Estimated income tax withheld and to be withheld (including income tax withholding on pensions, annuities, certain deferred income, etc.) during 1984 . . . . **15b**		
c Credit for Federal tax on gasoline and special fuels (see Form 4136) . . **15c**		
16 Total (add lines 15a, b, and c)	**16**	
17 Estimated tax (subtract line 16 from line 14). If $400 or more, fill out and file the payment-voucher along with your payment; if less, no payment is required at this time. If you are applying an overpayment from 1983 to 1984 estimated tax, see Instruction C.(2), page 1	**17**	

Caution: You are required to prepay at least 80% of your tax liability each year. If you prepay less than 80% of your actual tax liability, you will be subject to a penalty (see Instruction E). To avoid this, make sure your estimate is as accurate as possible. If you are unsure of your estimate, you may want to pay more than 80% of the amount you have estimated. In determining the amount of your estimated tax, you may take into account any of the exceptions to the underpayment penalty. For more information on these exceptions, please get **Publication 505.**

18 If the first payment you are required to make is due April 16, 1984, enter ¼ of line 17 (less any 1983 overpayment that you are applying to this installment) here and on line 1 of your payment-voucher. You may round off cents to the nearest whole dollar. If you wish to pay more estimated tax than is shown on line 17, you may do so	**18**	

-------------------------------------- **Tear off here** --------------------------------------

Form **1040-ES** | **1984**
Department of the Treasury | **Payment-**
Internal Revenue Service | **Voucher**

OMB No. 1545-0087

Return this voucher with check or money order payable to the Internal Revenue Service. Please do not send cash or staple your payment to this voucher.

(Calendar year—Due Jan. 16, 1985)

		Your social security number	Spouse's number, if joint payment
1 Amount of payment $_____			
	Please type or print	First name and middle initial (of both spouses if joint payment)	Last name
2 Fiscal year filers enter year ending			
_____ (month and year)		Address (Number and street)	
File only if you are making a payment of estimated tax.		City, State, and ZIP code	

1984 Tax Rate Schedules

Caution: Do not use these Tax Rate Schedules to figure your 1983 taxes. Use only to figure your 1984 estimated taxes.

SCHEDULE X—Single Taxpayers

If line 5 is: Over—	but not over—	The tax is:	of the amount over—
$0	$2,300	—0—	
2,300	3,400	------- 11%	$2,300
3,400	4,400	$121 + 12%	3,400
4,400	6,500	241 + 14%	4,400
6,500	8,500	535 + 15%	6,500
8,500	10,800	835 + 16%	8,500
10,800	12,900	1,203 + 18%	10,800
12,900	15,000	1,581 + 20%	12,900
15,000	18,200	2,001 + 23%	15,000
18,200	23,500	2,737 + 26%	18,200
23,500	28,800	4,115 + 30%	23,500
28,800	34,100	5,705 + 34%	28,800
34,100	41,500	7,507 + 38%	34,100
41,500	55,300	10,319 + 42%	41,500
55,300	81,800	16,115 + 48%	55,300
81,800	------	28,835 + 50%	81,800

SCHEDULE Z—Heads of Household

If line 5 is: Over—	but not over—	The tax is:	of the amount over—
$0	$2,300	—0—	
2,300	4,400	------- 11%	$2,300
4,400	6,500	$231 + 12%	4,400
6,500	8,700	483 + 14%	6,500
8,700	11,800	791 + 17%	8,700
11,800	15,000	1,318 + 18%	11,800
15,000	18,200	1,894 + 20%	15,000
18,200	23,500	2,534 + 24%	18,200
23,500	28,800	3,806 + 28%	23,500
28,800	34,100	5,290 + 32%	28,800
34,100	44,700	6,986 + 35%	34,100
44,700	60,600	10,696 + 42%	44,700
60,600	81,800	17,374 + 45%	60,600
81,800	108,300	26,914 + 48%	81,800
108,300	------	39,634 + 50%	108,300

SCHEDULE Y—Married Taxpayers and Qualifying Widows and Widowers

Married Filing Joint Returns and Qualifying Widows and Widowers

If line 5 is: Over—	but not over—	The tax is:	of the amount over—
$0	$3,400	—0—	
3,400	5,500	------- 11%	$3,400
5,500	7,600	$231 + 12%	5,500
7,600	11,900	483 + 14%	7,600
11,900	16,000	1,085 + 16%	11,900
16,000	20,200	1,741 + 18%	16,000
20,200	24,600	2,497 + 22%	20,200
24,600	29,900	3,465 + 25%	24,600
29,900	35,200	4,790 + 28%	29,900
35,200	45,800	6,274 + 33%	35,200
45,800	60,000	9,772 + 38%	45,800
60,000	85,600	15,168 + 42%	60,000
85,600	109,400	25,920 + 45%	85,600
109,400	162,400	36,630 + 49%	109,400
162,400	--------	62,600 + 50%	162,400

Married Filing Separate Returns

If line 5 is: Over—	but not over—	The tax is:	of the amount over—
$0	$1,700	—0—	
1,700	2,750	---------- 11%	$1,700
2,750	3,800	$115.50 + 12%	2,750
3,800	5,950	241.50 + 14%	3,800
5,950	8,000	542.50 + 16%	5,950
8,000	10,100	870.50 + 18%	8,000
10,100	12,300	1,248.50 + 22%	10,100
12,300	14,950	1,732.50 + 25%	12,300
14,950	17,600	2,395.00 + 28%	14,950
17,600	22,900	3,137.00 + 33%	17,600
22,900	30,000	4,886.00 + 38%	22,900
30,000	42,800	7,584.00 + 42%	30,000
42,800	54,700	12,960.00 + 45%	42,800
54,700	81,200	18,315.00 + 49%	54,700
81,200	------	31,300.00 + 50%	81,200

Form **1040-ES** | **1984**
Department of the Treasury | **Payment-**
Internal Revenue Service | **Voucher**

OMB No. 1545-0087

**Return this voucher with check or money order payable to the Internal Revenue Service.
Please do not send cash or staple your payment to this voucher.**

(Calendar year—Due Sept. 17, 1984)

		Your social security number	Spouse's number, if joint payment
1 Amount of payment $ _ _ _ _ _ _ _ _ _ _ _ _ _ _ _ _		First name and middle initial (of both spouses if joint payment)	Last name
2 Fiscal year filers enter year ending			
_ _ _ _ _ _ _ _ _ _ _ _ (month and year) _ _ _ _ _ _ _ _ _		Address (Number and street)	
File only if you are making a payment of estimated tax.		City, State, and ZIP code	

Please type or print

For Paperwork Reduction Act Notice, see instructions on page 1.

Tear off here

- -

Form **1040-ES** | **1984**
Department of the Treasury | **Payment-**
Internal Revenue Service | **Voucher**

OMB No. 1545-0087

**Return this voucher with check or money order payable to the Internal Revenue Service.
Please do not send cash or staple your payment to this voucher.**

(Calendar year—Due June 15, 1984)

		Your social security number	Spouse's number, if joint payment
1 Amount of payment $ _ _ _ _ _ _ _ _ _ _ _ _ _ _ _ _		First name and middle initial (of both spouses if joint payment)	Last name
2 Fiscal year filers enter year ending			
_ _ _ _ _ _ _ _ _ _ _ _ (month and year) _ _ _ _ _ _ _ _ _		Address (Number and street)	
File only if you are making a payment of estimated tax.		City, State, and ZIP code	

Please type or print

For Paperwork Reduction Act Notice, see instructions on page 1.

Tear off here

- -

Form **1040-ES** | **1984**
Department of the Treasury | **Payment-**
Internal Revenue Service | **Voucher**

OMB No. 1545-0087

**Return this voucher with check or money order payable to the Internal Revenue Service.
Please do not send cash or staple your payment to this voucher.**

(Calendar year—Due April 16, 1984)

		Your social security number	Spouse's number, if joint payment
1 Amount of payment $ _ _ _ _ _ _ _ _ _ _ _ _ _ _ _ _		First name and middle initial (of both spouses if joint payment)	Last name
2 Fiscal year filers enter year ending			
_ _ _ _ _ _ _ _ _ _ _ _ (month and year) _ _ _ _ _ _ _ _ _		Address (Number and street)	
File only if you are making a payment of estimated tax.		City, State, and ZIP code	

Please type or print

For Paperwork Reduction Act Notice, see instructions on page 1.

1 Control number	22222	For Paperwork Reduction Act Notice, see back of Copy D. OMB No. 1545-0008	For Official Use Only		
2 Employer's name, address, and ZIP code			3 Employer's identification number		4 Employer's State number
			5 Stat. employee ☐ Deceased ☐ Legal rep. ☐ 942 emp. ☐ Subtotal ☐ Void ☐		
			6 Allocated tips		7 Advance EIC payment
8 Employee's social security number		9 Federal income tax withheld	10 Wages, tips, other compensation		11 Social security tax withheld
12 Employee's name (first, middle, last)			13 Social security wages		14 Social security tips
			16 *		
			17 State income tax	18 State wages, tips, etc.	19 Name of State
15 Employee's address and ZIP code			20 Local income tax	21 Local wages, tips, etc.	22 Name of locality

Form **W-2 Wage and Tax Statement** **1984**   Copy A For Social Security Administration
* See Instructions for Forms W-2 and W-2P

Department of the Treasury
Internal Revenue Service

Notice to Employee:

You must file a tax return regardless of your income if any amount is shown in box 7, Advance EIC (earned income credit) payment.

File Copy B of this form with your 1984 Federal income tax return. Attach Copy 2 to your 1984 State or local income tax return. Please keep Copy C for your records. You can use it to prove your right to social security benefits. If your name, social security number, or address is incorrect, please correct Copies B, C, and 2 and tell your employer.

If you have already filed your tax return and the information from this W-2 was not included, please amend your Form 1040, 1040A, or 1040EZ by filing Form 1040X.

If you have nonwage income of more than $500 and will owe tax of $400 or more ($500 for 1985) you should file Form 1040-ES, Estimated Tax for Individuals, and pay the tax in installments during the year.

If you retired during 1984 or plan to retire soon, you may have to pay tax on your income either by filing Form 1040-ES or by having tax withheld from your pension or annuity. See **Publication 505,** Tax Withholding and Estimated Tax, for details.

Credit for Social Security (FICA) Tax.—If more than one employer paid you wages during 1984 and more than the maximum social security employee tax, railroad retirement (RRTA) tax, or combined social security and RRTA tax was withheld, you can claim the excess as a credit against your Federal income tax. (Please see your Federal income tax return instructions.) The social security rate of 6.7% (after allowance of a 0.3% credit) includes 1.3% for hospital insurance benefits and 5.4% for retirement, survivors, and disability insurance.

Instructions for Preparing Form W-2

The 6-part wage and tax statement is acceptable in most States. If you are in doubt, ask your appropriate State or local official.

Prepare Form W-2 for each of your employees to whom any of the following items applied during 1984:

(a)   You withheld income tax or social security (FICA) tax.

(b)   You would have withheld income tax if the employee had not claimed more than one withholding allowance.

(c)   You paid $600 or more.

(d)   You paid any amount for services, if you are in a trade or business. Include the cash value of any payment you made that was not in cash.

By January 31, 1985, give Copies B, C, and 2 to each person who was your employee during 1984. For anyone who stopped working for you before the end of 1984, you may give copies any time after employment ends. If the employee asks for Form W-2, give him or her the completed copies within 30 days of the request or the final wage payment, whichever is later. Send Copy A to the Social Security Administration by February 28, 1985. (For more information, please see Forms 941, 942, W-3, or Circular E. Farmers, see Circular A.)

See separate **Instructions for Forms W-2 and W-2P** for more information on how to complete Form W-2.

Paperwork Reduction Act Notice.— We ask for this information to carry out the Internal Revenue laws of the United States. We need it to ensure that taxpayers are complying with these laws and to allow us to figure and collect the right amount of tax. You are required to give us this information.

900

Appendix B

Form **W-4** (Rev. January 1984)	Department of the Treasury—Internal Revenue Service **Employee's Withholding Allowance Certificate**	OMB No. 1545-0010

1 Type or print your full name

2 Your social security number

Home address (number and street or rural route)

City or town, State, and ZIP code

3 Marital Status
- [ ] Single [ ] Married
- [ ] Married, but withhold at higher Single rate

Note: If married, but legally separated, or spouse is a nonresident alien, check the Single box.

4 Total number of allowances you are claiming (from line F of the worksheet on page 2) . . . . $

5 Additional amount, if any, you want deducted from each pay . . . .

6 I claim exemption from withholding because (see instructions and check boxes below that apply):

a [ ] Last year I did not owe any Federal income tax and had a right to a full refund of **ALL** income tax withheld, **AND**

b [ ] This year I do not expect to owe any Federal income tax and expect to have a right to a full refund of **ALL** income tax withheld. If both a and b apply, enter the year effective and "EXEMPT" here ▶ Year

c If you entered "EXEMPT" on line 6b, are you a full-time student? . . . . [ ] Yes [ ] No

Under penalties of perjury, I certify that I am entitled to the number of withholding allowances claimed on this certificate, or if claiming exemption from withholding, that I am entitled to claim the exempt status.

Employee's signature ▶   Date ▶ , 19

7 Employer's name and address (**Employer: Complete 7, 8, and 9 only if sending to IRS**)

8 Office code

9 Employer identification number

- - - - - - - - - - Detach along this line. Give the top part of this form to employer; keep the lower part for your records. - - - - - - - - - -

Privacy Act and Paperwork Reduction Act Notice.—If you do not give your employer a certificate, you will be treated as a single person with no withholding allowances as required by law. We ask for this information to carry out the Internal Revenue laws of the United States. We may give the information to the Dept. of Justice for civil or criminal litigation and to the States and the District of Columbia for use in administering their tax laws.

Purpose.—The law requires that you complete Form W-4 so that your employer can withhold Federal income tax from your pay. Your Form W-4 remains in effect until you change it or, if you entered "EXEMPT" on line 6b above, until February 15 of next year. By correctly completing this form, you can fit the amount of tax withheld from your wages to your tax liability.

If you got a large refund last year, you may be having too much tax withheld. If so, you may want to increase the number of your allowances on line 4 by claiming any other allowances you are entitled to. The kinds of allowances, and how to figure them, are explained in detail below.

If you owed a large amount of tax last year, you may not be having enough tax withheld. If so, you can claim fewer allowances on line 4, or ask that an additional amount be withheld on line 5, or both.

If the number of withholding allowances you are entitled to claim decreases to less than you are now claiming, you must file a new W-4 with your employer within 10 days.

The instructions below explain how to fill in Form W-4. **Publication 505**, Tax Withholding and Estimated Tax, contains more information on withholding. You can get it from most IRS offices.

For more information about who qualifies as your dependent, what deductions you can take, and what tax credits you qualify for, see the Form 1040 Instructions.

You may be fined $500 if you file, with no reasonable basis, a W-4 that results in less tax being withheld than is properly allowable. In addition, criminal penalties apply for willfully supplying false or fraudulent information or failing to supply information requiring an increase in withholding.

Line-By-Line Instructions

Fill in the identifying information in Boxes 1 and 2. If you are married and want tax withheld at the regular rate for married persons, check "Married" in Box 3. If you are married and want tax withheld at the higher Single rate (because both you and your spouse work, for example), check "Married, but withhold at higher Single rate" in Box 3.

Line 4 of Form W-4

Total number of allowances.—Use the worksheet on page 2 to figure your allowances. Add the number of allowances for each category explained below. Enter the total on line 4.

If you are single and hold more than one job, you may not claim the same allowances with more than one employer at the same time. If you are married and both you and your spouse are employed, you may not both claim the same allowances with both of your employers at the same time. To have the highest amount of tax withheld, claim "0" allowances on line 4.

A. Personal allowances.—You can claim the following personal allowances:

1 for yourself, 1 if you are 65 or older, and 1 if you are blind.

If you are married and your spouse either does not work or is not claiming his or her allowances on a separate W-4, you may also claim the following allowances: 1 for your spouse, 1 if your spouse is 65 or older, and 1 if your spouse is blind.

B. Special withholding allowance.—Claim the special withholding allowance if you are single and have one job or you are married, have one job, and your spouse does not work. You may still claim this allowance so long as the total wages earned on other jobs by you or your spouse (or both) is 10% or less of the combined total wages. Use this special withholding allowance only to figure your withholding. Do not claim it when you file your return.

C. Allowances for dependents.—You may claim one allowance for each dependent you will be able to claim on your Federal income tax return.

Note: If you are not claiming any deductions or credits, skip D and E, add lines A, B, and C, enter the total on line F and carry the total over to line 4 of W-4.

Before you claim allowances under D and E, total your non-wage taxable income (interest, dividends, self-employment, etc.) and subtract this amount from estimated deductions you would otherwise enter in D1. If your non-wage income is greater than the amount of estimated deductions, you cannot claim any allowances under D. Moreover, you should take one-third of the excess (non-wage income over estimated deductions) and add this to the appropriate "A" value in Table 1 if determining allowances under E.

D. Allowances for estimated deductions.—If you expect to itemize deductions, you can claim additional withholding allowances. See Schedule A (Form 1040) for deductions you can itemize.

You can also count deductible amounts you pay for (1) alimony (2) qualified retirement contributions including IRA and Keogh (H.R. 10) plans (3) moving expenses (4) employee business expenses (Part I of Form 2106) (5) the deduction for a married couple when both work (6) net losses shown on Schedules C, D, E, and F (Form 1040), the last line of Part II of Form 4797, and the net operating loss carryover (7) penalty on early withdrawal of savings and (8) charitable contributions for nonitemizers. **Note:** Check with your employer to see if any tax is being withheld on moving expenses or IRA contributions. Do not include these amounts if tax is not being withheld; otherwise, you may be underwithheld. For details, see **Publication 505.**

The deduction allowed a married couple when both work is 10% of the lesser of $30,000 or the qualified earned income of the spouse with the lower income.

Once you have determined these deductions, enter the total on line D1 of the worksheet on page 2 and figure the number of withholding allowances for them.

E. Allowances for tax credits.—If you expect to take credits like those shown on lines 41 through 48 on the 1983 Form 1040 (child care, residential energy, etc.), use the table on the top of page 2 to figure the number of additional allowances you can claim. You may estimate these credits. Include the earned income credit if you are not receiving advance payment of it, and any excess social security tax withheld. Also, if you expect to income average, include the amount of the reduction in tax because of averaging when using the table.

Form **W-4** (Rev. 1-84)

Line 5 of Form W-4

Additional amount, if any, you want deducted from each pay.—If you are not having enough tax withheld from your pay, you may ask your employer to withhold more by filling in an additional amount on line 5. Often, married couples, both of whom are working, and persons with two or more jobs need to have additional tax withheld. You may also need to have additional tax withheld because you have income other than wages, such as interest and dividends, capital gains, rents, alimony received, taxable social security benefits, etc. Estimate the amount you will be underwithheld and divide that amount by the number of pay periods in the year. Enter the additional amount you want withheld each pay period on line 5.

Line 6 of Form W-4

Exemption from withholding.—You can claim exemption from withholding only if last year you did not owe any Federal income tax and had a right to a refund of all income tax withheld, **and** this year you do not expect to owe any Federal income tax and expect to have a right to a refund of all income tax withheld. If you qualify, check Boxes 6a and b, write the year exempt status is effective and "EXEMPT" on line 6b, and answer Yes or No to the question on line 6c.

If you want to claim exemption from withholding next year, you must file a new W-4 with your employer on or before February 15 of next year. If you are not having Federal income tax withheld this year, but expect to have a tax liability next year, the law requires you to give your employer a new W-4 by December 1 of this year. If you are covered by social security, your employer must withhold social security tax.

Your employer must send to IRS any W-4 claiming more than 14 withholding allowances or claiming exemption from withholding if the wages are expected to usually exceed $200 a week. The employer is to complete Boxes 7, 8, and 9 only on copies of the W-4 sent to IRS.

Table 1—For Figuring Your Withholding Allowances For Estimated Tax Credits and Income Averaging (Line E)

Estimated Salaries and Wages from All sources	Single Employees		Head of Household Employees		Married Employees (When Spouse not Employed)		Married Employees (When Both Spouses are Employed)	
	(A)	(B)	(A)	(B)	(A)	(B)	(A)	(B)
Under $15,000	$ 90	$150	$ 30	$150	$ 50	$120	$ 0	$120
15,000-25,000	120	250	0	250	70	170	310	170
25,001-35,000	190	300	0	300	130	250	800	220
35,001-45,000	250	370	0	370	170	320	1,500	250
45,001-55,000	690	370	0	370	230	340	2,210	330
55,001-65,000	1,470	370	220	370	310	370	3,020	330
Over 65,000	2,460	370	920	370	680	370	3,400	370

Worksheet to Figure Your Withholding Allowances to be Entered on Line 4 of Form W-4

A Personal allowances . . . . ▶ **A** _____

B Special withholding allowance (not to exceed 1 allowance—see instructions on page 1) . . . . . . ▶ **B** _____

C Allowances for dependents . . . . ▶ **C** _____

If you are not claiming any deductions or credits, skip lines D and E.

D Allowances for estimated deductions:

  1 Enter the total amount of your estimated itemized deductions, alimony payments, qualified retirement contributions including IRA and Keogh (H.R. 10) plans, deduction for a married couple when both work, business losses including net operating loss carryovers, moving expenses, employee business expenses, penalty on early withdrawal of savings, and charitable contributions for nonitemizers for the year . . . ▶ **1** $ _____

  2 If you do not plan to itemize deductions, enter $500 on line D2. If you plan to itemize, find your total estimated salaries and wages amount in the left column of the table below. (Include salaries and wages of both spouses.) Read across to the right and find the amount from the column that applies to you. Enter that amount on line D2. . . . ▶ **2** $ _____

Estimated salaries and wages from all sources:	Single and Head of Household Employees (only one job)		Married Employees (one spouse working and one job only)		Employees with more than one job or Married Employees with both spouses working [1]	
Under $15,000	. . $2,800	. . . . .	. .$3,900	. . . . .	. . 40%	
15,000-35,000	. . 2,800	. . . . .	. . 3,900	. . . . .	. . 23%	of estimated salaries and wages
35,001-50,000	. . 8%	of estimated salaries and wages	. . 3,900	. . . . .	. . 20%	
Over $50,000	. . 10%		. . . . 7%	of estimated salaries and wages	. . 18%	

  3 Subtract line D2 from line D1 (But not less than zero) . . . . ▶ **3** $ _____

  4 Divide the amount on line D3 by $1,000 (increase any fraction to the next whole number). Enter here . . . ▶ **D** _____

E Allowances for tax credits and income averaging: use Table 1 above for figuring withholding allowances

  1 Enter tax credits, excess social security tax withheld, and tax reduction from income averaging $ _____

  2 Enter the column (A) amount from Table 1 for your salary range and filing status (single, etc.). However, enter 0 if you claim 1 or more allowances on line D4 . . . . $ _____

  3 Subtract line 2 from line 1 (If zero or less, do not complete lines 4 and 5) . . . . $ _____

  4 Find the column (B) amount from Table 1 for your salary range and filing status . . . . . $ _____

  5 Divide line 3 by line 4. Increase any fraction to the next whole number. This is the maximum number of withholding allowances for tax credits and income averaging. Enter here . . . . ▶ **E** _____

  Example: A taxpayer who expects to file a Federal income tax return as a single person estimates annual wages of $12,000 and tax credits of $650. The $12,000 falls in the wage bracket of under $15,000. The value in column (A) is 90. Subtracting this from the estimated credits of 650 leaves 560. The value in column (B) is 150. Dividing 560 by 150 gives 3.7. Since any fraction is increased to the next whole number, show 4 on line E.

F Total (add lines A through E). Enter total here and on line 4 of Form W-4 . . . . ▶ **F** _____

[1] If you earn 10% or less of your total wages from other jobs or one spouse earns 10% or less of the couple's combined total wages, you can use the "Single and Head of Household Employees (only one job)" or "Married Employees (one spouse working and one job only)" table, whichever is appropriate.

B-5   FORM 1120   U. S. CORPORATION INCOME
TAX RETURN

Form **1120**	**U.S. Corporation Income Tax Return**	OMB No. 1545-0123
Department of the Treasury Internal Revenue Service	For calendar year 1983 or other tax year beginning ...., 1983, ending .... 19 ..... ▶ For Paperwork Reduction Act Notice, see page 1 of the instructions.	**1983**

Check if a—	Use IRS label. Other-wise please print or type.	Name	D. Employer identification number
A. Consolidated return ☐			
B. Personal Holding Co. ☐		Number and street	E. Date incorporated
C. Business Code No. (See page 9 of Instructions)		City or town, State, and ZIP code	F. Total assets (see Specific Instructions) $

G. Check box if there has been a change in address from the previous year . . . . ▶ ☐

Gross Income	1 (a) Gross receipts or sales $............. (b) Less returns and allowances $............. Balance ▶	1(c)	
	2 Cost of goods sold (Schedule A) and/or operations (attach schedule)	2	
	3 Gross profit (subtract line 2 from line 1(c))	3	
	4 Dividends (Schedule C)	4	
	5 Interest	5	
	6 Gross rents	6	
	7 Gross royalties	7	
	8 Capital gain net income (attach separate Schedule D)	8	
	9 Net gain or (loss) from Form 4797, line 14(a), Part II (attach Form 4797) . . .	9	
	10 Other income (see instructions—attach schedule).	10	
	11 TOTAL income—Add lines 3 through 10 and enter here . . . . ▶	11	
Deductions	12 Compensation of officers (Schedule E)	12	
	13 (a) Salaries and wages $............. (b) Less jobs credit $............. Balance ▶	13(c)	
	14 Repairs (see instructions)	14	
	15 Bad debts (Schedule F if reserve method is used)	15	
	16 Rents	16	
	17 Taxes	17	
	18 Interest	18	
	19 Contributions (not over 10% of line 30 adjusted per instructions)	19	
	20 Depreciation (attach Form 4562) **20**		
	21 Less depreciation claimed in Schedule A and elsewhere on return . . **21(a)** ( )	21(b)	
	22 Depletion	22	
	23 Advertising	23	
	24 Pension, profit-sharing, etc. plans (see instructions)	24	
	25 Employee benefit programs (see instructions)	25	
	26 Other deductions (attach schedule)	26	
	27 TOTAL deductions—Add lines 12 through 26 and enter here . . . . ▶	27	
	28 Taxable income before net operating loss deduction and special deductions (subtract line 27 from line 11)	28	
	29 **Less:** (a) Net operating loss deduction (see instructions—attach schedule) . **29(a)**		
	(b) Special deductions (Schedule C) . . . . **29(b)**	29	
	30 Taxable income (subtract line 29 from line 28)	30	
Tax	31 TOTAL TAX (Schedule J).	31	
	32 **Credits: (a)** Overpayment from 1982 allowed as a credit .		
	(b) 1983 estimated tax payments		
	(c) Less refund of 1983 estimated tax applied for on Form 4466 ( )		
	(d) Tax deposited with Form 7004		
	(e) Credit from regulated investment companies (attach Form 2439). . .		
	(f) Federal tax on special fuels and oils (attach Form 4136). . . .	32	
	33 **TAX DUE** (subtract line 32 from line 31—If line 32 is greater than line 31, skip line 33 and go to line 34). See instruction C3 for depositary method of payment . . . . (Check ▶ ☐ if Form 2220 is attached. See instruction D.) ▶ $.............	33	
	34 **OVERPAYMENT** (subtract line 31 from line 32) . . . . ▶	34	
	35 Enter amount of line 34 you want: **Credited to 1984 estimated tax** ▶ Refunded ▶	35	

Please Sign Here	Under penalties of perjury, I declare that I have examined this return, including accompanying schedules and statements, and to the best of my knowledge and belief, it is true, correct, and complete. Declaration of preparer (other than taxpayer) is based on all information of which preparer has any knowledge.		
	▶ _____ Signature of officer	Date	▶ _____ Title

Paid Preparer's Use Only	Preparer's signature ▶	Date	Check if self-em-ployed ▶ ☐	Preparer's social security number
	Firm's name (or yours, if self-employed) and address ▶		E.I. No. ▶	
			ZIP code ▶	

Form 1120 (1983)   Page **2**

SCHEDULE A.—Cost of Goods Sold
(See instructions for Schedule A)

1 Inventory at beginning of year.	**1**	
2 Merchandise bought for manufacture or sale	**2**	
3 Salaries and wages	**3**	
4 Other costs (attach schedule).	**4**	
5 Total—Add lines 1 through 4	**5**	
6 Inventory at end of year.	**6**	
7 Cost of goods sold—Subtract line 6 from line 5. Enter here and on line 2, page 1	**7**	

8 **(a)** Check all methods used for valuing closing inventory:

   (i) ☐ Cost

   (ii) ☐ Lower of cost or market as described in Regulations section 1.471–4 (see instructions)

   (iii) ☐ Writedown of "subnormal" goods as described in Regulations section 1.471–2(c) (see instructions)

   (iv) ☐ Other (Specify method used and attach explanation) ▶ _____

   (b) Check if the LIFO inventory method was adopted this tax year for any goods (if checked, attach Form 970) . . . . ☐

   (c) If the LIFO inventory method was used for this tax year, enter percentage (or amounts) of closing inventory computed under LIFO . . . .

   (d) If you are engaged in manufacturing, did you value your inventory using the full absorption method (Regulations section 1.471–11)? . . . . ☐ Yes ☐ No

   (e) Was there any substantial change in determining quantities, cost, or valuations between opening and closing inventory? ☐ Yes ☐ No
   If "Yes," attach explanation.

SCHEDULE C.—Dividends and Special Deductions
(See instructions for Schedule C)

	(A) Dividends received	(B) %	(C) Special deductions: multiply (A) X (B)
1 Domestic corporations subject to 85% deduction		85	
2 Certain preferred stock of public utilities		59.13	
3 Foreign corporations subject to 85% deduction		85	
4 Wholly-owned foreign subsidiaries subject to 100% deduction (section 245(b)) . .		100	
5 Total—Add lines 1 through 4. See instructions for limitation			
6 Affiliated groups subject to the 100% deduction (section 243(a)(3))		100	
7 Other dividends from foreign corporations not included in lines 3 and 4			
8 Income from controlled foreign corporations under subpart F (attach Forms 5471) .			
9 Foreign dividend gross-up (section 78)			
10 DISC or former DISC dividends not included in line 1 (section 246(d))			
11 Other dividends			
12 Deduction for dividends paid on certain preferred stock of public utilities (see instructions)			
13 Total dividends—Add lines 1 through 11. Enter here and on line 4, page 1 . . ▶			
14 Total deductions—Add lines 5, 6 and 12. Enter here and on line 29(b), page 1 . . . . ▶			

SCHEDULE E.—Compensation of Officers (See instruction for line 12, page 1)
Complete Schedule E only if your total receipts (line 1(a), plus lines 4 through 10, of page 1, Form 1120) are $150,000 or more.

1. Name of officer	2. Social security number	3. Percent of time devoted to business	Percent of corporation stock owned		6. Amount of compensation
			4. Common	5. Preferred	
		%	%	%	
		%	%	%	
		%	%	%	
		%	%	%	
		%	%	%	
		%	%	%	
		%	%	%	

Total compensation of officers—Enter here and on line 12, page 1 . . . .

SCHEDULE F.—Bad Debts—Reserve Method (See instruction for line 15, page 1)

1. Year	2. Trade notes and accounts receivable outstanding at end of year	3. Sales on account	Amount added to reserve		6. Amount charged against reserve	7. Reserve for bad debts at end of year
			4. Current year's provision	5. Recoveries		
1978						
1979						
1980						
1981						
1982						
1983						

Form 1120 (1983)   Page **3**

SCHEDULE J.—Tax Computation
(See instructions for Schedule J on page 7)

1 Check if you are a member of a controlled group (see sections 1561 and 1563) . . . . . . ▶ ☐

2 If line 1 is checked, see instructions and enter your portion of the $25,000 amount in each taxable income bracket:

    (i) $ _ _ _ _ _ _ _ _ _ _   *(ii)* $ _ _ _ _ _ _ _ _ _ _   *(iii)* $ _ _ _ _ _ _ _ _ _   *(iv)* $ _ _ _ _ _ _ _ _ _

3 Income tax (see instructions to figure the tax; enter this tax or alternative tax from Schedule D, whichever is less). Check if from Schedule D ▶ ☐ **3**

4 **(a)** Foreign tax credit (attach Form 1118). . . . . |4(a)|
    (b) Investment credit (attach Form 3468) . . . . |(b)|
    (c) Jobs credit (attach Form 5884) . . . . |(c)|
    (d) Employee stock ownership credit (attach Form 8007) . . . . . . |(d)|
    (e) Research credit (attach Form 6765) . . . . |(e)|
    (f) Possessions tax credit (attach Form 5735) . . . . |(f)|
    (g) Alcohol fuel credit (attach Form 6478) . . . . |(g)|
    (h) Credit for fuel produced from a nonconventional source (see instructions) |(h)|

5 Total—Add lines 4(a) through 4(h) **5**

6 Subtract line 5 from line 3 . . . . **6**

7 Personal holding company tax (attach Schedule PH (Form 1120)) **7**

8 Tax from recomputing prior-year investment credit (attach Form 4255) **8**

9 Minimum tax on tax preference items (see instructions—attach Form 4626) **9**

10 Total tax—Add lines 6 through 9. Enter here and on line 31, page 1 . . . . **10**

Additional Information (See page 8 of instructions) |Yes|No|

H Did you claim a deduction for expenses connected with:
   (1) Entertainment facility (boat, resort, ranch, etc.)? . . . .
   (2) Living accommodations (except employees on business)? . .
   (3) Employees attending conventions or meetings outside the North American area? (See section 274(h))
   (4) Employees' families at conventions or meetings? . . . .
     If "Yes," were any of these conventions or meetings outside the North American area? (See section 274(h)) . . . .
   (5) Employee or family vacations not reported on Form W-2? . .

I (1) Did you at the end of the tax year own, directly or indirectly, 50% or more of the voting stock of a domestic corporation? (For rules of attribution, see section 267(c).)
     If "Yes," attach a schedule showing: (a) name, address, and identifying number; (b) percentage owned; (c) taxable income or (loss) before NOL and special deductions (e.g., If a Form 1120: from Form 1120, line 28, page 1) of such corporation for the tax year ending with or within your tax year; (d) highest amount owed by you to such corporation during the year ; and (e) highest amount owed to you by such corporation during the year.
   (2) Did any individual, partnership, corporation, estate or trust at the end of the tax year own, directly or indirectly, 50% or more of your voting stock? (For rules of attribution, see section 267(c).) If "Yes," complete (a) through (e) . . . . . .
     (a) Attach a schedule showing name, address, and identifying number.
     (b) Enter percentage owned ▶ _ _ _ _ _ _ _ _ _ _ _ _ _ _ _
     (c) Was the owner of such voting stock a person other than a U.S. person? (See instructions). . . . .
     If "Yes," enter owner's country ▶ _ _ _ _ _ _ _ _ _ _ _
     (d) Enter highest amount owed by you to such owner during the year ▶

       (e) Enter highest amount owed to you by such owner during the year ▶ _ _ _ _ _ _ _ _ _ _ _ _ _ _ _ |Yes|No|
     (Note: For purposes of I(1) and I(2), "highest amount owed" includes loans and accounts receivable/payable.)

J Refer to page 9 of instructions and state the principal:
   Business activity ▶ _
   Product or service ▶ _ _ _ _ _ _ _ _ _ _ _ _ _ _ _ _ _ _ _

K Were you a U.S. shareholder of any controlled foreign corporation? (See sections 951 and 957.) If "Yes," attach Form 5471 for each such corporation.

L At any time during the tax year, did you have an interest in or a signature or other authority over a bank account, securities account, or other financial account in a foreign country? (See page 8 for exceptions and filing requirements for Form 90-22.1.) . . .
   If "Yes," write the name of the foreign country ▶ _ _ _ _ _ _ _ _ _ _
_ _

M Were you the grantor of, or transferor to, a foreign trust which existed during the current tax year, whether or not you have any beneficial interest in it? . . . .
   If "Yes," you may have to file Forms 3520, 3520-A or 926.

N During this tax year, did you pay dividends (other than stock dividends and distributions in exchange for stock) in excess of your current and accumulated earnings and profits? (See sections 301 and 316) . . .
   If "Yes," file Form 5452. If this is a consolidated return, answer here for parent corporation and on Form 851, Affiliations Schedule, for each subsidiary.

O During this tax year did you maintain any part of your accounting/tax records on a computerized system? . . . .

P Check method of accounting: **(1)** ☐ Cash   **(2)** ☐ Accrual
     (3) ☐   Other (specify) ▶

Form 1120 (1983) Page **4**

SCHEDULE L.—Balance Sheets

Assets	Beginning of tax year		End of tax year	
	(A)	(B)	(C)	(D)
1 Cash				
2 Trade notes and accounts receivable . . .				
(a) Less allowance for bad debts				
3 Inventories				
4 Federal and State government obligations .				
5 Other current assets (attach schedule) . .				
6 Loans to stockholders				
7 Mortgage and real estate loans				
8 Other investments (attach schedule) . .				
9 Buildings and other depreciable assets . .				
(a) Less accumulated depreciation . . .				
10 Depletable assets				
(a) Less accumulated depletion				
11 Land (net of any amortization)				
12 Intangible assets (amortizable only) . . .				
(a) Less accumulated amortization . . .				
13 Other assets (attach schedule)				
14 Total assets				
Liabilities and Stockholders' Equity				
15 Accounts payable				
16 Mortgages, notes, bonds payable in less than 1 year				
17 Other current liabilities (attach schedule) . .				
18 Loans from stockholders				
19 Mortgages, notes, bonds payable in 1 year or more				
20 Other liabilities (attach schedule)				
21 Capital stock: **(a)** Preferred stock				
(b) Common stock				
22 Paid-in or capital surplus				
23 Retained earnings—Appropriated (attach schedule)				
24 Retained earnings—Unappropriated . . .				
25 Less cost of treasury stock		( )		( )
26 Total liabilities and stockholders' equity .				

SCHEDULE M-1.—Reconciliation of Income Per Books With Income Per Return

Do not complete this schedule if your total assets (line 14, column (D), above) are less than $25,000.

1 Net income per books.		7 Income recorded on books this year not included in this return (itemize)	
2 Federal income tax			
3 Excess of capital losses over capital gains		**(a)** Tax-exempt interest $_____	
4 Income subject to tax not recorded on books this year (itemize) _____		_____	
_____		8 Deductions in this tax return not charged against book income this year (itemize)	
5 Expenses recorded on books this year not deducted in this return (itemize)		**(a)** Depreciation . . . $_____	
(a) Depreciation . . . $_____		**(b)** Contributions carryover $ _____	
(b) Contributions carryover $ _____		_____	
_____		9 Total of lines 7 and 8	
6 Total of lines 1 through 5		10 Income (line 28, page 1)—line G less line 9. .	

SCHEDULE M-2.—Analysis of Unappropriated Retained Earnings Per Books (line 24 above)

Do not complete this schedule if your total assets (line 14, column (D), above) are less than $25,000.

1 Balance at beginning of year		5 Distributions: **(a)** Cash.	
2 Net income per books.		**(b)** Stock	
3 Other increases (itemize) _____		**(c)** Property.	
_____		6 Other decreases (itemize) _____	
_____		_____	
_____		7 Total of lines 5 and 6	
4 Total of lines 1, 2, and 3		8 Balance at end of year (line 4 less line 7) . .	

B–6   FORM 1120S   U. S. INCOME TAX RETURN FOR AN S CORPORATION

Form **1120S** Department of the Treasury Internal Revenue Service	**U.S. Income Tax Return for an S Corporation** For calendar year 1983 or other tax year beginning _____, 1983, ending _____, 19 _____ ▶ **For Paperwork Reduction Act Notice, see page 1 of the instructions.**	OMB No. 1545-0130 19**83**

A. Date of election as an S corporation	Use IRS label. Other-wise, please print or type.	Name	**C. Employer identification number**
B. Business Code No. (see Specific Instructions)		Number and street	**D.** Date incorporated
		City or town, State, and ZIP code	**E.** Total assets (see Specific Instructions) $

F. Check box if there has been a change in address from the previous year . . . . ▶ ☐

Income

1 **a** Gross receipts or sales $ _____ **b** Less returns and allowances $ _____ Balance ▶	1c	
2 Cost of goods sold and/or operations (Schedule A, line 7)	2	
3 Gross profit (subtract line 2 from line 1c)	3	
4 Nonqualifying interest and nonqualifying dividends	4	
5 Gross rents	5	
6 Gross royalties	6	
7 Net gain or (loss) from Form 4797, line 14(a), Part II	7	
8 Other income (see instructions—attach schedule)	8	
9 TOTAL income (loss)—Combine lines 3 through 8 and enter here . . . . ▶	9	

Deductions

10 Compensation of officers	10	
11 **a** Salaries and wages $_____ **b** Less jobs credit $_____ Balance ▶	11c	
12 Repairs	12	
13 Bad debts (Schedule F if reserve method is used)	13	
14 Rents	14	
15 Taxes	15	
16 **a** Total deductible interest expense not claimed elsewhere on return (see instructions)	16a	
b Interest expense required to be passed through to shareholders on Schedules K and K-1, lines 16a(2) and 16a(3)	16b	
c Subtract line 16b from line 16a	16c	
17 **a** Depreciation from Form 4562 (attach Form 4562)	17a	
b Depreciation claimed on Schedule A and elsewhere on return . .	17b	
c Subtract line 17b from line 17a	17c	
18 Depletion (**Do not deduct oil and gas depletion. See instructions**)	18	
19 Advertising	19	
20 Pension, profit-sharing, etc. plans (see instructions)	20	
21 Employee benefit programs (see instructions)	21	
22 Other deductions (attach schedule)	22	
23 TOTAL deductions—Add lines 10 through 22 and enter here . . . . . ▶	23	
24 Ordinary income (loss)—Subtract line 23 from line 9	24	

Tax

25 **a** Excess net passive income tax (attach schedule) . . .	25a	
b Tax from Schedule D (Form 1120S), Part IV.	25b	
c Add lines 25a and 25b	25c	
26 Payments: **a** Tax deposited with Form 7004	26a	
b Federal tax on special fuels and oils (attach Form 4136)	26b	
c Add lines 26a and 26b	26c	
27 **TAX DUE** (subtract line 26c from line 25c). See instructions for Paying the Tax. . . . . ▶	27	
28 **OVERPAYMENT** (subtract line 25c from line 26c) . . . . ▶	28	

Please Sign Here

Under penalties of perjury, I declare that I have examined this return, including accompanying schedules and statements, and to the best of my knowledge and belief, it is true, correct, and complete. Declaration of preparer (other than taxpayer) is based on all information of which preparer has any knowledge.

Signature of officer		Date	▶	Title

Paid Preparer's Use Only

Preparer's signature ▶	Date	Check if self-em-ployed ▶ ☐	Preparer's social security number
Firm's name (or yours, if self-employed) and address ▶		E.I. No. ▶	
		ZIP code ▶	

Form **1120S** (1983)

Form 1120S (1983)　　　　　　　　　　　　　　　　　　　　　　　　　　　　　　　　Page **2**

SCHEDULE A.—Cost of Goods Sold and/or Operations
(See instructions for Schedule A)

1 Inventory at beginning of year.	1	
2 Merchandise bought for manufacture or sale .	2	
3 Salaries and wages .	3	
4 Other costs (attach schedule).	4	
5 Total—Add lines 1 through 4 .	5	
6 Inventory at end of year.	6	
7 Cost of goods sold—Subtract line 6 from line 5. Enter here and on line 2, page 1 .	7	

8 **(a)** Check all methods used for valuing closing inventory:

    (i) ☐ Cost

    (ii) ☐ Lower of cost or market as described in Regulations section 1.471–4 (see instructions)

    (iii) ☐ Writedown of "subnormal" goods as described in Regulations section 1.471–2(c) (see instructions)

    (iv) ☐ Other (Specify method used and attach explanation) ▶ _____

  (b) Check if the LIFO inventory method was adopted this tax year for any goods (if checked, attach Form 970) . . . . . ☐

  (c) If the LIFO inventory method was used for this tax year, enter percentage (or amounts) of closing inventory

    computed under LIFO

  (d) If you are engaged in manufacturing, did you value your inventory using the full absorption method (Regulations section 1.471–11)? . . . . ☐ Yes ☐ No

  (e) Was there any substantial change in determining quantities, cost, or valuations between opening and closing inventory? ☐ Yes ☐ No
If "Yes," attach explanation.

Additional Information Required

	Yes	No
G Did you at the end of the tax year own, directly or indirectly, 50% or more of the voting stock of a domestic corporation? (For rules of attribution, see section 267(c).)		
If "Yes," attach a schedule showing: **(1)** name, address, and employer identification number;		
(2) percentage owned;		
(3) highest amount owed by you to such corporation during the year; and		
(4) highest amount owed to you by such corporation during the year.		
(Note: For purposes of G(3) and G(4), "highest amount owed" includes loans and accounts receivable/payable.)		
H Refer to the listing of Business Activity Codes and state your principal:		
Business activity ▶ _____ ; Product or service ▶ _____		
I Were you a member of a controlled group subject to the provisions of section 1561?		
J Did you claim a deduction for expenses connected with:		
1 Entertainment facilities (boat, resort, ranch, etc.)?		
2 Living accommodations (except for employees on business)?		
3 Employees attending conventions or meetings outside the North American area? (See section 274(h).) . . .		
4 Employees' families at conventions or meetings?		
If "Yes," were any of these conventions or meetings outside the North American area? (See section 274(h).) . .		
5 Employee or family vacations not reported on Form W-2?		
K At any time during the tax year, did you have an interest in or a signature or other authority over a bank account, securities account, or other financial account in a foreign country? (See instructions for exceptions and filing requirements for Form 90-22.1.)		
If "Yes," write the name of the foreign country ▶ _____		
L Were you the grantor of, or transferor to, a foreign trust which existed during the current tax year, whether or not you have any beneficial interest in it? If "Yes," you may have to file Forms 3520, 3520-A, or 926		
M During this tax year did you maintain any part of your accounting/tax records on a computerized system? . . .		
N Check method of accounting: (1) ☐ Cash (2) ☐ Accrual (3) ☐ Other (specify) ▶		

SCHEDULE F.—Bad Debts— Reserve Method (See instruction for line 13, page 1)

1. Year	2. Trade notes and accounts receivable outstanding at end of year	3. Sales on account	Amount added to reserve		6. Amount charged against reserve	7. Reserve for bad debts at end of year
			4. Current year's provision	5. Recoveries		
1978						
1979						
1980						
1981						
1982						
1983						

Form 1120S (1983)   Page **3**

SCHEDULE K.—Shareholders' Share of Income, Credits, Deductions, etc. (See Instructions.)

a. Distributive share items		b. Total amount

Income and Deductions

1	Ordinary income (loss) (page 1, line 24)	1	
2	Interest from All-Savers Certificates	2	
3	Dividends qualifying for the exclusion	3	
4	Net short-term capital gain (loss) (Schedule D (Form 1120S))	4	
5	Net long-term capital gain (loss) (Schedule D (Form 1120S))	5	
6	Net gain (loss) from involuntary conversions due to casualty or theft	6	
7	Other net gain (loss) under section 1231	7	
8	Other income (loss) (attach schedule)	8	
9	Charitable contributions: 50% ...., 30% ...., 20%	9	
10	Expense deduction for recovery property (section 179 expense)	10	
11	Other (attach schedule)	11	

Credits

12	Jobs credit	12	
13	Credit for alcohol used as fuel	13	
14	Other (see instructions)	14	

Tax Preference Items

15 a	Accelerated depreciation on nonrecovery real property or 15-year real property	15a	
b	Accelerated depreciation on leased personal property or leased recovery property other than 15-year real property	15b	
c	Depletion (other than oil and gas)	15c	
d (1)	Excess intangible drilling costs from oil, gas, or geothermal wells	15d(1)	
(2)	Net income from oil, gas, or geothermal wells	15d(2)	
e	Net investment income (loss)	15e	
f	Other (attach schedule)	15f	

Interest on Investment Indebtedness

16 a (1)	Interest on investment indebtedness incurred before 12-17-69	16a(1)	
(2)	Interest on investment indebtedness incurred before 9-11-75 but after 12-16-69	16a(2)	
(3)	Interest on investment indebtedness incurred after 9-10-75	16a(3)	
b	Net investment income or (loss)	16b	
c	Excess expenses from "net lease property"	16c	
d	Net capital gain attributable to investment property	16d	

Foreign Taxes

17a	Type of income		
b	Name of foreign country or U.S. possession		
c	Total gross income from sources outside the U.S. (attach schedule)	17c	
d	Total applicable deductions and losses (attach schedule)	17d	
e	Total foreign taxes (check one): ▶ ☐ Paid ☐ Accrued	17e	
f	Reduction in taxes available for credit (attach schedule)	17f	
g	Other (attach schedule)	17g	

Other Items

18	Total dividend distributions paid from retained earnings (lines 23 and 24 of Schedule L)	18	
19	Total property distributions (including cash) other than dividend distributions reported on line 18 above	19	
20	Other (attached schedule)		

Form 1120S (1983) Page **4**

SCHEDULE L.—Balance Sheets

Assets	Beginning of tax year		End of tax year	
	(A)	(B)	(C)	(D)
1 Cash				
2 Trade notes and accounts receivable				
(a) Less allowance for bad debts				
3 Inventories				
4 Federal and State government obligations				
5 Other current assets (attach schedule)				
6 Loans to stockholders				
7 Mortgage and real estate loans				
8 Other investments (attach schedule)				
9 Buildings and other depreciable assets				
(a) Less accumulated depreciation				
10 Depletable assets				
(a) Less accumulated depletion				
11 Land (net of any amortization)				
12 Intangible assets (amortizable only)				
(a) Less accumulated amortization				
13 Other assets (attach schedule)				
14 Total assets				
Liabilities and Shareholders' Equity				
15 Accounts payable				
16 Mortgages, notes, bonds payable in less than 1 year				
17 Other current liabilities (attach schedule)				
18 Loans from shareholders				
19 Mortgages, notes, bonds payable in 1 year or more				
20 Other liabilities (attach schedule)				
21 Capital stock				
22 Paid-in or capital surplus				
23 Retained earnings—Appropriated (attach schedule)				
24 Retained earnings—Unappropriated				
25 Shareholders' undistributed taxable income previously taxed				
26 Accumulated adjustments account				
27 Other adjustments account				
28 Less cost of treasury stock	(	)	(	)
29 Total liabilities and shareholders' equity				

SCHEDULE M.—Reconciliation of Shareholders' Undistributed Taxable Income Previously Taxed, Accumulated Adjustments Account, and Other Adjustments Account, lines 25, 26, and 27 above (see instructions).

	Shareholders' undistributed taxable income previously taxed	Accumulated adjustments account	Other adjustments account
1 Balance at beginning of year			
2 Ordinary income from page 1, line 24			
3 Other additions			
4 Total of lines 1, 2, and 3			
5 Distributions other than dividend distributions			
6 Loss from page 1, line 24			
7 Other reductions			
8 Add lines 5, 6, and 7			
9 Balance at end of tax year—Line 4 less line 8			

SCHEDULE K-1
(Form 1120S)

Department of the Treasury
Internal Revenue Service

Shareholder's Share of Income, Credits, Deductions, etc. For 1983 calendar year and fiscal year

beginning _____, 1983 and ending _____, 19____

(Complete a separate Schedule K-1 for each shareholder—See instructions)

OMB No. 1545-0130

1983

Shareholder's identifying number ▶ | Corporation's identifying number ▶

Shareholder's name, address, and ZIP code | Corporation's name, address, and ZIP code

A Shareholder's percentage of stock ownership for tax year . . . . ▶ _____ %

B Internal Revenue Service Center where corporation filed its return ▶

		a. Distributive share item	**b.** Amount	**c.** 1040 filers enter the amount in column b on:
Income (Losses) and Deductions	1	Ordinary income (loss)		Sch. E, Part II, col. (d) or (e)
	2	Interest from All-Savers Certificates		Sch. B, Part I, line 4
	3	Dividends qualifying for the exclusion		Sch. B, Part II, line 9
	4	Net short-term capital gain (loss)		Sch. D, line 4, col. f or g
	5	Net long-term capital gain (loss)		Sch. D, line 12, col. f or g
	6	Net gain (loss) from involuntary conversions due to casualty or theft . .		See attached instructions
	7	Other net gain (loss) under section 1231.		Form 4797, line 1
	8	Other income (loss) (attach schedule)		(Enter on applicable line of your return)
	9	Charitable contributions: 50% ____, 30% ____, 20% ____		See Form 1040 Instructions
	10	Expense deduction for recovery property (section 179 expense) . . .		Sch. E, Part II, line 34
	11	Other (attach schedule)		(Enter on applicable line of your return)
Credits	12	Jobs credit		Form 5884
	13	Credit for alcohol used as fuel		Form 6478
	14	Other (attach schedule)		(Enter on applicable line of your return)
Tax Preference Items	15a	Accelerated depreciation on nonrecovery real property or 15-year real property		Form 6251, line 4c
	b	Accelerated depreciation on leased personal property or leased recovery property other than 15-year real property		Form 6251, line 4d
	c	Depletion (other than oil and gas)		Form 6251, line 4i
	d (1)	Excess intangible drilling costs from oil, gas, or geothermal wells		See Form 6251 instructions
	(2)	Net income from oil, gas, or geothermal wells		
	e	Net investment income (loss)		Form 6251, line 2e(2)
	f	Other (attach schedule)		See attached instructions
Interest on Investment Indebtedness	16a	Investment interest expense on:		
	(1)	Indebtedness incurred before 12/17/69		Form 4952, line 1
	(2)	Indebtedness incurred before 9/11/75 but after 12/16/69 . . .		Form 4952, line 15
	(3)	Indebtedness incurred after 9/10/75		Form 4952, line 5
	b	Net investment income (loss)		See attached instructions
	c	Excess expenses from "net lease property"		Form 4952, lines 11 and 19
	d	Excess of net long-term capital gain over net short-term capital loss from investment property.		Form 4952, line 20
Foreign Taxes	17a	Type of income ▶		Form 1116, Check boxes
	b	Name of foreign country or U.S. possession ▶		Form 1116, Part I
	c	Total gross income from sources outside the U.S. (attach schedule) . .		Form 1116, Part I
	d	Total applicable deductions and losses (attach schedule)		Form 1116, Part I
	e	Total foreign taxes (check one): ▶ ☐ Paid ☐ Accrued . .		Form 1116, Part II
	f	Reduction in taxes available for credit (attach schedule).		Form 1116, Part III
	g	Other (attach schedule)		Form 1116 Instructions

For Paperwork Reduction Act Notice, see page 1 of Instructions for Form 1120S.   Schedule K-1 (Form 1120S) 1983

		a. Distributive share item			b. Amount	c. 1040 filers enter the amount in column b on:
Property Eligible for Investment Credit	18	Unadjusted basis of new recovery property	**a** 3-year.			See attached instructions
			b Other.			See attached instructions
		Unadjusted basis of used recovery property	**c** 3-year			See attached instructions
			d Other.			See attached instructions
	e	Nonrecovery property (see page 10 of instructions) (attach schedule) .				Form 3468, Instr., line 2
	f	New commuter highway vehicle.				Form 3468, line 3
	g	Used commuter highway vehicle.				Form 3468, line 4
	h	Qualified rehabilitation expenditures.				Form 3468, line 6a, b, or c
Property Subject to Recapture of Investment Credit	19	Properties:	**A**	**B**	**C**	
	a	Description of property (state whether recovery or nonrecovery property)				Form 4255, top
	b	Date placed in service .				Form 4255, line 2
	c	Cost or other basis . .				Form 4255, line 3
	d	Class of recovery property or original estimated useful life				Form 4255, line 4
	e	Date item ceased to be investment credit property				Form 4255, line 8
Other Items	20	Property distributions (including cash) other than dividend distributions reported to you on Form 1099-DIV				See attached instructions
	21	Amount of loan repayments for "Loans from Shareholders"				See attached instructions
	22	Other (attach schedule).				See attached instructions

Instructions for Shareholder

(To be attached to shareholder's copy of Schedule K-1)

(Section references are to the Internal Revenue Code, unless otherwise noted.)

Purpose of Schedule

The corporation uses Schedule K-1 (Form 1120S) to report to you your share of the corporation's income (reduced by any tax the corporation paid on the income), credits, deductions, etc. Please keep it for your records.

Although the corporation is subject to a capital gains tax and an excess net passive income tax, you, the shareholder, are liable for the income tax on your share of the corporation's income, whether or not distributed, and you must include your share on your tax return. Please read **Limitation on Aggregate Losses and Deductions** under line 1 instructions to figure how much of your share of the corporation's loss is deductible.

Schedule K-1 does not show the amount of actual dividend distributions the corporation paid to you. The corporation must report such amounts totaling $10 or more during the calendar year to you on Form 1099-DIV. You report actual dividend distributions on Schedule B (Form 1040).

General Instructions

Basis in Corporate Stock.—You are responsible for maintaining records to show the computation of your basis in stock of the corporation. Schedule K-1 provides you with information to help you make the computation at the end of each corporate tax year. Your basis in stock is adjusted as follows (this list is not all-inclusive):

Increased for:

(1) All income (including tax-exempt income) reported on Schedule K-1. Note: Taxable income must be reported on your tax return for it to increase your basis.

(2) The excess of the deduction for depletion over the basis of the property subject to depletion.

Decreased for:

(1) Property distributions made by the corporation (excluding dividend distributions reported on Form 1099-DIV and distributions in excess of basis) Schedule K-1, line 20.

(2) All items of loss and deductions (including nondeductible expenses) reported on Schedule K-1.

Inconsistent Treatment of Items.— You must treat corporate items on your return consistent with the way the corporation treated the items on its filed return. See sections 6242, 6243, and 6244 for more information.

If your treatment on your original or amended return is (or may be) inconsistent with the corporation's treatment, or if the corporation has not filed a return, you must file **Form 8082**, Notice of Inconsistent Treatment or Amended Return, with your original or amended return to identify and explain the inconsistency (or noting that a corporate return has not been filed).

If you are required to file Form 8082 but fail to do so, you may be subject to a penalty. Also, any deficiency that results from making the treatment of the inconsistent corporate item consistent with the corporate treatment may be assessed immediately.

Errors.—If you believe the corporation has made an error on your Schedule K-1, notify the corporation and ask for a corrected Schedule K-1. Do not change any items on your copy. Be sure that the corporation sends a copy of the corrected Schedule K-1 to the IRS. See Inconsistent Treatment of Items above.

Windfall Profit Tax.—If you are a producer of domestic crude oil, your corporation will inform you of your income tax deduction for windfall profit tax on **Form 6248**, Annual Information Return of Windfall Profit Tax, and not on this Schedule K-1. In addition, generally, you must determine if you are entitled to a refund of overpaid windfall profit tax. See **Form 6249**, Computation of Overpaid Windfall Profit Tax. You will not be notified of any overpayment on this Schedule K-1.

Elections.—Generally, the corporation decides how to figure taxable income from its operations. For example, it chooses the accounting method and depreciation methods it will use.

However, certain elections are made by you separately on your income tax return and not by the corporation. These elections are made under: a. section 901 (foreign tax credit); b. section 617 (deduction and recapture of certain mining exploration expenditures, paid or incurred); c. section 57(c) (net leases); d. section 163(d)(6) (limitation on interest on investment indebtedness); e. sections 108(b)(5) or 108(d)(4) (income from discharge of indebtedness); and f. section 58(i) (optional writeoff of certain tax preference items.)

Additional Information.—For more information on the treatment of S corporation income, credits, deductions, etc. see **Publication 589**, Tax Information on S Corporations, **Publication 535**, Business Expenses, **Publication 536**, Net Operating Losses and the At-Risk Limits, and **Publication 550**, Investment Income and Expenses.

Specific Instructions

Name, Address, and Identifying Number.— Your name, address, and identifying number, the corporation's name, address, and identifying number, and items A and B should be entered.

Lines 1—22

If you are an individual shareholder, take the amounts shown in column b and enter them on the lines on your tax return as indicated in column c. If you are an estate or trust, report the amounts shown in column b as instructed on **Form 1041**, U.S. Fiduciary Income Tax Return.

Note: The line number references are to forms in use for tax years beginning in 1983. If you are a calendar year shareholder in a fiscal year 1983/1984 corporation, enter these amounts on the corresponding lines of the tax form in use for 1984. Also, "(attach schedule)" means see the schedule which the corporation has attached to your copy of Schedule K-1.

Caution: If you have losses, deductions, credits, etc. from a prior year that were not deductible or useable because of certain may limitations, such as the at-risk rules, they may be taken into account in determining your income, loss, etc., for this year. However, do not combine the prior year amounts with any amounts shown on this Schedule K-1 to get a net figure to report on your return. Instead, report the amounts on your return on a year-by-year basis.

If you have amounts, other than line 1, to report on Schedule E (Form 1040), enter each item on a separate line of Part II of Schedule E, column (d) or (e), whichever applies. Enter any deduction items in column (d).

Line 1. Ordinary Income (loss).—The amount shown reflects your share of ordinary income (loss) from all corporate business operations, including at-risk activities, without reference to your adjusted basis in stock and debt of the corporation, or the amount you are at-risk.

Limitation on Aggregate Losses and Deductions.—Generally, your share of aggregate losses and deductions reported on Schedule K-1 is limited to your basis in stock and debt of the corporation. Your basis in stock is figured at year end. **See Corporate Basis in**

Stock in the General Instructions. Your basis in loans made to the corporation is the balance the corporation now owes you less any reduction for losses in a prior year. See the instructions for line 21. Any loss not allowed for the tax year because of this limitation is available for indefinite carryover, limited to your basis in stock and debt in each subsequent tax year. See section 1366(d) for details.

If you have (1) a loss from any activity (except the holding of real property, other than mineral property) carried on as a trade or business or for the production of income by the corporation, and (2) amounts in the activity for which you are not at risk, you will have to complete **Form 6198**, Computation of Deductible Loss from an Activity Described in Section 465(c), to figure the allowable loss to report on your return. Generally, your deductible loss from each activity for the tax year is limited to the amount you are at risk for the activity at the end of the corporation's tax year, or the amount of the loss, whichever is less.

You are not at risk for the following:

a. Your basis in stock of the corporation or basis in loans you made to the corporation if the cash or other property used to purchase the stock or make the loans was from a source covered by nonrecourse indebtedness or protected against loss by a guarantee, stop-loss agreement, or other similar arrangement, or that is covered by indebtedness from a person who is related to you or who has an interest in the activity other than a creditor.

b. Any cash or property contributed to a corporate activity, or your interest in the corporate activity, that is covered by nonrecourse indebtedness or protected against loss by a guarantee, stop-loss agreement, or other similar arrangement, or that is covered by indebtedness from a person who is related to you or who has an interest in the activity other than a creditor.

Any loss from a section 465 activity not allowed for this tax year will be treated as a deduction allocable to the activity in the next tax year.

Note: If the corporation sells or otherwise disposes of (1) an asset used in the activity to which the at-risk rules apply or (2) any part of its interest in such an activity (or if you sell or dispose of your interest), you should combine the gain or loss on the sale or disposition with the profit or loss from the activity to determine the net profit or loss from the activity. If this is a net loss, it may be limited because of the at-risk rules.

To help you complete Form 6198, if required, the corporation should give you your share of the total pre-1976 loss(es) from a section 465(c)(1) activity (i.e., film or videotapes, leasing section 1245 property, farm, or oil and gas property) for which there existed a corresponding amount of nonrecourse liability at the end of the year in which the loss(es) occurred. In addition, you should get a separate statement of income, expenses, etc. for each activity from the corporation.

Special transitional rules for movies, video tapes, and leasing activities can be found in section 204(c)(2) and (3) of the Tax Reform Act of 1976 and Publication 536.

Line 6. Net Gain (Loss) From Involuntary Conversions Due to Casualty or Theft.—The corporation will give you a schedule that shows the amounts to be reported on line 22, columns B(i), B(ii), and C of **Form 4684**, Casualties and Thefts. If there is an amount to be reported in column B(ii) of line 22, the corporation will tell you the amount to enter on line 10 of Form 4684, before entering it in Part II of Form 4684, and the amount to enter directly on line 22, column B(ii).

Line 8. Other Income.—Amounts on this line are other items of income, gain, or loss not included on lines 1-7 such as:

a. Wagering gains and losses (section 165(d)).

b. Recoveries of bad debts, prior taxes, or delinquency amounts (section 111).

The corporation should give you a description and the amount of your share of each of these items.

Line 10. Expense Deduction for Recovery Property Under Section 179.—See **Form 4562,** Depreciation and Amortization, for more information.

Line 11. Other Deductions.—Amounts on this line are other deductions not included on lines 9 or 10, such as:

a. Other itemized deductions (Form 1040 filers enter on Schedule A). If you have to use Form 4684, the corporation will give you a schedule that shows the amounts to be entered on line 10 of Form 4684 and the amount to be entered directly in column B(ii) of line 22, Form 4684.

b. Any penalty on early withdrawal of savings.

c. Soil and water conservation expenditures (section 175).

d. Deduction and recapture of certain mining exploration expenditures paid or incurred (section 617).

e. Intangible drilling costs (see Publication 535 for more information).

f. Section 58(i)(2) expenditures.

The corporation should give you a description and the amount of your share of each of these items.

Line 14. Other Credits.—Amounts on this line are credits other than investment credit and credits on lines 12 and 13, such as:

a. Credit for income tax withheld on dividends and interest (see Form 1040 instructions).

b. Nonconventional source fuel credit. Enter this credit on a schedule you prepare yourself to determine the allowed credit to take on your tax return. See section 44D for rules on how to figure the credit.

c. Unused credits from cooperatives.

d. Credit for increasing research activities (enter this credit on **Form 6765,** Credit for Increasing Research Activities).

The corporation will give you a description and the amount of your share of each of these items.

Line 15e. Net Investment Income (Loss).

Caution: Do not use any part of the amount shown on line 1 of this Schedule K-1 to complete Form 6251. This amount has been included in the amount shown on line 15e.

To determine the amount of net investment income to enter on Form 6251, add to the amount on line 15e, net investment income (loss) from all other sources including any investment from income (loss) items shown on lines other than 1 and 15e of this Schedule K-1.

Line 16. Investment Interest.—If the corporation paid or accrued interest on debts it incurred to buy or hold investment property, the amount of interest you can deduct may be limited. The corporation should have entered the interest on investment indebtedness; items

of investment income and expenses; and gains and losses from the sale or exchange of investment property.

For more information and the special provisions that apply to "out-of-pocket" expenses and rental income from property subject to a net lease, see section 163(d), Publication 550 and Form 4952.

Note: *Generally, if your total investment interest expense including investment interest expenses from all other sources (including carryovers, etc.) is less than $10,000 ($5,000 if married filing separately), you do not need to get Form 4952. Instead, you may enter the amounts of investment interest expense directly on Schedule A (Form 1040). The corporation will tell you if any of the amounts should be reported on Schedule E (Form 1040).*

Line 16b. Net Investment Income.— Caution: Do not use any part of the amount shown on line 1 of this Schedule K-1 to complete Form 4952. This amount has been included in the amount shown on line 16b.

To determine the amount of net investment income to enter on Form 4952, add to the amount on line 16b, net investment income (loss) from all other sources including any investment income (loss) items shown on lines other than 1 and 16b of this Schedule K-1.

Report the amount on line 16b as follows:

a. If (1) there is an entry on line 16a(1) or you had investment interest expense on debt incurred before 12/17/69; and (2) there is an entry on line 16b or you had investment income (loss) in 1983; combine the amount on line 16b with your other investment income (loss) from all sources and enter the result (but not less than zero) on line 2 of Form 4952. Complete lines 3 and 4 of Form 4952.

b. If there is not an entry on line 16a(1) and you do not have investment interest expense on debt incurred before 12/17/69; combine the amount on line 16b with your other investment income (loss) from all sources and enter the result (but not less than zero) on line 10a of Form 4952.

Line 18. Property Eligible for Investment Credit.—Your share of the corporation's investment in property that qualifies for the investment credit should be entered. You can claim a tax credit based on your pro rata share of this investment by filing **Form 3468,** Computation of Investment Credit. (For other information, see Form 3468 and the related instructions.)

In addition to the qualifying property reported on line 18, if applicable, the corporation will give you a separate schedule that:

a. Identifies, on a line-by-line basis, property on which it has reduced the basis and property on which it has elected to take a reduced credit. Report the amounts on Form 3468, line 1, as follows:

- Property on which the basis has been reduced. Enter the amount shown on: line 18a on line 1(a); line 18b on line 1(b); line 18c on line 1(c); and line 18d on line 1(d).

- Property on which an election has been made to take a reduced credit. Enter the amount shown on: line 18a on line 1(e); line 18b on line 1(f); line 18c on line 1(g); and line 18d on line 1(h).

b. Shows your share of the corporation's investment in energy property that qualifies for the credit, and where to report it.

c. Provides additional information on your share of line 18h expenditures and the Form 3468 lines on which to enter the expenditure(s) (line 6a, 6b, or 6c).

Line 19. Property Subject to Recapture of Investment Credit.—When investment credit property is disposed of or ceases to qualify before the "life-years category" or "recovery period" assigned, you will be notified. You may have to recapture (pay back) the investment credit taken in prior years. Use the information on line 19 to figure your recapture tax on **Form 4255,** Recapture of Investment Credit. See Form 3468 on which you took the original credit for other information you need to complete Form 4255.

You may also need Form 4255 if you disposed of more than one-third of your interest in the corporation. See **Publication 572,** Investment Credit, for more information.

Line 20.—Reduce your basis in stock of the corporation by the distributions on line 20. If these distributions exceed your basis in stock, the excess is treated as gain from the sale or exchange of property.

Line 21.—If the line 21 payments are made on indebtedness with a reduced basis, the repayments result in income to you to the extent the repayments are more than the adjusted basis of the loan. See section 1367(b)(2) for information on reduction in basis of a loan and restoration in basis of a loan with a reduced basis.

If the loan is repaid in installments, a breakdown of each payment must be made to show the computation of (1) return of capital and (2) income. (Revenue Ruling 64-162, 1964-1 (Part 1) C.B. 304 and Revenue Ruling 68-537, 1968-2 C.B. 372.)

Line 22.—If applicable, the corporation will give you a description and the amount of your share for each of the following:

a. Tax-exempt income realized by the corporation. This income is not reported on your tax return but it does increase your basis in stock. Tax-exempt interest earned by a fiscal year 1983/1984 corporation will be stated separately to assist certain retired individuals in figuring section 86 income.

b. Nondeductible expenses realized by the corporation. These expenses are not deducted on your tax return but decrease your basis in stock.

c. Taxes paid on undistributed capital gains by a regulated investment company. (Form 1040 filers enter your share of these taxes on line 63, and add the words "from Form 1120S". Also reduce your basis in stock of the S corporation by this tax.)

d. Your share of gross income from the property, share of production for the tax year, etc., needed to figure your depletion deduction for oil and gas wells. The corporation should also allocate to you a proportionate share of the adjusted basis of each corporate oil or gas property. The allocation of the basis of each property is made as specified in section 613A(c)(13). See Publication 535 for how to figure your depletion deduction.

e. Any item that certain retired individuals may need to complete **Schedules R&RP (Form 1040),** Credit for the Elderly.

B–7   FORM 1065   U. S. PARTNERSHIP RETURN OF INCOME

Form **1065**	**U.S. Partnership Return of Income**	OMB No. 1545-0099
Department of the Treasury Internal Revenue Service	▶ **For Paperwork Reduction Act Notice, see Form 1065 Instructions.** For calendar year 1983, or fiscal year beginning _____, 1983, and ending _____, 19__	**1983**

A Principal business activity (see page 4 of Instructions)	**Use IRS label. Otherwise, please print or type.**	Name	**D** Employer identification number
B Principal product or service (see page 16 of Instructions)		Number and street	**E** Date business started
C Business code number (see page 16 of Instructions)		City or town, State, and ZIP code	**F** Enter total assets at end of tax year $

		Yes	No
G Check method of accounting: (1) ☐ Cash (2) ☐ Accrual (3) ☐ Other	**N** (1) Was there a distribution of property or a transfer of a partnership interest during the tax year?		
H Check applicable boxes: (1) ☐ Final return (2) ☐ Change in address (3) ☐ Amended return	(2) If "Yes," is the partnership making an election under section 754? If "Yes," attach a statement for the election. (See page 4 of the Instructions before answering this question.)		
I Check if the partnership meets **all** the requirements shown on page 4 of the Instructions under **Question I** . . . . ▶ ☐	**O** At any time during the tax year, did the partnership have an interest in or a signature or other authority over a bank account, securities account, or other financial account in a foreign country (see page 4 of Instructions)? .		
J Number of partners in this partnership ▶ _____	**P** Was the partnership the grantor of, or transferor to, a foreign trust which existed during the current tax year, whether or not the partnership or any partner has any beneficial interest in it? If "Yes," you may have to file Forms 3520, 3520-A, or 926. (See page 5 of Instructions.)		
K Is this partnership a limited partnership (see page 3 of Instructions)?			
L Is this partnership a partner in another partnership? . .	**Q** Are there any specially allocated items of income, gain, loss, deduction, credit, etc. (see page 5 of Instructions)		
M Are any partners in this partnership also partnerships?			

Income

1a Gross receipts or sales $ _____ **1b** Minus returns and allowances $ _____ Balance ▶		**1c**
2 Cost of goods sold and/or operations (Schedule A, line 7)		**2**
3 Gross profit (subtract line 2 from line 1c) . . .		**3**
4 Ordinary income (loss) from other partnerships and fiduciaries		**4**
5 Nonqualifying interest and nonqualifying dividends		**5**
6a Gross rents $ _____ **6b** Minus rental expenses (attach schedule) $ _____		
c Balance net rental income (loss) . . . . ▶		**6c**
7 Net income (loss) from royalties (attach schedule)		**7**
8 Net farm profit (loss) (attach Schedule F (Form 1040))		**8**
9 Net gain (loss) (Form 4797, line 14)		**9**
10 Other income (loss)		**10**
11 **TOTAL** income (loss) (combine lines 3 through 10)		**11**

Deductions

12a Salaries and wages (other than to partners) $ _____ **12b** Minus jobs credit $ _____ Balance ▶		**12c**
13 Guaranteed payments to partners (see page 6 of Instructions)		**13**
14 Rent		**14**
15a Total deductible interest expense not claimed elsewhere on return (see page 6 of Instructions)	**15a**	
b Minus interest expense required to be passed through to partners on Schedule K-1, lines 13, 20a(2), and 20a(3) and Schedule K, lines 13, 20a(2), and 20a(3) (if Schedule K is required).	**15b**	
c Balance . . . . ▶		**15c**
16 Taxes		**16**
17 Bad debts (see page 7 of Instructions)		**17**
18 Repairs		**18**
19a Depreciation from Form 4562 (attach Form 4562) $ _____ **19b** Minus depreciation claimed on Schedule A and elsewhere on return $ _____ Balance . . . . ▶		**19c**
20 Depletion (**Do not deduct oil and gas depletion.** See page 7 of Instructions.)		**20**
21a Retirement plans, etc. (see page 7 of Instructions)		**21a**
b Employee benefit programs (see page 7 of Instructions)		**21b**
22 Other deductions (attach schedule)		**22**
23 **TOTAL** deductions (add amounts in column for lines 12c through 22)		**23**
24 Ordinary income (loss) (subtract line 23 from line 11)		**24**

Please Sign Here

Under penalties of perjury, I declare that I have examined this return, including accompanying schedules and statements, and to the best of my knowledge and belief it is true, correct, and complete. Declaration of preparer (other than taxpayer) is based on all information of which preparer has any knowledge.

▶ _____ Signature of general partner   ▶ _____ Date

Paid Preparer's Use Only	Preparer's signature ▶	Date	Check if self-employed ▶ ☐	Preparer's social security no.
	Firm's name (or yours, if self-employed) and address ▶		E.I. No. ▶	
			ZIP code ▶	

Form 1065 (1983) Page **2**

SCHEDULE A.—Cost of Goods Sold and/or Operations (See Page 7 of Instructions.)

1	Inventory at beginning of year	1	
2	Purchases minus cost of items withdrawn for personal use	2	
3	Cost of labor	3	
4	Other costs (attach schedule)	4	
5	Total (add lines 1 through 4)	5	
6	Inventory at end of year	6	
7	Cost of goods sold (subtract line 6 from line 5). Enter here and on page 1, line 2	7	

8a Check all methods used for valuing closing inventory:

   (i) ☐ Cost

   (ii) ☐ Lower of cost or market as described in regulations section 1.471-4 (see page 8 of Instructions)

   (iii) ☐ Writedown of "subnormal" goods as described in regulations section 1.471-2(c) (see page 8 of Instructions)

   (iv) ☐ Other (specify method used and attach explanation) ▶ ....

  b Check if the LIFO inventory method was adopted this tax year for any goods (if checked, attach Form 970) ☐

  c If you are engaged in manufacturing, did you value your inventory using the full absorption method (regulations section 1.471-11)? ☐ Yes ☐ No

  d Was there any substantial change in determining quantities, cost, or valuations between opening and closing inventory? ☐ Yes ☐ No
If "Yes," attach explanation.

SCHEDULE B.—Distributive Share Items (See Pages 8, 10-11, and 15 of Instructions.)

(a) Distributive share items		(b) Total amount
1 Net long-term capital gain (loss)	1	
2 Other net gain (loss) under section 1231 and specially allocated ordinary gain (loss)	2	
3a If the partnership had income from outside the United States, enter the name of the country or U.S. possession ▶		
b Total gross income from sources outside the United States	3b	

SCHEDULE L.—Balance Sheets
(See Pages 4 and 8 of Instructions and Question I on Page 1 Before Completing Schedules L and M.)

Assets	Beginning of tax year (a)	(b)	End of tax year (c)	(d)
1 Cash				
2 Trade notes and accounts receivable				
a Minus allowance for bad debts				
3 Inventories				
4 Federal and State government obligations				
5 Other current assets (attach schedule)				
6 Mortgage and real estate loans				
7 Other investments (attach schedule)				
8 Buildings and other depreciable assets				
a Minus accumulated depreciation				
9 Depletable assets				
a Minus accumulated depletion				
10 Land (net of any amortization)				
11 Intangible assets (amortizable only)				
a Minus accumulated amortization				
12 Other assets (attach schedule)				
13 TOTAL assets				
Liabilities and Capital				
14 Accounts payable				
15 Mortgages, notes, and bonds payable in less than 1 year				
16 Other current liabilities (attach schedule)				
17 All nonrecourse loans				
18 Mortgages, notes, and bonds payable in 1 year or more				
19 Other liabilities (attach schedule)				
20 Partners' capital accounts				
21 TOTAL liabilities and capital				

SCHEDULE M.—Reconciliation of Partners' Capital Accounts (See Page 8 of Instructions.)
(Show reconciliation of each partner's capital account on Schedule K-1, Item F.)

(a) Capital account at beginning of year	(b) Capital contributed during year	(c) Ordinary income (loss) from page 1, line 24	(d) Income not included in column (c), plus nontaxable income	(e) Losses not included in column (c), plus unallowable deductions	(f) Withdrawals and distributions	(g) Capital account at end of year

SCHEDULE K | **Partners' Shares of Income, Credits, Deductions, etc.** | OMB No. 1545-0099
(Form 1065)

▶ File this form if there are more than ten Schedules K-1 to be filed with Form 1065.
Do not complete lines 6, 8, 21b, and 21c. The amounts for these lines are shown on Schedule B, Form 1065.

Department of the Treasury
Internal Revenue Service

▶ Attach to Form 1065.   ▶ See Instructions for Schedule K (Form 1065).

1983

Name of partnership | Employer identification number

a. Distributive share items		b. Total amount	
Income (Loss)	1 Ordinary income (loss) (page 1, line 24)	1	
	2 Guaranteed payments	2	
	3 Interest from All-Savers Certificates	3	
	4 Dividends qualifying for exclusion	4	
	5 Net short-term capital gain (loss) (Schedule D, line 4)	5	
	6 Net long-term capital gain (loss) (Schedule D, line 9)		
	7 Net gain (loss) from involuntary conversions due to casualty or theft (Form 4684)	7	
	8 Other net gain (loss) under section 1231		
	9 Other (attach schedule)	9	
Deductions	10 Charitable contributions (attach list): 50%_____, 30%_____, 20%_____	10	
	11 Expense deduction for recovery property (section 179) from Part I, Section A, Form 4562	11	
	12a Payments for partners to an IRA	12a	
	b Payments for partners to a Keogh Plan (Type of plan ▶_____)	12b	
	c Payments for partners to Simplified Employee Pension (SEP)	12c	
	13 Other (attach schedule)	13	
Credits	14 Jobs credit	14	
	15 Credit for alcohol used as fuel	15	
	16 Credit for income tax withheld	16	
	17 Other (attach schedule)	17	
Other	18a Gross farming or fishing income	18a	
	b Net earnings (loss) from self-employment	18b	
	c Other (attach schedule)		
Tax Preference Items	19a Accelerated depreciation on nonrecovery real property or 15-year real property	19a	
	b Accelerated depreciation on leased personal property or leased recovery property other than 15-year real property	19b	
	c Depletion (other than oil and gas)	19c	
	d (1) Excess intangible drilling costs from oil, gas, or geothermal wells	19d(1)	
	(2) Net income from oil, gas, or geothermal wells	19d(2)	
	e Net investment income (loss)	19e	
	f Other (attach schedule)	19f	
Investment Interest	20a Investment interest expense:		
	(1) Indebtedness incurred before 12/17/69	20a(1)	
	(2) Indebtedness incurred before 9/11/75, but after 12/16/69	20a(2)	
	(3) Indebtedness incurred after 9/10/75	20a(3)	
	b Net investment income (loss)	20b	
	c Excess expenses from "net lease property"	20c	
	d Excess of net long-term capital gain over net short-term capital loss from investment property	20d	
Foreign Taxes	21a Type of income_____		
	b Foreign country or U.S. possession		
	c Total gross income from sources outside the U.S. (attach schedule)		
	d Total applicable deductions and losses (attach schedule)	21d	
	e Total foreign taxes (check one): ▶ ☐ Paid ☐ Accrued	21e	
	f Reduction in taxes available for credit (attach schedule)	21f	
	g Other (attach schedule)	21g	

For Paperwork Reduction Act Notice, see Form 1065 Instructions.   Schedule K (Form 1065) 1983

SCHEDULE K-1 (Form 1065)	Partner's Share of Income, Credits, Deductions, etc.	OMB No. 1545-0099
Department of the Treasury Internal Revenue Service	For calendar year 1983 or fiscal year beginning _____, 1983, and ending _____, 19___	1983

Partner's identifying number ▶	Partnership's identifying number ▶
Partner's name, address, and ZIP code	Partnership's name, address, and ZIP code

A Is partner a general partner (see page 3 of Instructions)? . . . . ☐ Yes ☐ No

B Partner's share of liabilities (see page 10 of Instructions):

Nonrecourse . . . . $ _____

Other . . . . $ _____

C What type of entity is this partner? ▶ _____

D Enter partner's percentage of:

	(i) Before decrease or termination	(ii) End of year
Profit sharing	_____%	_____%
Loss sharing	_____%	_____%
Ownership of capital	_____%	_____%

E IRS Center where partnership filed return ▶ _____

F Reconciliation of partner's capital account:

(a) Capital account at beginning of year	(b) Capital contributed during year	(c) Ordinary income (loss) from line 1	(d) Income not included in column (c), plus nontaxable income	(e) Losses not included in column (c), plus unallowable deductions	(f) Withdrawals and distributions	(g) Capital account at end of year

(a) Distributive share item	(b) Amount	(c) 1040 filers enter the amount in column (b) on:
Income (Loss)		
1 Ordinary income (loss)		Sch. E, Part II, col. (d) or (e)
2 Guaranteed payments		Sch. E, Part II, column (e)
3 Interest from All-Savers Certificates		Sch. B, Part I, line 4
4 Dividends qualifying for exclusion		Sch. B, Part II, line 9
5 Net short-term capital gain (loss)		Sch. D, line 4, col. f. or g.
6 Net long-term capital gain (loss)		Sch. D, line 12, col. f. or g.
7 Net gain (loss) from involuntary conversions due to casualty or theft .		See attached instructions
8 Other net gain (loss) under section 1231		Form 4797, line 1
9 Other (attach schedule)		(Enter on applicable lines of your return)
Deductions		
10 Charitable contributions: 50% _____, 30% _____, 20% _____		See Form 1040 instructions
11 Expense deduction for recovery property (section 179)		Sch. E, Part II, line 28
12 a Payments for partner to an IRA		See Form 1040 instructions
b Payments for partner to a Keogh Plan (Type of plan ▶ _____) . .		Form 1040, line 26
c Payments for partner to Simplified Employee Pension (SEP)		Form 1040, line 26
13 Other (attach schedule)		(Enter on applicable lines of your return)
Credits		
14 Jobs credit		Form 5884
15 Credit for alcohol used as fuel		Form 6478
16 Credit for income tax withheld		See Form 1040 instructions
17 Other (attach schedule)		(Enter on applicable lines of your return)
Other		
18 a Gross farming or fishing income		See attached instructions
b Net earnings (loss) from self-employment		Sch. SE, Part I
c Other (attach schedule)		(Enter on applicable lines of your return)
Tax Preference Items		
19 a Accelerated depreciation on nonrecovery real property or 15-year real property.		Form 6251, line 4c
b Accelerated depreciation on leased personal property or leased recovery property other than 15-year real property.		Form 6251, line 4d
c Depletion (other than oil and gas)		Form 6251, line 4i
d (1) Excess intangible drilling costs from oil, gas, or geothermal wells .		See Form 6251 instructions
(2) Net income from oil, gas, or geothermal wells		
e Net investment income (loss)		Form 6251, line 2e(2)
f Other (attach schedule)		See attached instructions

For Paperwork Reduction Act Notice, see Form 1065 Instructions.　　　　　　Schedule K-1 (Form 1065) 1983

		(a) Distributive share item			(b) Amount	(c) 1040 filers enter the amount in column (b) on:
Investment Interest	**20 a**	Investment interest expense:				
		(1) Indebtedness incurred before 12/17/69				Form 4952, line 1
		(2) Indebtedness incurred before 9/11/75, but after 12/16/69 . .				Form 4952, line 15
		(3) Indebtedness incurred after 9/10/75				Form 4952, line 5
	b	Net investment income (loss)				See attached instructions
	c	Excess expenses from "net lease property".				Form 4952, lines 11 and 19
	d	Excess of net long-term capital gain over net short-term capital loss from investment property				Form 4952, line 20
Foreign Taxes	**21 a**	Type of income _____				Form 1116, Checkboxes
	b	Name of foreign country or U.S. possession _____				Form 1116, Part I
	c	Total gross income from sources outside the U.S. (attach schedule) .				Form 1116, Part I
	d	Total applicable deductions and losses (attach schedule)				Form 1116, Part I
	e	Total foreign taxes (check one): ▶ ☐ Paid ☐ Accrued				Form 1116, Part II
	f	Reduction in taxes available for credit (attach schedule).				Form 1116, Part III
	g	Other (attach schedule)				Form 1116, instructions
Property Eligible for Investment Credit	**22**	Unadjusted basis of new recovery property	**a**	3-Year		See attached instructions
			b	Other		See attached instructions
		Unadjusted basis of used recovery property	**c**	3-Year		See attached instructions
			d	Other		See attached instructions
	e	Nonrecovery property (see page 15 of Instructions) (attach schedule)				Form 3468, instr., line 2
	f	New commuter highway vehicle				Form 3468, line 3
	g	Used commuter highway vehicle				Form 3468, line 4
	h	Qualified rehabilitation expenditures				Form 3468, line 6a,b,or c

		Properties:	A	B	C	
Property Subject to Recapture of Investment Credit	**23**					
	a	Description of property (state whether recovery or nonrecovery property)				Form 4255, top
	b	Date placed in service				Form 4255, line 2
	c	Cost or other basis				Form 4255, line 3
	d	Class of recovery property or original estimated useful life				Form 4255, line 4
	e	Date item ceased to be investment credit property				Form 4255, line 8

Instructions for the Partner

(Section references are to the Internal Revenue Code, unless otherwise noted.)

Purpose of Form

The partnership uses Schedule K-1 (Form 1065) to report to you your share of the partnership's income, credits, deductions, etc. Please keep it for your records. Do not file it with your income tax return. A copy has been filed with the IRS.

Although the partnership is not subject to income tax, you, the partner, are liable for tax on your share of the partnership income, whether or not distributed, and you must include your share on your tax return. Your share of any partnership income, credit, deduction, etc., must also be reported on your return. Please read *Limitation on Losses* under line 1 to figure how much of your share of any partnership loss is deductible.

General Information

Inconsistent Treatment of Items Shown on this Schedule (and Any Attached Schedules) or Similar Statement. You must treat partnership items on your return consistent with the way the partnership treated the items on its filed return. This rule does not apply if your partnership is within the "small partnership" exception and does not elect to have the new procedures apply. See sections 6222 and 6231 (a)(1) for more information.

If your treatment on your original or amended return is (or may be) inconsistent with the partnership's treatment, or if the partnership has not filed a partnership return, you must file **Form 8082**, Notice of Inconsistent Treatment or Amended Return, with your original or amended return to identify and explain the inconsistency (or note that a partnership return has not been filed).

If you are required to file Form 8082 but fail to do so, you may be subject to a penalty, and any deficiency that results from making the treatment of the inconsistent partnership item consistent with the partnership's treatment may be assessed immediately.

United States Persons with Interests in Foreign Partnerships. If you have an interest in a foreign partnership, you may be required to report changes in your partnership interest when: you acquire an interest in a foreign partnership; you dispose of any part of your interest in a foreign partnership; or your proportional interest in a foreign partnership changes substantially.

See **Form 5473**, Acquisitions and Dispositions of Interests in a Foreign Partnership, and the related instructions and section 6046A for more information.

In addition, if you are a U.S. person in a foreign partnership that fails to file a partnership return, any losses or credits from that partnership may be disallowed to you.

Regulated Futures Contracts and Straddles.— For information on how to report gains and losses from regulated futures contracts and straddles, see **Form 6781**, Gains and Losses From Regulated Futures Contracts and Straddles.

Windfall Profit Tax.—If you are a producer of domestic crude oil, your partnership will inform you on **Form 6248**, Annual Information Return of Windfall Profit Tax-1983, and not on this Schedule K-1, of your income tax deduction for the windfall profit tax.

In addition, generally, you will have to determine if you are entitled to a refund of overpaid windfall profit tax. File **Form 6249**, Computation of Overpaid Windfall Profit Tax, to obtain a refund. You will not be notified of any overpayment on this Schedule K-1.

Errors.—If you believe the partnership has made an error on your Schedule K-1, notify the partnership and ask for a corrected Schedule K-1. Do not change any items on your copy. Be sure that the partnership sends a copy of the corrected Schedule K-1 to the Internal Revenue Service. However, see **Inconsistent Treatment of Items Shown on this Schedule** above.

International Boycotts.—Every partnership that had operations in, or related to, a boycotting country, company, or national must file **Form 5713**, International Boycott Report. If this partnership did not cooperate with an international boycott and notifies you of that fact, you do not have to file Form 5713, unless you had other boycotting operations.

If the partnership cooperated with an international boycott, it must give you a copy of the Form 5713 that it filed. You also must file Form 5713 to report the activities of the partnership and any other boycott operations of your own. You may lose certain tax benefits if the partnership participated in, or cooperated with, an international boycott. Please see Form 5713 and the instructions for more information.

Definitions.—

a. General Partner. A general partner is a member of the organization who is personally liable for the obligations of the partnership.

b. Limited Partner. A limited partner is one whose potential personal liability for partnership debts is limited to the amount of money or other property that partner contributed or is required to contribute to the partnership.

c. Limited Partnership. A limited partnership is a partnership composed of at least one general partner and one or more limited partners.

d. Nonrecourse Loans. Nonrecourse loans are those liabilities of the partnership for which none of the partners have any personal liability.

Elections.—Generally, the partnership decides how to figure taxable income from its operations. For example, it chooses the accounting method and depreciation methods it will use.

However, certain elections are made by you separately on your income tax return and not by the partnership. These elections are made under: **a.** section 901 (foreign tax credit); **b.** section 617 (deduction and recapture of certain mining exploration expenditures, paid or incurred); **c.** section 57(c) (definition of net lease); **d.** section 163(d)(6) (limitation on interest on investment indebtedness); and **e.** sections 108(b)(5) or 108(d)(4) (income from discharge of indebtedness).

Additional Information.—For more information on the treatment of partnership income, credits, deductions, etc., see **Publication 541**, Tax Information on Partnerships, **Publication 535**, Business Expenses, **Publication 536**, Net Operating Losses and the At-Risk Limits, and **Publication 550**, Investment Income and Expenses.

Specific Instructions

Name, Address, and Identifying Number. Your name, address, and identifying number, as well as the partnership's name, address, and identifying number, should be entered.

Question B. Partner's Share of Liabilities. Question B should show your share of the partnership's nonrecourse liabilities and other liabilities as of the end of the year. Nonrecourse loans are those liabilities of the partnership for which none of the partners have any personal liability. If you terminated your interest in the partnership during the year, Question B should show the share that existed immediately before the total disposition. (A partner's "other liability" is any partnership liability for which a partner is personally liable.)

Use the total of the two amounts for computing the adjusted basis of your partnership interest. Use the amount shown on "Other" to compute your amount at risk. Do not include any amounts that are not at risk that may be included in "Other."

If your partnership is engaged in two or more different types of at-risk activities, or a combination of at-risk activities and any other activity, the partnership should give you a statement showing your share of nonrecourse liabilities and other liabilities for each activity.

See *Limitation on Losses* under line 1 for more information.

Lines 1-23

If you are an individual partner, take the amounts shown in column (b) and enter them on the lines on your tax return as indicated in column (c). If you are not an individual partner, report the amounts in column (b) as instructed on your tax return.

Note: *The line numbers are references to forms in use for calendar year 1983. If you file your tax return on a calendar year basis, but your partnership files a fiscal year 1983/1984 partnership return, enter these amounts on the corresponding lines of the tax form in use for 1984.*

Caution: If you have losses, deductions, credits, etc., from a prior year that were not deductible or useable because of certain limitations, such as the at-risk rules, they may be taken into account in determining your net income, loss, etc., for this year. However, do not combine the prior-year amounts with any amounts shown on this Schedule K-1 to get a net figure to report on any supporting schedules, statements, or forms (such as Schedule E (Form 1040)) attached to your return. Instead, report the amounts on the attached schedule, statement, or form on a year-by-year basis.

If you have amounts, other than line 1, to report on Schedule E (Form 1040), enter each item on a separate line of Part II of Schedule E, column (d) or (e), whichever applies. Enter any deduction items in column (d).

Line 1. Ordinary Income (Loss). The amount shown should reflect your share of ordinary income (loss) from all partnership business operations, including at-risk activities, without reference to the adjusted basis of your partnership interest or your amount at risk.

Limitation on Losses.—Generally, you may not claim your share of a partnership loss (including capital loss) that is greater than the adjusted basis of your partnership interest at the end of the partnership's tax year.

However, if you have (1) a loss (including losses from the disposition of assets or any part of an interest), or other deductions such as the expense deduction for recovery property (section 179), from any activity (except the holding of real property, other than mineral property) carried on as a trade or business or for the production of income by the partnership, and (2) amounts in the activity for which you are not at risk (described below), use **Form 6198**, Computation of Deductible Loss from an Activity Described in Section 465(c), to figure the allowable loss or deduction to report on your return. (If you have a loss or other deductions but do not have any amounts not at risk, or you have a loss from a non at-risk activity, deduct the amount of the loss and other deductions or the adjusted basis of your partnership interest, whichever is less.)

You are not at risk for the following amounts:
a. Nonrecourse loans used to finance the activity, to acquire property used in the activity, or to acquire your interest in the activity, that are not secured by your own property (other than that used in the activity).
b. Cash, property, or borrowed amounts used in the activity (or contributed to the activity, or used to acquire your interest in the activity) that are protected against loss by a guarantee, stop-loss agreement, or other similar arrangement (excluding casualty insurance and insurance against tort liability).
c. Amounts you borrowed to use in the activity, or to acquire your interest in the activity, from a person who is related to you under section 267(b) or who has an interest in the activity other than as a creditor.

To help you complete Form 6198, the partnership should give you your share of the total pre-1976 loss(es) from a section 465(c)(1) activity (i.e., film or video tapes, section 1245 property leasing, farm, or oil and gas property) for which there existed a corresponding amount of nonrecourse liability at the end of the year in which this loss(es) occurred. In addition, you should get a separate statement of income, expenses, etc., for each activity from the partnership.

Special transitional rules for movies, video tapes, and leasing activities can be found in section 204(c)(2) and (3) of the Tax Reform Act of 1976 and Publication 536.

Line 7. Net Gain (Loss) From Involuntary Conversions Due to Casualty or Theft. The partnership will give you a schedule that shows the amounts to be entered on **Form 4684**, Casualties and Thefts, Part II, line 22, columns B(i), B(ii), and C. If there is an amount to be reported in column B(ii) of line 22, the partnership will tell you the amount to enter on line 10, Part I of Form 4684 and the amount to enter on line 22, column B(ii).

Line 9. Other Income (Loss). Amounts on this line are other items of income, gain, or loss not included on lines 1–8 such as:

a. Interest from an All-Savers Certificate (ASC) (if in a prior year you excluded interest income from a partnership ASC and the partnership redeemed the ASC in the next year before its maturity, you must include in income any interest you excluded in a prior year from this ASC).

b. Partnership gains from disposition of farm recapture property (see **Form 4797**, Supplemental Schedule of Gains and Losses) and other items to which sections 1251 and 1252 apply.

c. Recoveries of bad debts, prior taxes, and delinquency amounts (section 111).

d. Gains and losses from wagers (section 165(d)).

e. Any income, gain, or loss to the partnership under section 751(b).

f. Specially allocated ordinary gain (loss). Report this amount on Form 4797, line 12

The partnership should give you a description and the amount of your share for each of these items.

Line 11. Expense Deduction for Recovery Property. See **Form 4562**, Depreciation and Amortization, for more information.

Line 12b. Payments for Partner to a Keogh Plan. If there is a defined benefit plan, the partnership should give you a statement showing the amount of the benefit accrued for the tax year.

Line 13. Other Deductions. Amounts on this line are other deductions not included on lines 10–12c such as:

a. Other itemized deductions (1040 filers enter on Schedule A). If you have to use Form 4684, the partnership will give you a schedule that shows the amounts to be entered on line 10, Part I and the amounts to be entered in column B(ii) of line 17, Part II, Form 4684.

b. Any penalty on early withdrawal of savings.

c. Soil and water conservation expenditures (section 175) and expenditures by farming partnerships for clearing land (section 182).

d. Deduction and recapture of certain mining exploration expenditures paid or incurred (section 617).

e. Intangible drilling costs (see Publication 535 for more information).

The partnership should give you a description and the amount of your share for each of these items.

Line 14. Jobs Credit. The amount shown is your share of the jobs credit. See **Form 5884** for definitions, special rules, and limitations.

Line 15. Credit for Alcohol Used as Fuel. Complete **Form 6478** and attach it to your return.

Line 17. Other Credits. Amounts on this line are other credits (other than investment credit which is reported on line 22) not included in lines 14–16, such as:

a. Nonconventional source fuel credit.

b. Unused credits from cooperatives.

c. The credit for increasing research activities (enter this credit on **Form 6765**, Credit for Increasing Research Activities).

d. Orphan drug credit.

The partnership should give you a description and the amount of your share for each of these items.

Line 18a. Gross Farming or Fishing Income. If you are an individual partner, enter the amount from this line on Schedule E (Form 1040), Part IV, line 40. You may also use this amount to figure self-employment income under the optional method on **Schedule SE (Form 1040)**, Part II.

Line 18b. Net Earnings (Loss) From Self-Employment. Before entering this amount on Schedule SE (Form 1040), net earnings (loss)

from self-employment must be adjusted by the section 179 expense claimed, unreimbursed partnership expenses claimed, and depletion claimed on oil and gas properties.

If the amount on this line is a loss, enter only the deductible amount on Schedule SE (Form 1040). See **Limitation on Losses** under the instructions for line 1.

Line 18c. Other. The partnership should give you a description and the amount of your share for each of the following:

a. Taxes paid on undistributed capital gains by a regulated investment company. (Form 1040 filers enter your share of these taxes on line 63, and add the words "From 1065.")

b. Number of gallons of the fuels used during the tax year for each type of use identified on **Form 4136**, Computation of Credit for Federal Tax on Gasoline, Special Fuels, and Lubricating Oil, and in the related instructions.

c. Gross non-farm income which is used by an individual partner to figure self-employment income under the optional method (Schedule SE (Form 1040), Part II).

d. Your share of gross income from the property, share of production for the tax year, etc., needed to figure your depletion deduction for oil and gas wells. The partnership should also allocate to you a proportionate share of the adjusted basis of each partnership oil or gas property. The allocation of the basis of each property is made as specified in section 613A(c)(7)(D). See Publication 535 for how to figure your depletion deduction.

e. If you are a corporation, any income allocable to you that is "timber preference income" under section 57(e).

f. Tax-exempt interest income earned by a fiscal year 1983/1984 partnership.

g. Recapture of expense deduction for recovery property (section 179). Include this amount on your Form 4797 to the extent that you took a deduction. You will have to look at your return for the year in which you took the deduction to determine how much to recapture.

h. Qualified expenditures to which an election under section 58(i) applies.

i. Any items you need to determine the basis of your partnership interest for purposes of section 704(d) because line F on Schedule K-1 is not completed; or any items you need to complete **Schedules R&RP (Form 1040)**; or any items (other than those shown in Question B) you need to figure your amount at risk.

j. Any information or statements you need to comply with section 6661.

Line 19e. Net Investment Income (Loss). **Caution:** Do not use any part of the amount shown on line 1 of this Schedule K-1 to complete **Form 6251.** This amount has been included in the amount shown on line 19e.

To determine the amount of net investment income to enter on Form 6251, add to the amount on line 19e, net investment income (loss) from all other sources including any investment income (loss) items shown on lines other than 1 and 19e of this Schedule K-1.

Line 19f. Other Tax Preference Items. Enter the information on the schedule attached by the partnership for line 19f on the applicable lines of Form 6251.

Line 20. Investment Interest. If the partnership paid or accrued interest on debts it incurred to buy or hold investment property, the amount of interest you can deduct may be limited. The partnership should have entered the interest on investment indebtedness and items of investment income and expenses, and gains and losses from the sale or exchange of investment property.

For more information and the special provisions that apply to "out-of-pocket" expenses and rental income from property subject to a net lease, see section 163(d) and Publication 550. (Individuals, estates, and trusts, also see **Form 4952**, Investment Interest Expense Deduction.)

Note: Generally, if your total investment interest expense including investment interest expense from all other sources (including carryovers, etc.) is less than $10,000 ($5,000 if married filing separately), you do not need to get Form 4952. Instead, you may enter the amounts of investment interest directly on Schedule A (Form 1040). The partnership will tell you if any of the amounts should be reported on Schedule E (Form 1040).

Line 20b. Net Investment Income (Loss). **Caution:** Do not use any part of the amount shown on line 1 of this Schedule K-1 to complete Form 4952. This amount has been included in the amount shown on line 20b. To determine the amount of net investment income to enter on Form 4952, add to the amount on line 20b, net investment income (loss) from all other sources including any investment income (loss) items shown on lines other than 1 and 20b of this Schedule K-1.

Report the amount on line 20b as follows:

● If (1) there is an entry on line 20a(1) or you had investment interest expense on indebtedness incurred before 12/17/69; and (2) there is an entry on line 20b or you had investment income (loss) in 1983; combine the amount on line 20b with your other investment income (loss) from all sources and enter the result (but not less than zero) on line 2 of Form 4952. Complete lines 3 and 4 of Form 4952. Then enter the amount from line 4 of Form 4952 on line 10a of Form 4952.

● If there is not an entry on line 20a(1) and you do not have investment interest expense on indebtedness incurred before 12/17/69, combine the amount on line 20b with your other investment income (loss) from all sources and enter the result (but not less than zero) on line 10a of Form 4952.

Lines 21a–21g. Foreign Taxes. Use the information on lines 21a through 21g to figure your foreign tax credit. For more information, see: **Form 1116**, Computation of Foreign Tax Credit—Individual, Fiduciary, or Nonresident Alien Individual, and the related instructions; or **Form 1118**, Computation of Foreign Tax Credit—Corporations, and the related instructions.

Line 22. Property Eligible for Investment Credit. Your share of the partnership's investment in property that qualifies for the investment credit should be entered. You can claim a tax credit based on your pro rata share of this investment by filing **Form 3468**, Computation of Investment Credit. (For other information, see Form 3468 and the related instructions.)

Lines 22a–22d. The partnership will give you a schedule that identifies, on a line-by-line basis, property on which it has reduced the basis and property on which it has elected to take a reduced credit. Report the amounts on Form 3468, line 1 as follows:

● Property on which the basis has been reduced. Enter the amount shown on: line 22a on line 1(a); line 22b on line 1(b); line 22c on line 1(c); and line 22d on line 1(d).

● Property on which an election has been made to take a reduced credit. Enter the amount shown on: line 22a on line 1(e); line 22b on line 1(f); line 22c on line 1(g); and line 22d on line 1(h).

In addition to the qualifying property reported on line 22, the partnership will give you a separate schedule that shows your share of the partnership's investment in energy property that qualifies for the credit, and where to report it.

Line 23. Property Subject to Recapture of Investment Credit. When investment credit property is disposed of or ceases to qualify before the "life-years category" or "recovery period" assigned, you will be notified. You may have to recapture (pay back) the investment credit taken in prior years. Use the information on line 23 to figure your recapture tax on **Form 4255**, Recapture of Investment Credit. See Form 3468 on which you took the original credit for other information you need to complete Form 4255.

You may also need Form 4255 if you disposed of more than one-third of your interest in a partnership. See **Publication 572**, Investment Credit, for more information.

B–8   FORM 2106   EMPLOYEE BUSINESS EXPENSES

Form **2106**	**Employee Business Expenses**	OMB No. 1545-0139
Department of the Treasury Internal Revenue Service	(Please use Form 3903 to figure moving expense deduction.) ▶ **Attach to Form 1040.**	**1983** 54

Your name	Social security number	Occupation in which expenses were incurred
Employer's name	Employer's address	

PART I.—Employee Business Expenses Deductible in Figuring Adjusted Gross Income on Form 1040, Line 32

1 Reimbursed and unreimbursed fares for airplane, boat, bus, taxicab, train, etc..	1	
2 Reimbursed and unreimbursed meal, lodging, and other expenses while away from your tax home. .	2	
3 Reimbursed and unreimbursed car expenses from Part II.	3	
4 Reimbursed and unreimbursed outside salesperson's expenses other than those shown on lines 1 through 3. **Caution:** *Do not use this line unless you are an outside salesperson (see instructions)*		

---	4	
5 Reimbursed expenses other than those shown on lines 1 through 3 (see instructions)	5	
6 Add lines 1 through 5	6	
7 Employer's payments for these expenses only if not included on Form W-2	7	
8 If line 6 is more than line 7, subtract line 7 from line 6. Enter here and on Form 1040, line 24 . .	8	
9 If line 7 is more than line 6, subtract line 6 from line 7. Enter here and on Form 1040, line 7 . .	9	

PART II.—Car Expenses (Use either your actual expenses or the mileage rate.)

	Car 1	Car 2	Car 3
A. Number of months you used car for business during 1983 .	_____ months	_____ months	_____ months
B. Total mileage for months on line A	_____ miles	_____ miles	_____ miles
C. Business part of line B mileage	_____ miles	_____ miles	_____ miles

Actual Expenses (Include expenses on lines 1 and 2 only for the months shown on line A, above.)

		Car 1	Car 2	Car 3
1 Gasoline, oil, lubrication, etc.	1			
2 Other	2			
3 Total (add lines 1 and 2)	3			
4 Divide line C by line B, above	4	%	%	%
5 Multiply line 3 by line 4	5			
6 Depreciation (see instructions)	6			
7 Section 179 deduction (see instructions)	7			
8 Business parking fees and tolls	8			
9 Total (add lines 5 through 8). Enter here and in Part I, line 3	9			

Mileage Rate

10 Enter the smaller of (a) 15,000 miles or (b) the total mileage (Car 1+ Car 2+ Car 3) from line C, above	10	miles
11 Multiply line 10 by 20½¢ (11¢ if applicable, see instructions)	11	
12 Enter the total mileage, if any (Car 1 + Car 2 + Car 3) from line C that is over 15,000 miles	12	miles
13 Multiply line 12 by 11¢ and enter here	13	
14 Business part of car interest, parking fees, tolls, and State and local taxes (except gasoline tax) . .	14	
15 Total (add lines 11, 13, and 14). Enter here and in Part I, line 3	15	

PART III.—Information About Educational Expenses Shown in Part I or on Schedule A (Form 1040)

1 Did you need this education to meet the basic requirements for your business or profession?   . . . . ☐ Yes   ☐ No

2 Will this study program qualify you for a new business or profession?   . . . . ☐ Yes   ☐ No

    Note: *If your answer to question 1 or 2 is ''Yes,'' stop here. You cannot deduct these expenses, even if you do not intend to change your business or profession.*

3 If ''No,'' list the courses you took and their relationship to your business or profession ▶ _____

For Paperwork Reduction Act Notice, see instructions on back.	Form **2106** (1983)

General Instructions

Paperwork Reduction Act Notice.—We ask for this information to carry out the Internal Revenue laws of the United States. We need it to ensure that taxpayers are complying with these laws and to allow us to figure and collect the right amount of tax. You are required to give us this information.

Purpose of Form.—This form is used to show employee business expenses. Use this form or a similar statement if you **are not an outside salesperson** and have reimbursed or unreimbursed transportation, travel away from home, and car expenses and other expenses that are reimbursed, or if you **are an outside salesperson** and have reimbursed and unreimbursed business expenses. You do not have to use this form or similar statement if you were required to and did account to your employer and any of the following apply to you:

● Expenses are equal to the total of your reimbursements and allowances,

● Expenses are more than the total of your reimbursements and allowances and you do not deduct the excess expenses, or

● Expenses are less than your reimbursements and allowances and your employer does not include the total reimbursements and allowances on Form W-2. In this case, include the amount by which the reimbursements and allowances are more than your expenses on line 7, Form 1040.

Also, complete and file Form 2106 if you have deductible educational expenses. See the instructions for Part III.

Expenses to include.—Only include expenses you paid or incurred in 1983 in connection with services you performed as an employee.

Outside salesperson.—You are an outside salesperson if you do your selling away from your employer's place of business. **You are not** an outside salesperson if your main duties are service and delivery or if you are required to sell at your employer's place of business.

Accounting to your employer.— This is giving your employer documentary evidence and an account book, diary, or similar record in which you entered each expense at or near the time you made it.

Tax home.—Generally, your tax home is your main place of business or post of duty, regardless of where you maintain your family home.

Publications.—See the following publications for more information about employee business expenses and the records you must keep: **Publication 463**, Travel, Entertainment, and Gift Expenses. **Publication 508**, Educational Expenses. **Publication 529**, Miscellaneous Deductions. **Publication 534**, Depreciation. **Publication 587**, Business Use of Your Home.

Specific Instructions

Part I

Line 1.—Fares include fares for local business transportation as well as fares for business travel away from home. **Do not include** fares for commuting to and from work. Also include tips, baggage charges, charges for transporting sample and display material, and similar expenses.

Line 2.—Other expenses include tips, cleaning and laundry, telephone and telegraph, public stenographer's fees, and similar expenses.

Standard meal allowance.—Instead of actual cost, you generally may include your expenses for meals at $14 a day when you are in a general area less than 30 days and at $9 a day if you are in a general area 30 days or more. For more information, see Publication 463.

Line 4.—Include all your expenses not shown on lines 1 through 3. These include entertainment, gift, publications, and similar expenses and expenses for employment-related education, such as tuition, books, supplies, lab fees, etc. See the instructions for Part III.

Line 5.—Include reimbursed expenses other than those shown on lines 1 through 3 (see line 4 instructions). **Do not use** this line for reimbursed outside salesperson expenses. If you were reimbursed in full, enter the total expenses. If you were partially reimbursed, enter the expenses to the extent of the reimbursement. Enter any excess expenses on Schedule A (Form 1040), line 24. If you received a partial reimbursement that was intended to cover all expenses described on lines 1, 2, 3, and 5 without specifying the amount for each expense, use the formula in Publication 463 to figure the amount to enter.

Part II

Generally, you may figure your car expenses using either:

a. The **actual cost** of your car expenses (such as gas, oil, repairs, depreciation, section 179 deduction, etc.); or

b. The **standard mileage rate** which gives you a fixed deduction per business mile. **Do not use** this method if any of the following apply:

● The car is leased or used for hire;

● More than one car is used in your business at a time;

● You take a section 179 deduction on line 7;

● You figured depreciation in an earlier year using ACRS (Accelerated Cost Recovery System) or a method other than straight-line; or

● You took additional first-year depreciation.

If you are eligible to use the standard mileage rate, you may want to figure your deduction under both methods and use whichever one gives you the larger deduction.

Note: *If you use the standard mileage rate, you cannot use ACRS for that car.*

Actual Expenses

Line 2.—Include on this line your actual expenses for repairs, tires, supplies, insurance, taxes, tags, licenses, interest, etc.

Line 6.—The method of depreciation you may use depends on when you started using your car (placed the car in service). Do not deduct depreciation in excess of your basis or if your car is fully depreciated.

Cars placed in service before 1981 or for which standard mileage was used.—If you used either straight-line depreciation or the standard mileage rate in earlier years, you may use either straight-line depreciation or the standard mileage rate this year. If you used a method of depreciation other than straight-line, continue to use that method. If you want to change to straight-line depreciation or to another method of depreciation, see Publication 534. You cannot change to ACRS.

Percentage of business use.— If line A shows 12 months, multiply the amount of depreciation for the entire year by the percentage on line 4. If line A shows less than 12 months, multiply the resulting amount from the preceding sentence by the percentage arrived at by dividing the months on line A by 12. Enter the appropriate amount on line 6.

Cars placed in service after 1980.—If you placed a car in service after 1980 and you do not use the standard mileage rate, you must use one of two methods for figuring depreciation under ACRS:

● One ACRS method lets you deduct the following percentages of the business cost or other basis of your car regardless of what month you placed the car in service—

1st year—25%
2nd year—38%
3rd year—37%

● The other ACRS method allows you to use a straight-line method over a recovery period of 3, 5, or 12 years with the half-year convention.

Do not consider salvage value in either of the ACRS methods.

Percentage of business use.—If you use ACRS, divide business miles by total miles for the year. If line A shows less than 12 months and you were not an employee all year, multiply the percentage on line 4 by the months on line A and divide by 12. If you sell (not trade) or stop using your car for business before the end of the year, line 6 is zero for that car.

Multiply the unadjusted basis of your car (generally cost) minus any amount on line 7, minus half of any investment credit you take in 1983 (unless you take the reduced credit) by the percentage determined above. Multiply the resulting amount by the ACRS percentage for the year and enter on line 6.

Investment credit.—If you placed a car in service during 1983, use **Form 3468**, Computation of Investment Credit, to determine the amount of investment credit you can take. If you take the investment credit, you will have to reduce your depreciation basis by ½ of the credit, unless you take the reduced investment credit.

Line 7.—You may deduct the cost related to the percentage of business use of your car up to $5,000 ($2,500 if you are married filing a separate return). This is the total section 179 deduction allowed for all property. Reduce the basis by the amount claimed. See Publication 534.

Mileage Rate

Use 20½¢ a mile for the first 15,000 miles of business use a year. Use 11¢ a mile for each mile over 15,000 business miles a year. You must also use 11¢ a mile if your car is fully depreciated. Generally, a car placed in service after 1979 is considered fully depreciated after 60,000 miles of business use at the maximum standard mileage rate.

Line 14.—The business part of parking and tolls is the amount you paid or incurred for business purposes. To figure the business part of interest and State and local taxes (except gasoline taxes) multiply the total of these items by the percentage you get by dividing line C by line B. For more information on the standard mileage rate, see Publication 463.

Part III

If you show educational expenses in Part I or on Schedule A (Form 1040), complete Part III.

You can deduct the cost of education that helps you keep or improve your skills for your business or profession. This includes education that your employer, the law, or regulations require you to get in order to keep your job or your salary. Do not deduct the cost of study that helps you meet the basic requirements for your business or profession or qualifies you for a new business or profession even if you do not intend to change to a new business or profession.

B–9   FORM 2119   SALE OR EXCHANGE OF PRINCIPAL RESIDENCE

Form **2119**	**Sale or Exchange of Principal Residence**	OMB No. 1545–0072
Department of the Treasury Internal Revenue Service	▶ See instructions on back. ▶ Attach to Form 1040 for year of sale (see instruction C).	**19****83** 22

Do not include expenses that you deduct as moving expenses.

Name(s) as shown on Form 1040.	Your social security number

1 (a) Date former residence sold ▶

(b) Enter the face amount of any mortgage, note (for example, second trust), or other financial instrument on which you will receive periodic payments of principal or interest from this sale ▶

2 (a) If you bought or built a new residence, enter date you occupied it; otherwise enter "none".

(b) Are any rooms in either residence rented out or used for business for which a deduction is allowed? . . . . . ☐ Yes ☐ No
(If "Yes" do not include gain in line 7 from the rented or business part; instead include in income on Form 4797.)

PART I.—Gain and Adjusted Sales Price

3 Selling price of residence. (Do not include selling price of personal property items.)	**3**
4 Commissions and other expenses of sale not deducted as moving expenses	**4**
5 Amount realized (subtract line 4 from line 3)	**5**
6 Basis of residence sold **6**	
7 Gain on sale (subtract line 6 from line 5). (If line 6 is more than line 5, enter zero and do not complete the rest of form.) If you bought another principal residence during the replacement period or if you elect the one time exclusion in Part III, continue with this form. Otherwise, enter the gain on Schedule D, line 2 or 10*. **7**	
If you haven't replaced your residence, do you plan to do so within the replacement period?. . ☐ Yes ☐ No (If "Yes" see instruction C.) .	
8 Fixing-up expenses (see instructions for time limits.)	**8**
9 Adjusted sales price (subtract line 8 from line 5)	**9**

PART II.—Gain to be Postponed and Adjusted Basis of New Residence

Do not complete this part if you check Yes to 14(d) to elect the Age 55 or over Exclusion in Part III.

10 Cost of new residence.	**10**
11 Gain taxable this year. (If line 9 is more than line 10, subtract line 10 from line 9. Do not enter more than line 7. Enter the gain from line 11 on Schedule D, line 2 or 10.*) (If line 10 is more than line 9, enter zero.) . . .	**11**
12 Gain to be postponed (subtract line 11 from line 7)	**12**
13 Adjusted basis of new residence (subtract line 12 from line 10)	**13**

PART III.—55 or over Exclusion, Gain to be Reported, and Adjusted Basis of New Residence

		Yes	No
14 (a)	Were you 55 or over on date of sale?.		
(b)	Was your spouse 55 or over on date of sale? . . . . (If you answered "No" to 14(a) and (b), do not complete this part.)		
(c)	Did the one who answered "Yes" to 14(a) or (b) own and use the property sold as his or her principal residence for a total of at least 3 years (except for short absences) of the 5-year period before the sale? . . . . (If "No," see Part II.)		
(d)	If you answered "Yes" to 14(c), do you elect to take the once in a lifetime exclusion of the gain on the sale?. . . . (If "Yes," complete the rest of Part III. If "No," see Part II.)		
(e)	At time of sale, was the residence owned by: ☐ you, ☐ your spouse, ☐ both of you?		
(f)	Social security number of spouse, at time of sale, if different from number on Form 1040 ▶ (Enter "none" if you were not married at time of sale.)		

15 Enter the smaller of line 7 or $125,000 ($62,500, if married filing separate return)	**15**
16 Part of gain included (subtract line 15 from line 7) (If the result is zero, do not complete the rest of form.) . .	**16**
17 Cost of new residence. If you did not buy a new principal residence, enter "None." Then enter the gain from line 16 on Schedule D, line 10,* and do not complete the rest of form	**17**
18 Gain taxable this year. (If line 9 is more than line 15 plus line 17, subtract line 15 plus line 17 from line 9. Do not enter more than line 16. *Enter the gain from line 18 on Schedule D, line 10.*) (If line 15 plus line 17 is more than line 9, enter zero.)	**18**
19 Gain to be postponed (subtract line 18 from line 16)	**19**
20 Adjusted basis of new residence (subtract line 19 from line 17)	**20**

***Caution:** If you completed Form 6252 for the residence in 1(a), do not enter your taxable gain from Form 2119 on Schedule D.

For Paperwork Reduction Act Notice, see back of form.   Form **2119** (1983)

Instructions

Paperwork Reduction Act Notice.—We ask for this information to carry out the Internal Revenue laws of the United States. We need it to ensure that taxpayers are complying with these laws and to allow us to figure and collect the right amount of tax. You are required to give us this information.

A. Purpose of Form.—Use Form 2119 to report gain from selling your principal residence, whether or not you buy another. A loss is not deductible. Use this form to postpone gain or make the one-time election to exclude it from your income.

Report any taxable gain on **Schedule D (Form 1040),** Capital Gains and Losses. However, if you sold your residence on the installment method, complete **Form 6252,** Computation of Installment Sale Income, in addition to Form 2119.

For more information, **see Publication 523,** Tax Information on Selling Your Home.

Principal Residence.—Postponement or exclusion of gain applies only to the sale of your principal residence. Usually, the home where you live is your principal residence. It can be for example, a house, houseboat, housetrailer, cooperative apartment, or condominium. If you have more than one residence, your principal residence is the one you physically occupy most of the time.

B. Postponing Gain on Sale of Principal Residence.—Unless you elect to exclude the gain in Part III, you may have to postpone it if you buy or build, and occupy another principal residence within 2 years before or after the sale.

If, after you sell your old residence, you are on active duty in the U.S. Armed Forces for more than 90 days, or you live and work outside the U.S., that time is not counted in figuring your replacement period. *However, this replacement period cannot extend beyond 4 years after the date of sale.*

If you sell the new residence in a later year and do not replace it, the postponed gain will be taxed then. If you do replace it, you may continue to postpone the gain. If you change your principal residence more than once during the replacement period, only the last residence you bought qualifies as your new residence for postponing gain, unless you sold the residence because of a job relocation and are allowed a moving expense deduction.

C. When to File.—File Form 2119 for the year of sale whether or not you replaced your principal residence.

In the following cases file 2 Forms 2119:

If you plan to replace your residence but have not done so by the time you file your return, and the replacement period has not expired, attach Form 2119 to Form 1040 for the year of sale, but complete lines 1 through 7 only. In that case, do not include the gain on Schedule D. If you replace it after you file your return, within the replacement period, and the new residence costs as much as the adjusted sales price of your old residence, write to notify the Director of the Internal Revenue Service Center where you filed your return. Attach a new Form 2119 for the year of sale.

If you replace your residence after you file your return, within the replacement period, and the new one costs less than the adjusted sales price of the old one, or you do not replace it within the replacement period, file **Form 1040X,** Amended U.S. Individual Income Tax Return, with a Schedule D and a new Form 2119 for the year of sale. Show the gain then. Interest will be charged on the additional tax due.

If you paid tax on the gain from selling your old residence and then buy a new one within the replacement period, file Form 1040X with Form 2119 to claim a refund.

D. Excluding Gain from Income.—You can elect to exclude from your income part or all of the gain from the sale of your principal residence if you meet the following tests:

1. You were 55 or over on the date of the sale.

2. Neither you nor your spouse has already elected this exclusion after July 26, 1978.

3. You owned and occupied your residence for periods totaling at least 3 years within the 5 years ending on the date of sale.

The exclusion election is a once-in-a-lifetime election, so you may choose not to make it now.

The gain excluded from your income is never taxed. The rest of your gain is taxed in the year of sale, unless you replace the residence and postpone that part of the gain. Generally, you can make or revoke the exclusion election within 3 years from the date the return for the year you sold the residence was due, including extensions. Use Form 1040X to amend your return.

Married Taxpayers.—If you and your spouse own the property jointly and file a joint return, only one of you must meet the age, ownership, and use tests for electing the exclusion. If you do not own the property jointly, only the owner must meet these tests, regardless of your filing status on Form 1040.

If you are married at the time of sale, both you and your spouse must make the election to exclude the gain. If you do not file a joint return with that spouse, that spouse must consent to the election by writing in the bottom margin of Form 2119 or on an attached statement, "I consent to Part III election," and signing.

The election does not apply separately to you and your spouse. If you and your spouse make an election during marriage and later divorce, no further elections are available to either of you or to your new spouse if you remarry.

E. Applying Separate Gain to Basis of New Residence.—If you own the old residence separately, but you and your spouse own the new residence jointly (or vice versa) you and your spouse may elect to divide the gain and the adjusted basis if both of you:

1. use the old and new residences as your principal residence; and

2. sign a consent that says, "We consent to reduce the basis of the new residence by the gain from selling the old residence." Write this statement in the bottom margin of Form 2119 or on an attached sheet, and sign it. If you both do not sign the consent, determine the recognition of gain in the regular way with no division.

Line-By-Line Instructions

Use Parts I and II to figure the gain that must be postponed. Complete Parts I and III if you elect the one-time exclusion.

Line 3. Selling Price of Residence.—Enter the amount of money you received, the amount of all notes, mortgages, or other liabilities to which the property was subject, and the fair market value of any other property you received.

Note: *Report interest from a note as income for the tax year in which the interest is received.*

Line 4. Commissions and Other Expenses of Sale.—This includes sales commissions, advertising expenses, attorney and legal fees, etc., incurred in order to sell the old residence. Loan charges, such as "loan placement fees" or "points" charged the seller are selling expenses. Do not include amounts deducted as moving expenses.

Line 6. Basis of Residence Sold.—Include the original cost of the property, commissions, and other expenses incurred in buying it, plus the cost of improvements. Subtract any depreciation allowed or allowable, any casualty loss or energy credit you took on the residence, and the postponed gain on the sale or exchange of a previous principal residence. For more information, see **Publication 551,** Basis of Assets.

Line 8. Fixing-up Expenses.—These are decorating and repair expenses incurred only to help sell the old property. You must have incurred them for work performed within 90 days before the contract to sell was signed, and paid for within 30 days after the sale. Do not include capital expenditures for permanent improvements or replacements that are added to the basis of the property sold.

Lines 10 and 17. Cost of New Residence.—The cost of your new residence includes one or more of the following:

(a) cash payments;

(b) the amount of any mortgage or other debt on the new residence;

(c) commissions and other purchase expenses you paid that were not deducted as moving expenses;

(d) construction costs (when you build your own residence) made within 2 years before and 2 years after the sale of the old residence;

(e) if you buy rather than build your new residence, all capital expenditures made within 2 years before and 2 years after the sale of the old residence.

B–10   FORM 2120   MULTIPLE SUPPORT DECLARATION

Form **2120** (Rev. Sept. 1981)	Department of the Treasury—Internal Revenue Service **Multiple Support Declaration**	OMB No. 1545-0071 Expires 8-31-84

During the calendar year 19............, I paid more than 10% of the support of

....**.**
(Name of person)

I could have claimed this person as a dependent except that I did not pay more than 50% of his or her support.

I understand that this person is being claimed as a dependent on the income tax return of ....
(Name)

...., and
(Address)

I agree not to claim an exemption for this person on my Federal income tax return for any tax year beginning in this calendar year.

....
(Your signature)   (Your social security number)

....
(Date)   (Address)

For Paperwork Reduction Act Notice, see back of form.

Instructions

Paperwork Reduction Act Notice.—The Paperwork Reduction Act of 1980 says we must tell you why we are collecting this information, how we will use it, and whether you have to give it to us. We ask for the information to carry out the Internal Revenue laws of the United States. We need it to ensure that you are complying with these laws and to allow us to figure and collect the right amount of tax. You are required to give us this information.

If two or more persons together paid more than 50% of the support of an individual for a calendar year and each could claim that person as a dependent except that they did not individually pay more than 50% of the support, one of the contributors can claim the person as a dependent if:

(1) the taxpayer claiming the person as a dependent paid more than 10% of the support, and

(2) each contributor (other than the taxpayer claiming the dependent) who paid more than 10% of the support of the dependent agrees not to claim that person as a dependent for any tax year beginning in that calendar year.

Each person (other than the taxpayer claiming the dependent) who paid more than 10% of the support of the dependent must complete this declaration and give it to the taxpayer claiming the dependent, who in turn must file the declarations with his or her return.

The taxpayer claiming an exemption for the dependent should be prepared to support the right to claim the exemption if requested.

☆U.S. G.P.O. 1981–343-224   E.I. 43-0787267

B–11 FORM 2210 UNDERPAYMENT OF ESTIMATED TAX BY INDIVIDUALS

Form **2210** Department of the Treasury Internal Revenue Service	**Underpayment of Estimated Tax by Individuals** ▶ See instructions on back ▶ Attach to Form 1040	OMB No. 1545-0140 **1983** 56

Name(s) as shown on Form 1040	Social security number

PART I.—Figuring Your Underpayment

**If you received interest and dividend income after June 30, 1983, and underpaid your April or June installment, check this box ▶ ☐
(See instructions under Interest and Dividend Income.)**

1	1983 tax (from Form 1040, line 56)	1
2	Add the amounts on lines 51, 53, 54, 59, and 62, Form 1040. Also add tax on an IRA from Part I or III, Form 5329, reported on line 55, Form 1040. Write the total here	2
3	Subtract line 2 from line 1	3
4	Add the amounts on lines 57 and 61, Form 1040. (Also add amount from Form 6249. See instructions.) Write the total here	4
5	Subtract line 4 from line 3. (If less than $300, stop here; do not complete the rest of this form.)	5
6	Multiply the amount on line 3 by .80 (80%) and enter result here	6

		Payment Due Dates			
		(a) Apr. 15, 1983	(b) June 15, 1983	(c) Sept. 15, 1983	(d) Jan. 15, 1984
7	Divide amount on line 6 by the number of payments required for the year (usually four). Enter the result in appropriate columns				
8	Estimated tax paid and tax withheld (see instructions)				
9	Overpayment (see instructions)				
10	Add lines 8 and 9				
11	Underpayment. (Subtract line 10 from line 7.) **OR** Overpayment. (Subtract line 7 from line 10.)				

PART II.—Exceptions to the Penalty

12	Total amount paid and withheld from January 1 through payment due date shown. (Do not include withholding after Dec. 31, 1983.)				
13	Exception 1.—(See instructions.) ▶ Enter 1982 tax	$ 25% of 1982 tax:	50% of 1982 tax:	75% of 1982 tax:	100% of 1982 tax:
14	Exception 2.—Tax on 1982 income using 1983 rates and exemptions. (See instructions and attach computation.)	Enter 25% of tax:	Enter 50% of tax:	Enter 75% of tax:	Enter 100% of tax:
15	Exception 3.—Tax on annualized 1983 income. (See instructions and attach computation.)	Enter 20% of tax:	Enter 40% of tax:	Enter 60% of tax:	Exceptions Do Not Apply
16	Exception 4.—Tax on 1983 income over 3-, 5-, and 8-month periods. (See worksheet on back.)	Enter 90% of tax:	Enter 90% of tax:	Enter 90% of tax:	

PART III.—Figuring the Penalty (Complete for any underpayment to which no exception applies.)

17 a	Number of days after payment due date through the date of payment or June 30, 1983, whichever is earlier. If June 30 is earlier, enter 76 and 15 respectively				
b	Number of days after payment due date or June 30, 1983, whichever is later, through date of payment or December 31, 1983, whichever is earlier. If December 31 is earlier, enter 184, 184, and 107 respectively				
c	Number of days after payment due date or December 31, 1983, whichever is later, through date of payment or April 15, 1984, whichever is earlier. If April 15 is earlier, enter 106, 106, 106, and 91 respectively				
18 a	$\dfrac{\text{Number of days on line 17a}}{365}$ × 16% × underpayment on line 11				
b	$\dfrac{\text{Number of days on line 17b}}{365}$ × 11% × underpayment on line 11				
c	$\dfrac{\text{Number of days on line 17c}}{366}$ × 11% × underpayment on line 11				

19	Penalty (add amounts on lines 18a, b, and c). Check the box below line 68 on Form 1040 and show this amount in the space provided. If you owe tax, add penalty to tax and show total on line 68. If you are due a refund, subtract penalty from overpayment on line 65	19

For Paperwork Reduction Act Notice, see back of form.   Form **2210** (1983)

B–12 FORM 2440 DISABILITY INCOME EXCLUSION

Form **2440**	**Disability Income Exclusion**	OMB No. 1545-0069
Department of the Treasury Internal Revenue Service	**(Applies Only to Disabled Retirees Under Age 65)** ▶ Attach to Form 1040. ▶ See instructions on back.	**1983** **23**

Name(s) as shown on Form 1040	Social security number

See Line 4 Instructions for Income Limits on Exclusion

Date you retired (if after December 31, 1976, also enter this date in the space after box (2) on physician's statement below)	Employer's name (also give payer's name, if other than employer)
Yourself	
Spouse	

Note: *To take the disability income exclusion, you must complete lines 1 through 5.*

Joint return filers use column (a) for wife and column (b) for husband. All other filers use column (b) only.

	(a)	(b)
1 Enter total disability pay you received during 1983		
2 Excludable disability pay (see instructions):		
(i) Multiply $100 by the number of weeks for which your disability payments were at least $100. Enter total		
(ii) If you received disability payments of less than $100 for any week, enter the total amount you received for all such weeks		
(iii) If you received disability payments for less than a week, enter the smaller amount of either the amount you received or the highest exclusion allowable for the period (see instructions)		
(iv) Add lines (i), (ii), and (iii). Enter total		
3 Add amounts on line 2(iv), columns (a) and (b). Enter total		
4 Limit on exclusion (see instructions):		
(i) Enter total income from Form 1040, line 22		
(ii) Add amounts on Form 1040, lines 23 through 28 and any write-in adjustments on line 31. Enter total		
(iii) Subtract line (ii) from line (i)		
(iv) Amount used to figure any exclusion decrease	$15,000.00	
(v) Subtract line (iv) from line (iii). If line (iv) is more than line (iii), enter zero		
5 Subtract line 4(v) from line 3. This is your disability income exclusion. Enter here and on Form 1040, line 30		

6 If you filed a physician's statement for this disability in an earlier year, please check this box. ▶ ☐ You do not have to file another statement. If you have not, you must file a physician's statement (see below).

For Paperwork Reduction Act Notice, see instructions on back.   Form **2440** (1983)

Physician's Statement of Permanent and Total Disability
▶ Please complete and return to taxpayer.

Name of disabled taxpayer	Social security number

I certify that the taxpayer named above was (check only one box—please see instructions below):

(1) ☐ Permanently and totally disabled on January 1, 1976, or January 1, 1977

(2) ☐ Permanently and totally disabled on the date he or she retired. Date retired ▶

Physician's name

Physician's address

Physician's signature   Date

Instructions for Statement

Taxpayer

Please enter your name and social security number. If you retired after December 31, 1976, enter your retirement date in the space after box (2).

Physician

Box (1) applies to taxpayers who retired before January 1, 1977.

Box (2) applies to taxpayers who retired after December 31, 1976.

What is Permanent and Total Disability?

A person is permanently and totally disabled when—

● He or she cannot engage in any substantial gainful activity because of a physical or mental condition; and

● A physician determines that the disability (a) has lasted or can be expected to last continuously for at least a year; or (b) can be expected to lead to death.

General Instructions

Paperwork Reduction Act Notice.—The Paperwork Reduction Act of 1980 says we must tell you why we are collecting this information, how we will use it, and whether you have to give it to us. We ask for the information to carry out the Internal Revenue laws of the United States. We need it to ensure that you are complying with these laws and to allow us to figure and collect the right amount of tax. You are required to give us this information.

A. Purpose.—If you retired on disability, you must include all of your disability income on Form 1040, line 7 (see Instruction D for exception). However, you may be able to exclude part of it from the income on which you are taxed. To do that, you must meet the tests explained below. For details, please see **Publication 522**, Disability Payments.

B. Who Can Exclude Disability Income.—You can take the exclusion for 1982 if you meet ALL these tests:

- You got disability pay.
- You were not yet 65 when your tax year ended.
- You retired on disability and were permanently and totally disabled when you retired. (See Instruction C, **What is Permanent and Total Disability?**) (See also instructions for **Physician's Statement.**)
- On January 1, 1982, you had not yet reached the age when your employer's retirement program would have required you to retire.
- You did not let IRS know that you chose to treat your disability income as a pension instead of taking the exclusion. (See Instruction D.)
- If you were married at the end of 1982, you must file a joint return. (This rule does not apply if you did not live with your spouse at any time in 1982. If this is the case, write on the Spouse line on page 1, "I did not live with my spouse during the tax year.")

If you meet these tests, you can take the exclusion until the earliest of the following dates:

(1) The first day of the tax year in which you turn 65.

(2) The first day of the tax year for which you choose to treat your disability income as a pension. (See Instruction D.)

(3) The day you reach the age when your employer's retirement program would have required you to retire.

C. What is Permanent and Total Disability?—A person is permanently and totally disabled when:

- He or she cannot engage in any substantial gainful activity because of a physical or mental condition; and
- A physician determines that the condition (1) has lasted or can be expected to last continuously for at least a year; or (2) can be expected to lead to death.

The examples below show substantial gainful activity. In such cases, the disability income exclusion cannot be taken.

Example (1): Bob worked at a hotel as a desk clerk. After retiring on disability, he got a desk clerk job at another hotel. Bob does all the duties of the job and is paid more than the minimum wage. Because Bob does the job on the same terms as the other desk clerks and is paid more than the minimum wage, he is considered engaged in a substantial gainful activity. He cannot take the disability income exclusion.

Example (2): Sue retired on disability as a sales clerk. She now works as a full-time babysitter for more than the minimum wage. Even though Sue does different work, she babysits on ordinary terms for more than the minimum wage. She cannot take the disability income exclusion.

Example (3): Mary, president of the XYZ Corporation, retired on disability because of terminal illness. However, her doctor advised her to work part time. She now works for another company as a part-time manager. She is paid more than the minimum wage and the employer sets her days and hours. Even though Mary's illness is terminal and she works part time, she is considered engaged in a substantial gainful activity. She cannot take the exclusion.

Example (4): Jane retired on disability and now works at an easier job in a full-time competitive work situation. She earns half of what she used to, but is paid more than the minimum wage. She is considered engaged in a substantial gainful activity. She cannot take the exclusion.

The following example shows a person who might not be considered to be engaged in a substantial gainful activity.

Example: John, who retired on disability, took a job with a former employer on a trial basis. The purpose of the job was to see if John could do the work. The trial period lasted for some time during which John was paid at a rate equal to the minimum wage. However, because of John's disability only light duties of a nonproductive make-work nature were given him. Unless the activity is both substantial and gainful, John is not engaged in substantial gainful activity. The activity was gainful because John was paid at a rate at or above the minimum wage. However, the activity was not substantial because the duties were of a nonproductive, make-work nature. Therefore, these facts do not, by themselves, establish John's ability to engage in substantial gainful activity.

D. Treating Disability Income as a Pension.—Instead of taking the exclusion, you can choose to treat your disability income as a pension. If you do, you cannot take the disability income exclusion in any later year.

It may help you more not to take the exclusion, but to treat the income as a pension instead. This may be so if:

(1) The income limits in line 4 lower your exclusion; or

(2) You reached minimum retirement age in 1982 and can take a **Credit for the Elderly** under the Schedule RP (Form 1040) rules; or

(3) Because of your condition, you do not expect to live long enough to recover the tax-free part (your cost) of the pension.

To treat your disability income as a pension, attach to your Form 1040 a statement that:

- You are eligible to take the exclusion; and
- You choose to treat the income as a pension and will not take the exclusion.

You must also attach a physician's statement (described in Specific Instructions) if you have not submitted one.

For more information, see instructions for Form 1040, line 17.

〜〜〜〜〜〜〜〜〜〜〜〜〜〜〜〜〜〜〜〜〜〜

Specific Instructions

Lines 2(i) and (ii).—You can exclude either your actual weekly disability pay or $100 a week, whichever is less. This table shows how to figure your weekly disability pay.

Pay period	Your weekly pay is the following part of what you receive each pay period
Weekly	All
Every 2 weeks . .	Half
Twice a month . .	Multiply your pay by 24, and divide the result by 52
Each month . . .	Multiply your pay by 12, and divide the result by 52
Other	Divide your yearly pay by 52

Line 2(iii).—If you received disability pay for part of a week, follow the steps below.

Step 1. Divide $100 by the number of days a week you normally worked before you retired.

Step 2. Divide the disability pay you got by the number of days it covered in that week.

Step 3. Compare the Step 1 and Step 2 amounts. The smaller amount is your daily rate. Your exclusion for the week is based on it.

Step 4. Multiply your daily rate by the number of days you received disability pay in the short week. The result is your exclusion for that week.

Step 5. Add your exclusion for that week to your exclusion for any other short weeks. Enter the total on line 2(iii).

Disability payments are made for part of a week when one of the following happens after the first day of the taxpayer's normal workweek:

(1) The disability retirement begins.

(2) The disability retirement ends because the taxpayer reaches required retirement age.

(3) The taxpayer dies.

Line 4.—Generally, the most a person can exclude is $5,200. This exclusion goes down, dollar for dollar, by any amount over $15,000 on line 4(iii). That line shows your adjusted gross income before you take the deduction for a married couple when both work and the disability income exclusion.

Generally, no exclusion is left if line 4(iii) is—

- $20,200 or more, and one person could take the exclusion.
- $25,400 or more, and both husband and wife could take the exclusion.

Treating your disability income as a pension may help you more than taking the exclusion. (See Instruction D.)

Physician's Statement.—Attach to Form 2440 a physician's statement of permanent and total disability. You can use the physician's statement on Form 2440 for this purpose. Please take it off the form and have your physician fill it in. Be sure to attach the completed statement to Form 2440 and file it with your tax return.

If both husband and wife take the exclusion, each must file a statement. If you filed a statement for the disability in an earlier year, do not file another. Instead, check the box on line 6 of Form 2440.

If you retired on disability before January 1, 1977, the physician's statement must show that you were permanently and totally disabled on January 1, 1976, or January 1, 1977.

If you retired on disability after 1976, the physician's statement must show that you were permanently and totally disabled when you retired.

If the Veterans Administration certifies that you are permanently and totally disabled, you can file Form 6004 instead of the physician's statement. Form 6004 must be signed by a physician on the VA disability rating board. You can get Form 6004 from the Veterans Administration.

B–13 FORM 2441 CREDIT FOR CHILD AND DEPENDENT CARE EXPENSES

Form **2441**	**Credit for Child and Dependent Care Expenses**	OMB No. 1545-0068
Department of the Treasury Internal Revenue Service	▶ Attach to Form 1040. ▶ See Instructions below.	19**83** 24

Name(s) as shown on Form 1040 — Your social security number

1 Write the number of qualifying persons who were cared for in 1983. (See the instructions below for the definition of qualifying persons.) ▶

2 If payments listed on line 3 were made to an individual, complete the following: — **Yes** | **No**
   a If you paid $50 or more in a calendar quarter to an individual, were the services performed in your home?
   b If "Yes," have you filed appropriate wage tax returns on **wages** for services in your home (see instructions for line 2)?
   c If the answer to **b** is "Yes," write your employer identification number. ▶

3 Write the amount of expenses you incurred and actually paid in 1983, but **do not** write more than $2,400 ($4,800 if you paid for the care of two or more persons) **3**

4 You **must** write your earned income on line 4. See the instructions for line 4 for the definition of earned income.
   ● If you were **unmarried** at the end of 1983, write your earned income on line 4, **OR**
   ● If you are **married**, filing a joint return for 1983,
   a write your earned income $ .... and
   b write your spouse's earned income $ .... and
   c compare amounts on lines 4a and 4b, and write the **smaller** of the two amounts on line 4. **4**

5 Compare amounts on lines 3 and 4, and write the **smaller** of the two amounts on line 5 **5**

6 Write the percentage from the table below that applies to the adjusted gross income on Form 1040, line 33. **6**

If line 33 is:		Percentage is:	If line 33 is:		Percentage is:
Over—	But not over—		Over—	But not over—	
0	$10,000	30% (.30)	$20,000	22,000	24% (.24)
$10,000	12,000	29% (.29)	22,000	24,000	23% (.23)
12,000	14,000	28% (.28)	24,000	26,000	22% (.22)
14,000	16,000	27% (.27)	26,000	28,000	21% (.21)
16,000	18,000	26% (.26)	28,000		20% (.20)
18,000	20,000	25% (.25)			

7 Multiply the amount on line 5 by the percentage shown on line 6, and write the result. **7**

8 Multiply any child and dependent care expenses for 1982 that you paid in 1983 by the percentage that applies to the adjusted gross income on Form 1040, line 33, for 1982. Write the result. (See line 8 instructions for the required statement.) **8**

9 Add amounts on lines 7 and 8, and write the total **9**

10 a Write the tax shown on Form 1040, line 40 **10a**
   b Add lines 41 through 44 of Form 1040, and write total. (See line 10 instructions.) **10b**
   c Subtract line 10b from line 10a, and write the result. (If line 10b is more than line 10a, write zero.) **10c**

11 Compare amounts on lines 9 and 10c, and write the **smaller** of the two amounts on line 11. Also, write this amount on Form 1040, line 45 **11**

General Instructions

Paperwork Reduction Act Notice.—We ask for this information to carry out the Internal Revenue laws of the United States. We need it to ensure that taxpayers are complying with these laws and to allow us to figure and collect the right amount of tax. You are required to give us this information.

What Is the Child and Dependent Care Expenses Credit?

You may be able to take a tax credit for amounts you paid someone to care for your child or other qualifying person so you could work or look for work in 1983. The credit will lower the amount of your tax. The credit is based on a percentage of the amount you paid during the year. The most you can take as a credit is $720 if you paid for the care of one qualifying person, or $1440 if you paid for the care of two or more qualifying persons.

Who is a qualifying person.— A qualifying person is any one of the following persons:
● Any person under age 15 whom you claim as a dependent (but see the special rule below for **Children of divorced or separated parents**).
● Your disabled spouse who is mentally or physically unable to care for himself or herself.
● Any disabled person who is mentally or physically unable to care for himself or herself and whom you claim as a dependent, or could claim as a dependent except that he or she had income of $1,000 or more.

Children of divorced or separated parents.—If you were divorced, legally separated, or separated under a written agreement, you may be able to claim the credit even if your child is not your dependent. Your child is a qualifying person if **all four** of the following apply:

1. You had custody for the longer period during the year, and
2. The child received over half of his or her support from one or both of the parents, and
3. The child was in the custody of one or both of the parents over half of the year, and
4. The child was under age 15, or was physically or mentally unable to care for himself or herself.

(Continued on back)

Form **2441** (1983)

Who Can Take the Credit?

To claim the credit **all five** of the following must apply:

1. You paid for the care so you (and your spouse if you were married) could work or look for work (but see the rules at the line 4 instructions for **Spouse who is a full-time student or is disabled**).

2. One or more qualifying persons lived in your home.

3. You (and your spouse if you were married) paid over half the cost of keeping up your home. The cost includes: rent; mortgage interest; property taxes; utilities; home repairs; and food eaten at home.

4. The person you paid to provide the care was not your spouse or a person you could claim as a dependent.

Note: *If the person you paid for the care was your child, he or she must have been 19 or over by the end of 1983.*

5. If you were married at the end of 1983, generally, you must file a joint tax return. However, there are two exceptions to this rule. You will be treated as unmarried and can file a separate return and still be eligible to take the credit if:

a. You were legally separated; or

b. You were living apart, and:
- The qualifying person lived in your home over 6 months, and
- You provided over half the cost of keeping up your home, and
- Your spouse did not live in your home during the last 6 months of the tax year.

What Are Qualified Expenses?

Qualified expenses include amounts paid for household services and care of the qualifying person.

Household services.—These services must be needed to care for the qualifying person as well as to run the home. They include, for example, the services of a cook, maid, babysitter, housekeeper, governess, or cleaning person if the services were at least partly for the benefit of the qualifying person.

Care of the qualifying person.—Care includes the cost of services for the qualifying person's well-being and protection.

Generally, care does not include food, clothing, or schooling expenses; but if you paid for care that included these items, and you cannot separate their cost from the total payment, you can count the total payment. However, you cannot count the cost of schooling for a child in the first grade or above.

Care outside the home.—You can count care provided outside your home if the care was for:

a. Your dependent under age 15; or

b. Any other qualifying person who regularly spends at least 8 hours each day in your home.

Care that is provided by a dependent care center may be counted if the center complies with all applicable state and local laws and regulations. A dependent care center is a place that provides care for at least seven persons (other than persons who live there), and receives a fee, payment, or grant for providing the services for any of those persons, regardless of whether the center is run for profit.

Medical expenses.—Some dependent care expenses may qualify as medical expenses. If you itemize deductions, you may want to take all or part of these medical expenses on Schedule A (Form 1040). If you cannot use all the medical expenses on Form 2441 because of the dollar limit or earned income limit (explained later), you can take the rest of these expenses on Schedule A. But if you deduct the medical expenses first on Schedule A, you cannot use any part of these expenses on Form 2441.

For more information, get **Publication 503,** Child and Disabled Dependent Care.

Specific Instructions

We have provided specific instructions for most of the lines on the form. Those lines that do not appear in the instructions are self-explanatory.

Line 2.—In general, if you paid cash wages of $50 or more in a calendar quarter for household services provided by a person such as a housekeeper, maid, babysitter, or cook, you must file an employment tax return. If you are not sure whether you should file an employment tax return, get **Form 942,** Employer's Quarterly Tax Return for Household Employees.

Note: *You should file a **Form 940,** Employer's Annual Federal Unemployment Tax Return, for 1983 by January 31, 1984, if you paid cash wages of $1,000 or more for household services in any calendar quarter in 1982 or 1983.*

Line 3. Dollar limit.—On line 3 write the amount of qualified child and dependent care expenses you incurred and actually paid in 1983. However, the most you can figure the credit on is $2,400 a year for one qualifying person, or $4,800 a year for two or more qualifying persons.

Note: *Do not include on line 3 qualified expenses that you incurred in 1983 but did not pay until 1984. Instead, you may be entitled to increase the amount of your 1984 credit when you pay the 1983 expenses in 1984.*

Line 4. Earned income limit.—Figure your earned income on line 4. The amount of your qualified expenses **cannot** be more than your earned income.

In general, earned income is wages, salaries, tips, and other employee compensation. It also includes net earnings from self-employment. For more information on what is earned income for purposes of the credit, see Publication 503.

Unmarried taxpayers.—If you were unmarried at the end of 1983 or are treated as being unmarried at the end of the year, write your earned income on line 4.

Married taxpayers.—If you are married, filing a joint return, figure each spouse's earned income separately and disregard community property laws. Write your earned income on line 4a and your spouse's earned income on line 4b. Then, write the **smaller** of your earned income or your spouse's earned income on line 4.

Spouse who is a full-time student or is disabled.—If your spouse was a full-time student or was mentally or physically unable to care for himself or herself, figure your spouse's earned income on a monthly basis to determine your spouse's earned income for the year. For each month that your spouse was disabled or a full-time student, your spouse is considered to have earned income of not less than $200 a month ($400 a month if more than one qualifying person was cared for in 1983).

If, in the same month, both you and your spouse were full-time students and did not work, you cannot use any amount paid that month to figure the credit. The same applies to a couple who did not work because neither was capable of self-care.

A full-time student is one who was enrolled in a school for the number of hours or classes that is considered full time. The student must have been enrolled at least 5 months during 1983.

Self-employment income.—You must reduce your earned income by any loss from self-employment. If your net earnings from self-employment are less than $1,600, and you use the optional method to figure your self-employment tax, you may be able to increase your net earnings to $1,600. See Publication 533, Self-Employment Tax, for details. If you only have a loss from self-employment, or your loss is more than your other earned income and you do not use the optional method, you cannot take the credit.

Line 8.—If you had qualified expenses for 1982 that you did not pay in 1983, you may be able to increase the amount of credit you can take in 1983. To do this, multiply the 1982 expenses you paid in 1983 by the percentage from the table on line 6 that applies to the adjusted gross income shown on your 1982 Form 1040, line 33. Your 1982 expenses must be within the 1982 limits. Attach a computation showing how you figured the increase. (Use the example in Publication 503 as a guide.)

Line 10.—Your credit cannot be more than your tax after subtracting certain credits. Write on line 10a your tax from Form 1040, line 40. Add the amounts, if any, from lines 41 through 44 of Form 1040, and write the total on line 10b. Also, add any WIN credit carryover you entered on Form 1040, line 46. Subtract line 10b from line 10a, and write the result on line 10c.

Line 11.—Compare amounts on lines 9 and 10c, and write the **smaller** of the two amounts on line 11. Also write this amount on Form 1040, line 45. This is your credit for child and dependent care expenses.

B–14   FORM 3468   COMPUTATION OF INVESTMENT CREDIT

Form **3468**	**Computation of Investment Credit**	OMB No. 1545-0155
Department of the Treasury Internal Revenue Service	▶ Attach to your tax return. ▶ Schedule B (Business Energy Investment Credit) on back.	19**83** 25

Name(s) as shown on return	Identifying number

PART I.—Elections (Check the box(es) below that apply to you (See Instruction D).)

A   I elect to increase my qualified investment to 100% for certain commuter highway vehicles under section 46(c)(6) . . . . ☐

B   I elect to increase my qualified investment by all qualified progress expenditures made this and all later tax years . . . . ☐

Enter total qualified progress expenditures included in column (4), Part II ▶ -

C   I claim full credit on certain ships under section 46(g)(3) (See **Instruction B** for details.) . . . . ☐

PART II.—Qualified Investment

1 Recovery Property		Line	(1) Class of Property	(2) Unadjusted Basis	(3) Applicable Percentage	(4) Qualified Investment (Column 2 x column 3)
Regular Percentage	New Property	**(a)**	3-year		60	
		(b)	Other		100	
	Used Property	**(c)**	3-year		60	
		(d)	Other		100	
Section 48(q) Election to Reduce Credit (instead of adjusting basis)	New Property	**(e)**	3-year		40	
		(f)	Other		80	
	Used Property	**(g)**	3-year		40	
		(h)	Other		80	

2 Nonrecovery property—Enter total qualified investment (See instructions for line 2)	2	
3 New commuter highway vehicle—Enter total qualified investment (See **Instruction D(1)**)	3	
4 Used commuter highway vehicle—Enter total qualified investment (See **Instruction D(1)**)	4	
5 **Total qualified investment in 10% property**—Add lines 1(a) through 1(h), 2, 3, and 4 (See instructions for special limits)	5	
6 Qualified rehabilitation expenditures—Enter total qualified investment for:		
a 30-year-old buildings	6a	
b 40-year-old buildings	6b	
c Certified historic structures (See instructions)	6c	

PART III.—Tentative Regular Investment Credit

7 10% of line 5	7	
8 15% of line 6a	8	
9 20% of line 6b	9	
10 25% of line 6c	10	
11 Credit from cooperative—Enter regular investment credit from cooperatives	11	
12 Current year regular investment credit—Add lines 7 through 11	12	
13 Carryover of unused credits	13	
14 Carryback of unused credits	14	
15 Tentative regular investment credit—Add lines 12, 13, and 14	15	

PART IV.—Tax Liability Limitations

16 **a** Individuals—From Form 1040, enter tax from line 38, page 2, plus any additional taxes from Form 4970
   b Estates and trusts—From Form 1041, enter tax from line 26a, plus any section 644 tax on trusts .
   c Corporations (1120 filers)—From Form 1120, Schedule J, enter tax from line 3 .
   d Other organizations—Enter tax before credits from return .
	16	

17 **a** Individuals—From Form 1040, enter credits from lines 41 and 42 of page 2 . . . . .
   b Estates and trusts—From Form 1041, enter any foreign tax credit from line 27a . .
   c Corporations (1120 filers)—From Form 1120, Schedule J, enter any foreign tax credit from line 4(a), plus any possessions tax credit from line 4(f) .
   d Other organizations—Enter any foreign or possessions tax credit . . . . . .
	17	

18 Income tax liability as adjusted (subtract line 17 from line 16)	18	
19 **a** Enter smaller of line 18 or $25,000. See instruction for line 19	19a	
b If line 18 is more than $25,000—Enter 85% of the excess	19b	
20 Regular investment credit limitation—Add lines 19a and 19b	20	
21 Allowed regular investment credit—Enter the smaller of line 15 or line 20	21	
22 Business energy investment credit limitation—Subtract line 21 from line 18	22	
23 Business energy investment credit—From line 14 of Schedule B	23	
24 Allowed business energy investment credit—Enter smaller of line 22 or line 23	24	
25 Total allowed regular and business energy investment credit—Add lines 21 and 24. Enter here and on Form 1040, line 43; Schedule J (Form 1120), line 4(b), page 3; or the proper line on other returns	25	

For Paperwork Reduction Act Notice, see separate instructions.   Form **3468** (1983)

Form 3468 (1983)　　　　　　　　　　　　　　　　　　　　　　　　　　　　　　　　　Page **2**

Schedule B.—Business Energy Investment Credit

1   Enter on lines 1(a) through 1(e) your qualified investment in business energy property that is the kind listed in the instructions for line 1, column (2).

Type of Property	Line	(1) Class of Property or Life Years	(2) Code	(3) Unadjusted Basis/ Basis	(4) Applicable Percentage	(5) Qualified Investment (Column 3 x column 4)
Recovery	(a)	3-year			60	
	(b)	Other			100	
Nonrecovery	(c)	3 or more but less than 5			33 ⅓	
	(d)	5 or more but less than 7			66 ⅔	
	(e)	7 or more			100	

2   Total 10% energy investment property—Add lines 1(a) through 1(e), column (5) **2**

3   Enter on lines 3(a) through 3(e) the basis in qualified hydroelectric generating property. Enter nameplate capacity of the property (see instructions for line 3) ▶

	Line	(1)	(2)	(3)	(4)	(5)
Recovery	(a)	3-year			60	
	(b)	Other			100	
Nonrecovery	(c)	3 or more but less than 5			33 ⅓	
	(d)	5 or more but less than 7			66 ⅔	
	(e)	7 or more			100	

4   Total 11% energy investment property—Add lines 3(a) through 3(e), column (5) **4**

5   Enter on lines 5(a) through 5(e) the basis in energy property that is solar equipment, wind equipment, ocean thermal equipment, or geothermal equipment. (See instructions for line 5, column (2).)

	Line	(1)	(2)	(3)	(4)	(5)
Recovery	(a)	3-year			60	
	(b)	Other			100	
Nonrecovery	(c)	3 or more but less than 5			33 ⅓	
	(d)	5 or more but less than 7			66 ⅔	
	(e)	7 or more			100	

6   Total 15% energy investment property—Add lines 5(a) through 5(e), column (5) **6**

7   Enter 10% of line 2 . . . .   **7**

8   Enter 11% of line 4 . . . .   **8**

9   Enter 15% of line 6 . . . .   **9**

10   Cooperative credit—Enter business energy investment credit from cooperatives **10**

11   Current year business energy investment credit—Add lines 7 through 10 . . . .   **11**

12   Carryover of unused credit(s) **12**

13   Carryback of unused credit(s) **13**

14   Tentative business energy investment credit—Add lines 11 through 13. Enter here and on line 23 of page 1 . . . .   **14**

Instructions for Schedule B (Form 3468)

Energy property must meet the same requirements as regular investment credit property, except that the provisions of sections 48(a)(1) and 48(a)(3) do not apply. See Instructions for Form 3468 for definitions and rules regarding regular investment credit property.

Energy property must be acquired new. See sections 46(a)(2)(C) and 48(l)(1) through (17) for details.

See section 48(l)(17) for special rules on public utility property, and section 48(l)(11) (as amended by the Crude Oil Windfall Profit Tax Act of 1980) for special rules on property financed by Industrial Development Bonds.

Specific Instructions

One Credit Only.—If property qualifies as more than one kind of energy property, you may take only one credit for the property.

Lines 1, 3, and 5—Type of Property.—For definition of recovery and nonrecovery property, see the separate Instructions for Form 3468.

Line 1—Column (2).—Use the code letters from the following list to indicate the kind of property for which you are claiming a credit. If you enter more than one kind of property on a line, enter the code letter for each kind of property in column (2) and the code letter and dollar amount of each kind of property in the right hand margin.

The code letters are:

a. Biomass property

b. Qualified intercity buses (see section 48(l)(16)(C) for the limitation on qualified investment for intercity buses based on the increase in operating seating capacity.)

Line 3.—Figure your qualified investment in hydroelectric generating property. If the installed capacity is more than 25

megawatts, the 11% energy credit is allowed for only part of the qualified investment. See section 48(l)(13)(C).

In the space provided in line 3, enter the megawatts capacity of the generator as shown on the nameplate of the generator.

Line 5—Column (2).—Use the code letters from the following list to indicate the kind of property for which you are claiming a credit. Be sure to put the code or codes on the line for the correct recovery period or life years as explained in the instruction for line 1, column (2).

c. Solar equipment (but not passive solar equipment)

d. Wind equipment

e. Ocean thermal equipment

f. Geothermal equipment

See sections 48(l)(4) and 48(l)(3)(A)(viii) and (ix) for definitions and special rules that apply to these kinds of property.

1983

Department of the Treasury
Internal Revenue Service

Instructions for Form 3468

Computation of Investment Credit

(Section references are to the Internal Revenue Code, unless otherwise noted.)

General Instructions

Paperwork Reduction Act Notice.—
We ask for this information to carry out the Internal Revenue laws of the United States. We need it to ensure that taxpayers are complying with these laws and so that we can figure and collect the correct amount of tax. You are required to give us this information.

A. Purpose of Form.—Use Form 3468 if you are an individual, estate, trust, or corporation claiming a regular or business energy investment credit or making certain elections. An exempt organization may also claim the credit if the property is used mainly in an unrelated trade or business whose income is taxed under section 511. **Caution:** *You may have to refigure the credit if you dispose of the property before the end of the property class life or life years shown in column (1) of either Form 3468, Schedule B, or the line 2 worksheet. This also applies if you change the use of the property so that it no longer qualifies as regular or energy investment credit property. See Form 4255, Recapture of Investment Credit.*

This credit does not apply to a Domestic International Sales Corporation (DISC), and is not divided among DISC shareholders.

A partnership or S corporation completes only the Part I elections; column (2) of line 1 and the line 2 worksheet; and columns (2) and (3) for lines 1, 3, and 5 of Schedule B, to figure the basis or cost of property to pass through to their individual partners or shareholders. Attach the form to the return to show the total cost or basis that is passed through.

If you are a partner, beneficiary, shareholder in an S corporation, or lessee, use Form 3468 to figure the credit based on your share of the investment by the partnership, estate, trust, S corporation, or lessor.

For detailed information on investment credit, see **Publication 572**, Investment Credit, and the regulations under sections 46 and 48.

B. How to Figure the Credit.—For recovery property, the class of property determines the percentage qualifying for investment credit. Even if you elect an alternate recovery period under section 168(b) of 5 or 12 years for 3-year property, the property is still treated as 3-year property, and the lower percentage applies.

For nonrecovery property the useful life of the property for investment credit must be the same as the useful life for depreciation or amortization.

See section 48(k) for special rules on figuring investment credit for movie and television films or tapes.

See section 46(e) for limitations on the investment credit for mutual savings institutions, regulated investment companies, and real estate investment trusts.

Generally, you may only take an investment credit of half of the regular investment credit for certain vessels. See sections 46(g)(1) through (6) for more information. If you claim the full credit, check box C in Part I of Form 3468.

C. Regular Investment Credit Property.—Generally, you may take the investment credit the first year you place qualified property in service, make qualified progress expenditures, or acquire an amortizable basis in qualified forestation or reforestation expenditures.

The property must be used in a trade or business and be either recovery property or other depreciable property with a life of 3 years or more. Enter only the business part of the investment in property that is for both business and personal use.

Examples of investment credit property are listed below. For more details see **Publication 572**.

Generally, investment credit property is:

(1) Tangible personal property as defined in section 48(a)(1).

(2) Elevators and escalators.

(3) Other tangible property, including certain real property, used as an integral part of manufacturing, production, or extraction, or used as a research facility or bulk storage facility for fungible commodities for these activities.

(4) Livestock other than horses as long as you do not sell or dispose of substantially identical livestock (not subject to recapture tax) during the 1-year period beginning 6 months before the date you got the livestock. Reduce the cost of the livestock you got by the amount you received on the disposition of the substantially identical livestock.

(5) Certain single-purpose agricultural or horticultural structures defined in section 48(p).

(6) Rehabilitation expenditures for qualified 30-year buildings, 40-year buildings, and certified historic structures. See sections 46(a)(2)(F) and 48(g) for details.

(7) Forestation and reforestation expenditures that are amortizable under section 194. See section 48(a)(1)(F) for more information.

(8) Petroleum storage facilities (but do not include buildings or their structural components).

*Exceptions.—*The regular investment credit generally does not apply to property that is:

(1) Used mainly outside the U.S.

(2) Used by a tax-exempt organization (other than a section 521 farmers' cooperative) unless the property is used mainly in an unrelated trade or business.

(3) Used by governmental units.

(4) Used for lodging or for furnishing the lodging (see section 48(a)(3) for exceptions, i.e., hotel or motel furnishings).

(5) Amortized or depreciated under sections 167(k), 184 and 188.

(6) Acquired or constructed with "excluded cost-sharing payments" from grants made after September 30, 1979, under any program listed in section 126(a) or by grants under the Energy Security Act.

(7) Expensed under section 179.

D. Elections.—There are certain elections you may make that affect the amount of investment credit you can claim. Some of these elections are made by checking the boxes in Part I of Form 3468. Others are made by attaching a statement to Form 3468. *(***Note:** *Contributions to an employee stock ownership plan made after 1982 are claimed on* **Form 8007**, *Credit for Employee Stock Ownership Plan.)*

*(1) Commuter Highway Vehicle.—*Employers may elect under section 46(c)(6) to claim the full investment credit for commuter highway vehicles which have a useful life of 3 years or more, or which are recovery property. Make this election by checking box A in Part I of Form 3468. See section 46(c)(6) for the definition of commuter highway vehicle and other details.

*(2) Qualified Progress Expenditures.—*You may elect under section 46(d) to increase your qualified investment for a year by qualified progress expenditures. Make this election by checking box B in Part I of Form 3468. The election applies to all progress expenditure property for the tax year it is made and all later tax years. On the line between blocks B and C, Part I, enter your 1983 qualified investment (column (4) of Part II) for progress expenditures for which you made an election in any tax year.

*(3) Election for Leased Property.—*If you lease property to someone else, you may elect to treat all or part of your investment in new property as if it were made by the person who is leasing it from you. See section 48(d) and related regulations for rules on making this election and special rules on leased property and the section 48(q) basis adjustment. For the limitation on the availability of the credit to certain owners of property for lease, see section 46(e)(3).

E. At Risk Limitation for Individuals and Closely Held Corporations.—The allowable basis or cost of property for investment credit purposes is limited to the amount a taxpayer is at risk for the property at the close of the taxpayer's tax year.

A person is generally considered at risk for property to the extent of the qualified loans and cash and the adjusted basis of property contributed for acquisition or construction of property. See **Publication 572** and sections 46(c)(8) and 465 for definitions, exceptions, and other details.

Specific Instructions

Lines 1(a)-1(h). Recovery Property.—Enter on the proper line the unadjusted basis of new or used recovery property. Do not include any amount that was expensed under section 179(a). Recovery property is tangible personal property used in a trade or business or held for the production of income, and depreciated under the Accelerated Cost Recovery System (ACRS). See sections 46(c)(7) and 168.

For property placed in service after December 31, 1982, you must reduce the depreciable basis of the property by one-half of the investment credit taken. Instead of adjusting the basis of the property, you may make an election to take a reduced credit. You make this election by listing the property on lines 1(e)-1(h) instead of on lines 1(a)-1(d). See **Publication 572** for more details.

Line 2. Nonrecovery Property.— Compute your qualified investment using the worksheet format below. Nonrecovery property includes:

- property placed in service before 1981;
- property you elect to depreciate using a method not expressed in terms of years;
- property you elect to amortize (e.g., leasehold improvements);
- property transferred or acquired merely to bring the property under ACRS;
- property acquired in certain nonrecognition transactions;
- certain property used outside the U.S.;
- public utility property if you do not use the normalization method of accounting.

See section 168(e) for further details.

Enter the amortizable basis in forestation and reforestation expenditures on line 2(c) of the worksheet. See section 48(a)(1)(F). See section 46(c)(5) for rules for certain pollution control facilities.

Lines 1(a), 1(b), 1(e), and 1(f) of Form 3468; lines 2(a), 2(b), and 2(c) of worksheet. Qualified Progress Expenditures.— Enter on the proper line the amount of qualified progress expenditures made in the tax year.

Do not take any qualified progress expenditures for the year in which the progress expenditure property is placed in service or for the year for which recapture is required for the property. The investment credit allowed for the year the property is placed in service is based on the entire qualified investment in the property reduced by the progress expenditures that were included as qualified investment in earlier years.

See section 46(d) for more information.

Lines 1(c), 1(d), 1(g), and 1(h) of Form 3468; lines 2(d), 2(e), and 2(f) of worksheet. Used Property Dollar Limitation.— In general, you may not take into account more than $125,000 of the cost of used property in any one year. The cost of used property does not include the basis of any property traded in unless the trade-in caused the recapture of all or part of an investment credit allowed earlier, or a reduction in an investment credit carryback or carryover. Determine the $125,000 amount before applying the percentages based on the class of property or useful life. On the proper line, enter the cost (subject to the dollar limitation) of used property

placed in service during the year. Property you inherited, received as a gift, or acquired from certain related persons does not qualify for the investment credit.

If a husband and wife file separate returns, each may claim up to $62,500. If one of them has no qualifying used property, the other may claim up to $125,000.

The $125,000 limitation applies to a partnership, S corporation, estate, or trust. The $125,000 must be divided among the estate or trust and its beneficiaries based on the income of the estate or trust allocable to each. The $125,000 limitation also applies to each partner, shareholder and beneficiary. Controlled corporate groups must divide the limitation among all component members. See section 48(c) and related regulations.

Lines 3 and 4. Commuter Highway Vehicle.— Enter 100% of basis in new vehicles on line 3, and 100% of cost (subject to the overall limitation) of used vehicles on line 4.

If you make the election to use the lower percentage in section 48(q)(4) instead of reducing the basis of the property, enter 80% (instead of 100%) on these lines. If you elect to take a reduced credit on all the vehicles on line 3 or 4, write "48(q)(4) election property" in the margin. If your election covers only certain vehicles, attach a schedule showing the breakdown.

Lines 6a, 6b, and 6c. Rehabilitation Expenditures.— Enter on the proper line the qualified investment in qualified rehabilitation expenditures for the tax year. The applicable percentage for qualified rehabilitation expenditures is 100%. The additions or improvements must have a recovery period of at least 15 years.

The increase in basis of the qualified rehabilitated building that would result from the expenditures must be decreased by 100% of the allowed credit (50% for certified historic structures). The increase in basis must be recovered by a straight line depreciation method over a recovery period of at least 15 years. See section 212(e)(2) of the Economic Recovery Tax Act of 1981 for transitional rules and code section 48(g) for other details. The qualified investment for rehabilitation expenditures that qualify under pre-1982 rules, but not under post-1981 rules, is figured separately and entered in the total for line 5. (Identify this amount in the margin.)

If you are claiming a credit for a certified historic structure on line 6(c), you must attach a copy of the first page of Part I or Part II of the Department of the Interior's "Historic Preservation Certification Application." (Do not do this if the line 6c credit is a flow-through from a partnership, S corporation, estate or trust because that entity will attach a copy to its return.)

Instead write "$_____ FROM PARTNERSHIP" (or "S CORP.," etc.) on the dotted line to the left of the entry column.)

Lines 5, 6, and 19a Limitations.— Mutual savings institutions, regulated investment companies, and real estate investment trusts are subject to special limitations for the amounts to be entered on lines 5, 6 a-c, and line 19a. See regulations section 1.46-4.

Line 11. Credit from Cooperative.— Section 1381(a) cooperative organizations may claim the regular and energy investment credits. If the cooperative cannot use any of the credit because of the tax liability limitation that applies, the unused credit from tax years ending after October 31, 1978, must be allocated to the patrons of the cooperative. The recapture provisions of section 47 apply as if the cooperative had kept the credit and not allocated it.

Patrons should enter their regular investment credit from a cooperative on line 11.

Lines 13 and 14. Carryover and Carryback of Unused Credits.— If you cannot use part of a regular or energy investment credit earned in any tax year ending after Dec. 31, 1973, because of tax liability limitations or the operation of the alternative minimum tax, you may carry it back 3 years, then forward 15 years.

If the basis of property was reduced under section 48(q), new section 196 permits the writeoff of one-half of the unused credit after the 15-year carryover period (or earlier if the taxpayer dies or goes out of business). See **Publication 572** for more details.

Line 19. Limitation.— If the tax liability (line 18) is $25,000 or less, the investment credit may not be more than the amount of the tax liability.

If the tax liability is more than $25,000, the credit may not be more than $25,000 plus 85% of the excess.

If you and your spouse file separate returns, each must use $12,500 instead of $25,000. However, if only one has any qualifying investment, that one may use the entire $25,000.

Controlled corporate groups (see section 46(a)(6)) must divide the $25,000 among all component members.

An estate or trust must allocate the $25,000 among itself and its beneficiaries in the same ratio as the qualified investment was allocated.

Line 22. Business Energy Investment Credit Limitation.— The energy credit is limited to the tax on line 18 minus the regular investment credit allowed on line 21. See the instructions for Schedule B on page 2 of Form 3468.

Line 2 Nonrecovery Property Worksheet	Line	(1) Life Years	(2) Basis or Cost	(3) Applicable Percentage	(4) Qualified Investment (Column 2 x column 3)
New	(a)	3 or more but less than 5		33⅓	
	(b)	5 or more but less than 7		66⅔	
	(c)	7 or more		100	
Used	(d)	3 or more but less than 5		33⅓	
	(e)	5 or more but less than 7		66⅔	
	(f)	7 or more		100	
Total—Add lines (a) through (f) and enter on line 2 of Form 3468				2	

B–15 FORM 3903 MOVING EXPENSE ADJUSTMENT

Form **3903**	**Moving Expense Adjustment**	OMB No. 1545-0062
Department of the Treasury Internal Revenue Service	▶ **Attach to Form 1040.**	**19**8**3** 62

Name(s) as shown on Form 1040	Your social security number

a What is the distance from your **old** residence to your **new** work place? _____ miles

b What is the distance from your **old** residence to your **old** work place? _____ miles

c If the distance in **a** above is 35 or more miles farther than the distance in **b** above, complete the rest of this form. If the distance is less than 35 miles, you may not take a deduction for moving expenses. This rule does not apply to members of the armed forces.

1	Transportation expenses in moving household goods and personal effects	**1**	
2	Travel, meal, and lodging expenses in moving from old to new residence	**2**	
3	Pre-move travel, meal, and lodging expenses in looking for a new residence after getting your job	**3**	
4	Temporary living expenses in new location or area during any 30 days in a row after getting your job	**4**	
5	Add lines 3 and 4	**5**	
6	Enter the smaller of line 5 or $1,500 ($750 if married, filing a separate return, and, at the end of the tax year, you lived with your spouse who also started work during the tax year)	**6**	
7	Expenses of (check one): a ☐ selling or exchanging your old residence; or b ☐ if renting, settling an unexpired lease on your old residence	**7**	
8	Expenses of (check one): a ☐ buying your new residence; or b ☐ if renting, getting a lease on your new residence	**8**	
9	Add lines 6, 7, and 8	**9**	
10	Enter the smaller of line 9 or $3,000 ($1,500 if married, filing a separate return, and, at the end of the tax year, you lived with your spouse who also started work during the tax year)	**10**	

Note: *Use any amount on line **7a** not deducted because of the $3,000 (or $1,500) limit to decrease the gain on the sale of your residence. Use any amount on line **8a** not deducted because of the limit to increase the basis of your new residence. See* **No Double Benefit** *in the instructions.*

11	Add lines 1, 2, and 10. This is your moving expense deduction. Enter here and on Form 1040, line 23 . ▶	**11**	

Note: *If your employer paid for any part of your move (including the value of any services furnished in kind), report that amount on* **Form 1040, line 7.** *See* **Reimbursements** *in the instructions.*

General Instructions

Paperwork Reduction Act Notice.—We ask for this information to carry out the Internal Revenue laws of the United States. We need it to ensure that taxpayers are complying with these laws and to allow us to figure and collect the right amount of tax. You are required to give us this information.

Purpose of Form.—Use Form 3903 if you moved to a new principal work place within the United States or its possessions and you qualify to deduct your moving expenses.

Note: *Use* **Form 3903F,** *Foreign Moving Expense Adjustment, instead of this form if you are a U.S. citizen or resident alien who moved to a new principal work place outside the United States or its possessions.*

Additional Information.—For more information about moving expenses, please get **Publication 521,** Moving Expenses.

Who May Deduct Moving Expenses.—If you moved your residence because of a change in the location of your job, you may be able to deduct your moving expenses. You may qualify for a deduction whether you are self-employed or an employee. However, you must meet certain tests of distance and time, explained below.

Distance Test.—Your new work place must be at least 35 miles farther from your old residence than your old work place was. For example, if your old work place was 3 miles from your old residence, your new work place must be at least 38 miles from that residence. If you did not have an old work place, your new work place must be at least 35 miles from your old residence. (The distance between two points is the shortest of the more commonly traveled routes between the points.)

Time Test.—If you are an employee, you must work full time for at least 39 weeks during the 12 months right after you move. If you are self-employed, you must work full time for at least 39 weeks during the first 12 months and a total of at least 78 weeks during the 24 months right after you move.

You may deduct your moving expenses for 1983 even if you have not met the time test before your 1983 return is due. You may do this if you expect to meet the 39-week test by the end of 1984 or the 78-week test by the end of 1985. If you have not met the test by then, you will have to do one of the following:

● Amend your 1983 tax return on which you deducted moving expenses. To do this, use **Form 1040X,** Amended U.S. Individual Income Tax Return.

● Report as income on your tax return for the year you cannot meet the test the amount you deducted on your 1983 return.

If you do not deduct your moving expenses on your 1983 return, and you later meet the time test, you may file an amended return for 1983, taking the deduction. To do this, use Form 1040X.

Exceptions to the Distance and Time Tests.—You do not have to meet the time

Form **3903** (1983)

936

Appendix B

test in case of death or if your job ends because of disability, transfer for your employer's benefit, or layoff or other discharge besides willful misconduct.

You do not have to meet the time test if you meet the requirements, explained below, for retirees or survivors living outside the United States.

If you are in the armed forces, you do not have to meet the distance and time tests if the move is due to a permanent change of station. A permanent change of station includes a move in connection with and within 1 year of retirement or other termination of active duty. In figuring your moving expenses, do not deduct any moving expenses for moving services that were provided by the military or that were reimbursed to you and that you did not include in income. However, you may deduct your unreimbursed moving expenses, subject to the dollar limits. If you and your spouse and dependents are moved to or from different locations, treat the moves as a single move.

Qualified Retirees or Survivors Living Outside the United States.—If the requirements below are met, retirees or survivors who move to a U.S. residence are treated as if they moved to a new work place located in the United States. You are subject to the dollar limits and distance test explained on this form. Use this form instead of Form 3903F to claim your moving expenses.

Retirees.—You may deduct moving expenses for a move to a new residence in the United States when you actually retire, if both your old principal work place and your old residence were outside the United States.

Survivors.—You may deduct moving expenses for a move to a residence in the United States if you are the spouse or dependent of a person whose principal work place at the time of death was outside the United States. In addition, the expenses must be: (1) for a move that begins within 6 months after the decedent's death; and (2) must be from a former residence outside the United States that you lived in with the decedent at the time of death.

Moving Expenses in General.—You may deduct most, but not all, of the reasonable expenses you incur in moving your family and dependent household members. You may not include moving expenses for employees such as a servant, governess, or nurse.

Examples of expenses you MAY deduct are:
- Travel, meal, and lodging expenses during the move to the new residence;
- Temporary living expenses in the new location; and
- Pre-move travel expenses.

Examples of expenses you MAY NOT deduct are:
- Loss on the sale of your residence;
- Mortgage penalties;
- Cost of refitting carpets and draperies; and
- Losses on quitting club memberships.

Reimbursements.—You must include any reimbursement of, or payment for, moving expenses in gross income as compensation for services. If your employer paid for any part of your move, you must report that amount as income on **Form 1040, line 7.** Your employer should include the amount paid in your total income on Form W-2. However, if you are not sure the reimbursements have been included in your Form W-2, check with your employer. Your employer must give you a statement showing a detailed breakdown of reimbursements or payments for moving expenses. Your employer may use **Form 4782,** Employee Moving Expense Information, to give you the required breakdown of reimbursements or your employer may use his or her own form.

No Double Benefit.—You may not take double benefits. For example, you may not use the moving expense on line 7 that is part of your moving expense deduction to lower the amount of gain on the sale of your old residence. You also may not use the moving expense on line 8 that is part of your moving expense deduction to add to the cost of your new residence. (Use **Form 2119,** Sale or Exchange of Principal Residence, to figure the gain, if any, you must report on the sale of your old residence and the adjusted cost of the new one.)

Dollar Limits.—Lines 1 and 2 (costs of moving household goods and travel expenses to your new residence) are not limited to any amount. All the other expenses (lines 3, 4, 7, and 8) together may not be more than $3,000. In addition, line 3 (househunting trip expenses) and line 4 (temporary living expenses) together may not be more than $1,500. These are overall per-move limits.

There are some special situations:
- If both you and your spouse began work at new work places and shared the same new residence at the end of the tax year, you must treat this as one move rather than two. If you file separate returns, each of you is limited to a total of $1,500 for lines 3, 4, 7, and 8; and to a total of $750 for lines 3 and 4.
- If both you and your spouse began work at new work places but each of you moved to separate new residences, this is treated as two separate moves. If you file a joint return, lines 3, 4, 7, and 8 are limited to a total of $6,000; and lines 3 and 4 are limited to a total of $3,000. If you file separate returns, each of you is limited to a total of $3,000 for lines 3, 4, 7, and 8; and to a total of $1,500 for lines 3 and 4.

Line-by-Line Instructions

To see whether you meet the distance test, fill in the number of miles for questions **a** and **b** at the top of the form. If you meet the test in **c,** continue with the items that follow.

We have provided specific instructions for most of the lines on the form. Those lines that do not appear in these instructions are self-explanatory.

Line 1.—Enter the actual cost of packing, crating, moving, storing in transit, and insuring your household goods and personal effects.

Line 2.—Enter the costs of travel from your old residence to your new residence. These include transportation, meals, and lodging on the way, including costs for the day you arrive. You may only include expenses for one trip. However, all the members of your household do not have to travel together or at the same time. If you use your own car, you may figure the expenses in either of the following two ways:
- Actual out-of-pocket expenses for gas and oil (keep records to verify the amounts); or
- At the rate of 9 cents a mile (keep records to verify your mileage).

You may add parking fees and tolls to the amount claimed under either method.

Line 3.—Include the costs of travel before you move in order to look for a new residence. You may deduct the costs only if:
- You began the househunting trip after you got the job; and
- You returned to your old residence after looking for a new one; and
- You traveled to the general location of the new work place primarily to look for a new residence.

There is no limit on the number of househunting trips made by you and members of your household that may be included on this line. Your househunting does not have to be successful to qualify for this deduction. If you used your own car, figure transportation costs the same way as in the instructions for line 2. If you are self-employed, you may deduct these househunting costs only if you had already made substantial arrangements to begin work in the new location.

Line 4.—Include the costs of meals and lodging while occupying temporary quarters in the area of your new work place. You may include these costs for any period of 30 days in a row after you get the job, but before you move into permanent quarters. If you are self-employed, you may count these temporary living expenses only if you had already made substantial arrangements to begin work in the new location.

Lines 7 and 8.—You may include most of the costs to sell or buy a residence or to settle or get a lease. Examples of expenses you MAY include are:
- Sales commissions;
- Advertising costs;
- Attorney's fees;
- Title and escrow fees;
- State transfer taxes; and
- Costs to settle an unexpired lease or to get a new lease.

Examples of expenses you MAY NOT include are:
- Costs to improve your residence to help it sell;
- Charges for payment or prepayment of interest; and
- Payments or prepayments of rent.

Check the appropriate box, **a** or **b,** for lines 7 and 8 when you enter the amounts for these two lines.

B–16 FORM 4255 RECAPTURE OF INVESTMENT CREDIT

Form **4255** (Rev. Nov. 1982) Department of the Treasury Internal Revenue Service	**Recapture of Investment Credit** (Including Energy Investment Credit) ▶ Attach to your income tax return	OMB No. 1545–0166 Expires 11–30–85 **65**

Name(s) as shown on return	Identifying number

Properties	Kind of property—State whether recovery or nonrecovery (see Form 3468 instructions for definitions). If energy property, show type. Also indicate if rehabilitation expenditure property.
A	
B	
C	
D	
E	

	Computation Steps: (see Specific Instructions)	Properties				
		A	B	C	D	E
Original Investment Credit	**1** Original rate of credit					
	2 Date property was placed in service					
	3 Cost or other basis					
	4 Original estimated useful life or class of property					
	5 Applicable percentage					
	6 Original qualified investment (line 3 times line 5)					
	7 Original credit (line 1 times line 6)					
	8 Date property ceased to be qualified investment credit property .					
	9 Number of full years between the date on line 2 and the date on line 8					
Computation of Recapture Tax	**10** Recapture percentage					
	11 Tentative recapture tax—Line 7 times line 10					

12 Add line 11, columns A through E . . . .

13 a Enter tax from disposed qualified progress expenditure property (attach separate computation) . . . . .

   b Enter tax from any part of property ceasing to be at risk (attach separate computation) . . . .

14 Total—Add lines 12, 13a and 13b . . . .

15 Portion of original credit (line 7) not used to offset tax in any year (Do not enter more than line 14—see instructions) . . . .

16 Total increase in tax—Subtract line 15 from line 14. Enter here and on the proper line of your tax return. Do not use this amount to reduce current year's investment credit figured on Form 3468, Computation of Investment Credit. Any unused credit on line 15 cannot be used in any year as a carryback or carryover . .

For Paperwork Reduction Act Notice, see instructions on back.   363–490–1   Form **4255** (Rev. 11–82)

General Instructions

References are to the Internal Revenue Code.

Paperwork Reduction Act Notice.—We ask for this information to carry out the Internal Revenue laws of the United States. We need it to ensure that you are complying with these laws and to allow us to figure and collect the right amount of tax. You are required to give us this information.

Purpose.—Use Form 4255 to figure the increase in tax for the recapture of investment credit for regular and energy property. You must refigure the credit if you took it in an earlier year, but disposed of the property before the end of the recapture period, or the useful life you used to figure the original credit. You must also refigure the credit if you changed the use of the property so that it no longer qualifies as regular or energy investment credit property. Also, see instructions for line 13b regarding recapture if property ceases to be at risk.

For tax years beginning after December 31, 1982, election of subchapter S status does not automatically trigger recapture of investment credit taken before the election was effective. However, on disposition of the assets, the subchapter S corporation continues to be liable for any recapture of investment credit taken before the election.

If property on which you took both the regular and energy investment credit ceases to be energy credit property, but still qualifies as regular investment credit property, you need only refigure the energy investment credit. However, if you took both credits, and you dispose of the property, or the property ceases to be both energy and regular investment credit property, you must refigure both credits.

If you are a subchapter S corporation, a partnership, or an estate or trust that allocated any or all of the investment credit to the beneficiaries, you must give your shareholders, partners, or beneficiaries the information they need to refigure the credit. See regulations sections 1.47–4, 1.47–5 and 1.47–6.

Special rules.—If you took the credit on the following kinds of property, see the sections listed below before you complete Form 4255:

Property	IRC section
Motion picture films and video tape	47(a)(8)
Ships	46(g)(4)
Commuter highway vehicles	47(a)(4)

If you dispose of property and you had elected the basic or basic and matching employee plan percentage for contributions to tax credit employee stock option plans, see section 48(n)(4).

If you took any credit for production of fuel from nonconventional sources, see section 44D(b)(4).

If, before the end of the recapture period, you dispose of recovery property placed in service after 1982, you must increase the basis of this property by 50% of the recapture amount before computing gain or loss on disposition. See section 48(q)(2) and (3). (This does not apply if you originally made the section 48(q)(4) election to take a reduced credit instead of reducing the basis of the property.)

For more information, see **Publication 572**, Investment Credit.

Specific Instructions

Note: *Do not figure the recapture tax for qualified progress expenditure property or for property ceasing to be at risk on lines 1 through 12. Figure the recapture tax for these properties on separate schedules and enter the recapture tax on lines 13a and 13b. Include any unused credit for these properties on line 15.*

Lines A through E.—Describe the property for which you must refigure the regular or energy investment credit.

Fill in lines 1 through 11 for each property on which you are refiguring the credit. Use a separate column for each item. If you must recapture both the energy investment credit and the regular investment credit for the same item, use a separate column for each credit. If you need more columns, use additional Forms 4255, or other schedules with all the information shown on Form 4255. Enter the total from the separate sheets on line 12.

Line 1.—Enter the rate you used to figure the original credit as determined from the tables below:

Regular Investment Property:

Property (including public utility property) acquired or constructed and placed in service after January 21, 1975 . . . . 10%

For property acquired or constructed before January 22, 1975, enter the rate used on your original Form 3468 (7% or 4%).

Be sure to include any basic and matching ESOP or other credits listed under the special rules above.

See section 46(a)(2)(F) for the rates for qualified rehabilitation expenditures made after December 31, 1981.

Energy Investment Property:

Alternative energy property, specially defined energy property, recycling equipment, shale oil equipment, equipment for producing natural gas from geopressured brine, cogeneration equipment, and intercity buses . . . 10%

Qualified hydroelectric generating equipment . 11%

Solar and wind equipment acquired or constructed after 1/1/80 . . . . . . 10%

Solar and wind equipment, ocean thermal equipment, and geothermal equipment acquired or constructed after 12/31/79 . . . 15%

Line 2.—For both recovery and nonrecovery property, enter the first day of the first month, and the year, that the property was available for service.

Line 3.—Enter the cost or other basis of nonrecovery property (unadjusted basis of recovery property) that you used to figure the original credit.

Line 4.—Enter the estimated useful life that you used to figure the original credit for nonrecovery property. Enter the class of property for recovery property.

Line 5.—Enter the applicable percentage that you used to figure the original qualified investment from the tables below:

Nonrecovery Property

Original estimated useful life:	Applicable percentage
3 or more but less than 5 years	33⅓%
5 or more but less than 7 years	66⅔%
7 or more years	100%

Recovery Property

Class of property	Applicable percentage
3-year	60%
Other	100%

Section 48(q) Election Recovery Property
(Placed in service after 12/31/82)

Class of property	Applicable percentage
3-year	40%
Other	80%

Line 8.—See regulations section 1.47–1(c) for more information.

Line 9.—Do not enter partial years. If property was held less than 12 months, enter zero.

Line 10.—Enter the recapture percentage from the following tables:

Nonrecovery Property

If number of full years on line 9 of Form 4255 is:	The recapture percentage for property with an original useful life of:		
	3 or more but less than 5 years is	5 or more but less than 7 years is	7 or more years is
0	100	100	100
1	100	100	100
2	100	100	100
3	0	50	66.6
4	0	50	66.6
5	0	0	33.3
6	0	0	33.3

Recovery Property

If number of full years on line 9 of Form 4255 is:	The recapture percentage for:	
	3-year property is	15-year, 10-year, and 5-year property is
0	100	100
1	66	80
2	33	60
3	0	40
4	0	20

Line 12.—If you have used more than one Form 4255, or separate sheets to list additional items on which you figured an increase in tax, write on the dotted line "Tax from attached, $................." Include the amount in the total for line 12.

Line 13a.—See section 47(a)(3) for information on recapturing investment credit on the disposal of qualified progress expenditure property. Attach a separate computation schedule and enter the recapture tax on line 13a.

Line 13b.—For certain taxpayers, the basis or cost of property placed in service after February 18, 1981, is limited to the amount the taxpayer is at risk for the property at year end. If property ceases to be at risk in a later year, recapture may be required. See section 47(d) for details. Attach a separate computation schedule to figure the recapture tax and enter the total tax on line 13b.

Line 15.—If you did not use all the credit you originally figured, either in the year you figured the credit or in a carryback or carryover year, you do not have to recapture the amount of the credit you did not use. You must also take into account the current year's increase in tax in figuring the increase in tax. See regulations section 1.47–1(d), Revenue Ruling 72–221, and Publication 572 for more information.

Figure the unused portion on a separate sheet and enter it on this line. Do not enter more than the recapture tax on line 14.

Line 16.—This is the total increase in tax. Enter it on the proper line of your tax return. Do not use this amount to reduce your current year's investment credit from Form 3468.

363–490–1

B-17 FORM 4562 DEPRECIATION AND AMORTIZATION

Form **4562**

Department of the Treasury
Internal Revenue Service

Depreciation and Amortization

▶ See separate instructions.

▶ Attach this form to your return.

OMB No. 1545-0172

19**83**

67

Name(s) as shown on return

Identifying number

Business or activity to which this form relates

PART I.—Depreciation

Section A.—Election to expense recovery property (Section 179)

A. Class of property	B. Cost	C. Expense deduction

1 Total (not more than $5,000). Enter here and on page 2, line 8 (Partnerships or S corporations—see the Schedule K and Schedule K-1 Instructions of Form 1065 or 1120S) . . . .

Section B.—Depreciation of recovery property

A. Class of property	B. Date placed in service	C. Cost or other basis	D. Recovery period	E. Method of figuring depreciation	F. Percentage	G. Deduction for this year
2 Accelerated Cost Recovery System (ACRS) (See instructions):						
(a) 3-year property						
(b) 5-year property						
(c) 10-year property						
(d) 15-year public utility property						
(e) 15-year real property— low-income housing						
(f) 15-year real property other than low-income housing						
3 Property subject to section 168(e)(2) election (See instructions):						

4 Total column G. Enter here and on page 2, line 9 . . . .

See Paperwork Reduction Act Notice on page 1 of the separate instructions.

Form **4562** (1983)

Section C.—Depreciation of nonrecovery property

A. Description of property	B. Date acquired	C. Cost or other basis	D. Depreciation allowed or allowable in earlier years	E. Method of figuring depreciation	F. Life or rate	G. Deduction for this year
5 Class Life Asset Depreciation Range (CLADR) System Depreciation					▶	
6 Other depreciation (See instructions):						

7 Total column G, Section C

8 Enter amount from Section A, line 1 (Partnerships and S corporations enter zero)

9 Enter amount from Section B, line 4

10 Total—Add lines 7, 8, and 9. Enter here and on the Depreciation line of your return

PART II.—Amortization of Property

A. Description of property	B. Date acquired	C. Cost or other basis	D. Amortization allowed or allowable in earlier years	E. Code section	F. Amortization period or percentage	G. Amortization for this year

1 Total column G. Enter here and on Other Deductions or Other Expenses line of your return

1983

**Department of the Treasury
Internal Revenue Service**

Instructions for Form 4562

Depreciation and Amortization

(Section references are to the Internal Revenue Code, unless otherwise noted.)

Paperwork Reduction Act Notice

We ask for this information to carry out the Internal Revenue laws of the United States. We need it to ensure that taxpayers are complying with these laws and to allow us to figure and collect the right amount of tax. You are required to give us this information.

Purpose of Form

Use Form 4562 to explain this year's deduction for depreciation and amortization, and to make the election to expense recovery property. In using this form, a taxpayer has the option of preparing and submitting either: a separate Form 4562 for each business or activity in the return, or a separate depreciation schedule for each business or activity along with one Form 4562 on which the taxpayer enters summary totals for each line of the form. If the second option is used, each separate schedule must be readily identifiable with the business or activity to which it relates.

For more information about depreciation (including the treatment of mass asset accounts) and the election to expense newly acquired recovery property, see **Publication 534,** Depreciation. For more information about amortization, see **Publication 535,** Business Expenses. You may be eligible to take investment credit on newly acquired depreciable property. See the Instructions for **Form 3468,** Computation of Investment Credit, for more information.

Specific Instructions
Part I.—Depreciation

Depreciation is an amount you can deduct each year for assets, except land, you buy to use in your business or hold to produce income. (Land is never depreciable.) Depreciation starts when you place the property in service. It ends when you take the property out of service or deduct all of your depreciable cost.

Generally, assets you place in service after December 31, 1980, are depreciated using the Accelerated Cost Recovery System (ACRS). These assets are called "recovery property." You may be able to elect to expense up to $5,000 of certain recovery property in Section A. Show your depreciation for recovery property in Section B. If you have an asset that is nonrecovery property, show your depreciation in Section C.

Section A—Election to expense recovery property.— You may choose to expense part of the cost of recovery property that would qualify for investment credit. To do so, you must have purchased (as defined in section 179(d)(2)) the property and placed it in service this year for use in your trade or business. If you take this deduction, the amount on which you figure your depreciation or amortization deduction and your investment tax credit must be reduced by the amount you deduct as a section 179 expense. This is because you may not depreciate, amortize, or take the investment tax credit on any amount deducted as a section 179 expense.

An estate or trust may not elect to expense recovery property. A partnership or S corporation may choose to expense and pass through to its partners or shareholders a maximum of $5,000. Partners or shareholders add their share of the partnership or S corporation amount to any other section 179 expense they choose to take, and deduct the combined amount up to the $5,000 (or $2,500 for married taxpayers filing separately) limit for each taxpayer. See **Publication 572,** Investment Credit, and Publication 534 for more information.

Column A.—Enter the class of recovery property (that is, 3-year, 5-year, etc.) for which you make the election and a brief description of the item.

Column B.—Enter the property's cost. Include only what you paid; omit any undepreciated basis on assets you traded in. For information about basis, see **Publication 551,** Basis of Assets.

Column C.—Enter the part of the cost you choose to expense. You can choose to expense part of the cost of an asset and depreciate the rest of it. (You may take the investment credit for the part of the cost you do not deduct as a section 179 expense.)

Line 1.—Enter the Column C total, up to $5,000 ($2,500 for married taxpayers filing separately). Partnerships should carry the line 1 amount to Schedule K-1 (Form 1065) and Schedule K (Form 1065) (if applicable). S corporations should carry the line 1 amount to Schedule K and Schedule K-1 of Form 1120S. All others carry it to line 8 of Section C.

Section B—Depreciation of recovery property.—

Column A.—Two factors determine the class of property: whether the property is section 1245 or section 1250 property; and what midpoint class life (if any) would have applied to it on January 1, 1981, if the asset depreciation range (ADR) system had been elected. The midpoint class lives are listed in the asset guideline period column of the table for depreciation in the back of Publication 534.

In each recovery class, except 15-year real property, group the property by the year you placed it in service. For example, list as one item all new and used 3-year property you bought in 1983. However, you must list separately:

- Property used mainly outside the United States.
- Retirement-replacement-betterment property.
- Qualified leased property.
- Property financed by tax-exempt obligations.

In the 15-year real property class, group property by the depreciation method elected and the month and year you placed it in service.

Column B.—For lines 2(a), (b), (c), and (d), enter the year you placed the property in service. For lines 2(e) and (f), enter the month and year you placed it in service.

Column C.—Enter the unadjusted basis of the assets you placed in service in the same year. To find unadjusted basis, subtract the part of the basis you elected to amortize or expense (section 179) from the basis you use to determine gain. Do not deduct salvage value in figuring your ACRS deduction. Also, the basis of property placed in service after December 31, 1982, may have to be reduced by one-half of any investment credit taken on it. See Instructions for Form 3468, and Publication 551.

Column D.—Enter the recovery period you are using. This is usually the class of property itself (that is, 3-year, 5-year, etc.); but you may instead elect an alternate percentage figured by using the straight-line method over one of the following periods.

For—	You may choose:
3-year property	3, 5, or 12 years
5-year property	5, 12, or 25 years
10-year property	10, 25, or 35 years
15-year real property	15, 35, or 45 years
15-year public utility property	15, 35, or 45 years

Also, for certain assets (described in Column E, below) you may be required to use a specified recovery period.

Column E.—For property for which you are using the prescribed percentages in Section B, lines 2(a) through 2(f) below, enter "PRE." If you elect an alternate percentage, as described above in Column D instructions, enter "SL." If the asset is used mainly outside the United States, enter "FP" and see section 168(f)(2). If the asset is retirement-replacement-betterment property, enter "RRB" and see section 168(f)(3). If the asset is qualified leased property, enter "QLP" and see sections 168(f)(8) and 168(i). If the asset is property financed by tax-exempt obligations, enter "TEO" and see section 168(f)(12).

Column F.—Unless you use an alternate percentage, or a special percentage required for certain types of property (as described above in Column E instructions), enter the prescribed percentage from the line instructions below. If you use an alternate percentage, enter the percentage based on the recovery period you chose. Except for 15-year real property and property requiring a special percentage (as described above), use the same alternate percentage for all property in the same class that you place in service in the same year.

If you elect an alternate percentage, do not figure depreciation by the number of months the property was in use; instead use the half-year convention. The half-year convention treats property as if it were placed in service, or retired, on the first day of the second half of the tax year. However, for the 15-year real property, you can elect an alternate percentage on a property-by-property basis, and the half-year convention does not apply.

Column G.—Multiply the amount in Column C by the percentage in Column F, and enter the result in Column G.

Section B, Line 2(a)—3-year property.— Includes section 1245 class property that:

- Has a midpoint class life of 4 years or less, or
- Is used for research and experimentation, or
- Is a race horse more than 2 years old when you place it in service, or any other horse that is more than 12 years old when you place it in service.

Some examples of 3-year property are: automobiles; light-duty trucks; and machinery and equipment used in connection with research and experiments.

The percentages prescribed for these assets are:

1st year	25%
2nd year	38%
3rd year	37%

Line 2(b)—5-year property.—Includes section 1245 class property that is not assigned to one of the other recovery classes.

The percentages prescribed for these assets are:

1st year	15%
2nd year	22%
3rd through 5th year	21%

Line 2(c)—10-year property.—Includes: public utility property (except 3-year property or section 1250 class property) that has a midpoint class life of more than 18 years and no more than 25 years; section 1250 class property that has a midpoint class life of 12.5 years or less (however, under a special rule for theme parks, etc., a building and its structural components shall not be treated as having a class life of 12.5 years or less by reason of any use other than the use for which that building was originally placed in service); manufactured homes; railroad tank cars; and qualified coal utilization property which would otherwise be 15-year public utility property.

The percentages prescribed for these assets are:

1st year	8%
2nd year	14%
3rd year	12%
4th through 6th year	10%
7th through 10th year	9%

Line 2(e). 15-year real property low-income housing.—

Year	Use the column for the month placed in service											
	1	2	3	4	5	6	7	8	9	10	11	12
1st	13%	12%	11%	10%	9%	8%	7%	6%	4%	3%	2%	1%
2nd	12%	12%	12%	12%	12%	12%	12%	13%	13%	13%	13%	13%
3rd	10%	10%	10%	10%	11%	11%	11%	11%	11%	11%	11%	11%

Line 2(f). 15-year real property other than low-income housing.—

Year	Use the column for the month placed in service											
	1	2	3	4	5	6	7	8	9	10	11	12
1st	12%	11%	10%	9%	8%	7%	6%	5%	4%	3%	2%	1%
2nd	10%	10%	11%	11%	11%	11%	11%	11%	11%	11%	11%	12%
3rd	9%	9%	9%	9%	10%	10%	10%	10%	10%	10%	10%	10%

Section B, Line 3.—Report property on line 3 that you elect, under section 168(e)(2), to depreciate by the units-of-production method or any other method not based on a term of years. If you use the retirement-replacement-betterment method, see section 168(f)(3).

Column A.—Describe the property and what depreciation method you elect that excludes the property from ACRS.

Column C.—Enter the depreciable basis (cost or other basis reduced, if applicable, by salvage value, half the investment credit, and the section 179 expense).

Column G.—Enter the depreciation deduction for the property in Column G.

Section C—Depreciation of nonrecovery property.— Use Section C for property you do not amortize, expense, or use ACRS to depreciate. This includes:

● Property placed in service before January 1, 1981; and

● Certain public utility property, which does not meet certain normalization requirements; and

Line 2(d)—15-year public utility property.—Includes section 1245 class property (except 3-year property or 15-year real property) that has a midpoint class life of more than 25 years.

The percentages prescribed for these assets are:

1st year	5%
2nd year	10%
3rd year	9%
4th year	8%
5th and 6th year	7%
7th through 15th year	6%

Lines 2(e) and (f)—15-year real property.—Includes section 1250 class property that does not have a midpoint class life of 12.5 years or less (however, under a special rule for theme parks, etc., a building and its structural components shall not be treated as having a class life of 12.5 years or less by reason of any use other than the use for which that building was originally placed in service). Within each line, enter property grouped by the depreciation method elected and the month and year you placed it in service.

Different percentages apply to low-income housing than to other 15-year real property. The percentage to enter in Column F each year depends on the month you placed the property in service. Publication 534 gives complete percentage tables for 15-year real property. The following chart shows the percentages prescribed for the first three years.

● Certain property acquired from related persons; and

● Property acquired in certain nonrecognition transactions.

Section C, Line 5.—The Class Life Asset Depreciation Range (CLADR) system does not apply to recovery property placed in service after December 31, 1980.

If you previously elected the CLADR system, you must continue to use it to depreciate assets left in your vintage accounts. You must continue to meet record-keeping requirements.

If you elect CLADR for assets that do not qualify for ACRS (see sections 168(e)(1) and (4)), attach a statement that specifies the items that still apply of those listed in Regulations section 1.167(a)-11(f)(2).

Section C, Line 6.—You may list each asset separately or group assets in depreciation accounts. Depreciate each asset or group of assets separately.

Note: Capital improvements made in 1983 to buildings placed in service prior to 1981 qualify as recovery property. However, the deduction must be computed over the same period and under the same method as that elected for the first capital improvement placed in service after 1980 with regard to the building. For the special rule for substantial improvements made to real property, see Publication 534 and section 168(f)(1)(C).

Column A.—Briefly describe each asset or group.

Column B.—For a single asset, enter the date you placed it in service. For a group of assets that you place in service on the same date, enter that date. Otherwise, leave Column B blank.

Column C.—Enter the depreciable basis (cost or other basis reduced by salvage value, if it applies). See Publication 551 for more information.

Part II.—Amortization of Property

Each year you may elect to deduct part of certain capital expenses over a fixed period. If you amortize property, the part you amortize does not qualify for the election to expense recovery property or depreciation.

Column A.—Describe the property you are amortizing. Amortizable property includes—

● Pollution control facilities (section 169, limited by section 291 for corporations).

● Expenses paid before January 1, 1982, for child-care facilities (section 188).

● Amounts paid for research or experiments (section 174), or for a trademark or trade name (section 177).

● Certain business startup costs paid or incurred after July 29, 1980 (section 195).

● Organizational expenses for a corporation (section 248) or partnership (section 709).

● Qualified forestation and reforestation cost (section 194).

● Construction period interest and taxes on real property (for exceptions, see section 189).

● Certain railroad property (section 185).

● Certain rehabilitation expenses of historic structures made before January 1, 1982 (section 191 (as before repeal by Public Law 97-34) and the transitional rule in Public Law 97-34, section 212(e)(2)).

● Optional 10-year write-off of certain tax preferences (section 58(i)).

Column B.—Enter the date you acquired or completed the property or spent the amount you are amortizing.

Column C.—Enter the total amount you are amortizing. See the applicable Code section for limits on the amortizable amount.

Column E.—Enter the Code section under which you amortize the property.

Attach any other information the Code and Regulations may require in order to make a valid election.

B–18   FORM 4684   CASUALTIES AND THEFTS

Form **4684**	**Casualties and Thefts**	OMB No. 1545-0177
Department of the Treasury Internal Revenue Service	▶ See separate instructions. ▶ To be filed with Form 1040, 1041, 1065, 1120, etc.	19**83** 27

Name(s) as shown on tax return	Identifying Number

PART I.—Casualty or Theft Gain or Loss (Use a separate Part I for each different casualty or theft.)

		Item or article	Item or article	Item or article	Item or article
1	(a) Kind of property and description				
	(b) Date of purchase or acquisition				
2	Cost or other basis of each item				
3	Insurance or other reimbursement you received or expect to receive for each item				
	Note: *If line 2 is more than line 3, skip line 4 and complete lines 5 through 16.*				
4	Gain from casualty or theft. If line 3 is more than line 2, enter difference here and on line 17 or 22, column C. However, see instructions for line 21. Also, skip lines 5 through 16				
5	Fair market value before casualty or theft				
6	Fair market value after casualty or theft				
7	Subtract line 6 from line 5				
8	Enter smaller of line 2 or line 7				
	Note: *If the loss was to property used in a trade or business, or for income-producing purposes, and it was totally destroyed by a casualty or it was a loss from theft, enter on line 8, in each column, the amount from line 2.*				
9	Subtract line 3 from line 8				
10	Casualty or theft loss. Add amounts on line 9. See instructions for **How Many Forms to Complete**				
11	Enter the part of line 9 that is from trade, business, or income-producing property here and on line 17 or 22				
12	Subtract line 11 from line 10				
13	Enter the amount from line 12 or $100, whichever is smaller				
14	Subtract line 13 from line 12. See instructions for **How Many Forms to Complete**				
15	Enter 10% of adjusted gross income (line 33, Form 1040). See instructions before completing this line.				
16	Subtract line 15 from line 14. If line 15 is more than line 14, enter zero. Enter here and on line 17 or 22, column (B)(ii)				

PART II.—Summary of Gains and Losses (From separate Parts I)

	(A) Identify casualty or theft	(B) Losses from casualties or thefts		(C) Gains from casualties or thefts includible in income
		(i) Trade, business, rental or royalty property	(ii) Other property	

Casualty or Theft of Property Held One Year or Less

17				
18	Totals. Add amounts on line 17 for each column			
19	Combine line 18, columns (B)(i) and (C). Enter the net gain or (loss) here and on Form 4797, Part II, line 9. (If Form 4797 is not otherwise required, see instructions.)			
20	Enter the amount from line 18, column (B)(ii) here and on line 21 of Schedule A (Form 1040). Estates, trusts, partnerships, and S corporations, see instructions.			

Casualty or Theft of Property Held More Than One Year

21	Casualty or theft gains from Form 4797, Part III, line 29			
22				
23	Total losses. Add amounts on line 22, columns (B)(i) and (B)(ii)			
24	Total gains. Add lines 21 and 22, column (C)			
25	Add amounts on line 23, columns (B)(i) and (B)(ii)			
	Partnerships and S corporations, see instructions before completing lines 26(a), 26(b), and 27.			
26	If the loss on line 25 is more than the gain on line 24:			
	(a) Combine line 23, column (B)(i) and line 24. Enter the net gain or (loss) here and on Form 4797, Part II, line 9. (If Form 4797 is not otherwise required, see instructions.)			
	(b) Enter the amount from line 23, column (B)(ii) here and on line 21 of Schedule A (Form 1040). See instructions before completing this line.			
27	If the loss on line 25 is equal to or smaller than the gain on line 24, combine lines 24 and 25. Enter the net gain here and on Form 4797, Part I, line 2. (If Form 4797 is not otherwise required, see instructions.)			

For Paperwork Reduction Act Notice, see page 1 of separate instructions.   Form **4684** (1983)

B-19 FORM 4797 SUPPLEMENTAL SCHEDULE OF GAINS AND LOSSES

Form **4797** Department of the Treasury Internal Revenue Service	**Supplemental Schedule of Gains and Losses** (Includes Gains and Losses From Sales or Exchanges of Assets Used in a Trade or Business and Involuntary Conversions) ▶ To be filed with Form 1040, 1041, 1065, 1120, etc.—See Separate Instructions	OMB No. 1545-0184 **1983** 28

Name(s) as shown on return	Identifying number

PART I.—Sales or Exchanges of Property Used in a Trade or Business, and Involuntary Conversions From Other Than Casualty and Theft — Property Held More Than 1 Year (Except for Certain Livestock)

Note: Use Form 4684 to report involuntary conversions from casualty and theft.

Caution: If you sold property on which you claimed the investment credit, you may be liable for recapture of that credit. See Form 4255 for additional information.

a. Description of property	**b.** Date acquired (mo., day, yr.)	**c.** Date sold (mo., day, yr.)	**d.** Gross sales price	**e.** Depreciation allowed (or allowable) since acquisition	**f.** Cost or other basis, plus improvements and expense of sale	**g.** LOSS (f minus the sum of d and e)	**h.** GAIN (d plus e minus f)
1							

2 Gain, if any, from Form 4684, line 27 . . . .

3 Section 1231 gain from installment sales from Form 6252, line 21 or 29 . . . .

4 Gain, if any, from line 29, Part III, on back of this form from other than casualty and theft. . . . . . .

5 Add lines 1 through 4 in column g and column h . . . . ( )

6 Combine columns g and h of line 5. Enter gain or (loss) here, and on the appropriate line as follows:

  (a) For all except partnership returns:

    (1) If line 6 is a gain, enter the gain as a long-term capital gain on Schedule D. See instruction E.

    (2) If line 6 is zero or a loss, enter that amount on line 7. (S corporations, enter on Schedule K (Form 1120S), line 7.)

  (b) For partnership returns: Enter each partner's share of line 6 above, on Schedule K-1 (Form 1065), line 8.

PART II.—Ordinary Gains and Losses

a. Description of property	**b.** Date acquired (mo., day, yr.)	**c.** Date sold (mo., day, yr.)	**d.** Gross sales price	**e.** Depreciation allowed (or allowable) since acquisition	**f.** Cost or other basis, plus improvements and expense of sale	**g.** LOSS (f minus the sum of d and e)	**h.** GAIN (d plus e minus f)
7 Loss, if any, from line 6(a)(2)							
8 Gain, if any, from line 28, Part III on back of this form							
9 Net gain or (loss) from Form 4684, lines 19 and 26a							
10 Ordinary gain from installment sales from Form 6252, line 20 or 28 . . .							
11 Recapture of section 179 deduction (see instructions)							
12 Other ordinary gains and losses (include property held 1 year or less):							

13 Add lines 7 through 12 in column g and column h . . . . ( )

14 Combine columns g and h of line 13. Enter gain or (loss) here, and on the appropriate line as follows:

  (a) For all except individual returns: Enter the gain or (loss) from line 14, on the return being filed. See instruction F for specific line reference.

  (b) For individual returns:

    (1) If the loss on line 7 includes a loss from Form 4684, Part II, column B(ii), enter that part of the loss here and on line 21 of Schedule A (Form 1040). Identify as from "Form 4797, line 14(b)(1)". . . . .

    (2) Redetermine the gain or (loss) on line 14, excluding the loss (if any) on line 14(b)(1). Enter here and on Form 1040, line 15 . . . .

For Paperwork Reduction Act Notice, see page 1 of separate instructions.   Form **4797** (1983)

Form 4797 (1983)

PART III.—Gain From Disposition of Property Under Sections 1245, 1250, 1251, 1252, 1254, 1255

Skip lines 23 and 24 if you did not dispose of farm property or farmland, or if a partnership files this form.

15 Description of sections 1245, 1250, 1251, 1252, 1254, and 1255 property:	Date acquired (mo., day, yr.)	Date sold (mo., day, yr.)
(A)		
(B)		
(C)		
(D)		

Relate lines 15(A) through 15(D) to these columns ► ► ► ►	Property (A)	Property (B)	Property (C)	Property (D)
16 Gross sales price				
17 Cost or other basis plus expense of sale				
18 Depreciation (or depletion) allowed (or allowable)				
19 Adjusted basis, subtract line 18 from line 17				
20 Total gain, subtract line 19 from line 16				
21 If section 1245 property:				
(a) Depreciation allowed (or allowable) after applicable date (see instructions)				
(b) Enter smaller of line 20 or 21(a)				
22 If section 1250 property: (If straight line depreciation used, enter zero on line 22(f).)				
(a) Additional depreciation after 12/31/75				
(b) Applicable percentage times the smaller of line 20 or line 22(a) (see instruction G.4)				
(c) Subtract line 22(a) from line 20. If line 20 is not more than line 22(a), skip lines 22(d) and 22(e)				
(d) Additional depreciation after 12/31/69 and before 1/1/76				
(e) Applicable percentage times the smaller of line 22(c) or 22(d) (see instruction G.4)				
(f) Add lines 22(b), and 22(e)				
23 If section 1251 property:				
(a) If farmland, enter soil, water, and land clearing expenses for current year and the four preceding years				
(b) If farm property other than land, subtract line 21(b) from line 20; if farmland, enter smaller of line 20 or 23(a)				
(c) Excess deductions account (see instruction G.5)				
(d) Enter smaller of line 23(b) or 23(c)				
24 If section 1252 property:				
(a) Soil, water, and land clearing expenses				
(b) Amount from line 23(d), if none enter zero				
(c) Subtract line 24(b) from line 24(a). If line 24(b) is more than line 24(a), enter zero				
(d) Line 24(c) times applicable percentage (see instruction G.5)				
(e) Subtract line 24(b) from line 20				
(f) Enter smaller of line 24(d) or 24(e)				
25 If section 1254 property:				
(a) Intangible drilling and development costs deducted after 12/31/75 (see instruction G.6)				
(b) Enter smaller of line 20 or 25(a)				
26 If section 1255 property:				
(a) Applicable percentage of payments excluded from income under section 126 (see instruction G.7)				
(b) Enter the smaller of line 20 or 26(a)				

Summary of Part III Gains (Complete Property columns (A) through (D) through line 26(b) before going to line 27)

27 Total gains for all properties (add columns (A) through (D), line 20) ....

28 Add columns (A) through (D), lines 21(b), 22(f), 23(d), 24(f), 25(b) and 26(b). Enter here and on Part II, line 8 .....

29 Subtract line 28 from line 27. Enter the portion from casualty and theft on Form 4684, line 21; enter the portion from other than casualty and theft on Form 4797, Part I, line 4 ....

PART IV.—Complete this Part Only if You Elect Out of the Installment Method And Report a Note or Other Obligation at Less Than Full Face Value

☐ Check here if you elect out of the installment method.

Enter the face amount of the note or other obligation ► ---

Enter the percentage of valuation of the note or other obligation ►

B–20 FORM 4868 APPLICATION FOR AUTOMATIC EXTENSION OF TIME TO FILE U. S. INDIVIDUAL INCOME TAX RETURN

Form **4868** Department of the Treasury Internal Revenue Service	**Application for Automatic Extension of Time to File U.S. Individual Income Tax Return**	OMB No. 1545-0188 **1983** 71

Please Type or Print	Your first name and initial (if joint return, also give spouse's name and initial)	Last name	Your social security number
	Present home address (Number and street, including apartment number, or rural route)		Spouse's social security no.
	City, town or post office, State, and ZIP code		

Note: File this form with the Internal Revenue Service Center where you must file your income tax return and pay the amount shown on line 6 below. **This is not an extension of time for payment of tax.** You will be charged a penalty for late payment of tax and late filing unless you show reasonable cause for not paying or filing on time (see instructions).

If you expect to file a gift tax return (Form 709 or Form 709-A) for 1983, generally due by April 16, 1984, check this box . . . . ▶ ☐

I request an automatic 4-month extension of time to August 15, 1984, to file Form 1040A or Form 1040 for the calendar year 1983 (or if a fiscal year Form 1040 to _____ , 19 _____ , for the tax year ending _____ , 19 _____).

1	Total income tax liability for 1983. (You may estimate this amount.) . . . . **Note:** *You **must** enter an amount on line 1. If you do not expect to owe tax, enter zero (0).*	**1**	
2	Federal income tax withheld	**2**	
3	1983 estimated tax payments (include 1982 overpayment allowed as a credit) .	**3**	
4	Other payments and credits you expect to show on Form 1040A or Form 1040 ·	**4**	
5	Add lines 2, 3, and 4	**5**	
6	Income tax balance due (subtract line 5 from line 1). Pay in full with this form. (If line 5 is more than line 1, enter zero (0).). . . . . ▶	**6**	
7	Total gift tax you expect to owe for 1983 (see instructions) . . . . ▶	**7**	

If you send only one check for both income and gift tax due, attach a statement showing how much of the check applies to each type of tax.

Signature and Verification

If Prepared by Taxpayer.—Under penalties of perjury, I declare that I have examined this form, including accompanying schedules and statements, and to the best of my knowledge and belief, it is true, correct, and complete.

_____   _____
Your signature   Date

_____   _____
Spouse's signature (if filing jointly, BOTH must sign even if only one had income)   Date

If Prepared by Someone Other Than Taxpayer.—Under penalties of perjury, I declare that I have examined this form, including accompanying schedules and statements, and to the best of my knowledge and belief, it is true, correct, and complete; and that I am authorized to prepare this form.

_____   _____
Signature of preparer other than taxpayer   Date

Note: The person who signs this form may be an attorney or certified public accountant qualified to practice before the IRS, a person enrolled to practice before the IRS, or a person holding a power of attorney. If the taxpayer cannot sign because of illness, absence, or other good cause, a person in a close personal or business relationship to the taxpayer may sign this form.

For Paperwork Reduction Act Notice, see back of form.   Form **4868** (1983)

General Instructions

Paperwork Reduction Act Notice.—We ask for this information to carry out the Internal Revenue laws of the United States. We need it to ensure that taxpayers are complying with these laws and to allow us to figure and collect the right amount of tax. You are required to give us this information.

Purpose of Form.—Use Form 4868 to ask for an automatic 4-month extension of time to file **Form 1040A** or **Form 1040**. The 4-month extension period includes the automatic 2-month extension granted to U.S. citizens and resident aliens who are living or traveling outside the United States and Puerto Rico on the due date for filing their returns. Do not file this form if:

● You want the IRS to figure your tax, or
● You are under a court order to file your return by the regular due date.

The extension will be granted if you complete this form properly, file it on time, **and pay with it the amount of tax shown on line 6.** We will notify you **only** if your request for an extension is denied.

Note: *Any extension of time granted for filing your 1983* **calendar** *year income tax return also extends the time for filing a gift tax return for 1983.*

Filing Form 2688.—Except in cases of undue hardship, we will not accept Form 2688, Application for Extension of Time to File U.S. Individual Income Tax Return, until you have first used Form 4868.

If you have filed Form 4868 and still need more time, use Form 2688 or write a letter of explanation. You must show reasonable cause. Send Form 2688 or the letter to the Internal Revenue Service Center where you file your Form 1040A or Form 1040. (See **Where to File,** below.)

If you need a further extension, ask for it early so that, if denied, you can still file your return on time.

When to File.—File Form 4868 by April 16, 1984. If you are filing a fiscal year Form 1040, file Form 4868 by the regular due date of your return. If you were granted the automatic 2-month extension explained above, file this form by the end of the 2-month period (June 15, 1984, for a 1983 calendar year return).

You may file Form 1040A or Form 1040 any time before the 4-month period ends.

Where to File.—Mail this form to the **Internal Revenue Service Center** for the place where you live.

If you are located in:	Use this address:
New Jersey, New York City and counties of Nassau, Rockland, Suffolk, and Westchester	Holtsville, NY 00501
New York (all other counties). Connecticut, Maine, Massachusetts, New Hampshire, Rhode Island, Vermont	Andover, MA 05501
Delaware, District of Columbia, Maryland, Pennsylvania	Philadelphia, PA 19255
Alabama, Florida, Georgia, Mississippi, South Carolina	Atlanta, GA 31101
Michigan, Ohio	Cincinnati, OH 45999
Arkansas, Kansas, Louisiana, New Mexico, Oklahoma, Texas	Austin, TX 73301

Alaska, Arizona, Colorado, Idaho, Minnesota, Montana, Nebraska, Nevada, North Dakota, Oregon, South Dakota, Utah, Washington, Wyoming	Ogden, UT 84201
Illinois, Iowa, Missouri, Wisconsin	Kansas City, MO 64999
California, Hawaii	Fresno, CA 93888
Indiana, Kentucky, North Carolina, Tennessee, Virginia, West Virginia	Memphis, TN 37501
American Samoa	Philadelphia, PA 19255
Guam	Commissioner of Revenue and Taxation Agana, GU 96910
Puerto Rico (or if excluding income under section 933) Virgin Islands: Nonpermanent residents	Philadelphia, PA 19255
Virgin Islands: Permanent residents	Bureau of Internal Revenue Charlotte Amalie St. Thomas, VI 00801
A.P.O. or F.P.O. address of:	Miami—Atlanta, GA 31101 New York—Holtsville, NY 00501 San Francisco—Fresno, CA 93888 Seattle—Ogden, UT 84201
Foreign country: U.S. citizens and those excluding income under section 911 or 931, or claiming the housing deduction under section 911	Philadelphia, PA 19255

Penalties.—You may be charged one or both of the following penalties.

Late payment penalty.—Form 4868 does not extend the time to pay income or gift tax. A penalty of 1/2 of 1% of any tax (other than estimated tax) not paid by the regular due date is charged for each month, or part of a month, that the tax remains unpaid. The penalty will not be charged if you can show reasonable cause for not paying on time. The penalty is limited to 25%.

You are considered to have reasonable cause for the period covered by this automatic extension if the amount you owe on Form 1040A, line 27, or Form 1040, line 68 (minus any estimated tax penalty):

● Is not more than 10% of the amount shown as total tax on Form 1040A, line 23, or Form 1040, line 56, and
● Is paid with Form 1040A or Form 1040.

If both of the above conditions are not met, the late payment penalty will apply, unless you show reasonable cause.

If you have reasonable cause, attach a statement to your return giving your reason.

If you cannot show reasonable cause, figure the penalty on the total tax due on Form 1040A, line 27, or Form 1040, line 68, from the regular due date of your return to the date of payment.

Late filing penalty.—A penalty is charged if your return is filed after the due date (including extensions), unless you can show reasonable cause for filing late. The penalty is 5% of the tax not paid by the regular due date for each month, or part of a month, that your return is late, but not more than 25%. If your return is more than 60 days late, the penalty will not be less than $100 or the balance of tax due on your return, whichever is smaller. If you file your return late, attach a full explanation with the return.

Interest.—Interest is charged from the regular due date of the return until the tax is paid. It will be charged even if:

● You have been granted an extension, or
● You show reasonable cause for not paying the tax on time.

Line-by-Line Instructions

At the top of this form, fill in the spaces for your name, address, social security number, and spouse's social security number if you are filing a joint return. If you expect to file a gift tax return **(Form 709** or **Form 709-A)** for 1983, generally due by April 16, 1984, check the box on the front of this form. Below that, if you are on a fiscal year, fill in the date on which your 4-month extension will end and the date your tax year ends.

We have provided specific instructions for most of the lines on the form. Those lines that do not appear in these instructions are self-explanatory.

Note: *If you were granted the automatic 2-month extension and are filing Form 4868 to ask for an additional 2-month extension, write "Taxpayer Abroad" across the top of this form.*

Line 1.—Enter the total amount of income tax you expect to owe for 1983 (the amount you expect to enter on Form 1040A, line 23, or Form 1040, line 56, when you file your return). Be sure to estimate the amount correctly. If you underestimate this amount, you may be charged a penalty as explained earlier under **Penalties.**

Line 6.—Form 4868 does not extend the time to pay your income tax. Therefore, you must pay the amount of income tax shown on line 6 in full with this form.

Line 7.—If you plan to use the extension of time to file your gift tax return, enter the amount of gift tax you expect to owe for 1983. To avoid the late payment penalty, you must pay this amount in full with Form 4868 unless you specifically request an extension to pay the gift tax. To request an extension to pay the gift tax only, you must attach a statement to this form that paying the gift tax on the due date would cause you undue hardship (not merely inconvenience).

If your spouse is filing a separate Form 4868, enter on your form only the total gift tax **you** expect to owe.

If you are filing Form 4868 with your spouse, enter on line 7 the total gift tax the two of you expect to owe. However, if each of you expects to file a gift tax return, also show in the space to the right of line 7 how much gift tax each expects to owe for 1983.

Below line 7, sign and date the form. If someone else prepares the form for you, that person must sign and date the form.

How to Claim Credit for Payment Made With This Form.— If you file Form 1040A, include the amount paid (line 6) with this form in the total on Form 1040A, line 25. Also write "Form 4868" and the amount paid in the space to the left of line 25. If you file Form 1040, enter the amount paid (line 6) with this form on Form 1040, line 60.

If you and your spouse file separate Forms 4868 for 1983, but file a joint income tax return for the year, enter on the appropriate line of your Form 1040A or Form 1040, the total of the amounts paid on the separate Forms 4868. Also enter the social security numbers of both spouses in the spaces on your return.

If you and your spouse file a joint Form 4868 for 1983, but file separate income tax returns for the year, you may claim the total tax payment (line 6) on your separate return or on your spouse's separate return or you may divide it in any agreed amounts. Be sure to enter the social security numbers of both spouses on the separate returns.

B–21   FORM 4972 SPECIAL 10-YEAR AVERAGING METHOD

Form **4972** Department of the Treasury Internal Revenue Service	**Special 10-Year Averaging Method** **(For Total Distribution from Qualified Retirement Plan)** ▶ Attach to Form 1040 or Form 1041. ▶ See separate instructions.	OMB No. 1545-0193 19**83** 74

Name(s) as shown on return	Identifying number

By checking this box ▶ ☐ , I agree, for this and all other lump-sum distributions I receive for the same employee, not to treat any part as capital gain. I know this decision cannot be changed. (See Instruction F.)

PART I.— Use Part I if You Have Not Filed Form 4972 for Any Year after 1977

1	Capital gain part from payer's statement (Form 1099R, box 2)	1	
	If you are using the 10-year averaging method for the capital gain from the distribution as well as for the ordinary income, leave line 1 blank and include the capital gain on line 2 (see instruction F). Otherwise, enter the capital gain from your payer's statement (Form 1099R, box 2). If you are filing Schedule D and cannot take the exclusion on line 4 below or do not have to decrease the capital gain for Federal estate tax, enter the capital gain on your Schedule D also. See the separate instructions for line 1.		
2	Ordinary income part from payer's statement (Form 1099R, box 3). Enter here instead of on Form 1040 or Form 1041	2	
3	Add lines 1 and 2	3	
4	Death benefit exclusion (see instructions for line 4)	4	
5	Total taxable amount (subtract line 4 from line 3)	5	
6	Current actuarial value of annuity, if applicable (from Form 1099R, box 9)	6	
7	Adjusted total taxable amount (add lines 5 and 6). If this amount is $70,000 or more, skip lines 8 through 11, and enter this amount on line 12 also	7	
8	50% of line 7, but not more than $10,000 8		
9	Subtract $20,000 from line 7. Enter difference. If line 7 is $20,000 or less, enter zero . . . 9		
10	20% of line 9 10		
11	Minimum distribution allowance (subtract line 10 from line 8)	11	
12	Subtract line 11 from line 7	12	
13	Federal estate tax attributable to lump-sum distribution. Do not deduct on Form 1040 or Form 1041 the amount entered on this line that is attributable to the ordinary income entered on line 2. (See instructions for line 13)	13	
14	Subtract line 13 from line 12	14	
15	$2,300 plus 10% of line 14	15	
16	Tax on amount on line 15. Use Tax Rate Schedule X (Single Taxpayer Rate) in Form 1040 Instructions	16	
17	Multiply line 16 by 10. If no entry on line 6, skip lines 18 through 23, and enter this amount on line 24 also	17	
18	Divide line 6 by line 7 (carry percentage to four places)	18	%
19	Multiply line 11 by percentage on line 18	19	
20	Subtract line 19 from line 6	20	
21	$2,300 plus 10% of line 20	21	
22	Tax on amount on line 21. Use Tax Rate Schedule X (Single Taxpayer Rate) in Form 1040 Instructions .	22	
23	Multiply line 22 by 10	23	
24	Subtract line 23 from line 17.	24	
25	Divide line 2 by line 3 (carry percentage to four places)	25	%
26	Tax on ordinary income part of lump-sum distribution (multiply line 24 by percentage on line 25). Show this amount on Form 1040, line 39, or Form 1041, line 26b . . . . ▶	26	

For Paperwork Reduction Act Notice, see separate instructions.   Form **4972** (1983)

Form 4972 (1983)   Page **2**

PART II.—Use Part II if You Filed Form 4972 for Any Other Year After 1977 or if You Received an Annuity Contract after 1977

		(a) Total received 1983	(b) Total received after 1977 and before 1983	(c) Total of columns (a) and (b)
1	Capital gain part from payer's statement (Form 1099R, box 2) . . . . [1]			
	If you are using the 10-year averaging method for the capital gain from the distribution as well as for the ordinary income, leave line 1 blank and include the capital gain on line 2 (see instruction F). Otherwise, enter the capital gain from your payer's statement (Form 1099R, box 2). If you are filing Schedule D and cannot take the exclusion on line 4 below or do not have to decrease the capital gain for Federal estate tax, enter the capital gain on your Schedule D also. See separate instructions for line 1.			
2	Ordinary income part from payer's statement (Form 1099R, box 3). Enter here instead of on Form 1040 or Form 1041 . . . . [2]			
3	Add lines 1 and 2 . . . . [3]			
4	Death benefit exclusion (see instructions for Part I, line 4) [4]			
5	Total taxable amount (subtract line 4 from line 3) . . [5]			
6	Current actuarial value of annuity if applicable (from Form 1099R, box 9) . . . . [6]			
7	Adjusted total taxable amount (add lines 5 and 6, column (c)). If this amount is $70,000 or more, skip lines 8 through 11, and enter this amount on line 12 also . . . . [7]			
8	50% of line 7, but not more than $10,000 . . . . [8]			
9	Subtract $20,000 from line 7. Enter difference. If line 7 is $20,000 or less, enter zero . . . . . [9]			
10	20% of line 9 . . . . [10]			
11	Minimum distribution allowance (subtract line 10 from line 8) . . . . . [11]			
12	Subtract line 11 from line 7. [12]			
13	Federal estate tax attributable to lump-sum distribution. Do not deduct on Form 1040 or Form 1041 the amount entered on this line that is attributable to the ordinary income entered on line 2. (See instructions for Part I, line 13) . . . . [13]			
14	Subtract line 13 from line 12. [14]			
15	$2,300 plus 10% of line 14 . . . . [15]			
16	Tax on amount on line 15. Use Tax Rate Schedule X (Single Taxpayer Rate) in Form 1040 Instructions . [16]			
17	Multiply line 16 by 10. If no entry on line 6, skip lines 18 through 23, and enter this amount on line 24 also . . . . [17]			
18	Divide line 6, column (c), by line 7 (carry percentage to four places) . . . . . [18]			%
19	Multiply line 11 by percentage on line 18 . . . . . [19]			
20	Subtract line 19 from line 6, column (c) . . . . . [20]			
21	$2,300 plus 10% of line 20 . . . . . [21]			
22	Tax on amount on line 21. Use Tax Rate Schedule X (Single Taxpayer Rate) in Form 1040 Instructions . [22]			
23	Multiply line 22 by 10 . . . . . [23]			
24	Subtract line 23 from line 17 . . . . . [24]			
25	Divide line 2, column (c), by line 3, column (c) (carry percentage to four places) . . . . . [25]			%
26	Tax on ordinary income parts of lump-sum distributions (multiply line 24 by percentage on line 25) [26]			
27	Tax on ordinary income part of lump-sum distribution shown on Form 4972, Part I or Part II, for 1978 through 1982 [27]			
28	Tax on ordinary income part of lump-sum distribution (subtract line 27 from line 26). Show this amount, but not less than zero, on Form 1040, line 39, or Form 1041, line 26b . . . . . ▶ [28]			

B–22 FORM 5695 RESIDENTIAL ENERGY CREDIT

Form **5695**	**Residential Energy Credit**	OMB No. 1545-0214
Department of the Treasury Internal Revenue Service	▶ Attach to Form 1040. ▶ See Instructions on back. ▶ For Paperwork Reduction Act Notice, see instructions on back.	**1983** 31

Name(s) as shown on Form 1040	Your social security number

Enter the address of your principal residence on which the credit is claimed if it is different from the address shown on Form 1040.

If you have an energy credit carryover from a previous tax year and no energy savings costs this year, skip to Part III, line 24.

PART I.—Fill in your energy conservation costs (but do not include repair or maintenance costs).

1 Was your principal residence substantially completed before April 20, 1977? (see instructions) ▶ ☐ Yes ☐ No
Note: You MUST answer this question. Failure to do so will delay the processing of your return. If you checked the "No" box, you CANNOT claim an energy credit under Part I and you should not fill in lines 2 through 12 of this form.

2 a Insulation	2a	
b Storm (or thermal) windows or doors	2b	
c Caulking or weatherstripping	2c	
d A replacement burner for your existing furnace that reduces fuel use	2d	
e A device for modifying flue openings to make a heating system more efficient	2e	
f An electrical or mechanical furnace ignition system that replaces a gas pilot light	2f	
g A thermostat with an automatic setback	2g	
h A meter that shows the cost of energy used	2h	
3 Total (add lines 2a through 2h)	3	
4 Enter the part of expenditures made from nontaxable government grants and subsidized financing	4	
5 Subtract line 4 from line 3	5	
6 Maximum amount of cost on which credit can be figured	6	$2,000 00
7 Enter the total energy conservation costs for this residence. Add line 2 of your 1978, 1979, and 1980 Forms 5695 and line 3 of your 1981 and 1982 Forms 5695	7	
8 Subtract line 7 from line 6	8	
9 Enter the total nontaxable grants and subsidized financing used to purchase qualified energy items for this residence. Add the amount on line 4 of this form and your 1981and 1982 Forms 5695	9	
10 Subtract line 9 from line 8. If zero or less, do not complete the rest of this part	10	
11 Enter the amount on line 5 or line 10, whichever is less	11	
12 Enter 15% of line 11 here and include in amount on line 23 below	12	

PART II.—Fill in your renewable energy source costs (but do not include repair or maintenance costs).

13 a Solar ____ 13 b Geothermal ____ 13 c Wind ____ Total ▶	13d	
14 Enter the part of expenditures made from nontaxable government grants and subsidized financing	14	
15 Subtract line 14 from line 13	15	
16 Maximum amount of cost on which the credit can be figured	16	$10,000 00
17 Enter the total renewable energy source costs for this residence. Add line 5 of your 1978 Form 5695, line 9 of your 1979 and 1980 Forms 5695, and line 13d of your 1981 and 1982 Forms 5695	17	
18 Subtract line 17 from line 16	18	
19 Enter the total nontaxable grants and subsidized financing used to purchase qualified energy items for this residence. Add the amount on line 14 of this form and your 1981 and 1982 Forms 5695	19	
20 Subtract line 19 from line 18. If zero or less, do not complete the rest of this part	20	
21 Enter the amount on line 15 or line 20, whichever is less	21	
22 Enter 40% of line 21 here and include in amount on line 23 below	22	

PART III.—Fill in this part to figure the limitation.

23 Add lines 12 and 22. If less than $10, enter zero	23	
24 Enter your energy credit carryover from a previous tax year. Caution—Do not make an entry on this line if your 1982 Form 1040, line 50, showed an amount of more than zero	24	
25 Add lines 23 and 24	25	
26 Enter the amount of tax shown on Form 1040, line 40	26	
27 Add lines 41 through 46 from Form 1040 and enter the total	27	
28 Subtract line 27 from line 26. If zero or less, enter zero	28	
29 Residential energy credit. Enter the amount on line 25 or line 28, whichever is less. Also, enter this amount on Form 1040, line 47. Complete Part IV below if this line is less than line 25	29	

PART IV.—Fill in this part to figure your carryover to 1984 (Complete only if line 29 is less than line 25).

30 Enter amount from Part III, line 25	30	
31 Enter amount from Part III, line 29	31	
32 Credit carryover to 1984 (subtract line 31 from line 30)	32	

General Instructions

Paperwork Reduction Act Notice.—We ask for this information to carry out the Internal Revenue laws of the United States. We need it to ensure that taxpayers are complying with these laws and to allow us to figure and collect the right amount of tax. You are required to give us this information.

Purpose of Form.—Use this form to figure your residential energy credit if you had qualified energy saving items installed in your principal residence. The instructions below list conditions you must meet to take the credit. If you have an energy credit carryover from the previous tax year and no energy saving costs this year, skip to Part III of the form. Attach Form 5695 to your tax return. For more information, please get **Publication 903,** Energy Credits for Individuals.

Two energy credits make up the residential energy credit, each with its own conditions and limits. These credits are based on: (1) Costs for home energy conservation, and (2) Costs for renewable energy source property.

The credit is based on the cost of items installed in your principal residence after April 19, 1977, and before January 1, 1986.

What is your principal residence?—To qualify as your principal residence, your residence must be the home in the United States where you live (you may own it or rent it from another person).

A summer or vacation home does not qualify.

Special Rules.—If you live in a condominium, cooperative apartment, occupy a dwelling unit jointly, or share the cost of energy property, see **Publication 903** for more details.

What are energy saving items?—You can take the credit for energy conservation and renewable energy source items.

Energy conservation items are limited to:

- insulation (fiberglass, cellulose, etc.) for ceilings, walls, floors, roofs, water heaters, etc.
- storm (or thermal) windows or doors for the outside of your residence.
- caulking or weatherstripping for windows or doors for the outside of your residence.
- a replacement burner for your existing furnace that reduces fuel use. The burner must replace an existing burner. It does not qualify if it is acquired as a component of, or for use in, a new furnace or boiler.
- a device for modifying flue openings to make a heating system more efficient.
- an electrical or mechanical furnace ignition system that replaces a gas pilot light.
- a thermostat with an automatic setback.
- a meter that shows the cost of energy used.

To take the credit for an energy conservation item, you must:

- install the item in your principal residence which was substantially completed before April 20, 1977,
- be the first one to use the item, and
- expect it to last at least 3 years.

The maximum **accumulated** credit for energy conservation items cannot be more than **$300** ($2,000 x 15%) for each principal residence.

Renewable energy source items include solar, wind, and geothermal energy items that heat or cool your principal residence or provide hot water or electricity for it.

Examples of solar energy items that may qualify include:

- collectors,
- rockbeds,
- heat exchangers, and
- solar panels installed on roofs (including those installed as a roof or part of a roof).

An example of an item that uses wind energy is a windmill that produces energy in any form (usually electricity) for your residence.

Geothermal energy property expenditures must be made in connection with a "geothermal deposit." A geothermal deposit is one having a temperature exceeding 50 degrees Celsius (122 degrees Fahrenheit) as measured at the wellhead or in the case of a natural hot spring (where no well is drilled), at the intake to the distribution system . Generally , the qualifying geothermal resources that are economically recoverable are located in States west of the Rocky Mountains (except for geothermal springs located in Arkansas).

To take the credit for a renewable energy source item, you must:

- be the first one to use the item, and
- expect it to last at least 5 years.

The maximum **accumulated** credit for renewable energy source items cannot be more than $4,000 ($10,000 x 40%) for each principal residence.

What items are NOT eligible for the energy credit?—Do not take credit for:

- carpeting;
- drapes;
- wood paneling;
- wood or peat-burning stoves;
- hydrogen fueled residential equipment;
- siding for the outside of your residence;
- heat pumps (both air and water);
- fluorescent replacement lighting systems;
- replacement boilers and furnaces; and
- swimming pools used to store energy.

Federal, State, or local government nontaxable grants and subsidized financing.—Qualified expenditures financed with nontaxable Federal, State, or local government grants cannot be used to figure the energy credit. Also, if Federal, State, or local government programs provide subsidized financing for any part of qualified expenditures, that part cannot be used to figure the energy credit. You must reduce the expenditure limits on energy conservation and renewable energy source property for a dwelling by the part of expenditures financed by Federal, State, or local government subsidized energy financing, as well as by the amount of nontaxable Federal, State, or local government grants used to purchase conservation or renewable energy source property.

Figuring the credit for more than one principal residence.—You can take the maximum credit for each principal residence you live in. If you use all of your credit for one residence and then move, you may take the maximum credit amount on your next residence.

To figure your 1983 energy credit for more than one principal residence:

(1) Fill out Part I or II on a separate Form 5695 for each principal residence.

(2) Enter the total of all parts on line 23 of one of the forms.

(3) In the space above line 23, write "More than one principal residence."

(4) Attach all forms to your return.

Caution: *You should keep a copy of each Form 5695 that you file for your records. For example, if you sell your principal residence, you will need to know the amount of the credit claimed in prior tax years. If the items for which you took the credit increased the basis of your principal residence, you must reduce the basis by the credit you took.*

If the credit is more than your tax.—If your energy credit for this year is more than your tax minus certain other credits, you can carry over the excess energy credit to the following tax year or until the maximum accumulated credit is used.

Specific Instructions

Part I, line 1.— For energy conservation items to qualify, your principal residence must have been substantially completed before April 20, 1977. A dwelling unit is considered substantially completed when it can be used as a personal residence even though minor items remain unfinished.

Part I, lines 2a through 2h.—Enter your energy conservation costs (including expenditures made with nontaxable government grants and subsidized financing) only for this tax year. Count the cost of the item and its installation in or on your principal residence. Do not include the cost of repairs or maintenance for energy conservation items.

Part I, line 4.—Enter the amount of nontaxable government grants and subsidized financing used to purchase the energy items on lines 2a through 2h. If you do not know the amount, check with the government agency that gave you the grant or subsidized financing.

Part I, line 7.—Enter your total energy conservation costs from 1978, 1979, 1980, 1981, and 1982 for this principal residence. If you had energy conservation costs in the previous tax year but could not take a credit because it was less than $10, enter zero.

Part I, line 9.—Enter the part of nontaxable government grants and subsidized financing received under Federal, State, or local programs to purchase energy items in 1981 through 1983. You must use the amounts received under these programs to reduce the maximum amount of cost used to figure the credit. If you do not know the amount of the nontaxable grant, check with the government agency which gave you the grant or subsidized financing.

Part II, lines 13a through 13d.—Enter your renewable energy source costs (including expenditures made with nontaxable government grants and subsidized financing) only for this tax year. Do not include the cost of repairs or maintenance for renewable energy source items.

Part II, line 14.—See Part I, line 4 for an explanation.

Part II, line 17.—Enter your total renewable energy source costs from 1978, 1979, 1980, 1981, and 1982 for this principal residence. If you had renewable energy source costs in the previous tax year but could not take a credit because it was less than $10, enter zero.

Part II, line 19.—See Part I, line 9 for an explanation.

Part III, line 24.—Generally, your energy credit carryover will be computed on your prior year Form 5695, Part IV. Exception—If the alternative minimum tax applied, see **Publication 909,** Minimum Tax and Alternative Minimum Tax.

Part IV.—Complete this part only if line 29 is less than line 25. You can carry over the amount entered on line 32 to your next tax year.

B–23   FORM 5884 JOBS CREDIT

Form **5884** Department of the Treasury Internal Revenue Service	**Jobs Credit** (and WIN credit carryover) ▶ Attach to your tax return.	OMB No. 1545-0219 19**83** 77

Name(s) as shown on return	Identifying number

PART I.—Jobs Credit

1   Enter the number of employees and total qualified wages paid or incurred during the tax year (up to $6,000 for each employee for each of the first two years) for services of employees who are certified as members of a targeted group. See instructions for special rules on qualified summer youth employees.

		Number of employees	Total qualified wages
First year	Do not include sum-	(a)	(b)
Second year	mer youth employees	(c)	(d)
Qualified summer youth employees		(e)	(f)

2   Enter 50% of line 1(b) **2**

3   Enter 25% of line 1(d) **3**

4   Enter 85% of line 1(f) **4**

5   Current year jobs credit—Add lines 2, 3, and 4. Enter here and include on Schedule C (Form 1040), line 28b; Form 1120, line 13(b), page 1; or the corresponding line on other returns. (Members of a group of trades or businesses under common control, see Specific Instructions) **5**

6   Flow-through jobs credits from other entities . . . .

If you are a—	Then enter total of current year jobs credit(s) from—
a Shareholder . .	Schedule K-1 (Form 1120S), line 12 . . . .
b Partner. . .	Schedule K-1 (Form 1065), line 14 . . .
c Beneficiary. .	Schedule K-1 (Form 1041), line 10 . . .
d Patron . . .	(see instructions for line 6d) . . . .

  6

7   Total jobs credit for current year—Add lines 5 and 6 (S corporations, partnerships, estates, trusts, and cooperatives, see instructions for line 7.) **7**

8   a   Individuals—From Form 1040, enter tax from line 38 plus any additional tax from Form 4970 .
   b   Estates and trusts —From Form 1041, enter tax from line 26a, plus any section 644 tax on trusts
   c   Corporations (1120 filers)—From Form 1120, Schedule J, enter tax from line 3 . . . . .
   d   Other organizations—Enter income tax before credits from return **8**

9   a   Individuals—From Form 1040, enter credits from lines 41 through 44 . . . . . .
   b   Estates and trusts—From Form 1041, enter credits from lines 27a and 27b . . . . . .
   c   Corporations (1120 filers)—From Form 1120, Schedule J, enter credits from lines 4(a), 4(b), and 4(f) . . . .
   d   Other organizations—Enter total of any foreign tax, possessions, and investment credits . .   **9**

10   Income tax liability as adjusted (subtract line 9 from line 8) **10**

PART II.—Allowed WIN Credit Carryover

11   WIN credit carryover from prior year . . . .   **11** |

12   Allowed WIN credit for 1983—Enter smaller of line 10 or line 11 . . . .   **12**

PART III.—Allowed Jobs Credit

13   Line 10 less any WIN credit taken on line 12 . . . .   **13**

14   Child care credit—Form 1040, line 45 (individuals only) · · · · · · · · · · ·   **14**

15   Income tax liability as adjusted—Subtract line 14 from line 13. . . .   **15** |

16   Jobs credit limitation—Multiply line 15 by 90% (line 15 x .90) **16**

17   Allowed jobs credit for 1983 tax year—Enter smaller of line 7 or line 16. If line 7 does not contain an entry, enter zero. (Section 1381(a) cooperatives: see line 7 instructions) **17**

   If you have an unused jobs credit from other years, complete lines 18–20. Otherwise, skip to line 21

18   Tax liability limit for unused jobs credits from other years—Subtract line 17 from line 16 . . . . .   **18**

19   Carryback and carryover of unused jobs credits from other years **19**

20   Allowed unused jobs credits from other years—Enter smaller of line 18 or line 19 . . . . . .   **20**

21   Allowed jobs and WIN credits from all sources—Add lines 12, 17, and 20. Enter here and on Form 1040, line 46; Schedule J (Form 1120), line 4(c), page 3; or the appropriate line on other returns . .   **21**

Instructions

(Section references are to the Internal Revenue Code, unless otherwise noted.)

Paperwork Reduction Act Notice.—We ask for this information to carry out the Internal Revenue laws of the United States. We need it to ensure that taxpayers are complying with these laws and to allow us to figure and collect the right amount of tax. You are required to give us this information.

Purpose of Form.— Use the 1983 Form 5884 if you had jobs credit employees and take an income tax credit for wages you paid or accrued for them during the tax year.

Mutual savings institutions, regulated investment companies, and real estate investment trusts can take a limited jobs credit. See section 52(e) and the related regulations.

You can take or revoke the jobs credit any time within 3 years from the date your return was due for the year. You can take the credit either on your original return or on an amended return. To revoke your jobs credit after you take it, file an amended return.

For more information, see **Publication 906,** Jobs and Research Credits.

How to Figure the Credit.—In general, you should figure your jobs credit based on the employee's wages subject to the Federal Unemployment Tax Act (FUTA) tax. Jobs credit wages, however, are limited to $6,000 for each employee ($3,000 for each qualified summer youth employee). Special rules apply in the following cases:

(1) You can take the jobs credit for *agricultural employees* who meet the other tests if their services qualify under FUTA as agricultural labor during more than half of any pay period. Base your jobs credit for each agricultural employee on the first $6,000 in wages subject to social security (FICA) tax you paid or accrued for that person during the year.

(2) You can take the jobs credit for *railroad employees* who meet the other tests if their wages qualify under the Railroad Unemployment Insurance Act (RUIA). Base your jobs credit for each employee on the first $500 a month you paid or accrued for that person during the year in wages subject to RUIA tax.

(3) Wages for *youths in a cooperative education program* are not subject to FUTA, but include their wages in the amount you use to figure your jobs credit. Base your jobs credit for each youth on the first $6,000 in wages you paid or accrued for that person during the year.

Your credit is based on a percentage of the wages for each employee in the following targeted groups:

- Referrals by a vocational rehabilitation program.
- Economically disadvantaged Vietnam-era veterans.
- Economically disadvantaged youths.
- Supplemental Security Income (SSI) recipients.
- General assistance recipients.
- Youths in a cooperative education program, who belong to an economically disadvantaged family.
- Economically disadvantaged ex-convicts.
- CETA employees whose jobs were involuntarily ended. (Only employees first beginning work between August 13, 1981, and January 1, 1983, can qualify as a member of this group.)
- Eligible work incentive employees.
- Qualified summer youth employees, age 16 or 17, who first worked for you between May 1 and September 15, 1983.

In addition, to claim a jobs credit on an employee's wages:

(1) more than half the wages received from you must be for working in your trade or business;

(2) the employee must be certified, as explained below, as belonging to a targeted group; and

(3) you may not claim a credit on wages that were repaid by a Federally funded on-the-job training program.

Effective for employees first beginning work after August 13, 1981, the employee cannot be:

(1) Your relative or dependent (see section 51(i)).

(2) Your rehired employee if he or she was not a targeted group member when employed earlier.

Certification is done by a local agency, generally an office of the State Employment Security Agency (Jobs Service). The agency gives the employer a form certifying that the employee is in a targeted group. The certification must be completed or the employer must request, in writing, a certification from the certifying agency by the date the employee begins work.

Certification of a Youth in a Cooperative Education Program.—For a youth in a cooperative education program, the certification is completed by the school administering the cooperative program. The school gives the employer a completed **Form 6199,** Certification of Youth Participating in a Qualified Cooperative Education Program.

Specific Instructions

Part I

On lines 1 through 5 figure your credit for wages you paid or accrued. If you have credits only from sources that shared a jobs credit (S corporations, partnerships, estates, trusts, or cooperatives), skip lines 1 through 5.

Whether or not you complete lines 1 through 5, enter on line 6 any credits you received from sources that share the credit. Complete the rest of the form to figure the credit to enter on your income tax return.

Controlled groups: The group member proportionately contributing the most first-year wages (or second-year wages if no first-year wages are involved) figures the group credit in Part I (lines 1–7 only) and skips Parts II and III.

On separate Forms 5884, that member and every other member of the group skips lines 1 through 4 and enters its share of the group credit on line 5. Each member then completes lines 6 through 21 on its separate form, entering any unused credit from other years on line 19. Each group member attaches to its Form 5884 a schedule showing how the group credit was divided among all the members. The members share the credit in the same proportion that they contributed qualifying wages.

Line 1(a).—Enter the number of employees for whom you have first-year wages.

Line 1(b).—Enter the first-year wages. They are limited to $6,000 of each employee's first-year wages. If you paid first-year wages to any of these employees last year, subtract those wages from the $6,000 limit.

For example, if a jobs credit employee started working in your business on September 1, 1982, and you are a calendar year taxpayer, you would have figured your 1982 jobs credit based on the first-year wages you paid between September 1 and December 31, 1982. You would figure your 1983 jobs credit on the rest of the first-year wages you paid between January 1 and August 31, 1983; and on the second-year wages you paid between September 1 and December 31, 1983.

For a vocational rehabilitation employee, count the years that person worked for you from the later of the date he or she began work or the date his or her rehabilitation plan started. For other jobs credit employees, count the years the person worked for you from the date he or she began work.

Line 1(c).—Enter the number of employees for whom you have second-year wages.

Line 1(d).—Enter the second-year wages. They are limited to $6,000 for each employee. If you paid second-year wages to any of these employees last year, subtract those wages from the $6,000 limit for that employee.

Line 1(f).—For each qualified summer youth employee, the wages are limited to those paid for any 90-day period between May 1 and September 15, up to $3,000. You cannot claim a credit for an employee who was your employee in any prior period.

Line 4.—**Taxpayers with qualified summer youth employees.**—Include 85% of the first $3,000 of wages paid to each qualified summer youth employee.

Line 5.—In general, you must subtract your current year jobs credit on line 5 from the deduction on your return for salaries and wages you paid or owe for 1983. This is true even if you cannot take the full credit this year and must carry part of it back or forward.

An exception is a jobs credit based on salaries and wages you capitalize for depreciation. If you have such a credit, reduce the amount on which you figure depreciation by the part of the current year jobs credit on line 5 that applies to the jobs credit wages you capitalize.

Another exception involves the full absorption method of inventory costing. See the proposed regulations under section 280C to reduce your basis in inventory for the jobs credit.

If either exception applies to you, attach a statement to your return to explain why the amount on line 5 differs from the amount you subtract from your salary and wage deduction. See **Publication 906** for details.

Line 6.—If you have flow-through credits from more than one entity or type of entity, add them up and enter the total on line 6.

Line 6d.—If you belong to a cooperative that has an excess jobs credit, the cooperative should have given you a statement that shows your share of the excess. Include on line 6 your total excess jobs credit from all cooperatives to which you belong.

Line 7.—*Estates and trusts:* The jobs credit on line 7 is shared between the estate or trust itself and the beneficiaries in proportion to the income allocable to each. On the dotted line to the left of the amount on line 7, the estate or trust should enter its own part of the total jobs credit. Please label it "1041 PORTION" and use *this amount* in Part III to figure the jobs credit to take on Form 1041.

S corporations and partnerships: Prorate the jobs credit on line 7 among the shareholders or partners. Attach Form 5884 to the return and on Schedule K-1 show the credit for each shareholder or partner.

Cooperatives: Most tax-exempt organizations cannot take the jobs credit; but a cooperative described in section 1381(a) takes the jobs credit to the extent it has tax liability. Any excess is shared among its patrons.

If the cooperative has unused jobs credits from tax years that ended before November 1, 1978, the cooperative can carry them back or forward. It cannot share them among its patrons.

Part III

Line 16.—The jobs credit you take for your 1983 tax year cannot be more than 90% of your tax for the year. The tax liability limit applies first to current and then to carryover jobs credits. You must make an entry on line 16 before figuring your allowed credit on lines 17 through 21.

Carryovers.—If the tax liability limit (line 16) prevents you from using your full jobs credit for your 1983 tax year, you can carry the excess back 3 years and forward 15 years, up to the tax liability limit for each year. To figure the amount of jobs credit that you may carry to other years, subtract line 16 from the total of lines 7 and 19. Apply any unused credit first to the earliest year to which it may be carried, and then to each later year in order.

If you have a carryover credit (new jobs credit or targeted jobs credit) from prior years that is more than the line 18 limit, you can carry it forward for 15 years from the tax year the credit was earned.

B–24   FORM 6251   ALTERNATIVE MINIMUM TAX COMPUTATION

Form **6251**	**Alternative Minimum Tax Computation**	OMB No. 1545-0227
Department of the Treasury Internal Revenue Service	▶ Attach to Forms 1040, 1040NR, 1041 or 990-T (Trust)	19**83** 33

Name(s) as shown on tax return	Identifying number

1	Adjusted gross income from Form 1040, or Form 1040NR, line 33 (estates and trusts, see instructions) · ·	**1**
2	Deductions (estates and trusts, see instructions):	
	a (1) Medical and dental expense from Schedule A, line 7 · · · **2a(1)**	
	(2) Multiply Form 1040, line 33 by 5% (.05) · · · · · · · **2a(2)**	
	(3) Subtract line 2a(2) from line 2a(1). (If less than zero, enter zero) · · · · · · · **2a(3)**	
	b Contributions from Schedule A, line 20 · · · · · · · · · · · **2b**	
	c Casualty and theft losses from Schedule A, line 21 · · · · · **2c**	
	d Interest expense on property used as a residence from Schedule A, line 13 · · · · **2d**	
	e (1) Interest, other than line 2d above, from Schedule A, line 16 **2e(1)**	
	(2) Net investment income · · · · · · · · · · · **2e(2)**	
	(3) Enter the smaller of line 2e(1) or line 2e(2) · · · · · · · **2e(3)**	
	f Gambling losses to the extent of gambling winnings from Schedule A, line 24 · · · **2f**	
	g Estate tax allowable under section 691(c) from Schedule A · · · · · · **2g**	
	h Add lines 2a(3), b, c, d, e(3), f, and g · · · · · · · · · · · · · · ·	**2h**
3	Subtract line 2h from line 1 ·	**3**
4	Tax preference items:	
	a All-savers interest exclusion, and dividend exclusion · · · · · **4a**	
	b 60% capital gain deduction · · · · · · · · · · · · · · · **4b**	
	c Accelerated depreciation on nonrecovery real property or 15-year real property · · **4c**	
	d Accelerated depreciation on leased personal property or leased recovery property	
	other than 15-year real property · · · · · · · · · · · · · **4d**	
	e Amortization of certified pollution control facilities · · · · · · · **4e**	
	f Mining exploration and development costs · · · · · · · · · **4f**	
	g Circulation and research and experimental expenditures · · · · · **4g**	
	h Reserves for losses on bad debts of financial institutions · · · · · **4h**	
	i Depletion · **4i**	
	j Incentive stock options · · · · · · · · · · · · · · · · · **4j**	
	k Intangible drilling costs · · · · · · · · · · · · · · · · · **4k**	
	l Add lines 4a through 4k ·	**4l**
5	Alternative minimum taxable income (add lines 3 and 4(l)) (short period returns, see instructions) · · · ·	**5**
6	Enter: $40,000, if married filing joint return or surviving spouse	
	$30,000, if single or head of household	**6**
	$20,000, if married filing separate return or estate or trust	
7	Subtract line 6 from line 5. If zero or less, do not complete the rest of this form · · · · · · · · ·	**7**
8	Enter 20% of line 7 ·	**8**
9	Amount from Form 1040, line 49 or Form 1040NR, line 51 (Do not include Form 1040, line 39 or 1040NR,	
	line 42.) (estates and trusts, see instructions) · · · · · · · · · · · · · · ·	**9**
10	Subtract line 9 from line 8. If zero or less, enter zero · · · · · · · · · · · · · · ·	**10**
11	Foreign tax credit ·	**11**
12	Alternative minimum tax (subtract line 11 from line 10). Enter on Form 1040, line 51, Form 1040NR, line	
	52, Form 1041, line 32, or Form 990-T, page 1, line 14 · · · · · · · · · · · · ·	**12**

Instructions

(Section References are to the Internal Revenue Code)

Paperwork Reduction Act Notice.— We ask for this information to carry out the Internal Revenue laws of the United States. We need it to ensure that taxpayers are complying with these laws and to allow us to figure and collect the right amount of tax. You are required to give us this information.

Purpose of Form.— Use this form to figure your alternative minimum tax, but file it only if you are liable. Individuals, estates or trusts may be liable if they have any tax preference items listed on line 4 or adjusted gross income of more than line 6.

If you made an election under section 58(i), enter zero on lines 4f, 4g, and 4k.

Minimum Tax Deferred From Earlier Year(s).— If a net operating loss carryover from an earlier year(s) reduces taxable income for 1983, and the net operating loss giving rise to the carryover resulted in the deferral of minimum tax in that earlier year(s), all or part of the deferred minimum tax may be includible as tax liability for 1983. Figure the deferred minimum tax at 15% and complete and attach a 1982 Form 4625, Computation of Minimum Tax—Individuals, lines 14 through 18. You may attach a schedule following the format of Form 4625. Enter the amount from line 18 on Form 1040, line 51, or Form 1041, line 32 and write "Form 4625."

Partners, Beneficiaries, etc.— If you are a:

(1) Partner or shareholder of an S corporation, take into account separately your distributive share of items of income and deductions that enter into the computation of tax preference items.

(2) Beneficiary of an estate or trust, see section 58(c).

(3) Participant in a common trust fund, see section 58(e).

(4) Shareholder or holder of beneficial interest in a regulated investment company or a real estate investment trust, see section 58(f).

Carryback and Carryover of Unused Credits.— It may be necessary to figure the carryback or carryover of unused credits. See section 55(c)(3).

(Continued on back)

Form **6251** (1983)

Line by Line Instructions

Line 1, Estates and Trusts.—Adjusted gross income is figured in the same way as for an individual except that the costs of the administration of the estate or trust are allowed in figuring adjusted gross income.

All taxpayers.—Do not include in adjusted gross income, interest expense incurred to purchase or carry a limited business interest in a partnership or S corporation.

Lines 2(a) through 2(g).—Do not include on these lines any deduction that can be carried back or forward as a net operating loss or forward as a charitable contribution.

Individuals.—Complete Schedule A (Form 1040) for any deduction listed on these lines, whether or not you completed it in figuring Form 1040, line 34(a).

Estates and Trusts.—Enter on the applicable line any deduction listed on these lines allowable to the estate or trust. Include on line 2h the deductions allowable under sections 642(c), 651(a), and 661(a).

Line 2(d).—Enter the part of Schedule A, line 13 that is from debts you incurred in acquiring, constructing, or substantially rehabilitating property, other than a houseboat, which you, or certain family members as listed in section 267(c)(4), use as a residence.

If you incurred the interest before July 1, 1982 the following applies. At the time you incurred the interest, it must have been secured by property which you, or certain family members as listed in section 267(c)(4), used as a residence.

Line 2(e)(2).—Enter your investment income minus investment expenses.

Investment income is your gross income from interest, dividends, rents, and royalties, and any amount treated as ordinary income under sections 1245, 1250, and 1254. Do not include income from a trade or business. Include as investment income, your capital gain net income from the sale or exchange of property held for investment. Also include as investment income, any income from a limited business interest, and the amount to be entered on line 4(a).

Investment expenses are those expenses allowable against the production of investment income provided they are allowed in figuring adjusted gross income and not includible in line 4.

Line 4(b), 60% Capital gain deduction.—
Individuals.—Enter your 60% capital gain deduction from your Schedule D (Form 1040), line 22, or Form 4798, line 9. If you had an entry on Form 1040, line 14, enter 60% of your capital gain distributions. Do not include the capital gain deduction attributable to a sale or exchange of a principal residence.

Estates and Trusts.—Enter the capital gain deduction taken into account on Form 1041 or 990-T. However, an amount paid or permanently set aside for a charitable purpose is not a tax preference item.

Lines 4(c) and 4(d), Accelerated depreciation on real property; Accelerated depreciation on leased personal property or leased recovery property other than 15-year real property.—If you use the Class Life Asset Depreciation Range (CLADR) System, use the asset guideline period as the straight-line useful life to figure lines 4(c) and (d).

For (c) but not (d), use any variance in useful life under section 167(m)(1) as the straight-line useful life.

Line 4(c).—For property other than recovery property, enter the amount you get (never less than zero) by subtracting the depreciation that would have been allowable for the year if you had used the straight-line method, from the depreciation or amortization actually allowable. Figure this amount separately for each property.

For 15-year real property, enter the amount by which the deduction allowed under section 168(a) (or section 167 for section 167(k) property) is more than the deduction which would have been allowable had the property been depreciated using a 15-year period and the straight-line method without salvage value.

Line 4(d).—For leased property other than recovery property, enter the amount you get (never less than zero) by subtracting the depreciation that would have been allowable for the year if you had used the straight-line method, from the depreciation or amortization actually allowable. Figure this amount separately for each property.

For leased recovery property other than 15-year real property, enter the amount by which your deduction under section 168(a) is more than the deduction allowable using the straight-line method with a half-year convention, no salvage value, and the following recovery period:

3 year property	5 years
5 year property	8 years
10 year property	15 years
15 year public utility property	22 years

Note: *If the recovery period actually used is longer than the recovery period in 4(c) or 4(d), do not complete line 4(c) or 4(d).*

Line 4(e), Amortization of certified pollution control facilities.—Enter the amount by which the amortization you took for 1983 is more than the depreciation deduction otherwise allowable.

Line 4(f), Mining exploration and development costs.—For each mine or other natural deposit (other than an oil or gas well), enter the amount by which the deductions you took under section 616(a) or 617 are more than the amount that would have been allowable if you had amortized the expenses over a ten-year period.

Line 4(g), Circulation and research and experimental expenditures.—Enter the amount by which the deductions you took for circulation and research and experimental expenditures under sections 173 or 174(a) are more than the amount that would have been allowable under section 58(i).

Line 4(h), Reserves for losses on bad debts of financial institutions.—Enter your share of the excess of the addition to the reserve for bad debts over the reasonable addition to the reserve for bad debts that would have been allowable if you had maintained the bad debt reserve for all tax years based on actual experience.

Line 4(i), Depletion.—In the case of mines, wells, and other natural deposits, enter the amount by which the deduction for depletion under section 611 (including percentage depletion for geothermal deposits), is more than the adjusted basis of such property at the end of the tax year. Figure the adjusted basis without regard to the depletion deduction and figure the excess separately for each property.

Line 4(j), Incentive stock options.—If you received stock by the exercise of an incentive stock option (as defined in section 422A), enter the amount by which the fair market value of the shares at the time of exercise was more than the option price.

Line 4(k), Intangible drilling costs.—Intangible drilling costs are a tax preference item to the extent that the excess intangible drilling costs are more than your net income from oil, gas, and geothermal properties.

Figure excess intangible drilling costs as follows: From the allowable intangible drilling and development costs (except for costs in drilling a nonproductive well), subtract the amount that would have been allowable if you had capitalized these costs and either amortized them over the 120 months that started when production began, or treated them according to any election you made under section 57(d)(2).

Your net income from oil, gas, and geothermal properties is your gross income from them, minus the deductions allocable to them, except for excess intangible drilling costs and nonproductive well costs.

Figure the line 4(k) amount separately for oil and gas properties which are not geothermal deposits and for all properties which are geothermal deposits.

Lines 5 and 8.—If this is a short period return, use the formula in section 443(d)(1) to determine the amount to enter on these lines.

Nonresident Alien Individuals.—If you disposed of U.S. real property interests at a gain, see Form 1040NR instructions for a special rule in figuring line 8.

Line 9, Estates and trusts.—Enter the amount from Form 1041, line 30. Do not include any tax from Forms 4970, 4972 or 5544.

Line 11, Foreign Tax Credit.—If line 10 is more than zero, and you incurred foreign taxes and elect to take them as a credit, enter on line 11 the foreign tax credit allowed against the alternative minimum tax. Figure this credit as follows:

(1) Use and attach a separate Form 1116 for each type of income specified at the top of Form 1116.

(2) Print across the top of each Form 1116 used: "ALT MIN TAX."

(3) Part I.—Fill in a new Part I using your income, deductions and tax preference items used in figuring alternative minimum taxable income from sources outside the U.S. Part II need not be completed.

(4) Part III.—
　(a) Skip lines 1 to 4.
　(b) Insert on line 5 the result of the following:
　　(i) the amount from Part III, line 5 of the Form 1116 used to figure the credit allowed against your regular tax, minus
　　(ii) the amount from Part III, line 17 of that Form 1116, plus
　　(iii) the smaller of (A) the amount from Part III, line 17 of that Form 1116, or (B) Form 6251, line 10 (or if more than one Form 1116 is being used, an allocable portion of Form 6251, line 10).
　(c) Complete lines 6 through 8, using the result of step 3 for line 6.
　(d) Skip lines 9 and 10.
　(e) Line 11.—Enter Form 6251, line 5.
　(f) Complete line 12 as indicated in Part III.
　(g) Skip lines 13 and 14.
　(h) Line 15.—Enter Form 6251, line 8.
　(i) Complete lines 16 and 17 as indicated in Part III.

(5) Part IV.—

Enter on line 11, Form 6251, the amount from line 6, Part IV of this Form 1116 (but not more than the amount on Form 6251, line 10).

For more information, see **Publication 909,** Minimum Tax and Alternative Minimum Tax.

APPENDIX C
GLOSSARY OF TAX TERMS

[NOTE: The words and phrases appearing below have been defined to reflect their conventional use in the field of taxation. Such definitions may therefore be incomplete for other purposes.]

–A–

Accelerated Cost Recovery System. An arbitrary means whereby the cost of tangible property is recovered over a prescribed period of time. Enacted by the Economic Recovery Tax Act (ERTA) of 1981, the approach disregards salvage value and imposes a period of cost recovery that depends upon the classification of the asset.

Accelerated depreciation. Various methods of depreciation that yield larger deductions in the earlier years of the life of an asset than the straight-line method. Examples include the double declining-balance and the sum-of-the-years' digits methods of depreciation. § 167(b)(2) and (3).

Accident and health benefits. Employee fringe benefits provided by employers through the payment of health and accident insurance premiums or the establishment of employer-funded medical reimbursement plans. Employers generally are entitled to a deduction for such payments, whereas employees generally exclude the fringe benefits from gross income.

Accounting income. The accountant's concept of income is generally based upon the realization principle. Financial accounting income may differ from taxable income (e. g., accelerated depreciation might be used for Federal income tax and straight-line depreciation for financial accounting purposes). Differences are included in a reconciliation of taxable and accounting income on Schedule M of Form 1120 for corporations.

Accounting method. The method under which income and expenses are determined for tax purposes. Major accounting methods are the cash basis and the accrual basis. Special methods are available for the reporting of gain on installment sales, recognition of income on construction projects (i. e., the completed contract and percentage of completion methods), and the valuation of inventories (i. e., last-in first-out and first-in first-out). §§ 446–472. See *accrual method, cash method, completed contract method, percentage-of-completion method,* etc.

Accounting period. The period of time, usually a year, used by a taxpayer for the determination of tax liability. Unless a fiscal year is chosen, taxpayers must determine and pay their income tax liability by using the calendar year (i. e., January 1 through December 31) as the period of measurement. An example of a fiscal year is July 1 through June 30. A change in accounting periods (e. g., from a calendar year to a fiscal year) generally requires the consent of the IRS. A new taxpayer, such as a newly formed corporation or an estate created upon the death of an individual taxpayer, is free to select either a calendar or a fiscal year without the consent of the IRS. § § 441–443.

Accrual method. A method of accounting that reflects expenses incurred and income earned for any one tax year. In contrast to the cash basis of accounting, expenses do not have to be paid to be deductible nor does income have to be received to be taxable. Unearned income (e. g., prepaid interest and rent) generally is taxed in the year of receipt regardless of the method of accounting used by the taxpayer. § 446(c)(2). See *accounting method* and *unearned income*.

Accumulated earnings tax. A special tax imposed on corporations that accumulate (rather than distribute) their earnings beyond the reasonable needs of the business. The tax is imposed on accumulated taxable income and is imposed in addition to the corporate income tax. § § 531–537.

Acquiescence. In agreement with the result reached. The IRS follows a policy of either acquiescing (i. e., *A, Acq.*) or non-acquiescing (i. e., *NA, Non-Acq.*) in the results reached in the Regular decisions of the U. S. Tax Court.

Additional first-year depreciation. Before 1981, taxpayers could elect to deduct additional depreciation equal to 20 percent of the cost of new or used tangible depreciable property with an estimated useful life of 6 or more years. The maximum cost that qualified was $10,000 ($20,000 for married persons filing a joint return), and the basis for regular depreciation was reduced by the amount of depreciation claimed under this rule. § 179 prior to ERTA amendment.

Adjusted basis. The cost or other basis of property reduced by depreciation allowed or allowable and increased by capital improvements. See *basis*.

Adjusted gross income. A determination peculiar to individual taxpayers. Generally, it represents gross income less business expenses, expenses attributable to the production of rent or royalty income, and the long-term capital gain deduction.

Ad valorem tax. A tax imposed on the value of property. The more common ad valorem tax is that imposed by states, counties, and cities on real estate. Ad valorem taxes can, however, be imposed upon personal property (e. g., a motor vehicle tax based on the value of an automobile). § § 164(a)(1) and (2).

Advance payments. In general, prepayments for services or goods are includible in gross income upon receipt of the advance payments (for both accrual and cash basis taxpayers). However, Rev.Proc. 71–21 (1971–2 C.B. 549) provides guidelines for the deferral of tax on certain advance payments providing specific conditions are met.

AFTR. Published by Prentice-Hall, *American Federal Tax Reports* contains all of the Federal tax decisions issued by the U. S. District Courts, U. S. Claims Court, U. S. Court of Appeals, and the U. S. Supreme Court.

AFTR2d. The second series of the *American Federal Tax Reports*.

Alimony payments. Alimony and separate maintenance payments are includible in the gross income of the recipient and are deductible by the payor. The payments must be periodic and made in discharge of a legal obligation arising from a marital or family relationship. Child support and voluntary payments are not treated as alimony. § § 62(13) and 71.

All events test. For accrual method taxpayers, income is earned when (1) all the events have occurred which fix the right to receive the income and (2) the amount can be determined with reasonable accuracy. Accrual of income cannot be postponed simply because a portion of the income may have to be returned in a subsequent period. The all events test also is utilized to determine when expenses can be deducted by an accrual basis taxpayer. The application of the test could cause a variation between the treatment of an item for accounting and for tax purposes. For example, a reserve for warranty expense may be properly accruable pursuant to generally accepted accounting principles but not be deductible under the Federal income tax law. Because of the application of the all events test, the deduction becomes available in the year the warranty obligation becomes fixed and the amount is determinable with reasonable certainty. Reg. § § 1.446–1(c)(1)(ii) and 1.461–1(a)(2).

Alternative minimum tax. The Tax Equity and Fiscal Responsibility Act of 1982 restructured and expanded the alternative minimum tax. The alternative minimum tax base (see Figure I, Chapter 12) is subject to a flat rate of 10 percent. The alternative minimum tax is imposed only to the extent it exceeds the regular income tax.

Alternative tax. An option allowed to corporations in computing the tax on net long-term capital gains. The rate is 28% of the net long-term capital gains. For corporate taxpayers, failure to use the alternative tax means all of the long-term capital gain will be taxed in the appropriate income tax bracket.

Alternate valuation date. Property passing from a person by death may be valued for death tax purposes as of the date of death or the alternate valuation date. The alternate valuation date is six months from the date of death or the date the property is disposed of by the estate, whichever comes first. The use of the alternate valuation date requires an affirmative election on the part of the executor or administrator of the estate.

Amortization. The allocation (and charge to expense) of the cost or other basis of an intangible asset over the asset's estimated useful life. Intangible assets which have an indefinite life (e. g., goodwill) are not amortizable. Examples of amortizable intangibles include patents, copyrights, and leasehold interests.

Amount realized. The amount received by a taxpayer on the sale or exchange of property. The measure of the amount realized is the sum of the cash and the fair market value of any property or services. Determining the amount realized is the starting point for arriving at realized gain or loss. The amount realized is defined in § 1001(b) and the Regulations thereunder. See *realized gain or loss* and *recognized gain or loss*.

Annuities. A fixed sum payable to a person at specified intervals for a specific period of time or for life. Payments represent a partial return of capital and a return (interest) on the capital investment. Therefore, an exclusion ratio must generally be used to compute the amount of nontaxable income. Special rules apply to annuities received by employees from qualified pension and profit sharing plans. § 72. See *qualified pension or profit sharing plan*.

Appellate court. For Federal tax purposes, appellate courts include the Courts of Appeals and the Supreme Court. If the party losing in the trial (or lower) court is dissatisfied with the result, the dispute may be carried to the appropriate appellate court. See *trial court*.

Arm's length transaction. The standard under which unrelated parties would determine an exchange price pursuant to a transaction. Suppose, for example, X Corporation sells property to its sole shareholder for $10,000. In testing whether the $10,000 is an "arm's length" price, one would ascertain the price which would have been negotiated between the corporation and an unrelated party in a bargained exchange.

Assignment of income. A procedure whereby a taxpayer attempts to avoid the recognition of income by assigning the property that generates the income to another. Such a procedure will not avoid the recognition of income by the taxpayer making the assignment if it can be said that the income was earned at the point of the transfer. In this case, usually referred to as an anticipatory assignment of income, the income will be taxed to the person who earns it.

Association. An organization treated as a corporation for Federal tax purposes even though it may not qualify as such under applicable state law. What is designated as a trust or a partnership, for example, may be classified as an association if it clearly possesses corporate attributes. Corporate attributes include centralized management, continuity of existence, free transferability of interests, and limited liability. § 7701(a)(3)

Attribution. Under certain circumstances, the tax law applies attribution rules to assign to one taxpayer the ownership interest of another taxpayer. If, for example, the stock of X Corporation is held 60 percent by M and 40 percent by S, M may be deemed to own 100 percent of X Corporation if M and S are mother and son. In such case, the stock owned by S is attributed to M.

Audit. Inspection and verification of a taxpayer's return or other transactions possessing tax consequences. An office audit is an audit by the IRS which is conducted in the agent's office. A field audit is conducted by the IRS on the business premises of the taxpayer or in the office of the tax practitioner representing the taxpayer. A correspondence audit is conducted by the IRS by mail.

Automatic mileage method. See *automobile expenses.*

Automobile expenses. Automobile expenses are generally deductible only to the extent the automobile is used in business or for the production of income. Personal commuting expenses are not deductible. The taxpayer may deduct actual expenses (including depreciation and insurance) or the standard (automatic) mileage rate may be used (20.5 cents per mile for the first 15,000 miles and 11 cents thereafter) during any one year. Automobile expenses relative to charitable activities and medical purposes and in connection with job-related moving expenses are deductible to the extent of actual out-of-pocket expenses or at the rate of 9 cents per mile.

–B–

Bad debts. A deduction is permitted if a business account receivable subsequently becomes worthless, providing the income arising from the debt previously was included in income. The deduction is allowed only in the year of worthlessness. If a reserve method is used, partially or totally worthless accounts are charged to the reserve. A nonbusiness bad debt deduction is allowed as a short-term capital loss if the loan did not arise in connection with the creditor's trade or business activities. Loans between related parties (family members) generally are classified as nonbusiness. § 166. See *nonbusiness bad debts.*

Basis. The amount assigned to an asset for income tax purposes. For assets acquired by purchase, basis would be cost (§ 1012). Special rules govern the basis of property received by virtue of another's death (§ 1014) or by gift (§ 1015), the basis of stock received on a transfer of property to a controlled corporation (§ 358), the basis of the property transferred to the corporation (§ 362), and the basis of property received upon the liquidation of a corporation (§ 334). See *adjusted basis.*

Bonus depreciation. See *additional first-year depreciation.*

Book value. The net amount of an asset after reduction by a related reserve. The book value of accounts receivable, for example, would be the face amount of the receivables less the reserve for bad debts.

Boot. Cash or property of a type not included in the definition of a nontaxable exchange. The receipt of boot will cause an otherwise tax-free transfer to become taxable to the extent of the lesser of the fair market value of such boot or the realized gain on the transfer. Examples of nontaxable exchanges that could be partially or completely taxable due to the receipt of boot include transfers to controlled corporations [§ 351(b)] and like-kind exchanges [§ 1031(b)]. See *realized gain or loss.*

Bribes and illegal payments. Section 162 denies a deduction for bribes or kickbacks, fines and penalties paid to a government for violation of law, and two-thirds of the treble damage payments made to claimants under violation of the antitrust law. Denial of a deduction for bribes and illegal payments is based upon the judicially established principle that allowing such payments would be contrary to public policy.

B.T.A. The Board of Tax Appeals was a trial court which considered Federal tax matters. This Court is now designated as the U. S. Tax Court.

Burden of proof. The requirement in a lawsuit to show the weight of evidence and thereby gain a favorable decision. Except in cases of tax fraud, the burden of proof in a tax case generally will be on the taxpayer.

Business energy tax credit. See *energy tax credit—business property*.

Business gifts. Business gifts are deductible only to the extent that each gift does not exceed $25 per person per year. Exceptions are made for gifts costing $4 or less and for certain employee awards under $100. § 274(b).

–C–

Canons of taxation. Tax criteria used in the selection of a tax base originally discussed by Adam Smith in *Wealth of Nations*. Canons of taxation include equality, convenience, certainty, and economy.

Capital asset. Broadly speaking, all assets are capital except those specifically excluded. Major categories of non-capital assets include property held for resale in the normal course of business (i. e., inventory), trade accounts and notes receivable, depreciable property, and real estate used in a trade or business (i. e., § 1231 assets). § 1221.

Capital contributions. Various means by which a shareholder makes additional funds available to the corporation (i. e., placed at the risk of the business) without the receipt of additional stock. Such contributions are added to the basis of the shareholder's existing stock investment and do not generate income to the corporation. § 118.

Capital expenditure. An expenditure which should be added to the basis of the property improved. For income tax purposes, this generally precludes a full deduction for the expenditure in the year paid or incurred. Any capital recovery in the form of a tax deduction would have to come in the form of depreciation. § 263.

Capital gain deduction. Noncorporate taxpayers are permitted to deduct from gross income 60% of the excess of net long-term capital gains over net short-term capital losses. The remainder of the gain is includible in gross income and is subject to the regular tax rates. § 1202.

Capital gain. The gain from the sale or exchange of a capital asset. See *capital asset*.

Capital gain or loss holding period. The requirement for long-term treatment is that the asset be held for more than one year.

Capital loss. The loss from the sale or exchange of a capital asset. See *capital asset.*

Cash basis. See *accounting method.*

Cash equivalent doctrine. Generally, a cash basis taxpayer does not report income until cash is constructively or actually received. Under the cash equivalent doctrine, cash basis taxpayers are required to report income if the equivalent of cash is received (e. g., property is received) in a taxable transaction.

Cash method. A method of accounting that generally reports income when cash is collected, and reports expenses when cash payments are made. However, for fixed assets, the cash basis taxpayer claims deductions through depreciation or amortization, the same as is done by an accrual basis taxpayer. Prepaid expenses must be capitalized and amortized if the life of the asset extends "substantially beyond" the end of the tax year.

Casualty loss. A casualty is defined as "the complete or partial destruction of property resulting from an identifiable event of a sudden, unexpected or unusual nature" (e. g., floods, storms, fires, auto accidents). Individuals may deduct a casualty loss only if the loss is incurred in a trade or business or in a transaction entered into for profit or is a loss arising from fire, storm, shipwreck, or other casualty or from theft. Individuals usually deduct personal casualty losses as itemized deductions subject to a $100 nondeductible amount and to a floor equal to 10 percent of adjusted gross income that applies after the $100 per casualty floor has been applied. Special rules are provided for the netting of certain casualty gains and losses. See *Section 1231 gains and losses.*

Cert. den. By denying the Writ of Certiorari, the U. S. Supreme Court refuses to accept an appeal from a U. S. Court of Appeals. The denial of certiorari does not, however, mean that the U. S. Supreme Court agrees with the result reached by the lower court.

Certiorari. Appeal from a U. S. Court of Appeals to the U. S. Supreme Court is by Writ of Certiorari. The Supreme Court does not have to accept the appeal and usually does not (i. e., *cert. den.*) unless there is a conflict among the lower courts that needs to be resolved or a constitutional issue is involved.

Change in accounting method. A change in the taxpayer's method of accounting (e. g., from FIFO to LIFO) generally requires prior approval from the IRS. Generally, a request must be filed within

180 days after the beginning of the taxable year of the desired change. In some instances, the permission for change will not be granted unless the taxpayer agrees to certain adjustments prescribed by the IRS.

Change in accounting period. A taxpayer must obtain the consent of the IRS before changing his or her tax year. Income for the short period created by the change is required to be annualized.

Charitable contributions. Contributions are deductible (subject to various restrictions and ceiling limitations) if made to qualified nonprofit charitable organizations. A cash basis taxpayer is entitled to a deduction solely in the year of payment. Accrual basis corporations may accrue contributions at year-end if payment is authorized properly prior to the end of the year and payment is made within 2½ months from the end of the year. § 170.

Child and dependent care credit. A tax credit ranging from 20 percent to 30 percent of employment-related expenses (child and dependent care expenses) for amounts of up to $4,800 is available to individuals who are employed on a full-time basis and maintain a household for a dependent child or disabled spouse or dependent. § 44A.

Child support payments. Payments for child support do not constitute alimony and are therefore not includible in gross income by the recipient or deductible as alimony by the payor. None of the amounts paid are regarded as child support unless the divorce decree or separation agreement specifically calls for child support payments. § 71(b).

Claim of right doctrine. A judicially imposed doctrine applicable to both cash and accrual basis taxpayers which holds that an amount is includible in income upon actual or constructive receipt if the taxpayer has an unrestricted claim to such amounts. For the tax treatment of amounts repaid when previously included in income under the claim of right doctrine, see § 1341.

Claims Court. One of three Federal trial courts that consider Federal tax controversy. Appeal from the U. S. Claims Court (formerly to the U. S. Supreme Court) now goes to the new Court of Appeals for the Federal circuit.

Clear reflection of income. The IRS has the authority to redetermine a taxpayer's income using a method which clearly reflects income if the taxpayer's method does not do so. § 446(b). In addition, the IRS may apportion or allocate income among various related businesses if income is not "clearly reflected." § 482.

Closely-held corporation. A corporation, the stock ownership of which is not widely dispersed. Instead, a few shareholders are in control of corporate policy and are in a position to benefit personally from such policy.

Completed contract method. A method of reporting gain or loss on certain long-term contracts. Under this method of accounting, gross income and expenses are recognized in the tax year in which the contract is completed. Reg. § 1.451-3. For another alternative, see *percentage of completion method.*

Condemnation. The taking of property by a public authority. The property is condemned as the result of legal action, and the owner is compensated by the public authority. The power to condemn property is known as the right of eminent domain.

Conduit concept. An approach the tax law assumes in the tax treatment of certain entities and their owners. Specific tax characteristics pass through the entity without losing their identity. For example, items of income and expense, capital gains and losses, tax credits, etc., pass through a partnership (a conduit) and are subject to taxation at the partner level. Also, in an S corporation, certain items pass through and are reported on the returns of the shareholders.

Constructive ownership. See *attribution.*

Constructive receipt. If income is unqualifiedly available, it will be subject to the income tax even though it is not physically in the taxpayer's possession. An example would be accrued interest on a savings account. Under the constructive receipt of income concept, such interest will be taxed to a depositor in the year it is available rather than the year actually withdrawn. The fact that the depositor uses the cash basis of accounting for tax purposes makes no difference. See Reg. § 1.451–2.

Convention expenses. Travel expenses incurred in attending a convention are deductible if the meetings are related to a taxpayer's trade or business or job related activities. If, however, the convention trip is primarily for pleasure, no deduction is permitted. Specific limitations are provided for foreign convention expenses. § 274(h).

Contributions to the capital of a corporation. See *capital contributions.*

Correspondence audit. An audit conducted by the IRS through the use of the mail. Typically, the IRS writes to the taxpayer requesting the verification of a particular deduction or exemption. The completion of a special form or the remittance of copies of records or other support is all that is requested of the taxpayer. To be distinguished from a *field audit* or an *office audit.*

Cost recovery allowance. The portion of the cost of an asset written off under the Accelerated Cost Recovery System (ACRS), which replaced the depreciation system as a method for writing off the cost of an asset.

Cost recovery period. A specified period (three, five, ten or fifteen years, depending on the type of asset) for writing off the cost of an asset under the Accelerated Cost Recovery System (ACRS).

Court of Appeals. Any of thirteen Federal courts which consider tax matters appealed from the U. S. Tax Court, U. S. Claims Court, or a U. S. District Court. Appeal from a U. S. Court of Appeals is to the U. S. Supreme Court by Writ of Certiorari.

–D–

Death benefits. A payment made by an employer to the beneficiary or beneficiaries of a deceased employee on account of the death of the employee. Under certain conditions, the first $5,000 of such payment will not be subject to the income tax. § 101(b)(1).

Death Tax. See *estate tax.*

Declaration of estimated tax. A procedure whereby individuals and corporations are required to make quarterly installment payments of estimated tax. Individuals are required to make the declaration and file quarterly payments of the estimated tax if certain requirements are met. In 1984, a declaration is not required for an individual if the estimated tax is reasonably expected to be less than $400.

Deductions for adjusted gross income. See *adjusted gross income.*

Deductions from adjusted gross income. See *itemized deductions.*

Deferred compensation. Compensation which will be taxed when received or upon the removal of certain restrictions on receipt and not when earned. An example would be contributions by an employer to a qualified pension or profit sharing plan on behalf of an employee. Such contributions will not be taxed to the employee until the funds are made available or distributed to the employee (e. g., upon retirement). See *qualified pension or profit sharing plan.*

Deficiency. Additional tax liability owed by a taxpayer and assessed by the IRS.

Depletion. The process by which the cost or other basis of a natural resource (e. g., an oil and gas interest) is recovered upon extraction and sale of the resource. The two ways to determine the depletion allowance are the cost and percentage (or statutory) methods. Under the cost method, each unit of production sold is assigned a portion of the cost or other basis of the interest. This is determined by dividing the cost or other basis by the total units expected to be recovered. Under the percentage (or statutory) method, the tax law provides a special percentage factor for different types of minerals and other natural resources. This percentage is multiplied by the gross income from the interest to arrive at the depletion allowance. § § 613 and 613A.

Depreciation. The write-off for tax purposes of the cost or other basis of a tangible asset over its estimated useful life. § 167. As to intangible assets, see *amortization*. As to natural resources, see *depletion*. Also see *estimated useful life*. The depreciation system was replaced by the Accelerated Cost Recovery System (ACRS) for assets acquired after 1980 but still applies for assets placed in service before 1981.

Determination letter. Upon the request of a taxpayer, a District Director will pass upon the tax status of a completed transaction. Determination letters are most frequently used to clarify employee status, to determine whether a pension or profit sharing plan "qualifies" under the Code, and to determine the tax-exempt status of certain nonprofit organizations.

Direct charge-off method. A method of accounting for bad debts whereby a deduction is permitted only when an account becomes partially or completely worthless. See *reserve for bad debts*.

Disaster loss. If a casualty is sustained in an area designated as a disaster area by the President of the United States, the casualty is designated a disaster loss. In such an event, the disaster loss may be treated as having occurred in the taxable year immediately preceding the year in which the disaster actually occurred. Thus, immediate tax benefits are provided to victims of a disaster. § 165(h). See *casualty loss*.

Dissent. To disagree with the majority. If, for example, Judge B disagrees with the result reached by Judges C and D (all of whom are members of the same court), Judge B could issue a dissenting opinion.

District court. A Federal District Court is a trial court for purposes of litigating (among others) Federal tax matters. It is the only trial court where a jury trial can be obtained.

Dividend exclusion. The $100 exclusion ($200 on a joint return) allowed individuals for dividends received from certain qualifying domestic corporations and financial institutions. § 116.

Dividends received deduction. A deduction allowed a corporate shareholder for dividends received from a domestic corporation. The deduction usually is 85 percent of the dividends received but could be 100 percent if an affiliated group is involved. § § 243–246.

–E–

Earned income. Income from personal services as distinguished from income generated by property. See § 911 and the Regulations thereunder.

Earned income credit. The earned income credit is 10% of earned income up to $5,000 (i. e., a maximum credit of $500). If either earned income or adjusted gross income exceeds $6,000, the $500 maximum credit must be reduced by 12.5% of the amount by which the greater of earned income or adjusted gross income exceeds $6,000. Therefore, no earned income credit is allowed if either earned income or adjusted gross income is $10,000 or more.

Earnings and profits. A tax concept peculiar to corporate taxpayers which measures economic capacity to make a distribution to shareholders that is not a return of capital. Such a distribution will result in dividend income to the shareholders to the extent of the corporation's current and accumulated earnings and profits.

Education expenses. Employees may deduct education expenses if such items are incurred either (1) to maintain or improve existing job-related skills or (2) to meet the express requirements of the employer or the requirements imposed by law to retain employment status. Such expenses are not deductible if the education is required to meet the minimum educational requirements for the taxpayer's job or the education qualifies the individual for a new trade or business. Reg. § 1.162–5.

Employee expenses. The deductions *for* adjusted gross income include travel, transportation, reimbursed expenses, outside salesperson's expenses, and moving expenses. All other employee expenses are deductible *from* adjusted gross income.

Energy Tax Act. Legislation that provides various income tax credits for certain energy conservation expenditures. See *energy tax credit—business property* and *energy tax credit—residential property*.

Energy tax credit—business property. A 10% to 15% tax credit is available to businesses that invest in certain energy property. The purpose of the credit is to create incentives for conservation and to penalize the increased use of oil and gas. The business energy tax credit applies to equipment with an estimated useful life of at least three years that uses fuel or feedstock other than oil or natural gas (e. g., solar, wind, coal). If the property also qualifies for the investment tax credit, a total credit of 20% to 25% is allowed. § § 46(a) and 48(e). See *energy tax credit—residential property, estimated useful life,* and *investment tax credit.*

Energy tax credit—residential property. The Energy Tax Act provides individual homeowners and renters with two separate tax credits: one for energy conservation expenditures and the other for renewable energy source property. All such expenditures must be made for property installed in or on a taxpayers' principal residence. Energy conservation expenditures include installation of insulation, storm windows, and certain other energy-conserving components. The amount of this tax credit is 15% of the first $2,000 of qualifying expenditures (i. e., a maximum credit of $300). Renewable energy source property includes solar, wind, and geothermal energy devices. The amount of the credit is 40% of the first $10,000 of qualifying expenditures (i. e., the ceiling limitation is $4,000). Expenditures made on or after April 20, 1977, and through 1985 will qualify for the credits. § 44C. See *energy tax credit—business property.*

Entertainment expenses. Such expenses are deductible only if they are directly related to or associated with a trade or business. Various restrictions and documentation requirements have been imposed upon the deductibility of entertainment expenses to prevent abuses by taxpayers. § 274.

Estate tax. A tax imposed on the right to transfer property by death. Thus, an estate tax is levied on the decedent's estate and not on the heir receiving the property. § § 2001–2009.

Estimated useful life. The period over which an asset will be used by a particular taxpayer. Although such period cannot be longer than the estimated physical life of an asset, it could be shorter if the taxpayer does not intend to keep the asset until the asset wears out. Assets such as goodwill do not have an estimated useful life. The estimated useful life of an asset is essential to measuring the annual tax deduction for depreciation and amortization. An asset subject to ACRS is written off over a specified cost recovery period rather than over its estimated useful life.

Excise tax. A tax on the manufacture, sale, or use of goods or on the carrying on of an occupation or activity. Also a tax on the transfer of property. Thus, the Federal death and gift taxes are, theoretically, excise taxes.

–F–

Fair market value. The amount at which property would change hands between a willing buyer and a willing seller, neither being under any compulsion to buy or sell and both having reasonable knowledge of the relevant facts. Reg. § 20.2031–1(b).

F.2d. An abbreviation for the Second Series of the *Federal Reporter,* the official series wherein decisions of the U. S. Claims Court and the U. S. Courts of Appeals are published.

F. Supp. The abbreviation for *Federal Supplement,* the official series wherein the reported decisions of the U. S. Federal District Courts are published.

Field audit. An audit by the IRS conducted on the business premises of the taxpayer or in the office of the tax practitioner representing the taxpayer. To be distinguished from a *correspondence audit* or an *office audit.*

First-in first-out (FIFO). An accounting method for determining the cost of inventories. Under this method, the inventory on hand is deemed to be the sum of the cost of the most recently acquired units.

Foreign earned income exclusion. The foreign earned income exclusion is a relief provision which applies to U. S. citizens working in a foreign country. To qualify for the exclusion, the taxpayer must be either a bona fide resident of the foreign country or present in the country for 330 days during any 12 consecutive months. The exclusion is limited to $85,000 in 1984 and increases by $5,000 per year until 1986, when it reaches $95,000.

Foreign tax credit or deduction. Both individual taxpayers and corporations may claim a foreign tax credit on income earned and subject to tax in a foreign country or U. S. possession. As an alternative to the credit, a deduction may be taken for the foreign taxes paid. § § 33, 164, and 901–905.

Franchise. A franchise is an agreement which gives the transferee the right to distribute, sell, or provide goods, services, or facilities within a specified area. The cost of obtaining a franchise may be amortized over the life of the agreement. In general, a franchise is a capital asset and results in capital gain or loss if all significant powers, rights, or continuing interests are transferred pursuant to the sale of a franchise. § 1253.

Fringe benefits. Compensation or other benefits received by an employee which are not in the form of cash. Some fringe benefits (e. g., accident and health plans, group-term life insurance) may be excluded from the employee's gross income and therefore not subject to the Federal income tax.

Fruit and the tree doctrine. The courts have held that an individual who earns income from property or services cannot assign that income to another. For example, a father cannot assign his earnings from commissions to his son and escape income tax on such amounts.

–G–

Gasoline tax. See *sales tax*.

Gift. A transfer of property for less than adequate consideration. Gifts usually occur in a personal setting (such as between members of the same family). § § 2501–2524.

Gift tax. A tax imposed on the transfer of property by gift. Such tax is imposed upon the donor of a gift and is based upon the fair market value of the property on the date of the gift.

Goodwill. The ability of a business to generate income in excess of a normal rate on assets due to superior managerial skills, market position, new product technology, etc. In the purchase of a business, goodwill represents the difference between the purchase price and the value of the net assets. Goodwill is an intangible asset which possesses an indefinite life and cannot, therefore, be amortized for Federal income tax purposes. Reg. § 1.167(a)–3.

Government bonds issued at a discount. Certain U. S. government bonds (Series E and EE) are issued at a discount and do not pay interest during the life of the bond. Instead, the bonds are redeemable at increasing fixed amounts. Thus, the difference between the purchase price and the amount received upon redemption represents interest income to the holder. A cash basis taxpayer may defer recognition of taxable income until such bonds are redeemed. As an alternative, the taxpayer may elect to include in gross income on an annual basis the annual increase in the value of the bond. § 454.

Gross income. Income subject to the Federal income tax. Gross income does not include income such as interest on municipal bonds. In the case of a manufacturing or merchandising business, gross income means gross profit (i. e., gross sales or gross receipts less cost of goods sold). § 61 and Reg. § 1.61–3(a).

Group-term life insurance. Life insurance coverage permitted by an employer for a group of employees. Such insurance is renewable on a year-to-year basis and does not accumulate in value (i. e., no cash surrender value is built up). The premiums paid by the employer on such insurance are not taxed to an employee on coverage of up to $50,000 per year. § 79 and Reg. § 1.79–1(b).

–H–

Head of household. An unmarried individual who maintains a household for another and satisfies certain conditions set forth in § 2(b). Such status enables the taxpayer to use a set of income tax rates [see § 1(b)] that are lower than those applicable to other unmarried individuals [§ 1(c)] but higher than those applicable to surviving spouses and married persons filing a joint return [§ 1(a)]. See *tax rate schedules*.

Hobby loss. A nondeductible loss arising from a personal hobby as contrasted with an activity engaged in for profit. Generally, the law provides a presumption that an activity is engaged in for profit if profits are earned during any two or more years during a five-year period. § 183.

Holding period. The period of time property has been held for income tax purposes. The holding period is crucial in determining whether gain or loss from the sale or exchange of a capital asset is long- or short-term. § 1223.

HR 10 plan. See *self-employment retirement plan*.

–I–

Imputed interest. In cases of certain long-term sales of property, the IRS has the authority to convert some of the gain from the sale into interest income if the contract does not provide for a minimum rate of interest to be paid by the purchaser. The application of this procedure has the effect of forcing the seller to recognize less long-term capital gain and more ordinary income (i. e., interest income). § 483 and the Regulations thereunder.

Income averaging. A special method whereby the income tax of an individual is determined by taking into account the taxable income of the past four years. The income averaging procedure provides relief from the annual accounting period concept when a taxpayer attains a "rags to riches" income position and has a relatively large amount of income "bunched" in a particular year. See Schedule G of Form 1040 and § § 1301–1305.

Individual retirement account (IRA). Employees, whether or not covered by qualified pension or profit sharing plans, are permitted to set aside up to 100 percent of their salary per year (generally not to exceed $2,000) for a retirement account. The amount set aside can be deducted by the employee and will be subject to income tax only upon withdrawal. Specific requirements are established for the withdrawal of such amounts, and penalties are provided for failure to comply. § 219. See *simplified employee pensions*.

Installment method. A method of accounting enabling a taxpayer to spread the recognition of gain on the sale of property over the payout period. Under this procedure, the seller computes the gross profit percentage from the sales (i. e., the gain divided by the contract price) and applies it to each payment received to arrive at the gain to be recognized. § 453.

Intangible drilling and development costs. Taxpayers may elect to expense or capitalize (subject to amortization) intangible drilling and development costs. However, ordinary income recapture provisions now apply to oil and gas properties on a sale or other disposition if the expense method is elected. § 263(c) and § 1254(a).

Interest on life insurance proceeds. Interest of up to $1,000 per year earned on insurance proceeds which are retained by an insurance company for making periodic payments to a surviving spouse are exempt from Federal income tax. § 101(d).

Investigation of a new business. Expenditures by taxpayers who are not engaged in a trade or business incurred in the evaluation of prospective business activities (i. e., acquiring an existing business or entering into a new trade or business activity). If the expenditures are general, it is the position of the IRS that no deduction is permitted even if the investigation is abandoned because the taxpayer is not engaged in a trade or business. The courts, however, have permitted a loss deduction providing the expenditures were specific.

Investment indebtedness. If funds are borrowed by noncorporate taxpayers for the purpose of purchasing or continuing to hold investment property, some portion of the interest expense deduction may be disallowed. Interest is generally limited to $10,000 plus net investment income. Amounts which are disallowed may be carried forward and treated as investment interest of the succeeding year. § 163(d).

Investment tax credit. A special tax credit usually equal to 10 percent of the qualified investment in tangible personalty used in a trade or business. If the tangible personalty has a recovery period of five years or more, the full cost of the property qualifies for the credit. Only 60 percent qualifies for property with a recovery period of three years. § 38, 46–50. See *recapture of investment tax credit.*

Involuntary conversion. The loss or destruction of property through theft, casualty, or condemnation. Any gain realized on an involuntary conversion can, at the taxpayer's election, be considered nonrecognizable for Federal income tax purposes if the owner reinvests the proceeds within a prescribed period of time in property that is similar or related in service or use. § 1033.

IRA. See *individual retirement account.*

Itemized deductions. Certain personal expenditures allowed by the Code as deductions *from* adjusted gross income if they exceed the zero bracket amount. Examples include certain medical expenses, interest on home mortgages, state sales tax, and charitable contributions. Itemized deductions are reported on Schedule A of Form 1040.

–K–

Keogh plan. See *self-employed retirement plan.*

–L–

Last-in first-out (LIFO). An accounting method for valuing inventories for tax purposes. Under this method, it is assumed that the inventory on hand is valued at the cost of the earliest acquired units. § 472 and the Regulations thereunder.

Lessee. One who rents property from another. In the case of real estate, the lessee is also known as the tenant.

Lessor. One who rents property to another. In the case of real estate, the lessor is also known as the landlord.

Life insurance proceeds. Generally, life insurance proceeds paid to a beneficiary upon the death of the insured are exempt from

Federal income tax. An exception is provided when a life insurance contract has been transferred for valuable consideration to another individual who assumes ownership rights. In such case, the proceeds are income to the assignee to the extent that the proceeds exceed the amount paid for the policy plus any subsequent premiums paid. Insurance proceeds may be subject to the Federal estate tax if the decedent retained any incidents of ownership in the policy prior to death or if the proceeds are payable to the decendent's estate. § § 101 and 2042.

Like-kind exchange. An exchange of property held for productive use in a trade or business or for investment (except inventory and stocks and bonds) for property of the same type. Unless different property is received (i. e., boot) the exchange will be nontaxable. § 1031. See *boot*.

Liquidation of a corporation. In a complete or partial liquidation of a corporation, amounts received by the shareholders in exchange for their stock are usually treated as a sale or exchange of the stock resulting in capital gain or loss treatment. Special rules apply to one-month liquidations under § 333, twelve-month liquidations under § 337, and the liquidation of a subsidiary under § 332.

Lump-sum distribution. Payment of the entire amount due at one time rather than in installments. Such distributions often occur from qualified pension or profit sharing plans upon the retirement or death of a covered employee. The recipient of a lump-sum distribution may recognize both long-term capital gain and ordinary income upon the receipt of the distribution. The ordinary income portion is subject to a special ten-year income averaging provision.

–M–

Marital deduction. A deduction allowed upon the transfer of property from one spouse to another. The deduction is allowed under the Federal gift tax for lifetime (i. e., inter vivos) transfers or under the Federal death tax for death (i. e., testamentary) transfers. § § 2056 and 2523.

Medical expenses. Medical expenses of an individual, spouse, and dependents are allowed as an itemized deduction to the extent that such amounts (less insurance reimbursements) exceed 5 percent of adjusted gross income.

Mitigation of the annual accounting period concept. Various tax provisions that provide relief from the effect of the finality of the annual accounting period concept. For example, income averaging provisions provide relief for taxpayers with a large and unusual amount of income concentrated in a single tax year. See *accounting period*.

Moving expenses. A deduction *for* AGI is permitted to employees and self-employed individuals providing certain tests are met (e. g., the taxpayer's new job must be at least 35 miles farther from the old residence than the old residence was from the former place of work). In addition, an employee must be employed on a full-time basis at the new location for 39 weeks. Ceiling limitations are placed on direct moving expenses (e. g., expenses of moving personal belongings and traveling) and on indirect expenses (e. g., house-hunting trips and temporary living expenses). § 217.

-N-

Necessary. Appropriate and helpful in furthering the taxpayer's business or income-producing activity. §§ 162(a) and 212. See *ordinary*.

Net operating loss. To mitigate the effect of the annual accounting period concept, § 172 allows taxpayers to use an excess loss of one year as a deduction for certain past or future years. In this regard, a carryback period of three years and a carryforward period of fifteen years is allowed. See *mitigation of the annual accounting period concept*.

Net worth method. An approach used by the IRS to reconstruct the income of a taxpayer who fails to maintain adequate records. Under this approach, the gross income for the year is the increase in net worth of the taxpayer (i. e., assets in excess of liabilities) with appropriate adjustment for nontaxable receipts and nondeductible expenditures. The net worth method often is used when tax fraud is suspected.

Nonbusiness bad debts. A bad debt loss not incurred in connection with a creditor's trade or business. Such loss is deductible as a short-term capital loss and will be allowed only in the year the debt becomes entirely worthless. In addition to family loans, many investor losses fall into the classification of nonbusiness bad debts. § 166(d). See *bad debts*.

Nonqualified deferred compensation plans. Compensation arrangements which are frequently offered to executives. Such plans may include stock options, restricted stock, etc. Often, an executive may defer the recognition of taxable income. The employer, however, does not receive a tax deduction until the employee is required to include the compensation in income. See *restricted property.*

Nonrecourse debt. An obligation on which the endorser is not personally liable. An example of a nonrecourse debt is a mortgage on real estate acquired by a partnership without the assumption of any liability on the mortgage by the partnership or any of the partners. The acquired property generally is pledged as collateral for the loan.

–O–

Office audit. An audit by the IRS of a taxpayer's return which is conducted in the agent's office. To be distinguished from a *correspondence audit* or a *field audit.*

Office in the home expenses. Employment and business-related expenses attributable to the use of a residence (e. g., den or office) are allowed only if the portion of the residence is exclusively used on a regular basis as a place of business of the taxpayer or as a place of business which is used by patients, clients, or customers. If the expenses are employment related, the use must be for the convenience of the employer as opposed to being merely appropriate and helpful. § 280A.

Open transaction. A judicially imposed doctrine which allows the taxpayer to defer all gain until he or she has collected an amount equal to the adjusted basis of assets transferred pursuant to an exchange transaction. This doctrine has been applied where the property received in an exchange has no ascertainable fair market value due to the existence of contingencies.

Options. The sale or exchange of an option to buy or sell property results in capital gain or loss if the property is a capital asset. Generally, the closing of an option transaction results in short-term capital gain or loss to the writer of the call and the purchaser of the call option. § 1234.

Ordinary. Common and accepted in the general industry or type of activity in which the taxpayer is engaged. It comprises one of the tests for the deductibility of expenses incurred or paid in connection with a trade or business; for the production or collection of income; for the management, conservation, or maintenance of property held for the production of income; or in connection with the determination, collection, or refund of any tax. § § 162(a) and 212. See *necessary.*

Organizational expenses. A corporation may elect to amortize organizational expenses over a period of 60 months or more. Certain expenses of organizing a company do not qualify for amortization (e. g., expenditures connected with issuing or selling stock or other securities). § 248.

Outside salesperson. An outside salesperson is one who solicits business away from the employer's place of business on a full-time basis. If an employee qualifies as an outside salesperson, all employment-related expenses are deductible *for* AGI.

–P–

Partnerships. Partnerships are treated as a conduit and are not subject to taxation. Various items of partnership income, expenses, gains, and losses flow through to the individual partners and are reported on the partners' personal income tax returns.

Passive investment income. As defined in § 1372(e)(5)(C), "passive investment income" means gross receipts from royalties, certain rents, dividends, interest, annuities, and gains from the sale or exchange of stock and securities. Revocation of the S corporation election may occur in certain cases when the S corporation has passive investment income in excess of 25 percent of gross receipts for a period of three consecutive years.

Patent. A patent is an intangible asset which may be amortized over its remaining life. The sale of a patent usually results in favorable long-term capital gain treatment. § 1235.

Percentage of completion method. A method of reporting gain or loss on certain long-term contracts. Under this method of accounting, the gross contract price is included in income as the contract is completed. Reg. § 1.451–3. See *completed contract method.*

Personal expenses. Expenses of an individual for personal reasons which are not deductible unless specifically provided for under the tax law. § 262.

Personal property. Generally, all property other than real estate. It is sometimes designated as personalty when real estate is termed realty. Personal property also can refer to property which is not used in a taxpayer's trade or business or held for the production or collection of income. When used in this sense, personal property could include both realty (e. g., a personal residence) and personalty (e. g., personal effects such as clothing and furniture).

Personal residence. The sale of a personal residence generally results in the recognition of capital gain (but not loss). However, the gain may be deferred if the adjusted sales price of the old residence is reinvested in the purchase of a new residence within certain prescribed time periods. Also, taxpayers age 55 or older may exclude $125,000 of the gain from tax providing certain requirements are met. § § 1034 and 121.

Personal and dependency exemptions. The tax law provides a $1,000 exemption for each individual taxpayer and an additional $1,000 exemption for his or her spouse if a joint return is filed. Additional personal exemptions are provided for old age (65) and blindness. An individual may also claim a $1,000 dependency exemption for each dependent providing certain tests are met. Before 1979, the amount allowed for each personal and dependency exemption was $750. § 151.

Personalty. All property other than realty (real estate). Personalty usually is categorized as tangible or intangible property. Tangible personalty includes such assets as machinery and equipment, automobiles and trucks, and office equipment. Intangible assets include stocks and bonds, goodwill, patents, trademarks, and copyrights.

Points. Loan origination fees which are generally deductible as interest by a buyer of property. A seller of property who pays points is required to reduce the selling price and therefore does not receive an interest deduction.

Political contributions. Individuals can claim a tax credit equal to one-half of certain qualifying political contributions. The credit is limited to $50 ($100 on a joint return). § 41.

Pollution control facilities. A certified pollution control facility, the cost of which may be amortized over a 60-month period if elected by the taxpayer. § 169.

Prepaid expenses. Cash basis as well as accrual basis taxpayers usually are required to capitalize prepayments for rent, insurance, etc., that cover more than one year. Deductions are taken during the period the benefits are received. See *prepaid interest.*

Prepaid interest. In effect, the Tax Reform Act of 1976 placed cash basis taxpayers on an accrual basis for purposes of recognizing a deduction for prepaid interest. Thus, interest paid in advance is deductible as an interest expense only as it accrues. The one exception to this rule involves the interest element when a cash basis taxpayer pays points to obtain financing for the purchase of a principal residence (or to make improvements thereto) if the payment of points is an established business practice in the area in which the indebtedness is incurred and the amount involved is not excessive. § 461(g). See *points* and *prepaid expenses.*

Prizes and awards. The fair market value of a prize or award generally is includible in gross income. Certain exceptions are provided where the prize or award is made in recognition of religious, charitable, scientific, educational, artistic, literary, or civic achievement and providing certain other requirements are met. § 74.

Public policy limitation. See *bribes and illegal payments.*

–Q–

Qualified pension or profit sharing plan. An employer-sponsored plan that meets the requirements of § 401. If these requirements are met, none of the employer's contributions to the plan will be taxed to the employee until distributed to him or her [§ 402]. The employer will be allowed a deduction in the year the contributions are made [§ 404].

–R–

RAR. A revenue agent's report which reflects any adjustments made by the agent as a result of an audit of the taxpayer. The RAR is mailed to the taxpayer along with the 30-day letter which outlines the appellate procedures available to the taxpayer.

Realized gain or loss. The difference between the amount realized upon the sale or other disposition of property and the adjusted basis of such property. § 1001. See *adjusted basis* and *recognized gain or loss.*

Realty. All real estate, including land and buildings. Permanent improvements to a building (i. e., fixtures) become realty if their removal would cause significant damage to the property. An example of a fixture might be the installation of a central air conditioning or heating system to a building. Thus, personalty could become realty through the fixture reclassification.

Reasonable needs of the business. See *accumulated earnings tax.*

Recapture. To recover the tax benefit of a deduction or a credit previously taken. See *recapture of depreciation* and *recapture of investment tax credit.*

Recapture of depreciation. Upon the disposition of depreciable property used in a trade or business, gain or loss is determined measured by the difference between the consideration received (i. e., the amount realized) and the adjusted basis of the property. Before the enactment of the recapture of depreciation provisions of the Code, any such gain recognized could be § 1231 gain and usually qualified for long-term capital gain treatment. The recapture provisions of the Code (e. g., § § 1245 and 1250) may operate to convert some or all of the previous § 1231 gain into ordinary income. The justification for recapture of depreciation is that it prevents a taxpayer from converting a dollar of deduction (in the form of depreciation) into forty cents of income (§ 1231 gain taxed as a long-term capital gain). The recapture of depreciation rules do not apply when the property is disposed of at a loss. See *Section 1231 gains and losses.*

Recapture of investment tax credit. When investment credit property is disposed of or ceases to be used in the trade or business of the taxpayer, some of the investment tax credit claimed on such property may be recaptured as additional tax liability. The amount of the recapture is the difference between the amount of the credit originally claimed and what should have been claimed in light of the length of time the property was actually held or used for qualifying purposes. § 47. See *investment tax credit.*

Recapture potential. Reference is to property which, if disposed of in a taxable transaction, would result in the recapture of depreciation [§ § 1245 or 1250] and/or of the investment tax credit [§ 47].

Recognized gain or loss. The portion of realized gain or loss that is considered in computing taxable income. See *realized gain or loss.*

Regulations. Treasury Department Regulations represent the position of the IRS as to how the Internal Revenue Code is to be interpreted. Their purpose is to provide taxpayers and IRS personnel with rules of general and specific application to the various provisions of the tax law. Regulations are published in the Federal Register and in all tax services.

Rehabilitation expenditures. A special five-year amortization election is provided for rehabilitation expenditures on low-income housing. The expenditures must exceed $3,000 per dwelling unit over two consecutive years and in the aggregate may not exceed $20,000 per dwelling unit. § 167(k).

Related-party transactions. The tax law places restrictions upon the recognition of gains and losses between related parties due to the potential for abuse. For example, restrictions are placed on the deduction of losses from the sale or exchange of property between related parties. A related party includes a corporation controlled by the taxpayer. § 267.

Research and experimentation expenditures. Three alternative methods are provided in the Code. The expenditures may be expensed in the year paid or incurred, deferred subject to amortization, or capitalized. If an election is not made to expense such costs or to defer the expenditures subject to amortization (over 60 months), the research and experimentation costs must be capitalized. § 174. Incremental research and experimentation expenditures qualify for a 25 percent credit.

Reserve for bad debts. A method of accounting whereby an allowance is permitted for estimated uncollectible accounts. Actual write-offs are charged to the reserve, and recoveries of amounts previously written off are credited to the reserve. § 166(c).

Reserves for estimated expenses. Except in the case of bad debts, reserves for estimated expenses (e. g., warranty service costs) are not permitted for tax purposes, even though such reserves are appropriate for financial accounting purposes. See *all events test.*

Residential energy tax credit. See *energy tax credit—residential property.*

Restricted property. An arrangement whereby an employer transfers property (usually stock) to an employee at a bargain price (i. e., for less than its fair market value). If the transfer is accompanied by a substantial risk of forfeiture and the property is not transferable, no compensation results to the employee until such restrictions disappear. An example of a substantial risk of forfeiture would be a requirement that the employee return the property if his or her employment is terminated within a specified period of time. § 83. See *nonqualified deferred compensation plans.*

Retirement of corporate obligations. The retirement of corporate and certain government obligations is considered to be a sale or exchange. Gain or loss, therefore, is treated as capital gain or loss upon the retirement of a corporate obligation rather than as ordinary income or loss. § 1232.

Return of capital doctrine. When a taxable sale or exchange occurs, the seller may be permitted to recover his or her investment (or other adjusted basis) in the property before gain or loss is recognized. See *open transaction.*

Revenue Procedure. A matter of procedural importance to both taxpayers and the IRS concerning the administration of the tax laws is issued as a Revenue Procedure (abbreviated as "Rev.Proc."). A Revenue Procedure is first published in an Internal Revenue Bulletin (I.R.B.) and later transferred to the appropriate Cumulative Bulletin (C.B.). Both the Internal Revenue Bulletins and the Cumulative Bulletins are published by the U. S. Government.

Revenue Ruling. A Revenue Ruling (abbreviated "Rev.Rul.") is issued by the National Office of the IRS to express an official interpretation of the tax law as applied to specific transactions. Unlike a Regulation, it is more limited in application. A Revenue Ruling is first published in an Internal Revenue Bulletin (I.R.B.) and later transferred to the appropriate Cumulative Bulletin (C.B.).

–S–

Sales tax. State and local taxes are deductible if such taxes are separately stated and imposed upon the taxpayer (consumer). Unless business related, sales tax is deductible *from* AGI. The IRS issues optional state sales tax tables for individuals to use. § 164(a)(4).

Scholarships and fellowships. Scholarships and fellowships are generally excluded from gross income of the recipient unless the payments are a disguised form of compensation for services rendered. Special rules apply when the payments are for dual motives (i. e., to aid the recipient and to benefit the grantor). § 117.

S corporation *status.* An elective provision permitting certain small business corporations (§ 1371) and their shareholders to elect (§ 1372) to be treated for income tax purposes in accordance with the operating rules of § § 1373–1379. Of major significance is the fact that S status usually avoids the corporate income tax, and corporate losses can be claimed by the shareholders.

Section 38 property. Property which qualifies for the investment tax credit. Generally, this includes all tangible property (other than real estate) used in a trade or business. § 48.

Section 1231 assets. Section 1231 assets are depreciable assets and real estate used in a trade or business and held for more than one year. Under certain circumstances, the classification also includes timber, coal, domestic iron ore, livestock (held for draft, breeding, dairy, or sporting purposes), and unharvested crops. § 1231(b).

Section 1231 gains and losses. If the net result of the combined gains and losses from the taxable dispositions of § 1231 assets plus the net gain from involuntary conversion (of both § 1231 assets and long-term capital assets) is a gain, the gains and losses from § 1231 assets are treated as long-term capital gains and losses. In arriving at § 1231 gains, however, the depreciation recapture provisions (e. g., § § 1245 and 1250) are first applied to produce ordinary income. If the net result of the combination is a loss, the gains and losses from § 1231 assets are treated as ordinary gains and losses. § 1231(a).

Section 1244 stock. Stock issued under § 1244 by qualifying small business corporations. If § 1244 stock becomes worthless, the shareholders may claim an ordinary loss rather than the usual capital loss.

Section 1245 property. Property which is subject to the recapture of depreciation under § 1245. For a definition of § 1245 property see § 1245(a)(3). See *recapture of depreciation* and *Section 1245 recapture.*

Section 1245 recapture. Upon a taxable disposition of § 1245 property, all depreciation claimed on such property after 1962 will be recaptured as ordinary income (but not to exceed recognized gain from the disposition).

Section 1250 property. Real estate which is subject to the recapture of depreciation under § 1250. For a definition of § 1250 property see § 1250(c). See *recapture of depreciation* and *Section 1250 recapture.*

Section 1250 recapture. Upon a taxable disposition of § 1250 property, some of the excess depreciation (amounts in excess of straight-line) claimed on the property may be recaptured as ordinary income. Various recapture rules apply depending upon the type of property (i. e., residential or commercial real estate) and the date acquired. Generally, the excess depreciation (amounts in excess of what would have been claimed under the straight-line method) is recaptured in full to the extent of the gain recognized.

Self-employment tax. A tax of 14 percent (subject to a 2.7 percent credit) in 1984 is levied on individuals with net earnings from self-employment (up to $37,800) to provide Social Security benefits for such individuals. If a self-employed individual also receives wages from an employer which are subject to FICA, the self-employment tax is reduced.

Self-employment retirement plan. Also known as HR 10 and Keogh plans. Under such plans, a taxpayer may deduct each year up to either 15 percent of net earnings from self-employment or $30,000, whichever is less.

Short sales. A short sale occurs when a taxpayer sells borrowed property (usually stock) and repays the lender with substantially identical property either held on the date of the short sale or purchased after the sale. No gain or loss is recognized until the short sale is closed, and such gain or loss is generally short term. § 1233.

Simplified employee pensions. An employer may make contributions to an employee's individual retirement account (IRA) in amounts not exceeding the lesser of 15% of compensation or $30,000 per individual. These employer-sponsored simplified employee pensions are permitted only if the contributions are nondiscriminatory and are made on behalf of all employees who have attained age 25 and have worked for the employer during at least three of the five preceding calendar years. § 219(b)(7). See *individual retirement account.*

Small business corporation. A corporation which satisfies the definition of § 1371(a), § 1244(c)(2), or both. Satisfaction of § 1371(a) permits an S corporation election, while satisfaction of § 1244 enables the shareholders of the corporation to claim an ordinary loss on the worthlessness of the stock.

Standard deduction. Replaced by the zero bracket amount. See *zero bracket amount.*

State and local taxes. See *sales tax.*

Statute of limitations. Provisions of the law which specify the maximum period of time in which action may be taken on a past event. Code § § 6501–6504 contain the limitation periods applicable to the IRS for additional assessments, while § § 6511–6515 relate to refund claims by taxpayers.

Statutory notice of deficiency. Commonly referred to as the 90-day letter, this notice is sent to a taxpayer upon request, upon the expiration of the 30-day letter, or upon exhaustion by the taxpayer of his or her administrative remedies before the IRS. The notice gives the taxpayer 90 days in which to file a petition with the U. S. Tax Court. If such a petition is not filed, the IRS will issue a demand for payment of the assessed deficiency. § § 6211–6216. See *thirty-day letter.*

Stock redemptions. The redemption of the stock of a shareholder by the issuing corporation will be treated as a sale or exchange of the stock if the redemption is not a dividend. § § 301 and 302.

–T–

Targeted jobs tax credit. Employers are allowed a tax credit equal to 50 percent of the first $6,000 of wages (per eligible employee) for the first year of employment and 25 percent of such wages for the succeeding year. Eligible employees include certain hard-to-employ individuals (e. g., youths from low-income families, handicapped persons). The employer's deduction for wages is reduced by the amount of the credit taken. For qualified summer youth employees, the credit is 85 percent of the first $3,000 of qualified wages.

Tax avoidance. The minimization of one's tax liability by taking advantage of legally available tax planning opportunities. Tax avoidance may be contrasted with tax evasion, which entails the reduction of tax liability by using illegal means.

Tax benefit rule. A rule which limits the recognition of income from the recovery of an expense or loss properly deducted in a prior tax year to the amount of the deduction that generated a tax benefit. Assume for example, that in 1983 T (an individual) had medical expenses of $1,800 and adjusted gross income of $30,000. Due to the 5 percent limitation, T was able to deduct only $300 of these expenses [i. e., $1,800 − (5 percent × $30,000)]. If, in 1984, T is reimbursed by his insurance company for $400 of these expenses, the tax benefit rule limits the amount of income from the reimbursement to $300 (i. e., the amount previously deducted with a tax benefit).

Tax Court. The U. S. Tax Court is one of three trial courts of original jurisdiction which decides litigation involving Federal income, death, or gift taxes. It is the only trial court wherein the taxpayer need not first pay the deficiency assessed by the IRS. The Tax Court will not have jurisdiction over a case unless the statutory notice of deficiency (i. e., 90-day letter) has been issued by the IRS and the taxpayer files the petition for hearing within the time prescribed.

Tax credit for elderly. An elderly taxpayer (age 65 and over) may receive a tax credit amounting to 15 percent of $2,500 ($3,750 for married individuals filing jointly). This amount is reduced by Social Security benefits, excluded pension benefits, and one-half of the taxpayer's adjusted gross income in excess of $7,500 ($10,000 for married taxpayers filing jointly). § 37.

Tax-free exchange. Transfers of property specifically exempted from Federal income tax consequences. Examples are a transfer of property to a controlled corporation under § 351(a) and a like-kind exchange under § 1031(a).

Tax home. Since travel expenses of an employee are deductible only if the taxpayer is away from home, the deductibility of such expenses rests upon the definition of "tax home." The IRS position is that tax home is the business location, post, or station of the taxpayer. If an employee is temporarily reassigned to a new post for a period of one year or less, the taxpayer's home should be his or her personal residence and the travel expenses should be deductible. The courts are in conflict regarding what constitutes a person's home for tax purposes.

Tax preference items. Those items set forth in § 57 which may result in the imposition of the alternative minimum tax. See *alternative minimum tax.*

Tax rates—corporations. See *normal tax* and *surtax.*

Tax rate schedules. Rate schedules appearing in Appendix A–1 which are used by upper income taxpayers and those not permitted to use the Tax Table. Separate rate schedules are provided for married individuals filing jointly, unmarried individuals who maintain a household, single taxpayers, and estates and trusts and married individuals filing separate returns.

Tax table. A tax table appearing in Appendix A–2 is provided for taxpayers with less than $50,000 of taxable income. Separate columns are provided for single taxpayers, married taxpayers filing jointly, head of household, and married taxpayers filing separately.

Thin corporation. When debt owed by a corporation to its shareholders is large in relationship to its capital structure (i. e., stock and shareholder equity), the IRS may contend that the corporation is thinly capitalized. In effect, this means that some or all of the debt will be reclassified as equity. The immediate result is to disallow any interest deduction to the corporation on the reclassified debt. To the extent of the corporation's earnings and profits, interest payments and loan repayments are treated as dividends to the shareholders. § 385.

Thirty-day letter. A letter which accompanies a revenue agent's report (RAR) issued as a result of an IRS audit of a taxpayer (or the rejection of a taxpayer's claim for refund). The letter outlines the taxpayer's appeal procedure before the IRS. If the taxpayer does not request any such procedures within the 30-day period, the IRS will issue a statutory notice of deficiency (the "90-day letter").

Timber. Special rules apply to the recognition of gain from the sale of timber. A taxpayer may elect to treat the cutting of timber, which is held for sale or use in a trade or business, as a sale or exchange. If the holding period requirements are met, the gain is recognized as § 1231 gain and may therefore receive favorable long-term capital gain treatment. § 631.

Trade or business expenses. Deductions *for* AGI which are attributable to a taxpayer's business or profession. Some employee expenses may also be treated as trade or business expenses. See *employee expenses.*

Transportation expenses. Transportation expenses for an employee include only the cost of transportation (taxi fares, automobile expenses, etc.) in the course of employment when the employee is not away from home in travel status. Commuting expenses are not deductible. See *automobile expenses.*

Travel expenses. Travel expenses include meals and lodging and transportation expenses while away from home in the pursuit of a trade or business (including that of an employee). See *tax home.*

Trial court. The court of original jurisdiction; the first court to consider litigation. In Federal tax controversies, trial courts include U. S. District Courts, the U. S. Tax Court, and the U. S. Claims Court. See *appellate court.*

–U–

Unearned (prepaid) income. For tax purposes, prepaid income (e. g., rent) is taxable in the year of receipt. In certain cases involving advance payments for goods and services, income may be deferred. See Rev.Proc. 71–21 (1971–2 C.B. 549) and Reg. § 1.451–5.

Unreasonable compensation. Under § 162(a)(1) a deduction is allowed for "reasonable" salaries or other compensation for personal services actually rendered. To the extent compensation is "excessive" (i. e., "unreasonable"), no deduction will be allowed. The problem of unreasonable compensation usually is limited to closely-held corporations where the motivation is to pay out profits in some form deductible to the corporation. Deductible compensation, therefore, becomes an attractive substitute for nondeductible dividends when the shareholders are also employees of the corporation.

USTC. Published by Commerce Clearing House, *U. S. Tax Cases* contain all of the Federal tax decisions issued by the U. S. District Courts, U. S. Claims Court, U. S. Courts of Appeals, and the U. S. Supreme Court.

–V–

Vacation home. The Code places restrictions upon taxpayers who rent their residences or vacation homes for part of the tax year. The restrictions may result in a scaling down of expense deductions for such taxpayers. § 280A. See *hobby loss.*

–W–

Wash sale. A loss from the sale of stock or securities which is disallowed because the taxpayer has within 30 days before or after the sale acquired stock or securities which are substantially identical to those sold. § 1091.

Worthless securities. A loss (usually capital) is allowed for a security that becomes worthless during the year. The loss is deemed to have occurred on the last day of the year. Special rules apply to securities of affiliated companies and small business stock. § 165. See *Section 1244 stock*.

Writ of certiorari. See *certiorari*.

–Z–

Zero bracket amount. A deduction generally available to all individual taxpayers in arriving at taxable income. Unlike the standard deduction which it replaced, the zero bracket amount is not determined as a percentage of adjusted gross income but is a flat amount. This amount is $2,300 for single persons and heads of household, $3,400 for married persons filing jointly, and $1,700 for married persons filing separate returns. The zero bracket amount does not have to be computed separately but is built into the tax tables and the tax rate schedules.

APPENDIX D–1
TABLE OF CODE SECTIONS CITED

[See Title 26 U.S.C.A.]

APPENDIX D-2
TABLE OF PROPOSED REGULATIONS AND REGULATIONS CITED

PROPOSED REGULATIONS

REGULATIONS

APPENDIX D-3
TABLE OF REVENUE PROCEDURES AND REVENUE RULINGS CITED

REVENUE PROCEDURES

REVENUE RULINGS

APPENDIX E
CITATOR EXAMPLE

ILLUSTRATION OF THE USE OF THE P–H CITATOR

Background

The Prentice-Hall *Federal Tax Citator* is a separate service with a loose-leaf current matters section. Cases that are reported by the *Citator* are divided into the various issues involved. Since the researcher may be interested in only one or two issues, only those cases involving the particular issue need to be checked.

The volumes of the P–H *Federal Tax Citator* and the period of time covered by each are:

Volume 1 (1919–1941)

Volume 2 (1942–1948)

Volume 3 (1948–1954)

Volume 1, Second Series (1954–1977)

Loose-leaf volume, Second Series (1977 to present)

Through the use of symbols, the *Citator* indicates whether a decision is followed, explained, criticized, questioned, or overruled by a later court decision. These symbols are reproduced in Figure 1.

Figure 1

Prentice-Hall Citator Symbols*

COURT DECISIONS

Judicial History of the Case

a	affirmed (by decision of a higher court)
d	dismissed (appeal to a higher court dismissed)
m	modified (decision modified by a higher court, or on rehearing)
r	reversed (by a decision of a higher court)
s	same case (e. g., on rehearing)
rc	related case (companion cases and other cases arising out of the same subject matter are so designated)
x	certiorari denied (by the Supreme Court of the United States)
(C or G)	The Commissioner or Solicitor General has made the appeal
(T)	Taxpayer has made the appeal
(A)	Tax Court's decision acquiesced in by Commissioner
(NA)	Tax Court's decision nonacquiesced in by Commissioner
sa	same case affirmed (by the cited case)
sd	same case dismissed (by the cited case)
sm	same case modified (by the cited case)
sr	same case reversed (by the cited case)
sx	same case-certiorari denied

Syllabus of the Cited Case

iv	four (on all fours with the cited case)
f	followed (the cited case followed)
e	explained (comment generally favorable, but not to a degree that indicates the cited case is followed)
k	reconciled (the cited case reconciled)
n	dissenting opinion (cited in a dissenting opinion)
g	distinguished (the cited case distinguished either in law or on the facts)
l	limited (the cited case limited to its facts. Used when an appellate court so limits a prior decision, or a lower court states that in its opinion the cited case should be so limited)
c	criticized (adverse comment on the cited case)
q	questioned (the cited case not only criticized, but its correctness questioned)
o	overruled

Example

Determine the background and validity of *Adda v. Comm.*, 37 AFTR 654, 171 F.2d 457 (CA–4, 1948).

Solution

Turning directly to the case itself (reproduced as Figure 2), note the two issues involved (i. e., "1." and "2."). For purposes of emphasis,

---

* Reproduced from the Federal Taxes Citator with the permission of the publisher, Prentice-Hall, Inc., Englewood Cliffs, N.J. 07632

Figure 2

ADDA v. COMMISSIONER OF INTERNAL REVENUE

Cite as 171 F.2d 457

ADDA v. COMMISSIONER OF INTERNAL REVENUE

No. 5796.

United States Court of Appeals
Fourth Circuit.

Dec. 3, 1948.

1. Internal revenue ⟜792

ISSUE 1.
Where nonresident alien's brother residing in United States traded for alien's benefit on commodity exchanges in United States at authorization of alien, who vested full discretion in brother with regard thereto, and many transactions were effected through different brokers, several accounts were maintained, and substantial gains and losses realized, transactions constituted a "trade or business," profits of which were "capital gains" taxable as income to the alien. 26 U.S.C.A. § 211(b).

See Words and Phrases, Permanent Edition, for other judicial constructions and definitions of "Capital Gains" and "Trade or Business".

2. Internal revenue ⟜792

ISSUE 2.
The exemption of a nonresident alien's commodity transactions in the United States provided for by the Internal Revenue Code does not apply where alien has agent in United States using his own discretion in effecting transactions for alien's account. 26 U.S.C.A. § 211(b).

On Petition to Review the Decision of The Tax Court of the United States.

Petition by Fernand C. A. Adda to review a decision of the Tax Court redetermining a deficiency in income tax imposed by the Commissioner of Internal Revenue.

Decision affirmed.

Rollin Browne and Mitchell B. Carroll, both of New York City, for petitioner.

Irving I. Axelrad, Sp. Asst. to Atty. Gen. (Theron Lamar Caudle, Asst. Atty. Gen., and Ellis N. Slack and A. F. Prescott, Sp. Assts. to Atty. Gen., on the brief), for respondent.

Before PARKER, Chief Judge, and SOPER and DOBIE, Circuit Judges.

PER CURIAM.

[1, 2] This is a petition by a non-resident alien to review a decision of the Tax Court. Petitioner is a national of Egypt, who in the year 1941 was residing in France. He had a brother who at that time was residing in the United States and who traded for petitioner's benefit on commodity exchanges in the United States in cotton, wool, grains, silk, hides and copper. This trading was authorized by petitioner who vested full discretion in his brother with regard thereto, and it resulted in profits in the sum of $193,857.14. The Tax Court said: "While the number of transactions or the total amount of money involved in them has not been stated, it is apparent that many transactions were effected through different brokers, several accounts were maintained, and gains and losses in substantial amounts were realized. This evidence shows that the trading was extensive enough to amount to a trade or business, and the petitioner does not contend, nor has he shown, that the transactions were so infrequent or inconsequential as not to amount to a trade or business." We agree with the Tax Court that, for reasons adequately set forth in its opinion, this income was subject to taxation, and that the exemption of a non-resident alien's commodity transactions in the United States, provided by section 211(b) of the Internal Revenue Code, 26 U.S.C.A. § 211 (b), does not apply to a case where the alien has an agent in the United States using his own discretion in effecting the transactions for the alien's account. As said by the Tax Court, "Through such transactions the alien is engaging in trade or business within the United States, and the profits on these transactions are capital gains taxable to him." Nothing need be added to the reasoning of the Tax Court in this connection, and the decision will be affirmed on its opinion.

Affirmed.

Figure 3

» Adamson — Adler «   5505

ADAMSON, JAMES H. & MARION C. v U. S., — F Supp —, 36 AFTR 1529, 1946 P.-H. ¶ 72,418 (DC Calif) (See Adamson v U. S.)

ADAMSON, R. R., MRS., — BTA —, 1934 (P.-H.) BTA Memo. Dec. ¶ 34,370

ADAMSON v U. S., 26 AFTR 1188 (DC Calif, Sept 8, 1939)
iv—Coggan, Linus C., 1939 (P.-H.) BTA Memo. Dec. page 39—806

ADAMSON; U. S. v, 161 F(2d) 942, 35 AFTR 1404 (CCA 9)
1—Lazier v U. S., 170 F(2d) 524, 37 AFTR 545, 1948 P.-H. page 73,174 (CCA 8)
1—Grace Bros., Inc. v Comm., 173 F(2d) 178, 37 AFTR 1014, 1949 P.-H. page 72,433 (CCA 9)
1—Briggs; Hofferbert v, 178 F(2d) 744, 38 AFTR 1219, 1950 P.-H. page 72,267 (CCA 4)
1—Rogers v Comm., 180 F(2d) 722, 39 AFTR 115, 1950 P.-H. page 72,531 (CCA 3)
1—Lamar v Granger, 99 F Supp 41, 40 AFTR 270, 1951 P.-H. page 72,945 (DC Pa)
1—Herbert v Riddell, 103 F Supp 383, 41 AFTR 975, 1952 P.-H. page 72,383 (DC Calif)
1—Hudson, Galvin, 20 TC 737, 20-1953 P.-H. TC 418

ADAMSON v U. S., — F Supp —, 36 AFTR 1529, 1946 P.-H. ¶ 72,418 (DC Calif, Jan 28, 1946)

ADAMS-ROTH BAKING CO., 8 BTA 458
1—Gunderson Bros. Engineering Corp., 16 TC 129, 16-1951 P.-H. TC 72

ADAMSTON FLAT GLASS CO. v COMM., 162 F(2d) 875, 35 AFTR 1579 (CCA 6)
4—Forrest Hotel Corp. v. Fly, 112 F Supp 789, 43 AFTR 1080, 1953 P.-H. page 72,856 (DC Miss)

ADDA v COMM., 171 F(2d) 457, 37 AFTR 654, 1948 P.-H. ¶ 72,655 (CCA 4, Dec 3, 1948)
Cert. filed, March 1, 1949 (T)
No cert. (G) 1949 P-H ¶ 71,050
x—Adda v Comm., 336 US 952, 69 S Ct 883, 93 L Ed 1107, April 18, 1949 (T)
sa—Adda, Fernand C. A., 10 TC 273 (No. 33), ¶ 10.33 P.-H. TC 1948
iv—Milner Hotels, Inc., N. Y., 173 F (2d) 567, 37 AFTR 1170, 1949 P.-H. page 72,528 (CCA 6)
1—Nubar; Comm. v, 185 F(2d) 588, 39 AFTR 1315, 1950 P.-H. page 73,423 (CCA 4)
g-1—Scottish Amer. Invest. Co., Ltd., The, 12 TC 59, 12-1949 P.-H. TC 32
g-1—Nubar, Zareh, 13 TC 579, 13-1949 P.-H. TC 318

ADDA, FERNAND C. A., 10 TC 273 (No. 33), ¶ 10.33 P.-H. TC 1948 (A) 1948-2 CB 1
a—Adda v Comm., 171 F(2d) 457, 37 AFTR 654, 1948 P.-H. ¶ 72,655 (CCA 4)
1—Nubar; Comm. v, 185 F(2d) 588, 39 AFTR 1315, 1950 P.-H. page 73,423 (CCA 4)
g-1—Scottish Amer. Invest. Co., Ltd., The, 12 TC 59, 12-1949 P.-H. TC 32
g-1—Nubar, Zareh, 13 TC 579, 13-1949 P.-H. TC 318

ADDA, FERNAND C. A., 10 TC 1291 (No. 168), ¶ 10.168 P.-H. TC 1948 (A) 1953-1 CB 3, 1953 P.-H. ¶ 76,453 (NA) 1948-2 CB 5, 1948 P.-H. ¶ 76,434 withdrawn
1—Scottish Amer. Invest. Co., Ltd., The, 12 TC 59, 12-1949 P.-H. TC 32

ADDA INC., 9 TC 199 (A) 1949-1 CB 1, 1949 P.-H. ¶ 76,260 (NA) 1947-2 CB 6 withdrawn
a—Adda, Inc.; Comm. v, 171 F(2d) 367, 37 AFTR 641, 1948 P.-H. ¶ 72,654 (CCA 2)
a—Adda, Inc.; Comm. v, 171 F(2d) 367, 37 AFTR 641, 1949 P.-H. ¶ 72,303 (CCA 2)
e-1—G.C.M. 26069, 1949-2 CB 38, 1949 P.-H. page 76,226
3—Koshland, Execx.; U.S. v, 208 F(2d) 640, — AFTR —, 1953 P.-H. page 73,597 (CCA 9)
4—Kent, Otis Beall, 1954 (P. H.) TC Memo. Dec. page 54—47

ADDA, INC.; COMM. v, 171 F(2d) 367, 37 AFTR 641, 1948 P.-H. ¶ 72,654 (CCA 2, Dec 6, 1948)
sa—Adda, Inc., 9 TC 199
s—Adda, Inc.; Comm. v, 171 F(2d) 367, 37 AFTR 641, 1949 P.-H. ¶ 72,303 (CCA 2) reh. den.
e-1—G.C.M. 26069, 1949-2 CB 39, 1949 P.-H. page 76,227
e-2—G.C.M. 26069, 1949-2 CB 39, 1949 P.-H. page 76,227

ADDA, INC.; COMM. v, 171 F(2d) 367, 37 AFTR 641, 1949 P.-H. ¶ 72,303 (CCA 2, Dec 6, 1948) reh. den.
sa—Adda, Inc., 9 TC 199
s—Adda, Inc.; Comm. v, 171 F(2d) 367, 37 AFTR 641, 1948 P.-H. ¶ 72,654 (CCA 2)

ADDISON-CHEVROLET SALES, INC. v CHAMBERLAIN, L. A. & NAT. BANK OF WASH., THE, — F Supp —, 1954 P.-H. ¶ 72,550 (DC DC) (See Campbell v Chamberlain)

ADDISON v COMM., 177 F(2d) 521, 38 AFTR 821, 1949 P.-H. ¶ 72,637 (CCA 8, Nov 3, 1949)
sa—Addison, Irene D., — TC —, 1948 (P.-H.) TC Memo. Dec. ¶ 48,177
1—Roberts, Supt. v U. S., 115 Ct Cl 439, 87 F Supp 937, 38 AFTR 1314, 1950 P.-H. page 72,292
1—Cold Metal Process Co., The, 17 TC 934, 17-1951 P.-H. TC 512
1—Berger, Samuel & Lillian, 1954 (P.-H.) TC Memo. Dec. page 54—232
2—Urquhart, George Gordon & Mary F., 20 TC 948, 20-1953 P.-H. TC 536

ADDISON, IRENE D., — TC —, 1948 (P.-H.) TC Memo. Dec. ¶ 48,177
App (T) Jan 14. 1949 (CCA 8)
a—Addison v Comm., 177 F(2d) 521, 38 AFTR 821, 1949 P.-H. ¶ 72,637 (CCA 8)
1—Urquhart, George Gordon & Mary F., 20 TC 948, 20-1953 P.-H. TC 536

ADDITON, HARRY L. & ANNIE S., 3 TC 427
1—Lum, Ralph E., 12 TC 379, 12-1949 P.-H. TC 204
1—Christie, John A. & Elizabeth H., — TC —, 1949 (P.-H.) TC Memo. Dec. page 49—795

ADDRESSOGRAPH - MULTIGRAPH CORP., 1945 (P.-H.) TC Memo. Dec. ¶ 45,058
f-10—Rev. Rul. 54-71, 1954 P.-H. page 76,453

ADDRESSOGRAPH-MULTIGRAPH CORP. v U. S., 112 Ct Cl 201, 78 F Supp 111, 37 AFTR 53, 1948 P.-H. ¶ 72,504 (June 1, 1948)
No cert (G) 1949 P.-H. ¶ 71,041
1—New Oakmont Corp., The v U. S., 114 Ct Cl 686, 86 F Supp 901, 38 AFTR 924, 1949 P.-H. page 73,181

ADELAIDE PARK LAND, 25 BTA 211
g—Amer. Security & Fidelity Corp., — BTA —, 1940 (P.-H.) BTA Memo. Dec. page 40—571

ADELPHI PAINT & COLOR WORKS, INC., 18 BTA 436
1—Neracher, William A., — BTA —, 1939 (P.-H.) BTA Memo. Dec. page 39—69
1—Lyman-Hawkins Lumber Co., — BTA —, 1939 (P.-H.) BTA Memo. Dec. page 39—350

ADEMAN v U. S., 174 F(2d) 283, 37 AFTR 1406 (CCA 9, April 25, 1949)

ADICONIS, NOELLA L. (PATNAUDE), 1953 (P.-H.) TC Memo. Dec. ¶ 53,305

ADJUSTMENT BUREAU OF ST. LOUIS ASSN., OF CREDIT MEN, 21 BTA 232
1—Cook County Loss Adjustment Bureau, — BTA —, 1940 (P.-H.) BTA Memo. Dec. page 40—331

ADKINS, CHARLES I., — BTA —, 1933 (P.-H.) BTA Memo. Dec. ¶ 33,457

ADLER v COMM., 77 F(2d) 733, 16 AFTR 162 (CCA 5)
g-2—McEuen v Comm., 196 F(2d) 130, 41 AFTR 1172, 1952 P.-H. page 72,604 (CCA 5)

these issues have been bracketed and identified as such by a marginal notation added to Figure 2. The reason for the division of the issues becomes apparent when the case is traced through the *Citator*.

Refer to Volume 3 for the AFTR Series (covering the period from October 7, 1948, through July 29, 1954) of the P–H *Federal Tax Citator*. Reference to the case is located on page 5505. This page is reproduced in Figure 3.

Correlating the symbols reproduced in Figure 3 with the shaded portion of Figure 3, reveals the following information about *Adda v. Comm.*:

Application for certiorari (i. e., appeal to the U. S. Supreme Court) filed by the taxpayer (T) on March 1, 1949.

Certiorari was denied (x) by the U. S. Supreme Court on April 18, 1949.

The trial court decision is reported in 10 T.C. 273 and was affirmed on appeal (sa) to the Fourth Court of Appeals.

During the time frame of Volume 3 of the *Citator* (October 7, 1948, through July 29, 1954), one decision *(Milner Hotels, Inc.)* has agreed "on all fours with the cited case" (iv). One decision *(Comm. v. Nubar)* has and two decisions *(The Scottish American Investment Co., Ltd.* and *Zareh Nubar)* have distinguished the cited case on issue number one (g–1).

Reference to Volume 1 of the Citator Second Series (covering the period from 1954 through 1977) shows the *Adda v. Comm.* case on page 25. This page is reproduced in Figure 4.

Correlating the symbols reproduced in Figure 3 with the shaded portion of Figure 4 reveals the following additional information about *Adda v. Comm.*

The case was cited without comment in two rulings and two cases: *Rev.Rul. 56–145*, and *Rev.Rul. 56–392, Balanovski* and *Liang*.

It was followed in *Asthmanefrin Co.* (f–1).

It was distinguished in *deVegvar* and *Purvis* (g–1).

It was recorded in *deKrause* (k–1).

Reference to the loose-leaf volume for the Citator Second Series covering the period from 1977 to the present shows that *Adda v. Comm.* was cited by *Security Bancorp, Inc. v. U. S.* and *Robert E. Cleveland*, but no symbol was given opposite the citing cases. This absence of a symbol means that the language of the decision is without express comment to fit directly within the meaning of a symbol or that the case was cited in a concurring opinion. Be sure to search the "Current Monthly Supplement" near the back of this volume; otherwise you may miss the latest citation.

Except as otherwise noted, it would appear that *Adda v. Comm.* has withstood the test of time.

Figure 4

ADASKAVICH, STEPHEN A. v U.S., 39 AFTR2d 77-517, 422 F Supp 276 (DC Mont) (See Wiegand, Charles J., Jr. v U.S.)
AD. AURIEMA, INC., 1943 P-H TC Memo ¶ 43,422
 e-1—Miller v U.S., 13 AFTR2d 1515, 166 Ct Cl 257, 331 F2d 859
ADAY v SUPERIOR CT. OF ALAMEDA COUNTY, 8 AFTR2d 5367, 13 Cal Reptr 415, 362 P2d 47 (Calif, 5-11-61)
ADCO SERVICE, INC., ASSIGNEE v CYBERMATICS, INC., 36 AFTR2d 75-6342 (NJ) (See Adco Service, Inc., Assignee v Graphic Color Plate)
ADCO SERVICE, INC., ASSIGNEE v GRAPHIC COLOR PLATE, 36 AFTR2d 75-6342 (NJ, Supr Ct, 11-10-75)
ADCO SERVICE, INC., ASSIGNEE v GRAPHIC COLOR PLATE, INC., 36 AFTR2d 75-6342 (NJ) (See Adco Service. Inc., Assignee v Graphic Color Plate)
ADDA v COMM., 171 F2d 457, 37 AFTR 654 (USCA 4)
 Rev. Rul. 56-145, 1956-1 CB 613
 1—Balanovski; U.S. v, 236 F2d 304, 49 AFTR 2013 (USCA 2)
 1—Liang, Chang Hsiao, 23 TC 1045, 23-1955 P-H TC 624
 f-1—Asthmanefrin Co., Inc., 25 TC 1141, 25-1956 P-H TC 639
 g-1—de Vegvar, Edward A. Neuman, 28 TC 1061, 28-1957 P-H TC 599
 g-1—Purvis, Ralph E. & Patricia Lee, 1974 P-H TC Memo 74-669
 k-1—deKrause, Piedad Alvarado, 1974 P-H TC Memo 74-1291
 1—Rev. Rul. 56-392, 1956-2 CB 971
ADDA, FERNAND C.A., 10 TC 273, ¶ 10,133 P-H TC 1948
 1—Balanovski; U.S. v, 236 F2d 303, 49 AFTR 2012 (USCA 2)
 1—Liang, Chang Hsiao, 23 TC 1045, 23-1955 P-H TC 624
 g-1—de Vegvar, Edward A. Neuman, 28 TC 1061, 28-1957 P-H TC 599
 g-1—Purvis, Ralph E. & Patricia Lee, 1974 P-H TC Memo 74-669
 k-1—deKrause, Piedad Alvarado, 1974 P-H TC Memo 74-1291
ADDA, INC., 9 TC 199
 Pardee, Marvin L., Est. of, 49 TC 152, 49 P-H TC 107 [See 9 TC 206-208]
 f-1—Asthmanefrin Co., Inc., 25 TC 1141, 25-1956 P-H TC 639
 1—Keil Properties, Inc. (Dela), 24 TC 1117, 24-1955 P-H TC 615
 1—Saffan, Samuel, 1957 P-H TC Memo 57—701
 1—Rev. Rul. 56-145, 1956-1 CB 613
 1—Rev. Rul. 56-392, 1956-2 CB 971
 4—Midler Court Realty, Inc., 61 TC 597, 61 P-H TC 368
ADDA, INC.; COMM. v, 171 F2d 367, 37 AFTR 641 (USCA 2)
 1—Pardee, Marvin L., Est. of, 49 TC 152, 49 P-H TC 107
 1—Saffan, Samuel, 1957 P-H TC Memo 57-701
 2—Midler Court Realty, Inc., 61 TC 597, 61 P-H TC 368
ADDELSTON, ALBERT A. & SARAH M., 1965 P-H TC Memo ¶ 65,215
ADDISON v COMM., 177 F2d 521, 38 AFTR 821 (USCA 8)
 g-1—Industrial Aggregate Co. v U.S., 6 AFTR2d 5963, 284 F2d 645 (USCA 8)
 1—Sturgeon v McMahon, 155 F Supp 630, 52 AFTR 789 (DC NY)
 1—Gilmore v U.S., 16 AFTR2d 5211, 5213, 245 F Supp 384, 386 (DC Calif)
 1—Waldheim & Co., Inc., 25 TC 599, 25-1955 P-H TC 332
 g-1—Galewitz, Samuel & Marian, 50 TC 113, 50 P-H TC 79
 1—Buder, G. A., Est. of, 1963 P-H TC Memo 63-345
 e-1—Rhodes, Lynn E. & Martha E., 1963 P-H TC Memo, 63-1374
 2—Shipp v Comm., 217 F2d 402, 46 AFTR 1170 (USCA 9)

ADDISON—Contd.
 g-2—Industrial Aggregate Co. v U.S., 6 AFTR2d 5964, 284 F2d 645 (USCA 8)
 e-2—Buder, Est. of v Comm., 13 AFTR2d 1238, 330 F2d 443 (USCA 8)
 2—Iowa Southern Utilities Co. v Comm., 14 AFTR2d 5063, 333 F2d 385 (USCA 8)
 2—Kelly, Daniel, S.W., 23 TC 687, 23-1955 P-H TC 422
 f-2—Morgan, Joseph P., Est. of, 37 TC 36, 37, 37-1961 P-H TC 26, 27
 n-2—Woodward, Fred W. & Elsie M., 49 TC 385, 49 P-H TC 270
ADDISON, IRENE D., 1948 P-H TC Memo ¶ 48,177
 1—Waldheim & Co., Inc., 25 TC 599, 25-1955 P-H TC 332
 f-1—Morgan, Joseph P., Est. of, 37 TC 36, 37, 37-1961 P-H TC 26, 27
 1—Buder, G. A., Est. of, 1963 P-H TC Memo 63-345
 e-1—Rhodes, Lynn E. & Martha E., 1963 P-H TC Memo 63-1374
ADDISON, JOHN MILTON, BKPT; U.S. v, 20 AFTR2d 5630, 384 F2d 748 (USCA 5) (See Rochelle Jr., Trtee; U.S. v)
ADDRESSOGRAPH - MULTIGRAPH CORP., 1945 P-H TC Memo ¶ 45,058
 Conn. L. & P. Co., The v U.S., 9 AFTR2d 679, 156 Ct Cl 312, 314, 299 F2d 264
 Copperhead Coal Co., Inc., 1958 P-H TC Memo 58-33
 1—Seas Shipping Co., Inc. v Comm., 19 AFTR2d 596, 371 F2d 529 (USCA 2)
 e-1—Hitchcock, E. R., Co., The v U.S., 35 AFTR2d 75-1207, 514 F2d 487 (USCA 2)
 f-2—Vulcan Materials Co. v U.S., 25 AFTR2d 70-446, 308 F Supp 57 (DC Ala)
 f-3—Marlo Coil Co. v U.S., 1969 P-H 58,133 (Ct Cl Comr Rep)
 4—United Gas Improvement Co. v Comm., 240 F2d 318, 50 AFTR 1354 (USCA 3)
 10—St. Louis Co. (Del) (in Dissolution) v U.S., 237 F2d 156, 50 AFTR 257 (USCA 3)
ADDRESSOGRAPH - MULTIGRAPH CORP. v U.S., 112 Ct Cl 201, 78 F Supp 111, 37 AFTR 53
 f-1—St. Joseph Lead Co. v U.S., 9 AFTR2d 712, 299 F2d 350 (USCA 2)
 e-1—Central & South West Corp. v U.S., 1968 P-H 58,175 (Ct Cl Comr Rep)
 1—Smale & Robinson, Inc. v U.S., 123 F Supp 469, 46 AFTR 375 (DC Calif)
 1—St. Joseph Lead Co. v U.S., 7 AFTR2d 401, 190 F Supp 640 (DC NY)
 1—Eisenstadt Mfg. Co., 28 TC 230, 28-1957 P-H TC 132
 f-2—St. Joseph Lead Co. v U.S., 9 AFTR2d 712, 299 F2d 350 (USCA 2)
 f-3—Consol, Coppermines Corp. v U.S., 8 AFTR2d 5873, 155 Ct Cl 736, 296 F2d 745
ADELAIDE PARK LAND, 25 BTA 211
 g—Custom Component Switches, Inc. v U.S., 19 AFTR2d 560 (DC Calif) [See 25 BTA 215]
 O'Connor, John C., 1957 P-H TC Memo 57-190
ADELBERG, MARVIN & HELEN, 1971 P-H TC Memo ¶ 71,015
ADELMAN v U.S., 27 AFTR2d 71-1464, 440 F2d 991 (USCA 9, 5-3-71)
 sa—Adelman v U.S., 24 AFTR2d 69-5769, 304 F Supp 599 (DC Calif)
ADELMAN v U.S., 24 AFTR2d 69-5769, 304 F Supp 599 (DC Calif, 9-30-69)
 a—Adelman v U.S., 27 AFTR2d 71-1464, 440 F2d 991 (USCA 9)
ADELSON, SAMUEL; U.S. v, 52 AFTR 1798 (DC RI) (See Sullivan Co., Inc.; U.S. v)
ADELSON v U.S., 15 AFTR2d 246, 342 F2d 332 (USCA 9, 1-13-65)
 sa—Adelson v U.S., 12 AFTR2d 5010, 221 F Supp 31 (DC Calif)
 g-1—Greenlee, L. C. & Gladys M., 1966 P-H TC Memo 66-985
 f-1—Cochran, Carol J., 1973 P-H TC Memo 73-459
 f-1—Marchionni, Siro L., 1976 P-H TC Memo 76-1321
 f-2—Krist, Edwin F. v Comm., 32 AFTR2d 73-5663, 483 F2d 1351 (USCA 2)
 f-2—Fugate v U.S., 18 AFTR2d 5607, 259 F Supp 401 (DC Tex) [See 15 AFTR2d 249, 342 F2d 335]

APPENDIX F
COMPREHENSIVE TAX RETURN PROBLEMS

Ronald M. and Susan J. Bradford

(1) Ronald M. and Susan J. Bradford, both age 45, are married and file a joint income tax return. Ronald is employed as an engineer, and Susan is a self-employed attorney. They have three dependent children: John, age 12; Paul, age 14; and George, age 17. Since June 15, 1983, Susan's nephew, Eric, has lived with them. Eric, whose parents were killed in an automobile accident, is 19 years old and is a full-time student at Purdue University. Eric works part-time and earned $1,400 during 1983. Ronald and Susan provided over half of Eric's support during the year. The Bradfords currently live at 1864 Southern Avenue, Lafayette, Indiana, 47902. Ronald's Social Security number is 233-45-6789 and Susan's is 345-67-8910. Ronald and Susan both specify that $1 is to be directed to the Presidential Election Campaign Fund.

(2) During 1983, Ronald earned a salary of $30,000 from Research Corporation, Orlando, Florida. Research Corporation withheld Federal income tax of $7,962, state income tax of $900, and FICA (Social Security) of $2,010. Ronald received a better offer from Hi-Tech Corporation of Lafayette, Indiana, and began working for Hi-Tech on June 1, earning $49,000 in his new job. Hi-Tech withheld Federal income tax of $13,737, state income tax of $1,470, and FICA (Social Security) of $2,392. On December 20, Ronald received a year-end bonus of $1,000 from Hi-Tech. This amount was not included on his W-2 Form.

(3) Susan was employed until May 31, 1983, as a staff attorney by Ketchum and Company, a law firm in Orlando, Florida. Her salary during that time was $25,000. Her employer withheld $6,883 of Federal income tax, $750 of state income tax, and FICA (Social Security) of $1,675.

(4) Ronald and Susan received the following interest income during 1983:

First National Bank (Ronald's account)	$ 450
Second National Bank (Susan's account)	1,200
Lafayette Savings & Loan (joint account)	965

(5) The Bradfords received the following dividend income during the year:

Abner Corporation (Ronald's stock)	$ 680
Bailey Corporation (Susan's stock	330
Crown Corporation (jointly owned stock)	700

On December 10, they give 100 shares of Edwards Corporation stock to their oldest son, George. The stock's basis was $5,000, and its fair market value was $8,000. On December 15, Edwards Corporation declared a dividend of $10 per share. The dividend was payable December 30 to shareholders of record as of December 20.

(6) Upon moving to Lafayette, Susan was unable to find suitable employment with a law firm. As a result, she established her own practice, beginning July 1, 1983. Her office is located at 234 Lahr Street, Lafayette, Indiana, 47902. Her employer identification number is 12-3456789. She elected to use the cash basis of accounting. The following items relate to her practice during 1983:

Gross receipts from clients	$ 60,000
Expenses	
Advertising	1,200
Bank service charges	68
Dues and publications	550
Insurance	2,500
Interest	1,370
Legal and professional services	900
Office rent	6,300
Office supplies	960
Utilities and phone	620
Secretary's wages	5,400
Miscellaneous expenses	375

Susan used her personal automobile for business purposes, accumulating a total of 4,000 business miles from July 1 to December 31, 1983. She acquired the following equipment for use in her business (with all assets being placed in service on July 1, 1983):

Office furniture	$ 8,000
Microcomputer	4,200
Printer	1,500

Susan elected to expense $5,000 of the cost of the office furniture under the provisions of § 179. She elected to compute her cost recovery allowance on all of the assets using the ACRS statutory percentage method. To compute the investment credit, she will make the reduced credit election.

On November 15, a client who owed Susan $1,000 was declared bankrupt. Susan feels there is no chance for future collection of the account.

(7) The Bradfords were involved in several property transactions during 1983:

(a) On March 5, they acquired 100 shares of Simpson Corporation common stock for $162 a share. The company experienced financial difficulties and did not pay the regular semiannual dividend in June. As a result, Ronald and Susan decided to sell the stock before matters got worse. On November 23, 1983, they sold the stock for $125 a share.

(b) On May 6, 1968, Susan inherited a vacation home from her Uncle Marvin. Marvin's adjusted basis for the property was $38,000. The fair market value at the date of Marvin's death was $52,000 (the value elected by the executor of Marvin's estate). Because the Bradfords felt they would not be able to return to Florida frequently enough to justify keeping the home, they sold it on August 12, 1983, for $157,000.

(c) When they decided to move from Orlando to Lafayette, they sold their Florida residence. The selling price of the home was $200,000, and the broker charged a five-percent sales commission. The Bradfords incurred fixing-up expenses of $2,000 on the residence, which they had owned since October 4, 1975. Their basis in the residence was $110,000. In Lafayette, they acquired a new residence for $166,000. The closing date on the sale of their Orlando residence was May 30, 1983. They moved into the new residence on June 1, 1983.

(d) On September 12, Ronald wrote a call option on his Abner Corporation stock. The option gives the holder the right to buy the stock for $9,000 during the following six-month period. Ronald's basis in the stock, which he acquired in 1981, is $6,500. He received a call premium of $600 for writing the option.

(e) On November 29, Susan sold a one-acre lot in Orlando to her sister Sarah. Susan's basis in the lot was $15,000. She sold the lot for $10,000. Susan had purchased the lot on April 17, 1978.

(f) During 1981 and 1982, Ronald had a part-time practice as a consulting engineer. Anticipating a change of employment and a move, he decided to discontinue the practice, doing so on March 8, 1983. At that time, he sold the following equipment, all of which had been acquired on January 3, 1981:

Item	Cost
Drafting equipment	$ 3,200
Microcomputer	4,500
Printer	1,800
Office furniture	2,600

Ronald sold the drafting equipment for $2,600, the microcomputer for $2,500, the printer for $1,000, and the office furniture for $2,000. All of the equipment was five-year ACRS property, and Ronald had used the statutory percentage method in computing cost recovery allowances. He had taken investment credit on all the property on his 1981 tax return.

(8) In 1980, Susan wrote a monograph on tax-planning aspects of divorce and separation agreements. During 1983, she received royalties of $6,400 from her publisher. (Royalty income is not subject to self-employment tax.)

(9) The Bradfords own a rental house in Florida. The rental unit was occupied during all of 1983, producing rental income of $14,000. To avoid managerial duties with regard to the property, the Bradfords

paid a commission of $1,400 to a property management company. The only other expenditures related to the property were $2,000 for real property taxes and $800 for real estate insurance on the property. The property was acquired on January 2, 1979, at a cost of $100,000, of which $10,000 was allocated to the lot. The rental house is being depreciated over a 25-year period using the straight-line method. Estimated salvage value is zero.

(10) In 1981, Ronald loaned $3,000 to his friend, George, who signed a note agreeing to repay the loan on June 30, 1982. George declared bankruptcy in March 1982. Ronald deducted the amount as a non-business bad debt on his 1982 tax return. In 1983, George inherited a large amount of money from his mother and repaid the loan. Because they were such good friends, Ronald refused to accept any interest from George.

(11) Because their income is unusually high this year, the Bradfords decided to invest in a tax shelter. They invested as partners in XYZ Realty Limited, a limited partnership that develops and manages apartment buildings. Their share of the partnership's loss for 1983 was $20,000. The loss is fully deductible by the Bradfords.

(12) The Bradford family incurred the following expenses in moving from Orlando to Lafayette:

Cost of moving household goods	$ 3,500
Travel, meals, and lodging	600
House-hunting expenses	1,000
Temporary living expenses (5 days)	700
Cost of fitting drapes in new house	900

Hi-Tech Corporation reimbursed Ronald for $3,000 of the moving expenses. The reimbursement was not included on Ronald's W-2 Form.

(13) Ronald attended an engineering convention in Boston in October, incurring the following unreimbursed expenses:

Airfare	$ 460
Taxi fares	35
Meals and lodging	200

(14) Ronald and Susan each contributed the maximum allowable amount for 1983 to their separate Individual Retirement Accounts. In addition, Susan contributed $4,000 to her Keogh plan. All contributions were made in December 1983.

(15) The Bradfords had the following expenditures during the year:

Prescription medicines and drugs	$ 880
Medical insurance premiums	1,440
Doctor and hospital bills	2,350
Real estate taxes on residence	6,440
General sales tax (use this amount rather than computing the amount from the sales tax table)	732

Sales tax on new car	1,350
Excise tax on home phone	38
Home mortgage interest	7,630
Credit card interest	748
Cash contributions	
Community Church	2,000
United Way	1,500
Purdue University	1,000
Professional dues and subscriptions	850
Tax return preparation fee	500

(16) On August 1, the Bradfords acquired a rundown garage apartment for $15,000. Their plan was to have the apartment restored to good condition and hold it as rental property. On October 5, the electrician they had hired to rewire the house accidentally left his soldering iron on while he was away for lunch. When he returned, fire had destroyed the apartment. Unfortunately, the Bradfords had not insured the building. Between August 1 and October 5, they had spent $1,700 on repairs on the house.

(17) A review of their tax returns for the past four years shows the following amounts: line 34 of 1979 return, $30,000; line 34 of 1980 return, $41,000; line 34 of 1981 return, $46,000; and line 37 of 1982 return, $52,000. This information is needed if the Bradfords elect to compute their tax using the income averaging method. They claimed five exemptions during each of the four years.

(18) Ronald contributed $100 to the Democratic party's state campaign fund. Susan contributed $100 to the Republican party's state campaign fund.

(19) The Bradfords paid $500 each month for household and child care expenses. Their employer identification number is 22-3344556.

(20) To prepare for the cold Indiana winters, they installed insulation at a cost of $900 and storm doors and windows at a cost of $1,500. The residence was built in 1976. In 1982, the Bradfords claimed a residential energy credit for $1,800 of qualified expenditures on their residence in Florida.

(21) The Bradfords made timely estimated federal income tax payments of $13,500 during the year.

Requirements

You are to complete the Bradfords' Federal income tax return for 1983. If they have a refund due, they would like to have it credited to their 1984 tax. You will need Forms 1040, 2106, 2119, 2441, 3468, 3903, 4255, 4562, 4684, 4797, and 5695 and Schedules A, B, C, D, E, G, SE, and W.

Paul J. and Judy L. Vance

(1) Paul J. and Judy L. Vance are married and file a joint return. Paul is 54 years of age, and Judy is 51. Paul is self-employed as a dentist, and Judy is a college professor. Paul's Social Security number is 333-45-6666, and Judy's is 666-77-8888. They live at 621 Franklin Avenue, Cincinnati, Ohio, 45211. Both of the Vances designate that

$1 is to go to the Presidential Election Campaign Fund. They have one child, Vince, age 23, who lives at home. Vince is a law student at the University of Cincinnati and worked part-time during 1983, earning $1,500, which he spent for his own support. In addition, he received a $2,000 scholarship from the University of Cincinnati. Paul and Judy provided $2,000 toward Vince's support. They also provided over half the support of their daughter, Joan, age 19, who is a full-time student at Edgecliff College. Joan worked part-time during 1983, earning $1,200. She filed a joint return with her husband, Patrick, who earned $4,000 during 1983.

(2) Paul's mother, Vera, age 87, lives with the Vances. Vera received $900 in Social Security benefits and $950 of interest in 1983, all of which she used for her own support. Paul and his brother George each incurred out-of-pocket costs of $900 for Vera's support. In addition, Paul provided lodging for Vera during all of 1983. Paul estimates the fair rental value of the lodging is $1,200. George is willing to do whatever is necessary to enable Paul to claim Vera as a dependent.

(3) Judy is a professor at Xavier University in Cincinnati, where her salary for 1983 was $30,000. The University withheld Federal income tax of $5,100, Social Security tax of $2,010, state income tax of $600, and Cincinnati city income tax of $300.

(4) The Vances received $1,100 of interest from State Savings Bank on a joint account. They received interest of $1,000 on City of Cincinnati bonds they bought in January with the proceeds of a loan from Fifth Third Bank of Cincinnati. They paid interest of $1,200 on the loan. Paul received a dividend of $440 on General Bicycle Corporation stock he owns. Judy received a dividend of $380 on Acme Clothing Corporation stock she owns. General Bicycle and Acme Clothing are both domestic corporations. Paul and Judy received a dividend of $965 on jointly owned stock in Maple Leaf Brewing Company, a Canadian corporation.

(5) Paul practices under the name "Paul J. Vance, DDS." His business is located at 645 West Avenue, Cincinnati, Ohio, 45211, and his employer identification number is 01-2222222. Paul's gross billings during 1983 were $170,000. Accounts receivable were $3,600 at the beginning of the year and $4,200 at the end of the year. The end-of-year balance does not include a $700 account from a customer who declared bankruptcy on November 9, 1983. The $700 was billed in July 1983 for work done during the previous two months. Paul uses the cash method of accounting for his business.

Paul's business expenses are listed below:

Advertising	$ 1,200
Bank service charges	108
Professional dues	490
Professional journals	360
Contributions to employee benefit plans	2,000
Malpractice insurance	1,200
Fine for overbilling State of Ohio for work performed on welfare patient	5,000

Insurance on office contents	720
Interest on money borrowed to refurbish office	900
Accounting services	1,800
Miscellaneous office expense	388
Office rent	6,000
Dental supplies	8,672
Utilities and telephone	3,360
Wages	30,000

Included in the $30,000 of wages is $8,000 paid to a new receptionist Paul hired on March 1, 1983. The receptionist is handicapped and qualifies as a member of a targeted group for purposes of the targeted jobs credit.

In June, Paul decided to refurbish his office. This project was completed and the assets placed in service on July 1. Paul's expenditures included $8,000 for new office furniture, $6,000 for new dental equipment, and $1,000 for a new typewriter. All three assets have a recovery period of five years. Paul elects to compute his cost recovery allowance using the statutory percentage method. He elects to use the full ten-percent rate for computing investment credit on the property. He also elects immediate expensing of $5,000 of the cost of the office furniture under § 179.

On July 1, Paul sold his old office furniture and old typewriter, both acquired on January 3, 1979. The office furniture, which cost $5,000, had been depreciated using the straight-line method with a ten-year estimated useful life and an estimated salvage value of zero. It was sold for $2,000. The typewriter, which cost $900, had been depreciated using the straight-line method with an estimated useful life of five years and estimated salvage value of zero. It was sold for $500. Paul took investment credit on both items in the year they were placed in service.

(6) Judy's mother, Sarah, died on July 2, 1973, leaving Judy her entire estate. Included in the estate was Sarah's residence. Sarah's basis in the residence was $30,000. Fair market value of the residence on July 2, 1973, was $40,000. The property was distributed to Judy on September 9, 1973. From March 1, 1974, until April 30, 1983, the house was rented to the same tenant. The tenant was transferred to a branch office in California and moved out at the end of April. Since they did not want to bother finding a new tenant, Paul and Judy decided to sell the house, which they did on June 2, 1983. They received $150,000 for the house, less a six-percent commission charged by the broker. They had depreciated the house using the straight-line method of depreciation with an estimated useful life of 20 years and an estimated salvage value of zero. In computing depreciation, they had allocated a value of $4,000 to the lot on which the house was located. The broker estimated that the value of the lot on the date of sale was $30,000. The Vances collected rent of $1,200 a month during the four months the house was occupied in 1983. They incurred the following related expenses during this period:

property insurance, $200; property taxes (paid by buyer of the property but allocated to the Vances), $550; maintenance, $220.

(7) The Vances sold 1,000 shares of Capp Corporation stock they had received as a wedding present on June 25, 1953. The stock was worth $95 a share in January. By September 3, its value had dropped to $81 per share, and the Vances sold the stock on that date. They had been given the stock by Paul's father, who had paid $1 per share for it in 1950. Its value at the date of gift was $4.50 per share. No gift tax was paid on the gift.

(8) Judy purchased a computer on July 1, 1982, for $4,000. The computer, which was used exclusively for business purposes, was being written off as five-year recovery property using the statutory percentage method under ACRS. Judy claimed investment credit on the property on their joint return for 1982. On September 6, 1983, a severe electrical storm caused a power surge that damaged the computer beyond repair. A computer dealer estimated that the computer, which was uninsured, was worth $3,500 before the casualty. Judy replaced the computer on October 1 with a new computer costing $3,500. Judy intends to use this new computer exclusively for business purposes. To insure that a similar casualty would not recur, Judy also acquired a power surge protector for $300. Cost recovery allowances for both assets will be computed using a five-year recovery period. Judy elects the straight-line method and elects to compute investment credit using the reduced rate of eight percent.

(9) On December 30, 1982, as he was leaving the grocery store, Paul found an Ohio state lottery ticket someone apparently had dropped. On January 4, 1983, when the lottery held its weekly drawing, Paul found he had won $10,000, which he received on January 7.

(10) Paul and Judy each contributed $2,000 to their separate Individual Retirement Accounts and plan to deduct these amounts on their 1983 tax return. However, since they were short of cash, they were unable to make the contributions until March 15, 1984. Paul contributed $10,000 to his Keogh plan on December 30, 1983. The Vance's are cash basis taxpayers.

(11) Judy is required by her employer to visit several high schools in the Cincinnati area to evaluate Xavier University students who are doing their practice teaching. However, she is not reimbursed for the expenses she incurs in doing this. During 1983, she drove her personal automobile 6,200 miles in fulfilling this obligation.

(12) Paul and Judy have given you a file containing the following receipts for expenditures during 1983:

Medicines and drugs	$ 376
Doctor and hospital bills	1,148
Medical insurance premiums	1,320
1982 state income tax paid when filing 1982 return on April 15, 1983	560
Penalty for underpayment of 1981 state tax	362
Real estate taxes on personal residence	4,762
State sales tax on new furniture	280
State sales tax on new sailboat	230

Interest on home mortgage (paid to Home State Savings & Loan)	8,250
Interest on credit cards	495
Cash contribution to St. Matthew's church	2,080
Payroll deductions for Judy's contributions to the United Way	150
Professional dues (Judy)	325
Professional subscriptions (Judy)	245
Fee for preparation of 1982 tax return	500

(13) Examination of the Vances' tax returns for the previous four years shows an amount from Form 1040, line 34, of $48,000 in 1979, $53,000 in 1980, and $58,000 in 1981. The amount reported on line 37 of their 1982 return was $60,000. They claimed exemptions for Paul, Judy, Vince, and Joan in 1979, 1980, 1981, and 1982. They also claimed Vera as a dependent on their 1981 and 1982 returns. You will need this information if you use the income averaging method in computing the Vances's tax.

(14) Paul and Judy contributed $500 to the campaign fund of Senator John Glenn, presidential candidate.

(15) In addition to the previously mentioned expenditures incurred on Vera's behalf, the Vance's paid $600 a month to a licensed practical nurse to stay with Vera for three months while she was at home recovering from surgery. Their employer identification number is 66-6677889.

(16) Paul and Judy had storm doors and windows installed in their residence in October at a cost of $1,400. In 1982, they had insulation installed at a cost of $1,000. They acquired and moved into the house in September, 1975.

(17) The Vances made quarterly estimated Federal income tax payments of $12,000 each in 1983. They made estimated state income tax payments of $1,400 and estimated city income tax payments of $700.

Requirements

You are to prepare Paul and Judy Vance's 1983 Federal income tax return. You will need Forms 1040, 2106, 2210, 2441, 3468, 4255, 4562, 4684, 4797, 5695, and 5884 and Schedules A, B, C, D, E, G, SE, and W.

J. D. and Gloria McVey

In December 1982, J. D. McVey graduated from the University of Minnesota (Minneapolis) and immediately accepted employment with Union Valve Corporation, a West Virginia corporation and a manufacturer and distributor of mining and drilling equipment. Under the terms of the employment agreement, J. D. was to assume responsibility (effective February 1, 1983) for the sales region comprising the States of Montana and Wyoming. Since Union Valve Corporation had not yet established an office in the region, J. D. was to conduct all business from his home. J. D. was expected to locate his home in either Montana or Wyoming, and he chose Searcy, Wyoming, because of its central location and available housing.

J. D. McVey is 22 years of age and has been a full-time student at the University of Minnesota since his graduation from high school four years ago. He married Gloria, age 25, during his junior year in college. Gloria has one child, Anthony, age 3, by a former marriage.

During 1983, the McVeys had the following receipts:

(1) Salary of $22,000 from Union Valve Corporation of which $1,474 was withheld for FICA and $3,162.39 for Federal income tax purposes (all reflected on Form W–2). Although J. D. received a bonus of $3,500 for his sales in 1983, such bonus was not declared and paid by Union Valve Corporation until February of 1984.

(2) Commissions of $14,300 earned by Gloria from the sale of real estate from early June through December 31, 1983. Gloria operates this business out of her apartment and as a sole proprietor. No taxes have been paid on the amounts earned.

(3) In early 1983, the McVeys won $10,000 in a contest sponsored by a national chain of fast-food franchises. Although the winning ticket was registered in Gloria's name, she placed the proceeds in a savings account with Anthony listed as the owner. Interest on this account for 1983 amounted to $540, none of which was withdrawn.

(4) Receipts of $4,200 from the lessee of property in Ypsilanti, Michigan. The property, a two-story brick house located in a residential area, was acquired by J. D. when his aunt died on December 1, 1982. As executor and sole heir of his aunt's estate, J. D. assumed control over the property on December 15, 1982. On December 16, 1982, he listed the house as being for rent but was not able to find a suitable tenant until late May. Under the terms of the two-year lease, the lessee was required to pay the following amounts: rent of $500 per month (beginning on June 1, 1983), the last month's rent of $500 in advance (i. e., the rent for May of 1985), and a damage deposit of $200.

The Ypsilanti property had a value of $150,000 and an adjusted basis to the aunt of $50,000 on the date of her death. Gloria, who has had considerable training and experience in matters dealing with real estate, estimates that 20 percent of the value of the property is attributable to the land. (The "anti-churning" rules do not apply to inherited property. Therefore, the house qualifies as ACRS recovery property.)

(5) Cash of $500 received by Gloria from the estate of J. D.'s aunt. The amount was paid by J. D., acting in his capacity as executor, to Gloria in return for the services she performed in appraising estate assets. Indications are that the charge was reasonable for the services rendered.

(6) Upon the final dissolution of the aunt's estate and after the payment of all expenses and taxes, J. D. received the following:

	Fair Market Value on Date of Death	Adjusted Basis to Aunt
Cash	$ 15,000	$ 15,000
Household furnishings	6,000	?
1957 Chevrolet convertible	12,000	3,200
Jewelry (mainly gold and silver)	8,000	?
Personal effects (e.g., clothing)	1,200	?

The dissolution and final distribution occurred on March 26, 1983. Under the aunt's will, J. D. was not entitled to any commission for serving as the executor of the estate. As executor, J. D. did not elect the alternate valuation date for the estate.

On June 26, 1983, J. D. received in the mail a check for $5,725.25 from the United Insurance Company. Unknown to him, J. D. was the designated beneficiary of an insurance policy on the life of his aunt. The policy had a maturity value of $5,000, and an enclosed statement from the company reflected that the aunt had paid premiums thereon of $2,600. Of the amount received, $725.25 was designated as being interest accrued since the date of the aunt's death.

(7) On August 4, 1983, J. D. received $18,200 from the sale of the 1957 Chevrolet [see item (6)]. Although the car was in good condition when the aunt died, it needed certain repairs to place it in "top" condition for resale. After J. D. received several estimates from mechanics who specialized in such restorations, he decided to do the work himself. In this connection, J. D. spent $2,400 on replacement parts and devoted considerable spare time to their installation. Based on the estimates received from the mechanics, the value of J. D.'s services was $2,100.

(8) On September 25, 1983, J. D. sold his aunt's jewelry for $7,600. For sentimental reasons, J. D. wanted to keep these items, but he was concerned about their safekeeping.

(9) Throughout 1983, Gloria received child support of $300 per month (for a total of $3,600) from her ex-husband. Although the divorce decree awards the dependency exemption for Anthony to the ex-husband, the McVeys can prove that they furnished more than 50 percent of the support of the child.

(10) Since beginning employment with Union Valve Corporation, J. D. has been covered under their group-term life insurance policy. The policy applicable to J. D. provides for coverage of $100,000 and designates Gloria as the beneficiary.

(11) Union Valve Corporation follows a policy of allowing its employees to choose between coverage in its noncontributory accident and health care plan *or* the receipt of an annual award of $1,500 in additional wages. For 1983, J. D. chose the medical insurance option. [Note: Neither item (10) nor item (11) is reflected in the salary information furnished in (1).]

(12) Federal income tax refund of $140 received on March 6, 1983. In January of 1983, the McVeys had filed a Form 1040A and a State of Minnesota income tax return for 1982 to recover some of the withholdings from Gloria's wages from a part-time job, as the tax liabilities proved to be less than the amounts withheld. A refund of $40 was received from the Department of Revenue of the State of Minnesota on March 20, 1983.

(13) Dividends from domestic corporations of $250 and interest on a savings account of $420. The dividends were received on stock owned by Gloria, while the interest was from a joint savings account that J. D. had established with some of the funds inherited from his aunt. None of the interest was withdrawn by the McVeys.

(14) During 1983, Gloria had the following receipts involving the sales of marketable securities:

Asset	Date Acquired	Date Sold	Selling Price
100 shares of common stock in Y Corporation	3/18/78	7/15/83	$ 5,200
500 shares of preferred stock in Z Corporation	7/30/79	10/2/83	6,500

The selling price listed is net of brokerage commissions. In other words, it represents the amount Gloria actually received.

On March 18, 1978, Gloria had received as a wedding present from her father 100 shares of common stock in Y Corporation. The stock, which had been acquired by her father on November 10, 1973, had an adjusted basis to him of $3,000 and a fair market value of $3,800 on the date of the gift. No gift tax was due or paid as a result of the transfer.

Upon the receipt of a cash property settlement from her first husband, Gloria had purchased 500 shares of preferred stock in Z Corporation for $10,000. Shortly after the purchase, she received a nontaxable two-for-one stock split.

(15) In January, J. D. received a check from Union Valve Corporation for $457.28 which represented reimbursement for a trip he made to the home office in West Virginia. The trip for the job interview was made in November of 1982 and led to the offer of employment that J. D. later accepted. It was the understanding of the parties that the company would reimburse J. D. for reasonable expenses actually incurred. The $457.28 was not claimed as a deduction on the McVey's joint return filed for 1982, nor was the reimbursement shown on the Form W–2 (for 1983) sent to J. D. by the employer in early 1984.

(16) A check for $492.17 received on March 19, 1983, from Union Valve Corporation which represented reimbursement for some of the McVeys' moving expenses [see item (a)]. This amount was included in the W–2 sent to J. D. for tax year 1983.

(17) A check for $420 received in February of 1983 from Ajax Casualty Insurance Company which represented the amount due on a policy covering Gloria's 1975 automobile. In December of 1982, J. D. had totalled the automobile on the way to class. When the accident occurred, the car had an adjusted basis of $1,800 and a fair market value of $520.

During 1983, the McVeys had the following disbursements:

(a) On January 12–13, 1983, the McVeys drove to Searcy, Wyoming, to find a suitable place to live. After several days of narrowing the alternatives, they leased an apartment [see item (c)]. The return trip to Minneapolis took place on January 16–17.

On January 30–31, 1983, the McVeys drove to Searcy with their personal belongings. Per the lease agreement, the McVeys occupied the apartment in Searcy on February 1, 1983.

Expenses incurred in connection with the January 12–17 and the January 30–31 trips are summarized below.

	January 12– 17 Trip	January 30– 31 Trip
Meals while in transit	$ 36.75	$ 19.25
Meals in Searcy	38.23	15.40
Lodging while in transit	48.16	24.10
Lodging in Searcy	76.18	24.10
Trailer rental	—	210.00

The distance between Minneapolis and Searcy (one way) is 1,100 miles. In addition, the McVeys drove 140 miles while in Searcy during their January 14–15 stay while looking for an apartment. As noted in item (16), the employer reimbursed the McVeys for $492.17 of the above expenses. Under company policy, however, mileage is not covered under the reimbursement plan in the case of new employees.

(b) As a graduation present from his parents, J. D. received $3,000 for a down payment on a new automobile. On January 2, he purchased a small Buick station wagon for $9,000 through an automobile dealer in Montana with delivery in Detroit. Shortly thereafter, Gloria took a bus to Detroit and picked up the car (the dealer had provided Montana license plates). The reason J. D. used a Montana dealer was to avoid either the Minnesota or the Wyoming sales tax (Montana has no sales tax). The scheme backfired, however, when J. D. registered his car in Wyoming in early March of 1983. On that occasion, he was assessed and had to pay a Wyoming use tax of $400.

Not including the two trips mentioned in (a), the station wagon was used as follows during 1983:

	Miles
Business	19,465
Medical	380
Charitable	900
Personal	8,326

In addition, J. D. spent $82 on parking while in business travel status.

The station wagon has an estimated useful life to the McVeys of less than three years.

(c) On January 15, 1983, the McVeys leased a three-bedroom apartment in Searcy for one year (occupancy as of February 1). In addition to paying a $100 damage deposit, they paid the following amounts for this facility during 1983:

Rent ($400 per month)	$ 4,400.00
Utilities	1,320.12
Telephone	1,209.56

When they moved in on February 1, J. D. converted one of the bedrooms (approximately 20 percent of the total available floor space) into an office. The office was furnished with office equipment obtained from a local furniture-leasing concern. All lease charges were billed directly to Union Valve Corporation. The office was used exclusively for business, either by J. D. or by Gloria when she began her real estate activities in June.

The McVeys estimate that they used their phone 40 percent of the time for business.

Except for the lease charges on the office furniture, none of these expenses were paid for by J. D.'s employer.

(d) To facilitate her real estate operations, in June Gloria leased a used automobile for $210 per month. Lease payments by the McVeys during 1983 totalled $1,260. The car was used 80 percent for business and 20 percent for personal. Operating expenses on the automobile (e. g., gas and oil) were the responsibility of the lessee and amounted to $450.28.

(e) During 1983, the McVeys incurred the following additional expenses in connection with their business activities:

	Gloria	J. D.
Dues to professional organizations	$ 75.00	$ 110.00
Expenses for attending professional meetings (e. g., business seminars)	150.00	— *
Subscriptions to professional journals	48.00	95.00
Entertainment (e. g., business lunches)	140.00	— *
Business gifts	200.00	— *

(* These items were billed directly to Union Valve Corporation.)

Except as indicated, none of J. D.'s expenses were reimbursed by his employer. All of these expenses are properly substantiated and satisfy the requirements of § 274 of the Code. Before Christmas of 1983, Gloria made gifts (worth $40 apiece) to each of five families that had purchased residential property through her during the year. The gifts were of such a nature that none of the cost was attributable to gift wrapping.

(f) During 1983, J. D. paid the following amounts regarding the Ypsilanti rental property [see item (4)]:

Repairs	$ 1,280.00
Management fee	350.00
Leasing costs (e. g., advertising)	240.00
Property taxes (not chargeable to the estate)	1,392.01
Special street-paving assessment	520.00

The special paving assessment was made by the City of Ypsilanti against all property owners in a four-block area. The assessment was made in December of 1983 for paving repairs and replacement that would be carried out in early 1984.

(g) During 1983, the McVeys had the interest expense summarized below:

Montgomery Ward revolving account	$ 295.86
J. C. Penney revolving account	121.52
First National Bank of Searcy	396.39

The Montgomery Ward and J. C. Penney accounts were used to purchase clothes, toys, and certain household items.

The interest paid to the First National Bank of Searcy was for amounts J. D. borrowed to help pay for Gloria's dental work [see item (h)].

(h) Medical expenses paid during 1983 were as follows:

Payee	Amount
U of M Memorial Hospital	$ 1,875.00
Dr. Peter Lyons (diagnostician)	450.00
Dr. Richard Spain (radiologist)	370.00
Dr. Kenneth Wolford (general dentistry)	3,500.00
Dr. James Myers (orthodontia)	2,400.00
Bone and Joint Clinic of Searcy	750.00

The first three charges were incurred in December of 1982 and were the result of J. D.'s automobile accident [item (17)]. Because J. D. was a student at the University, however, the parties involved allowed him to defer payment until 1983. No interest was charged for the privilege of late payment.

Because of a lack of funds while J. D. was a student, Gloria had been postponing some necessary dental restoration (e. g., crowns, bridges). She also needed braces to improve her appearance. These procedures were initiated and partially carried out in the last half of 1983 by Drs. Wolford and Myers working as a team. Although the orthodontia correction only was 50 percent complete by the end of 1983, the McVeys paid Dr. Myers the full amount that would be due. Full payment for orthodontia work before all of the services are rendered is not an uncommon practice.

As a result of moving from Minneapolis to Searcy, J. D. began experiencing discomfort in his back. Ultimately he went to the Bone and Joint Clinic of Searcy for a series of X-rays and orthopedic therapy. Although the McVeys were under the employer's medical insurance plan [see item (11)], the expenses resulting from the December 1982 automobile accident occurred before J. D. became an employee of Union Valve Corporation. Unfortunately, the coverage of the plan does not extend to dental work. In late December 1983, however, J. D. remembered about the plan and promptly filed a claim with Central Insurance Company (the carrier of the Union Valve Corporation plan) for the orthopedic charges. On January 22, 1984, J. D.

received a check from the carrier for $650 (the policy had a $100 deductible feature for out-patient treatment). The McVeys do not keep a record of their drug expenditures.

(i) Cash charitable contributions for 1983 included: Searcy United Way Campaign ($450), First Methodist Church of Searcy ($350), and the Italian Red Cross ($100).

Shortly after moving to Searcy, J. D. donated his aunt's personal effects [see item (6)] to the local branch of the Salvation Army.

Requirements

Based on the assumptions appearing below, prepare a joint income tax return for the McVeys for calendar year 1983. The return should be in good form and should include all necessary supporting schedules.

Assumptions and Additional Requirements

A. The McVeys use the cash method of accounting and the calendar year for tax purposes.

B. Wyoming imposes a three-percent general sales tax, and the City of Searcy another one percent. To simplify the state sales tax computation, assume all purchases during the year occurred in Searcy.

C. Wyoming does not impose a state income tax. No state income taxes were paid or are due for 1983 to Minnesota or Michigan.

D. The McVeys do not qualify for income averaging as to tax year 1983.

E. Do not make assumptions not supported by the facts. For example, under (b), you must use the automatic mileage method allowed by the IRS, as you cannot determine all of the operating expenses (gasoline purchases are unknown).

F. Allocate the full office in the home expenses to J. D.

G. Prepare a Form 1040–ES for 1984, basing the estimated tax on the 1983 income tax liability.

H. Other relevant information concerning the McVeys and their affairs is summarized below:

—Gloria's Social Security number is 371-42-5207.

—J. D.'s Social Security number is 371-09-7846.

—In Minneapolis, the McVeys lived at 1318 Queensbury Street (Apt. 12H), 55440.

In Searcy, the McVeys live at 492 Commerce Street (Apt. 4), 82190.

The rental property in Ypsilanti is located at 789 University Drive, 48197.

APPENDIX G
TABLE OF CASES CITED

A

Aagaard, Robert W., 591.
Aitkin v. Commissioner, 271.
Allen, Mary Francis, 284.
Allison, Kenneth W., 378.
American Auto. Ass'n v. United States, 158.
American Dental Co., Helvering v., 218.
Anderson, Commissioner v., 206.
Anton, M. G., 161.
Arcade Realty Co., 405.
Armentrout, William F., 439.
Armstrong v. Phinney, 205.
Arnold v. United States, 192.
Artnell Co. v. Comm'r, 158.
Automated Marketing Systems, Inc. v. Comm'r, 158.
Automobile Club of Michigan v. United States, 158.

B

Baird Publishing Co., 601.
Balistrieri, Joseph P., 580.
Basset, Robert S., 424.
Basye, United States v., 785.
Bedell v. Comm'r, 151.
Bhalla, C. P., 199.
Biggs, Franklin B., 601.
Bilder, Comm'r v., 394.
Bingler v. Johnson, 199.
Bissett & Son, Inc., F. D., 80.
Black Ltd., E. E. v. Alsup, 716.
Black Motor Co. v. Comm'r, 278, 300, 304.
Bolton, Doranee D. v. Comm., 250.

Bonaire Development Co. v. Comm'r, 241.
Boise Cascade Corp. v. United States, 158.
Borsody, Frank J., 258.
Bradford v. Comm'r, 403.
Briggs v. United States, 205.
Brown v. Helvering, 151.
Bruun, Helvering v., 191.
Burnet v. Sanford & Brooks Co., 151, 709.

C

Calhoun v. United States, 703.
California Federal Life Insurance, Co., 616.
Camp Wolters Enterprises, Inc. v. Comm'r, 823.
Cannon, Geraldine G., 378.
Cannon, John M., 378.
Carter, Estate of Sydney J. v. Comm'r, 196.
Church, Wade E., 202.
Clapham, Robert G., 591, 614.
Clark v. Comm'r, 148.
Coates Trust v. Comm., 851.
Cohan v. Comm'r, 258, 369, 394.
Cohen, Theodore H., 154.
Collins v. United States, 810.
Colston v. Burnet, 405.
Consolidated-Hammer Dry Plate & Film Co. v. Comm'r, 158.
Continental Trust Co., 405.
Cook, Charles D., 168.
Corn Products Ref. Co., 621.
Correll, United States v., 355.
Cowden v. Comm'r, 154.
Crane v. Comm'r, 217, 529, 570.

SUBJECT INDEX

A

Abandoned Spouse Rule, 131
Accelerated Cost Recovery System
    (ACRS), 38
  Anti-churning rules, 326
  Election to expense assets, 325–326,
    337
  Eligible property, 319–320
  General considerations, 319
  Investment tax credit, 322–323,
    337–338, 481
  Involuntary conversions, 327
  Like-kind exchanges, 327
  Personalty, 320–323
  Pre-ERTA depreciation rules, 319
  Real property, 671–673, 690–691
  Realty, 323–324
  Recapture, 671–673, 690–691
  Recovery periods and methods, 320–
    324
  Related-party transactions, 326–327
  Special rules, 326–327
  Statutory percentage method of
    recovery, 320–322, 323, 324, 335,
    337
  Straight-line election, 324–325, 335
  Tax planning, 332–338, 690–691
  TEFRA, 322
Accelerated Depreciation, See also
    Depreciation and Amortization,
    313, 316–317, 320, 819
Accident and Health Benefits, See also
    Employee Fringe Benefits, 193,
    203–205, 220–221
Accounting Income, Reconciliation with
    Taxable Income, 820–821
Accounting Income Concept, 144–145
Accounting Method Changes, 279,
    710–715
  Correction of error, 279, 710–715
  Depreciation methods,
  Involuntary, 712–714
  LIFO, 742
  Net adjustments, 711–712
  Taxable income, 713
  Tax deferral, 742
  Voluntary, 714–715
Accounting Methods, 149–152 and
    Chapter 18
  Accrual method, 150, 151–152, 240,
    241–242, 405, 707, 708, 709–710

Accounting Methods—Cont'd
  Cash receipts and disbursements
    method (cash basis), 150–151,
    240–241, 707, 708–709
  Change of method, 279, 710–715
  Claim of right doctrine, 151–152,
    706–707
  Clear reflection of income concept,
    150, 707–708, 710, 712, 714, 735,
    736
  Completed contract method, 150,
    716–719
  Constructive receipt of income, 152–
    155, 175, 708
  Deferral of advance payments, 158–
    159
  Determination of IRS, 149–150, 707–
    708
  Election to expense assets under
    ACRS, 325–326, 337
  Erroneous method, 711
  Exceptions applicable to accrual basis
    taxpayers, 157–159
  Exceptions applicable to cash basis
    taxpayers, 152–157, 709
  Farming, 679–680
  Hybrid method, 150, 707, 710
  Installment method, 150, 719–734,
    742–743
  Inventories, 735–742
  Partnerships, 836
  Percentage of completion method,
    150, 718–719
  Permissible methods, 707–708
  Prepaid expenses, 708
  Prepaid income, 157–158
  Recovery periods, 320–324
  Reserve for bad debts, 277–278, 279,
    300, 742
  Reserve for estimated expenses, 710
  Special methods, 715–734
  Straight-line under ACRS, 324–325,
    335
  Tax planning, 742–743
  Tax Reform Act of 1976, p. 405
  Timing of expense recognition, 240–
    242
Accounting Period Changes, 703–704
Accounting Periods, See also Chapter
    18
  Annual accounting period, 45–48,
    149, 705–707
  Annualization of income, 704–705

C

F

H

1054   Index

Self-Employed Retirement Plans, See
   also Keogh Plans
   Comparison with corporate pension
      plans, 779–780
   Contribution limitations, 778–779
   Coverage requirements, 777–778
   Deduction, 347
   Tax planning, 376, 796–797
   TEFRA, 779, 796
Self-Employed Versus Employee Status,
   345–347, 376
Self-Employment Tax, 467–468
   Declaration of estimated tax, 115,
      465–466
Separate Maintenance Payments, See
   also Alimony, 165–168, 178
Separate Property, see Community
   Property
Separately Stated Items of Income and
   Loss to S Corporations, 832, 833,
   834
Series E and EE Savings Bonds
   Gross income, 155–156
   Tax planning, 175, 176
Series HH Savings Bonds, 156, 175
Settlement Procedures, 29
Severance Damages, 581–582
Severance Taxes, 11
Sham Transactions, 255
Shifting Deductions, 263, 376–377
Shifting of Income, see Assignment of
   Income Doctrine
Shifting Income to Relatives, 176–177
Short Periods, see Accounting Periods,
   Taxable periods of less than one
   year
Short Sales, 635–637
Short-Term Government Bonds, 626,
   627
Short Year, 704
Sick Pay, see Disability and Sick Pay
Simplified Employee Pension (SEP)
   Plan, 771, 797
Simplified LIFO, 740–741
Simplified Pension Plans, 781–782
Single-Pool LIFO, 741–742
Sixteenth Amendment, 2
Small Business Corporations, See also S
   Corporations, Section 1244 Stock;
   Small Business Stock
   Special tax treatment, 41–42
Small Business Stock, 282
Small Claims Division, (U. S. Tax
   Court), 68
Social Considerations of the Tax Law,
   42–43, 54

Social Security Benefits, 193, 467, 767
   Gross income, 173–174
   New laws, 173–174
   Received by dependent, 109
   Tax credit for the elderly, 502, 503
Social Security Tax, See also Federal
   Insurance Contributions Act, 376,
   399
Soil and Water Conservation
   Expenditures, 680
Special Accounting Methods, 715–734
Special Interest Legislation, 48–49
Specific Charge-off Method, see Bad
   Debts
Sponge Tax, 15, 16
Sports Franchises, 632
Spreading Capital Gains, 647
Stale Claims, 29
Standard Cost Method, see Inventory
   Methods
Standard Deduction, see Zero Bracket
   Amount
Stare Decisis Doctrine, 68
State and Local Influences on Tax
   Laws, 49–50
State and Local Taxes, 21–22
   Itemized deductions, 237
   Miscellaneous, 26
Statute of Limitations
   Assessment by IRS, 29–30
   Fraud, 30
   Refunds, 30–31
   Sale of a residence, 595
Statutory Depletion, 329–330, 338
Statutory Percentage Method of
   Recovery, 320–322, 323, 324, 335,
   337, 690
Statutory Tax Law, 53–54
Step-Up in Basis, 543, 558, 678, 825,
   843
Stock
   Small business, 282
   Stock dividends and dividend
      reinvestment plans, 214–216, 222
Stock Bonus Plans, see Qualified
   Pension and Profit Sharing Plans
Stock Options, 755
   Advantages and disadvantages of
      nonqualified stock options, 794–
      795
   Alternative minimum tax, 452, 790
   Holding period, 791–792, 794, 799
   Incentive stock options, 790–793
   Issue limitation, 793
   Nonqualified stock options, 793–795,
      799–800

Withholding—Cont'd
  State income taxes, 21
  Tax planning, 470
  TEFRA, 48, 464
  Wage bracket tables, 458–462
  Zero bracket amount, 458
Workers' Compensation, 202–203
Worthless Securities, 282, 624
Writ of Certiorari, 72

Y

Year-End Tax Planning, 647

Z

Zero Bracket Amount, 20–21, 101, 103–104
Adjustment, 122
Charitable contributions, 416–417
Dependent child, 105–106
Filing requirements, 117
Filing status, 131
Increasing amount, 51
Net operating losses, 293, 294, 297
Partnerships, 839
Tax planning, 127–128, 131, 422, 426
Unused, 104–107
Withholding, 458

†